UNDERSTANDING CIVIL PROCEDURE

THE CALIFORNIA EDITION

UNDERSTANDING CIVIL PROCEDURE

THE CALIFORNIA EDITION

Walter W. Heiser
Professor of Law
University of SanDiego School of Law

Gene R. Shreve
Richard S. Melvin Professor of Law
Indiana University Maurer School of Law

Peter Raven-Hansen
Glen Earl Weston Research Professor of Law
George Washington University Law School

Charles Gardner Geyh
John F. Kimberling Professor of Law
Indiana University Maurer School of Law

ISBN: 978-0-7698-5156-3 (print)
ISBN: 978-0-7698-8852-1 (eBook)

Library of Congress Cataloging-in-Publication Data

Heiser, Walter W., author.
Understanding civil procedure / Walter W. Heiser, Professor of Law, University of SanDiego School of Law; Gene R. Shreve, Richard S. Melvin Professor of Law, Indiana University Maurer School of Law; Peter Raven-Hansen Glen Earl Weston Research Professor of Law, George Washington University Law School; Charles Gardner Geyh, John F. Kimberling Professor of Law, Indiana University Maurer School of Law. -- The California Edition.
pages cm.
Includes index.
ISBN 978-0-7698-5156-3
1. Civil procedure--California. 2. Civil procedure--California--Cases. 3. Civil procedure--United States. I. Shreve, Gene R., author. II. Raven-Hansen, Peter, 1946- author. III. Geyh, Charles Gardner, author. IV. Title.
KFC995.H455 2014
347.794'05--dc23

2013036348

NOTE TO USERS
To ensure that you are using the latest materials available in this area, please be sure to periodically check the LexisNexis Law School web site for downloadable updates and supplements at www.lexisnexis.com/lawschool.

Editorial Offices
121 Chanlon Rd., New Providence, NJ 07974 (908) 464-6800
201 Mission St., San Francisco, CA 94105-1831 (415) 908-3200
www.lexisnexis.com

MATTHEW◆BENDER

Acknowledgments

In preparing the *California Edition* of *Understanding Civil Procedure*, I benefited greatly from my collaboration with coauthors Peter Raven-Hansen and Charles Geyh. In particular, I would like to thank Professor Raven-Hansen for his comments and suggestions with respect to the initial manuscript. I would also like to express my gratitude to my wife, Susan, for her support and patience throughout this project.

San Diego, California

September, 2013

Preface to the California Edition

These materials discuss the entire subject of civil procedure as practiced in the federal courts and in the California state courts. This book contains the entire text of the Fifth Edition of *Understanding Civil Procedure*. In addition, it includes analysis of the relevant California procedural laws and doctrines at the end of each chapter. Although this book is primarily intended as a reference for law school civil procedure students in California, practitioners in California and elsewhere may also find it useful.

The emphasis of the California materials is often on those areas where California civil procedure departs from the general or federal rules. Accordingly, the discussion of California civil procedure makes frequent comparisons to analogous Federal Rules of Civil Procedure and federal court practice. In this manner, this book seeks to provide readers with an understanding of civil procedure in the federal courts and in the California courts, as well as appreciation of the important differences between the procedural laws in these two systems.

San Diego, California

September, 2013

Preface to the First Edition of Understanding Civil Procedure

This text treats the entire subject of civil procedure. It is primarily intended as a reference for law school civil procedure students. However, its treatment of recent developments in areas like Federal Rules of Civil Procedure 11, 16 and 26, personal jurisdiction and res judicata may make it useful to some practitioners as well.

If the law of contracts, torts or property reflects the substantive values of our society, civil procedure is the process for making those values real. The law of civil procedure governs the manner in which cases enter, transit, and leave the judicial process. It establishes the authority of courts to hear cases, opportunities for litigants to create and use a record of decision, and the force and effect of judgments.

We believe that the key to understanding the principles of civil procedure is knowing why: why they were created and why they are invoked. To these ends we have used a variety of means. History is the key to personal jurisdiction and the Erie doctrine, and we have explained them accordingly by tracing their historical evolution. Pragmatic concerns chiefly shape the civil procedure of pretrial discovery and motion practice, as well as trial practice, and we start discussion of these subjects by assessing why a lawyer is interested in them.

Federal Rule 11, discovery controls under Federal Rules 26(b)(1), 26(f), and 26(g), and expanded pretrial management under Federal Rule 16, are subjects so new that neither history nor pragmatic considerations are sufficient to anticipate their development. Using theory as well as both reported and unreported opinions available through early 1988, we have compensated by giving more prominence to these subjects than they presently enjoy in the typical civil procedure curriculum. This reflects our conviction that the subjects will grow in importance over the next few years. Finally, throughout the book we identify the latest sources which will enable readers with specialized needs to supplement the information we provide.

We have followed the practice of almost all civil procedure courses in using the Federal Rules of Civil Procedure as our model. However, we have also referred to different state rules and doctrines where appropriate, striving to use a representative cross-section of state models. We have also referred frequently to major civil procedure treatises, using a short form for citations explained in § 5.

Bloomington, Indiana

Washington, D.C.

May, 1988

TABLE OF CONTENTS

TABLE OF CONTENTS

TABLE OF CONTENTS

TABLE OF CONTENTS

TABLE OF CONTENTS

TABLE OF CONTENTS

TABLE OF CONTENTS

TABLE OF CONTENTS

TABLE OF CONTENTS

TABLE OF CONTENTS

TABLE OF CONTENTS

TABLE OF CONTENTS

TABLE OF CONTENTS

TABLE OF CONTENTS

TABLE OF CONTENTS

TABLE OF CONTENTS

TABLE OF CONTENTS

TABLE OF CONTENTS

TABLE OF CONTENTS

TABLE OF CONTENTS

TABLE OF CONTENTS

TABLE OF CONTENTS

TABLE OF CONTENTS

TABLE OF CONTENTS

Chapter 1

INTRODUCTION

§ 1.01 WHAT IS CIVIL PROCEDURE?

[1] Approaching the Subject

Like all law, the law of civil procedure can be seen as a series of expedients to influence, punish, reward, and authoritatively explain human behavior. Perhaps the reason that beginning students sometimes find civil procedure especially difficult is that it is preoccupied with *litigation* behavior, and students come to the course with little sense of what litigation is.

Litigation is sometimes described as a game, and procedural maneuvering is described as gamesmanship. Litigants do look like players and judges like umpires. The litigation game is remorselessly competitive and seems to have winners and losers. Its rules, like those of many other games, are difficult to understand in the abstract. They are given life and meaning by the experience of the game itself. Thus, the more we understand the phenomenon of civil litigation, the easier it will be to understand civil procedure.

Litigation differs from most games, however, in at least two important respects.

First, most games exist for the pleasure they give to participants or spectators. So long as they are relatively harmless, they are not difficult to justify. In contrast, the litigation game carries a heavy burden of justification. The game may impose onerous costs upon the parties, the court and the public, and frequently has only one enthusiastic player — the plaintiff.

Civil procedure cases and problems can therefore appropriately be considered from the perspective of cost control or resource allocation. Could the factual dispute between the parties have been resolved by any means that would have eliminated the need for litigation? Should particular tactics employed by litigants be viewed as legitimate procedural means to substantive ends, or unreasonably burdensome means that are disproportionate to the ends? What should the balance be between litigant autonomy and judicial control?

Inquiry about the most appropriate use of judicial resources also requires a developing appreciation of the different roles trial and appellate courts play. The law of civil procedure recognizes that some issues resolved by trial judges should rarely, if ever, be reviewed,[1] because appellate courts have an inferior vantage

---

[1] When the losing party can appeal a trial judge's procedural order and does so, the appellate court must decide whether the order under review should be upheld. Whatever it decides, the appellate court

1

point or because redecision does not seem to justify expenditure of scarce appellate resources. Where and how the line should be drawn between matters freely reviewable and matters committed to the trial court's discretion (hence, largely unreviewable) is a recurring question in the civil procedure course.

A second difference between litigation and most games is that games are usually not of central importance to (at least amateur) participants or to society. In contrast, the plaintiff may be forced to play the litigation game in order to avert or recover from a crushing setback in life. To deny claimants opportunities to become effective players in the litigation game might make meaningless the rights secured by substantive law (*e.g.*, torts, contracts, civil rights).

Readers of Dickens' *Bleak House* will recall how the redundant and prolonged Chancery procedure consumed the merits of the case. And, as Kafka's *The Trial* suggests, too little procedure can be just as bad. At its worst, procedure displaces or blocks substance. This can happen either when the expense and delay of too much procedure makes it impossible for a player to stay in the game long enough to reach the merits, or when potential players are shut out of the game because there is too little procedure. We must also be sensitive to possible differences between rules in theory and in application. As Anatole France observed, "the law in its majestic equality forbids the rich as well as the poor to sleep under bridges, to beg in the streets and to steal bread."

Ultimately, then, the game analogy must be used cautiously because it risks trivializing both the costs and the stakes of litigation. Unlike a game, civil litigation does not exist for its own sake. Civil Procedure works best when it validates substantive law (the merits) in the most expeditious, accessible, and unobtrusive way possible.

[2] Substance and Procedure

The study of the formation and content of substantive rules of decision — the standards by which society controls and affects "primary decisions respecting human conduct"[2] — is the subject of the traditional first year law courses of contracts, torts, property, and substantive criminal law. Civil procedure concerns itself with enforcing substantive rules through civil lawsuits. Roughly speaking, substantive rules of decision control conduct outside the courtroom, and procedural rules control conduct within.[3]

The latter determine in what courts lawyers file lawsuits; how they frame claims, denials and defenses; how the lawsuits progress from commencement to judgment; when and how judgments can be appealed; and the effect judgments have on subsequent lawsuits.

---

acts by issuing an order of its own, *e.g.*, to affirm, to reverse, or to vacate and remand for further proceedings. It often explains its order in an accompanying opinion. Most of the edited opinions civil procedure students read are appellate rather than trial court opinions.

[2] *Hanna v. Plumer*, 380 U.S. 460, 475 (1965) (Harlan, J., concurring).

[3] For a detailed and illuminating discussion of distinctions between the two, see Walter Wheeler Cook, *"Substance" and "Procedure" in the Conflict of Laws*, 42 YALE L.J. 333 (1933).

[3]   Civil Procedure in the United States

Civil procedure in the United States has three distinctive features. First, it follows an adversarial model of dispute resolution. Parties initiate and propel litigation in this model, and the judge, historically and at least in theory, plays the relatively passive role of umpire. The burden is on the parties to present their grievances and defenses. Unlike in so-called *inquisitorial* models of dispute resolution,[4] the judge rarely makes independent inquiries. The burden is also on the parties to prosecute their grievances and defenses; litigation stops unless the parties pursue it. Indeed, some scholars have argued that recent procedural rule changes have "undermined judicial evaluation of the merits of lawsuits and thereby vastly expanded attorneys' opportunities to twist procedure and substance on behalf of their clients."[5] These characteristics of our system of dispute resolution place a heavy responsibility on lawyers for assuring justice and mastering civil procedure.

Second, civil procedure in the United States is dominated by *positive law*: codified rules enacted by legislatures or their delegates. In contrast, the substantive rules of decision taught in the other traditional first year courses are more often doctrinal: declared by courts as part of the *common law* — legal doctrines declared, applied, and sometimes modified by judges in judicial opinions.

One difference between positive and common law lies in the materials containing the legal rules. The common-law materials are almost entirely judicial opinions, and the appropriate inquiry is: what rule best fits the case? In contrast, positive law materials are enacted laws or procedural rules and legislative history. Emphasis in administering the latter is on their plain words and (sometimes) legislative intent, in recognition of the superior lawmaking authority of legislatures and their delegates. In other words, judges have more freedom in construing and applying common law than they have in interpreting and applying positive law.

It is not always easy for the first year student to subordinate the comparatively freewheeling policy-oriented analysis of common law taught in many substantive courses to the plain language of positive law, principles of statutory construction, and reading of legislative history. But mastery of the latter lays the groundwork not just for understanding much of civil procedure, but also for understanding upper level law courses. Significantly, practicing lawyers rank "knowledge of statutory law" as the most important knowledge for practice, just ahead of "knowledge of procedural rules."[6]

---

[4] *See, e.g.*, John H. Langbein, *The German Advantage in Civil Procedure*, 52 U. CHI. L. REV. 823 (1985).

[5] Jonathan T. Molot, *How Changes in the Legal Profession Reflect Changes in Civil Procedure*, 84 VA. L. REV. 955, 958 (1998).

[6] Leonard L. Baird, *A Survey of the Relevance of Legal Training to Law School Graduates*, 29 J. LEGAL EDUC. 264, 273 (1978) (explaining that knowledge of common law, constitutional law, ethics, and regulations were all ranked lower by practitioners). More recent studies suggest that practitioners still consider knowledge of substantive law and procedural rules to be vital traits for young lawyers, *see* AMERICAN BAR ASSOCIATION TASK FORCE ON LAW SCHOOLS AND THE PROFESSION: NARROWING THE GAP, LEGAL EDUCATION AND PROFESSIONAL DEVELOPMENT AN EDUCATIONAL CONTINUUM (Robert MacCrate ed., 1992) (identifying ten skills that the "well-trained generalist" should have; prominent among these skills were

Finally, the purpose of civil procedure is, as the Federal Rules of Civil Procedure state, "to secure the just, speedy, and inexpensive determination of every action and proceeding."[7] Presumably, decisions are more likely to be just when they reach the merits (we say, "on the merits"). But the adversarial character of civil dispute resolution in the United States, the number of lawyers, and perhaps a national tendency to look too readily to the courts to solve disputes that other societies settle politically, administratively or privately,[8] have made the goals of "speedy and inexpensive" determinations increasingly difficult to attain.[9] As a result, there is constant pressure for more active judicial management of litigation and for judicial intervention to dispose of litigation without trial, if possible. Thus, the 1993 amendment to Rule 1 requires the rules not just to be "construed" (the original term), but also "administered" — "to secure just, speedy, and inexpensive determination of every action and proceeding." No one foresees the replacement of our adversarial model by the inquisitorial model of dispute resolution (in which the judge, not the parties, drives the litigation process), yet our model is undergoing significant change in response to widespread criticisms of the cost and efficiency of civil litigation.

"legal analysis and reasoning," and "litigation and alternative dispute-resolution procedures"). There is some evidence, however, that recognition of the importance of procedural and statutory knowledge has waned over the past few decades, see Bryant G. Garth & Joanne Martin, Law Schools and the Construction of Competence, 43 J. LEGAL EDUC. 469 (1993) (noting that, fifteen years after the study cited in Baird's article, surveyed hiring partners believed that knowledge of substantive and procedural law ranked well behind more esoteric eras — like "ability to obtain and keep clients," and "instilling others' confidence in you" — when it came to hiring decisions and partnership selections). One wonders whether those who believe that substantive and procedural acumen is of lesser importance feel the same way when selecting an associate to draft a key appellate brief!

[7] See, e.g., FED. R. CIV. P. 1. Hereinafter we will cite to a Federal Rule of Civil Procedure as "Rule."

[8] See PATRICK M. GARRY, A NATION OF ADVERSARIES: HOW THE LITIGATION EXPLOSION IS RESHAPING AMERICA (1997); WALTER K. OLSON, THE LITIGATION EXPLOSION: WHAT HAPPENED WHEN AMERICA UNLEASHED THE LAWSUIT (1991); JETHRO KOLLER LIEBERMAN, THE LITIGIOUS SOCIETY (1983); see also Nicola Faith Sharpe, Corporate Cooperation Through Cost-Sharing, 16 MICH. TELECOMM. & TECH. L. REV. 109, 116 (2009) ("The 1960s and early 1970s saw technological changes that led to an increase in discovery volume, burden, and costs, and has since been characterized by some as a litigation explosion. The widespread use of computers and digital communication has spawned a similar escalation."). We say "perhaps," because scholars have raised serious doubts whether the data support claims of a "litigation explosion," especially when one considers the number of lawsuits in proportion to the world's largest economy. See, e.g., Arthur R. Miller, The Pretrial Rush to Judgment: Are the "Litigation Explosion," "Liability Crisis," and Efficiency Clichés Eroding Our Day in Court and Jury Trial Commitments?, 78 N.Y.U. L. REV. 982 (2003); Marc S. Galanter, The Day After the Litigation Explosion, 46 MD. L. REV. 3 (1986); see also Richard M. Calkins, Mediation: A Revolutionary Process That Is Replacing the American Judicial System, 13 CARDOZO J. CONFLICT RESOL. 1 (2011).

[9] See, e.g., Arthur R. Miller, The Adversary System: Dinosaur or Phoenix, 69 MINN. L. REV. 1 (1984); David M. Trubek et al., The Costs of Ordinary Litigation, 31 U.C.L.A. L. REV. 72 (1983); Rand Inst., The Costs of Asbestos Litigation (1983), excerpted in LEGAL TIMES OF WASHINGTON, Aug. 8, 1983, at 26, Table 6.2 (reporting that of every dollar expended per claim, 37 cents were attributable to defendant's litigation expenses, 26 cents attributable to plaintiff's litigation expenses, and 37 cents attributable to net compensation to plaintiffs). Litigation delays vary tremendously between courts. In federal trial courts, the median time between commencement of civil litigation and disposition at trial was 23.4 months, with many of the dispositions at trial taking much longer. 2011 ADMIN. OFFICE U.S. COURTS ANNUAL REPORT OF THE DIR., Table C-59. See also Bruce Moyer, Congress and the Courts: The Outlook for 2011, 58 FED. LAW. 8 (2011) ("[S]ignificant budget cuts for the federal courts could result in job furloughs and reductions in court personnel. That could slow down court operations and create litigation delays.").

[4]   Some Common Misperceptions of Civil Procedure

The study of civil procedure is often impeded by misperceptions formed before law school or by comparison of civil procedure with the substantive first year courses.

One is that civil procedure is, as scholars once labeled it, strictly *adjective* law that "exists for the sake of something else."[10] However, while it is true that civil procedure is not an end in itself, it does not follow that procedural law is less significant than substantive law. At least one federal appellate court has suggested that procedures can have value independent of the merits, such that a lawyer's negligent waiver of the procedure may give rise to malpractice liability even when the procedure would not necessarily have improved the outcome.[11] Appellate cases all reach courts by procedural initiatives, and the procedural posture in which an issue is presented to the appellate court often determines how much attention it will receive.[12] Moreover, a judge may sometimes manipulate procedure in order to reach a "just" result in spite of inhospitable substantive law.[13] Procedure also interacts with substantive law outside the courtroom, as illustrated by the effect of the procedural device of class actions[14] on the substantive elements of securities fraud claims,[15] and the effect of the procedural requirement that plaintiffs pay for the cost of sending notice of the class action to class members on the effective enforcement of consumer laws.[16] Law has not escaped "the tendency of all modern scientific and philosophic thought . . . to emphasize the importance of method, process, or procedure."[17]

---

[10] Charles M. Hepburn, The Historical Development of Code Pleading in America and England with Special Reference to the Codes of New York, Missouri, California, Kentucky, Iowa, Minnesota, Indiana, Ohio, Oregon, Washington, Nebraska, Wisconsin, Kansas, Nevada, North Dakota, South Dakota, Idaho, Montana, Arizona, North Carolina, South Carolina, Arkansas, Wyoming, Utah, Colorado, Connecticut, and Oklahoma ___ (1897).

[11] *Jones Motor Co. v. Holtkamp, Liese, Beckemeier & Childress P.C.*, 197 F.3d 1190 (7th Cir. 1999) (asserting that failure to perfect jury demand may be such a procedure, but affirming judgment for malpractice defendant because plaintiffs had not proven resulting damages to a reasonable certainty).

[12] *See* §§ 13.09 & 13.10 (scope and intensity of review), *infra*.

[13] Fleming James Jr. et al., Civil Procedure § 1.1 (4th ed. 1992) (quotation marks supplied) (hereinafter *James, Hazard, & Leubsdorf*). *See* Robert M. Cover, *For James Wm. Moore: Some Reflections on a Reading of the Rules*, 84 Yale L.J. 718 (1975).

[14] Suits which may be brought by representative parties on behalf of a defined class of members who are not themselves participants in the litigation but may be bound by its outcome. *See* § 9.09 (class actions), *infra*.

[15] *See* Hal S. Scott, Comment, *The Impact of Class Actions on Rule 10b-5*, 38 U. Chi. L. Rev. 337, 338 (1971) (arguing that class actions permit some class members to recover who would fail to satisfy reliance and materiality requirements in individual actions for securities fraud).

[16] *See* Kenneth E. Scott, *Two Models of the Civil Process*, 27 Stan. L. Rev. 937, 944 (1975) (noting that the expense of such notice dooms most consumer actions because, if the cost precludes maintenance of a class action, the expense of suing individually exceeds the benefits that they could confer on individual plaintiffs). That is, it just isn't worth it unless the class action rules permit the individual plaintiffs to join together as a class.

[17] Morris R. Cohen, *The Process of Judicial Legislation, in* Law and the Social Order: Essays in Legal Philosophy 112 (2001).

Another common misperception is that civil procedure is nothing more than the unimaginative and routine application of black-letter law to dry procedural issues. This may be a law student's initial reaction to the positive law materials from which civil procedure is primarily taught. Yet positive law is more dynamic than the black letter of a rule or statute might indicate. Moreover, important parts of civil procedure, including personal jurisdiction (court's power to bind particular defendants) and *res judicata* (the effect of prior judgments on subsequent litigation), are based primarily on judicial doctrine, rather than written rules.

Furthermore, such written rules or statutes governing procedural questions are not self-applying. Problems often elude solution by plain-language tests or application of simple canons of statutory construction. Statutes over time acquire their own judicial gloss. The legislative product may be inarticulate, forcing courts to finish the lawmaking process. Or the legislature may deliberately create a rule that can never be completed in the abstract. Rules of the latter kind place courts at procedural crossroads, supplying general criteria for decision and leaving the result to courts' appreciation of the facts in particular cases.[18]

In addition, many, if not most, procedural questions are susceptible to more than one answer. Civil procedure, hence effective litigation, consists less of finding black-letter answers than of making choices among tactical options. These choices turn not just on the rules and procedural posture of litigation, but also on the relative strengths and attitudes of the parties, the relationships between lawyers and judge, and all the other subtle factors that make lawyering an art as well as a profession.

A third misperception is that civil procedure is trial practice.[19] This may cause some law students who cannot picture themselves as trial lawyers to approach their civil procedure course with less enthusiasm. But even a brief glance at litigation statistics refutes this perception. For example, of all the federal civil actions terminated in the year ending Sept. 30, 2000, 72% ended before the pretrial conference that often precedes trial in federal court[20] (one in four of these ended without court action of any kind), 8% ended during or after pretrial, and only 1.4% made it to trial.[21] Just under one third of these were tried to a judge rather than a jury,[22] calling upon far different lawyering skills than far more rare jury trial practice. State civil disposition statistics[23] send the same message: *civil procedure is not about trial.* Litigation in the United States is predominantly *pretrial*

---

[18] *See, e.g.*, § 9.05 (discussing Rules 19 and 20 dealing with compulsory and permissive joinder), *infra*.

[19] For treatment of trial practice (jury selection, opening statements, presentation of evidence, closing argument, jury deliberation, and preservation of points for appeal), see MARILYN J. BERGER, JOHN B. MITCHELL & RONALD H. CLARK, TRIAL ADVOCACY: PLANNING ANALYSIS & STRATEGY (3d ed. 2011); D. SHANE READ, WINNING AT TRIAL (2007).

[20] *See* § 12.03 (pretrial conference), *infra*.

[21] 2005 ADMIN. OFFICE U.S. COURTS ANNUAL REPORT OF THE DIR., note 9, *supra*, Table C-4A.

[22] 2005 ADMIN. OFFICE U.S. COURTS ANNUAL REPORT OF THE DIR., note 9, *supra*, Table C-4A.

[23] *See* LYNN LANGTON & THOMAS H. COHEN, BUREAU OF JUSTICE STATISTICS, CIVIL BENCH AND JURY TRIALS IN STATE COURTS, 2005 (2008), *available at* http://www.bjs.gov/content/pub/pdf/cbjtsc05.pdf (indicating that 3% of all tort, contract, and real property cases in state courts were disposed of through a jury or bench trial in 2005).

practice. In the pretrial phase of litigation, it is not theatrics, charisma, or trial tactics that carry the day, but mastery of pretrial procedure, the ability to communicate effectively to the court, and a command of the details of the lawsuit — skills accessible even to those who lack a flair for the melodramatic.

§ 1.02   SOURCES OF CIVIL PROCEDURE

Constitutional law sets the outer limits of civil procedure. The United States Constitution limits the subject matter of the cases that federal courts may hear,[24] determines the effect courts of one state must give to the judgments of another,[25] and preserves the right to jury trial in certain categories of cases in federal court.[26] In addition, the Due Process Clause of the Fifth Amendment to the United States Constitution guarantees some minimum level of process to litigants in federal courts, and the Due Process Clause of the Fourteenth Amendment gives a comparable guarantee to litigants in state courts. Due process has helped shape procedural requirements for personal jurisdiction (meaning the power of a court to enter judgments that are binding on particular defendants or property),[27] notice, and the opportunity to be heard in litigation.[28] Given their potential procedural reach, in fact, it is curious that the Due Process Clauses have not been invoked more frequently as sources of procedure.[29]

Statutes are a second source of positive procedural law. In both the federal and state systems, they define the power of various courts to hear particular cases[30] and the convenient forums for litigation.[31] In all states, statutes also help define the personal jurisdiction of state courts.[32] In addition, a declining minority of states have enacted statutory procedural codes.[33]

The most important sources of positive procedural law, however, are formally adopted rules of civil procedure. The federal courts and forty states have adopted them, usually by a judicial rulemaking process authorized by a statute.[34] As of 1986, twenty-three states had copied, with minor modifications, the Federal Rules of Civil

---

[24] U.S. CONST. art. III. *See* Ch. 5 (subject matter jurisdiction), *infra.*

[25] U.S. CONST. art. IV. *See* §§ 15.10–15.11 (full faith and credit and inter-system preclusion), *infra.*

[26] U.S. CONST. amend. VII. *See* § 12.07[1] (right to a jury), *infra.* Most state constitutions have analogous procedural provisions governing state courts.

[27] *See* Ch. 3 (personal jurisdiction), *infra.*

[28] *See* Ch. 4 (notice and opportunity to be heard) & § 9.09[4] (due process requirements in class actions), *infra.*

[29] *See* John Leubsdorf, *Constitutional Civil Procedure*, 63 TEX. L. REV. 579 (1984).

[30] *See* §§ 5.01[2] (citing federal statutes illustratively), 13.02–13.04 (federal appeals), *infra.*

[31] *See* Ch. 6 (venue), *infra.*

[32] *See* § 3.07[1] (long-arm statutes), *infra.*

[33] Approximately thirty-five states now mirror the federal rules in their state procedural rules. *See* John B. Oakley, *A Fresh Look at the Federal Rules in State Courts*, 3 NEV. L.J. 354 (2003). Even states that have clung onto their own, more unique procedural rules (like California and New York) have adopted the federal rules' cornerstones: relaxed pleading; broad discovery; a willingness to turn to summary judgment; and forgiving joinder rules. *See id.*

[34] Oakley, note 33, *supra.*

Procedure,[35] and almost two-thirds of the states based their procedures substantially on the federal model (although several of the most populated states — including New York and California — substantially diverged from it).[36] As a result, almost all first year civil procedure courses and casebooks focus primarily on the federal rules, as we will here. At the same time, you should remember that the rules of the state in which you eventually practice may well differ, and that you cannot assume that even a state rule that is apparently modeled on a federal rule is the same as the federal "source" rule, or that it has been interpreted the same way as a matter of state law.

Some understanding of the federal rulemaking process[37] is essential to understanding the effect of the Federal Rules of Civil Procedure in federal courts. The Rules Enabling Act delegates lawmaking authority to the Supreme Court to make rules governing "general rules of practice and procedure" for cases in the federal courts.[38] The Judicial Conference of the United States, comprised of the Chief Justice of the Supreme Court and designated judges from other federal courts, oversees the rulemaking process. The Advisory Committee on Civil Rules to the Judicial Conference's Standing Committee on Rules of Practice and Procedure is charged with the actual work of drafting and recommending rules of civil procedure. The Advisory Committee is comprised of judges, practitioners and law professors. The Chief Justice appoints a Reporter who monitors developments in the field and aids the Advisory Committee.

Federal procedural rulemaking typically begins when the Advisory Committee notes a procedural need or problem. If the Committee so directs, the Reporter prepares a preliminary draft of responsive rule changes with "committee notes" explaining their purpose. The Committee meets and revises these materials and

---

[35] Oakley, note 33, *supra* (listing Alabama, Alaska, Arizona, Colorado, District of Columbia, Hawaii, Indiana, Kentucky, Maine, Massachusetts, Minnesota, Montana, New Mexico, North Dakota, Ohio, Rhode Island, South Dakota, Tennessee, Utah, Vermont, Washington, West Virginia, and Wyoming). This statement tends to understate the influence of the federal rules, because four of the states with statutory procedural codes have codified versions of the federal rules (Georgia, Kansas, North Carolina, and Oklahoma), and three other states have rules that "show strong affinity to the content and organization of the Federal Rules . . . ." (Idaho, Michigan, and Nevada). *See* Kenneth W. Graham Jr., *State Adaptation of the Federal Rules: The Pros and Cons*, 43 OKLA. L. REV. 293 (1990). Even states that replicated the federal rules have not necessarily kept pace with federal rule amendments, however. *See* Stephen N. Subrin, *Federal Rules, Local Rules, and States Rules: Uniformity, Divergence and Emerging Procedural Patterns*, 137 U. PA. L. REV. 1999, 2037 (1989).

[36] Oakley, note 33, *supra*; *see also* John B. Oakley, *A Fresh Look at the Federal Rules in State Courts*, 3 NEV. L.J. 354 (2003).

[37] *See generally* Thomas E. Baker, *An Introduction to Federal Court Rulemaking Procedure*, 22 TEX. TECH. L. REV. 323 (1991); WINIFRED R. BROWN, FEDERAL RULEMAKING: PROBLEMS AND POSSIBILITIES (Federal Judicial Center 1981); Benjamin Kaplan, *Amendments of the Federal Rules of Civil Procedure 1961–1963 (I)*, 77 HARV. L. REV. 601, 601–02 (1964); Laurens Walker, *A Comprehensive Reform for Federal Civil Rulemaking*, 61 GEO. WASH. L. REV. 455 (1993).

[38] 28 U.S.C. §§ 2071–2074. *See generally* Stephen B. Burbank, *The Rules Enabling Act of 1934*, 130 U. PA. L. REV. 1015 (1982). The Act expressly mandates that such rules "shall not abridge, enlarge or modify any substantive right," thus reserving substantive lawmaking to the Congress and to the state legislatures within their proper spheres. *See generally* §§ 7.01–7.04 (the laws applied in federal courts and the applicability of federal procedural rules), *infra*. *See also* Paul D. Carrington, *"Substance" and "Procedure" in the Rules Enabling Act*, 1989 DUKE L.J. 281 (1989).

then reports them to the Standing Committee. If the Standing Committee approves the draft for publication, it is published in the *Federal Register* and the federal reporters[39] for public comment. In addition, the Advisory Committee usually holds public hearings on the draft in diverse locations. After reviewing public comments, the Committee may make revisions and then submit the proposed rule changes and final comments[40] to the Standing Committee of the Judicial Conference. The latter reviews and ultimately forwards the proposal, revised if necessary, to the members of the Judicial Conference.

If the Conference approves the proposal, it sends the rule changes to the Supreme Court. In theory, the Supreme Court conducts a substantive review of the change. In fact, the Justices have differed about their true role. Justice Douglas, for example, described it as "merely perfunctory" and the Court as "a mere conduit" for transmittal of the rules to Congress.[41] Individual justices may make statements concerning the rule changes. The Court then transmits the changes to Congress no later than May 1 of the year in which they are to become effective. The change becomes effective no earlier than December 1 of that year, unless Congress by statute modifies or rejects the rule.[42]

However, not all written rules governing federal practice are promulgated in this fashion. Rule 83 authorizes a majority of the judges of each district court to promulgate local rules "consistent" with the formal federal rules of civil procedure. Many district courts have exercised this authority to issue housekeeping rules governing the length of briefs and the availability of oral hearings, attorney admissions, procedures for submitting requests for attorneys' fees, and other matters.[43] The result has been a proliferation of local rules, some of them

---

[39] Selected opinions of federal courts are published in the *Federal Supplement* (district courts), *Federal Reporter* (courts of appeals), and *United States Reporter* (Supreme Court).

[40] When rule changes are adopted, the advisory committee's notes become an important source of legislative history for construing the changes. They are published in the *Federal Rules Decisions*, the principal civil procedure treatises, and in many rulebooks.

[41] *See* Statement of Douglas, 409 U.S. 1132 (1972) (Douglas, J., dissenting). More recently, Justice White has said that the Court's role "is to transmit the Judicial Conference's recommendations without change and without careful study, as long as there is no suggestion that the committee system has not operated with integrity." Statement of J. White, 113 S. Ct. CCC, CCCIV (1993).

[42] Except for rules affecting an evidentiary privilege, Section 2074 contemplates (but does not require) a passive role for Congress: "[i]nertia means approval." David D. Siegel, 28 U.S.C.A. § 2074 commentary (1988). Congress usually remains silent, but has shown a greater tendency to become active in recent years. *Cf.* John Hart Ely, *The Irrepressible Myth of Erie*, 87 Harv. L. Rev. 693, 693–94 (1974) (describing congressional resistance to the Court's proposed federal rules of evidence), and § 4.03[1] (describing congressional substitution of its own enactment for the Court's proposed amendment to Rule 4), *infra*. Congress' constitutional authority to change the rules is not undisputed. *Compare* Linda S. Mullinex, *Judicial Power and the Rules Enabling Act*, 46 Mercer L. Rev. 733 (1995) (questioning such authority to supercede procedural rulemaking by the judiciary), *with* Martin H. Redish, *Federal Judicial Independence: Constitutional and Political Perspectives*, 46 Mercer L. Rev. 697 (1995) (supporting such authority on majoritarian principles).

[43] *See* Charles Alan Wright & Arthur R. Miller, Federal Practice and Procedure § 3154 (giving examples). The scope of local rulemaking authority is a matter of continuing debate. *See, e.g.*, Samuel P. Jordan, *Local Rules and the Limits of Trans-Territorial Procedure*, 52 Wm. & Mary L. Rev. 415 (2010); Steven Flanders, *Local Rules in Federal District Courts: Usurpation, Legislation, or Information?*, 14 Loy. L.A. L. Rev. 213 (1981); A. Leo Levin, *Local Rules as Experiments: A Study in the Division of*

contradicting or altering the uniform federal rules in apparent disregard of Rule 83's insistence on consistency.[44] Indeed, one civil procedure scholar lamented that "[p]rocedural anarchy is now the order of the day."[45]

Individual judges may also establish rules governing procedures for scheduling and argument in their courtrooms. Rule 83 expressly provides that when there is no controlling law, a judge "may regulate practice in any manner consistent with federal law, rules adopted under 28 U.S.C. §§ 2072 and 2075, and the district's local rules."[46] Furthermore, judges always have what has been called "individual calendar" discretion over scheduling and hearing practice in a particular case.[47]

The parties themselves can also be an important source of procedural rules often overlooked by law students. A few federal rules expressly authorize parties themselves to stipulate to departures from some rules,[48] and parties can make other agreements that supplement and sometimes modify positive procedural law. They often agree by contract, for example, to the appropriate forum for litigation under the contract, the mode of service of the complaint and summons, or the applicable substantive law for such litigation, superseding the otherwise applicable law.[49] At a more mundane level, litigation counsel schedule many pretrial activities among themselves.

Finally, ethical rules bearing on civil litigation are promulgated as codes of professional conduct or rules of the bar by courts acting in conjunction with bar associations. The American Bar Association's *Model Rules of Professional Conduct*,[50] substantially adopted by the majority of the states,[51] contain several rules concerning the zeal with which a lawyer may represent a client in litigation.[52] Although historically there have been serious doubts concerning the organized bar's capacity for self-enforcement of such rules,[53] it is probable that the majority of

---

Power, 139 U. Pa. L. Rev. 1567 (1991). In 1988, Congress acted to subject such rulemaking to closer scrutiny. *See* 28 U.S.C. § 2071; David D. Siegel, 28 U.S.C.A. § 2071 commentary (1988).

[44] *See* Stephen N. Subrin, *Federal Rules, Local Rules, and State Rules: Uniformity, Divergence, and Emerging Procedural Patterns*, 137 U. Pa. L. Rev. 1999 (1989).

[45] Charles Alan Wright, *Forward: The Malaise of Federal Rulemaking*, 14 Rev. Litig. 1, 11 (1994).

[46] *See, e.g.*, William W. Schwarzer (J., N.D. Cal.), *Guidelines for Discovery, Motion Practice and Trial*, 117 F.R.D. 273 (1987). Judge Schwarzer's *Guidelines* admonish counsel to observe not only the Federal Rules of Civil Procedure and the District Court's Local Rules, but also "the rules and practices of the particular judge to whom the case is assigned." The latter are available "[b]y obtaining from the judge's courtroom deputy copies of the standing orders used by that judge; and [b]y inquiring of the deputy (not the law clerks) how the judge wants things done." Schwarzer, at 273.

[47] David D. Siegel, 28 U.S.C.A. § 2077 commentary (1988).

[48] *See* Rules 15(a) (stipulation in lieu of court permission to amend pleadings), 26(f) (changes in discovery limitations), and Rule 29 (stipulation of discovery procedure).

[49] *See, e.g.*, *National Equip. Rental, Ltd. v. Szukhent*, 375 U.S. 311 (1964) (enforcing contract that designated agent to receive service).

[50] Model Rules of Prof'l Conduct (2011).

[51] *See* ABA Center for Professional Conduct, Status of State Review of Professional Conduct Rules (chart), *available at* http://www.americanbar.org/content/dam/aba/migrated/cpr/pic/ethics_2000_status_chart.authcheckdam.pdf (current as of September 14, 2011).

[52] *See, e.g.*, Model Rules 3.1–3.6, note 50, *supra*.

[53] American Bar Ass'n, Special Committee on Evaluation and Disciplinary Enforcement, Problems and

lawyers abide by them. Moreover, several Federal Rules of Civil Procedure underscore professional responsibilities in federal courts and may become a vehicle for enforcement of some of the ethical rules adopted by the bar.[54]

§ 1.03   BRIEFING A CIVIL PROCEDURE CASE

The primary vehicles for class discussion in most civil procedure courses are assigned cases. These are judicial opinions, usually written by judges to accompany their orders (rulings) on civil procedure motions. An *order* may dispose of the lawsuit or simply resolve a skirmish between the litigants and leave the lawsuit to continue. Typically, the order simply says who won — for example: "Plaintiff's motion for summary judgment is granted [denied]." The *opinion* is written by the judge to accompany the order and to explain why the judge decided to rule in favor of the prevailing party (or, in appellate opinions, why the ruling below was reversed or affirmed).

Virtually all the orders in cases we consider were on contested matters. That is to say, the parties urged upon the court opposing choices of judicial conduct before the court decided how to rule in the order. Not all orders are accompanied by opinions, and not all opinions are designated by the court for publication. Opinions are most likely to accompany orders which decide contested matters, because judges feel greater pressure to justify what they have done under such circumstances. In this sense, judges are advocates, too. The judicial opinions we read are the judges' means of arguing that their orders reflect decisions most likely to advance the rule and logic of civil procedure and to do justice in the individual case.

The primary purpose of case briefing is to enable students to get the most out of class. Briefing helps students prepare by giving structure to their consideration of cases before class begins. It also provides a working paper during class, making it easier for students to follow developments and to advance the discussion when called upon by the professor. On the other hand, briefs may not be terribly useful tools for course review. This is because they are made before class, before thoughts about the material have matured. Comments and addenda students make on their briefs during and after classroom discussion of the case are likely to be far more useful for exam study.

Casebooks and study aids suggest how to brief a case, and many students are taught briefing in first semester orientation lectures or legal methods classes. Our concern here is to explain how the generic briefing technique should be adapted for civil procedure cases.

Most briefs and many reported judicial opinions begin with a *recitation of the pre-litigation facts* which gave rise to the claims or defenses in the litigation. These are always important, if for no other reason than to remind the reader of the real world, flesh-and-blood implications of the legal issues put by the case. But they are often of less significance in civil procedure decisions than in those focusing on points of substantive law.

Recommendations on Disciplinary Enforcement 1 (final draft, 1970).

[54] *See* Rule 11, *discussed in* § 8.05[2] *infra*, and Rule 26(g), *discussed in* § 10.13[1] *infra*.

Instead, the crucial facts for us are *procedural facts*: what happened to the case after it was filed. The chronology of procedural steps taken by the litigants and the court is often important. For example, the pattern might be commencement of the litigation by the filing of a complaint, defendant's filing of a motion to dismiss the complaint for some reason, argument on the motion leading to its denial, fact-finding by the parties, trial, judgment for the plaintiff, and appeal by defendant (raising, among others, the same issue presented previously by motion). Retracing procedural steps is essential to understanding who's who, what has happened in the case, and how ripe procedural rulings are for review. It is also important to an appreciation of the tactical aspects of litigation.[55] It facilitates reconstruction of the alternatives available to the parties as the litigation progresses.

Thus, while an elaborate general fact description may be unnecessary in briefing most civil procedure cases, students should include a full statement of facts setting the *procedural posture* of the case. This statement should ordinarily indicate who is suing whom, facts which may be easier to diagram in the margin of the brief or the casebook itself. The student might use arrows to represent claims (and sometimes defenses) instead of describing the process narratively. Here is an illustration:

Figure 1-1

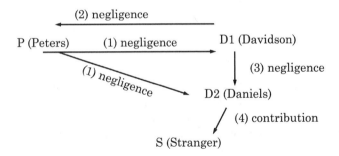

(Diagram shows that (1) Peters sued Davidson and Daniels for negligence, whereupon (2) Davidson counterclaimed against Peters and (3) cross-claimed against Daniels for negligence, and (4) Daniels impleaded Stranger on a theory of contribution.)

The chronology of procedural facts can be suggested by numbering the facts in the brief (as illustrated above) or in the case excerpt itself.

Next, it is useful to *identify the statutes or rules involved in the case.* Some study aids omit this step in briefing because they are geared primarily to briefing cases applying common law, not positive law (statutes or codified rules of procedure).[56]

---

[55] *See* § 1.01[1], *supra.*

[56] Since procedural decisions often turn on rules of positive law, a routine search for this material is a good briefing step. *Never rely on a paraphrase of the positive law;* good lawyers always read the original on the theory that you cannot ascertain the "plain meaning" of words without reading them. Here there simply is no substitute for the actual language of the statute or rule.

Nor is it enough to consider this kind of material in the abstract or in bulk at sporadic intervals during

For example, when you encounter positive federal law, consider the following approach. Read the cited statute or rule carefully, going to your rulebook if the text is not reproduced in the case itself. Is it clear from a reading of the provision how Congress or the rulemakers intended to apply it to the case at hand? If so, has the court's decision given it that application? If it is not clear from a reading of the provision how Congress or the rulemakers intended it to apply to the case at hand, has the court resolved the provision's ambiguity in a satisfactory way? Often, to answer these questions, it is necessary not just to read the provision in question, but to read around it to grasp the context in which it appears and to compare it with like provisions (sometimes called construing a statute or rule "in pari materia" (the principle that when a statutory provision or rule is ambiguous, its meaning can be ascertained by comparing it with others on the same or similar subjects)).

Third, the brief should *frame the issues presented by the case*. Many opinions do this expressly, but when the opinion is unclear, framing the issue is often the crucial step towards understanding the court's decision and its reasoning. If you are just annotating a casebook, and can identify the issue in the opinion, marking it with a "Q" may do the job, but sometimes you must frame the issue yourself.

Fourth, the brief should *describe the court's decision on the issue at two levels*. The court will both supply an *answer* to the issue put by the case and make a formal *disposition* of the case, as noted often in the final paragraph. For example, when the issue is whether the plaintiff's complaint has stated a claim upon which relief can be granted, the court may decide that it does not and then grant the motion to dismiss and enter an order of dismissal. But this latter disposition — an order of dismissal — need not go hand-in-hand with the decision of the issue. The court might instead grant the motion to dismiss with leave (permission) to plaintiff to amend his complaint.

Fifth, the brief should *describe and critique the reasoning articulated for the decision*. In describing the reasoning, the student should take full advantage of dissenting and concurring opinions, sometimes expressly written to limit the applicability of the court's reasoning. Presumptuous as it might seem at first, you must also evaluate the court's reasoning. This may take some effort, since students often arrive at law school believing that the laws they will study exist as part of a static natural order — like laws of physics. Unfortunately, this attitude permits no more than a superficial grasp of the law in civil procedure or other courses. It makes the student easy prey for the rhetoric in many judicial opinions that the result reached by the court is obvious. On the contrary, many cases — particularly those selected for casebook treatment — pose close and difficult questions. Great jurists may produce illuminating opinions, but they cannot make hard cases easy. What one often finds is "not a matter of right against wrong, but of right against right."[57] And, of course, judges often get it wrong. In fact, your casebooks sometimes include wrong or doubtful decisions because they provoke useful class discussion.

---

the semester. Students can best learn and understand statutes and rules of procedure in the context of particular case applications. It goes without saying that cases must be read with the rulebook close at hand.

[57] Maurice Rosenberg, *Devising Procedures That Are Civil to Promote Justice That Is Civilized*, 69 MICH. L. REV. 797, 797 (1971).

This critical side of analysis and discussion is a good deal of what makes the course (and the professor) tick. Civil procedure professors strive to illustrate and teach the proposition that civil procedure involves hard choices. In turn, answers to examination questions must reflect judgment seasoned by an appreciation of both sides of the issue.[58] To respond, students cannot afford a passive approach to assigned materials.

The critique of the court's reasoning will be the most ambitious portion of your brief, the part most likely to require revision during and after civil procedure class. Don't worry. As noted earlier, unrevised case briefs are ultimately unreliable, anyway. The purpose of briefing is to enable you to get the most out of class and to stimulate (and ultimately reward) your critical thought. A marked up brief is evidence that the purpose was accomplished.

§ 1.04   OUTLINING IN CIVIL PROCEDURE

Outlining in preparation for examinations is an art that goes beyond the scope of this book. But a few principles of that art are especially pertinent to Civil Procedure.

First, a descriptive outline that paraphrases rules, summarizes cases, and condenses lecture notes in more or less chronological order may help you prepare for classes, but is unlikely to be very useful in preparing for exams. It may, more or less, describe the black letter law, but it does not help you "operationalize" it — synthesize it into an orderly process or template for solving problems. Even if you make a descriptive outline for day-to-day classes, you would need to reorganize (and probably shorten) it to make it a useful tool for problem-solving on exams.

What is more useful is an "attack outline" — often consisting of a sequential series of inquiries or steps, or, for the engineers among you, even a flow chart or decision tree — for each particular type of problem (e.g., amendment; motions to dismiss for lack of personal jurisdiction; choice of federal or state law) in the course. To determine the proper inquiries or steps and their logical order, you need to synthesize rules and principles of cases and reorganize them after your own fashion. The process is arduous but rewarding. It will not only provide an approach to the kind of problems that are posed in exam questions (especially essay questions), and a guide to identifying the relevant facts, but also an outline for writing your answer.

Second, an attack outline should not simply paraphrase a rule. In the first place, it is always dangerous to paraphrase positive law — the plain words matter and often control; your paraphrases do not, as we said above. It bears repetition: You should always consult the actual language of pertinent rules and statutes instead of relying on a paraphrase or summary. In addition, the rules are not themselves always organized operationally — that is, in the sequence of steps by which they are applied — and sometimes key factors in the application of the rules are found not

---

[58] Contrary to what beginning students might assume, students rarely get the bottom line wrong, at least in essay examinations. The difference between an "A" and a "C" examination more often lies in the imagination and agility demonstrated in applying course rules and concepts in a new setting, than in differences in bottom line conclusions. This demonstration is possible only with an approach to civil procedure that is both descriptive *and* critical.

in the rule itself, but in the judicial gloss on the rule. You will therefore often need to reorganize a rule and add to it from the cases in order to operationalize it.

Finally, even if you choose not to outline or decide to outline in a different fashion, you should realize that you unavoidably do it anyway when you apply the rules to solve a civil litigation problem. The written attack outline is simply a map of a logical thought process or decision tree that informs legal analysis of a problem.

§ 1.05   RESEARCH AND DRAFTING IN CIVIL PROCEDURE

The starting point for research on any legal problem is to frame the issue tentatively, something that students rehearse in their preparation of case briefs. For law students and beginning lawyers, even this step will sometimes prove difficult. When it does, it may be helpful to consult a civil procedure treatise like this one to frame the issue correctly and to identify relevant statutes or rules.

The second step is to read carefully any statutes or rules of procedure involved in your problem, noting when necessary any time frame for acting under them. It is difficult to overstate the importance of rereading the text of a rule or statute with each succeeding problem. This is because these provisions are drafted to cover a variety of situations arising in cases. A subsequent case thus may be governed by the same rule of procedure, yet the demands of the new controversy may illuminate a different portion of the text. As a result, even experienced lawyers take the trouble to reread rules and statutes carefully.

For federal civil procedure problems, the third step is to consult the two federal practice treatises: J. Moore, *Moore's Federal Practice* (Matthew Bender) and C. Wright & A. Miller et al., *Federal Practice and Procedure* (West), both of which are now on-line. Both treat the federal rules sequentially and also cover statutory issues of procedure, such as jurisdiction and venue. They also reproduce the Advisory Committee's notes that accompanied the rule and represent most of its legislative history. Federal courts often cite analyses and conclusions from these treatises, in recognition of their thoroughness and quality. Finally, both supply voluminous case citations that are frequently updated. Coverage overlaps considerably; yet style, analysis, and case coverage in the two are sufficiently distinct to justify examination of both in researching the typical problem of federal civil procedure. For the typical federal procedural issue, it is rarely wise to go to the cases directly without reading the relevant sections of the treatises. Their unusual thoroughness and authority sometimes supplies an answer without need of additional case research, and they will at least focus the case search and thus ultimately save time for the issues that they address. (Treatises on state procedural law also exist, although they tend to be less thorough and to be updated less frequently.) These steps will help reframe the problem, suggest a more or less detailed analysis, and generate lists of possibly relevant cases for further research.

Civil procedure problems that turn on statutes or rules are particularly well-suited to computer research, because it is easy to frame a search request around the statute or rule number. Students are cautioned, however, that there is no uniformity in judicial citation to such procedural law, and a complete search request must include in the alternative all of the likely variants. With regard to the

Federal Rules of Civil Procedure, for example, these variants include at least "FRCP," "F. R. C. P.," "Fed. R. Civ. P.," "Rule," and "R." with the relevant number, and, ideally, some generic phrase to help exclude like-numbered federal rules of appellate or criminal procedure from the search.

For drafting problems involving the Federal Rules of Civil Procedure, students should consult the official appendix of forms immediately following the rules. These forms have been declared sufficient in federal practice by Rule 84. Students may also wish to examine unofficial form books. These may offer guidance in both state and federal practice.[59] They are collections of prior pleadings, motions or discovery requests. Most have passed muster at some time in a relevant court and may therefore serve as a form for current papers of the same kind. The advent of the Internet age has also ushered in a veritable cottage industry that offers download-able templates of an array of legal pleadings. Depending on the type of pleading sought, one might find what one needs free of charge,[60] or for a (handsome) price.[61]

For several reasons, such form books must be used with extreme caution and a heavy dose of common sense. First, unlike those in the official appendix to the federal rules, most published forms do not carry the imprimatur of any court system. All that stands behind many items memorialized as forms is that they worked once in a case. Close perusal of the fine print in the form books that give citations may reveal that the most recent approval of a particular form came in the nineteenth century. Arcane and dated wording in forms provides another danger signal. Second, because forms were originally created to meet the facts and demands of a different case, substantial adaptation is often necessary to make forms usable. Finally, a form may not have been selected for its brilliance, but for its (one-time) sufficiency. It may represent no more than the lowest common denominator. Still, form books (and, particularly in large law firms today, internally-generated forms and prior papers) are often a helpful starting point for procedural drafting.

§ 1.06 CIVIL PROCEDURE BIBLIOGRAPHY AND SHORT FORM CITATIONS

We cite in footnotes to the textbooks and articles on civil procedure that are useful sources for further reading. Several are cited often enough to warrant use of a short form citation. The following list gives the full citation for each such work, followed by the manner in which we cite it. We supply only the section numbers for

---

[59] *See, e.g.*, AMERICAN JURISPRUDENCE PLEADING AND PRACTICE FORMS ANNOTATED (Lawyers Co-op.); LOUIS R. FRUMER & IRWIN HALL ET AL., BENDER'S FEDERAL PRACTICE FORMS (Matthew Bender); BENDER'S FORMS OF DISCOVERY (Matthew Bender); FEDERAL PROCEDURAL FORMS LAWYERS EDITION (Lawyers Co-op); NICHOLS CYCLOPEDIA OF FEDERAL PROCEDURE FORMS (Callaghan); WEST'S FEDERAL FORMS (West).

[60] *See* Joan Indiana Rigdon, *Pro Bono Goes Online*, D.C. BAR (May 2002), *available at* http://www.dcbar.org/for_lawyers/resources/publications/washington_lawyer/may_2002/probono.cfm (offering select free pleading templates online for pro bono litigators).

[61] *See California Pleading Templates Package*, CNET, *available at* http://download.cnet.com/California-Pleading-Templates-Package/3000-2073_4-10421944.html (last visited June 12, 2012) (Offering "a pleading software and template package for major California and Federal District & Appellate courts" for the low, low price of $349!).

these sources because the page numbers vary with succeeding editions.

I. *Hornbooks*

RICHARD D. FREER, INTRODUCTION TO CIVIL PROCEDURE (3d ed. 2012)

JACK H. FRIEDENTHAL, ARTHUR R. MILLER, JOHN E. SEXTON & HELEN HERSHKOFF, CIVIL PROCEDURE (10th ed. 2009).

FLEMING JAMES, JR., GEOFFREY C. HAZARD, JR. & JOHN LEUBSDORF, CIVIL PROCEDURE (5th ed. 2001).

LARRY L. TEPLY & RALPH U. WHITTEN, CIVIL PROCEDURE (4th ed. 2009).

CHARLES ALAN WRIGHT & MARY KAY KANE, LAW OF FEDERAL COURTS (6th ed. 2002).

II. *Treatises*

CHARLES ALAN WRIGHT ET AL., FEDERAL PRACTICE AND PROCEDURE (4th ed. 2008, updated online 2012) (*WRIGHT & MILLER*). In rare cases where quoted material is taken from a prior edition, we have left a full citation.

JAMES W. MOORE, MOORE'S FEDERAL PRACTICE (3d ed. 1997, updated online 2012) (*MOORE*; volume number omitted where section number is keyed to a Federal Rule of Civil Procedure). In rare cases where quoted material is taken from a prior edition of *MOORE*, we have left a full citation.

§ 1.07   CIVIL PROCEDURE IN THE CALIFORNIA COURTS

[1]   Introductory Note on California Civil Procedure

California Civil Procedure refers to the rules, doctrines, and policies that govern civil litigation in the California courts. Like civil procedure in other states and in the federal courts, civil procedure in the California courts is dominated by *positive law*, in particular, by statutes or *codes* enacted by the California Legislature. Also like other jurisdictions, civil procedure in California is not about trial. Litigation in the California courts is predominantly pretrial practice. The vast majority of civil actions are resolved prior to trial, often because the court granted a dispositive pretrial motion or because the parties agreed to settle the dispute. California court statistics for fiscal year 2010-11 indicate that 81% of civil cases involving claims of more than $25,000 ("unlimited civil cases"), and 93% of civil cases involving claims for a lesser amount ("limited civil cases"), were disposed of before trial.[62]

Despite these general similarities, there are some specific differences between civil procedure in the federal and the California courts. Some are merely matters of form. For example, the California courts use different terminology. A federal court "motion to dismiss the plaintiff's complaint for failure to state a claim upon which relief can be granted" is called a "general demurrer" in California procedure, and the federal joinder devices of "counterclaim," "cross-claim," and "impleader" which

---

[62] *See* Judicial Council of California, *2012 Court Statistics Report*, Superior Courts, Fig. 21: Caseflow Management Data, Fiscal Year 2010-11.

determine the size of civil litigation are all referred to as "cross-complaints" in California. However, the main focus of this book is not on the formal differences between California and other jurisdictions. Instead, the emphasis is on those aspects of California civil procedure that may make a significant difference in the preparation, presentation, and ultimate outcome of a civil case in the California courts as opposed to the federal system.

[2]   A Brief History of Civil Procedure in California

The history of civil procedure in California provides insight into the state's current reliance on procedural *codes*. Spanish-Mexican settlement of California began in 1769, when an expedition established the first mission in San Diego.[63] In 1781, the "Regulations for Governing the Province of the Californias" were approved by the King of Spain. These regulations provided detailed rules for the organization and administration of the pueblos, the civilian settlements which began to spring up in California; and provided that each village have a local judge, an "alcalde." Even though the Spanish Civil Law technically governed his decisions, the alcalde had no legal training at all, so he simply used common sense and the advice of "two good men" from the town. Yet, the alcalde system was the beginning of the judiciary in California. The Spanish-Mexican period in California lasted until the Mexican-American war in 1846.

California adopted the first California Constitution when it became a state in 1850. This new Constitution provided for a complex judiciary with a Supreme Court, district and county courts, and justices of the peace. However, the judicial provisions of the Constitution were not implemented by the California Legislature until 1851, when Stephen Field was elected to the California Legislature. His greatest contribution during his term as a legislator was the Civil Practice Act of 1851. This was Stephen Field's version of the "Field Code of Civil Procedure," created in New York by his older brother David Dudley Field. California's Civil Practice Act incorporated all of the important changes in civil procedure brought about by the Field Code, including abolishing the procedural distinction between law and equity, and abolishing the more restrictive traditional forms of pleading and joinder. The common law and the new procedure were accepted very quickly in a state which, at least theoretically, was governed by the civil law only years before.[64]

California further codified its law in 1872 by enacting four codes — Civil, Civil Procedure, Political, and Penal. Since then, the Code of Civil Procedure has been frequently revised to reflect litigation concerns in a rapidly growing judicial system.[65] In modern times, amendments to the Code have been greatly influenced by the Federal Rules of Civil Procedure. For example, the federal rules regarding joinder of claims and parties and for discovery of information during litigation have

---

[63] *See generally* RICHARD R. POWELL, COMPROMISES OF CONFLICTING CLAIMS: A CENTURY OF CALIFORNIA LAW, 1760 TO 1860, 19–59 (1977).

[64] *See* POWELL, COMPROMISES OF CONFLICTING CLAIMS, *supra* at 138–42.

[65] *See* Ralph N. Kleps, *The Revision and Codification of California Statutes 1849–1953*, 42 CAL. L. REV. 766 (1954).

been substantially incorporated into the California Code of Civil Procedure. However, despite the strong influence of the Federal Rules, California Civil Procedure can be quite different from federal civil procedure in many important respects.

§ 1.08   SOURCES OF CALIFORNIA PROCEDURAL LAWS

[1]   "Written Law"

According to the California Code of Civil Procedure, all laws in California are either "written" or "unwritten." This distinction corresponds to the more familiar one between *positive law* (codified rules enacted by legislatures or their delegates) and *common law* (legal doctrines declared by judges in judicial opinions). The written law is contained in the California Constitution and statutes, and in the United States Constitution and statutes.[66] Unwritten law is "observed and administered in the courts" and "is collected from the reports of the decisions of the courts."[67]

[a]   The United States Constitution and Laws

Although the origins of specific California procedural laws lie elsewhere, the United States Constitution is in one sense the ultimate source. Both as a conceptual proposition and an actual check when challenged, all state procedural laws must be consistent with the requirements of the Fourteenth Amendment. The federal Due Process Clause provides the ultimate "fairness" standard by which state procedural statutes, rules, and court actions are measured. A California procedural law which violates this federal standard is invalid and unenforceable.[68]

Article VI of the United States Constitution makes federal statutes, as well as the federal constitution, the "supreme Law of the Land." Consequently, state courts are generally obligated to enforce *substantive* claims based on federal statutes.[69] However, most federal *procedural* statutes apply only to claims litigated in the federal courts.

[b]   The California Constitution

In addition to a general Due Process provision which mirrors that of the United States Constitution, the California Constitution contains a number of more specific sections which help define the civil litigation process in the California courts. For example, Section 16 of Article I provides the following with respect to civil jury

---

[66] CAL. CODE CIV. PROC. § 1897.

[67] CAL. CODE CIV. PROC. § 1899.

[68] *See, e.g., Kulko v. Superior Court*, 436 U.S. 84 (1978) (holding California state court's exercise of personal jurisdiction over nonresident parent in child support action violated federal Due Process Clause); *Randone v. Appellate Dept.*, 5 Cal. 3d 536, 96 Cal. Rptr. 709, 488 P.2d 13 (1971), *cert. denied*, 407 U.S. 924 (1972) (holding then-existing California attachment statute, which authorized prejudgment attachment without notice and an opportunity for a hearing, violated Due Process Clause).

[69] *Testa v. Katt*, 330 U.S. 386 (1947).

trials: "Trial by jury is an inviolate right and shall be secured to all, but in a civil cause three-fourths of the jury may render a verdict." Other provisions specify the judicial power of the state courts, the structure of the court system, basic trial and appellate court jurisdiction, and the election and the removal of judges. Section 13 of Article VI imposes a prejudicial error ("miscarriage of justice") requirement as a prerequisite to overturning an erroneous judgment, and Section 14 requires that appellate decisions be in writing and with reasons stated.

[c] The California Code of Civil Procedure

The California Code of Civil Procedure (often cited as "CAL. CODE CIV. PROC." in the footnotes of this book) is the primary source of procedural law for California state courts. This Code, consisting of hundreds of statutes, covers such topics as subject matter jurisdiction, statutes of limitations, joinder of parties and claims, service of process, pleadings and motions, attachment, trial and pretrial motions, extraordinary writs, appeals, and judgments and enforcement of judgments. Unlike the relatively succinct Federal Rules of Civil Procedure which apply in federal trial courts, the California Code of Civil Procedure is lengthy, comprehensive, and quite detailed. In addition to this Code, other California codes contain important procedural provisions, often limited to particular types of cases.[70] The code approach employed by California usually means that most specific procedural questions can be answered by simply locating the relevant Code sections.

[d] California Rules of Court

Pursuant to the authority contained in the California Constitution and in various statutes, the Judicial Council of California — the policy-making branch of the California courts — has adopted numerous state-wide rules of practice and procedure. These Rules of Court supplement statutory and constitutional provisions, and have the force of law. The scope of the numerous and detailed California Rules of Court is difficult to characterize. Some rules govern procedures in the appellate courts, others fine-tune civil pretrial and trial procedures in the trial courts. Some Rules cover seemingly mundane topics, such as the form and size requirements of papers presented for filing; others provide essential information on important matters not covered elsewhere, such as the time deadlines for filing a notice of appeal. For example, the criteria for publication of appellate opinions are found in the Rules of Court and no place else.[71]

[e] Local Rules of Court

You might think a detailed Code of Civil Procedure plus hundreds of state-wide Rules of Court would provide sufficient bases for the regulation of civil procedure. Apparently, the California courts do not. The Superior Court (the trial court) in

---

[70] *E.g.*, CAL. GOV'T CODE § 900 *et seq.* (procedures for presentation of claims against public entities and officials under the California Government Claims Act); CAL. FAM. CODE §§ 200–291 (procedures relating to dissolution of marriage and related proceedings); CAL. CIVIL CODE §§ 3274–3424 (monetary and other judicial relief); CAL. EVID. CODE §§ 450–460 (judicial notice); CAL. BUS. & PROF. CODE §§ 6146–6149 (limitations on contingent fee agreements).

[71] CAL. CT. R. 8.1100–8.1125.

each county has promulgated numerous local rules applicable to civil actions. Typically these rules govern such areas of local variation as the filing requirements for papers, the procedures for scheduling hearings, telephonic rulings, and special rules for specific departments. A local court rule has the force of a procedural statute, provided it does not conflict with statutory law or with state-wide court rules.

With the advent of the California's Trial Court Delay Reduction Act, local rules have taken on increased importance. This Act requires the Superior Court in each county to adopt local rules of procedure, including time standards for the completion of all critical stages of the litigation process, to meet the standards for delay reduction imposed by the Act. These local delay reduction rules, commonly referred to as "Fast Track" rules, are designed to achieve compliance with the case disposition time standards for civil litigation promulgated by the California Judicial Council.[72] Failure to comply with local fast track rules may lead to sanctions, usually monetary fines but in appropriate circumstances case-dispositive penalties such as dismissal of the plaintiff's lawsuit.

[2] "Unwritten" Law

[a] Judicial Decisions

Judicial decisions are a prevalent source of procedural law. The California courts not only interpret the written law, but possess the inherent power to make procedural law. For example, in the absence of a comprehensive statute, the California Supreme Court has adopted judge-made standards and procedures for class actions in the California courts.[73] Other examples are the important doctrines of *stare decisis* (the role of precedent), *res judicata* (claim preclusion), and *collateral estoppel* (issue preclusion), which determine the effect of prior court judgments on subsequent litigation.[74]

[b] Publication of Appellate Court Opinions

Decisions on the merits by the California Supreme Court and California Courts of Appeal must be in writing with the court's reasons stated.[75] All such written opinions of the California Supreme Court are published in the Official Reports (*i.e.*, the multi-volume *California Reports*). However, an opinion of the California Court

---

[72] Under the current case disposition goals, unlimited civil cases — generally, those with more than $25,000 in controversy — should be resolved as follows: (1) 75% disposed of within 12 months after filing; (2) 85% disposed of within 18 months after filing; (3) 100% disposed of within 24 months after filing. CAL. CT. R. 3.714(b)(1); STANDARDS OF JUDICIAL ADMINISTRATION, CAL. CT. R. APP. § 2.1(f)(1).

[73] *See, e.g., La Sala v. Am. Sav. & Loan Ass'n*, 5 Cal. 3d 864, 872, 97 Cal. Rptr. 849, 489 P.2d 1113 (1971) (adopting procedures for class actions); *Green v. Obledo*, 29 Cal. 3d 126, 145–46, 172 Cal. Rptr. 206, 624 P.2d 256 (1981) (same).

[74] *See, e.g., Slater v. Blackwood*, 15 Cal. 3d 791, 126 Cal. Rptr. 225, 543 P.2d 593 (1975) (claim preclusion); *Lucido v. Superior Court*, 51 Cal. 3d 335, 272 Cal. Rptr. 767, 795 P.2d 1223 (1990) (issue preclusion); *Auto Equity Sales, Inc. v. Superior Court*, 57 Cal. 2d 450, 455, 20 Cal. Rptr. 321, 369 P.2d 937 (1962) (stare decisis).

[75] CAL. CONST. art. VI, § 14.

of Appeal is published in the Official Reports (*i.e.*, the multi-volume *California Appellate Reports*) only if it satisfies one of the criteria for publication set forth in the California Rules of Court, which include the following: the opinion establishes a new rule of law, addresses or creates an apparent conflict in the law, involves a legal issue of continuing public interest, invokes a previously overlooked rule of law. Because these criteria discourage publication, only 18% of the opinions rendered by the various Courts of Appeal in civil appeals were punished in 2010-11.[76] Generally, subject to certain limited exceptions, an unpublished opinion cannot be cited or relied on by a court or a party in any other action or proceeding.[77] Because an unpublished opinion cannot be cited, it has no precedential value.[78]

[c] Secondary Authorities ("Learned Treatises")

Secondary authorities, such as learned treatises, are not themselves law and do not have the binding force of statutes, court rules, or judicial precedents. Nevertheless, they can be quite persuasive. The California courts often rely on legal treatises, scholarly publications, and secondary authorities to illuminate gray areas of the law. The most authoritative treatise by far is the ten-volume *California Procedure* authored by Bernard E. Witkin, now in its Fifth edition (2008) and supplemented annually. Other influential treatises include two loose-leaf publications that are updated annually: *California Civil Procedure Before Trial* (CEB 4th ed.) and Weil, Brown, Rylaarsdam & Edmon, *Civil Procedure Before Trial* (The Rutter Group).

---

[76] *See* Judicial Council of California, *2012 Court Statistics Report*, Courts of Appeal, Fig. 30: Civil Appeals for 2010-11.

[77] CAL. CT. R. 8.1115(a).

[78] *See, e.g., Nelson v. Justice Court*, 86 Cal. App. 3d 64, 66, 150 Cal. Rptr. 39 (1978); *Heaton v. Marin Cnty. Emp. Retirement Bd.*, 63 Cal. App. 3d 421, 431, 133 Cal. Rptr. 809 (1976).

Chapter 2

SELECTING A COURT — AN INTRODUCTION

§ 2.01 THE CHOICES: STATE AND FEDERAL JUDICIAL SYSTEMS

After a lawyer has agreed to represent a prospective plaintiff and tentatively identified one or more legal "theories" of recovery, she must select the court in which to sue. This decision is enriched and complicated in the United States by the existence not only of fifty-one separate state judicial systems,[1] but also of the federal judicial system. Before we can introduce the factors that affect the choice, we need to describe these alternatives.

It is easiest to start with the federal system, because it is simplest. There are three layers of federal courts. At the bottom lie the federal district courts. These are courts of *original jurisdiction*, so called because they are where judicial cases originate — where they are filed and initially tried.[2] The district courts, like all federal courts, are also courts of *limited subject matter jurisdiction*, in that statutes authorize them to hear only certain kinds of cases.[3] The most important are those involving questions of federal law ("federal question cases") and those involving state law claims valued at more than $75,000 between citizens of different states ("diversity cases").[4] The district courts are assigned to districts whose geographic boundaries correspond with those of the smallest states or with parts of the larger states.[5] For example, the federal trial courts for New York are the United States District Courts for the Southern, Eastern, Western and Northern Districts of New York.

United States Courts of Appeals make up the middle layer.[6] They are courts of *appellate jurisdiction*, so called because they are authorized only to review decisions which come to them on appeal from district courts,[7] certain specialized

---

[1] The District of Columbia was given its own judicial system by District of Columbia Court Reform and Criminal Procedure Act of 1970, Pub. L. 91-358, 84 Stat. 473 (codified in scattered sections of 28 U.S.C.).

[2] Cases may also originate in administrative agencies or in certain specialized courts created by Congress. *E.g.*, 28 U.S.C. §§ 171–179 (Court of Federal Claims); 28 U.S.C. §§ 1581–1585 (Court of International Trade).

[3] *See* § 5.01 (subject matter jurisdiction), *infra*.

[4] *See* § 5.01[2] (federal jurisdiction in general); §§ 5.02–5.06 (particulars of federal question and diversity jurisdiction), *infra*.

[5] *See* 28 U.S.C. § 133.

[6] On appellate systems generally, see § 13.07, *infra*.

[7] *See* 28 U.S.C. §§ 1291–1292.

federal courts, or federal administrative agencies. The country is divided into twelve geographic circuits,[8] and appeals from the district courts in each circuit are taken to the court of appeals for that circuit. Appeals from many of the administrative agencies go to the Court of Appeals for the D.C. Circuit, while appeals from various specialized federal courts[9] are taken to a thirteenth circuit called the Court of Appeals for the Federal Circuit.[10]

The United States Supreme Court sits atop the federal system. It has original jurisdiction over cases affecting ambassadors and in which states are parties, and appellate jurisdiction in all others.[11] While most appellate jurisdiction exercised by federal courts of appeal is *mandatory*, meaning that a court of appeals must accept a properly filed appeal, the Supreme Court's appellate jurisdiction is chiefly *discretionary*, meaning that it is free to decide whether to hear an appeal by granting a party's petition to it for a *writ of certiorari* ("granting cert"). In other words, a party who loses a final judgment in the district court has a *right* to appeal that judgment to the court of appeals. But a party who loses in the court of appeals usually can only ask ("petition") the Supreme Court to exercise its discretion to hear his appeal. (It usually declines.)[12]

State judicial systems have three or four layers. At the bottom are usually a variety of courts of *limited or special subject matter jurisdiction*, authorized, for example, to hear only traffic, landlord-tenant, small claims or probate cases. All states also have one court of original and *general jurisdiction* that hears all claims not exclusively vested in courts of limited jurisdiction. These claims may include state claims and most federal question claims, which a plaintiff can assert either in state or in federal district courts. (The state and federal courts are said to have *concurrent jurisdiction* over such federal claims.) State courts of general jurisdiction often exist at the county level, but their designations differ widely. In the District of Columbia, for example, they are called the superior courts, in Virginia circuit courts, and in New York (somewhat perversely) supreme courts. To add to the confusion, in some states these courts also enjoy some form of appellate jurisdiction over cases originally brought in state courts of limited jurisdiction.

State systems have at least one more layer, a court of exclusively or predominantly appellate jurisdiction at the top of their judicial systems, variously called the supreme court, the court of appeals, or, in Massachusetts, the Supreme Judicial Court. Many more populous states also have an intermediate appellate layer, roughly corresponding to courts of appeals in the federal system. Intermediate state appellate courts are created to relieve the caseload burden on the highest state court. Jurisdiction in inferior state appellate courts is usually mandatory, leaving the highest state court in the system to exercise considerable discretion in selecting cases for further review, much like the United States Supreme Court.

---

[8] *See* 28 U.S.C. § 41.

[9] *See* note 2, *supra*.

[10] *See* 28 U.S.C §§ 1292(c), 1295.

[11] U.S. Const. art. III, § 2.

[12] On appellate systems generally, *see* § 13.07, *infra*.

On matters of state law, the highest state court has the last word. However, the United States Supreme Court has the authority to review state court rulings on the meaning and application of federal law (including, of course, the United States Constitution). This creates the possibility of a level above state high courts in federal question adjudications. In practice, the possibility is remote because, as we noted above, the Supreme Court usually denies review.[13] This means that the highest state courts, as well as the federal courts of appeal, are, as a practical matter, courts of last resort in many federal question cases.[14]

The coexistence of state and federal judicial systems may present the claimant with a choice of forums. A federal court option exists if the claim exceeds $75,000, and the prospective plaintiff and defendants are from different states, or if the claim involves certain questions of federal law.[15] The option of trial in state court is less restricted, available except in the relatively few situations where federal courts enjoy exclusive subject matter jurisdiction.[16] And, as we shall examine in the next section, geographic affiliations of the parties or claims may offer the claimant the choice of state and federal courts in more than one state.

---

[13] The Supreme Court has traditionally kept abreast of its workload. Yet the Court has managed this in recent years only by refusing to review a large number of cases properly within its appellate jurisdiction. *See generally* Paul M. Bator, *What Is Wrong with the Supreme Court?*, 51 U. Pitt. L. Rev. 673 (1990) (noting the Supreme Court's high rate of review denial, and positing that this may be a symptom of a system that is no longer "acceptable and adequate . . . for the essential professional tasks of stabilizing, clarifying, and improving the national law"); *see also* Arthur D. Hellman, *The Shrunken Docket of the Rehnquist Court*, 1996 Sup. Ct. Rev. 403 (1996) (identifying a few of the more restrictive changes in the Supreme Court's case selection process).

[14] Due to its sparing exercise of its discretionary certiorari jurisdiction, the Supreme Court hears only a small number of federal question cases. Even as early as 1976, scholars asserted that "Supreme Court review has become an exceedingly unlikely event in most federal litigation." Paul D. Carrington, Daniel J. Meador & Maurice Rosenberg, Justice on Appeal 209 (1976) (citations omitted). The numbers still bear this out. In a 12-month period ending September 30, 2011, the Supreme Court reviewed only 0.57% of federal appeals court dispositions of civil suits, and only 2.2% of cases in which petitions for certiorari were filed. Of the over 12,000 appeals terminated, petitions were filed in 3,193 cases, and review was granted in only 70. *See* Administrative Office of U.S. Courts, Judicial Business of the United States Courts, in Annual Report of the Director, Administrative Office of the U.S. Courts, tables B-1A, B-2 (2011). The Court seldom explains *why* review was denied in a particular case — but a few Justices have acknowledged that a common reason is that an issue lacked sufficient "percolation," which is Supreme Court slang that signifies a situation in which at least two Circuit Courts of Appeals interpret the same federal law in a different manner. *See* Todd J. Tiberi, Comment, *Supreme Court Denials of Certiorari in Conflicts Cases: Percolation or Procrastination?*, 54 U. Pitt. L. Rev. 861 (1993) (citing H.W. Perry, Jr., Deciding to Decide 230 (1991)). Fewer data exist on Supreme Court supervision of federal question decisions in state courts, but the lack of effective supervision there appears to be at least as pronounced. *See generally* Preble Stolz, *Federal Review of State Court Decisions of Federal Questions: The Need for Additional Appellate Capacity*, 64 Calif. L. Rev. 943 (1976).

[15] *See* § 5.03 *infra*.

[16] Plaintiffs can bring certain cases (federal antitrust, patent and copyright, bankruptcy, etc.) only in federal court. For a discussion of the scope and intended purposes of exclusive federal jurisdiction, see Martin H. Redish, Federal Jurisdiction: Tensions in the Allocation of Judicial Power 149–56 (2d ed. 1990); ALI, Study of the Division of Jurisdiction Between State and Federal Courts 182–86 (1969); *see also* John F. Preis, *Reassessing the Purposes of Federal Question Jurisdiction*, 42 Wake Forest L. Rev. 247 (2007) (identifying the traditional reasoning for the existence of exclusive federal jurisdiction, and positing a few rationales for its continued relevance)

§ 2.02 FACTORS INFLUENCING THE SELECTION OF A COURT

Every first year law student intuitively senses that it would be unfair to require a Vermonter who has never been to or had contact with Alaska to defend a lawsuit brought there. The law acknowledges that unfairness by conditioning a court's *personal jurisdiction* (the power to issue a judgment binding a person or affecting his property) on some voluntary contact or political affiliation between the defendant and the *forum state* in which the action is brought. Historically, the principal basis for and limitation upon personal jurisdiction was territorial (essentially, presence within the state), hence our adoption of the term *territorial jurisdiction* as a generic description for this requirement. Chapter 3 discusses this essential factor in selecting a court.

We considered in the last section how the coexistence of state and federal judicial systems creates the possibility of choice within the same geographical area, choice limited by the constraints of *subject matter* jurisdiction. Chapter 5 discusses this factor. Of obvious interest to the plaintiff's lawyer, it also controls opportunities for the defendant to *remove* the action against him from state to federal court, as discussed in § 5.07.

The defendant's concerns over the convenience of the forum selected by plaintiff are also entitled to recognition. Beyond that, the judicial system as a whole has an efficiency interest in shifting litigation to the most generally convenient locations. These interests are served by the law of *venue*, discussed in Chapter 6.

Lawyers take these legal constraints into account in deciding where to file suit. They also consider a variety of tactical factors.[17] When legal constraints permit a choice, tactical factors should control the decision where to file.

One obvious tactical factor is the identity of the judge who will preside over the litigation. The manner in which cases are assigned to particular judges is often too random to permit accurate prediction. Yet lawyers frequently can make useful comparisons about the quality of judges in different kinds of courts. Some have argued, for example, that the kinds of cases brought in federal court, as well as the appointment process, life tenure, prestige, salary, and research resources of federal judges attract persons to the federal bench who are more capable and less susceptible to majoritarian pressures than those attracted to the state bench.[18]

---

[17] *See generally* James A. Dooley, *Selecting the Forum — Plaintiff's Position*, 3 Am. Jur. Trials 553 (1963); Victor E. Flango, *Attorneys' Perspectives on Choice of Forum in Diversity Cases*, 25 Akron L. Rev. 41 (1991); Josh H. Groce, *Selecting the Forum — Defendant's Position*, 3 Am. Jur. Trials 611 (1963); Ralph C. McCullough & James L. Underwood, Civil Trial Manual 2 at 89–140 (2d ed. 1980); Marvin R. Summers, *Analysis of Factors That Influence Choice of Forum in Diversity Cases*, 47 Iowa L. Rev. 933 (1962); Note, *Forum Shopping Reconsidered*, 103 Harv. L. Rev. 1677 (1990).

[18] *Compare, e.g.*, Thomas B. Marvell, *The Rationales for Federal Question Jurisdiction: An Empirical Examination of Student Rights Litigation*, 1984 Wis. L. Rev. 1315 (lawyers representing students select federal courts because they are more protective of student rights), *and* Burt Neuborne, *The Myth of Parity*, 90 Harv. L. Rev. 1105 (1977) (federal courts are superior to state courts in protecting federal rights), *with* Michael E. Solimine & James L. Walker, *Constitutional Litigation in Federal and State Courts: An Empirical Analysis of Judicial Parity*, 10 Hastings Const. L.Q. 213 (1983) (state courts are no more hostile to vindication of federal rights than federal courts).

Lawyers given a choice thus tend to file civil rights actions in federal rather than state courts.[19]

The court's calendar can also be a tactical concern. During the 12-month period preceding September 30, 2011, for example, the median time from commencement of a civil action to disposition at trial in federal district courts ranged from just under 18 months in the fastest district to over five years in the slowest.[20] A plaintiff's lawyer who is anxious to move the case through trial might file it in one of the faster federal district courts or opt instead for a state court with a shorter trial calendar.

Sundry procedural differences between courts may also influence court selection.[21] Extensive provision in the federal rules for discovery — court-supported fact-gathering by the parties — may attract some lawyers who need discovery to develop their cases and discourage others who already command the facts or whose clients are averse to discovery of *their* facts. Many other procedural factors — including the availability of jury trial, the composition of jury panels (for example, are they selected from predominantly urban populations — which some think will be more liberal in granting money judgments — or rural populations — which some think will be more conservative?), the required level of agreement for verdicts (unanimous or majority?), the applicable rules of evidence (will they admit or exclude a crucial piece of evidence?), and the availability of appellate review — can influence court selection. Of course, a lawyer's familiarity with procedures of particular courts also influences her choice of court. The "home court advantage" doesn't apply just to sports teams; lawyers typically opt for their home courts, not necessarily because the judge will lean their way, but because they know their way around and the court is convenient for them.

Client characteristics may also be an important consideration in choice of court. Some lawyers prefer federal courts when their client is from outside the state.[22] One study suggests that client characteristics, together with the quality of judges and the convenience of the court, in fact, are the most important reasons lawyers choose one forum over another, outweighing procedural considerations.[23]

Finally, the substantive law that courts will apply can be a crucial factor in forum choice. Although there is much support in modern choice-of-law theory for the idea that the law chosen in a case should not vary according to where the case is tried, local choice-of-law ("conflicts") rules and the manner in which they are applied do not always reflect this idea. This can be an enormous incentive for interstate forum-shopping in search of favorable substantive law.[24] Chapter 7 discusses the

---

[19] *See, e.g.*, Neuborne, note 18, *supra*.

[20] 2011 ADMIN. OFF. U.S. COURTS ANNUAL REPORT OF THE DIR. Table C-5 (with the Eastern District of Pennsylvania having the "fastest" time to trial disposition, and the District of the Virgin Islands the "slowest").

[21] *See generally* Dooley, note 17, *supra*, §§ 19–39; Groce, note 17, *supra*, §§ 9–15.

[22] *See* Flango, note 17, *supra*, at 105. *See* § 5.04, *infra*.

[23] Flango, note 17, *supra*, at 105.

[24] For a survey of developments, see Gene R. Shreve, *Choice of Law and the Forgiving Constitution*, 71 IND. L.J. 271 (1996).

choice of applicable law in federal court, while the conflict of laws in general is treated in a companion to this volume.[25]

Although every plaintiff looks for an advantageous forum in selecting a court in which to sue (given a choice), courts sometimes decry such "forum-shopping," almost imbuing it with a sense of impropriety. But as long as the intersection of jurisdictional rules and venue provides forum choices, parties will necessarily have to make them, and, of course, will make them to benefit their clients and themselves. Indeed, the *Model Rules of Professional Conduct* comment that a lawyer has a "duty to use legal procedure for the fullest benefit of the client's cause,"[26] leading one scholar to assert that this duty "may include selecting a forum with little connection to the events giving rise to a cause of action if that forum is an acceptable forum under the law, despite the fact that the attorney may be accused of taking advantage of 'loopholes' or 'technicalities.' "[27] To return to the game analogy from Chapter One, "The rules in litigation include the plaintiff's ability to choose which set of rules will govern the game" by choosing the forum.[28] These rules guard against any resulting unfairness, as we shall see. If they waste resources by providing too many choices, the best solution is probably to go after the rules, not the lawyers who use them.

§ 2.03   THE CALIFORNIA JUDICIAL SYSTEM

[1]   The California Judicial Branch

The California court system — the largest in the nation, with more than 2,000 judicial officers, 19,000 court employees, and nearly 10 million cases per year — serves over 38 million people.[29] The California Constitution vests the judicial power of California in the Supreme Court, Courts of Appeal, and Superior Courts. The Constitution also provides for the formation and functions of the Judicial Council, the policy-making body for the state courts.

[a]   Superior Courts — California's Trial Courts

The vast majority of cases in California are commenced in one of the Superior Courts, which are located in each of the state's 58 counties. Superior Courts have trial jurisdiction over all criminal cases and over all civil cases including family law, probate, juvenile, and general civil matters. Over one million civil cases are filed in the Superior Courts each year, and a roughly equal number are disposed of on an

---

[25] *See generally* William M. Richman & William L. Reynolds, Understanding Conflict of Laws Ch. 4 (3d ed. 2002).

[26] American Bar Ass'n, Model Rules of Professional Conduct and Code of Judicial Conduct Rule 3.1 cmt. 1 (1983).

[27] Mary Garvey Algero, *In Defense of Forum Shopping: A Realistic Look at Selecting a Venue*, 78 Neb. L. Rev. 79, 106 (1999).

[28] Debra Lyn Bassett, *The Forum Game*, 84 N.C. L. Rev. 333, 336 (2006).

[29] Judicial Council of California, *2012 Court Statistics Report*, The California Court System.

annual basis.[30] Despite their heavy caseload, the superior courts are reasonably efficient. In fiscal year 2010-11, 70% of all unlimited civil cases (generally, cases where the amount in controversy exceeds $25,000) were disposed of within 12 months, 85% within 18 months, and 92% within 24 months.[31]

[b]　California Courts of Appeal

The Courts of Appeal are California's intermediate courts of review. Courts of Appeal have appellate jurisdiction over decisions of the Superior Courts and in certain other cases prescribed by statute. California statutes divide the state geographically into six appellate districts, each containing a Court of Appeal. Each district has a presiding justice and two or more associate justices. Cases are decided by three-judge panels. Decisions of Courts of Appeal are published in the *California Appellate Reports*, but only if they meet certain criteria for publication.[32] During fiscal year 2010-11, only 18% of Court of Appeal opinions in civil appeals were certified as meeting the criteria for publication, generally the same as in prior years.

In the vast majority of civil appeals, the decision of the Superior Court is affirmed by the Court of Appeal. For example, with respect to the over 3,000 civil appeals disposed of by written opinion during fiscal year 2010-11, the Superior Court was affirmed in full in 69% of the cases and affirmed with modification in another 10%.[33] Despite the large number of appeals, the Courts of Appeal are fairly efficient, at least when compared to some other jurisdictions. Statewide, the median time for civil appeals disposed of by written opinion in 2010-11 was 442 days from notice of appeal to decision, and 90% of civil appeals were resolved within 690 days.[34]

[c]　California Supreme Court

The Supreme Court of California, consisting of one Chief Justice and six Associate Justices, is the state's highest court. The California Constitution gives the Supreme Court the authority to review decisions of the state Courts of Appeal. Supreme Court review in civil cases and in most criminal cases is discretionary.[35]

---

[30] Judicial Council of California, *2012 Court Statistics Report*, Superior Courts, Fig. 3, Civil Filings and Dispositions, Fiscal Years 2001-02 through 2010-11.

[31] Judicial Council of California, *2012 Court Statistics Report*, Superior Courts, Civil Case Processing Time. The case processing times for limited civil cases (cases involving less than $25,000) were shorter: 86% were disposed of within 12 months, 95% within 18 months, and 98% within 24 months.

[32] In general, the opinion is published if it establishes a new rule of law, involves a legal issue of continuing public interest, criticizes existing law, or makes a significant contribution to legal literature. CAL. CT. R. 8.1105(c).

[33] Judicial Council of California, *2012 Court Statistics Report*, Courts of Appeal, Appeals Terminated by Written Opinion.

[34] Judicial Council of California, *2012 Court Statistics Report*, Courts of Appeal, Fig. 33.

[35] CAL. CONST. art. VI, § 12; CAL. CT. R. 8.500. However, the California Supreme Court must review all cases in which a judgment of death has been pronounced by the Superior Court. CAL. CONST. art. VI, § 11. Such cases are automatically appealed directly from the Superior Court to the California Supreme Court. CAL. PENAL CODE § 1239(b).

The Supreme Court also has the discretion to review an entire Court of Appeal decision or only selected issues, leaving the decision undisturbed on the remaining issues.[36] A party who seeks review of a lower court decision must file a timely petition for review in the Supreme Court. Only a small percentage of these petitions are granted. For example, the Court granted 5% of the petitions for review in civil matters during fiscal year 2010-11.[37] As a result, even combining civil and criminal cases, the Supreme Court typically issues a total of only 100–125 written opinions per year.[38]

[d] California Judicial Council

Chaired by the Chief Justice, the Judicial Council is the governing body of the California courts. The California Constitution directs the Judicial Council to provide policy guidelines to the courts, to make recommendations annually to the Governor and Legislature, and to adopt and revise California Rules of Court in the areas of court administration, practice and procedure.

[2] Factors Influencing the Selection of the California Courts

[a] Interstate Selection: The California Courts vs. The Courts of Another State

Although the doctrine of personal jurisdiction may impose some legal constraints, often a plaintiff has the option to choose a court in one of several states within which to litigate a civil action. Numerous tactical factors may influence a plaintiff to select a court in California rather than in some other state. Often the decision is based on a comparison of each state's substantive law or of its statute of limitations. A rational plaintiff will choose a state whose courts will apply the substantive law that is most favorable to the plaintiff's case. Likewise, a plaintiff will choose a state where the plaintiff's action is not barred by the statute of limitations. There may also be differences in the procedures applied by the courts in each state, which in some instances may be of sufficient importance that a plaintiff will choose to litigate in one state rather than another.

California is often said to be a "plaintiff-friendly" state. This depiction may be accurate with respect to personal injury cases, where California's substantive tort law is more favorable to plaintiffs as a class than is the law of many other states. Likewise, California's procedural law may be more advantageous to plaintiffs than that of many other states. For these and other tactical reasons, a plaintiff may choose to litigate in a California court as opposed to in some other state.

---

[36] *See* Cal. Const. art. VI, § 12; Cal. Ct. R. 8.516.

[37] Judicial Council of California, *2012 Court Statistics Report*, Supreme Court, Table 1.

[38] Judicial Council of California, *2012 Court Statistics Report*, Supreme Court, Fig. 15.

[b]   Intrastate Selection: The California Courts vs. the Federal Courts

In many cases, a plaintiff has the option of filing an action in either a federal court or a California state court. The rules of subject matter jurisdiction, which determine what types of cases a court has the power to hear, often permit an action to be brought in either court. For example, nearly all actions alleging a violation of a federal law ("federal question" cases) may be litigated in either a federal or a state court. In addition, many actions alleging a violation of state law may be brought in either court, although the federal court's jurisdiction is limited to those cases where the plaintiff and the defendant are from different states and the amount in controversy exceeds $75,000 ("diversity cases"). When the option of litigating in either a federal or a California court is available, tactical factors will likely influence the plaintiff's selection of one court over the other.

Unlike the decision to litigate in one state rather than in another state, considerations regarding substantive law are usually not relevant when choosing between a federal and a state court. This is because in cases where the federal and state courts have concurrent jurisdiction, both courts must apply the same substantive law. In federal question cases, the federal substantive law applied is the same regardless of the court. In diversity cases, the state substantive law applied must be the same as would be applied by a court of the state in which the federal court sits.[39] But each court will apply its own procedural law, which may not necessarily be the same with respect to some important issues. For example, California's procedural rules and court decisions encourage litigation of certain types of class actions in state court which, pursuant to the corresponding provisions of the Federal Rules of Civil Procedure, could not be maintained in federal court. In such cases, the plaintiff would obviously prefer to litigate in a California superior court rather than a federal district court, even if the federal court is located in California. Of course, the defendant would prefer to litigate such cases in federal court and, if authorized by the federal jurisdictional statutes, would undoubtedly remove the action from state to federal court. In this manner, such procedural differences influence each party's selection of a California state court as opposed to a federal court.

---

[39] This result is dictated by federalism principles commonly referred to as the "*Erie* doctrine." The *Erie* doctrine is discussed in considerable detail in §§ 7.01–7.07, *infra*.

Chapter 3

A COURT WITH JURISDICTION OVER PERSONS AND THINGS

§ 3.01 PERSONAL JURISDICTION BASICS

[1] How and Why Personal Jurisdiction Problems Arise

The function of civil litigation is to dispose of controversies by subjecting them to a formal, authoritative process. The process works by ultimately producing binding judgments.[1] For reasons that shall become clear, however, courts cannot be free to issue binding judgments in every civil action filed, without regard to where the cause of action arose or where the defendant resides. Courts are restrained by limitations on territorial jurisdiction (courts' jurisdiction over persons and things). In this chapter we will substitute for "territorial jurisdiction," the term "personal jurisdiction," which historically referred to one subset of territorial jurisdiction but is now widely used as a synonym for territorial jurisdiction in all its forms.[2]

Consider the following example. A, a citizen of Hawaii, travels to New York City on business. A steps off of a curb into the path of an automobile driven by B. A receives medical treatment in New York, returns to Hawaii and files suit there for medical expenses incurred in New York resulting from the accident. Service of process in the Hawaii case reaches B in New York by mail. B is a lifetime citizen of New York State. He does no business in Hawaii, owns no property there, and has never visited the state.

Can a Hawaii court entertain this case? No. The Hawaii court would clearly lack personal jurisdiction. Even without benefit of details of the law of personal jurisdiction that follow, we can see why a Hawaii court should not have the power to hear the case. It would add substantially to B's burden of being a defendant for him to have to defend against A's claim in far-away Hawaii. Neither B nor the facts of the controversy have any connection with Hawaii to suggest that imposition of

---

[1] *See generally* Chapter 15, *infra.* This is true unless the case settles or is dismissed without prejudice prior to final judgment.

[2] The term "personal jurisdiction" derives from *in personam* jurisdiction, one of three traditional categories of territorial jurisdiction. The other two are *in rem* and *quasi in rem* jurisdiction. *See* § 3.01[3], *infra.* By far the largest number of cases entertained by courts are founded on *in personam* jurisdiction. The Supreme Court's decisions setting limits on *in personam* jurisdiction have added importance because it has extended them to all forms of territorial jurisdiction. *See* § 3.09. These developments have encouraged interchangeable use of the terms territorial jurisdiction and personal jurisdiction. We follow this approach in the text when context permits.

Hawaii jurisdiction would be justified. B could go to Hawaii and question the Hawaii court's personal jurisdiction there, but even this would unfairly burden him. The law of personal jurisdiction should and does permit B to sit tight in New York, take no part in the Hawaii proceeding, and successfully resist a Hawaii default judgment[3] if A ever presents it for enforcement in New York (which A must do to satisfy his Hawaii judgment if B's assets are in New York).[4]

But what if we change the facts of the example? Suppose that B (not A) was the traveler, that B struck A while B was driving a rented car in Hawaii. Now the Hawaii court clearly has personal jurisdiction. Can you see why?[5] Or suppose we leave the accident in New York, but give B a condominium in Hawaii. Could B still safely assume that the Hawaii court lacked jurisdiction?[6] Even if B had a substantial personal jurisdiction argument to make, would it still be wise for him to refuse to appear and raise it in the Hawaii case?[7]

[2] Law that Limits the Reach of Personal Jurisdiction

[a] State Courts — Due Process and "Long Arm" Statutes

The primary restraint on the territorial jurisdiction of state courts is the Due Process Clause of the Fourteenth Amendment to the United States Constitution. In "opaque few words,"[8] the Clause provides that "[n]o State shall . . . deprive any person of life, liberty, or property, without due process of law." A claim is "property" within the meaning of the Clause, which cannot be forfeited through state proceedings lacking due process.[9] The protections of due process are similarly available to those against whom claims are made.[10]

The Due Process Clause also affords litigants rights to notice and the opportunity to be heard in state court.[11] These rights, however, are secured by a branch of due process doctrine separate and distinct from that which governs personal jurisdiction.[12] The concerns that give the Due Process Clause life in the personal

---

[3] A default judgment may be entered when a defendant fails to respond to the complaint in any manner. *See* FED. R. CIV. P. 55.

[4] *See* § 3.10, *infra.*

[5] Hawaii's authority to impose jurisdiction on B derives from a regulatory concern over acts committed in the forum state. *See* § 3.04[2], *infra* (specific jurisdiction).

[6] Maybe not. *See* § 3.08, *infra.*

[7] No. *See* § 3.10[2], *infra.*

[8] Kevin M. Clermont, *A Global Law of Jurisdiction and Judgments: Views from the United States and Japan*, 37 CORNELL INT'L L.J. 1, 2 (2004).

[9] *Logan v. Zimmerman Brush Co.*, 455 U.S. 422, 428–29 (1982).

[10] "Any claim asserted by a plaintiff is simply the reverse side of what is at stake to the defendant; the same property is at stake for both." James R. Pielemeier, *Due Process Limitations on the Application of Collateral Estoppel Against Nonparties to Prior Litigation*, 63 B.U.L. REV. 383, 398 (1983). *See also World-Wide Volkswagen Corp. v. Woodson*, 444 U.S. 286, 291–94 (1980) ("[d]ue process requires that the defendant[s] be . . . subject to the personal jurisdiction of the court").

[11] *See* Chapter 4, *infra.*

[12] The Supreme Court explained and compared the two branches of due process doctrine in *Phillips*

jurisdiction setting are more elusive and less agreed upon by courts and commentators.[13]

There is agreement, however, that the Due Process Clause should protect the nonresident[14] defendant from suffering unreasonably from plaintiff's choice of forum. To uphold jurisdiction in the forum selected by plaintiff at the very least forces the defendant to go there and move for a *forum non conveniens* dismissal: a dismissal on the ground that there is a more convenient place for the litigation.[15] When a court exercises its considerable discretion to deny the motion, defendant is forced to litigate the merits in the courts of that state.

State law may set additional limits on the reach of state courts' territorial jurisdiction. Most state courts enjoy only as much territorial jurisdiction over nonresident defendants as their legislatures have chosen to confer by statute.

It is therefore possible that the statutory scheme could leave the courts of a state short of the full scope of authority over nonresident defendants permitted under federal constitutional law. In practice, however, this does not seem to be much of a problem. All states now have so-called *long-arm statutes*, which endow their courts with all, or nearly all the jurisdictional authority permitted by due process.

Long arm statutes provide personal jurisdiction over nonresident defendants who cannot be found and served in the forum state. They have generally taken one of two forms. The first is a laundry-list approach that attempts to specify factual circumstances likely to satisfy due process requirements and authorizes the court to exercise jurisdiction over nonresidents in cases where such circumstances arise.[16] The second takes a blanket approach, conferring all jurisdiction permitted by state and federal constitutional law.[17]

Petroleum Co. v. Shutts, 472 U.S. 797 (1985), concluding that the passive members of plaintiffs' nationwide class were entitled to due process protections of notice and the opportunity to be heard, but that the minimum contacts constraint imposed by due process on personal jurisdiction did not apply to their claims. For discussions of the case, see Arthur R. Miller & David Crump, *Jurisdiction and Choice of Law in Multistate Class Actions After* Phillips Petroleum Co. v. Shutts., 96 YALE L.J. 1 (1986); John E. Kennedy, *The Supreme Court Meets the Bride of Frankenstein:* Phillips Petroleum Co. v. Shutts *and the State Multistate Class Action*, 34 U. KAN. L. REV. 255 (1985); § 9.09[1], *infra.*

[13] Critics include A. Benjamin Spencer, *Jurisdiction to Adjudicate: A Revised Analysis*, 73 U. CHI. L. REV. 617, 618 (2006) ("[T]he law of personal jurisdiction has blossomed into an incoherent and precarious doctrine that many commentators have long vilified as being in need of reform."), and Linda S. Simard, *Meeting Expectations: Two Profiles for Specific Jurisdiction*, 38 IND. L. REV. 343, 344 (2005) ("[T]he doctrine of personal jurisdiction is largely in a state of disarray.").

[14] Most significant territorial jurisdiction cases involve defendants who do not reside in the forum state. The distinction between the concepts of *residence* and *citizenship* is unclear. However, it is at least true that the Due Process Clause poses no significant obstacle to the forum state's exercise of territorial jurisdiction over its own citizens.

[15] *See* § 6.02[1], *infra.*

[16] *E.g.*, NEW YORK CIV. PRAC. LAW AND RULES § 302(a); 735 ILL. COMP. STAT. ANN. 512-209.

[17] *E.g.*, CAL. CIV. PROC. CODE § 410.10 (2006); N.J. COURT RULES 1969 R. 4:4-4(b)(1) (2006); R.I. GEN. LAWS ANN. § 9-5-33. For example, the California provision states: "A court of this state may exercise jurisdiction on any basis not inconsistent with the Constitution of this state or of the United States."

Neither approach is ideal.[18] Implicit in the assumption of lawmaking authority by state legislatures is a judgment that they have a special function to perform in determining the appropriate reach of their court's personal jurisdiction. They may be abdicating that responsibility when they enact blanket long-arm statutes. Moreover, in declining to be specific, the legislature withholds guidance from those wishing to learn in advance whether their in-state activities will expose them to personal jurisdiction.[19] On the other hand, legislatures enacting categorical long-arm statutes (sometimes also called "enumerated long-arm statutes") may unwittingly omit some legitimate factual category, impairing their courts' useful range of personal jurisdiction.[20]

Differences between the two approaches, however, have not turned out to be great in application. The state courts have tended to interpret their statutes to confer all or virtually all jurisdiction permitted by due process, regardless of the statutes' language.[21]

[b]   Federal Courts — Due Process and Rule 4

The Fourteenth Amendment does not apply to federal courts. The Due Process Clause in the Fifth Amendment to the Constitution limits the authority of federal courts. But the Constitution does not limit federal courts to the same degree as their state counterparts. It is at least arguable that the Fifth Amendment permits federal courts to exercise territorial jurisdiction over all United States citizens,[22] permitting greater geographical reach than the Fourteenth Amendment permits state courts.[23]

---

[18] For a review of the strengths and weaknesses of each approach, see Douglas D. McFarland, *Dictum Run Wild: How Long-Arm Statutes Extended to the Limits of Due Process*, 84 B.U. L. Rev. 491, 531–36 (2004).

[19] Two recent commentators argue against the blanket approach. McFarland, note 18, *supra*, at 536; Patrick J. Borchers, *Internet Libel: The Consequences of a Non-Rule Approach to Personal Jurisdiction*, 98 Nw. U. L. Rev. 473, 474 (2004).

[20] Russell J. Weintraub, Commentary on the Conflict of Laws 219-20 (6th ed. 2010).

[21] Robert H. Abrams & Paul R. Dimond, *Toward a Constitutional Framework for the Control of State Court Jurisdiction*, 69 Minn. L. Rev. 75, 84 n.43 (1984). For one such example, see Carole L. Baab, Note, *Current Status of Personal and General Jurisdiction in Minnesota*, 16 Wm. Mitchell L. Rev. 309, 334 (1990). *But cf.* M. Glannon, Civil Procedure 31 (6th ed. 2008) ("Unfortunately, courts have not always grasped [the] distinction between broad interpretation of . . . enumerated acts and absorbing the whole constitutional sphere.").

[22] The principle that defendants submit to personal jurisdiction in exchange for the benefits of forum citizenship is most fully developed in the law of state court jurisdiction. *See* § 3.04[2] (suit in defendant's home state), *infra*. But the Supreme Court has also applied the principle to uphold a federal court's territorial jurisdiction over a United States citizen. *Blackmer v. United States*, 284 U.S. 421 (1932).

[23] For differing views, *compare* Robert H. Abrams, *Power, Convenience, and the Elimination of Personal Jurisdiction in the Federal Courts*, 58 Ind. L.J. 1 (1982) (supporting the point), James, Hazard & Leubsdorf § 2.34 (same), *with* Maryellen Fullerton, *Constitutional Limits on Nationwide Personal Jurisdiction in the Federal Courts*, 79 Nw. U. L. Rev. 1 (1984) (questioning whether the Fifth Amendment should permit a federal court to exercise territorial jurisdiction if the Fourteenth Amendment would prevent exercise of territorial jurisdiction by a state court in the same locale), *and* Lea Brilmayer & Charles Norchi, *Federal Extraterritoriality and Fifth Amendment Due Process*, 105 Harv. L. Rev. 1217, 1262 (1992) (arguing that Fifth Amendment constraints should in significant part be "parallel to those of the Fourteenth Amendment").

The current difference in the reach of process, however, is not great. This is because federal courts, like the state courts, are dependent on the legislative branch to delineate the reach of territorial jurisdiction,[24] and Congress has created nationwide territorial jurisdiction for federal courts in only a few special circumstances.[25] Absent such a statute, federal courts will in most cases be limited to the jurisdictional reach of a local state court. This limitation results from Rule 4's provision that service or waiver of service will establish jurisdiction over any defendant "who is subject to the [territorial] jurisdiction of a court of general [subject matter] jurisdiction in the state where the district court is located. . . ."[26] This provision effectively incorporates the forum state's law of personal jurisdiction (including its long-arm statutes), as well as the constitutional limitations upon it. By this indirect route, federal judges usually find themselves laboring under the same Fourteenth Amendment due process and state law limitations as their state court counterparts.[27] This means that federal courts often do not direct their concerns over territorial jurisdiction to a body of distinctly federal law.[28] This is in marked contrast to the preeminent role federal law plays in resolving questions of federal subject matter jurisdiction.[29]

---

[24] G.W. Foster, Jr., *Long-Arm Jurisdiction in Federal Courts*, 1969 Wis. L. Rev. 9, 11. *Cf.* Note, *Alien Corporations and Aggregate Contacts: A Genuinely Federal Jurisdictional Standard*, 95 Harv. L. Rev. 470, 470 (1981) ("[I]n federal cases it is for Congress to determine whether a defendant is amenable to service and to establish the manner in which process may be served."). *Accord, Omni Capital Int'l v. Rudolf Wolff & Co., Ltd.*, 484 U.S. 97 (1987).

[25] Thus, 28 U.S.C. § 2361 permits nationwide service of process in federal statutory interpleader proceedings. For a discussion of additional federal statutes authorizing nationwide service of process, see Jon Heller, Note, *Pendent Personal Jurisdiction and Nationwide Service of Process*, 64 N.Y.U. L. Rev. 113 (1989).

Even when Congress gives a statute nationwide reach, however, federal courts may yet delve deeper to ensure that parties' due process rights are protected. *See, e.g., Republic of Panama v. BCCI Holdings (Lux.) S.A.*, 119 F.3d 935, 947 (11th Cir. 1997) ("minimum contacts with the United States do not . . . automatically satisfy . . . due process requirements" when a federal statute permits the assertion of nationwide territorial jurisdiction); *see also Eleventh Circuit Holds That Minimum Contacts with the United States Do Not Automatically Confer Jurisdiction over a Defendant Served Via a Nationwide Service of Process Statute*, 111 Harv. L. Rev. 1359 (1998).

[26] Rule 4(k)(1)(A). In limited circumstances involving parties added by impleader or compulsory joinder, Rule 4(k)(1)(B) permits service of process up to 100 miles from the federal court — whether or not the same service would have been possible in a local state case.

[27] *See generally* Robert C. Casad, *Personal Jurisdiction in Federal Question Cases*, 70 Tex. L. Rev. 1589 (1992). With a limited exception discussed *infra*, Rule 4 makes no distinction between federal diversity and federal question cases. While incorporation of state court jurisdictional limitations has been applauded in the former, Arthur T. von Mehren & Donald T. Trautman, *Jurisdiction to Adjudicate: A Suggested Analysis*, 79 Harv. L. Rev. 1121, 1123–25 n.6 (1966), it has been criticized as too confining in federal question cases, particularly those involving alien defendants. *Alien Corporations*, note 24, *supra*; Ronan E. Degnan & Mary K. Kane, *The Exercise of Jurisdiction over and Enforcement of Judgments Against Alien Defendants*, 39 Hastings L.J. 799 (1988); Brian B. Frasch, Comment, *National Contacts as a Basis for In Personam Jurisdiction over Aliens in Federal Question Suits*, 70 Cal. L. Rev. 686 (1982).

[28] *See, e.g., Burger King v. Rudzewicz*, 471 U.S. 462 (1985) (sufficiency of a federal court's territorial jurisdiction measured under Florida's long-arm statute); *Keeton v. Hustler Magazine*, 465 U.S. 770 (1984) (the same under New Hampshire's long-arm statute).

[29] For a particularly helpful discussion of the differences between territorial jurisdiction and subject

The situation described above changed to a slight degree with the 1993 amendment of Rule 4 authorizing nationwide service of process in some cases brought under federal courts' federal question jurisdiction.[30] Relatively few cases, however, are likely to be affected by the amendment. It represents a "narrow extension of the federal reach. . . ."[31]

[3] Traditional Categories of Jurisdiction

Historically, American courts have enjoyed three types of territorial jurisdiction: *in personam*,[32] *in rem*,[33] and *quasi in rem*.[34] The United States Supreme Court once distinguished the three as follows:

> A judgment *in personam* imposes a personal liability or obligation on one person in favor of another. A judgment *in rem* affects the interests of all persons in designated property. A judgment *quasi in rem* affects the interests of particular persons in designated property.[35]

---

matter jurisdiction in the federal courts, see *Insurance Corp. of Ireland, Ltd. v. Compagnie des Bauxites de Guinee*, 456 U.S. 694 (1982).

[30] Rule 4(k)(2) now states:

> For a claim that arises under federal law, serving a summons or filing a waiver of service establishes personal jurisdiction over a defendant if: (A) the defendant is not subject to jurisdiction in any state's courts of general jurisdiction; and (B) exercising jurisdiction is consistent with the United States Constitution and laws.

[31] Rule 4 Advisory Committee notes (1993). The relative unimportance of the change can be explained as follows. Since defendants incorporated in or citizens of a state are subject to jurisdiction in that state, *see* § 3.04[2], *infra*, only aliens appear to fit within the category created in Rule 4(k)(2). Moreover, aliens would be subject to the new subsection only when minimum contacts existed between them and the United States *but* did not exist between them and any state. William M. Richman, *Carnival Cruise Lines: Forum Selection Clauses in Adhesion Contracts*, 40 AM. J. COMP. L. 977, 977 n.1 (1992). For a survey of lower federal court decisions under Rule 4(k)(2), see Dora A. Corby, *Putting Personal Jurisdiction Within Reach: Just What Has Rule 4(k)(2) Done for the Personal Jurisdiction of Federal Courts?*, 30 MCGEORGE L. REV. 167 (1998). A particularly helpful approach can be found in *ISI Int'l, Inc. v. Borden Ladner Gervais LLP*, 256 F.3d 548, 552 (7th Cir. 2001). The court stated that "[a] defendant who wants to preclude use of Rule 4(k)(2) has only to name some other state in which the suit could proceed. Naming a more appropriate state would amount to a consent to personal jurisdiction there." The court added: "If, however, the defendant contends that he cannot be sued in the forum state and refuses to identify any other where suit is possible, then the federal court is entitled to use Rule 4(k)(2)." For a rare application of the rule to a case that satisfies these requirements, see *Graduate Admission Council v. Raju*, 267 F. Supp. 2d 505 (E.D. Va. 2003) (Rule 4(k)(2) satisfied where an Indian defendant allegedly infringed federal copyright and trademark laws with a website that targeted United States customers generally, but where "there are no specific contacts with any state other than Virginia, and the Virginia contacts are not sufficient to support jurisdiction in Virginia").

[32] *See* Joseph J. Kalo, *Jurisdiction as an Evolutionary Process: The Development of Quasi In Rem and In Personam Principles*, 1978 DUKE L.J. 1147; Philip B. Kurland, *The Supreme Court, the Due Process Clause and the In Personam Jurisdiction of State Courts — From Pennoyer to Denckla: A Review*, 25 U. CHI. L. REV. 569 (1958).

[33] *See* Hans Smit, *The Enduring Utility of In Rem Rules: A Lasting Legacy of* Pennoyer v. Neff, 43 BROOK. L. REV. 600 (1977).

[34] *See* Kalo, note 32, *supra*; William R. Slomanson, *Real Property Unrelated to Claim: Due Process for Quasi In Rem Jurisdiction?*, 83 DICK. L. REV. 51 (1978).

[35] *Hanson v. Denckla*, 357 U.S. 235, 246 n.12 (1958).

The relative significance of these categories has changed since the Court's observation. But each has survived into contemporary law and the essential features of each remain unchanged.

[a] *In Personam* Jurisdiction

In personam jurisdiction, also called personal jurisdiction (a term that is also used more broadly to refer to all forms of territorial jurisdiction) or jurisdiction over the person, provides courts with a basis for entirely determining controversies involving personal obligations. Because the court's jurisdiction is over the person of the defendant, it can impose judgment indebtedness upon him to the full extent of the wrong done to the plaintiff. If an *in personam* judgment for damages cannot be fully satisfied where rendered,[36] plaintiff may collect the unsatisfied portion of the judgment in any other state or federal court in a state where the defendant has assets.[37]

[b] *In Rem* Jurisdiction

In rem jurisdiction focuses not on the person of the defendant but on some of the defendant's property located within the forum. Courts use this form of jurisdiction to adjudicate questions concerning the ownership and control of such property — to settle questions, it is sometimes said, against the whole world. "Examples of such actions include suits to quiet title to real estate that purport to conclude all adverse claims, and in rem libels in admiralty."[38] Theoretically, the function of *in rem* jurisdiction is to act upon — dispose of — the thing, or *res*, itself, rather than to act directly upon rights of individuals. This is an artificial distinction, since both types affect the rights of others to the property.

[c] *Quasi in Rem* Jurisdiction

Like *in rem* jurisdiction, *quasi in rem* jurisdiction operates on property located within the forum and not directly against the person of individual defendants. Like an *in rem* judgment, a *quasi in rem* judgment binds the parties only with reference to their interests in the property (*res*) upon which jurisdiction is based.[39] Thus, the

---

[36] For the manner in which judgments are enforced, see § 15.02, *infra.*

[37] "The Full Faith and Credit Clause makes the valid *in personam* judgment of one State enforceable in all other States." *Shaffer v. Heitner*, 433 U.S. 186, 210 (1977). Federal statutory law requires that the same respect be given to state judgments in federal court and to federal judgments in either state or other federal courts. *See* § 15.10, *infra.*

[38] R. CASAD & R. RICHMAN, JURISDICTION IN CIVIL ACTIONS § 1-1[3] (3d ed. 1998).

[39] Thus, in contrast to *in personam* judgments (*see* note 37 and related text, *supra*), *in rem* and *quasi in rem* judgments usually have no effect elsewhere. A judgment *in rem* or *quasi in rem* only authorizes liquidation or alteration of the legal status of the *res* underpinning jurisdiction. In a few cases, courts limited to one of these two forms of jurisdiction have presumed to adjudicate the entire dollar amount of defendant's personal obligation to plaintiff. Courts elsewhere, however, are under no obligation to recognize such judgments. For example, in *Combs v. Combs*, 60 S.W.2d 368 (Ky. 1933), a Kentucky court refused to give effect to an Arkansas *in rem* judgment that not only adjudicated the status of Arkansas real estate, but also presumed to fix the entire sum defendant owed to plaintiff. But see *Harnischfeger Sales Corp. v. Sternberg Dredging Co.*, 191 So. 94 (Miss. 1939), where a Mississippi court noted that a prior Louisiana judgment was *in rem*, but gave it preclusive effect. However, "[t]here is scant judicial

value of a *quasi in rem* judgment cannot exceed the value of the *res*.

Like *in personam* jurisdiction, however, *quasi in rem* jurisdiction can be used to adjudicate personal obligations.[40] *Harris v. Balk*,[41] perhaps the most famous *quasi in rem* case, provides an illustration. A Maryland plaintiff sued nonresident defendant Balk by serving one Harris to garnish[42] a debt owed by Harris to Balk. The *res* was the debt, deemed present wherever the debtor could be found. The plaintiff prevailed and recovered the *res* — the amount of Harris' debt. Thereafter, Balk sued Harris in North Carolina on the debt. Harris argued that he had discharged his obligation to Balk by paying the sum in the earlier case. Harris prevailed because the United States Supreme Court concluded that the Maryland court had properly exercised *quasi in rem* jurisdiction.[43]

Eventually the Supreme Court decided that exercises of *quasi in rem* jurisdiction must satisfy the same due process standards applicable to personal jurisdiction, and the form of *quasi in rem* jurisdiction exemplified by *Harris* lost its special appeal.[44] Plaintiffs no longer obtain any jurisdictional advantage by attaching nonresident defendants' property and proceeding under a *quasi in rem* theory; they may just as well proceed directly and assert personal jurisdiction. Other forms of *quasi in rem* jurisdiction, however, continue to have application where the property at issue is related to the dispute.[45]

---

authority for this position." Richard W. Bourne, *The Demise of Foreign Attachment*, 21 CREIGHTON L. REV. 141, 151 n.84 (1987).

Quasi in rem jurisdiction has enjoyed a recent return to prominence in the context of anticybersquatting litigation, where the property at issue (for example, a domain name) may be "located" in a jurisdiction far from its owner. *See, e.g.*, John A. Greer, *If the Shoe Fits: Reconciling the International Shoe Minimum Contacts Test with the Anticybersquatting Consumer Protection Act*, 61 VAND. L. REV. 1861 (2008); *see also* Jason W. Callen, *Asserting in Personam Jurisdiction over Foreign Cybersquatters*, 69 U. CHI. L. REV. 1837, 1840 (2002) (discussing *quasi in rem* jurisdiction in the cybersquatting context, concluding that it "is of questionable value to plaintiffs").

[40] But, this use is now quite limited. *See* § 3.09[1][a], *infra.*

[41] 198 U.S. 215 (1905). For an illuminating discussion of this case, see WILLIAM M. RICHMAN & WILLIAM L. REYNOLDS, UNDERSTANDING CONFLICT OF LAWS § 42[b] (3d ed. 2002).

[42] *Garnishment* is the seizure of a debt by service of process on the debtor with a warning not to pay the debt pending litigation. *Attachment* is the actual or constructive seizure of real property using judicial process. Property may also be seized before judgment to provide security for an eventual judgment, rather than to confer territorial jurisdiction, or after judgment to execute upon the judgment. Pre-judgment seizures are subject to strict due process protection, *see* § 4.02[2], *infra*, while post-judgment seizures are typically subject to detailed local procedures, even in federal courts. *See generally* § 15.02 (enforcing money judgments), *infra.*

[43] For a further illustration of this form of *quasi in rem* jurisdiction, see the discussion of the *Seider* doctrine at § 3.09[1][b], *infra.*

[44] For discussion of these developments, see § 3.09, *infra.*

[45] For example, an action against named defendants to remove a cloud on the title to real estate. RICHMAN & REYNOLDS, note 41, *supra*, at § 41[b].

§ 3.02   *PENNOYER v. NEFF*: AN ERA OF RIGID TERRITORIAL LIMITS

[1]   *Pennoyer* and its Rationale

In 1877, the constitutional framework for regulating personal jurisdiction of state courts was uncertain.[46] Then, in *Pennoyer v. Neff*,[47] the United States Supreme Court rendered a decision applying "principles of public law" that laid the groundwork for a due process analysis restricting the effect of judgments. Although the Due Process Clause did not control the Court's decision in *Pennoyer*, because events giving rise to the original suit predated the adoption of the Fourteenth Amendment, the Court took pains to emphasize that the recently adopted Due Process Clause furnished an additional basis upon which to contest jurisdiction in cases such as this.[48] It thus became clear after *Pennoyer* that, while the Full Faith and Credit Clause compelled interstate enforcement of state judgments, it did not purge those judgments of any problems they might have under the Due Process Clause. Rather, the same federal due process grounds available to resist enforcement of a state judgment locally would also be available if enforcement was sought for that judgment in federal court or in the court of a sister state.

---

[46] Albert A. Ehrenzweig, *The Transient Rule of Personal Jurisdiction: The "Power" Myth and Forum Conveniens*, 65 YALE L.J. 289, 303, 308 (1956). *See generally* the historical studies by Professors Weinstein, Kogan & Trangsrud, note 48, *infra*.

[47] 95 U.S. 714 (1878). Overviews of *Pennoyer*, its precursors, and developments after the case, include James Weinstein, *The Federal Common Law Origins of Judicial Jurisdiction: Implications for Modern Doctrine*, 90 VA. L. REV. 169 (2004); Patrick J. Borchers, *Jurisdictional Pragmatism: International Shoe's Half-Buried Legacy*, 28 U.C. DAVIS L. REV. 561 (1995); John B. Oakley, *The Pitfalls of "Hint and Run" History: A Critique of Professor Borchers's "Limited View"* of Pennoyer v. Neff, 28 U.C. DAVIS L. REV. 591 (1995); Patrick J. Borchers, *Pennoyer's Limited Legacy: A Reply to Professor Oakley*, 29 U.C. DAVIS L. REV. 115 (1995); Geoffrey C. Hazard, Jr., *A General Theory of State-Court Jurisdiction*, 1965 SUP. CT. REV. 241; Philip B. Kurland, *The Supreme Court, the Due Process Clause and the In Personam Jurisdiction of State Courts from* Pennoyer *to Denckla: A Review*, 25 U. CHI. L. REV. 569 (1958). For an account of the principals in the case, see Wendy C. Perdue, *Sin, Scandal, and Substantive Due Process: Personal Jurisdiction and* Pennoyer *Reconsidered*, 62 WASH. L. REV. 479 (1987).

[48]

> Since the adoption of the Fourteenth Amendment to the Federal Constitution, the validity of such judgments may be directly questioned, and their enforcement in the State resisted, on the ground that proceedings in a court of justice to determine the personal rights and obligations of parties over whom the court has no jurisdiction, do not constitute due process of law.

95 U.S. at 733. Most see the *Pennoyer* case as a milestone, a view reflected in *Burnham v. Superior Court*, 495 U.S. 604 (1990).

There has been some interest in the legal history surrounding *Pennoyer*. Some contend that the requirement of in-state service on nonresident defendants existed well before *Pennoyer*. James Weinstein, *The Early American Origins of Territoriality in Judicial Jurisdiction*, 37 ST. LOUIS U. L.J. 1 (1992); Terry S. Kogan, *A Neo-Federalist Tale of Personal Jurisdiction*, 63 S. CAL. L. REV. 257 (1990). Another commentator has maintained that *Pennoyer* is best seen as a federal common law decision that later informed development of the due process test, accounting in large part for the persistence of territorial minimum contacts. Roger H. Trangsrud, *The Federal Common Law of Personal Jurisdiction*, 57 GEO. WASH. L. REV. 849 (1989).

It remained for the Court to give content to its standard. The approach reflected in *Pennoyer* would dominate the law of personal jurisdiction for nearly seventy years. State courts could entertain suits against their citizens. They could also entertain suits against nonresidents so long as they consented or if they could be found and served within the forum state. But due process prevented suit against nonresident defendants who could only be found and served elsewhere.

Pennoyer involved two lawsuits. In the first, Mitchell obtained a default judgment in an Oregon state court against Neff for attorney's fees. Neff's Oregon property was seized and sold by the sheriff to Pennoyer in order to satisfy this judgment. In the second lawsuit, Neff sued Pennoyer in federal court for recovery of his property, and Pennoyer defended by claiming title under the sheriff's deed of sale.

Pennoyer's problem was that, when the Oregon court had entered a default judgment, Neff was neither a citizen of the forum nor had he been served there. Concluding that Oregon could not exercise personal jurisdiction over Neff, the United States Supreme Court invalidated the default judgment and resulting sheriff's sale. The Court held that if a state court attempts to exercise *in personam* jurisdiction over the defendant, that is, to adjudicate a case "that involves merely a determination of the personal liability of the defendant, he must be brought within its jurisdiction by service of process within the State, or his voluntary appearance."[49] The Court recognized that *quasi in rem* jurisdiction was an alternative when the defendant had property in the jurisdiction, but stressed that this form of territorial jurisdiction required a proper pre-judgment attachment of the property. Because Neff's property was first seized to enforce a judgment already obtained, *quasi in rem* jurisdiction was unavailable to save the Oregon judgment.

The boundaries of the forum state had transcendent importance in *Pennoyer*, as reflected in the two principles of public law that the Court announced: First, that "every State possesses exclusive jurisdiction and sovereignty over persons and property within its territory,"[50] and second, that "no State can exercise direct jurisdiction and authority over persons or property without its territory."[51] The Court drove the point home. "Process from the tribunals of one State cannot run into another State, and summon parties there domiciled to leave its territory and respond to proceedings against them."[52]

The Court's approach in *Pennoyer* was in tune with the times. Justice Holmes was to observe somewhat later that "[t]he foundation of jurisdiction is physical power."[53] He was speaking of a court's physical power over the defendant. While it was no longer necessary for the defendant to be under the court's physical control,[54] the power concept remained. Writing for the Court in *Pennoyer*, Justice

---

[49] 95 U.S. at 733.

[50] 95 U.S. at 722.

[51] 95 U.S. at 722.

[52] 95 U.S. at 727.

[53] *McDonald v. Mabee*, 243 U.S. 90, 91 (1917).

[54] In earlier times, "the power of a court to enter a judgment was dependent upon the actual physical

Field was greatly influenced by the theories of Joseph Story.[55] Story urged a strong relationship between territory and legal authority. One of the ideas he advanced was that the geographical origin of case facts determined when or if legal authority materialized. This notion grew in appeal in the second half of the nineteenth century. However, belief in detached legal principles then began to lose ground in American legal thought to "a growing perception that legal principles were in fact nothing more than doctrines found in . . . local law."[56]

[2]   The Aftermath of *Pennoyer*

Pennoyer's power rationale became outmoded over time. It was a formalistic doctrine and as such reflected a view of the law as a "static and closed logical system."[57] Increasingly, *Pennoyer*'s analysis seemed inadequate either to explain the Court's rule or — perhaps more importantly — to accommodate the needs of an era of increasing interstate activity. Two developments put particular strain on the *Pennoyer* doctrine: the growth of national corporate activity and the advent of the automobile.

Pennoyer made some provision for personal jurisdiction over foreign corporations and others who did business in the forum state but could not be found and served there. The Court made clear that states could require them to appoint an in-state agent to receive court process. Moreover, when these potential defendants refused to appoint someone, states appeared to have authority to designate a state official to accept service for them.[58]

Unfortunately, the Supreme Court was never able to develop an intelligible standard for determining when the forum involvement of the out-of-state defendant was sufficient to justify substituted service on a state officer. The Court invoked concepts of implied consent[59] and presence,[60] each leading to an inquiry

---

presence of the defendant before the court." Joseph J. Kalo, *Jurisdiction as an Evolutionary Process: The Development of Quasi In Rem and In Personam Principles*, 1978 Duke L.J. 1147, 1148.

[55]   Hazard, note 47, *supra*, at 262. *See generally* J. Story, Commentaries on the Conflict of Laws (1834).

[56]   T. Freyer, Harmony & Dissonance: The *Swift* & *Erie* Cases in American Federalism 74 (1981). As Holmes said of the common law, it "is not a brooding omnipresence in the sky but the articulate voice of some sovereign . . . ." *Southern Pac. Co. v. Jensen*, 244 U.S. 205, 222 (1917) (Holmes, J., dissenting).

[57]   Robert S. Summers, *Pragmatic Instrumentalism in Twentieth Century American Legal Thought — A Synthesis and Critique of Our Dominant General Theory About Law and Its Use*, 66 Cornell L. Rev. 861, 867 n.4 (1981). *Cf.* Kenneth J. Vandevelde, *Ideology, Due Process and Civil Procedure*, 67 St. John's L. Rev. 265, 276 (1993) ("The law of personal jurisdiction articulated in *Pennoyer* . . . was consistent with the formalist ideology of late nineteenth century conservatives."). Restlessness under *Pennoyer* represented only part of a larger movement away from procedural formalism and toward a functional or instrumental understanding of civil procedure. The trend, which continues, is described in Gene R. Shreve, *Pragmatism Without Politics — A Half Measure of Authority for Jurisdictional Common Law*, 1991 BYU L. Rev. 767, 793–96; Robert G. Bone, *Mapping the Boundaries of a Dispute: Conceptions of Ideal Lawsuit Structure from the Field Code to the Federal Rules*, 89 Colum. L. Rev. 1 (1989).

[58]   *Pennoyer*, 95 U.S. at 735. "States that had no statutes of this sort soon enacted them." Hazard, note 47, *supra*, at 272. This arrangement honored, at least technically, *Pennoyer*'s limitation that service of process be completed within the forum state.

[59]   *E.g.*, *Simon v. Southern Ry.*, 236 U.S. 115 (1915).

about the amount of business done by the defendant in the forum state.[61] The results were arbitrary and unsatisfactory.[62] Ambiguity inherent in the nature of corporate identity compounded the problem. Legal confections, corporations did not literally exist anywhere. Thus, it was particularly difficult to subject them to *Pennoyer*'s legal metaphor based on geographical whereabouts and physical movement.[63]

Professor Hazard observed that *Pennoyer* "had a less secure place in particular application than it did in general theory."[64] The famous accident case, *Hess v. Pawloski*,[65] illustrates this point. Hess, a Pennsylvanian, struck and injured Pawloski while driving in Massachusetts. After Hess returned to Pennsylvania, Pawloski filed suit against him in a Massachusetts court. It was impossible to serve Hess personally in Massachusetts. Pawloski instead used a Massachusetts statute declaring that, by using Massachusetts's highways, nonresident motorists constructively appointed a state officer to accept in-state service for them in Massachusetts's accident cases. Hess challenged the appointment as fictitious, which, of course, it was. The Supreme Court nonetheless upheld personal jurisdiction.

The *Hess* Court acknowledged *Pennoyer*'s requirement that "actual service within the state" be made on the defendant "or upon someone authorized to accept service for him."[66] It also noted a previous case in which it had invalidated as fictitious an analogous use of the concept of implied consent.[67] However, it upheld jurisdiction under the statute because of the strong interest Massachusetts had in highway safety:

> Motor vehicles are dangerous machines; and, even when skillfully and carefully operated, their use is attended by serious dangers to persons and property. In the public interest the State may make and enforce regulations reasonably calculated to promote care on the part of all, residents and non-residents alike, who use its highways. The measure in question operates to require a non-resident to answer for his conduct in the State where arise causes of action alleged against him, as well as to provide for a claimant a convenient method by which he may sue to enforce his rights.[68]

---

[60] *E.g., International Harvester Co. v. Kentucky*, 234 U.S. 579 (1914).

[61] *E.g., St. Louis Sw. Ry. v. Alexander*, 227 U.S. 218 (1913). *See* Kurland, note 47, *supra*, at 577–86; Austin W. Scott, *Jurisdiction over Nonresidents Doing Business Within a State*, 32 HARV. L. REV. 871 (1919); Note, *Recent Interpretations of "Doing Business" Statutes*, 44 IOWA L. REV. 345 (1959).

[62] *See* Kurland, note 47, *supra*, at 584–86; *Developments in the Law-State-Court Jurisdiction*, 73 HARV. L. REV. 909, 919–23 (1960).

[63] *Developments*, note 62, *supra*, at 919. *See generally* William A. Holby, Note, *"Doing Business": Defining State Control over Foreign Corporations*, 32 VAND. L. REV. 1105 (1979); Note, *Jurisdiction Over Foreign Corporations — An Analysis of Due Process*, 104 U. PA. L. REV. 381 (1955).

[64] Hazard, note 47, *supra*, at 272.

[65] 274 U.S. 352 (1927). *See generally* Austin W. Scott, *Jurisdiction over Nonresident Motorists*, 39 HARV. L. REV. 563 (1926).

[66] 274 U.S. at 355.

[67] 274 U.S. at 355 (*citing Flexner v. Farson*, 248 U.S. 289 (1919)).

[68] 274 U.S. at 356.

Most commentators would agree that the Court reached the best result in *Hess* and, in the language above, offered the best of reasons. It is impossible, however, to square this rationale for personal jurisdiction with *Pennoyer.* However desirable it might be for Massachusetts courts to have an opportunity to adjudicate Pawloski's claim, this has nothing to do with whether Hess was served there, or whether he may be regarded as having consented to suit through appointment of an in-state agent.

This dichotomy reveals the legal climate in which *Hess* was decided. Lower courts and the United States Supreme Court were growing disenchanted with an interpretation of due process that denied states the opportunity to address by judicial proceedings conduct occurring within their borders. The language from *Hess* quoted above says as much.[69] But there was little room in the approach of *Pennoyer* for this kind of sentiment. *Hess* reveals the schizophrenia eventually created in the law of personal jurisdiction by *Pennoyer*'s territorial limitations.

The weight upon the old rule eventually became intolerable. As a result, the Court quietly overthrew the restraints of *Pennoyer* in *International Shoe Co. v. Washington.*[70]

§ 3.03　*INTERNATIONAL SHOE CO. v. WASHINGTON*: THE SHIFT TO MINIMUM CONTACTS

[1]　Due Process and the Reasonableness of Plaintiff's Forum Choice

The International Shoe Company was incorporated in Delaware and had its principal place of business in Missouri. International Shoe employed Washington residents to solicit orders there. They reported directly to the company's main office in St. Louis. Washington sued International Shoe to collect unemployment compensation tax upon salaries defendant had paid to its Washington employees. International Shoe challenged personal jurisdiction in Washington. The Washington Supreme Court ruled that personal jurisdiction existed over the defendant. It relied on United States Supreme Court doctrine[71] to conclude that International Shoe's Washington activities constituted a sufficient in-state presence to make it amenable to suit.

The United States Supreme Court affirmed on significantly different grounds. Noting that "the corporate personality is a fiction," the Court proceeded to divest

---

[69]　*Henry L. Doherty & Co. v. Goodman*, 294 U.S. 623 (1935), provides another example. The Court permitted personal jurisdiction over a nonresident individual who had operated a securities business in the forum state. Plaintiff had invoked an implied consent statute which was about as tenuous as the one in *Hess.* As in *Hess*, the Court cited but refused to follow *Flexner. See* note 67 and related text, *supra.* The real reason for the decision in *Doherty* seems to be the Court's observation that "Iowa treats the business of dealing in corporate securities as exceptional, and subjects it to special regulation." 294 U.S. at 627. *See* Willis L. M. Reese & Nina M. Galston, *Doing an Act or Causing Consequences as Bases of Judicial Jurisdiction*, 44 Iowa L. Rev. 249 (1959).

[70]　326 U.S. 310 (1945).

[71]　For discussion of the doctrine and illustrative cases, see § 3.02, *supra.*

corporate "presence" of its special significance:

> To say that the corporation is so far "present" [in a state] as to satisfy due
> process requirements . . . is to beg the question to be decided. For the
> terms "present" or "presence" are used merely to symbolize those activities
> of the corporation's agent within the state, which courts will deem to be
> sufficient to satisfy the demands of due process. . . . Those demands may
> be met by such contacts of the corporation with the state of the forum as
> make it reasonable, in the context of our federal system of government, to
> require the corporation to defend the particular suit which is brought
> there.[72]

This language from the Court's opinion is illuminating in several respects. First, it reminds the reader why due process protection is necessary. Without it, plaintiff can "require" the defendant "to defend the particular suit" wherever plaintiff chooses to bring it. The guarantee of due process permits defendant to minimize the ordeal created by plaintiff's forum choice by giving defendant a means of attacking it directly at the outset of suit.[73] Due process also provides defendant an alternative by tempering the effect of full faith and credit, permitting defendant to ignore plaintiff's case altogether and to collaterally attack the resulting default judgment if plaintiff tries to enforce it in defendant's home state.[74] Thus, plaintiff's power to require defendant to participate where plaintiff chooses is limited by the due process constraints on the scope of personal jurisdiction.[75]

Second, the above passage from *International Shoe* indicates that due process will limit plaintiff to "reasonable" choices and tells us that an important focus for determining jurisdiction will be on the "contacts" the corporate defendant has with the forum state. This is a pragmatic, fact-centered approach to setting limits on personal jurisdiction.[76] It differs from the formalistic approach of *Pennoyer* and lacks *Pennoyer*'s preoccupation with whether service of process has been completed within the territorial limits of the forum. Most important, the Supreme Court approved personal jurisdiction in *International Shoe* based upon service of process outside Washington's boundaries.[77]

---

[72] 326 U.S. at 316–17.

[73] For a discussion of the dynamics of direct attack, see § 3.10[1], *infra.*

[74] *E.g., Hanson v. Denckla,* 357 U.S. 235, 255 (1958) ("Delaware is under no obligation to give full faith and credit to a Florida judgment invalid in Florida because offensive to the Due Process Clause of the Fourteenth Amendment."). For a discussion of collateral attack and of how direct and collateral attack options combine to secure due process protection, see § 3.10, *infra.*

[75] *See Ruhrgas AG v. Marathon Oil Co.,* 526 U.S. 574, 584 (1999).

[76] The Court notes this: "It is evident that the criteria by which we mark the boundary line between those activities which justify the subjection of a corporation to suit, and those which do not, cannot be simply mechanical or quantitative." *International Shoe,* 326 U.S. at 319.

[77] "In suggesting that service outside of the state without more would suffice, the opinion offered the states an opportunity to dispense with the cumbersome procedure of service on a state official plus extraterritorial notice, the method suggested in *Pennoyer* and utilized extensively by the states since." Philip B. Kurland, *The Supreme Court, the Due Process Clause and the In Personam Jurisdiction of State Courts from Pennoyer to Denckla: A Review,* 25 U. CHI. L. REV. 569, 590 (1958). *See also* Peter Hay, *Refining Personal Jurisdiction in the United States,* 35 INT'L & COMP. L.Q. 32, 61 (1986) (observing that the case "freed American jurisdictional thinking from the territorial strait jacket of the historical

For a nonresident defendant who cannot be found and served within the forum state, *Shoe* announced that good personal jurisdiction requires that the defendant "have certain *minimum contacts* with [the forum], such that the maintenance of the suit does not offend 'traditional notions of fair play and substantial justice.' "[78]

[2] The Advent of Minimum Contacts

International Shoe's "minimum contacts" test has dominated the law of personal jurisdiction.[79] Absent consent, waiver, or personal service in the forum,[80] minimum contacts between the forum and the defendant are necessary to make plaintiff's choice a constitutional forum.[81] When plaintiff selects defendant's home forum, the reasonableness of the choice will usually be so obvious as to gainsay the minimum contacts question.[82] But when and how is the minimum contacts test satisfied when plaintiff selects another forum?

For several reasons, *International Shoe* does not provide a complete answer to this question. To an extent, the problem is inherent in the approach announced by the case. Fairness is a vague concept. It is one thing to declare that due process permits jurisdiction over nonresident defendants when fair under the circumstances. It is another to sift the facts of cases in an effort to apply the standard. Beyond that, the Court's analysis in *International Shoe* is blurred by reluctance to break sharply with prior decisions.[83] Finally, the facts of the case were not especially demanding. Washington state courts probably would have had personal jurisdiction over the case even under the Court's earlier, more restrictive case law.[84]

The broader jurisdictional implications of the minimum contacts test would become clear only in later cases. However, the Court's opinion did offer principles that were to provide much of the foundation for modern doctrine. A geographical outlook concerning jurisdictional facts would be as important under *International Shoe* as it was under *Pennoyer.* The former simply attached clearer, more decisive importance to the location within the forum of facts about the controversy and about the defendant, and far less importance to whether service of process was completed there.[85]

---

requirement that the defendant be present in the forum at the time of service").

[78] 326 U.S. at 316, *quoting Milliken v. Meyer*, 311 U.S. 457, 463 (1940) (emphasis added).

[79] *E.g., Burger King, Inc. v. Rudzewicz*, 471 U.S. 462, 474 (1985) ("[T]he constitutional touchstone remains whether the defendant purposefully established 'minimum contacts' in the forum State" [*citing International Shoe*]).

[80] *See* § 3.01[3] (traditionally accepted forms of personal jurisdiction), *supra.*

[81] On how contacts function in the test, see § 3.06, *infra.*

[82] *See* § 3.04, *infra.*

[83] "That the Supreme Court was cautious in developing the new approach and was unwilling to cut off precedent directly in *International Shoe* is not surprising. The history of jurisdiction has been one of gradual evolution, of new ideas growing out of old, until the new completely supplants the old." Joseph J. Kalo, *Jurisdiction as an Evolutionary Process: The Development of Quasi In Rem and In Personam Principles*, 1978 DUKE L.J. 1147, 1184 n.234.

[84] Kurland, note 77, *supra*, at 592.

[85] While the case established the principle that personal jurisdiction would not necessarily require

[3] Justifications for *Shoe*'s Extension of Personal Jurisdiction

The Supreme Court laid down three justifications for the Washington court's personal jurisdiction over International Shoe. Each provided a reason for attaching importance to defendant's contact with the forum; each would figure significantly in later cases.

First, the Court suggested that, given sufficient contacts, it would be reasonable to subject the defendant to suit as a fair exchange for the advantages it received from the forum.

> [T]o the extent that a corporation exercises the privilege of conducting activities within a state, it enjoys the benefits and protection of the laws of that state. The exercise of that privilege may give rise to obligations. . . .[86]

This suggests an analogy to forum citizenship as a basis for personal jurisdiction.[87] Granted, the nonresident defendant's enjoyment of forum benefits and protection is not likely to be as pervasive as that of a forum citizen, and thus the case for personal jurisdiction over the former may not be as easy to establish. However, the process of reasoning toward a conclusion of personal jurisdiction is much the same.[88] Under this rationale, a nonresident defendant's contacts with the forum (understood as advantages conferred by the forum state) could be so extensive as to support personal jurisdiction for causes of action arising elsewhere.[89]

Second, personal jurisdiction will be possible even when advantages conferred on a nonresident defendant by the forum are so small as to strain the idea of amenability to suit as a fair exchange, so long as defendant acted within the forum to cause the controversy. The forum is entitled to exercise jurisdiction in such cases

---

service of process to be completed within the forum, it was silent concerning the converse — whether service on the defendant within the forum would invariably create good personal jurisdiction. For recent developments on this issue, see § 3.09, *infra.*

[86] 326 U.S. at 319. This line of argument casts the nonresident defendant and the forum state into a relationship similar to that of contracting parties. Defendant thus bargains with the state by accepting benefits in return for consent to jurisdiction. "Consent is a seductive notion because it seems to explain obligations in terms of the obligated individual's voluntary choice." Lea Brilmayer, *Consent, Contract, and Territory,* 74 MINN. L. REV. 1, 21 (1989). Note, however, that such jurisdiction does not require defendant's knowing and actual consent. Consent has less descriptive power in this context than where plaintiff has expressly contracted for defendant's consent to jurisdiction. This is why consent-to-jurisdiction clauses in contracts pose little analytic difficulty and are freely enforced. *See* § 3.11[4], *infra.*

[87] On forum citizenship as a basis for personal jurisdiction, see § 3.04[2], *infra.* It is significant that *International Shoe* describes its due process standard by quoting from *Milliken v. Meyer,* note 78 and related text, *supra,* an earlier case where the Supreme Court had confirmed a forum state's jurisdictional power over its own citizen.

[88] *Compare* the language from *International Shoe,* text accompanying note 78, *supra, with* the following from *Milliken v. Meyer,* 311 U.S. 457 (1940): "Domicile in the state is alone sufficient to bring an absent defendant within the reach of the state's jurisdiction . . . ." *Milliken,* 311 U.S. at 462. "The state which accords him privileges and affords protection to him and his property by virtue of his domicile may also exact reciprocal duties." 311 U.S. at 463.

[89] The Supreme Court confirmed this possibility in *Perkins v. Benguet Consol. Mining Co.,* 342 U.S. 437 (1952), *discussed in* § 3.08[1], *infra.*

in furtherance of a regulatory interest. The passage from *International Shoe* quoted above continues:

> . . . so far as those obligations arise out of or are connected with the activities within the state, a procedure which requires the corporation to respond to a suit brought to enforce them can, in most instances, hardly be said to be undue.[90]

Finally, the Court suggested another way of evaluating defendant's relationship with the forum. The burden in having to defend away from home will vary depending, among other things, on how unfamiliar or inconvenient the forum really is to the defendant. The Court thus observed that "[a]n estimate of the inconveniences which would result to the corporation from a trial away from its home or principal place of business is relevant" to an examination of defendant's contacts with the forum.[91] It may again be useful to make an analogy between personal jurisdiction over nonresidents and the same over forum citizens. A further reason supporting near automatic jurisdiction over the latter is that citizens usually experience the least disorientation and inconvenience when defending at home.[92] Significant contacts between the nonresident defendant and the forum may suggest that the place for suit selected by plaintiff bears at least some resemblance to defendant's home turf. This may be true even if defendant's contacts with the forum are unrelated to the controversy.[93]

§ 3.04 SPECIFIC AND GENERAL JURISDICTION

[1] The Four Scenarios from *International Shoe*

International Shoe identified four scenarios encountered in prior cases. Two of those scenarios concerned circumstances in which the defendant's contacts with the forum state gave rise to the claims sued upon: When contacts are extensive, precedent showed that the case for jurisdiction is strong;[94] conversely, when such

---

[90] 326 U.S. at 319. The Court gave this regulatory rationale greater attention later in *McGee v. International Life Ins. Co.*, 355 U.S. 220 (1957), *discussed* in § 3.05[1], *infra*.

[91] 326 U.S. at 317, *citing Hutchinson v. Chase & Gilbert*, 45 F.2d 139, 141 (2d Cir. 1930). This concern may now stand apart from the minimum contacts test. *Asahi Metal Ind. Co., Ltd. v. Superior Court*, 480 U.S. 102 (1987), indicates that a forum may have minimum contacts with a nonresident defendant yet be so inconvenient that due process prevents exercise of personal jurisdiction. Five Justices in *Asahi* suggested minimum contacts between the forum and the defendant may have existed. But they joined three other members of the Court to conclude that forcing a Japanese litigant to defend in California against a Taiwanese claimant would (in language drawn from *International Shoe*) violate "traditional notions of fair play and substantial justice." 480 U.S. at 113. On *Asahi*, see generally § 3.07[2], *infra*.

[92] *See* § 3.04[2], *infra*.

[93] "If the primary purpose of jurisdiction is to protect defendants from unfair litigation burdens, it is probably not oppressive for a defendant to be sued in a state where the defendant conducts highly regularized activities, even if those activities are unrelated to the plaintiff's particular claim." Kathleen Waits, *Values, Intuitions, and Opinion Writing: The Judicial Process and State Court Jurisdiction*, 1983 U. ILL. L. REV. 917, 940. *Accord*, R. LEFLAR ET AL., AMERICAN CONFLICTS LAW § 22 (4th ed. 1986).

[94] 326 U.S. at 317 (jurisdiction "has never been doubted when the activities of the corporation there have not only been continuous and systematic, but also give rise to the liabilities sued on").

contacts are more isolated, the case for jurisdiction is less certain.[95] In addition to these two "specific jurisdiction" scenarios in which the plaintiff's claims arise out of the defendant's specific contacts with the forum, the Court alluded to two additional scenarios, in which the defendant's contacts with the forum do not give rise to the plaintiff's claims (scenarios that implicate what would later be dubbed "general jurisdiction"): When a defendant's contacts with the forum are pervasive, they will sometimes be sufficient to establish jurisdiction despite the fact that such contacts did not give rise to the claim sued upon;[96] when, however, the defendant's unrelated forum contacts are less extensive, jurisdiction may fail.[97] The *International Shoe* Court classified the case before it as fitting the first scenario: The company's general activities in the forum had been substantial, "systematic and continuous."[98] At the same time, "[t]he obligation . . . sued upon arose out of [the] very activities" of the defendant.[99] Taken together, these four scenarios provide a useful tool for subdividing personal jurisdiction cases into specific and general jurisdiction variations.

[2] Specific and General Jurisdiction Compared[100]

As the *International Shoe* scenarios reveal, a nonresident defendant may have contacts with the forum sufficient to support personal jurisdiction when those contacts are either related or unrelated to the controversy. Personal jurisdiction based on the first type of contacts is sometimes called *specific* jurisdiction. Personal jurisdiction based on the second is called *general* jurisdiction.[101] As

---

[95] 326 U.S. at 318 ("although the commission of some single or occasional acts of the corporate agent in a state sufficient to impose an obligation or liability on the corporation has not been thought to confer upon the state authority to enforce it, . . . other such acts, because of their nature and quality and the circumstances of their commission, may be deemed sufficient to render the corporation liable to suit").

[96] 326 U.S. at 318 ("there have been instances in which the continuous corporate operations within a state were thought so substantial and of such a nature as to justify suit against it on causes of action arising from dealings entirely distinct from those activities").

[97] 326 U.S. at 318 ("it has been held . . . that continuous activity of some sorts within a state is not enough to support the demand that the corporation be amenable to suits unrelated to that activity").

[98] 326 U.S. at 320.

[99] 326 U.S. at 320.

[100] For studies explaining and comparing specific and general jurisdiction, see ROBERT C. CASAD & WILLIAM B. RICHMAN, JURISDICTION IN CIVIL ACTIONS § 2-5[2][b] (Lexis 3d ed. 1998); Charles W. Rhodes, *The Predictability Principle in Personal Jurisdiction Doctrine: A Case Study on the Effects of a "Generally" Too Broad, but "Specifically" Too Narrow Approach to Minimum Contacts*, 57 BAYLOR L. REV. 135 (2005); Patrick J. Borchers, *The Problem with General Jurisdiction*, 2001 U. CHI. LEGAL F. 119.

[101] The Supreme Court used these terms in *Helicopteros Nacionales de Colombia v. Hall*, 466 U.S. 408, 414 n.8–9 (1984), describing specific jurisdiction as that "in a suit arising out of or related to the defendant's contacts with the forum" and general jurisdiction as that "in a suit not arising out of or related to the defendant's contacts with the forum." *See* Mary Twitchell, *The Myth of General Jurisdiction*, 101 HARV. L. REV. 610, 680 (1988) ("The Supreme Court's recent use of the general/specific terminology suggests that this typology will continue to play a central role in personal jurisdiction decisions."). *See generally* Robert L. Theriot, Note, *Specific and General Jurisdiction — The Reshuffling of Minimum Contacts Analysis*, 59 TUL. L. REV. 826 (1985). To date, however, the Supreme Court has been far less informative about general jurisdiction. One writer has gone so far as to suggest: "The development of general jurisdiction analysis . . . seems to have atrophied at its 1945 level." B. Glenn George, *In Search of General Jurisdiction*, 64 TUL. L. REV. 1097, 1141 (1990).

discussed in § 3.08, the Supreme Court has indicated that a defendant's unrelated contacts need to be such that he is essentially at home in the forum to establish general jurisdiction. While such a test raises as many questions as it answers, it is clear that general jurisdiction requires far more extensive contact between the forum and the defendant than does specific jurisdiction.

General jurisdiction proceeds from a relationship between the forum and defendant that is so extensive that defendant's submission to jurisdiction there is a fair exchange for the considerable privileges and protections that the forum state has extended to defendant. General jurisdiction is indifferent to where the controversy arose and its significance as a jurisdictional option comes in those cases where the controversy arose outside the forum. Citizenship of defendant in the forum provides the strongest case for general jurisdiction,[102] so strong that jurisdiction of the forum over its own citizens is unquestioned.

The central question concerning general jurisdiction is: if a noncitizen defendant cannot be found and served within the forum, and if the cause of action arises entirely outside the forum, when do connections between the defendant and the forum (from purposeful acts by defendant taken in the forum or directed into the forum) become so extensive that the forum can exercise the same general jurisdiction that it does over its own citizens?

Specific jurisdiction proceeds from a relationship between the forum and the noncitizen defendant funneled through the facts of the controversy. One question central to the application of specific jurisdiction is: How related must defendant's forum acts be to the controversy? In *International Shoe*, the requisite relationship was established by showing that the employer's activities in the forum gave rise to the claim that the state sued upon. While showing that a defendant's forum contacts gave rise to the plaintiff's claim there is clearly sufficient, is it necessary? Or might a lesser showing of relationship suffice? Suppose that the plaintiff's claim would not have arisen but for the defendant's activities in the forum state, even though those activities, by themselves, did not give rise to the plaintiff's claim. The issue raises interesting questions of proximate cause. Consider two scenarios: (1) Plaintiff sues defendant cruise line in Washington State, where defendant sold plaintiff his cruise tickets, but for which plaintiff would not have taken the Caribbean cruise where he was injured due to defendant's negligent maintenance of the ship. (2) Plaintiff sues defendant in Washington state, where defendant was conceived forty years earlier, but for which he could not have caused the plaintiff negligent injury on board a Caribbean cruise. Finding specific jurisdiction seems more plausible in the first scenario than the second, because in the first, the forum events are closely connected to the claim that followed.[103] Unfortunately, the Supreme Court declined to explore the issue of "but for" causation in *Helicopteros*

---

[102] *Cf.* Patrick J. Borchers, *The Problem with General Jurisdiction*, 2001 U. Chi. Legal F. 119, 119–20 ("[A]ssertions of jurisdiction based upon . . . the defendant's domicile are assertions of general jurisdiction because they apply without regard to the nature of the dispute.").

[103] In *Shute v. Carnival Cruise Lines*, 897 F.2d 377 (9th Cir. 1990), the Ninth Circuit found that specific jurisdiction was satisfied on similar facts. The Supreme Court reversed on other grounds. 499 U.S. 585 (1991). *See* Flavio Rose, Comment, *Related Contacts and Personal Jurisdiction: The "But For" Test*, 82 Cal. L. Rev. 1545 (1994).

Nacionales de Colombia, S.A. v. Hall, choosing instead to treat the case as presenting a question of general jurisdiction only, leaving commentators to speculate as to why.[104]

A second question is: How purposeful must the defendant's contacts with the forum be in order to support specific jurisdiction? In a plurality opinion, Justice O'Connor opined that a defendant's conduct in the forum state is sufficiently purposeful if it designs the product for the forum state, advertises the product there, establishes channels for providing in-state customers with product advice, or markets the product through a distributor who has agreed to serve as a sales agent in the state.[105] The Court has been less clear in elaborating on whether or when lesser showings of purposefulness will suffice, such as where the defendant does not market its wares in the forum but is aware that its products are regularly sold there via the chain of distribution.[106]

§ 3.05   SPECIFIC JURISDICTION — THE EMERGING, MULTIFACTOR ANALYSIS

[1]   *McGee v. International Life Ins. Co.*[107]

The Court noted in *International Shoe* that a corporation's "single or isolated items of activities in a state . . . are not enough to subject it to suit on causes of action *unconnected* with the activities there."[108] At the same time, the *International Shoe* Court appeared to place a premium on the fact that the defendant's activities giving rise to the suit against it were conducted in the forum state.[109] What would happen if a foreign corporation's contacts with the forum state were "single or isolated," but the case arose out of those very contacts? The Supreme Court did not have to answer the question, because International Shoe's overall contacts with Washington were "systematic and continuous."[110] The Court subsequently answered the question in *McGee* and, in so doing, realized some of the more liberating implications of the minimum contacts approach.

McGee, as the beneficiary of her deceased son's life insurance policy, sued defendant International Life in California. Defendant was served by mail in Texas, its corporate home. International Life declined to appear in the case, and plaintiff obtained a default judgment. Plaintiff took the California judgment to Texas and attempted to enforce it. International Life collaterally attacked the judgment, arguing that California did not have personal jurisdiction. Texas courts agreed. The United States Supreme Court did not question defendant's right to argue that the

---

[104] *See* § 3.08[2].

[105] *Asahi Metal Industry Co., Ltd. v. Superior Court,* 480 U.S. 102, 112 (1987).

[106] *See* § 3.07.

[107] 355 U.S. 220 (1957).

[108] 326 U.S. at 317 (emphasis added); *see* § 3.06[1][b].

[109] *See* note 90 and related text, *supra.*

[110] *See* note 89 and related text, *supra.*

California court lacked jurisdiction in an effort to resist the California judgment,[111] but found the argument without merit and reversed.

The facts revealed that defendant conducted virtually no business in California. Decedent's policy had been the only one in force there. It would be hard to imagine a clearer example of "single or isolated" corporate activity in the forum state. The Court nonetheless held that California had validly exercised jurisdiction over International Life, demonstrating that minimum contacts can be minimal indeed — so long as they are sufficiently related to the lawsuit:

> [W]e think it apparent that the Due Process Clause did not preclude the California court from entering a judgment binding on respondent. It is sufficient for purposes of due process that the suit was based on a contract which had substantial connection with that State. . . . The contract was delivered in California, the premiums were mailed from there and the insured was a resident of that State when he died.[112]

The Court explained why it mattered that defendant's forum contacts were related to the controversy. "It cannot be denied that California has a manifest interest in providing effective means of redress for its residents when their insurers refuse to pay claims."[113] "These residents would be at a severe disadvantage if they were forced to follow the insurance company to a distant State in order to hold it legally accountable."[114] And the Court suggested that, on the whole, California might have been the most logical place to try the case.[115] There might have been some inconvenience for International Life, "but certainly nothing which amounts to a denial of due process."[116]

The most enduring aspect of *McGee* is that it established beyond question the forum's authority to exercise jurisdiction over nonresident defendants in lawsuits resulting from their forum-directed activities.[117] On the other hand, it is difficult to say how much reliance can safely be placed on some of the more freewheeling

---

[111] Defendant was able to raise the personal jurisdiction issue only because it had not taken any part in the California proceeding. But, while defaulting in California preserved defendant's opportunity to litigate the personal jurisdiction question later in Texas, it also made everything turn on winning the issue. Because International Life lost, it was never able to present the substantial case it apparently had on the merits — that the policy was inapplicable because the insured died by suicide. 355 U.S. at 223. Such are the risks of favoring collateral over direct attack as a means of raising personal jurisdiction issues. For a discussion of direct and collateral attack on personal jurisdiction and considerations in choosing between the two, see § 3.04, *supra*.

[112] 355 U.S. at 223.

[113] 355 U.S. at 223.

[114] 355 U.S. at 223.

[115] "Often the crucial witnesses — as here on the company's defense of suicide — will be found in the insured's locality." 355 U.S. at 223.

[116] 355 U.S. at 224.

[117] When, as in *McGee*, the cause of action arises entirely from activities of the defendant directed at the forum, it is universally accepted that due process does not prevent the forum from exercising jurisdiction. *Cf.* RESTATEMENT (SECOND) OF CONFLICTS § 35 comment e (1971) ("It is always reasonable for a State to exercise judicial jurisdiction over an individual as to causes of action arising from business done by him within its territory."). *See, e.g., Burger King Corp. v. Rudzewicz*, 471 U.S. 462, 473 (1985) (applying the principle and citing *McGee*). *See generally* § 3.06 (discussing *Burger King*), *infra*.

arguments made by the Court in support of its conclusion. The Supreme Court has neither questioned *McGee*, nor been reluctant to cite the case. Yet it may be true that Supreme Court decisions on personal jurisdiction represent more a spectrum of opinion than a single point of view. If this is so, then *McGee* exists at one end of the spectrum.[118] As Professor Weintraub observed, the case "was the high-water mark of personal jurisdiction."[119]

[2] *Hanson v. Denckla*[120]

Hanson v. Denckla was decided one year after *McGee*. The facts of *Hanson v. Denckla* were quite complicated.[121] Two factions fought over distribution of a $400,000 estate. The Denckla group claimed that the money passed to them through decedent's will. The Hanson group claimed that the funds were not affected by the will because they were the subject of a trust (with the Hanson group as beneficiaries) created by the decedent before her death. The Denckla group brought suit in Florida to have the trust declared invalid. The Florida Supreme Court eventually ruled that it was. It also ruled that personal jurisdiction existed over two Delaware trust companies, defendants in the case who had been appointed trustees for the disputed trust. On review, a narrowly divided Supreme Court disagreed, finding that the Florida courts lacked personal jurisdiction over the trustees.

First reaching the somewhat surprising conclusion that defendants properly within the Florida courts' jurisdiction could question jurisdiction over the absent trustees,[122] the Court proceeded to the due process issue. Clearly, the case for personal jurisdiction was weaker in *Hanson* than in previous cases decided by the Court after *International Shoe*. Unlike the defendant in *International Shoe*, the

---

[118] *E.g.*, compare the *McGee* Court's recognition of the forum's interest in providing a means for its citizens to sue and of the significance of the forum as a generally convenient place for suit with the Court's rejection of the same concerns in *Hanson v. Denckla*, 357 U.S. 235 (1958). It may be possible to reconcile the results in the two cases, *see* § 3.05[2], *infra*, yet they do seem to reflect differences in philosophy.

[119] Russell J. Weintraub, *Due Process Limitations on the Personal Jurisdiction of State Courts: Time for Change*, 63 OR. L. REV. 485, 489 (1984).

[120] 357 U.S. 235 (1958).

[121] For more detailed statements of the case, see Austin W. Scott, *Hanson v. Denckla*, 72 HARV. L. REV. 695 (1959); Philip B. Kurland, *The Supreme Court, the Due Process Clause and the In Personam Jurisdiction of State Courts from Pennoyer to Denckla: A Review*, 25 U. CHI. L. REV. 569, 610–23 (1958).

[122] Most of the Hanson-group defendants were Florida domiciliaries and were served there. However, the Delaware-trustee defendants were foreign corporations who maintained no office in Florida and had to be served out of state by mail. They refused to participate and ultimately defaulted. The challenge concerning Florida jurisdiction over the trustees was not raised by the trustees themselves, but by the Hanson group. Traditionally, the Court has been reluctant to permit litigants, whose own constitutional rights have not been injured, to object to the proceedings by raising the rights of others. The Court got around this in *Hanson* by reading Florida procedural law to make the Delaware trustees indispensable parties to the lawsuit. Thus, it reasoned, the case could not proceed if Florida was incapable of exercising jurisdiction over them. 357 U.S. at 254–55. *See* § 9.05[2] (compulsory joinder), *infra*. Dissenting, Justice Black questioned this interpretation of Florida law and argued that at the very least the case should have been remanded to the Florida courts to give them an opportunity to pass on the indispensability question. 357 U.S. at 257–62 (Black, J., dissenting).

Delaware trust companies did not conduct "continuous and systematic" operations in the forum. Indeed, they had no offices in Florida and transacted no business there.[123] The controversy centered on the validity of the trust, and the trust was created in Delaware. Therefore, unlike the defendant in *McGee*,[124] the trustees directed little if any of their activities at the forum state.[125]

What divided the Court was that two theories, which previously combined to support personal jurisdiction, seemed in *Hanson* to pull in opposite directions. The first of these, a power theory, was refined in *International Shoe*[126] from earlier cases. Under this theory, submission to suit is a fair exchange for the benefits and protection a nonresident defendant receives from the forum state. The second, which received more glancing treatment in *International Shoe*,[127] focused on the logic or convenience of plaintiff's forum choice. The burden on defendant from litigating there is a factor. Other factors are the degree of difficulty for plaintiff in suing elsewhere and possible interest the forum state might have in making its courts available to hear the case. The Court had utilized both theories in intervening cases.[128] Never before *Hanson* had they seemed at odds.

Dissenting from the Court's refusal to permit personal jurisdiction, Justice Black argued the convenience theory: that Florida would be a logical and convenient place to adjudicate the lawsuit.[129] The question of the trust's validity bore not only on the trust itself but also on the scope and effect of decedent's will. And the will was probated in Florida. Thus, contended Justice Black, "Florida was seriously concerned with winding up Mrs. Donner's estate and with finally determining what property was to be distributed under her will."[130]

However, the *Hanson* majority adopted the power theory. In so doing, the majority did not really dispute the relative convenience of Florida as a place for suit, or the interest of the plaintiffs and the State of Florida in a Florida adjudication. It simply concluded that, without minimum contacts between the nonresident defendants and the forum capable of supporting the power theory, these other considerations did not come into play.

First, the majority brushed aside the convenience of a Florida forum. The protections of due process, it said,

---

[123] Scott, note 121, *supra*, at 702.

[124] *See* § 3.05[1], *supra*.

[125] On the other hand, Justice Black contended that the Delaware trustees were not altogether free of contact with Florida. The last time the decedent exercised her power under the trust instrument to redirect the remainder, she did so from Florida. 357 U.S. at 258 (Black, J. dissenting). Presumably, this required the assistance of at least one of the trustees. Also, at least one of the trustees transmitted trust income to the decedent while she was living in Florida. 357 U.S. at 257. The latter contact would have been more significant if the case concerned whether the trustee had breached its duty under the trust instrument, instead of whether the trust itself was valid.

[126] *See* § 3.03, *supra*.

[127] *See* § 3.03, *supra*.

[128] The Court consolidated its analysis of these factors in *Burger King*. *See* § 3.06, *infra*.

[129] "Florida, the home of the principal contenders for Mrs. Donner's largess, was a reasonably convenient forum for all." 357 U.S. at 259 (Black, J., dissenting).

[130] 357 U.S. at 259.

are more than a guarantee of immunity from inconvenient or distant litigation. They are a consequence of territorial limitations on the power of the respective States. However minimal the burden of defending in a foreign tribunal, a defendant may not be called upon to do so unless he has had the "minimal contacts" with that State that are a prerequisite to its exercise of power over him.[131]

The *Hanson* majority similarly discounted the significance of contacts between the plaintiffs and the forum, stating that the "unilateral activity of those who claim some relationship with a nonresident defendant cannot satisfy the requirement of contact with the forum State."[132] The Court also refused to attach importance to Florida's interest in adjudicating this kind of lawsuit.[133]

The majority left no doubt that (1) focus on the relationship between the forum and *defendant* was both central and indispensable to its minimum contacts inquiry, and (2) contacts would achieve the minimum only if they were sufficient to support the power theory:

> The application of that rule will vary with the quality and nature of the defendant's activity, but it is essential in each case that there be some act by which the defendant purposefully avails itself of the privilege of conducting activities within the forum State, thus invoking the benefits and protections of its laws.[134]

Hanson's history as precedent reflects a reversal of the usual pattern. The later force of the case is far greater than were its immediate effects.[135] For a long time, *Hanson*'s chief importance seemed to lie in confirming *International Shoe*'s admonition that due process "does not contemplate that a state may make binding a judgment *in personam* against an individual or corporate defendant with which the state has no contacts, ties, or relations."[136] Perhaps this was significant in itself, providing "a stopping place . . . on what had been the road toward nationwide in

---

[131] 357 U.S. at 251 (citing *International Shoe*).

[132] 357 U.S. at 253.

[133] The *Hanson* Court entertained the possibility that the facts of the controversy might so involve Florida state interests as to justify application of Florida substantive law, but stated flatly: "The issue is personal jurisdiction, not choice of law." 357 U.S. at 254. Granted, there are situations where a court constitutionally capable of applying its own substantive law to a controversy may lack contacts with the defendant necessary for personal jurisdiction. *See* the example provided in Gene R. Shreve, *Interest Analysis as Constitutional Law*, 48 Oᴴɪᴏ Sᴛ. L.J. 51, 60 n.60 (1987). In *Hanson*, however, it might have been difficult for the Supreme Court to have upheld as constitutional the Florida court's rejection of Delaware trust law in favor of its own. Frederic L. Kirgis, Jr., *The Roles of Due Process and Full Faith and Credit in Choice of Law*, 62 Cᴏʀɴᴇʟʟ L. Rᴇᴠ. 94, 144–46 (1976); Gene R. Shreve, *In Search of a Choice-of-Law Reviewing Standard — Reflections on* Allstate Insurance Co. v. Hague, 66 Mɪɴɴ. L. Rᴇᴠ. 327, 334 (1982). Because of its ruling of no personal jurisdiction, it was unnecessary for the Court to reach the choice-of-law question.

[134] 357 U.S. at 253 (citing *International Shoe*).

[135] The case was to underpin modern decisions regulating extraterritorial jurisdiction more stringently. *E.g., Shaffer v. Heitner*, 433 U.S. 186, 215–16 (1977); *World-Wide Volkswagen Corp. v. Woodson*, 444 U.S. 286, 294–99 (1980).

[136] *International Shoe Co. v. Washington*, 326 U.S. 310, 319 (1945).

personam jurisdiction for state courts."[137]

The case left unanswered important questions concerning how the "quality and nature of defendant's activity" should be measured in order to determine whether minimum forum contacts existed. The Court's failure to address these questions in *Hanson*, or to return to them until 1977, left considerable ambiguity in its due process doctrine. Isolated, the authority of the *Hanson* case also suffered from its complicated and somewhat bizarre facts and from the Court's questionable judgment that there was a due process issue in the case at all.[138] As one scholar has observed, "[i]n the ensuing years many commentators and courts distinguished or effectively ignored it, while suggesting or taking a more expansive approach to jurisdiction. And there the Supreme Court let things lie for two decades."[139]

[3]   *World-Wide Volkswagen v. Woodson*[140]

In 1977, the Supreme Court revisited personal jurisdiction for the first time in twenty years, in a *quasi in rem* case.[141] It was not until 1980 that the Supreme Court decided another, more traditional *in personam* jurisdiction case. Plaintiffs purchased an Audi automobile from defendant retailer Seaway Volkswagen in New York. Seaway had obtained the car from defendant World-Wide Volkswagen, a regional distributor. Plaintiffs thereafter moved from New York, traveling in their Audi toward a destination in Arizona. The gas tank ignited in an Oklahoma collision, seriously injuring several members of the family. Plaintiffs brought suit in an Oklahoma state court against manufacturer Audi, importer Volkswagen of America, World-Wide Volkswagen and Seaway.

Plaintiffs made a substantial case for personal jurisdiction. Since product failure and injuries were alleged to have occurred in the forum, it seemed a natural place for plaintiff to bring suit. Moreover, the fact of injury in the forum appeared to provide Oklahoma with a regulatory interest in adjudicating the case. Nonetheless, the Supreme Court upheld the challenges of retailer Seaway and regional distributor World-Wide Volkswagen.[142] Noting that these "defendants' only connection with Oklahoma is the fact that an automobile sold in New York to New York residents became involved in an accident in Oklahoma,"[143] the Court held that Oklahoma courts were without minimum contacts necessary to assert personal jurisdiction.[144]

---

[137] Kurland, note 121, *supra*, at 622.

[138] *See* note 122, *supra.*

[139] Kevin M. Clermont, *Restating Territorial Jurisdiction and Venue for State and Federal Courts*, 66 Cornell L. Rev. 411, 419 (1981).

[140] 444 U.S. 286 (1980).

[141] *Shaffer v. Heitner*, 433 U.S. 186 (1977). *See* § 3.09[1][a], *infra.*

[142] Audi does not appear to have challenged jurisdiction. Volkswagen of America dropped its jurisdictional objection prior to Supreme Court review. 444 U.S. at 288 n.3.

[143] 444 U.S. at 287.

[144] The Oklahoma court lacked jurisdiction,

[e]ven if the defendant would suffer minimal or no inconvenience from being forced to litigate before the tribunals of another State; even if the forum State has a strong interest in applying

The problem to the Court was the lack of contacts between the defendants and the Oklahoma forum.[145] Granted, defendants could have foreseen that so mobile a product might reach Oklahoma highways, but "'foreseeability' alone has never been a sufficient benchmark for personal jurisdiction under the Due Process Clause."[146] The Court did not wish to discard the concept of foreseeability, but emphasized that it was a different kind of foreseeability that mattered.

> [T]he foreseeability that is critical to due process analysis is not the mere likelihood that a product will find its way into the forum State. Rather, it is that the defendant's conduct and connection with the forum State are such that he should reasonably anticipate being haled into court there.[147]

The Court reasoned that the conduct of the retailer and wholesaler in *World-Wide Volkswagen* was not such as to cause them to anticipate being haled into court in Oklahoma. Neither sold cars, advertised, or carried on any other activity in the state. And the conduct of the Robinsons in driving the car to Oklahoma did not help. The mere "unilateral activity of those who claim some relationship with a nonresident defendant cannot satisfy the requirement of contact with the forum State," the Court said.[148]

---

its law to the controversy; even if the forum State is the most convenient location for litigation. 444 U.S. at 294.

[145] As it had in *Hanson*, the Court stressed that "the Due Process Clause does not contemplate that a state may make binding a judgment *in personam* against an individual or corporate defendant with which the state has no contacts, ties, or relations." 444 U.S. at 294 (*quoting* from *International Shoe Co. v. Washington*, 326 U.S. 310, 319 (1945)).

[146] 444 U.S. at 295. If it was, said the Court, failures in such products as tires, automobile jacks and soft drinks would expose local retailers to suit wherever plaintiff might transport the product. "Every seller of chattels would in effect appoint the chattel his agent for service of process. His amenability to suit would travel with the chattel." 444 U.S. at 296.

[147] 444 U.S. at 297. Then it is reasonable to impose personal jurisdiction because a corporation purposefully directing its activities at the forum

> has clear notice that it is subject to suit there, and can act to alleviate the risk of burdensome litigation by procuring insurance, passing the expected costs on to customers, or, if the risks are too great, severing its connection with the State.

444 U.S. at 297.

[148] The Court cited *Hanson v. Denckla*, 357 U.S. 235 (1958). Other modern cases, including *Shaffer v. Heitner*, 433 U.S. 186 (1977), discussed at § 3.09[1][a], *infra; Rush v. Savchuk*, 444 U.S. 320 (1980), discussed at § 3.09[1][b], *infra*, and *Kulko v. Superior Court*, 436 U.S. 84 (1978), also refurbished *Hanson's* authority. *Kulko* involved a California custody and child support proceeding. The Supreme Court held that the fact that the New York father provided his daughter with a one-way ticket to California did not establish requisite minimum contacts between the defendant-father and the forum. California's interest in adjudicating the case was real, deriving from the presence there of the mother and two children. To the Court, however, the lack of contacts between California and the defendant made California's interest academic. Quoting *Hanson*, the Court stated:

> The unilateral activity of those who claim some relationship with a nonresident defendant cannot satisfy the requirement of contact with the forum State. . . . [I]t is essential in each case that there be some act by which the defendant purposefully avails [him]self of the privilege of conducting activities within the forum State.

436 U.S at 93–94. For more on personal jurisdiction in the domestic relations setting, see Rosemarie T. Ring, *Personal Jurisdiction and Child Support: Establishing the Parent-Child Relationship as*

Finally, it was no answer either that the defendants may have had the resources (or insurance) to defend in Oklahoma, or even that Oklahoma had a strong forum interest in hearing the claim. "Even if the defendant would suffer minimal or no inconvenience from being forced to litigate before the tribunals of another State; even if the forum State has a strong interest in applying its law to the controversy; even if the forum State is the most convenient location for litigation, the Due Process Clause, acting as an instrument of interstate federalism, may sometimes act to divest the State of its power to render a valid judgment."[149] In short, interstate federalism requires minimum contacts even when suit is otherwise reasonable and fair to the defendant.

[4] *Keeton v. Hustler Magazine*[150]

It is clear that sufficient claim-related contacts between the forum and a nonresident defendant make the defendant amenable to suit on a theory of specific jurisdiction,[151] and that sufficient contacts between the two which are unrelated to the controversy will produce the same result on a theory of general jurisdiction.[152] There will be cases, however, where the forum has both types of contacts with a nonresident defendant, but neither in sufficient quantity to alone support personal jurisdiction. May the forum satisfy due process in such cases by aggregating all of defendant's forum contacts?

The question once divided commentators[153] but now may be resolved in a way broadening opportunities for personal jurisdiction. Without endorsing general use of the technique, the Supreme Court appeared to combine related and unrelated contacts in holding that jurisdiction was proper in *Keeton v. Hustler Magazine.*

Plaintiff Keeton sued Hustler Magazine in New Hampshire federal court for libel. The First Circuit Court of Appeals upheld Hustler's objection to personal jurisdiction. It ruled that due process prevented New Hampshire's long-arm statute from reaching Hustler,[154] an Ohio corporation with its principal place of business in California. The Supreme Court reversed.

Hustler had some contacts with the New Hampshire forum both related and unrelated to the controversy. It had circulated in New Hampshire copies of the

---

Minimum Contacts, 89 CAL. L. REV. 1125 (2001); Rhonda Wasserman, *Parents, Partners, and Personal Jurisdiction*, 1995 U. ILL. L. REV. 813.

[149] *World-Wide Volkswagen*, 444 U.S. at 294, *quoting Hanson v. Denckla*, 357 U.S. at 251, 254.

[150] 465 U.S. 770 (1984).

[151] *See* §§ 3.03 & 3.04[2], *supra*.

[152] *See* § 3.08.

[153] *Compare, e.g.*, Harold S. Lewis, Jr., *A Brave New World for Personal Jurisdiction: Flexible Tests Under Uniform Standards*, 37 VAND. L. REV. 1, 34 (1984) (arguing the possibility of establishing personal jurisdiction through "partial satisfaction of both versions of the contacts tests"), *with* Lea Brilmayer, *How Contacts Count: Due Process Limitations on State Court Jurisdiction*, 1980 SUP. CT. REV. 77, 88 ("These two bases are independent threshold tests, so that a greater quantum of unrelated activity does not compensate for attenuated related contacts."). For the latter view, see also K. A. Lambert, Comment, *De Reyes v. Marine Management & Consulting, Ltd.: The Abuse of General Jurisdiction*, 66 TUL. L. REV. 2085, 2093 (1992) (criticizing a recent Louisiana case for "merging the two doctrines").

[154] *Keeton v. Hustler Magazine*, 682 F.2d 33 (1st Cir. 1982).

magazine alleged to have libeled plaintiff, and it had circulated other unrelated issues there in a continuous and systematic fashion. There is some indication, however, that neither defendant's related nor unrelated contacts would have alone been sufficient to support personal jurisdiction. The Court noted that the magnitude of the alleged libel was the total circulation of the offending issues and that "only a small portion" of that circulation occurred in New Hampshire.[155] Similarly, Hustler's activities in New Hampshire "may not" have been "so substantial as to support jurisdiction over a cause of action unrelated to those activities."[156] However, the combination of defendant's related and unrelated contacts with the forum proved enough. "[R]espondent is carrying on a 'part of its general business' in New Hampshire, and that is sufficient to support jurisdiction when the cause of action arises out of the very activity being conducted, in part, in New Hampshire."[157] Although the plaintiff had no meaningful contact with the state, the Court did not regard that as critical, because the focus of personal jurisdiction analysis is on the defendant's due process rights, which is evaluated with reference to the defendant's purposeful minimum contacts with the forum.[158]

It may be that the Court was simply aggregating the contacts to reach a quantitative threshold in a case like *Keeton*, but, if so, it backtracked from its disavowal in *International Shoe* of any "simply mechanical or quantitative" test.[159] A more plausible theory for "hybrid" cases (combining related with unrelated contacts to uphold personal jurisdiction) rests on the suggestion that general and specific jurisdiction are simply opposite ends of a sliding scale, by which the quantity and quality of the defendant's contacts and the relatedness of the contacts to the claim are inversely related.[160] The availability of unrelated contacts can therefore compensate for the paucity of related contacts, even though the case is "a near-miss"[161] on both — it does not reach either end of the scale.

---

[155] 465 U.S. at 775.

[156] 465 U.S. at 779.

[157] 465 U.S. at 780 (*quoting Perkins v. Benguet Mining Co.*, 342 U.S. 437, 438 (1952)). The Court added that, "Where, as in this case, respondent has continuously and deliberately exploited the New Hampshire market, it must reasonably anticipate being haled into court there in a libel action based on the contents of its magazine." 465 U.S. at 781. The Supreme Court had given earlier indication that related and unrelated contacts might have combined effect. For example, in *World-Wide Volkswagen Corp. v. Woodson*, 444 U.S. 286 (1980), the Court concluded that Oklahoma lacked jurisdiction only after finding that defendants' claim-related contacts with the forum were slight *and* that defendants had no contacts unrelated to the controversy. *World-Wide Volkswagen Corp.*, 444 U.S. at 295.

[158] 465 U.S. at 779.

[159] *International Shoe*, 326 U.S. at 319. *See RAR, Inc. v. Turner Diesel Ltd.*, 107 F.3d 1272, 1277 (7th Cir. 1997):

> We cannot simply aggregate all of a defendant's contacts with a state — no matter how dissimilar in terms of geography, time, or substance . . . . [W]hen doing business with a forum in one context, potential defendants should not have to wonder whether some aggregation of other past or future forum contacts will render them liable to suit there.

[160] *See* William M. Richman, *A Sliding Scale to Supplement the Distinction Between General and Specific Jurisdiction*, 72 Cal. L. Rev. 1328 (1984).

[161] Richman, note 160, *supra*.

An alternative theory is that the causally unrelated contacts with the forum state (distributing magazines other than the offending issue) are of the same kind as the causally related, though slight contact (distributing the particular offending issue of the magazine) that the defendant could reasonably foresee having to defend some libel action based on its magazines distributed there and that the state has a regulatory interest in the content of magazines distributed there. As one commentator has put it, "if . . . the defendant could have foreseen its forum contact resulting in factual circumstances similar to those that gave rise to the plaintiff's cause of action, then the defendant's contact should form the basis for asserting . . . jurisdiction in the forum."[162]

[5] *Calder v. Jones*[163]

In *Calder*, a California plaintiff brought a libel suit there against a number of defendants concerning publication of a story about the plaintiff in a national tabloid. The defendant who wrote and the defendant who edited the story (both Floridians) attacked the California court's personal jurisdiction. The highest California court ruling on the matter concluded that jurisdiction over the defendants was valid, and the United States Supreme Court affirmed.

Calder is superficially similar to *Keeton*,[164] in that both concerned specific jurisdiction over an alleged libelist. The defendant in *Keeton*, however, was a publisher, which had purposefully availed itself of the forum state in a conventional way — by selling magazines there that allegedly defamed the plaintiff. Once the Court decided that it was unnecessary for the plaintiff to have any meaningful contacts with the forum state to establish personal jurisdiction, over the defendant, *Keeton* was an easy case. The critical difference in *Calder* is that the defendants who challenged personal jurisdiction were the writer and editor, not the publisher. The writer and the editor were differently situated: they worked for a publisher that availed itself of the California market, but neither the writer nor the editor had any control over where their employer sold its magazines. Moreover, their traditional, claim-related "contacts" with the forum were minimal: the editor had visited California once for pleasure, and while the writer had visited California several times on business, he relied on telephone calls to gather information for the article in question.

The Court nonetheless concluded that the California courts could exercise personal jurisdiction over the writer and editor. In so holding, the Court focused on the effects of the defendant's article on the plaintiff in California. "The plaintiff's lack of 'contacts' will not defeat otherwise proper jurisdiction," the Court observed, citing *Keeton*, "but they may be so manifold as to permit jurisdiction when it would not exist in their absence."[165] In this case, "California is the focal point both of the

---

[162] Linda S. Simard, *Hybrid Personal Jurisdiction: It's Not General Jurisdiction, or Specific Jurisdiction, but Is It Constitutional?*, 48 Case W. Res. L. Rev. 559, 590 (1998).

[163] 465 U.S. 783 (1984).

[164] *Keeton v. Hustler Magazine*, 465 U.S. 770 (1984), discussed at § 3.05[4], *supra*.

[165] 465 U.S. at 788. Plaintiff's contacts most often derive from forum citizenship. Just as defendants usually prefer to litigate at home (*see* § 3.04[2], *supra*), so do plaintiffs. The interest in litigating at home

story and the harm suffered. Jurisdiction over petitioners is therefore proper based on the 'effects' of their Florida conduct in California."[166]

On the one hand, *Calder* need not be interpreted as representing a complete break from mainstream minimum contacts analysis: "intentional, and allegedly tortious, actions . . . expressly aimed" at a plaintiff in the forum state are a form of purposeful activity directed at the forum state that give rise to the claims sued upon. On the other hand, the contacts in *Calder* did not involve purposeful availment in a traditional sense, which has the potential to open Pandora's box, if interpreted broadly to permit personal jurisdiction over a defendant wherever the effects of a defendant's conduct can be felt. The internet in particular, has given rise to a new wave of "effects-test" cases, that require courts to determine when a defendant's website has targeted a plaintiff in his or her home state with sufficient awareness and specificity to justify jurisdiction over the defendant there, and some scholars have cautioned against reading *Calder* broadly.[167]

§ 3.06   SPECIFIC JURISDICTION — GIVING STRUCTURE TO THE EMERGING, MULTI-FACTOR ANALYSIS: *BURGER KING CORP. v. RUDZEWICZ*[168]

International Shoe and the cases that followed its lead made clear that specific jurisdiction is contingent upon a minimum contacts analysis that should be analyzed with reference to a number of factors. *International Shoe* focused on the need for the defendant to have minimum contacts with the forum state, making the nature and extent of those contacts a relevant factor in the analysis. In *International Shoe*, the Court concluded that this factor was met when the defendant's contacts with the forum were systematic and continuous. *McGee*, however, stands for the proposition that even an isolated contact — renewing a contract — may be enough, if that contact is so closely related to the case that it gives rise to the claim sued upon, making the relationship between the defendant's contacts with the forum state and the plaintiff's claim critical to specific jurisdiction analysis. But *Hanson* warned that isolated contacts giving rise to the claim are not enough; the defendant must have *purposefully* directed its activities at the forum state, making "purposeful availment" an important part of the minimum contacts equation. *World-Wide Volkswagon*, in turn, added a criterion that the defendant's contacts with the forum must make it foreseeable that it will be haled into court there. *Keeton* adds the nuances that for a defendant, related and unrelated forum activities can be germane to assessing the nature and extent of the defendant's contacts with the forum state,

---

is most compelling for plaintiffs lacking the mobility, resources, or sophistication to sue nonresident defendants elsewhere. *See* Arthur T. von Mehren, *Adjudicatory Jurisdiction: General Theories Compared and Evaluated*, 63 B.U. L. Rev. 279, 311–14 (1983); Arthur T. von Mehren & Donald T. Trautman, *Jurisdiction to Adjudicate: A Suggested Analysis*, 79 Harv. L. Rev. 1121, 1150 (1966); Note, *Jurisdiction over Foreign Corporations — An Analysis of Due Process*, 104 U. Pa. L. Rev. 381, 383 (1955).

[166] *Id.*

[167] *See* Cassandra Burke Robertson, *The Inextricable Merits Problem in Personal Jurisdiction*, 45 U.C. Davis L. Rev. 1301 (2012).

[168] 471 U.S. 462 (1985).

while the plaintiff's forum contacts are of lesser consequence. And *Calder* adds that with intentional tort claims, at least, the defendant's awareness that the "effects" of its conduct will be felt in the forum state can be a proxy for purposeful availment.

Then there are still other factors: *International Shoe* identified "traditional notions of fair play and substantial justice" as the goal of due process — a standard that is satisfied if the defendant's forum contacts are such as to "make it reasonable" to defend suit there. In that regard, *International Shoe* observed that "an 'estimate of the inconveniences' which would result to the corporation from a trial away from its 'home' " was a relevant consideration. In *McGee*, however, the Court dismissed the significance of this factor given the convenience of modern travel, but hung its hat two others: the plaintiff's interest in a convenient forum and the forum state's interest in protecting its citizens. And yet, in *Worldwide Volkswagon*, the Court found personal jurisdiction lacking for reasons that did not factor into its analysis the inconvenience to the defendant, the convenience to the plaintiff, or the forum state's interest in litigating the dispute.

The net effect is that personal jurisdiction analysis had evolved to comprise a jumble of factors, with some seeming more dispensable than others, and no clear relationship among them. In *Burger King*, the Court sought to impose a structure on specific jurisdiction analysis. Through negotiation with Burger King's regional office in Michigan, Rudzewicz and another Michigan defendant obtained a franchise in that state. Defendants failed to make payments, and Burger King brought a federal diversity suit on the franchise agreement in Florida, its headquarters and place of incorporation. Rudzewicz appealed a judgment against him. Reversing, the Eleventh Circuit Court of Appeals held Rudzewicz to be beyond the constitutional reach of Florida's long-arm statute.[169] The Court of Appeals based its decision upon a determination that the bulk of the contacts giving rise to the controversy were with Michigan rather than Florida.[170]

The United States Supreme Court reversed. The Court began with a survey of its precedents, on the basis of which it observed that personal jurisdiction analysis included two steps. The first step and the "constitutional touchstone" is whether "the defendant purposefully established minimum contacts within the forum state."[171] This purposeful minimum contacts step calls upon the Court to evaluate whether the defendant purposely engaged in activities within the forum that made it foreseeable the defendant would be haled into court for claims related to those activities.[172]

The Court then addressed the second step. "Once it has been decided that a defendant purposefully established minimum contacts within the forum State, these

---

[169] *Burger King Corp. v. Macshara*, 724 F.2d 1505 (11th Cir. 1984).

[170] The two-judge majority stated that Rudzewicz had no office in Florida, nor did it appear that he had ever been there. Contract negotiations were conducted between Rudzewicz and Burger King's district representative entirely in Michigan. Anticipated profits from the franchise were to derive exclusively from Michigan food sales. Justice Stevens would later observe in his dissent: "Throughout the business relationship, appellee's principal contacts with appellant were with its Michigan office." 471 U.S. at 487.

[171] 471 U.S. at 474.

[172] *Id.* at 474–76.

contacts may be considered in light of other factors to determine whether the assertion of personal jurisdiction would comport with 'fair play and substantial justice.' "[173] In this "fair play" step, factors to be considered include: the burden on the defendant; the forum state's interest in adjudicating the dispute; the plaintiff's interest in a convenient forum; and the interstate judicial system's interest in efficient resolution of controversies.[174] The Court made it clear that this second step was largely reserved for close cases — like *Keeton* and *McGee*, where the sufficiency of minimum contacts was uncertain. In these cases, the "fair play" factors could affect case outcomes in either of two ways. First, "[t]hese considerations sometimes serve to establish the reasonableness of jurisdiction upon a lesser showing of minimum contacts than would otherwise be required."[175] Second, it is possible that a "defendant who purposefully directs as activities at forum residents" could defeat jurisdiction if he "present[s] a compelling case that the presence of some other considerations would render jurisdiction unreasonable."[176]

Turning to the facts of the case, the Court acknowledged the threshold importance of minimum contacts between defendant and the Florida forum — the first step in the personal jurisdiction analysis that it set out earlier in its opinion. The Court held that there were enough Florida contacts related to the controversy to satisfy the test. Defendants at times dealt directly with Burger King's Miami headquarters; they contracted with Burger King to have Florida law govern the franchise agreement;[177] and they promised to send their franchise payments to Burger King's Florida address. Under the circumstances, the Court refused to attach importance to the fact that Rudzewicz had not been in the forum state.

> Although territorial presence frequently will enhance a potential defendant's affiliation with a State and reinforce the reasonable foreseeability of suit there, it is an inescapable fact of modern commercial life that a substantial amount of business is transacted solely by mail and wire communications across state lines, thus obviating the need for physical presence within a State in which business is conducted. So long as a commercial actor's efforts are "purposefully directed" toward residents of another State, we have consistently rejected the notion that an absence of physical contacts can defeat personal jurisdiction there.[178]

The Court then turned to the second step of the personal jurisdiction analysis. It concluded that the defendant had not "pointed to other factors that can be said persuasively to outweigh the considerations discussed above and to establish the

---

[173] *Id.* at 476.

[174] *Id.* at 477.

[175] Id.

[176] Id.

[177] This is not to be confused with contractual consent to jurisdiction. Had Rudzewicz consented to Florida jurisdiction, his only basis for resistance presumably would have been to argue that the clause was unconscionable, or represented a contract of adhesion, and hence was unenforceable. For discussion of this point, see § 3.11[4], *infra.*

[178] 471 U.S. at 476.

unconstitutionality of Florida's assertion of jurisdiction."[179] In so concluding, it rejected arguments that Florida had no legitimate interest in the dispute, and that plaintiff had taken unfair advantage of defendants.[180]

On final analysis, *Burger King* may represent a realistic accommodation between the minimum contacts requirement of due process and the fact that controversy-related contacts are often spread over more than one state.[181] In this case, the defendants knowingly reached out to a Florida corporation in a variety of ways, as the price for establishing a Michigan franchise. To recognize specific jurisdiction only in the place that is the predominant source of related contacts would often deny forums the legitimate expression of their regulatory interests. More fundamentally, perhaps, and irrespective of its holding, *Burger King* synthesized the multi-factor personal jurisdiction analysis into a useful, two-step structure for analyzing specific jurisdiction cases in the future.

§ 3.07   THE "STREAM OF COMMERCE" PROBLEM

[1]   The Stream of Commerce

Product liability cases can pose a special problem in applying personal jurisdiction's minimum contacts test — the measurement of defendant's activities purposefully (knowingly) directed into the forum state.[182] Recall the assumption of the Supreme Court and commentators that minimum contacts analysis can be divided into the subcategories of specific and general jurisdiction.[183] This has proved a useful distinction and accommodates most personal jurisdiction cases. But the distinction can be problematic when applied to product liability cases.[184]

The problem comes from the nature and scope of product liability recovery. Liability for harm to consumers typically stems from faulty product design or manufacture. Manufacturers of the completed product (along with producers of

---

[179] *Id.* at 482.

[180] *Id.* at 483–86.

[181] *See also Keeton v. Hustler Magazine*, 465 U.S. 770 (1984). The Court permitted jurisdiction under the New Hampshire long-arm statute in a defamation action, although only a small percentage of defendant's total circulation of the offending magazine issue occurred in the forum state. However, the facts of *Keeton* furnished added jurisdictional support not present in *Burger King*. Defendant had carried on continuous and systematic activity (albeit unrelated to the controversy) in New Hampshire. For discussion of *Keeton*, see § 3.05[4], *supra.* For further discussion of *Burger King*, see Rex R. Perschbacher, *Minimum Contacts Reapplied: Mr. Justice Brennan Has It His Way in* Burger King Corp. v. Rudzewicz, 1986 Ariz. St. L.J. 585; Martin B. Louis, *Jurisdiction over Those Who Breach Their Contracts: The Lessons of Burger King*, 72 N.C. L. Rev. 55 (1993).

[182] Extended discussion of the minimum contacts test appears in § 3.06, *supra.*

[183] *See* § 3.04, *supra.*

[184] The chain-of-distribution problem and the response offered by the stream of commerce doctrine features most prominently in personal jurisdiction issues arising in product liability cases. However, the same situation may also arise in "tort, contract, domestic relations, fraud, antitrust, intellectual property, libel, defamation, unfair competition — to name a few." Diane S. Kaplan, *Paddling Up the Wrong Stream: Why the Stream of Commerce Theory Is Not Part of the Minimum Contacts Doctrine*, 55 Baylor L. Rev. 503, 506–07 (2003) (case citations omitted).

product ingredients or component parts involved in the failure) may therefore be liable. So may others responsible for moving the product along to the consumer (wholesalers, distributers, retailers). The points of origin for creation of the product, its component parts, or, ingredients may be distant from the point where a consumer purchases the product from a retailer. Those at the beginning of the chain may not have purposefully directed their product into the state where it failed inasmuch as they do not and could not purposefully direct any particular unit of the product anywhere.

Consider an example. A lawn mower injures consumer X in California, who bought it from retailer Y there. The cause is failure of a component part produced by Alabama Company A and incorporated into the lawn mower by B, a large lawn mower manufacturer in New Jersey. Y and anyone in the distribution chain who purposefully moved the offending lawn mower into or through the California market will clearly be within the California court's specific jurisdiction. But, while the particular products of A and B have failed in California so as to make them liable to X, neither can be said to have purposefully directed the particular lawn mower that failed into California. When that lawn mower left B's plant, it entered a nationwide distribution network, the details of which were beyond B's knowledge or control. B knew that its lawn mowers were in use in California, but A (and B) had no way of knowing which of A's lawn mowers would end up there.

Can a California court exercise personal jurisdiction over A and B? B did not knowingly direct the offending lawn mower into California. A and B have no purposefully-directed contacts with California related to the controversy, therefore nothing to support a theory of specific jurisdiction. Nor, we will assume, are B's California activities unrelated to the controversy so systematic, continuous and substantial as to provide a basis for general jurisdiction. All X has to work with to establish jurisdiction is the fact that A and B know that some of B's lawn mowers were ultimately sold and used in California.

At first, personal jurisdiction for such product liability cases seemed relatively secure under law straddling the specific/general distinction: the so-called stream of commerce doctrine. The doctrine is often associated with landmark case, *Gray v. American Radiator & Standard Sanitary Corp.*[185] One of the defendants challenged personal jurisdiction in an Illinois suit for injuries from a water heater that had exploded there. Defendant had manufactured the safety valve on the exploding heater, but it did no business in Illinois. It manufactured the valve in question in Ohio and sold it to another defendant who assembled the water heater in Pennsylvania. The Illinois Supreme Court stated in *Gray* that, while the defendant may have been unaware that the valve that failed was destined for use in Illinois, "it is a reasonable inference that its commercial transactions, like those of other manufacturers, result in substantial use and consumption in this State."[186] Defendant did not purposefully direct the offending valve into Illinois, but the court

---

[185] 176 N.E.2d 761 (Ill. 1961).

[186] 176 N.E.2d at 766. "To the extent that its business may be directly affected by transactions occurring here it enjoys benefits from the laws of this State, and it has undoubtedly benefited, to a degree, from the protection which our law has given to the marketing of hot water heaters containing its valves." *Id.*

found personal jurisdiction possible when "liability arises, as in this case, from the manufacture of products presumably sold in contemplation of use here."[187] Then, "it should not matter that the purchase was made from an independent middleman or that someone other than the defendant shipped the product into this State."[188] It was enough that defendant placed the defective valve into the stream of interstate commerce with the realization that some of its valves came to rest in the forum state.[189]

The stream of commerce doctrine laid down in *Gray* had much to recommend it[190] and, for over twenty-five years, it received widespread if not unanimous[191] acceptance. As recently as 1980, the United States Supreme Court cited *Gray* with apparent approval, stating: "The forum state does not exceed its powers under the Due Process Clause if it asserts personal jurisdiction over a corporation that delivers its products into the stream of commerce with the expectation that they will be purchased by consumers in the forum State."[192]

[2] *Asahi Metal Industry Co., Ltd. v. Superior Court*

In *Asahi*, the plaintiff sued in California over a serious accident there, allegedly caused by failure of the rear tire of plaintiff's motorcycle. Defendant Cheng Shin manufactured the tire in Taiwan. It attempted to bring Asahi, a Japanese concern and manufacturer of the tire's valve assembly, into the case on a theory of indemnification. Rejecting Asahi's jurisdictional challenge, the California Supreme Court held that it could exercise personal jurisdiction over Asahi without violating the Due Process Clause.[193] The United States Supreme Court reversed.

---

[187] 176 N.E.2d at 766.

[188] 176 N.E.2d at 766.

[189] "[I]t is not unreasonable, where a course of action arises from alleged defects in his product, to say that the use of such products in the ordinary course of commerce is sufficient contact with this State to justify a requirement that he defend here." 176 N.E.2d at 766.

[190] Stream of commerce theory enables the state to investigate through exercise of personal jurisdiction whether citizens have been harmed locally. And the latter has the incidental and salutary effect of permitting courts to adjudicate in one case the interests of more (perhaps all) defendants in the chain of distribution. A leading authority described stream of commerce as "a useful contribution to the developing law of jurisdiction; without it, an out-of-state enterprise could reap substantial rewards from goods sold in the forum, yet insulate itself from amenability by using middlemen." ROBERT C. CASAD & WILLIAM B. RICHMAN, JURISDICTION IN CIVIL ACTIONS § 2-5[4][b][v] (3d ed. 1998). *But see* Diane S. Kaplan, *Paddling up the Wrong Stream: Why the Stream of Commerce Theory is Not Part of the Minimum Contacts Doctrine*, 55 BAYLOR L. REV. 503 (2003) (arguing forcefully and at length against the stream of commerce doctrine).

[191] A few courts found *Gray*'s stream of commerce approach too expansive. *E.g.*, *In-Flight Devices Corp. v. Van Dusen Air, Inc.*, 466 F.2d 220 (6th Cir. 1972); *Beaty v. M. S. Steel Co.*, 276 F. Supp. 259 (D. Md. 1967).

[192] *World-Wide Volkswagen Corp. v. Woodson*, 444 U.S. 286, 297–98 (1980).

[193] The California Supreme Court sought to neutralize *World-Wide Volkswagen* by finding in the case a "distinction between businesses that serve a local market and those that serve a broader market," deeming Asahi to be the latter. 702 P.2d 543, 547 (Cal. 1985), *rev'd*, 480 U.S. 102 (1987). In other words, while "a secondary distributor and retailer" was protected under *World-Wide Volkswagen*, "a manufacturer or primary distributor" was not. 702 P.2d at 548. The United States Supreme Court's decision in *Asahi* makes clear that this categorical distinction does not work.

Consistent with the two-step structure articulated in *Burger King*,[194] the plurality opinion, written by Justice O'Connor and joined by three other Justices, maintained that minimum contacts did not exist. They did so by narrowing significantly the stream of commerce theory. It was not enough that the third-party defendant placed the product in the stream of commerce and was aware that its products were in use in the forum state.[195] A stream of commerce basis for personal jurisdiction would be acceptable only if there were additional acts of the defendant directed into the forum state. Justice O'Connor offered as examples

> designing the product for the market in the forum State, advertising in the forum State, establishing channels for providing regular advice to custom-ers in the forum State, or marketing the product through a distributor who has agreed to serve as the sales agent in the forum State.[196]

Justice Brennan and three other Justices, on the other hand, concluded that minimum contacts did exist. For the Brennan four, it was enough that the Japanese manufacturer knew its components were being incorporated into a Taiwanese company's tires bound for resale in the United States. In that way, Justice Brennan concluded, the Japanese corporation had availed itself of the U.S. market and could foresee that it would be subject to suit in California for problems relating to the valves that had been incorporated into tires sold there.[197]

The final member of the Court, Justice Stevens, declared that it was unnecessary to reach a conclusion as to minimum contacts, because he agreed with both Justice O'Connor and Justice Brennan that considerations of reasonableness and fair play tipped the balance against jurisdiction.[198] However, he added that, "in most circumstances I would be inclined to conclude that a regular course of dealing that results in deliveries of over 100,000 units annually over a period of several years would constitute 'purposeful availment.' "[199]

With respect to the minimum contacts component of the personal jurisdiction analysis, the Court was deadlocked; as a consequence, the second step in the *Burger King* analysis[200] — the fair play factors — would prove decisive. Seven Justices joined in Justice O'Connor's conclusion that, whether or not minimum contacts existed between the forum and Asahi, California's attempt to assert personal jurisdiction exceeded what the distinct "reasonableness" standard of due process. It drew the standard from language in *International Shoe* confining personal jurisdiction over nonresident defendants to "traditional notions of fair play and

---

[194] *See* § 3.06.

[195] Justice O'Connor wrote: "The placement of a product into the stream of commerce, without more, is not an act of the defendant purposefully directed toward the forum State." 480 U.S. at 112. She added: "a defendant's awareness that the stream of commerce may or will sweep the product into the forum State does not convert the mere act of placing the product into the stream into an act purposefully directed toward the forum State." 480 U.S. at 112.

[196] 480 U.S. at 112.

[197] 480 U.S. at 120–21 (Brennan, concurring).

[198] 480 U.S. at 121 (Stevens, concurring).

[199] 480 U.S. at 122 (Stevens, concurring).

[200] *See* § 3.06.

substantial justice."[201] The Court noted that

> the determination of the reasonableness of the exercise of jurisdiction in
> each case will depend on an evaluation of several factors. A court must
> consider the burden on the defendant, the interests of the forum state, and
> the plaintiff's interest in obtaining relief. It must also weigh in its
> determination "the interstate judicial system's interest in obtaining the
> most efficient resolution of controversies; and the shared interest of the
> several States in furthering fundamental substantive social policies."[202]

The Supreme Court found California's exercise of jurisdiction over Asahi to be
unreasonable on balance. On one hand, "the interests of the plaintiff and the forum
in California's assertion of jurisdiction over Asahi" were "slight." On the other hand,
Asahi's burden from defending in California was "severe."[203]

Asahi's significance as a minimum contacts case is at best uncertain. No opinion
on the issue commanded a majority; however, the Court invalidated jurisdiction in
a due process holding divorced from minimum contacts analysis — and that is
significant. The result in *Asahi* confirmed that in close cases, minimum contacts
between the forum and a nonresident defendant do not guarantee that assertion of
personal jurisdiction comports with due process. In such cases, the plaintiff must
still show reasonableness of personal jurisdiction under the criteria listed in *Asahi*.

The net effect is that *Asahi* left the law concerning stream of commerce in limbo.
The previously accepted view that a seller that puts its products into the chain of
distribution purposely avails itself of the forum where those products are ultimately
sold was cast in doubt. A solid majority of the Court agreed that application of a
"fair play" or reasonableness analysis tipped the balance against jurisdiction, but
that analysis is so case-sensitive that it offers little guidance in future cases.
Unsurprisingly, *Asahi* generated lower-court uncertainty about stream of commerce theory[204] — to the consequent dismay of many commentators.[205]

---

[201] *International Shoe Co. v. Washington*, 326 U.S. 310, 316 (1945), quoted in *Asahi*, 480 U.S. at 105.

[202] 480 U.S. at 113 (*quoting World-Wide Volkswagen*, 444 U.S. at 292). The Court confuses matters,
however, by relying directly on *World-Wide Volkswagen* for its reasonableness test. When the Court
raised the same concerns in *World-Wide Volkswagen*, it was discussing "the concept of minimum
contacts." 444 U.S. at 291. The *Asahi* Court shifted these concerns into a separate, free-standing due
process test. *World-Wide Volkswagen* did not portend this development, but the intervening *Burger King*
case did: "Once it has been decided that a defendant purposefully established minimum contacts within
the forum State, these contacts may be considered in light of other factors to determine whether the
assertion of personal jurisdiction would comport with fair play and substantial justice." *Burger King
Corp. v. Rudzewicz*, 471 U.S. 462, 476 (1985) (quoting *International Shoe*). For an attempt to sort out the
new test, see Leslie W. Abramson, *Clarifying "Fair Play and Substantial Justice": How the Courts
Apply the Supreme Court Standard for Personal Jurisdiction*, 18 HASTINGS CONST. L.Q. 441 (1991).

[203] 480 U.S. at 114.

> Asahi has been commanded not only to traverse the distance between Asahi's headquarters in
> Japan and the Superior Court of California but also to submit its dispute with Cheng Shin to
> a foreign nation's judicial system. The unique burdens placed upon one who must defend
> oneself in a foreign legal system should have significant weight in assessing the reasonable-
> ness of stretching the long arm of personal jurisdiction over national borders.

480 U.S. at 114.

[204] *Compare, e.g., Luv n' Care, Ltd. v. Insta-Mix, Inc.*, 438 F.3d 465 (5th Cir. 2006); *Barone v. Rich*

[3] *J. McIntyre Machinery, Ltd. v. Nicastro*[206]

In 2011, the Supreme Court revisited the "stream of commerce" problem in *J. McIntyre Machinery, Ltd. v. Nicastro*. There, the plaintiff was injured on the job in New Jersey while operating a shearing machine that had been manufactured in England by the defendant, J. McIntyre Machinery, Ltd.[207] Nicastro filed suit against J. McIntyre in New Jersey state court. J. McIntyre sold its machines to United States customers through an Ohio-based distributer, and to promote U.S. sales, sent corporate representatives to trade shows in several major U.S. cities, though none in New Jersey.[208] The record below reflected that Nicastro's New Jersey employer learned about J. McIntyre's shearing machine at a trade show defendant attended, and that the machine that injured Nicastro was sold by defendant to its Ohio distributor, which sold it to Nicastro's employer.[209] It is unclear how many machines defendant sold in New Jersey: Justice Kennedy reported that "up to four" machines had been sold there.[210]

The New Jersey Supreme Court held that J. McIntyre was subject to personal jurisdiction in New Jersey, but the U.S. Supreme Court reversed. Writing for a plurality of four, Justice Kennedy declared that "the principal inquiry" in personal jurisdiction cases is "whether the defendant's activities manifest an intention to submit to the power of a sovereign." "In other words," he continued, "the defendant must purposefully avail itself of the privilege of conducting activities within the forum state, thus invoking the benefits and protections of its laws."[211] Justice Kennedy deduced two principles from his analysis: "First, personal jurisdiction requires a forum-by-forum, or sovereign-by-sovereign, analysis"; and second, "a corollary of the first," "[b]ecause the United States is a distinct sovereign, a defendant may in principle be subject to the jurisdiction of the courts of the United States but not of any particular state."[212]

Bros. Interstate Display Fireworks Co., 25 F.3d 610 (8th Cir. 1994) (following the pre-*Asahi* formula), *with Bridgeport Music, Inc. v. Still N the Water Publ'g*, 327 F.3d 472 (6th Cir. 2003); *Rodriguez v. Fullerton Tires Corp.*, 115 F.3d 81 (1st Cir. 1997) (imposing Justice O'Connor's added requirement).

[205] "The most ominous aspect of the *Asahi* opinion is that four Justices joined in the finding that Asahi did not have minimum contacts with California." Russell J. Weintraub, *Asahi Sends Personal Jurisdiction Down the Tubes*, 23 TEX. INT'L L.J. 55, 66 (1988). *Cf.* William M. Richman, *Understanding Personal Jurisdiction*, 25 ARIZ. ST. L.J. 599, 625 (1993) (the opinion poses an "ominous limitation" on the stream-of-commerce justification for personal jurisdiction); Christine M. Wiseman, *Reconstructing the Citadel: The Advent of Jurisdictional Privity*, 54 OHIO ST. L.J. 403, 405–06 (1993) (criticizing the plurality for applying a "narrowly-defined jurisdictional privity" test).

[206] For a symposium that generated a collection of articles addressing the implications of *McIntyre*, see Howard B. Stravitz, *Personal Jurisdiction for the 21st Century: The Implications of* McIntyre *and* Goodyear Dunlop Tires, 63 S.C. L. REV. 463-466 (2012).

[207] 131 S. Ct. 2780 (2011).

[208] *Id.* at 2786.

[209] *Nicastro v. McIntyre Mach. Am., Ltd.*, 987 A.2d 575, 577–78 (N.J. 2010).

[210] 131 S. Ct. at 2790.

[211] 131 S. Ct. at 2788.

[212] 131 S. Ct. at 2789.

Applying these principles to the facts of the case, Justice Kennedy concluded that J. McIntyre had "directed marketing and sales efforts at the United States," but not at New Jersey.[213] He noted that J. McIntyre had no offices in New Jersey, owned no property there, did not advertise there, sent no employees there, paid no taxes there, and accepted the trial court's finding that "defendant does not have a single contact with New Jersey short of the machine in question ending up in this state."[214] Accordingly, Justice Kennedy concluded that it would violate due process for the New Jersey courts to adjudge the rights and liabilities of J. McIntyre.

Justice Kennedy explained that the Court's purpose in hearing *McIntyre* was to clarify "decades-old questions left open in *Asahi*." As to *Asahi*, Justice Kennedy rejected Justice Brennan's concurrence, which focused on fairness and foreseeability, and aligned himself more closely with Justice O'Connor's plurality opinion.[215] Justice Kennedy's approach adds to or differs from Justice O'Connor's however, in several important respects. First, Justice Kennedy's focus on whether a defendant has manifested an intention to submit to a particular sovereign is new and somewhat puzzling, insofar as it harkens back to cases decided before *International Shoe*, that evaluated personal jurisdiction over corporate defendants with reference to whether the corporation's activities within a forum manifested its implied consent to be sued there — an approach the *International Shoe* Court abandoned as a "legal fiction."[216] Second, *Asahi* concerned a foreign components manufacturer that did not market its wares in the United States, unlike J. McIntyre that manufactured a final product it concededly sought to sell in the United States. This distinction is what led the Kennedy four to conclude that a foreign defendant that purposefully directs its marketing activities at all fifty states does not necessarily direct its marketing activities at any one state. Third, the Kennedy four resisted resort to considerations of fairness or reasonableness that Justice O'Connor applied in *Asahi*, in the only part of her opinion that garnered majority support. Fourth, Justice Kennedy appears to have rejected the foreseeability of being haled into court in the forum as a relevant consideration; although his critique was focused on Justice Brennan's concurrence in *Asahi*, it reflects no awareness that the factor had been a part of the Court's personal jurisdiction analysis since *Worldwide Volkswagen*.[217]

Justice Breyer, joined by Justice Alito, concurred in the judgment. Justice Breyer agreed with Justice Kennedy's conclusion that personal jurisdiction over J. McIntyre was lacking, but argued that "the outcome of this case is determined by our precedents," and that "I think it unwise to announce a rule of broad applicability without full consideration of the modern-day consequences."[218] For Justice Breyer, it was enough to note that "[n]one of our precedents finds that a single isolated sale, even if accompanied by the kind of sales effort indicated here,

---

[213] 131 S. Ct. at 2790.

[214] 131 S. Ct. at 2790.

[215] 131 S. Ct. at 2788.

[216] *International Shoe Company v. Washington*, 326 U.S. 310, 318 (1945) (citing earlier cases using such a "legal fiction").

[217] *World-Wide Volkswagen Corp. v. Woodson*, 444 U.S. 286, 297 (1980).

[218] 131 S. Ct. at 2791 (Breyer, concurring).

is sufficient."[219] In so concluding, Justice Breyer did not reference *McGee*, where the Court found that an Arizona corporation was subject to personal jurisdiction in California on the basis of an isolated contract renewal with the California plaintiff, although *McGee* could be distinguished on the grounds that it was not a stream of commerce case in which the corporate defendant was acting through a distributor. Ultimately, Justice Breyer was unprepared to go further: *McIntyre* presented a traditional scenario best resolved by traditional means, and was "an unsuitable vehicle for making broad pronouncements that refashion basic jurisdictional rules" in ways that could bear on modern commercial practices not at issue here, most notably internet sales.[220]

Justice Ginsburg, joined by Justices Sotomayor and Kagan, dissented. Because J. McIntyre purposefully sought to "reach customers for its products 'anywhere in the United States,' " and sold a machine to a New Jersey business "not randomly or fortuitously, but as a result of the . . . distribution system that McIntyre UK deliberately arranged," Justice Ginsburg would have held that J. McIntyre was subject to personal jurisdiction in New Jersey.[221]

In short, a majority of justices in *McIntyre* concluded that a state does not have personal jurisdiction over a foreign corporation when the corporation's only contact with the forum state is the isolated sale of a product through a distributor to a purchaser in the state where the product causes injury, even though the corporation has availed itself of the U.S. market as a whole. In the absence of a majority opinion, further extrapolation to other settings is problematic, and the uncertainties created by *Asahi* remain largely unresolved. Would a majority of the Court have concluded that minimum contacts were present: if one of the national trade shows J. McIntyre attended had been hosted in Newark?; if J. McIntyre had sold a higher volume of units to New Jersey customers through its domestic distributor?; or if J. McIntyre had sold only one unit in New Jersey, but done so directly, via the internet? Do consideration of reasonableness and fair play remain a part of the personal jurisdiction calculation in close cases? In short, insofar as the *McIntyre* Court sought to resolve the "decades-old questions left open in *Asahi*," this was not an especially successful outing.

§ 3.08 GENERAL JURISDICTION

As summarized in § 3.04, general jurisdiction exists over a nonresident defendant when his contacts with the forum are so extensive that it is possible to overlook the fact that the cause of action arose elsewhere — that no contacts related to the controversy exist between the forum and the defendant.[222] The Supreme Court

---

[219] 131 S. Ct. at 2792 (Breyer, concurring).

[220] 131 S. Ct. at 2793 (Breyer, concurring).

[221] 131 S. Ct. at 2797 (Ginsburg, dissenting).

[222] For further commentary on general jurisdiction, see ROBERT C. CASAD & WILLIAM B. RICHMAN, JURISDICTION IN CIVIL ACTIONS § 2-5[3] (Lexis 3d ed. 1998); Charles W. Rhodes, *Clarifying General Jurisdiction*, 34 SETON HALL L. REV. 807 (2004); Friedrich K. Juenger, *The American Law of General Jurisdiction*, 2001 U. CHI. LEGAL F. 141. *See also* Charles W. Rhodes, *Nineteenth Century Personal Jurisdiction Doctrine in a Twenty-First Century World*, 64 FLA. L. REV. 387 (2012) (discussing the

alluded to this scenario in *International Shoe*,[223] and subsequently addressed it in the three cases discussed here.

[1] *Perkins v. Benguet Consolidated Mining Co.*[224]

Benguet was a Philippine corporation whose operations there were disrupted by World War II. Benguet's president moved to an office in Ohio and transacted "a continuous and systematic, but limited, part of its general business" in Ohio.[225] Perkins sued Benguet in Ohio over corporate obligations arising outside the forum. Believing that due process prevented personal jurisdiction over Benguet, the Ohio courts refused to hear the case. The United States Supreme Court reversed.

The Court considered whether Ohio was under an obligation to provide Perkins with a forum for suit against Benguet and concluded that it was not. It also considered:

> whether, as a matter of federal due process, the business done in Ohio by the respondent mining company was sufficiently substantial and of such a nature as to *permit* Ohio to entertain a cause of action against a foreign corporation, where the cause of action arose from activities entirely distinct from its activities in Ohio.[226]

Invoking *International Shoe*, the Supreme Court set out to answer the question by examining Benguet's unrelated contacts with the forum. Noting that the corporate president "carried on in Ohio a continuous and systematic supervision of the necessarily limited wartime activities of the company,"[227] the Court concluded that due process would permit Ohio courts to exercise personal jurisdiction over Perkins' claim.

Some commentators read *Perkins* to suggest the possibility of personal jurisdiction wherever a corporation carries on activities capable of the "continuous and systematic" description.[228] Others argued a narrower reading of the case, pointing to exceptional circumstances that made Ohio the most feasible (perhaps the only)

---

problems of applying dated general jurisdiction jurisprudence in the modern world).

[223] The Court speculated that "continuous corporate operations within a state" could be "so substantial and of such a nature as to justify suit against it on causes of action arising from dealings entirely distinct from those activities." *International Shoe Co. v. Washington*, 326 U.S. 310, 318 (1945). *See* § 3.04[1], *supra*.

[224] 342 U.S. 437 (1952).

[225] 342 U.S. at 438.

[226] 342 U.S. at 447 (emphasis in original).

[227] 342 U.S. at 448.

> He kept there office files . . . carried on there correspondence . . . drew and distributed there salary checks . . . used and maintained in Clermont County, Ohio, two active bank accounts carrying substantial balances of company funds. . . . Several directors' meetings were held at his office or home in Clermont County. From that office he supervised policies dealing with the rehabilitation of the corporation's properties in the Philippines and he dispatched funds to cover purchases of machinery for such rehabilitation.

342 U.S. at 448.

[228] *See* the authorities cited in note 93, *supra*.

forum in which Perkins could have sued Benguet.[229] It is at least true that, like the facts of *International Shoe*, the facts of *Perkins* were so sympathetic to a finding of jurisdiction that the Court was not driven to explain what might satisfy due process in closer, more difficult cases.

[2] *Helicopteros Nacionales de Colombia v. Hall*[230]

Respondents brought this Texas state wrongful death action as the result of the Peruvian crash of a helicopter operated by Helicopteros, a Colombian corporation. In their claims against Helicopteros, respondents alleged that pilot error caused the crash. Appearing specially, Helicopteros moved to dismiss for lack of personal jurisdiction. The trial court denied the motion, and respondents obtained a jury award in excess of one million dollars. The Texas Supreme Court eventually decided that the Texas court had personal jurisdiction over Helicopteros.[231] The United States Supreme Court reversed.

Helicopteros sent a representative to Texas to contract with a Texas helicopter manufacturer for the purchase and transport of most of its helicopter fleet, and for the training of its pilots, management, and maintenance personnel.[232] Helicopteros also used a Texas bank account. The Supreme Court refused to consider whether these contacts provided a basis for specific jurisdiction because the plaintiffs apparently failed to argue this form of jurisdiction.[233] It framed the issue instead as one of general jurisdiction: whether contacts between Helicopteros and the

---

[229] Arthur T. von Mehren & Donald T. Trautman, *Jurisdiction to Adjudicate: A Suggested Analysis*, 79 HARV. L. REV. 1121, 1144 (1966); Note, *Developments in the Law — State Court Jurisdiction*, 73 HARV. L. REV. 909, 932 (1960); RESTATEMENT (SECOND) OF JUDGMENTS introduction at 25 (1982).

[230] 466 U.S. 408 (1984).

[231] 638 S.W.2d 870 (Tex. 1982). For a detailed account of the Texas decisions in the case, see Dennis G. Terez, *The Misguided Helicopteros Case: Confusion in the Courts over Contacts*, 37 BAYLOR L. REV. 913 (1985).

[232] The helicopter that crashed was manufactured in Texas and the pilot was trained there. 466 U.S. at 409–12.

[233] "All parties to the present case," said the Court, "concede that respondents' claims against [Helicopteros] did not 'arise out of,' and are not related to, [Helicopteros'] activities within Texas." 466 U.S. at 415. *See generally* § 13.08, *infra*, on the necessity of preserving and presenting a question for appeal. Dissenting, Justice Brennan would have found the case properly within Texas's specific jurisdiction. Several commentators have agreed. Russell J. Weintraub, *Due Process Limitations on the Personal Jurisdiction of State Courts: Time for Change*, 63 OR. L. REV. 485, 530 (1984); Louise Weinberg, *The Helicopter Case and the Jurisprudence of Jurisdiction*, 58 S. CAL. L. REV. 913, 915 (1985); William J. Knudsen, Jr., *Keeton, Calder, Helicopteros and Burger King — International Shoe's Most Recent Progeny*, 39 U. MIAMI L. REV. 809, 832 (1985). For example, Professor Weintraub wrote: "The deaths in Peru 'arose out of' [Helicopteros'] Texas business contacts in the broadest 'but for' sense." Weintraub, *Due Process Limitations, supra.*

There may be problems, however, with so broad a conception of specific jurisdiction. Granted, Helicopteros' Texas contacts were not entirely isolated from the claims brought there. Yet an indiscriminate "but for" approach to specific jurisdiction seems capable of attaching significance to contacts which do not really provide the forum with regulatory concerns necessary to justify specific jurisdiction. *See* § 3.10[1], *infra*. In *Helicopteros*, "Texas probably has little interest in a wrongful death that occurred in Peru, especially when equipment manufactured and purchased in Texas was not at fault. . . ." Terez, note 231, *supra*, at 938. *See generally* Flavio Rose, *Related Contacts and Personal Jurisdiction: The "But For" Test*, 82 CAL. L. REV. 1545 (1994).

Texas forum were sufficient when seen as unrelated to the controversy. Invoking *International Shoe* and *Perkins*, the Court concluded that the case failed the minimum contacts test. Helicopteros lacked "the kind of continuous and systematic general business contacts" with Texas necessary to satisfy due process.[234] Since Helicopteros flew no commercial routes in Texas and kept no personnel there, the conclusion that no general jurisdiction existed was not difficult to reach.

[3] *Goodyear Dunlop Tires Operations v. Brown*[235]

In *Goodyear*, two boys from North Carolina were killed in a Paris bus accident. The boys' parents attributed the accident to tire failure, and filed suit in North Carolina state court against Goodyear USA and three foreign Goodyear subsidiaries, including Goodyear-Turkey, which had manufactured the tires. Goodyear USA did not challenge personal jurisdiction, but its foreign subsidiaries did. The North Carolina Supreme Court ruled that the foreign subsidiaries were subject to general jurisdiction in North Carolina, because a small percentage of their tires were distributed in North Carolina through the stream of commerce.[236]

A unanimous Supreme Court reversed. The Court noted that specific jurisdiction was lacking because the subsidiaries' limited contacts with North Carolina did not give rise to the claims sued upon.[237] The Court then opined that general jurisdiction was available to hold a corporation answerable for all claims within the state, only if "their affiliations with the state are so 'continuous and systematic' as to render them essentially at home in the forum state."[238] Unlike the defendant in *Perkins*, "whose sole wartime business activity was conducted in Ohio," Goodyear's foreign affiliates were "in no sense at home," in North Carolina, and hence were not subject to general jurisdiction there.[239]

The Court's opinion in *Goodyear* raised at least two questions it did not answer. First, while the Court opined that the paradigmatic homes for a corporation are the states where it is incorporated and where its principal place of business is located, might there be others? For example, would Goodyear USA — an Ohio Corporation with its principal place of business there — be subject to general jurisdiction in North Carolina, where it maintains a pervasive retail presence? On the one hand, the Court's statement that a corporation's activities must be "so" systematic and continuous as to render it essentially at home indicates that a

---

[234] 466 U.S. at 416. Relying on an early case, *Rosenberg Bros. & Co. v. Curtis Brown Co.*, 260 U.S. 516 (1923), the Court added that the fact that the defendant purchased goods from the forum contributed little to respondent's case for jurisdiction. "[W]e hold that mere purchases, even if occurring at regular intervals, are not enough to warrant a State's assertion of *in personam* jurisdiction over a nonresident corporation in a cause of action not related to those purchase transactions." 466 U.S. at 418.

[235] 131 S. Ct. 2846 (2011). For a discussion of *Goodyear* and its implications, see Michael H. Hoffheimer, *General Personal Jurisdiction After* Goodyear Dunlop Tires Operations, S.A. v. Brown, 60 U. Kan. L. Rev. 549 (2012); Allan R. Stein, *The Meaning of "Essentially at Home" in* Goodyear Dunlop, 63 S.C. L. Rev. 527 (2012).

[236] 131 S. Ct. at 2852.

[237] 131 S. Ct. at 2855.

[238] 131 S. Ct. at 2851.

[239] 131 S. Ct. at 2857.

systematic and continuous presence alone is insufficient. On the other hand, characterizing two sites as the "paradigm" of a corporation's home does not foreclose the possibility that other forums might be sufficiently home-like to create general jurisdiction. Second, should a foreign subsidiary be deemed to share the "home" of its parent corporation? Are Goodyear USA's subsidiaries subject to general jurisdiction in North Carolina, if their parent company is? Although the plaintiff raised that issue in *Goodyear*, the Court dismissed the argument on the grounds that it had first been raised too late in the proceeding.

Clearly, minimum contacts necessary to support general jurisdiction are greater than those for specific jurisdiction.[240] But how much greater? In the aftermath of *Goodyear*, general jurisdiction turns on whether a corporation's contacts with the forum state are so pervasive as to render the corporation "essentially" at home there. What the essentials of a corporation's home are remain uncertain pending further litigation. In the meantime, the two safe harbors for general jurisdiction are the states where a corporation is incorporated and where its principal place of business is located.

§ 3.09 *PENNOYER* REVISITED: THE LINGERING RELEVANCE OF TERRITORIAL PRESENCE

International Shoe and the early cases following it were first and most easily seen as a force for expanding courts' personal jurisdiction. *International Shoe* relaxed the stringent territorial limits *Pennoyer v. Neff*[241] had imposed: It was no longer necessary for a defendant or the defendant's property to be physically present in the forum when served or seized, as long as the defendant had sufficient purposeful minimum contacts with the forum state. But was it still sufficient? In other words, was the principle of public law articulated in *Pennoyer* — that courts had jurisdiction over people and property within state boundaries — still good law? Or had that principle been eclipsed under the Due Process Clause as construed by *International Shoe* and its progeny, so that physical presence of persons or property would be insufficient to establish personal jurisdiction, absent minimum contacts? As elaborated upon in this section, the Court's answers are inconsistent. With respect to the physical presence of property, Supreme Court rulings in *Shaffer v. Heitner*[242] and *Rush v. Savchuk*[243] extended the minimum contacts standard to *quasi in rem* cases, stripping that jurisdictional category of much of its discrete significance and appeal to plaintiffs. On the other hand, with respect to the physical presence of persons, the Supreme Court's ruling in *Burnham v. Superior Court*[244] effectively preserved the tradition that a defendant is subject to jurisdiction in the state where she is served.

---

[240] *See* § 3.04[2], *supra*; Lea Brilmayer, *Related Contacts and Personal Jurisdiction*, 101 Harv. L. Rev. 1444 (1988); Alfred Hill, *Choice of Law and Jurisdiction in the Supreme Court*, 81 Colum. L. Rev. 960, 980–81 (1981).

[241] For a discussion of *Pennoyer*, see § 3.02.

[242] 433 U.S. 186 (1977).

[243] 444 U.S. 320 (1980).

[244] 495 U.S. 604 (1990).

[1]   Presence of Property: The Decline of *Quasi in Rem* Jurisdiction

[a]   *Shaffer v. Heitner*[245]

Plaintiff brought a shareholder derivative suit[246] against officers and directors of the Greyhound Corp. and its subsidiary, Greyhound, Inc. Plaintiff filed the suit in Delaware, alleging that the individual defendants had caused Greyhound and its subsidiary to incur substantial expenses from civil antitrust damages and a fine for criminal contempt. The defendants neither resided in Delaware nor received service there. Moreover, the alleged wrongful acts occurred outside Delaware. Delaware may have lacked minimum contacts necessary to support personal jurisdiction over the defendants.[247] Plaintiff attempted to avoid the problem, however, by proceeding upon a *quasi in rem* (rather than *in personam*) theory of jurisdiction.[248] There seems little question that plaintiff's case met traditional *quasi in rem* standards.[249] Each of the defendants held stock in Greyhound. Greyhound was a Delaware corporation, and plaintiff relied on a Delaware statute that conferred *quasi in rem* jurisdiction over stock issued by corporations chartered there. The Delaware state courts rejected defendant's jurisdictional attack.

Reversing, the United States Supreme Court set out two propositions. First, exercises of *quasi in rem* jurisdiction would henceforth satisfy due process only if they met *International Shoe*'s minimum contacts test. Second, *Shaffer* failed that test. The first of the two propositions was *Shaffer*'s lasting contribution. In contrast, the Court's conclusion that Delaware lacked minimum contacts with the defendants and the controversy is open to question.[250]

Concerning the first proposition, the Court flatly stated that "all assertions of state-court jurisdiction must be evaluated according to the standards set forth in *International Shoe* and its progeny."[251] This did not make *quasi in rem* jurisdiction unconstitutional per se. However, because the Court found defendant's in-state

---

[245] A useful study of this case by Professor Wendy Perdue appears in Civil Procedure Stories Ch. 3 (Kevin M. Clermont ed., Foundation 2d ed., 2008).

[246] Shareholders bring this suit to assert rights of the corporation when its directors will not. *See* Rule 23.1. It is usually brought against the officers and directors of the corporation for fraud, breach of fiduciary duties and other mismanagement.

[247] However, that was by no means clear. *See* note 250, *infra.*

[248] For discussion of these two types of territorial jurisdiction and the third (*in rem*), see § 3.03 (traditional categories of territorial jurisdiction), *supra.*

[249] *See* § 3.01[3], *supra.*

[250] Inasmuch as Greyhound was a Delaware corporation, the alleged dissipation of the worth of the corporation by the defendants was at least arguably forum-related. *See* Robert C. Casad, *Shaffer v. Heitner: An End to Ambivalence in Jurisdictional Theory?*, 26 U. Kan. L. Rev. 61, 74 (1977); David H. Vernon, *Single-Factor Bases of In Personam Jurisdiction — A Speculation on the Impact of* Shaffer v. Heitner, 1978 Wash. U. L. Q. 273, 316. The Court's arguments to the contrary are somewhat clouded.

[251] 433 U.S. at 212. The Court's choice of words seemed calculated to make its rule as applicable to exercises of *in rem* jurisdiction as to the *quasi in rem* case at hand. Elsewhere in *Shaffer*, the Court made it clear that it was referring to "the minimum-contacts standard elucidated in *International Shoe.*" 433 U.S. at 207. In *Rush v. Savchuk*, 444 U.S. 320, 327 (1980), the Court reiterated that its purpose in

property to be "completely unrelated to the plaintiff's cause of action," it held that "the presence of the property alone would not support the State's jurisdiction."[252]

The impact of the Court's decision on prejudgment attachments should not be overstated. So long as minimum contacts exist, suits begun by attachment — whether called *in personam*[253] or *quasi in rem*[254] — survive *Shaffer*. In the first place, the property is itself always one contact, although it is now no longer sufficient by itself when it is unrelated to the claim.

The fact remains, however, that *Shaffer* divested *quasi in rem* jurisdiction of much of its special appeal. A great lure of *quasi in rem* for plaintiffs had been that it provided an end run around the minimum contacts requirements of personal jurisdiction. The availability of *quasi in rem* jurisdiction in courts incapable of exercising personal jurisdiction made them attract litigation, even though the scope of *quasi in rem* judgments cannot exceed the worth of forum property upon which jurisdiction is based.[255] Once the *Shaffer* principle was recognized, however, it was evident that plaintiff had to make the same minimum contacts showing for *quasi in rem* (or *in rem*) jurisdiction that he did for personal jurisdiction. This means that plaintiff will usually have a case for personal jurisdiction if he has a jurisdictional case at all.[256] Given a choice, naturally plaintiff will invoke personal over *quasi in rem* jurisdiction in order to obtain a judgment compensating him for defendant's entire wrong.[257]

The Court's decision in *Shaffer* was overdue. Insulation of *quasi in rem* jurisdiction from *Shoe*'s minimum contacts test was indefensible. It was arbitrary to suggest that the concern for fairness to defendants explicit in *Shoe*'s approach provided a basis for restricting only *in personam* jurisdiction. To so confine due process protection under *Shoe* was to engage in a kind of formalism and artificiality at odds with the Court's modern cases.[258]

---

invoking *International Shoe* in *Shaffer* was to give across-the-board application to the minimum contacts test.

[252] 433 U.S. at 209. For discussion of the effect of this ruling on subsequent cases, see Michael B. Mushlin, *The New Quasi in Rem Jurisdiction: New York's Revival of a Doctrine Whose Time Has Passed*, 55 Brook. L. Rev. 1059 (1990).

[253] Courts exercising *in personam* jurisdiction may still under appropriate circumstances authorize security attachments to enhance the prospect of an enforceable judgment, should plaintiff prevail. *See* Linda J. Silberman, *Shaffer v. Heitner: The End of an Era*, 53 N.Y.U. L. Rev. 33, 54 (1978).

[254] A case may be capable of satisfying the minimum contacts test yet be beyond the amount of personal jurisdiction over nonresident defendants conferred by the state's long-arm statute. If the same state has a *quasi in rem* statute or common law rule which does apply, the court may continue to use it in such cases. *See Vernon*, note 250, *supra*, at 280–81.

[255] This makes them less valuable than *in personam* judgments. *See* § 3.01[3], *supra*.

[256] In the event (now rare) that minimum contacts are present but no personal jurisdiction statute reaches the case, plaintiff might have access only to *quasi in rem* jurisdiction. *See* note 253, *supra*.

[257] *See* § 3.01[3], *supra*.

[258] Thus, reasoned the *Shaffer* Court, "if a direct assertion of personal jurisdiction over the defendant would violate the Constitution, it would seem that an indirect assertion of that jurisdiction should be equally impermissible." 433 U.S. at 209.

[b] *Rush v. Savchuk*[259]

Some of the most egregious exercises of *quasi in rem* jurisdiction prior to *Shaffer* occurred through application of the so-called *Seider* doctrine.[260] In *Harris v. Balk*,[261] the Court had earlier sanctioned *quasi in rem* jurisdiction based on the obligation of another to pay money to the defendant. A contemporary manifestation of this idea, the *Seider* doctrine permitted *quasi in rem* jurisdiction in accident cases where courts lacked minimum contacts with nonresident driver defendants. Courts reasoned that service within the forum on the nonresident driver's insurer[262] conferred *quasi in rem* jurisdiction. The property attached was the insurer's duty or "debt" under the policy to defend and indemnify the nonresident motorist.

Jurisdiction over nonresident drivers in these cases was unattainable under *International Shoe*'s minimum contacts test. So it should have been obvious after *Shaffer* that continued reliance on the *Seider* doctrine would run afoul of due process. However, several of the jurisdictions that had used the device refused to give it up.[263] The Supreme Court responded by squarely rejecting the *Seider* doctrine in *Rush v. Savchuk*.[264]

Plaintiff in *Rush* was injured in an automobile accident in Indiana. Defendant was a resident of Indiana. Plaintiff was also an Indiana resident at the time of the accident, but later moved to Minnesota and sued the defendant there for his injuries. The Minnesota courts applied the *Seider* doctrine to reach the nonresident defendant through his insurer. Reversing, the Supreme Court held that jurisdiction over the defendant exceeded due process.

The Supreme Court applied the minimum contacts test. This meant that, "[i]n determining whether a particular exercise of state-court jurisdiction is consistent with due process, the inquiry must focus on the relationship among the defendant, the forum, and the litigation."[265] The Court concluded that defendant had no contact with the forum state, through the subject matter of the litigation or otherwise. The Court also rejected plaintiff's attempt to skirt the minimum contacts problem by arguing the existence of a "direct action" against the insurer.[266]

---

[259] 444 U.S. 320 (1980).

[260] The case giving name to the doctrine is *Seider v. Roth*, 216 N.E.2d 312 (N.Y. 1966). For other examples, *see Simpson v. Loehmann*, 234 N.E.2d 669 (N.Y. 1967); *Minichiello v. Rosenberg*, 410 F.2d 106 (2d Cir. 1968).

[261] 198 U.S. 215 (1905), *discussed in* § 3.01[3], *supra*.

[262] Usually the insurer did not issue the policy in question in the forum state, but was thought to have sufficient unrelated contacts by doing business there to support personal jurisdiction over the insurer. The sufficiency of personal jurisdiction under such circumstances may be more open to question today. With the demise of the *Seider* doctrine, however, the question became academic.

[263] *See Baden v. Staples*, 383 N.E.2d 110 (N.Y. 1978); *O'Connor v. Lee-Hy Paving Corp.*, 579 F.2d 194 (2d Cir.), *cert. denied*, 439 U.S. 1034 (1978); *Savchuk v. Rush*, 272 N.W.2d 888 (Minn. 1978).

[264] 444 U.S. 320 (1980).

[265] 444 U.S. at 327 (*quoting from Shaffer*, 433 U.S. at 204).

[266] 444 U.S. at 330–31. *Seider* doctrine courts had frequently used "direct action" arguments to bolster their decisions. The argument proceeds from the assumption that governing substantive law makes the insurer directly liable for harm to the plaintiff caused by the insured. The court has good personal jurisdiction over the insurer, and, goes the argument, its jurisdiction over the nonresident

[2] Presence of Persons — The Retention of Transient Jurisdiction: *Burnham v. Superior Court of California*

When *Shaffer* subjected all assertions of personal jurisdiction to minimum contacts scrutiny,[267] it seemed to cast a shadow over transient jurisdiction, a form of personal jurisdiction under fire even before *Shaffer*. Transient jurisdiction occurs when a nonresident defendant is actually found and served within the forum state, when defendant's presence there is (1) only intended to be brief and (2) is unrelated to the controversy raised by plaintiff's claim. In the well-known case of *Grace v. McArthur*,[268] transient jurisdiction was found to exist when defendant was served on an aircraft flying over the airspace of the forum state.

This means of bypassing minimum contacts was widely criticized, called by one commentator a "blot on American law."[269] Transient jurisdiction was valid prior to *International Shoe* because service was completed within the forum state — which satisfied *Pennoyer v. Neff*'s requirement of physical presence within the state's territorial limits.[270] So long as *Shoe* seemed only a means of adding to the jurisdictional reach of courts, transient jurisdiction was not in danger. Moreover, *Shoe* itself used language that implied that minimum contacts were required only if a defendant "be not present within the territory of the forum,"[271] thereby suggesting the continuing viability of transient jurisdiction. *Shaffer* demonstrated unequivocally, however, that due process doctrine emerging from *Shoe* and later cases was also capable of shortening the reach of courts. Transient jurisdiction seemed vulnerable to some commentators, because defendant's contacts with the forum were typically slight and unrelated to the controversy.

Worry over the continuing validity of transient jurisdiction lessened considerably, however, after the Supreme Court's decision in *Burnham v. Superior Court of California*.[272] Burnham was served as defendant in a California action for

---

driver is not a worry because the latter has nothing to lose. The *Rush* Court, however, felt that the insured would have something to lose, "if, for example, multiple plaintiffs sued in different States for an aggregate amount in excess of the policy limits, or if a successful claim would affect the policyholder's insurability." 444 U.S. at 331 n.20.

[267] *See* note 251 and related text, *supra*. On the application of the minimum contacts test to assertions of personal jurisdiction generally, see § 3.06, *supra*.

[268] 170 F. Supp. 442 (E.D. Ark. 1959). For further examples, see SCOLES, HAY, BORCHERS & SYMEONIDES, CONFLICT OF LAWS § 6.2 (4th ed. 2004).

[269] Albert A. Ehrenzweig, *From State Jurisdiction to Interstate Venue*, 50 OR. L. REV. 103, 108 (1971). In addition, see Vernon, note 250, *supra*, at 302–03; Joseph J. Kalo, *Jurisdiction as an Evolutionary Process: The Development of Quasi In Rem and In Personam Principles*, 1978 DUKE L.J. 1147, 1191.

[270] Prior to *Shoe*, the Supreme Court was preoccupied with completion of service within the forum. *See* § 3.02, *supra*.

[271] *International Shoe Co. v. Washington*, 326 U.S. 310, 316 (1945).

[272] 495 U.S. 604 (1990). The case prompted a good deal of commentary. *E.g.*, Patrick J. Borchers, *The Death of the Constitutional Law of Personal Jurisdiction: From Pennoyer to Burnham and Back Again*, 24 U.C. DAVIS L. REV. 19 (1990); Peter Hay, *Transient Jurisdiction, Especially over International Defendants: Critical Comments on* Burnham v. Superior Court of California, 1990 U. ILL. L. REV. 593; Symposium, *The Future of Personal Jurisdiction: A Symposium on* Burnham v. Superior Court, 22 RUTGERS L.J. 559 (1991) (articles by Brilmayer, Silberman, Stein, Weintraub, Kogan, Twitchell, Redish, and Maltz); Phillip F. Cramer, *Constructing Alternative Avenues of Jurisdictional Protection: By*

separation, child support, and spousal support during his brief visit there on business and to visit his children (in other words, the claims were not for divorce, which carries its own personal jurisdiction at the residence of either spouse). The case seemed to present two basic questions. First, would applications of transient jurisdiction be subject to the standards of *International Shoe*? Second, if so, how would transient jurisdiction cases fare under *Shoe*?

All the Justices agreed in *Burnham* that California's attempt to exercise transient jurisdiction was permissible. They split, however, over whether the question should be resolved through minimum contacts analysis. Four Justices, with Scalia writing the opinion, found it unnecessary to test the case under *International Shoe*. They were willing to uphold transient jurisdiction because it was satisfactory as a matter of tradition, under the old *Pennoyer* doctrine.[273] Disagreeing, Justice Brennan, writing on behalf of four other Justices, applied *Shoe*. Yet the disagreement may not have been very significant, for Justice Brennan posed a test under *Shoe* that should be quite easy to satisfy in most cases — and which bore little similarity to the minimum contacts analysis the Court normally employed.[274] Rather, for Justice Brennan, it was enough that Burnham had deliberately partaken (however briefly) of "significant benefits provided by the State," such as using its roadways — despite the fact that those activities were unrelated to the plaintiff's claims in any meaningful way. While Justice Brennan criticized Justice Scalia for relying on tradition alone, tradition ultimately controlled Justice Brennan's hybridized minimum contacts analysis too, because for Brennan, the tradition of transient jurisdiction meant that a defendant could foresee being haled into court where served. While disagreement persists as to the viability of transient jurisdiction in rare cases (for example, service over a state's airspace) where a person's presence in a jurisdiction is unknowing,[275] overall, the effect of the opinions in *Burnham* was to give transient jurisdiction new life.[276]

Passing Burnham's Roadblock via § 1404(a), 53 Vand. L. Rev. 311 (2000).

For a variety of reasons, many of these writers are troubled by the manner in which *Burnham* gives free play to transient jurisdiction. Professor Earl Maltz, on the other hand, views matters more favorably. Earl M. Maltz, *Personal Jurisdiction and Constitutional Theory — A Comment on* Burnham v. Superior Court, 22 Rutgers L.J. 689 (1991); Earl M. Maltz, *Sovereign Authority, Fairness, and Personal Jurisdiction: The Case for the Doctrine of Transient Jurisdiction*, 66 Wash. U. L.Q. 671 (1988).

[273] For discussion of the doctrine of *Pennoyer v. Neff*, see § 3.02, *supra*. Justice Scalia, in an opinion joined by the Chief Justice and Justice Kennedy, gave transient jurisdiction a ringing endorsement under the *Pennoyer* doctrine. Joining their opinion in part, Justice White left room for the theoretical possibility of an example of transient jurisdiction "so arbitrary and lacking in common sense" that a due process problem might arise. He added, however, that a due process problem is unlikely "where presence in the forum state is intentional." 495 U.S. at 638. He concluded: "Here, personal service in California, without more, is enough." 495 U.S. at 638.

[274] 495 U.S. at 637.

[275] In his opinion, Justice Brennan left open the possibility of a different result under *Shoe* when defendant's "presence in a State" is "involuntary or unknowing." 495 U.S. at 637 n.11 (Brennan concurring), and on that point, Justice White appeared to agree with the Brennan four. 495 U.S. at 628 (White, concurring).

[276] In contrast, transient jurisdiction is rejected as a basis for personal jurisdiction in European courts. *See* Friedrich K. Juenger, *Traveling to the Hague in a Worn-Out Shoe*, 29 Pepp. L. Rev. 7, 7 (2001); Linda J. Silberman & Andreas F. Lowenfeld, *A Different Challenge for the ALI: Herein of*

§ 3.10   LITIGATING JURISDICTION: TIMING THE CHALLENGE

Two avenues have long been open to a defendant wishing to challenge the court's personal jurisdiction. First, defendant may use his challenge to keep the court from reaching the merits of the case. The defendant must participate in the lawsuit to use this option, called *direct attack*. Or the defendant may use his jurisdictional challenge later to argue that a default judgment rendered against him is not entitled to enforcement. Defendant must avoid participating or making any kind of appearance in the case underlying judgment in order to use this option, called *collateral attack*.

[1]   Direct Attack

Federal and state courts make ample opportunities available for a nonresident defendant to question personal jurisdiction prior to trial. Moreover, if the defendant is careful to observe the niceties of the local procedural system, he usually will be able to join with his jurisdictional attack other reasons why plaintiff's suit should be dismissed[277] and (if necessary) to contest the plaintiff's claim on the merits as well.[278] This is the great attraction of direct attack; it can be used with an array of other grounds for attacking plaintiff's case that are available in the initial forum.

The problem with direct attack is that it forces the defendant to give up part of the protection secured by due process. He experiences the increased burden of defending in a distant and inconvenient forum as soon as he begins participating in the case. The difference in hardship between traveling to the forum in order to get the suit dismissed for lack of personal jurisdiction and remaining there to defend on the merits is one only of degree.

From a tactical standpoint, the direct attack may be preferable in a number of circumstances. If the defendant has assets in the forum and must eventually travel to the forum to make his jurisdictional challenge anyway, he is better off doing it earlier by direct attack, so that he can challenge other aspects of plaintiff's case, too. Likewise, if the amount in controversy is high, if the defendant's argument on the merits is strong, or if the defendant's personal jurisdiction argument is less than ironclad, a direct attack — which affords the defendant an opportunity to challenge personal jurisdiction without forsaking other options should he lose — is ordinarily preferable.

[2]   Collateral Attack

The hardship of forcing the defendant to travel to the forum in order to challenge personal jurisdiction requires that defendant have the second option of collateral attack. Collateral attack is founded on the principle that, if plaintiff's

Foreign Country Judgments, an International Treaty, and an American Statute, 75 Ind. L.J. 635, 641 (2000).

[277] *See, e.g.,* Rule 12(b).

[278] *See, e.g.,* Rule 56.

choice of forum is so unfair as to violate defendant's right to due process, defendant's complete refusal to participate there should not preclude him from later questioning personal jurisdiction.[279] The United States Supreme Court has noted that: "[a] defendant is always free to ignore the judicial proceedings, risk a default judgment, and then challenge that judgment on jurisdictional grounds in a collateral proceeding."[280]

For an illustration, suppose that New Yorker B takes no part in A's Hawaii lawsuit. A obtains a default judgment for $100,000 against B. Since B has no assets in Hawaii to satisfy the judgment, A must sue on the judgment in a court of B's home state of New York.[281] B defends against the judgment in New York court on the ground that the Hawaii court lacked personal jurisdiction. B wins, the court ruling (as it must on these facts) that the Hawaii judgment is not entitled to enforcement. If A wishes a judgment against B enforceable in New York, A will have to sue B all over again in New York.

The problems with the collateral attack are that it is often unavailable and, when available, often risky to use. Courts will usually entertain collateral attack for lack of personal jurisdiction only if the defendant took no part whatsoever in the initial proceeding. If the defendant participated in the first case without questioning the court's personal jurisdiction, he cured any defect by waiver.[282] If the defendant did challenge the court's personal jurisdiction in the first case, he is precluded from relitigating the question in the judgment-enforcement proceeding. The Supreme Court's decision in *Baldwin v. Iowa State Traveling Men's Ass'n*[283] is a prominent example of the latter. Defendant appeared specially in the initial case and attacked the court's personal jurisdiction. When the trial court denied defendant's motion to dismiss, defendant withdrew from any further participation in the case and default judgment was thereafter entered against him. Defendant later attempted to relitigate his objection to personal jurisdiction by collaterally attacking the judgment. However, the Court refused to permit the challenge.

> The special appearance gives point to the fact that the respondent entered the Missouri court for the very purpose of litigating the question of jurisdiction over its person. It had the election not to appear at all. . . . It had also the right to appeal from the decision of the Missouri District Court.[284]

---

[279] Under these circumstances, the "right to challenge jurisdiction makes" the defendant "an instrument for confining judicial authority to its prescribed limits." RESTATEMENT (SECOND) OF JUDGMENTS § 65 comment (b) (1982).

[280] *Insurance Corp. of Ireland, Ltd. v. Compagnie des Bauxites de Guinee*, 456 U.S. 694, 706 (1982). The position taken under American law is thus at variance with that of the European Community, where "jurisdictional challenges are not permitted in the State in which enforcement is sought, even with respect to default judgments." LINDA J. SILBERMAN, ALLAN R. STEIN & TOBIAS B. WOLFF, CIVIL PROCEDURE: THEORY AND PRACTICE 930 (Aspen 2d ed. 2006).

[281] The process for suing on judgments is described in § 15.02, *infra*.

[282] *See generally* § 3.11[1], *infra*.

[283] 283 U.S. 522 (1931).

[284] 283 U.S. at 525. *See also Underwriters Nat'l Assurance Co. v. North Carolina Life & Accident & Health Ins. Guar. Ass'n*, 455 U.S. 691 (1982); *Stoll v. Gottlieb*, 305 U.S. 165, 172 (1938).

The grounds upon which a defendant can base a collateral attack are quite limited. Two that are clearly available — lack of notice[285] and the unenforceablity of the judgment where rendered[286] — require unusual supporting facts. Courts have occasionally permitted collateral attack on other grounds, but their availability in any given case is uncertain.[287] So, if defendant's collateral attack for lack of personal jurisdiction fails, there will usually be nothing to shield him from an obligation to pay the default judgment.[288]

Tactically, collateral attack is a risky gambit that will be a wise course under only limited circumstances. If the stakes are relatively low and the expense and inconvenience of travel to the forum is significant, the advantages of a collateral attack may outweigh the risks — at least when the defendant's argument against personal jurisdiction is strong or his defense on the merits is weak. The intangible "home court advantage" may also factor into the defendant's calculations, if the state where the plaintiff will seek to execute the judgment — typically, the defendant's home state — is perceived to be friendlier to the defendant and his personal jurisdiction argument than the distant forum.[289]

§ 3.11 WAIVER OF OR CONSENT TO PERSONAL JURISDICTION

[1] How Waiver Operates

State courts do not have the same authority to impose personal jurisdiction over nonresident defendants as they have over defendants who make their home in the forum state. But when the former have due process objections, they must take care to preserve them. The Supreme Court has observed that "[b]ecause the

---

[285] Defendants may assert denial of the notice and opportunity to be heard guaranteed by due process. RESTATEMENT (SECOND) OF JUDGMENTS, at 18. See generally § 4.01, infra.

[286] Defendants may invoke the sensible rule that a court need not enforce a foreign judgment if the rendering system would not. See Ford v. Ford, 371 U.S. 187 (1962) (full faith and credit does not obligate courts to give greater preclusive effect to a judgment than the rendering court). See generally § 15.11, infra.

[287] Cases like Huntington v. Attrill, 146 U.S. 657 (1892), raise the possibility that a judgment penal in character might be unenforceable, but "it is very possible that there is not much left of this penalty rule." Lawrence H. Averill, Jr., Choice-of-Law Problems Raised by Sister-State Judgments and the Full-Faith-and-Credit Mandate, 64 Nw. U. L. REV. 686, 694 (1970). Similarly, the modern trend is away from permitting collateral attacks on subject matter jurisdiction grounds. See generally Karen N. Moore, Collateral Attack on Subject Matter Jurisdiction: A Critique of the Restatement (Second) of Judgments, 66 CORNELL L. REV. 534, 562 (1981).

[288] Default judgments are judgments on the merits (see § 15.05, infra), and it is axiomatic that collateral attack may not be used to question the merits underlying a judgment. E.g., Fauntleroy v. Lum, 210 U.S. 230 (1908); Milliken v. Meyer, 311 U.S. 457 (1940). After objections that a default judgment is void for lack of personal jurisdiction or lack of notice, the only questions left for the judgment enforcement proceeding are: is defendant in fact the person named in the judgment, and how soon can defendant pay? See § 15.02, infra.

[289] Federal court diversity jurisdiction is built on this idea. Gene R. Shreve, Pragmatism Without Politics — A Half Measure of Authority for Jurisdictional Common Law, 1991 B.Y.U. L. REV. 767, 787; Wythe Holt, "To Establish Justice": Politics, the Judiciary Act of 1789, and the Invention of Federal Courts, 1989 DUKE L.J. 1421, 1458. See generally § 5.04[1], infra (justification for diversity jurisdiction).

requirement of personal jurisdiction represents first of all an individual right, it can, like other such rights, be waived."[290]

Waiver need not be express. It is enough that a party act in a way which is incompatible with his argument that the forum lacks a basis for asserting personal jurisdiction over him. This is why nonresident plaintiffs waive due process objections to the court's jurisdiction by filing suit.[291] Note how the nonresident plaintiff's act of filing makes his relationship to the forum more intimate. He has now availed himself of the protection and benefits of the forum's judicial process. By setting up legal shop in the forum, plaintiff makes the forum a more convenient place not only to litigate his claim but also to defend against such cross-claims or counterclaims as the forum might permit against him.[292]

Waiver of the right to challenge personal jurisdiction does not work quite so simply for nonresident *defendants*. Since it is unlikely that a court will respond to a defect in personal jurisdiction on its own initiative, defendant must move for dismissal. To say that the defendant waives his due process objection to personal jurisdiction by appearing in the case to press that objection as a ground for dismissal would trap the defendant in a Catch-22. Instead, procedural systems provide mechanisms for the defendant to appear and question the court's personal jurisdiction without curing plaintiff's problem in the process.

In the federal system, the Federal Rules of Civil Procedure enable a defendant to enter an appearance and raise an objection to the court's personal jurisdiction, but add that the objection is waived if it is not included in a motion filed prior to the answer, or in the answer itself.[293] State systems modeled after the federal rules include similar provisions, but some states employ other mechanisms, discussed in the subsections that follow.

[2] Special and Limited Appearances

Once, the standard way for defendant to protect himself against waiver was to file a *special appearance*. The special appearance permitted defendant to participate in the case without submitting to the court's personal jurisdiction. It was crucial, however, that defendant styled his entry into the suit as a special appearance and that he was careful not to question anything but the court's personal jurisdiction. If the defendant used this opportunity to urge any other reason why the case should be dismissed or to dispute the merits of plaintiff's case, his entry took on the character of a *general appearance*,[294] which functioned as a

---

[290] *Insurance Corp. of Ireland, Ltd. v. Compagnie des Bauxites de Guinee*, 456 U.S. 694, 703 (1982).

[291] *See* RESTATEMENT (SECOND) OF CONFLICTS.

[292] RESTATEMENT (SECOND) OF CONFLICTS. The Court upheld personal jurisdiction under such circumstances in *Adam v. Saenger*, 303 U.S. 59 (1938).

[293] Rules 12(b)(2) & 12(h)(1).

[294]

> A general appearance is one where the defendant either enters an appearance in an action without limiting the purpose for which he appears or where he asks for relief which the court may give only if it has jurisdiction over him. An appearance which falls into either of these two categories is a general appearance even though the defendant protests at the same time that

submission to the court's jurisdiction.[295]

Today most state courts have followed the lead of federal courts and dispensed with special appearances.[296] This means that the defendant will not prejudice his motion to dismiss by joining with it other grounds for dismissal.[297] However, care must be taken even in courts that follow the federal model. Defendant will waive his challenge to personal jurisdiction if he either fails to include it in a motion to dismiss made on other grounds, or fails to raise the matter by motion or pleading.[298] Moreover, the Supreme Court held that defendant might also lose his personal jurisdiction challenge as a penalty for failure to comply with an order compelling discovery.[299]

Students sometimes confuse special appearances with *limited appearances.* Many jurisdictions permitted a defendant whose property was attached through *quasi in rem* jurisdiction to appear and resist a judgment on the merits against the property without, by so doing, submitting to the court's *in personam* jurisdiction. This was called a limited appearance. Recall that a *quasi in rem* judgment bound the defendant only with reference to his interest in the *res* upon which jurisdiction was based.[300] In contrast, an *in personam* judgment bound the defendant to the full measure of damages for his wrong to the plaintiff.[301]

Limited appearances thus differed from special appearances in that the former were not a means of raising the personal jurisdiction issue but were instead designed to permit the defendant a full opportunity to litigate the case on the merits, while limiting the size of an adverse judgment to the value of the property.

Limited appearances have lost much of their importance. As soon as the Supreme Court required that *quasi in rem* cases satisfy more rigorous standards previously associated only with *in personam* jurisdiction,[302] the popularity of *quasi in rem* jurisdiction (and, hence, the necessity for limited appearances) declined dramatically.

---

he does not submit himself to the jurisdiction of the court.

RESTATEMENT (SECOND) OF CONFLICTS, § 33 comment d.

[295] ROBERT C. CASAD & WILLIAM B. RICHMAN, JURISDICTION IN CIVIL ACTIONS § 3-1[5][a] (3d ed. 1998).

[296] CASAD & RICHMAN, note 295, *supra*, at ¶ 3.01[5][b]. For one example of special appearance practice, see Newton & Wicker, *Personal Jurisdiction and the Appearance to Challenge Jurisdiction in Texas*, 38 BAYLOR L. REV. 491 (1986).

[297] *See* Rule 12(g). A majority of states have adopted the Rule 12 model. *See generally* John B. Oakley & Arthur F. Coon, *The Federal Rules in State Courts: A Survey of State Court Systems of Civil Procedure*, 61 WASH. L. REV. 1367 (1986).

[298] Rule 12(h)(1). *See generally* § 8.07[2][b] (waivable defenses), *infra*.

[299] *Insurance Corp. of Ireland, Ltd. v. Compagnie des Bauxites de Guinee*, 456 U.S. 694 (1982). Plaintiff sought discovery of facts supporting personal jurisdiction.

[300] *See* § 3.01[3][c].

[301] *Id.*

[302] *See* § 3.09[1].

[3]   Litigating Jurisdiction as Partial Consent or Waiver

As discussed in § 3.10, when defendants are sued in remote forums and wish to challenge the court's personal jurisdiction, they have a choice: they may default, and challenge personal jurisdiction later when the plaintiff seeks to execute the judgment, typically in a court of the defendant's home state; or they may enter an appearance and challenge personal jurisdiction in the forum that they contend lacks personal jurisdiction. If they choose the latter course, the defendants are, in effect, waiving their objections to personal jurisdiction for the limited purpose of enabling the court to decide whether it has such jurisdiction. In *Bank of Ireland, Ltd. v. Compagnie des Bauxites de Guinee*,[303] a Pennsylvania company sued foreign insurers in Pennsylvania federal district, who challenged personal jurisdiction in their answer. When the defendants refused to comply with discovery requests relevant to deciding their personal jurisdiction objection, the court sanctioned the defendants by finding that it had personal jurisdiction. The Supreme Court affirmed. A defendant may waive its personal jurisdiction defense by entering an appearance and failing to comply with rules requiring it to lodge a timely objection, the Court reasoned. So too, a defendant may waive a personal jurisdiction defense by entering an appearance, raising the objection, and failing to comply with applicable discovery rules, the violation of which include waiver as an available sanction.

If the defendant challenges personal jurisdiction where suit is filed and the challenge succeeds, the court will order plaintiff's case dismissed, pursuant to Rule 12(b)(2). Absent a successful appeal, plaintiff will have to refile against defendant[304] in a forum where jurisdictional requirements are satisfied. But what if the trial court rules against the defendant?

Many systems do not permit defendant to appeal immediately because denial of a motion to dismiss for lack of personal jurisdiction is an interlocutory (nonfinal) order, and such systems confine most appeals to those from final judgment.[305] This could place the defendant in a dilemma. If his further participation in the case constitutes a submission to jurisdiction, defendant will lose his jurisdictional challenge by pressing other reasons for dismissal or disputing the merits of plaintiff's case. To preserve the jurisdictional issue for appeal, he would have to stop participating at the trial level once the court rejects his jurisdictional challenge. This would draw a default judgment on the merits for plaintiff, and defendant could renew his jurisdictional challenge by appealing that final judgment. The risk in this option is that defendant will be bound on the merits, should he lose the jurisdictional argument.

Fortunately, most systems do not pose this hard choice. They permit the defendant to renew his objection to the court's personal jurisdiction on appeal of

---

[303]   456 U.S. 694 (1982).

[304]   A dismissal for lack of personal jurisdiction has no preclusive effect on plaintiff's claim in a different court outside the forum state. *See* § 15.05, *infra*. It does, however, prejudice a subsequent attempt by plaintiff to refile the case in the same state. *See* § 15.06.

[305]   *See* § 13.03.

the final judgment, even though he has fully contested the case during the interim.[306]

[4]   Jurisdiction by Pre-Litigation Consent

Under a rule similar to waiver, it has long been true that defendants could consent to a court's personal jurisdiction in advance of suit. Such consent, if expressly made, still functions to cure any jurisdictional defects that might otherwise exist.[307]

A leading express consent case is *National Equipment Rental v. Szukhent.* The Supreme Court upheld New York jurisdiction over Michigan defendants in a federal breach of contract suit. It did so on the ground that one of the clauses of the contract signed by the defendants named an individual in New York to receive service there on their behalf. "[I]t is settled," said the Court, "that parties to a contract may agree in advance to submit to the jurisdiction of a given court."[308] Of course, the contract must be valid and enforceable. The only line of escape in such cases may be for defendant to argue that the provision is deceptive, unconscionable or a contract of adhesion.[309]

States may require foreign corporations to file documents with state authorities expressly consenting to the jurisdiction of that state's courts as a condition for doing business in the forum.[310] At the very least, such consent effectively confers personal jurisdiction over the corporation for the adjudication of all claims arising

---

[306] Professor Casad offers representative cases from a number of states taking this view, and citations from three states (New Hampshire, Idaho and South Dakota) that do not. He observes that California also requires defendants to waive their jurisdictional challenge in order to contest the merits, but notes that defendants in California instead do have the option of interlocutory review of the jurisdictional question before they must proceed to the merits at trial. CASAD & RICHMAN, note 295, *supra*, at § 3-1[5][a][i]. Federal courts rarely permit interlocutory review but have long permitted defendants to renew their personal jurisdictional arguments on appeal, after fully litigating the case prior to final judgment. *Harkness v. Hyde*, 98 U.S. 476 (1879).

In limited circumstances, parties in federal court have been permitted to raise *initial* objections to personal jurisdiction on appeal. *See, e.g., Buchanan v. Manley*, 145 F.3d 386, 387 (D.C. Cir. 1998) (per curiam) (holding parties may raise initial objections to personal jurisdiction on appeal when they lacked an opportunity to do so in the trial court, such as when a case was dismissed *sua sponte* at an early stage).

[307] FRIEDENTHAL, KANE & MILLER § 3.5. On the other hand, it is doubtful whether the fictitious concept of implied consent continues to provide a sufficient basis for personal jurisdiction. *See* E. SCOLES & P. HAY, CONFLICT OF LAWS § 9.5 (2d ed. 1992).

[308] 375 U.S. 311, 315–16 (1964).

[309] Dissenting in *Szukhent*, Justice Black argued that the consent-to-jurisdiction portion of the contract was a "sham" and should be deemed unenforceable. 375 U.S. at 323–26.

[310]

> All states have statutes that require nonresident corporations that intend to conduct business in the state to comply with a registration procedure and to appoint a resident agent for the service of process. . . . Such statutes reach not only the in-state conduct of nonresident corporations, but potentially any claim — irrespective of its relationship with the . . . jurisdiction — pressed against a registered nonresident corporation.

Lee S. Taylor, *Registration Statutes, Personal Jurisdiction, and the Problem of Predictability*, 103 COLUM. L. REV. 1163, 1164–65 (2003).

within the forum. Once it seemed equally clear that filing operated as consent to personal jurisdiction over claims arising elsewhere, if the sweep of the state consent statute was broad enough.[311] The position still seems to have wide acceptance,[312] but several courts have questioned whether this form of filing provides a basis for the adjudication of nonforum controversies against foreign corporations sufficient to satisfy due process.[313] Commentators have criticized the practice.[314]

Some forum-selection provisions in contracts may include prorogation clauses.[315] That is, they not only consent to jurisdiction in a particular court, but also bar litigation in any other court. Unwilling to be ousted of what would otherwise be proper personal jurisdiction, some courts once refused to honor prorogation clauses. But the recent trend has been in favor of enforcing them. The Supreme Court stated in *M/S Bremen v. Zapata Off-Shore Co.*[316] that "such clauses are prima facie valid and should be enforced unless enforcement is shown by the resisting party to be 'unreasonable' under the circumstances."[317] Similarly, the American Law Institute's *Restatement (Second) of Conflicts* regards a prorogation agreement to be effective "unless it is unfair or unreasonable."[318] This now appears to be the standard in federal[319] and most state courts.[320]

---

[311] *Pennsylvania Fire Ins. Co. v. Gold Issue Mining & Milling Co.*, 243 U.S. 93 (1917) (opinion per Holmes, J.); *Smolik v. Philadelphia & Reading Coal & Iron Co.*, 222 F. 148 (1915) (opinion per L. Hand, J.). These decisions are criticized in William L. Walker, *Foreign Corporation Laws: A Current Account*, 47 N.C. L. Rev. 733, 735–37 (1969).

[312] Restatement (Second) of Conflicts, § 44 & comment (c); Scoles & Hay, note 307, *supra*, at 455. *But see* Alfred Hill, *Choice of Law and Jurisdiction in the Supreme Court*, 81 Colum. L. Rev. 960, 981–82 (1981).

[313] *Wenche Siemer v. Learjet Acquisition Corp.*, 966 F.2d 179 (5th Cir. 1992); *In re Mid-Atlantic Toyota Antitrust Litig.*, 525 F. Supp. 1265 (D. Md. 1981); *Schreiber v. Allis-Chalmers Corp.*, 448 F. Supp. 1079 (D. Kan. 1978), *rev'd on other grounds*, 611 F.2d 790 (10th Cir. 1979); *Cedar Inv. Co. v. Canal Ins. Co.*, 262 F. Supp. 337 (E.D. Mo. 1966). In *Bendix Autolite Corp. v. Midwesco Enterprises, Inc.*, 486 U.S. 888 (1988), the Supreme Court limited the authority of states to require foreign corporations to submit to jurisdiction in controversies arising outside the forum. However, the Court's constitutional ruling rested on Commerce Clause rather than due process grounds.

[314] *E.g.*, Mark Schuck, *Foreign Corporations and the Issue of Consent to Jurisdiction Through Registration to Do Business in Texas: Analysis and Proposal*, 40 Hous. L. Rev. 1455 (2004); Lee S. Taylor, *Registration Statutes, Personal Jurisdiction, and the Problem of Predictability*, 103 Colum. L. Rev. 1163 (2003).

[315] *Moore* § 108.53[5][a].

[316] 407 U.S. 1 (1972).

[317] 407 U.S. at 10.

[318] Section 80 (1971).

[319] Casad & Richman, note 295 *supra*, at § 1-7. In all federal cases, federal (as opposed to state) law determines the enforcement of prorogation clauses. *Stewart Org., Inc. v. Ricoh Corp.*, 487 U.S. 22, 32 (1988).

[320] "The state courts are free to adopt their own standards with respect to whether to honor a choice-of-forum clause, but it is fair to say that most state courts appear to have adopted something close to the *Zapata* standard." Linda J. Silberman, *The Impact of Jurisdictional Rules and Recognition Practice on International Business Transactions: The U.S. Regime*, 26 Hous. J. Int'l L. 327, 347 (2004).

Yet how do we determine when enforcement of the prorogation agreement would be unreasonable? *Bremen* appeared to offer a useful guide in that case: "a private international prorogation agreement will be honored . . . [i]f the agreement was freely negotiated, unaffected by fraud, undue influence, or overweening bargaining power."[321] But later, in *Carnival Cruise Lines, Inc. v. Shute*, the Supreme Court upheld a prorogation clause appearing on the back of a passenger's steamship ticket[322] — circumstances many observers regarded to be unfair.[323] There was an "obvious distinction between the freely negotiated commercial contract in *The Bremen* and the consumer adhesion contract in *Carnival Cruise Lines.*"[324]

§ 3.12   ISSUES ON THE FRONTIER OF PERSONAL JURISDICTION

[1]   Pendent or Supplemental Personal Jurisdiction

In the cases summarized to this point in the chapter, there was no question that jurisdiction over all claims in a given case case were subject to the same analysis. But in litigation, that is not always the case. Suppose that an Indiana plaintiff brings a diversity action against a Wisconsin defendant in Illinois district court, that includes two claims: a tort claim arising out of an automobile accident in Illinois, and an unrelated claim arising out of a contract for the sale of real estate in Wisconsin that was negotiated and executed in Wisconsin. Clearly, the defendant's contacts with Illinois gave rise to the automobile accident there and would be sufficient to support specific jurisdiction over the tort claim; but just as clearly, the defendant's contacts with Illinois had nothing to do with the real estate transaction, and hence would be insufficient to confer jurisdiction over the contract claim. In such cases, it would seem that the court has no choice but to analyze the claims separately and dismiss the contract claim for lack of personal jurisdiction.

Suppose instead that the claims are related, and that personal jurisdiction can be established as to some, but not all claims. To litigate different claims arising out of the same events in different forums in different states would be inefficient and risk inconsistent and potentially unjust results. Chapter 5 discusses supplemental subject matter jurisdiction, whereby to promote judicial economy, courts can hear supplemental claims outside the court's original subject matter jurisdiction, if they are joined with other claims within the court's original jurisdiction, as long as all claims arise out of the same nucleus of events. By the same logic, may courts exercise supplemental personal jurisdiction?

---

[321] Casad & Richman, note 38 *supra*, § 1-7.

[322] 499 U.S. 585 (1991).

[323] *See, e.g.*, Mullenix, *Another Easy Case, Some More Bad Law: Carnival Cruise Lines and Contractual Personal Jurisdiction*, 27 Tex. Int'l L.J. 323 (1992).

[324] Richman & Reynolds, note 41, *supra*, at § 30[2]. "[P]laintiff's right to a reasonable forum . . . should not be so easily defeated by sharp drafting practices." *Id.*

Federal courts have applied supplemental personal jurisdiction principles in different settings. One setting is where federal statutes have authorized nationwide service of process for a federal question claim, which confers jurisdiction on federal courts to hear that claim in a state that lacks personal jurisdiction over a related claim.[325] A second setting where courts have brought supplemental personal jurisdiction principles to bear is where the applicable state's long arm statute authorizes courts to exercise jurisdiction over, say, a contract claim, but not a closely related tort claim.[326] A third setting is where minimum contacts analysis can yield different results when applied to factually related claims. For example, in one case, a Massachusetts plaintiff filed a diversity action in Massachusetts against a Virginia surgeon. The action included a tort claim for botched plastic surgery in Virginia, and a contract claim for breach of the surgeon's agreement to pay for corrective surgery. The court ruled that the defendant had minimum contacts with Massachusetts for purposes of the contract claim (because the contract had been negotiated and breached in telephone calls between Virginia and Massachusetts) but not the tort claim (because all relevant events giving rise to the claim had occurred in Virginia).[327] The court held that the defendant was subject to personal jurisdiction in Massachusetts for all claims.

Pendent or supplemental personal jurisdiction has been widely accepted among the lower federal courts in nationwide service of process cases, but less so in other settings.[328] The parallel to supplemental subject matter jurisdiction is superficially appealing, insofar as both promote judicial efficiency by enabling the same court to hear claims falling outside its jurisdiction if they are closely related to other claims within its jurisdiction. It bears emphasis, however, that federal subject matter jurisdiction is a matter of judicial power delegated by Article III of the United States Constitution. Constitutional authority for supplemental subject matter jurisdiction is derived from an interpretation of Article III, which (the Supreme Court has held) authorizes federal courts to hear supplemental claims outside the scope of their original jurisdiction as long as those claims are part of the same constitutional case or controversy as a claim within the courts' original jurisdiction. Personal jurisdiction, in contrast, has nothing to do with judicial power under Article III, but concerns the due process rights of defendants to a constitutionally reasonable forum, and the territorial limits of state sovereignty. Whether courts should be permitted to exercise personal supplemental jurisdiction in the name of promoting efficiency, thus turns on a fundamentally different set of issues. Accordingly, final word on whether the Due Process Clause tolerates the exercise of supplemental personal jurisdiction must await Supreme Court resolution.

---

[325] *See, e.g., ESAB Group, Inc. v. Centricut, Inc.*, 126 F.3d 617 (4th Cir. 1997) (nationwide service of process conferred jurisdiction over a federal RICO claim; despite defendant's lack of minimum contacts with the forum state, supplemental personal jurisdiction authorized the court to hear related state law claims).

[326] *Hargrave v. Oki Nursery*, 646 F.2d 716 (2d Cir. 1980) (New York long arm statute authorized court to hear some but not all related claims; pendent personal jurisdiction authorized the court to hear the entire case).

[327] *Salpoglou v. Widder*, 899 F. Supp. 835 (D. Mass. 1995).

[328] Linda Sandstrom Simard, *Exploring the Limits of Specific Personal Jurisdiction*, 62 Ohio St. L.J. 1619 (2001) (surveying supplemental personal jurisdiction cases).

[2] Jurisdiction in Cyberspace

Increasingly, personal jurisdiction issues arise in controversies based entirely, or in significant part, on internet activity. The question in such cases is whether or how the rules and reference points of personal jurisdiction law can be made to work concerning defendant's cyberspace activity. One of the authors of this book posed the problem in this way:

> [P]ersonal jurisdiction retains a strong geographical dimension, typically resting on physical acts that were purposefully directed at a forum state. But cyberspace is structurally indifferent to geography. Internet addresses are logical addresses on the network, rather than geographic addresses in real space. Neither party to a transaction in cyberspace (by E-mail, Usenet post, or Worldwide Website) may know or care where the other is geographically located. If they transact in goods, their goods are likely to be digitized information products, not physical goods. And in many — if not most — cyberspace transactions, the remote party who is subsequently sued can hardly be said to have purposefully directed the information product or communication at a particular forum, except in the sense that she directed it at every forum.[329]

On the other hand, if cyberspace is indifferent to geography, "it does not and cannot change the fact that parties themselves exist in physical space."[330] This fact sounds a caution against any effort to jettison traditional personal jurisdiction law just because a suit arises out of a cyber transaction.

The subject of personal jurisdiction in cyberspace has produced extensive commentary.[331] The United States Supreme Court has not yet ruled in an internet jurisdiction case. But lower courts are grappling with the problem, and their decisions may offer some guidance. Many Courts have been influenced by the decision in *Zippo Manufacturing Co. v. Zippo Dot Com, Inc.*,[332] categorizing cyber

---

[329] P. Raven-Hansen, *Newsletter of the Section on Civil Procedure, Association of American Law Schools* at 2 (Fall, 1998). For a comprehensive study of commercial activity on the internet, see John Rothchild, *Protecting the Digital Consumer: The Limits of Cyberspace Utopianism*, 74 IND. L.J. 893 (1999).

[330] American Bar Association Jurisdiction in Cyberspace Project, *Achieving Legal and Business Order in Cyberspace: A Report on Global Jurisdiction Issues Created by the Internet* 8 (1999 draft) (hereinafter "ABA Cyberspace Report").

[331] *E.g.*, ABA Cyberspace Report, note 330, *supra*; A. Benjamin Spencer, *Jurisdiction and the Internet: Returning to Traditional Principles to Analyze Network-Mediated Contacts*, 2006 U. ILL. L. REV. 71; Joel R. Reidenberg, *Technology and Internet Jurisdiction*, 153 U. PA. L. REV. 1951 (2005); Patrick J. Borchers, Symposium, *Personal Jurisdiction in the Internet Age*, 98 NW. U. L. REV. 473 (2004); Note, *A "Category-Specific" Legislative Approach to the Internet Personal Jurisdiction Problem in U.S. Law*, 117 HARV. L. REV. 1617 (2004); Jack L. Goldsmith, *Against Cyberanarchy*, 65 U. CHI. L. REV. 1199 (1998); Dan L. Burk, *Federalism in Cyberspace*, 28 CONN. L. REV. 1095 (1996); Mark S. Kende, *Lost in Cyberspace: The Judiciary's Distracted Application of Free Speech and Personal Jurisdiction Doctrines to the Internet*, 77 OR. L. REV. 1125 (1998); Christine E. Mayewski, *The Presence of a Web Site as a Constitutionally Permissible Basis for Personal Jurisdiction*, 73 IND. L.J. 297 (1997).

[332] 952 F. Supp. 1119 (W.D. Pa. 1997). "*Zippo* has earned a place in history as one of the most-cited district court opinions ever." Patrick J. Borchers, *Internet Libel: The Consequences of a Non-Rule Approach to Personal Jurisdiction*, 98 NW. U. L. REV. 473, 478 (2004). For extensive discussion of *Zippo*

contacts by whether they were passive, commercially transactional, or interactive.

For example, it appears that due process does not permit exercise of personal jurisdiction based just on the fact that defendant's website is passive — merely accessible to internet users in the forum state.[333] Refusing personal jurisdiction in such circumstances, the Ninth Circuit observed:

> So far as we are aware, no court has ever held that an Internet advertisement alone is sufficient to subject the advertiser to jurisdiction in the plaintiff's home state. . . . Rather [in the internet cases permitting jurisdiction], there has been "something more" to indicate that the defendant purposefully (albeit electronically) directed his activity in a substantial way to the forum state.[334]

Any other rule would subject the sponsor of a passive website to personal jurisdiction the world over, because its website can be accessed by connected computers anywhere. The website's passive presence is ubiquitous and beyond its control.[335]

But when, as in the case of *CompuServe Inc. v. Patterson*,[336] the defendant directs particular internet activity into the forum state that is related to the controversy, the forum acquires specific jurisdiction.[337] The Sixth Circuit in *CompuServe* ruled that defendant's contacts with the Ohio forum, while "almost entirely electronic in nature,"[338] were sufficient to support personal jurisdiction. The court noted that defendant

> was on notice that he had made contracts, to be governed by Ohio law, with an Ohio-based company. Then, he repeatedly sent his computer software, via electronic links, to the CompuServe system in Ohio, and he advertised that software on the CompuServe system. Moreover, he initiated the events

---

and cases following it, see A. Benjamin Spencer, *Jurisdiction and the Internet: Returning to Traditional Principles to Analyze Network-Mediated Contacts*, 2006 U. ILL. L. REV. 71, 78–85.

[333] *See, e.g., Bensusan Restaurant Corp. v. King*, 937 F. Supp. 295 (S.D.N.Y. 1996), *aff'd*, 126 F.3d 25 (2d Cir. 1997); *Cybersell, Inc. v. Cybersell*, Inc., 130 F.3d 414 (9th Cir. 1997); *Weber v. Jolly Hotels*, 977 F. Supp. 327 (D.N.J. 1997). *See also ABA Cyberspace Report*, note 330, *supra*, at 18 ("Personal or prescriptive jurisdiction should not be asserted based solely on the accessibility in the state of a passive web site that does not target the state").

[334] *Cybersell*, 130 F.3d at 418.

[335] *ABA Cyberspace Report*, note 330, *supra*, at 59.

[336] 89 F.3d 1257 (6th Cir. 1996). The case is featured in Bryce A. Lenox, *Personal Jurisdiction in Cyberspace: Teaching the Stream of Commerce Dog New Internet Tricks:* CompuServe, Inc. v. Patterson,, *89 F.3d 1257 (6th Cir. 1996)*, 22 U. DAYTON L. REV. 331 (1997); Daniel V. Logue, *If the International Shoe Fits, Wear It: Applying Traditional Personal Jurisdiction Analysis to Cyberspace in* CompuServe, Inc. v. Patterson, 42 VILL. L. REV. 1213 (1997); Aaron A. VanderLaan, CompuServe, Inc. v. Patterson: *Civil Procedure Enters the Cyber-Age*, 41 ST. LOUIS U. L.J. 1399 (1997); David D. Tyler, *Personal Jurisdiction via E-Mail: Has Personal Jurisdiction Changed in the Wake of* CompuServe, Inc. v. Patterson?, 51 ARK. L. REV. 429 (1998).

[337] For a discussion of specific jurisdiction as a subcategory of personal jurisdiction, see § 3.04.

[338] 89 F.3d at 1262.

that led to the filing of this suit by making demands of CompuServe via electronic and regular mail messages.[339]

The court was therefore able to conclude that defendant "purposefully availed himself of CompuServe's Ohio-based services."[340] This will generally be true of commercially transactional websites, through which the sponsor directs a product to a specified forum in exchange for payment by a purchaser in the forum.

The *Zippo* categorization is less helpful for the category in between these cases: the interactive website. How much interaction is required for jurisdiction and why? An American Bar Association report on jurisdiction and cyberspace offers this explanation:

> Jurisdiction is about chosen contacts between the defendant and the forum. . . . [T]he sponsor of a passive web site has no way to control which fora she is "connected to" by the site. On the other hand, the site sponsor who does business electronically knows or can take reasonable steps to discover the location of the party with whom she is interacting. The provision of the interactive site, alone, may express the sponsor's willingness to become connected to all fora in which the site is accessible (assuming it does not contain any disclaimers, etc.) but it does not constitute that connection. Nor, of course, does the mere accessing of the site by forum residents. . . .

> Reliance, then, on the nature of the web site alone is misplaced. If an interactive site is not targeted to a specific forum, courts should focus on how the site is actually used. Knowing and willing use of it by a nonpresent party to enter into dealings with persons or business in the forum demonstrates a chosen contact with the forum, provides the forum with an interest in the relationships thus created, and makes it less likely that multiple fora with different applicable laws will attempt to regulate the site and assert jurisdiction over its sponsor.[341]

This analysis suggests that *Zippo*'s categorization is superficial, or, at least, just the beginning of the inquiry.[342] The real inquiry ought to be how the website is used, whether it targets the forum, and the defendant's intent or willingness to contact

---

[339] 89 F.3d at 1264.

[340] 89 F.3d at 1264. For a similar case, see *Panavision Int'l v. Toeppen*, 141 F.3d 1316 (9th Cir. 1998).

[341] *ABA Cyberspace Report*, note 330, *supra*, at 60–61.

[342] For recent criticisms of *Zippo*, see A. Benjamin Spencer, *Jurisdiction and the Internet: Returning to Traditional Principles to Analyze Network-Mediated Contacts*, 2006 U. Ill. L. Rev. 71, 87–88; Allan R. Stein, *Personal Jurisdiction and the Internet: Seeing Due Process Through the Lens of Regulatory Precision*, 98 Nw. U.L. Rev. 411, 430–32 (2004); Patrick J. Borchers, *Internet Libel: The Consequences of a Non-Rule Approach to Personal Jurisdiction*, 98 Nw. U.L. Rev. 473, 479–80 (2004). More sympathetic treatment of *Zippo* appears in Note, *A "Category-Specific" Legislative Approach to the Internet Personal Jurisdiction Problem in U.S. Law*, 117 Harv. L. Rev. 1617, 1619–24 (2004); Dennis T. Yokoyama, *You Can't Always Use the Zippo Code: The Fallacy of a Uniform Theory of Internet Personal Jurisdiction*, 54 DePaul L. Rev. 1147 (2005); Bunmi Awoyemi, Zippo *Is Dying, Should It Be Dead?: The Exercise of Personal Jurisdiction by U.S. Federal Courts over Non-Domiciliary Defendants in Trademark Infringement Lawsuits Arising Out of Cyberspace*, 9 Marq. Intell. Prop. L. Rev. 37 (2005).

forum users — in a word (or, more accurately, two words): "purposeful availment." It remains to be seen, however, whether the courts will probe beyond *Zippo*'s categories to stay abreast of new developments in internet technology.[343]

[3]   Globalization and Personal Jurisdiction

The assorted human affairs giving rise to civil litigation are becoming increasingly global in character. This affects personal jurisdiction as well as other civil procedure topics.[344]

The law of personal jurisdiction in American courts is outwardly unaffected by whether the defendant is a citizen of a sister state or of a foreign country. That law is shaped by the Due Process Clause, which protects *all* defendants. At the same time, problems arising under personal jurisdiction law may become more acute when the defendant is abroad. For example, "the remoteness of a foreign defendant makes the motion to dismiss for lack of personal jurisdiction an extremely powerful tool in the context of transnational litigation."[345] And the international character of internet activity can accentuate problems of determining jurisdiction in cyberspace.[346]

The United States is not a party to any international treaty on personal jurisdiction.[347] The absence of a treaty leaves American courts considerable latitude to refuse to enforce the judgments of foreign courts and vice versa. United States courts have on the whole been willing to enforce foreign judgments, but foreign courts have often been reluctant to enforce U.S. judgments.[348] Among the numerous idiosyncrasies of American civil procedure[349] that account for what one

---

[343] For example, a recent commentator suggests that advances in information technology permit targeting of the forum producing an "interactivity [giving] the victim's state a greater nexus with offending acts and [providing] a direct relationship with the offender for purposes of personal jurisdiction." Joel R. Reidenberg, *Technology and Internet Jurisdiction*, 153 U. Pa. L. Rev. 1951, 1953 (2005). *Accord* A. Benjamin Spencer, *Jurisdiction and the Internet: Returning to Traditional Principles to Analyze Network-Mediated Contacts*, 2006 U. Ill. L. Rev. 71.

[344] These are surveyed in § 15.12, *infra*.

[345] Thomas Main, Global Issues in Civil Procedure 63 (2006). "Indeed, unlike a purely domestic litigation matter where plaintiff must refile in another *state* when the court lacks personal jurisdiction over the defendant, the plaintiff must commence litigation in another *country*. Dreading the inconvenience or fearing the unfamiliar, that case may simply never be pursued elsewhere once the action is dismissed in the United States." *Id.*

[346] *See* § 3.12[2], *supra*. In international litigation, "assertions of national authority have raised many . . . legal conundrums regarding nation-state sovereignty, territorial borders, and legal jurisdiction." Paul Schiff Berman, *The Globalization of Jurisdiction*, 151 U. Pa. L. Rev. 311, 317 (2002). *See also* Patricia L. Bellia Et Al., Cyberlaw: Problems of Policy and Jurisprudence in the Information Age ch. 3 (4th ed. 2011).

[347] Kevin M. Clermont, *A Global Law of Jurisdiction and Judgments: Views from the United States and Japan*, 37 Cornell Int'l L.J. 1, 2 (2004).

[348] "[C]ompanies often do not sue in the United States when the assets are elsewhere because they fear the uncertainty of subsequent enforcement of a United States judgment overseas." Louise Ellen Teitz, *The Hague Choice of Court Convention: Validating Party Autonomy and Providing an Alternative to Arbitration*, 53 Am. J. Comp. L. 543, 548 (2005).

[349] Richard L. Marcus, *Putting American Procedural Exceptionalism into a Globalized Context*, 53 Am. J. Comp. L. 709, 709–10 (2005).

writer has called "the nasty aroma American litigation seems to elicit in much of the rest of the world,"[350] differences over personal jurisdiction are prominent. Some applications of personal jurisdiction accepted in the U.S. are rejected elsewhere as invalid.[351] More generally, tension arises from differences between the common law and civil law approaches to the subject.[352]

§ 3.13   PERSONAL JURISDICTION IN THE CALIFORNIA COURTS

[1]   The California Long-Arm Statute

Unlike many states which limit the bases of their courts' personal jurisdiction by reference to specific statutory categories, the California long-arm statute, Code of Civil Procedure § 410.10, broadly states that "[a] court of this state may exercise jurisdiction on any basis not inconsistent with the Constitution of this state or of the United States."[353] Therefore, the "minimum contacts" analysis of *International Shoe Co. v. Washington* and its progeny, as well as the subsidiary considerations of "fair play and substantial justice" (or "reasonableness"), directly prescribe the exercise of personal jurisdiction by the California courts.[354]

[2]   Due Process: General vs. Specific Jurisdiction

[a]   *Vons Companies, Inc. v. Seabest Foods, Inc.*: The "Substantial Connection" Test

In *Vons Companies, Inc. v. Seabest Foods, Inc.*,[355] the California Supreme Court attempted to clarify the personal jurisdiction concept of "specific jurisdiction" by defining the circumstances under which a cause of action "arises out of or relates to" a defendant's contacts with the forum.[356] The facts in *Vons* are complicated, involving multiple parties and claims. What follows is a brief, somewhat simplified,

---

[350] *Id.* at 710.

[351] Thus, "United States courts' assertions of 'general jurisdiction' on grounds of 'tag' and 'doing business' are often viewed as excessive and exorbitant by other countries." Linda J. Silberman & Andreas F. Lowenfeld, *A Different Challenge for the ALI: Herein of Foreign Country Judgments, an International Treaty, and an American Statute*, 75 IND. L.J. 635, 639 n.22 (2000).

[352] Teitz, *supra* n. 348, at 549, noting "theoretical divisions between common law and civil law approaches to jurisdiction. The civil law's rejection of broad discretion in the exercise of jurisdiction lends itself to detailed provisions covering all contingencies which will easily produce inconsistencies and hinder compromise."

[353] Section 410.10 manifests the intent that California courts exercise the broadest possible personal jurisdiction over nonresidents, limited only by constitutional considerations. *Sibley v. Superior Court*, 16 Cal. 3d 442, 445, 128 Cal. Rptr. 34, 546 P.2d 322 (1976).

[354] *See, e.g., Vons Companies, Inc. v. Seabest Foods, Inc.*, 14 Cal. 4th 434, 58 Cal. Rptr. 2d 899, 926 P.2d 1085 (1996) (applying the "minimum contacts" and fairness tests); *Snowney v. Harrah's Entm't, Inc.*, 35 Cal. 4th 1054, 29 Cal. Rptr. 3d 33, 112 P.3d 28 (2005) (same). The "minimum contacts" test is discussed at length in §§ 3.03–3.09, *supra*; the "reasonableness factors" in § 3.06 and § 3.07[2], *supra*.

[355] 14 Cal. 4th 434, 58 Cal. Rptr. 2d 899, 926 P.2d 1085 (1996).

[356] Specific jurisdiction is discussed in detail in §§ 3.04–3.06, *supra*.

summary. In 1993, costumers of two Jack-in-the Box restaurants in Washington State suffered from exposure to E. coli bacteria traced to hamburgers sold at these two restaurants. Some fell ill and some died. Jack-in-the-Box is a division of Foodmaker, Inc., which has its principle place of business in California. Foodmaker blamed the E. coli contamination on its meat supplier, Vons Companies, Inc. (Vons). Vons processed hamburger patties in its California plant and shipped them to Foodmaker for use in Jack-in-the-Box restaurants.

Eighty-five Jack-in-the-Box franchisees from California, whose customers had *not* been injured, sued Foodmaker and Vons in a California superior court, alleging causes of action for negligence and breach of contract and seeking substantial damages for loss of business caused by the adverse publicity that followed the E. coli outbreak. Vons then filed a third-party claim against Seabest Foods, Inc. (Seabest) and Washington Restaurant Management, Inc. (WRMI), owners of the Jack-in-the-Box franchises in Washington at which E. coli contamination had injured or killed Jack-in-the-Box customers. Vons alleged the injuries caused by the E. coli contamination would have been avoided if Seabest and WRMI cooked the hamburgers at the proper temperature, and sought damages for its own loss of business and for indemnification. Third-party defendants Seabest and WRMI moved to quash on the ground of lack of personal jurisdiction.

Seabest had considerable contacts with the State of California through its business dealings with its franchiser, Foodmaker. Pursuant to the franchise agreement, Seabest officers conducted some of its business with Foodmaker at its corporate headquarters in California, attended training sessions in California, and made monthly rent and royalty payments to Foodmaker's California headquarters. Seabest also purchased most its hamburger patties from Foodmaker, and received delivery from Foodmaker's Washington warehouse. WRMI had similar contacts with Foodmaker in California. However — and significantly — neither Seabest nor WRMI had direct business dealings or other contacts with Vons, the plaintiff in the third-party claim filed against them. Nor were their contacts sufficiently "continuous and systematic" to establish general jurisdiction. The superior court granted the motion to quash, and the Court of Appeal affirmed.

The main focus of the California Supreme Court's analysis in *Vons* was on the nature of the nexus between the defendants' forum activities and the plaintiff Von's cause of action. The defendants argued for the adoption of the proximate cause test formulated by the Court of Appeal, *i.e.*, unless the defendants' forum contacts *proximately caused* the occurrence that injured the plaintiff, the connection between the contacts and the claim is insufficient to permit the exercise of specific jurisdiction. The Supreme Court rejected the proximate cause test as too narrow and as inconsistent with fairness rationale underlying the specific jurisdiction doctrine.

Plaintiff Vons argued that the required relationship between the defendants' forum contacts and the plaintiff's cause of action should be determined by an expansive "but for" test, which focuses on whether the plaintiff's injury would have occurred "but for" the defendants' forum contacts. The plaintiff pointed out that the U.S. Court of Appeals for the Ninth Circuit employed the "but for" test in its specific jurisdiction analysis.[357] Despite the federal court precedent, the *Vons* Court determined that the "but for" test was too broad and amorphous.[358]

The California Supreme Court in *Vons* ultimately concluded that the appropriate inquiry for specific jurisdiction was whether the plaintiff's cause of action has a "substantial connection" with the defendant's forum activities. Although this "substantial connection" standard does little by itself to clarify the nature of the specific jurisdiction analysis, the manner in which the Court applied this standard in *Vons* is very instructive. In particular, the Court ruled that the defendants' forum activities need not be directed at the *plaintiff* in order to give rise to specific jurisdiction. The nexus required to establish specific jurisdiction is between the defendant, the forum, and the litigation, not between the plaintiff and the defendant. Consequently, a claim need not arise directly from the defendant's forum contacts in order to be sufficiently related to those contacts to warrant the exercise of specific jurisdiction.

The *Vons* Court defined "substantial connection" by reference to the facts of an earlier California Supreme Court decision, *Cornelison v. Chaney*,[359] where the Court held that a California resident could sue a Nebraska defendant in California for wrongful death in connection with an accident that occurred in Nevada. The defendant in *Cornelison* was engaged in the business of hauling goods by truck and made fairly frequent deliveries in California. The accident occurred while the defendant was en route to California for further deliveries. The Supreme Court in *Cornelison* found the nexus between plaintiff's cause of action and defendant's activities in California sufficient to support specific jurisdiction, explaining that the appropriate inquiry is whether the plaintiff's cause of action "arises out of or has a substantial connection with a business relationship defendant has purposefully established with California."[360] In applying the reasoning of *Cornelison*, the *Vons* Court emphasized that under the substantial connection test, the defendants' forum activities need not be directed at the plaintiff (Vons) in order to give rise to specific jurisdiction.[361]

---

[357] *See, e.g., Shute v. Carnival Cruise Lines*, 897 F.2d 377, 385 (9th Cir. 1990); *Ballard v. Savage*, 65 F.3d 1495, 1500 (9th Cir. 1995).

[358] *Vons, supra*, 14 Cal. 4th at 467–68. The Court wryly observed that "if the defendant is a lawyer who was received his or her legal education in the forum, that legal education may be said to be a 'but for' cause of any malpractice the lawyer commits anywhere in the nation, yet it hardly seems a sufficient basis for the forum to exercise jurisdiction." *Id.* at 467.

[359] 16 Cal. 3d 143, 127 Cal. Rptr. 352, 545 P.2d 264 (1976).

[360] *Cornelison, supra*, 16 Cal. 3d at 149. The Court observed that the defendant's activities in California were not so wide ranging as to justify general jurisdiction, but that the plaintiff's wrongful death cause of action had a substantial connection with those activities and therefore justified specific jurisdiction. *Id.* at 147–49.

[361] *Vons, supra*, 14 Cal. 4th at 458. In other words, there need be no "plaintiff-specific link" between a defendant's California activities and a plaintiff's cause of action. *See, e.g., Cassiar Mining Corp. v. Superior Court*, 66 Cal. App. 4th 550, 78 Cal. Rptr. 2d 167 (1998) (applying *Vons*' "substantial connection" test to find sufficient contacts to justify the exercise of specific jurisdiction over Canadian company that sold raw asbestos fiber directly to California manufacturers who incorporated the asbestos into finished products even though no evidence in the record that plaintiffs were actually exposed to the asbestos fibers it sold in California).

The "substantial connection" test developed by the California Supreme Court in *Vons* blurs the line between specific and general jurisdiction. Under traditional due process analysis, "general jurisdiction" refers to those cases in which the plaintiff's cause of action did *not* "arise out of or relate to" the defendant's forum activities, and therefore requires (at least) "continuous and systematic" forum contacts to satisfy the due process requirements for personal jurisdiction.[362] In light of the broad definition of specific jurisdiction adopted in *Vons*, the circumstances in which a defendant will be subject to general jurisdiction in a California court are far from clear. The *Vons* definition generally favors plaintiffs. Because specific jurisdiction requires a lesser quantum of contacts with the forum state than general jurisdiction, a plaintiff may now be able to convince a California court to sustain personal jurisdiction in circumstances where the court may have been unwilling to do so before *Vons*.

[b] *Snowney v. Harrah's Entertainment, Inc*

Recently, the California Supreme applied the "substantial connection" test in *Snowney v. Harrah's Entertainment, Inc.*,[363] where the plaintiff, a California resident, filed a class action against a group of Nevada hotels for failing to provide notice of an energy surcharge imposed on hotel guests. Although these hotels conducted no business and had no bank accounts or employees in California, they did advertise heavily in California and obtained a significant percentage of their business from California residents. The advertising activities included billboards located in California, print ads in California newspapers, ads aired on California radio and television stations, and an internet web site and toll-free phone number where visitors or callers may obtain room quotes and make reservations.

Based on the defendants' purposeful and successful solicitation of business from California residents through a website that specifically targeted these residents, the California Supreme Court concluded that superior court may properly exercise personal jurisdiction over the Nevada hotels. The Court also found a "substantial connection" between the defendants' forum activities and the plaintiff's causes of action — unfair competition, breach of contract, unjust enrichment, and false advertising alleging that defendants failed to provide notice of an energy surcharge during the reservation process and in their advertising — sufficient for specific jurisdiction.

[c] Recent Lower Court Decisions

The California Courts of Appeal frequently confront difficult and interesting personal jurisdiction questions. For example, in one recent case, the court held that the defendant Florida automobile seller's maintenance of a website was not

---

[362] *Vons, supra*, 14 Cal. 4th at 445–46; *Helicopteros Nacionales de Columbia, S.A. v. Hall*, 466 U.S. 408, 415, n.9 & 416 (1984); *but see Goodyear Dunlop Tires Operations, S.A. v. Brown*, ___ U.S. ___, 131 S. Ct. 2846 (2011) (indicating the paradigm forum for the exercise of general jurisdiction is an individual defendant's domicile and for a corporation an equivalent place where the corporation is fairly regarded as "at home," such as place of incorporation or principal place of business). General jurisdiction is discussed in more detail in § 3.08, *supra*.

[363] 35 Cal. 4th 1054, 29 Cal. Rptr. 3d 33, 112 P.3d 28 (2005).

sufficient to establish personal jurisdiction because it did not target California residents and there was no ongoing business relationship between the parties, despite fact that the plaintiff California buyer purchased an allegedly defective vehicle advertised on the defendant seller's web site.[364] In another case, the court found insufficient minimum contacts to establish personal jurisdiction over an out-of-state defendant whose only contact with California was a single purchase from a California vendor of goods for delivery out of state, even though the vendor supplied financing to the buyer. The court explained that although regular purchasing activities in California may be a basis for jurisdiction over an out-of-state buyer, the general rule in California is that a non-resident making a one-time purchase of goods from a seller in the forum state cannot be constitutionally subject to the exercise of personal jurisdiction by the courts of the seller's state.[365]

[3] The "Reasonableness" Factors

The United States Supreme Court has developed a subsidiary due process consideration in addition to the "minimum contacts" test. In rare but appropriate cases, a state court should not assert personal jurisdiction over a nonresident defendant, even one who has purposely established minimum contacts in the forum state, where the exercise of jurisdiction would not be "fair and reasonable."[366] This "reasonableness" consideration includes evaluation of several factors, such as the burden on the defendant, the interests of the forum state, the plaintiff's interest in obtaining relief, the interstate judicial system's interest in obtaining the most efficient resolution of controversies, and the shared interest of the several states in furthering fundamental substantive social policies.[367] Because "reasonableness" is a constitutional limitation, the California courts have incorporated these factors into their personal jurisdiction analysis.[368]

[4] "Stream of Commerce"

In *Asahi Metal Industry Co. v. Superior Court*, the United States Supreme Court was evenly divided over how minimum contacts and purposeful availment applied in the so-called "stream of commerce" context, and more recently in *J. McIntyre Machinery, Ltd. v. Nicastro* the Court was again unable to muster a

---

[364] *Shisler v. Sanfer Sports Cars, Inc.*, 146 Cal. App. 4th 1254, 53 Cal. Rptr. 3d 335 (2006).

[365] *Hunt v. Superior Court*, 81 Cal. App. 4th 901, 97 Cal. Rptr. 2d 215 (2000).

[366] *Asahi Metal Indus. Co. v. Superior Court*, 480 U.S. 102, 113 (1987).

[367] *Asahi, supra*, 480 U.S. at 113; *Burger King Corp. v. Rudzewicz*, 471 U.S. 462 (1985); *World-Wide Volkswagen v. Woodson*, 444 U.S. 286 (1980); *see Epic Commc'n, Inc. v. Richwave Tech., Inc.*, 179 Cal. App. 4th 314, 317–18, 336–37, 101 Cal. Rptr. 3d 572 (2009) (a refusal to exercise personal jurisdiction cannot be justified by the mere fact that a claim arising from California contacts is brought by a nonresident; while the plaintiff's foreign status might reduce the state's interest in adjudicating the dispute, that is at most a subsidiary consideration which cannot by itself justify a denial of access to the California courts); *but see Goodyear Dunlop Tires, supra*, 131 S. Ct. at 2857, n.5 (noting that the plaintiff's residence in the forum may strengthen the case for the exercise of specific, but not general, jurisdiction).

[368] *E.g., Vons, supra*, 14 Cal. 4th at 449, 475–78; *Snowney, supra*, 35 Cal. 4th at 1070; *Bridgestone Corp. v. Superior Court*, 99 Cal. App. 4th 767, 778–79, 121 Cal. Rptr. 2d 673 (2002).

majority opinion on this issue.[369] This uncertainty left the law concerning stream of commerce in limbo, and opened the door for a state court to choose which side of the *Asahi* "split" it prefers. This is exactly what the California Court of Appeal did in *Bridgestone Corp. v. Superior Court*,[370] a recent case whose facts are similar to those in *Asahi*. In *Bridgestone*, the plaintiff truck driver sued his employer and Firestone, a Tennessee company that distributed Bridgestone tires in California, seeking damages for personal injuries sustained when one of the tires failed. The defendant employer then filed a cross-complaint for equitable indemnity against the Bridgestone Corporation, the manufacturer of the allegedly defective tire. Cross-defendant Bridgestone is a Japanese company that manufactures and sells its tires only in Japan for resale by various distributers, including Firestone. Bridgestone moved to quash, arguing that merely placing goods in the stream of commerce with knowledge that they may be purchased in California does not constitute sufficient contacts to support personal jurisdiction.

The Court of Appeal rejected this argument, and concluded that a manufacturer's placement of goods in the stream of commerce with the expectation that they will be purchased from a distributor by consumers in California constitutes purposeful availment if the income earned by the manufacturer from the sale of its product in California is substantial. In so holding, the court declined to follow contrary dicta regarding purposeful availment in Justice O'Connor's plurality opinion on minimum contacts in *Asahi*.[371] The *Bridgestone* court also found the exercise of personal jurisdiction would be fair and reasonable because, unlike *Asahi*, the cross-plaintiffs are California residents whose common interest in convenient and effective relief is best served in a California forum, and California has an interest in providing a convenient forum for its residents to redress injuries caused by out-of-state parties.

[5]   Due Process: The "Effects" Test

In *Calder v. Jones*, the United States Supreme Court recognized a variant of the minimum contacts analysis for determining purposeful availment, referred to as the "effects" test.[372] In *Pavlovich v. Superior Court*,[373] the California Supreme Court applied the *Calder* "effects" test in the context of the posting of information on an internet web site.[374] The defendant website operator, a resident of Texas,

---

[369] The various opinions in *Asahi* and *McIntyre* are discussed in detail in § 3.07, *supra*.

[370] 99 Cal. App. 4th 767, 121 Cal. Rptr. 2d 673 (2002).

[371] *Asahi, supra*, 480 U.S. at 108–113 (1987) (O'Connor, J., plurality opinion).

[372] *Calder v. Jones*, 465 U.S. 783, 104 S. Ct. 1482, 79 L. Ed. 2d 804 (1984) (holding California court could exercise personal jurisdiction over Florida reporter and editor who in an article defamed plaintiff, a well-known actress who lived and worked in California, based on the harmful "effects" of their Florida conduct in California). *Calder v. Jones* is discussed in more detail in § 3.05[5], *supra*.

[373] 29 Cal. 4th 262, 127 Cal. Rptr. 2d 329, 58 P.3d 2 (2002).

[374] Other recent California decisions applying the "effects test" include *Archdiocese of Milwaukee v. Superior Court*, 112 Cal. App. 4th 423, 5 Cal. Rptr. 3d 154 (2003), *cert. denied*, 542 U.S. 919 (2004) (upholding personal jurisdiction over Wisconsin archdiocese in an action alleging sexual molestation by a catholic priest under the "effects test" because the defendant archdiocese knew the priest was a convicted pedophile and purposely reassigned him to California), and *In re Automobile Antitrust Cases*,

posted the source code of a computer program designed to defeat the copy protection system employed to encrypt and protect copyrighted motion pictures contained on digital versatile discs (DVD's). The plaintiff, a California trade association created by the DVD industry to control and administer licensing of encryption technology, filed an action in a California court for misappropriation of trade secrets.

In a 4-3 decision, the California Supreme Court held that the trial court's exercise of personal jurisdiction was inconsistent with due process. The Court ruled that the "effects" test requires intentional conduct expressly aimed at or targeting the forum state in addition to the defendant's knowledge that his intentional conduct would cause harm in the forum. But the majority concluded that the defendant's knowledge that his tortious conduct may harm certain industries centered in California — *i.e.*, the motion picture, computer, and consumer electronics industries — was insufficient to establish express aiming at California and, by itself, cannot establish purposeful availment under the effects test.[375]

The dissent agreed that the mere operation of an internet website cannot expose the operator to suit in any jurisdiction where the site's contents might be read, or where resulting injury might occur. However, the dissent viewed the defendant's internet website posting as "expressly aimed" at California because his illegal conduct intentionally targeted the movie and the computer industries, which he knew were centered in California: "[D]efendants who aim conduct at particular jurisdictions, expecting and intending that injurious effects will be felt in those specific places, cannot shield themselves from suit there simply by using the Internet, or some other generalized medium of communication, as the means of inflicting the harm."[376]

The *Pavlovich* Court's division over the "expressly aimed" requirement demonstrates the uncertain nature of the "effects test" when applied in such internet cases. This doctrine needs further judicial clarification before it can be confidently applied to intentional torts other than defamation (the type of tortuous conduct alleged in *Calder v. Jones*). To date, neither the United States nor the California Supreme Court has provided this additional guidance.

[6] Transient Jurisdiction

Another constitutional basis for personal jurisdiction is transient (or "tag service") jurisdiction, which depends solely on service of the complaint and summons on a nonresident defendant while present in the forum state, regardless of whether that defendant otherwise has any minimum contacts with the forum

---

135 Cal. App. 4th 100, 37 Cal. Rptr. 3d 258 (2005) (ruling that mere foreseeability that the defendant knew or should have known that its intentional acts could cause harm in California is not sufficient to establish jurisdiction under the effects test, instead the plaintiff must demonstrate that the defendant expressly aimed or targeted its tortious conduct at plaintiffs in California).

[375] *Pavlovich, supra*, 29 Cal. 4th at 273–78.

[376] *Pavlovich, supra*, 29 Cal. 4th at 289 (Baxter, J., dissenting).

state.[377] The California courts endorse transient jurisdiction. For example, in one case, the Court of Appeal held personal jurisdiction proper where a nonresident defendant was served with process while present in California at a mandatory settlement conference in a different action, ruling that California no longer recognizes immunity from service for nonresident witnesses or parties.[378]

[7] Nonresident Parent Corporations

[a] Alter Ego and Agency Doctrines

A recurring issue is whether, and under what circumstances, a nonresident parent corporation is subject to personal jurisdiction in California based solely on the contacts of its California subsidiary. The general rule is that a parent company's ownership or control of a subsidiary corporation does not, without more, subject the parent corporation to the jurisdiction of the state where the subsidiary does business.[379] However, most California courts recognize two principles under which the contacts of the subsidiary doing business in California are attributed to the parent corporation: the "alter ego doctrine" and the "agency theory."[380] The assertion of jurisdiction under either theory requires a fact-specific examination of numerous elements.

When the elements of the alter ego doctrine are present, the court will disregard the parent's and the subsidiary's independent corporate existence for purposes of jurisdiction. The main inquiry is whether there is such a unity of control, interest, and ownership between the parent and subsidiary corporations that their separate corporate personalities do not really exist. According to a summary of the alter ego doctrine provided by one Court of Appeal, the California courts consider numerous factors "including inadequate capitalization, commingling of funds and other assets of the two entities, the holding out by one entity that it is liable for the debts of the other, identical equitable ownership in the two entities, use of the same offices and employees, use of one as a mere conduit for the affairs of the other, disregard of

---

[377] *Burnham v. Superior Court*, 495 U.S. 604 (1990); *see* § 3.09[2], *supra*; Barbara Surtees Goto, Comment, *International Shoe Gets the Boot:* Burnham v. Superior Court *Resurrects the Physical Power Theory*, 24 Loy. L.A. L. Rev. 851 (1991);

[378] *Silverman v. Superior Court*, 203 Cal. App. 3d 145, 150, 249 Cal. Rptr. 724 (1988); *but see Tri-West Ins. Serv., Inc. v. Seguros Monterrey Aetna, S.A.*, 78 Cal. App. 4th 672, 676, 93 Cal. Rptr. 2d 78 (2000) (holding service of the complaint and summons on the California Insurance Commissioner pursuant to the Insurance Code, which provide that certain specified acts by a foreign insurer shall constitute the appointment of the Commissioner as the insurer's agent for service of process, does not provide a basis for personal jurisdiction over such defendant insurer under the concept of transient jurisdiction).

[379] *See, e.g., DVI, Inc. v. Superior Court*, 104 Cal. App. 4th 1080, 1092, 128 Cal. Rptr. 2d 683 (2002); *Sonora Diamond Corp. v. Superior Court*, 83 Cal. App. 4th 523, 540, 99 Cal. Rptr. 2d 824 (2000). For example, in *Sammons Enter., Inc. v. Superior Court*, 205 Cal. App. 3d 1427, 253 Cal. Rptr. 261 (1988), the court held that a foreign corporation is not subject to personal jurisdiction based solely on the independent activities of its wholly owned local subsidiary even where the parent exercises general executive responsibility for the operations of the subsidiary and reviews its major policy decisions.

[380] *See, e.g., Sonora Diamond Corp., supra*, 83 Cal. App. 4th at 537–42; *BBA Aviation PLC v. Superior Court*, 190 Cal. App. 4th 421, 429, 433–35,117 Cal. Rptr. 3d 914 (2010); *Rollins Burdick Hunter of So. Cal., Inc. v. Alexander & Alexander Serv., Inc.*, 206 Cal. App. 3d 1, 9–11, 253 Cal. Rptr. 338 (1988).

corporate formalities, lack of segregation of corporate records, and identical directors and officers."[381]

Under the principal/agent theory, if the forum may assert jurisdiction over the subsidiary, the forum may extend its jurisdiction to the parent if the parent exerts a sufficiently high degree of control over its subsidiary to reasonably deem the subsidiary the agent of the parent under traditional agency principles. Only when the degree of control reflects the parent's purposeful disregard of the subsidiary's independent corporate existence by moving beyond the establishment of general policy and direction for the subsidiary and in effect taking over performance of the subsidiary's day-to-day operations in carrying out that policy, will the principal/agent theory apply.[382]

Some California courts have questioned whether principles of "alter ego" and "agency" can justify the exercise of specific personal jurisdiction over a nonresident parent company. For example, in one case, the Court of Appeal reasoned that reliance on state substantive law of agency and alter ego to determine the constitutional limits of specific personal jurisdiction is unnecessary and is an imprecise substitute for the appropriate jurisdictional questions, and concluded that the proper due process inquiry is as follows: "A parent company purposely avails itself of forum benefits through the activities of its subsidiary, as required to justify the exercise of specific personal jurisdiction, if and only if the parent deliberately directs the subsidiary's activities in, or having a substantial connection with, the forum state."[383]

[b] Representative Services Doctrine

The California courts also recognize the "representative services" doctrine, a variation of the general agency theory discussed above.[384] However, unlike the general agency theory, the narrow representative services doctrine does not depend on whether the parent company enjoys pervasive and continuous control over the subsidiary. Instead, personal jurisdiction may be exercised over a foreign parent corporation when the local agent/subsidiary exists only to further the business of the parent and but for the local agent's existence, the parent would be performing those functions in the forum itself.

---

[381] *VirtualMagic, supra*, 99 Cal. App. 4th at 245.

[382] *Sonora Diamond Corp., supra*, 83 Cal. App. 4th at 541–42; *VirtualMagic, supra*, 99 Cal. App. 4th at 245.

[383] *HealthMarkets, Inc. v. Superior Court*, 171 Cal. App. 4th 1160, 1169, 90 Cal. Rptr. 3d 527 (2009).

[384] *See, e.g., BBA Aviation PLC v. Superior Court*, 190 Cal. App. 4th 421, 429–33,117 Cal. Rptr. 3d 914 (2010) (ruling the representative services doctrine is inapplicable where foreign parent corporation is a holding company and the requisite high level of control over the subsidiary not shown); *In re Automobile Antitrust Cases I & II*, 135 Cal. App. 4th 100, 37 Cal. Rptr. 3d 258 (2005) (holding that the foreign parent company defendants are not subject to personal jurisdiction under representative services doctrine because no evidence that defendants controlled the day-to-day activities of their local subsidiaries); *Dorel Indus., Inc. v. Superior Court*, 134 Cal. App. 4th 1267, 1269–80, 36 Cal. Rptr. 3d 742 (2005) (finding personal jurisdiction proper with respect to defendant foreign grandparent corporation based on agency theory of representative services doctrine where defendant used local subsidiary to engage in business the defendant would otherwise have done itself).

[8]   Raising the Personal Jurisdiction Defense

[a]   Waivable Due Process Right

The due process personal jurisdiction requirement recognizes and protects an individual liberty interest.[385] Because the requirement of personal jurisdiction represents an individual right, it can, like other such rights, be waived. Such waiver may be express or implied, and traditionally occurs when a defendant does not raise this due process right in the proper procedural manner.

[b]   Timely Motion to Quash Required

Pursuant to a 2003 amendment to Code of Civil Procedure § 418.10, the California practice with respect to raising an objection to personal jurisdiction conforms generally, but not entirely, to the practice in the federal courts under federal Rule 12.[386] An objection to personal jurisdiction must be made by filing a motion to quash on or before the last day to plead in response to the complaint.[387] The defendant need not raise the objection by a "special appearance" but may simultaneously answer, demur, or move to strike at the same time the objection is raised by a timely motion to quash.[388]

However, unlike the federal practice, the California statute does not give a defendant the option to plead lack of personal jurisdiction as a defense in an answer and reserve determination of that issue until as late as trial. Instead, section 418.10 continues to require a timely *motion to quash* as the means of raising the lack of personal jurisdiction service of process. The defendant may move to quash and simultaneously file an answer containing defenses to the action, but "the latter is not a substitute for the former."[389] If the defendant makes a general appearance, such as by filing an answer, demurrer, or motion to strike, *before* filing a motion to quash objecting to personal jurisdiction, the defendant waives his right to contest personal jurisdiction.[390]

---

[385] *Insurance Corp. of Ireland, Ltd. v. Compagnie des Bauxites de Guinee*, 456 U.S. 694, 702 (1982).

[386] Federal Rule 12 and waiver of the personal jurisdiction defense in federal court are discussed in § 3.11, *supra*.

[387] CAL. CODE CIV. PROC. § 418.10(a) & (b). Generally, the defendant must respond to the complaint within 30 days after service of the complaint and summons. CAL. CODE CIV. PROC. § 412.20(a)(3).

[388] *See* CAL. CODE CIV. PROC. § 418.10(e) (effective Jan. 1, 2003).

[389] *Roy v. Superior Court*, 127 Cal. App. 4th 337, 345, 25 Cal. Rptr. 3d 488 (2005). The *Roy* court also expressed its preference for the California practice over the federal practice, noting section 418.10 requires that the jurisdictional issue be raised and finally resolved at an early stage. *Id.* at 343–44.

[390] *See* CAL. CODE CIV. PROC. § 418.10(e)(3); *Fireman's Fund Ins. Co. v. Sparks Constr., Inc.*, 114 Cal. App. 4th 1135, 8 Cal. Rptr. 3d 446 (2004) (ruling a defendant who makes a general appearance forfeits any objection to defective service, even when the defendant does not know at the time that such an objection is available). Under California law, a defendant generally appears in an action when he answers, demurs, files a motion to strike or to transfer venue, gives notice of appearance, seeks affirmative relief on the merits, or in some other manner recognizes the authority of the court to proceed. CAL. CODE CIV. PROC. § 1014; *Factor Health Mgmt. v. Superior Court*, 132 Cal. App. 4th 246, 33 Cal. Rptr. 3d 599 (2005); *Dial 800 v. Fesbinder*, 118 Cal. App. 4th 32, 12 Cal. Rptr. 3d 711 (2004). For a very thorough review of the California cases determining what activity constitutes a general appearance even though

When a defendant moves to quash service of process on jurisdictional grounds, the plaintiff has the initial burden of demonstrating facts justifying the exercise of jurisdiction.[391] Once the facts showing "minimum contacts" with the forum state have been established, however, the burden to demonstrate that the exercise of jurisdiction would be "unreasonable" shifts to the defendant.[392]

[c] Appellate Review: Writ of Mandate

The general rule in federal court is that a defendant must wait until the district court enters a final judgment on the merits to seek appellate review of the denial of a properly raised personal jurisdiction defense.[393] In contrast to the federal approach, Code of Civil Procedure § 418.10(c) authorizes immediate, interlocutory appellate review of a superior court order denying a motion to quash by a *writ of mandate*.[394] Failure to timely seek such interlocutory review precludes appeal later by defendant after a decision on the merits.[395] The benefit of the California approach over the federal approach is that the threshold personal jurisdiction issue is fully and finally resolved before the litigation proceeds beyond the pleading stage.[396]

[9] Forum Selection Agreements in the California Courts

[a] Forum Selection Clauses, Generally

The California courts, like the federal courts and those of all but a handful of other states, will enforce a freely negotiated forum selection clause unless the resisting party shows that enforcement would be "unreasonable."[397] The test for

---

the defendant has filed a timely motion to quash for lack of personal jurisdiction, see *Dial 800 v. Fesbinder, supra*, 118 Cal. App. 4th at 50–55.

[391] *See, e.g., Vons Companies, Inc. v. Seabest Foods, Inc.*, 14 Cal. 4th 434, 449, 58 Cal. Rptr. 2d 899, 926 P.2d 1085 (1996); *Floveyor Intl., Ltd. v. Superior Court*, 59 Cal. App. 4th 789, 69 Cal. Rptr. 2d 457 (1997) (upholding a motion to quash because the plaintiff failed to produce any evidence that the defendant had any contacts with California).

[392] *Vons, supra*, 14 Cal. 4th at 449.

[393] *See, e.g., Burger King Corp. v. Rudzewicz*, 471 U.S. 462 (1985). The order of a federal district court denying a motion to dismiss for lack of personal jurisdiction is not an appealable "final decision" within the meaning of 28 U.S.C. § 1291, *see Catlin v. United States*, 324 U.S. 229, 236 (1945); although in rare cases the district court may certify the order for interlocutory appeal pursuant to 28 U.S.C. § 1292(b). *E.g., Klinghoffer v. S.N.C. Achille Lauro*, 921 F.2d 21 (2d Cir. 1990).

[394] The defendant must petition the appellate court for a writ of mandate within 10 days (extendable by the trial court for up to 20 days) after service of written notice of entry of the trial court's order denying the motion to quash. CAL. CODE CIV. PROC. § 418.10(c). Filing a timely writ of mandate extends the defendant's time to plead until 10 days after notification of the final decision in the mandate proceeding. *Id.*

[395] *See Danzig v. Jack Grynberg & Assoc.*, 161 Cal. App. 3d 1128, 1141, 208 Cal. Rptr. 336 (1984), *cert. denied*, 474 U.S. 819 (1985); *Roy v. Superior Court*, 127 Cal. App. 4th 337, 343–44, 25 Cal. Rptr. 3d 488 (2005). Of course, an order *granting* a motion to quash is an appealable order. CAL. CODE CIV. PROC. § 904.1(a)(3).

[396] *Roy v. Superior Court, supra*, 127 Cal. App. 4th at 343–44 (expressing preference for the California practice over the federal practice).

[397] *E.g., Smith, Valentino & Smith, Inc. v. Superior Court*, 17 Cal. 3d 491, 131 Cal. Rptr. 374, 551 P.2d

reasonableness includes such factors as whether the forum selection clause is the result of unfair use of unequal bargaining power or fraud, the forum selected would be unavailable or unable to accomplish substantial justice, or would bring about a result contrary to the public policy of the forum.[398] However, neither inconvenience nor additional expense in litigating in the selected forum is part of this test.

[b] Forum Clauses and Forum Non Conveniens

When a plaintiff commences an action in a court other than the contractually mandated forum, a forum non conveniens motion is the proper procedural vehicle to enforce a forum selection clause.[399] In such circumstances, the only relevant consideration is whether the forum selection clause is unreasonable or unfair. The presumptions and discretionary weighing of private and public interest factors pertinent to a forum non conveniens motion in the absence of a contractual forum provision are irrelevant.[400] However, when a plaintiff commences an action in the contractually designated forum, an argument can be made that the existence of the forum clause does not preclude an attempt by the defendant to change the forum via a forum non conveniens motion. Because the parties lack the power to contractually waive the public (as opposed to the private) interest factors associated with forum non conveniens, a court arguably retains the power to grant the motion in appropriate cases.[401]

[c] Validity of Forum Clauses in Consumer Contracts

The first Supreme Court (both United States and California) cases to approve the modern rule favoring enforcement of forum selection clauses involved freely negotiated contracts between commercial entities of roughly equal bargaining power.[402] Subsequently, the United States Supreme Court in *Carnival Cruise Lines, Inc. v. Shute* extended this modern rule to enforcement of forum clauses in nonnegotiated standard form consumer contracts, at least where the consumers had notice of the clause.[403] For the most part, the California courts have adopted the *Carnival Cruise Lines* approach.[404] The fact the forum selection clause is contained

---

1206 (1976); *Cal-State Bus. Prod. & Serv., Inc. v. Ricoh*, 12 Cal. App. 4th 1666, 16 Cal. Rptr. 2d 417 (1993).

[398] *Smith, Valentino & Smith, supra*, 17 Cal. 3d 494–96, *Cal-State Bus. Prod., supra*, 12 Cal. App. 4th at 1679. For a discussion of these and related issues, see Walter W. Heiser, *Forum Selection Clauses in State Courts: Limitations on Enforcement After Stewart and Carnival Cruise*, 45 Fla. L. Rev. 361 (1993).

[399] *Cal-State Bus. Prod., supra*, 12 Cal. App. 4th at 1680; *Smith, Valentino & Smith, supra*, 17 Cal. 3d at 494.

[400] *Cal-State Bus. Prod., supra*, 12 Cal. App. 4th at 1682–83; *see Berg, supra*, 61 Cal. App. 4th at 358–64 (ruling the factors that apply generally to a forum non conveniens motion do not apply to enforcement of a mandatory, as opposed to a permissive, forum selection clause).

[401] *See* Heiser, *Forum Selection Clauses in State Courts, supra*, 45 Fla. L. Rev. at 393–401.

[402] *The Bremen v. Zapata Off-Shore Co.*, 407 U.S. 1 (1972); *Smith, Valentino & Smith, supra; see* § 3.11[4], *supra*.

[403] *Carnival Cruise Lines, Inc. v. Shute*, 499 U.S. 585 (1991) (finding clause reasonable and enforcing it even though clause required Washington consumers to litigate in Florida courts).

[404] *See, e.g., Net2Phone, Inc. v. Superior Court*, 109 Cal. App. 4th 583, 135 Cal. Rptr. 2d 149 (2003) (enforcing forum selection clause between customers and defendant telecommunications services

in a form consumer contract and was not the subject of bargaining does not defeat enforcement as a matter of law, where there is no evidence of unfair use of superior power to impose the contract upon the consumer and the consumer had adequate notice of the clause.[405] However, in one case, the Court of Appeal refused to enforce a forum selection clause in a consumer contract where to do so would constitute a contractual waiver of the California's consumer protection statute, "thereby violating an important public policy underlying California's consumer protection law."[406]

The California Legislature has recently added some protection for consumers with respect to enforcement of forum selection clauses in certain actions where the amount in controversy is less than $5,000;[407] and has also placed some limits on forum clause enforcement in other specific types of contracts.[408]

---

provider designating New Jersey courts, where clause accessed via hyperlink in defendant's internet website); *Lu v. Dryclean-U.S.A. of Cal., Inc.*, 11 Cal. App. 4th 1490, 14 Cal. Rptr. 2d 906 (1992) (enforcing forum selection clause in franchise agreement requiring plaintiffs, individual franchisees, to litigate in Florida); *but see Aral v. Earthlink, Inc.*, 134 Cal. App. 4th 544, 36 Cal. Rptr. 3d 229 (2005) (refusing to enforce a forum selection clause designating Georgia as the forum because that clause required the plaintiff consumer to travel 2,000 miles to recover a small sum and therefore is not reasonable).

[405] *See, e.g., Intershop Commc'n AG v. Superior Court*, 104 Cal. App. 4th 191, 201–02, 127 Cal. Rptr. 2d 847 (2002) (forum selection clause within an adhesion contract, which required plaintiff employee to litigate breach of stock options exchange agreement in Germany, will be enforced so long as the clause provided adequate notice to the plaintiff that he was agreeing to the jurisdiction cited in the contract); *Lu v. Dryclean-U.S.A of Cal., Inc., supra; Bos Material Handling, Inc. v. Crown Controls Corp.*, 137 Cal. App. 3d 99, 186 Cal. Rptr. 740 (1982) (enforcing forum clause in standardized contract which required arbitration in Ohio, even though contract deemed adhesive).

[406] *American Online, Inc., v. Superior Court*, 90 Cal. App. 4th 1, 5, 108 Cal. Rtpr. 2d 699 (2001).

[407] CAL. CODE CIV. PROC. § 116.225 (an agreement establishing a forum outside California for an action arising from the provision of goods, services, property, or extensions of credit primarily for personal, family or household purposes that is otherwise within the jurisdiction of the small claims court of California is contrary to public policy and is void and unenforceable).

[408] *E.g.,* CAL. CODE CIV. PROC. § 410.42 (construction subcontracts); CAL. COM. CODE § 10106(b) (consumer leases); CAL. CORP. CODE § 15627.5 (partnership agreements).

Chapter 4

NOTICE AND OPPORTUNITY TO BE HEARD

§ 4.01 THE DUE PROCESS GUARANTEE OF NOTICE AND THE OPPORTUNITY TO BE HEARD

Federal and state adjudications are binding only when they satisfy the Due Process Clauses of the United States Constitution.[1] Having seen how the clauses impose limits on courts' territorial jurisdiction,[2] we will now consider how they deny effect to adjudications unless those to be bound were given prior notice and an opportunity to participate.[3]

Notice is tied to the procedure for service of process. The United States Supreme Court has reemphasized the importance of service of process, stating that "[s]ervice of process, under longstanding tradition in our system of justice, is fundamental to any procedural imposition on a named defendant."[4] As the Court observed in another case, "the core function of service is to supply notice of the pendency of a legal action, in a manner and at a time that affords the defendant a fair opportunity to answer the complaint and present defenses and objections."[5]

Process usually consists of a summons, directing defendant to respond or appear in court on penalty of default, and a copy of the complaint. *Service* is the formal means by which process is delivered to a defendant. Assurance of a quality of notice sufficient to satisfy due process is an important function of every system's service procedure.[6] We shall see that actual notice is not an invariable due process requirement. That is, it is possible under the right circumstances for defendant to be bound by an adjudication, although he neither participated in it nor made an

---

[1] Restricting federal and state courts respectively, the Fifth and Fourteenth amendments protect against deprivation of "life, liberty or property, without due process of law." A cause of action is "property" within the meaning of the amendments and cannot be forfeited through proceedings lacking in due process. Due process similarly protects litigants who are claimed against. For elaboration of these points, see § 3.01[2] (law limiting the court's reach), *supra*.

[2] Chapter 3, *supra*.

[3] These two branches of due process doctrine are explained and compared in *Phillips Petroleum Co. v. Shutts*, 472 U.S. 797 (1985). *See* § 3.01, *supra*. For restatement of the due process principle of notice and the opportunity to be heard, see *Nelson v. Adams USA, Inc.*, 529 U.S. 460, 466 (2000) (voiding a judgment without requisite prior notice). On the contemporary importance of the principle, see Patrick Woolley, *Rethinking the Adequacy of Adequate Representation*, 75 Tex. L. Rev. 571 (1997).

[4] *Murphy Bros., Inc. v. Michetti Pipe Stringing, Inc.*, 526 U.S. 344, 350 (1999).

[5] *Henderson v. United States*, 517 U.S. 654, 672 (1996).

[6] *E.g., Jones v. Flowers*, 547 U.S. 220 (2006).

informed decision to forgo participation.[7] At the same time, due process places a heavy burden of justification on attempts to bind those who have not received actual notice.

The Court laid down the modern standard in *Mullane v. Central Hanover Bank & Trust Co.*[8]

> An elementary and fundamental requirement of due process in any proceeding which is to be accorded finality is notice reasonably calculated, under all the circumstances, to apprise interested parties of the pendency of the action and afford them an opportunity to present their objections. . . . The notice must be of such nature as reasonably to convey the required information . . . , and it must afford a reasonable time for those interested to make their appearance. . . . But if with due regard for the practicalities and peculiarities of the case these conditions are reasonably met, the constitutional requirements are satisfied.[9]

Mullane involved adjudication by a New York state court of the interests of trust beneficiaries. The beneficiaries fell into three categories: (1) those whose names and addresses were known; (2) those who were unknowable; (3) and those whose names and addresses could be ascertained at considerable expense. The Court refused to permit notice by publication to the first category, "because under the circumstances it is not reasonably calculated to reach those who could easily be informed by other means at hand."[10] When addresses were known, "the reasons disappear for resort to means less likely than the mails to apprise them of [the] pendency [of the proceeding]."[11] Since a substantial number of beneficiaries would thus have actual (individual) notice, the Court was willing to dispense with a requirement of individualized notice for beneficiaries in categories two and three.

> This type of trust presupposes a large number of small interests. The individual interest does not stand alone but is identical with that of a class. The rights of each in the integrity of the fund and the fidelity of the trustee are shared by many other beneficiaries. Therefore notice reasonably certain to reach most of those interested in objecting is likely to safeguard the interest of all, since any objection sustained would inure to the benefit of all. We think that under such circumstances reasonable risks that notice might not actually reach every beneficiary are justifiable.[12]

Accordingly, the Court approved constructive notice by publication to the beneficiaries for whom individualized notice was impractical.[13]

---

[7] *E.g., Dusenbery v. United States,* 534 U.S. 161 (2002).

[8] 339 U.S. 306 (1950).

[9] 339 U.S. at 314–15.

[10] 339 U.S. at 319.

[11] 339 U.S. at 318.

[12] 339 U.S. at 319.

[13] Similarly, the Supreme Court recently observed that "the Due Process Clause does not require . . . heroic efforts" to give defendant actual notice. *Dusenbery v. United States,* 534 U.S. 161, 170 (2002). Discussions of the case appear in David F. Benson, *United States v. Dusenbery: Supreme*

Mullane and its progeny "radically modified" the historical notice requirement.[14] *Mullane* curtailed notice by publication, holding that it could not substitute for individual notice when the latter was practicable.[15] On the other hand, *Mullane* authorized service by the best alternative means, possibly publication,[16] in some situations where individual notice was impracticable. The Court did not offer a comprehensive list of these situations and has not since. However, the manner in which the Court reacted to the circumstances in *Mullane* suggests that something less than individual notice is most likely to satisfy due process when proof of the impracticability of individual notice is accompanied by proof that (1) the suit is in the interest of the absentees, (2) they will be adequately represented by one before the court, and (3) the value of their individual interests is not too great.

The Supreme Court has subsequently adhered to the *Mullane* reasonableness-under-the-circumstances approach to notice. In *Greene v. Lindsey*,[17] it rejected a Kentucky state service of process scheme permitting notice of eviction proceedings to be left at the homes of defendants under circumstances where there was substantial possibility that passers-by would remove the notices before defendants knew of them. In *Greene* and in the subsequent case of *Mennonite Board of Missions v. Adams*,[18] the Court seemed to suggest that constitutional defects in service could have been cured through the additional step of mailing a copy of court process to the due process claimant.[19] Similarly, the Court recently held in *Jones v.*

Court Silence and the Lingering Echo of Due Process Violations in Civil Forfeiture Actions, 78 CHI.-KENT L. REV. 409 (2003); W. Alexander Burnett, *Dusenbery v. United States: Setting the Standard for Adequate Notice*, 37 U. RICH. L. REV. 613 (2003).

[14] RESTATEMENT (SECOND) OF JUDGMENTS 27 (introductory note to Ch. 2) (1982).

[15] 339 U.S. at 318.

[16] "The rule in *Mullane* recognizes that persons can be bound even if they cannot be found through reasonably diligent search. Assuming that such a search has been made, the fiction is indulged that publication notifies the absentee." RESTATEMENT (SECOND) OF JUDGMENTS, note 14, *supra*, § 2 comment g. "Publication of notice creates an additional possibility of bringing the proceeding to the absentee's attention. Perhaps more important, however, publication of notice is a ceremony whose performance assures that the termination of the absentee's rights is not done in secret." RESTATEMENT (SECOND) OF JUDGMENTS, note 14, *supra*, § 2 comment g.

[17] 456 U.S. 444 (1982). For a discussion of *Greene*, see Arthur F. Greenbaum, *The Postman Never Rings Twice: The Constitutionality of Service of Process by Posting After Greene v. Lindsey*, 33 AM. U. L. REV. 601–41 (1984).

[18] 462 U.S. 791 (1983). The case is examined in Linda S. Akchin, Note, *Mennonite Board of Missions v. Adams: Expansion of the Due Process Notice Requirements*, 46 LA. L. REV. 311 (1985). Later, in *Tulsa Professional Collection Services, Inc. v. Pope*, 485 U.S. 478 (1988), the Supreme Court again found circumstances requiring actual notice. Attention has turned to the constitutionality of internet service. *See* Matthew R. Schreck, *How Service of Process By E-Mail Does Not Meet Constitutional Procedural Due Process Requirements*, 38 J. MARSHALL L. REV. 1121 (2005); Jeremy A. Colby, *The Modern Trend Towards Universal Electronic Service of Process*, 51 BUFF. L. REV. 337 (2003); Rachel Cantor, *Internet Service of Process: A Constitutionally Adequate Alternative?* 66 U. CHI. L. REV. 943 (1999).

[19] It seems desirable to permit the party initiating service to cure through informal mailing a constitutional insufficiency in the formal scheme. However, in *Wuchter v. Pizzutti*, 276 U.S. 13 (1928), the Court struck down a judgment on due process notice grounds because the statute failed to require service on the defendant, even though the defendant in the case had in fact received actual notice. The Supreme Court has not expressly overruled *Wuchter*, but the continuing authority of the case is in some doubt. *See* SCOLES, HAY, BORCHERS & SYMEONIDES, CONFLICT OF LAWS § 12.3 (4th ed. 2004). "The more discerning cases have recognized that the requirement is adequate notice and that it is fulfilled by actual

Flowers[20] that, when notice by certified mail was returned to defendant as undelivered, due process required defendant to take other practical steps to attempt to notify plaintiff of the case.[21]

§ 4.02 SPECIAL DUE PROCESS CONCERNS ARISING FROM CLASS ACTIONS AND PREJUDGMENT ATTACHMENTS

[1] Class Actions

While class actions and special due process considerations pertaining to them are discussed elsewhere,[22] it is useful to make a few observations here. The special contribution of the class action device is to conclude simultaneously the interests of a far greater number of persons than could actively participate in the case. Those who do not actively participate but are nonetheless bound by the adjudication of class issues are called *passive* members of the class.

Due process does not (and, for class actions to exist, could not) require the active participation of each person to be bound in a civil action. The Supreme Court's classic standard for applying the Due Process Clauses to class actions is "that there has been a failure of due process only in those cases where it cannot be said that the procedure adopted, fairly insures the protection of the interests of absent parties who are to be bound by it."[23] Read broadly, this might suggest that the due process touchstone for class actions is adequate representation, rather than actual notice. However, since class actions are fully subject to *Mullane*'s due process requirement of best notice practicable,[24] so broad a reading would be unwise. Actual notice is clearly the best notice, and due process requires it to be given to class members whenever practicable.[25]

---

notice whose tenor indicates it ought to be taken seriously." Restatement (Second) of Judgments, note 14, *supra*, § 2 comment d.

[20] 547 U.S. 220 (2006).

[21] Defendant could "resend the notice by regular mail, so that a signature was not required." 547 U.S. at 234. "Other reasonable followup measures . . . would have been to post notice on the front door, or to address otherwise undeliverable mail to 'occupant.' " 547 U.S. at 235.

[22] *See* § 9.09, *infra.*

[23] *Hansberry v. Lee*, 311 U.S. 32, 42 (1940) (citation omitted).

[24] For discussion of *Mullane*'s requirements, see § 4.01, *supra*. The Supreme Court has consistently applied *Mullane* to class actions. *E.g.*, *Phillips Petroleum Co. v. Shutts*, 472 U.S. 797 (1985).

[25] In addition, federal class action Rule 23 and the rules of many states require actual notice to class members in some situations whether or not actual notice would be required by due process. *See* § 9.09[2], *infra*. Neither the rule, nor due process, requires notice in some class actions when it is impracticable. *See* § 9.09[2], *infra*.

[2] Prejudgment Attachments

In theory, post-judgment attachment of the real or personal property of one against whom judgment is rendered (the judgment debtor) helps the judgment creditor to realize all or part of the value of the judgment.[26] The procedure is worthless, however, when the judgment debtor has little or nothing of value to attach. Pre-judgment attachment provides some hedge against this possibility because it "prevent[s] the defendant from disposing of or otherwise impairing the value of property that might be used to satisfy the judgment in an action."[27] Absent settlement, property remains frozen by prejudgment attachment until the plaintiff wins on the merits and is able to enforce his judgment against the property, or until defendant recaptures the property by having the attachment dissolved, posting surety, or winning on the merits.

At first glance, the due process law of notice[28] seems to restrain prejudgment attachments less than it does judicial proceedings generally. Current due process doctrine permits some decisions authorizing prejudgment attachments to be made after *ex parte* proceedings — proceedings conducted without notice to or participation by the defendant.[29] Defendant in such cases usually learns of the existence of suit only when prejudgment attachment separates him from his property. Earlier notice would make it possible for defendant to appear and contest plaintiff's application before the court decides to issue the attachment order. Since defendants in such cases typically are easy to find and notify prior to the attachment proceeding,[30] earlier notice might seem practicable in the *Mullane* sense and hence required by due process.[31]

Given the purpose of prejudgment attachments, however, requiring plaintiff to give notice to defendant before the fact of attachment might be impracticable in a different sense. Recall that prejudgment attachments exist to secure defendant's property to which plaintiff can look if he prevails on the merits. Alerting defendant to the attachment proceedings (or even to the existence of suit) may defeat this purpose. Defendant may transfer his interest in property to another, remove it from the jurisdiction, hide it, or otherwise diminish its value,[32] leaving little to attach.

---

[26] *See* § 15.02 (enforcement of judgments), *infra.*

[27] FRIEDENTHAL, KANE & MILLER § 15.2. Garnishment, another so-called provisional remedy, functions the same way. Sometimes the latter term is favored to describe seizure of defendant's liquid assets, including wages and debts owed him by others. *See, e.g., Sniadach v. Family Fin. Corp.*, 395 U.S. 337 (1969). For discussion of a different provisional remedy, the temporary injunction, see § 14.02[2], *infra.*

[28] When prejudgment attachment cases proceed on a theory of *quasi in rem* jurisdiction, a second branch of due process doctrine (regulating the exercise of territorial jurisdiction over nonresident defendants) may also be a factor. *See* § 3.01[3][c], *supra.*

[29] The Court upheld such a procedure in *Mitchell v. W.T. Grant Co.*, 416 U.S. 600 (1974).

[30] Indeed, plaintiff will probably be required to notify defendant quite soon *after* the attachment.

[31] *See* § 4.01 (notice), *supra.*

[32] Not only is there a possibility of transfer or malicious waste of the property, but also decline in value through ordinary continued use by the defendant during the pendency of the case. This may be of special concern to plaintiff when it holds a security interest in the property, a factor noted in *Mitchell v. W.T. Grant Co.*, 416 U.S. 600, 608 (1974).

It is unwise to ban *ex parte* attachments altogether for the reasons noted above. On the other hand, any use of the judicial process depriving one of notice and property in so calculated a fashion must be subjected to careful scrutiny. The Supreme Court has struggled in four decisions to strike the proper balance. Whether these decisions, *North Georgia Finishing, Inc. v. Di-Chem, Inc.*,[33] *Mitchell v. W.T. Grant Co.*,[34] *Fuentes v. Shevin*,[35] and *Sniadach v. Family Finance Corp.*,[36] are entirely compatible is an open question.[37] The approach in each, however, centers on two inquiries.

First, what is the nature of the *ex parte* proceeding? The Supreme Court has made clear that the fact that only the plaintiff participates should not decide the outcome. Rather, procedures for deciding an *ex parte* application for attachment should take into account the interests of the defendant *in absentia* and carry the possibility that the application would be refused in appropriate cases. When the Court struck down prejudgment attachment procedures in *Fuentes* and *Di-Chem*, therefore, it gave considerable weight to the fact that the applications required of plaintiffs were undemanding in form and content,[38] and that issuance of attachment was left to clerical employees. The Court noted that circumstances were different in *Grant*. A sworn and factually detailed showing was necessary under Louisiana law. Moreover, the decision to issue the writ was made by a judge — an official more used to saying "no" to attorneys. Overall, the Court was able to conclude in *Grant* that "[t]he system protects the debtor's interest in every conceivable way, except allowing him to have the property to start with . . . ."[39]

The second inquiry is: how long is defendant likely to be separated from custody or control of the property? Even systems invalidated in *Fuentes* and *Di-Chem* provided some procedure for defendant to recapture the property prior to the conclusion of the case. The problem was that the procedures were insufficiently prompt and accessible. *Grant* noted that the procedure available to defendants in *Fuentes* was too obscure, leaving them "in limbo to await a hearing that might or might not 'eventually' occur. . . . "[40] The scheme upheld in *Grant* did not suffer from this problem. "Louisiana law," the Court stated, "expressly provides for an immediate hearing and dissolution of the writ 'unless the plaintiff proves the

---

[33] 419 U.S. 601 (1975).

[34] 416 U.S. 600 (1974).

[35] 407 U.S. 67 (1972).

[36] 395 U.S. 337 (1969).

[37] *See* Robert S. Catz & Edmund H. Robinson, *Due Process and Creditor's Remedies: From Sniadach and Fuentes to Mitchell, North Georgia and Beyond*, 28 RUTGERS L. REV. 541 (1975); Comment, *A Confusing Course Made More Confusing: The Supreme Court, Due Process, and Summary Creditor Remedies*, 70 NW. U. L. REV. 331 (1975). In *Lugar v. Edmondson Oil Co., Inc.*, 457 U.S. 922, 927 (1982), the Court said that the four decisions could be read together as due process law governing prejudgment attachments.

[38] For example, Florida law in *Fuentes* required merely "the bare assertion of the party seeking the writ that he is entitled to one." 407 U.S. at 74.

[39] 416 U.S. at 618.

[40] 416 U.S. at 618. "Nor was it apparent in *Sniadach* with what speed the debtor could challenge the validity of the garnishment." 416 U.S. at 614.

grounds upon which the writ was issued.' "[41]

The Supreme Court's message continues to be that state legislatures must beef up defendant's side of the formal adversary process. In *Grant*, the quality of procedure before and after the attachment was clearly superior to that in *Sniadach, Fuentes*, and *Di-Chem*. Returning to the subject in 1991, the Court in *Connecticut v. Doehr* faulted a Connecticut statute for failing to reach the standard set in *Grant*. Instead, the statute permitted issuance of an *ex parte* attachment on "only a skeletal affidavit" constituting "one-sided, self-serving, and conclusory submissions."[42]

Yet, while the procedural scheme was best for the defendant in *Grant*, the question remains: was the defendant there treated fairly enough to satisfy what should be the requirements of due process? Greater protection before and after issuance of the *ex parte* order is a procedural advantage theoretically available to all defendants facing attachment. But will low-income debtors such as the defendant in *Grant* be as likely as other debtors to exploit the advantage?[43]

§ 4.03   RULES REGULATING SERVICE OF PROCESS

[1]   The Interplay of Constitutional Law and Rules or Statutes; Diversity of Local Approaches

We have seen that the Constitution does no more than set a pragmatic general standard for the quality of service of process.[44] Important as due process doctrine is, it does not create the particular structure and detail necessary for service-of-process rules or statutes. Because constitutional notice can take different forms, and because nothing stops legislatures from creating service requirements more demanding than those required by due process, approaches to service vary.[45] The net effect is that the adequacy of service in any given case must be evaluated with

---

[41]   416 U.S. at 618 (*quoting* state statute).

[42]   501 U.S. 1, 14 (1991). Plaintiff in *Doehr* sought a real estate attachment against defendant pursuant to his claim for assault and battery. The fact that plaintiff wanted to attach real estate rather than movables of the defendant appeared to work against plaintiff. The Court noted that the "[p]laintiff had no existing interest in Doehr's real estate when he sought the attachment" and that "there was no allegation that Doehr was about to transfer or encumber his real estate. . . . " The Court concluded that "plaintiff's interest in attaching the property does not justify the burdening of Doehr's ownership rights without a hearing to determine the likelihood of recovery." 501 U.S. at 16. An illuminating study of this case by Professor Robert G. Bone appears in Civil Procedure Stories Ch. 4 (Kevin M. Clermont ed. Foundation 2d ed., 2008).

[43]   For an argument that the United States Supreme Court relies unduly on adversary formalities in its attempt to secure due process objectives, see Jerry L. Mashaw, *The Management Side of Due Process: Some Theoretical and Litigation Notes on the Assurance of Accuracy, Fairness, and Timeliness in the Adjudication of Social Welfare Claims*, 59 Cornell L. Rev. 772 (1974). In prejudgment attachment and other legal contexts, equality in theory may not be equality in fact. *See generally* Jason Parkin, *Adaptable Due Process*, 160 U. Pa. L. Rev. 1309 (2012) (arguing that the "conversation about procedural justice that went silent many years ago" must be "reinvigorate[d]" to ensure due process before welfare benefits are revoked).

[44]   *See* § 4.01 (due process guarantee of notice), *supra*.

[45]   *See, e.g.*, the comparison between Massachusetts law (requiring service in hand) and Rule 4(d)(1)

reference to the requirements of due process and the applicable service of process rule or statute.

The legal consequences attached to service also vary. Some states use *service* to define commencement of civil suit for statute of limitations and other purposes. Other states use *filing* to define commencement, as do federal courts under Rule 3. When a state uses service to define commencement for limitations purposes, however, federal courts in diversity cases must follow the state law in determining whether state law claims are time-barred.[46]

[2] The Federal Rule Model

Federal court service is said to have "changed drastically"[47] with the 1983 amendments to Rule 4. The process leading to this development was unusual in itself. A year earlier, the Supreme Court proposed to Congress extensive changes in Rule 4.[48] Congress did not follow its usual practice of remaining silent, thereby permitting the Court's recommendation to become law.[49] Instead, Congress first postponed the effective date of the Court's rule, then amended the rule by statute.[50]

The 1983 amendment to Rule 4 attempted to make two fundamental changes urged by the Supreme Court in its unsuccessful proposal.[51] The first was to give plaintiff (or plaintiff's attorney) control over service of process. The second was to permit service by mail as a form of federal service.

(permitting process to be left at defendant's home under certain circumstances) as interpreted by the Supreme Court in *Hanna v. Plumer*, 380 U.S. 460 (1965).

[46] *Compare Walker v. Armco Steel Corp.*, 446 U.S. 740 (1980) (Rule 3 gave way to Oklahoma's service-based definition of commencement), *with Schiavone v. Fortune*, 477 U.S. 21 (1986) (Rule 3 followed when New Jersey law also used a filing-based definition of commencement). For more on the interplay of state law and the Federal Rules of Civil Procedure, see § 7.04, *infra*.

[47] WRIGHT § 64. *See generally* Kent Sinclair, *Service of Process: Rethinking the Theory and Procedure of Serving Process Under Federal Rule 4(c)*, 73 VA. L. REV. 1183 (1987).

[48] The Chief Justice's letter appears at 456 U.S. 1014 (1982). The Advisory Committee note intended to explain the Court's revision of Rule 4 appears at 93 F.R.D. 255, 262–63 (1982).

[49] The Rules Enabling Act, 28 U.S.C. § 2072, contemplates (but does not require) a passive role for Congress. Congress usually remains silent, but has shown a greater tendency to become actively involved in recent years. *Cf.* John H. Ely, *The Irrepressible Myth of Erie*, 87 HARV. L. REV. 693, 693–94 (1974) (describing congressional resistance to the Court's proposed Federal Rules of Evidence). For a general description of the federal procedural rule-making process, see § 1.02 (sources of civil procedure), *supra*.

[50] The Federal Rules of Civil Procedure Amendments Act of 1982, Public Law 97-462, 96 Stat. 2527 (Jan. 12, 1983). Since Congress discarded the work of the Advisory Committee, no Advisory Committee notes accompany this amendment to Rule 4. However, the legislative history for Public Law 97-462 offers some help in interpreting the amendment and is reprinted in David D. Siegel, *Practice Commentary on Amendment of Federal Rule 4 (Eff. Feb. 26, 1983) With Special Statute of Limitations Precautions*, 96 F.R.D. 88, 116–30 (1983) [hereinafter *1983 Commentary*]. For discussion of subsequent practice under Rule 4, *see* David D. Siegel, 28 U.S.C.A. Fed. R. Civ. P. 4, practice commentaries (1992) [hereinafter *1992 Commentary*].

[51] *See generally* Rachel Cantor, *Internet Service of Process: A Constitutionally Adequate Alternative?*, 66 U. CHI. L. REV. 943 (1999); Linda S. Mullenix, *The New Federal Express: Mail Service of Process Under Amended Rule 4*, 4 REV. LITIG. 299 (1985); Note, *Service of Process by First-Class Mail Under Rule 4 of the Federal Rules of Civil Procedure*, 15 RUTGERS L.J. 993 (1984).

Prior to the 1983 amendment, federal marshals had usually been responsible for service of plaintiff's summons and complaint. "The principal purpose of the amendments adopted in 1983 was to end this."[52] Responsibility was placed "squarely on the plaintiff."[53]

The change made sense. Federal marshals and their deputies have always had many responsibilities involving both civil and criminal litigation. Even with provision in the prior rule for special appointment of process servers, backlogs in summons and complaint service were common prior to 1983. It is usually in plaintiff's best interest to move the case along. Plaintiff's attorney can therefore be expected to handle responsibilities under Rule 4 quickly and correctly. To provide an end point for cases in which service is not completed promptly — because the plaintiff is not predisposed to act quickly, or because the defendant is evading service — the rule gives the plaintiff 120 days from filing the complaint to serve the summons and complaint on defendant or (absent "good cause" for delay) suffer dismissal without prejudice.[54]

The 1983 provision for mail service was less successful than its proponents had hoped. The procedure for return of the acknowledgment form confused plaintiffs and defendants alike, and its applicability outside the forum state was unclear.[55] Moreover, defendants had little incentive to cooperate in the 1983 mail service because the only sanction for failure to return the acknowledgment form was the payment of usually insignificant costs of alternative service, and because the expense of collecting these costs discouraged enforcement of even this modest sanction.[56]

The 1993 rule amendment addressed all of these shortcomings. First, it substituted the language of waiver for acknowledgment, making its operation and effect clearer to all parties.[57] Plaintiff or plaintiff's attorney may now mail the complaint, a request for waiver of formal service, and a form explaining the consequences of waiver to the defendant by first class mail. Second, the new procedure was clearly made applicable to service outside the state.[58] Third, it imposed on the defendant "a duty to avoid unnecessary expenses of serving the summons" and provided new incentives to defendant to discharge that duty. The

---

[52] *Wright* § 64.

[53] *Moore*, 1987 Rules Part 1, at 44. *Cf.* Siegel, *1983 Commentary*, note 50, *supra*, at 94 ("The main purpose of the 1983 revision was to take the marshals out of the summons serving business almost entirely."). In a limited number of situations stated in Rule 4, the marshal retains authority to make service of the summons and complaint when requested by the party wishing service.

[54] Rule 4(m).

[55] Rule 4 advisory committee's notes (1993).

[56] Rule 4 advisory committee's notes (1993). *See generally* David S. Welkowitz, *The Trouble with Service by Mail*, 67 Neb. L. Rev. 289 (1988); Mullenix, note 51, *supra*; Note, *Service of Process*, note 51, *supra*; *Report of the Committee on Federal Courts of the New York State Bar Association on Service of Process by Mail Pursuant to Rule 4(c)(2)(C)(ii) of the Federal Rules of Civil Procedure*, 116 F.R.D. 169 (1987).

[57] Rule 4(d).

[58] Rule 4(k)(1) ("filing a waiver of service establishes personal jurisdiction" over defendant who could be subjected to jurisdiction of forum state courts).

defendant who returns a waiver of service form gets 60 days after the request for waiver was sent to answer the complaint instead of the usual 20. The defendant who does not is made liable not only for the costs of alternative service, but also for attorney's fees incurred in any motion to collect the costs of service.[59]

Changes in Rule 4 brought about by the 1993 amendment extend well beyond service by mail. The rule was almost completely rewritten. Much of the pre-1993 substance was preserved, but the amendment rearranged the sequence of matters discussed and worked a number of changes. These include authorization to use the service procedures of the state in which service is made as well as those of the forum state,[60] nationwide service of process in some cases founded on federal question jurisdiction,[61] and express reference to the Hague Convention.[62]

When it comes to serving individuals, corporations, partnerships, and associations under Rule 4, plaintiffs in federal court have three choices: they may follow the service of process law for the state where the action is filed; they may follow the service of process law for the state where the defendant is served; or they may follow a default service of process procedure embedded in Rule 4 itself.[63] For service on individuals, the default procedure authorizes service by delivery of the summons and complaint to the defendant personally, by leaving the summons and complaint with someone of "suitable age and discretion" residing at the defendant's home, or by delivering a copy of the summons and complaint to the defendant's authorized agent.[64] For corporations, partnerships, and associations, the default procedure requires service upon an officer, managing agent, or other authorized agent.[65] Plaintiffs are likewise afforded a choice when serving state or local governments: they may follow that state's service rule; or they may follow the default rule of serving the summons and complaint on the chief executive officer.[66] When serving the United States government, the plaintiff must send copies of the summons and complaint by certified or registered mail to the Attorney General; to the administrative agency (when applicable); and to the civil process clerk of the U.S. Attorney's office (or, with respect to the latter, may serve the U.S. Attorney or

---

[59] Rule 4(d), (2). Prior to the 1993 amendment to Rule 4, courts disagreed concerning the availability of attorney's fees necessitated by additional service arrangements. *E.g.*, compare *Premier Bank v. Ward*, 129 F.R.D. 500 (D. La. 1990) (attorney's fees available), *with McCarthy v. Wolfeboro Res. Serv.*, 132 F.R.D. 613 (D. Mass. 1990) (attorney's fees unavailable). Much turned on this. "Without attorney's fees, costs awards will usually be paltry, depriving defendants of incentive to acknowledge mail service voluntarily." Siegel, *1992 Commentary*, note 50, *supra*.

[60] Rule 4(e)(1).

[61] Rule 4(k)(2) states:

> For a claim that arises under federal law, serving a summons or filing a waiver of service establishes personal jurisdiction over a defendant if: (A) the defendant is not subject to jurisdiction in any state's courts of general jurisdiction; and (B) exercising jurisdiction is consistent with the United States Constitution and laws.

[62] Rule 4(f)(1).

[63] Rule 4(e) and (h).

[64] Rule 4(e)(2).

[65] Rule 4(h)(1)(B).

[66] Rule 4(j).

her designee personally).[67] That leaves service upon individuals and entities in foreign countries, which raises special concerns discussed next.

[3] Service Abroad; The Hague Convention

Rule 4(f) offers means for effecting service of process in foreign countries. However, it does not in itself eliminate the risk that a federal court judgment might be denied enforcement abroad. This matters most in cases where assets sufficient to satisfy a judgment exist only in the foreign defendant's home country. Then it is essential that service on the defendant there comport with that foreign country's service requirements. Otherwise, the courts there may refuse for that reason to enforce the judgment.

For cases to which it applies, the Hague Convention[68] may offer a means of stabilizing international service of process from American courts. For example, each signatory to the Convention designates a "Central Authority" to process service in that country,[69] and the treaty makes some provision for service by mail.[70]

At the same time, the treaty does not completely cure problems in international service of process. Not all countries are signatories to the Hague Convention. Moreover, those that have joined have often attached conditions to their participation.[71] It is useful, then, to note alternatives to the Hague Convention.[72] First, there may be means of effecting service abroad apart from that treaty.[73]

---

[67] Rule 4(i).

[68] Hague Convention on Service Abroad of Judicial and Extrajudicial Documents in Civil and Commercial Matters, Nov. 15, 1965, 20 U.S.T. 361, 658 U.N.T.S. 163. *See generally* SCOLES, HAY, BORCHERS & SYMEONIDES, CONFLICT OF LAWS § 12.7 (4th ed. 2004); Pamela M. Parmalee, Note, *International Service of Process: A Guide to Serving Process Abroad Under the Hague Convention*, 39 OKLA. L. REV. 287 (1986); Robert M. Hamilton, *An Interpretation of the Hague Convention on the Service of Process Abroad of Judicial and Extrajudicial Documents Concerning Personal Service in Japan*, 6 LOY. L.A. INT'L & COMP. L.J. 143 (1983).

The United States has also joined the Inter-American Convention on Letters Rogatory. 14 INT'L LEG. MAT. 339 (1975); 18 INT'L LEG. MAT. 1238 (1979). *See generally* Anne-Marie Kim, *The Inter-American Convention and Additional Protocol on Letters Rogatory: The Hague Service Conventions "Country Cousins"?*, 36 COLUM. J. TRANSNAT'L L. 687 (1998); Lucinda A. Low, *International Judicial Assistance Among the American States — The Inter-American Conventions*, 18 INT'L LAW 705 (1984).

[69] Art. 2.

[70] Art. 10(a). Federal decisions are divided over whether 10(a) authorizes direct service abroad by mail without using the foreign country's central authority or diplomatic channels. *Compare Ackermann v. Levine*, 788 F.2d 830 (2d Cir. 1986) (yes); *Eli Lilly & Co. v. Roussel Corp.*, 23 F. Supp. 2d 460 (D.N.J. 1998) (yes) *with Bankston v. Toyota Motor Corp.*, 889 F.2d 172 (8th Cir. 1989) (no); *Knapp v. Yamaha Motor Corp.*, 60 F. Supp. 2d 566 (S.D. W. Va. 1999) (no).

[71] These reservations, called declarations, are used by countries to modify or negate obligations set out in the treaty. For examples, *see* DAVID BORN & GARY B. WESTIN, INTERNATIONAL CIVIL LITIGATION IN THE UNITED STATES 1100–05 (3d ed. 1996).

[72] *See generally* THOMAS O. MAIN, GLOBAL ISSUES IN PROCEDURE 124–47 (Thomson/West 2006).

[73] "The Convention is not, as has occasionally been supposed, automatically preemptive of all methods that may be used for service abroad." Siegel, *1992 Commentary*, note 50, *supra*. Professor Siegel adds: "As long as the nation concerned has not, in its ratification or in any other part of its law, imposed any limits on other methods, these others remain available and the Convention and its local implementing

Second, it will be possible in some cases to establish jurisdiction over foreign nationals without resorting to service of process abroad.

The availability of the second option was greatly enhanced by the Supreme Court's decision in *Volkswagenwerk v. Schlunk*.[74] The Court suggested the Hague Convention does not require jurisdiction to be established through service of process abroad when the facts of the case support a local theory of personal jurisdiction. That is, whenever the joint due process requirements of minimum contacts and of reasonableness are satisfied, jurisdiction exists in state (or federal) courts over foreign nationals — just as it does over Americans residing outside the forum in sister states. The Court held in *Schlunk* that service upon a German corporation was permissible under the Illinois long-arm statute. State law permitted substituted service on the defendant's subsidiary located in the United States. State law and federal due process provided the appropriate tests, and those tests were satisfied.[75]

§ 4.04 SERVICE OF PROCESS IN THE CALIFORNIA COURTS

[1] Introductory Note on Manner of Service

The California Jurisdiction and Service of Process Act (Code of Civil Procedure § 410.10 *et seq.*) governs service of process in the California courts. Generally speaking, the proper manner of service, and the person upon whom service must be made, depends on the place where process is to be served (*i.e.*, within California, in another state, or outside the United States) and the type of party to be served (*e.g.*, an individual defendant, a corporation or association, or a public entity). The Act contains service provisions applicable to each of these variables, and often the most difficult task is finding the relevant statute.

---

materials serve as supplements." Siegel, *1992 Commentary*, note 50, *supra*. Electronic service (i.e., via e-mail or social networking sites) is one method that is often cited as an appealing alternative to physical service abroad. *See* Yvonne A. Tamayo, *Catch Me If You Can: Serving United States Process on an Elusive Defendant Abroad*, 17 HARV. J.L. & TECH. 211 (2003); *see also Rio Props., Inc. v. Rio Int'l Interlink*, 284 F.3d 1007 (9th Cir. 2002) (e-mail service of a federal court summons and complaint on a Costa Rican gambling operation complied with federal statutory and constitutional requirements for adequate notice).

[74] 486 U.S. 694 (1988). The decision is discussed in Kenneth M. Minesinger, Note, *The Supreme Court Interprets the Hague Service Convention*, 23 GEO. WASH. J. INT'L L. & ECON. 769 (1990); Brenda L. White, Note, *Service of Process: Application of the Hague Service Convention in the United States*, 30 HARV. INT'L L.J. 277 (1989).

[75] "Where service on a domestic agent is valid and complete under both state law and the Due Process Clause, our inquiry ends and the Convention has no further implications." 486 U.S. at 707. *But see* Stephen R. Burbank, *The United States' Approach to International Civil Litigation: Recent Developments in Forum Selection*, 19 U. PA. J. INT'L ECON. L. 1, 5–8 (1998) (endorsing recent lower court opinions requiring compliance with Hague Convention even after service was made in-state on foreign agent).

[2] Service Within California: Personal Service and Substituted Service

[a] Personal Service Preferred for Individual Defendants

Personal delivery of a copy of the complaint and summons is the preferred manner of service upon individual defendants within California, and must be attempted before a plaintiff may resort to substituted service.[76] In contrast, Rule 4(e) of the Federal Rules of Civil Procedure authorizes substituted service on someone residing at an individual defendant's place of abode as an unqualified alternative to personal service. Likewise, the vast majority of states recognize substituted "abode" service as a primary method of service; only California and a few other states relegate it to a secondary method of service.[77] The California rule has been criticized as an unnecessary restriction on the use of substituted service that does not significantly improve the likelihood that the defendant will actually receive notice.[78]

[b] Substituted Service on Individuals

Substituted service on an individual defendant is authorized only when process cannot with "reasonable diligence" be personally delivered.[79] In this context, ordinarily two or three attempts at personal service at a proper place constitutes "reasonable diligence."[80] If such efforts are unsuccessful, substituted service is appropriate. The plaintiff may then serve an individual defendant by leaving a copy of the complaint and summons at that person's "dwelling house, usual place of abode, usual place of business" with a competent member of the household or a person apparently in charge of his or her office or place of business, who is at least 18 years of age, and "by thereafter mailing a copy of the summons and of the complaint (by first-class mail, postage prepaid) to the person to be served at the

---

[76] CAL. CODE CIV. PROC. § 415.10.

[77] *See* Philip Craig Starti, Note, *Substituted Service of Process on Individuals: California Code of Civil Procedure Section 415.20(b)*, 21 HASTINGS L.J. 1257, 1278 (1970).

[78] *See* Starti, *Substituted Service of Process on Individuals, supra.*

[79] CAL. CODE CIV. PROC. § 415.20(b); *see Earl W. Schott, Inc. v. Kalar*, 20 Cal. App. 4th 943, 24 Cal. Rptr. 2d 580 (1993) (ruling the failure to comply with due diligence requirements rendered attempted service on individual defendant and subsequent default judgment unenforceable); *Stafford v. Mach*, 64 Cal. App. 4th 1174, 1182–83, 75 Cal. Rptr. 2d 809 (1998) (holding "drop service" on the actual defendant, on the sixth attempt to serve him at his home, was proper where the defendant answered the door but refused to identify himself); *Bein v. Brechtel-Jochim Group, Inc.*, 6 Cal. App. 4th 1387, 8 Cal. Rptr. 2d 351 (1992) (approving substituted service on gate guard proper where access denied to defendant residing in gated community).

[80] *Bein v. Brechtel-Jochim Group, supra*, 6 Cal App. 4th at 1391–92; *Hearn v. Howard*, 177 Cal. App. 4th 1193, 99 Cal. Rtpr. 3d 642 (2009) (upholding substituted service on a defendant whose business address was a private post office box rental store where, after three unsuccessful attempts to personally serve the defendant, the complaint and summons were left with the mail store clerk); *Espindola v. Nunez*, 199 Cal. App. 3d 1389, 245 Cal. Rptr. 596 (1988) (finding that three unsuccessful attempts to personally serve defendant at home within four days constituted reasonable diligence sufficient to uphold substituted service on defendant's wife at home).

place where a copy of the summons and of the complaint were left."[81]

[c]   Substituted Service on Entities

Service on a defendant corporation may be accomplished by one of several options: (1) by delivering a copy of the complaint and summons to the president, vice-president, general manager, or other officer; (2) by delivering a copy to the person designated by the corporation as the agent for service of process; or (3) by leaving a copy with the person who is apparently in charge of the corporate office during usual office hours and mailing a copy to the officer sought to be served.[82] Attempted personal service on the corporation's designated agent or on an officer is not a prerequisite to substitute service on someone in charge of the office during usual office hours.[83] Nor is attempted service on the designated agent a prerequisite to service on an officer of the corporation.[84] Similar service options and rules apply when the defendant is an unincorporated association (including a partnership) or a public entity.[85]

[3]   Constructive Service by Publication

California's Jurisdiction and Service of Process Act permits constructive service by publication only where the court is satisfied that the party to be served cannot with "reasonable diligence" be served personally or by substituted service.[86] The "reasonable diligence" necessary to uphold an order for service by publication requires more exhaustive attempts to locate the defendant than is sufficient to uphold substituted service on an individual defendant. At a minimum, the standard of diligence required includes recent inquiries of all relatives, friends, and other persons likely to know defendant's whereabouts; searches of city directories, telephone directories, tax roles, and register of voters; and other inquiries relevant to the particular litigation.[87] A plaintiff must not only *exercise* due diligence as a prerequisite for an order of publication, but must also *show* due diligence in the application to the court by properly asserting the relevant facts by an affidavit of someone with personal knowledge.[88]

---

[81] CAL. CODE CIV. PROC. § 415.20(b). Service of a summons in this manner is deemed complete on the 10th day after the mailing. *Id.*

[82] CAL. CODE CIV. PROC. §§ 415.20(a), 416.10.

[83] CAL. CODE CIV. PROC. § 415.20(a); *see Earl W. Schott, Inc. v. Kalar, supra*, 20 Cal. App. 4th at 945 (distinguishing § 415.20(a), applicable to corporations and not requiring due diligence, from § 415.20(b), applicable to individuals).

[84] *Bein v. Brechtel-Jochim Group, supra*, 6 Cal App. 4th at 1394.

[85] CAL. CODE CIV. PROC. §§ 415.20(a), 416.40, 416.50.

[86] CAL. CODE CIV. PROC. § 415.50.

[87] *See Olvera v. Olvera*, 232 Cal. App. 3d 32, 283 Cal. Rptr. 271 (1991); *Espindola v. Nunez*, 199 Cal. App. 3d 1389, 1392–93, 249 Cal. Rptr. 596 (1988); *Donel, Inc. v. Badalian*, 87 Cal. App. 3d 327, 150 Cal. Rptr. 885 (1978) (ruling that a single act of searching telephone directories insufficient diligence).

[88] CAL. CODE CIV. PROC. § 415.50. *See Olvera, supra*, 232 Cal. App. 3d at 42–43 (finding plaintiffs' affidavit failed to demonstrate they employed any of the usual means to find the defendant); *Sanford v. Smith*, 11 Cal. App. 3d 991, 90 Cal. Rptr. 256 (1970) (ruling that declaration of the attorney was hearsay and not adequate to establish due diligence for publication order).

[4]   Discretionary Relief from Default When Service Provides No "Actual Notice"

So long as the requirements for substituted or constructive service are followed, such service is valid even though the defendant does not actually receive the complaint and summons. Recognizing this possibility, Code of Civil Procedure section 473.5 permits the trial court to vacate a default judgment when service, even though valid and proper, has not resulted in "actual notice" to the defendant. If the trial court finds that the defaulting party's lack of actual notice was not caused by avoidance of service or inexcusable neglect, the trial court may, in its discretion, set aside the default judgment.

The statutory reference to "actual notice" has been strictly construed, with the aim of implementing the policy of liberally granting relief so that cases may be resolved on their merits.[89] The question of what constitutes "actual notice" often arises in a motion to vacate a default judgment entered after service by publication. Some courts suggest that "actual notice" in this context exists only where the defendant has actual knowledge of the summons as the result of reading the published summons in the newspaper or actually receiving a copy.[90] A defendant who does not receive actual notice of the complaint and summons as a result of service, but acquired actual knowledge of the lawsuit from some other source, is not precluded from seeking discretionary relief under section 473.5.[91] Moreover, some cases hold that even if the defendants have received copies of the complaint and summons, they had no actual knowledge when they had neither the English language competency nor business sophistication to understand these documents.[92]

---

[89]   *See, e.g., Rosenthal v. Garner*, 142 Cal. App. 3d 891, 895, 191 Cal. Rptr. 300 (1983) (holding service on an attorney representing defendant in a related prior litigation does not constitute "actual notice" where the attorney did not inform the defendant); *Tunis v. Barrow*, 184 Cal. App. 3d 1069, 1077–80, 229 Cal. Rptr. 389 (1986) (same); *but see Boland v. All Persons*, 160 Cal. 486, 490, 117 P. 547 (1911) (finding defendant, although not personally served, had actual notice of the complaint and summons posted on her front door).

[90]   *Olvera, supra*, 232 Cal. App. 3d at 40; *Ellard v. Conway*, 94 Cal. App. 4th 540, 114 Cal. Rptr. 2d 399 (2001); *see also Rosenthal v. Garner, supra*, 142 Cal. App. 3d at 895 (allowing relief under section 473.5 where, in addition to service by publication, plaintiff had sent a copy of the summons and complaint to defendants' counsel, because this imputed knowledge is not equivalent to the actual knowledge required by the statute).

[91]   *See, e.g., Olvera, supra*, 232 Cal. App. 3d at 40–41 (ruling defendant served by publication did not have "actual notice" of the complaint and summons even though she knew of the lawsuit as a result of the filing of a lis pendens notice); *Ellard v. Conway, supra*, 94 Cal. App. 4th at 547–48 (explaining that although actual knowledge from a source other than service of summons does not *preclude* a defendant from seeking relief from a default judgment under section 473.5, such knowledge may provide a proper basis for denying relief where the defendants had actual knowledge of the lawsuit in time to defend the action but failed to file an answer due to inexcusable neglect).

[92]   *Goya v. P.E.R.U. Enter.*, 87 Cal. App. 3d 886, 151 Cal. Rptr. 258 (1978) (setting aside default for these reasons).

[5] Service by Mail Within California

The Jurisdiction and Service of Process Act authorizes a very limited form of service by mail within California. The plaintiff must mail copies of the complaint and summons, along with two copies of the "Notice and Acknowledgment of Receipt of Summons," and a prepaid self-addressed return envelope, to the defendant.[93] Service is not deemed complete unless the defendant executes and returns the acknowledgment. Consequently, if the defendant fails to execute or return the acknowledgment form, the plaintiff must serve the defendant in some other proper method. The defendant may, however, be liable for reasonable expenses incurred by plaintiff in serving defendant by another method.

[6] Special Service Statutes

Numerous specific statutes require or authorize service of process in a manner different from, or in addition to, that of the general service statutes for particular causes of action. For example, special service statutes apply to tort actions against the State of California or against a public agency, quiet title actions, condemnation actions, and unlawful detainer actions.[94]

[7] Service in Another State

[a] Service Options

A plaintiff has many options when required to serve a defendant located in another state. California's Jurisdiction and Service of Process Act authorizes service of process on a defendant in another state in any manner provided by the Act for in-state service, and also authorizes service by mail.[95] Additionally, the Act authorizes service in another state in accordance with the law of the state where the defendant is to be served.[96]

[b] Service by Mail, Return Receipt Required

The Jurisdiction and Service of Process Act authorizes service by first-class mail, requiring a return receipt, on a person in another state when actual delivery is established by the signed return receipt or by "other evidence."[97] Service by mail on an out-of-state defendant does not require a signed "Notice and Acknowledgment of Receipt of Summons," as is required under the very limited form of service by mail within California.

---

[93] CAL. CODE CIV. PROC. § 415.30.

[94] CAL. GOV'T CODE §§ 955.4, 955.6–.8 (State), 960.2–.8 (public agency); CAL. CODE CIV. PROC. §§ 416.50 (public entity), 763.010–.030 (quiet title), 1250.130 &.140 (condemnation), 415.45–.47 (unlawful detainer). For a more complete list of these special manner of service statutes, see ANN SCHWING, CALIFORNIA AFFIRMATIVE DEFENSES, *Lack of Proper or Effective Service* § 2.2 (2012).

[95] CAL. CODE CIV. PROC. § 415.40.

[96] CAL. CODE CIV. PROC. § 413.10(b).

[97] CAL. CODE CIV. PROC. § 415.40 & § 417.20(b).

The California courts often address the issue of what constitutes sufficient "other evidence" in this context.[98] For example, in one case, the appellate court concluded that a letter written by the attorney for an Arkansas defendant acknowledging the defendant's receipt of the complaint and summons constituted sufficient "other evidence" of actual delivery.[99] However, in another case, the court ruled that while a return receipt signed by someone authorized by a nonresident defendant to sign for his mail is sufficient, the plaintiff must provide separate evidence establishing the authority of the person who signed the return receipt on defendant's behalf.[100]

[8] Substituted Service on Agent Within California

In a wide variety of situations, California statutes authorize substituted service on a designated agent of the defendant within California. For example, corporations, partnerships, and other entities doing business in California must designate an agent for service of process within the state. If no such agent for service of process is designated by the entity, substitute service may be made upon the California Secretary of State or other appropriate governmental agent.[101] Upon receipt of process, the Secretary of State must mail a copy to the corporation at its principal executive office. Also, the parties to a contract may agree to designate an agent for service of process within the state.[102]

In some circumstances, an in-state agent may be implied by operation of law. For example, the California Vehicle Code provides that ownership or operation of a motor vehicle within California by a nonresident is the equivalent to an appointment of the Director of the California Department of Motor Vehicles as agent for service of process in any action arising from an accident resulting from operation of the motor vehicle in California.[103] If the plaintiff serves process on the Director pursuant to this section, the plaintiff must also mail a copy to the defendant.[104]

---

[98] *E.g.*, *Dill v. Berquist Constr. Co.*, 24 Cal. App. 4th 1426, 29 Cal. Rptr. 2d 746 (1994) (holding that although postal receipt indicated that some employee of nonresident defendant corporation had signed and acknowledged delivery, service was invalid because not mailed to one of the corporate officers specified to receive service in Cal. Code Civ. Proc. § 416.10 and no other evidence that the summons was actually received by one of these officers); *Cruz v. Fagor Am., Inc.*, 146 Cal. App. 4th 488, 52 Cal. Rptr. 3d 862 (2007) (upholding service by mail on out-of-state defendant corporation where addressed to proper corporate official but return receipt signed by another employee because plaintiff's attorney submitted a declaration attesting that the attorney had received confirmation from a representative of the U.S. Postal Service that the individual who signed the return receipt was an employee of the defendant corporation who regularly received mail on the corporation's behalf).

[99] *In re Marriage of Tusinger*, 170 Cal. App. 3d 80, 215 Cal. Rptr. 838 (1985).

[100] *Taylor-Rush v. Multitech Corp.*, 217 Cal. App. 3d 103, 265 Cal. Rptr. 672 (1990).

[101] CAL. CORP. CODE §§ 1702, 2111, 15800(b). For a more complete list of statutes which authorize such substitute service on a governmental official, see ANN SCHWING, CALIFORNIA AFFIRMATIVE DEFENSES, *Lack of Proper or Effective Service* § 2.8 (2012).

[102] CAL. CODE CIV. PROC. § 416.90; *see National Equip. Rental, Ltd. v. Szukhent*, 375 U.S. 311 (1964) (service on contractually appointed agent constitutionally adequate under due process).

[103] CAL. VEH. CODE § 17451.

[104] CAL. VEH. CODE §§ 17454, 17455.

Substituted service on a designated or implied agent is alternative to, not exclusive of, the other statutorily authorized methods of service on a defendant.[105]

[9] Service Outside the United States

A plaintiff is authorized to serve a defendant in another country in a manner prescribed by the California service statutes or the law of the other country, or as directed by the court in which the action is pending or by the relevant foreign authority in response to a letter rogatory.[106] However, these service options are subject to preemption by the provisions of certain multinational international agreements, such as the Hague Convention on the "Service Abroad of Judicial and Extrajudicial Documents" (the Hague Service Convention) and the Inter-American Convention on Letters Rogatory.[107]

The United States Supreme Court in *Volkswagenwerk AG v. Schlunk*[108] indicated in dicta that, by virtue of the Supremacy Clause, the Hague Service Convention preempts inconsistent methods of service prescribed by state law in all cases to which the Convention applies. However, the *Schlunk* Court also explained that the Convention applies only where there is occasion for "service abroad," but not where service on a foreign defendant within the territory of the United States is complete and valid under domestic law. Resort to the Convention is not required, for example, where service on the domestic agent of a foreign corporation constitutes complete and valid service under state law, as illustrated by the recent decision in *Yamaha Motor Co., Ltd. v. Superior Court.*[109] In *Yamaha*, the plaintiff in a products liability action served the defendant manufacturer, a Japanese corporation, through its American subsidiary's agent for service of process. Applying the holding in *Schlunk*, the California Court of Appeal held that the Hague Service Convention's provisions were not implicated because California law

---

[105] *M. Lowenstein & Sons, Inc. v. Superior Court*, 80 Cal. App. 3d 762, 145 Cal. Rptr. 814 (1978) (explaining that a plaintiff serving nonresident corporation may serve designated agent pursuant to Cal. Code Civ. Proc. § 416.10 or, alternatively, may serve by mail pursuant to Cal. Code Civ. Proc. § 415.40); *Anderson v. Sherman*, 125 Cal. App. 3d 228, 235–37, 178 Cal. Rptr. 38 (1981) (ruling an injured California resident may serve nonresident motorist pursuant to Cal. Veh. Code §§ 17454 & 17455, or Cal. Code Civ. Proc. § 415.40).

[106] CAL. CODE CIV. PROC. § 413.10(c).

[107] CAL. CODE CIV. PROC. § 413.10(c). For commentary and analysis of the Hague Service Convention, see DAVID EPSTEIN & JEFFREY L. SNYDER, INTERNATIONAL LITIGATION: A GUIDE TO JURISDICTION, PRACTICE AND STRATEGY, §§ 4.01–4.05 (1993); Leonard A. Leo, Note, *The Interplay Between Domestic Rules Permitting Service Abroad by Mail and the Hague Convention on Service: Proposing an Amendment to the Federal Rules of Civil Procedure*, 22 CORNELL INT'L L.J. 335 (1989); Pamela R. Parmalee, Note, *International Service of Process: A Guide to Serving Process Abroad Under the Hague Convention*, 39 OKLA. L. REV. 287 (1986). For commentary on the Inter-American Convention, see Lucinda A. Low, *International Judicial Assistance Among the American States — The Inter-American Conventions*, 18 INT'L LAW. 705 (1984); Richard D. Kearney, *Developments in Private International Law*, 81 AM. J. INT'L LAW 724 (1987) (comparing Inter-American Convention and Hague Service Convention).

[108] 486 U.S. 694, 699 (1988).

[109] 174 Cal. App. 4th 264, 94 Cal. Rptr. 3d 494 (2009); *see also Kott v. Superior Court*, 45 Cal. App. 4th 1126, 53 Cal. Rptr. 2d 215 (1996) (indicating that service on a Canadian resident by publication in a Los Angeles newspaper did not implicate the Hague Service Convention because such service does not require the transmission of documents outside the United States).

provides for service of process on a foreign corporation by serving its domestic subsidiary as agent and does not necessarily require transmittal of the relevant documents to the defendant in Japan.

[10]   Motion to Quash for Lack of Proper Service

A challenge to the validity of service of process must be made by filing a *motion to quash* on or before the last day to plead in response to the complaint. Pursuant to a 2003 amendment to Code of Civil Procedure § 418.10, the California practice with respect to challenging the validity of service of process conforms generally, but not entirely, to the practice in the federal courts under federal Rule 12. The defendant need not raise an objection to service by a "special appearance," but may simultaneously file an answer, demurrer, or motion to strike along with a timely motion to quash.

However, unlike the federal practice, the California statute does not give a defendant the option to plead lack of proper service as a defense in an answer and reserve determination of that issue until as late as trial. Instead, section 418.10 continues to require a timely motion to quash as the means of challenging the validity of service of process. The defendant may move to quash and simultaneously file an answer containing defenses to the action, but "the latter is not a substitute for the former."[110] If the defendant makes a general appearance, such as by filing an answer, demurrer, or motion to strike, *before* filing a motion to quash objecting to lack of proper service, the defendant waives his right to contest the validity of the service.[111]

When a defendant properly moves to quash service of process, the burden is on the plaintiff to prove the facts establishing valid service.[112] However, the return of a registered process server establishes a presumption, affecting the burden of producing evidence, of the truth of the facts stated in the return.[113] This presumption arises only if the proof of service complies with the statutory requirements regarding such proofs. For example, proof of service which shows that the complaint was mailed solely to the defendant corporation but not to any of the corporate officers statutorily required to be served on behalf of the corporation raised no presumption of proper service.[114]

If a motion to quash is granted, the service is quashed but the action is not dismissed. The plaintiff may attempt to perfect the court's jurisdiction by obtaining

---

[110] *Roy v. Superior Court*, 127 Cal. App. 4th 337, 345, 25 Cal. Rptr. 3d 488 (2005).

[111] *See* CAL. CODE CIV. PROC. § 418.10(e)(3) & § 410.50(a) ("A general appearance by a party is equivalent to personal service of summons on such party."); *Fireman's Fund Ins. Co. v. Sparks Constr., Inc.*, 114 Cal. App. 4th 1135, 8 Cal. Rptr. 3d 446 (2004) (ruling that a defendant who makes a general appearance forfeits any objection to defective service, even when the defendant does not know at the time that such an objection is available).

[112] *Dill v. Berquist Constr. Co.*, 24 Cal. App. 4th 1426, 1441–43, 29 Cal. Rptr. 2d 746 (1994); *Taylor-Rush v. Multitech Corp.*, *supra*, 217 Cal. App. 3d at 110–11; *Kroopf v. Guffey*, 183 Cal. App. 3d 1351, 1356, 228 Cal. Rptr. 807 (1986).

[113] CAL. EVID. CODE § 647.

[114] *See Dill*, *supra*, 24 Cal. App. 4th at 1441–42.

valid service, subject to applicable time limits for service. If a motion to quash is denied, the defendant may obtain immediate appellate review by a *writ of mandate*.[115] If the motion is granted, the plaintiff has the right to appeal the order.[116]

[11]   Time Limits on Service of Process

The complaint and summons must be served upon a defendant within three years after the action is commenced against the defendant.[117] This statutory time-for-service requirement does not apply if the defendant enters into a written stipulation or does some other act which constitutes a general appearance.[118] Failure to serve within the prescribed time will result in mandatory dismissal of the action.[119] Moreover, service not made within two years after the action is commenced against the defendant may result in discretionary dismissal for delay in prosecution.[120]

The mandatory and discretionary dismissal statutes set out the outer time limits for service of process. In modern California practice, in most cases, the rules of court rather than the dismissal statutes provide the effective time limits for service of process. The California Government Code grants the California Judicial Council, the governing body of the California courts, the authority to develop and adopt state-wide time standards for the completion of all critical steps in the civil litigation process.[121] Adopted pursuant to this authority, the California Rules of Court require service of the complaint on all named defendants, and proofs of service filed, within 60 days after the filing of the complaint, unless the court orders an extension of time.[122] Likewise, many local "fast track" rules require service of the complaint within 60 days of its filing.

---

[115] CAL. CODE CIV. PROC. § 418.10(c).

[116] CAL. CODE CIV. PROC. § 904.1(a)(3).

[117] CAL. CODE CIV. PROC. §§ 583.210(a), 583.110. Return of summons or other proof of service must be made within 60 days after this required time for service of the summons and complaint. CAL. CODE CIV. PROC. § 583.210(b).

[118] CAL. CODE CIV. PROC. Other exceptions and time exclusions are set forth in Code of Civil Procedure § 583.230 and § 583.240.

[119] CAL. CODE CIV. PROC. § 583.250; *see, e.g., Perez v. Smith*, 19 Cal. App. 4th 1595, 24 Cal. Rptr. 2d 186 (1993) (explaining that an action must be dismissed if complaint and summons not served within three years unless plaintiff can demonstrate defendant was not amenable to process during some portion of this period).

[120] CAL. CODE CIV. PROC. §§ 583.410, 583.420(a)(1); CAL. CT. R. 3.1342(e). *See, e.g., Williams v. Los Angeles Unified Sch. Dist.*, 23 Cal. App. 4th 84, 28 Cal. Rptr. 2d 219 (1994) (discussing factors relevant to dismissal determination).

[121] CAL. GOV'T CODE §§ 68603, 68612–68619.

[122] CAL. CT. R. 3.110.

Chapter 5

A COURT WITH JURISDICTION OVER THE SUBJECT

§ 5.01 INTRODUCTION

[1] Subject Matter Jurisdiction Generally

Subject matter jurisdiction refers to a court's power or "competence" to decide a particular kind of controversy. To render a binding decision, the court must be "competent by its constitution — that is, by the law of its creation — to pass upon the subject-matter of the suit."[1] Typically, that law will include the organic law (the constitution) of the sovereign, any implementing jurisdictional legislation, and the common law gloss placed on such legislation by the courts. Because the constitutions and jurisdictional statutes of the states and the federal government differ, so does the subject matter jurisdiction of their respective courts.

Subject matter jurisdiction can, however, be described by certain generic terms. All states have courts of *limited, special, or inferior jurisdiction*, which are vested with the power only to hear cases of a particular kind. Small claims courts or traffic courts are courts of limited jurisdiction, the former limited to cases of a particular amount in controversy and the latter obviously limited to traffic violation cases. Virtually every state has at least one court of *general jurisdiction*, which is vested with a comprehensive residual subject matter jurisdiction to hear all cases not exclusively allocated to courts of limited jurisdiction. Such general jurisdiction courts, frequently established at the county level, are the workhorses of the state judicial systems, hearing the majority of significant civil and criminal cases.

Another generic distinction is between *original* and *appellate jurisdiction*. Those courts in which suits are first filed have original jurisdiction; the cases originate there. Courts that review cases that originate elsewhere, either in lower courts or in administrative agencies, are vested with appellate jurisdiction, usually but not always requiring some degree of deference to the original decision and hence a limited intensity of review.[2]

Finally, subject matter jurisdiction can be *concurrent* — shared between several different kinds of courts — or *exclusive*, restricted to a particular kind of court. State courts of general jurisdiction and federal district courts, for example, have concurrent jurisdiction of most cases involving questions of federal constitutional

---

[1] *Pennoyer v. Neff*, 95 U.S. 714, 733 (1878).

[2] *See* § 13.09 (intensity of review on appeal), *infra*.

or statutory law, but the latter are vested with exclusive jurisdiction over *some* topics, including admiralty, maritime, patent, plant variety protection, copyright,[3] and certain cases in which the United States is a defendant.[4]

It is more difficult to generalize about the timing and mode of challenging subject matter jurisdiction. These procedural incidents often differ depending upon whether the jurisdiction is general or limited. Strict rules for challenging subject matter jurisdiction have developed in federal courts because they are courts of limited jurisdiction. Subject matter jurisdiction implicates the distribution of federal judicial power and the separation of powers between the branches, rather than the personal rights of the parties to a litigation. Consequently, the parties cannot enlarge a federal court's subject matter jurisdiction by consent or waiver.[5] Any other rule would effectively enable the parties by their acts to amend Article III of the Constitution or federal jurisdictional statutes. Parties may therefore challenge a federal court's subject matter jurisdiction at any point in the litigation,[6] including appeal.[7] Moreover, a federal court is required on its own motion (*sua sponte*) to consider whether it has subject matter jurisdiction when the litigants have not raised the question.[8] Finally, in courts of limited jurisdiction the burden of

---

[3] 28 U.S.C. §§ 1333, 1338.

[4] 28 U.S.C. § 1346(f).

[5] Nor may a federal rule, because Congress has not given the rulemakers authority to extend or restrict the subject matter jurisdiction conferred by statute. *See Willy v. Coastal Corp.*, 503 U.S. 131 (1992). Rule 82 acknowledges this fact expressly.

[6] However, a subject matter jurisdiction challenge does not necessarily take precedence over a challenge to personal jurisdiction; "there is no unyielding jurisdictional hierarchy." *Ruhrgas AG v. Marathon Oil Co.*, 526 U.S. 574, 578 (1999). In *Ruhrgas*, a unanimous Court held that a federal court has discretion to decide personal ahead of subject matter jurisdiction when the former question is more easily and readily resolved. This discretion helps the courts avoid unnecessary determination of complex and novel questions of subject matter jurisdiction. In contrast, the Court has emphasized that a court must decide subject matter jurisdiction before ruling on the merits. *Steel Co. v. Citizens for a Better Environment*, 523 U.S. 83 (1998). *See generally* Jack H. Friedenthal, *The Crack in the Steel Case*, 68 Geo. Wash. L. Rev. 258 (2000) (comparing *Steel* and *Ruhrgas*).

[7] In *Capron v. Van Noorden*, 6 U.S. (2 Cranch) 126 (1804), for example, the plaintiff lost at trial and then successfully appealed the judgment on the grounds that the court that *he* had selected lacked subject matter jurisdiction over his claim. However, collateral attacks on subject matter jurisdiction — challenges made not at trial or on direct appeal but in a separate litigation, such as one brought to enforce a prior judgment — are not allowed except in extraordinary circumstances, given the strong public interest in the finality of judgments. *Des Moines Navigation & R.R. Co. v. Iowa Homestead Co.*, 123 U.S. 552 (1887). *See generally* Robert J. Martineau, *Subject Matter Jurisdiction as a New Issue on Appeal: Reining in an Unruly Horse*, 1988 B.Y.U. L. Rev. 1 (1988); Karen Nelson Moore, *Collateral Attack on Subject Matter Jurisdiction: A Critique of the Restatement (Second) of Judgments*, 66 Cornell L. Rev. 534 (1981); Dan B. Dobbs, *Beyond Bootstrap: Foreclosing the Issue of Subject Matter Jurisdiction Before Final Judgment*, 51 Minn. L. Rev. 491 (1967). *The Restatement (Second) of Judgments* would permit collateral attacks for lack of subject matter jurisdiction, just as they are permitted for lack of personal jurisdiction, but it acknowledges that few courts have agreed. *Compare* Restatement (Second) of Judgments § 65 (1982) *with* Restatement (Second) of Judgments § 12 cmt. f.

[8] "If the court determines at any time that it lacks subject-matter jurisdiction, the court must dismiss the action." Rule 12(h)(3). The parties can assert the defense by a motion to dismiss for lack of jurisdiction over the subject matter. Rule 12(b)(1). *See* § 8.07[2][c] (challenging pleadings on the basis of non-waivable defenses), *infra*.

pleading and proving jurisdiction rests on the party who invokes jurisdiction.[9] Disputes about facts that are relevant to deciding subject matter jurisdiction — issues of "jurisdictional fact" — are ordinarily for the judge to decide, looking to the pleadings, any record evidence, affidavits, deposition testimony, and even live evidence.[10]

While some states apply similar rules, many have more relaxed attitudes towards subject matter jurisdiction. Some treat the objection to subject matter jurisdiction as waivable,[11] and most place the burden of raising the issue of subject matter jurisdiction on the party who challenges it.[12]

[2] Subject Matter Jurisdiction of the Federal Courts

The United States Constitution sets out the permissible scope of the judicial power of federal courts in Article III, § 2. It lists the following types (sometimes called "heads") of federal subject matter jurisdiction:

- cases "arising under this Constitution, the Laws of the United States, and Treaties made . . . under their Authority," popularly known as *federal question* jurisdiction;

- cases affecting ambassadors and other official representatives of foreign sovereigns;

- admiralty and maritime cases;

- controversies to which the United States is a party;

- controversies between states and between a state and citizens of another state;

- cases between citizens of different states, popularly known as *diversity* jurisdiction;

- cases between citizens of the same state claiming lands under grants of different states;

- and cases between a state or its citizens and foreign states and their citizens or subjects, sometimes known as *alienage* jurisdiction.[13]

Article III directly vests the Supreme Court with original jurisdiction of cases affecting ambassadors and other foreign officials and those to which a state is a party, and such appellate jurisdiction as Congress may create. In contrast, Article III vests no jurisdiction directly in lower federal courts; in other words, it is not self-executing. Instead, it authorizes Congress to create and endow them with

---

[9] Rule 8(a) & Form 7.

[10] *See MOORE* § 12.30[3]. *See, e.g., Valentin v. Hospital Bella Vista*, 254 F.3d 358, 362–65 (1st Cir. 2001) (court may, but is not required to, order discovery, consider extrinsic evidence, and hold evidentiary hearing to determine its own jurisdiction).

[11] *See Dobbs, note 7, supra,* at 504.

[12] *See JAMES, HAZARD, & LEUBSDORF* § 2.22.

[13] U.S. CONST. art. III, § 2.

subject matter jurisdiction.[14] Congress therefore has the constitutional authority to decide by legislation how much of the federal subject matter jurisdiction available under Article III shall be vested in the lower federal courts.[15]

While it established lower federal courts in the very first jurisdictional legislation, Congress has never vested them with as much subject matter jurisdiction as Article III permits. Except for the short-lived "Midnight Judges Act" in 1801,[16] the lower federal courts were not given general federal question jurisdiction until 1875.[17] They have never been given the whole of Article III diversity jurisdiction, as Congress has always limited this head of jurisdiction to cases that involve a specified amount in controversy. In other words, while Article III authorizes federal jurisdiction over *any* claim between citizens of different states, Congress has also set some dollar floor on such claims, apparently reasoning that some are too small to be worth federal court time.[18] Today, the main heads of federal jurisdiction are federal question jurisdiction and diversity jurisdiction, usually concurrent with state court jurisdiction, giving plaintiffs the choice in most cases of whether to file in federal or state courts.[19]

---

[14] "The judicial power of the United States, shall be vested . . . in such inferior Courts as the Congress *may* from time to time ordain and establish." U.S. CONST. art. III, § 1 (emphasis added).

[15] How little federal subject matter jurisdiction can be vested in the lower federal courts is a hotly debated question that arises from time to time in connection with proposed jurisdiction-stripping legislation. *See, e.g.*, Lawrence Gene Sager, *The Supreme Court 1980 Term, Foreword: Constitutional Limitations on Congress' Authority to Regulate the Jurisdiction of the Federal Courts*, 95 HARV. L. REV. 17 (1981); Ronald D. Rotunda, *Congressional Power to Restrict the Jurisdiction of the Lower Federal Courts and the Problem of School Busing*, 64 GEO. L.J. 839, 842–43 (1976); Martin H. Redish & Curtis E. Woods, *Congressional Power to Control the Jurisdiction of the Lower Federal Courts: A Critical Review and a New Synthesis*, 124 U. PA. L. REV. 45, 52–55 (1975); Theodore Eisenberg, *Congressional Authority to Restrict Lower Federal Court Jurisdiction*, 83 YALE L.J. 498 (1974).

[16] Act of Feb. 13, 1801, 2 Stat. 89, *repealed by* Act of March 8, 1802, 2 Stat. 132.

[17] Act of March 3, 1875, ch. 137, 18 Stat. 470. *See generally* FELIX FRANKFURTER & JAMES M. LANDIS, THE BUSINESS OF THE SUPREME COURT (1928) (history of federal judicial system).

[18] *See* 28 U.S.C. §§ 1332(a) (more than $75,000) & 1335(a) (disputed money or property of a value greater than $500 in interpleader actions). *See* § 9.07 (interpleader), *infra*.

[19] Federal diversity jurisdiction is always concurrent. Federal subject matter jurisdiction is presumptively concurrent unless it is expressly made exclusive by statute or impliedly "by incompatibility in its exercise arising from the nature of the particular case." *Claflin v. Houseman*, 93 U.S. 130, 136 (1876); *see also Tafflin v. Levitt*, 493 U.S. 455, 459 (1990); *Charles Dowd Box Co. v. Courtney*, 368 U.S. 502 (1962). For examples of exclusive federal jurisdiction, see 28 U.S.C. §§ 1333 (admiralty, maritime, and prize cases), 1337 (antitrust; exclusive by implication), & 1338(a) (patent, plant variety protection, and copyright). *See generally* ERWIN CHEMERINSKY, FEDERAL JURISDICTION § 5.2 (6th ed. 2012).

PART A.
Federal Question Jurisdiction

§ 5.02 CONSTITUTIONAL SCOPE

The most important federal subject matter jurisdiction today is federal question jurisdiction. This head of jurisdiction is premised on the belief that federal courts should have the authority to interpret and apply federal law because of their expertise in that law, their relative insulation from local and majoritarian pressures (and correspondingly more protective attitude toward federal rights), and their ability to give federal law more uniform application than state courts.[20] In *Osborn v. Bank of the United States*,[21] Chief Justice Marshall suggested in dicta the outer constitutional limits of federal question jurisdiction. He reasoned that Article III federal question jurisdiction extends not only to the federal question in a lawsuit, but "to a whole case" and all the questions in it.[22]

> [W]hen a question to which the judicial power of the Union is extended by the constitution, forms an ingredient of the original cause, it is in the power of Congress to give the Circuit Courts [which were trial courts at the time] jurisdiction of that cause, although other questions of fact or of law may be involved in it.[23]

That is, Marshall suggested that Congress could authorize a court, that has before it a case involving some federal question, to decide other questions and claims in the same case, even if they were not themselves federal. Marshall did not define what he meant by "ingredient," but suggested that it is at least sufficient that the right or title asserted by a party may be defeated by one construction of federal law and sustained by the opposite.[24]

He went on to suggest that it did not matter whether federal questions were actually put forth by the parties, as long as they were potentially available in the action.[25] Justice Frankfurter later explained that by this theory, federal question

---

[20] *See* Burt Neuborne, *The Myth of Parity*, 90 Harv. L. Rev. 1105 (1977). These premises have not gone unchallenged. *See, e.g.*, Paul M. Bator, *The State Courts and Federal Constitutional Litigation*, 22 Wm. & Mary L. Rev. 605 (1981) (noting practical inevitability of state court decision of federal law and resulting need to expand experience of state judges with federal law). For reviews of factors that are or should be considered in the allocation of business between federal and state courts, see Martin H. Redish, *Reassessing the Allocation of Judicial Business Between State and Federal Courts: Federal Jurisdiction and "The Martian Chronicles,"* 78 Va. L. Rev. 1769 (1992); Barry Friedman, *Under the Law of Federal Jurisdiction: Allocating Cases Between Federal and State Courts*, 104 Colum. L. Rev. 1211 (2004).

[21] 22 U.S. (9 Wheat.) 738, 822 (1824).

[22] By this reasoning, Marshall helped lay the groundwork for the subsequent development of the judicial doctrines of pendent and ancillary jurisdiction and the codification of supplemental jurisdiction over non-federal claims and parties in cases that also present federal questions. *See* § 5.08 (overview of supplemental jurisdiction and its antecedents), *infra*.

[23] *Osborn*, 22 U.S. at 823.

[24] 22 U.S. at 823.

[25] 22 U.S. at 825. *See Pacific R.R. Removal Cases*, 115 U.S. 1 (1885) (federal question jurisdiction

jurisdiction would be extended "whenever there exists in the background some federal proposition that might be challenged, despite the remoteness of the likelihood of actual presentation of such a federal question."[26]

Finally, Marshall extended his logic even to federal questions that had already been definitively answered by prior cases. Reasoning that the federal character of a legal question is not transformed by its having been answered, and that an answered federal question might well be renewed, he concluded that it is still an ingredient of the case sufficient to confer *constitutional* federal question jurisdiction.[27]

The Supreme Court has not again explored the reach of Article III's federal question jurisdiction as fully as Chief Justice Marshall did in *Osborn*. But in 1983, it endorsed *Osborn* as "[t]he controlling decision" on the scope of that jurisdiction.[28] The most frequently debated questions remaining involve less the theoretical scope of that jurisdiction than how much of it Congress has actually vested in the federal courts.

§ 5.03 STATUTORY SCOPE[29]

Although Congress approximated the language of Article III in vesting statutory federal question jurisdiction in the lower federal courts,[30] the courts have been reluctant, in light of the limited character of the federal judicial power in general, to construe their own authority expansively. They have therefore given a narrower scope to statutory federal question jurisdiction than Chief Justice Marshall gave constitutional federal question jurisdiction in *Osborn*. Congress, after all, could "correct" what it finds to be too narrow a judicial construction of statutory jurisdiction by amending a jurisdictional statute; it obviously has no equivalent power to amend a narrow construction of Article III.

---

upheld over purely state law claims asserted by federally chartered railroads because federal questions concerning their charter could potentially arise).

[26] *Textile Workers Union of America v. Lincoln Mills*, 353 U.S. 448, 471 (1957) (Frankfurter, J., dissenting).

[27] *Osborn*, 22 U.S. at 825.

[28] *Verlinden B.V. v. Central Bank of Nigeria*, 461 U.S. 480, 492 (1983).

[29] *See generally* Alan D. Hornstein, *Federalism, Judicial Power and the "Arising Under" Jurisdiction of the Federal Courts: A Hierarchical Analysis*, 56 IND. L.J. 563 (1981); William Cohen, *The Broken Compass: The Requirement That A Case Arise "Directly" Under Federal Law*, 115 U. PA. L. REV. 890 (1967); Paul J. Mishkin, *The Federal "Question" In The District Courts*, 53 COLUM. L. REV. 157 (1953); Ray Forrester, *The Nature Of A "Federal Question,"* 16 TUL. L. REV. 362 (1942).

[30] "The district courts shall have original jurisdiction of all civil actions arising under the Constitution, laws, or treaties of the United States." 28 U.S.C. § 1331. Similar language is also employed in 28 U.S.C. §§ 1337 and 1338(a) and they are usually given the same interpretation as § 1331. *See Carlson v. Coca-Cola Co.*, 483 F.2d 279 (9th Cir. 1973). *But see T.B. Harms Co. v. Eliscu*, 339 F.2d 823, 828 (2d Cir. 1964), *cert. denied*, 381 U.S. 915 (1965) (arguing that exclusivity of § 1338(a) jurisdiction justifies narrower construction). *See generally* Amy B. Cohen, *"Arising Under" Jurisdiction and the Copyright Laws*, 44 HASTINGS L.J. 337 (1993). At least one commentator has argued that the drafters of the 1875 federal question statute intended to vest the full constitutional federal question jurisdiction in the lower federal courts. *See, e.g.*, Forrester, note 29, *supra*, at 374–75.

There is no "single, precise definition" of the statutory jurisdiction.[31] Many federal courts today cite Justice Cardozo's reformulation of Chief Justice Marshall's suggestion in *Osborn*:

> [A] right or immunity created by the Constitution or laws of the United States must be an element, and an essential one, of the plaintiff's cause of action. The right or immunity must be such that it will be supported if the Constitution or laws of the United States are given one construction or effect, and defeated if they receive another.[32]

But their recitation of this test or other language from prior cases is often formulaic, "a substitute for analysis of the case that is actually before them."[33]

Still, the cases together suggest three statutory filters for federal question jurisdiction. First, all federal courts are agreed that the federal question must be "substantial" in the sense that it is not frivolous, that the basis for jurisdiction set out in the complaint is colorable — the "substantial question" filter. Second, a federal question must be part of a "well-pleaded" complaint (one shorn of anticipated defenses and other allegations not necessary to state a claim) — the "well-pleaded complaint" filter. Finally, the federal question must implicate a sufficiently significant federal interest to warrant a federal forum — the "significance" filter. In other words, the substantial question filter tests whether the federal question is too frivolous to serve as a basis for federal jurisdiction; the well-pleaded complaint filter tests whether the federal question is properly found in the complaint; and the significance filter tests whether the question is "federal enough" to justify the federal forum.[34]

[1]   The Substantial Question Filter

A "substantial" federal question is one that is not "so attenuated and insubstantial as to be absolutely devoid of merit," "wholly insubstantial," "obviously frivolous," "plainly insubstantial," or "unsound[] . . . [because] previous decisions . . . foreclose the subject and leave no room for the inference that the questions sought to be raised can be the subject of controversy."[35] This filter for federal question jurisdiction is uncontroversial and understandable: a litigant should not be permitted to invoke federal jurisdiction and consume a federal court's valuable resources with a wholly contrived and plainly phony federal question. Nevertheless, the substantiality requirement can be confusing because it may seem that if the court deems a federal claim to be frivolous, it should dismiss on the merits for failure to state a claim. Nevertheless, the rule is well established: if the basis for federal jurisdiction is "insubstantial" — frivolous — then the dismissal is

---

[31] *Franchise Tax Bd. v. Construction Laborers Vacation Trust*, 463 U.S. 1, 8 (1983).

[32] *Gully v. First Nat'l Bank*, 299 U.S. 109, 112 (1936) (citations omitted). Professor Mishkin's formulation is also popular: whether plaintiff asserts a "substantial claim founded 'directly' upon federal law." Mishkin, note 29, *supra*, at 1268.

[33] 13D *Wright & Miller* § 3562.

[34] *See* Richard D. Freer, *Of Rules and Standards: Reconciling Statutory Limitations on "Arising Under" Jurisdiction*, 82 Ind. L. Rev. 309, 317, 320–21 (2007).

[35] *Hagans v. Lavine*, 415 U.S. 528, 536–38 (1974) (quoting cases; citations omitted).

for want of jurisdiction. If not — if there is a colorable basis for federal jurisdiction — then the decision must go to the merits, whether on a Rule 12(b)(6) motion to dismiss for failure to state a claim, on a Rule 56 motion for summary judgment, or by trial. A court could therefore deny a motion to dismiss for want of subject matter jurisdiction, yet grant a motion to dismiss for failure to state a claim. Jurisdiction would not disappear just because the court ultimately decides that a federal claim is without merit.[36] Thus, the Supreme Court explained in *Bell v. Hood*,[37]

> Jurisdiction . . . is not defeated as respondents seem to contend, by the possibility that the averments might fail to state a cause of action on which petitioners could actually recover. For it is well settled that the failure to state a proper cause of action calls for a judgment on the merits and not for a dismissal for want of jurisdiction. Whether the complaint states a cause of action on which relief could be granted is a question of law and just as issues of fact it must be decided after and not before the court has assumed jurisdiction over the controversy. If the court does later exercise its jurisdiction to determine that the allegations in the complaint do not state a ground for relief, then dismissal of the case would be on the merits, not for want of jurisdiction.

[2] The Well-Pleaded Complaint Filter[38]

Although we have seen that in *Osborn*, Chief Justice Marshall suggested that *constitutional* federal question jurisdiction extended even to potential or anticipated federal questions,[39] the federal courts have rejected the proposition that the mere potentiality of a federal question will suffice for *statutory* jurisdiction. It is not enough that there is a *potential* federal question in a case to satisfy the jurisdictional statute; it must appear in plaintiff's complaint. A plaintiff cannot invoke the original jurisdiction of the federal courts either by anticipating a federal defense or otherwise importing a federal question into his complaint that is not essential to his case, and the federal court will examine only so much of the complaint as is "well-pleaded" — confined to the essential elements — to decide its federal question jurisdiction.[40]

Operation of the well-pleaded complaint filter is illustrated by *Louisville & Nashville Railroad Co. v. Mottley.*[41] In 1871, the Mottleys settled a claim against the railroad in exchange for free lifetime passes. But in 1907, the railroad declined

---

[36] 13D *Wright & Miller* § 3564.

[37] 327 U.S. 678, 682 (1946).

[38] *See generally* Arthur R. Miller, *Artful Pleading: A Doctrine in Search of Definition*, 76 Tex. L. Rev. 1781 (1998); Robert A. Ragazzo, *Reconsidering the Artful Pleading Doctrine*, 44 Hastings L.J. 273, 317–27 (1993); Donald L. Doernberg, *There's No Reason for It; It's Just Our Policy: Why the Well-Pleaded Complaint Rule Sabotages the Purposes of Federal Question Jurisdiction*, 38 Hastings L.J. 597 (1987).

[39] *See* § 5.02 (constitutional scope), *supra*.

[40] The Supreme court has endorsed this rule repeatedly. *See, e.g., Franchise Tax Bd. v. Construction Laborers Vacation Trust*, 463 U.S. 1 (1983).

[41] 211 U.S. 149 (1908).

to renew the passes, citing a new federal statute allegedly prohibiting free passes. The Mottleys then sued in federal court for specific performance of the settlement agreement, alleging alternatively that the federal statute did not prohibit free passes or that, if it did, it offended the Fifth Amendment.

Neither party raised the issue of subject matter jurisdiction, but when the case reached the Supreme Court, the Court considered the issue on its own motion. Although the federal statute presented a potential and even likely federal defense by the railroad, "[i]t is not enough that the plaintiff alleges some anticipated defense to his cause of action and asserts that the defense is invalidated by . . . the Constitution."[42] Well-pleaded, *i.e.*, shorn of the anticipated federal defense, the Mottley complaint merely stated a state common law claim for specific performance of the settlement agreement and therefore presented no federal question.

The "well-pleaded complaint rule" has its advantages. Because subject matter challenges go to the heart of federal judicial competence, they must be addressed promptly. The rule facilitates this, relieving the court of the burden of speculating what federal questions might later enter into the case. It also assures that a federal court will not waste its time and effort on a case that it is ultimately without jurisdiction to decide because the potential federal question fails to materialize. Consider, for example, the outcome if a federal court had taken jurisdiction of the Mottleys' complaint, only to find that the railroad never asserted the federal statute defense. The well-pleaded complaint rule also promotes federalism by leaving to state courts those cases that turn entirely or predominantly on state law. Finally, it reduces, if crudely, the federal question caseload burden on the federal courts by excluding cases in which the federal question is posed as a defense.

These advantages have been achieved at some cost, however. First, the rule may substantially delay eventual federal decision of a federal defense or other post-complaint federal question. Such delay may seriously prejudice federal rights. In *Mottley*, for example, the railroad did assert the federal statute defense to the Mottleys' lawsuit in state court after the Supreme Court decision, and the case ultimately came back to the Supreme Court for review,[43] resulting in a ruling for the railroad.[44] The well-pleaded complaint rule posits that when Congress conferred original federal question jurisdiction on the district courts, it withheld from the district courts the power to adjudicate federal questions raised by defendants in defenses or counterclaims. In contrast, when Congress conferred appellate jurisdiction over federal questions raised in state court proceedings, it authorized the United States Supreme Court to hear appeals from cases decided by state supreme courts that raised any federal question, including but not limited

---

[42] 211 U.S. at 152.

[43] If the plaintiff is confined to state court, any resulting judgment may thereafter have preclusive effect in federal court — that is, the federal court will treat the state court judgment as binding and the parties will not be permitted to relitigate it. *See* § 15.10[2], *infra*. This limits the prospect of federal adjudication when the plaintiff is confined to state court to United States Supreme Court review of the state court's decision — a possibility in some cases, but by no means a certainty. *See* Preble Stoltz, *Federal Review of State Decisions of Federal Questions*, 64 CALIF. L. REV. 943 (1976).

[44] *Louisville & Nashville R.R. Co. v. Mottley*, 219 U.S. 467 (1911).

to those raised in the plaintiff's complaint.[45] Hence, in *Mottley*, application of the well-pleaded complaint rule delayed for four years a federal court decision of the federal question.

Second, the rule can place a premium on pleading technicalities and distinctions between forms of action[46] that otherwise have no place in federal courts.[47] For example, it results in federal jurisdiction over an action to remove a specific cloud over title, but not over an action to quiet title, when defendant claims adversely under federal law. The difference is that in an action to remove a cloud, the plaintiff is required to plead facts showing the invalidity of the adverse claim that is dependent on federal law. But in an action to quiet title, the source and nature of the adverse claim is not an essential element of plaintiff's cause of action. Hence, the well-pleaded claim to quiet title has no federal ingredient.[48]

These consequences of the well-pleaded complaint rule[49] could be mitigated by allowing a party to "remove" (effectively, to transfer)[50] to federal court any state court action in which a federal defense or other post-complaint federal question is actually presented.[51] Presently, however, the removal statute restricts removal to those cases that could have been brought in federal court originally, *i.e.*, those presenting federal questions in the well-pleaded complaint.[52]

---

[45] *Compare* 28 U.S.C. § 1331 (conferring general federal question jurisdiction on the district courts over civil actions "arising under" federal law) *and* 28 U.S.C. § 1257 (conferring appellate jurisdiction on the Supreme Court over any state supreme court decision in which the constitutionality of state or federal statutes is "drawn in question," or that concern "any title, right, privilege, or immunity . . . claimed under the Constitution or the treaties or statutes of . . . the United States").

[46] *See* § 8.02[1] (common law pleading), *infra*.

[47] *See* Rule 8(e)(1) ("No technical form [of pleading] is required."); § 8.04 (modern notice pleading), *infra*.

[48] *See* Moore § 2.03[1]. *See also Additive Controls & Measurements Sys., Inc. v. Flowdata, Inc.*, 986 F.2d 476, 478–79 (Fed. Cir. 1993) (deciding federal question jurisdiction by whether the state allocates burden of pleading truth or falsity of assertions of federal patent infringement to plaintiff or defendant in state-created business disparagement suit).

[49] *See* Doernberg, note 38, *supra*, for fuller discussion of negative consequences.

[50] *See* § 5.07 (removal jurisdiction).

[51] In its study of federal jurisdiction, the American Law Institute (ALI) recommended that the law be changed to permit removal of these cases. Criticizing the well-pleaded complaint rule, the ALI observed that "[t]he alignment of parties to a lawsuit is often quite fortuitous," and that "[t]he dangers against which jurisdiction guards are as likely to be met when federal law is relied on defensively as when it is relied on offensively." ALI, Study of the Division of Jurisdiction Between State and Federal Courts 189 (1969). *See also* Mary P. Twitchell, *Characterizing Federal Claims: Preemption, Removal, and the Arising-Under Jurisdiction of the Federal Courts*, 54 Geo. Wash. L. Rev. 812 (1986); Michael G. Collins, *The Unhappy History of Federal Question Removal*, 71 Iowa L. Rev. 717 (1986).

[52] *See* § 5.07 (removal), *infra*. *See generally* Ragazzo, note 38, *supra*; Note, *Artful Pleading and Removal Jurisdiction: Ferreting Out the True Nature of a Claim*, 35 UCLA L. Rev. 315 (1987). The well-pleaded complaint rule has also substantially diminished the remedial scope of declaratory judgments. The federal Declaratory Judgment Act, 28 U.S.C. § 2201, was intended to help parties like the railroad in *Mottley*, which had no way to test its belief that federal law prohibited its renewal of the Mottleys' free pass other than to refuse renewal and invite suit by the Mottleys for breach of contract. Instead of waiting for that suit, under the Declaratory Judgment Act, the railroad could have obtained a declaration of its rights from a federal court by suing there for a "declaratory judgment." In *Skelly Oil Co. v. Phillips Petroleum Co.*, 339 U.S. 667 (1950), however, the Supreme Court reasoned that because

The undesirable consequences of the well-pleaded complaint rule can also be avoided by looking beyond a pleading in which the plaintiff has attempted to defeat removal to federal court by artfully leaving out a substantial federal question. The Supreme Court has used the "artful pleading doctrine" to look past such a pleading "when federal legislation reveals an intent by Congress to preempt a field completely, which means that regardless of what the plaintiffs plead, a federal claim — by definition raising a substantial federal question — has been raised."[53] Thus, the formalism of the well-pleaded complaint rule can sometimes be softened by the artful pleading doctrine to enable federal courts to take jurisdiction of real but omitted federal questions.

[3] The Significance Filter

That a substantial federal question appears in the well-pleaded complaint is not enough to justify statutory federal question jurisdiction unless it is "federal enough"[54] to require the expert and sympathetic attention of a federal forum. The courts have used both the "creation test" and the "embedded federal question test" for deciding the significance of the federal question.

[a] The Creation Test

A question is presumptively federal enough when federal law actually creates the plaintiff's right to sue. Justice Holmes so concluded in *American Well Works Co. v. Layne & Bowler Co.*,[55] applying what has since become known as the "creation test" for federal question jurisdiction. There the Court was asked to decide whether federal jurisdiction was available for a claim that defendants had libeled and slandered plaintiff by falsely stating that plaintiff's pump infringed the defendants' federally granted patent. Justice Holmes reasoned that "[a] suit arises under the law that creates the cause of action," and therefore found federal jurisdiction lacking, since libel and slander are state-created causes of action.[56] By this reasoning, causes of action created expressly[57] or "impliedly" under a federal statute[58] or "impliedly" under the Constitution[59] are presumptively within the

---

the Declaratory Judgment Act did not alter the federal courts' jurisdiction, it should not be construed to allow jurisdiction over a suit like the railroad's if, applying the well-pleaded complaint rule, there would be no jurisdiction over the coercive suit that would have been brought by the Mottley's had declaratory relief been unavailable. The Court has since extended *Skelly* to state declaratory judgment complaints that defendants attempt to remove to federal court, explaining that at this late date it is for Congress, not the courts, to change the rule. *Franchise Tax Bd. v. Construction Laborers Vacation Trust*, 463 U.S. 1 (1983). *See generally* TEPLY & WHITTEN Ch. 2, § C(5).

[53] *See* Miller, note 38, *supra*, at 1818. The Court has explained that "Congress may so completely pre-empt a particular area that any civil complaint raising this select group of claims is necessarily federal in character." *Metropolitan Life Ins. Co. v. Taylor*, 481 U.S. 58, 63–64 (1987). It reaffirmed the vitality of this branch of the artful pleading doctrine in *Rivet v. Regions Bank*, 522 U.S. 470, 476 (1998) (dictum).

[54] The term is Freer's. *See* Freer, note 34, *supra* at 320.

[55] 241 U.S. 257 (1916).

[56] 241 U.S. at 260.

[57] *E.g.*, 42 U.S.C. § 1983 (civil rights actions).

[58] *E.g.*, *Cannon v. University of Chicago*, 441 U.S. 677 (1979) (citing legislative intent to approve an

statutory federal question jurisdiction of the federal courts. If federal law created the right to sue, it is reasonable to presume that there is a sufficient federal interest to justify a federal forum. This is true whether or not the defendant challenges the existence of the cause of action by filing a Rule 12(b)(6) motion — whether or not the complaint states a cognizable claim. "The question whether a cause of action exists," the Court has said, "is not a question of jurisdiction, and therefore may be assumed without being decided."[60] The creation test works well for the majority of federal question cases.

[b] The Embedded Federal Question Test

However, the creation test is not conclusive. Even a state-created claim could turn on a question that may, in rare cases, be significant enough — "federal enough" — to "justify resort to the experience, solicitude, and hope of uniformity that a federal forum offers."[61] Just five years after *American Well Works*, the Court decided *Smith v. Kansas City Title & Trust Co.*[62] The plaintiff sought to enjoin the defendant trust company from investing its funds in federal farm loan bonds on the grounds that their issuance was unconstitutional. The cause of action clearly arose under state law, which prohibited the company's directors from making any investment not authorized by a valid law. Nevertheless, citing *Osborn*, the Court declared that "where it appears . . . that the right to relief depends upon the construction or application of [federal law] . . . , the District Court has jurisdiction."[63] Because the plaintiff shareholders would prevail if the federal law authorizing the bonds was found unconstitutional and lose on the opposite construction, the district court had jurisdiction of the case; the federal question embedded in plaintiff's state law claim was pivotal to that claim. The *embedded federal question test* applied in the *Smith* case reached beyond Holmes' *creation test*, which has since appropriately been described as "more useful for inclusion than for the exclusion for which it was intended."[64] In other words, a claim that passes the creation test presumptively qualifies for federal question jurisdiction, but a claim that does not pass the creation test is not necessarily disqualified for such jurisdiction because it may still contain a qualifying pivotal federal question.

At the same time, the Court has cautioned that the mere presence of a federal issue in a state-created cause of action — even one that is pivotal to the claim —

---

implied cause of action for damages under federal statute).

[59] *E.g., Bivens v. Six Unnamed Agents of Federal Bureau of Narcotics*, 403 U.S. 388 (1971) (approving an implied cause of action for damages as a necessary remedy for violation of plaintiff's Fourth Amendment rights).

[60] *Burks v. Lasker*, 441 U.S. 471, 476 n.5 (1979). *See also Bell v. Hood*, 327 U.S. 678 (1946). Rule 12 (identifying defenses that may be asserted by motion to dismiss) thus distinguishes between the defense of lack of subject matter jurisdiction (12(b)(1)) and the defense of failure to state a claim (12(b)(6)). *See* § 5.03[1], *supra*.

[61] *Grable & Sons Metal Prods. v. Darue Eng'g & Mfg.*, 545 U.S. 308, 312 (2005).

[62] 255 U.S. 180 (1921).

[63] 255 U.S. at 199. *See also Franchise Tax Bd. v. Construction Laborers Vacation Trust*, 463 U.S. 1, 13 (1983) (federal question jurisdiction appropriate when "it appears that some substantial, disputed question of federal law is a necessary element of one of the well-pleaded state claims").

[64] *T.B. Harms Co.*, 339 F.2d at 827 (2d Cir. 1964), *cert. denied*, 381 U.S. 915 (1965).

does not automatically confer federal question jurisdiction. Its availability depends in part on "an evaluation of the nature of the federal interest at stake":[65] whether it is sufficiently significant to require a federal trial forum. Unfortunately, the Court has been less than clear about how a district court is to evaluate the nature of the federal interest.

In *Merrell Dow Pharmaceuticals, Inc. v. Thompson*,[66] the plaintiffs sued the defendant on a state claim of negligence, among others. They alleged also that the defendant had "misbranded" its products in violation of federal law, creating a rebuttable presumption of negligence under state law. The Supreme Court found that the federal issue thus incorporated into state law was "insufficiently substantial"[67] to confer federal question jurisdiction,[68] a conclusion suggested in part — if not compelled, according to the majority — by the fact that Congress had created no private cause of action for violations of the federal law at issue.[69]

Merrell Dow usefully focused on the significance of the federal question, but its terminology was confusing and its logic questionable. The *Merrell Dow* majority appeared to conflate the question whether Congress intended to create a private right of action with the question of whether plaintiff's state law claim included a pivotal federal question. Yet it hardly followed from Congress' intention to leave a statute's enforcement to public authorities that, when a federal statutory question arises as part of a state-created right of action, Congress also intended to leave the question to state court interpretation (subject only to the statistically remote possibility of Supreme Court review). On this score, the dissent may have had the better argument. Congress' intent to rely on public enforcement "reflects congressional concern with obtaining more accurate implementation and more coordinated enforcement of a regulatory scheme." These are concerns which, if anything, strengthen the argument for federal jurisdiction over the embedded question of compliance with federal product regulations.[70]

---

[65] *Merrell Dow Pharm., Inc. v. Thompson*, 478 U.S. 804, 804–15 n.12 (1986) (endorsing this characterization by commentators of the Supreme Court's cases regarding federal question jurisdiction).

[66] 478 U.S. 804.

[67] 478 U.S. at 814. The Court's choice of the word "substantial" in *Merrell Dow* was unfortunate because, as we have seen, the word is already used in the law of subject matter jurisdiction to mean not "wholly insubstantial and frivolous" or "patently without merit." *Bell v. Hood*, 327 U.S. 678, 682–83 (1946). *See infra* § 5.03[1], *supra*. But in the context of the *Merrell Dow* decision, the Supreme Court's use of "substantial" was clearly intended to suggest the significance of the federal interest.

[68] *See also Moore v. Chesapeake & Ohio Ry. Co.*, 291 U.S. 205 (1934). In fact, the Court has sometimes denied jurisdiction over even federally-created causes of action "because of an overwhelming predominance of state-law issues." *Merrell Dow*, 478 U.S. at 814–15 n.12, *citing Shulthis v. McDougal*, 225 U.S. 561, 569–70 (1912); *Shoshone Mining Co. v. Rutter*, 177 U.S. 505, 507 (1900) (both involving federally-created causes of action to vindicate property claims under state law). This is why we said that federally-created claims only "presumptively" invoke federal jurisdiction under the creation test.

[69] *Merrell Dow*, 478 U.S. at 810–12, 817. Insofar as such federal questions may eventually need federal appellate review, they are still subject to such review on appeal of the highest state court decision to the United States Supreme Court. 478 U.S. at 816 n.14, *citing Moore*, 291 U.S. at 214–15.

[70] 478 U.S. at 832. *See generally* Patti Alleva, *Prerogative Lost: The Trouble with Statutory Federal Question Doctrine After Merrell Dow*, 52 Ohio St. L.J. 1477 (1991); Note, *The Supreme Court, 1985 Term*, 100 Harv. L. Rev. 100, 230–40 (1986).

More recently, the Court tried to clarify the significance filter for embedded federal questions. In *Grable & Sons Metal Products, Inc. v. Darue Engineering & Manufacturing*,[71] Grable sued Darue in state court on a state-created claim to quiet title. The Internal Revenue Service (IRS) had seized Grable's land for its failure to pay taxes, sent Grable notice of the seizure by mail, and then sold the seized land to Darue. Grable argued that the sale was invalid because federal law did not permit service by mail.

Darue removed the case to federal court on federal question grounds. As we discuss below,[72] to invoke federal jurisdiction by removal Darue had to show that Grable's case could have been brought originally in federal court — that there was federal question jurisdiction over Grable's claim. Darue argued that although state law created the right to sue, the state law claim of invalidity turned on the answer to a federal question: whether federal law permitted service by mail. The lower courts and the Supreme Court agreed, finding jurisdiction.

But how was *Grable* different from *Merrell Dow*? The Court explained that "even when the state action discloses a contested and substantial federal question, the exercise of federal jurisdiction is subject to a possible veto . . . [f]or the federal issue will ultimately qualify for a federal forum only if federal jurisdiction is consistent with congressional judgment about the sound division of labor between state and federal courts . . . ."[73] This "federalism veto" did not apply to *Grable*, because the narrow issue of mail notice that it posed was unlikely to arise as part of state law claims very often, yet cried out for a uniform answer to facilitate IRS tax-enforcement administration. The rarity with which it arose in state claims suggested that "federal jurisdiction to resolve genuine disagreement over federal tax title provisions will portend only a microscopic effect on the federal-state division of labor."[74] In contrast, the federalism veto applied to prevent jurisdiction in *Merrell Dow* because allowing jurisdiction there for the federal question embedded in the plaintiff's state-created negligence per se claim would open the federal courthouse doors to thousands of similar routine state tort claims, a result that would distort the traditional allocation of tort business between state and federal courts, and one that Congress surely never intended.[75]

Grable thus adds a further layer to the significance filter. In evaluating the nature of the federal interest presented by an embedded federal question, a court must decide not only the significance of the federal question to the parties (whether it is pivotal to a claim) and to federal interests, but also whether taking jurisdiction would distort the allocation of business between state and federal courts and thus invoke the "federalism veto." Whether this nuance clarifies analysis is debatable,[76]

---

[71] 545 U.S. 308 (2005).

[72] *See* § 5.07, *infra*.

[73] 545 U.S. at 313.

[74] 545 U.S. at 315.

[75] 545 U.S. at 318 ("[I]f the federal labeling standard without a federal cause of action could get a state claim into federal court, so could any other federal standard without a federal cause of action. And that would have meant a tremendous number of cases.").

[76] *Compare* Freer, note 34, *supra* at 344 (yes; its "sensible balancing" puts the statutory test for

and it seems unlikely that this will be the Court's last word.

PART B.
Diversity Jurisdiction

§ 5.04 IN GENERAL

[1] Rationale and the Modern Critique

The traditional justification for diversity jurisdiction[77] is that it protects out-of-state litigants from local bias.[78] With the passage of time and the decline in the intensity of state allegiances, many have criticized the continued availability of diversity jurisdiction.[79] First, they argue that local bias is no longer a serious concern in most cases. They add that even if it were, existing diversity jurisdiction is too broad in affording the choice of federal court even to a plaintiff who sues an out-of-state citizen in plaintiff's home state.[80] Advocates of diversity jurisdiction respond that some bias still exists, often exacerbated by the selection of state juries from a single county as opposed to district or state-wide jury pools. They add that, in any event, out-of-state litigants still need the protection of federal courts to avoid the prejudice inherent in their lack of familiarity with local judicial procedures.

---

federal question jurisdiction "in better shape now than it has been in a generation"), *and* Rory Ryan, *No Welcome Mat, No Problem?: Federal-Question Jurisdiction After Grable*, 80 St. John's L. Rev. 621 (2006) (yes; *Grable* established a four-pronged test: (1) necessity; (2) actually disputed; (3) substantiality; and (4) disruptiveness), *with* Douglas D. McFarland, *The True Compass: No Federal Question in a State Claim*, 55 U. Kan. L. Rev. 1 (2006) (no; courts should exclusively use the creation test for the clarity it provides).

[77] 28 U.S.C. § 1332(a) confers jurisdiction *inter alia* over all civil actions between "citizens of different States" when the matter in controversy exceeds $75,000.

[78] Neither the records of the Constitutional Convention nor the records of the First Congress, which vested the federal courts with diversity jurisdiction of cases involving more than $400, describe this or any other justification in any detail. The historical reasons for the jurisdiction must therefore be gleaned from ratification debates and contemporary judicial opinions. *See, e.g.*, Henry J. Friendly, *The Historic Basis of Diversity Jurisdiction*, 41 Harv. L. Rev. 483 (1928). Chief Justice Marshall explained that "the constitution itself either entertains apprehensions" about the impartiality of state courts towards non-resident litigants, "or views with . . . indulgence thei[r] possible fears and apprehensions." *Bank of the United States v. Deveaux*, 9 U.S. (5 Cranch) 61, 87 (1809). Subsequently the Court opined that the protection of diversity jurisdiction was intended principally to "give security to all contracts [and] stability to credit" by protecting out-of-state creditors from the bias of local courts. *Ogden v. Saunders*, 25 U.S. (12 Wheat.) 213, 237 (1827).

[79] The arguments for and against diversity jurisdiction have been rehearsed in a succession of congressional hearings and sundry articles. A typical collection of statements, from which the arguments in the text are drawn, may be found in *Diversity of Citizenship Jurisdiction 1982: Hearings on H.R. 6691 Before the Subcomm. on Courts, Civil Liberties and the Administration of Justice of the House Comm. on Judiciary*, 97th Cong., 2d Sess. (1982) (hereinafter cited as *1982 Diversity Hearings*).

[80] Even Chief Justice Rehnquist urged abolition of at least this much of diversity jurisdiction. William H. Rehnquist, *Remarks of the Chief Justice*, 21 St. Mary's L.J. 5, 7–9 (1989).

Second, critics of diversity cite the caseload burden it imposes on the federal courts, interfering with their primary role in construing and protecting federal rights. Historically diversity cases have accounted for between 18 and 30% of the federal district court civil caseload.[81] Moreover, they remain on the dockets longer, require more pretrial proceedings, go to trial more often, and require jury trials more frequently than other civil cases in the federal courts.[82] Diversity proponents respond that abolition of diversity jurisdiction would only shift the burden to equally taxed state courts.[83] They contend that the solution to the federal caseload is instead to create more federal judges and magistrates and to reform federal pretrial process.

Third, critics of diversity jurisdiction emphasize the hopelessly complex procedural, jurisdictional, and choice-of-law problems that it creates. Courts must now spend substantial time analyzing and applying elaborate, abstract, and often quite arbitrary rules in determining citizenship, aggregating claims for purposes of computing the amount in controversy, properly aligning parties, determining the effect of joinder and intervention in diversity cases, judging the propriety of separate and independent claim removal, and unmasking prohibited devices to manufacture diversity, all of which would be largely unnecessary were diversity to be eliminated.[84] Perhaps more significantly, the *Erie* doctrine requires federal courts sitting in diversity to apply state law as rules of decision, a task easier for their state court brethren to perform.[85]

Diversity advocates respond that much of the complexity could be avoided by the elimination of the statutory requirement of *complete diversity*[86] in favor of minimal diversity,[87] and argue that the *Erie* problem is exaggerated. Moreover, they contend that diversity jurisdiction results in "cross-pollination" of state and federal courts to the lasting benefit of both.

At a time when federal caseloads are excessive and federal question cases must compete for scarce judicial resources with diversity cases, the critics of diversity

---

[81] DAVID NEUBAUER & HENRY FRADELLA, AMERICA'S COURTS AND THE CRIMINAL JUSTICE SYSTEM 70 (2011).

[82] *1982 Diversity Hearings* at 10 (statement of J. Rose, Assistant Attorney General). This may be explained in part by the fact that nearly one-half of diversity cases are personal injury lawsuits in which the plaintiff expects to obtain a larger award from a jury than from the court JUDICIAL BUSINESS OF THE UNITED STATES COURTS 125–27, Table C-2 (2011).

[83] Indeed, a statistical study conducted by the National Center for State Courts found that the abolition of just in-state plaintiff diversity jurisdiction, as urged by Chief Justice Rehnquist, *see* note 80, *supra*, "would have a surprisingly burdensome effect on state court caseloads . . . nearly as much . . . as would . . . total abolition of diversity jurisdiction." Victor E. Flango & Craig Boersema, *Changes in Federal Diversity Jurisdiction: Effects on State Court Caseloads*, 15 U. DAYTON L. REV. 405, 455 (1990).

[84] *See* Thomas D. Rowe, *Abolishing Diversity Jurisdiction: Positive Side Effects and Potential for Further Reforms*, 92 HARV. L. REV. 963, 980–81 (1979). For a discussion of some of these rules, see §§ 5.04[2]–[3], 5.05, 5.06, *infra*.

[85] *See* § 7.02[3] (ascertaining the content of state law), *infra*.

[86] Complete diversity refers to the statutory requirement that every plaintiff be diverse from every defendant. *See* § 5.04[2], *infra*.

[87] *Minimal diversity* refers to the constitutional requirement that at least one plaintiff and one defendant be of diverse citizenship. *See* § 5.04[2], *infra*.

appear to have the better of the arguments. It is both most efficient and most faithful to a federal scheme of dual judicial systems that the subject matter of litigation be allocated according to the systems' comparative advantages and the sovereigns' primary interests and responsibilities. Federal courts are best at and have a special protective interest in determining and applying federal law. The continuation of broad diversity jurisdiction diverts them from their primary mission to no better end, in most cases today, than assuring some litigants a tactical choice of forum. Yet, as long as practicing lawyers value that choice,[88] and lobby to retain diversity jurisdiction more energetically and effectively than those who support its abolition, it is unlikely that diversity will be abolished.[89]

[2]   Diversity Between Whom?

While Congress has not yet acted to eliminate general diversity, the federal courts have often taken the matter into their own hands by construing diversity legislation narrowly.

> The policy of the [diversity] statute calls for its strict construction. The power reserved to the states, under the Constitution, to provide for the determination of controversies in their courts may be restricted only by the action of Congress in conformity to [Article III]. Due regard for the rightful independence of state governments, which should actuate federal courts, requires that they scrupulously confine their own jurisdiction to the precise limits which the statute has defined.[90]

This is most apparent in the requirement for complete diversity. Although the Supreme Court has held that Article III requires only minimal diversity[91] (that at least one party be a citizen of a different state from at least one opposing party), in *Strawbridge v. Curtiss*[92] it construed the general diversity *statute* to require complete diversity (that no party may share citizenship with any opposing party).[93]

---

[88] *See* Victor E. Flango, *Attorneys' Perspectives on Choice of Forum in Diversity Cases*, 25 Akron L. Rev. 41, 56, 105 (1991) (finding that fear of bias against non-resident clients was a significant factor in choice of forum for more than 60% of attorneys surveyed).

[89] Of course, it will never be wholly abolished. All agree that *alienage diversity*, jurisdiction over suits between citizens and foreign nationals, must remain in the federal courts. It is likely, too, that diversity jurisdiction will be continued over multi-party lawsuits that could otherwise not be brought in any single state court. *See* Report of the Federal Courts Study Comm. 38–42 (1990); *1982 Diversity Hearings*, note 79, *supra*, at 263 (multidistrict mass tort litigation consolidated under 28 U.S.C. § 1407; 28 U.S.C. § 1397 (interpleader).

[90] *Healy v. Ratta*, 292 U.S. 263, 270 (1934).

[91] *State Farm Fire & Casualty Co. v. Tashire*, 386 U.S. 523 (1967) (upholding constitutionality of federal interpleader statute, 28 U.S.C. § 1397, which requires only minimal diversity).

[92] 7 U.S. (3 Cranch) 267 (1806). *See* Howard P. Fink, *Supplemental Jurisdiction — Take It to the Limit!*, 74 Ind. L.J. 161 (1998) (calling for elimination of rule of complete diversity); David P. Currie, *The Federal Courts and the American Law Institute*, 36 U. Chi. L. Rev. 1, 18–21 (1968) (criticizing the complete diversity rule).

[93] Although Congress has not overridden the Supreme Court's construction of the general diversity statute, 28 U.S.C. § 1332(a), to require complete diversity, it has adopted minimal diversity for some claims. *See, e.g.*, 28 U.S.C. §§ 1332(d)(2) (authorizing federal jurisdiction for class action claims where "any member of a class of plaintiffs is a citizen of a State different from any defendant" and aggregate

In modern multi-party litigation, the statutory requirement for complete diversity is in theory quite restrictive; it defeats jurisdiction whenever any plaintiff is a citizen of the same state as any defendant.

The courts have further narrowed the availability of diversity jurisdiction by looking behind the pleadings in some disputes and "realigning" the parties according to their real interests. Assume, for example, that a mortgagee sues its mortgagor and a city with whom the mortgagor has a contract for specific performance of a contract. Since the mortgagee and mortgagor have the same interest in specific performance, they should be aligned together, which will destroy complete diversity if the mortgagor and the city are citizens of the same state.[94] Realignment is more difficult when interests are shared on some issues and divided on others. But in such cases, the court will look to the "principal purpose of the suit" and the "primary and controlling matter in dispute" for purposes of alignment.[95]

[3]   Further Limitations on Diversity Jurisdiction

Deferring to state courts, federal courts have traditionally declined to exercise jurisdiction in certain *in rem* (regarding title to property),[96] probate cases, and domestic relations cases, even when the parties satisfy the requirements for diversity jurisdiction. In addition, they are also obliged by statute to deny jurisdiction which has been "improperly or collusively made."[97]

Considerations of respect owed state courts and of reciprocity — which courts lump under the phrase "comity" — have motivated federal courts to decline jurisdiction over diversity suits in which, in order to give effect to their judgments, they must take control of property that is already in the custody of a state court of competent jurisdiction. Such suits may include "suits . . . brought to marshal assets, administer trusts, or liquidate estates."[98] In part, similar considerations have supported the "probate exception."

> The probate exception reserves to state probate courts the probate or annulment of a will and the administration of a decedent's estate; it also precludes federal courts from endeavoring to dispose of property that is in the custody of a state probate court.[99]

---

amount in controversy exceeds $5,000,000); 1335(a)(1) (providing federal jurisdiction for interpleader claims when "[t]wo or more adverse claimants [are] of diverse citizenship" and amount at stake is $500 or more).

[94] *See Dawson v. Columbia Trust Co.*, 197 U.S. 178 (1905).

[95] *See, e.g., Indianapolis v. Chase Nat'l Bank*, 314 U.S. 63, 69 (1941), *citing East Tennessee, V. & G. R.R. v. Grayson*, 119 U.S. 240, 244 (1886), *and Merchants' Cotton Press & Storage Co. v. Insurance Co.*, 151 U.S. 368, 385 (1894). In *Chase Nat'l Bank*, the Court dismissed several secondary issues on which the mortgagor and mortgagee were divided as mere "window-dressing designed to satisfy the requirements of diversity jurisdiction." 314 U.S. at 72. In a case which presents multiple issues of equal importance, it is arguable that a court should not realign parties who are truly divided on any one of the issues, but the case law is divided on this point. *See* Wright § 30.

[96] *See* § 3.01[3][b] (*in rem* jurisdiction), *supra*.

[97] 28 U.S.C. § 1359.

[98] *Princess Lida v. Thompson*, 305 U.S. 456, 466 (1939).

[99] *Marshall v. Marshall*, 547 U.S. 293 (2006).

A time-honored but possibly erroneous construction of the diversity statute, as well as recognition that the "whole subject of the domestic relations of husband and wife, parent and child, belongs to the laws of the States," account for the long-standing exclusion of domestic relations actions from diversity jurisdiction.[100] In *Ankenbrandt v. Richards*,[101] the Supreme Court traced the domestic relations exception to the historical assumption that alimony and divorce lay outside the jurisdiction of the chancery courts in England and therefore outside the diversity jurisdiction "in suits of a civil nature at common law or in equity" conferred by the Judiciary Act of 1789. Without confirming this assumption, the Court deferred to "Congress' apparent acceptance of this construction of the [early] diversity jurisdictional provisions" and its subsequent reenactment of diversity jurisdiction without substantive change.[102] This statutory conclusion has modern-day appeal. State courts are more closely associated with state and local governmental units dedicated to monitoring compliance with domestic relations decrees, and federal judges understandably lack enthusiasm for burdensome, fact-bound, and often protracted domestic relations disputes.[103]

On the other hand, the *Ankenbrandt* Court stressed the relatively narrow scope of the domestic relations exception. It divests the federal courts of the power to issue divorce, alimony, and child custody decrees. It does not encompass other intra-family legal claims, including ordinary tort or contract claims.[104]

Finally, the courts are barred by statute from asserting jurisdiction when a party contrives to create diversity. Assignments of claims between non-diverse parties to diverse parties for purposes of manufacturing diversity were outlawed in the very first Judiciary Act, but poor drafting invited evasion.[105] Today the statute prohibits this by denying jurisdiction when a party "by assignment or otherwise, has been improperly or collusively made or joined to invoke the jurisdiction of such court."[106] Appointment of out-of-state administrators to represent infants, incompetents, or the estates of decedents was also a popular device to create diversity. Since 1988, the diversity statute defeats this device by deeming the citizenship of a legal

---

[100] *In re Burrus*, 136 U.S. 586, 593–94 (1890) (dictum). In a full account of the history of the "domestic relations" exception, Judge Friendly has also traced it and the exception for probate actions to the belief that such cases were not "suits of a civil nature in law and equity" within the language of the first diversity jurisdiction statute because they were historically within the jurisdiction of ecclesiastical courts. *See Phillips, Nizer, Benjamin, Krim & Ballon v. Rosenstiel*, 490 F.2d 509, 513 (2d Cir. 1973).

[101] 504 U.S. 689 (1992).

[102] 504 U.S. at 700.

[103] 504 U.S. at 703 (noting sound policy considerations supporting the exception); *Rosenstiel*, 490 F.2d at 516 n.8 (Friendly, J.) (candidly opining that taking jurisdiction would be a "waste" of scarce federal judicial resources).

[104] *See, e.g., Ankenbrandt*, 504 U.S. at 704 (finding that diversity jurisdiction exists over physical and sexual abuse claims by children against a parent).

[105] *See generally* WRIGHT § 31.

[106] 28 U.S.C. § 1359. The statutory bar on collusive or improperly made diversity jurisdiction literally only applies to devices to "invoke" jurisdiction. The courts, however, are increasingly refusing to give effect to comparable devices to *defeat* diversity jurisdiction, typically arising in response to attempted removals of actions from state to federal court. WRIGHT § 31.

representative to be that of the infant, incompetent, or decedent.[107]

§ 5.05   CITIZENSHIP

In deciding diversity jurisdiction, the courts look to the citizenship of the parties at the time of filing of the complaint. As the Supreme Court has said,

> This time-of-filing rule is hornbook law (quite literally) taught to first-year law students in any basic course on federal civil procedure. It measures all challenges to subject-matter jurisdiction premised upon diversity of citizenship against the state of facts that existed at the time of filing — whether the challenge be brought shortly after filing, after the trial, or even for the first time on appeal.[108]

This measuring point provides precision because the clerk time-stamps and dockets the complaint on filing, and stability, because the existence of diversity jurisdiction is unaffected by the vicissitudes of the subsequent litigation. Post-commencement changes in citizenship of the parties can neither create jurisdiction where none existed at commencement, nor divest the court of jurisdiction that was proper at commencement. However, realignment of the parties during the litigation[109] may show that diversity was or was not present at commencement of the suit. In addition, the Court has long recognized an exception to the time-of-filing rule by which incomplete diversity at filing can be cured by dropping the non-diverse parties during the litigation pursuant to Rule 21,[110] if they are dispensable.[111]

Citizenship for diversity purposes requires a party to be a citizen of both the United States and of a state. United States citizenship ordinarily poses no analytic difficulties, since it is usually conferred by birth to citizen parents or birth on United States soil, but state citizenship can be more problematic. The courts have equated the state citizenship of natural persons with *domicile* in a state. Domicile itself, however, is a legal fiction imposed on persons in order to simplify legal determinations, unlike *residence*, which has a practical meaning outside the law. "The very meaning of domicile is the technically pre-eminent headquarters that every person is compelled to have in order that certain rights and duties that have been attached to it by the law may be determined."[112]

Domicile is created by the concurrent establishment of physical residence in a state and an intent to remain there indefinitely[113] — that is, we look to residence and intent at the same point in time. Although a person can have more than one

---

[107] 28 U.S.C. § 1332(c)(2).

[108] *Grupo Dataflux v. Atlas Global Group, L.P.*, 541 U.S. 567, 570–71 (2004).

[109] *See* § 5.04[2] (diversity between whom), *supra*.

[110] *Grupo Dataflux*, 541 U.S. at 572–73. Defective allegations of jurisdiction can also be amended during the litigation, provided that jurisdiction in fact existed at commencement. *See* 28 U.S.C. § 1653.

[111] *See* Rule 19, discussed at § 9.05[2], *infra*.

[112] *Williamson v. Osenton*, 232 U.S. 619, 625 (1914) (Holmes, J.).

[113] The requisite intent has also been characterized as the intent to return to the residence when one is absent, *WRIGHT* § 26, and the absence of any present intention to live elsewhere. *Williamson*, 232 U.S. at 623.

residence at one time, he can by definition only form the requisite intent with respect to a single state at one time, and therefore can have only one domicile at a time.[114] Neither residence nor intent alone will suffice to establish domicile; both must be established concurrently. Accordingly, once established, domicile continues until a person has concurrently changed both her state of residence and her intent to remain. A mere change of residence without a concurrent formation of an intent to remain indefinitely in the state of new residence, or the mere formation of an intent to go elsewhere unaccompanied by a change in residence, will not alter a previously established domicile. Indeed, although the burden of pleading and proving citizenship is on the party invoking diversity jurisdiction, she enjoys a presumption in favor of her last-established domicile which must be rebutted by the party alleging a change in domicile.[115]

Because the requisite intent is a state of mind, it can only be shown circumstantially. Sundry affiliating circumstances may be offered in evidence of that intent: place of employment, voter or vehicle registration, driver's license, current residence, presence of other property or intangible interests, bank accounts, club memberships, mailing address, etc.[116] The courts once shortcut such proof in some instances, however, by adopting the "now vanishing fiction of identity of person,"[117] by which the domicile of the husband was attributed to the wife and domicile of parent attributed to child. Modern courts have been increasingly willing to discard this fiction when appropriate and to determine the domicile of each of the parties on his or her individual facts.

This trend and many of the foregoing principles are well-illustrated by *Mas v. Perry*.[118] Mr. and Mrs. Mas, graduate students studying at Louisiana State University, sued their landlord, a Louisiana citizen, in federal court for damages resulting from his spying on their bedroom through a two-way mirror. The landlord challenged diversity jurisdiction. The challenge was clearly unsound as to Mr. Mas; he was a French national whose suit fell within alienage jurisdiction as it then existed.[119] By the fiction of identity of person, however, diversity was arguably lacking as to Mrs. Mas, as she would be assigned the French domicile of her husband but, as a United States citizen, would not qualify for alienage jurisdiction.

---

[114] 232 U.S. at 623. Thus, it is not usually sufficient for a plaintiff to allege mere residence of the parties in order to allege citizenship for diversity purposes. *See, e.g., Rosenquist v. Gustafson*, 803 F. Supp. 1325 (N.D. Ill. 1992). *See* Form 7.

[115] *Bank One, Texas, N.A. v. Montle*, 964 F.2d 48, 50 (1st Cir. 1992); *Janzen v. Goos*, 302 F.2d 421 (8th Cir. 1962).

[116] *See, e.g., Tanzymore v. Bethlehem Steel Corp.*, 457 F.2d 1320 (3d Cir. 1972) (affirming dismissal for lack of diversity, when deposition of plaintiff showed none of these affiliating circumstances); *Simmons v. Skyway of Ocala*, 592 F. Supp. 356, 360 (S.D. Ga. 1984) ("grab-bag of indicia having to do with everyday life" established Florida domicile).

[117] *Williamson*, 232 U.S. at 625.

[118] 489 F.2d 1396 (5th Cir. 1974).

[119] 28 U.S.C. § 1332(a)(2). The diversity statute now provides, however, that diversity of citizenship is destroyed in actions between citizens of a state and permanent resident aliens who are "domiciled in the same state." 28 U.S.C. § 1332(a). In other words, Mr. Mas would be deemed a citizen of the state where he was domiciled.

Instead, the court discarded the fiction and traced her last established domicile to Mississippi, where she had lived with her parents before her marriage. Neither her establishment of a Louisiana residence as a student, nor her candid admission that she did not intend to return to Mississippi, changed her Mississippi domicile because she had not yet formed an intent to remain indefinitely in Louisiana or any other state. Moreover, the Mas' change of residence to Illinois *after* commencement of the action was immaterial to jurisdiction. Not only had they formed no intent to remain indefinitely in Illinois, but Mrs. Mas' domicile at commencement of the action remained Mississippi. Thus, there was diversity at commencement of the action, and the landlord's challenge failed.

Two legal fictions, domicile and the corporate entity, complicate the process of determining citizenship for corporations. But the amendment of the diversity statute to deem a corporation to be the citizen of "any State by which it has been incorporated *and* of the state where it has its principal place of business"[120] has simplified matters greatly. Because corporations often have dual citizenship under the statute, the party invoking diversity must plead not only its citizenship by incorporation, but also its citizenship by principal place of business.[121]

Incorporation is a definite and ascertainable legal act, but determining the "principal place of business" can become difficult when a corporation conducts business in multiple states. The statute contemplates a single principal place of business; how should a pleader and the court choose among them? Over years, the lower courts developed different tests for determining the site of a corporation's principal place of business. Some courts looked to the corporation's "muscle center" — the locus of the bulk of the corporation's activities, measured by corporate assets, sales or other physical measures.[122] Other courts applied a home office — or "nerve center" — test, looking to the locus of the corporation's operating headquarters.[123]

In 2010, the Supreme Court resolved this disagreement in favor of the nerve center test in *Hertz Corporation v. Friend:*[124]

> In an effort to find a single, more uniform interpretation of the statutory phrase, this Court returns to the 'nerve center' approach: '[P]rincipal place of business' is best read as referring to the place where a corporation's officers direct, control, and coordinate the corporation's activities. In practice it should normally be the place where the corporation maintains its

---

[120] 28 U.S.C. § 1332(c)(1) (emphasis added). Some unnecessary ambiguity may have been perpetuated by the amendment's use of "any state" instead of "every state," but most courts and commentators are agreed that the latter is the intended meaning of the amendment. *See* WRIGHT § 27.

[121] *Canton v. Angelina Casualty Co.*, 279 F.2d 553 (5th Cir. 1960). *See* Form 7 (plaintiff is [a citizen of State A] and "defendant is [a corporation incorporated under the laws of State [B with its principal place of business in State B]").

[122] *See, e.g., Anniston Soil Pipe Co. v. Central Foundry Co.*, 329 F.2d 313 (5th Cir. 1964) (locus of plant and production facilities rather than of executive offices); *Kelly v. United States Steel Corp.*, 284 F.2d 850 (3d Cir. 1960) (locus of largest number of executive officers and corporate operating committee, as well as of largest percentage of employees and assets); *United States Fid. & Guar. Co. v. DiMassa*, 561 F. Supp. 348 (E.D. Pa. 1983) (locus of corporate operations as well as main computer).

[123] *See, e.g., Scot Typewriter Co. v. Underwood Corp.*, 170 F. Supp. 862 (S.D.N.Y. 1959).

[124] 130 S. Ct. 1181 (2010).

headquarters — provided that the headquarters is the actual center of direction, control, and coordination, i.e., the 'nerve center,' and not simply an office where the corporation holds its board meetings.[125]

Finally, the federal courts have traditionally held that unincorporated associations, such as partnerships and labor unions, take the citizenship of each of their members.[126] This rule reflects the historical assumption that such organizations are not juridical persons and therefore must be disregarded for citizenship purposes. In 1990, the Court reaffirmed this view and distinguished an apparently contrary decision as going to the question whether parties who were natural persons were real parties to the controversy, not whether an artificial entity is a citizen.[127] However, the rule has not been applied to class actions; diversity is determined by the citizenship of the representative parties, without regard to the absent class members.[128]

§ 5.06   AMOUNT IN CONTROVERSY

[1]   The "Legal Certainty Test" and the Single Claim

Since the First Judiciary Act, Congress has imposed a monetary limitation on diversity jurisdiction.[129] The present amount in controversy is $75,000, exclusive of interest and costs.[130] The purpose of the limitation has always been to ration federal judicial resources by screening out penny-ante cases. Like citizenship, jurisdictional amount must be pled and (if challenged) proven by the plaintiff, and is determined as of the time of commencement of the action.[131] The Supreme Court stated the proper test for amount in controversy in the leading case of *St. Paul Mercury Indemnity Co. v. Red Cab Co.:*[132]

---

[125] 130 S. Ct. at 1184.

[126] *See, e.g., Carden v. Arkoma Assocs.*, 494 U.S. 185 (1990); *United Steelworkers v. R.H. Bouligny, Inc.*, 382 U.S. 145, 150–51 (1965).

[127] *Carden*, 494 U.S. 185 (distinguishing *Navarro Sav. Ass'n v. Lee*, 446 U.S. 458 (1980)).

[128] *Supreme Tribe of Ben-Hur v. Cauble*, 255 U.S. 356 (1921). Unincorporated associations or other entities that may be unable to satisfy diversity requirements due to the citizenship of their members may therefore be able to avoid diversity problems by suing through representative members in class actions. *See* Rule 23.2 (permitting such suits if representative parties will fairly and adequately protect the interests of the association and its members). *See generally* § 9.09 (class actions), *infra*.

[129] Until 1980, Congress also imposed a monetary limitation on general federal question jurisdiction. However, dissatisfaction with its application to constitutional claims of incalculable monetary value and resulting relaxed applications of the requirement in many federal question cases led to the abandonment of the requirement. Act of Dec. 1, 1980, Pub. L. No. 96-486, 94 Stat. 2369. Nevertheless, many of the old federal question cases are still relevant authority for ascertaining amount in controversy in diversity cases.

[130] 28 U.S.C. § 1332(a).

[131] It is the direct effect of the immediate lawsuit that is relevant for ascertaining the jurisdictional amount, not its collateral effects or importance to strangers or society at large. *See, e.g., Healy v. Ratta*, 292 U.S. 263, 267 (1934) (collateral effect via *stare decisis* may not be considered). *See generally* MOORE § 102.106.

[132] 303 U.S. 283 (1938).

> [T]he sum claimed by the plaintiff controls if the claim is apparently made
> in good faith. It must appear to a legal certainty that the claim is really for
> less than the jurisdictional amount to justify dismissal. The inability of
> plaintiff to recover an amount adequate to give the court jurisdiction does
> not show his bad faith or oust the jurisdiction. Nor does the fact that the
> complaint discloses the existence of a valid defense to the claim.[133]

Jurisdictional amount is thus ordinarily computed from the plaintiff's viewpoint
without regard to possible defenses, and plaintiff's good faith pleading controls
unless the court concludes to "a legal certainty" that he cannot recover the pleaded
amount.

When plaintiff seeks only liquidated — arithmetically ascertainable — damages,
the amount is easily determined. Suits seeking unliquidated damages, equitable
relief, or inherently unquantifiable relief have proven more difficult.

In suits seeking unliquidated damages, *legal certainty in law*[134] is established by
the legal unavailability of relief necessary to reach the jurisdictional amount. For
example, if the applicable law requires aggravating circumstances before punitive
damages can be recovered in a contract action, and the plaintiff has not and cannot
in good faith allege such circumstances, his prayer for punitive damages must be
disregarded as a matter of law.[135] Similarly, the applicable law may place a
statutory ceiling on the recovery[136] or may limit special damages to interest on
property in a suit to recover personal property.[137] As the Supreme Court put it as
early as 1798,[138] "where the law gives the rule, the legal cause of action, and not the
Plaintiff's demand, must be regarded."

Legal certainty in fact is much more difficult to find, because it requires a court
to appraise the evidentiary basis for plaintiff's claim. The court must chart a course

> between a rule on the one hand that allows some cases involving inflated
> claims for relief to be brought in a federal forum in order to insure access
> to that forum for all those cases that properly may be brought there, and,
> on the other hand, a rule that closes the doors to the federal forum in the
> face of some claims that properly could be brought there in order to insure
> the denial of the forum to cases involving inflated claims.[139]

The cases divide between the two approaches.

---

[133] 303 U.S. at 288–89 (footnotes omitted). However, if plaintiff fails at the end to recover the
jurisdictional amount, the court has the discretion to reverse the usual award of costs. 28 U.S.C.
§ 1332(b).

[134] *Kahal v. J.W. Wilson Assocs. Inc.*, 673 F.2d 547, 548 (D.C. Cir. 1982) (distinguishing between legal
certainty in law and in fact).

[135] *Kahal*, 673 F.2d at 549 (dismissing contract claim in which compensatory damages were below the
jurisdictional amount).

[136] *See, e.g., Ringsby Truck Lines, Inc. v. Beardsley*, 331 F.2d 14 (8th Cir. 1964).

[137] *See Vance v. W.A. Vandercook Co.*, 170 U.S. 468 (1898).

[138] *Wilson v. Daniel*, 3 U.S. (Dall.) 401, 408 (1798).

[139] *Deutsch v. Hewes St. Realty Corp.*, 359 F.2d 96, 100 (2d Cir. 1966).

Some courts give presumptive effect to plaintiff's claim of amount in controversy, no matter how unlikely it is that she will prevail on the facts at trial.[140] These courts reason that any other approach would run the risk of depriving the plaintiff of her right to a jury trial by converting the jurisdictional inquiry into a mini-trial of the merits.

Other courts test plaintiff's claim of amount in controversy for reasonableness in light of the evidence adduced in an evidentiary hearing on the motion to dismiss for lack of jurisdiction.[141] These courts assert that the focus on plaintiff's right to a jury trial begs the question whether she *has* a right to come into the federal court room to try her claim. Since judges may, through their power to set aside excessive verdicts,[142] place upper limits on jury awards, they should not be timid in relating that upper limit to the jurisdictional floor for purposes of deciding diversity jurisdiction.[143]

Actions for equitable relief pose special problems. In *Mississippi & Mo. R.R Co. v. Ward*,[144] a suit by a steamboat owner to abate the nuisance posed by a bridge over the Mississippi River, the Supreme Court declared that "removal of the obstruction is the matter of controversy, and the value of the object must govern." This rule focuses on the value of the object of the equitable relief, but value to whom? The value to plaintiff of having the obstruction removed will rarely be the same as the cost to defendant of having to remove it. A majority of courts have looked at the cost to the plaintiff if relief is not afforded,[145] while a minority have considered the greater of "the pecuniary result[s] to *either* party which the judgment would directly produce."[146] The minority rule seems preferable because otherwise a suit in which plaintiff seeks an injunction to remove a 50-story office building encroaching on a few inches of his land would fall outside the diversity jurisdiction of the federal courts despite the enormous expense to the defendant. Since "[t]he purpose of an amount in controversy requirement is to ensure the substantiality of the suit itself, not solely the amount which the plaintiff stands to recover," a federal court should

---

[140] *See, e.g.*, Deutsch v. Hewes St. Realty Corp., 359 F.2d 96, 100 (2d Cir. 1966).

[141] *See, e.g., Nelson v. Keefer*, 451 F.2d 289, 293 (3d Cir. 1971).

[142] *See* § 12.09[2][b] (new trials), *infra*.

[143] *Nelson*, 451 F.2d 289. *See also Jimenez Puig v. Avis Rent-A-Car Sys.*, 574 F.2d 37 (1st Cir. 1978) ("brief embarrassment" of having defendant's agent erroneously seize and destroy plaintiff's credit card for non-payment will not factually support punitive damages claim necessary to satisfy jurisdictional amount); *Sierra v. Lidchi*, 651 F. Supp. 1019 (D.P.R. 1986) (counterclaim for defamation based on hearsay allegation that plaintiff called defendant a thief will not support jurisdictional amount).

[144] 67 U.S. 485, 492 (1863).

[145] *See, e.g., City of Milwaukee v. Saxbe*, 546 F.2d 693, 702 (7th Cir. 1976); *cf. Glenwood Light & Water Co. v. Mutual Light, Heat & Power Co.*, 239 U.S. 121, 125 (1915) (measuring amount by harm to plaintiff's business rather than by defendant's cost of removal, without, however, expressly endorsing "plaintiff viewpoint" as the only test). The "plaintiff viewpoint" rule does not avail a defendant who seeks removal of a case brought in state court when the plaintiff's injury is below the jurisdictional amount. A few courts have therefore suggested that jurisdictional amount be measured from the viewpoint of the party who invokes federal jurisdiction. *See* Moore § 102.109[5].

[146] *Ronzio v. Denver & R.G.W.R. Co.*, 116 F.2d 604, 606 (10th Cir. 1940) (emphasis supplied). *See also McCarty v. Amoco Pipeline Co.*, 595 F.2d 389 (7th Cir. 1979) (discussing four tests for amounts in controversy in equitable actions); Moore § 102.109[1].

look to the largest effect on either party and take jurisdiction of such a suit, according to the minority view.[147]

Finally, the courts have found some claims involving inherently unquantifiable relief to fall outside monetarily limited jurisdiction grants. An early Supreme Court decision suggested that amount in controversy could be satisfied only "where the rights of property are concerned, and where the matter in dispute has a known and certain value, which can be proved and calculated, in the ordinary mode of a business transaction."[148] While the Court has since rejected any distinction between personal and property rights for jurisdictional purposes,[149] some courts still insist on susceptibility of the claim to ready pecuniary appraisal. In a suit by the Senate Watergate Committee to compel President Nixon to give up the Watergate tapes, for example, the court refused to place any monetary value on the interference with the Committee's constitutional obligations and therefore denied jurisdiction.[150] Courts have reached the same result in suits to compel inspection of a corporation's books and records, to prohibit divulging of telephone intercepts, to adjudicate lunacy, and to declare marital status.[151]

[2] Aggregating Multiple Claims

The discussion of amount in controversy to this point has assumed that plaintiff asserts a single claim against a single defendant. But liberal modern joinder rules encourage multiple claims, posing the question whether the amounts in controversy on such claims can be aggregated to satisfy the jurisdictional amount.[152] Unfortunately, the judge-made aggregation rules do not track the joinder rules and do not follow transactional or any other apparent logic. Consequently, "it is not altogether easy to say what the law is in this area, and it is quite hard to say why it is as it seems to be."[153] Consider three joinder situations: the plaintiff joins multiple claims against a single defendant; multiple parties, whether plaintiffs or defendants or both, are joined on one or more claims; defendant counterclaims against plaintiff.

It is well-established that a plaintiff may aggregate all the claims he asserts against a single defendant, whether or not they are transactionally related and whether or not any of them alone satisfies the jurisdictional amount.[154] Thus, in

---

[147] See MOORE § 102.109[4].

[148] Barry v. Mercein, 46 U.S. (5 How.) 103, 120 (1847).

[149] Lynch v. Household Fin. Corp., 405 U.S. 538 (1972).

[150] Senate Select Comm. on Presidential Campaign Activities v. Nixon, 366 F. Supp. 51, 59 (D.D.C. 1973). The amount in controversy requirement has since been abolished in general federal question cases. See note 129, supra.

[151] See cases cited in J. MOORE, MOORE'S FEDERAL PRACTICE ¶ 0.92[5] (2d. ed.).

[152] See generally WRIGHT § 36; Note, The Federal Jurisdictional Amount and Rule 20 Joinder of Parties: Aggregation of Claims, 53 MINN. L. REV. 94 (1968).

[153] WRIGHT § 36, at 209. But see Jeffrey L. Rosenberger, The Amount in Controversy: Understanding the Rules of Aggregation, 26 ARIZ. ST. L.J. 925 (1994) (asserting that aggregation rules are more firmly rooted in policy than commentators have supposed).

[154] MOORE § 102.108[1].

this joinder situation, aggregation is co-extensive with joinder under Rule 18.[155]

The rule is different, however, when plaintiff joins several defendants to the same claim or several plaintiffs join in the same claim against one or more defendants pursuant to Rule 20.[156] Aggregation is possible if several parties have a common undivided interest or title, but not if they have separate and independent interests.[157] For example, when multiple plaintiffs sue on the basis of common title, or multiple defendants assert common title as a defense to a suit to recover land, the matter in controversy is the entire tract of land, not just its several parts. Aggregation is therefore permitted.[158] On the other hand, the necessary common and undivided interest is not established merely because claims derive from a single instrument or because multiple parties share a community of interest.[159] Nor will the fact that defendants are joint tortfeasors justify aggregation; plaintiff's claim against each tortfeasor is ordinarily separate and distinct and must therefore stand alone for purposes of satisfying the jurisdictional amount.[160] The aggregation rules are thus more restrictive than Rule 20, governing joinder of parties, and are essentially artifacts of a bygone era before the liberalization of joinder in federal courts.

As discussed at greater length in § 5.11, supplemental jurisdiction can blunt the impact of diversity jurisdiction aggregation rules in limited circumstances. For example, suppose that A and B, joined as co-plaintiffs under rule 20, file $100,000 and $20,000 claims, respectively, against the defendant for injuries sustained in the same auto accident. Assuming complete diversity of citizenship, traditional, § 1332 aggregation rules would forbid B from adding her claim to A's to reach the required amount in controversy. But § 1367 supplemental jurisdiction rules characterize B as a party supplemental to A, which confers authority on the court to hear B's claim

---

[155] *See* § 9.02 (claim joinder), *infra.*

[156] *See* § 9.05[1] (permissive party joinder), *infra.*

[157] Wright §§ 36, 102.108[2]–[3]. The circuit courts are divided about whether punitive damages among plaintiff class members can be aggregated on the theory that they share a common and undivided interest in punishing the defendant and deterring the offending conduct. *See* Christopher J. Willis, *Aggregation of Punitive Damages in Diversity Class Actions: Will the Real Amount in Controversy Please Stand Up*, 30 Loy. L.A. L. Rev. 775 (1997). The answer is important in consumer class actions where the class members' individualized compensatory damages fall below $75,000 and there is no federal question jurisdiction.

[158] *Cornell v. Mabe*, 206 F.2d 514, 516 (5th Cir. 1953).

[159] Wright § 36.

[160] These rules applied to class actions as well and therefore required that each class member satisfy the jurisdictional amount when their claims are separate and distinct. *Zahn v. International Paper Co.*, 414 U.S. 291 (1973); *Snyder v. Harris*, 394 U.S. 332 (1969). However, the Supreme Court has now ruled that if a representative class member satisfies the amount in controversy, the court can exercise "supplemental jurisdiction" under 28 U.S.C. § 1367 over the below-amount claims of other class members. *See* § 5.11, *infra* (discussing impact of supplemental jurisdiction on the no-aggregation rule). In addition, in the Class Action Fairness Act of 2005, codified at 28 U.S.C. § 1332(d), Congress provided that an aggregate total of claims exceeding $5,000,000 would suffice for federal jurisdiction in certain class actions in which any member of the class is diverse from any defendant, thus superseding the usual requirement for such actions that all members, and even the requirement for supplemental jurisdiction that at least one class member assert a claim exceeding $75,000.

as a matter of supplemental jurisdiction.[161]

Finally, the logic of computing the amount in controversy from plaintiff's complaint alone and the separate and distinct nature of original claims and counterclaims suggest that their aggregation should not be permitted.[162] But in *Horton v. Liberty Mutual Insurance Co.*,[163] the Court held 5-4 that the then-$10,000 jurisdictional amount was satisfied when the plaintiff insurer alleged that defendant would counterclaim for $14,035, even though the insurer actually sued to set aside a workmen's compensation award of only $1050. Under Texas law, however, the insurer's suit reopened the entire compensation claim below regardless of the award and might therefore be viewed as an action for a judgment declaring the insurer's non-liability as to the entire $14,035 workmen's compensation claim. Most federal decisions have read the case as involving a quirk of Texas law and confined it to its facts.[164] But until the Supreme Court distinguishes or overrules *Horton* it leaves uncertain the question whether (and when) claims and counterclaims can be aggregated to satisfy the amount in controversy.

PART C.
Removal and Supplemental Jurisdiction

§ 5.07   REMOVAL JURISDICTION

[1]   In General

Removal jurisdiction is an exception to the usual rule that plaintiff chooses the court.[165] Although the Constitution makes no express provision for removal, it is now well-established that a defendant may, pursuant to statute,[166] remove a civil

---

[161] *Exxon Mobil Corp. v. Allapattah Services, Inc.*, 545 U.S. 546 (2005).

[162] On the other hand, a no-aggregation rule interacts with the removal provisions to permit a party with a small claim to force his adversary to litigate his much larger counterclaim in state court, provided that the former wins the race to the courthouse. WRIGHT § 37. It also risks a wasteful minuet whereby a plaintiff's complaint is dismissed despite a compulsory counterclaim that satisfies the jurisdictional amount, and then is reinstated as a compulsory counterclaim, now within the court's supplemental jurisdiction, to the defendant's now independently standing claim. 1 J. MOORE, MOORE'S FEDERAL PRACTICE ¶ 0.98[1] (2d ed.). This minuet, however, does serve to give the original defendant the choice whether to stay in the federal forum, which he would be denied by a rule of aggregation. 1 J. MOORE, MOORE'S FEDERAL PRACTICE ¶ 0.98[1] (2d ed.).

[163] 367 U.S. 348 (1961).

[164] *See* WRIGHT § 37.

[165] *See* Chapter 2, *supra*.

[166] The general removal statute is 28 U.S.C. § 1441, which is discussed in this section. Congress has also provided for removal of specific civil actions not discussed here. *See, e.g.*, 28 U.S.C. § 1442 (suits against federal officers); 28 U.S.C. § 1442a (suits against members of the armed forces); 28 U.S.C. § 1443 (suits in which civil rights are denied); 28 U.S.C. § 2679(d) (suits against federal employees arising out of motor vehicle accidents within the scope of employment). In addition, Congress has guaranteed plaintiffs their choice of forum by prohibiting removal in certain cases. *See, e.g.*, 28 U.S.C. § 1445(a)

action from a state court. The state court does not need to have either subject matter jurisdiction[167] or personal jurisdiction[168] in order for defendant to remove the case to federal court, although she is free to challenge personal jurisdiction when she gets there. The purpose of removal is to make the option of suit in federal court as available to defendants (except for resident defendants in a diversity-only case) as it is to plaintiffs.[169] This purpose has been given effect in several ways by the provisions of the general removal statute and by the judicial gloss upon them.

First, because removal is a protective option for defendants, only defendants may invoke it.[170] The courts have read this limitation strictly, prohibiting a plaintiff who is sued upon a federal counterclaim from removing on that account.[171] When there is more than one defendant, to secure removal to federal court all defendants must join in the notice of removal. A related statute creates an exception to this requirement in certain class actions.[172] Section 1441(c) includes a second exception. There, removal is authorized when the plaintiff's complaint combines a claim within the court's federal question jurisdiction with a state law claim over which the federal courts lack original or supplemental jurisdiction. In such cases, only those defendants subject to the federal question claim must join in the notice of removal because, pursuant to the statute, the state law claims will never be heard in federal court anyway.[173]

Second, because removal is intended just to make existing federal jurisdiction available to defendants, only civil actions "of which the district courts . . . have original jurisdiction . . . may be removed."[174] Thus, civil actions grounded in federal question and diversity jurisdiction (subject to an exception for in-state defendants discussed in the third point below) are eligible for removal, as are civil actions grounded in original jurisdiction that are accompanied by claims within the court's supplemental jurisdiction, which together could be filed in federal court originally.[175] Removal jurisdiction is therefore keyed to original jurisdiction, and all the rules and principles previously discussed concerning federal question and diversity jurisdiction apply. That is, the court decides on the facts as they existed at

---

(Federal Employers' Liability Act suits); 28 U.S.C. § 1445(c) (workmen's compensation suits); 46 U.S.C. § 30104 (Jones Act suits).

[167] 28 U.S.C. § 1441(f).

[168] *See Lambert Run Coal Co. v. Baltimore & Ohio R.R. Co.*, 258 U.S. 377 (1922).

[169] *See* Neal Miller, *An Empirical Study of Forum Choices in Removal Cases Under Diversity and Federal Question Jurisdiction*, 41 Am. U. L. Rev. 369 (1992) (finding that fear of local bias against out-of-state litigants is a significant factor in removal).

[170] 28 U.S.C. § 1441(a) (civil actions "may be removed by the defendant or the defendants").

[171] *See Shamrock Oil & Gas Corp. v. Sheets*, 313 U.S. 100 (1941). Realignment of the parties may affect designation of the "defendant." *See* § 5.04[2] (diversity between whom), *supra*.

[172] 28 U.S.C. § 1453(b).

[173] 28 U.S.C. § 1441(c).

[174] 28 U.S.C. § 1441(a).

[175] *Halmekangas v. State Farm Fire and Cas. Co.*, 603 F.3d 290 (5th Cir. 2010) (relying on *City of Chicago v. International College of Surgeons*, 522 U.S. 156, 164–65 (1997) ("with the right ingredients, § 1367 and 1441 can combine to bring into federal court a state claim originally filed in state court. Indeed, if a plaintiff files suit in state court alleging both federal and state claims arising out of the same controversy, the entire action may be removed to federal court").

the time the notice of removal was filed whether the action would have satisfied the requirements for federal jurisdiction had it originally been filed in federal court.[176] A court, however, may consider post-removal evidence of what those facts were at the time of filing.[177] Furthermore, the plaintiff may cure problems in a case nonremovable when filed by amending to increase the amount in controversy or to add a removable claim or by dismissing a non-diverse defendant, because removal jurisdiction is measured at the filing of the notice of removal, not the complaint.[178]

The interaction of the time-of-filing-notice rule with the well-pleaded complaint rule[179] creates an anomaly (some might say, perversity) of removal law: that a defendant who asserts a federal defense or counterclaim to a non-diverse plaintiff's state claim cannot remove (unless federal law has completely preempted state law in this area), inasmuch as a federal court would not have had original jurisdiction over the plaintiff's claim. The anomaly is that some important federal questions — those arising by way of defense — are stuck in state court, without rescue by removal.[180] On the other hand, the Court has repeatedly held that a plaintiff cannot defeat removal by artfully failing to plead potentially preemptive federal law.[181] "If the only remedy available to plaintiff is federal, because of preemption or otherwise, and the state court necessarily must look to federal law in passing on the claim, the case is removable regardless of what is in the pleading."[182]

---

[176] Ordinarily, therefore, the court does not have jurisdiction if it is only *after* removal that facts necessary to establish jurisdiction come into existence (for example, that the parties become diverse). In *Caterpillar Inc. v. Lewis*, 519 U.S. 61 (1996), however, the Supreme Court held that when incomplete diversity at the filing of the notice of removal was cured by dismissal of the non-diverse party before final judgment, that judgment could stand. It explained that once a case has been tried, "considerations of finality, efficiency, and economy become overwhelming." *Caterpillar Inc.*, 519 U.S. at 75. Setting aside a judgment entered when there was complete diversity would waste the federal resources expended in reaching the judgment and possibly impose the costs of retrying the case on state courts.

Subsequently, the Court explained that *Caterpillar* made only a limited exception for perfection of jurisdiction by dismissal of the non-diverse party and therefore "did not augur a new approach to deciding whether a jurisdictional defect has been cured." *Grupo Dataflux v. Atlas Global Group, L.P.*, 541 U.S. 567, 572 (2004). The exception, it asserted, is authorized by Rule 21, permitting dismissal of the jurisdiction-destroying party by motion or by the court *sua sponte*. *Grupo Dataflux*, 541 U.S. at 572–73.

[177] *See e.g.*, *Sierminski v. Transouth Fin. Corp.*, 216 F.3d 945 (11th Cir. 2000).

[178] Moore § 107.14[2][h]. As noted above, the removing party may also move to drop a jurisdiction-defeating party under Rule 21 even after removal, under a limited exception to the usual time-of-filing-notice rule. *See* n.176, *supra*.

[179] *See* § 5.03[2], *supra*.

[180] *See, e.g.*, *Oklahoma Tax Comm'n v. Graham*, 489 U.S. 838 (1989) (holding the case not removable despite the federal defense of tribal immunity to state tax claims). The Supreme Court has acknowledged that a rational jurisdictional system might well discard the equation of original and removal jurisdiction in these circumstances, since "the defendant's petition for removal could furnish the necessary guarantee that the case necessarily presented a substantial question of federal law." *Franchise Tax Bd.*, 463 U.S. at 11 n.9. But the Supreme Court also has noted that removal is statutory and that reform must therefore come from the Congress. 463 U.S. at 10–11.

[181] *See, e.g.*, *Avco Corp. v. Aero Lodge No. 735*, 390 U.S. 557 (1958); § 5.03[2], *supra*.

[182] 14B Wright & Miller § 3722. *See generally* Arthur R. Miller, *Artful Pleading: A Doctrine in Search of Definition*, 76 Tex. L. Rev. 1781 (1998); Robert A. Ragazzo, *Reconsidering the Artful Pleading Doctrine*, 44 Hastings L.J. 273 (1993). The courts, however, have increasingly distinguished "ordinary preemption" cases, which often fall outside federal question jurisdiction when plaintiff chooses to frame his claim purely in terms of state law, from "complete preemption" cases, in which the federal law is so

Third, because the protective rationale for removal is inapplicable to a defendant sued upon state law claims in his own state court, diversity cases are removable "only if none of the parties in interest properly joined and served as defendants is a citizen of the State in which such action is brought."[183] Thus, a citizen of Virginia sued in a Virginia state court by a citizen of Maryland may not remove the case to federal court — he does not need protection from his own state's court. In this respect, removal jurisdiction is narrower than original jurisdiction. Note, however, that a corresponding argument could be made against permitting plaintiffs to file original diversity claims in the federal courts of their home states, where the protective rationale is inapplicable to them, but no such bar exists. As a consequence, when it comes to diversity claims, plaintiffs and defendants have asymmetrical access to federal courts.

The procedure for removal is clearly laid out by statute.[184] Within thirty days after receipt of the pleading or other paper affording grounds for removal,[185] defendant must file a notice of removal in the federal court for the district encompassing the place where the state court action is pending,[186] setting forth a short and plain statement of the grounds for removal, together with all filings from the state court action. Filing of a copy of the notice with the state court perfects removal and ousts that court of all further jurisdiction; no permission of either court is required. The federal court thereafter proceeds under the Federal Rules of Civil Procedure[187] as if the case had been filed with it originally, without regard to the usual venue requirements.[188] Plaintiff may oppose the removal by a motion to remand, or the court will decide its jurisdiction *sua sponte*. If there is any doubt of removability, the court should *remand* — send the case back to state court — in accord with the rule of strict construction of jurisdictional statutes.[189] A decision to remand the case is unreviewable, except for remands in civil rights cases removed under a special statute.[190] Denial of a motion to remand is, of course, reviewable on appeal of the final judgment by the federal court.

Finally, removal is one-way, from state to federal court. While an improperly removed case can be sent back to state court by remand, there is no procedure for moving a case originally filed in federal court to state court. If for any reason, the

---

controlling that it necessarily substitutes a federally created cause of action for the state claim, however the latter is framed. 14B WRIGHT & MILLER § 3722.1.

[183] 28 U.S.C. § 1441(b).

[184] 28 U.S.C. §§ 1446–50.

[185] 28 U.S.C. § 1446(b). In addition, actions removed on grounds of diversity must be removed no more than one year after they were commenced in state court.

[186] 28 U.S.C. § 1441(a). This provision thus provides venue for the removed action, superseding the other federal venue statutes. *Polizzi v. Cowles Magazines, Inc.*, 345 U.S. 663, 665–66 (1953).

[187] *See* Rule 81(c).

[188] *See* 14C WRIGHT & MILLER § 3726.

[189] *See* WRIGHT § 41.

[190] 28 U.S.C. § 1447(d) (exempting remand of civil rights cases removed under 28 U.S.C. § 1443 from the bar on appeal). A remand for other reasons may be reviewed for abuse of discretion. *Thermtron Prods., Inc. v. Hermansdorfer*, 423 U.S. 336 (1976). Commentators have criticized the statutory bar on appeal as anachronistic and destructive of federal rights. *See* Rhonda Wasserman, *Rethinking Review of Remands: Proposed Amendments to the Federal Statute*, 43 EMORY L.J. 83 (1994).

federal court lacks jurisdiction, it can only dismiss the case, not send it to state court. (Nor, as we will see in Chapter 6, can it transfer the case to state court. *Transfer* is a term of art for changing the *venue* within a court system — for moving a case from a court within a state to another court within the same state, or from one federal district court to another federal district court, for reasons of convenience. There is no transfer *between* states, between the state and federal courts, or between U.S. and foreign courts.)

Congress, of course, can change the foregoing restrictions on removal and did in the Class Action Fairness Act of 2005.[191] In response to alleged abuses of class action rules in state courts, Congress made removal of such actions to federal court easier by abolishing the restriction against removal by in-state defendants, the requirement that all defendants join in the notice of removal, the one-year time limit on removal, and the bar on appellate review of decisions to remand. Instead, it carved out some exceptions for local and for certain other controversies, and gave the court discretion to refuse removal in certain other circumstances.[192]

[2] Removal of Joined Federal and State Law Claims

Suppose that P, a citizen of Virginia, joins a state law claim to a federal question claim against D, also a citizen of Virginia. Should we allow D only to remove the latter to federal court? If partial removal is not allowed, plaintiffs will have an incentive to join non-removable claims to removable claims in state court in order to defeat removal of the case. On the other hand, if partial removal is allowed, it would put each claim in its "own" court system, which could promote inefficiently duplicative litigation, at least in cases where the claims are factually related.

Congress originally responded by authorizing removal of "the entire case" containing one or more "separate and independent claim[s] or cause[s] of action which would be removable if sued upon alone," vesting discretion in the federal judge to retain the entire case or to remand the independently non-removable claims. "Separate and independent" was originally given a restrictive interpretation by the Supreme Court in a diversity case,[193] and the lower court case law is complex and often inconsistent. Today it can perhaps best be generalized as construing the requirement to mean "factually unrelated."[194] In 1990, Congress restricted separate and independent claim removal to cases in which the independently removable claim poses a federal question. Congress authorized the federal court, in the judge's discretion, to retain the whole removed case or to remand "all matters in which State law predominates." However, Congress may have largely mooted this branch of removal jurisdiction by enacting

---

[191] Codified at 28 U.S.C. § 1332(d)(11).

[192] *See generally* William B. Rubenstein, Understanding the Class Action Fairness Act of 2005, *available at* http://www.classactionprofessor.com/cafa-analysis.pdf. For further discussion of the impact of the Act on class action litigation, see § 9.09, *infra*.

[193] *American Fire & Cas. Co. v. Finn*, 341 U.S. 6 (1951) (claims arising from a "single wrong" are not separate and independent).

[194] *See* Moore § 107.14[6][d] (discussing cases which appear to apply this interpretation).

supplemental jurisdiction at the same time.[195] If the otherwise non-removable state law claim is part of the same constitutional case or controversy as the federal question claim (essentially, arising from the same transaction, as we discuss below), then the state law claim falls within the supplemental jurisdiction of the court[196] and can be removed pursuant to sections 1441(a) & (b) of the statute.

If the state law claim does not fall within the same constitutional case or controversy as the federal question claim (that is, it arises from a different transaction), then the removal of the state law claim to federal court may present a serious constitutional question: whether Article III permits jurisdiction if the claim is unsupported by federal question, diversity, or supplemental jurisdiction.[197] In 2011, Congress resolved the issue by revising the removal statute to retain separate and independent claim removal (under the new name, "joinder of federal law claims and state law claims") but requiring the district court to remand those claims that lack jurisdictional support.[198] In effect, the 2011 legislation authorizes partial removal, enabling a defendant to remove cases that include federal question claims to federal court while requiring the district court to remand to the state courts any joined state claims that are unsupported by original or supplemental jurisdiction.

§ 5.08   OVERVIEW OF SUPPLEMENTAL JURISDICTION AND ITS ANTECEDENTS

All cases that fall within the subject matter jurisdiction of the federal courts must begin with the allegation of at least one claim capable of invoking a statutory grant of federal subject matter jurisdiction. Many federal cases are made up entirely of these claims. But sometimes a federal court will use its statutory subject matter jurisdiction over one such predicate or "anchor" claim to justify its adjudication of one or more related claims that would not independently satisfy subject matter jurisdictional requirements. Such extended jurisdiction[199] histori-

[195] David D. Siegel, 28 U.S.C.A. § 1441 commentary (1990).

[196] See § 5.11 infra.

[197] See TEPLY & WHITTEN, Chap. 2, § C(5); William Cohen, Problems in the Removal of a Separate and Independent Claim or Cause of Action, 46 MINN. L. REV. 1, 20–25 (1961). But see Joan Steinman, Supplemental Jurisdiction in § 1441 Removed Cases: An Unsurveyed Frontier of Congress' Handiwork, 35 ARIZ. L. REV. 305 (1993). In Twentieth Century-Fox Film Corp. v. Taylor, 239 F. Supp. 913 (S.D.N.Y. 1965), the court suggested that the prior version of § 1441(c) gave it removal jurisdiction over the independent claims and was a valid exercise of Congress' authority under the Necessary and Proper Clause. The Supreme Court has yet to rule on the question.

[198] 28 U.S.C. § 1441(c).

[199] See, e.g., Richard D. Freer, A Principled Statutory Approach to Supplemental Jurisdiction, 1987 DUKE L.J. 34; Richard A. Matasar, Rediscovering "One Constitutional Case": Procedural Rules and the Rejection of the Gibbs Test for Supplemental Jurisdiction, 71 CAL. L. REV. 1399, 1402 n.3 (1983) ("supplemental jurisdiction . . . suggests an extension of power over claims normally outside federal jurisdiction in order to serve important federal interests that supplement the purposes underlying the decision of the original federal claims"); Note, A Closer Look at Pendent and Ancillary Jurisdiction: Toward a Theory of Incidental Jurisdiction, 95 HARV. L. REV. 1935 (1982) [hereinafter cited as Incidental Jurisdiction]. Neel K. Chopra, Valuing the Federal Right: Reevaluating the Outer Limits of Supplemental Jurisdiction, 83 N.Y.U.L. REV. 1915 (2008).

cally evolved under the separate labels of *pendent* and *ancillary* jurisdiction, although the courts' terminology was often inconsistent.[200] In 1990, Congress codified much of the prior law of pendent and ancillary jurisdiction as *supplemental jurisdiction.*[201] After introducing the terminology in this section, in succeeding sections we explore pendent, ancillary and supplemental jurisdiction in greater detail.

As used here, *pendent jurisdiction* refers to the courts' extension of jurisdiction from a claim that independently falls within federal (usually federal question) jurisdiction — the anchor claim — [202] to an otherwise jurisdictionally insufficient (usually state law) claim by a plaintiff or plaintiffs. Since the latter thus depends on the anchor claim for jurisdiction, it is commonly called the *pendent claim.* Pendent jurisdiction applied, for example, to a state claim for unauthorized use of a play that plaintiff joins with an anchor federal claim for copyright violation against a non-diverse defendant. Commentators also coined the phrase *pendent party jurisdiction* to describe jurisdiction extended from the anchor claim to a pendent claim against a new party that would not independently fall within the court's subject matter jurisdiction.

A rationale of convenience supported pendent jurisdiction.[203] It avoided piecemeal lawsuits and the unnecessary decision of federal questions in federal courts by allowing them to hear and decide related state law questions. It also avoided duplicative litigation in state courts that might otherwise have resulted from the plaintiff's splitting of related federal and state law claims between the two court systems. But convenience was not the sole rationale for pendent jurisdiction. It also promoted the protective purposes of federal jurisdiction by giving the plaintiff with related federal and state claims unimpeded access to the federal forum.[204] Without pendent jurisdiction, plaintiff would have to (1) split her claims between federal and state courts, running the risk that a state court judgment would preclude her from relitigating common issues in the federal action; (2) forgo one of her claims in favor of litigating just the other in one forum; or (3) pursue both claims in state court, when the federal claim is not within the exclusive jurisdiction of the federal court, thereby forgoing the protection of federal court jurisdiction.[205]

---

[200] *See, e.g., County of Oakland v. City of Berkley,* 742 F.2d 289, 296 (6th Cir. 1984) (court expresses uncertainty whether lower court exercised pendent or ancillary jurisdiction); *By-Prod Corp. v. Armen-Berry Co.,* 668 F.2d 956, 962 (7th Cir. 1982) (discussing ancillary jurisdiction over defendant's counterclaim as "pendent jurisdiction").

[201] 28 U.S.C. § 1367.

[202] *See generally* § 5.03 (statutory scope), *supra.* Various federal jurisdictional grants will support the anchor claim, including admiralty jurisdiction. *See, e.g., Leather's Best, Inc. v. S.S. Mormaclynx,* 451 F.2d 800 (2d Cir. 1971) (admiralty). At least one court has held that even diversity jurisdiction will support the anchor. *See Seybold v. Francis P. Dean, Inc.,* 628 F. Supp. 912 (W.D. Pa. 1986) (diversity, where pendent claim was jurisdictionally insufficient federal claim).

[203] *See, e.g.,* Richard A. Matasar, *A Pendent and Ancillary Jurisdiction Primer: The Scope and Limits of Supplemental Jurisdiction,* 17 U.C. Davis L. Rev. 103, 152 (1983); Note, *Unraveling the "Pendent Party" Controversy: A Revisionist Approach to Pendent and Ancillary Jurisdiction,* 64 B.U. L. Rev. 895, 900, 927 n.170 (1985) [hereinafter cited as *Revisionist Approach*].

[204] Matasar, note 199, *supra,* at 1402 n.3, 1404–07 n.6; Friedenthal, Kane & Miller § 2.12.

[205] Matasar, note 199, *supra,* at 1402 n.3, 1404–07 n.6.

In contrast, *ancillary jurisdiction* extended jurisdiction from the anchor (often diversity) claim to an otherwise jurisdictionally insufficient claim by the defendant(s) or similarly situated parties such as intervenors as of right,[206] who, as a practical matter, did not choose the forum. The latter was often called the *ancillary claim*. In a diversity action, for example, ancillary jurisdiction supported a compulsory counterclaim or cross-claim for less than the jurisdictional amount or an impleader of a non-diverse party. The rationale was one of fairness and necessity. Ancillary jurisdiction permitted the federal courts to give full and effective relief by hearing claims and deciding rights that might be lost or compromised if forced into another forum.[207] This is particularly necessary as a matter of fairness to parties who are involuntarily in the federal forum and who assert essentially defensive claims.[208]

Whether a court could exercise either pendent or ancillary jurisdiction was initially a question of constitutional power. Article III sets the constitutional boundaries on federal subject matter jurisdiction and appears to confine it to the nine listed heads of jurisdiction.[209] Yet Article III speaks to judicial power over "cases" arising under federal law and "controversies" between diverse citizens, not over questions or issues. Thus, provided that a civil action has within it at least one jurisdictionally sufficient anchor claim, a federal court arguably has the constitutional power to hear any otherwise jurisdictionally insufficient claims which are part of the same constitutional case.[210] The trick is to define the parameters of a constitutional case: to determine what relationship is required between the anchor claim and the jurisdictionally dependent claims for them to be considered part of the same case. The focal point of analysis is therefore the particular relationship between the anchor claim,[211] which is jurisdictionally self-sufficient, and the dependent (pendent or ancillary) claim, which is not.

Even if a court has constitutional power to extend its jurisdiction, it must still satisfy itself that it has statutory power and that it should exercise its power in the circumstances. If so, then it may hear and decide additional claims without regard to venue over them.[212] Personal jurisdiction over each of the parties is also still required, but is often obtained for pendent or ancillary claims by plaintiff's reliance on the 100-mile bulge rule,[213] federal statutory provision for nationwide service of

---

[206] *See* § 9.08[1], *infra*.

[207] *Revisionist Approach*, note 203, *supra*, at 900; Matasar, note 199, *supra*, 17 U.C. Davis L. Rev. at 151–52.

[208] *See, e.g., Incidental Jurisdiction*, note 199, *supra*, at 1937.

[209] *See* § 5.01[2] (federal subject matter jurisdiction), *supra*.

[210] *United Mine Workers v. Gibbs*, 383 U.S. 715, 725 (1966). *See also Osborn*, 22 U.S. at 821, discussed in § 5.02, *supra*.

[211] The cases and commentators regularly refer to the anchor claim as a "federal" claim, and the dependent claim as the "nonfederal claim." *See, e.g., Owen Equip. & Erection Co. v. Kroger*, 437 U.S. 365, 372 n.11 (1978). Because the anchor claim can be an admiralty or a state claim within diversity jurisdiction, this usage is somewhat confusing and is therefore not followed here.

[212] Wright §§ 9 & 19.

[213] Rule 4(k) (allowing service within 100 miles of courthouse). *See generally* §§ 4.03[2] (service), *supra*, 9.05[2] (compulsory joinder) & 9.06 (impleader), *infra*.

process on the federal claims,[214] or defendants' waiver of personal jurisdiction.

§ 5.09   PENDENT JURISDICTION

[1]   Pendent Claim Jurisdiction

The leading case of pendent jurisdiction is *United Mine Workers v. Gibbs*.[215] Gibbs sued the non-diverse United Mine Workers in federal court for violations of the federal Labor Management Relations Act and of the common law of Tennessee as a result of its interference with his hauling contract during a labor dispute. After the jury decided for Gibbs on both claims, the trial court set aside the verdict on the federal claim, reasoning that the union interference was not cognizable under federal law, but entered judgment on the state law claim. The Court of Appeals affirmed, and the Supreme Court was presented the question whether the federal courts had jurisdiction over the pendent state claim in the absence of diversity. The Court held that constitutional power exists to decide the pendent claim whenever it is so related to the federal claim that they comprise "but one constitutional 'case.' "[216] It suggested a three-part test for *constitutional case*.

First, to anchor such a case, plaintiff must assert a federal claim that has "substance sufficient to confer subject matter jurisdiction on the court."[217] Gibbs's anchor claim met the requirements for federal question jurisdiction,[218] asserting a right to relief created by the federal Labor Management Relations Act. That is, he presented a substantial federal question in a well-pleaded complaint that passed the creation test for federal question jurisdiction.

Second, the anchor and pendent claims "must derive from a common nucleus of operative fact."[219] In so ruling, the Court discarded as "unnecessarily grudging" a "cause of action" test for constitutional case which confined the term *case* to alternative federal and nonfederal grounds for the same cause of action.[220] Since Gibbs' federal anchor and pendent state law claims involved overlapping facts concerning the union's actions, the common nucleus requirement was satisfied. But it would also be consistent with an expansive exposition of Article III power over "cases" to find the requirement satisfied by less than substantial overlap, even just a common origin in the same-transaction-or-occurrence or simply a logical relationship between the claims, like that required for several forms of joinder

---

[214] *Wright* § 9 (noting split of authority concerning whether availability of nationwide service confers ancillary jurisdiction over jurisdictionally insufficient claims).

[215] 383 U.S. 715 (1966).

[216] 383 U.S. at 725.

[217] 383 U.S. at 725.

[218] *See* § 5.03, *infra*.

[219] *Gibbs*, 383 U.S. at 725.

[220] The cause of action test was set forth in the pre-rules case of *Hurn v. Oursler*, 289 U.S. 238 (1933). But the concept of "cause of action" has presented serious ambiguities in all of its applications, *see, e.g.*, § 15.03 (res judicata), *infra*, causing the drafters of the rules to reject it in favor of "civil action." Rule 2. The *Gibbs* court noted this history in discarding *Hurn*. *Gibbs*, 383 U.S. at 722–25.

under the federal rules of civil procedure.[221] Most courts have opted for this definition of common nucleus.[222]

Third, *Gibbs* seemed also to require that the federal and nonfederal claims be such that the plaintiff "would ordinarily be expected to try them all in one judicial proceeding."[223] This apparently referred to a plaintiff's anticipation of the possible claim-preclusive effects of a federal judgment on the anchor claim in subsequent state court suits asserting the jurisdictionally insufficient claims. Under the modern law of claim preclusion or res judicata,[224] a plaintiff is expected to try all transactionally-related claims together, in that he is precluded by a final judgment on any of them from subsequently trying the others. The expected-to-try part of the *Gibbs* test for constitutional case was therefore perhaps best viewed as a restatement of the common nucleus requirement rather than an independent requirement.[225]

Constitutional power to exercise pendent jurisdiction was decided on the pleadings. But *Gibbs* also held that the "power need not be exercised in every case in which it is found to exist."[226] "Needless decisions of state law should be avoided" to assure both comity and "surer-footed reading" of state law.[227] In addition,

---

[221] Joinder under Rules 13(a) (compulsory counterclaims), 13(g) (cross-claims), and 20 (permissive joinder of parties) requires that the joined claim arise out of the same transaction or occurrence that is the subject matter of existing claims. Most modern courts have interpreted this transactional nexus to mean simply a "logical relationship" between the claims. *See, e.g., Great Lakes Rubber Corp. v. Herbert Cooper Co.*, 286 F.2d 631 (3d Cir. 1961). *See generally* §§ 9.02–9.05 (simple joinder), *infra*.

Professor Matasar illustrates the difference between factual overlap and logical relationship by positing an action by a welfare recipient from whom a social worker has gathered confidential information and then disclosed the same to third persons. *See* Matasar, note 199, *supra*, at 129–32. If the federal claim is that the information was gathered in violation of federal regulations, and the state claim is that it was disclosed in violation of state privacy law, there is neither factual identity nor overlap between the claims. They arguably arise out of the same transaction and are logically related, however, which would permit pendent jurisdiction under the broadest interpretation of "common nucleus of operative fact." Matasar, at 132; *cf. Reyes v. Edmunds*, 416 F. Supp. 649 (D. Minn. 1976). *But cf. Mason v. Richmond Motor Co., Inc.*, 625 F. Supp. 883 (E.D. Va. 1986) (rejecting "[m]ere commonality of facts" in favor of a stricter test).

[222] At least one court has suggested that the "common nucleus of operative fact" test is broader than the "transaction or occurrence" test of the federal rules. *See Ambromovage v. United Mine Workers*, 726 F.2d 972, 990 (3d Cir. 1984). The Supreme Court has also implied that the constitutional case may include factually unrelated claims whose resolution is necessary and proper to give full effect to a federal court's federal subject matter jurisdiction. *See* § 5.10, *infra*.

[223] *Gibbs*, 383 U.S. at 725.

[224] *See* §§ 15.02–15.05, *infra*. The older law of claim preclusion gave preclusive effect only to those claims which were part of the same "cause of action," § 15.03, *infra*, precisely the test that *Gibbs* expressly rejected in adopting the common nucleus test.

[225] Matasar, note 199, *supra*, at 138. *But see* 13D WRIGHT & MILLER § 3567.1 (requirements are cumulative).

[226] 383 U.S. at 726.

[227] 383 U.S. at 726. Federal court decision of unsettled state law questions poses at least two serious federalism concerns. There is no mechanism by which federal errors of state law can be corrected on appeal by state courts, and state courts may be reluctant in later cases to reject even "lead-footed" federal decisions of state law because of intervening public reliance on the latter. *See Financial Gen. Bankshares, Inc. v. Metzger*, 680 F.2d 768, 772–75 (D.C. Cir. 1982) (explaining why trial court abused its

justification for pendent jurisdiction lay "in considerations of judicial economy, convenience and fairness to litigants," which differ from case to case and from one stage of a single case to another. Whether a court should exercise its power of pendent jurisdiction was therefore a question of discretion open throughout the case.

The factors that guided the exercise of discretion reflected these considerations and comity concerns. Timing of the disposition of the anchor claim was a key factor. Ordinarily if the anchor claim was resolved early in the litigation, refusing jurisdiction over pendent state claims would not result in wasteful duplication of effort and could well yield a "surer-footed" decision of state law from the state court in which the refused claims would then have to be brought. In fact, dictum in *Gibbs* stated that state claims "[c]ertainly . . . should be dismissed" without prejudice if the federal claims were dismissed before trial.[228] The Court subsequently backed away from its dictum,[229] however, and most lower courts recognized that the timing of dismissal was only a surrogate for a more basic factor: the likelihood of wasteful duplication of effort should pendent jurisdiction be refused.[230]

Predominance of state claims — in terms of proof, scope or remedy — was also a factor weighing against pendent jurisdiction. Exercising pendent jurisdiction when the state claims predominate and the federal claims drop out of the case before trial "smacks of the tail wagging the dog."[231]

The possibility of jury confusion was another factor, since the possible cure of ordering separate trials on the anchor and pendent claims[232] could sacrifice the judicial economy that in part justified pendent jurisdiction.

On the other hand, these factors could be outweighed by a close connection between the state claims and federal policy. For example, in *Gibbs* itself there was a substantial question whether the state law claim was preempted by federal labor law, which "afforded a special reason for the exercise of pendent jurisdiction."[233]

[2] Pendent Party Jurisdiction[234]

Gibbs presented the classic case of pendent jurisdiction, in which the plaintiff appended state law claims to an anchor federal law claim against the same defendant. But *Gibbs* also acknowledged that "[u]nder the [federal] [r]ules, the

---

discretion in exercising jurisdiction over pendent claim involving unsettled state law after pretrial disposition of federal claims). On the difficulty of ascertaining the meaning of state law, see generally § 7.06, *infra*.

[228] 383 U.S. at 726.

[229] *See Rosado v. Wyman*, 397 U.S. 397 (1970) (approving pendent jurisdiction after federal claims became moot before trial, where substantial time and energy had been expended on case).

[230] *See, e.g., Financial Gen. Bankshares, Inc.*, 680 F.2d at 773–74 (and cases there cited).

[231] *McFaddin Express, Inc. v. Adley Corp.*, 346 F.2d 424, 427 (2d Cir. 1965), *cert. denied*, 382 U.S. 1026 (1966).

[232] *See* Rule 42(a) (separate trials).

[233] 383 U.S. at 729.

[234] *See generally* David P. Currie, *Pendent Parties*, 45 U. Chi. L. Rev. 753 (1978).

impulse is toward entertaining the broadest possible scope of action consistent with fairness to the parties; joinder of claims, *parties* and remedies is strongly encouraged."[235] Accordingly, some plaintiffs invoked *pendent party jurisdiction* to assert claims against new parties over whom independent federal subject matter jurisdiction was unavailable.

Such jurisdiction, for example, was invoked in diversity cases to add a defendant on a claim for less than the jurisdictional amount in controversy.[236] This form of pendent party jurisdiction, however, offends the rule against aggregating claims for amount in controversy in diversity cases.[237] In *Zahn v. International Paper Co.*,[238] the Court applied the rule forbidding aggregation of the plaintiffs' claims against different defendants (absent suit upon a joint and undivided interest) to deny pendent party jurisdiction in a class action in which the parties did not all meet the amount in controversy requirement. *Zahn* thus suggested, though it did not decide, that pendent party jurisdiction generally could not be used to avoid the rule against aggregation.[239]

Pendent party jurisdiction was also invoked in federal question cases to add non-diverse parties to state law claims. In *Aldinger v. Howard*,[240] however, the Court cast doubt over this form of extended jurisdiction. Plaintiff had brought a civil rights action against the county treasurer and then appended a transactionally-related state law claim against the county and its commissioners. The Court refused jurisdiction over the state claim despite its factual overlap with the federal claims. It explained first that there is a difference between simply adding a state law claim against a defendant already in court on a jurisdictionally sufficient federal question and adding a new defendant on a pendent claim. Arguably the latter is a further, and often more burdensome, extension of jurisdiction than the former. The Court then noted that jurisdiction over the county was, in any event, expressly negated by a fair reading of the Civil Rights Act.[241]

At the same time, the Court in *Aldinger* was careful not to rule out pendent party jurisdiction altogether. "Other statutory grants and other alignments of parties and claims might call for a different result."[242] For example, the Court suggested[243] that if an anchor claim was within the exclusive jurisdiction of the

---

[235] 383 U.S. at 724 (emphasis added).

[236] *See, e.g., F.C. Stiles Contracting Co. v. Home Ins. Co.*, 431 F.2d 917 (6th Cir. 1970).

[237] *See* § 5.06[2] (aggregating multiple claims), *supra*.

[238] 414 U.S. 291 (1973).

[239] *See* Darell D. Bratton, *Pendent Jurisdiction in Diversity Cases — Some Doubts*, 11 San Diego L. Rev. 296, 322–23 (1974).

[240] 427 U.S. 1 (1976).

[241] 427 U.S. at 16. It later changed its mind about the Act. *Monell v. New York City Dep't of Social Servs.*, 436 U.S. 658 (1978). The Court also denied pendent party jurisdiction in a diversity case in which plaintiff tried to assert a state law claim against a non-diverse third party defendant. The statutory requirement of complete diversity negated the existence of pendent party jurisdiction in such circumstances. *Kroger*, 437 U.S. at 365. *See* § 5.10, *infra*, for further discussion of *Kroger* as an ancillary jurisdiction case; § 9.06, *infra*, for further discussion of third-party practice.

[242] 427 U.S. at 18.

[243] 427 U.S. at 18.

federal courts, then *only* in federal court can all the claims be heard together. Allowing pendent party jurisdiction in this case would arguably effectuate the special protective purpose of exclusive federal jurisdiction. Consequently, *Aldinger* may still have held open the door of the federal court to pendent party jurisdiction when the anchor and pendent claims share a common nucleus of operative fact, and when jurisdiction, given the alignment of the parties, was not expressly or impliedly negated by the anchoring jurisdictional statute.[244]

To the general surprise of commentators, however, the Court slammed that door shut in *Finley v. United States*.[245] *Finley* presented precisely the case about which the *Aldinger* Court had speculated: plaintiff asserted an anchor claim within the exclusive jurisdiction of the federal courts[246] and sought to join transactionally-related state law claims against non-diverse defendants. Absent pendent party jurisdiction, plaintiff would be forced to forgo her state law claims against the non-diverse parties or to bring separate actions in federal and state court. The Court acknowledged the inefficiency and inconvenience of this result, yet denied pendent party jurisdiction because the underlying jurisdictional statute contained no "affirmative grant of pendent-party jurisdiction."[247] The Court thus turned the *Aldinger* search for implied congressional negation of pendent jurisdiction into a requirement for congressional affirmation of such jurisdiction.[248] Because Section 1331 (general federal question jurisdiction) and most other federal jurisdictional statutes are silent about pendent jurisdiction, the logic of *Aldinger* imperiled all pendent (and all ancillary) jurisdiction,[249] notwithstanding the Court's disclaimer of any "intent to limit or impair" the *Gibbs* line of cases.[250]

---

[244] Every circuit but the Ninth upheld exercises of pendent party jurisdiction after *Aldinger*. *See Feigler v. Tidex, Inc.*, 826 F.2d 1435, 1438 (5th Cir. 1987) (so noting). *See generally* Samuel Hoar, Note, *Unraveling the "Pendent Party" Controversy: A Revisionist Approach to Pendent and Ancillary Jurisdiction*, 64 B.U. L. REV. 895, 938 (1985) (suggesting the test whether fairness in the circumstances compels a statutory interpretation that would allow jurisdiction); Matasar, note 199, *supra*, at 163–65 (expressing doubt that there is a practical difference between a claim and a party in light of possible net efficiency to judicial system of joining the latter).

[245] 490 U.S. 545 (1989).

[246] 28 U.S.C. § 1346(b) (conferring exclusive jurisdiction of "civil actions on claims against the United States").

[247] 490 U.S. at 553.

[248] *See, e.g.*, Richard D. Freer, *Compounding Confusion and Hampering Diversity: Life After Finley and the Supplemental Jurisdiction Statute*, 40 EMORY L.J. 445, 465–66 (1991) ("In *Finley*, the presumption [of congressional authorization for pendent jurisdiction] is turned 180 degrees.").

[249] Some courts read *Finley* "as sounding the death knell" for at least pendent party jurisdiction, *see, e.g., Sarmiento v. Texas Bd. of Veterinary Med. Exam'rs*, 939 F.2d 1242, 1247 (5th Cir. 1991), and the commentators went further. *See, e.g.*, Thomas M. Mengler, *The Demise of Pendent and Ancillary Jurisdiction*, 1990 BYU L. REV. 247 (1990); Wendy Collins Perdue, *Finley v. United States: Unstringing Pendent Jurisdiction*, 76 VA. L. REV. 539 (1990).

[250] 490 U.S. at 556. *See also* C. Douglas Floyd, *Three Faces of Supplemental Jurisdiction After the Demise of* United Mine Workers v. Gibbs, 60 FLA. L. REV. 277 (2008).

§ 5.10   ANCILLARY JURISDICTION

Ancillary jurisdiction originally developed independently of pendent jurisdiction. In *Freeman v. Howe*,[251] a United States marshal had seized certain railroad cars under a writ of attachment issued by a federal court sitting in diversity. The railroad's mortgagees sought replevin (return of property) against the marshal in state court, but were ultimately rebuffed when the Supreme Court held that the state court was powerless to interfere with property under federal judicial control. They were therefore left without a forum in which to pursue their claims to the property unless they could get into federal court. Despite their lack of diversity to the marshal and the absence of any federal question, the Court said that they could have asserted their claims in federal court on the theory that their claim was "ancillary and dependent, supplementary merely to the original suit, out of which it had arisen."[252] The justification for this extension of jurisdiction was clearly fairness — necessity from the perspective of the mortgagees — in that they were otherwise unable to assert their rights to the property in any forum.

Subsequently in *Moore v. New York Cotton Exchange*,[253] the Court extended ancillary jurisdiction in a federal antitrust action to a transactionally-related state law counterclaim, emphasizing the close, mirror-image relationship between the claims.[254] The necessity or fairness to a defendant of having such a counterclaim heard in federal court was not comparable to the necessity presented by the mortgagees in *Freeman*. Presumably the convenience of litigating the claims at the same time supported ancillary jurisdiction in this setting, although the Court did not elaborate or even characterize the jurisdiction as ancillary. But by premising the extension of jurisdiction on the close factual relationship between the claims, *Moore* led the eventual expansion of ancillary jurisdiction to transactionally-related joinders of claims and parties under the Federal Rules of Civil Procedure.

The expansion was summarized, and perhaps slowed, by the 1978 decision in *Owen Equipment & Erection Co. v. Kroger*.[255] There the Court found two broad requirements for ancillary jurisdiction in diversity cases.

First, ancillary jurisdiction, like pendent jurisdiction, required constitutional power to hear the jurisdictionally insufficient claims. The Court "assume[d] without deciding" that the *Gibbs* common nucleus requirement delineates the outer constitutional boundaries of federal diversity as well as federal question jurisdiction.[256]

---

[251]   65 U.S. (24 How.) 450 (1860).

[252]   65 U.S. (24 How.) at 460.

[253]   270 U.S. 593 (1926).

[254]   270 U.S. at 610 ("[I]t only needs the failure of the [antitrust claim] to establish a foundation for the [counterclaim].").

[255]   437 U.S. 365 (1978).

[256]   437 U.S. at 372. The Court wisely declined to decide the question because its own prior cases suggest that a common nucleus of operative fact is only a sufficient and not a necessary predicate for constitutional power. *Freeman* itself allowed apparently unrelated claims to be asserted against the property under the court's ancillary jurisdiction, 65 U.S. (24 How.) 450, and the Court has approved ancillary jurisdiction over unrelated claims by a receiver to collect a debtor's assets and by and against

Second, ancillary jurisdiction required a court to determine that Congress had neither expressly nor impliedly negated the exercise of jurisdiction, a determination based upon "the posture in which the nonfederal claim is asserted" and an examination of the anchoring jurisdictional statute.[257] In *Kroger*, the plaintiff was attempting to assert a state law claim against a non-diverse third-party defendant in a diversity case. Unlike the defendant who had brought the third-party defendant into the case, however, the plaintiff had voluntarily chosen the federal forum. "By contrast, ancillary jurisdiction typically involves claims by a defending party haled into court against his will, or by another person whose rights might be irretrievably lost unless he could assert them in an ongoing action in a federal court."[258] Thus, the posture in which the dependent claim was asserted did not suggest such unfairness to plaintiff from denying ancillary jurisdiction as to overcome the usual statutory requirement of complete diversity.[259] On the other hand, the Court's analysis would presumably have supported a transactionally-related claim by the involuntary third-party defendant against the plaintiff, and, once such a claim is entertained, perhaps any claim by the plaintiff in the nature of a transactionally-related counterclaim, since such a claim would then be asserted defensively.[260]

The Court's analysis of ancillary jurisdiction explains the doctrine's extension to at least impleader under Rule 14,[261] presented by *Kroger* itself, cross-claims under Rule 13(g), compulsory counterclaims under Rule 13(a), parties added under Rule 13(h) to cross-claims and compulsory counterclaims, and sometimes intervention as of right under Rule 24(a).[262] Each of these kinds of joinder requires a transactional nexus under the rules between the joined and the anchor claim (thus presumptively satisfying the common nucleus requirement), and each is invoked defensively by a defendant or another party who has no practical choice of forum. Conversely, ancillary jurisdiction was not extended to permissive counterclaims under Rule 13(b),[263] permissive joinder of parties under Rule 20 or permissive intervention

---

trustees in bankruptcy. *See* cases cited in Richard A. Matasar, *Rediscovering "One Constitutional Case": Procedural Rules and the Rejection of the Gibbs Test for Supplemental Jurisdiction*, 71 CAL. L. REV. 1401, 1465–74 (1983). If these claims fall within the concept of constitutional case, it must be because they are either necessary and proper to give full effect to a particular subject matter jurisdiction or, more doubtfully in light of Rule 82, because the constitutional case extends as far as the scope of permissible joinder under the rules. Matasar, 71 CAL. L. REV. at 1477–90 (proposing the latter solution).

[257] *Kroger*, 437 U.S. at 373 (*citing Aldinger v. Howard*, 427 U.S. 1 (1976), discussed in § 5.09[2], *supra*).

[258] 437 U.S. at 366.

[259] *See* § 5.04[2] (diversity between whom), *supra*.

[260] FRIEDENTHAL, KANE & MILLER § 2.12 (suggesting that a majority of courts have found ancillary jurisdiction for these claims and citing cases).

[261] For detailed analysis of joinder under Rule 14 and the other rules mentioned in the text, *see* §§ 9.02–9.08 (joinder), *infra*.

[262] *Kroger*, 437 U.S. at 375 n.18. The overlap between Rules 19 and Rule 24(a) led to an anomaly in ancillary jurisdiction. Because it is not available for required parties under Rule 19, *see* § 9.05[2], *infra*, the courts reasoned that it must also be unavailable when such a party tries to intervene as of right under Rule 24(a). *See generally* 7 WRIGHT & MILLER § 1610; John E. Kennedy, *Let's All Join In: Intervention Under Federal Rule 24*, 57 KY. L.J. 329, 362–63 (1969).

[263] *But see* Matasar, note 256, *supra*, at 1474–75 (noting that it has sometimes been extended to setoffs for liquidated claims). *See* § 9.03 note 28, *infra* (defining set-offs).

under Rule 24(a). These kinds of joinder either involve transactionally-unrelated claims and/or are invoked by parties who voluntarily chose the forum, and thus fail the *Kroger* test.

Once a court satisfied itself of constitutional power to assert ancillary jurisdiction, and that Congress had not negated such jurisdiction, there remained the question whether it *should* assert it as a matter of discretion. Some commentators and courts, stressing the historical roots of ancillary jurisdiction in "necessity," treated the doctrine as mandatory once power was found.[264] But as the rationale for ancillary jurisdiction evolved from strict necessity to a mixture of fairness and convenience, the better view was that a court had the discretion to decide whether to exercise ancillary jurisdiction.[265] The factors that the courts should consider were those identified in *Gibbs*,[266] except that there was ordinarily no federal policy interest in a diversity case. "Necessity," or related considerations of fairness and convenience of involuntary parties, meant only that the discretionary part of the analysis should less often result in denial of ancillary jurisdiction, not that this jurisdiction was mandatory.

So the law stood when *Finley v. United States*[267] was decided. As we noted in the prior section, *Finley*'s insistence on affirmative evidence of congressional approval for pendent jurisdiction logically extended to ancillary jurisdiction as well. Some lower federal courts therefore began to restrict ancillary jurisdiction. Some even disallowed ancillary jurisdiction over third-party (impleader) claims[268] by defendants, despite the Supreme Court's endorsement of that application of ancillary jurisdiction in *Kroger*.[269] Other lower courts, however, confined *Finley* to its context — plaintiff's invocation of pendent party jurisdiction — and continued to uphold ancillary jurisdiction in other contexts. A few courts continued to uphold pendent party jurisdiction under different statutes.[270]

---

[264] *See, e.g.*, Matasar, note 199, *supra*, at 184 (it is unclear whether discretionary factors apply at all and few courts have considered the question); Arthur R. Miller, *Ancillary and Pendent Jurisdiction*, 26 S. Tex. L.J. 1, 7 (1985) (noting that the issue "has never been seriously adjudicated" and that there is an inconsistency between jurisdictional discretion and lack of discretion in the court in permitting compulsory counterclaims under Rule 13(a)).

[265] *See, e.g.*, Matasar, note 199, *supra*, at 187–88; Friedenthal, Kane & Miller § 2.12; Wright § 76. Since the Court found no statutory power in *Kroger*, it never reached the question of discretion. Justices White and Brennan, dissenting, assumed that the trial court had discretion, as it would in a case of pendent jurisdiction. *Kroger*, 437 U.S. at 382 n.4 (White, J., dissenting).

[266] *See* § 5.09[1] (pendent claims), *supra*.

[267] 490 U.S. 545 (1989).

[268] *See* § 9.06 (impleader), *infra*.

[269] *See, e.g., Aetna Cas. & Sur. Co. v. Spartan Mech. Corp.*, 738 F. Supp. 664, 675 (E.D.N.Y. 1990) (finding that a defendant's third-party claim against a non-diverse defendant "comes under the prohibition of *Finley*" because the diversity statute does not affirmatively grant jurisdiction).

[270] *See* Freer, note 248, *supra*, at 467–69 (finding that most courts were reading *Finley* narrowly).

§ 5.11 STATUTORY SUPPLEMENTAL JURISDICTION[271]

The Court ended its opinion in *Finley* with the reminder that "[w]hatever we say regarding the scope of jurisdiction conferred by a particular statute can of course be changed by Congress."[272] Congress accepted the Court's invitation in 1990 by enacting the supplemental jurisdiction statute.[273] The House Report accompanying the statute explained that it "would authorize jurisdiction in a case like *Finley*, as well as essentially restore the pre-*Finley* understandings of the authorization for and limits on other forms of supplemental jurisdiction."[274] The law professors who helped write the bill added that the measure was intended "to repair *Finley*'s damage in a noncontroversial manner without expanding the scope of diversity jurisdiction" and "was therefore framed to restore and regularize jurisdiction, not to revamp it."[275] Whether Congress accomplished all it set out to do remains to be seen, but it definitely did not avoid controversy. Here we first consider what the supplemental jurisdiction statute has accomplished and how it works, and then consider several apparent problems it poses.

[1] The Three-Part Test for Supplemental Jurisdiction

Section 1367's subsections suggest three stages of inquiry in deciding the availability of supplemental jurisdiction over a claim for which there is no independent jurisdiction. The first is whether the claim qualifies for supplemental jurisdiction under § 1367(a) by falling within the same constitutional case or controversy as the anchor claim that enjoys independent jurisdiction.[276] If § 1367(a) is satisfied, but the anchor claim is based only on diversity, the second stage of inquiry is whether the supplemental claim is disqualified for supplemental jurisdiction by § 1367(b). If not, the third stage of inquiry is whether the court should nonetheless decline to exercise supplemental discretion for any of the reasons listed in § 1367(c).

---

[271] For a thorough review of the initial commentary about and issues posed by statutory supplemental jurisdiction, see Denis F. McLaughlin, *The Federal Supplemental Jurisdiction Statute — A Constitutional and Statutory Analysis*, 24 Ariz. St. L.J. 849 (1992). The statute engendered a heated debate between its first critics and the three law professors who helped to draft it, published in the articles cited by McLaughlin, 24 Ariz. St. L.J. at 854 n.6. For a later reappraisal, see articles collected in *Symposium: A Reappraisal of the Supplemental Jurisdiction Statute: Title 28 U.S.C. § 1367*, 74 Ind. L.J. 1–250 (1998) (hereinafter "*Reappraisal*").

[272] 490 U.S. 545, 556 (1989).

[273] 28 U.S.C. § 1367.

[274] Federal Courts Study Committee Implementation Act of 1990, H.R. Rep. No. 101-734, 101st Cong., 2d Sess. 28 (1990) [hereinafter *H.R. Rep.*].

[275] Thomas M. Mengler et al., *Congress Accepts Supreme Court's Invitation to Codify Supplemental Jurisdiction*, 74 Judicature 213, 214–15 (1991).

[276] We continue to call the "anchor claim" a claim that would be jurisdictionally viable by itself. *See* § 5.08, *supra*. Jurisdictional support for such a claim may come from one of several federal statutes. *E.g.*, 28 U.S.C. § 1331 (federal question jurisdiction). In contrast, a claim for which jurisdiction is sought under § 1367 is never viable alone. Rather, jurisdiction over such a claim depends upon whether it relates to an anchor claim in a way that satisfies § 1367. We therefore call such a claim the "supplemental" claim.

[a] Qualifying Under Section 1367(a)

Subsection 1367(a) codifies the authority for the extension of jurisdiction that *Finley* found lacking. Subsection 1367(a) overrules *Finley* by expressly providing that "supplemental jurisdiction shall include claims that involve joinder or intervention of parties," thereby authorizing jurisdiction over what were formerly called pendent party claims. Authority for supplemental jurisdiction is extended to any claim satisfying this subsection, unless it is one of the claims in diversity-only cases for which supplemental jurisdiction is withdrawn by subsection 1367(b), or jurisdiction is expressly negated by another federal statute.

Moreover, the new statutory jurisdiction "go[es to] the constitutional limit."[277] Despite legislative history suggesting that Congress intended to codify only the familiar transaction-or-occurrence test for extending jurisdiction,[278] subsection 1367(a) expressly extends federal jurisdiction from anchor claims within the original jurisdiction of the federal court to supplemental claims that are "so related [to the anchor claims] . . . that they form part of the same case or controversy under Article III of the United States Constitution." Whatever Congress's intent, its plain words refrain from creating yet another gap between statutory and constitutional jurisdiction. Assuming that the constitutional case is broader than same-transaction-or-occurrence, subsection 1367(a) apparently leaves scope for the exercise of supplemental jurisdiction over transactionally unrelated but logically related claims in the rare case where it may be appropriate.[279]

Despite Congress's adoption of the vague "same case or controversy" test for supplemental jurisdiction instead of the familiar "same transaction or occurrence" test which appeared in earlier legislative drafts of section 1367(a), the latter should still suffice for deciding to *include* a supplemental claim. Thus, most courts have found that claims which satisfy the same transaction or occurrence standard for joinder under Rules 13(a) (compulsory counterclaim),[280] 13(g) (crossclaim), or 20 (joinder of parties) also qualify for supplemental jurisdiction. As one court explained in deciding ancillary jurisdiction before section 1367 was enacted, "[t]he tests are the same because Rule 13(a) and the doctrine of ancillary jurisdiction are designed to abolish the same evil, viz., piecemeal litigation in the federal courts."[281]

---

[277] David S. Siegel, 28 U.S.C.A. § 1367 practice commentary (1990).

[278] *See* TEPLY & WHITTEN, Chap. 2, § C(4)(d) (arguing for this intent by tracing § 1367(a) to Federal Courts Study Committee Report, but conceding that "Congress may have inadvertently exercised" the full Article III power).

[279] *See* § 5.10 note 256, *supra* (citing cases); MOORE §§ 106.24[1][2] (noting division in courts about logical-relation test for supplemental jurisdiction and rejection of mere "but for" relationship); TEPLY & WHITTEN Chap. 2, § C(4)(d) (asserting that the "better approach" to deciding the scope of a constitutional case would be "to examine every grant of authority over factually unrelated federal and nonfederal claims to determine whether Congress has sound reasons, grounded in the fair and efficient operation of federal subject-matter jurisdiction grants, for providing such authority"). Teply and Whitten, however, opt for a narrow transaction-or-occurrence construction of section 1367(a) to avoid " 'inconvenient' effects." TEPLY & WHITTEN Chap. 2, § C(4)(d).

[280] *See* § 9.03, *infra*.

[281] *Great Lakes Rubber Corp. v. Herbert Cooper Co.*, 286 F.2d 631, 633 (3d Cir. 1961).

But a claim which does not meet the same transaction test is not necessarily *excluded* from supplemental jurisdiction. A court may properly take a narrower view of "transaction or occurrence" in the counterclaim context, because of the harsh result of finding that a previously unasserted claim was compulsory (it cannot be asserted later), than in the supplemental jurisdiction context, where the results are less draconian (the claim can still be heard in state court).[282] Thus, for example, one court has said that even if a supplemental counterclaim does not arise from the same transaction or occurrence as plaintiff's anchor original claim (so that it is a permissive, not a compulsory counterclaim), it can still qualify for supplemental jurisdiction if it bears even a loose factual relationship to the anchor claim.[283]

[b] Disqualifying Under § 1367(b)

Subsection 1367(b) provides that in diversity-only cases, the courts do not have supplemental jurisdiction over claims by plaintiffs against persons made parties by Rules 14, 19, 20 or 24, when exercising such jurisdiction "would be inconsistent with the jurisdictional requirements of subsection 1332." The House Report explains that the "net effect of subsection (b) is to implement the principal rationale of *Owen Equipment & Erection Co. v. Kroger.*"[284]

The subsection would thus deny supplemental jurisdiction for the Rule 14(a) claim that plaintiff Kroger asserted against the non-diverse third-party defendant, as well as other claims that a plaintiff might add to evade the complete diversity requirement of § 1332. As the House Report explains,

> [i]n diversity-only actions the district courts may not hear plaintiffs' supplemental claims when exercising supplemental jurisdiction would encourage plaintiffs to evade the jurisdictional requirement of 28 U.S.C. § 1332 by the simple expedient of naming initially only those defendants whose joinder satisfies § 1332's requirements and later adding claims not within original federal jurisdiction against other defendants who have intervened or been joined on a supplemental basis.[285]

A good case can be made for overruling *Kroger*, or, conversely, for mooting it by eliminating diversity altogether.[286] However, if it is to be left largely intact, the statute is generally faithful to the task,[287] although it suffers from several problems

---

[282] *See Moore* § 106.25 (arguing that different purposes of test for joinder and test for supplemental jurisdiction justify different applications, but acknowledging that "courts have generally continued to equate the factual identity required for supplemental jurisdiction with that required for the presence of a compulsory counterclaim"); Mary Kay Kane, *Original Sin and the Transaction in Federal Civil Procedure*, 76 Tex. L. Rev. 1723, 1730–33 (1998) (noting different policy purposes animating use of transaction test in different settings).

[283] *Polaris Pool Sys. v. Letro Prods., Inc.*, 161 F.R.D. 422, 425 (C.D. Cal. 1995). *See also Channell v. Citicorp Nat'l Servs., Inc.*, 89 F.3d 379, 385–86 (7th Cir. 1996) (endorsing loose factual connection as sufficient for supplemental jurisdiction).

[284] *H.R. Rep.*, note 274, *supra*, at 29 n.16. For discussion of *Kroger*, see § 5.10, *supra*.

[285] *H.R. Rep.*, note 274, *supra*, at 29.

[286] *See* § 5.04[1] (reviewing the arguments for and against diversity jurisdiction), *supra*.

[287] Subsection 1367(b) makes what the House Report characterizes as "one small change" in *Kroger* and pre-*Finley* practice. *H.R. Rep.*, note 274, *supra*, at 29. *Kroger* noted that ancillary jurisdiction had

discussed below.[288]

[c]   Discretion Under § 1367(c)

Subsection 1367(c) codifies a discretionary step in what was pendent jurisdiction analysis. Although the subsection includes only some of the factors identified in the pendent jurisdiction cases, it invites courts, "in exceptional circumstances," to consider "other compelling reasons for declining jurisdiction."[289] Subsection 1367(c) thus serves as a counterweight to subsection 1367(a). It gives courts discretion to refuse jurisdiction within the outer limits of their power, when dismissal of the anchor claim on other than jurisdictional grounds,[290] the novelty or predominance of state law issues in federal question cases, or other good reasons suggest that the supplemental claims would more appropriately be decided by state courts. The Supreme Court has indicated that the statute reflects the understanding that a federal court " 'should consider and weigh in each case, and at every stage of the litigation, the values of judicial economy, convenience, fairness, and comity.' "[291]

On the other hand, the mandatory "shall" in § 1367(a) and § 1367(c)'s reference to "exceptional circumstances" and "compelling reasons" for declining supplemental jurisdiction has led some courts to conclude that § 1367(c) gives less discretion to decline jurisdiction than courts enjoyed under *Gibbs*. By this view, § 1367(a) effectively *requires* the court to exercise supplemental jurisdiction *unless* the court finds one of the listed grounds, or other *exceptional* circumstances, to be a *compelling* reason to decline.[292] A court could not therefore decline to exercise jurisdiction for an unlisted reason just because it promotes "economy, convenience, fairness, and comity," absent especially compelling circumstances. Another way of stating this view is that qualification for supplemental jurisdiction creates a presumption in favor of its exercise which can only be rebutted by one of the "compelling" reasons listed in § 1367(c).

---

been extended to Rule 24(a) intervenors as of right, 437 U.S. at 375 n.18, subject to the anomaly that jurisdiction was denied intervenors as of right who also qualified as necessary parties under Rule 19. Subsection 1367(b) "cures" the anomaly by denying supplemental jurisdiction to *all* plaintiff-intervenors. Critics have charged that this cure runs the wrong way and is worse than the anomaly, cutting off access to federal court for intervenors whose interest forces them into the federal forum without any intent to evade complete diversity. *See, e.g.*, McLaughlin, note 271, *supra*, at 960–70; Freer, note 248, *supra*, at 476–78.

[288]   *See* § 5.11[2], *infra.*

[289]   *See* McLaughlin, note 271, *supra*, at 975–76.

[290]   Dismissal of the putative anchor claim for lack of subject matter jurisdiction deprives the court of supplemental jurisdiction because it eliminates the constitutional case or controversy. Dismissal of the anchor claim for other reasons leaves the court the power to hear the supplemental claims at its discretion under subsection 1367(c)(3). *See* McLaughlin, note 271, *supra*, at 979 (citing cases).

[291]   *City of Chicago v. International Coll. of Surgeons*, 522 U.S. 156, 173 (1997) (quoting *Carnegie-Mellon Univ. v. Cohill*, 484 U.S. 343, 350 (1988)).

[292]   MOORE §§ 106.60–106.61. *See, e.g.*, *Executive Software N. Am., Inc. v. United States Dist. Court*, 24 F.3d 1545 (9th Cir. 1994) ("declining jurisdiction outside of subsection (c)(1)–(3) should be the exception, rather than the rule").

[2] Problems With Subsection 1367(b)

It is chiefly what the statute did not say that generated much initial criticism. We identify only some of its alleged omissions here.

[a] Overinclusiveness?

We noted in § 5.10 that *Kroger*'s focus on the posture in which the supplemental claim is asserted did not necessarily foreclose the assertion in a diversity-only case of jurisdiction over a plaintiff's essentially defensive claims (*e.g.*, compulsory counterclaims or cross-claims against non-diverse parties), and some courts so held.[293] Does subsection 1367(b)'s restriction now prohibit even defensive claims by plaintiffs? That would require plaintiffs to bring separate state court actions for indemnification or contribution from non-diverse defendants, with the possibility that their transactionally-related federal claims could be precluded by state court judgments.[294]

One solution is to read subsection 1367(b) to reach only plaintiff's original claims, not counterclaims, cross-claims, or third-party claims added after the original complaint.[295] This facile reading, however, is hard to square with subsection 1367(a)'s use of the generic "claims." Arguably, it is also unnecessary. Subsection 1367(b)'s restriction on claims by the plaintiff is not absolute. It applies only "when exercising supplemental jurisdiction over such claims would be inconsistent with the jurisdictional requirements of section 1332." The plaintiff who asserts a defensive claim against a non-diverse party is typically not attempting to evade the complete diversity requirement; therefore, exercising supplemental jurisdiction over that claim would not be inconsistent with the requirements of diversity as they were articulated in *Kroger*. So federal courts reasoned before enactment of supplemental jurisdiction, and the qualifying clause in subsection 1367(b) permits that precedent to continue undisturbed, although courts have not observed this nuance.[296]

[b] Underinclusiveness?

A second troublesome omission in subsection 1367(b) concerned the joinder of claims by persons made parties by Rule 23, the class action rule.[297] We noted in subsection 5.09[2] that the Supreme Court had denied pendent party jurisdiction in

---

[293] *See* Freer, note 248, *supra*, at 463 & n.103 (citing cases).

[294] *See* Freer, note 248, *supra*, at 482–83.

[295] Richard Freer, in *Reappraisal*, note 271, *supra*, at 5, 12–15; Siegel, note 277, *supra*; Mengler, et al., note 275, *supra*, at 215 n.17. A comparable solution is to read "plaintiff" in subsection 1367(b) to mean only a party who files an aggressive pleading rather than a defensive pleading. The rules themselves do not use "plaintiffs" this way, however. When they are intended to apply more generally, they use "parties asserting a claim" or "opposing parties." *Compare* Rule 20(a) *with* Rules 13 & 18.

[296] *See generally* Peter Raven-Hansen, *The Forgotten Provison of § 1367(b) (And Why We Forgot)*, in *Reappraisal*, note 271, *supra*, at 197. *See also* Darren J. Gold, *Supplemental Jurisdiction over Claims by Plaintiffs in Diversity Cases: Making Sense of 28 U.S.C. § 1367(b)*, 93 MICH. L. REV. 2133, 2163–66 (1995) (positing that "it is not unrealistic to assume that plaintiffs will [use this precedent to] engage in . . . strategic gamesmanship" to elude the complete diversity requirement).

[297] *See* § 9.09 (class actions), *infra*.

plaintiff class actions over claims by class members that did not individually satisfy the amount in controversy.[298] Subsection 1367(b), however, omits joinder of such claims from its qualified restriction on supplemental jurisdiction. The inference is that supplemental jurisdiction is available pursuant to the general grant in subsection 1367(a). This inference contradicts the indications of congressional intent found in the statute's legislative history. Commentators and some courts have therefore favored the intent over the letter of the statute.[299] It is at least arguable that resort to the legislative history is warranted by subsection 1367(b)'s silence about Rule 23 joinder.

On the other hand, the principle of *expressio unius est exclusio alterius* (the expression of one thing is the exclusion of another) could be applied to uphold supplemental jurisdiction over supplemental plaintiff class action claims. Moreover, upholding such jurisdiction makes sense. In effect, the Supreme Court now allows supplemental jurisdiction over non-diverse class members in plaintiff class actions.[300] A plain language reading of subsection 1367(b) to allow supplemental jurisdiction over class members' monetarily insufficient claims would be perfectly consistent with the treatment of the diversity requirement in plaintiff class actions.[301]

In *Exxon Mobil Corp. v. Allapattah Services, Inc.*,[302] the Supreme Court adopted the plain language reading to find supplemental jurisdiction over monetarily insufficient class claims as long as there was at least one monetarily sufficient anchor class claim. In *Allapattah*, plaintiffs filed a class action complaint[303] against Exxon on behalf of 10,000 Exxon dealers, alleging that Exxon had employed a scheme to overcharge them for fuel. Although at least one of the representative class members had a claim exceeding the amount in controversy for diversity jurisdiction, many did not. The district court held, and the Court of Appeals affirmed, that it had supplemental jurisdiction over the monetarily insufficient claims, thus finding that the supplemental jurisdiction statute had overruled *Zahn*, notwithstanding the inconsistent legislative history. The Supreme Court agreed.

> When the well-pleaded complaint contains at least one claim that satisfies the amount-in-controversy requirement, and there are no other relevant jurisdictional defects, the district court, beyond all question, has original jurisdiction over that claim. The presence of other claims in the complaint, over which the district court may lack original jurisdiction, is of no moment. If the court has original jurisdiction over a single claim in the

---

[298] *Zahn v. International Paper Co.*, 414 U.S. 291 (1973) (denying aggregation of amounts to satisfy jurisdictional requirement).

[299] *See* McLaughlin, note 271, *supra*, 972–74 (citing *H.R. Rep.*, note 274, *supra*, at 29); *cf. Griffin v. Dana Point Condo. Ass'n*, 768 F. Supp. 1299, 1301–02 (N.D. Ill. 1991) (refusing to exercise supplemental jurisdiction over co-plaintiffs' jurisdictionally insufficient claims).

[300] *See Supreme Tribe of Ben-Hur v. Cauble*, 255 U.S. 356 (1921) (counting only the citizenship of the representative class action plaintiffs for purposes of diversity).

[301] *See* § 9.09[4][b] (discussing problems of federal class actions after *Zahn*), *infra*.

[302] 545 U.S. 546 (2005).

[303] *See* Rule 23; § 9.09, *infra*.

complaint, it has original jurisdiction over a "civil action" within the meaning of § 1367(a), even if the civil action over which it has jurisdiction comprises fewer claims than were included in the complaint. Once the court determines it has original jurisdiction over the civil action, it can turn to the question whether it has a constitutional and statutory basis for exercising supplemental jurisdiction over the other claims in the action.[304]

Because at least one of the class action representative's claims exceeded the amount in controversy required for diversity jurisdiction, and thus qualified, standing alone, for diversity jurisdiction, the federal courts had original jurisdiction over the civil action of which that claim was a part. It therefore had a basis for exercising supplemental jurisdiction over the monetarily insufficient dealers' claims in the same action (clearly based on the same fuel sale transaction). The Supreme Court found no ambiguity in the plain language of section 1367 that would justify resort to some legislative history eschewing a congressional intent to overrule *Zahn*.[305]

The same reasoning resolved another problem in section 1367(b) caused by the absence of any reference in it to Rule 20 joinder of plaintiffs. While the subsection denies jurisdiction for supplemental claims made *against* persons made parties under Rule 20 in diversity-only cases, it does *not* deny supplemental jurisdiction over joinder of non-diverse or below-amount claims *by* persons who join as plaintiffs under Rule 20. In a companion case decided with *Allapattah*, *Ortega v. Star-Kist Foods, Inc.*,[306] a nine-year old plaintiff had invoked diversity jurisdiction for serious injuries suffered when she cut her finger severely on a tunafish can, and her family members had joined as co-plaintiffs[307] with monetarily insufficient claims for emotional distress and medical expenses. The court of appeals ruled that there was no supplemental jurisdiction over the joined claims, reasoning that section 1367 did not overrule the long-standing rules against aggregation notwithstanding its language. The Court disagreed. Because the nine-year-old plaintiff's claims satisfied the amount-in-controversy requirements for diversity jurisdiction, the district court had jurisdiction over the entire case (civil action) of which they were part, and section 1367(b) did not withdraw supplemental jurisdiction over her family's joined claims (obviously arising from the same tuna can accident).

What then of supplemental jurisdiction for claims by *non-diverse* plaintiffs who join under Rule 20? Suppose, for example, that although the nine-year-old plaintiff was diverse from defendant, one of the joined family members was not. Now, reading the plain words of section 1367(b) to allow supplemental jurisdiction would destroy the hoary *Strawbridge v. Curtiss* rule of complete diversity,[308] a statutory interpretation that Congress has been content to leave undisturbed for more than

---

[304] 545 U.S. at 559. Note that this analysis still requires an anchor claim exceeding the jurisdictional amount. If no claim does so, then the amount requirement cannot be met by aggregating the claims. *Allapattah* did not abolish the no-aggregation rule, and on these facts, there is no anchor for the supplemental claims.

[305] 545 U.S. at 567–71. It added that the legislative history, in any event, was "far murkier than selective quotation" from a single report would indicate. 545 U.S. at 569.

[306] 545 U.S. 546 (2005).

[307] *See* Rule 20.

[308] *See* § 5.04[2], *supra*.

200 years. The answer, the Court said, is that complete diversity is necessary to confer the original jurisdiction that section 1367(a) requires before you even get to section 1367(b).

> In order for a federal court to invoke supplemental jurisdiction under *Gibbs*, it must first have original jurisdiction over at least one claim in the action. Incomplete diversity destroys original jurisdiction with respect to all claims, so there is nothing to which supplemental jurisdiction can adhere.

> In contrast to the diversity requirement, most of the other statutory prerequisites for federal jurisdiction, including the federal-question and amount-in-controversy requirements, can be analyzed claim by claim.[309]

The Court's analysis can be defended as a matter of plain language construction. Whether it comports in both cases with what Congress thought it was doing by enacting the supplemental jurisdiction statute is less clear (assuming that we can divine what "Congress" thought it was doing). In any event, the flaws of section 1367 should not be allowed to obscure its virtues. The statute did *most* of what it set out to do from the start, and the Supreme Court's construction in *Allapattah* has clarified two of its central ambiguities. The result is both a firmer basis for extended jurisdiction and greater clarity in its most common applications.

§ 5.12   SUBJECT MATTER JURISDICTION OF THE CALIFORNIA COURTS

[1]   Introductory Note

The federal courts are courts of limited jurisdiction — they may hear only those actions which are within the constitutional grant of judicial power delineated by Article III of the United States Constitution, and even then only to the extent that Congress by statute authorizes the assertion of federal court jurisdiction over such actions.[310] When a federal court determines that it lacks statutory or constitutional authority to assert subject matter jurisdiction, the court must dismiss the claim.

The California state courts, by contrast, are courts of general jurisdiction.[311] Except for those actions within the exclusive jurisdiction of the federal courts — *e.g.*, 28 U.S.C. § 1338 (patents and copyrights), § 1346 (actions against United States), 15 U.S.C. § 78aa (federal securities claims) — a California state court or tribunal has the authority to decide all causes of action presented by the parties.

---

[309] 545 U.S. at 554.

[310] *See, e.g., Marbury v. Madison*, 5 U.S. (1 Cranch) 137, 2 L. Ed. 60 (1803) (holding that Art. III defines outer limits of federal judicial power); *Sheldon v. Sill*, 49 U.S. (8 How.) 441, 12 L. Ed. 1147 (1850) (holding that the lower federal courts have no jurisdiction except as Congress confers by statute). The subject matter jurisdiction of the federal courts is discussed in detail in § 5.01–§ 5.10, *supra*.

[311] *See* CAL. CONST. art. VI, § 10.

[2] Superior Court Jurisdiction

[a] California Trial Court Unification

Prior to 1998, California's trial courts consisted of superior and municipal courts, each with its own jurisdiction and number of judges fixed by the California Legislature. Subsequently, the California voters approved Proposition 220 in June 1998 and Proposition 48 in November 2002, that amended the California Constitution to eliminate references to the constitutional authority to vest judicial power in the municipal courts.[312] As a result of these constitutional amendments, the superior court now has jurisdiction in all matters that were previously under the jurisdiction of either the superior or municipal courts.[313] However, even after unification, the jurisdictional differences between the superior courts and the former municipal courts remain relevant for purposes of certain trial court procedures, such as the size of the jury, and for purposes of the proper court for appellate review.[314]

The California Courts of Appeal have appellate jurisdiction as to the type of cases that were within the original jurisdiction of the superior courts on June 30, 1995, and in other cases as prescribed by statute.[315] As to all other cases — referred to in the legislation implementing Prop. 220 as "limited civil cases"—the appellate division of the superior court has appellate jurisdiction.[316] Under the current statutory scheme, the definition of "limited civil cases" corresponds to the type of cases that could only be heard in municipal court prior to unification — generally, civil cases in which the amount in controversy is $25,000 or less.[317]

[b] "Limited" vs. "Unlimited" Civil Cases

Generally speaking, a "limited civil case" is an action in which the amount in controversy does not exceed $25,000.[318] An "unlimited civil case" is an action which seeks more than $25,000, or one designated as an unlimited civil case by statute regardless of the amount in controversy.[319] Although the procedural laws applicable to civil actions generally also apply to limited civil cases, there are some provisions applicable only to limited civil cases. These include limitations on pleadings, simplified discovery, admissibility of affidavits or declarations in lieu of direct

---

[312] CAL. CONST. art. VI, § 5 (repealed), § 6, § 8, § 16 & § 23 (repealed).

[313] CAL. CONST. art. VI, § 10.

[314] CAL. CONST. art. I, § 16; art. VI, § 11.

[315] CAL. CONST. art. VI, § 11.

[316] CAL. CONST. art. VI, § 11; CAL. CODE CIV. PROC. §§ 77–86, 904.2.

[317] CAL. CODE CIV. PROC. § 86. The Legislature has the authority to change appellate jurisdiction of the Courts of Appeal, and therefore necessarily of the appellate division of the superior court, by changing the jurisdictional amount in controversy. CAL. CONST. art. VI, § 11.

[318] CAL. CODE CIV. PROC. §§ 85(a), 86(a) (designating various specific actions as limited civil cases).

[319] E.g., CAL. CODE CIV. PROC. § 88 (defining an unlimited civil case); CAL. FAM. CODE §§ 200, 4900–4976, 8500–9206 (dissolution of marriage, adoption, and support proceedings); CAL. PROB. CODE §§ 2200, 7050 (guardianship, conservatorship, and probate proceedings).

testimony, lower filing fees, and appeal to the appellate division of the superior court instead of the Court of Appeal.[320]

The clerk of court makes the initial jurisdictional classification of a civil case based on the plaintiff's classification designation in the caption of the complaint. A party or the court on its own motion may move for reclassification of a case that is erroneously classified.[321] If a party files an amended pleading or a cross-complaint that causes the action to exceed the maximum amount in controversy or otherwise fail to satisfy the requirements for a limited civil case, and pays a reclassification fee, the clerk must change the jurisdictional classification from limited to unlimited.[322] An order reclassifying a case is not an appealable order; a party seeking appellate review of such an order must file a timely petition for a writ of mandate.[323]

The "amount in controversy" means the amount of the demand, or the recovery sought, or the value of the property, that is in controversy in an action, "exclusive of attorneys' fees, interest, and costs."[324] The superior court must deny a motion to reclassify a civil case as "limited" (and thus keep the matter in the "unlimited" classification) unless it appears to a legal certainty that the plaintiff's damages will necessarily be less than $25,000.[325]

The changes in court organization, procedure, and nomenclature caused by trial court unification have not altered the prior law governing the computation of that amount.[326] Therefore, when a single plaintiff alleges multiple causes of action against a single defendant, the demands of all the claims are aggregated in computing the amount in controversy.[327] Aggregation is not permitted, however, when a single plaintiff has separate claims against several defendants.[328] When properly-joined multiple plaintiffs have joint causes of action against a single defendant, their joint claims are aggregated in computing the amount in controversy.[329] However, where the joined plaintiffs' causes of action are separate, their

---

[320] CAL. CODE CIV. PROC. §§ 92–96, 98, 904.2; CAL. GOV'T CODE §§ 70613, 70614.

[321] CAL. CODE CIV. PROC. § 403.040; *see Stern v. Superior Court*, 105 Cal. App. 4th 223, 231–33, 129 Cal. Rptr. 2d 275 (2003) (holding trial court abused its discretion in reclassifying the case without giving plaintiffs notice and an opportunity to contest the reclassification).

[322] CAL. CODE CIV. PROC. §§ 403.020, 403.030; *see also* CAL. CODE CIV. PROC. § 403.050 (reclassification pursuant to parties' stipulation).

[323] CAL. CODE CIV. PROC. § 403.080; *Garau v. Torrance Unified School Dist.*, 137 Cal. App. 4th 192, 40 Cal. Rptr. 3d 108 (2006).

[324] CAL. CODE CIV. PROC. § 85(a).

[325] *See Ytuarte v. Superior Court*, 129 Cal. App. 4th 266, 276–79, 28 Cal. Rptr. 3d 474 (2005) (explaining that to defeat a motion to reclassify from unlimited to limited, the party opposing reclassification must present evidence to demonstrate a possibility that the verdict will exceed $25,000); *Stern, supra*, 105 Cal. App. 4th at 233–34 (reversing trial court's reclassification from unlimited to limited action because it failed to make requisite finding that the matter would necessarily result in a verdict below the jurisdictional minimum).

[326] *Stern, supra*, 105 Cal. App. 4th at 227, 230–31.

[327] *Hammell v. Superior Court*, 217 Cal. 5, 7–8, 17 P.2d 101 (1932).

[328] *Myers v. Sierra Valley Stock & Agric. Ass'n*, 122 Cal. 669, 55 P. 689 (1898).

[329] *Frost v. Mighetto*, 22 Cal. App. 2d 612, 71 P.2d 932 (1937).

separate claims are not aggregated.[330]

When a good faith demand in a complaint exceeds the amount necessary for classification as an unlimited civil case but the subsequent judgment is one that could have been rendered in a limited civil case, the court is not required to reclassify the action as a limited civil action but may refuse to award costs to the prevailing plaintiff.[331] Likewise, when a plaintiff in a limited civil case recovers an amount within the jurisdictional limit of the small claims court, the court may deny costs to the prevailing plaintiff or may allow them in any amount it deems proper.[332]

[c] Small Claims Court

Each superior court must have a small claims division. Generally, the small claims court has jurisdiction in actions for recovery of money if the amount of the demand does not exceed $5000, and also has jurisdiction in an action brought by a natural person if the amount of the demand does not exceed $10,000.[333] The jurisdiction of small claims courts is concurrent with that of the superior courts.

A plaintiff who files an action in small claims court waives any damages above the jurisdictional limit, and has no right to appeal an adverse judgment on the plaintiff's claim.[334] However, the defendant with respect to the plaintiff's claim, and a plaintiff with respect to a claim of the defendant, may appeal the judgment to the superior court. The appeal consists of a trial *de novo* before a superior court judge.[335]

[d] Probate Court

The superior courts in many larger counties in California have separate departments for probate matters. Such departments have primary jurisdiction relating to certain probate matters assigned to such court by statute.[336] The probate court in such proceedings is, however, a court of general jurisdiction with all the powers of the superior courts.

---

[330] *Colla v. Carmichael U-Drive Autos*, 111 Cal. App. Supp. 784, 294 P. 378 (1930).

[331] CAL. CODE CIV. PROC. §§ 403.040(e), 1033(a).

[332] CAL. CODE CIV. PROC. § 1033(b); *see, e.g., Chavez v. City of Los Angeles*, 47 Cal. 4th 970, 982–89, 104 Cal. Rptr. 3d 710, 224 P.3d 41 (2010) (holding the trial court did not abuse its discretion in denying successful plaintiff statutory attorney fees as costs in an action brought as an unlimited civil case because the plaintiff recovered an amount that could have been recovered in a limited civil case).

[333] CAL. CODE CIV. PROC. §§ 116.220(a) & 116.221. A small claims court is also authorized to grant equitable relief in the form of rescission, restitution, reformation, and specific performance. CAL. CODE CIV. PROC. § 116.220(b).

[334] CAL. CODE CIV. PROC. §§ 116.220(d), 116.710(a).

[335] CAL. CODE CIV. PROC. § 116.770.

[336] *See* CAL. PROB. CODE § 7050 (administration of decedents' estates); *Saks v. Damon Raike & Co.*, 7 Cal. App. 4th 419, 428–30, 8 Cal. Rptr. 2d 869 (1992) (holding that pursuant to Prob. Code § 17000(a), the probate department has exclusive jurisdiction of proceedings concerning the internal affairs of trusts).

[3] Superior Court vs. Administrative Tribunal Jurisdiction

[a] Exclusive Agency Jurisdiction

A statute may vest exclusive original jurisdiction in an administrative agency over controversies within its grant of power, subject to appellate judicial review, and thereby deny jurisdiction to the superior court.[337] For example, pursuant to California Labor Code § 5955 the California Workers' Compensation Appeals Board (WCAB) has exclusive jurisdiction, not concurrent with the superior courts, over actions by employees against employers for work-related injuries. Of course, a superior court has jurisdiction to determine questions of whether the court or an administrative agency has exclusive jurisdiction over a particular claim.[338]

[b] Exhaustion of Administrative Remedies

Even when a statutory scheme does not divest the superior courts of initial exclusive jurisdiction, the provisions may require claimants to exhaust available administrative remedies prior to commencing an action in superior court.[339] Although some applications of this exhaustion requirement may not implicate the superior courts' fundamental subject matter jurisdiction because the requirement may be waived or be subject to judicial exceptions, the exhaustion requirement often postpones the superior court's jurisdiction during the pendency of the administrative proceeding.[340] Moreover, even where a claim is originally cognizable in the courts and not in an administrative agency, under the doctrine of primary jurisdiction a superior court may stay judicial proceedings pending resolution of administrative proceedings on the claim.[341]

---

[337] Such statutes and agencies include the following: Agricultural Labor Relations Board, CAL. LABOR CODE § 1160.8 & § 1160.9 (exclusive original jurisdiction over certain unfair labor practices); Public Employment Relations Board (PERB), CAL. GOV'T CODE § 3541.5 (granting the PERB exclusive initial jurisdiction of charges of unfair practices in public employment); Public Utilities Commission (PUC), CAL. PUB. UTIL. CODE § 1759 (providing that no court, except the Supreme Court and the courts of appeal, shall have jurisdiction to review a decision of the PUC); *but see* CAL. PUB. UTIL. CODE § 2106 (the superior court has jurisdiction to award damages for unlawful acts of a public utility, but limited to those situations in which an award of damages would not hinder or frustrate the PUC's declared supervisory and regulatory policies).

[338] *E.g., Scott v. Indus. Accident Comm'n,* 46 Cal. 2d 76, 81–89, 293 P.2d 18 (1956).

[339] *E.g.,* CAL. GOV'T CODE § 11523 (judicial review of agency decision based on agency record, pursuant to California Administrative Procedure Act); CAL. CODE CIV. PROC. § 1094.5 (administrative mandamus for judicial review of final administrative hearing decision); *see, e.g., Anton v. San Antonio Cmty. Hosp.,* 19 Cal. 3d 802, 140 Cal. Rptr. 442, 567 P.2d 1162 (1977) (applying administrative mandamus prerequisites to decision of private community hospital); *Abelleira v. Dist. Court of Appeal,* 17 Cal. 2d 280, 293, 109 P.2d 942 (1941) (holding exhaustion of statutory administrative remedy a jurisdictional prerequisite to resort to the courts).

[340] *See, e.g., Abelleira, supra,* 17 Cal. 2d at 292–306; *Green v. City of Oceanside,* 194 Cal. App. 3d 212, 222, 239 Cal. Rptr. 470 (1987) (holding the exhaustion doctrine did not implicate subject matter jurisdiction but rather was a procedural prerequisite to suit); *County of Contra Costa v. State of Cal.,* 177 Cal. App. 3d 62, 222 Cal. Rptr. 750 (1986) (holding when no exception or waiver applied, exhaustion of an administrative remedy was a jurisdictional prerequisite to resort to the courts).

[341] *Farmers Ins. Exch. v. Superior Court,* 2 Cal. 4th 377, 6 Cal. Rptr. 2d 487, 826 P.2d 730 (1992) (invoking primary jurisdiction doctrine to suspend court action pending resolution of administrative

[4] No Waiver of Jurisdictional Defense

The defense of lack of subject matter jurisdiction may be raised at any time, and by any party or by the court.[342] However, in the interests of judicial economy, the California courts sometimes suggest that counsel may have a duty to raise this fundamental objection at an early time.[343] Nevertheless, subject matter jurisdiction cannot be conferred by estoppel, waiver, or consent.[344]

---

agency proceedings on complex insurance regulations issues).

[342] CAL. CODE CIV. PROC. §§ 430.10, 430.80(a); *Unruh v. Truck Ins. Exch.*, 7 Cal. 3d 616, 622, 102 Cal. Rptr. 815, 498 P.2d 1063 (1972) (ruling lack of subject matter jurisdiction may be asserted at any time, even for the first time on appeal); *Barnick v. Longs Drug Stores, Inc.*, 203 Cal. App. 3d 377, 379–80, 250 Cal. Rptr. 10 (1988) (same).

[343] *E.g., Rowland v. Cnty. of Sonoma*, 220 Cal. App. 3d 331, 335, 269 Cal. Rptr. 426 (1990).

[344] *Summers v. Superior Court*, 53 Cal. 2d 295, 298, 1 Cal. Rptr. 324, 347 P.2d 668 (1959); *Rowland, supra*, 220 Cal. App. 3d at 333 (ruling a court must dismiss action if it lacks subject matter jurisdiction; parties cannot confer jurisdiction on civil courts by stipulation or estoppel).

Chapter 6

A CONVENIENT COURT

§ 6.01 TRADITIONAL BASES FOR VENUE

[1] In General

The law of venue is founded on the realization that a court with subject matter and territorial jurisdiction can still be an inefficient, inconvenient location for litigation. Justice Scalia has observed that

> [v]enue is often a vitally important matter, as is shown by the frequency with which parties contractually provide for and litigate the issue. Suit might well not be pursued, or might not be as successful, in a significantly less convenient forum. Transfer to such a less desirable forum is, therefore, of sufficient import that plaintiffs will base their decisions on the likelihood of that eventuality when they are choosing whether to sue in state or federal court.[1]

Rules of *venue* are rules of convenience for allocating cases territorially, usually among state courts (typically by county) within a state's judicial system or among federal judicial districts and their divisions within the federal judicial system. That is, venue involves the choice of court *within* a state or federal judicial system, not between or among them.

Venue differs from subject matter jurisdiction in several ways. Objection to improper venue is waived if not promptly asserted; but objections to subject matter jurisdiction are non-waivable.[2] Similarly, a court is not obliged to question venue on its own initiative, and parties can stipulate or contract to an otherwise improper venue; but a court must consider whether it has subject matter jurisdiction even if no party raises the issue, and the parties cannot stipulate to such jurisdiction any more than they can waive it. While venue questions are likely to be resolved at the outset of a lawsuit, courts typically entertain objections to subject matter jurisdiction throughout. While improper venue can frequently be cured by transfer of the action to another court within the same judicial system, jurisdictional defects usually require dismissal of a lawsuit. Finally, improper venue does not subject a judgment to collateral attack, unlike some jurisdictional defects.

---

[1] *Stewart Org., Inc. v. Ricoh Corp.*, 487 U.S. 22, 39–40 (1988) (Scalia, J., dissenting).

[2] *See, e.g.*, Rule 12(h)(1). Note, however, that Rule 12 only governs the defense of "improper venue." Motions to transfer venue from one proper venue to another that is better — more convenient — may be made at any time. WRIGHT § 44.

Venue also differs from personal jurisdiction in several respects. Venue applies chiefly to original claims (the general federal venue statute speaks of where a "civil action may be brought"),[3] and not to claims added later, unlike personal jurisdiction.[4] The original parties, already present and litigating, are unlikely to be inconvenienced by litigating additional claims. Claims against additional parties usually enjoy what might be termed "ancillary," "pendent,"[5] or "derivative" venue[6] if those claims are sufficiently related to the original claims. Finally, although a defendant must plead the defenses of improper venue and lack of personal jurisdiction, improper venue is treated like an affirmative defense which the defendant must prove, while personal jurisdiction must be demonstrated by the party invoking it.

In short, venue is a more lenient requirement for choice of court than either subject matter jurisdiction or personal jurisdiction and thus less likely to result in dismissal. (Furthermore, in commercial contracts, the parties often choose the venue by a "forum selection clause.")

As statutory rules, venue requirements differ from judicial system to system, but similarities predominate. Subsection 2 describes the usual statutory bases for venue, using the general federal venue statute to illustrate some of them. Subsection 3 then discusses several judge-made exceptions to venue requirements.

[2]   Bases for Venue

To promote party and forum convenience, most venue statutes are based on some logical relationship between the parties or subject matter of the lawsuit and the place of trial. A comprehensive survey of typical venue statutes identified the following kinds of relationships as typical:

(1)   the locus of the *res* (property) or event that is the subject of the lawsuit;

(2)   where the claim arose;

(3)   where the defendant resides, does business, or retains an agent;

(4)   where the plaintiff resides; or,

(5)   in suits by or against government parties, where the seat of government is located.[7]

---

[3]   28 U.S.C. § 1391(b).

[4]   *Moore* § 110.06. *See, e.g., United States v. Acord*, 209 F.2d 709, 713–14 (10th Cir. 1954). However, if the plaintiff amends its complaint, the amended complaint is treated as a new action for venue purposes. The plaintiff could otherwise avoid venue requirements by artful pleading.

[5]   *Wright & Miller* § 3808. *See, e.g., Garrel v. NYLCare Health Plans, Inc.*, 1999 U.S. Dist. LEXIS 9778, *8 (S.D.N.Y. June 24, 1999) ("The doctrine of pendent venue is ordinarily employed where venue is lacking for a state law claim that arises from the same nucleus of operative facts as a 'properly venued' federal claim"). If separate venue statutes govern each claim, then the problem may be more complicated. *Id.* at *12.

[6]   William D. Underwood, *Reconsidering Derivative-Venue in Cases Involving Multiple Parties and Multiple Claims*, 56 Baylor L. Rev. 579 (2004).

[7]   *See* George Neff Stevens, *Venue Statutes: Diagnosis and Proposed Cure*, 49 Mich. L. Rev. 307, 331–32 (1951).

"The most common provision," the survey concluded, "and the basic one, appears to be venue based upon the residence of the defendant."[8] But venue provisions are also based on other criteria, usually designed to facilitate suit, such as where the defendant is served or may be found.[9]

The general federal venue provision[10] illustrates some of the common criteria.[11] It provides two general alternatives for venue and a fallback provision keyed to the limits of personal jurisdiction.

First, section 1391(b)(1) lays venue literally at the doorstep of a single defendant, or multiple defendants who reside in the same state, by allowing suit to be brought in the judicial district where any of them reside.[12] The residence of a natural person is defined as her domicile,[13] a concept we have already encountered in defining citizenship for diversity subject matter jurisdiction purposes. In the context of diversity subject matter jurisdiction, domicile is defined as where a person last lived or resided with the intention to remain indefinitely. Thus, a student who is born and raised in Virginia and moves to Indiana for college with no plans to remain in Indiana after graduation, remains a domiciliary of Virginia — and hence a "resident" of Virginia for venue purposes — during her college years. That will be the case even if she has no plans to return to Virginia after college: Virginia is the last place she lived with the intention to remain indefinitely, and will remain her domicile for purposes of determining *both* venue and citizenship, unless and until she moves to a new state with the requisite intent to remain there. In short, "domicile" means the same in both the diversity statute and the venue statute, but "residency" does not.

The residence of an entity like a corporation is more complicated. Such an entity is deemed a resident of any district in which it would be subject to personal jurisdiction with respect to the civil action in question.[14] In using the general phrase "personal jurisdiction," the subsection appears to subsume both specific and general jurisdiction.[15] The courts are divided about whether to measure personal jurisdiction under section 1391(c) by the constitutional minimum contacts test alone, by the forum state's long arm statute, or by other jurisdictional provisions as well. Because section 1391 venue is a question of federal law, the better view is that it is the former alone which controls.[16] Thus, if the entity has contacts with a district such that it would be subject to specific personal jurisdiction with respect

---

[8] *Id.* at 315.

[9] *See id.* at 332.

[10] 28 U.S.C. § 1391. In addition to 28 U.S.C. § 1391, there are numerous special federal venue statutes. *See* 28 U.S.C. §§ 1394–1403, 1407–1410. For discussion of 28 U.S.C. § 1407, authorizing venue consolidation for multidistrict litigation, see § 9.10[1][b] (multidistrict litigation), *infra.*

[11] *See generally* Christian E. Mammen, Note, *Here Today, Gone Tomorrow: The Timing of Contacts for Jurisdiction and Venue Under* 28 U.S.C. § 1391, 78 CORNELL L. REV. 707 (1993); David D. Siegel, Commentary on 1990 Revision of Subdivisions (a), (b), and (e), 28 U.S.C. § 1391 (Supp. 1993).

[12] 28 U.S.C. §§ 1391(b)(1).

[13] 28 U.S.C. § 1391(c)(1).

[14] 28 U.S.C. § 1391(c)(2).

[15] *See* § 3.09[2] (specific and general jurisdiction), *supra.*

[16] *See MOORE* § 110.03[4][c].

to the claim against it, or subject to general personal jurisdiction for any claim (including, therefore, the specific claim against it), it is deemed a resident of that district, as well as of any other district where the same holds true.

However, if the defendant entity is a corporation (as opposed, say, to an unincorporated organization or a partnership) that is subject to personal jurisdiction in a state that has more than one district, then it is deemed to reside just in any district within the state in which its contacts would be sufficient to subject it to personal jurisdiction if we treated that district as if it were a state, or if there is no district in which that would be true, then the district where it has the most contacts.[17] Consider, for example, Acme Corporation, a defendant in a product liability suit, which manufactures the product at a plant in Buffalo. Based on this claim-related contact, Acme would be subject to personal jurisdiction in any state or federal district court in New York. However, because New York is a multi-district state, section 1391(d) deems Acme only to reside — *for venue purposes* — in the Western District of New York (which includes Buffalo) and not in the other three New York districts. This provision, it seems, is designed to provide some additional venue protection to the corporation that does business only in one district of the state, although it is doubtful that the benefit it affords is worth the costs of re-targeting the contacts analysis to the weird "district-as-if-it-were-a-state" construct of the statute. Alternatively, if Acme had enough operations in all four New York districts to confer general personal jurisdiction, even though not enough contact with any one district alone to subject it to personal jurisdiction there if that district were treated as if it were a state, then the corporation would still be deemed to reside in the district in which it has "the most significant contacts."

Section 1391(b)(2) provides a handy alternative to residence-based venue. A plaintiff may lay venue in "a judicial district in which a substantial part of the events or omissions giving rise to the claim occurred, or a substantial part of property that is the subject of the action is situated."[18] Under a prior version of the statute, this venue alternative depended, like many state venue statutes, on the district where "the claim arose."[19] But identifying the single district in which the claim arose would be problematic for many cases in which the facts giving rise to the claim occurred in two or more districts.[20] By substituting "a" for "the" district, and looking to "a substantial part" of the events or omissions giving rise to the claim, the new subsection eases the problem by enlarging the number of permissible venues. For example, in a civil racketeering suit against a California-based defendant who phoned a party in Kansas and sent mail there, the court held these contacts substantial enough under subsection 1391(b)(2) to make the District

---

[17] 28 U.S.C. § 1391(d).

[18] 28 U.S.C. § 1391(b)(2).

[19] Act of Nov. 2, 1966, Pub. L. No. 89-714, 80 Stat. 1111, *amending* 28 U.S.C. §§ 1391(a) & (b). *See* WRIGHT & MILLER § 3806.

[20] *See, e.g., Leroy v. Great W. United Corp.*, 443 U.S. 173 (1979) (involving claims arising out of public tender offer by Delaware-incorporated and Texas-based corporation trying to take over publicly-listed Washington-incorporated corporation with executive offices and assets in Idaho and business in New York and Maryland).

of Kansas a proper venue, even though defendant's activities in California "might have been more substantial, or the most substantial."[21] "Events or omissions giving rise to the claim" has been given a common sense construction. Courts have looked at where a contract was made, executed, or to be performed, where breach occurred, where tortious acts took place, where the harms were felt, and where communications were transmitted or received, among many other factors.[22]

Finally, *if and only if* neither of these venue alternatives is available, section 1391(b)(3) affords the plaintiff a "fallback" venue. In this rare circumstance, plaintiffs may sue in "a judicial district in which any defendant is subject to personal jurisdiction at the time the action is commenced."[23] The original legislative history of section 1391 indicates that the purpose of the fallback provision was to provide a venue "safety net" in cases "in which no substantial part of the events happened in the United States and in which all the defendants do not reside in the same state."[24]

Of course, all of this statutory construction is often besides the point, because, instead of a statutory venue, parties may select a venue by including a forum selection clause in their contract. In *Bremen v. Zapata*,[25] the Supreme Court held that federal courts sitting in admiralty should enforce such clauses absent a showing that doing so "would be unreasonable and unjust, or that the clause was invalid for such reasons as fraud or overreaching."[26] It has since enforced even non-negotiable forum selection clauses.[27]

The applicability of this law to forum selection clauses in the Internet era is illustrated by *Caspi v. The Microsoft Network, L.L.C.*[28] There, a state appellate court upheld enforcement of such a clause in an online subscriber agreement because it found that the plaintiffs had validly assented to it by a mouse click. Notwithstanding disparity in size between the plaintiff class and Microsoft, the court found that the on-line computer service industry offered plaintiffs competitive choices, and that they were free to scroll through computer screens presenting the terms of the bargain before clicking their assent. Finally, it dismissed the plaintiffs' lack-of-notice argument. It concluded that nothing in the content, size, or placement of the clause in the online subscriber agreement was unusual or obfuscatory. Since the vast majority of web surfers click assent indiscriminately without reading the terms of online subscriber agreements, the court's analysis makes it clear that it is the *opportunity* to notice, comprehend, and reject the agreement containing the forum selection clause that counts.[29]

---

[21] *See Merchants Nat'l Bank v. Safrabank*, 776 F. Supp. 538, 541 (D. Kan. 1991).

[22] WRIGHT & MILLER § 3806.1

[23] 28 U.S.C. § 1391(b)(3).

[24] H.R. Rep. No. 101-734, 101st Cong., 2d Sess. 23 (1990).

[25] 407 U.S. 1 (1972).

[26] *Id.* at 15.

[27] *See Carnival Cruise Lines, Inc. v. Shute*, 499 U.S. 585 (1991). A more extended discussion of forum selection clauses appears in § 3.03[2][d], *supra*.

[28] 732 A.2d 528 (N.J. Super.), *cert. denied*, 743 A.2d 851 (N.J. 1999).

[29] *But see Hoffman v. Supplements Togo Mgmt., LLC*, 18 A.3d 210, 212 (N.J. Super. Ct. App. Div.

[3] Judge-Made Exceptions

Courts have carved several exceptions out of the usual venue statutes. They have held that actions properly removed to federal courts need not satisfy federal venue requirements because the removal statute itself[30] specifies the district to which the case must be removed.[31] (This is not so much an "exception," as it is simply a different venue statute.) As we noted above, courts usually have not applied federal venue requirements to supplemental claims when venue was proper on the anchor claim, partly on the theory that convenience was already taken into account in the jurisdictional analysis in such cases.[32]

A broader exception, made by most state courts, as well as federal courts before the 2012 amendment to the venue statutes, is for real property-based actions. Under the common law *local action rule*, the only proper venue for such an action is the locus of the property which is the subject of the action. This exception is an artifact of history, tracing its origin to an era in which juries were selected for their knowledge of the case. When an action involved real property, the only proper venue was necessarily where the property was located because only juries from that location knew enough about the property to decide the facts.[33] In contrast, all other actions — called *transitory actions* — can be heard wherever they arise. Distinguishing local from transitory actions, however, was no easy task. At English common law, the former included not only *in rem* and real actions for possession, ejectment, partition, foreclosure and quieting title, but also certain actions for trespass, and the states differ in their incorporation of this law.[34] Partly because of the haziness of such distinctions, Congress has now provided that federal venue

---

2011) (holding forum selection clause "presumptively unenforceable . . . because defendants' website was . . . structured in an unfair manner so that the clause would not appear on a purchaser's computer screen unless he or she scrolled down to display the 'submerged' clause"). *Compare* Paul J. Morrow, *Cyberlaw: The Unconscionability/Unenforceability of Contracts (Shrink-Wrap, Clickwrap, and Browse-wrap) on the Internet: A Multijurisdictional Analysis Showing the Need for Oversight*, 11 U. Pitt. J. Tech. L. & Pol'y 7 (2011) (arguing "clickwrap" contracts like those found in *Caspi* and *Hoffman* are invalid because they "are not communicated, definitive, or the product of negotiation," and calling for a more pronounced "meeting of the minds" analysis when such agreements are reviewed) *with* Nathan J. Davis, *Presumed Assent: The Judicial Acceptance of Clickwrap*, 22 Berkeley Tech. L.J. 577 (2007) (noting the "recognized benefits of standard form contracting in the electronic environment," and arguing widespread invalidation of "clickwrap" contracts "for lack of assent would have significant negative effects on electronic commerce").

[30] 28 U.S.C. § 1441(a) (qualifying cases "may be removed by the defendant or the defendants, *to the district court of the United States for the district and division embracing the place where such action is pending*") (emphasis added).

[31] *Wright & Miller* § 3804. On removal, *see generally* § 5.07, *supra*. Once the case has been removed, however, any party may seek a transfer of venue in accord with 28 U.S.C. § 1404. *See* § 6.02[2] (transfer), *infra*.

[32] *Moore* § 110.06.

[33] *See, e.g.*, *Wright* § 42. The local action exception was also historically based on judicial reluctance, for reasons of sovereignty and ability, to decide disputes concerning foreign property. *Cf. Reasor-Hill Corp. v. Harrison*, 249 S.W.2d 994 (Ark. 1952) (questioning application of this reasoning to interstate disputes about property, in rejecting the "majority [local action] rule").

[34] *See, e.g.*, *Livingston v. Jefferson*, 15 F. Cas. 660 (C.C.D. Va. 1811) (No. 8,411) (applying local action rule to dismiss suit in Virginia federal court against former President Jefferson for trespass to property in Louisiana Territory).

"shall be determined without regard to whether the action is local or transitory in nature,"[35] but most state courts continue to make this exception to their statutory venue requirements.

§ 6.02 CHANGE OF VENUE

[1] Dismissal and Forum Non Conveniens[36]

Objection to improper venue is ordinarily made by a preliminary motion to dismiss, and the indicated remedy is, therefore, dismissal of the action without prejudice. If, however, the statute of limitations has since expired,[37] a dismissal effectively extinguishes the plaintiff's right of action without reaching the merits. To avoid this harsh result, the plaintiff will usually seek the transfer of the action to a proper venue within the same judicial system as an alternative to dismissal. Most venue laws permit such transfers in the alternative.

In the federal system, for example, a court in which venue has improperly been laid may dismiss, "or if it be in the interest of justice, transfer [the] case to any district or division in which it could have been brought."[38] As federal courts have interpreted this provision, a court with subject matter jurisdiction, whether or not it has personal jurisdiction over the parties,[39] may transfer a case laying improper venue to any federal forum which would have had personal jurisdiction over the defendant and would have been a proper venue initially. Almost all states have similar or less restrictive provisions for transfer in lieu of dismissal, if there is a proper alternative venue within the state judicial system.

Suppose, however, that the alternative forum is outside the state's judicial system or even outside the United States. State courts have no power to transfer cases to the courts of other states, and neither state nor federal courts have the power to transfer cases to the courts of foreign countries.[40] In such cases, most judicial systems permit dismissal of suits under the common law doctrine of *forum non conveniens*, in anticipation that the plaintiff will recommence the suit in the

---

[35] 28 U.S.C. § 1391(a)(2).

[36] *See generally* David W. Robertson & Paula K. Speck, *Access to State Courts in Transnational Personal Injury Cases: Forum Non Conveniens and Antisuit Injunctions*, 68 Tex. L. Rev. 937 (1990); Allan R. Stein, *Forum Non Conveniens and the Redundancy of Court-Access Doctrine*, 133 U. Pa. L. Rev. 781 (1985); Margaret G. Stewart, *Forum Non Conveniens: A Doctrine in Search of a Role*, 74 Cal. L. Rev. 1259 (1986).

[37] Under some statutes, the pendency of the lawsuit — even in an improper venue — tolls the statute. *See generally* § 8.08[2][b] (limitations defense), *infra*.

[38] 28 U.S.C. § 1406(a).

[39] *See Goldlawr, Inc. v. Heiman*, 369 U.S. 463 (1962).

[40] Nor can federal courts transfer cases onto the dockets of state courts. However, there is less need for transfer in this setting. A state court in the state where the federal court is sitting usually will not be appreciably more convenient than the federal court there. The court of a second state might be more convenient, but so too would a federal court in the second state. The federal court where suit originated can affect intra-system transfer to the latter under 28 U.S.C. § 1404. *See* § 6.02[2] (transfer of venue), *infra*.

alternative foreign venue.[41] The Supreme Court has characterized the doctrine as "a supervening venue provision, permitting displacement of the ordinary rules of venue when, in light of certain conditions, the trial court thinks that jurisdiction ought to be declined."[42] To obtain a *forum non conveniens* dismissal, defendant must satisfy two requirements.

First, he must show that an adequate alternative forum is available.[43] Since *forum non conveniens* presupposes a proper original venue, it would be unfair to plaintiff who correctly chose it and would frustrate the purposes of venue law to dismiss a case for which there was no adequate alternative forum. In *Piper Aircraft Co. v. Reyno*,[44] the plaintiff argued that his case should not be dismissed from a proper federal venue under the doctrine of *forum non conveniens* when the alternative Scottish forum would apply less favorable substantive law. The Supreme Court held that the mere possibility of an unfavorable change in the applicable law does not bar a *forum non conveniens* dismissal, unless the change makes the remedy "so clearly inadequate or unsatisfactory that it is no remedy at all."[45] In another case, a federal district court ruled that alleged defects and disadvantages of the Indian legal system, including allegedly high filing fees, serious case backlogs occasioned in part by frequent interlocutory appeals, and underdeveloped tort laws,[46] did not render an Indian forum inadequate in the litigation spawned by the catastrophic Bhopal pesticide leak.[47] On the other hand,

---

[41] The federal courts have asserted an inherent common law power to dismiss on *forum non conveniens* grounds. *But see* Elizabeth T. Lear, *Congress, the Federal Courts, and Forum non Conveniens: Friction on the Frontier of the Inherent Power*, 91 Iowa L. Rev. 1147 (2006) (arguing that courts' assumption of inherent *forum non conveniens* power to dismiss cases satisfying statutory venue requirements is unconstitutional).

[42] *Am. Dredging Co. v. Miller*, 510 U.S. 443, 453 (1994).

[43] *Gulf Oil Corp. v. Gilbert*, 330 U.S. 501, 506–07 (1947). *See generally* Joel H. Samuels, *When Is an Alternative Forum Available? Rethinking the Forum Non Conveniens Analysis*, 85 Ind. L.J. 1059 (2010); Annotation, *Forum Non Conveniens in State Court as Affected by Availability of Alternative Forum*, 57 A.L.R.4th 973 (1987); Ann Alexander, Note, *Forum Non Conveniens in the Absence of an Alternative Forum*, 86 Colum. L. Rev. 1000 (1986). A few courts have treated the availability of an adequate alternative forum as just one factor to weigh in a *forum non conveniens* decision, rather than a prerequisite to such a decision. *E.g.*, *Islamic Republic of Iran v. Pahlavi*, 467 N.E.2d 245 (N.Y. 1984).

[44] 454 U.S. 235 (1981).

[45] *Id.* at 254.

[46] *See generally* Marc Galanter, *Legal Torpor: Why So Little Has Happened in India After the Bhopal Tragedy*, 20 Tex. Int'l L.J. 273 (1985); James Stewart, *Why Suits for Damages Such as Bhopal Claims Are Very Rare in India*, Wall St. J., Jan. 23, 1985, at 1.

[47] *In re Union Carbide Corp. Gas Plant Disaster at Bhopal, India*, 634 F. Supp. 842 (S.D.N.Y. 1986), *aff'd as modified*, 809 F.2d 195 (2d Cir. 1987) (hereinafter cited as Bhopal Litigation). On the Bhopal Litigation generally, see Tim Covell, *The Bhopal Disaster Litigation: It's Not Over Yet*, 16 N.C. J. Int'l L. & Com. Reg. 279 (1991); Stephen J. Darmody, *An Economic Approach to Forum Non Conveniens Dismissals Requested by U.S. Multinational Corporations — The Bhopal Case*, 22 Geo. Wash. J. Int'l L. & Econ. 215 (1988); Ved P. Nanda, *For Whom the Bell Tolls in the Aftermath of the Bhopal Tragedy: Reflections on Forum Non Conveniens and Alternative Methods of Resolving the Bhopal Dispute*, 15 Denv. J. Int'l L. & Pol'y 235 (1987); Richard Schwadron, Note, *The Bhopal Incident: How the Courts Have Faced Complex International Litigation*, 5 B.U. Int'l L.J. 445 (1987); *see also* Kathryn Lee Boyd, *The Inconvenience of Victims: Abolishing Forum Non Conveniens in U.S. Human Rights Litigation*, 39 Va. J. Int'l L. 41, 49 (1998) (arguing that "unique federal interests embodied in the legislative creation of rights for human rights plaintiffs to sue their victimizers in the United States override convenience

a lack of subject matter jurisdiction in the alternative forum clearly renders it inadequate for *forum non conveniens* purposes.[48]

Second, the defendant must show that considerations of party and forum convenience override the plaintiff's choice of forum and justify dismissal. Typical party or "private" considerations include relative ease of access to proof, availability of compulsory process for attendance of witnesses, the cost of obtaining their attendance, the possibility of obtaining a jury view of the scene of the accident or property which is the subject of the action, and the enforceability of any eventual judgment in the original forum.[49] Ordinarily the plaintiff's choice of forum enjoys a strong presumption of convenience. When these factors indicate that the alternative forum would be more convenient for the parties, however, then the plaintiff's choice was presumably tactical, or even harassing, and may therefore be disturbed. This is more likely to be true when the plaintiff is a foreign party than when he is someone suing on his "home turf."[50]

Forum or "public" considerations reflect the relative burdens and benefits of imposing the litigation on the contending forums, including effect on judicial calendars, imposition of jury duty on the forum community, local interest in the controversy, and the choice of law.[51] Clearly, forum convenience — the public interest — is best served by localizing the litigation and assigning it to the forum most familiar with the applicable law.

The *forum non conveniens* determination is committed to the sound discretion of the trial court,[52] and, as such, is largely immune from effective appellate review.[53] The Supreme Court has held, moreover, that where the normally predicate issues of subject matter or personal jurisdiction are difficult (or require extensive discovery), and convenience points to an adequate foreign forum, a district court may by-pass them and take the "less burdensome course" of dismissing on *forum non conveniens* grounds.[54] Included within the court's discretion is the power to condition dismissal on a defendant's satisfaction of various conditions that will ensure the adequacy of the alternative forum (such as agreement to waive a limitations defense to a refiled suit or to submit to the

---

concerns," citing the Bhopal incident as an example).

[48] *Piper Aircraft*, 454 U.S. at 254 n.22 (ordinarily amenability of defendants to suit in the alternative forum evidences its adequacy, while lack of subject matter jurisdiction in the alternative forum makes it inadequate).

[49] *See, e.g., id.* at 257–58; *Gulf Oil*, 330 U.S. at 508.

[50] In some states, a resident plaintiff's interest in having his case heard by his own courts trumps all other private and public considerations and bars dismissal. *See, e.g., Ferreira v. Ferreira*, 512 P.2d 304 (Cal. 1973); *Iacouzze v. Iacouzze*, 672 P.2d 949 (Ariz. Ct. App. 1983). *See generally* Peter G. McAllen, *Deference to the Plaintiff in Forum Non Conveniens*, 13 S. Ill. U. L.J. 191 (1989).

[51] *Piper Aircraft*, 454 U.S. at 259–61; *Gulf Oil*, 330 U.S. at 508–09.

[52] *Piper Aircraft*, 454 U.S. at 257.

[53] *See* Stein, note 36, *supra*, at 831–32; Christina Melady Morin, Note, *Review and Appeal of Forum Non Conveniens and Venue Transfer Orders*, 59 Geo. Wash. L. Rev. 715 (1991); § 13.04[2] (noting unavailability of statutory interlocutory appeal under 28 U.S.C. § 1292(b) for review of venue transfer decisions), *infra*.

[54] *Sinochem Int'l Co. Ltd. v. Malaysia Int'l Shipping Corp.*, 549 U.S. 422, 436 (2007).

personal jurisdiction of the alternative forum)[55] or conditions that will enhance the party convenience of that forum (such as defendant's agreement to provide certain discovery).[56]

[2] Transfer of Venue

In § 2.02 we discussed factors influencing the plaintiff's choice of court. But defendants also forum shop by moving to transfer venue. Indeed, one commentator alleges that "the transfer motion has become a common, almost reflexive defendant response to a lawsuit."[57] Because courts lack the power to transfer cases outside their own judicial system, the doctrine of *forum non conveniens* is still used as a substitute for inter-system "transfer" from state or federal courts to state or foreign courts.[58] For intra-system transfers, however, relaxed versions of the doctrine have been codified in many jurisdictions.

The statutory provision for transfer of venue within the federal system[59] is probably typical. Unlike the common law *forum non conveniens* doctrine, the statute provides for transfer to a district where the case might have been brought,[60] instead of dismissal. Unlike section 1406, however, section 1404 transfers can be made not just to a district court or division where the action "might have been brought," but also to one to which all parties have consented. Since defendants can waive defenses of improper venue and lack of personal jurisdiction by consenting to a forum, this means that a court can order a 1404 transfer to a court that has neither if all consent. Furthermore, because the statute provides this milder remedy of transfer instead of dismissal, it is available upon a lesser showing[61] than required for *forum non conveniens* dismissal. The relaxed showing is phrased generally and unhelpfully as "the convenience of parties and witnesses, [or] in the interest of justice."[62] The parties' contractual choice of forum is an important factor for a court to consider in making this decision, but it is not

---

[55] *Bhopal Litigation*, 809 F.2d at 203–04 (conditioning dismissal in part on defendant's consent to personal jurisdiction of Indian courts and waiver of limitations defenses).

[56] *See Piper Aircraft*, 454 U.S. at 257 n.25. *See generally* John Bies, *Conditioning Forum Non Conveniens*, 67 U. Chi. L. Rev. 489 (2000).

[57] Stowell R.R. Kelner, Note, *"Adrift on an Uncharted Sea": A Survey of Section 1404(a) Transfer in the Federal System*, 67 N.Y.U. L. Rev. 612, 615 (1992).

[58] *See* note 40 and accompanying text, *supra*. It is not the only inter-system venue device, however. Some courts will stay proceedings before them until the plaintiff has refiled and defendant has submitted in a better foreign venue, and others will entertain actions by parties who are defendants in an inconvenient foreign venue to enjoin the plaintiff from prosecuting her action there. *See generally* Robertson & Speck, note 35, *supra*; Comment, *Forum non Conveniens, Injunctions Against Suit and Full Faith and Credit*, 29 U. Chi. L. Rev. 740, 741 (1962).

[59] 28 U.S.C. § 1404. *See generally* Maryellen Corna, Note, *Confusion and Dissension Surrounding the Venue Transfer Statutes*, 53 Ohio St. L.J. 319 (1992); Kelner, note 57, *supra*; David E. Steinberg, *The Motion to Transfer and the Interests of Justice*, 66 Notre Dame L. Rev. 443 (1990).

[60] 28 U.S.C. § 1404(a).

[61] *See Piper Aircraft*, 454 U.S. at 253; *Norwood v. Kirkpatrick*, 349 U.S. 29, 29–33 (1955) (noting section 1404 is not merely a codification of *forum non conveniens*, but adopts a more relaxed test for transfer in the federal system).

[62] 28 U.S.C. § 1404(a).

dispositive.[63] Moreover, unlike *forum non conveniens* dismissals, transfers of venue between federal courts are available to plaintiffs and defendants alike.[64]

The effect of a transfer is also different from the effect of a dismissal. Statutory transfer is intended only to change the place of trial and not the applicable law or the availability of limitations defenses. Accordingly, the Supreme Court has held that a federal transferee court must apply the law that would have been applied in the transferor court, whether the movant was the plaintiff or the defendant.[65] But courts have applied this holding only to section 1404 transfers, and not section 1406 transfers for improper venue,[66] for otherwise it would be too easy for a plaintiff to shop for favorable law by intentionally filing in an improper venue.

The law the transferor court would have applied includes choice of law rules. Thus, if a federal court in the Northern District of California transfers a diversity action asserting a tort claim arising from an accident in Ohio to the Middle District of Pennsylvania, the latter must ordinarily apply California's choice of law rules. If those rules apply the law of the place where the accident took place to such a tort claim, then the federal court for the Middle District of Pennsylvania, as the transferee, must apply the tort law of Ohio, just as the Northern District of California, the transferor court, would have. In short, the transferor law rule does not automatically mean that the transferee court will end up applying the substantive law of the transferor forum; it must apply the law that the transferor would apply following the transferor's choice of law rules. Only in this way do the courts assure that the transfer changes only the place of trial, not the applicable law.

After the transfer, the transferee court takes up the litigation where the transferor court left it, and no recommencement of the action is necessary, which preserves to plaintiff the date of the original commencement of the lawsuit for purposes of satisfying the statute of limitations.

The interaction of liberal federal venue, relaxed federal transfer standards, the uncertain effects of the parties' contractual choice of forum, and the general absence of effective appellate supervision of transfer decisions has bred substantial confusion in the case law and new opportunities to forum shop.[67] Whether a given

---

[63] *See Stewart Org., Inc. v. Ricoh Corp.*, 487 U.S. 22 (1988). *See generally* Leandra Lederman, Note, *Viva Zapata! Toward a Rational System of Forum-Selection Clause Enforcement in Diversity Cases*, 66 N.Y.U. L. REV. 422, 450–64 (1991).

[64] *See Ferens v. John Deere Co.*, 494 U.S. 516 (1990) (discussing choice of law after plaintiff-initiated transfer).

[65] *Ferens*, 494 U.S. at 516 (plaintiff's transfer under 28 U.S.C. § 1404); *Van Dusen v. Barrack*, 376 U.S. 612, 639 (1964) (defendant's transfer under 28 U.S.C. § 1404). *See generally* § 7.05[3] (*Klaxon* and § 1404(a)), *infra*. It is unclear whether the rule applies when a federal court transfers under circumstances in which a forum state court would have dismissed under the doctrine of *forum non conveniens*. *See* WRIGHT § 44; John D. Currivan, Note, *Choice of Law in Federal Court After Transfer of Venue*, 63 CORNELL L. REV. 149 (1977).

[66] *See* MOORE § 111.38[1].

[67] *See, e.g.*, Kimberly Jade Norwood, *Double Forum Shopping and the Extension of Ferens to Federal Claims that Borrow State Limitation Periods*, 44 EMORY L.J. 501 (1995); Corna, note 59, *supra*; Kelner, note 57, *supra*.

court will transfer is unpredictable.[68] The rule applying the law that the transferor court would apply lets plaintiffs forum-shop for the statute of limitations in some cases; less obviously, the willingness of at least some transferee courts to overrule the law of the case (that is, re-decide interlocutory decisions by the transferor court)[69] lets defendants forum-shop for reconsideration of adverse interlocutory decisions.[70] Critics of the current system, however, are undecided whether closer appellate supervision or statutory reform is the better solution.

§ 6.03 PROPOSALS REGARDING THE RELATIONSHIP OF PERSONAL JURISDICTION AND VENUE

A careful reader of Chapters 3 and 6 cannot help but note the similarities between personal jurisdiction and venue. Both address in part the reasonableness of the forum from defendant's perspective and the forum interests in the locus of suit. More generally, these doctrines of court access share common historical roots and purposes and have similar analytic structures.[71] Little wonder that students and lawyers alike occasionally have difficulty understanding how a court that may "reasonably" exercise personal jurisdiction over a defendant can be too inconvenient to the defendant to serve as an appropriate venue.

Critics have attempted to reformulate these court-access doctrines to eliminate or explain their overlap within a judicial system. One approach is capsulated in the prediction, "jurisdiction must become venue."[72] Proponents of this reformulation urge a system of nationwide service of federal process, under which the venue rules alone carry the full burden of assuring a reasonably convenient forum.[73]

"Venue must become jurisdiction" summarizes another alternative. Its approach is to abolish federal venue requirements and look solely to a federal long-arm statute to ensure a reasonably convenient forum.[74] Long-arm jurisdiction would be available in any district where a substantial part of the events giving rise to suit occurred or where defendant resides. To a significant degree, the 1990 amendments to the general federal venue statute moved in this direction, by laying venue in the

---

[68] *See, e.g., Carijano v. Occidental Petroleum Corp.*, 643 F.3d 1216 (9th Cir. 2011), *pet. for reh'g en banc denied*, 686 F.3d 1027 (9th Cir. 2012) (2-1 decision reversing district court's dismissal on *forum non conveniens* grounds because that court did not consider all the relevant public and private factors and failed to impose conditions on the dismissal, over a dissent arguing that the court did not abuse its discretion in weighing the relevant factors and refusing to impose conditions).

[69] *See* § 15.14 (law of the case), *infra*.

[70] *See* Kelner, note 57, *supra*, at 636–42; Joan Steinman, *Law of the Case: A Judicial Puzzle in Consolidated and Transferred Cases and in Multidistrict Litigation*, 135 U. Pa. L. Rev. 595 (1987).

[71] *See* Kevin M. Clermont, *Restating Territorial Jurisdiction and Venue for State and Federal Courts*, 66 Cornell L. Rev. 411, 430–34 (1981).

[72] Albert A. Ehrenzweig, *From State Jurisdiction to Interstate Venue*, 50 Or. L. Rev. 103, 113 (1971).

[73] *See* Edward L. Barrett, Jr., *Venue and Service of Process in the Federal Courts — Suggestions for Reform*, 7 Vand. L. Rev. 608, 627–35 (1954); David E. Seidelson, *Jurisdiction of Federal Courts Hearing Federal Cases: An Examination of the Propriety of the Limitations Imposed by Venue Restrictions*, 37 Geo. Wash. L. Rev. 82, 84 (1968).

[74] *See* David P. Currie, *The Federal Courts and the American Law Institute* (pt. 2), 36 U. Chi. L. Rev. 268, 299–311 (1969).

district in which significant contacts occur, or, for corporate defendants, where they are subject to personal jurisdiction, or, when these venues are unavailable, in the district in which the defendants are subject to personal jurisdiction.[75]

Alternatively, and more modestly, the *forum non conveniens* doctrine alone could be eliminated from venue law in favor of an expanded jurisdictional inquiry that expressly takes into account the private and public interests now canvassed under that doctrine.[76] Courts in Texas, for example, have taken this approach, finding themselves prohibited by statute from entertaining *forum non conveniens* motions and therefore importing *forum non conveniens* considerations into the law of personal jurisdiction.[77]

Another approach is to retain an assortment of access doctrines, but redefine their content to minimize overlap. This approach proposes a three-part inquiry: power (requiring only some contact with the forum), reasonableness (a constitutional due process requirement), and subconstitutional convenience (all other restrictions on geographic choice of forum, including the local action rule).[78] No system has yet adopted these approaches, and it remains to be seen whether any would respond more effectively to concerns treated by current law.

§ 6.04   PROPER VENUE IN THE CALIFORNIA COURTS

[1]   Introductory Note on Proper Venue in the California Courts

The rules of venue allocate cases territorially within a judicial system.[79] In the California state court system, venue determines the appropriate county within which to commence an action. The general concern of California's venue statutes is that litigation be conducted in a location convenient to the defendant. Despite advances in technology, the burden of defending in a distant county remains an important consideration for parties and their attorneys. Venue considerations may have a substantial impact on an attorney's decision to undertake representation. This is particularly true in a large state like California, where urban centers and their courthouses are hundreds of miles from each other.

[2]   General Venue Rules and Exceptions

Various statutory provisions govern the determination of proper venue in California. These provisions often overlap in a conflicting manner, but may be reduced to one fundamental premise, as stated in California Code of Civil Procedure § 395: A defendant is entitled to have an action tried in the county of his

---

[75] *See* 28 U.S.C. § 1391, discussed in § 6.02, *supra*.

[76] Stein, note 36, *supra*, at 844–45.

[77] *See generally* Alex Wilson Albright, *In Personam Jurisdiction: A Confused and Inappropriate Substitute for Forum Non Conveniens*, 71 Tex. L. Rev. 351 (1992).

[78] Clermont, note 71, *supra*, at 437–43.

[79] The rules of venue applicable within the federal court system are discussed in §§ 6.01–6.03, *supra*.

residence unless the action falls within some statutory exception to this general venue rule. The residence of an individual is defined as the one place where a person remains and to which he or she returns in seasons of repose; the residence of a corporation is its principal place of business.[80] When there are multiple defendants, venue is generally proper in any county where at least one of them resides. If none of the defendants resides in California, venue is generally proper in any county which the plaintiff may designate in the complaint.[81] However, there are a number of statutory exceptions to these general venue rules, and these exceptions in turn may be subject to more specific exceptions.[82] Some of the most common exceptions are discussed below.

Exceptions to the general venue rule usually reflect legislative policy to consider the plaintiff's convenience interests as well as the defendant's or, in some instances, a systemic concern for judicial efficiency. For example, in an action for "injury to person" or for wrongful death, the proper venue is either the county where the injury occurred or the county in which the defendants or some of them reside.[83] However, the California courts define "injury to person" narrowly to include physical or bodily injuries but not injuries to character, reputation, mental or emotional distress because they have no definite situs.[84] Another example is an action for recovery of real property or some interest in the property, where venue is proper only in the county in which the real property, or some part of the property, is located.[85] The California courts traditionally refer to such actions involving real property as "local actions," and to all other actions as "transitory actions," a distinction no longer made by the federal venue statute.

In an action against a corporation or an association, the legislative policy is to permit a wider choice of venue than is available in suits against an individual defendant. This policy is based on the assumption that an entity defendant has greater financial resources than an individual defendant or a plaintiff. Therefore, the venue statutes afford several venue options in order to permit the plaintiff chose the county he or she deems the most appropriate and convenient: the county where the obligation or liability arises, or where the contract was made or is to be performed or where breach occurs, or of the corporation's principal place of

---

[80] CAL. GOV'T CODE § 244(a); CAL. CODE CIV. PROC. § 395.2. In *Rosas v. Superior Court*, 25 Cal. App. 4th 671, 30 Cal. Rptr. 2d 609 (1994), the court discussed the factors relevant to the determination of a corporation's principal place of business and ruled that, for purposes of venue, a corporation is deemed bound by its designation of a principal place of business in the corporate documents it filed with the California Secretary of State.

[81] CAL. CODE CIV. PROC. § 395.

[82] *See generally* CEB, *California Civil Procedure Before Trial, Venue* §§ 8.1–8.78 (4th ed. 2012); 3 BERNARD E. WITKIN, CALIFORNIA PROCEDURE, *Actions* §§ 779–904 (5th ed. 2008) (hereinafter, WITKIN, CALIFORNIA PROCEDURE).

[83] CAL. CODE CIV. PROC. § 395.

[84] *E.g., Cacciaguidi v. Superior Court*, 226 Cal. App. 3d 181, 276 Cal. Rptr. 465 (1990) (abuse of process action not one for "injury to person"); *Carruth v. Superior Court*, 80 Cal. App. 3d 215, 145 Cal. Rptr. 344 (1978) (damage action for malicious prosecution); *Cubic Corp. v. Superior Court*, 186 Cal. App. 3d 622, 231 Cal. Rptr. 18 (1986) (action for intentional infliction of emotional distress).

[85] CAL. CODE CIV. PROC. § 392.

business.[86] Likewise, in a contract action, the plaintiff may bring suit in the county where the obligation is to be performed or in which the contract was entered into, where any defendant resides or, in certain consumer transactions for the sale of goods or services, where the buyer or lessee resided at the time of the contract or at the time of commencement of the action.[87]

The county in which the cause of action or some part of it arose is generally the proper venue for actions against a public officer for an official act.[88] However, notwithstanding any other statute, where the State of California is named as a defendant in an action for death or injury to person or personal property, the proper venue is the county where the injury occurred.[89] This provision is mandatory and, in multi-defendant actions, overrides any otherwise applicable venue provisions.[90] The proper venue for an action against the State for taking or damaging private property for public use is the county in which the property is situated.[91] In actions by or against a county, venue is governed by a complicated statute which includes a "removal" provision designed to avoid local prejudice by permitting transfer to a neutral county for trial.[92]

[3] Proper Venue in "Mixed Actions"

The general statutory venue rules and exceptions often overlap and conflict when a lawsuit involves multiple parties or causes of action. Such "mixed actions" may occur when plaintiffs permissively join transitory and local actions or multiple transitory actions, governed by conflicting venue statutes; or when one cause of action is brought but the complaint seeks different forms of relief, some local and others transitory. Because the venue statutes do not provide any general approach for resolving these conflicts, the California courts have developed their own general rules. As is often the case with venue analysis, these general judge-made rules may be subject to specific exceptions in particular cases.[93]

---

[86] CAL. CODE CIV. PROC. § 395.5.

[87] CAL. CODE CIV. PROC. § 395(a) & (b).

[88] CAL. CODE CIV. PROC. § 393(b). The California courts liberally construe "public officer" to include many agencies, departments, institutions, and boards. *See Regents of Univ. of Cal. v. Superior Court*, 3 Cal. 3d 529, 91 Cal. Rptr. 57, 476 P.2d 457 (1970).

[89] CAL. GOV'T CODE § 955.2.

[90] *State of Cal. v. Superior Court*, 193 Cal. App. 3d 328, 238 Cal. Rptr. 315 (1987).

[91] CAL. GOV'T CODE § 955.

[92] CAL. CODE CIV. PROC. § 394. *See, e.g., Delgado v. Superior Court*, 74 Cal. App. 3d 560, 141 Cal. Rptr. 528 (1977) (ruling Cal. Code Civ. Proc. § 394 controls over the general provisions of § 395); *Tutor-Saliba-Perini Joint Venture v. Superior Court*, 233 Cal. App. 3d 736, 285 Cal. Rptr. 1 (1991) (discussing when change of venue required under § 394 with respect to action against local agency based on negligent injury to person or property).

[93] *See generally* Arlo Van Alstyne, *Venue of Mixed Actions in California*, 44 CAL. L. REV. 685 (1956).

[a] The "Main Relief" Rule

When a complaint joins local and transitory causes of action against a defendant, the California courts usually disregard the local causes of action to establish proper venue.[94] Whether a complaint asserts a single or multiple causes of action is determined by the same "primary rights" analysis used to define a cause of action for purposes of California's res judicata doctrine.[95]

However, when a complaint alleges a single cause of action but seeks both local and transitory relief, the court will ascertain the primary object or "main relief" sought by the action to establish proper venue.[96] For example, in *Turlock Theatre Co. v. Laws*,[97] the plaintiff lessor brought an action against defendant lessees, residents of San Francisco County, to recover unpaid rentals under a lease of a theatre located in Stanislaus County and to terminate the lease and recover possession of the property. The action was commenced in Stanislaus County, but the trial court granted the defendants' motion to transfer venue to San Francisco County. On review, the California Supreme Court held that the plaintiff's action is "transitory" because the primary object of the action is to recover unpaid money and proper venue was therefore San Francisco County, the county of defendants' residence.

[b] Mixed Action Rules: Single Defendant and Multiple Causes of Action

The "mixed action" venue rules recognize a preference for trial in the county of a defendant's residence. Where a complaint naming one defendant alleges multiple transitory causes of action subject to conflicting venue provisions, in most cases the court must grant a change of venue on the entire complaint whenever the defendant is entitled to a change of venue — to the county of the defendant's residence — on any one cause of action.[98]

[c] Mixed Action Rules: Multiple Defendants and Causes of Action

Various mixed action venue rules apply in cases involving multiple defendants and causes of action subject to conflicting venue provisions. In such cases, when venue is proper in the county in which one of the defendants resides as to one cause

---

[94] *E.g., Peiser v. Mettler*, 50 Cal. 2d 594, 603–06, 328 P.2d 953 (1958); *Turlock Theatre Co. v. Laws*, 12 Cal. 2d 573, 86 P.2d 345 (1939).

[95] The "primary rights" doctrine is discussed in more detail in § 15.16, *infra*.

[96] *See, e.g., Peiser v. Mettler*, 50 Cal. 2d 594, 603–06, 328 P.2d 953 (1958) (in action by lessor for breach of farm lease seeking return of improvements and damages for loss of use and waste, court determined that main relief sought was transitory for venue purposes); *Massae v. Superior Court*, 118 Cal. App. 3d 527, 533, 173 Cal. Rptr. 527 (1981) (in an action by trustors under deed of trust seeking declaratory relief, reformation, and damages, court determined main relief to be for reformation and therefore the action local for venue purposes).

[97] 12 Cal. 2d 573, 86 P.2d 345 (1939).

[98] *See Brown v. Superior Court*, 37 Cal. 3d 477, 208 Cal. Rptr. 724, 691 P.2d 272 (1984) (and cases cited therein); *Ah Fong v. Sternes*, 79 Cal. 30, 33, 21 P. 381 (1889).

of action, venue is proper in that county as to all properly joined causes of action and defendants.[99] This mixed action rule applies even if some of the causes of action name only nonresidents of the county selected by plaintiff, so long as a resident defendant is named in others. This rule makes it easier for a plaintiff to select an appropriate county for venue when two or more inconsistent venue provisions appear to be concurrently applicable in the same case.

A different mixed action rule applies when the plaintiff commences an action involving multiple defendants and causes of action in a county where *no* defendant resides. In such cases, the court must grant a change of venue whenever a defendant is entitled to a change of venue — to the county of that defendant's residence — on any one cause of action.[100] For example, in *Gallin v. Superior Court*,[101] the plaintiff commenced a class action in San Diego County on behalf of purchasers of "Milli Vanilli" recordings against several defendants, including the performers, their manager, record producers, and distributors. Plaintiff claimed that the defendants committed deceptive consumer practices in violation of the California Consumer Legal Remedies Act, and common law fraud and breach of contract, when they failed to disclose that the Milli Vanilli rock group did not perform its own vocals in their recordings. Defendant Gallin, the group's manager, moved to transfer venue to Los Angeles County on the basis that he resides there and none of the defendants reside in San Diego County, relying on Code of Civil Procedure § 395 and various mixed action rules. Plaintiff argued that venue in San Diego County was proper under the special venue provision of the Consumer Legal Remedies Act, which authorizes venue in the county where the consumer sales transaction occurred. The superior court denied the motion and defendant sought appellate review. The Court of Appeal held that the defendant was entitled to a transfer of venue under the mixed action rules, and directed the superior court to grant the motion.

However, this mixed action rule is subject to exceptions, such as where the strong countervailing policy of a special venue statute outweighs that preference for trial in the county of the defendant's residence. For example, in *Brown v. Superior Court*,[102] three former employees brought an action against their former employers, both corporate and individual defendants, seeking damages for alleged racial discrimination in violation of California's Fair Employment and Housing Act

---

[99] *See, e.g., Monogram Co. v. Kingsley*, 38 Cal. 2d 28, 237 P.2d 265 (1951); *Tutor-Saliba-Perini Joint Venture v. Superior Court*, 233 Cal. App. 3d 736, 742, 285 Cal. Rptr. 1 (1991). This mixed action rule becomes more complicated when the action includes individual and corporate defendants. *See, e.g., Mosby v. Superior Court*, 43 Cal. App. 3d 219, 226, 117 Cal. Rptr. 588 (1974) (when a plaintiff brings an action against several defendants, both individual and corporate, in a county which is neither the residence nor principal place of business of any defendant, an individual defendant may change venue to the county of his residence even though venue initially laid may otherwise be proper on one of the alternative grounds provided in Cal. Code Civ. Proc. § 395.5); *Capp Care, Inc. v. Superior Court*, 195 Cal. App. 3d 504, 241 Cal. Rptr. 741 (1987) (holding defendant corporation is entitled to a transfer of venue from Los Angeles County to Orange County pursuant to a special venue statute for corporate dissolutions, despite the fact that individual defendants resided in Los Angeles County).

[100] *See Brown v. Superior Court, supra*, 37 Cal. 3d at 487–89 (discussing mixed action rules).

[101] 230 Cal. App. 3d 541, 281 Cal. Rptr. 304 (1991).

[102] 37 Cal. 3d 477, 208 Cal. Rptr. 724, 691 P.2d 272 (1984).

(FEHA), as well as for intentional infliction of emotional distress and wrongful discharge. All three claims rested on the same factual allegations and were based on the same allegedly discriminatory practices. The action was filed in Alameda County, the county in which the alleged discriminatory employment practices took place, as provided by the special venue provision of the FEHA. The defendants moved for a transfer of venue to Sacramento County on the grounds that the individual and corporate defendants resided there, and none of the defendants resided in the Alameda County where the action was filed. The trial court applied the "mixed action" venue rule and granted the motion to transfer, and the plaintiffs sought appellate review.

The California Supreme Court in *Brown* held that the special provisions of the FEHA venue statute control in cases involving FEHA claims joined with non-FEHA claims arising from the same facts. Therefore, the FEHA's special venue statute governed the entire action, and the county in which the alleged discriminatory practices occurred was the proper county for the trial of the lawsuit. In reaching this conclusion, the Court ruled that the mixed action rule, which recognizes a preference for trial in the county of the defendant's residence, is outweighed by the important public policy of the FEHA which favors a plaintiff's choice of venue.

[4] Importance of the Complaint

The general rule in California is that venue must be determined based on the allegations of the complaint on file at the time the motion to transfer venue was made, and not based on subsequent amendments.[103] A plaintiff may exercise considerable control over a determination of proper venue based on the causes of action and theories the plaintiff chooses to assert in the complaint, the parties named as defendants, and the relief sought. However, if a plaintiff *improperly* joins a defendant solely for the purpose of establishing venue in the county of that defendant's residence, that defendant's residence will not be considered in determining proper venue.[104]

[5] Raising Improper Venue: Motion to Transfer Required

A defendant who wishes to contest the plaintiff's choice of venue as not the proper county must "at the time he or she answers, demurs, or moves to strike, or, at his or her option, without answering, demurring, or moving to strike and within the time otherwise allowed to respond to the complaint," move to transfer the action to the proper court.[105] Otherwise, the defendant's objection to improper venue is waived, and the action may be tried in the court where commenced.

---

[103] *Turlock Theatre Co. v. Laws*, 12 Cal. 2d 573, 575, 86 P.2d 345 (1939); *Peiser v. Mettler, supra*, 50 Cal. 2d at 603.

[104] CAL. CODE CIV. PROC. § 395(a); *Peiser v. Mettler, supra*, 50 Cal. 2d at 601–03 (in deciding a motion for transfer of venue, the trial court must determine whether the plaintiff had reasonable grounds for the belief in good faith that plaintiff had a cause of action against the resident defendant).

[105] CAL. CODE CIV. PROC. § 396b.

The California procedure is similar, but not identical, to that of Rule 12 of the Federal Rules of Civil Procedure with respect to raising improper venue. An objection to venue is not waived in federal court by being joined with other objections or defenses, so long as the objection is raised by pleading or motion at the defendant's first appearance. However, unlike federal Rule 12, the California venue statutes require that the defendant make a *motion to transfer venue* at the time defendant files the first responsive pleading.[106] Failure to file a separate motion to transfer at time of answer waives the objection to venue in the improper court; only raising the issue by affirmative defense in an answer is inadequate.[107] Also, unlike federal Rule 12, dismissal — as opposed to transfer — for lack of proper venue is not an option under the California venue statutes.

[6] Change of Venue for Convenience of Witnesses, Etc.

Pursuant to California Code of Civil Procedure § 397, a trial court also has discretionary authority upon motion to change the place of trial "[w]hen the convenience of witnesses and the ends of justice would be promoted by the change." Unlike the federal discretionary transfer of venue statute, 28 U.S.C. § 1404(a), section 397 does not authorize consideration of the convenience of parties or employees of parties except when employees of one party are called as witnesses by the adverse party or when a party's physical condition makes it impossible for the party to travel to a distant county to give material evidence.[108] When a court orders discretionary change of venue pursuant to section 397, the action must be transferred to a court which the parties may agree upon by stipulation or, if they do not so agree, to the nearest court where the cause for making the order does not exist.[109]

[7] Contractual Venue Provisions

The California courts are unwilling to enforce contractual provisions which specify the county for contract-related litigation.[110] The courts distinguish between an *interstate* forum selection clause, which is enforceable if reasonable, and an

---

[106] CAL. CODE CIV. PROC. § 396b(a).

[107] *E.g., Northern Cal. Dist. Council of Hod Carriers v. Penn. Pipeline, Inc.*, 103 Cal. App. 3d 163, 173–74, 162 Cal. Rptr. 851 (1980); *Dugar v. Happy Tiger Records, Inc.*, 41 Cal. App. 3d 811, 819–20, n.11, 116 Cal. Rptr. 412 (1974).

[108] *See, e.g., Peiser v. Mettler*, 50 Cal. 2d 594, 612, 328 P.2d 953 (1958); *Lieberman v. Superior Court*, 194 Cal. App. 3d 396, 401–02, 239 Cal. Rptr. 450 (1987); *see* 2 CEB, *California Civil Procedure Before Trial, Motions to Change Venue* §§ 20.1–20.42 (4th ed. 2012); 3 WITKIN, CALIFORNIA PROCEDURE, *Actions* §§ 905–958 (5th ed. 2008).

[109] CAL. CODE CIV. PROC. § 398. The factors relevant to transfer of venue in federal court pursuant to 28 U.S.C. § 1404(a) are discussed in § 6.02[2], *supra*.

[110] *See, e.g., General Acceptance Corp. v. Robinson*, 207 Cal. 285, 277 P. 1039 (1929) (holding intrastate contract venue provision void when the county specified for litigation not proper one under statutory provisions); *Alexander v. Superior Court*, 114 Cal. App. 4th 723, 8 Cal. Rptr. 3d 111 (2003) (holding contractual venue selection clause that stipulates venue in a county not a proper county under Cal. Code Civ. Proc. § 395 is invalid and unenforceable); *Arntz Builders v. Superior Court*, 122 Cal. App. 4th 1195, 19 Cal. Rptr. 3d 346 (2004) (ruling invalid a contractual venue provision purporting to waive

intrastate venue selection clause, which is invalid. They also distinguish a waiver of the right to transfer venue to a proper county by failing to file a timely motion after an action has been instituted from a contractual provision entered into before the action has been filed designating an improper venue, which is against public policy and void. A few special statutes specifically declare such venue provisions void and unenforceable when included in certain consumer contracts.[111] The existence of these explicit statutory restrictions would seem to suggest that such venue agreements may be enforceable in contracts not governed by these special statutes, but the California courts have consistently rejected such arguments.

[8] California's Forum Non Conveniens Doctrine

[a] Relevant Factors Under the California Doctrine

The California doctrine of forum non conveniens is virtually identical to the federal doctrine applied by the United States Supreme Court in *Piper Aircraft Co. v. Reyno*,[112] and *Gulf Oil Corp. v. Gilbert*.[113] In *Stangvik v. Shiley Inc.*,[114] the California Supreme Court described the California doctrine in the following manner:

> In determining whether to grant a motion based on forum non conveniens, a court must first determine whether the alternate forum is a "suitable" place for trial. If it is, the next step is to consider the private interests of the litigants and the interests of the public in retaining the action for trial in California. The private interest factors are those that make trial and the enforceability of the ensuing judgment expeditious and relatively inexpensive, such as the ease of access to sources of proof, the cost of obtaining attendance of witnesses, and the availability of compulsory process for attendance of unwilling witnesses. The public interest factors include avoidance of overburdening local courts with congested calendars, protecting the interests of potential jurors so that they are not called upon to decide cases in which the local community has little concern, and weighing

---

defendant's right to transfer action brought by county to a neutral forum pursuant to Cal. Code Civ. Proc. § 394).

[111] *E.g.,* CAL. CODE CIV. PROC. § 395(b) & (c) (actions arising out of most consumer transactions); CAL. CIV. CODE § 1804.1 (Unruh Retail Installment Sales Act); § 2983.7(f) (Rees-Levering Motor Vehicle Sales and Finance Act); CAL. COM. CODE § 10106(b) (limitation on power of parties to consumer lease to contractually designate county for litigation).

[112] 454 U.S. 235, 259–61 (1981). The federal common law doctrine of forum non conveniens applicable in the federal courts is discussed in § 6.02[1], *supra*.

[113] 330 U.S. 501, 507–09 (1947).

[114] 54 Cal. 3d 744, 1 Cal. Rptr. 2d 556, 819 P.2d 14 (1991). The *Stangvik* court identified several private and public interest factors that a trial court must consider in determining a forum non conveniens motion, which fit roughly into three broad categories: the relationship of the case and the parties to each forum, concerns of judicial administration, and convenience to the parties and witnesses. *See Ford Motor Co. v. Ins. Co. of N. Am.*, 35 Cal. App. 4th 604, 41 Cal. Rptr. 2d 342 (1995); *Great No. Ry. Co. v. Superior Court*, 12 Cal. App. 3d 105, 113–15, 90 Cal. Rptr. 461 (1970) (listing 25 factors to be considered when resolving a forum non conveniens motion).

the competing interests of California and the alternate jurisdiction in the litigation.[115]

Similar to — but stated more definitively than — the federal doctrine, the California doctrine does not accord the possibility of an unfavorable change in the law *any* weight in deciding a motion provided, however, that "some remedy is afforded."[116]

[b] Adequate Alternate Forum

As *Stangvik v. Shiley, supra*, indicates, a California court will not dismiss an action based on forum non conveniens unless a suitable alternate forum is available to the plaintiff for trial of the action. Generally, this simply means that the alternative forum will not preclude the plaintiff from proceeding there due to lack of personal jurisdiction or the bar of the statute of limitations. Because defendants can always offer to stipulate to submit to an alternative forum's jurisdiction and to waive any applicable statutes of limitations, these threshold requirements are usually insignificant.[117]

[c] The "No Remedy at All" Exception

In *Stangvik v. Shiley, supra*, the California Supreme Court indicated that an unfavorable change in law is a relevant consideration only where the remedy in the alternative forum is so clearly inadequate or unsatisfactory that it is "no remedy at all." The California courts interpret this "no remedy at all" exception very narrowly. For example, in *Shiley, Inc. v. Superior Court*,[118] several nonresident plaintiffs commenced actions in California against defendant Shiley seeking damages for alleged emotional distress they suffered as a result of the knowledge that their implanted heart valves may be defective and malfunction, causing death. California law recognized a viable cause of action for fraud in such circumstances; but none of the various states of plaintiffs' domiciles recognized any cause of action for injuries caused by a product which had not yet malfunctioned.

On appeal after a forum non conveniens dismissal, the Court of Appeal in *Shiley* held that the "no remedy at all" exception was inapplicable and the plaintiffs' home states constituted suitable forums. The court reasoned that the "no remedy at all" exception "applies only in 'rare circumstances,' such as where the alternative forum is a foreign country whose courts are ruled by a dictatorship, so that there is no independent judiciary or due process of law. . . . The exception has never been applied to a sister state, and we decline to apply it here."[119]

---

[115] *Stangvik, supra*, 54 Cal. 3d at 751.

[116] *Stangvik, supra*, 54 Cal. 3d at 753, n.5.

[117] *See, e.g., Stangvik, supra*, 54 Cal. 3d at 752 (ruling the action may be suitably tried in Norway and Sweden because defendant stipulated that they would submit to jurisdiction there and that the statute of limitations was tolled).

[118] 4 Cal. App. 4th 126, 6 Cal. Rptr. 2d 38 (1992).

[119] *Shiley, supra*, 4 Cal. App. 4th at 133–34.

After *Shiley*, the "no-remedy-at-all" exception is practically meaningless in interstate litigation. As one California court noted, the fact that a plaintiff will be disadvantaged by the law of the other jurisdiction, or that the plaintiff will probably or even certainly lose, does not render the alternative forum "unsuitable."[120]

[d] Effect of Plaintiff's Residency: Dismissal vs. Stay

Under the California doctrine, the effect of the plaintiff's residence in deciding a motion to dismiss for forum non conveniens is essentially the same as under the federal doctrine. Although a trial court must accord substantial deference to a resident plaintiff's choice of a California court, a nonresident plaintiff's choice of a California court is not a significant factor in favor of retaining jurisdiction.[121] One area where the California and federal doctrines may differ is over the treatment of a resident plaintiff when the defendant seeks a *stay* as opposed to a *dismissal*.

A court that dismisses a suit on grounds of forum non conveniens loses jurisdiction over the action. A court that stays the action retains jurisdiction over the parties and the cause, and can protect the interests of the parties pending the final decision of the foreign court. Several recent California decisions have relied on the distinction between a dismissal and a stay to affirm a forum non conveniens stay even though the plaintiffs are California residents.[122] Other cases have found this distinction relevant to the threshold issue of whether there is a suitable alternative forum.[123] However, from the parties' perspective, a stay has the same effect as a dismissal — the action must be re-filed by the plaintiff and litigated in a forum other than the court in California where the action was originally commenced.

[e] Procedures for Raising Forum Non Conveniens

A defendant may move to stay or dismiss on the ground of inconvenient forum within the time available for pleading to the complaint. If the motion is denied, the defendant may seek immediate appellate review by writ of mandate. However, the right to raise forum non conveniens is not waived by failure to make the motion prior to a responsive pleading.[124] Even after the defendant has made a general appearance, either party or the court may move for stay or dismissal based on

---

[120] *Boaz v. Boyle & Co.*, 40 Cal. App. 4th 700, 46 Cal. Rptr. 2d 888 (1995).

[121] *Stangvik, supra*, 54 Cal. 3d at 754–55.

[122] *E.g., Berg v. MTC Elec. Tech. Co.*, 61 Cal. App. 4th 349, 71 Cal. Rptr. 2d 523 (1998); *Century Indem. Co. v. Bank of Am., FSB*, 58 Cal. App. 4th 408, 68 Cal. Rptr. 2d 132 (1997).

[123] *E.g., Hansen v. Owens-Corning Fiberglas Corp.*, 51 Cal. App. 4th 753, 59 Cal. Rptr. 2d 229 (1996) (holding the moving party seeking a forum non conveniens *stay* is not required to show all defendants are subject to personal jurisdiction in a particular alternative forum); *American Cemwood Corp. v. Am. Home Assurance Co.*, 87 Cal. App. 4th 431, 104 Cal. Rptr. 2d 670 (2001) (holding the failure of the moving party to demonstrate that all defendants are subject to jurisdiction in British Columbia precludes a forum non conveniens *dismissal*, and that *Hansen* is inapposite because there the moving party only sought a *stay*).

[124] CAL. CODE CIV. PROC. § 410.30; *see Marriage of Tucker*, 226 Cal. App. 3d 1249, 1257, 277 Cal. Rptr. 403 (1991) (observing that under both state and federal law, a forum non conveniens defense need not be raised prior to filing a responsive pleading); *Britton v. Dallas Airmotive, Inc.*, 153 Cal. App. 4th 127, 62 Cal. Rptr. 3d 487 (2007) (ruling a defendant does not waive the forum non conveniens issue by failing to file a preappearance forum non conveniens motion).

forum non conveniens. In most cases, this is the preferable procedure because it may be necessary to conduct discovery to develop the factual underpinnings for a forum non conveniens motion. A trial court order granting such a motion, filed after a general appearance, is an appealable order.

[f] Forum Non Conveniens and Forum Selection Clauses

The California courts, like the federal courts and those of all but a handful of other states, will enforce a freely negotiated interstate forum selection clause unless the resisting party shows that enforcement would be "unreasonable."[125] When a plaintiff commences an action in a California court but the contractually mandated forum is in another state or country, the proper procedural vehicle to enforce a forum selection clause is a forum non conveniens motion.[126] In such circumstances, the only relevant consideration is whether the forum selection clause is unreasonable or unfair. The presumptions and discretionary weighing of private and public interest factors pertinent to a forum non conveniens motion in the absence of a contractual forum provision are irrelevant.[127]

However, when a plaintiff commences an action in the contractually designated forum, an argument can be made that the existence of the forum clause does not preclude an attempt by the defendant to change the forum via a forum non conveniens motion. Because the parties lack the power to contractually waive the public (as opposed to the private) interest factors associated with forum non conveniens, a court arguably retains the power to grant the motion based on those factors in appropriate cases.[128]

---

[125] *E.g., Smith, Valentino & Smith, Inc. v. Superior Court*, 17 Cal. 3d 491, 131 Cal. Rptr. 374, 551 P.2d 1206 (1976); *Cal-State Bus. Prod. & Serv., Inc. v. Ricoh*, 12 Cal. App. 4th 1666, 16 Cal. Rptr. 2d 417 (1993).

[126] *Cal-State Bus. Prod., supra*, 12 Cal. App. 4th at 1680; *Smith, Valentino & Smith, supra*, 17 Cal. 3d 494.

[127] *Cal-State Bus. Prod., supra*, 12 Cal. App. 4th at 1682–83; *see Berg, supra*, 61 Cal. App. 4th at 358–64 (ruling the factors that apply generally to a forum non conveniens motion do not apply to enforcement of a mandatory, as opposed to a permissive, forum selection clause).

[128] *See* Walter W. Heiser, *Forum Selection Clauses in State Courts: Limitations on Enforcement After Stewart and Carnival Cruise*, 45 Fla. L. Rev. 361, 393–401 (1993).

Chapter 7

ASCERTAINING THE APPLICABLE LAW

§ 7.01 OVERVIEW

This chapter explores the duty of federal courts to ascertain and apply state law when deciding cases within their diversity jurisdiction, and claims within their supplemental jurisdiction.[1] The source of the obligation is the *Erie* doctrine,[2] which reads the federal Rules of Decision Act[3] to require use of state law when the difference between state and federal law might invite forum shopping or result in inequitable administration of state law.

Section 7.02 of this chapter examines the origins of the *Erie* doctrine and the policies responsible for its creation that have contemporary significance. Section 7.03 considers subsequent developments in the doctrine and offers some suggestions for understanding and applying the various tests that have emerged from United States Supreme Court decisions. Section 7.04 looks at how federal courts have used the *Erie* doctrine to resolve tensions between the federal rules of procedure and state law.

To decide that *Erie* requires a federal court to look to state rather than federal law may be only the first step toward decision. Difficult questions can also arise concerning which of the conflicting laws of two or more states should govern the case and concerning the content of state law. These questions are discussed in Sections 7.05 and 7.06, respectively.

Erie eliminated general federal common law, but left specific federal common law undisturbed in federal question cases. Section 7.07 examines when that law applies and how it is determined.

---

[1] General diversity jurisdiction exists for federal courts under 28 U.S.C. § 1332. For a discussion of federal diversity jurisdiction, see § 5.04, *supra*. Supplemental jurisdiction is authorized by 28 U.S.C. § 1367, and is discussed in § 5.11, *supra*.

[2] *See Erie R.R. Co. v. Tompkins*, 304 U.S. 64 (1938), and its progeny, discussed in §§ 7.03–7.04, *infra*.

[3] 28 U.S.C. § 1652:

> The laws of the several states, except where the Constitution or treaties of the United States or Acts of Congress otherwise require or provide, shall be regarded as rules of decision in civil actions in the courts of the United States, in cases where they apply.

§ 7.02 THE EVOLUTION FROM *SWIFT* TO *ERIE*[4]

[1] *Swift v. Tyson*

The Supreme Court held in *Swift v. Tyson*,[5] a federal diversity case, that the Rules of Decision Act[6] did not require it to follow New York state judicial decisions concerning the law of negotiable instruments. Writing for the Court, Justice Story stated that, at least with regard to "contracts and other instruments of a commercial nature," federal diversity courts were free to follow their own best understanding of the "general principles and doctrines of commercial jurisprudence."[7] In such cases, said Justice Story, state judicial decisions to the contrary were not part of the "laws of the several states," as that term was used in the Rules of Decision Act. The Act's mandate that state laws be followed "as rules of decision" did not apply because the *Swift* Court regarded its application to be limited

> to state laws strictly *local*, that is to say, to the positive statutes of the state, and the construction thereof adopted by the local tribunals, and to rights and titles to things having a permanent locality . . . . It never has been supposed by us, that the section did apply, or was designed to apply, to questions of a more *general* nature.[8]

[2] The Controversial Reign of the *Swift* Doctrine

Swift and the succeeding cases that made up the *Swift* doctrine permitted federal judges to displace state with federal common law simply because the federal court's diversity jurisdiction had been invoked. Law that federal judges made and applied under these circumstances came to be called *federal general common law*. At the time *Swift* was decided, assertion of this lawmaking authority does not seem to have been questioned.[9] During nearly a century when the *Swift* doctrine was in force, attitudes toward it changed and the doctrine became increasingly controversial. Two developments help explain this.

First, federal general common law expanded to rival state common law in a growing number of fields. The "general" and local categories created in *Swift* left many points of law unaccounted for, and usually it was the general law category into which the new problems were placed. Moreover, the Supreme Court

---

[4] For an extended version of this Section, see Gene R. Shreve, *From Swift to Erie: An Historical Perspective*, 82 Mich. L. Rev. 869 (1984).

[5] 41 U.S. (16 Pet.) 1 (1842).

[6] The statute was enacted as § 34 of the Judiciary Act of 1789. It has been amended in respects which do not bear on this discussion and now appears as 28 U.S.C. § 1652. Section 1652 is reproduced in § 7.01, *supra*.

[7] 41 U.S. at 19.

[8] 41 U.S. at 18 (emphasis added).

[9] *See* Tony Freyer, Harmony & Dissonance: The *Swift* and *Erie* Cases in American Federalism 36 (1981); Grant Gilmore, The Ages of American Law 33–34 (1977).

increasingly tended to displace state law even within the sanctuary of "local" matters originally defined in *Swift*.[10]

Second, it became relatively easy for corporate litigants to gain access to a federal court by invoking its diversity jurisdiction. Corporations had grown enormously as a class of litigants since the time of *Swift*. They frequently found federal general common law more congenial than state common law.[11] Through tactical selection of the place of incorporation, a corporation was often able to forum shop — to ensure that suits by or against it would be litigated in a federal diversity court — which gave it the benefit of federal general common law. This was especially true after Congress enlarged the scope of general diversity jurisdiction and removal in 1875.[12]

The *Swift* doctrine was never without its champions, who hoped it would promote uniformity among state and federal courts. By the twentieth century, however, it drew strong criticism from the legal community. Many saw federal diversity courts as protectors of the monied, corporate interests. But at the heart of the problem was the more basic issue of federalism. Which sovereign should have authority to create rules of decision to govern federal diversity cases? Forceful arguments were made in Supreme Court dissents that only states had such authority.[13]

[3]   *Erie R.R. Co. v. Tompkins*

The reign of *Swift* was finally brought to an end in 1938 by the Supreme Court's decision in *Erie Railroad Co. v. Tompkins*.[14] Plaintiff there sought to recover for injuries he received when struck by an object protruding from defendant's passing train. Plaintiff was on a path adjacent to the tracks at the time of the accident. The defendant railroad argued that the common law of Pennsylvania regarded the plaintiff as a trespasser under such circumstances and therefore imposed upon the defendant railroad only the duty to refrain from acts of wanton negligence. Plaintiff countered that the federal diversity court was free under *Swift* to disregard Pennsylvania judicial precedents and to regard plaintiff as an invitee to

---

[10] The most significant example was the withdrawal of state cases interpreting state statutes or constitutions from the preserve of "local" law created by *Swift*. *See Rowan v. Runnels*, 46 U.S. (5 How.) 134 (1847); *Watson v. Tarpley*, 59 U.S. (18 How.) 517 (1855); *Gelpcke v. City of Dubuque*, 68 U.S. (1 Wall) 175 (1863); *Burgess v. Seligman*, 107 U.S. 20 (1882). These cases are discussed in Robert H. Jackson, *The Rise and Fall of Swift v. Tyson*, 24 A.B.A.J. 609, 611–13 (1938).

[11] *See* JAMES WILLARD HURST, THE GROWTH OF AMERICAN LAW — THE LAW MAKERS 190 (1950); Alfred B. Teton, *The Story of Swift v. Tyson*, 35 ILL. L. REV. 519, 529–30 (1941).

[12] FREYER, note 9, *supra*, at 55–56.

[13] *See, e.g., Black & White Taxicab & Transfer Co. v. Brown & Yellow Taxicab & Transfer Co.*, 276 U.S. 518 (1928) (dissenting opinion of Justices Holmes, Brandeis and Stone). For a survey of other attacks on the *Swift* doctrine by Supreme Court dissenters, *see* William R. Casto, *The Erie Doctrine and the Structure of Constitutional Revolutions*, 62 TUL. L. REV. 907, 914–27 (1988); Shreve, note 4, *supra*, at 875 n.41.

[14] 304 U.S. 64. For an illuminating discussions of the facts and procedural history of *Erie*, see Irving Younger, *What Happened in Erie*, 56 TEX. L. REV. 1011 (1978); and Edward A. Purcell, Jr., *Governing Law — The Story of Erie: How Litigants, Lawyers, Judges, Politics, and Social Change Reshape the Law, in* CIVIL PROCEDURE STORIES, Ch. 1 (Kevin M. Clermont ed., 2d ed. 2008).

whom defendant owed a duty of ordinary care under federal general common law.

When the case finally reached the United States Supreme Court, the Court ruled in favor of the defendant and, in so doing, overruled *Swift*'s interpretation of the Rules of Decision Act. Writing for the Court, Justice Brandeis stated:

> Except in matters governed by the Federal Constitution or by Acts of Congress, the law to be applied in any case is the law of the State. And whether the law of the State shall be declared by its Legislature in a statute or by its highest court in a decision is not a matter of federal concern. There is no federal general common law.[15]

Brandeis noted that the uniformity of law sought by the advocates of the *Swift* doctrine had not materialized. State courts continued to make and adhere to their own precedents, while federal diversity courts were free to disregard them. Moreover, Brandeis observed that *Swift* had actually produced three undesirable results. First, the inability of courts to draw a clear line between local and general law had led to considerable confusion. Second, *Swift* worked mischief by providing non-citizens the forum-shopping advantage of invoking diversity jurisdiction to evade state common law rules, when plaintiffs who shared the citizenship of their defendants could not.[16] Furthermore, the non-citizen defendant sued by a diverse plaintiff in a state court can either stay or remove to federal court, while the citizen defendant is prevented from removing by the "forum defendant rule."[17] Third and most important, *Swift* had eroded the states' legitimate authority to regulate their own affairs, and effectively deprived state citizens of the benefits and protections of their own laws.[18]

---

[15] 304 U.S. at 78. Of course, Justice Brandeis did not suggest that federal courts should entirely give up making common law. "[T]he same justice the same day in another case pointed out that there may be questions of 'federal common law' upon which state statutes and decisions cannot be conclusive, such as the apportionment between two states of the water of an interstate stream." Charles E. Clark, *State Law in the Federal Courts: The Brooding Omnipresence of Erie v. Tompkins*, 55 YALE L.J. 267, 273 (1946) (*citing Hinderlider v. La Plata River and Cherry Creek Ditch Co.*, 304 U.S. 92, 110 (1938)). Federal common law is discussed in § 7.07, *infra*.

[16] In overruling *Swift*, *Erie* deprived litigants of their greatest gain from manipulating federal diversity jurisdiction — access to federal general common law. But *Erie* did not actually restrict the manipulation itself. Congress has since addressed the problem by barring the exercise of diversity jurisdiction when a party "has been improperly or collusively made or joined to invoke the jurisdiction of such court," 28 U.S.C. § 1359, and by rendering jurisdictional manipulation through incorporation, *see* note 12 and accompanying text *supra*, more difficult by extending the citizenship of a corporation to the additional state, if any, "where it has its principal place of business." 28 U.S.C. § 1332(c). On developments in federal diversity jurisdiction generally, *see* § 5.04, *supra. See also* § 5.05 (corporate citizenship), *supra*.

[17] 28 U.S.C. § 1441(b). *See* § 5.07[1].

[18] Brandeis suggested that *Swift* was simply wrong in reading the Rules of Decision Act to permit federal diversity courts to disregard state common law. He based this part of his attack on *Swift* upon Professor Charles Warren's research and argument that Justice Story had misconstrued the original purpose of the Rules of Decision Act. Charles Warren, *New Light on the History of the Federal Judiciary Act of 1789*, 37 HARV. L. REV. 49, 51–52, 81–88, 108 (1923). Brandeis's reliance upon this article was to cast a slight shadow over *Erie*, since Warren's methods and conclusions were, in time, roundly attacked. *See* the authorities cited in WRIGHT § 54; FREYER, note 9, *supra*, at 178 n.21. *Erie*'s authority was undamaged, however, because the principle of state lawmaking autonomy it vindicated rested upon a foundation

Erie was a momentous decision for several reasons. *Erie* not only overruled *Swift* and the long line of Supreme Court decisions adhering to it, it also invalidated hundreds — perhaps thousands — of federal general common law precedents in torts, commercial law and many other fields. In so doing, *Erie* repudiated the Court's prior settled interpretation of an act of Congress — something the Court does only with great reluctance.[19] This may explain why, despite the strong policy arguments for the result in *Erie* previously discussed, the Court found it necessary to further justify its decision by suggesting that the *Swift* doctrine was constitutionally suspect. Justice Brandeis wrote, "If only a question of statutory construction were involved, we should not be prepared to abandon a doctrine so widely applied throughout nearly a century. But the unconstitutionality of the course pursued has now been made clear and compels us to do so."[20] Finally, *Erie* worked a lasting change in the judicial arrangements of federalism. The case "announces no technical doctrine of procedure or jurisdiction but goes to the heart of the relations between the federal government and the states and returns to the states a power that had for nearly a century been exercised by the federal government."[21]

---

broader than Warren's work. The principle was extended in decisions beginning with *Guaranty Trust Co. v. York*, 326 U.S. 99 (1945).

[19] *See, e.g.*, EDWARD H. LEVI, AN INTRODUCTION TO LEGAL REASONING 32 (1948).

[20] *Erie*, 304 U.S. at 77–78. Concurring separately, Justice Reed saw no need to raise a constitutional question in order to overrule *Swift*. 304 U.S. at 9092. The Supreme Court has not chosen since to clarify or refine *Erie*'s constitutional dimension beyond the cryptic observation that *Erie* "indicated that Congress does not have the constitutional authority to make the law that is applicable to controversies in diversity of citizenship cases." *Bernhardt v. Polygraphic Co. of Am., Inc.*, 350 U.S. 198, 202 (1956). *See generally* Bradford R. Clark, *Erie's Constitutional Source*, 95 CALIF. L. REV. 1289 (2007).

The matter has been much debated in the literature. A number of commentators have endorsed the suggestion in *Erie* that the Constitution required the result there. *See, e.g.*, Paul J. Mishkin, *Some Further Last Words on Erie — The Thread*, 87 HARV. L. REV. 1682 (1974); Henry J. Friendly, *In Praise of Erie — and of the New Common Law* 39 N.Y.U. L. REV. 383, 392–98 (1964); Henry M. Hart, Jr., *The Relations Between State and Federal Law*, 54 COLUM. L. REV. 489, 509–10 (1954); Herbert Wechsler, *Federal Jurisdiction and the Revision of the Judicial Code*, 13 LAW AND CONTEMP. PROBS. 216, 239 n.121 (1948); Note, *The Competence of Federal Courts to Formulate Rules of Decision*, 77 HARV. L. REV. 1084, 1086 (1964). *But see, e.g.*, Charles E. Clark, *State Law in the Federal Courts: The Brooding Omnipresence of Erie v. Tompkins*, 55 YALE L.J. 267, 278–79 (1946); Philip B. Kurland, *Mr. Justice Frankfurter, The Supreme Court and the Erie Doctrine in Diversity Cases*, 67 YALE L.J. 187, 197 (1957); *cf.* John H. Ely, *The Irrepressible Myth of Erie*, 87 HARV. L. REV. 693 (1974) (suggesting a less restrictive role for the Constitution and a commensurately greater range of options for Congress); American Law Institute, Study of the Division of Jurisdiction Between State and Federal Courts 442 (1969) ("[I]t does not necessarily follow that the *Erie* holding was constitutionally compelled in the technical sense of being legally imposed by the fundamental instrument."). One scholar notes that the majority opinion in *Erie* rested on three grounds: "a new interpretation of the Rules of Decision Act, the 'defects' of *Swift*, and the 'unconstitutionality of the course pursued' under *Swift*" — and argues that "the Court was mistaken on each ground." *See* Suzanna Sherry, *Wrong, Out of Step, and Pernicious*: Erie *as the Worst Decision of All Time*, 39 PEPP. L. REV. 129 (2011).

[21] WRIGHT § 55. This is part of a broader principle. "Today, in our post-*Erie* world, . . . law in American courts must be positivistically attributable to a relevant sovereign, a sovereign with a legitimate interest in governing the particular issue presented in the particular circumstances." Louise Weinberg, *Back to the Future: Tne New General Common Law*, 35 J. MAR. L. & COM. 523, 526 (2004).

Most commentators have supported *Erie*, but not all. *See, e.g.*, John B. Corr, *Thoughts on the Vitality of Erie*, 41 AM. U. L. REV. 1087 (1992) (suggesting that *Swift* was preferable to *Erie*). *Cf.* Patrick J. Borchers, *The Origins of Diversity Jurisdiction, The Rise of Legal Positivism, and a Brave New World*

Some of the implications of this power shift are still being worked out by the courts, and the resulting *Erie* doctrine questions will be the subject of the sections that follow.

§ 7.03   TESTS FOR APPLYING *ERIE*

[1]   Substance-Versus-Procedure and the Outcome Determination Tests

The choice between state and federal common law in *Erie* involved competing standards of duty in tort law — what was then and is now understood to be substantive law.[22] It was never doubted that substantive law was most directly and obviously contemplated by the term "rules of decision" in the Rules of Decision Act. Therefore, once the Supreme Court reached the conclusion that the Act extended to state common law, *Erie* was easy to decide.

Subsequent litigants, however, were not content to confine their state law arguments under *Erie* to matters of torts or contracts. They argued that conflicting federal law must give way to local state law not only to determine the content of rights, but also to decide how and under what circumstances rights would be vindicated. These questions, which concern the processes by which the claims of rights are examined, are resolved according to a body of law often regarded as *procedural* rather than substantive in character.[23]

Those wishing to check the expansion of *Erie* attempted to use the distinction between substance and procedure as a dividing line. Under a substance-versus-procedure test, matters characterized as substantive would be governed by state law, and those characterized as procedural would be governed by federal law. Indeed, concurring in *Erie*, Justice Reed had said, "[n]o one doubts federal power over procedure."[24]

With the Supreme Court's decision in *Guaranty Trust Co. v. York*,[25] however, it became clear that this test would not be adequate to resolve all issues arising under the Rules of Decision Act.

---

for *Erie and Klaxon*, 72 TEX. L. REV. 79 (1993) (questioning the continued desirability of *Erie*). *See* Sherry, *supra* note 20.

[22] *Swift* and virtually all intervening cases had, in the same sense, also involved substantive law. *See, e.g., Black & White Taxicab & Transfer Co. v. Brown & Yellow Taxicab & Transfer Co.*, 276 U.S. 518 (1928) (a federal diversity action in which a contract, unenforceable under Kentucky state common law, was enforced under federal general common law).

[23] *See* § 1.01[2] (substance and procedure), *supra*.

[24] 304 U.S. at 92. The institution most obviously empowered to make federal procedural law is Congress. *Cf.* Riyaz A. Kanji, Note, *The Proper Scope of Pendent Appellate Jurisdiction in the Collateral Order Context*, 100 YALE L.J. 511, 522 (1990) ("Congress' Article III power to create the lower federal courts enables it to organize their operations as it sees fit."). When no statute interferes with their power to do so, federal courts may also make federal procedural law. For examples, see *Byrd v. Blue Ridge Rural Elec. Coop., Inc.*, 356 U.S. 525 (1958); *Chambers v. NASCO, Inc.*, 501 U.S. 32 (1991).

[25] 326 U.S. 99 (1945). For extended discussion of *York*, see Philip B. Kurland, *Mr. Justice Frankfurter, the Supreme Court and the Erie Doctrine in Diversity Cases*, 67 YALE L.J. 187 (1957).

Plaintiff in *York* brought a class action alleging that defendant breached its fiduciary duty as trustee in a corporate financing transaction. *Erie* left no doubt that the scope of defendant's fiduciary duty to plaintiff was to be determined under New York state law. Defendant urged, however, that *Erie* also required application of the state statute of limitations, which barred the action.[26] Plaintiff countered that the limitations question was instead governed by federal law. The Court sided with the defendant and, in a majority opinion written by Justice Frankfurter, held *Erie* to be fully applicable. Justice Frankfurter did not, however, adopt the defendant's argument that *Erie* was applicable because the limitations issue in *York* was substantive in character. He found the substance-versus-procedure test inadequate to explain the result in the case, observing that " 'substance' and 'procedure' are the same key-words to very different problems . . . . Each implies different variables depending upon the particular problem for which it is used."[27] This is not to say that he regarded the substance-procedure distinction as irrelevant to the Court's analysis; rather, Frankfurter explained, it was a particular kind of substance-procedure distinction that mattered — one that turned on whether applying federal rather than state law would affect the outcome of the case:

> The question is whether [the state law] concerns merely the manner and the means by which a right to recover, as recognized by the State, is enforced, or whether such statutory limitation is a matter of substance in the aspect that alone is relevant to our problem, namely, does it significantly affect the result of a litigation for a federal court to disregard a law of a State that would be controlling in an action upon the same claim by the same parties in a State court?[28]

This came to be regarded as the *outcome-determination* test. Under it, state rules controlled if the choice between state or federal law could be outcome-determinative in the case.

Clearly, the *York* decision carried the rule of *Erie* well beyond the facts of the *Erie* case. But just how far? One commentator observed that "to such a principle there is no apparent stopping place."[29] In three cases decided after *York*, the Supreme Court indeed seemed unable to find a stopping place in applying the outcome-determination test. These cases seemed to suggest that federal law could not be employed to decide questions of *procedure*[30] in diversity cases if state law conflicted and the choice could possibly affect the outcome. Then, in *Byrd v. Blue Ridge Rural Electric Cooperative, Inc.*,[31] the Supreme Court further massaged the

---

[26] On statutes of limitation generally, see § 8.08[2][b], *infra*.

[27] 326 U.S. at 108.

[28] 326 U.S. at 109.

[29] WRIGHT § 59.

[30] *Ragan v. Merchants Transfer & Warehouse Co.*, 337 U.S. 530 (1949) (time of commencement for purpose of tolling limitations); *Cohen v. Beneficial Indus. Loan Corp.*, 337 U.S. 541 (1949) (whether plaintiff must post security-for-expenses bond); *Woods v. Interstate Realty Co.*, 337 U.S. 535 (1949) (whether corporate plaintiff must meet state business qualification requirement in order to sue). *Ragan* and *Cohen* are discussed in § 7.04, *infra*.

[31] 356 U.S. 525 (1958).

test.

[2] *Byrd* and the Assessment of State and Federal Interests

The plaintiff in *Byrd* brought a federal diversity action for negligence, alleging injury while working on defendant's power line. The defendant argued that the work undertaken by plaintiff was the same as that done by defendant's own employees; therefore, plaintiff's only remedy was under the South Carolina worker's compensation act. Plaintiff contended that his work was not sufficiently like that of defendant's employees to satisfy the statute and sought a jury trial of this and other factual issues. Had plaintiff sued in South Carolina state court, a jury trial would not have been available on the statutory coverage issue. The defendant argued that the *Erie* doctrine operated to bar a federal jury trial as well.

The Supreme Court held that the plaintiff was entitled to a jury trial, notwithstanding the possibility "that in the instant personal-injury case the outcome would be substantially affected by whether the issue . . . is decided by a judge or a jury."[32] The Court did not repudiate the outcome-determination test, but made clear that outcome determination would not settle the *Erie* question in all cases.

Byrd added a new mode of analysis: an assessment of governmental interests behind the rules contending for application. The Court concluded that important policies supporting the federal jury rule would be sacrificed if plaintiff could not claim a jury in *Byrd*, but that it was far from clear that policies accounting for the South Carolina rule would be offended if plaintiff got his jury trial. Thus, it might be said that only the federal government was demonstrably interested in the application of its rule.

Byrd is the most perplexing of the *Erie* doctrine cases, in part because of the innate difficulty of interest-balancing analysis[33] and in part because portions of the Court's opinion in *Byrd* are not altogether clear. To begin with, the Court did not say that plaintiff had a constitutional right to a federal jury trial under the Seventh Amendment.[34] Rather, it favored plaintiff because neither the outcome-determination implication of the case nor the policy force behind South Carolina's rule against jury trials was sufficient to displace "[a]n essential characteristic of the [federal court system:] . . . the manner in which . . . it distributes trial functions between judge and jury . . . ."[35] Given the Supreme Court's approach in *Byrd*, the result might have been different if the policy interests of the federal courts had

---

[32] 356 U.S. at 537.

[33] *See* Joseph P. Bauer, *The Erie Doctrine Revisited: How a Conflicts Perspective Can Aid the Analysis*, 74 NOTRE DAME L. REV. 1235, 1281–99 (1999) (suggesting refinements in interest balancing).

[34] "Our conclusion makes unnecessary the consideration of — and we intimate no view upon — the constitutional question whether the right of jury trial protected in federal courts by the Seventh Amendment embraces the factual issue . . . here . . . ." 356 U.S. at 537 n.10. If the Court had found that plaintiff had a Seventh Amendment right to a jury trial, the *Erie* issue would not have arisen because the Constitution would control. For a discussion of the Seventh Amendment right to jury trials in federal court, see § 12.07[1], *infra*.

[35] 356 U.S. at 537.

been weaker, or those of South Carolina stronger.[36] *Byrd* shortened the reach of *York*'s outcome-determination test. At least in close cases, *Erie* questions were to be answered by assessing the state and federal interests behind the laws vying for application.

[3] *Hanna* and the Modified Outcome-Determination Test

The Supreme Court completed its modification of the outcome-determination test in *Hanna v. Plumer*.[37] The plaintiff there suffered personal injuries in an automobile accident and brought a federal diversity action against the estate of the alleged wrongdoer. The administrator of the estate was served by leaving a copy of the papers at his home in compliance with what was then federal Rule (4)(d)(1). The defendant-administrator argued, however, that the action could not be maintained because he had not been personally served as required by Massachusetts law. The Supreme Court rejected this argument and held service under Rule 4(d)(1) adequate.

The *Hanna* Court dismissed defendant's outcome-determination argument as too literal-minded. Granted, once the lawsuit was filed, plaintiff would lose if the state rule applied, while the litigation would continue if the federal rule applied. "[I]n this sense," observed the Court, "*every* procedural variation is 'outcome determinative.' "[38] The Court made clear, however, that such differences alone were insignificant. The real question was

> whether application of the [state] rule would make so important a differ-
> ence to the character or result of the litigation that failure to enforce it
> would unfairly discriminate against citizens of the forum state, or whether
> application of the rule would have so important an effect upon the fortunes
> of one or both of the litigants that failure to enforce it would be likely to
> cause a plaintiff to choose the federal court.[39]

Applying this more subdued version of the outcome determination test, the *Hanna* Court found the difference between the state and federal rules to be too insubstantial to raise the danger of inequitable administration of law posed in *Erie*.

This part of *Hanna*, however, was an alternative holding (or arguably dictum). It rested on the assumption that *Erie* and *York* governed cases such as this, where the federal law at issue was a Federal Rule of Civil Procedure. As discussed in § 7.04,

---

[36] The Court indicated in *Byrd* that no strong state policy would be sacrificed by refusal to follow the South Carolina rule in a federal diversity case. *Id.* at 535–36.

[37] 380 U.S. 460 (1965).

[38] 380 U.S. at 468 (emphasis in original).

[39] 380 U.S. at 468 n.9. The Court reiterated these points in *Chambers v. NASCO, Inc.*, 501 U.S. 32, 52 (1991). Note, however, that the *Erie* doctrine will require choice of the state rule in some cases where plaintiff does not appear to have shopped for the federal rule. The Court subsequently held a federal diversity court to a state law definition of "commencement" of suit, even though there was "no indication that when petitioner filed his suit in federal court he had any reason to believe that he would be unable to comply with the service requirements of Oklahoma law or that he chose to sue in federal court in an attempt to avoid those service requirements." *Walker v. Armco Steel Corp.*, 446 U.S. 740, 753 n.15 (1980). *Walker* is discussed more fully in § 7.04[2], *infra*.

the *Hanna* Court went on to conclude that this assumption was incorrect, and that a different mode of analysis was necessary when analyzing whether to apply federal rules promulgated under the Rules Enabling Act in diversity cases.

[4] Later *Erie* Issues

A subsequent issue involving *Erie* has been whether federal diversity courts will enforce state statutory requirements that certain claims must be submitted in the first instance to state administrative tribunals. After some initial resistance,[40] several federal courts have concluded that *Erie* requires the enforcement of such provisions.

Typical of these cases is the First Circuit's decision in *Feinstein v. Massachusetts General Hospital.*[41] The plaintiff sued defendant hospital for medical malpractice, invoking the federal court's diversity jurisdiction. Defendant moved to refer plaintiff's claim to a medical malpractice panel appointed under a Massachusetts statute. The purpose of the panel was to screen malpractice claims, reviewing plaintiff's proof by a standard similar to that used for directed verdicts.[42] If the panel found for defendant, plaintiff was to post a bond payable to defendant in the event plaintiff did not prevail at trial. The plaintiff conceded that the statute would have applied had he filed his malpractice case in Massachusetts state court, but argued that it was without effect in federal proceedings.

The First Circuit, however, agreed with defendant that *Erie* required that the Massachusetts statute be followed. The court observed that "[t]he statute's referral procedure and associated provisions were designed to serve . . . substantive policy objectives . . . ."[43]

The approach taken in *Feinstein* has been viewed sympathetically.[44] At least part of the motivation for state creation of administrative panel prerequisites is to reduce the size and incidence of recoveries obtained through either trial or settlement, and some plaintiffs may have shopped for a federal forum in order to avoid this consequence. State statutes establishing administrative prerequisites to suit are somewhat analogous to state "door-closing" rules which operate to prevent certain types of cases from being heard altogether. The *Feinstein* approach thus may draw support from the fact that the Supreme Court has interpreted the *Erie*

---

[40] *See Wheeler v. Shoemaker*, 78 F.R.D. 218 (D.R.I. 1978) (denying defendant's motion to refer plaintiff's claim to a state malpractice panel).

[41] 643 F.2d 880 (1st Cir. 1981). *See also DiAntonio v. Northampton-Accomack Mem'l Hosp.*, 628 F.2d 287 (4th Cir. 1980); *Hines v. Elkhart Gen. Hosp.*, 603 F.2d 646 (7th Cir. 1979).

[42] *See generally* § 12.09[1] (directed verdicts and judgments n.o.v.), *infra.*

[43] *Feinstein*, 643 F.2d at 885. The Court described the objectives as "providing for a prompt determination of the likely merits of a claim and requiring that a plaintiff who is unsuccessful before the malpractice tribunal post a bond" if he wishes to continue suit. Therefore, stated the Court, "[i]n the absence of any overriding federal interest in not applying the statute . . . we conclude that the Rules of Decision Act requires that federal courts to apply the state rules at issue here." 643 F.2d at 885.

[44] Vincent C. Alexander, *State Medical Malpractice Screening Panels in Federal Diversity Actions*, 21 ARIZ. L. REV. 959 (1979).

doctrine to mean that state door-closing doctrine bars federal diversity litigation.[45]

At the same time, to graft administrative referrals (or other satellite procedures contemplated by state litigation) onto federal cases creates "significant burdens on the parties and on the federal courts" in diversity litigation "of a sort inconsistent with the concept of those courts as an independently functioning judicial system."[46] Until federal courts are willing to view this concern as overriding, however, *Byrd*'s interest assessment test is unlikely to lead to a refusal to honor state administrative law in medical malpractice cases.

In *Gasperini v. Center for Humanities, Inc.*,[47] the United States Supreme Court invoked the Rules of Decision Act to require use of a state-law standard to determine whether a verdict was so excessive as to warrant a new federal trial under Rule 59(a)(1).[48] That provision authorizes a new trial "for any reason for which a new trial has heretofore been granted in an action at law in federal court." The Rule does not offer a test for determining when new trial orders (or conditional new trial orders)[49] are warranted in response to excessive jury verdicts, and federal courts have often applied a "shocks the conscience" test.[50] But defendant in *Gasperini* invoked the more favorable New York state law standard permitting court intervention whenever the verdict "deviates materially from what would be reasonable compensation."[51]

---

[45] *Angel v. Bullington*, 330 U.S. 183 (1947). "[D]iversity jurisdiction must follow State law and policy. A federal court in North Carolina, when invoked on grounds of diversity of citizenship, cannot give that which North Carolina has withheld." *Angel*, 330 U.S. at 192. Despite the breadth of this language, the reach of Angel is limited in at least two respects. First, the constitutionality of a state closing its doors to particular litigation may be open to question. RUSSELL J WEINTRAUB, COMMENTARY ON THE CONFLICT OF LAWS § 10.6B (4th ed. 2001). Naturally, if a state court could not constitutionally close its doors to a lawsuit, *Erie* cannot require a federal diversity court to do so. Second, the door-closing rule must reflect state substantive rather than procedural policies. If, for example, the state door-closing rule rests on a concern of *forum non conveniens, see* § 6.02[1], *supra, Erie* should impose no obligation on a federal diversity court to follow it. WEINTRAUB, at 576. *Stewart Org., Inc. v. Ricoh Corp.*, 810 F.2d 1066 (11th Cir. 1987), *aff'd* 487 U.S. 22 (1988), presents the converse situation where Alabama law opens its courts to suit, notwithstanding an agreement between the parties to confine suit to New York. The Eleventh Circuit invokes a federal law principle to honor the agreement.

[46] PAUL M. BATOR, PAUL J. MISHKIN, DAVID L. SHAPIRO, & HERBERT WECHSLER, THE FEDERAL COURTS AND THE FEDERAL SYSTEM 171 (2d ed. 1981 supplement).

A similar issue is whether a federal diversity judge must defer to a state arbitration award when a state court would have been required to do so. *See Towey v. Catling*, 743 F. Supp. 738, 740 (D. Hawaii 1990) (following state law to enforce an arbitration award, because that law was "an integral, substantive part of state policy . . ."). *Towey* is featured in John S. Mackey, Note, *Enforcement of State Annexed-arbitration Rules in Federal Courts with Diversity Jurisdiction*, 1991 J. DISP. RESOL. 397.

[47] 518 U.S. 415 (1996).

[48] *See* § 12.09, *infra* (new trial motions).

[49] That is, when the trial judge grants the motion for new trial unless the opposing party agrees to a reduction (remittitur) of the verdict. *See* § 12.09(2)(b), *infra*.

[50] *E.g., Abrams v. Lightolier*, 841 F. Supp. 584 (D.N.J. 1994). For additional cases, see 11 WRIGHT & MILLER § 2807 n.7.

[51] N.Y. CIV. PRAC. L. & R. § 5501(c).

Once it ruled that Rule 59 did not govern the issue,[52] the Supreme Court was able to turn to the question whether application of the state court "deviates materially" standard was required by the Rules of Decision Act. The Court concluded that it was, because New York's "objective is manifestly substantive."[53] Apart from this observation, the majority's opinion in *Gasperini* is not terribly clear. One commentator has observed: "It is possible that *Gasperini* employs an overarching RDA [Rules of Decision Act] approach similar to that embraced in *Byrd*. But such an interpretation is more the result of the reader's speculation than the Court's explanation."[54]

[5] Analytical Summary: Three Contemporary Tests Under the *Erie* Doctrine

Byrd's interest-dominated inquiry is analytic labor of the most demanding sort. It requires a determination of the nature and force of state and federal policies that might be implicated in the case. Often, only the policy (or policies) supporting one of the two rules will actually be at stake in the outcome. Then only the source (federal or state) providing that rule is really interested in having its law applied. This level of interest analysis may be sufficient to account for most or all of the Court's actual work under the *Byrd* branch of the *Erie* doctrine.[55] There is, however, the specter of cases even more taxing, those where *both* a state and the federal government would be interested in having their conflicting rules applied.[56]

---

[52] Had Rule 59 itself provided the federal-law standard, any conflicting state law would have given way as a result of Rules Enabling Act analysis. *See* § 7.04, *infra*.

[53] 518 U.S. at 429.

[54] Richard D. Freer, *Some Thoughts on The State of Erie After Gasperini*, 76 TEX. L. REV. 1637, 1641 (1998). *See also* Thomas D. Rowe, Jr., *Not Bad for Government Work: Does Anyone Else Think the Supreme Court is Doing a Halfway Decent Job in its Erie-Hanna Jurisprudence?*, 73 NOTRE DAME L. REV. 963 (1998); C. Douglas Floyd, *Erie Awry: A Comment on Gasperini v. Center for Humanities, Inc*, 1997 BYU L. REV. 267. A recent appraisal of *Gasperini* and other *Erie* doctrine cases appears in Earl C. Dudley, Jr. & George Rutherglen, *Deforming the Federal Rules: An Essay on What's Wrong With the Recent Erie Decisions*, 92 VA. L. REV. 707 (2006).

[55] The opposing results in two cases illustrate the point. The Supreme Court seemed to question in *Byrd* whether South Carolina was much if at all interested in application of its no-jury rule. Since the interests behind the federal jury rule were strongly implicated by the case (*see* § 7.03[2], *supra*), *Byrd* directed choice of the federal rule. In *Walker v. Armco Steel Corp.*, 446 U.S. 740 (1980), the situation was reversed and the Supreme Court therefore applied state law. Policies behind the Oklahoma state statute of limitations were at stake in the case and no federal interest supported a refusal to treat the action as time-barred. The Court concluded:

> There is simply no reason why . . . an action based on state law which concededly would be barred in the state courts by the state statute of limitations should proceed through litigation to judgment in federal court solely because of the fortuity that there is diversity of citizenship between litigants. The policies underlying diversity jurisdiction do not support such a distinction between state and federal plaintiffs, and *Erie* and its progeny do not permit it.

Walker, 446 U.S. at 753.

[56] Difficulties in determining whether law sources are interested and, if two or more are, which law to choose, are also at the center of modern choice-of-law analysis. Gene R. Shreve, *Conflicts Law — State or Federal?*, 68 IND. L.J. 907 (1993); EUGENE F. SCOLES, PETER HAY, PATRICK J. BORCHERS & SYMEON C. SYMEONIDES, CONFLICT OF LAWS ch. 3 (4th ed. 2004); Gene R. Shreve, *Teaching Conflicts, Improving the Odds*, 90 MICH. L. REV. 1672, 1673–75 (1992). The main difference between mainstream choice-of-law

Yet it would exaggerate the difficulty of the *Erie* doctrine to assume that the *Byrd* test need be applied in every case. Actually, all three tests that we have considered — substance-versus-procedure, modified outcome-determination, and the assessment of state and federal interests — have some role in contemporary analysis. It is only those cases that cannot be decided by one of the first two tests that require resort to *Byrd*-type interest assessment.

The substance-versus-procedure test serves as a first-stage screening device in modern *Erie* analysis. It is true that the words of the test still carry a stigma from their unsympathetic reception in *York*.[57] It is also true that the closer the *Erie* question, the more unreliable the substance-versus-procedure distinction becomes. For all that, however, the difference between substance and procedure, between the body of "rules which define legal rights" and rules "structuring and regulating the judicial process"[58] retains importance under the Rules of Decision Act.[59] In many cases, application of the distinction is all that will be necessary to resolve the *Erie* issue.[60]

Some cases eluding treatment under a substance-versus-procedure test will be appropriate for decision under the modified outcome-determination test. This test will suffice for statute of limitations problems, as in *York*, where the state law is not grounded entirely on substantive or procedural policies but instead derives from both.[61] Absent compelling circumstances for applying the federal rule, the modified outcome-determination test should advance state law when that law serves substantive interests at least in part. The *Byrd* interest assessment test is available as a last resort, when state substantive policies become more difficult to discern, or when policies supporting federal law approach overriding importance.

Functionally, the three tests can be linked as follows. Substance-versus-procedure marked the initial boundaries of the *Erie* doctrine and remains an easy and useful means for demonstrating why law made possible through exercise of

---

cases and those under the *Erie* doctrine is that sovereigns providing conflicting laws in the former are roughly co-equal, *e.g.*, a conflict between New York and Colorado. Yet the parallel is stronger than one might think. A federal diversity judge using *Byrd*'s interest analysis might give federal law the nod when both federal and state sources are interested; similarly, state judges are free under the Constitution to favor their own law over that of a sister state when both states are interested. *See* Louise Weinberg, *Choice of Law and Minimal Scrutiny*, 49 U. CHI. L. REV. 440 (1982); Gene R. Shreve, *Interest Analysis as Constitutional Law*, 48 OHIO ST. L.J. 51 (1987).

[57] *See* § 7.03[1], *supra*.

[58] Note, *The Law Applied in Diversity Cases: The Rules of Decision Act and the Erie Doctrine*, 85 YALE L.J. 678, 696 (1976).

[59] The substance-procedure distinction continues to command attention in commentary on the *Erie* doctrine. *E.g.*, Allan R. Stein, *Erie and Court Access*, 100 YALE L.J. 1935, 1942–46 (1991); Richard D. Freer, *Erie's Mid-Life Crisis*, 63 TUL. L.REV. 1087, 1131–34 (1989); Gregory Gelfand & Howard B. Abrams, *Putting Erie on the Right Track*, 49 U. PITT. L. REV. 937, 958–64 (1988). Jay Tidmarsh, *Procedure, Substance, and* Erie, 64 VAND. L. REV. 877 (2011).

[60] For example, in *Stineman v. Fontbonne College*, 664 F.2d 1082 (8th Cir. 1981), the Eighth Circuit held that a federal diversity judge was required to follow state law to decide whether damages in a tort action were excessive, but was not required to follow state law requiring that instructions be given to the jury in writing. The first issue was clearly substantive, and the second clearly procedural.

[61] *Cf. Walker v. Armco Steel Corp.*, 446 U.S. 740, 751 (1980) (referring to Oklahoma law defining its statute of limitation as "a statement of a substantive decision by that State").

federal diversity jurisdiction cannot displace state law created to advance substantive interests. The modified outcome-determination test recognizes that a state law which is both substantive and procedural in purpose should be honored under *Erie* whenever possible because of its substantive, result-affecting dimension. *Byrd*'s interest assessment test requires more precise calibration of the substantive state interests and the procedural federal interests underlying the competing rules. It can lead (as in *Byrd*) to nullification of the result of the outcome-determination test and application of federal law.

It is useful to remember that, for all their quirks, the cases making up the *Erie* doctrine have never strayed far from the notions of reason and justice central to *Erie* itself. When a federal diversity judge makes victory possible for a plaintiff who could not have won in state court, that judge must be saying to the defendant: "You lost because you and the plaintiff live in different states." That is an unacceptable reason for choosing winners and losers in our legal system. It is unacceptable because it is substantively grotesque to use the accident of diversity to shrink or swell rights, because it blocks the legitimate efforts of states to regulate local conduct through substantive laws, and because forum shopping would exacerbate these evils and hold federal courts up to ridicule.

§ 7.04 STATE LAW VERSUS FEDERAL PROCEDURAL STATUTES AND RULES PROMULGATED UNDER THE RULES ENABLING ACT

[1] Early Uncertainty

The Federal Rules of Civil Procedure were promulgated in 1938, the same year in which *Erie* was decided. The new rules promised sweeping reforms.[62] The emerging *Erie* doctrine, however, was to cast a shadow over their operation in diversity cases.

York and the outcome-determination cases which followed it appeared to suggest that state law controlled whenever the outcome of a diversity case might conceivably be affected by the choice of state, as opposed to federal law.[63] In two post-*York* cases, the Supreme Court invoked the outcome-determination test in refusing to apply a Federal Rule of Civil Procedure. In *Ragan v. Merchants Transfer & Warehouse Co.*,[64] the Court used the Kansas rule that suit commenced with service of process to conclude that plaintiff failed to sue within the time permitted by Kansas' statute of limitations. Plaintiff unsuccessfully argued that the

---

[62] On the effect of the Federal Rules of Civil Procedure on existing practice, see WRIGHT § 62; Robert G. Bone, *Mapping the Boundaries of a Dispute: Conceptions of Ideal Lawsuit Structure From the Field Code to the Federal Rules*, 89 COLUM. L. REV. 1 (1989); Stephen N. Subrin, *How Equity Conquered Common Law: The Federal Rules of Civil Procedure in Historical Perspective*, 135 U. PA. L. REV. 909 (1987). For contemporary assessments of the Rules, see Symposium, *The 50th Anniversary of the Federal Rules of Civil Procedure, 1938–1988*, 137 U. PA. L. REV. 1874 (1989); Symposium, *The Fiftieth Anniversary of the Federal Rules of Civil Procedure*, 63 NOTRE DAME L. REV. 597 (1988).

[63] *See* § 7.03[1], *supra*.

[64] 337 U.S. 530 (1949).

definition of commencement contained in Federal Rule 3 should govern.[65] In *Cohen v. Beneficial Indus. Loan Corp.*,[66] the Supreme Court imposed a New Jersey requirement that plaintiff in a stockholder's derivative suit must post a bond. The Court rejected plaintiff's argument that federal Rule 23.1, which did not require a bond, should govern.

These cases led many observers to fear that the Federal Rules of Civil Procedure would be thwarted in diversity cases, unless they coincided with state law. The Supreme Court eventually put these fears to rest in *Hanna v. Plumer*.[67]

[2] *Hanna, Walker, Woods*, and *Shady Grove*: The Resilience of Federal Rules of Procedure

Hanna rests on alternative grounds. We have already seen how the first ground, that *Erie* did not require the application of state law, was notable because it softened the outcome-determination test.[68]

The second ground, that *Erie* did not even apply, bolstered the authority of the Federal Rules of Civil Procedure in diversity cases. The Supreme Court called "incorrect" the "assumption that the rule of *Erie* constitutes the appropriate test of the validity and therefore the applicability of a Federal Rule of Civil Procedure."[69] Instead, the *Hanna* Court asserted, the proper test of the validity of a Federal Rule is provided by the Rules Enabling Act: whether the rule is a "rule of practice and procedure" that the Act authorizes the Supreme Court to prescribe,[70] and, if so, whether the rule violates the Act's mandate that a rule "not abridge, enlarge or modify any substantive right."[71] Applying this test, the Court found what was then Rule 4(d)(1) to be valid because it "neither exceeded the congressional mandate embodied in the Rules Enabling Act[72] nor transgressed constitutional bounds."[73] Since the rule applied — that is, it answered the service question in *Hanna* — Massachusetts state law had to give way.

The majority did not fully explain its reasoning, but the message conveyed by the Court's opinion in *Hanna* was clear. When challenged under *Erie*, federal rules of procedure were to receive different and more protective treatment than that given to federal doctrine. The Court stated that the constitutional authority to

---

[65] Rule 3 states that "[a] civil action is commenced by filing a complaint with the court." Plaintiff filed his action within the applicable limitations period, but served the complaint after it had run. Regarding statutes of limitations generally, see § 8.08[2][b], *infra*.

[66] 337 U.S. 541 (1949).

[67] 380 U.S. 460 (1965). *See generally* John C. McCoid, II, *Hanna v. Plumer: The Erie Doctrine Changes Shape*, 51 Va. L. Rev. 884 (1965).

[68] *See* § 7.03[3], *supra*.

[69] 380 U.S. at 469–70.

[70] 28 U.S.C. § 2072(a).

[71] 28 U.S.C. § 2072(b).

[72] 28 U.S.C. § 2072. On the process of rule creation and revision under the Rules Enabling Act, see note 104, *infra*, and § 1.02, *supra*.

[73] 380 U.S. at 464.

make a federal court system, augmented by the Necessary and Proper Clause of the United States Constitution,

> carries with it congressional power to make rules governing the practice and pleading in those courts, which in turn includes a power to regulate matters which, though falling within the uncertain area between substance and procedure, are rationally capable of classification as either.[74]

Compared to the "relatively unguided *Erie* choice"[75] used when neither a federal statute nor rule of procedure is involved, the approach of the majority in *Hanna* seemed simple and direct. So long as it is constitutional and complies with the Rules Enabling Act, the Federal Rule of Civil Procedure controls.[76]

In 1980, the Supreme Court again considered whether state law or a Federal Rule of Civil Procedure should apply in a diversity case, this time deciding in favor of state law. In *Walker v. Armco Steel Corp.*,[77] plaintiff sued for injuries he received while using defendant's product. Relying on the definition of commencement found in federal Rule 3, plaintiff argued that he had filed suit within the Oklahoma statute of limitations. The defendant argued that *Erie* required the court to follow the Oklahoma law defining commencement as service of process, and that service of process had not been made within the limitations period. The defendant relied on the Court's decision in *Ragan v. Merchant's Transfer & Warehouse Co.*[78] While *Ragan* appeared indistinguishable, plaintiff's argument proceeded on the assumption — shared by many observers — that *Ragan* had been weakened, if not overruled, by *Hanna v. Plumer.*

The Supreme Court did not agree. It refused to apply the Rules Enabling Act approach it announced in *Hanna* because it found "no direct conflict between the Federal Rule and the state law."[79] For there to be a conflict, refusal to apply Rule 3 would have to thwart some purpose the federal rule was intended to achieve. This did not happen in *Walker*, since "Rule 3 governs the date from which various timing requirements of the Federal Rules begin to run,[80] but does not affect state statutes of limitations."[81]

Walker is a useful reminder that favored treatment for federal procedural rules under the Rules Enabling Act is only appropriate *when the rules apply*. Because Rule 3 did not bear on the case, "the *Hanna* analysis does not apply. Instead, the

---

[74] 380 U.S. at 472.

[75] 380 U.S. at 471.

[76] 28 U.S.C. § 2072. For extended discussion of developments under the Act, see Karen N. Moore, *The Supreme Court's Role in Interpreting the Federal Rules of Civil Procedure*, 44 Hast. L.J. 1039, 1041–53 (1993); Stephen B. Burbank, *The Rules Enabling Act of 1934*, 130 U. Pa. L. Rev. 1015 (1982).

[77] 446 U.S. 740 (1980).

[78] *See* note 64 and accompanying text, *supra.*

[79] *Walker*, 446 U.S. at 752. But Rule 3 probably would be used to measure commencement within the running of the statute of limitations had the case rested on the court's federal question jurisdiction. *See Henderson v. United States*, 517 U.S. 654, 657 (1990).

[80] The Court presumably had in mind the use of Rule 3's definition of commencement for timing requirements contained in such rules as 13(a), 14(a), 30(a), 31(a) and 33(a).

[81] *Walker*, 446 U.S. at 751.

policies behind *Erie* . . . control the issue . . . ."[82] This permitted the substantive purpose behind Oklahoma's definition of commencement to become more of a factor in the decision.[83] The choice of Oklahoma law became clear once *Erie* and the Rules of Decision Act came into play.[84]

> There is simply no reason why, in the absence of a controlling federal rule, an action based on state law which concededly would be barred in the state courts by the state statute of limitations should proceed through litigation to judgment in federal court solely because of the fortuity that there is diversity of citizenship between the litigants.[85]

The case settled the question whether Rule 3 has any effect on state statute of limitations questions.[86]

Although *Walker* applied state law, it accepted the principle announced in *Hanna* that validly enacted and properly applied Federal Rules of Civil Procedure control. This raises the possibility that, no matter how substantive applicable state law may be, the *Erie* doctrine offers it no protection when a Federal Rule applies.

The Supreme Court did nothing to negate this suggestion in a later decision, *Burlington Northern Railroad v. Woods*.[87] *Woods* presented the Court with a choice between Federal Rule of Appellate Procedure 38 (giving federal courts of appeal discretion to award damages for frivolous appeals) and Alabama state law (making damages in such cases mandatory). Unlike *Walker*, the Court found the federal rule applicable. Faced with a "direct collision" between the federal and state rules, the *Woods* Court returned to the two-part test it used in *Hanna*. Because the issue before the court was within the scope of Federal Rule 38, that rule "must . . . be applied if it represents a valid exercise of Congress' rule-making authority, which originates in the Constitution and has been bestowed on this Court by the Rules Enabling Act . . . ."[88]

---

[82] 446 U.S. at 752.

[83] The Court noted that "the Oklahoma statute is a statement of a substantive decision by that State that actual service on, and accordingly actual notice by, the defendant is an integral part of the several policies served by the statute of limitations." *Id.* at 751. It read Oklahoma law to have substantially the same statute-of-limitations effect as Kansas law did in *Ragan*; therefore, *Walker* followed *Ragan* in holding plaintiff's claim to be time-barred.

[84] For more on the relationship between the Rules of Decision Act and the Rules Enabling Act, see § 7.04[3][b], *infra*.

[85] 446 U.S. at 753.

[86] *See, e.g., Cambridge Mut. Fire Ins. Co. v. City of Claxton*, 720 F.2d 1230 (11th Cir. 1983) (use of Rule 3 to enlarge the Georgia statute of limitations refused upon the authority of *Walker*). Applications of the *Walker* case are confined to exercises of federal diversity jurisdiction. When plaintiff's claim is based on federal law, "the action is not barred if it has been 'commenced' in compliance with Rule 3 within the . . . [limitations] period." *West v. CONRAIL*, 481 U.S. 35, 39 (1987).

[87] 480 U.S. 1 (1987). For discussions of the case, see Ralph U. Whitten, *Erie and the Federal Rules: A Review and Reappraisal After Burlington Northern Railroad v. Woods*, 21 CREIGHTON L. REV. 1 (1987); Kurt M. Saunders, *Plying the Erie Waters: Choice of Law in the Deterrence of Frivolous Appeals*, 21 GA. L. REV. 653 (1987).

[88] 480 U.S. at 5.

Beginning with the constitutional phase of its test, the Court noted that "constitutional constraints on the exercise of this rulemaking authority define a test of reasonableness . . . ," and that "[r]ules regulating matters indisputably procedural are *a priori* constitutional."[89] The Court seemed to see no constitutional problem in the fact that damage to state substantive interests might occur in the process. Quoting *Hanna*, it observed, "Rules regulating matters which, though falling within the uncertain area between substance and procedure, are rationally capable of classification as either, also satisfy this constitutional standard."[90]

Turning to the Rules Enabling Act, it interpreted the Act's limitation that federal rules "shall not abridge, enlarge or modify any substantive right . . . ."

> The cardinal purpose of Congress in authorizing the development of a uniform and consistent system of rules governing federal practice and procedure suggests that *rules which incidentally* affect litigants' substantive rights do not violate this provision if reasonably necessary to maintain the integrity of that system of rules.[91]

Note that the key word in this test is "incidental" — not "insignificant." This suggests that any impact upon state substantive interests (no matter how serious) is tolerable, so long it is a byproduct of (incidental to) advancement of a federal procedural policy. Thus, at both the constitutional and Rules Enabling Act levels, the *Woods* Court seems to accept disruption of state substantive interests, so long as application of federal law would advance clear procedural interests.

Tension between a state law and a federal rule of civil procedure was again at issue in *Shady Grove Orthopedic Associates, P.A. v. Allstate Ins. Co.*,[92] where the Supreme Court's analysis took a turn for the complicated. Shady Grove filed a federal class action against Allstate on behalf of Allstate customers, that sought statutory interest penalties for late insurance payments, in the teeth of a New York statute, which provided that "an action to recover a penalty . . . created or imposed by statute may not be maintained as a class action." Writing for a majority of five, Justice Scalia concluded that federal and state law were in conflict, because Rule 23 did not forbid plaintiffs from maintaining a class action to recover statutory penalties as the New York statute did. Proceeding from there with a plurality of four, Justice Scalia explained that Rule 23 will trump conflicting state law if it does

---

[89] 480 U.S. at 5.

[90] 480 U.S. at 5.

[91] 480 U.S. at 5. (emphasis added). *Cf. Business Guides v. Chromatic Commc'ns Ent.*, 498 U.S 533, 552 (1991) ("There is little doubt that Rule 11 is reasonably necessary to maintain the integrity of the system of federal practice and procedure, and that any effect on substantive rights is incidental.").

[92] 130 S. Ct. 1431 (2010). For a discussion of the Court's decision in *Shady Grove*, see Stephen B. Burbank & Tobias Barrington Wolff, *Redeeming the Missed Opportunities of Shady Grove*, 159 U. PA. L. REV. 17 (2010); Kevin M. Clermont, *The Repressible Myth of* Shady Grove, 86 NOTRE DAME L. REV. 987 (2011); Allan Ides, *The Standard for Measuring the Validity of a Federal Rule of Civil Procedure: The* Shady Grove *Debate Between Justices Scalia and Stevens*, 86 NOTRE DAME L. REV. 1041 (2011); Linda S. Mullenix, *Federal Class Actions: A Near-Death Experience in a Shady Grove*, 79 GEO. WASH. L. REV. 448 (2011); Adam N. Steinman, *Our Class Action Federalism: Erie and the Rules Enabling Act After* Shady Grove, 86 NOTRE DAME L. REV. 1131 (2011); Catherine T. Struve, *Institutional Practice, Procedural Uniformity, and as-Applied Challenges Under the Rules Enabling Act*, 86 NOTRE DAME L. REV. 1181 (2011).

not abridge or enlarge a substantive right in derogation of Rules Enabling Act. The federal rule will be upheld, Justice Scalia continued, if it "really regulate[s] procedure."[93] Thus, the rule is valid if it governs "the manner and the means by which the litigants rights are enforced," but not if it changes "the rules of decision by which [the] court will adjudicate those rights."[94] Justice Scalia concluded that Rule 23, like other rules that permit consolidation of multiple claims or multiple parties in one forum merely alters "how the claims are processed."[95] Hence, the rule represented a valid exercise of Rules Enabling Act authority and authorized the plaintiffs to proceed with their class action in federal court, state statute to the contrary notwithstanding.

Justice Stevens agreed with the plurality that Rule 23 conflicted with state law, but argued that whether the Rule abridged or enlarged a substantive right in violation of the Rules Enabling Act depends upon whether the state law that the federal rule would displace is "part of a State's framework of substantive rights or remedies." If it is, "federal courts must consider whether the rule can reasonably be interpreted to avoid that impermissible result," and if it cannot, the federal rule must not be applied.[96] Justice Stevens concluded that in this case, the state law "is a procedural rule that is not part of New York's substantive law," and hence Rule 23's displacement of state law did not abridge a substantive right.[97]

Justice Ginsburg, writing on behalf of four dissenters, argued that Rule 23 did not conflict with state law, because Rule 23 "describes a method of enforcing a claim for relief, while § 901(b) defines the dimensions of the claim itself."[98] Turning then to the Rules of Decision Act as interpreted in *Erie* and *York*, the dissent concluded that "the application of the [state] rule would have so important an effect upon the fortunes of one or both of the litigants that failure to apply it would likely [cause] a plaintiff to choose the federal court," and hence that the state statute foreclosing plaintiffs from recovering statutory penalties in class actions should apply.

On the one hand, *Shady Grove* is another in an uninterrupted series of cases that has upheld the application of a federal rule of civil procedure in the teeth of a conflicting state law. On the other hand, only a four-justice plurality embraced the formalistic approach of prior cases that perfunctorily resolved tension between state laws and federal rules in favor of the latter. Five members of the Court actively sought to accommodate state prerogatives: the four dissenters, by struggling to read the federal and state laws harmoniously, so that both could apply; and the concurrence, by reading the Rules Enabling Act to bar federal rules from displacing substantive state law.

---

[93] *Id.* at 1442.

[94] *Id.*

[95] *Id.* at 1442–43.

[96] *Id.* at 1452 (Stevens, concurring).

[97] *Id.* at 1448 (Stevens, concurring).

[98] *Id.* at 1466 (Ginburg, dissenting).

[3] Modern Analysis

[a] Matters "Procedural" Within the Meaning of the Rules Enabling Act

Rules validated as properly procedural in *Hanna* (service of process) and in *Woods* (regulation of frivolous appeals) are but some of those protected by the Rules Enabling Act.[99] Recall the Court's description in *Woods* of congressional intent in the Rules Enabling Act to create "a uniform and consistent system of rules governing federal practice and procedure." Consider the purpose of the Federal Rules of Civil Procedure: "to secure the just, speedy, and inexpensive determination of every action and proceeding."[100] The breadth of such mandates suggests that a rule regulating any aspect of judicial administration is probably procedural within the meaning of the Rules Enabling Act.

To illustrate, note that the Supreme Court's refusal to follow a federal rule in *Walker* was based on the conclusion that the particular federal rule had no application concerning statutes of limitation.[101] *Walker* did not say that a Federal Rule of Civil Procedure was incapable of nullifying a state statute of limitations in diversity cases. Rule 15(c) in fact does just that, allowing plaintiff under certain circumstances to amend her complaint by claiming against a new defendant, even though the statute of limitations[102] has run since the suit was originally filed.[103] This "relation-back" feature of Federal Rule 15[104] reflects a strong procedural policy favoring liberal pleading.[105] State law in direct collision with Rule 15(c) has thus given way in diversity cases.[106]

---

[99] The Supreme Court recently has invoked *Woods* and *Hanna* to give broad application to Rule 11. *Business Guides v. Chromatic Commc'ns Ent.*, 498 U.S. 533 (1991). In *Business Guides*, a diversity case, the Court read Rule 11 to impose a form of liability on represented parties that did not exist under state law.

[100] Rule 1.

[101] *See* § 7.04[2], *supra.*

[102] On statutes of limitations generally, see § 8.08[2][b], *infra.*

[103] *See generally* § 8.10[3][b] (relation back of amendments changing parties), *infra.*

[104] *See* § 8.10[3], *infra.*

[105] *See* § 8.10[3], *infra.*

[106] "Application of Rule 15(c) will mean in some instances that the action can go forward against the new defendant even though in state court that party would have a good defense of limitations. In this situation the courts have uniformly held . . . that Rule 15(c) can be applied and that to do so does not violate the substantive rights' proviso of the Enabling Act." WRIGHT § 59. *Cf. Freund v. Nycomed Amersham*, 347 F.3d 752 (9th Cir. 2003) (imposing the requirement under FED. R. CIV. P. 50 that a prior motion for directed verdict was a prerequisite for moving for judgment notwithstanding the verdict, even though California state law would impose no such prerequisite for testing punitive damage awards, and even though the court found California law rooted in public policy).

But see Douglas v. NCNB Texas Nat'l Bank, 979 F.2d 1128 (5th Cir. 1992). Invoking the substantive abridgement clause of § 2072, *Douglas* refused to give effect to the compulsory counterclaim requirement of Rule 13(a). Texas state law made clear that a secured lender's opportunity to recover could not be cut off through preclusion by rule. "Application of rule 13(a)", stated the court, "would abridge the lender's substantive rights and enlarge the debtor's substantive rights." *Id.* at 1130. While the case

[b] The Relationship Between the Rules Enabling Act and the Rules of Decision Act

Subsequent cases have confirmed Professor Ely's distinction:

> [W]here there is no relevant Federal Rule of Civil Procedure or other Rule promulgated pursuant to the Enabling Act and the federal rule in issue is therefore wholly judge-made, whether state or federal law should be applied is controlled by the Rules of Decision Act, the statute construed in *Erie* and *York*. Where the matter in issue is covered by a Federal Rule, however, the Enabling Act — and not the Rules of Decision Act itself or the line of cases construing it — constitutes the relevant standard.[107]

This distinction can alter the choice between state and federal law. For example, consider what would happen if the relation-back principle was not embedded in Rule 15(c), as discussed above,[108] but instead derived from federal judicial doctrine. Because the Rules Enabling Act would then be inapplicable, it would not insulate federal law from scrutiny under the Rules of Decision Act. Enforcement of the Rules of Decision Act through the *Erie* doctrine would likely lead to the choice of state over federal law.[109]

State substantive interests clearly receive less respect under the Rules Enabling Act approach of *Hanna* and *Woods* than they would under the *Erie* doctrine and the Rules of Decision Act. Some have questioned this discrepancy, suggesting a role for *Erie* and the Rules of Decision Act even when federal diversity courts are presented with applicable and valid rules of procedure.[110] More basically, the language of the Rules Enabling Act simply fails to support the conclusion that federal rules of procedure fare better against state law than does judge-made federal law. On the contrary, the provision in the Act denying federal rules authority to "abridge . . . any substantive right . . . ." would seem to vindicate substantive state interests even at the sacrifice of federal procedural objectives.[111] Neverthe-

---

involves a different federal rule, the position on § 2072 taken in *Douglas* is difficult to reconcile with the Rule 15(c) cases surveyed by Professor Wright.

[107] John H. Ely, *The Irrepressible Myth of Erie*, 87 HARV. L. REV. 693, 698 (1974).

[108] *See* § 7.04[3][a], *supra* (state statutes of limitation yield to the relation-back principle in Rule 15(c)).

[109] Defendant need merely demonstrate that the state statute of limitations functions at least in part to secure substantive policies. The Court in *Walker* enforced a state statute of limitations upon such a showing, once it concluded that the federal rules did not require the result sought by plaintiff.

[110] *See, e.g.*, Justice Harlan's concurrence in *Hanna*, entertaining the possibility that "*Erie* and the Constitution" might "require that the state rule prevail, even in the face of a conflicting federal rule." 380 U.S. at 475; Martin H. Redish & Carter G. Phillips, *Erie and the Rules of Decision Act: In Search of the Appropriate Dilemma*, 91 HARV. L. REV. 356 (1977) (advocating an interest-weighing approach for *Hanna*).

[111] Despite its apparent clarity, this passage of the Rules Enabling Act "has been a source of substantial controversy in the courts and among commentators over the years." Moore, note 76, *supra*, at 1042. Thus, while there is much support in the literature for the view that "Congress' concern in formulating the procedure/substance dichotomy was the preservation of an enclave of state law in diversity cases," Burbank, note 76, *supra*, at 1110, Burbank himself disagrees. He argues that the purpose of the dichotomy was to protect laws made by Congress from abridgment through court-generated rulemaking. Burbank, note 76, *supra*, at 1122–23. For more on substantive-abridgement

less, the Supreme Court reads the Act differently, vindicating federal procedural objectives even at the sacrifice of state substantive interests.[112] The position taken by the Court is not altogether surprising. It is natural for the Court to be concerned about the resilience of procedural law governing federal litigation.[113] Moreover, the Rules Enabling Act assigns to the Supreme Court a major role in the creation of most rules. The Court must give serious thought — albeit in the abstract — to the constitutionality and Rules Enabling Act validity of rules before it transmits them to Congress for final approval.[114] All this may explain why the Supreme Court has never invoked the abridging-substance limitation of the Act to deny effect to a Federal Rule of Civil Procedure.[115]

[4]   Other Federal Procedural Statutes

The philosophy underlying *Hanna* and its progeny is that when rules properly promulgated under the Rules Enabling Act are at issue, federalism concerns embodied in the Rules of Decision Act, and elaborated upon in *Erie* and *York*, must yield to the supremacy of congressional power and federal law. Logically, then, the deference the Court has shown Federal Rules of Civil Procedure adopted pursuant

---

provision of the Rules Enabling Act, see Leslie M. Kelleher, *Taking "Substantial Rights" (in the Rules Enabling Act) More Seriously*, 74 NOTRE DAME L. REV. 47 (1998); Paul D. Carrington, *Substance and Procedure in the Rules Enabling Act*, 1989 DUKE L.J. 281 (1989).

[112] *See* note 91 and related text, *supra*. *See also Shady Grove Orthopedic Assocs., P.A. v. Allstate Ins. Co.*, 130 S. Ct. 1431 (2010) (holding federal court should apply the federal class-action rule even when a state's procedural code would have barred the same case from proceeding on a class-wide basis in state court).

[113] To give as much play to state substantive interests as the language of the Act suggests would create considerable uncertainty over application of federal rules of procedure in diversity cases. *Cf.* Ely, note 107, *supra*, at 698 ("The Court has correctly sensed that [the Enabling Act] cannot be construed to protect state prerogatives as strenuously as the Rules of Decision Act protects them in the absence of a Federal Rule."). *But see* Whitten, note 87, *supra*, at 42 (criticizing the approach of Court and concluding: "the one constant in the Court's decisions dealing with Federal Rules-state law conflicts . . . has been its refusal to provide significant content to the Act's substantive rights restriction."); Leslie M. Kelleher, *Amenability to Jurisdiction as a "Substantive Right": The Invalidity of Rule 4(k) Under the Rules Enabling Act*, 75 IND. L.J. 1191 (2000) (similar conclusion).

[114] "[T]he recommendations of the [Judicial] Conference pass to the Court; any rule changes finally adopted by the Court are laid on the tables of Congress in accordance with the Rules Enabling Act." Benjamin Kaplan, *Amendments of the Federal Rules of Civil Procedure, 1961–63 (I)*, 77 HARV. L. REV. 601, 602 (1964). *See generally* § 1.02 (the federal rulemaking process), *supra*.

[115] As the Court observed, one challenging a federal rule under the Rules Enabling Act "has a large hurdle to get over." *Business Guides v. Chromatic Commc'ns Ent.*, 498 U.S. 533, 552 (1991). That hurdle has proven insurmountable in cases before the United States Supreme Court, although there have been close calls. The first was in *Sibbach v. Wilson & Co., Inc.*, 312 U.S. 1 (1941). The Court ruled 5 to 4 there that (notwithstanding the substantive-abridgment provision of the Rules Enabling Act) state law protecting litigants from physical examinations had to yield to federal discovery Rule 35. Three justices who dissented in *Business Guides* raised the substantive-abridgment provision to argue for a narrower interpretation of Rule 11, but they reserved opinion "[w]hether or not Rule 11 as construed by the majority exceeds our rule-making authority . . . ." 498 U.S. at 568. The second was in *Shady Grove Orthopedic Associates, P.A. v. Allstate Ins. Co*, 130 S. Ct. 1431 (2010), another 5-4 decision, in which the Court held that Rule 23 displaced a state law that foreclosed plaintiffs from maintaining class actions to recover statutory penalties, but where five members of the Court manifested a heightened level of interest in reducing tensions between federal rules and state law when possible. *See* § 7.04[2].

to Rules Enabling Act procedures would apply with equal force to other procedural statutes enacted by Congress.

In *Stewart Organization, Inc. v. Ricoh Corp.*,[116] an Alabama plaintiff entered into a dealership agreement that included a forum selection clause identifying Manhattan as the site for litigation arising under the contract. Plaintiff later filed suit for breach in Alabama federal court, and the defendant moved to transfer venue to the southern district of New York. The federal transfer of venue statute provides that transfer decisions are guided by "the convenience of parties and witnesses" and "the interest of justice," which the Supreme Court noted, would make the forum selection clause a "significant factor that figures centrally in the district court's calculus."[117] The district court, however, denied the motion to transfer venue, concluding that Alabama transfer of venue law, which disregarded forum selection clauses, should apply.

The circuit court reversed the district court and the Supreme Court affirmed. The Court began by citing *Hanna* for the proposition that "a district court's decision whether to apply a federal statute such as § 1404(a) in a diversity action . . . involves a considerably less intricate analysis than that which governs the 'relatively unguided *Erie* choice.' "[118] Turning first to whether state and federal law conflicted, the Court reframed the inquiry in terms of whether the federal statute "covers the point in dispute." The Court concluded that it did: the federal statute afforded the district court the flexibility to take the forum selection clause into account and Alabama law did not. Once it was determined that the federal statute covered the dispute, the "unguided" analysis of *Erie* and *York* played no role: if the federal transfer of venue statute was a valid exercise of congressional power — and the Court concluded that it was — federal law controlled. Of course, it is not the Rules Enabling Act that elevates a statute over inconsistent state law; it is the Supremacy Clause of the Constitution.[119]

In short, when federal law derives from a statute or rule promulgated pursuant to a statute, the analysis is governed by the *Hanna* line of cases, which asks whether federal and state law conflict, and if so, whether the statute is constitutional or whether the procedural rule is a valid exercise of Rules Enabling Act authority. *Erie* and *York* retain currency in cases where the source of federal law is a matter of informal practice, common law, or local district court rule. They likewise have a role to play when the federal law at issue is a statute or Federal Rule of Civil Procedure that does not conflict with state law. In these latter cases, the question is whether the court must apply the state law in addition to the federal law, with the answer turning on whether application of the state law (or not) would lead to forum shopping or inequitable administration of state law under *Erie*.

---

[116] 487 U.S. 22 (1988).

[117] *Id.* at 29.

[118] *Id.* at 26.

[119] U.S. Const. art. VI, cl. 2.

§ 7.05 WHICH STATE'S LAW?

[1] The Conflict-of-Laws Problem

When the parties come from different states or when facts creating the controversy occur in more than one state, the source of governing law may become one of the issues in the case. This happens when laws of different states appear to produce contradictory results. For example, the same facts may make defendant liable to plaintiff under the law of New York but not under the law of California.

The variety of approaches courts use to resolve conflicts can lead to differences in the law chosen.[120] It thus becomes important to determine which body of choice-of-law rules apply to resolve a given conflict. State courts usually apply their own common law of conflicts. Federal courts apply their own conflicts law in federal question cases.[121] Prior to *Erie*, federal conflicts doctrine governed in diversity cases as well. That changed with *Klaxon Co. v. Stentor Electric Manufacturing*,[122] where the Supreme Court extended the *Erie* principle to choice of law.

[2] The *Klaxon* Rule

Klaxon ended brief uncertainty whether federal conflicts doctrine was still available to federal courts sitting in diversity or was part of the federal general common law that *Erie* invalidated.[123] Ruling it to be the latter, *Klaxon* required federal diversity courts to administer the conflicts law of the states in which they were sitting ("forum states"). Reasoning from *Erie*, *Klaxon* held that a plaintiff should not be permitted to use federal diversity jurisdiction to obtain a more favorable conflicts law.

The *Klaxon* rule has been both criticized and defended.[124] Critics note that it forces federal judges to use a kind of state law (conflicts doctrine) that is particularly difficult to fathom[125] and that it imported local state bias into federal

---

[120] For surveys of approaches currently in use, see SCOLES, ET AL., CONFLICT OF LAWS, note 56 *supra*, at §§ 2.18–2.25; Hermer H. Kay, *Theory into Practice: Choice of Law in the Courts*, 34 MERCER L. REV. 521 (1983); Gene R. Shreve, *In Search of a Choice-of-Law Reviewing Standard-Reflections on Allstate Insurance Co. v. Hague*, 66 MINN. L. REV. 327, 341–44 (1982). *See also* § 7.03[6], *supra* (comparing the choice-of-law process with certain applications of the *Erie* doctrine).

[121] *E.g.*, *United States v. Little Lake Misere Land Co.*, 412 U.S. 580 (1973); *Siegelman v. Cunard White Star, Ltd.*, 221 F.2d 189 (2d Cir. 1955).

[122] 313 U.S. 487 (1941).

[123] *See* § 7.02[3], *supra*.

[124] *Compare* RANDALL BRIDWELL & RALPH V. WHITTEN, THE CONSTITUTION AND THE COMMON LAW: THE DECLINE OF THE DOCTRINES OF SEPARATION OF POWERS AND FEDERALISM 135 (1977), and the authorities appearing in *WRIGHT* § 57 (attacking *Klaxon*), *with* David F. Cavers, *The Changing Choice-of-Law Process and the Federal Courts*, 28 LAW & CONTEMP. PROBS. 732 (1963); American Law Institute, Study of the Division of Jurisdiction of State and Federal Courts 379 n.7 (1969) (defending *Klaxon*). *Cf.* Earl M. Maltz, *Choice of Forum and Choice of Law in the Federal Courts: A Reconsideration of Erie Principles*, 79 KY. L.J. 231 (1990–91) (*Klaxon* defensible when decided but incompatible with modern conflicts doctrine).

[125] Ascertaining state law when the same is "confused or nonexistent" is a chronic problem in administering the *Erie* doctrine. Charles E. Clark, *State Law in the Federal Courts: The Brooding*

court decision-making.[126] Nonetheless, conflicts rules do determine the content of *substantive* law governing the case. It would therefore seem outcome-determinative[127] in the clearest, forum-shopping sense for federal diversity courts to be able to declare a different winner by choosing different law. The Supreme Court has since reaffirmed the *Klaxon* rule in *Day & Zimmerman, Inc. v. Challoner.*[128]

[3] *Klaxon* and § 1404(a)

Consider the interplay of *Klaxon* and federal change-of-venue law in the following example. A New York plaintiff files a federal diversity action in New York against a California defendant. The case is transferred under § 1404(a)[129] to a federal diversity court in California. Assume that applicable tort laws from New York and California conflict. Assume further that New York conflicts doctrine would require application of New York tort law, while California conflicts doctrine would require California tort law. Does the state conflicts law of the transferor forum (New York) or that of the transferee forum (California) govern? Current law reads *Erie, Klaxon,* and § 1404(a) to require the governing state conflicts doctrine to be that of the transferor forum (New York). As the Supreme Court stated in a leading case, *Van Dusen v. Barrack,*

> . . . the transferee district court must be obligated to apply the state law that would have been applied if there had been no change of venue. A change of venue under § 1404(a) generally should be, with respect to state law, but a change of courtrooms.[130]

Van Dusen left open the question whether the same rule applied to actions which, if originally filed in state court, would have been dismissed there[131] on *forum non conveniens* grounds.[132] Some lower federal courts have applied the rule in such

---

Omnipresence of Erie v. Tompkins, 55 YALE L.J. 267, 290 (1946). *See generally* § 7.06, *infra.* The problem is especially great in ascertaining state conflicts law under *Klaxon,* due in part to the innate difficulty of conflicts doctrine. *Cf.* Max Rheinstein, *How to Review a Festschrift,* 11 AM. J. COMP. L. 632, 655 (1962) (calling conflicts the "most difficult and most confused of all branches of the law").

[126] "At bottom, the argument that federal courts should always apply their own conflict rules assumes that federal courts, being by nature less parochial than the courts of the state in which they are sitting, are more likely to evolve better choice-of-law rules . . . ." RUSSELL J. WEINTRAUB, COMMENTARY ON THE CONFLICT OF LAWS 745 (6th ed. 2010).

[127] On the contemporary use of the outcome-determination test, see § 7.03[5], *supra.*

[128] 423 U.S. 3 (1975).

[129] For a discussion of the federal change-of-venue statute, 28 U.S.C. § 1404(a), see § 6.02[2] *supra.* The focus here will be on § 1404(a) transfers in diversity cases, although the statute governs transfer of cases under other forms of federal subject matter jurisdiction.

[130] 376 U.S. 612, 639 (1964). The Court applied the rule to " 'ensure that the accident' of federal diversity jurisdiction does not enable a party to utilize a transfer to achieve a result in federal court which could not have been achieved in the courts of the State where the action was filed." *Id.* at 638 (quoting *York*). The Supreme Court reiterated the *Van Dusen* rule and rationale in *Ferens v. John Deere Co.,* 494 U.S. 516 (1990).

[131] *Van Dusen,* 376 U.S at 640.

[132] On the doctrine generally, see § 6.02[1], *supra.*

cases.[133] Yet to do so may actually frustrate *Erie* by permitting plaintiffs to use federal diversity jurisdiction to shop for favorable substantive law. Two points explain this.

First, it is useful to understand why plaintiff might want to shop for conflicts doctrine. Return to the example. Assume that the New York plaintiff wants New York tort law applied because it is easier to recover under that law. The plaintiff also wants New York's own state conflicts doctrine to be used because that doctrine happens to use litigant citizenship as a tool for choosing law and would permit plaintiff to use his New York citizenship to obtain application of New York tort law.[134]

Second, the *Erie* problem arises if our plaintiff is unable to obtain application of New York conflicts doctrine (and hence favorable New York substantive law) in any state court but is able to obtain New York conflicts doctrine in a federal diversity case originating in New York and transferred to California. To understand how state *forum non conveniens* doctrine can bring this about, note that our plaintiff can file his case in one of four courts: (1) a state or (2) federal diversity court in New York, or (3) a state or (4) federal diversity court in California.

Assume that plaintiff begins with option (1). New York state courts lack authority to transfer cases to the docket of another court system; therefore, if plaintiff runs afoul of New York state *forum non conveniens* doctrine, his New York state case would simply be dismissed without prejudice. Naturally, plaintiff in this situation would not last long enough in New York state court to benefit from favorable New York tort law.

If plaintiff files (or refiles) the same case in California state court, the suit would be governed by California conflicts law. California conflicts law will also govern if plaintiff files (or refiles) in California federal district court — this time under *Klaxon*'s directive.

Only through strategic use of the *Van Dusen* rule could our plaintiff sidestep the application of California conflicts doctrine. Plaintiff's route would be to begin with a federal diversity action in New York, and then either finesse defendant into seeking a § 1404(a) transfer or move for one himself.[135] In short, rigid application of *Van Dusen*'s requirement that conflicts law of the transferor forum governs would permit plaintiff to exploit the availability of diversity jurisdiction in New York to alter eventual decision on the merits in California.

---

[133] *See, e.g., In re Korean Air Lines Disaster of September 1, 1983*, 664 F. Supp. 1478 (D.D.C. 1986); *In re Air Crash Disaster at Boston, Mass.*, 399 F. Supp. 1106 (D. Mass. 1975).

[134] For an illustrative New York case, *see Tooker v. Lopez*, 249 N.E.2d 394 (N.Y. 1969). The practice has been criticized, John H. Ely, *Choice of Law and the State's Interest in Protecting Its Own*, 23 Wm. & Mary L. Rev. 173 (1981). But it is constitutional (and common) for a state to advance through its conflicts law the object that its citizens be compensated. For discussion how and why this controversial principle dominates modern conflicts doctrine, see Gene R. Shreve, *Conflicts Law — State or Federal?*, 68 Ind. L.J. 907 (1993).

[135] In *Ferens v. John Deere Co.*, 494 U.S. 516 (1990), the Supreme Court required application of the conflicts law of the transferor forum even though plaintiff initiated the transfer. Thus, "the legal system allowed the plaintiffs to shop for Mississippi law . . . ." George D. Brown, *The Ideologies of Forum Shopping — Why Doesn't A Conservative Court Protect Defendants?*, 71 N.C. L. Rev. 649, 655 (1993).

Commentators have urged more sensitivity in determining whether transferor or transferee law should be applied regarding § 1404(a) transfers.[136] Federal courts should at least have flexibility to choose transferee over transferor law in situations where plaintiff uses federal diversity jurisdiction to orchestrate a choice-of-law result. The Supreme Court's decision in *Ferens v. John Deere Co.*,[137] however, does not support a flexible approach. Plaintiffs there filed in a federal forum (Mississippi) where apparently they never intended to litigate. Rather, plaintiffs moved successfully under § 1404(a) for transfer to a Pennsylvania federal court and sought to use Mississippi (transferor) law to maintain an action barred under Pennsylvania (transferee) law. The Supreme Court followed its *Van Dusen* rule and rewarded plaintiffs with Mississippi law. The dissent observed,

> one must be blind to reality to say that it is the *Mississippi* federal court in which these plaintiffs have chosen to sue. That was merely a way station in route to suit in the Pennsylvania federal court. The plaintiffs were seeking to achieve exactly what Klaxon was designed to prevent: the use of a Pennsylvania federal court instead of a Pennsylvania state court in order to obtain application of a different substantive law.[138]

§ 7.06 ASCERTAINING THE CONTENT OF STATE LAW

[1] The Elusive Model of the Highest State Court

State law controlling in federal court under *Erie*[139] must be determined and applied as it would have been if the case had, instead, been adjudicated by the highest state court whose law is being applied. This rule reflects the fact that the ultimate authority on the meaning of state law is the state's highest court,[140] just as the United States Supreme Court is the ultimate authority on the meaning of federal law.

The problem is that a federal diversity court may not know how a state high court would rule on the case at hand because it is often impossible or impracticable for federal judges to certify state law questions to state courts in order to find out.[141] This leaves federal courts in an awkward position, particularly when state

---

[136] Michael B. Rodden, Comment, *Is 28 U.S.C. § 1404(a) a Federal Forum-Shopping Statute?*, 66 Wash. L. Rev. 851 (1991); Ursula M. Henninger, Comment, *The Plaintiff's Forum Shopping Gold Card: Choice of Law in Federal Courts After Transfer of Venue Under § 1404(a) — Ferens v. John Deere Co.*, 26 Wake Forest L. Rev. 809 (1991); Scoles & Hay, note 120, *supra*, at § 3.46; Maltz, note 124, *supra*.

[137] 494 U.S. 516 (1990).

[138] 494 U.S. at 535.

[139] The process for determining state law discussed in this section also applies in federal court searches for the meaning of state laws that are not required under *Erie*. For examples, see § 7.07, *infra*.

[140] The principle is well-established. *E.g., Exxon Corp. v. Eagerton*, 462 U.S. 176, 181 n.3 (1983); *Commissioner v. Estate of Bosch*, 387 U.S. 456, 465 (1967). *See generally* Paul L. Caron, *The Role of State Court Decisions in Federal Tax Litigation: Bosch, Erie, and Beyond*, 71 Or. L. Rev. 781 (1992). *Cf. City of Chi. v. Morales*, 527 U.S. 41, 61 (1999) ("We have no authority to construe the language of a state statute more narrowly than the instruction given by that State's highest court.").

[141] "Except in those few jurisdictions permitting a federal court to certify an unsettled question of

law is unsettled. No federal court can give genuinely authoritative meaning to state law.[142] Yet federal courts usually cannot avoid the ambiguities of state law by declining jurisdiction.[143] Instead, they must "vicariously"[144] create enough state law to decide the case at hand by attempting to "forecast" the state's law "as it would be expressed by its highest court."[145]

[2] Data to Be Used in Forecasting State Law

The most authoritative indication of how the state's high court would rule on the same case frequently will be found in that court's opinions. In keeping with the principle of *stare decisis*, a court usually can be expected to adhere to its own precedents.[146] If the precedent of the state's highest court is indistinguishable, a federal diversity court usually will have no choice but to follow it.[147] Since, however, all appellate courts overrule some of their own precedents over time, the requirement that federal diversity courts follow apposite state high court cases is not ironclad. Federal diversity courts have refused to follow state high court precedents when they are convinced that the state high court would not follow them either.[148] At least by negative implication, the Supreme Court lent support to

---

state law to the state's highest court, a federal court's decision on state law cannot be corrected, for the benefit of the litigants in the particular case, by the state's authoritative tribunal." *Factors Etc., Inc. v. Pro Arts, Inc.*, 652 F.2d 278, 282 (2d Cir. 1981), *cert. denied*, 456 U.S. 927 (1982).

The Supreme Court gave guarded approval to the technique of certification in *Salve Regina College v. Russell*, 499 U.S. 225, 237 (1991). *See generally* Deborah J. Challner, *Distinguishing Certification From Abstention in Diversity Cases, Postponement Versus Abdication of the Duty of Exercise Jurisdiction*, 38 Rutgers L.J. 847 (2007); Geri J. Yonover, *A Kinder, Gentler Erie: Reining in the Use of Certification*, 47 Ark. L. Rev. 305 (1994); Richard M. Chase, *A State Court's Refusal to Answer Certified Questions: Are Inferences Permitted?*, 66 St. John's L. Rev. 407 (1992); John B. Corr & Ira P. Robbins, *Interjurisdictional Certification and Choice of Law*, 41 Vand. L. Rev. 411 (1988); Carroll Seron, Certifying Questions of State Law: Experience of Federal Judges (Federal Judicial Center 1983).

For examples where certification was workable, see *Reyes-Cardona v. J.C. Penney Co.*, 694 F.2d 894 (1st Cir. 1982); *Strange v. Krebs*, 658 F.2d 268 (5th Cir. 1981).

[142] At times, a federal decision on the meaning of state law has been followed by a subsequent federal court. *E.g., Factors Etc., Inc. v. Pro Arts, Inc.*, 652 F.2d 278, 282 (2d Cir. 1981), *cert. denied*, 456 U.S. 927 (1982). But it is clear that the courts of the state are free to disregard all federal court pronouncements — even those of the Supreme Court — concerning the meaning of state law. The Supreme Court has acknowledged on numerous occasions the need to look to state courts for "an authoritative construction" of state law. *See, e.g., Babbitt v. United Farm Workers Nat'l Union*, 442 U.S. 289, 308 (1979).

[143] *Meredith v. City of Winter Haven*, 320 U.S. 228 (1943). For instances where extraordinary circumstances required federal diversity courts to abstain from decision, see *Burford v. Sun Oil Co.*, 319 U.S. 315 (1943); *Louisiana Power & Light Co. v. City of Thibodaux*, 360 U.S. 25 (1959).

[144] The term is from 19 Wright & Miller § 4507.

[145] *McKenna v. Ortho Pharm. Corp.*, 622 F.2d 657, 662 (3d Cir.), *cert. denied*, 449 U.S. 976 (1980).

[146] On stare decisis generally, see § 15.13, *infra*.

[147] "[T]he duty rests upon federal courts to apply state law under the Rules of Decision statute in accordance with the then controlling decision of the highest state court." *Vandenbark v. Owens-Illinois Glass Co.*, 311 U.S. 538, 543 (1941). *Vandenbark* held that a federal circuit court was not free to disregard an apposite decision handed down by the Ohio Supreme Court while the federal case was on appeal.

[148] *See Rock Island Improvement Co. v. Helmerich & Payne, Inc.*, 698 F.2d 1075 (10th Cir.), *cert. denied*, 461 U.S. 944 (1983) (refusing to follow an Oklahoma Supreme Court case because of an intervening declaration of policy by the Oklahoma legislature); *Mason v. American Emery Wheel Works*,

this view in *Bernhardt v. Polygraphic Co. of America.*[149] It was aided in part in reaching its decision to follow a 40-year old Vermont Supreme Court precedent by the fact that

> there appears to be no confusion in the Vermont decisions, no developing line of authorities that casts a shadow over the established ones, no dicta, doubts or ambiguities in the opinions of Vermont judges on the question, no legislative development that promises to undermine the judicial rule.[150]

When no decision of the highest state court is on point, federal courts must base their forecasts on other material. Decisions of intermediate state appellate courts carry considerable weight in such situations. The rule was once that federal diversity courts "must follow the decisions of intermediate state courts in the absence of convincing evidence that the highest court of the state would decide differently."[151] While some federal circuit courts have restated the rule,[152] the Supreme Court appeared to relax it in *Commissioner v. Estate of Bosch.*[153] The Court noted that "under some conditions, federal authority may not be bound by an intermediate state appellate court ruling."[154] An influential circuit court opinion has read *Bosch* to permit a wide-ranging examination of legal sources in order to forecast the Ohio Supreme Court's position when none of its decisions were on point:

> The primary source that must be analyzed, of course, is the decisional law of the Ohio Supreme Court. In the absence of authority directly on point, decisions by that court in analogous cases provide useful indications of the court's probable disposition of a particular question of law . . . . Considered dicta by the state's highest court may also provide a federal court with reliable indicia of how the state tribunal might rule on a particular question . . . . Of somewhat less importance to a prognostication of what the highest state court will do are decisions of lower state courts and other federal courts. Such decisions should be accorded "proper regard" of course, but not conclusive effect . . . . Additionally, federal courts may consider scholarly treatises, the Restatement of Law, and germane law review articles . . . .[155]

---

241 F.2d 906 (1st Cir.), *cert. denied*, 355 U.S. 815 (1957) (refusing to follow a thirty-year-old Mississippi Supreme Court case, noting that the liability limitation imposed by the case had been discredited in other state jurisdictions and reasoning that the Mississippi Supreme Court would overrule it).

[149]   350 U.S. 198 (1956).

[150]   350 U.S. at 205.

[151]   *Stoner v. New York Life Ins. Co.*, 311 U.S. 464, 467 (1940).

[152]   *E.g.*, *Silverberg v. Paine, Webber, Jackson & Curtis, Inc.*, 710 F.2d 678, 690 (11th Cir. 1983); *Delano v. Kitch*, 663 F.2d 990, 996 (10th Cir. 1981), *cert. denied*, 456 U.S. 946 (1982).

[153]   387 U.S. 456 (1967).

[154]   387 U.S. at 465. Citing *Bernhardt*, the Court went on to observe, "If there be no decision by [the state's highest court] then federal authorities must apply what they find to be the state law after giving 'proper regard' to relevant rulings of other courts of the State." 387 U.S. at 465.

[155]   *McKenna v. Ortho Pharm. Corp.*, 622 F.2d 657, 662 (3d Cir.) (*quoting Bosch*, 387 U.S. at 471), *cert. denied*, 449 U.S. 976. For discussion of the uses and limitations of state high-court dicta in forecasting state law, see *Moore* § 124.22[3]. Federal diversity courts also may be influenced by broad trends in the

[3] How Much Freedom Do Federal Judges Have in Handling State Law?

The inability of federal courts to make truly authoritative pronouncements of state law and the constraints of the *Erie* doctrine make it impossible to reduce the process of forecasting state law to a simple formula. Federal judges use state law in a way that is not comparable to how either trial or appellate judges use it within the state judicial system.

On one hand, federal judges — whether trial or appellate[156] — require greater freedom than state trial judges in handling state precedents. State trial judges are controlled by precedents created by their superiors in the state judicial hierarchy.[157] Federal courts similarly constrained would not really be applying state law as state courts would, since state adjudication carries the possibility of review by a state appellate court powerful enough to overrule the state precedent.

On the other hand, federal courts cannot have as much freedom to react to state precedents as the state appellate courts which created them. All courts have the power to repudiate their own precedents at any time, although the doctrine of *stare decisis* usually restrains them.[158] However, forecasts whether or when a state appellate court will overrule its own precedent are likely to be speculative.[159] Moreover, guesses by federal diversity judges that state precedents would be overruled are likely to be colored by their own convictions about what the law ought to be. This kind of forecasting is dangerously akin to the federal general common law approach banned by *Erie*.[160]

All this explains why, in discharging the obligation to apply state law, federal diversity judges do not function as exact equivalents of either state lower or high court judges. They exercise instead a degree of authority somewhere between the two. When required to forecast whether the highest state court would overrule its

---

development of a substantive field of law. *See, e.g., Michelin Tires Ltd. v. First Nat'l Bank of Boston*, 666 F.2d 673, 682 (1st Cir. 1981); *Mason v. American Emery Wheel Works*, 241 F.2d 906, 908 (1st Cir.), *cert. denied*, 355 U.S. 815 (1957). On sources for determining state law, *see* Jed I. Bergman, *Putting Precedent in Its Place: Stare Decisis and Federal Predictions of State Law*, 96 Colum. L. Rev. 969 (1996); Note, *Federal Interpretation of State Law — An Argument for Expanded Scope of Inquiry*, 53 Minn. L. Rev. 806 (1969).

[156] In *Salve Regina College v. Russell*, 499 U.S. 225 (1991), the Supreme Court ruled that determinations by federal trial judges of the meaning of state law are to receive no special weight. Rather, state law issues are reviewable *de novo* in federal courts of appeals.

Salve seems correctly decided. As we argued in the first edition of this book, the distinction between federal trial and federal appellate judges is unimportant in this context. Both address the same issue: how would the highest state court rule? *See* note 140 and accompanying text, *supra*. A federal appellate court may reverse because it disagrees with the federal district court's answer to this question, but both are alike in their inability to give authoritative meaning to state law. *See* note 142, *supra*.

[157] *See* § 15.13, *infra*.

[158] *Id.*

[159] The lines of the doctrine of *stare decisis* are indistinct and departures from it are episodic and frequently controversial. *See, e.g.*, Chief Justice Bell's vigorous dissent to the Pennsylvania Supreme Court's overruling of its decisions which had limited recovery for negligently inflicted emotional distress. *Niederman v. Brodsky*, 261 A.2d 84, 90 (Pa. 1970).

[160] *See* § 7.02, *supra*.

own cases, federal courts should — and usually do — proceed with caution.[161] They have more latitude in resolving state law questions of first impression.[162] Even then, however, federal courts should weigh matters carefully before vicariously creating new state law. A noted circuit decision reflects this view.

> Like many other plaintiffs in diversity cases filed in federal courts, the appellant here is asking that we anticipate the birth of a state law doctrine in the womb of time, but whose birth is distant. We have been asked to deliver prematurely a new doctrine of Pennsylvania tort law, and as a federal court we are unwilling to do so.[163]

When particularly close questions arise over the content of state law, there is something to be said for resolving them against the litigant invoking federal diversity jurisdiction.[164] This seems fair since, by directing the case to federal rather than state court, that litigant has effectively avoided authoritative state court decision in favor of what will be at best an informed federal court guess how the highest state court would rule.[165] This approach is also in keeping with the *Erie* doctrine's objective of keeping litigants from obtaining a substantive law advantage simply because they are capable of invoking federal diversity jurisdiction.[166]

§ 7.07   FEDERAL COMMON LAW[167]

The same day that Justice Brandeis declared in *Erie R.R. v. Tompkins*[168] that "[t]here is no federal general common law,"[169] he wrote that "whether the water of an interstate stream must be apportioned between the States is a question of 'federal common law' upon which neither the statutes nor the decisions of either State can be conclusive."[170] Justice Jackson subsequently explained this apparent

---

[161] *See* § 7.06[2], *supra.*

[162] *Cf. Moore* § 124.22[3].

[163] *Vargus v. Pitman Mfg. Co.*, 675 F.2d 73, 76 (3d Cir. 1982).

[164] The litigant may be either a plaintiff who has invoked the federal court's original diversity jurisdiction under 28 U.S.C. § 1332, *see* §§ 5.04–5.06, *supra*, or a defendant who has removed the case on federal diversity grounds under 28 U.S.C. § 1441. *See* § 5.07, *supra.*

[165] There are some cases, however, where uncertainty over the meaning of state law will be as perplexing for state judges. In conflict-of-laws situations, a state court may be called upon to ascertain the meaning of the law of another state. *See* § 7.05[1], *supra*. In grappling with the law of another state, state judges face essentially the same analytic difficulties as federal judges do in administering the *Erie* doctrine. *See* Corr & Robbins, note 141, *supra.*

[166] *See* § 7.02 (evolution from *Swift* to *Erie*), *supra.*

[167] *See generally Federal Courts Symposium*, 12 Pace L. Rev. 227–357 (1992); Martha A. Field, *Sources of Law: The Scope of Federal Common Law*, 99 Harv. L. Rev. 881 (1986); Thomas W. Merrill, *The Common Law Powers of Federal Courts*, 52 U. Chi. L. Rev. 1 (1985); Martin H. Redish, *The Power of the Federal Courts to Fashion Federal Common Law, in* Federal Jurisdiction: Tensions in the Allocation of Judicial Power 119 (2d ed. 1990). Caleb Nelson, *The Persistence of General Law*, 106 Colum. L. Rev. 503 (2006); Jay Tidmarsh & Brian J. Murray, *A Theory of Federal Common Law*, 100 Nw. U.L. Rev. 585 (2006).

[168] 304 U.S. 64 (1938), discussed in § 7.02[3], *supra.*

[169] 304 U.S. at 78.

[170] *Hinderlider v. La Plata River & Cherry Creek Ditch Co.*, 304 U.S. 92, 110 (1938).

inconsistency:

> The federal courts have no *general* common law, as in a sense they have no general or comprehensive jurisprudence of any kind, because many subjects of private law which bulk large in the traditional common law are ordinarily within the province of the states and not of the federal government. But this is not to say that wherever we have occasion to decide a federal question which cannot be answered from federal statutes alone we may not resort to all of the source materials of the common law, or that when we have fashioned an answer it does not become a part of the federal non-statutory or common law.[171]

Whenever a federal court is free to decide for itself what rule of decision to apply, it is making or applying federal common law.[172] Federal common law has been applied to interstate water disputes,[173] as Justice Brandeis noted, other interstate disputes,[174] questions regarding the proprietary (commercial) interests of the United States,[175] foreign relations questions,[176] maritime and admiralty questions,[177] questions regarding the defenses available to federal officials sued in private actions,[178] statute of limitations questions when relevant federal statutes are silent,[179] and the question whether a plaintiff has an implied cause of action under a federal statute[180] or constitutional provision.[181] Despite this range of subjects, the Supreme Court has said that applications of federal common law are "few and restricted."[182] Once it applies, however, it is controlling under the Supremacy Clause of the Constitution,[183] whether the forum is state or federal,[184] and whether

---

[171] *D'Oench, Duhme & Co. v. FDIC*, 315 U.S. 447, 469 (1942) (Jackson, J., concurring) (emphasis in original).

[172] WRIGHT § 60. *See generally* Jay Tidmarsh & Brian J. Murry, *A Theory of Federal Common Law*, 100 Nw. U. L. Rev. 585 (2006).

[173] Including questions of interstate pollution. *See Illinois v. City of Milwaukee*, 406 U.S. 91 (1972).

[174] *See, e.g., Texas v. New Jersey*, 379 U.S. 674 (1965).

[175] *See, e.g., United States v. Kimbell Foods, Inc.*, 440 U.S. 715 (1979) (priority of federal lien over private liens); *Clearfield Trust Co. v. United States*, 318 U.S. 363 (1943) (effect of late notice of forgery on U.S. rights as drawee to recover on guaranty of endorsements on check).

[176] *See, e.g., Banco Nacional de Cuba v. Sabbatino*, 376 U.S. 398 (1964) (effect of act of state doctrine on private litigation).

[177] *See, e.g., Edmonds v. Compagnie Generale Transatlantique*, 443 U.S. 256 (1979).

[178] *See, e.g., Howard v. Lyons*, 360 U.S. 593 (1959) (availability of privilege as defense to libel action).

[179] *See, e.g., Johnson v. Railway Express Agency, Inc.*, 421 U.S. 454, 462–66 (1975). *See generally* Note, *Limitation Borrowing in Federal Courts*, 77 MICH. L. REV. 1127 (1979) [hereinafter called *Limitation Borrowing*]; § 8.08[2][b] (the affirmative defense of limitations), *infra*.

[180] *See Cort v. Ash*, 422 U.S. 66, 78 (1975); § 5.03[1] (creation test for federal question jurisdiction), *supra*.

[181] *See Bivens v. Six Unknown Named Agents of Fed. Bureau of Narcotics*, 403 U.S. 388 (1971).

[182] *City of Milwaukee v. Illinois*, 451 U.S. 304, 313 (1981) *citing Wheeldin v. Wheeler*, 373 U.S. 647, 651 (1963). *See also* Redish, note 167, *supra*, at 80; Field, note 167, *supra*, at 885 (federal common law is usually said to be the exception, not the rule).

[183] U.S. Const. art. VI.

[184] Field, note 167, *supra*, at 897.

the federal jurisdiction is diversity or federal question,[185] until and unless Congress overrides it by legislation.[186]

Beyond these generalizations, there is little clarity. Federal common law can be viewed as posing three questions, although they are not distinct in practice: (1) whether a federal court may make common law, (2) when it should make such law, and (3) what law it should make?

The threshold problem is that there is no general authority for federal common lawmaking. The federal government, unlike the state governments, is a government of limited powers. Its limitations are reflected in the Rules of Decision Act, which provides that the laws of the states shall be regarded as rules of decision in cases where they apply, "except where the Constitution or treaties of the United States or Acts of Congress otherwise require or provide."[187] The most common rationale for federal common lawmaking is that it is interstitial; it "implements the federal Constitution and statutes, and is conditioned by them," by filling gaps in such law.[188] These positive laws can be read as "requiring" such common lawmaking in the sense of the Rules of Decision Act because the gaps must be filled to decide cases. Another rationale for federal common lawmaking is that Congress or the Constitution has delegated lawmaking for particular subjects to the courts.[189] The positive laws can be read as "providing" for delegated judicial lawmaking in the sense of the Rules of Decision Act.

Whether a bare jurisdictional grant can alone serve as a delegation of lawmaking authority is unclear. Article III's grant of original jurisdiction to the Supreme Court to decide interstate disputes, and its authorization of lower court jurisdiction over admiralty and maritime cases and over controversies to which the United States is a party are sometimes cited as authority for federal common lawmaking in these areas.[190] Yet the analogous theory of delegated authority under the grant of diversity jurisdiction was rejected in *Erie*.[191] Arguably something more than just the jurisdictional grant is required, whether it is a practical necessity created by the absence of any logically applicable state law (to decide, for example, foreign relations questions or interstate boundary disputes), or "a bit of legislative history"

---

[185] *See, e.g., Banco Nacional de Cuba*, 376 U.S. at 421; *Howard*, 360 U.S. 593.

[186] Redish, note 167, *supra*, at 97. *See, e.g., City of Milwaukee*, 451 U.S. at 313 (acknowledging "paramount authority of Congress" to override federal common law announced just one year earlier).

[187] 28 U.S.C. § 1652.

[188] *D'Oench, Duhme*, 315 U.S. at 471–72 (Jackson, J., concurring). *See generally* Kevin R. Johnson, *Bridging the Gap: Some Thoughts About Interstitial Lawmaking and the Federal Securities Laws*, 48 WASH. & LEE L. REV. 879 (1991). One commentator has characterized the process as "preemptive lawmaking," by which a court "finds that some federal policy specifically intended by an enacting body 'preempts' the application of state law to some collateral or subsidiary point about which the enacting body has been silent." Merrill, note 167, *supra*, at 36. *See generally* Henry M. Hart, Jr., *The Relations Between State and Federal Law*, 54 COLUM. L. REV. 489 (1954).

[189] *See, e.g., Textile Workers Union of Am. v. Lincoln Mills*, 353 U.S. 448, 451 (1957) (§ 301(a) of the Labor Management Relations Act of 1947, 29 U.S.C. § 185, "authorizes federal courts to fashion a body of federal law for the enforcement of . . . collective bargaining agreements").

[190] *See* Field, note 167, *supra*, at 916, 953–54 n.309 (citing authorities); Redish, note 167, *supra*, at 81–82.

[191] *See* Field, note 167, *supra*, at 916.

consistent with federal common lawmaking.[192]

When a court *should* make federal common law is also unclear. The predicate for making it appears to be a showing that the choice of the substantive legal rule will significantly affect an "identifiable federal policy or interest."[193] More recently, the Court has endorsed the description of the predicate or "precondition" for making federal common law as "a significant conflict between some federal policy or interest and the use of state law."[194] In the leading case of *Clearfield Trust Co. v. United States*,[195] for example, the issue was whether late notice by the United States of a forged signature on its check kept it from recovering against guarantor Clearfield Trust. Under state law, prejudice to Clearfield from the late notice was presumed and recovery by the United States barred, while under pre-*Erie* federal commercial law Clearfield had the burden of proving prejudice. A web of federal statutes and regulations governed the rights and duties of the United States on commercial paper, but none addressed the precise issue in the case. Citing these laws to demonstrate the federal interest in the subject, the Supreme Court held that in the absence of an applicable statute, "it is for the federal courts to fashion the governing rule of law according to their own standards."[196] Clearly, here the federal interest in recovering from the guarantor absent prejudice from late notice was in conflict with the state's presumption of prejudice.

In contrast, the Court held in *Bank of America National Trust & Savings Ass'n. v. Parnell*[197] that state law rather than federal common law set the burden of proof on the issue of good faith in the purchase of bearer bonds guaranteed by the United States. The suit involved only private parties and the Court saw no significant federal interest at stake. *Parnell* demonstrated that analysis of the federal interest must proceed on an issue-by-issue basis, for the Court simultaneously upheld application of federal common law to the collateral issue of overdueness of the bonds.[198]

---

[192] Henry J. Friendly, *In Praise of Erie — and of the New Federal Common Law*, 39 N.Y.U. L. Rev. 383, 413 (1964) (suggesting that for federal common lawmaking it is sufficient that there is a "grant of federal jurisdiction . . . adorned with a bit of legislative history"). *See also* Nelson, *supra* note 167

[193] *See Wallis v. Pan Am Petroleum Corp.*, 384 U.S. 63, 68 (1966). *See* Redish, note 167, *supra*, at 80. Some scholars have attempted to refine these interests in order to escape the "enclave approach" to federal common law, which simply lists subjects to which it applies. One such effort suggests that federal common law should only be made when the transactions to which it will apply fall beyond the legislative competence of the states, and when making federal law promotes a constitutional structure or relationship such as the separation of powers (e.g., the "exclusive" foreign relations authority of the political branches) or the constitutional equality of the states (e.g., interstate disputes). *See* Bradford R. Clark, *Federal Common Law: A Structural Reinterpretation*, 144 U. Pa. L. Rev. 1245, 1251–52 (1996).

[194] *Atherton v. FDIC*, 519 U.S. 213 (1997) (*quoting O'Melveny & Myers v. FDIC*, 512 U.S. 79, 87 (1994)).

[195] 318 U.S. 363 (1943).

[196] 318 U.S. at 367. Whether the background federal statutes and regulations truly declared any identifiable policy or interest has been questioned. *See* Note, *Clearfield: Clouded Field of Federal Common Law*, 53 Colum. L. Rev. 991, 1002–05 (1953).

[197] 352 U.S. 29 (1956).

[198] 352 U.S. at 34.

Finally, when the federal common lawmaking authority is exercised, the question of the content of the law remains. In fact, the phrase federal common law is somewhat misleading. It is more accurately called the "law of independent federal judicial decision,"[199] because once a court is satisfied that it should exercise lawmaking power, it is free to choose state law, fashion distinct federal law, or create some hybrid of the two.[200] Because states do not make their laws with federal interests in mind, the choice of state law as the content of federal common law would sometimes frustrate federal policy. But if a court finds as a threshold matter that the choice of state law would not frustrate federal policy, it may then consider such additional factors as the need for uniformity, the strength of a state's interest in having its own rules govern, the availability of developed state law, and the feasibility of judicially fashioning a substitute.[201] For example, this analysis has generally led the federal courts to "borrow" state limitations periods in federal causes of action for which Congress has not expressly provided limitations, and at the same time caused them to fashion distinct federal equitable tolling rules[202] in order to give effect to federal interests in the underlying cause of action.[203] Similarly, the Court concluded there was no federal interest in a uniform rule for determining the res judicata effect of a federal diversity judgment and therefore chose, as the applicable federal common law, the res judicata rule that would be applied by the forum state's courts.[204] At the same time, it was careful to note "the federal reference to state law will not obtain, of course, in situations in which the state law is incompatible with federal interests," such as a state law which would deny res judicata effect to a federal court dismissal for wilful violation of discovery orders.[205]

Of course, state law borrowed to supply the content of federal common law does not apply of its own force or by force of the Rules of Decision Act. It applies only because the federal court chose it. By the same token, the authority of state law as such is unaffected by its adoption (or later displacement) as federal common law.[206]

---

[199] *United States v. Standard Oil Co.*, 332 U.S. 301, 308 (1947).

[200] *United States v. Kimbell Foods, Inc.*, 440 U.S. 715, 728 (1979). The Supreme Court has described federal common law "in the strictest sense" as a "rule of decision that amounts, not simply to an interpretation of a federal statute or a properly promulgated administrative rule, but, rather, to a judicial 'creation' of a specific federal rule of decision." *Atherton*, 519 U.S. at 218.

[201] *See Wallis*, 384 U.S. at 68–69. *See generally* Field, note 167, at 953–62, *supra*. The borrowing court applies federal law to decide which state's law it will borrow. *De Sylva v. Ballentine*, 351 U.S. 570 (1956).

[202] Equitable tolling rules stop the running of the statute limitations because of the defendant's conduct. *See* § 8.08[2][b] (the affirmative defense of limitations), *infra*.

[203] *See generally Limitation Borrowing*, note 179, *supra*.

[204] *Semtek Int'l Inc.v. Lockheed Martin Corp.*, 531 U.S. 497, 508 (2001).

[205] *Semtek Int'l Inc.*, 531 U.S. at 508.

[206] Field, note 167, *supra*, at 887.

Chapter 8

SIMPLE PLEADING AND PRACTICE

§ 8.01 OVERVIEW: THE FUNCTIONS AND HISTORY OF PLEADING

Pleading is the exchange of written allegations to ascertain the subject for decision in a civil action. A pleading is a document — called the complaint, the answer and, where permitted, the reply — containing statements (allegations or averments), or denials of facts as well as statements of claims or defenses.[1] Legal objections to pleadings are made by filing a *demurrer* (in some state courts) or a *motion* (in federal and some state courts) attacking the pleading and asking the court to dismiss or alter the pleading.[2] Arguments about the law or how it applies to the facts are presented by memoranda of law called *briefs*, supporting or opposing a motion. This chapter introduces the basics of pleading in the simple case of a single claim by a single plaintiff against a single defendant. Chapter 9 treats the more common and complex case in which multiple parties or claims are *joined* together in the litigation.

To understand fully the requirements of pleading and their evolution, it is necessary to understand the functions of the pleading process — the filing of pleadings and responses to them. First, pleading can *give notice* to the parties of the nature of claims and defenses, helping them prepare their case. Second, pleading can help a court identify and weed out *sham or insufficient claims or defenses*, conserving scarce judicial resources and protecting litigants against harassing litigation. Third, pleading can help to *narrow the issues*, streamlining a case for trial and efficiently focusing the attention of the decision makers. Fourth, pleading can *guide the parties and the court in the conduct of the case*, helping them to define the scope of pretrial factual preparation and of evidentiary relevance at trial. Finally, pleading can *supply a record* for judgment, permitting the eventual application of the law of *res judicata* to preclude relitigation of already-decided claims and issues.[3]

The priority assigned these systemic functions of pleading determines the rules of pleading. Historically in Anglo-American law, the most important function of pleading was issue identification and narrowing. *Common law pleading* and practice developed elaborate and arcane judge-made rules to this end, until it grew so technical and arbitrary that it was discarded by most states in favor of simplified rules of procedure codified in pleading codes. The primary functions of *code*

---

[1] *See* Rule 7(a); §§ 8.06 & 8.08–8.09, *infra*.

[2] *See* Rule 7(b); § 8.07, *infra*.

[3] *See generally* Chapter 15, *infra*.

pleading were notice and guidance. To these ends, it emphasized the pleading of facts constituting a *cause of action* (legal theory of liability), but it eventually also bogged down in disputation about the required specificity of fact pleading and the meaning of the term "cause of action."

In 1938, the Federal Rules of Civil Procedure abolished fact pleading and the concept of cause of action in favor of what some courts and commentators (though not the rules themselves) originally called *notice pleading*. As this term suggested, modern federal pleading — since copied in whole or part by a majority of states[4] — at least in the beginning, served the function of giving notice to the opposing party. Other procedural devices such as discovery (fact-gathering), summary judgment (pretrial disposition on the law when the material facts are undisputed), and pretrial conferences serve the remaining functions.

No American jurisdiction requires pure common law pleading today, and a declining number follow code pleading. Yet exposure to these systems of pleading aids the understanding of modern pleading for several reasons. Much of the terminology of modern pleading is inherited from common law or code pleading. Many of the rules of modern pleading are best understood as attempts to cure problems that dogged common law or code pleading. Moreover, the focus of both common law and code pleading on the pleader's legal theory is still important. Finally, as the father of the federal rules observed, "by a kind of Gresham's Law, the bad or harsh procedural decisions drive out the good, so that in time a rule becomes entirely obscured by its interpretive barnacles."[5] To the extent that some of the barnacles on modern pleading are of ancient lineage, it is worth tracing that lineage at least in outline.

Accordingly, sections 8.02 and 8.03 sketch some of the essential elements of common law/equity and code pleading, respectively. Section 8.04 then introduces and briefly traces the evolution of modern federal pleading, and section 8.05 discusses the candor and care requirements of modern pleading. The remaining sections trace the modern pleading process chronologically from complaint, to responses, to amendment.

§ 8.02 PRE-CODE PLEADING AND PRACTICE

[1] Common Law Issue Pleading and Practice[6]

Pleading in early English history consisted of oral exchanges before feudal and communal courts. The difficulty of remembering long oral presentations probably compelled pleaders to exchange short allegations until they had reduced the

---

[4] John B. Oakley & Arthur F. Coon, *The Federal Rules in State Courts: A Survey of State Court Systems of Civil Procedure*, 61 WASH. L. REV. 1367, 1369 (1986).

[5] Charles E. Clark, *Special Problems in Drafting and Interpreting Procedural Codes and Rules*, 3 VAND. L. REV. 493, 498 (1950).

[6] The outline of historical pleading requirements and practices given in this section is drawn largely from JOSEPH H. KOFFLER & ALISON REPPY, HANDBOOK OF COMMON LAW PLEADING (1969), and BENJAMIN J. SHIPMAN, HANDBOOK OF COMMON-LAW PLEADING (H. Ballantine 3d ed. 1923), except as otherwise noted.

dispute to a specific issue that the decider and the pleaders could easily keep in mind.[7]

Two developments transpired over a period of centuries to mature this system. In the fourteenth century, written pleadings were introduced, permitting the elaboration of pleading allegations and the formalization of the oral practice of "pleading to the issue" — an iterative pleading and response process designed to reduce the dispute to a simple factual or legal issue. The necessity for pleading to a single issue became the driving force of an increasingly formalistic common law pleading system.

A plaintiff in the royal courts began his action by obtaining a *writ* from the king's representative ordering a sheriff to compel the defendant to satisfy the plaintiff's claim or to appear in court to defend himself. As long as feudal and communal courts still heard the major share of the judicial business, such writs were limited to a small number of claims on which the king could give relief. The writ, in effect, conferred a limited subject matter jurisdiction on the royal courts, and the plaintiff's claim had to fall within the writ — the particular royal court's jurisdiction — or it would fail. The royal courts gradually expanded their jurisdiction by issuing new writs or by stretching the limits of existing writs through legal fictions — effectively aggrandizing their power by tolerating partly fictitious pleading to fit old writs.

Eventually, each permitted writ became associated with its own substantive legal theory and developed its own procedural incidents. Each resulting *form of action* thus came to embrace[8] not just the appropriate writ, but also the forms of pleas, modes of trial, and forms of judgment.[9] "The primary question before the [common law] courts has not been the general one whether the plaintiff's statement of his case showed a right in him and a violation by the defendant; it has rather been whether the case presented facts which constituted a 'cause of action' in 'trespass,' 'assumpsit,' or other particular form attempted to be used."[10] Once the writ was issued, the plaintiff would begin the pleading process by filing a *declaration*, describing his case in the formalistic and often fictitious language held necessary under the particular writ and associated with the attendant form of action. Consistent with the objective of reducing the case to a single issue, no hypothetical (if, then) or alternative (either/or) pleading was permitted. From the outset, the plaintiff had to elect a particular set of facts, and by virtue of the form of action he invoked, a particular legal theory. Any deviation between the writ selected and the declaration, or between the declaration and eventual proof at trial, was termed a *variance* and forbidden.[11] Any pleading *departure* from the

---

[7] JAMES STEPHEN, THE PRINCIPLES OF PLEADING IN CIVIL ACTIONS 37, 147–50 (Tyler ed. 1882).

[8] The forms of action evolved gradually. They included, at different points in time, trespass, trespass on the case (encompassing various indirect injuries and non-physical torts), trover (for the return of property), ejectment, detinue (return of property and damages for its wrongful detention), replevin, debt, and special assumpsit. *See* KOFFLER & REPPY, note 6, *supra*, Chs. 7–13, 16.

[9] *See generally* FREDERIC WILLIAM MAITLAND, EQUITY, ALSO THE FORMS OF ACTION AT COMMON LAW (1909); CECIL HERBERT STUART FIFOOT, HISTORY AND SOURCES OF THE COMMON LAW — TORT AND CONTRACT (1949).

[10] SHIPMAN, note 6, *supra*, § 27.

[11] KOFFLER & REPPY, note 6, §§ 26–27; SHIPMAN, note 6, *supra*, § 82.

previously pleaded facts or legal theory was fatal to the pleading, because it was inconsistent with narrowing the issues.[12] Relief was limited to that sought in the declaration upon the facts and legal theory there asserted. The harshness of these principles is illustrated by a decision reversing a judgment for plaintiff because he had pleaded a debt of $2,579.57, but proved a debt of $2,579.57 1/2![13]

The drive toward a single issue was also reflected in the requirements for further pleading. There were three possible responses to a claim.

First, a party could *demur*, asserting that, even if true, the claimant's allegations state no legal claim. The demurrer had to attack a pleading on its face; so-called *speaking demurrers*, which relied on additional matter beyond the four corners of the pleading, were prohibited. At first, the demurrer did not specify the defect in the pleading that it attacked. This left the pleader in the dark as to whether his legal theory was deficient, he had omitted some necessary ritualistic language, or he had simply committed some other minor and easily corrected error of form. After a 16th century reform, however, defects of form had to be attacked by *special demurrer* specifying the defect or they were waived. The *general demurrer* was reserved for substantive legal defects.

Second, a party could respond with a *dilatory plea*, asserting some legal reason, incidental to the merits, why the court could not hear the case.[14] *Pleas to the court's jurisdiction* challenged the court's subject matter jurisdiction and, if sustained, required dismissal of the case. *Pleas in suspension* sought to suspend the action until some problem, such as the plaintiff's legal disability through outlawry, had been removed. *Pleas in abatement* challenged defects in the pleading itself, going to the capacity of the pleader, misjoinder of claims or parties, etc.

Third, the party could respond on the merits with a *plea in bar*, also called a *peremptory plea*, asserting a defense that could bar recovery. By asserting the plea in bar called the *traverse*, the pleader denied the allegations of the claim against him, creating a factual issue for trial. To assure singleness of issue, however, treacherous rules evolved concerning the precise form of denials in a traverse. The traps which these rules set for the unwary eventually made a different form of traverse popular — the *general issue*, essentially the civil version of a "not guilty" plea. By filing the general issue, a defendant could contest liability and even assert various defenses without having to specify which allegations of the complaint he denied or which of the defenses he would assert at trial.[15] The plea of the general issue neither gave notice nor helped to reduce the case to a single issue, but its "popularity . . . with the common law pleaders may be in part explained on the theory that it was a practical method of simplifying a system of pleading which had grown too technical for successful application."[16] Finally, an alternative plea in bar

---

[12] SHIPMAN, note 6, *supra*, §§ 217–229.

[13] *Spangler v. Pugh*, 21 Ill. 85 (1859).

[14] Most such pleas asserted curable preliminary defects or problems and would only delay rather than permanently bar an action by a persistent plaintiff — hence the generic term, *dilatory pleas*. KOFFLER & REPPY, note 6, *supra*, § 203.

[15] *See* KOFFLER & REPPY, note 6, *supra*, § 224.

[16] Charles Liebert Crum, *Scope of the General Denial*, 27 N.D. L. REV. 11, 14 (1951).

was the *plea in confession and avoidance*. It required defendant to admit (confess) plaintiff's claim and to plead an excuse: new matter that avoided the claim.

Both the demurrer and the dilatory plea created legal issues, while the traverse created a factual issue. Additional pleading was necessary to raise an issue on the plea of confession and avoidance, since no issue was created by the confession of plaintiff's claim. To achieve singleness in pleading, the demurrer, traverse and plea in confession and avoidance were mutually exclusive; combining pleas or otherwise raising more than one issue in a pleading was prohibited as *duplicity*.[17]

Once the defendant had answered, it was the plaintiff's turn to respond by filing a *replication*, asserting one of the three possible analytic responses described above. If the issue was still not joined, the defendant then filed a *rejoinder*. Additional rounds of pleading by way of *surrejoinder, rebutter, surrebutter* and theoretically beyond were also possible until issues had been joined. At the conclusion of this usually protracted and procedurally land-mined pleading process, trial with fact-finding by a jury was often "something of an afterthought."[18]

Complicated as this outline sounds, it does not begin to portray the true technicality of the common law pleading system in its heyday, or to illustrate the extent of the legal fictions which permeated the forms of action. Professor Charles Alan Wright pronounced a just and fitting verdict on the system: "This system was wonderfully scientific. It was also wonderfully slow, expensive and unworkable. The system was better calculated to vindicate scientific rules of pleading than it was to dispense justice."[19]

[2] Equity Pleading and Practice[20]

For dispensation of justice frustrated by the scientific complexities of the common law system or by the unavailability of a suitable writ or of adequate law relief in the traditional form of damages,[21] plaintiffs petitioned the king directly. He sent them to his chief minister, the chancellor, and by the 16th century, a *court of chancery* had developed to hear such petitions or *bills of complaint*.[22] The predicate for seeking equity in the chancery court was a showing of inadequate remedy at law. The remedy at equity was a decree ordering the respondent

---

[17] KOFFLER & REPPY, note 6, *supra*, §§ 234–35.

[18] Richard L. Marcus, *The Revival of Fact Pleading Under the Federal Rules of Civil Procedure*, 86 COLUM. L. REV. 433, 437 (1986) (citations omitted).

[19] *WRIGHT* § 68.

[20] *See generally* FREDERIC WILLIAM MAITLAND, EQUITY (2d rev. ed. 1936); JOHN NORTON POMEROY, CODE REMEDIES (5th ed. 1929). The following outline is drawn primarily from these sources, except as otherwise noted.

[21] Actually the law courts granted relief by declaring a legal relationship between plaintiff and defendant, usually that plaintiff was entitled to a sum of money ("damages") from the defendant. *See generally* § 14.01 (damages remedies), *infra*.

[22] Some scholars date the development of equity as a separate system to the 14th century. *See, e.g.*, Harold Dexter Hazeltine, *The Early History of English Equity, in* ESSAYS IN LEGAL HISTORY 261–85 (P. Vinogradoff ed. 1913).

personally and directly to do or not to do something, *i.e.*, a decree of specific performance or an injunction.[23]

As an alternative to the common law system, equity developed its own procedures. First, the bill of complaint consisted of a repetitive narrative of evidentiary facts culminating in *interrogatories* to respondent. The bill of complaint, framed partly to force disclosure of the defendant's case by his sworn answer and partly to serve as evidence in lieu of oral testimony at trial to the chancellor,[24] thus served as an early form of discovery of evidence from the adversary, unknown at common law. Eventually it gave rise to a *bill of discovery*, which could be brought in equity in aid of an action or defense at law — a forerunner of modern discovery.

Second, in order to do full justice, equity permitted the joinder (adding) of parties who could not be joined in a common law suit. *Cross-bills* in equity permitted claims between co-defendants, by defendant against the plaintiff, and against some third parties, while *interpleaders* and *derivative suits* permitted even more sophisticated forms of joinder. Equity procedures, then, were the forerunners of modern complex joinder devices.[25]

Third, equity did not ordinarily use the jury as a fact-finder. The trial was instead to the chancellor on the pleadings, answers to interrogatories, depositions (written examinations of witnesses under oath), and documentary evidence, rather than on oral testimony. The role of the chancellor as fact-finder led eventually to a different degree of appellate deference to his findings than to jury findings, which is today reflected in the federal standards of appellate review.[26]

Despite equity's origins as a flexible alternative to the rigidities of common law practice and procedure, it became encrusted with its own procedural barnacles. One study of equity practice concluded that equity actions were frequently interminable and that even in those which came to a successful conclusion, "the honest suitor emerged from the ordeal victorious rather than triumphant, for too often he had been ruined by the way."[27]

---

[23] *See generally* § 14.02 (equitable relief), *infra*.

[24] MAITLAND, note 20, *supra*, Lecture 1, at 5.

[25] *See generally* Chapter 9 (complex pleading and practice), *infra*.

[26] *See* § 13.10[2][b] (clearly erroneous standard of review), *infra*.

[27] Baron Bowen, *Progress in the Administration of Justice During the Victorian Period*, *in* 1 SELECT ESSAYS IN ANGLO-AMERICAN LEGAL HISTORY 516, 526–27 (E. Freund et al. eds. 1907).

§ 8.03   CODE FACT PLEADING AND PROCEDURE[28]

[1] In General

Neither common law nor equity pleading was imported in all its technical glory to the colonies. But enough was adopted to prompt reform by the mid-19th century. New York led the way in 1848 with the legislative adoption of the *Field Code of Civil Procedure*. It became a model for pleading reforms in more than half the states, and the *code pleading* — that is, pleading rules enacted in a statutory code — which it introduced is still retained in a few.[29]

The *Field Code* abolished the forms of action and the distinction between law and equity actions in favor of "one form of action, denominated a civil action."[30] It also discarded all existing pleading rules that were inconsistent with its provisions. The hallmark of the code was *fact pleading*: the requirement that the complaint state "facts constituting a cause of action, in ordinary and concise language."[31] Formalistic or fictitious pleading was to be replaced by straightforward pleading of facts. Issue-narrowing was no longer the primary function of pleading. Its objective, instead, was "three-fold: to present the facts on which the court is to pronounce the law; to present them in such a manner, as that the precise points in dispute shall be perceived, to which the proofs may be directed; and to preserve the record of the rights determined."[32] Since pleading no longer had to generate a single issue, multiple rounds of pleading were no longer required or permitted. Pleadings were instead limited to a complaint, answer, and, in rare cases, reply, which were all to be liberally construed.[33]

The adoption of code pleading brought with it two major problems: what constituted a cause of action, and how specifically did plaintiff have to plead facts constituting a cause of action? These are explored in the discussion which follows.

---

[28] *See generally* CHARLES E. CLARK, HANDBOOK OF THE LAW OF CODE PLEADING (2d ed. 1947), by any measure the leading authority on the subject, from which the following outline is drawn, except as otherwise noted.

[29] For example, California, Oklahoma, South Carolina, and Virginia have retained fact pleading requirements among other code pleading rules at the same time that they have adapted discovery, amendment and sometimes summary judgment provisions from the Federal Rules of Civil Procedure. FRIEDENTHAL, KANE & MILLER, § 5.1. *See, e.g.*, Va. Code Ann. § 8.01 (West 2012); *see generally* Ian Wilson & William Payne, Note, *The Specificity of Pleading in Modern Civil Practice*, 25 U. RICH. L. REV. 135 (1990) (discussing Virginia fact pleading).

[30] N.Y. Code Civ. Proc. § 69 (1848) (hereinafter *Field Code*).

[31] *Field Code* § 142(2).

[32] FIRST REPORT OF THE COMMISSIONERS ON PRACTICE AND PLEADINGS, 123–24, 137–38, 140–41, 144 (1848) (report which led to promulgation of the Field Code).

[33] *Field Code* §§ 156 & 159.

[2] The Cause of Action and the Theory of the Pleadings

The code drafters agreed that "[i]n some manner it is necessary to state the limits to which relief for a number of grievances or one severe and long-continued grievance may be accorded in a *single* suit."[34] The common law, of course, established narrow and seemingly precise limits through the forms of action and the attendant pleading niceties. But the abolition of the forms and old pleading rules made it unnecessary and arguably improper to plead the discarded common law allegations in order to set forth facts constituting a cause of action. On the other hand, conclusory pleading would not do either, in view of the code's emphasis on facts.

Between these extremes, at least two approaches to limiting the suit developed. The first equated a cause of action with a right of action or the legal or primary right suggested by the facts relied upon by the plaintiff.[35] The second looked to the "aggregate of operative facts," "limited as a lay onlooker would to a single occurrence or affair, without particular reference to the resulting legal right or rights."[36] The latter pragmatically anticipated the unit of facts that would most naturally and conveniently be presented at trial. But it was ahead of its time. Its very flexibility appeared to threaten the objective of notice by leaving unclear which legal rights arose from the aggregate of operative facts and therefore what law applied.

Consequently, most observers agreed on the need for some sort of legal right as the measuring stick for the plaintiff's pleading.[37] The result was a *theory-of-pleadings* approach to defining a cause of action in many, though not all, code states, by which the plaintiff was expected to identify a legal theory of recovery and to plead acts supporting the identified theory. Unfortunately, a wooden insistence on the identified theory, however, helped perpetuate much of the rigidity of formulary pleading and its corresponding rules against variance and departure. In *Jones v. Winsor*,[38] for example, the plaintiffs sued for return of money deposited with their attorney, alleging in part that his fee was unjust, unlawful and fraudulent. The complaint failed to state a cause of action for conversion because of plaintiffs' omission of allegations of ownership or possession of the money entrusted to the attorney. If, however, the cause of action was considered to be a contractual one for money had and received, the complaint would have been sufficient, and the allegations of fraudulent conversion would have been mere surplusage. The court upheld a demurrer, reasoning that

> [a] complaint should be framed upon the theory that it is either a complaint in tort or one *ex contractu*, and the two theories cannot be combined in one action; neither can an action at law and an action in equity be combined in

---

[34] CLARK, note 28, *supra*, § 19, at 128 (emphasis in original). Because such limits are also necessary to define the scope of a final judgment for purposes of the law of claim preclusion, detailed discussion of them is deferred until Chapter 15. *See* § 15.03 (claim preclusion), *infra*.

[35] *See* CLARK, note 28, *supra*, § 19; JOHN NORTON POMEROY, 1 EQUITY JURISPRUDENCE § 347 (5th ed. 1941).

[36] CLARK, note 28, *supra*, § 19, at 130, 137.

[37] *Id.*

[38] 118 N.W. 716 (S.D. 1908). *See also Mescall v. Tully*, 91 Ind. 96, 99 (1883).

one count in the same action. . . . "On demurrer to a complaint, or any count thereof, the court must determine what cause of action such complaint or count is designed to state, and then whether it states facts sufficient to constitute such a cause of action; and, if not, the demurrer must be sustained, though facts may be stated sufficient to show that plaintiff has a cause of action of a different character."[39]

In other words, the court held the plaintiff to the (insufficient) theory of conversion, even though the complaint could have been sustained on the alternative theory of contract. This arid insistence of one theory of the pleadings could hardly be said to construe the complaint to do substantial justice.

Similarly, other courts held that if a complaint stated a cause of action on one legal theory, the action would fail if that legal theory was not proven at trial, even though allegations in the complaint and proof at trial would have supported a cause of action on a different legal theory.[40] Plaintiff had, in effect, made a fatal departure or variance from the legal theory articulated by his complaint; he should have elected the successful legal theory before trial. Other courts rejected such harsh applications of the theory-of-the-pleadings approach by considering whether defendants were adequately apprised of the theory plaintiff ultimately argued at trial or whether they were surprised — considerations more in keeping with the objectives of fact pleading under the codes. Yet even these courts gave defendants the option of moving before trial to strike surplusage from the complaint and "to compel the plaintiff to make it more definite, or to elect in regard to the *form of action*."[41] As the italicized phrase in this "progressive" ruling reveals, in many states the forms of action still ruled code pleading from the grave.

[3] The Specificity of Fact Pleading Under the Codes

In reaction to the often fictitious quality of common law pleading, the codes required the pleading of only "dry, naked, actual facts,"[42] to which the court would apply the substantive law. Plaintiff was therefore obliged to avoid pleading a conclusory legal evaluation of his facts. At the same time, he was charged with pleading concisely. In short, he could plead neither too little nor too much, but just the so-called *ultimate facts* from which an appropriate cause of action could be inferred.

Pleading too little — bare conclusions of law — subjected the complaint to demurrer. But the dividing line between improper conclusions of law and proper ultimate facts proved evanescent. Typically nettlesome allegations included the following: plaintiff and defendant mutually agreed; plaintiff is the owner of property; defendant's servant was acting within the scope of his employment;

---

[39] *Jones v. Winsor*, 118 N.W. at 718 (*quoting Supervisors of Kewaunee County v. Decker*, 30 Wis. 624 (1872)).

[40] *See Ross v. Mather*, 51 N.Y. 108 (1872).

[41] *Conaughty v. Nichols*, 42 N.Y. 83, 88 (1870) (emphasis supplied) (permitting plaintiff to amend his complaint after trial by striking language of conversion, in order to recover on a contractual theory). *Contra, Jones*, 118 N.W. 716.

[42] *Wright* § 68 (quoting JOHN NORTON POMEROY, CODE REMEDIES 640 (1929)).

defendant was in charge of the construction. Sometimes the allegations as a group were held conclusory. In *Gillespie v. Goodyear Service Stores*,[43] plaintiff alleged that

> [o]n or about May 5, 1959, and May 6, 1959, the defendants, *without cause or just excuse and maliciously* came upon and trespassed upon the premises occupied by the plaintiff as a residence, and by the use of harsh and threatening language and physical force directed against the plaintiff assaulted the plaintiff and placed her in great fear, and humiliated and embarrassed her by subjecting her to public scorn and ridicule, and caused her to be seized and exhibited to the public as a prisoner, and to be confined in a public jail.[44]

The appellate court affirmed dismissal of the complaint on a demurrer, reasoning that it stated no facts upon which the italicized "legal conclusions" could be predicated.[45] "Plaintiff's allegations do not disclose *what* occurred, *when* it occurred, *where* it occurred, *who did what*, the relationships between defendants and plaintiff or of defendants *inter se*, or any other factual data that might identify the occasion or describe the circumstances."[46]

The plaintiff who sought to avoid such a result by pleading detailed *evidentiary facts*, however, risked pleading too much. Although this vice was rarely fatal, because the court could usually still draw the necessary legal inferences from the collective evidentiary facts, the plaintiff could never be sure that the consequences would not be more serious. In *McCaughey v. Schuette*,[47] the appellate court actually reversed a judgment for plaintiff because his complaint seeking possession of property contained only "a statement of evidentiary facts, which, if proven at the trial, would authorize the court in finding the ultimate fact of ownership and right to possession in the plaintiff."[48] Why was this bad? The court explained:

> The complaint here is argumentative — that is to say, the affirmative existence of the ultimate fact is left to inference or argument. Such pleading was bad at common law, and is none the less so under our code system. To uphold such a pleading is to encourage prolixity, and a wide departure from that definiteness, certainty, and perspicuity which it was one of the paramount objects sought to be enforced by the code system of pleading, and that, too, with no resultant effect, except to encumber the record with verbiage and enhance the cost of litigation.[49]

Though this explanation speaks of economy, it arguably gives away its real reasoning when it says "[s]uch pleading was bad at common law." It's still a court haunted by the ghosts of hypertechnical common law pleading.

---

[43] 128 S.E.2d 762 (N.C. 1963).

[44] *Id.* at 763 (emphasis supplied).

[45] *Id.* at 766.

[46] *Id.*

[47] 46 P. 666 (Cal. 1896).

[48] *Id.*

[49] *Id.*

The codes attempted to distinguish among legal conclusions, ultimate facts, and evidentiary facts, that was "one of degree only," not of kind.[50] Even frequent appellate treatments of the distinction furnished no guidance to the trial courts because they were inescapably ad hoc. When the issue was essentially whether the pleader had pleaded too little or too much, most precedents were distinguishable, most pleadings were fair game, and form was again elevated over substance as it had been under the common law.

§ 8.04 MODERN FEDERAL PLEADING

The drafters of the Federal Rules of Civil Procedure attempted to adopt the successes and avoid the failures of code pleading. In prescribing the basic federal pleading requirement, they therefore rejected both the phrases "facts" and "cause of action" in favor of the rule that a pleading contain "a short and plain statement of the claim showing that the pleader is entitled to relief."[51] Under the federal rules, issue-narrowing, fact development and guidance, and screening of sham or insufficient claims or defenses are accomplished chiefly by devices other than pleading. The primary remaining function of modern pleading is to give notice of claims or defenses. "The real importance of the Rules dealing with pleadings is that they make pleadings, in and of themselves, relatively unimportant. Cases are to be decided on their merits."[52]

We will examine four questions surrounding federal pleading. First, how specific must the pleading be? Second, has the theory-of-the-pleadings doctrine been finally abandoned? Third, what form must pleading take? Finally, what more specific pleading rules have survived and why?

[1] The Specificity of Federal Pleading

The required specificity of federal pleading has evolved over time. From the rhetoric (if not always the reality) of "notice pleading," it evolved in many courts to a more demanding "elements pleading" standard and in a few to a quite demanding "heightened pleading" standard, before the Supreme Court seemed to call halt. More recently, however, the Court has sown renewed confusion by seeming to endorse a "plausible pleading" standard for at least some cases.

[a] Notice Pleading

The phrase "notice pleading" suggests more the spirit than the letter of a sufficient pleading and was disavowed by the federal rulemakers themselves.[53] But Rule 8(a)(2)'s requirement of a "short and plain statement of the claim showing that the pleader is entitled to relief" is hardly more helpful. On one hand, it could mean that a sufficient pleading could inform defendant of little more than that she has been sued. On the other hand, it could contemplate a detailed statement of facts

---

[50] Clark, note 28, *supra*, § 38.

[51] Rule 8(a)(2).

[52] James William Moore, Moore's Federal Practice § 8.02 (2d ed. 1979).

[53] *See* Charles E. Clark, *Two Decades of the Federal Civil Rules*, 58 Colum. L. Rev. 435, 450–51 (1958).

making out each and every element of a claim.

The Supreme Court lent some support to the first view in *Conley v. Gibson*[54] by endorsing what it called "simplified 'notice pleading'" and "the accepted rule that a complaint should not be dismissed for failure to state a claim unless it appears beyond doubt that the plaintiff can prove no set of facts in support of his claim which would entitle him to relief."[55] *Dioguardi v. Durning*,[56] cited with approval in *Conley* and penned by the chief drafter of the federal rules, appeared to set a very modest standard for the statement of such matter and illustrates the leniency of the *Conley* statement. Plaintiff's "obviously home drawn" complaint against the Collector of Customs alleged cryptically that certain "medicinal extracts" imported by plaintiff had disappeared and that others had been given to a third party "with my betting [bidding?] price of $110: and not their price of $120."[57] Judge Clark reversed the dismissal of the action for failure to state a claim, concluding that the plaintiff had stated claims against the collector for conversion and improper public sale, "however inartistically."[58]

Read together, *Conley* and *Dioguardi* appeared to embrace a liberal view of notice pleading whereby no complaint will be held insufficient for failure to state a claim unless "the pleader makes allegations that show on the face of the complaint some insuperable bar to relief."[59] By this view, a plaintiff does not have to allege all the facts necessary to prove its claim.[60] Nor does he have to "set out the legal theory on which the claim is based,"[61] so long as there exists some theory that would entitle the claimant to relief on the allegations made. The test for the sufficiency of a pleading is whether the pleader has stated a claim under *any* legal theory, not just under *his* asserted theory of the pleadings. This is consistent with a theory of pleading that emphasizes notice and notice alone as the essential function of pleadings.

[b]   Elements Pleading

While *Conley* gave the most oft-quoted rule, it could hardly be taken literally, or (as the Supreme Court later critically commented), "a wholly conclusory statement of claim would survive a motion to dismiss whenever the pleadings left open the possibility that a plaintiff might later establish some 'set of [undisclosed] facts' to support recovery."[62] Read literally, *Conley*'s no-set-of-facts standard would permit

---

[54]   355 U.S. 41 (1957).

[55]   *Id.* at 45–46, 48.

[56]   139 F.2d 774 (2d Cir. 1944).

[57]   *Id.* at 775 (bracketed material in original). The full amended complaint is reproduced in John J. Cound, Jack H. Friedenthal, Arthur R. Miller & John E. Sexton, Civil Procedure: Cases and Materials 502–03 n.1 (7th ed. 1997).

[58]   *Dioguardi*, 139 F.2d at 775.

[59]   Wright § 68 (citations omitted).

[60]   *See, e.g., Sparrow v. United Air Lines, Inc.*, 216 F.3d 1111 (D.C. Cir. 2000).

[61]   *Siegelman v. Cunard White Star, Ltd.*, 221 F.2d 189, 196 (2d Cir. 1955) (Harlan, J.).

[62]   *Bell Atl. Corp. v. Twombly*, 550 U.S. 544, 561 (2007), discussed in § 8.04[1][d], *infra*. Many prior courts and commentators had made the same observation. *See Car Carriers, Inc. v. Ford Motor Co.*, 745

plaintiff to allege nothing but that defendant was liable to plaintiff and pass muster. The allegations in *Conley* itself went well beyond this, and the form complaints accompanying the federal rules and declared to "suffice" thereunder by Rule 84 also supply some specific factual matter in addition to the conclusory statements that "defendant owes plaintiff money" or that "defendant negligently drove a motor vehicle against plaintiff."[63] In other words, they imply that the complaint should state the circumstances, occurrences, and events that give rise to the claim, even though they can be stated quite generally.[64]

The inclusion of such factual matter in both the case and the forms provided support for the view that screening sham or legally insufficient complaints is still a proper secondary function. As Judge Richard Posner put it, the purpose of the federal pleading rule under this view is less to give defendant information with which to prepare his defense "than to allow the court to determine at the outset . . . whether the plaintiff has any tenable theory or basis of suit, so that if he does not the case can be got rid of immediately without clogging the court's docket and imposing needless expense on the defendant."[65]

Taking this view of modern pleading, some courts have required that "a complaint must . . . contain either direct or inferential allegations respecting all the material elements necessary to sustain a recovery under *some* viable legal theory."[66] Bare notice is insufficient; the pleader must at least allege sufficient factual detail to set out all the elements necessary to establish a claim — usually duty, breach, injury, and causation.[67] Such a complaint is said to state a *prima facie* claim. The Supreme Court, however, seemed to reject the idea that a complaint had to plead facts corresponding to all the elements of a claim, asserting that a *prima facie* case is an evidentiary standard, not a pleading standard.[68]

Still, although a plaintiff may not be required to plead facts "in support of every arcane element of his claim," he should not omit those facts that "would clearly

---

F.2d 1101, 1106 (7th Cir. 1984), *cert. denied*, 470 U.S. 1054 (1985); Richard L. Marcus, *The Revival of Fact Pleading Under the Federal Rules of Civil Procedure*, 86 COLUM. L. REV. 433, 434 (1986) ("Taken literally, it might have precluded dismissal in any case where the plaintiff invoked a valid legal theory.").

[63] Forms 10–15.

[64] WRIGHT § 68 (citations omitted). The best explanation for the seeming inconsistency of the "no-set-of-facts" language and the specific factual matter supplied in Form 11's complaint is that the former stated a standard for the legal sufficiency of the complaint rather than its factual sufficiency to give notice. The forms, instead, suggest the standard of factual sufficiency. *See, e.g.*, Wendy Gerwick Couture, Conley v. Gibson's *"No Set of Facts" Test: Neither Cancer Nor Cure*, 114 PENN ST. L. REV. PENN STATIM 19, 25 (2010); Patricia W. Hatamyar, *The Tao of Pleading: Do* Twombly *and* Iqbal *Matter Empirically?*, 59 AM. U. L. REV. 553, 560–61 (2010); *Hearing on Whether the Supreme Court Has Limited Americans' Access to Court Before the Comm. On the Judiciary*, 111 TH CONG. 11 (2009) (statement of Stephen B. Burbank, Univ. of Pa.).

[65] *Ryan v. Mary Immaculate Queen Ctr.*, 188 F.3d 857, 860 (7th Cir. 1999).

[66] *In re Plywood Antitrust Litigation*, 655 F.2d 627, 641 (5th Cir. 1981) (emphasis in original), *cert. denied*, 462 U.S. 1125 (1983). *See Car Carriers, Inc. v. Ford Motor Co.*, 745 F.2d 1101 (7th Cir. 1984), *cert. denied*, 470 U.S. 1054 (1985). *See generally* Marcus, note 62, *supra*, at 459–65.

[67] *See* § 8.06[2], *infra*.

[68] *Swierkiewicz v. Sorema N.A.*, 534 U.S. 506, 510–12 (2002). *See MOORE* § 8.04[1a] (3d ed. 2007).

dominate the case," or else the court may fairly assume that they do not exist.[69] Some even suggested that a plaintiff allege facts establishing a civil analogue to probable cause in criminal proceedings — probable cause to believe in the existence of a claim entitling plaintiff to relief.[70] This view of pleading leaves most of the work of discovery, preparation guidance, and merits dispositions to other procedural devices under the rules, but still affords appropriately limited scope for merits dispositions on the pleadings to screen undeserving cases. On the other hand, it does not require the plaintiff to identify a specific theory of the pleadings; if she has pleaded facts that would support *some* theory, it should be sufficient.

[c] Heightened Pleading

Until at least 1993, however, some circuits went beyond even elements pleading and selectively used an especially demanding version of this approach to dispose of disfavored actions on the pleadings. The *heightened pleading* standard was essentially a revival of fact pleading[71] as the courts insisted on very specific factual pleading of the elements in such actions. Typically these actions were disfavored because judges believed that a disproportionate number of them were frivolous. Tightening the screws of pleading meant that fewer of the actions would survive motions to dismiss to burden the judicial system. The heightened pleading standard, for example, was often applied to prisoners' complaints, many of which were frivolous because incarcerated plaintiffs are uninhibited by the usual practical and ethical restraints on frivolous suits against governmental officials.[72] Some circuits also applied it to other civil rights actions,[73] citing the volume of such cases, the number that were thought to be frivolous, and a consequential "public policy to weed out the [latter] at an early stage in the litigation."[74] Less systematically, courts applied the heightened pleading standard to securities fraud and antitrust complaints[75] and complaints against government action.[76]

From the start, this trend raised problems that had been associated with fact pleading under the codes.[77] Imposing special fact pleading requirements on disfavored actions introduces the same ad hoc differences of degree in pleading that

---

[69] *O'Brien v. Di Grazia*, 544 F.2d 543, 545 n.3 (1st Cir. 1976). *See also Daves v. Hawaiian Dredging Co.*, 114 F. Supp. 643, 645 (D. Haw. 1953); WRIGHT & MILLER § 1216. This proposition is reinforced by the care and candor requirements of Rule 11. *See* § 8.05[2] (certification), *infra*.

[70] *See* JAMES, HAZARD & LEUBSDORF § 3.6.

[71] *See* Marcus, note 62, *supra*, at 433.

[72] *See* James Dickson Phillips, Jr., *Foreword*, 39 WASH. & LEE L. REV. 425, 428 (1982).

[73] *See* Douglas A. Blaze, *Presumed Frivolous: Application of Stringent Pleading Requirements in Civil Rights Litigation*, 31 WM. & MARY L. REV. 935 (1990); Keith Wingate, *A Special Pleading Rule for Civil Rights Complaints: A Step Forward or a Step Back?*, 49 MO. L. REV. 677 (1984); Marcus, note 62, *supra*, at 449–50.

[74] *Rotolo v. Borough of Charleroi*, 532 F.2d 920, 922 (3d Cir. 1976) (quoting *Valley v. Maule*, 297 F. Supp. 958 (D. Conn. 1968)).

[75] Marcus, note 62, *supra*, at 447–49.

[76] *Id.* (noting use of special "fact" pleading rules to resolve questions of standing in such challenges). *See, e.g., Lujan v. Nat'l Wildlife Fed'n*, 497 U.S. 871 (1990) (finding that individualized injury was not pled with sufficient specificity to establish standing to challenge government action).

[77] *See* § 8.03[3], *supra*, discussing *Gillispie v. Goodyear Serv. Stores*, 128 S.E.2d 762 (N.C. 1963).

created such uncertainty under the codes,[78] and thus invites a sufficiency attack on the complaint in every disfavored action. Selective application of heightened pleading requirements also may reflect hidden judicial value preferences about the rights being asserted.[79] Not only are such preferences often contrary to those reflected by the congressional grant of federal jurisdiction to hear the judicially disfavored actions, but they may also be based on erroneous assumptions about the proportion of claims that are frivolous.[80] It is arguably for the legislature and the rulemakers to articulate and implement such preferences, not the courts.[81] Furthermore, more affluent (hence well-counseled) litigants can almost always meet a special pleading requirement whereas the pro se litigant often cannot. The difference will not necessarily reflect differences between the merits of their claims.

The Supreme Court's decision in *Leatherman v. Tarrant County Narcotics Intelligence and Coordination Unit*[82] finally slowed — though it did not halt — the trend towards applying heightened pleading. There, the district court had applied the Fifth Circuit's heightened pleading standard to dismiss two civil rights complaints alleging municipal liability. In a brief opinion, the Court unanimously found it "impossible to square the 'heightened pleading standard' . . . with the liberal system of 'notice pleading' set up by the Federal Rules."[83] Rule 9(b) *does* impose specific pleading requirements in certain listed instances, but its very existence precludes applying them to other instances. This reasoning applies with equal force to other applications of the heightened pleading standard and therefore may hasten its demise.

Nonetheless, scholars have remarked on "the puzzling persistence of pleading practice" into the next millennium, concluding that, in a small but significant number of cases, heightened pleading and its enforcement by Rule 12 motion practice help to implement substantive law and dispose of unsupportable claims.[84]

---

[78] *See Rotolo*, 532 F.2d at 924–25 (Gibbons, J., dissenting) (faulting majority for introducing "puzzling" standard of pleading sufficiency that evidently contemplates the pleading of evidence "beyond any prior holding of this court").

[79] *Id.* at 927 ("The explanation . . . for the imposition of a fact pleading requirement in [civil rights] cases . . . must be found in the attitude of the court toward the rights being asserted.").

[80] *Id.* at 927. *See, e.g.*, Eisenstadt, *Section 1983: Doctrinal Foundations and an Empirical Study*, 67 CORNELL L. REV. 482, 537 (1982) ("The vast majority of nonprisoner section 1983 cases involve classic rights of obvious importance; the trivial claims are a sideshow.").

[81] The federal rulemakers have already set out a few special pleading requirements in Rule 9. *See* § 8.04[4], *infra*. Arguably, the omission of other special pleading requirements was intentional and should be cured by the rulemakers, subject to congressional disapproval, *see* § 1.02 (the rulemaking process), *supra*, rather than by the courts.

[82] 507 U.S. 163 (1993).

[83] *Id.* at 168.

[84] Richard L. Marcus, *The Puzzling Persistence of Pleading Practice*, 76 TEX. L. REV. 1749 (1998).

[d] Plausible Pleading

The Supreme Court muddied the pleading waters in 2007 with its decision in *Bell Atlantic Corp. v. Twombly*.[85] In *Twombly*, plaintiffs brought an antitrust claim under the Sherman Act charging that a group of regional telephone companies ("Baby Bells") had conspired to restrain competition. They alleged that the Baby Bells had conspired to engage in parallel conduct to inhibit the growth of certain upstart local companies and to refrain from competing with one another in contiguous markets. Except for "a few stray statements [that] speak directly of agreement,"[86] plaintiffs relied on an inference of agreement from their allegations of defendants' conscious parallel conduct. In other words, the complaint essentially asserted that if they acted in parallel, they must have agreed to do so. The lower court granted a motion to dismiss for failure to state a claim, observing that defendants' parallel conduct could equally be explained by their lawful self-interests. The Court of Appeals reversed, asserting that it could not conclude that "there is no set of facts that would permit a plaintiff to demonstrate that the particular parallelism asserted was the product of collusion rather than coincidence,"[87] a seemingly straightforward application of the *Conley v. Gibson* no-set-of-facts notice pleading formula.

The Supreme Court reversed. Stressing that Rule 8(a) itself requires a "showing," rather than just a blanket assertion, of entitlement to relief, it held that "stating . . . a [Sherman Act § 1] claim requires a complaint with enough factual matter (taken as true) to suggest that an agreement was made" — "plausible grounds to infer an agreement."[88] It acknowledged that the *Conley* no-set-of-facts formula seemed to set a lower pleading standard, but found that such a standard, literally read, would permit the survival of claims on the basis of the mere possibility that a plaintiff might later find facts to support them. In part to avoid the massive discovery costs that this reading could unleash, the Court reasoned that a plaintiff in federal court must plead more than mere possibility, if less than probability. She must plead "enough facts to state a claim to relief that is plausible on its face," that crosses the "line from conceivable to plausible."[89]

Applying this "plausibility standard" to the complaint, the Court found that the parallel conduct alleged was perfectly consistent with natural, lawful economic conduct of the defendants. Observing that mere conscious parallelism can be "consistent with conspiracy, but just as much in line with a wide swath of rational and competitive business strategy unilaterally prompted by common perceptions of the market,"[90] the Court concluded that the complaint plausibly asserted no more.

---

[85] 550 U.S. 544 (U.S. 2007). *See generally* Saritha Komatireddy Tice, *A "Plausible" Explanation of Pleading Standards: Bell Atlantic Corp. v. Twombly*, 31 HARV. J.L. & PUB. POL'Y 827 (2008); Benjamin Spencer, *Plausibility Pleading*, 49 B.C. L. Rev. 431 (2008); Keith Bradley, *Pleading Standards Should Not Change After Bell Atlantic v. Twombly*, 102 Nw. U. L. REV. COLLOQUY 117 (2007); Amy J. Wildermuth, *What Twombly and Mead Have in Common*, 102 Nw. U. L. REV. COLLOQUY 276 (2007).

[86] 550 U.S. at 564.

[87] 425 F.3d 99, 114 (2d Cir. 2005).

[88] 550 U.S. at 556.

[89] *Id.* at 570.

[90] *Id.* at 554.

It therefore was properly dismissed.

Was *Twombly* merely an application of the pre-existing federal notice standards? Or, just the opposite, did it announce a new higher, possibly "heightened," federal pleading standard? Or did it do something in between, raising the bar for conspiracy claims in antitrust suits and possibly for similarly inferential and circumstantial claims in other cases as well?

The first alternative — that *Twombly* changed nothing[91] — was hard to square with its language. Not only did it expressly reject the *Conley* no-set-of-facts standard, but it also called into question two venerable corollaries. First, it dismissed plaintiffs' scattered allegations of actual agreement as "merely legal conclusions."[92] But the federal rules had been thought to have discarded the no-legal-conclusion rule of code pleading (*see* Form 11), as long the pleading also showed some facts entitling relief. Second, it seemingly refused to draw a plaintiff-favoring inference from allegations that supported both conspiracy and coincidental parallel conduct. Most importantly, the majority used "plausible" or variations on it fifteen times. *Twombly* seems to require something more than allegations that could, conceivably, support a claim.[93]

On the other hand, the opposite conclusion — that *Twombly* introduced a new, *generally* applicable higher standard[94] — also seemed hard to square with its language and antitrust context. The Court went out of its way twice to stress that it was not requiring "any 'heightened' pleading standard" or "heightened fact pleading of specifics," and added that it was not seeking to broaden the scope of Rule 9 either. In disavowing *Conley*'s no-set-of-facts language, the Court left untouched the rest of *Conley* and other court formulae consistent with federal notice pleading. Indeed, just two weeks later, the Court stated that a complaint need only " 'give the defendant fair notice of what the . . . claim is and the grounds upon which it rests,' " quoting *Conley*, as quoted in *Twombly*, without ever mentioning "plausibility."[95]

---

[91] *See, e.g., Equal Employment Opportunity Comm'n v. Concentra Health Servs., Inc.*, 496 F.3d 773, 779, 783 n.4 (7th Cir. 2007) (asserting, after *Twombly*, that "Rule 8(a)(2)'s 'short and plain statement of the claim' must contain a minimal level of factual detail, although that level is indeed very minimal"); Bradley, note 85, *supra* (arguing that "plausibility" is "antitrust jargon" and *Twombly* must be read in the context of antitrust law).

[92] 550 U.S. at 564.

[93] *Moore* § 8.04[1][a] (2008).

[94] *See, e.g.,* Tice, note 85, *supra*, at 832 ("*Twombly* seems to have created a more stringent pleading standard"); Scott Dodson, *Pleading Standards after* Bell Atlantic Corp. v. Twombly, 93 VA. L. REV. IN BRIEF 135, 138 (2007), *available at* www.virginialawreview.org/inbrief/2007/07/09/dodson.pdf ("The best reading of *Bell Atlantic* is that the new standard is absolute, that mere notice pleading is dead for all cases and causes of action"); Spencer, note 85, *supra* at 447 ("the Court's plausibility pleading is a new, more stringent pleading standard that deprives plaintiffs the benefits of inferences in their favor when the pleaded facts are consistent with alternate explanations that do not involve wrongdoing").

[95] *Erickson v. Pardus*, 551 U.S. 89, 93 (2007), quoting *Twombly*, 550 U.S. at 559 n. 14 (citing *Leatherman* and authority quoting it). *Erickson* was a pro se complaint, for which pleading rules have traditionally been relaxed, but the Court stated the "fair notice" pleading standard before turning to relaxed pleading for pro se litigants.

With the dry understatement that "these conflicting signals create some uncertainty as to the intended scope of the Court's decision," the Second Circuit Court of Appeals charted a third course in *Iqbal v. Hasty*, somewhere in between.[96] "[W]e believe the Court is not requiring a universal standard of heightened fact pleading, but is instead requiring a flexible 'plausibility standard,' which obligates a pleader to amplify a claim with some factual allegations in those contexts where such amplification is needed to render the claim *plausible.*"[97]

If this approach is read to limit the plausible pleading requirement to antitrust actions, it was wrong. On appeal of *Iqbal*, the Supreme Court said, such an approach "is not supported by *Twombly* and is incompatible with the Federal Rules of Civil Procedure," which govern "all civil actions and proceedings in the United States district courts."[98] The Court also rejected the argument that plausible pleading is inconsistent with Rule 9, by requiring particularity in pleading (heightened pleading) in circumstances where the rule does not. True, the Court said, Rule 9 only requires particularity in pleading fraud or mistake and allows other states of mind to be pled generally, but " 'generally' is a relative term."[99] The rule does not "give [the pleader] license to evade the less rigid — though still operative — strictures of Rule 8,"[100] the rule that the Court had construed in *Twombly*.

The Court in *Iqbal* then restated the new plausible pleading requirement. It requires three steps (though the first of these is un-enumerated in the Court's opinion). "[W]e begin by taking note of the elements a plaintiff must plead to state a claim," there a claim of unconstitutional discrimination by government officials.[101] Next, "a court must accept as true" just the non-conclusory allegations of the complaint; "[t]hreadbare recitals of the elements of a cause of action, supported by mere conclusory statements, do not suffice." Finally, the court must determine whether these "well-pleaded" (e.g., non-conclusory) allegations plausibly give rise to an entitlement to relief in light of the elements of the claim. This step of the analysis *is* "a context-specific task," as the Court of Appeals suggested in *Iqbal*, "that requires the reviewing court to draw on its judicial experience and common sense."[102] But if the facts "do not permit the court to infer more than the mere possibility of misconduct," or if, as in *Twombly*, they are equally consistent with lawful conduct, then the complaint fails the plausibility test.

The Court then found that a key element of the discrimination claim was that the defendant government official through his own individual action acted with discriminatory purpose. Next, it rejected plaintiff's allegations that the defendant officials knew of or condoned a policy of discrimination on the theory that "[t]hese bare assertions, much like the pleading of conspiracy in *Twombly*, amount to nothing

---

[96] *Iqbal v. Hasty*, 490 F.3d 143, 157 (2d Cir. 2007).

[97] *Iqbal*, 490 F.3d at 158. Some commentators call this a "notice-plus" pleading standard for certain types of cases. *See* Dodson, note 94, *supra*, at 138.

[98] *Ashcroft v. Iqbal*, 556 U.S. 662, 684 (2009) (quoting Rule 1).

[99] *Id.* at 686.

[100] *Id.* at 686–87.

[101] *Id.* at 675.

[102] *Id.* at 678–79.

more than a 'formulaic recitation of the elements' of a constitutional discrimination claim," and were not entitled to be assumed true.[103] Finally, taking as true the remaining non-conclusory allegations regarding the targeting of certain individuals for detention in the 9/11 investigations, the Court found that it was as likely that they were targeted because of a suspected link to the Arab Muslim disciples of bin Laden as it was that they were impermissibly targeted *because* they were Arab Muslims. "As between that 'obvious alternative explanation' for the arrests, and the purposeful, invidious discrimination respondent asks us to infer, discrimination is not a plausible conclusion."[104]

Criticisms of *Iqbal* and plausibility pleading start with the majority's arguable disbelief, based on "judicial experience and common sense," that the Attorney General or FBI Director could harbor discriminatory intent. Plausibility pleading requires comparative judgments that "depend . . . on a judge's background knowledge and assumptions, which seem every bit as vulnerable to the biasing effect of that individual's cultural predispositions as are judgments about adjudicative facts [who did what when]."[105] Would a judge who had previously been a civil rights litigator, or whose relatives had suffered the Japanese-American internments during World War II, have perceived the plausibility of discriminatory intent differently?[106] Should concern about such unconscious bias cause us to leave such judgments to the jury, which is presumably more representative than a single judge?

> [T]he Court[] instructed district judges to compare the challenged conduct to a hypothesized innocent explanation for the defendant's actions, which sounds very much like an invitation to evaluate the case's merits based on a single document — the complaint — without having the benefit of discovery let along anything remotely approximating a trial or a jury. The result is a process that appeals too much to judicial subjectivity.[107]

To be sure, a judge also applies her experience and common sense on a motion for summary judgment to decide whether a material fact is genuinely disputed, but at that stage of the litigation she is constrained by the record created by discovery. There is no such constraint on her determination of the plausibility of the complaint.[108] In fact, aggressive deployment of plausibility pleading arguably could

---

[103] *Id.* at 679–81.

[104] *Id.* at 682.

[105] *Hearing on Whether the Supreme Court Has Limited Americans' Access to Court Before the Senate Comm. On Judiciary*, 111 TH CONG., 1 ST SESS. 14 (2009) (statement of Stephen B. Burbank). Professor Arthur Miller asks, "Does [this] mean that a newly appointed judge has no judicial experience to employ, and are we supposed to believe that common sense is generously and equally distributed among the federal judges?" Arthur R. Miller, *Are They Closing the Courthouse Doors?*, New York University School of Law University Professorship Lecture 9 (Mar. 19, 2012), *available at* http://www.law.nyu.edu/ecm_dlv2/groups/public/@nyu_law_website__communications/documents/docu ments/ecm_pro_072088.pdf.

[106] *See* Janet Cecilia Walthall, *Iqbal, Twombly Pleading Standards Hotly Debated by Conference Panelists*, 78 U.S.L.W. 2782 (2010).

[107] Miller, *supra* note 105, at 9.

[108] Burbank, *supra* note 64, at 13.

intrude on the plaintiff's constitutional right to a jury.

Another critique goes to what we have called the second step of the plausible pleading standards: weeding out the conclusory allegations. But these are often state-of-mind allegations that are uniquely within the defendant's control and accessible only to the plaintiff by discovery, discovery which typically would follow rather than precede the defendant's motion to dismiss. How could Iqbal know Ashcroft's state of mind without deposing him or obtaining discovery of documents he authored regarding the detentions? This pleading standard may deny court access for meritorious claims of plaintiffs who can't meet the standard because they "lack the resources to engage in extensive pre-filing investigation or because of informational asymmetries."[109] If so, it has "shifted the information access balance in favor of those defendants best able to keep their records, conduct, and institutional secrets to themselves."[110]

One rebuttal is that post-filing discovery has become so expensive that the courts must do some serious gatekeeping at the pleading stage out of fairness to defendants. Thus, *Twombly* worried that "a plaintiff with 'a largely groundless claim' be allowed to 'take up the time of a number of other people, with the right to do so representing an *in terrorem* increment of the settlement value.' "[111] This is a fancy way of saying that overly lenient notice pleading invited plaintiffs to blackmail deep-pocket defendants by permitting costly discovery for unmeritorious claims.[112] By this view, the plausibility pleading standard simply restores the gatekeeping function that federal courts were always charged to perform under the federal rules, now made all the more necessary by the costly expansion of discovery. A counterpoint, however, is that because the new pleading standard applies to all cases, it may also affect "a wide swath of relatively simple lawsuits that do not need detailed pleading or extensive gatekeeping with their attendant cost, delay, and risk of premature termination."[113]

[e] Plausible Pleading After *"Twiqbal"*

We predicted in the last edition that any defense counsel worth her salt would invoke *"Twiqbal"* to attack the complaint (when doing so would be consistent with Rule 11, of course). The numbers support that prediction. The Federal Judicial Center (FJC) reports that there has been a substantial increase in the rate of filing Rule 12(b)(6) motions after *Twiqbal*,[114] and the *Twiqbal* decisions have been cited more than 125,000 times (and not just in federal court) — more often than *International Shoe*!

Whether *Twiqbal* motions have had much effect on the actual disposition of cases, however, is less clear. The same FJC study found that despite a general increase in

---

[109] Hearing, *supra*, note 105.

[110] Miller, *supra* note 105, at 11.

[111] 550 U.S. at 557–58 (internal citation omitted).

[112] *See generally* Douglas G. Smith, *The Twombly Revolution?*, 36 Pepp. L. Rev. 1063, 1094 (2009).

[113] Miller, *supra* note 105, at 11.

[114] Joe S. Cecil, George W. Cort, Margaret S. Williams & Jared J. Bataillon, *Motions to Dismiss for Failure to State a Claim After* Iqbal vii (Federal Judicial Center March 2011).

the rate of *filing* Rule 12(b)(6) motions after *Twiqbal*, there was no increase in the rate of *granting* the motion without leave to amend (except in cases challenging mortgage loans).[115] If this study is correct, then *Twiqbal* is not (yet) a get-out-of-jail-free card. On the other hand, a separate study speculates that this finding may reflect the exclusion of pro se and governmental immunity cases (like *Iqbal* itself) from the FJC study, and instead, this study reports a substantial *increase* in the number of motions granted after *Twiqbal*, especially in civil rights cases.[116] The author concludes that "district courts are taking [*Twiqbal*] to heart," which is "hasten[ing] the death of notice pleading."[117] Maybe *Twiqbal* is a get-out-of-jail card for defendants in civil rights cases.[118]

In any case, the dispositional success of a *Twiqbal*-based motion to dismiss is not a complete measure of its impact. Neither of the foregoing studies fully explores changes *in practice* occasioned by *Twiqbal*. Plaintiffs may often be preempting *Twiqbal* challenges by doing greater pre-filing investigation and pleading more facts from the start, thus discouraging a motion, or, more likely, preventing its success. A 2012 survey of plaintiffs' lawyers found that half reported changing their pleading practice after *Twiqbal*, of which 92% reported that they were including more factual detail in their complaints.[119] A motion may also cause the plaintiff voluntarily to amend before the court rules.[120] And, of course, most plaintiffs will not gamble that a Rule 12(b)(6) motion will fail; they will instead try to assure that outcome by filing a brief in opposition, raising the cost of litigation even where the motions fail. If *Twiqbal* has changed practice in these ways even without insignificantly changing the rate at which motions are granted, then the decisions have raised the cost of litigation in federal courts, especially to plaintiffs. This difficult-to-measure, but likely substantial, increase in the cost of litigation is one reason that critics have charged that *Twiqbal* has cut back on access to the courts.[121]

As to how *Twiqbal* is to be applied, there is not yet any consensus in the reported cases. There is broad agreement that the application of *Twiqbal* is *context-sensitive*, even though the Court said that it applied to all civil actions. The more complex the

---

[115] *Id.*

[116] Patricia Hatamyar Moore, *An Updated Quantitative Study of* Iqbal's *Impact on 12(B)(6) Motions*, 46 U. Rich. L. Rev. 603 (2012); Patricia W. Hatamyar, *The Tao of Pleading: Do* Twombly *and* Iqbal *Matter Empirically?*, 59 Am. U.L. Rev. 553 (2010). *See also* Statement of Stephen B. Burbank, note 64, *supra*, at 3.

[117] *Id.* at 624. *See also* Lonny Hoffman, Twombly *and* Iqbal's *Measure: An Assessment of the Federal Judicial Center's Study of Motions to Dismiss* (draft Aug. 3, 2011) (finding that *Twiqbal* has led to a higher absolute number of dismissals).

[118] *See* Victor D. Quintanilla, *Beyond Common Sense: A Social Psychological Study of* Iqbal's *Effect on Claims of Race Discrimination*, 17 Mich. J. Race & L. 1 (2011) (finding a significant uptick in dismissals by white judges).

[119] Emery G. Lee III, *Early Stages of Litigation Attorney Survey* 8 (Federal Judicial Center Mar. 2012).

[120] *See, e.g.*, Anand Agneshwar & Paige Sharpe, *Making the Most of* Twombly/Iqbal *in Product Liability Cases*, 80 U.S.L.W. 1765, 1767 (2012) (so arguing but also emphasizing the flipside: "it can tip your hand to the plaintiff, giving him or her an early opportunity to begin developing an opposing strategy to your specific arguments," as well as a roadmap for strengthening the complaint).

[121] *See, e.g.*, Burbank, *supra* note 6; Miller, *supra* note 105.

claim, the harder it is to meet the plausibility standard. "In other words, the height of the pleading requirement is relative to circumstances," commented the Seventh Circuit, in ruling that when plaintiff has alleged a vast conspiracy, she "must meet a high standard of plausibility."[122] On the other hand, when the relevant facts are in the defendant's knowledge or control (such as facts regarding the defendant's intent), some courts tolerate less specific pleading in the complaint.[123] Even after *Twombly*, the Second Circuit reiterated that "[p]leading on the basis of information and belief is generally appropriate under such circumstances."[124] Other circuits have been less generous, finding that after *Twiqbal*, plaintiffs "must allege specific facts of [their claim] . . . even if those facts are only within the head or hands of the defendants," and even though they are denied pre-motion discovery as *Twiqbal* instructs.[125]

The courts also are still agreed that *Twiqbal* does not require a plaintiff to identify a legal theory in her complaint, as long as she has pled facts that will support one. Thus, the Supreme Court reiterated after *Twiqbal* that, though a particular complaint was "not a model of the careful drafter's art, . . . a complaint need not pin plaintiff's claim for relief to a precise legal theory."[126]

But there is no agreement on what allegations are too conclusory to be considered on a motion to dismiss. One commentator reports that when he asked a roomful of judges to state whether particular statements were conclusory, they split 50-50.[127] "One person's 'factual allegation' is another's conclusion."[128] Thus, the risk-adverse plaintiff will still opt to plead with greater specificity than the pre-*Twiqbal* notice pleading regime (and the forms themselves) seemed to require.

Nor, finally, is there yet any consensus about the plausibility standard. The First Circuit has instructed lower courts not to apply it to each discrete allegation. "No single allegation" needs to make the standard, if the allegations "as a whole" make plaintiff's claim plausible.[129] This holistic, pleadings-as-a-whole approach comports with Justice Souter's expressed view that "[t]he make-or-break standard . . . is that

---

[122] Cooney v. Rossiter, 583 F.3d 967 (7th Cir. 2009); *Total Renal Care, Inc. v. W. Nephrology and Metabolic Bone Disease*, 2009 U.S. Dist. LEXIS 80821 (D. Colo. Aug. 21, 2009); JAMES W. MOORE, MOORE'S FEDERAL PRACTICE § 8.04[1][d] ("more complex claims will call for more complex allegations in order to establish 'plausibility' ").

[123] *See, e.g., Riley v. Vilsack*, 665 F. Supp. 2d 994 (W.D. Wis. 2009).

[124] *Boykin v. KeyCorp*, 521 F.3d 202, 215 (2d Cir. 2008); *Arista Records LLC v. Doe 3*, 604 F.3d 110, 120 (2d Cir. 2010).

[125] *See New Albany Tractor, Inc. v. Louisville Tractor, Inc.*, 650 F.3d 1046, 1051 (6th Cir. 2011) ("It may be that only [the defendants] have knowledge of whether [one defendant] exercises control over the terms and conditions of [the other's] sales to retailers. . . . The plaintiff apparently can no longer obtain the factual detail necessary because the language of *Iqbal* specifically directs that *no* discovery may be conducted in cases such as this, even when the information needed to establish a claim of discriminatory pricing is solely within the purview of the defendant or a third party, as it is here.").

[126] *Skinner v. Switzer*, 131 S. Ct. 1289, 1296 (2011).

[127] *Panelists Re-examine* Twombly *and* Iqbal: *Gamechangers, or Necessary Clarification?*, 79 U.S.L.W. 1658 (2010).

[128] Burbank, note 64, *supra*, at 12. Professor Burbank asserts that *Twiqbal's* standard of "conclusory" "lacks predictability, rationality or fairness." *Id.* at 9.

[129] *Ocasio-Hernandez v. Fortuno-Burset*, 640 F.3d 1, 14–15 (1st Cir. 2011).

the *combined* allegations, taken as true, must state a plausible, not a merely conceivable, case for relief."[130] But even that approach has not been expressly adopted across the circuits.

From a practical perspective, however, this state of judicial uncertainty does not leave a good litigator in a pleading quandary. However often the courts reiterate that a complaint need not identify a specific legal theory, no good lawyer would leave the task of finding one to the judge's clerk. The practice question is not how little the plaintiff can allege to meet the pleading standard, but what allegations and legal theories safely pass the *Twiqbal* bar or are necessary for other, practical purposes.

> For example, an attorney setting out the client's cause in writing for the first time may not want the simplest statement of the claim possible. This pleader may well desire to impress the client, the opponent, the opponent's insurance adjuster, the opponent's counsel, and, in appropriate cases, the public. Pleaders want pleadings to make a statement that draws attention to the claim and impresses with its seriousness; and pleaders may resort to unnecessary legal theorizing or statements of impressive but unnecessary evidentiary facts to make the desired impression.[131]

At the end of the day, factually specific "elements pleading" (or "checklist pleading") may well be the de facto "good" post-*Twiqbal* practice in federal court, whether or not it is required by *Twiqbal* or the rules.

[2] Consistency and the Theory of the Pleadings in Modern Pleading

The de-emphasis of pleading under modern notice pleading has substantially eliminated the theory-of-the-pleadings approach[132] and the related concepts of variance and election of remedies. Rule 8(d) expressly permits the pleading of alternative or hypothetical claims and defenses and as many claims or defenses as a party has "regardless of consistency," and Rule 8(a) permits demands for alternative types of relief. The rulemakers recognized that a party often does not know enough to elect a legal theory at the start of the litigation, and that a compelled election by the pleadings would either encourage needlessly verbose pleading, defeating the objective of short and plain statements, or entrap the uninformed.

If the pleadings are of reduced significance before trial, after trial they "lose such little significance as they had before, and judgment is to be in accordance with the evidence."[133] Rule 15(b) permits amendment of the pleadings to conform to the evidence at trial, and indeed provides for constructive amendment when the parties have consented to any variance from the pleadings.[134] As discussed in more detail

---

[130] *Sepulveda-Villarini v. Dept. of Educ. of Puerto Rico*, 628 F.3d 25, 29 (1st Cir. 2010) (Souter, J., sitting on circuit).

[131] MOORE § 8.04[7a].

[132] *See* § 8.03[2] (cause of action and theory of pleadings in code pleading), *supra*.

[133] WRIGHT § 68.

[134] *See* § 8.10[2] (amendment during and after trial), *infra*.

below,[135] the focus of the rule on amendment is properly now on possible prejudice to the opposing parties, rather than on the initial intent of the pleader in electing his legal theory. Moreover, Rule 54(c) provides that "[e]very . . . final judgment should grant the relief to which each party is entitled, even if the party has not demanded that relief in its pleadings."[136]

For several reasons, however, the theory of the pleadings doctrine is not wholly dead. First, the substantive law may require a party to elect his remedies. Thus a party that started by seeking one remedy or asserting one theory may be estopped from switching in mid-stream to another when defendant has reasonably relied in some fashion on the initial election.[137] The election is not compelled as a matter of pleading form in such a case; it is rooted in the substantive law of estoppel.[138]

Second, the theory of the pleadings may determine which statute of limitations is applicable to the action[139] and whether the pleader is entitled to a jury trial as a matter of right.[140] Limitations periods vary by type of action, and constitutional and some statutory guarantees of jury trial are often tied to historical forms of action or other particular kinds of suit.[141]

Third, federal judges are authorized by Rule 16 to frame pretrial orders that may require the parties to exchange pretrial briefs in which they commit to particular legal theories.[142] Such orders are binding unless modified, and the last pretrial order may be modified "only to prevent manifest injustice."[143] These orders are typically entered after discovery has been completed on the eve of trial, however — not at the pleading stage in the front end of the lawsuit.

Fourth, obligations of candor and care may also restrict a pleader's freedom to plead inconsistently, change his legal theory, or introduce new lines of proof. "[A]lternative pleading is not permitted when in the nature of things the pleader must know which of the inconsistent averments is true and which is false."[144]

---

[135] See § 8.10, infra.

[136] See, e.g., Webb v. Arresting Officers, 749 F.2d 500 (8th Cir. 1984) (plaintiff was entitled to judgment on his post-trial theory that defendants had a duty to intervene for his protection, as long as it was tried and proven, even though this theory was never alleged in the pleadings and his pleaded theory of unnecessary force was not proven).

[137] See generally CHARLES E. CLARK, HANDBOOK OF THE LAW OF CODE PLEADING § 77 (2d ed. 1947).

[138] Id.

[139] See generally § 8.08[2][b] (the statute of limitations), infra.

[140] See § 12.07[1] (right to jury trial), infra.

[141] For example, the Seventh Amendment provides that "[i]n suits at common law, where the value in controversy shall exceed twenty dollars, the right of trial by jury shall be preserved." U.S. CONST. amend. VII. It thus ties the right to a jury trial to actions that originated in the common law or are analogous to common law actions and is inapplicable to equitable actions. See § 12.07[1] (right to a jury trial), infra.

[142] See § 12.03[3] (pretrial orders), infra.

[143] Rule 16(e).

[144] Church v. Adler, 113 N.E.2d 327, 332 (Ill. App. Ct. 1953). See § 8.05[2] (certification), infra.

[3]　The Form of Pleading Under the Federal Rules

Modern pleading requires no "technical form" of pleading.[145] While sufficient under the rules, the form pleadings that accompany the federal rules are only examples.[146] A pleading need only include a caption, numbered paragraphs containing averments "limited as far as practicable to a statement of a single set of circumstances," and separate counts for different claims or defenses ("[i]f doing so would promote clarity").[147] Averments may be incorporated by reference and by documents attached to the pleading.[148] None of these requirements is strictly enforced because "[a]ll pleadings shall be so construed as to do substantial justice."[149]

[4]　Special Pleading Rules in Modern Pleading

"Short plain statement" pleading is the norm. Yet most modern pleading jurisdictions retain a few idiosyncratic special pleading rules, in addition to judge-made special pleading requirements for disfavored litigation. Special pleading rules are adopted for practical reasons which are reflected in Rule 9. They may be enforced by motions to strike or dismiss or for more definite statements.[150]

Some special pleading rules were adopted to discourage disfavored litigation. Fraud suits, for example, are disfavored because of the injury they may do to reputations and their potential to intimidate.[151] Claims of mistake are also disfavored because they upset the normal business expectations underlying contract law. As a result, Rule 9(b) requires that a party "state with particularity the circumstances constituting fraud or mistake." It must be harmonized, however, with the general pleading directives of Rule 8; Rule 9(b) "does not require nor make legitimate the pleading of detailed evidentiary matter."[152] The Supreme Court has also reminded us to harmonize Rule 9(b) with "the flexibility provided by Rule 11(b)(3),"[153] which allows anticipatory pleading: pleading of contentions "likely [to] have evidentiary support after a reasonable opportunity for further investigation or discovery,"[154] what many courts and lawyers still call pleading on "information and belief." As a result, what a specific pleading requirement like Rule 9(b) really achieves is probably only a marginal increase in the trial court's

---

[145] Rule 8(d)(1).

[146] *See* Rule 84.

[147] Rule 10(a)-(b).

[148] Rule 10(c).

[149] Rule 8(e).

[150] *See* § 8.07[2][a] (challenging defects of form), *infra*.

[151] *See, e.g., Ross v. A. H. Robins Co.*, 607 F.2d 545 (2d Cir. 1979), *cert. denied*, 446 U.S. 946 (1980) (citing importance of fair notice, of protecting defendants from harm to reputation and goodwill, and of reducing possibility that plaintiffs will pursue largely groundless fraud claims for their *in terrorem* settlement value).

[152] *Id.* at 557 n.20.

[153] *Rotella v. Wood*, 528 U.S. 549, 560 (2000).

[154] *See* § 8.05[2][b], *infra*.

discretion to use the pleadings to screen disfavored litigation, usually without much lasting effect.[155]

Legislatures are also free, of course, to impose special pleading requirements by statute to discourage disfavored litigation. An example is the 1995 Private Securities Litigation Reform Act,[156] which was passed to curb alleged abuses in federal securities litigation. The Act requires the plaintiff to "state with particularity facts giving rise to a strong inference that the defendant acted with the required state of mind" for liability.[157] It also requires specific pleading for alleging false or misleading statements. The Act appears not to have had a dramatic effect on pleading practice, but it certainly encourages courts to take a closer look at securities fraud complaints.[158]

Other special pleading rules promote pleading efficiency and convenience. Under the law of contract, the plaintiff usually must have performed all conditions precedent to defendant's contractual obligations before he may complain of a breach. But in the typical case in which defendant does not dispute performance of such conditions precedent, it would be wasteful to require plaintiff to plead them compendiously. Rule 9(c) therefore permits plaintiff to aver generally the performance of all conditions precedent and requires defendant to deny performance "with particularity."[159] The same rationale accounts for the requirement in Rule 9(a) that defendant specifically challenge the legal existence or capacity of a party to sue. That is, the rule casts the burden of disputing these matters on the defendant, because, in most cases, there is no dispute. Leaving it on the plaintiff would needlessly clutter up the complaint.

Special pleading is also sometimes required to avoid surprise. The averment of injury or breach of contract puts defendant fairly on notice that the plaintiff will seek the kinds of damages usually associated with injury (pain and suffering) or with breach (lost profits on the contract). No special pleading of such *general damages* is required. But general pleading is insufficient to put defendant on notice of unusual or unanticipated damages of a sort not ordinarily associated with the alleged injury or breach. Rule 9(g) therefore requires that items of *special damage* "be specifically stated." For example, the failure specifically to plead damages for higher blood pressure said to have been caused by an automobile collision prevented their recovery in *Ziervogel v. Royal Packing Co.*,[160] because this kind of damage, unlike damages for back or neck injuries, is not a normal and expected consequence of such an accident.

---

[155] *See generally* William M. Richman et al., *The Pleading of Fraud: Rhymes Without Reason*, 60 S. CAL. L. REV. 959 (1987); William C. Baskin III, Note, *Using Rule 9(b) to Reduce Nuisance Securities Litigation*, 99 YALE L.J. 1591 (1990).

[156] Pub. L. 104-52, 109 Stat. 737 (codified in scattered sections of 15 U.S.C. (Supp. I 1995)).

[157] *Id.*

[158] Marcus, note 84, *supra*, at 1765–67.

[159] *See generally* § 8.06[2], *infra*, for discussion of the allocation of pleading burdens.

[160] 225 S.W.2d 798 (Mo. Ct. App. 1949). Other special damages include medical expenses; unusual injuries such as induced abortion, epilepsy and insanity; expenses incurred in mitigation; and losses of use and income. *See Restatement (Second) of Torts* § 904 cmt. b (1979).

Finally, special pleading may reflect the requirements of the substantive law.[161] The usual rule of contract law, for example, is that plaintiff may only recover those damages within the contemplation of the parties at the time that the contract was made.[162] The pleading of "specials" in a contract case is therefore required to state the plaintiff's *prima facie* case. Similarly, the law's solicitude for free expression and competition, and its suspicion of intangible injuries to reputation, are reflected in the common substantive requirement that a plaintiff suing for defamation, slander, libel or disparagement show special damages and their proximate causation by the tort.[163] A pleading that omits such specific allegations not only offends special pleading rules, but fails to state a claim for relief.

§ 8.05   CANDOR AND CARE REQUIREMENTS IN MODERN PLEADING

The simplicity and flexibility of modern notice pleading has expanded opportunity for the careless or sharp practitioner to abuse pleading to bluff, bargain, delay, or harass. Motion practice[164] has been the most effective tool for coping with such abuses. However, most jurisdictions have also imposed candor or care standards on litigants and/or their attorneys, requiring *verification or certification* of pleadings.[165]

[1] Verification

Verification of a pleading attests under oath to the truth of its contents, effectively transforming it into an affidavit usable as evidence at trial when the averments are made on the pleader's personal knowledge. Jurisdictions that still require verification reserve it for pleadings in actions that turn uniquely on allegations whose truth or falsity are known only to the parties, such as domestic relations actions. Verification is not generally required of federal pleadings[166] because it would defeat the intentions of the federal rulemakers by either preventing the unsure plaintiff from filing at all or forcing her into a premature election of facts. Moreover, the requirement that *parties* verify their pleadings is ineffective to encourage good faith and reasonable inquiry by their *attorneys*, whom many regard as the principal source of procedural abuse in modern litigation.

---

[161] *See* Jeffrey A. Parness et al., *The Substantive Elements in the New Special Pleading Laws*, 78 Neb. L. Rev. 412 (1999).

[162] *See, e.g., Hadley v. Baxendale*, [1854] 156 Eng. Rep. 145.

[163] *See, e.g., Fairyland Amusement Co. v. Metromedia, Inc.*, 413 F. Supp. 1290 (W.D. Mo. 1976) (defamation, slander and libel complaint dismissed for plaintiff's failure to plead specifically its loss of patronage as a result of the false publication).

[164] *See* § 8.07 (motion practice), *infra*.

[165] In addition, federal courts have both statutory and inherent power to punish attorney and litigant misconduct. *See* § 8.05[2][e] (sanctions), *infra*.

[166] *But see* Rule 23.1; *cf.* Rules 27, 65 & 68. *See Surowitz v. Hilton Hotels Corp.*, 383 U.S. 363 (1966) (purpose of verification for shareholder derivative suits under Rule 23.1 is to discourage "strike suits," filed to coerce settlement regardless of their truth).

[2] Certification and Rule 11

A certification requirement suffers neither of these defects. Instead of verifying the allegations of the pleading, the signatory — usually the attorney of record or pro se litigant — certifies only to proper purpose and reasonable care in filing the pleading. Rule 11 is an example of a particularly strong certification requirement. Many states have modeled their own certification requirements on some version of the federal rule.[167]

[a] Rule 11 in General[168]

Prior to 1983, Rule 11 provided that by signing a pleading, motion or other paper, an attorney or party certified that he had read the pleading, that "to the best of his knowledge, information, and belief" there was "good ground to support it," and that it was "not interposed for delay." The rule authorized, but did not mandate, unspecified "disciplinary action" for "*wilful* violation[s]."[169] The implied prerequisite of subjective intent and the absence of any mandatory sanctions for a violation, however, rendered the pre-1983 rule of little use in federal courts. Only 19 cases involving Rule 11 motions were reported between 1938 and 1983.[170]

Concluding that "[e]xperience shows that in practice Rule 11 has not been effective in deterring abuses,"[171] the Advisory Committee on Civil Rules completely revised the rule in 1983. The 1983 revision provided that by signing a pleading or other paper, the attorney or party certified that, "to the best of his knowledge, information, and belief formed after reasonable inquiry it is well-grounded in fact and warranted by existing law or a good faith argument for the extension,

---

[167] Gerald F. Hess, *Rule 11 Practice in Federal and State Court: An Empirical, Comparative Study*, 75 MARQ. L. REV. 313, 315 n.8, 316 n.9 (1992); *Report of the Special Committee to Consider Sanctions for Frivolous Litigation in New York State Courts*, 18 FORDHAM URB. L.J. 3, 32–33 (1990) (comparing state approaches to abusive litigation).

[168] Probably more has been written about Rule 11 since 1983 than any other civil procedure rule. *See generally Hearing on H.R. 966, the Lawsuit Abuse Reduction Act Before the H. Comm. On Judiciary Subcomm. on the Constitution*, 112TH CONG. APPENDIX (2011) (statement of Lonny Hoffman, Univ. of Houston); Georgene M. Vairo, Symposium, *Happy (?) Birthday Rule* 11, 37 LOY. L.A. L. REV. 515 (2004). The rule has spawned its own looseleaf service, *id.*, its own newsletter, *see Attorney Sanctions Newsletter* (Shepard's), several book-length analyses, *see, e.g.*, GREGORY P. JOSEPH, SANCTIONS: THE FEDERAL LAW OF LITIGATION ABUSE (2008), and a host of empirical studies. *See, e.g.*, Lawrence C. Marshall et al., *The Use and Impact of Rule 11*, 86 NW. U. L. REV. 943 (1992); FEDERAL JUDICIAL CENTER, RULE 11: FINAL REPORT TO THE ADVISORY COMM. ON CIVIL RULES OF THE JUD. CONF. OF THE U.S. (undated), *summarized in* Elizabeth Wiggins *et al., The Federal Judicial Center's Study of Rule 11*, 2 FJC DIRECTIONS (1991); STEPHEN B. BURBANK, AMER. JUDICATURE SOC'Y, RULE 11 IN TRANSITION: THE REPORT OF THE THIRD CIRCUIT TASK FORCE ON FEDERAL RULE OF CIVIL PROCEDURE 11 (1989).

[169] *WRIGHT & MILLER* § 1331 (emphasis added).

[170] D. Michael Risinger, *Honesty in Pleading and Its Enforcement: Some "Striking" Problems With Federal Rule of Civil Procedure 11*, 61 MINN. L. REV. 1, 35–37 (1976). Most Rule 11 motions are unreported. *See* Wiggins, note 168, *supra*, at (finding that only 6.6% of district court cases involving Rule 11 activity were reported, and that reporting practices were highly variable); BURBANK, note 168, *supra*, at 59 (only 9% of dispositions involving Rule 11 were reported in Third Circuit sample; only 33% were available on Lexis). But even if ten times as many cases were decided as were reported prior to 1983, the reported case data would indicate fewer than 200 Rule 11 cases over forty-five years.

[171] Rule 11 advisory committee's notes (1983).

modification, or reversal of existing law, and that it is not interposed for any improper purpose." Under the 1983 rule, it was not only what an attorney actually believed (subjective good faith) that mattered, but what he should have believed as a competent attorney after reasonable pre-filing inquiry (objective reasonableness).[172] The substitution of an objective for a subjective standard made it easier for courts to find violations, and the mandatory sanction provision of the 1983 rule appeared to require them to punish such violations.

Practice under the 1983 rule, however, suggested to some that the pendulum had swung too far. Between 1983 and 1993, there were 6000 reported Rule 11 cases.[173] Eighty-one percent of the federal judges surveyed in one study thought that the 1983 rule had a positive effect,[174] and the actual percentage of cases in which Rule 11 activity occurred was reported at only 2–3%.[175] Yet critics charged that enforcement was inconsistent and unpredictable; that the rule was enforced disproportionately against plaintiffs in general (and civil rights plaintiffs in particular) with chilling effects on novel plaintiffs' claims; that courts relied almost exclusively on fee-shifting and compensation as sanctions, effectively turning the American rule against fee-shifting on its head; that sanctions were often imposed without fair procedure; and that Rule 11 motion practice had generated a Kafkaesque nightmare of satellite litigation (including Rule 11 motions against Rule 11 motions).[176] These criticisms were not always supported by the empirical data, and some may have been premature (reflecting transitional problems in judicial applications of the 1983 rule revisions), but enough persisted to prompt another rule revision in 1993.

As discussed in subsections [b] and [c] below, the 1993 rule equalized the burdens imposed by the rule on plaintiffs and defendants. As discussed in subsection [d] below, it abolished mandatory sanctions in favor of discretionary non-monetary

---

[172] *See* Rule 11 advisory committee's notes (1983). Although the text of the 1983 rule contained both objective and subjective components, the rulemakers clearly intended to eliminate the necessity for a finding of subjective bad faith as a predicate for sanctions, in a deliberate departure from prior case law. *See, e.g., Eastway Constr. Co. v. City of New York*, 762 F.2d 243, 253 (2d Cir. 1985). The no-improper-purpose requirement also prohibited, for example, the filing of tactical pleadings or motions to upset settlement negotiations in order to obtain fee-related concessions from defendant in other litigation, *In re Itel Sec. Litig.*, 596 F. Supp. 226 (N.D. Cal. 1984), *aff'd*, 791 F.2d 672 (9th Cir. 1986); motions to disqualify opposing counsel for the purpose of harassing the other side and increasing the costs of litigation, *Wold v. Minerals Eng'g Co.*, 575 F. Supp. 166 (D. Colo. 1983) (imposing attorney's fees on party who made the motion for these purposes); or attempts to continue the "economic and political warfare" of labor negotiations by using litigation to intimidate. *WSB Elec. Co. v. Rank & File Comm. to Stop the 2-Gate Sys.*, 103 F.R.D. 417, 421 (N.D. Cal. 1984).

[173] Mark Spiegel, *The Rule 11 Studies and Civil Rights Cases: An Inquiry Into the Neutrality of Procedural Rules*, 32 CONN. L. REV. 155, 157 (2000). This number of *reported* cases indicates that there may have been as many as 17,000 Rule 11 cases altogether in this decade. *See* Mark Spiegel, *The Rule 11 Studies and Civil Rights Cases: An Inquiry Into the Neutrality of Procedural Rules*, 32 CONN. L. REV. 155, 157 (1999).

[174] Wiggins, note 168, *supra*, at 34.

[175] Wiggins, note 168, *supra*, at 6.

[176] *See, e.g.*, Hoffman, *supra*, note 168; WRIGHT & MILLER § 1332; BURBANK, note 168, *supra*, at 57, 65; Melissa L. Nelken, *Has the Chancellor Shot Himself in the Foot? Looking for a Middle Ground on Rule 11 Sanctions*, 41 HASTINGS L.J. 383 (1990); William W. Schwarzer, *Rule 11 Revisited*, 101 HARV. L. REV. 1013 (1988).

sanctions. It also made several other significant changes, several of which are noted in the remainder of this subsection.

First, Rule 11(b) expanded the scope of certification from a pleading or other paper to individual "claims, defenses, and other legal contentions" and "factual contentions." It thus rejected the pleading-as-a-whole approach to Rule 11 taken by some courts, by which they found a violation only when the pleading as a whole (and not just a particular claim defense, or factual allegation) violated the good grounds and proper purposes requirements.[177] Still, the 1983 Advisory Committee cautioned that Rule 11 motions "should not be made or threatened for minor, inconsequential violations."[178] Inclusion of a minor ungrounded allegation or argument in an otherwise well-grounded paper thus should not be treated as a violation. Furthermore, the relative importance in the paper of the offending part may still be considered in deciding the severity of any sanction, as we discuss below in section [d].

Second, the 1993 rule amendments compromised on the issue whether of litigants have a continuing duty to correct or even withdraw papers in light of post-filing events. Most courts under the 1983 rule had rejected the concept of continuing duty in favor of a "snapshot rule." This focused only on whether a paper complied with the rule in "the instant when a picture is taken — when the signature is placed on the document."[179] These courts rejected the concept of continuing duty both because of the phrasing of the 1983 rule and the updating burden that such a duty would impose. In contrast, a few courts had imposed such a duty to effectuate the purpose of the rule.[180] The 1993 amendments provided that the rule is violated by "signing, filing, submitting, *or later advocating*" a paper when the litigant knows that it is no longer well-grounded.[181] Thus a lawyer who during a pretrial conference presses a claim or defense would be subject to the rule's obligations "measured as of that time" — not only as of the time she signed the paper containing the claim or defense.[182] On the other hand, the 1993 rule amendments did not saddle a litigant with the burden of curing pleadings by formal amendments to correct or withdraw such claims or defenses.[183]

Nevertheless, a litigant may formally withdraw such a claim or defense to bring itself into the rule's "safe harbor." Rule 11(c)(2) grants a litigant 21 days between

[177] *See, e.g.*, Carl Tobias, *Civil Rights Plaintiffs and the Proposed Revision of Rule 11*, 77 Iowa L. Rev. 1775, 1780 (1992). The majority of courts that had considered the issue had rejected the pleadings-as-a-whole approach. *See* Section of Litig., note 168, *supra*, at 3.

[178] Rule 11 advisory committee's notes (1983).

[179] *See, e.g.*, *Thomas v. Capital Sec. Servs., Inc.*, 836 F.2d 866, 874 (5th Cir. 1988).

[180] *See cases cited in* Neal Klausner, Note, *The Dynamics of Rule 11: Preventing Frivolous Litigation by Demanding Professional Responsibility*, 61 N.Y.U. L. Rev. 300, 325–26 n.195 (1986).

[181] Rule 11(b) (emphasis added).

[182] Rule 11(b) advisory committee's notes (1993). The 1993 amendments thus make it clear that Rule 11 applies to the complaint in a case that has been removed from state to federal court once the plaintiff "advocates" the claims in that complaint in federal court.

[183] *See* James R. Simpson, Note, *Why Change Rule 11? Ramifications of the 1992 Amendment Proposal*, 29 Cal. W. L. Rev. 495, 508 (1993).

service and filing of a Rule 11 motion[184] to correct or withdraw the offending paper. This provision is intended to reduce the amount of satellite litigation under the rule by letting rule offenders moot Rule 11 motions before they are filed in court. It may only codify what some lawyers are doing already by letting their adversaries know in advance that they will seek Rule 11 sanctions. On the other hand, some critics view this informal practice of "threat and retreat" as "problematic," concluding that its codification will accentuate "one of [the former] Rule's worst features."[185] Justice Scalia, for example, objected to the safe-harbor provision on the ground that it will encourage abusers, because they "will be able to file thoughtless, reckless, and harassing pleadings, secure in the knowledge that they have nothing to lose."[186]

[b]   Evidentiary Support

Rule 11(b)(3) requires litigants to certify that their factual allegations "have evidentiary support or, if specifically so identified, will likely have evidentiary support after a reasonable opportunity for further investigation or discovery." Rule 11(b)(4) also requires that "the denials of factual contentions are warranted on the evidence or, if specifically so identified, are reasonably based on belief or a lack of information." These provisions clarify and expand the 1983 rule in several respects.

Because Rule 11(b)(4) extends to *denials* of factual allegations, the 1993 rule has helped equalize the burden imposed on plaintiffs and defendants. By insisting just on *evidentiary support*, the Rules 11(b)(3) and 11(b)(4) also make clear that the litigant is not required to certify that its factual contentions will prevail.[187] Moreover, by authorizing certification of allegations that "likely" will have such support, Rule 11(b)(3) gives plaintiffs the same option of "information-and-belief" pleading now afforded defendants by Rules 8(b)(5) and 11(b)(4). This provision slightly relaxes the former rule's ban on "file now, check later" practice, by affording "a reasonable [post-filing] opportunity for further investigation" of specifically identified information-and-belief contentions, so long as the litigant has done its best before filing.[188] If that investigation turns up no evidentiary support for such contentions, then the litigant may not continue to advocate them.

At the same time, this new tolerance of anticipatory, "likely-to-have-support" pleading poses a dilemma for the pleader. On one hand, the pleader is not expressly

---

[184] The safe harbor is available only against Rule 11 motions and does not apply to show cause orders issued at the court's own initiative. Rule 11(c)(3). The 1993 Advisory Committee reasoned that show cause orders will ordinarily only be issued in extreme situations akin to contempt of court, which do not deserve any safe harbor. Rule 11 advisory committee's notes (1993). Relying on this language, the Second Circuit Court of Appeals reasoned that a court should apply a "bad faith" standard when it *sua sponte* sanctions a lawyer for a paper long after the offender has had an opportunity to correct or withdraw it, despite the absence of any bad faith requirement in the rule. *In re Pennie & Edmonds LLP*, 323 F.3d 86 (2d Cir. 2003). *Contra Jenkins v. Methodist Hospitals of Dallas, Inc.*, 478 F.3d 255 (5th Cir. 2007).

[185] Carl Tobias, *Reconsidering Rule 11*, 46 U. MIAMI L. REV. 855, 877 (1992).

[186] Dissenting statement of Justice Scalia on Amendments to the Federal Rules of Civil Procedure, 113 S. Ct. CCCVI, CCCVII (1993). *Accord*, Lonnie T. Brown, Jr., *Ending Illegitimate Advocacy: Reinvigorating Rule 11 Through Enhancement of the Ethical Duty to Report*, 62 OHIO ST. L.J. 1555 (2001).

[187] Rule 11(b) & (c) advisory committee's notes (1993).

[188] *Id.*

required to have that support at the time of the pleading, provided he specifically identifies the "likely-to-have-support" contentions as such. On the other hand, the Advisory Committee warned that this tolerance "is not a license to join parties, make claims, or present defenses without any factual basis or justification."[189] What must the pleader do to engage in such anticipatory pleading without running afoul of the rule? The Advisory Committee's notes, coupled with the rule, suggest an answer.[190] First, he must still conduct a prefiling inquiry which is reasonable in the circumstances. Second, he must have some "factual basis" for his contentions, even if it is not yet in evidentiary form. Third, he must, if challenged, be able to demonstrate that there was a need and reasonable opportunity for further discovery, by showing that circumstances beyond his control — such as time constraints or his adversary's or a third party's control of the information — prevented him from obtaining evidentiary support before filing.

Reasonableness of the required inquiry both before and after filing takes into account the litigant's access to necessary factual information and time available in which to make inquiry. Since the litigant's state of mind is not controlling, reasonableness is open to empirical verification. The focus is upon the facts of the pre-filing investigation, although the 1983 Advisory Committee expressly cautioned the courts against using hindsight in making that examination.[191]

The cases suggest that the requisite pre-filing factual investigation must at least include a thorough interview with the client and the key witnesses, if they are available.[192]

> To decide if the attorney may rely solely on his client, he should determine if his knowledge is direct or hearsay and check closely the plausibility of the client's account. When an attorney must rely on his client, he should question him thoroughly, not accepting the client's version on faith alone. However, "if all the attorney has is his client's assurance that facts exist or do not exist, when a reasonable inquiry would reveal otherwise, he has not satisfied his obligation."[193]

It follows that when an attorney can obtain factual information from public sources, he must do so and cannot rely solely on his client.[194] On the other hand, if the necessary information is primarily within the control of the prospective defendants,

---

[189] *Id.*

[190] *See* Lisa Pondrom, Comment, *Predicting the Unpredictable Under Rule 11(b)(3): When Are Allegations "Likely" to Have Evidentiary Support?*, 43 UCLA L. Rev. 1393 (1996) (suggesting the answer in the text).

[191] Rule 11 advisory committee's notes (1983).

[192] *See Wold v. Minerals Eng'g Co.*, 575 F. Supp. 166, 167 (D. Colo. 1983); *Rhinehart v. Stauffer*, 638 F.2d 1169, 1171 (9th Cir. 1979) (decision under pre-1983 Rule 11).

[193] *Nassau-Suffolk Ice Cream, Inc. v. Integrated Res., Inc.*, 114 F.R.D. 684, 689 (S.D.N.Y. 1987) (quoting *Coburn Optical Indus., Inc. v. Cilco, Inc.*, 610 F. Supp. 656, 659 (M.D.N.C. 1985); other citations omitted). *See generally* James E. Ward IV, Note, *Rule 11 and Factually Frivolous Claims — The Goal of Cost Minimization and the Client's Duty to Investigate*, 44 Vand. L. Rev. 1165 (1991).

[194] *Kendrick v. Zanides*, 609 F. Supp. 1162, 1172–73 (N.D. Cal. 1985); *Mohammed v. Union Carbide Corp.*, 606 F. Supp. 252 (E.D. Mich. 1985).

reliance on the client is reasonable under the rule.[195]

[c]   Legal Support

Reasonable inquiry into the law is what any competent attorney would make into the standard legal research sources. She must determine that any legal position asserted in a filing is warranted by existing law. Alternatively, in order not to chill advocacy for change in the law, Rule 11(b) shelters "nonfrivolous argument for extending, modifying, or reversing existing law . . . ."[196] Critics argued that this shelter was insufficient for civil rights plaintiffs, who often advocate the recognition of new rights.[197] The 1993 amendments to the rule therefore added "[arguments for the] . . . establishment of new law" to the shelter.

Must such plaintiffs flag such claims as novel to alert the court and the opposing parties? Some courts concluded that they must, but the 1993 Advisory Committee said that "arguments for a change of law are not required to be specifically so identified, [although] a contention that is so identified should be viewed with greater tolerance under the rule."[198]

Does the duty of legally-warranted argument imposed by Rule 11(b)(2) carry with it a corollary duty of candor, for example, to disclose contrary legal authority in the papers? Assuming *arguendo* that the uncited authority was directly contrary, the Ninth Circuit Court of Appeals nevertheless concluded that

> neither Rule 11 nor any other rule imposes a requirement that the lawyer, in addition to advocating the cause of his client, step first into the shoes of opposing counsel to find all potentially contrary authority, and finally into the robes of the judge to decide whether the authority is indeed contrary or whether it is distinguishable.[199]

The court acknowledged that the ethical rules proposed by the American Bar Association prohibit an attorney from knowingly failing to disclose "legal authority in the controlling jurisdiction known to the lawyer to be directly adverse to the position of the client and not disclosed by opposing counsel."[200] But it concluded that Rule 11 should not be used for broad-spectrum enforcement of ethical obligations.[201]

---

[195]   *See, e.g., Kamen v. Am. Telephone & Telegraph Co.*, 791 F.2d 1006 (2d Cir. 1986).

[196]   For examples of frivolous legal claims, *see, e.g., Heimbaugh v. City & Cnty. of San Francisco*, 591 F. Supp. 1573 (N.D. Cal. 1984) (complaint alleged that city's ban on playing softball on field reserved for hardball violated First Amendment right to advocate democracy in sports); *Blair v. Shenandoah Women's Ctr., Inc.*, 757 F.2d 1435 (4th Cir. 1985) (attorney for a man who filed suit against a women's shelter in which his wife sought refuge from his abuse was properly assessed attorney's fees in view of the complaint's scandalous accusations and frivolous legal positions).

[197]   See critics cited and analyzed in Mark Spiegel, *The Rule 11 Studies and Civil Rights Cases: An Inquiry in the Neutrality of Procedural Rules*, 32 CONN. L. REV. 155, 158 n.12 (1999).

[198]   Rule 11(b) & (c) advisory committee's notes (1993).

[199]   *Golden Eagle Distrib. Corp. v. Burroughs Corp.*, 801 F.2d 1531, 1542 (9th Cir. 1986).

[200]   *Burroughs Corp.*, 801 F.2d at 1539 (citing American Bar Ass'n, *Model Rules of Professional Conduct* R. 3.3(a)(3) (1983)).

[201]   *Id.* at 1542. *But see* Daisy Hurst Floyd, *Candor Versus Advocacy: Courts' Use of Sanctions to*

Arguably, the court of appeals ignored both the language and the history of the Rule.[202] Focusing only on the requirement that a filing be warranted by existing law, the court disregarded the independent requirement that it not be interposed for *any* improper purpose.[203] A knowing omission of directly contrary authority within the controlling jurisdiction evidences an intent to mislead the court. Filing with that intent is surely filing with an improper purpose. Moreover, a filing would appear to be unwarranted when it is directly contrary to the legal authority within the controlling jurisdiction. Courts have therefore divided over the duty of candor that was rejected by the Ninth Circuit.[204]

Does a court's eventual rejection of a legal argument necessarily suggest that its proponent violated Rule 11? The rule's express embrace of the word "nonfrivolous" suggests the contrary; nonfrivolous is not the same as correct. On the other hand, the same phrase focuses more judicial attention on the quality of a litigant's legal argument than on its pre-filing inquiry. Indeed, one judge has suggested that "the submissions of the parties are to be marked on a scale of 'A' through 'F.' Anything falling on the far side of 'C' merits not only loss of one's case but loss of one's shirt as well."[205] This kind of standard invites rulings that are based on product rather than on conduct, and rulings that risk conflating the merits of claims and defenses with the care with which they are asserted.[206] The Advisory Committee acknowledges this risk and tries to guard against it by directing a court to take into account a litigant's pre-filing conduct: "the extent to which a litigant has researched the issues and found some support for its theories even in minority opinions, in law review articles, or through consultation with other lawyers . . . ."[207]

[d] Improper Purpose

The converse question has divided the courts — whether a court's acceptance of a legal argument or, more broadly, finding that a paper is well-founded, necessarily suggests that Rule 11 was *not* violated. The Seventh Circuit may have rejected this proposition by asserting that it may be necessary to explore the filer's subjective intent even if the paper was objectively well-founded.[208] Several other appellate courts have taken the opposite view, holding that the filing of a well-founded

---

Enforce the Duty of Candor Toward the Tribunal, 29 GA. L. REV. 1035 (1995) (endorsing such use of Rule 11).

[202] *See Golden Eagle Distrib. Corp. v. Burroughs Corp.*, 809 F.2d 584, 586 (9th Cir. 1987) (Noonan, Sneed, Anderson, & Kozinski, JJ., dissenting from denial of reh'g *en banc*).

[203] *See* § 8.05[d], *infra*.

[204] *See, e.g.*, cases cited in Klausner, note 180, *supra*, at 321 n.164; *De Sisto Coll., Inc. v. Line*, 888 F.2d 755, 766 (11th Cir. 1989) (rule imposes duty of candor); *Cousin v. Dist. of Columbia*, 142 F.R.D. 574, 577 (D.D.C. 1992) (imposing sanctions for failing to disclose and discuss adverse authority).

[205] *Szabo Food Serv., Inc. v. Canteen Corp.*, 823 F.2d 1073, 1085 (7th Cir. 1987) (Cudahy, J., concurring in part and dissenting in part). *See* Samuel J. Levine, *Seeking a Common Language for the Application of Rule 11 Sanctions: What Is "Frivolous"?*, 78 NEB. L. REV. 677, 679–85 (1999) (criticizing inconsistency of courts' interpretation of frivolous legal arguments and urging a graduated standard instead).

[206] *See generally* BURBANK, note 168, *supra*, at 10–13; Stephen B. Burbank, *The Transformation of American Civil Procedure: The Example of Rule 11*, 137 U. PA. L. REV. 1925, 1933–34 (1989).

[207] Rule 11(b) & (c) advisory committee's notes (1993).

[208] *Szabo Food*, 823 F.2d at 1083.

complaint is not ordinarily sanctionable under the improper purpose standard (at least absent unusual circumstances, such as multiple filings amounting to harassment).[209]

The latter holdings reflect several problems in finding a violation of Rule 11's improper purpose provision. The first is that the rule generally tests papers by objective, reasonable lawyer standards, rather than by the signer's subjective intent. The Ninth Circuit has concluded that "because of the objective standard applicable to Rule 11 analysis, a complaint that is found well-grounded in fact and law cannot be sanctioned as harassing regardless of the attorney's subjective intent."[210] Second, even if subjective intent may be appropriately considered in deciding whether a filing has an improper purpose, its proof is circumstantial and problematic. It must necessarily be inferred from the paper itself, as well as from the consequences of filing. When the paper is well-founded, the circumstantial evidence is in conflict even if the consequences are delay or expense to opponents. Finally, sanctioning colorable claims may raise constitutional questions by deterring the presentation of grievances to the courts.[211] The Second Circuit has also suggested that filing to generate adverse publicity for the defendants may be constitutionally protected under the First Amendment. "It is not the role of Rule 11 to safeguard a defendant from public criticism that may result from the assertion of nonfrivolous claims."[212] On the other hand, assertion of an *unfounded* claim to use the judicial forum for a public protest has been held sanctionable by the D.C. Circuit.[213] Clearly, it is easier to infer improper purpose from an unfounded paper.

But if improper purpose can be inferred only from unfounded filings, the improper purpose provision of the rule would be superfluous. Such papers already violate the warranted-by-law and evidentiary-support provisions of the rule. For the improper purpose standard to play any independent role, it must be applicable to even well-founded papers in unusual circumstances which circumstantially prove an improper intent. The most common circumstances involve multiple filings and a pattern of harassment. Courts have also inferred improper purposes from the timing of filing when it results in strategic delays.[214] In other words, though improper purpose cannot be inferred from a well-founded paper, some courts have inferred it from *other* circumstances in connection with filing.

---

[209] *Moore* § 11.11[8][d] (citing 2d, 5th and 9th Circuits).

[210] *Hudson v. Moore Bus. Forms, Inc.*, 836 F.2d 1156, 1159 (9th Cir. 1987).

[211] *Moore* § 11.11[8][d].

[212] *Sussman v. Bank of Israel*, 56 F.3d 450, 459 (2d Cir.), *cert. denied sub nom. Bank of Israel v. Lewin*, 516 U.S. 916 (1995).

[213] *Saltany v. Reagan*, 886 F.2d 438 (D.C. Cir. 1989).

[214] *See, e.g., Aetna Life Ins. Co. v. Alla Med. Servs., Inc.*, 855 F.2d 1470, 1476 (9th Cir. 1988) (emphasizing pattern of abusive litigation and successive papers in approving sanctions, even when papers were nonfrivolous); cases cited in *Moore* § 11.11[8][a].

[e]　Sanctions

Rule 11 formerly provided that, after finding a violation, a court "shall impose appropriate sanctions," including reasonable attorney's fees. Although it also authorized nonmonetary sanctions, 95% of all sanctions imposed under the rule were monetary, including some very substantial fee awards.[215] Courts under the former sanctions regime appeared to have lost sight of the fact that Rule 11's purpose is deterrence rather than compensation.[216] Rule 11(c)(4) attempts to correct this by making sanctions discretionary and by expressly reminding the court of the availability of nonmonetary sanctions, including orders to pay penalties into court. The 1993 Advisory Committee presented examples of orders striking the offending paper; admonishing, reprimanding, or censuring the offender; requiring the offender to participate in educational programs; or referring the matter to disciplinary authorities. Courts have imaginatively developed others. (Our personal favorite: an order that the offending attorney take and pass a law school course on federal jurisdiction, remanded for further consideration because it might impose too great a burden *on the law school!*)[217] Moreover, when the court on motion does impose a monetary sanction, the sanction is limited to the reasonable attorney's fees and other expenses "incurred as a direct result of the violation" and may not be awarded against a represented party for violations of Rule 11(b)(2) — the warranted-by-the-law certification requirement.

The court's discretion in awarding sanctions is limited. Although the 1993 Advisory Committee apparently rejected a least-severe sanction standard,[218] it did provide in Rule 11(c)(4) that sanctions "must be limited to what suffices to deter repetition of [the violative conduct] or comparable conduct by others similarly situated." It suggested that the factors that should inform discretion include

> [w]hether the improper conduct was willful, or negligent; whether it was part of a pattern of activity, or an isolated event; whether it infected the entire pleading, or only one particular count or defense; whether the person has engaged in similar conduct in other litigation; whether it was intended to injure; what effect it had on the litigation process in time or expense; whether the responsible person is trained in the law; what amount, given the financial resources of the responsible person, is needed to deter that person from repetition in the same case; [and] what amount is needed to deter similar activity by other litigants. . . .[219]

The 1993 amendment also assures a minimum of procedural fairness in the sanctioning process. All motions for sanctions may be made only "after notice and

---

[215] *See, e.g., Avirgan v. Hull*, 932 F.2d 1572 (11th Cir. 1991) (over $1 million); *Brandt v. Schal Assocs., Inc.*, 131 F.R.D. 485 (N.D. Ill. 1990) (over $350,000).

[216] Rule 11 advisory committee's notes (1983) (noting that "the word 'sanctions' in the [rule] caption . . . stresses a deterrent orientation in dealing with improper pleadings, motions or other papers").

[217] *See Willhite v. Collins*, 459 F.3d 866, 869–71 (8th Cir. 2006) (trial court should consider requiring continuing legal education instead).

[218] *See* Tobias, note 185, *supra*, at 881.

[219] Rule 11(c) advisory committee's notes (1993).

a reasonable opportunity to respond," and a court may impose sanctions on its own initiative only after issuing an order directing a party to show cause why the party has not violated the rule.[220] In addition, Rule 11(c)(6) requires the court in a sanctions order to describe the offending conduct and "to explain the basis for the sanction" imposed. This provision assures an adequate basis for appellate review, which was not always provided under the former Rule 11 practice.[221]

Finally, the advisory committee's notes to the 1993 amendment reaffirm that Rule 11 is not the exclusive source of sanctioning authority in federal court. Congress has by statute authorized courts to assess costs, including attorney's fees, against an attorney who "multiplies the proceedings in any case unreasonably and vexatiously."[222] This statute differs significantly from Rule 11. It is broader because it applies to the whole course of counsel's litigation conduct (not just filing papers) and imposes a continuing duty to avoid dilatory tactics. But it is also narrower because it requires subjective bad faith by counsel and does not apply to clients.[223] The Supreme Court has also held that federal courts retain inherent power to discipline attorneys and parties who appear before them.[224] Although Rule 11's procedures ordinarily supersede the courts' inherent powers in cases to which the rule applies, these powers may be used to punish in-court conduct and inappropriate oral remarks beyond the reach of the rule.

[f] Assessment

In the first edition of this book, we suggested that vigorous enforcement of Rule 11 could make kitchen-sink pleadings and mechanical Rule 12 motions[225] endangered species, while over-zealous enforcement of Rule 11 risked a return to the problems of unfairness and inefficiency that plagued code pleading. In the second edition, we predicted that the 1993 amendments made both outcomes less likely, because, first, the de-emphasis of monetary sanctions would diminish incentives to file Rule 11 motions, and, second, the authorization of information-and-belief pleading, coupled with the safe harbor provision, would give litigants more leeway in pleading.

Assessments of the amendment's effect appear to be consistent with these predictions. Commentators have noted a "marked decline in formal Rule 11 activity" and in corresponding satellite litigation, as well as an amelioration of the rule's chilling effect on novel claims and arguments.[226] A 1995 survey of judges and

---

[220] Rule 11(c)(1) & (3). Previously, courts had not always afforded fair notice and an opportunity to be heard when they imposed sanctions *sua sponte*. *See* Wiggins, note 168, *supra*, at 17.

[221] *See, e.g., Brown v. Fed'n of State Med. Bds.*, 830 F.2d 1429, 1438–40 (7th Cir. 1987).

[222] 28 U.S.C. § 1927 (2012).

[223] *See United States v. Int'l Bhd. of Teamsters*, 948 F.2d 1338, 1344 (2d Cir. 1991). The statute also lacks Rule 11's safe harbor and separate motion provisions.

[224] *See Chambers v. NASCO, Inc.* 501 U.S. 32 (1991).

[225] *See* § 8.07 (motions practice), *infra*.

[226] *See, e.g.,* Georgene Vairo, *Rule 11 and the Profession*, 67 Ford. L. Rev. 589, 626, 643 (1998); *cf.* Theodore C. Hirt, *A Second Look at Amended Rule 11*, 48 Am. U. L. Rev. 1007 (1999) (noting "anecdotal evidence" of these effects but concluding that it may be premature to declare complete success).

lawyers provided lukewarm support for these assessments.[227] While most thought "groundless litigation" a "small" problem which had not changed much since the amendments, 14% of the judges and 11–13% of the lawyers thought it had declined. Substantial majorities supported the safe harbor provision and more than one-third of the judges thought it had reduced Rule 11 activity on their dockets, a conclusion which individual courts have stated in their reported opinions.[228] These assessments shows that Justice Scalia's fear that the 1993 amendments would "gut[]" the rule[229] has not materialized.

On the other hand, a majority of judges and lawyers in the 1995 survey supported changing the rule to make compensation, as well as deterrence, a purpose of sanctions. Perhaps, the more rigorous pre-filing inquiry is intercepting *negligently* prepared papers, or the safe harbor is being used to correct or withdraw them, with the result that the unsupported papers that remain are the kind that intentionally violate the rule? If so, they are papers for which non-monetary sanctions seem inadequate to lawyers who incur uncompensated expenses in opposing them. This conclusion is consistent with the claim that other, less circumscribed sanctions, such as those afforded by 28 U.S.C. § 1927 or the courts' inherent power,[230] are being used with increasing frequency since the 1993 amendments.[231]

Finally, the 1993 amendments do not fully address a serious problem of certification: its tendency to focus judicial sanctioning attention on a litigant's product rather than her conduct. It has sometimes proven difficult to draw a bright line between unsuccessful or merely inept papers and factually unwarranted or frivolous papers. But, as one critic puts it, Rule 11 was never intended as "an open-ended charter for upgrading the legal profession."[232] The proper focus of a certification rule is on a litigant's conduct in investigating the facts and researching the law before filing; other motions are available to test the merits and other devices (such as continuing legal education) to improve the bar's competency.

§ 8.06 THE COMPLAINT

In most modern pleading systems, the complaint (and any other pleading that sets out a claim for relief) should contain a statement of jurisdiction when necessary, a statement of the claim, and a demand for relief.[233] The federal complaint is illustrative.

---

[227] JOHN SHAPARD ET AL. (FEDERAL JUDICIAL CENTER), REPORT OF A SURVEY CONCERNING RULE 11, FEDERAL RULES OF CIVIL PROCEDURE (1995).

[228] *See* cases cited by Hirt, note 226, *supra*, at 1030–31. Whether the safe harbor also has revived professional collegiality and civility by making lawyers talk to each other, as some had hoped, is more doubtful. *See id.* at 1031, 1041 (citing judicial opinions expressing this hope); Vairo, note 226, *supra*, at 643–47 (raising doubts).

[229] Dissenting statement of Justice Scalia on amendments to the Federal Rules of Civil Procedure, 113 S. Ct. CCCVI, CCCVIX (1993).

[230] *See* § 8.05[2][e], *supra*.

[231] Vairo, note 226, *supra*, at 643.

[232] BURBANK, note 168, *supra*, at 13.

[233] *See* Rule 8(a).

[1] Statement of Jurisdiction

Rule 8(a) requires the claimant to include a statement of the "grounds for the court's jurisdiction," unless the court already has jurisdiction and the claim needs no independent grounds. This requirement reflects the limited jurisdiction of the federal courts,[234] and similar requirements apply to state courts of limited jurisdiction as well. Because the chief workhorses of state judicial systems are usually courts of general jurisdiction, no such jurisdictional statement is required for claims filed there, unless a jurisdictional requirement is built into the substantive claim itself.

The content of the jurisdictional statement depends upon how the court's subject matter jurisdiction is defined.[235] In federal courts, jurisdictional allegations that track the language of Form 7 are sufficient. Technical forms of pleading are no more necessary to plead jurisdiction than to plead a claim. Even with respect to jurisdictional allegations, pleadings should be construed liberally to do substantial justice. The court should search not just the pleading, but the whole record, to see if it will support subject matter jurisdiction.[236] By statute, defects in the pleading of jurisdiction can also be cured through amendment in the trial court or on appeal.[237] Note, however, that these rules apply only to the cure of defects in the *allegation* of jurisdiction; they cannot be invoked to supply jurisdiction that was not present at the commencement of the action.[238]

[2] Statement of Claim and the Burden of Pleading

Matters of form and detail in modern claim pleading were discussed in section 8.04. Here we will consider what elements must be pleaded and by whom. The substantive law from which the claim arises provides an answer to the first question. Special pleading rules like Rules 8(c) and 9 or precedent generally supply an answer to the second question. "Precedent as such," however, "does nothing for the inquiring mind."[239] Thus it is useful to consider the logic of allocating burdens in pleading (if any). We start with the burden of producing evidence at trial, which the burden of pleading usually follows.

A plaintiff has the burden of producing evidence at trial that would enable a rational trier of fact to find for him (1) *if* he also carries his burden of persuasion, *i.e.*, persuades the trier of fact that it is more probable than not that he is correct, (2) *unless* defendant in turn carries *her* burden of producing evidence that would enable the trier of fact to find that she has a defense.[240] When the plaintiff does not

---

[234] *See* § 5.01[2] (federal subject matter jurisdiction), *supra*.

[235] *See* §§ 5.03 (federal question jurisdiction) & 5.04–5.06 (diversity), *supra*.

[236] WRIGHT § 69 (citations omitted).

[237] 28 U.S.C. § 1653.

[238] *See* § 5.01[1] (subject matter jurisdiction generally), *supra*.

[239] Edward W. Cleary, *Presuming and Pleading: An Essay on Juristic Immaturity*, 12 STAN. L. REV. 5, 10 (1959).

[240] *Id.* at 15–16. "Burden of proof" is often used as a shorthand reference for the burdens of production and persuasion together. *See generally* § 12.04 (burdens and standards of proof), *infra*.

carry his initial burden of production at trial, the court can dismiss the action and enter judgment as a matter of law for the defendant.[241]

To the plaintiff typically (though not invariably) goes the burden of pleading matters for which he has the initial burden of production at trial: the *prima facie* case.[242] One reason is that the plaintiff is challenging the status quo and may fairly be asked to demonstrate why. Another is the assumption that if he is unable with due candor and care to plead such matters, he will probably also be unable to satisfy his burden of production at trial. If his case would be dismissed at trial, it would be wasteful to let it get that far. Requiring the plaintiff to plead those elements as to which he would have the burden of production at trial forces him to expose any basic infirmity in the case at the pleading stage, permitting its dismissal at the front of the litigation.

The defendant has the burden of pleading the elements as to which she carries the burden of production at trial. This allocation is efficient because it relieves the plaintiff of the task of pleading the negative of every possible defense, including many on which the defendant might never rely. It also forces the defendant to identify the specific defenses on which she will rely, information that would be withheld from plaintiff and the court until trial were the burden of pleading the nonexistence of all possible defenses placed on plaintiff.

Whether a jurisdiction classifies a particular element as part of the plaintiff's *prima facie* case or as part of a defense depends upon a highly variable mix of policy, fairness, convenience and probability considerations, as well as history and accident.[243] *Gomez v. Toledo*[244] illustrates the interplay of some of these. Gomez sued a public official for violating his civil rights. The Supreme Court had held that such officials are entitled to a qualified immunity from liability for acts performed in the reasonable belief that they were lawful. *Gomez* posed the question whether a civil rights plaintiff has the burden of pleading the defendant's bad faith and unreasonable belief as part of his *prima facie* case, or whether the defendant has the burden of pleading good faith and reasonable belief as part of his defense. The Court placed the burden on the defendant, reasoning in part that "whether such immunity has been established depends on facts peculiarly within the knowledge and control of the defendant."[245] Not only would it therefore be more convenient for defendant to assume the burden, but it would be unfair to ask the plaintiff to plead a state of mind that turns on factors "which [he] cannot reasonably be expected to know."[246] In a later case, the Supreme Court placed the burden of pleading a claimant's failure to exhaust his administrative remedies on the defendant, in part because the statute containing the exhaustion requirement was "not a source of a [claimant's] claim," suggesting another factor in allocating

---

[241] *See* Rules 41(b) & 50(a), and §§ 11.04[2] & 12.09[1], *infra* respectively.

[242] *See* § 8.04[1] (notice pleading), *supra*.

[243] *See generally* Cleary, note 239, *supra*. Some of these we have already considered in analyzing special pleading rules. *See* § 8.04[4], *supra*.

[244] 446 U.S. 635 (1980).

[245] *Id.* at 641.

[246] *Id.*

burdens of pleading.[247] It added that "[t]he argument that screening [complaints] would be more effective if exhaustion had to be shown in the complaint proves too much; the same could be said with respect to any affirmative defense."[248]

[3] Demand for Relief

The demand for relief has lost much of the significance it held at common law because most modern pleading systems frequently require a court to "grant the relief to which each party is entitled, even if the party has not demanded that relief in its pleadings."[249] Any other rule would be a reversion to the discarded doctrines of the theory of the pleadings and election of remedies.[250]

Nevertheless, the demand for relief is useful even under modern notice pleading. When the court's subject matter jurisdiction is limited by an amount in controversy,[251] the demand for monetary relief, or *ad damnum*, may determine the grounds for jurisdiction. The type of relief demanded also has jurisdictional significance in those systems that have maintained the division between law and equity. It can bear on the availability of a jury trial, which is often tied to particular kinds of actions.[252]

Finally, the prayer for relief may set a ceiling on the plaintiff's recovery in the event of default — an adverse judgment against defendant resulting from his failure to appear or otherwise defend.[253] Default, after all, is sometimes strategic, reflecting defendant's cost-benefit analysis of defending an action. To perform that analysis, defendant must know the maximum cost of not defending, information that is conveyed by the demand for judgment contained in the complaint. If, after defendant's default, the judgment could exceed the demand in the complaint, this cost-benefit analysis would be impossible to perform reliably, and default would cease to be a viable strategic option. Rule 54(c) therefore provides that "[a] default judgment must not differ in kind from, or exceed in amount, what is demanded in the pleadings."

---

[247] *Jones v. Bock*, 549 U.S. 199 (2007).

[248] *Id.* at 215.

[249] Rule 54(c). *See, e.g., Bail v. Cunningham Bros., Inc.*, 452 F.2d 182 (7th Cir. 1971).

[250] *See* § 8.04[2] (consistency and the theory of the pleadings in modern pleading), *supra*.

[251] *See* § 5.06 (amount in controversy), *supra*.

[252] *See* § 12.07[1] (right to a jury), *infra*.

[253] *See* § 11.02 (default), *infra*.

§ 8.07 CHALLENGING PLEADINGS: MOTION PRACTICE

[1] Motion Practice in General

One of the principal reforms carried forward from code pleading to the federal rules was the reduction of the many responsive pleadings at common law[254] to just three responses: motion, answer, and (when permitted) reply.[255] A *motion* is not a pleading; it is an application to the court for an order. It must state with particularity the grounds upon which it relies. A supporting memorandum of authorities (brief) and a proposed form of order often accompany a motion.[256] Like pleadings, motions are subject to the candor and care requirements of Rule 11 and do not require any technical forms.[257]

The federal rules and many state rules in notice pleading jurisdictions permit the defendant to file a motion attacking the complaint in lieu of an answer. Federal Rule 12(g), however, contemplates just one pre-answer motion in most cases (sometimes called the "omnibus motion rule") by forbidding subsequent motions under Rule 12 raising a defense or objection "that was available to the party but omitted from its earlier motion." This rule eliminates the undesirable practice of successive, "nickel-and-dime," pre-answer motions in favor of an omnibus pre-answer motion presenting all then-available Rule 12(b) defenses and objective at once.

At the same time, Rule 12(b) provides that no defense or objection is waived by being joined with others. This eliminates the risk in federal courts that a defendant who attacks personal jurisdiction at the same time he moves to dismiss for failure to state a claim will be deemed to have made a general appearance, waiving the former defense. It thus also eliminates any need for defendant to make a *special appearance* in order to present the defense of personal jurisdiction.

The pre-answer motion may be used to present what the common law called dilatory defenses, including matters in abatement and challenges to jurisdiction.[258] In some jurisdictions, some of these defenses can only be presented by motion; in federal court, all the Rule 12(b) defenses can be asserted by motion or in a responsive pleading. Such attacks do not go to the merits, or, ordinarily, to the sufficiency of the pleading alone. Therefore, a motion presenting them may be decided on the basis of materials submitted by the parties, as well as on the pleadings.

In contrast, a pre-answer motion that presents the defense of failure to state a claim (Rule 12(b)(6)) attacks the substantive content of a pleading and must usually

---

[254] *See* § 8.02[1] (common law pleading), *supra.*

[255] *See* § 8.09 (the reply), *infra.*

[256] *See* Rule 7(b)(1) & Form 40. Motions are usually written, but can be made orally in the course of a recorded hearing. Rule 7(b)(1) is often implemented by more detailed local rules, promulgated under the authority of Rule 83. *See, e.g.,* Local Civil Rule 7 of the United States District Court for the District of Columbia (establishing page limits and requirements for included matter).

[257] *See* Rules 11 & 8(d)(1).

[258] *See* § 8.02[1] (common law practice), supra.

be decided upon the face of the pleading alone — that is, on the basis of the allegations in the pleading, and not any additional factual matter from "outside the four corners of the pleading," in the common parlance. However, the court may take judicial notice of the law, other pleadings, its own records, and universally undisputed facts.[259] Moreover, in federal courts, the submission of materials outside the pleadings in support of or opposition to a Rule 12(b)(6) motion is not forbidden. It simply converts the Rule 12(b)(6) motion into a motion for summary judgment subject to the usual procedural safeguards of Rule 56.[260] Thus, the common law rule against "speaking demurrers"[261] has been discarded by the federal rules.

After the pleadings have closed in federal court, either side may seek judgment on the pleadings under Rule 12(c). This motion goes to the merits insofar as they appear from the pleadings. Whereas the scope of a Rule 12(b)(6) defense, when raised in a motion that is filed prior to the answer, is confined to the face of the complaint, a Rule 12(c) motion takes in all the pleadings on file. Thus, a 12(c) motion is available both to the defendant, who may use it to raise defenses such as 12(b)(6) failure to state a claim (if it was not already raised and resolved in a pre-answer motion), and to the plaintiff, who may use it to challenge the legal sufficiency of the defendant's answer. Submission of materials outside the pleadings converts the Rule 12(c) motion to a motion for summary judgment. In fact, Rule 12(c) motions have been largely superseded by motions for summary judgment and are today "little more than . . . relic[s] of the common law and code eras."[262]

Some have suggested that the de-emphasis of pleading in modern civil practice has made Rule 12(b)(6) motions relics as well, infrequently made and rarely dispositive.[263] Data from selected district courts in 1975 and 1988 indicate that Rule 12(b)(6) motions were made in 13–15% of the sampled cases, granted in 8–12% of the sampled cases (*e.g.*, 52–65% of the time), and dispositive in 3–6% of the sampled cases (*e.g.*, 51–72% of the granted cases).[264] These data support the assertion that Rule 12(b)(6) motions are rarely dispositive, although they apparently dispose of approximately as many cases as does trial.

---

[259] This is an over-simplification of the nuances of judicial notice. *See* Fed. R. Evid. 201.

[260] *See* § 11.03[2] (procedure for summary judgment), *infra.* Submission of such materials in support of a Rule 12 motion asserting defenses 12(b)(1)–(5) or (7) does not convert it into a summary judgment motion. These defenses "only challenge the propriety of the court adjudicating the claim before it and do not reach the validity of the claim itself." *Wright & Miller* § 1366. *See, e.g., Weidner Commc'ns, Inc. v. H.R.H. Prince Bandar Al Faisal*, 859 F.2d 1302, 1306 n.6 (7th Cir. 1988) (noting that Rule 12(b)(2) motion cannot be converted into summary judgment motion); *Haase v. Sessions*, 835 F.2d 902, 905–07 (D.C. Cir. 1987) (holding that Rule 12(b)(1) motion cannot be converted to summary judgment motion, although defendant may challenge standing by formally moving for summary judgment).

[261] *See* § 8.02[1] (common law practice), *supra.*

[262] *Wright & Miller* § 1369.

[263] *Wright* § 66; Arthur R. Miller, The August 1983 Amendments to the Federal Rules of Civil Procedure: Promoting Effective Case Management and Lawyer Responsibility 7–8 (1984).

[264] Thomas E. Willging, Use of Rule 12(b)(6) in Two Federal District Courts 6–8 (Federal Judicial Center 1989). These data are inflated by the inclusion of prisoners' cases, which are probably more vulnerable to 12(b)(6) dismissal than other cases. *Id.* at 7 & Table 2, 8 n.19.

But it does not follow that they are useless relics. Even if a motion does not finally dispose of a case, it may eliminate some marginal claims and parties, or at the very least signal the defendant's determination to litigate with immeasurable but real effect on settlement dynamics. A Rule 12(b)(6) motion "that whittles a complaint with twenty claims down to two viable claims has not been a failure in terms of merits dispositions."[265] Moreover, if heightened pleading requirements survive the Supreme Court's decision in *Leatherman v. Tarrant County Narcotics Intelligence and Coordination Unit* or are required by statute,[266] Rule 12(b)(6) motions may be effective in the sub-set of cases to which such standards are applied. Finally, there is some evidence that *Twiqbal's* "plausible pleading" standard[267] has incrementally revitalized Rule 12(b)(6) practice, although the early returns suggest that any such revitalization is confined chiefly to civil rights and employment discrimination cases.

[2] Bases for Motions

[a] Defects of Form

Because modern notice pleading does not require technical forms of pleading, attacks on pleadings for defects of form are virtually extinct in modern pleading jurisdictions. Under the federal rules, the only defects of form that can be challenged are that the complaint is unintelligible or that it contains "redundant, immaterial, impertinent, or scandalous matter."[268]

A complaint that is too vague, ambiguous or confused to enable the defendant to respond may be attacked by a Rule 12(e) motion for more definite statement in the federal courts, or by a special demurrer in states that retain this nomenclature.[269] In a notice pleading jurisdiction, however, discovery, and not pleading, is the device intended to obtain information about an adversary's case. Accordingly, a Rule 12(e) motion should not be granted just because the movant wants to know more than enough to prepare some response. In light of the leeway afforded by the rules to formulate responses,[270] few litigants are able to make the necessary showing.[271]

---

[265] Richard L. Marcus, *The Puzzling Persistence of Pleading Practice*, 76 Tex. L. Rev. 1749, 1756 (1998). Such a whittling effort may also encourage settlement.

[266] 507 U.S. 163 (1993). *See* § 8.04[1] (specificity of modern pleadings), *supra.*

[267] *See* § 8.04[1][d].

[268] Rule 12(f).

[269] *See, e.g.*, Cal. Civ. Proc. Code § 430.10(f).

[270] *See, e.g., Hodgson v. Va. Baptist Hosp., Inc.*, 482 F.2d 821 (4th Cir. 1973) (denying Rule 12(e) motion because Rule 8(b) permitted the response that defendant lacks knowledge or information sufficient to form a belief as to the truth of an averment in complaint). *See generally* § 8.08[1] (denials), *infra.*

[271] Rule 12(e) motions have been used in two other limited settings. They have been invoked to enforce Rule 9(b) requirements for special pleading of fraud and mistake. *See* Moore § 12.36; Wright & Miller § 1300; *see generally* § 8.04[4], *supra.* This use of the motion makes a reasonable accommodation between these requirements and Rule 8(a)'s requirement for a "short and plain statement," without requiring dismissal of a complaint. Rule 12(e) motions are also sometimes used to uncover threshold defenses such as the statute of limitations or fraud. *See* Wright & Miller § 1376.

Rule 12(f) motions to strike (delete) any of the various kinds of improper matter from a pleading are even less likely to be granted than Rule 12(e) motions. As long as pleadings are not shown to the jury, quibbling about how immaterial, nasty, or gratuitous they are is a waste of everyone's time unless their availability in the public record is likely to prejudice the movant. Rule 12(f) motions by defendants to strike improper matter are therefore often disfavored.[272] Usually the allegations that have been stricken were obviously prejudicial: describing a car as a "death trap," or plaintiff's co-conspirators as "strong arm men" and "racketeers."[273]

[b]   Waivable Preliminary Defenses

Lack of personal jurisdiction,[274] improper venue,[275] insufficiency of process (the papers served on the parties),[276] and insufficiency of service (the means of service)[277] are typical defenses that can or must be asserted by pre-answer motion. They are personal to the defendants, and their availability is usually clear from the outset of litigation. In almost all jurisdictions, therefore, defendants are required, on penalty of waiver,[278] to raise them preliminarily, before the court and the parties invest much time in the litigation or reach the merits. Federal Rules 12(g) and 12(h)(1) provide that these defenses are waived unless they are asserted in a single pre-answer motion, or, if none is filed, in an answer or reply or any amendment thereto permitted as a matter of course.

Rule 12's treatment of waivable defenses suggests a simple rule of thumb in federal court: a party should assert them in her first defensive paper. The same applies in many state courts as well. In some states, all of these defenses except improper venue can be asserted by *motions to quash* service. In a few, the assertion of defenses to the complaint constitutes a general appearance, submitting to the jurisdiction of the court. It is therefore necessary to *appear specially* to assert the defense of lack of personal jurisdiction.[279] As noted above, Rule 12(b) effectively eliminates the need for special appearances in federal court by expressly providing that "[n]o defense or objection is waived by joining it" with any other in a responsive pleading or motion.

---

[272] Such motions by plaintiffs serve a different purpose — to strike legally insufficient defenses.

[273] *See* Stephen C. Yeazell, Civil Procedure 453 n.7 (4th ed. 1996) (citing cases). *Cf. Theriault v. Silber*, 574 F.2d 197 (5th Cir. 1978) (striking "vile and insulting" references to trial judge in appellant's notice of appeal). Rule 12(f) may also be used to attack the substantive sufficiency of an answer or reply, *see* § 8.07[2][c] (failure to state defense), *infra*, and, in a few courts, to strike averments of fraud or mistake that violate Rule 9(b). *See* Wright & Miller § 1300.

[274] Rule 12(b)(2). *See* Chapter 3, *supra*.

[275] Rule 12(b)(3). *See* Chapter 6, *supra*.

[276] Rule 12(b)(4). *See* § 4.03, *supra*.

[277] Rule 12(b)(5). *See* § 4.03, *supra*.

[278] *See* § 3.03[2] (waiver of personal jurisdiction defense), *supra*.

[279] For more extensive discussion of opportunities in state and federal court to question personal jurisdiction, see § 3.03[2][b] (special and general appearances), *supra*.

[c]   Failure to State a Claim (or Defense) and Other Nonwaivable Defenses

The defenses of failure to state a claim or defense, lack of subject matter jurisdiction, and, in federal courts, failure to join a party under Rule 19[280] are not waived by their omission from a pre-answer motion.[281] Rule 12(h)(3), in fact, provides that if the court determines that it lacks subject matter jurisdiction, it must dismiss the action regardless of when the issue is raised, while Rule 12(h)(2) states that the other nonwaivable defenses may be asserted in any pleading, by motion for judgment on the pleadings, or even "at trial."[282] Were the rule otherwise, judgments could be recovered on claims or defenses unrecognized by the law, and courts would be unable to protect absent parties whose indispensability to the litigation first becomes evident as it progresses.

The most common nonwaivable defense is the failure to state a claim. It is asserted by a Rule 12(b)(6) motion in federal court and by general demurrer in many state courts. The test for disposition of the motion depends on the jurisdiction's requirement for stating a claim or cause of action.[283] All well-pleaded facts (*e.g.*, not legal conclusions, rank opinion, or speculation) in the challenged pleading are taken as true for purposes of the motion or demurrer, and all reasonable inferences are drawn in favor of the pleader.[284] The province of Rule 12(b)(6) motions and demurrers is to question the availability of a legal formula justifying relief on the alleged facts, not to test or determine the facts themselves. On the other hand, "courts are not . . . required to speculate that factual propositions unmentioned, or evidentiary links unrevealed, are among the facts plaintiff intends to prove at trial."[285]

In some code pleading states, a demurrer was overruled unless the entire pleading was defective.[286] This is no longer true in most jurisdictions, and a litigant can attack part of the complaint, usually a count, for failure to state a claim.

---

[280]   *See* § 9.05[2] (compulsory joinder), *infra.*

[281]   Rule 12(h)(2)-(3).

[282]   A failure to state a claim is usually raised at trial by a motion for dismissal (or judgment as a matter of law in federal courts) in a trial to the court, Rule 52(c), *see* §§ 11.04[2] & 12.10, *infra*; and by a motion for a directed verdict (or for judgment as a matter of law in federal courts) in a trial to a jury. Rule 50(a). *See* § 12.09[1] (directed verdicts), *infra.* The phrasing of Rule 12(h)(2) suggests that a post-answer 12(b)(6) motion is not a proper vehicle for asserting the defense.

[283]   *See generally* Yoichiro Hamabe, *Functions of Rule 12(b)(6) in the Federal Rules of Civil Procedure: A Categorization Approach*, 15 CAMPBELL L. REV. 119 (1993); §§ 8.03 (code pleading), 8.04[1] (modern notice pleading), & 8.06[2] (statement of claim), *supra.*

[284]   *See* MOORE § 12.34. The same standards are applied in the determination of Rule 12(c) motions for judgment on the pleadings. MOORE § 12.38. *Cf.* § 12.09[3][c] (comparing these with motions for directed verdict), *infra.* As noted in Section 8.04[1][d], in *Twombly*, 550 U.S. 544, the Supreme Court appeared unwilling to draw an inference of collusion from allegations of conscious parallel conduct by the defendant corporations, when the inference of independently motivated conduct was equally reasonable. It seems improbable that the Court meant to reject the plaintiff-favoring rule generally, however.

[285]   *ACLU Found. S. Cal. v. Barr*, 952 F.2d 457, 472 (D.C. Cir. 1991) (stating also that "[a] court must take care not to put words into counsel's mouth by reading into a complaint factual allegations not fairly comprehended within what is actually asserted.").

[286]   *See* CHARLES E. CLARK, HANDBOOK OF THE LAW OF CODE PLEADING § 79 (2d ed. 1947).

Technically, perhaps, a Rule 12(f) motion to strike the defective count or claim is the correct vehicle under the federal rules.[287] However, since Rule 8(d)(1) abolished technical forms of motions, a Rule 12(b)(6) motion should be equally effective.

The phrasing of the latter ("failure to state a *claim* upon which relief can be granted"), suggests its unsuitability for attacking the legal insufficiency of a *defense*. Instead, a Rule 12(f) motion to strike (or a motion for judgment on the pleadings or for summary judgment) is used for this purpose. The test for rejecting a defense for legal insufficiency is analogous to that used in deciding a Rule 12(b)(6) motion for failure to state a claim.[288]

[3]   Consequences of Challenging a Pleading

[a]   Successful Challenge

One reason why Rule 12(b)(6) motions appear so ineffective is that a plaintiff will often moot a strong pre-answer motion by amending his defective complaint. Rule 15(a) allows a party to amend his pleading once "as a matter of course" at any time before a responsive pleading is filed, and a pre-answer *motion* is not a responsive *pleading*.[289] Depending upon the federal circuit, amendment as of right or by permission is available even *after* a motion to dismiss has been granted, unless the court indicates that no curative amendment is possible.[290]

If plaintiff opts to amend, he runs the risk of waiving his argument that the original complaint was sufficient. Both state and federal courts are divided on this question of waiver. The better federal rule appears to be that such a plaintiff waives his objection to the court's dismissal order only insofar as it applies to technical defects in the original complaint. He may still argue, on appeal of an unfavorable final judgment after trial of the amended complaint, that the erroneous grant of the Rule 12(b)(6) motion against his original complaint "struck a vital blow" to a substantial portion of his case.[291]

If the plaintiff stands on his original complaint and takes a successful appeal from its dismissal, the complaint will be reinstated and the defendant will have to file a responsive pleading. If the appellate court affirms the dismissal, however, the plaintiff will have forfeited his opportunity to amend[292] unless the appellate

---

[287]   *See, e.g., Mills v. Fox*, 421 F. Supp. 519 (E.D.N.Y. 1976) (striking punitive damages not recoverable under state law); *Fry v. Lamb Rental Tools, Inc.*, 275 F. Supp. 283 (W.D. La. 1967) (striking demand for damages for losses not recoverable under state law).

[288]   *See, e.g., Donovan v. Robbins*, 99 F.R.D. 593 (N.D. Ill. 1983). *But see generally* Robert D. Loomis, *Motion to Strike Affirmative Defenses — The Equivalent of Partial Summary Judgment*, 13 Am. J. Trial Advocacy 645 (1989) (asserting that the no-genuine-issue standard for summary judgment (*see* § 11.03[3], *infra*) is different, but used by some courts to decide Rule 12(f) motions to strike affirmative defenses, even though the rule does not provide for converting such motions to summary judgment).

[289]   Rule 7(a). *See generally* § 8.10[1] (amendment before trial), *infra*.

[290]   *See* § 8.10[1] (amendment before trial), *infra*, noting split in the circuits.

[291]   *See, e.g., Wilson v. First Houston Inv. Corp.*, 566 F.2d 1235, 1238 (5th Cir. 1978), *vacated on other grounds*, 444 U.S. 959 (1979); *Blazer v. Black*, 196 F.2d 139, 143–44 (10th Cir. 1952) (dictum).

[292]   Some appellate courts have taken the view that the plaintiff-appellant also waives the right to

mandate preserves it.[293]

[b] Unsuccessful Challenge

The options posed by denial of defendant's motion to dismiss are simpler. She may, of course, file an answer, although in federal court she cannot include the waivable defenses if they were omitted from her motion.[294] By answering, she forgoes the opportunity to obtain immediate appellate review of the denial of her motion, unless the jurisdiction permits interlocutory appeals, because there is no final judgment from which to take an appeal.[295]

Depending upon the jurisdiction, she may also waive her preliminary defenses by going forward. But she can preserve the defense that the complaint fails to state a claim by raising it by motion at trial for dismissal, directed verdict, or, in federal courts, for judgment as a matter of law, and after trial, for judgment notwithstanding the verdict, and by appropriate evidentiary objections at trial. It will thereby be preserved on appeal of an eventual final judgment. In federal courts, it is preserved by the original Rule 12 motion.[296]

Alternatively, the defendant may elect to stand on her motion and refuse to answer. This course will result in the entry of a default judgment[297] against her, from which she can appeal. If the appellate court agrees with her, it should remand with leave for plaintiff to amend. But if the court affirms, defendant may lose the opportunity to defend on the merits.

§ 8.08 THE ANSWER

The answer may contain three kinds of responses: denials controverting the pleader's allegations, defenses, and claims by the defendant.[298]

[1] Denials

In all jurisdictions, the defendant must in her answer admit or deny all the well-pleaded allegations of the complaint. An admission takes the issue from the fact-finder and is conclusive at trial. The old common law plea of the general issue theoretically survives as a *general denial* of each and every allegation of the complaint,[299] but it will almost always be impossible to square with candor and care

---

argue any alternative legal theories that might have formed the basis of an amended complaint. *See Mitchell v. Archibald & Kendall, Inc.*, 573 F.2d 429, 433 (7th Cir. 1978) ("By appealing, the plaintiffs-appellants elected to stand on their original complaint and thereby relinquished the legal theory they now assert.").

[293] Federal appellate courts have broad remedial powers. *See* 28 U.S.C. § 2106 (2012).

[294] *See* § 8.07[2][b] (waivable preliminary defenses), *supra*.

[295] *See* § 13.03 (final judgment rule), *infra*.

[296] *See* Rule 46.

[297] *See* § 11.02 (default), *infra*.

[298] *See* Form 30.

[299] *See* Rule 8(b)(3) (expressly authorizing general denial).

requirements like those of Rule 11.[300] Instead, most defendants *specifically deny* particular paragraphs or sentences of the complaint. In fact, Rule 8(b) commands that a "denial must fairly respond to the substance of the allegation. . . . A party that does not intend to deny all the allegations must either specifically deny designated allegations or generally deny all except those specifically admitted." Failure to deny an allegation in a required responsive pleading, other than an allegation of the amount of damages, is deemed an admission.[301] But answers do not require technical forms and are construed, like all pleadings, to do substantial justice.

A well-known case, *Zielinski v. Philadelphia Piers, Inc.*,[302] illustrates some of these principles. In a personal injury suit, defendant generally denied a paragraph in the complaint that alleged that a forklift "owned, operated and controlled" by it and its employees was negligently driven so that it hit and injured the plaintiff. In fact, unknown to plaintiff, defendant had sold its business and transferred its employees to a third party prior to the accident, retaining only ownership of the forklift. By the time that plaintiff learned of these facts, it was too late under the applicable statute of limitations to sue the third party. Plaintiff therefore argued that the defendant's denial was ineffective and should be treated as an admission for purposes of the action.

The court ruled that defendant's failure to deny specifically the "operated and controlled" allegations in the quoted paragraph deprived plaintiff of warning that he had sued the wrong defendant. Although defendant's denial was literally true,[303] it did not "fairly meet the substance of the averments denied."[304] Moreover, not only should defendant have admitted ownership, but it should also have admitted that the forklift hit and injured the plaintiff, which was known to it from an accident report. Although a defective denial should not automatically be deemed an admission under the federal rules, the circumstances (compounded by a misleading and inaccurate answer to interrogatories during discovery) justified finding the defendant equitably estopped from denying ownership and agency for purposes of the action.

When a defendant neither knows nor can learn whether an averment in the complaint is true or false, most jurisdictions permit him to say so in the answer with the effect of a denial.[305] But he cannot blind himself to what he should know,

---

[300] *See, e.g., Williamson v. Clapper*, 199 P.2d 337, 339 (Cal. Ct. App. 1948) ("[L]oose practice of pleading [the general denial] which results in the incorporation in the answer of known false denials is to be condemned."). Rule 8(b) takes some pains to warn counsel of the danger of such "known false denials" by reminding him that a general denial controverts even routine jurisdictional allegations in the complaint. That is, it asks, "Can you really deny your client's your name or address consistently with Rule 11?"

[301] Rule 8(b)(6). *See Lipton Indus., Inc. v. Ralston Purina Co.*, 670 F.2d 1024, 1030 (C.C.P.A. 1982).

[302] 139 F. Supp. 408 (E.D. Pa. 1956).

[303] Because plaintiff used conjunctions to connect different averments, the entire paragraph was true literally only if all of its conjoined averments were true.

[304] *Zielinski*, 139 F. Supp. at 411–12 (quoting Fed. R. Civ. P. 8(b) (1993)).

[305] Rule 8(b)(5) (defendant "lacks knowledge or information sufficient to form a belief about the truth").

and facts presumptively within the control or knowledge of the defendant may be deemed admitted if he responds with an empty-headed denial of knowledge or information.[306] Moreover, Rule 11(b)(4) imposes a duty of reasonable inquiry on defendant by which he may obtain the necessary knowledge or information and explicitly applies to "denials of factual contentions."

[2] Other Defenses

[a] Preliminary, Nonwaivable and Affirmative Defenses

Besides admissions and denials, an answer should contain "in short and plain terms" other defenses to each claim in the complaint. Unless they have been waived by their omission from a pre-answer motion, some or all of the preliminary defenses may be asserted by an answer or, when permitted, a reply.[307] The nonwaivable defenses may also be asserted.

A defendant should also plead his *affirmative defenses*, if any. An affirmative defense is the lineal descendant of the common law plea in confession and avoidance[308] — in effect, an excuse or justification for his action that would avoid plaintiff's claim, even if that claim is proven at trial. It differs from its ancestor in that confession is no longer a predicate for avoidance, because a defendant may combine denials and affirmative defenses in his answer under modern pleading rules.[309] It differs from a counterclaim in that an affirmative defense makes no claim against any party and seeks no relief other than the defeat of plaintiff's claim.[310] Finally, it differs from a denial in that it does not tend to controvert the plaintiff's *prima facie* case, but instead affirmatively asserts new matter outside that case and beyond the plaintiff's claim.

Because such matter is new, it is not put in issue by a defendant's general or specific denials of the plaintiff's allegations. Affirmative defenses must be pleaded "as a condition to the admissibility of such evidence at the trial."[311] When defendant has failed to plead an affirmative defense, the admissibility of some tendered evidence will depend upon whether it goes to the plaintiff's *prima facie* case or whether it is truly new matter. If the latter, it may not come in unless the opposing party fails to object or the court permits amendment of the pleadings during trial.[312] One traditional test for deciding this question — and thus for identifying affirmative defenses — is whether the tendered evidence "tend[s] *to destroy* rather

---

[306] *See, e.g.*, *Mesirow v. Duggan*, 240 F.2d 751, 756 (8th Cir. 1957); *Oliver v. Swiss Club Tell*, 35 Cal. Rptr. 324 (Cal. Ct. App. 1963).

[307] Rule 12(b); Form 30.

[308] *See* § 8.02[1] (common law pleading), *supra*.

[309] *See, e.g.*, Rule 8(d)(2).

[310] In any event, the federal rules are merciful to the defendant who confuses an affirmative defense and a counterclaim in his pleading, requiring the court to treat the pleading "as though it were correctly designated." Rule 8(c)(2).

[311] *Layman v. Sw. Bell Tel. Co.*, 554 S.W.2d 477, 480 (Mo. Ct. App. 1977).

[312] *See* § 8.10[2], *infra*.

than *avoid* the cause of action as alleged by the complaint."[313] Another formulation is whether it arises by logical inference from the allegations of plaintiff's complaint.[314]

For example, when the complaint is for trespass and alleges plaintiff's ownership of the property and defendant's entry, evidence of defendant's title by adverse possession is logically related to ownership and tends to destroy an essential allegation of plaintiff's complaint. It is therefore admissible under a general denial, and the defendant need not plead an affirmative defense of adverse possession.[315] On the other hand, evidence of an easement is not admissible in defense of a trespass action unless defendant has pleaded an easement as an affirmative defense. Such evidence does not controvert ownership, but only goes to show justification for disturbing it.[316]

The distinction between evidence supporting defendant's denials and evidence that is admissible only in support of a pled affirmative defense, however, is not always easy to follow. This only reflects the fact that the underlying question is simply one of allocating pleading burdens. It is therefore decided less often by logic or formula than by precedent, itself based upon idiosyncratic considerations that vary from jurisdiction to jurisdiction.[317] For this same reason, however, the problem is today more theoretical than real. Most state jurisdictions have identified affirmative defenses by precedent, rule, or statute. The picture is not as clear in federal court. Rule 8(c) lists many of the affirmative defenses available there. But federal courts also borrow from the forum state's laws or rules to identify affirmative defenses not listed in Rule 8(c).[318]

The risk that the evidence will be excluded or that amendment will be denied dictates pleading an issue as an affirmative defense when in doubt.[319] In a few jurisdictions, the danger of this strategy is that by pleading an issue as an affirmative defense, defendant may be considered to have assumed the burden of proof, even if it would otherwise rest on the plaintiff.[320] This result is unsound because it elevates the form of pleading over the often substantive policy underlying the allocation of the burden of proof.[321] It will often be wise even in such jurisdictions for defendant to plead the matter as an affirmative defense. Otherwise,

---

[313] *Denham v. Cuddeback*, 311 P.2d 1014, 1016 (Or. 1957) (emphasis in original).

[314] CHARLES E. CLARK, HANDBOOK OF THE LAW OF CODE PLEADING § 96 (2d ed. 1947).

[315] *Denham*, 311 P.2d at 1017.

[316] *Layman*, 554 S.W.2d 477.

[317] *See* § 8.06[2] (statement of claim and burden of pleading), *supra*.

[318] Such local law is not binding because, under the *Erie* doctrine, the allocation of the burden of pleading is a procedural matter to be decided as a matter of federal law. *See Palmer v. Hoffman*, 318 U.S. 109, 117 (1943) (implying that burden of pleading is controlled by Rule 8(c), though burden of proof is a question of local law in diversity cases) (dictum). *See generally* WRIGHT & MILLER § 1272; § 7.04, *supra*. On the nature and effect of the *Erie* doctrine generally, *see* Chapter 7, *supra*.

[319] *See* WRIGHT & MILLER § 1278 (footnote omitted).

[320] *See* JAMES, HAZARD & LEUBSDORF § 4.7.

[321] *See* MOORE § 8.07.

he risks exclusion of the relevant evidence altogether.[322]

Most modern pleading jurisdictions do not permit a reply to defenses asserted by answer unless the court orders one.[323] Absent a reply, allegations supporting a defense are simply taken as denied by plaintiff.[324] Challenges to the legal sufficiency of defenses are made initially by a Rule 12(f) motion to strike in federal courts or by demurrer in states that retain the device, although they can also be made later by motions for summary judgment or judgment as a matter of law or directed verdict.[325]

On such Rule 12(f) challenges should a court insist that an affirmative defense be plausible? That is, should the *Twiqbal* pleading standard apply to affirmative defenses? The courts are divided.[326] Arguments why it should apply include that: (1) what's good for the goose (the defendant on a Rule 12(b)(6) motion) is good for the gander (the plaintiff on a Rule 12(f) motion); (2) Rule 8(b)(1)(A) echoes Rule 8(a)(2) in requiring a party to "state in short and plain terms its defenses"; and (3) insisting on plausible defense-pleading will help screen frivolous defenses and provide better notice to the plaintiff.

But Rule 8(b)(1)(A) is not identical to Rule 8(a)(2), because the latter requires the plaintiff to "show[] that the pleader is entitled to relief." Furthermore, Rule 8(c) simply requires the defendant to "affirmatively state" an affirmative defense, which sounds like something less than "showing." In addition, the practice in many federal courts has long been to tolerate conclusory "shot gun" pleading of affirmative defenses,[327] for which Form 30 provides some support. Finally, some argue that defendants should be allowed a lower pleading standard because they have less time to investigate the case than the typical plaintiff, who, having investigated and pled the transaction or occurrence that gave rise to her claims presumably needs less notice concerning defenses (and possibly faces a lower discovery burden for the same reason).

---

[322] There will usually be no reason why defendant cannot raise the matter in his answer *both* by specific denial and by affirmative defense.

[323] *See, e.g.*, Rule 7(a).

[324] Rule 8(b)(6).

[325] *See* §§ 8.07[2][c], *supra*, 12.09, *infra*.

[326] *See generally* Tom Tinkham & Eric Janus, *Plausible Answers and Affirmative Defenses*, 79 U.S.L.W. 2271 (2011). *Compare F.T.C. v. Hope Now Modifications, LLC*, 2011 U.S. Dist. LEXIS 24657 (D.N.J. Mar. 10, 2011) (Refusing to apply *Twiqbal* to affirmative defenses in part because "A defendant asserting an affirmative defense is not 'unlock[ing] the doors of discovery' in the same way that a plaintiff does by bringing a complaint in the first place. The Defendants here are already subjected to discovery.") (citation omitted) *and Charleswell v. Chase Manhattan Bank, N.A.*, 2009 U.S. Dist. LEXIS 116358 (D.V.I. Dec. 8, 2009) (refusing to apply *Twiqbal* to affirmative defenses and reviewing the case split) *with Palmer v. Oakland Farms, Inc.*, 2010 U.S. Dist. LEXIS 63265 (W.D. Va. June 24, 2010) (applying *Twiqbal* to afford plaintiff adequate notice) *and HCRI TRS Acquirer, LLC v. Iwer*, 708 F. Supp. 2d 687 (N.D. Ohio 2010) (applying *Twiqbal* in part because "[b]oilerplate affirmative defenses that provide little or no factual support can have the same detrimental effect on the cost of litigation as poorly worded complaints").

[327] *See, e.g.*, *United States ex rel. Smith v. Boeing Co.*, 2009 U.S. Dist. LEXIS 71625 (D. Kan. Aug. 13, 2009).

Yet, despite *Twiqbal*, a central mission of federal pleading on both sides of the "v" is still giving notice to the opposing party. Though the verdict is still out, *as long as Twiqbal is undisturbed*, we are inclined to agree with the magistrate who found:

> Despite these relevant countervailing arguments, the considerations of fairness, common sense and litigation efficiency underlying *Twombly* and *Iqbal* strongly suggest that the same heightened pleading standard should also apply to affirmative defenses. With complaints and with defenses, the purpose of pleading requirements is the same. It is to give fair notice to the opposing party that there is some plausible, factual basis for the assertion and not simply to suggest some possibility that it might apply to the case. To require less of a defendant sets the pleading bar far too low.[328]

[b]   A Note on the Affirmative Defense of the Statute of Limitations

This common affirmative defense merits further discussion because of its significance to procedure. Statutes of limitation require claimants to file their claims within a given time period or lose them. They reflect a conviction that, after the passage of the limitations period, realization of the substantive goals underpinning the claim is less important than protecting opposing parties from the frustrations of coping with stale claims. Chief among these frustrations are the loss from delay of evidence that might have defeated the claim and the emotional stress and financial uncertainty generated by the specter of future litigation.[329] The availability of statutes of limitations defenses depends upon three factors.

The first factor is when the claim *accrued* or came into existence. In most jurisdictions, tort actions accrue at the time of the injury[330] and contract actions accrue at the time of the breach,[331] but there are many nuances in the law governing accrual of actions. In particular, many courts have adopted a discovery/diligence rule of accrual for some torts (especially medical malpractice), by which the action accrues when the plaintiff should, by exercise of reasonable diligence, have discovered his injury (and, some courts add, its connection to defendant).[332] Using this rule of accrual protects a patient who is injured from some medical instrument or sponge misplaced during surgery, the presence of which she does not discover until years later when another doctor accurately diagnoses her stomach pain.

The second factor is the *period of limitation*. This also varies enormously from jurisdiction to jurisdiction, although short (one year) periods are commonly associated with intentional torts and disfavored actions like defamation,[333] inter-

---

[328] *Palmer v. Oakland Farms, Inc.*, 2010 U.S. Dist. LEXIS 63265, at *15 (W.D. Va. June 24, 2010).

[329] *See, e.g., Elkins v. Derby*, 525 P.2d 81 (Cal. 1974). *See generally* 51 Am. Jur. 2d *Limitation of Actions* §§ 17–18 (1970 & Supp. 1999).

[330] *See, e.g., Roberts v. Richard & Sons, Inc.*, 304 A.2d 364 (N.H. 1973); 51 Am. Jur. 2d *Limitation of Actions* § 135 (1970 & Supp. 1999).

[331] *See, e.g., Struthers Wells-Gulfport, Inc. v. Bradford*, 304 So. 2d 645 (Miss. 1974); 51 Am. Jur. 2d *Limitation of Actions* § 126 (1970 & Supp. 1999).

[332] 51 Am. Jur. 2d *Limitation of Actions* § 167 (2000).

[333] *See, e.g.*, Md. Cts. & Jud. Proc. Code Ann. § 5-105 (1984) (assault, slander, libel).

mediate (two or three year) periods with negligence and oral contract claims,[334] and longer periods (five or six years) with actions involving written contracts and instruments.[335] The longest periods are associated with claims to enforce previously awarded judgments.[336]

The last factor is when the period *tolls* or stops running. In most statutes, the period is tolled by the commencement of an action in court, but the rules defining commencement vary. Some statutes define commencement as filing plus service on the defendant. Others state that the period is tolled by filing, if service on defendant is accomplished within some additional short period — "service tail" — after filing.[337] Because of the potentially harsh application of a statute of limitations, many jurisdictions have statutory exceptions[338] or *equitable tolling* doctrines, whereby defendant's fraudulent concealment of his wrongdoing or other good reason is said to toll the period until plaintiff knew or should have known of her injury or that she had an action against defendant.[339] By statute, periods are also often tolled during the legal incapacity of a plaintiff to sue as a result of her minority or incompetency.[340]

State statutes of limitations are regarded as substantive law for *Erie* purposes, and therefore control in federal diversity actions.[341] Because there is no federal statute of limitations for many federal claims, courts often borrow state statutes of limitations in federal question cases,[342] if they are not inconsistent with the purpose of the federal law.[343] Federal equitable tolling doctrines are still applied to borrowed periods, creating an often confusing hybrid law of limitations in federal courts.[344]

When the ground for a limitations defense is obvious from the face of the complaint, it can be raised by a Rule 12(b)(6) motion, or in some state courts, by demurrer.[345] This procedure is disfavored by many courts, however, because it complicates plaintiff's offer of factual matter in avoidance of the defense, such as

---

[334] *E.g., id.* § 5-101 (contracts).

[335] *E.g., id.* § 5-102(a) (1) (twelve years for instruments under seal).

[336] *See, e.g.,* N.Y. Civ. Prac. L. & R. 211 (McKinney 2000) (twenty years).

[337] *See, e.g.,* Okla. Stat. tit. 12, § 97 (repealed 1984), analyzed in *Walker v. Armco Steel Corp.,* 446 U.S. 740, 751–52 (1980) and § 7.04[2], *supra.*

[338] *See, e.g.,* N.Y. Civ. Prac. L. & R. 213(8) (McKinney 2000).

[339] 51 Am. Jur. 2d *Limitation of Actions* §§ 146–69 (1970 & Supp. 1999).

[340] *See, e.g.,* N.Y. Civ. Prac. L. & R. 208 (McKinney 2000) (infancy and insanity toll the statute).

[341] *See* § 7.03[1] (analyzing the *York* decision), *supra.*

[342] *See* § 5.03 (statutory scope of federal question jurisdiction), *supra.*

[343] *See, e.g., Banks v. Chesapeake & Potomac Tel. Co.,* 802 F.2d 1416 (D.C. Cir. 1986). *See generally* Note, *Limitation Borrowing in Federal Courts,* 77 Mich. L. Rev. 1078 (1979); § 7.07 (federal common law), *supra.*

[344] *See Banks,* 802 F.2d at 1420. *See also Holmberg v. Armbrecht,* 327 U.S. 392 (1946) (fraudulent concealment tolls borrowed state statute of limitations).

[345] *See* Comment, *Raising Defense of Statute of Limitations by Demurrer, Equivalent Motion to Dismiss, or by Motion for Judgment on Pleadings,* 61 A.L.R.2d 300 (1999).

fraudulent concealment under the doctrine of equitable tolling.[346] Even when the defense appears on the face of the complaint, therefore, these courts have urged that it be raised by answer (which presents plaintiff the opportunity to seek leave to reply) and that it be presented for decision by motion for summary judgment.[347]

[3]   Claims by Way of Answer

A defendant may also respond to the complaint by asserting claims against the plaintiff, other defendants or third parties.[348] Claims against existing parties are usually asserted in the answer.[349] Claims against new parties have to be served with a complaint and summons, just as the original defendants must be served.

§ 8.09   THE REPLY AND OTHER PLEADINGS

Under the federal rules, further pleading is necessary after an answer only if the latter introduces a claim. Such a claim is tantamount to a complaint. Rule 7(a) therefore requires a reply to a counterclaim[350] denominated as such and answers to all other claims[351] included in the original answer. No other pleadings are allowed as of right, and all averments in the last required pleading are deemed denied or avoided.[352] The abandonment of issue-identification as the primary function of pleading accounts for this early cut-off; the complaint, answer, and reply suffice to give fair notice.

On rare occasions, the defendant may want the plaintiff to respond to an answer in order to ascertain what issues plaintiff will contest at trial. More rarely, the plaintiff herself may wish to respond affirmatively to new matter pleaded as an affirmative defense in the answer, by, for example, pleading facts showing fraud in response to the affirmative defense of release. Replies in these circumstances are not required or permitted as of right. Rule 7(a) does, however, give courts discretion to allow a reply, and on rare occasions they do so.[353] Although some states once

---

[346] *See* Richard L. Marcus, *Fraudulent Concealment in Federal Court: Toward a More Disparate Standard?*, 71 Geo. L.J. 829, 902–04 (1983).

[347] *See, e.g., Richards v. Mileski*, 662 F.2d 65, 73 (D.C. Cir. 1981). *See generally* Rhynette Northcross Hurd, *The Propriety of Permitting Affirmative Defenses to Be Raised by Motions to Dismiss*, 20 Memphis St. U. L. Rev. 411 (1990). The Supreme Court has permitted a trial court to dismiss a case on limitation grounds *sua sponte*, even where the defendant (respondent) failed to raise the affirmative defense, explaining that the trial judge could just have brought the oversight to the defendant's attention and invited an amendment of its answer, but also cautioning that before it dismisses, the court must give the plaintiff (petitioner) fair notice and an opportunity to be heard. *Day v. McDonough*, 547 U.S. 198 (2006).

[348] *See generally* §§ 9.04 (cross-claims), 9.05 (permissive and compulsory party joinder), & 9.06 (impleader), *infra*.

[349] *See, e.g.*, Rules 13 (counterclaims and cross-claims) and 22 (interpleader); Form 30.

[350] *See* § 9.03, *infra*.

[351] *See* §§ 9.04 (cross-claims), 9.05[1] (permissive party joinder), & 9.06, (impleader), *infra*.

[352] Rule 8(b)(6).

[353] "[O]ccasions when this power should be or has been exercised are extremely rare." Wright § 66. "The theory is that by the complaint and the answer each of the parties will have indicated the general position he is taking in the litigation, and that further pleading is not worth the trouble." *Id.*

mandated a reply to affirmative defenses,[354] today the pleading rules in most modern pleading jurisdictions do not require replies.

The only other pleading contemplated under federal and many state rules is a supplemental pleading "setting out any transaction, occurrence, or event that happened after the date of the pleading to be supplemented."[355] Such pleadings are most commonly used to allege new damages,[356] or affirmative defenses that have accrued since filing of the complaint, such as discharge in bankruptcy, release, or *res judicata*. Before a supplemental pleading may be filed, the court must grant leave and may set conditions designed to minimize its complicating or prejudicial impact on the pending litigation.[357] To the same ends, no responsive pleading is required or permitted to a supplemental pleading unless the court so orders.[358]

§ 8.10   AMENDMENT OF PLEADINGS

One reason that pleading in modern procedure is less perilous than it was in the common law is the availability of liberal amendment: the pleader is rarely stuck with his first effort. Most modern pleading jurisdictions allow amendment without permission early in litigation, and almost all provide liberal opportunities for amendment by permission later. The remaining constraints on amendment are functional rather than formalistic, imposed by concerns for efficient judicial administration, prejudice to opposing parties, and, where applicable, the policy of the statute of limitations. Widely copied in the states, Rule 15 accommodates these concerns and is therefore the focus of this section.

[1]   Amendment Before Trial

The earlier an amendment is made, the less likely it is to disrupt judicial administration or prejudice opposing parties. Rule 15(a)(1) therefore provides that a party may amend "once as a matter of course" (without permission from the court or consent of other parties) within twenty-one days of service, or, if a responsive pleading is required, within twenty-one days of service of the responsive pleading or Rule 12 motion, whichever is earlier. The rule thus permits one amendment as a matter of course to cure defects raised by such a motion before the court hears and rules on the motion. Rule 15(a)(1)'s "freebie amendment" not only can spare the court the effort of ruling on the motion, but also promotes efficient judicial administration without prejudice to opposing parties who have usually not yet invested significant resources in litigating the action and who are

---

[354] *Id.*

[355] Rule 15(d). Amendment, in contrast, deals with events that occurred *prior* to the date of the pleading sought to be amended. *See generally* § 8.10 (amendment), *infra*.

[356] *See, e.g., Fritz v. Standard Sec. Life Ins. Co. of N.Y.*, 676 F.2d 1356, 1358 & nn.3 & 4 (11th Cir. 1982) (supplemental complaint for insurance payments that accrued after filing of complaint); *McHenry v. Ford Motor Co.*, 269 F.2d 18 (6th Cir. 1959) (complaint to enjoin flooding of plaintiff's land; supplemental pleading to recover for new damage to plaintiff's house).

[357] The relevant factors are comparable to those considered in granting leave to amend. *See* § 8.10[1] (amendment before trial), *infra*.

[358] Rule 15(d).

typically given ample time to respond[359] to the amended pleading.[360]

Once issues have been joined by the filing of a responsive pleading (that is, allegations have been denied and defenses asserted, showing what is in dispute), amendment will often make that pleading moot and require the opposing party to prepare a new responsive pleading. In light of this inefficiency and the possible prejudice to the opposing parties, leave of court is required to amend.[361] The rule closes the window of opportunity for a freebie amendment because it assumes that with the passage of time, the opposing parties have invested significant resources in responding to the original pleading and are more likely to suffer prejudice from having to start over with an amended pleading. The same rationale explains why the rule only allows one freebie amendment ("A party may amend its pleading once as a matter of course."). Rule 15(a)(2) provides, however, that "[t]he court should freely give leave when justice so requires." Provided that amendment will promote disposition of the action on the merits, there is effectively a presumption favoring it. This presumption can only be rebutted by the opposing party's showing that the amendment is unreasonably dilatory, futile (e.g., amendment cannot cure the problem or presents a claim or defense that is legally insufficient on its face), or in bad faith, or that the opposing party will be unduly prejudiced.[362] This standard is a judicial gloss on the "justice so requires" formula of the rule.

Beeck v. Aquaslide 'N' Dive Corp.[363] illustrates the standard. In its answer to a complaint for personal injury, the defendant admitted design and manufacture of the water slide alleged to have caused the injury. Subsequently, after the statute of limitations on plaintiff's personal injury claim had expired, defendant sought to amend its answer because it belatedly discovered that it had not manufactured the defective slide. The trial court granted defendant leave to amend its answer in order to deny design and manufacture. Plaintiff appealed from a judgment on an

---

[359] Rule 15(a)(3) provides that a response shall be made within the original time remaining for response or fourteen days after service of the amended pleading, whichever is longer.

[360] After a motion to dismiss has been granted, some of this efficiency is lost because the court has already ruled. The Second Circuit therefore holds that the right to amend without permission terminates unless the court, in ruling on the motion, explicitly grants leave to amend. *See Elfenbein v. Gulf & Western Indus., Inc.*, 590 F.2d 445, 448 & n.1 (2d Cir. 1978). In contrast, some circuits distinguish dismissal of the complaint from dismissal of the action, and read Rule 15(a) literally to allow a plaintiff to amend once as of right after dismissal of the complaint pursuant to a pre-answer motion. *See Ruby v. Sec'y of Navy*, 365 F.2d 385, 387 (9th Cir. 1966), *cert. denied*, 386 U.S. 1011 (1967); *222 E. Chestnut St. Corp. v. Lakefront Realty Corp.*, 256 F.2d 513 (7th Cir.), *cert. denied*, 358 U.S. 907 (1958). The Eleventh Circuit has taken the intermediate position that plaintiff may amend with leave of court after dismissal, unless the court either holds that no amendment is possible or that dismissal of the complaint also constitutes dismissal of the action. *See Czeremcha v. Int'l Ass'n of Machinists & Aerospace Workers, AFL-CIO*, 724 F.2d 1552 (11th Cir. 1984).

[361] Leave is requested by filing a motion to amend accompanied by the proposed amendment. WRIGHT & MILLER § 1485.

[362] *See Foman v. Davis*, 371 U.S. 178, 182 (1962); *Espey v. Wainwright*, 734 F.2d 748, 750 (11th Cir. 1984) ("This policy of Rule 15(a) in liberally permitting amendments to facilitate determination of claims on the merits circumscribes the exercise of the trial court's discretion; thus, '[u]nless there is a substantial reason to deny leave to amend, the discretion of the district court is not broad enough to permit denial.' ") (citations omitted).

[363] 562 F.2d 537 (8th Cir. 1977).

eventual verdict for defendant, asserting that the grant of leave to amend was error. The appellate court affirmed.

The amendment was not futile, for it presented what proved to be a winning defense, and it permitted the parties to litigate a material factual issue on the merits. In addition, there was no evidence of bad faith or unreasonable delay. Defendant had relied on the conclusions of three different insurance companies in preparing its initial answer and had promptly sought amendment upon discovering their error in identifying the slide's manufacturer.

Plaintiffs were also unable to show undue prejudice sufficient to overcome these justifications for the amendment. They were, of course, disadvantaged on the merits by the amendment, which interjected a new and difficult fact issue into the litigation. But this kind of prejudice cannot be "undue" because it is inherent in every amendment: if the amending party would not gain some advantage from the amendment, it would not seek amendment. This kind of what we might call "merits prejudice" to the opposing party is therefore built into every amended pleading. Instead, undue prejudice ordinarily consists of "preparation prejudice" flowing from delay in offering the amendment — a substantial disadvantage in preparing to litigate the amended matter that the opposing party would not have faced had the amended pleading been filed originally. In *Beeck*, for example, plaintiffs tried to make this showing by arguing that the amendment came too late for them to sue other parties (including the real manufacturer of the slide) because the applicable statute of limitations had expired during the defendant's delay in changing its answer. But the trial court found no preparation prejudice because claims for fraud or breach of contract might still be available against other parties, and because such parties might also be equitably estopped[364] from asserting a limitations defense.[365] On this record, the appellate court found no abuse of discretion and affirmed the judgment for defendants.

Even when a proposed amendment may prejudice opposing parties, the court may impose conditions upon the amendment that mitigate the prejudice. For example, allowance of the amendment may be accompanied by a grant to the party opposing it of additional discovery, continuances, or time extensions. Financial prejudice may be controlled by conditioning amendment upon payment of costs.[366]

[2] Amendment During and After Trial

At common law, evidence offered outside the issues framed by the pleadings was inadmissible because *variance* from the pleadings was forbidden.[367] Rule 15(b), in deliberate contrast, anticipates such variance and authorizes curing amendments by consent and over objection, during trial and even after judgment, "to conform [the pleadings] to the evidence."[368]

---

[364] *See* § 8.08[2][b] (the statute of limitations defense), *supra*.

[365] 67 F.R.D. 411, 415 (S.D. Iowa 1975).

[366] *See* WRIGHT & MILLER § 1486.

[367] *See* § 8.02[1] (common law practice), *supra*.

[368] A more functional version of the doctrines of variance and of the theory of the pleadings, *see*

[a]   Conforming Amendment by Consent

The parties may always expressly consent to the trial of issues outside the pleadings. Rule 15(b)(2) provides that the issues will then be treated as if they had been raised in the pleadings. Unpleaded issues may also be tried by implied consent of the parties. In either case, a party may move at any time, even after judgment, to amend the pleadings to conform to the evidence, although amendment is not necessary.

Implied consent presupposes both knowledge that an unpleaded issue has been injected into the litigation and a meaningful opportunity to litigate the issue.[369] Usually the offer of evidence bearing upon an unpleaded issue gives the requisite notice, and a failure to object signifies implied consent. This basis for inferring consent fails, however, when the evidence is also applicable to pleaded issues, because then its proffer does not necessarily alert the opposing party to the insertion of a new issue into the litigation.

In *Moore v. Moore*,[370] for example, after trial of a husband's complaint for child custody, the trial court granted the wife's motion to amend her answer to include counterclaims for custody, child support, separate maintenance, and attorney's fees. On appeal, the appellate court reasoned that the complaint for custody necessarily raised the issues of which parent was entitled to custody and of support for that custody, putting the husband on notice of these claims. The court also concluded that the husband had impliedly consented to trial of these issues by introducing evidence on them and failing to object to the wife's offer of evidence of the child's financial needs. However, the issue of separate maintenance, involving the marital relationship, is not normally litigated in a suit focused on child custody.

> While evidence of [the wife's] financial needs was admitted without objection relatively late in the proceedings, we cannot conclude that this evidence was so uniquely pertinent to her support alone, in contrast with the custody or the child support issues, that it justifies our concluding that appellant had adequate, timely notice of, and an opportunity to contest, a claim by his wife for her own support.[371]

The appellate court therefore ruled that the trial court abused its discretion in granting the amendment to add the separate maintenance claim.

A failure to object to evidence that is apposite to both pleaded and unpleaded issues, however, may evidence consent when combined with other indicia. The test for implied consent searches the entire record and considers a party's conduct in all the circumstances. In *Nielson v. Armstrong Rubber Co.*,[372] the plaintiff moved at

---

§ 8.04[2], *supra*, is now embodied in the provision for binding pretrial orders. *See* Rule 16(e); § 12.03[3] (binding effect of pretrial orders), *infra*.

[369] *See Moore v. Moore*, 391 A.2d 762, 768 (D.C. 1978).

[370] *Id.*

[371] *Id.* at 770. *See also DCPB, Inc. v. City of Lebanon*, 957 F.2d 913, 917 (1st Cir. 1992) ("The introduction of evidence directly relevant to a pleaded issue cannot be the basis for a founded claim that the opposing party should have realized that a new issue was infiltrating the case.").

[372] 570 F.2d 272 (8th Cir. 1978).

the close of the evidence to amend his simple negligence complaint to include a claim of strict products liability. While the defendant had not objected at trial to evidence of dangerousness and of failure to include a warning, defendant argued that this evidence applied to the negligence claim as well as the unpleaded claim of strict products liability and therefore had not provided him notice that the strict product liability claim had been added to the litigation. Yet the defendant had received plaintiff's pretrial memorandum citing the law of products liability, introduced evidence to rebut a strict liability claim, and been present when the trial court said, "it seems to me that we have now amended our pleadings."[373] On the whole record, defendant therefore clearly had notice and an opportunity to litigate the unpleaded issue, and the amendment to conform to the evidence was proper.

[b] Conforming Amendment Over Objection

The functional approach to amendment is most dramatically reflected by the provision for conforming amendment over the objection that evidence is outside the issues framed by the pleadings. Rule 15(b)(1) encourages the federal courts to grant such amendments "freely . . . when doing so will aid in presenting the merits" and the objecting party fails to show prejudice in maintaining his action or defense upon the merits. This provision offers further proof of the sympathetic climate for amendment generally.[374]

Nevertheless, the presumption favoring amendment is slightly weakened once trial has begun, given the lateness of the amendment and its effect on the on-going trial.[375] To the extent that the objecting party complains that he needs more preparation time to litigate the unpleaded issue, Rule 15(b) expressly authorizes continuances. In jury cases, however, a mid-trial continuance may not be a realistic option.

[c] The Objecting Party's Tactical Dilemma

When evidence apposite to an unpleaded issue is introduced at trial, the adverse party may feel, under Rule 15(b), that he is damned if he objects and damned if he does not. By objecting, he invites a motion by the opposing party for a conforming amendment, which the court will often grant under the liberal standard embodied in the rule. The most an objecting party usually stands to gain is a continuance to prepare to meet the new evidence and/or conditions on amendment, such as the payment of costs. On the other hand, by not objecting, he runs a substantial risk that his silence will be taken as implied consent to the interjection of the new issue.

The safe course in these circumstances is to object and defend. This is also the course most in keeping with the purposes of modern pleading, because it promotes decision on the merits and rejects sandbagging and pretense as litigation tactics.

---

[373] *Id.* at 275.

[374] *See* § 8.10[1] (amendment before trial), *supra*.

[375] These same considerations account for the restrictive "only-to-prevent-manifest-injustice" test for amending final pretrial orders. *See* Rule 16(e), discussed in § 12.03[3], *infra*.

[3] Amendment and the Statute of Limitations

[a] Relation Back of Amendments Amending Claims Against the Same Parties

When the applicable statute of limitations expires between the date of an original pleading and the date of a proposed amendment to it, is the amendment time-barred or does it take (*relate back* to) the date of the original pleading? In federal and most state courts, the answer to this question depends on the nature of the amendment. Under Rule 15(c)(1)(A), an amendment amending claims relates back if relation back is permitted by the state or federal law that provides the applicable statute of limitations.

It also relates back if it arises out of the same transaction or occurrence as the original pleading. When the amendment presents a claim that is completely new and factually unrelated to the original claims, it operates, in effect, as an independent original action brought after the applicable limitations period has expired. Allowing it to relate back would offend the policy of limitations — to protect against stale claims and assure repose[376] — no less than would an original action brought beyond the limitations period. But when the amendment presents a matter that is closely related to a timely-filed original pleading, allowing it to relate back would not offend the policy of limitations. In that case, the filing of the original pleading gives defendant notice to start gathering evidence before it grows stale and to plan for the possibility of liability under any closely related pleading. In other words, relation back is permitted because, if the original pleading gave timely notice of the litigation-provoking transaction or occurrence, there should be no prejudice from later-filed claims or defenses as long as they arise from the same transaction or occurrence. Almost all jurisdictions therefore today permit relation back in these circumstances. This policy, which is implicit in Rule 15(c)(1)(B) and (C) is made explicit by the corresponding North Carolina rule: a claim added by amendment "is deemed to have been interposed at the time the claim in the original pleading was interposed, unless the original pleading does not give notice of the transactions, occurrences, or series of transactions or occurrences, to be proved pursuant to the amended pleading."[377]

The problem is to determine how close the relationship between the original pleading and its amendment must be before the jurisdiction will allow relation back of the latter. In code pleading jurisdictions, the solution was to allow relation back of amendments as long as they did not change the cause of action originally pleaded.[378] When cause of action is defined narrowly in terms of legal right or a particular legal theory, this approach to relation back is correspondingly restrictive. For example, some courts deny relation back to an amendment in a malpractice action adding a claim of failure to obtain informed consent to an original complaint sounding only in negligence.[379]

---

[376] *See* § 8.08[2][b] (the affirmative defense of limitations), *supra*.

[377] N.C. R. Civ. P. 15(c).

[378] *See* § 8.03[2] (the cause of action in code pleading), *supra*.

[379] *See, e.g., Keenan v. Yale New Haven Hosp.*, 355 A.2d 253 (Conn. 1974).

Rule 15(c)(1)(B) rejects the cause of action concept[380] and instead premises relation back on a transactional relationship between the original pleading and the amendment. It allows relation back, *inter alia*, when "the amendment asserts a claim or defense that arose out of the conduct, transaction, or occurrence set out — or attempted to be set out — in the original pleading."[381] In a modern notice pleading jurisdiction, a complaint gives the defendant notice "that the whole transaction described in it will be fully sifted, by amendment if need be,"[382] and that liability for claims arising out of the transaction may be premised not only on the legal theory articulated in the complaint, but also on any other legal theory that the transaction might support.[383] The wise defendant therefore gathers evidence concerning and prepares to defend the transaction and not just against the theory of recovery articulated in the complaint.

The transactional relationship test clearly permits relation back of amendments that merely change the legal theory on which plaintiff seeks relief for the identical transaction. An example is an amendment adding a strict products liability claim to a complaint that originally asserted a simple negligence claim arising out of injuries received in the use of a product, or an amendment adding a claim for failure to obtain informed consent to a malpractice claim.[384]

On the other hand, Rule 15(c)'s general concern with fairness and notice to the party opposing the pleading informs the liberality with which courts should apply the transactional standard. *McGregor v. Louisiana State University Board of Supervisors*,[385] supplies a good illustration. A handicapped law student sued the school and its officials for violating the Rehabilitation Act of 1973 by denying him advancement to his second year. His original, timely complaint asserted that the school discriminated against him by insisting that he take a full-time schedule, have in-class exams, and attain a certain GPA before he advanced. After the statute of limitations had run, he sought to amend his complaint by adding due process claims on the ground that the school had provided no written procedure concerning his right to appeal denial of his petitions to the school. Although an expansive reading of Rule 15(c) might view this claim as arising from the same transaction as his original claim (his failure to advance), the appellate court agreed with the district court that the original complaint had not put defendant on notice of the due process claim. That complaint made no mention whatever of any appeals procedures or policy, and therefore, the court concluded, the amendment "set forth new and

---

[380] *See* § 8.04[2] (theory of pleadings in modern pleadings), *supra*.

[381] Rule 15(c)(1)(B). Transactional relationship is also the nexus for many joinder provisions of the federal rules, *see* §§ 9.03–9.08[1], *infra*, one possible test for identifying a constitutional "case or controversy" for purposes of supplemental jurisdiction, *see* §§ 5.08 & 5.11, *supra*, and the modern test for the scope of claim preclusion. *See* § 16.03[2], *infra*. *But see* Mary Kay Kane, *Original Sin and the Transaction in Federal Civil Procedure*, 76 TEX. L. REV. 1723 (1998) (arguing that different purposes of these provisions and doctrines call for different interpretations of "same transaction").

[382] *Barthel v. Stamm*, 145 F.2d 487, 491 (5th Cir. 1944), *cert. denied*, 324 U.S. 878 (1945).

[383] *See* §§ 8.04[1] & [2] (modern notice pleading), *supra*.

[384] *See, e.g., Neeriemer v. Superior Court*, 477 P.2d 746 (Ariz. Ct. App. 1970). *See also De Malherbe v. Int'l Union of Elevator Constructors*, 449 F. Supp. 1335 (N.D. Cal. 1978) (adding constitutional claim to statutory discrimination claim).

[385] 3 F.3d 850, 863–64 (5th Cir. 1993).

distinct conduct, transactions, or occurrences not found in the original complaint."[386] The court clearly applied the transaction standard "with an eye toward what legitimately should have been known or recognized within the scope of the litigation as a result of the initial pleadings."[387]

[b] Relation Back of Amendments Amending Parties

Amendments seeking to change parties beyond the applicable period of limitations are more problematic because the original pleading — served only on the original parties — did not formally put the new party on notice. As a stranger to the original lawsuit, he was not served. When the new party is a defendant, relation back of the late-filed claim against him is far more likely to be prejudicial than relation back of an additional claim against one who is already a defendant.[388] As a general rule, then, such amendments are disallowed in many jurisdictions. Exceptions are made to the general rule when the amendment arises out of the same transaction as the original pleading and the new party had some form of timely notice of the original pleading. In federal court, again, an amendment changing parties relates back if relation back is permitted by the state or federal law that provides the applicable statute of limitations, or if it is permitted by Rule 15(c)(1)(C).[389]

Many jurisdictions permit relation back of an amendment that simply corrects a *misnomer* — a reasonable mistake in the name of the party intended to be sued.[390] In such a case, the party intended to be sued received notice of the action from the original complaint. No real change in parties is made and no offense is done the policy of limitations by what is in effect a typographical correction to the pleadings.

Relation back is also permitted in some jurisdictions when there is sufficient *identity of interests* between the party originally sued and the new party such that notice to the former can be imputed to the latter. In *Stauffer v. Isaly Dairy Co.*,[391]

---

[386] *Id.* at 864.

[387] Kane, note 381, *supra*, at 1728.

[388] Relation back of amendments substituting new plaintiffs may not present comparable problems because a substitution will often cause no prejudice to the defendant. *See e.g.*, *Staggers v. Otto Gerdau Co.*, 359 F.2d 292, 297 (2d Cir. 1966). The relation back of additional plaintiffs, however, may in some cases allow tardy plaintiffs to increase geometrically defendant's potential liability and the tactical complexity of their defenses long after the statute of limitations has run. *See Leachman v. Beech Aircraft Corp.*, 694 F.2d 1301, 1309 (D.C. Cir. 1982). In these cases, the courts have imposed requirements for relation back approximating those of Rule 15(c)(1)(C). *See, e.g., Andujar v. Rogowski*, 113 F.R.D. 151 (S.D.N.Y. 1986).

[389] *But see Arroyo v. Pleasant Garden Apartments*, 14 F. Supp. 2d 696 (D.N.J. 1998) (finding that state law forbidding relation back of amendment adding parties is controlling under *Erie* (see § 7.04, *supra*), despite Rule 15(c)(1)(C)). Because this rule is "arguably procedural," commentators have argued that it should prevail over inconsistent state law and most courts have so ruled. *See* Moore § 15.20[2] (citing cases). On the other hand, its effect on the state's substantive law of limitations might be thought sufficient to raise a question whether it runs afoul of the Rules Enabling Act.

[390] *See, e.g., Grooms v. Greyhound Corp.*, 287 F.2d 95 (6th Cir. 1961) (amendment to change name from "Pennsylvania Greyhound Lines, Inc." to "The Greyhound Corporation"); *Clark v. S. Ry. Co.*, 87 F.R.D. 356 (N.D. Ill. 1980) (amendment to change name from "Southern Railway Systems" to "Southern Railway Company").

[391] 211 N.E.2d 72 (Ohio Ct. App. 1965).

for example, the plaintiff timely sued the Isaly Dairy Company of Pittsburgh, a corporation maintaining the same address as the proper defendant, the Isaly Dairy Company, and served a common officer of both corporations. The court held that an amendment to name the proper defendant related back because the intermingling of the corporations gave the impression that they were one and the same. The rationale is both imputed notice and equitable estoppel.[392]

Rule 15(c)(1)(C) takes an approach in some respects broader and in some respects narrower than that suggested by these exceptions. Under the rule, an amendment changing the parties relates back if (1) it asserts a claim arising out of the same conduct, transaction, or occurrence set out in the original pleading, and (2) within the 120-day period provided by Rule 4(m) for service of process,[393] the party added by amendment (3) received such notice of the institution of the action that he would not be prejudiced in defending on the merits and (4) knew or should have known that the action would originally have been brought against him, but for a mistake in identity of the proper party.

The first requirement is the core transactional relationship requirement for any relation back, and the third and fourth requirements encompass most misnomer and identity of interests cases, although they are not confined to them. The second requirement was revised in 1991 to change the result reached by the Supreme Court in *Schiavone v. Fortune*.[394] Under the prior version of Rule 15(c), the party added by amendment had to receive the requisite notice "within the period provided by law." *Schiavone* posed the question whether the "period provided by law" referred literally only to the applicable limitations period or whether it included any reasonable period tacked on for service of the complaint as well.[395] The Court ruled that it referred only to the limitations period, even though the original complaint was filed within the limitations period and the amended party had received the notice of the filing within the 120-day period provided by Rule 4 for service of process. The 1991 amendment to Rule 15(c) clearly changes this result by expressly adding that 120-day period to the period within which the amended party must receive the requisite notice of the institution of the original action.[396]

The Supreme Court considered the application of the amended rule in *Krupski v. Costa Crociere S.p.A.*[397] Krupski was injured on a cruise ship and filed a timely

---

[392] The estoppel theory extends beyond the identity of interests case to any case in which the proper defendant has lulled plaintiff into suing the wrong defendant. *See Zielinski v. Philadelphia Piers, Inc.,* 139 F. Supp. 408 (E.D. Pa. 1956), *discussed in* § 8.08[1] (denials) *supra. See generally* WRIGHT & MILLER § 1500.

[393] *See* § 4.03[2], *supra.*

[394] 477 U.S. 21 (1986).

[395] *See* § 8.08[2][b] (statute of limitations), *supra.* The question arose under statutes that provide that the limitations period is tolled by filing of the complaint, provided that service is perfected within some additional number of days or "tail period" after filing. *See Ingram v. Kumar,* 585 F.2d 566 (2d Cir. 1978), *cert. denied,* 440 U.S. 940 (1979) (relation back permitted when service is accomplished within a reasonable time allowed under the federal rules for service of process but after the period has run).

[396] *See, e.g., Worthington v. Wilson,* 790 F. Supp. 829 (C.D. Ill. 1992).

[397] 130 S. Ct. 2485 (2010). *See generally* Robert A. Lusardi, *Rule 15(C) Mistake: The Supreme Court in* Krupski *Seeks to Resolve a Judicial Thicket,* 49 U. LOUISVILLE L. REV. 317 (2011).

complaint against "Costa Cruise Lines." The defendant answered, denying that the named defendant was a proper defendant, ultimately seeking summary judgment on this basis. Before the district court ruled on this motion, but after the relevant limitations period had expired, Krupski moved for leave to amend her complaint to add as a defendant "Costa Crociere S.p.A.," the entity with the capacity to be sued. Did her amended complaint relate back to her timely original complaint?

The timing of notice posed no real problem. Costa Crociere had at least "constructive notice" from service of the original complaint on its agent within the period of limitations.[398] Notice of the original complaint itself is the best "notice of the action," but the Advisory Committee's notes to the rule state that notice "need not be formal."[399] For example, a letter from the mistakenly named defendant to the proper one advising of the pendency of the lawsuit, and warning of the possibility that the latter might be drawn into the lawsuit, has been held sufficient.[400] Often notice of the original action is imputed through a shared agent or attorney, and sometimes through shared (identity of) interests.[401] On the other hand, a mere demand letter threatening to sue has been held insufficient.[402]

The more difficult question was whether Costa Crociere — the "new" party — "knew or should have known that the action would have been brought against it, but for a mistake concerning the proper "party's identity." The Court held, first, that the question is what the new party knew or should have known, not what Krupski knew. Second, because Krupski's complaint showed clearly that she meant to sue the company that "owned, operated, managed, supervised and controlled" the ship, Costa Crociere should have known that she meant to sue it but for her "misunderstanding about which 'Costa' entity was in charge of the ship."[403]

But was her "misunderstanding" of the Costa entities' capacity to be sued a "mistake" within the meaning of Rule 15(c)(1)C)? "The classic example of mistake is misnomer,"[404] when plaintiff names the right party by the wrong name (using trade name instead of corporate name, naming subsidiary instead of parent, or even simply misspelling the name). In such cases, the "correct" defendant is actually served and should know that, but for plaintiff's misnomer, the action would have been brought against it, so it suffers no prejudice from relation back. On the other hand, the Court stated in *Krupski* that a party's "deliberate choice to sue one party over another . . . is the antithesis of making a mistake concerning the proper party's identity."[405] Thus, if a plaintiff sues deep-pocket defendant X and deliberately chooses not to join prospective defendant Y because it thinks Y has no assets,

---

[398] 130 S. Ct. at 2497.

[399] Rule 15(c) advisory committee's notes (1966).

[400] *Loveall v. Employer Health Servs., Inc.*, 196 F.R.D. 399 (D. Kan. 2000).

[401] 266 F.3d at 196–200. It was the identity of interests between the "Costa" entities that led the district court to find constructive notice to the right Costa from the original service on the wrong Costa. *See Krupski v. Costa Crociere S.p.A.*, 2008 U.S. Dist. LEXIS 112213, at *10 (S.D. Fla. Oct. 21, 2008).

[402] *See Schrader v. Royal Caribbean Cruise Line, Inc.*, 952 F.2d 1008, 1012–13 (8th Cir. 1991).

[403] 130 S. Ct. at 2497.

[404] *Moore* § 15.19[3][d].

[405] 130 S. Ct. at 2494.

the plaintiff cannot later, after the statute of limitations runs, change its mind and amend to add Y. The plaintiff is stuck with its deliberate choice of defendants because it was not a mistake. The Court held that Krupski had not made this kind of choice. Even if Krupski knew of the existence of both "Costa" entities, she did not make a *tactical* choice among possible defendants. Instead, she mistakenly thought that the wrong one was the legally responsible company. The Court held that this kind of mistake qualified for relation back under the rule.

Its analysis still leaves it unclear whether another kind of deliberate choice could also qualify. For example, in *Singletary v. Pennsylvania Department of Corrections*,[406] the plaintiff had sued certain "John Doe" defendants, and then sought to replace them with real names when he learned them after the limitations period had run. The court of appeals held that his amendment substituting the real names related back, even though his failure to name them in the original complaint stemmed from lack of knowledge, not a mistake. The court acknowledged case law denying relation back in similar "John Doe" situations,[407] but reasoned that allowing it was consistent with the policy of the rule, as long as the named defendant also received the notice required by the rule. The Supreme Court's approval in *Krupski* of "deliberate but mistaken" choices of defendants does not necessarily cover this "deliberate but ignorant" choice of fictitious "place-holder" defendants.[408]

Finally, Costa Crociere also argued that relation back should have been denied because Krupski delayed too long from when she was served with its answer until she filed her motion to amend. The Court said that a plaintiff's diligence is not one of the requirements for relation back listed in Rule 15(c)(1)(C), but should instead be considered separately under Rule 15(a)(2) in deciding leave to amend. It then found that she had not delayed too long. The Court's ruling is a reminder that Rules 15(a) and 15(c)(1)(C) involve distinct inquiries, although they overlap to the extent that the denial of relation back makes amendment futile and that both require consideration of prejudice to the opposing party.

[c] Responding to Amendment

The Supreme Court has also reminded us that the propriety of amendment depends not only on "the state of affairs prior to amendment" — presumably including the reasons for and timing of the amendment — "but also on what happens afterwards."[409] Because amendment may change the claims or defenses asserted against a party, the rule directs that she be given at least fourteen days to respond.[410] This can apply even to amendments after trial. In *Nelson v. Adams, USA, Inc.*,[411] the district court amended a judgment to add a new (though closely

---

[406] 266 F.3d 186 (3d Cir. 2001).

[407] *See* Moore § 15.19[3][d] (noting that most courts have held that plaintiff's lack of knowledge of identity of defendant does not constitute mistake).

[408] *See* Howard Wasserman, *Belated Thoughts on Relating Back*, Prawfsblawg (June 10, 2010), http://prawfsblawg.blogs.com/prawfsblawg/2010/06/belated-thoughts-on-relation-back.html.

[409] *Nelson v. Adams, USA, Inc.*, 529 U.S. 460, 466 (2000).

[410] Rule 15(a)(3).

[411] 529 U.S. 460 (2000).

affiliated) party without giving him an opportunity to respond and the court of appeals affirmed, finding no prejudice. The Supreme Court reversed, holding that the new party was entitled to be served with the amendment and to respond, unless he had consented to the amendment. In dictum, it added that the same is true for amendments that relate back.

§ 8.11 A CONCLUDING NOTE ON COMMON SENSE IN PLEADING

Professor Moore once said that "what was a good pleading before [the federal rules] continues to be good pleading" today.[412] By this assertion, he was stating more than the uninteresting truism that the federal rules are no more demanding than code pleading or the common law. He was also emphasizing that good pleading, as distinguished from technically sufficient pleading, obeys the rules of common sense and good practice, as well as the formal procedural rules of the jurisdiction.

For example, despite the rejection of the doctrine of the theory of the pleadings in modern jurisdictions, no competent attorney files a pleading without having formulated a primary legal theory of recovery or defense.[413] Ordinarily, the attorney formulates that theory after preliminary factual investigation of her client's story and initial legal research into alternative legal theories available in the jurisdiction. She then drafts her pleadings to reflect at least the primary theory of recovery or defense. She may also include alternative theories as well, as a precaution against dismissal and factual surprises during discovery.

Moreover, she ordinarily will plead each and every element of her legal theories. Less might suffice, but the complaint is intended not only to give minimal notice that would survive motions to dismiss, but also to create impressions in the minds of the defendant and the judge. A full complaint helps educate the defendant about his potential exposure in the litigation and to prepare him for settlement negotiations. It also helps justify the judge's investment of time in the action. Furthermore, a full complaint can provide the plaintiff's first discovery; "a plaintiff who includes rifle-shot allegations may be rewarded with precise admissions and denials that advance the case."[414]

Common sense also cautions against pleading or motion practice aimed at trapping, surprising, or delaying your opponent. The pleader who seeks to divert the parties and the court from the merits more often than not succeeds only in alienating them, and in encouraging satellite litigation culminating in sanctions under amended Rule 11 or its state counterpart. The pay-off from deploying modern pleading rules in service of functions for which they were not intended is rarely worth the effort. Real pay-offs lie in marrying the persuasive power of careful pleading with effective discovery, well-researched and analyzed legal theories, and

---

[412] JAMES W. MOORE, MOORE'S FEDERAL PRACTICE § 8.02 (2d ed. 1979).

[413] See WRIGHT & MILLER § 1219.

[414] Richard L. Marcus, *The Puzzling Persistence of Pleading Practice*, 76 TEX. L. REV. 1749, 1768 (1998).

a thorough practical understanding of the parties' willingness and ability to litigate the merits.

The rules of pleading — like all rules of procedure — are never a substitute for common sense. They are just a framework within which it must be applied.

§ 8.12 PLEADINGS IN THE CALIFORNIA COURTS

[1] Introduction to California Code Pleading

California is often referred to as a "code pleading" state. California's pleading system derives from the Field Code reforms of the mid-19th century. The Field Code abolished the common law forms of action, merged law and equity, limited the types of pleadings and the effects of technical errors, and required pleading only the "facts constituting the cause of action."[415] California remains nominally a "code pleading" state, but this reference is somewhat misleading. The California courts have liberalized many of the code pleading requirements and even adopted some aspects of notice pleading.

By statute, only four types of pleadings are allowed in civil actions in the California courts: complaints, demurrers, answers, and cross-complaints.[416] (Although technically considered a pleading, the procedural rules generally treat a demurrer like a motion.) Each of these pleadings is discussed in more detail below.

[2] The Complaint

[a] Pleading Ultimate Facts

California Code of Civil Procedure section 425.10(a) requires the complaint to contain "a statement of the facts constituting the cause of action, in ordinary and concise language." Two issues are present in evaluating the sufficiency of a complaint, and by analogy any pleading in California's pleading system. Since the complaint must contain "a statement of the *facts* constituting the *cause of action*," it must be both formally sufficient — the "facts" must be in the appropriate style of "ultimate facts" — and these facts must present each of the elements of one or more "causes of action." Under traditional code pleading, the pleader can err by being either too general — pleading conclusions of law — or too specific — pleading evidence. However, the California courts have relaxed these requirements. Case law reflects a reduced concern with pleading ultimate facts in precisely the correct format. Although the elements of a cause of action must be present in a pleading, if the allegations give sufficient notice of plaintiff's factual theory, this is usually sufficient.[417]

---

[415] *See* CAL. CODE CIV. PROC. §§ 307, 422.10, 425.10, 475. Code pleading under the Field Code is discussed in more detail in § 8.03, *supra.*

[416] CAL. CODE CIV. PROC. § 422.10.

[417] *See, e.g.,* Leet v. Union P. R. Co., 25 Cal. 2d 605, 619, 155 P.2d 42 (1944) (observing fairness in pleading is to give the defendant such notice by the complaint that he may prepare his case); *Holmes v. Cal. Nat. Guard,* 90 Cal. App. 4th 297, 314, 109 Cal. Rptr. 2d 154 (2001) (finding complaint adequate

The oft-cited opinion in *Semole v. Sansoucie*[418] illustrates California's modern approach to code pleading. The plaintiffs in *Semole* filed a wrongful death complaint against the defendant, a fellow employee of their deceased son, seeking damages for their son's death that occurred while he was working. The California Labor Code authorizes such a cause of action, but only if the death was caused by a fellow employee's act "which evinces a reckless disregard for the safety of the employee injured and a calculated and conscious willingness to permit injury or death to such employee." The plaintiffs' complaint alleged that the defendant failed to inspect the area into which he was backing a tractor and trailer and, using the very words of the Labor Code, further alleged that the defendant operated the vehicle "in a reckless disregard for the safety and calculated and conscious willingness to permit injury or death" to fellow employees. The defendant filed a general demurrer — the California equivalent of a motion to dismiss for failure to state a claim — objecting that this allegation lacked factual content and should be disregarded as merely a conclusion of law. The trial court sustained the demurrer, and plaintiffs appealed.

The California Court of Appeal ruled that the plaintiffs' "complaint, though hardly a model of pleading, stated a cause of action." Quoting from several prior decisions, the *Semole* court explained that under the California pleading standards the allegations of the complaint must be liberally construed with a view to attaining substantial justice among the parties: "we assume the truth of all properly pleaded material allegations of the complaint and give it a reasonable interpretation by reading it as a whole and its parts in their context." The court then set forth the following pleading standard:

> The [California] Supreme Court has consistently stated the guideline that "a plaintiff is required only to set forth the essential facts of his case with reasonable precision and with particularity sufficient to acquaint a defendant with the nature, source and extent of his cause of action." It has also been stated that "[the] particularity required in pleading facts depends on the extent to which the defendant in fairness needs detailed information that can be conveniently provided by the plaintiff; less particularity is required where the defendant may be assumed to have knowledge of the facts equal to that possessed by the plaintiff."[419]

As to the defendant's contention that by using the language of the Labor Code the plaintiff's key allegation was a conclusion of law and not one of ultimate fact, the *Semole* court responded that the "conclusion of law-ultimate fact" dichotomy is not an absolute pleading principle. Instead, "the fair import of language used in the pleading must be received to determine whether the adversary has been fairly apprised of the factual basis of the claim against him." In endorsing this "fairly apprised" standard, the court noted that the modern discovery procedures necessarily affect the amount of detail that should be required in a pleading.

---

because it put defendants on notice of the nature of plaintiff(s claims); *Estate of Archer*, 193 Cal. App. 3d 238, 245, 239 Cal. Rptr. 137 (1987) (ruling that a useful test for determining adequacy is whether the complaint as a whole apprises the defendant of the factual basis of the claim).

[418] 28 Cal. App. 3d 714, 104 Cal. Rptr. 897 (1972).

[419] *Semole v. Sansoucie, supra*, 28 Cal. App. 3d at 719.

[b]   Federal Court Pleading Standard Compared

For several decades, pleading a fact-based cause of action was not necessary in the federal courts as long as the pleading gives the defendant "fair notice of what the plaintiff's claim is and the grounds upon which it rests."[420] However, two recent United States Supreme Court decisions construing federal Rule 8(a)(2), *Bell Atlantic Corp. v. Twombly*[421] and *Ashcroft v. Iqbal*,[422] disapproved of this traditional "notice" pleading approach. Instead, the Supreme Court adopted the following new standard for federal courts: To survive a motion to dismiss for failure to state a claim, a complaint must contain sufficient factual matter, accepted as true, to "state a claim to relief that is plausible on its face." "A claim has facial plausibility," the Supreme Court explained, "when the plaintiff pleads factual content that allows the court to draw the reasonable inference that the defendant is liable for the misconduct alleged." Under this standard, a federal court considering a motion to dismiss must first disregard conclusory allegations in a complaint because they are not entitled to the assumption of truth, and then determine whether well-pleaded factual allegations — whose veracity is assumed for purposes of the motion — plausibly give rise to an entitlement to relief in light of the elements of the claim.[423]

Ironically, the new federal pleading standard may require more fact-based pleading than does the current California standard. For example, the complaint in *Semole* — whose allegation of an essential element of the wrongful death cause of action simply repeated the relevant statutory language — may not have survived a demurrer if the California court had applied the new federal standard. Once that conclusory allegation is disregarded, the remaining factual allegations in the *Semole* complaint would likely not have stated a cause of action under the "reckless and willful" liability standard. Moreover, unlike the court in *Semole*, the United States Supreme Court in *Twombly* and *Iqbal* did not relax the plaintiffs' fact-pleading obligation, even though in each of those cases the facts necessary to support an essential element of the relevant cause of action were in the sole possession of, and known only to, the defendants.

[c]   Heightened Specificity Requirements in Pleading

In addition to its generally higher standard of factual specificity, code pleading, like notice pleading, requires heightened specificity for certain types of disfavored causes of action. For example, causes of action based on fraud must be specifically pleaded. Each of the elements of fraud — false representation of a material fact, knowledge of its falsity, intent to defraud, justifiable reliance, and resulting damage — must be alleged in full, factually and specifically.[424] However, less specificity is

---

[420] *Conley v. Gibson*, 355 U.S. 41 (1957).

[421] 550 U.S. 544 (2007).

[422] 556 U.S. 662 (2009).

[423] *Ashcroft v. Iqbal, supra*, 556 U.S. at 678–79. The Supreme Court explained that "[w]hile legal conclusions can provide the framework of a complaint, they must be supported by factual allegations." *Id.* at 678. The new federal plausibility standard is discussed in more detail in § 8.04[1][d], *supra*.

[424] *See, e.g., Small v. Fritz Companies, Inc.*, 30 Cal. 4th 167, 183–85, 132 Cal. Rptr. 2d 490, 65 P.3d 1255 (2003); *Stansfield v. Starkey*, 220 Cal. App. 3d 59, 72–73, 269 Cal. Rptr. 337 (1990) (ruling that in

required where the allegations show defendant must necessarily possess full information concerning the facts of the controversy. For example, in *Committee on Children's Television, Inc. v. General Foods Corp.*,[425] the California Supreme Court held that a complaint alleging deceptive advertising with respect to sugared breakfast cereals was sufficiently specific because defendants had more ready access to the information — the actual broadcast advertisements — and pleading complete details of each advertisement, the identity of the speaker and listener, and specifying its time, place, and medium would be impractical.

[d]   Special Pleading Rules for Punitive Damages

California statutes impose numerous procedural and substantive restrictions on claims for punitive damages, including a pre-pleading hurdle for plaintiffs in medical malpractice actions.[426] Before a medical malpractice plaintiff can even *plead* a claim for punitive damages, she must first demonstrate to the trial court, via affidavits containing specific facts, that there is a "substantial probability" that she will prevail on the punitive damages claim. This pre-pleading hurdle does not authorize the trial court to weigh the evidence or assess its relative strength, but does require the plaintiff to show that she possesses a legally sufficient claim for punitive damages which is supported by competent, admissible evidence.[427] A plaintiff will not be permitted to amend the complaint to include a punitive damages claim unless the court is satisfied the plaintiff has made the required statutory showing.

[3]   Inconsistent and Alternative Pleading

The general rule in California is that a pleader may assert inconsistent allegations subject to certain good faith limitations.[428] Where the exact nature of the facts is in doubt, or where the exact legal nature of the plaintiff's right and defendant's liability depend on facts not well known to the plaintiff, the pleadings may properly set forth alternative theories in varied and inconsistent counts. However, a party cannot both assert and deny a fact that that party must know.

---

alleging fraud against a corporation, plaintiff must allege "the names of the persons who made the allegedly fraudulent representations, their authority to speak, to whom they spoke, what they said or wrote, and when it was said or written"); *Wilhelm v. Pray, Price, Williams & Russell*, 186 Cal. App. 3d 1324, 231 Cal. Rptr. 355 (1986) (holding complaint which failed to specifically plead factual basis for knowledge of falsity and justifiable reliance did not to state fraud cause of action).

[425]   35 Cal. 3d 197, 197 Cal. Rptr. 783, 673 P.2d 660 (1983).

[426]   Cal. Code Civ. Proc. § 425.13.

[427]   *College Hosp., Inc. v. Superior Court*, 8 Cal. 4th 704, 715–22, 34 Cal. Rptr. 2d 898, 882 P.2d 894 (1994) (examining the facts alleged in the amended complaint and the evidence from plaintiffs' declarations and deposition testimony submitted in support of these allegations and concluding that no basis appears for assessing punitive damages against the defendant hospital and that the plaintiffs failed to satisfy the requirements of section 425.13(a) when they sought to plead a punitive damages claim against the hospital).

[428]   *Rader Co. v. Stone*, 178 Cal. App. 3d 10, 233 Cal. Rptr. 806 (1986) (holding plaintiff not precluded from alleging in one cause of action the breach of a contract and an inconsistent theory of recovery in another case of action); *Lawson v. Superior Court*, 180 Cal. App. 4th 1372, 1385, n.13, 103 Cal. Rptr. 3d 934 (2010) ("A plaintiff may plead inconsistent facts and legal theories in alternative counts.").

For example, a breach of contract action is not properly pleaded where the plaintiff generally alleges satisfaction of conditions precedent but also alleges facts which demonstrate these conditions were not fully performed.[429]

These rules carry through to trial. Neither party is required generally to make an election when introducing evidence.[430] (However, from a tactical standpoint, a party may decide to select one theory of the case so as not to confuse the fact-finder.) The California rule regarding inconsistent pleadings is similar to Rules 8(d)(2) & (3) of the Federal Rules of Civil Procedure, which permit a party in federal court to "set out two or more statements of a claim or defense alternatively or hypothetically," and to state "as many separate claims or defenses as it has, regardless of consistency."

[4] Prayer for Relief

A defective prayer for relief, or even the entire lack of a prayer, does not make a complaint subject to demurrer so long as the averments in the complaint state a cause of action. Likewise, the averments contained in the pleading determine the maximum sum which may be awarded the plaintiff in a contested action; the prayer of the pleading is not controlling. For example, in one case, the plaintiff was awarded compensatory damages in excess of those requested in the prayer for relief, and the complaint was never amended to conform to the proof offered at trial. Because the parties actually tried issues of damages in amounts beyond those stated in the complaint, the court held that the relief granted was consistent with the issues made by the complaint and voluntarily tried by the parties.[431] The same result would occur in federal court under Rule 15(b)(2) of the Federal Rules of Civil Procedure, which provides that when an issue not raised by the pleadings is tried by the parties' consent, it must be treated as if raised by the pleadings.

[5] Statement of Damages in Personal Injury Actions

One of the peculiarities of California pleading is that a complaint in an action seeking to recover actual or punitive damages for personal injury or wrongful death must *not* state the amount of the damages sought.[432] Instead, the nature and amount of damages must be stated in a separate (and private) "statement of damages" which, even if not requested by the defendant, must be served on the defendant before trial or default.[433] The purpose of this confidential statement of damages is to avoid publicizing inflated claims against defendants, particularly

---

[429] *See, e.g., Careau & Co. v. Sec. Pac.*, 222 Cal. App. 3d 1371, 272 Cal. Rptr. 387 (1990).

[430] In *Shepard & Morgan v. Lee & Daniel, Inc.*, 31 Cal. 3d 256, 182 Cal. Rptr. 351, 643 P.2d 968 (1982), the California Supreme Court confirmed that the plaintiff in a civil action cannot be forced to choose between two or more inconsistent causes of action; instead, the plaintiff is entitled to introduce evidence upon all such causes and submit to the trier of fact the question as to which, if any, counts are sustained by the proof.

[431] *Castaic Clay Mfg. Co. v. Dedes*, 195 Cal. App. 3d 444, 449–50, 240 Cal. Rptr. 652 (1987).

[432] Cal. Code Civ. Proc. § 425.10; *see also* Cal. Code Civ. Proc. § 425.115 (statement preserving right to seek punitive damages).

[433] Cal. Code Civ. Proc. § 425.11.

health care providers. Failure to properly serve this statement may invalidate a judgment even where the defendant was apprised by other pretrial communications of the amount sought by the plaintiff.[434]

[6]   California's "Truth in Pleadings" Statutes

In 1981, the California Legislature passed Code of Civil Procedure § 128.5, which authorized trial courts to order a party or the party's attorney to pay any reasonable expenses, including attorney's fees, incurred by another party as a result of *"bad faith actions or tactics* that are frivolous or solely intended to cause unnecessary delay."[435] Section 128.5 has had very little impact because, to be considered frivolous, a bad faith action or tactic had to be totally and completely without merit or for the sole purpose of harassing an opposing party. As a result of this and other limitations, in 1994 the Legislature added a new section 128.7, which is patterned directly on Rule 11 of the Federal Rules of Civil Procedure.[436]

The heart of this statute, section 128.7(b), imposes on the attorney or party a series of "certifications" any time the attorney or party makes a "presentation" to the court. These include that, "after an inquiry reasonable under the circumstances," the pleading or other court paper is (1) not being presented primarily for an improper purpose, (2) the claims, defenses, and other legal contentions therein are "warranted by existing law or by a nonfrivolous argument for the extension, modification, or reversal of existing law or the establishment of new law," (3) the allegations and other factual contentions have "evidentiary support or, if specifically so identified, are likely to have evidentiary support after a reasonable opportunity for further investigation or discovery," and (4) the denials of factual contentions are "warranted on the evidence or, if specifically so identified, are reasonably based on a lack of information or belief."

Like the current version of federal Rule 11, sanctions under section 128.7 are discretionary with the court, not mandatory, upon finding a violation of one of the certifications. Also like Rule 11, there is a "safe harbor" provision. A party served with a motion for section 128.7 sanctions ordinarily has 21 days in which to withdraw or correct the challenged paper before the motion is filed. If the pleading is withdrawn, the motion for sanctions may not be filed with the court. If the pleading is not withdrawn, the motion for sanctions may then be filed. Sanctions are "limited to what is sufficient to deter" repetition of the conduct. Accordingly, paying the injured party's attorneys' fees as a sanction is limited to specified circumstances and when "warranted for effective deterrence."[437]

---

[434] *See, e.g., Schwab v. Rondel Homes, Inc.*, 53 Cal. 3d 428, 280 Cal. Rptr. 83, 808 P.2d 226 (1991) (vacating default judgment for $200,000 because plaintiff did not serve defendant with a § 425.11 statement of damages); *Debbie S. v. Ray*, 16 Cal. App. 4th 193, 19 Cal. Rptr. 2d 814 (1993) (vacating default judgment after defendant failed to appear at trial because plaintiff failed to serve a statement of damages within 60 days of trial as required by § 425.11).

[435] CAL. CODE CIV. PROC. § 128.5(a) (emphasis added).

[436] Federal Rule 11 is discussed in detail in § 8.05, *supra*.

[437] CAL. CODE CIV. PROC. § 128.7(d).

Generally, if a plaintiff's complaint is dismissed during the 21-day safe harbor period, either voluntarily or involuntarily, the trial court no longer has the authority to award section 128.7 sanctions.[438] As one appellate court astutely observed, allowing a party to serve and file a sanctions motion after the conclusion of the case would completely defeat the purpose of the safe harbor provision which is to deter frivolous filings, not to punish parties, by allowing the offending party to avoid sanctions by correcting the sanctionable conduct after being alerted to the violation.[439]

[7] Amendments to Pleadings in the California Courts

[a] Liberal Amendment Policy

The California courts will ordinarily exercise liberality in permitting amendments to pleadings at any stage of the proceedings.[440] Code of Civil Procedure § 473 provides that "in furtherance of justice" a trial court may allow a party to amend its pleadings and, if necessary, postpone trial. Whether an amendment should be allowed rests in the sound discretion of the trial court. Two primary factors are relevant to the determination of whether to permit an amended complaint: whether the plaintiff has unreasonably delayed the presentation of the motion to amend, and whether this delay has resulted in substantial prejudice to the defendant.[441] Some courts apply these factors pragmatically to permit an amendment unless it will unfairly surprise, and thereby unduly prejudice, the defendant in preparation for trial.[442] The most important inquiry to these courts is whether as a result of pretrial discovery, the defendant is already prepared to respond to the new allegations in the proposed amendment.

[b] Amendments to Conform to Proof

The California decisional and statutory law on the subject of variances is extremely liberal in allowing amendments to conform to proof. The objective is to avoid the use of technicalities to defeat recovery by a plaintiff who has pleaded, no

---

[438] *See, e.g., Hart v. Avetoom*, 95 Cal. App. 4th 410, 115 Cal. Rptr. 2d 511 (2002); *Malovec v. Hamrell*, 70 Cal. App. 4th 434, 82 Cal. Rptr. 2d 712 (1999).

[439] *Hart v. Avetoom, supra*, 95 Cal. App. 4th at 414–15 ("It is difficult to imagine a more 'appropriate correction' than voluntary dismissal."); *but see Eichenbaum v. Alon*, 106 Cal. App. 4th 967, 131 Cal. Rptr. 2d 296 (2003) (noting the availability of § 128.7 sanctions against an offending plaintiff who has voluntarily dismissed his action depends upon whether the sanctions motion was filed before or after dismissal).

[440] *E.g., Hulsey v. Koehler*, 218 Cal. App. 3d 1150, 1159, 267 Cal. Rptr. 523 (1990); *California Cas. Gen. Ins. Co. v. Superior Court*, 173 Cal. App. 3d 274, 279, 218 Cal. Rptr. 817 (1985).

[441] *See* Walter W. Heiser, *Relation Back of Amended Complaints: The California Courts Should Adopt a More Pragmatic Approach*, 44 Santa Clara L. Rev. 643, 647–60 (2004) (discussing numerous cases). These same factors, unreasonable delay and prejudice to the other party, inform a trial court's discretion to allow an amended answer. *Hulsey v. Koehler, supra*, 218 Cal. App. 3d at 1159; *Permalab-Metalab Equip. Corp. v. Maryland Cas. Co.*, 25 Cal. App. 3d 465, 472, 102 Cal. Rptr. 26 (1972).

[442] *See, e.g., Mesler v. Bragg Mgmt. Co.*, 39 Cal. 3d 290, 297, 216 Cal. Rptr. 443, 702 P.2d 601 (1985); *Honig v. Fin. Corp. of America*, 6 Cal. App. 4th 960, 965–66, 7 Cal. Rptr. 2d 922 (1992); *see also* Heiser, *Relation Back of Amended Complaints, supra* at 650–56 (collecting cases).

matter how unskillfully, sufficient facts to warrant recovery from a defendant. Where recovery is sought "on the same general set of facts" as pled in the complaint, and there is no prejudice to opposing party, an amendment to conform to the evidence will be granted even though the amendment gives rise to a separate and distinct cause of action.[443] However, where a party alleges facts amounting to one cause of action and the evidence sets forth an entirely separate set of facts constituting a different cause of action from the one pled, the result is not an immaterial variance but a failure of proof. For example, when a cause of action is based on one contract and the proof establishes an entirely different contract, the case is one of failure of proof; but where the written contract pleaded and the oral contract proved are essentially the same, the judgment will stand.[444]

[8] Amended Complaints and California's Relation Back Doctrine, Generally

The *relation back doctrine* permits an amended complaint to relate back to the date of the original complaint and thereby avoid a statute of limitations bar. California's relation back doctrine is the product of judge-made law and provides, in general terms, that an amended complaint relates back if it: (1) rests on the "same general set of facts" as the original complaint; and (2) refers to the "same accident," the "same injuries," and the "same offending instrumentality" as the original complaint.[445] The fact that a plaintiff's amended complaint rests on a different legal theory and states a different cause of action is irrelevant if the two complaints relate to the same general set of facts.[446] For example, in *Grudt v. City of Los Angeles*,[447] the initial complaint alleged that plaintiff's husband was wrongfully killed by the city police, and pleaded liability of the city on a theory of *respondeat superior*. The California Supreme Court held that the amended complaint alleging an additional theory of active negligence by the city in retaining employees known to be dangerous related back to the filing of the original complaint because the underlying cause of death was always the conduct of the police officers in the same shooting incident.

The vagueness of the "same general set of facts" standard makes it susceptible to inconsistent applications. For example, in *Honig v. Financial Corporation of*

---

[443] *See* CAL. CODE CIV. PROC. §§ 469, 470; *General Credit Corp. v. Pichel*, 44 Cal. App. 3d 844, 849–50, 118 Cal. Rptr. 913 (1975); *Walker v. Belvedere*, 16 Cal. App. 4th 1663, 1670, 20 Cal. Rptr. 2d 773 (1993).

[444] *Johnson v. DeWaard*, 113 Cal. App. 417, 298 P. 92 (1931); *see Fineberg v. Niekerk*, 175 Cal. App. 3d 935, 939, 221 Cal. Rptr. 106 (1985) (holding causes of action for breach of contract stated in pleading and declaratory relief sought at trial are not so different that the court cannot grant the latter relief based on the evidence actually produced at trial).

[445] *See, e.g., Smeltzley v. Nicholson Mfg. Co.*, 18 Cal. 3d 932, 934, 136 Cal. Rptr. 269, 559 P.2d 624 (1977); *Barrington v. A.H. Robins Co.*, 39 Cal. 3d 146, 216 Cal. Rptr. 405, 702 P.2d 563 (1985); *Branick v. Downey Sav. & Loan Ass'n*, 39 Cal. 4th 235, 243–44, 46 Cal. Rptr. 3d 66, 138 P.3d 214 (2006).

[446] *Austin v. Massachusetts Bonding & Ins. Co.*, 56 Cal. 2d 596, 15 Cal. Rptr. 817, 364 P.2d 681 (1961) (adopting the modern relation back rule); *Goldman v. Wilsey Foods, Inc.*, 216 Cal. App. 3d 1085, 1094, 265 Cal. Rptr. 294 (1989) (holding statutory civil rights claim for emotional distress related back to common law claim as both based upon defendant's discrimination).

[447] 2 Cal. 3d 575, 86 Cal. Rptr. 465, 468 P.2d 825 (1970).

America,[448] the court took an expansive view of this standard and held that an amended complaint alleging wrongful discharge and defamation related back to the plaintiff's original complaint alleging harassment and intimidation by the defendant employer. However, in *Lee v. Bank of America*,[449] another court held that an amended complaint alleging wrongful termination from employment did not relate back to the plaintiff's original complaint alleging wrongful demotion because it was not based on the same general set of facts. The *Lee* court found the *Honig* facts indistinguishable, but declined to follow *Honig* because it was not faithful to the traditional relation back doctrine.

[a] The "Same Accident" and "Same Instrumentality" Requirements

The California Supreme Court's decision in *Barrington v. A.H. Robins Co.*,[450] demonstrates how the "same accident" and "same offending instrumentality" requirements limit relation back. The plaintiff in *Barrington* filed suit against her doctor, the manufacturer of Darvon, and several fictitious ("Doe")[451] defendants, alleging medical malpractice and negligent failure to warn of the dangers involved in taking the drug. Plaintiff subsequently substituted A.H. Robins Company for one of the fictitious defendants, and filed an amended complaint alleging a new cause of action against Robins. This new cause alleged that the instrument causing her injury was a defective Dalkan Shield intrauterine device manufactured by Robins. The California Supreme Court concluded that the amended complaint did not relate back because the new cause of action in the amended complaint involved separate and distinct "offending instrumentalities" and "accidents."

The original complaint alleged that the offending instrumentality was the doctor's negligent medical treatment and the failure of the doctor and the Darvon manufacturer to warn of the dangers involved in taking the prescription drug Darvon. The alleged accident was her ingestion of that drug. By contrast, the amended complaint alleged that the offending instrumentality was a defective and unsafe Dalkon Shield designed, manufactured, and sold by Robins. The alleged accident was tubal-ovarian abscesses and an infection resulting from her use of the Dalkon Shield.

Likewise, the amended complaint in *Coronet Manufacturing Co. v. Superior Court*,[452] a wrongful death action, did not relate back and was barred by the applicable statute of limitations. The original complaint alleged death from electrocution by a hairdryer, but the amended complaint changed the cause of death to

---

[448] 6 Cal. App. 4th 960, 7 Cal. Rptr. 2d 922 (1992).

[449] 27 Cal. App. 4th 197, 32 Cal. Rptr. 2d 388 (1994).

[450] 39 Cal. 3d 146, 216 Cal. Rptr. 405, 702 P.2d 563 (1985).

[451] *Introductory Note on Fictitious ("Doe") Defendants.* The relation back doctrine often applies to amended complaints which not only allege new causes of action, but also substitute new actual defendants for ones named fictitiously as placeholder or "Doe" defendants in the original complaint. Because of the unique nature of California's "Doe" defendant doctrine and its importance in California civil litigation, such use of the relation back doctrine to extend applicable statutes of limitations is discussed in detail in § 8.13, *infra*.

[452] 90 Cal. App. 3d 342, 153 Cal. Rptr. 366 (1979).

electrocution by a table lamp. The court concluded that although both pleadings related to a single death at a single location, they alleged different accidents and involved different offending instrumentalities.

[b] The "Same Injury" Requirement

Even where an amended complaint refers to the "same accident" and "same offending instrumentality" as the original complaint, the amended complaint will not relate back unless it also alleges the "same injury."[453] For example, an amended complaint seeking recovery of personal injury damages caused by an automobile accident will not relate back to an original complaint seeking property damages caused by the same accident, because the amended complaint does not seek recovery for the "same injury."[454]

The "same injury" requirement is ambiguous. A more fundamental criticism is that it makes California's a relation back doctrine more restrictive than that utilized by the federal courts and by the vast majority of other jurisdictions. The reasons for this requirement are largely historical and likely based on out-dated restrictions on code pleading and joinder of claims.[455] It also appears to rely on the "primary rights" theory used to define a "cause of action" for purposes of California's res judicata (claim preclusion) doctrine, and therefore to resurrect the traditional "same cause of action" restriction on relation back seemingly rejected years ago by the California Supreme Court.[456] Nonetheless, the "same injury" requirement is frequently repeated by the California courts and should be considered a relevant component of California's modern relation back doctrine.

[c] Federal Rule 15(c)(1)(B) Compared

By requiring an amended complaint to refer to the "same injury" in addition to the "same general set of facts," the California relation back rule is more restrictive than its federal counterpart under Rule 15(c)(1)(B) of the Federal Rules of Civil Procedure, which authorizes relation back in federal court when the amended complaint refers to the "same conduct, transaction, or occurrence" set out in the original pleading. For example, assume in our car crash example that the plaintiff files a timely complaint against the defendant seeking recovery of property damages to plaintiff's vehicle. After the statute of limitations has expired, the plaintiff files an amended complaint seeking personal injury damages caused by the same accident. The amended complaint would relate back to the original complaint under federal Rule 15(c)(1)(B) because they both refer to the same occurrence — the car crash — but would not relate back under the California doctrine because it

---

[453] *See, e.g., Dudley v. Dept. of Transp.*, 90 Cal. App. 4th 255, 266, 108 Cal. Rptr. 2d 739 (2001); *Goldman v. Wilsey Foods, Inc.*, 216 Cal. App. 3d 1085, 1094, 265 Cal. Rptr. 294 (1989); *Rowland v. Superior Court*, 171 Cal. App. 3d 1214, 217 Cal. Rptr. 786 (1985).

[454] *See Sidney v. Superior Court*, 198 Cal. App. 3d 710, 717, n.4, 244 Cal. Rptr. 31 (1988).

[455] *See* Heiser, *Relation Back of Amended Complaints, supra* at 660–97 (discussing and criticizing the "same accident," "same injury," and "same instrumentality" restrictions on relation back).

[456] *See Austin, supra,* 56 Cal. 2d at 610–03 (rejecting the use of same "cause of action" for the modern relation back standard); *see also* Heiser, *Relation Back of Amended Complaints, supra* at 666–68.

alleges a different injury than the original complaint.[457]

§ 8.13 CALIFORNIA'S FICTITIOUS ("DOE") DEFENDANT PRACTICE

[1] Introductory Note

The effect of California's fictitious ("Doe") defendant practice can be explained as follows: A plaintiff who timely filed a complaint against named defendants and properly alleged Doe defendants may have up to three years after the original complaint is filed to ascertain additional defendants and add them into the lawsuit by an amended complaint which substitutes the new defendant for a Doe defendant. The plaintiff must serve the amended complaint upon the new defendant within the statutory period (up to three years) for service of the original complaint. If these simple procedural hurdles are cleared, the amended complaint will relate back to the date of the original complaint as to the newly added party, for statute of limitation purposes, so long as the general relation back test is satisfied (*i.e.*, the amended complaint rests on the same general set of facts as the original complaint and refers to the same injuries).

California's "Doe defendant practice" is significantly more liberal than that recognized in other jurisdictions and in federal practice.[458] California allows a plaintiff to name as fictitious ("Doe") defendants parties whom the plaintiff has no reason to believe even exist solely as insurance against the statute of limitations bar. Designed to mitigate the harsh effects of California's short statutes of limitations, particularly in personal injury actions, California's Doe practice permits relation back to the date of the original pleading in a broad variety of circumstances unknown to the federal courts under Rule 15(1)(C) of the Federal Rules of Civil Procedure.

California's Doe defendant practice has evolved through case law interpreting three sections of the California Code of Civil Procedure: Section 474, which permits designation of a fictitious defendant the complaint when the plaintiff is ignorant of his or her true name; section 350, which states that an action is "commenced" for purposes of satisfying the statute of limitations "when the complaint is filed"; and section 583.210, which requires that a summons and complaint shall be served upon a defendant within three years after the action is commenced. The fictitious defendant doctrine is not obvious from the text of these statutes. But when infused with some creative common law interpretations, including a relation back concept, these sections provide the basis for a unique method of extending the statute of limitations.

---

[457] *See Sidney, supra*, 198 Cal. App. 3d at 710, 717, n.4.

[458] *See* James E. Hogan, *California's Unique Doe Defendant Practice: A Fiction Stranger Than Truth*, 30 Stan. L. Rev. 51, 88–101 (1977).

[2] Requirements for Use of Doe Defendant Practice

The California courts have developed five basic requirements for the use of Doe defendant practice.[459] First, the plaintiff must file the original complaint naming at least one actual defendant before the applicable statute of limitations has expired. Second, the plaintiff must be "ignorant of the name" of any defendant designated by a fictitious name in the original complaint. Third, the plaintiff must plead this ignorance in the original complaint. Fourth, the plaintiff must allege a cause of action against the fictitious defendants in the original complaint based on the same general set of facts as the cause of action later asserted against the actually named defendants in the amended complaint. Fifth, the plaintiff must serve the amended complaint naming the actual defendants on those newly named defendants within the maximum period of three years of filing of the original complaint, and make return of service within 60 days after service of the complaint and summons.

Although each of these five requirements is important for the successful use of Doe defendant practice, the one that deserves the most attention is that the plaintiff must be "ignorant of the name" of any defendant designated by a fictitious name in the original complaint. An examination of the required "ignorance" really illuminates the advantages conferred on plaintiffs by California's Doe practice. Indeed, the advantages are so significant that a prudent plaintiff should include Doe defendant allegations in *every* complaint as a precaution, even though the plaintiff does not anticipate the need to add new parties to the lawsuit at the time the original complaint is filed.

[3] Ignorance of the Defendant's "Name"

[a] Ignorance of the Defendant's Actual Name

When the plaintiff knows the defendant's general identity, but does not know his name, the plaintiff is clearly "ignorant of the name" of the defendant within the meaning of Code of Civil Procedure § 474 and can sue him as a Doe defendant. Likewise, section 474 would be applicable even if the plaintiff knows that the defendant exists, but does not know his name or even his general identity. Such limited use of fictitious defendant pleading is typical of its use in many other jurisdictions. Moreover, as the court observed in *Day v. Western Loan & Building Co.*,[460] section 474 does not require a plaintiff, when suing a fictitious defendant, to plead a description identifying the person intended to be sued. The *Day* Court also rejected the theory that only names, and not defendants, may be fictitious, and concluded that section 474 is applicable even though the plaintiff admittedly did not know the defendant's name, identity, or existence when the original complaint was filed. This broad use of "ignorance" is now established practice in the California courts.

---

[459] *See* Hogan, *California's Unique Doe Defendant Practice, supra*, at 69–87.

[460] 42 Cal. App. 2d 226, 108 P.2d 702 (1940).

[b] Ignorance of the Facts Giving Rise to the Cause of Action

A plaintiff can also utilize Doe defendant practice even when the plaintiff knew the individual's name and identity but was ignorant of the facts giving the plaintiff a cause of action against that individual at the time the original complaint was filed.[461] This often occurs where the original complaint containing Doe allegations alleges negligence theories against certain defendants and the amended complaint alleges warranty and products liability claims against newly named ones. For example, in *Streicher v. Tommy's Electric Co.*,[462] the plaintiff sued a general contractor, a subcontractor, and several fictitiously named defendants for negligently causing personal injuries he sustained when a radio-controlled overhead garage door opened unexpectedly, causing him to fall from the scaffolding where he was working. More than two years later, the plaintiff amended his complaint to add the manufacturer of the door opener and allegations that the opener was negligently designed. Although the plaintiff knew the door had opened and knew it was radio-controlled, his amended complaint was held to relate back because he did not know at the time he filed the original complaint any facts that would indicate the possibility that the door openers were defectively designed.

Likewise, in *General Motors Corp. v. Superior Court*,[463] the plaintiff driver was seriously injured when her car was rear-ended. She was wearing a seat belt that remained fastened and did not break, but which did not prevent her from striking her head on the steering wheel. Within one year, plaintiff sued the driver of the other car and several Doe defendants. More than two years after the accident, plaintiff filed an amended complaint that substituted the seat belt manufacturer, General Motors, for a Doe defendant, alleging the seat belt was defective. The California Court of Appeal held that the amended complaint related back because the plaintiff did not initially know the basic facts necessary to plead a products liability claim against the seat belt manufacturer when she filed the original complaint, and was thus entitled to substitute the manufacturer for a Doe defendant when she later learned the seat belt might have been defectively designed. The *General Motors* court reasoned that it is not commonly understood that a driver wearing a seat belt will hit his or her head on the steering wheel when the car is rear-ended only if there was something wrong with the seat belt. Where the alleged defect is not externally visible, the court explained, it may not be said that the plaintiff had actual knowledge of any fact or circumstance suggesting a defect in the manner in which the belt was designed.

---

[461] *E.g., Larson v. Barnett*, 101 Cal. App. 2d 282, 225 P.2d 297 (1950); *Barrows v. Am. Motors Corp.*, 144 Cal. App. 3d 1, 192 Cal. Rptr. 380 (1983); *Day v. West. Loan & Bldg. Co.*, 42 Cal. App. 2d 226, 108 P.2d 702 (1940).

[462] 164 Cal. App. 3d 876, 211 Cal. Rptr. 22 (1985).

[463] 48 Cal. App. 4th 580, 55 Cal. Rptr. 2d 871 (1996).

[c]   Ignorance That the Law Provides a Cause of Action

A plaintiff can also utilize Doe defendant practice in circumstances where the substantive law did not provide a cause of action against the (unnamed) defendant at the time the original complaint was filed, but subsequently changed to authorize a cause of action.[464] However, section 474 is inapplicable where the plaintiff is ignorant of the law because she simply failed to discover that the existing substantive law provided a cause of action against the defendant at the time of the original complaint.[465]

[d]   The Requirement of Actual Ignorance

As the above discussion indicates, Code of Civil Procedure § 474 has been construed quite broadly with respect to the requisite ignorance. However, as often noted by the California courts, the ignorance must be "genuine and not feigned."[466] In other words, the plaintiff must actually be "ignorant" of the defendant's true name when the original complaint is filed.[467] The California cases make it clear that a plaintiff is "ignorant" even when a reasonably diligent plaintiff could have easily determined the defendant's true name.[468] As early as 1886, the California Supreme Court rejected the argument that relation back is precluded where a plaintiff could have easily ascertained the defendant's name and existence, for example, by searching the public records before the original complaint was filed.[469] Instead, the Court held that section 474 applies when the plaintiff is actually ignorant of a certain fact, noting that "whether his ignorance is from misfortune or negligence, he is alike ignorant, and that is all the statute requires."[470]

Still, there are some limits as to how "ignorant" a plaintiff can be and still use Doe defendant practice. Where the facts indicate that the plaintiff did not possess

---

[464] *See Marasco v. Wadsworth*, 21 Cal. 3d 82, 145 Cal. Rptr. 843, 578 P.2d 90 (1978) (holding plaintiff properly deemed "ignorant of the name" of the defendant even though she knew the defendant's name and all the facts but was unaware the law gave her a cause of action against the fictitiously named defendant and discovered that right by reason of a change in the relevant law after the commencement of the action).

[465] *Von Gibson v. Estate of Lynch*, 197 Cal. App. 3d 725, 730, 243 Cal. Rptr. 50 (1988).

[466] *E.g., General Motors Corp. v. Superior Court*, 48 Cal. App. 4th 580, 594–95, 55 Cal. Rptr. 2d 871 (1996) (citing several cases); *Streicher v. Tommy's Elec. Co.*, 164 Cal. App. 3d 876, 882, 211 Cal. Rptr. 22 (1985).

[467] *See, e.g., Munoz v. Purdy*, 91 Cal. App. 3d 942, 154 Cal. Rptr. 472 (1979) (explaining that a plaintiff must actually be ignorant of the facts giving him a cause of action against a defendant, at the time of filing of the complaint); *Parker v. Robert McKee, Inc.*, 3 Cal. App. 4th 512, 4 Cal. Rptr. 2d 347 (1992) (holding section 474 applied where the plaintiff knew the defendant's name and identity, but not the capacity in which the defendant acted at the time the original complaint filed).

[468] *E.g., Marasco v. Wadsworth, supra*, 21 Cal. 3d at 88; *General Motors, supra*, 48 Cal. App. 4th 580, 596 & n.15, 55 Cal. Rptr. 2d 871 (1996) (citing several cases); *Fuller v. Tucker*, 84 Cal. App. 4th 1163, 101 Cal. Rptr. 2d 776 (2000) (holding trial court erred in finding that a medical malpractice plaintiff, who had failed to conduct a reasonable investigation to discover an anesthesiologist's name prior to filing the original complaint, was barred by the statute of limitations from amending the complaint to substitute the anesthesiologist for a Doe defendant).

[469] *Irving v. Carpentier*, 70 Cal. 23, 11 P. 391 (1886).

[470] *Irving, supra*, 70 Cal. at 26.

good faith actual ignorance of a defendant's name when the original complaint was filed, the courts have not hesitated to hold that relation back under section 474 is unavailable. For example, in one case, the plaintiff was not permitted to use section 474 to amend a prior complaint and substitute a developer for a Doe defendant where the original complaint included minutes of city council meetings that disclosed the developer's identity.[471] In another, the court held that the plaintiff could not utilize section 474 where the plaintiff's pre-lawsuit demand letter demonstrated he lacked the requisite ignorance when the original complaint was filed.[472]

[4] Policy Reason for California's Doe Defendant Practice

The California courts often state that there is no requirement in using Doe defendant practice that a plaintiff must exercise reasonable diligence in discovering either the true identity of fictitious defendants or the facts giving rise to a cause of action against such persons.[473] In contrast, the applicable statute of limitations imposes on a plaintiff the duty to exercise diligence by discovering facts and commencing an action within a specified period of time. Moreover, under California decisional law, ignorance of the legal significance of known facts or the identity of the wrongdoer will not delay the running of the statute of limitations.

At first blush, the no-duty-of-diligence standard of California's Doe defendant practice seems inconsistent with the duty-of-diligence required by the statute of limitations. However, the California courts observe that "the interjection of a discovery standard into section 474 would lead to the harmful practice in all litigation of requiring that all persons who might conceivably have some connection with the lawsuit be specifically named" in the original complaint.[474] In other words, so long as at least one actual defendant is named in a timely filed original complaint, the plaintiff need not name all other potential defendants at that time in order to avoid the statute of limitations bar. Rather than speculate and name as defendants everyone who might remotely be liable, the plaintiff can utilize formal discovery to identify other actual defendants and add them later.

This no-duty-of-diligence policy applies even after the original complaint is filed. A plaintiff is under no obligation to diligently discover either the true identity of fictitious defendants or the facts giving rise to a cause of action *after* the original complaint is filed, so long as the amended complaint adding actual defendants is filed and served within the relevant time limit for service of process.[475] However,

---

[471] *Beresford v. City of San Mateo*, 207 Cal. App. 3d 1180, 255 Cal. Rptr. 434 (1989).

[472] *Optical Surplus, Inc. v. Superior Court*, 228 Cal. App. 3d 776, 279 Cal. Rptr. 194 (1991).

[473] *See, e.g., Streicher, supra*, 164 Cal. App. 3d at 882–83; *General Motors, supra*, 48 Cal. App. 4th 580 at 596 & n.15, 55 Cal. Rptr. 2d 871 (1996); *Fuller v. Tucker, supra*, 84 Cal. App. 4th at 1172 (trial court erred in finding that a medical malpractice plaintiff, who had failed to conduct a reasonable investigation to discover an anesthesiologist's name prior to filing the original complaint, was barred by the statute of limitations from amending the complaint to substitute the anesthesiologist for a Doe defendant).

[474] *Munoz, supra*, 91 Cal. App. 3d at 947–48; *see General Motors, supra*, 48 Cal. App. 4th at 595–96 (discussing the delayed discovery rule and Doe defendant practice, and concluding that section 474 does not impose a duty of inquiry).

[475] *See, e.g., Streicher, supra*, 164 Cal. App. 3d at 882–83; *Barrows v. Am. Motors Corp.*, 144 Cal. App.

there is authority for the proposition that a plaintiff must not unreasonably delay filing the *amended* complaint after the plaintiff actually discovers the true identity of the defendant who was fictitiously named in the original complaint. Unreasonable delay in filing the amendment may bar a plaintiff's resort to the Doe defendant procedure, but only where the newly named defendant shows not just that the plaintiff was dilatory but also that the defendant suffered "specific prejudice" due to the delay and not simply the prejudice generally presumed from the policy of the statute of limitations.[476] An example of "specific prejudice" in this context is where the plaintiff waited two years after learning the defendant's identity to file the amended complaint bringing the new defendant into the case one month before trial and that defendant would have difficulties in preparing a defense on such short order.[477]

[5]   Time Limits for Service of the Amended Complaint

Under California's Doe defendant practice, the amended complaint must be served upon the newly named (actual) defendant within the statutory maximum of three years from the date of the filing of the *original* complaint. However, as a result of the various state and local "fast track" rules promulgated pursuant to the Trial Court Delay Reduction Act, the time within which to serve a complaint may as a practical matter be significantly less than three years. To ensure that trial courts do not use these rules to negate the advantages of Doe defendant practice, the Act prohibits dismissal of fictitious defendants prior to the conclusion of the introduction of evidence at trial, except on stipulation or motion of the parties.[478]

[6]   Federal Procedure Compared

Under Rule 15(c)(1)(C) of the Federal Rules of Civil Procedure, an amended complaint adding a new party may relate back only if that party had timely notice of the action (generally, within 120 days of filing of the original complaint) and knows his omission from the original complaint was due to a naming mistake by the plaintiff.[479] By contrast, California's Doe defendant practice authorizes relation back regardless of whether the newly named defendant had *any* knowledge of the original complaint or lawsuit. In fact, often the first time the newly named defendant learns of the lawsuit is when he or she is served with the amended complaint and summons. Nor is California's Doe defendant practice concerned with the reason why the newly named defendant was not named in the original

---

3d 1, 10, n.4, 192 Cal. Rptr. 380 (1983); *Munoz, supra,* 91 Cal. App. 3d at 947–48.

[476] *Barrows, supra,* 144 Cal. App. 3d at 9; *see Sobeck & Assoc., Inc. v. B & R Inv. No. 24,* 215 Cal. App. 3d 861, 264 Cal. Rptr. 156 (1989) (noting an amendment will relate back if made within three years of filing the original complaint, unless there is evidence of unreasonable delay by the plaintiff or specific prejudice to the defendant).

[477] *See A.N. v. Cnty. of Los Angeles,* 171 Cal. App. 4th 1058, 90 Cal. Rptr. 3d 293 (2009).

[478] Cal. Gov't Code § 68616(h).

[479] *See* § 8.10[3], *supra.* For a discussion of these differences between the federal and California standards for relation back with respect to fictitious defendants, see Walter W. Heiser, *Relation Back of Amended Complaints: The California Courts Should Adopt a More Pragmatic Approach,* 44 Santa Clara L. Rev. 643, 678–83 (2004).

complaint. Doe practice applies regardless of whether this omission was due to a naming mistake, lack of knowledge of the name or the existence of the newly named defendant, or lack of knowledge of the facts giving rise to a cause of action against that defendant.

In some cases, California's liberal Doe defendant practice may also apply in federal court. Rule 15(c)(1)(A) of the Federal Rules of Civil Procedure authorizes relation back of an amended complaint in federal court whenever "the law that provides the applicable statute of limitations allows relation back." Essentially, if state law provides the controlling statute of limitations and affords a more forgiving principle of relation back than is provided under federal Rules 15(c)(1)(B) and (C), the state doctrine should be available to save the cause of action. Therefore, where California law provides the statute of limitations applicable to a cause of action in federal court, California's Doe defendant practice also applies to that cause of action.[480]

§ 8.14   RESPONSIVE PLEADINGS AND MOTIONS IN THE CALIFORNIA COURTS

[1]   The Demurrer

[a]   Introductory Note on Demurrers

A demurrer presents an objection to a complaint, cross-complaint, or answer when the ground for objection appears on the face of such pleading and from any matter of which the court may take judicial notice.[481] The grounds for objection to a complaint or cross-complaint by demurrer are set forth in Code of Civil Procedure § 430.10, and include the following: (a) the court has no jurisdiction of the subject of the cause of action alleged in the pleading; (b) the person who filed the pleading does not have the legal capacity to sue; (c) there is another action pending between the same parties on the same cause of action; (d) there is a defect or misjoinder of parties; (e) the pleading does not state facts sufficient to constitute a cause of action (typically referred to as a "general demurrer"); and (f) the pleading is uncertain. These objections may also be raised by an answer, although an objection whose resolution requires consideration of new or additional facts — facts not appearing on the face of the complaint or judicially noticeable — *must* be raised by an answer.[482]

---

[480] *See, e.g., Kreines v. United States*, 959 F.2d 834, 836–38 (9th Cir. 1992) (applying California Doe defendant practice to allow relation back of amended complaint substituting in named federal agents in federal constitutional claim based on Fourth Amendment); *Motley v. Parks*, 198 F.R.D. 532 (C.D. Cal. 2000) (applying California's Doe defendant practice in a federal civil rights action); David D. Siegel, *The Recent (Dec. 1, 1991) Changes in the Federal Rules of Civil Procedure*, 142 F.R.D. 359, 362–66 (1992).

[481] CAL. CODE CIV. PROC. § 430.30(a).

[482] CAL. CODE CIV. PROC. § 430.30(b). A party objecting to a complaint or cross-complaint may demur and answer at the same time. CAL. CODE CIV. PROC. § 430.30(c).

[b]   Procedures

Although technically considered a pleading, the procedural rules generally treat a demurrer like a motion. A demurrer may be taken to the whole complaint or cross-complaint, or to any causes of action stated therein. A party must demur to a complaint or cross-complaint within 30 days after service. Failure to timely object to a pleading by demurrer or answer constitutes a waiver of all grounds for objection except an objection that the court lacks subject matter jurisdiction or that the pleading does not state facts sufficient to constitute a cause of action or a defense.[483] When a demurrer is sustained, the court must state in the order the specific grounds upon which the decision is based.

[c]   Federal Rules Compared

Rule 7(c) of the Federal Rules of Civil Procedure abolished the use of demurrers in federal courts, although other federal rules authorize various motions which perform similar functions. Federal Rules 12(b)(1), 12(b)(7), and 12(e), for example, provide grounds for dismissal nearly identical to a demurrer for lack of subject matter jurisdiction, misjoinder of parties, and uncertain pleading, respectively. And Rule 12(b)(6), which authorizes a motion to dismiss for failure to state a claim upon which relief can be granted, corresponds to a general demurrer.

[2]   Standards for General Demurrers

A demurrer does not test the truth of the allegations in a pleading, only the legal sufficiency of the pleading.[484] The court must "assume the truth of all properly pleaded material allegations of the complaint and give it a reasonable interpretation by reading it as a whole and its parts in their context."[485] Consequently, a demurrer must be denied where the factual allegations state a cause of action but the defendant contests their accuracy.[486] A general demurrer may consider not only the facts appearing upon the face of the complaint but also any matter of which the court is required to, or may, take judicial notice.[487] Use of judicial notice permits the court to consider dispositive matter — such as official

---

[483] Cal. Code Civ. Proc. § 430.80; see Collins v. Rocha, 7 Cal. 3d 232, 239, 102 Cal. Rptr. 1, 497 P.2d 225 (1972) (holding defendant's failure to raise uncertainty of complaint by a timely special demurrer deemed a waiver of such pleading defect).

[484] See Committee on Children's Television, Inc. v. Gen. Foods Corp., 35 Cal. 3d 197, 197 Cal. Rptr. 783, 673 P.2d 660 (1983).

[485] Phillips v. Desert Hosp. Dist., 49 Cal. 3d 699, 702, 263 Cal. Rptr. 119, 780 P.2d 349 (1989).

[486] See, e.g., Committee on Children's Television, supra, 35 Cal. 3d at 213–15 (holding defendants' contention that the words and images of their television commercials were not misrepresentations, as plaintiffs had alleged in the complaint, framed a factual issue for resolution by trial, not demurrer); Selleck v. Globe Intl., Inc., 166 Cal. App. 3d 1123, 212 Cal. Rptr. 838 (1985) (holding trial court erred in sustaining demurrer where the complaint stated the contents of the article and alleged that the article was libelous on its face because the article was reasonably susceptible of a defamatory meaning on its face and therefore is libelous per se).

[487] Cal. Code Civ. Proc. § 430.30; Dryden v. Tri-Valley Growers, 65 Cal. App. 3d 990, 997, 135 Cal. Rptr. 720 (1977) (citing cases); Legg v. Mut. Benefit Health & Accident Ass'n, 184 Cal. App. 2d 482, 487–89, 7 Cal. Rptr. 595 (1960). A court must take judicial notice of certain specified California and federal laws, as well as "[f]acts and propositions of generalized knowledge that are so universally known

government publications, local codes and regulations, and court records in the same or other cases — not alleged in the complaint.[488]

[3] Amendment After Sustained Demurrer

A demurrer may be granted with or without leave to amend. An order sustaining a demurrer *without leave to amend* will constitute an abuse of discretion if there is any reasonable possibility that the defect can be cured by an amendment.[489] This rule is liberally applied to permit further amendment not only where the defect is one of form but also where it is one of substance, provided the pleader did not have "a fair prior opportunity to correct the substantive defect."[490] To meet the burden of showing abuse of discretion, the pleader must demonstrate how the pleading can be amended to state a cause of action.[491] What a plaintiff must demonstrate to establish abuse of discretion will vary with the ground for the demurrer.[492] For example, in one case, the appellate court reversed a general demurrer without leave to amend with respect to a contract cause of action because the plaintiff could amend the complaint to allege more specifically the facts necessary to establish the existence of a binding contract, but sustained the demurrer with respect to tort recovery for bad faith denial of the existence of the

---

that they cannot reasonably be the subject of dispute"; and *may* take judicial notice of a variety of other laws such as local and federal rules, foreign state rules and acts, and federal regulations; as well as "[f]acts and propositions that are not reasonably subject to dispute and are capable of immediate and accurate determination by resort to sources of reasonably indisputable accuracy." Cal. Evid. Code §§ 451, 452.

[488] *See, e.g., Beresford Neighborhood Ass'n v. City of San Mateo*, 207 Cal. App. 3d 1180, 1191, 255 Cal. Rptr. 434 (1989) (ruling trial court properly took judicial notice of city municipal code governing bidding procedures when considering demurrer); *Arce v. Kaiser Found. Health Plan, Inc.*, 181 Cal. App. 4th 471, 482–85, 104 Cal. Rptr. 3d 545 (2010) (taking judicial notice of pleadings filed in other cases and of a report of a legislative commission, but not of a transcript and videotaped recording of a television interview); *Carleton v. Tortosa*, 14 Cal. App. 4th 745, 753, n.1, 17 Cal. Rptr. 2d 734 (1993) (ruling brochures and summaries by private corporations not properly subjects of judicial notice, but official publications and bulletin of California Department of Real Estate are not reasonably subject to dispute).

[489] *Cooper v. Leslie Salt Co.*, 70 Cal. 2d 627, 636, 75 Cal. Rptr. 766, 451 P.2d 406 (1969); *Goodman v. Kennedy*, 18 Cal. 3d 335, 349, 134 Cal. Rptr. 375, 556 P.2d 737 (1976); *Careau & Co. v. Sec. Pac. Bus. Credit, Inc.*, 222 Cal. App. 3d 1371, 1386–88, 272 Cal. Rptr. 387 (1990); *see Blank v. Kirwan*, 39 Cal. 3d 311, 318, 216 Cal. Rptr. 718, 703 P.2d 58 (1985).

[490] *Leach v. Drummond Med. Grp., Inc.*, 144 Cal. App. 3d 362, 368, 192 Cal. Rptr. 650 (1983).

[491] *Goodman v. Kennedy, supra*, 18 Cal. 3d 335, 349; *Careau, supra*, 222 Cal. App. 3d at 1387–91. However, such a showing need not be made in the trial court so long as it is made to the reviewing court. Cal. Code Civ. Proc. § 472c; *Nestle v. City of Santa Monica*, 6 Cal. 3d 920, 939, 101 Cal. Rptr. 568, 496 P.2d 480 (1972). An appellate court may more readily find an abuse of discretion where a general demurrer is sustained without leave to amend as to an initial, as opposed to a previously amended, complaint. *See 1119 Delaware v. Cont'l Land Title Co.*, 16 Cal. App. 4th 992, 998, 20 Cal. Rptr. 2d 438 (1993) (holding demurrer sustained without leave to amend constituted abuse of discretion where original complaint did not show on its face it was incapable of stating cause of action upon amendment).

[492] *See, e.g., Blank v. Kirwan*, 39 Cal. 3d 311, 318, 216 Cal. Rptr. 718, 703 P.2d 58 (1985) (affirming general demurrer without leave to amend because plaintiff unable to demonstrate how an amended complaint could establish the elements of an action for unfair competition); *Sirott v. Latts*, 6 Cal. App. 4th 923, 8 Cal. Rptr. 2d 206 (1992) (sustaining special demurrer without leave to amend affirmed where matters subject to judicial notice showed complaint cannot be amended to overcome statute of limitations bar).

contract because the plaintiff did not demonstrate that an amended complaint would sufficiently allege the facts necessary to support that tort claim.[493]

When the trial court makes an order sustaining a demurrer without leave to amend, the question of whether the court abused its discretion in making this order is open on appeal even though no request to amend the pleading was made. When a trial court sustains a demurrer with leave to amend a complaint and the plaintiff fails to do so, the court must enter a judgment of dismissal upon motion by either party. As a tactical matter, a plaintiff may decide not to amend and then move for dismissal in order to seek appellate review of the validity of the cause of action pleaded in the complaint. If the dismissal is appealed, the appellate court must strictly construe the complaint and presume that the plaintiff has stated as strong a case as she can.[494]

[4] Motion to Strike

A trial court may, upon motion by a party or at any time in its discretion, strike out any irrelevant, false, or improper matter inserted in any pleading; or strike any part of a pleading not filed in conformity with court rules, orders, or other laws.[495] A motion to strike is generally used to reach defects in a pleading which are not subject to demurrer. For example, a motion to strike does not lie to attack a complaint for insufficiency of allegations to justify relief because that is the basis for a general demurrer. The grounds for a motion to strike must appear on the face of the challenged pleading or in matter which the court may judicially notice. A common use of the motion is to strike punitive damage allegations from a medical malpractice complaint when the plaintiff failed to comply with the statutory pre-pleading requirements, or to strike an amount of personal injury or punitive damages inappropriately stated in a complaint instead of in a separate (and private) statement of damages.[496]

[5] The Answer

[a] Introductory Note

A defendant served with a complaint has three principal choices: (1) do nothing and risk entry of default and a default judgment, (2) attack the complaint and seek a partial or complete dismissal of the action through use of the demurrer and other related motions, or (3) respond to the complaint on its own terms through the *answer*. Conceptually, preparing and filing an answer is the normal procedural response; whether in practice it is the most common response is not at all clear.

The answer is a pleading that responds to the allegations in the complaint. Except in those instances where a defending party can file a general denial, answers contain three types of responses. First, portions of the complaint may be admitted,

---

[493] *Careau & Co. v. Sec. Pac. Bus. Credit, Inc.*, 222 Cal. App. 3d 1371, 272 Cal. Rptr. 387 (1990).

[494] *Gonzales, supra*, 68 Cal. App. 3d at 635.

[495] CAL. CODE CIV. PROC. §§ 435, 436(a) & (b), 437(a).

[496] *See* CAL. CODE CIV. PROC. § 425.10(b); CAL. CIV. CODE § 3295(e).

either by express admission or by failure to deny. Second, allegations in the complaint may be controverted by general or specific denials, on the basis of information or belief, or on the ground of lack of information or belief. Third, the answer may respond by stating defenses that provide a defense to the complaint even if its allegations are true. If the defending party seeks affirmative relief against the party filing the complaint, the defending party must proceed by a separate pleading referred to as "cross-complaint."

[b] Denials

Failure to properly deny a material allegation constitutes an admission.[497] The pleading statutes require specific and positive denials when answering a verified complaint, but permit a general denial in lieu of an answer when the complaint is not verified or in a limited civil case.[498] A general denial simply states: "Defendant denies each and every allegation in plaintiff's complaint." The advantage of a general denial is that the defendant is not required to admit any of the allegations in the complaint prior to discovery. The disadvantage is that a general denial only puts into issue the material allegations of the complaint which comprise the plaintiff's cause of action, and therefore may not put into issue the defendant's relevant defenses and affirmative defenses.[499] For example, the general denial of a complaint pleading a cause of action on a promissory note encompasses such defenses as the contract is wholly void, the note was not executed, and payment by defendant; but does not put into issue the defense that the note was a sham transaction.[500]

An answer delineates the contested issues of fact through admissions and denials, and requires the plaintiff to prove all material allegations in the complaint controverted by the answer. A timely filed answer also prevents the plaintiff from obtaining a default judgment against the answering defendant. Generally, a defendant must file an answer within 30 days after service of a complaint or cross-complaint, unless the defendant obtains an extension or files a demurrer, motion to quash, or some other responsive motion. The answer also provides the vehicle for raising objections to pleadings that cannot be taken by demurrer because the ground does not appear on the face of the pleading, and for stating defenses.

---

[497] Code of Civil Procedure § 431.20(a) states "[e]very material allegation of the complaint or cross-complaint, not controverted by the answer, shall, for purposes of the action, be taken as true." *See Valerio v. Andrew Youngquist Constr.*, 103 Cal. App. 4th 1264, 1271–72, 127 Cal. Rptr. 2d 436 (2002) (ruling an admission in a pleading is conclusive on the pleader).

[498] Cal Code Civ. Proc. §§ 431.30(d), 431.40; *see, e.g., Conley v. Lieber*, 97 Cal. App. 3d 646, 158 Cal. Rptr. 770 (1979) (holding that in light of the liberality afforded answers under § 431.30, defendant's answer, which denied "generally and specifically each and every allegation contained" in the complaint, effectively denied plaintiff's allegations regarding causation and damages).

[499] *See* Cal Code Civ. Proc. § 431.30(d); *Carranza v. Noroian*, 240 Cal. App. 2d 481, 488, 49 Cal. Rptr. 629 (1966) (holding a general denial constituted waiver of defendant's right to prove setoff based on independent and different contract).

[500] *FPI Dev., Inc. v. Nakashima*, 231 Cal. App. 3d 367, 282 Cal. Rptr. 508 (1991).

[c] Affirmative Defenses ("New Matter")

Under California Code of Civil Procedure § 431.30(b)(2), the answer to a complaint must include a statement of any "new matter constituting a defense." The phrase "new matter" refers to something relied on by a defendant which is not put in issue by the plaintiff. Where the answer sets forth facts showing some essential allegation of the complaint is not true, such facts do not constitute "new matter" but only a denial. Accordingly, what is put in issue by such a denial is limited to the allegations of the complaint.[501] Therefore, a defendant who wishes to raise matters that are not responsive to allegations of the complaint must raise them in the answer as an *affirmative defense.*

Failure to plead an affirmative defense ("new matter") waives that defense.[502] Because the reply is not recognized as a pleading in California, a plaintiff need not answer affirmative defenses raised in defendant's answer to the complaint. Affirmative defenses are deemed controverted and a plaintiff may introduce evidence on the issue at trial.[503] For example, a plaintiff need not answer an affirmative defense of statute of limitations raised in the defendant's answer in order to contest this defense at trial.[504]

[d] Brief Note on the Affirmative Defense of Statute of Limitations

Perhaps the most frequently raised affirmative defense is that the plaintiff's cause of action is barred by the applicable statute of limitations. Extended discussion this affirmative defense is beyond the scope of these materials. What follows is a brief overview of some of the various aspects of statutes of limitations in the California courts.

From a litigant's perspective, the first step in the statute of limitations analysis is to ascertain the length of the statutorily prescribed period for a cause of action. Code of Civil Procedure § 312 then requires that the action be commenced within that period after the cause of action has "accrued." (Pursuant to section 350, an action is commenced "when the complaint is filed.") The next question is to determine when a cause of action has "accrued" such that the statutory limitation period begins to run. The answer to this question can be quite complex. The Code of Civil Procedure does not provide a general definition of "accrual" applicable to all statutes of limitations.[505] Instead, the California courts have traditionally provided

---

[501] *FPI Dev., Inc. v. Nakashima,* 231 Cal. App. 3d 367, 383–85, 282 Cal. Rptr. 508 (1991); *Walsh v. West Valley Mission Cmty. Coll. Dist.,* 66 Cal. App. 4th 1532, 1546, 78 Cal. Rptr. 2d 725 (1998); *State Farm Mut. Auto Ins. Co. v. Superior Court,* 228 Cal. App. 3d 721, 725, 279 Cal. Rptr. 116 (1991).

[502] *See, e.g., Hulsey v. Koehler,* 218 Cal. App. 3d 1150, 267 Cal. Rptr. 523 (1990) (explaining that failure to assert a compulsory cross-complaint in prior action is a special defense which, like res judicata, is waived if not raised in the instant action); *Minton v. Cavaney,* 56 Cal. 2d 576, 581, 15 Cal. Rptr. 641, 364 P.2d 473 (1961) (holding defendant waived statute of limitations defense by failing to plead that defense in the answer or by demurrer).

[503] CAL CODE CIV. PROC. § 431.20(b).

[504] *Aerojet General Corp. v. Superior Court,* 177 Cal. App. 3d 950, 953, 223 Cal. Rptr. 249 (1986).

[505] However, the Legislature has defined the accrual point for certain specific causes of action, such

the general rules regarding accrual, including the "delayed discovery rule."

Under the delayed discovery rule, the statute of limitations begins to run "when the plaintiff suspects or should suspect that her injury was caused by wrongdoing, that someone has done something wrong to her."[506] Once the plaintiff has a suspicion of wrongdoing, and therefore an incentive to sue, she must decide whether to file suit or sit on her rights. "So long as a suspicion exists, it is clear that the plaintiff must go find the facts; she cannot wait for the facts to find her."[507] The need for diligence on the part of the plaintiff is further underscored by a well-established California rule: Ignorance of the identity of the wrongdoer or the legal significance of known facts will not delay the running of the statute of limitations. Consequently, the statute of limitations begins to run when the plaintiff knows of her injury, its cause, and suspects wrongdoing, even though the plaintiff does not know *who* caused her injury or whether the wrongdoing is actionable.

After a cause of action has accrued, there are a number of situations in California that will toll (*i.e.*, suspend) the running of a statutory limitation period. Many of these general tolling provisions are defined in the Code of Civil Procedure. For example, if a person has a "disability" (*e.g*, is "under the age of majority" or "insane") at the time a cause of action accrues, the applicable statute of limitations is suspended during the time of such "disability."[508] Also, in some limited situations the statute of limitations is tolled during the time that a defendant is absent from California.[509]

In addition to the statutory tolling provisions, the California courts have created equitable tolling doctrines based on concepts of fairness, typically when the plaintiff has filed a timely action against the defendant but in the wrong court or tribunal.[510] For example, in *Addision v. State of California*,[511] the California Supreme Court held that the statute of limitations was tolled during the period that the plaintiff's state law claims were pending before a federal court and until that court declined

---

as medical malpractice, legal malpractice, childhood sexual abuse, injury due to exposure to asbestos, and breach of contract for sale of goods. *See, e.g.*, CAL CODE CIV. PROC. §§ 340.1, 340.2, 340.5 & 340.6.

[506] *Jolly v. Eli Lilly & Co.*, 44 Cal. 3d 1103, 1110, 245 Cal. Rptr. 658, 751 P.2d 923 (1988).

[507] *Jolly, supra*, 44 Cal. 3d at 1111.

[508] CAL CODE CIV. PROC. § 352.

[509] CAL CODE CIV. PROC. § 351; *see, e.g.*, *Filet Menu, Inc. v. Cheng*, 71 Cal. App. 4th 1276, 84 Cal. Rptr. 2d 384 (1999) (tolling statutory periods for the duration of out-of-state travel unrelated to interstate commerce, such as for vacation trips or to attend college); Walter W. Heiser, *Can the Tolling of Statutes of Limitations Based on the Defendant's Absence from the State Ever Be Consistent with the Commerce Clause?*, 76 Mo. L. REV. 385 (2011) (discussing constitutional limitations on the use of section 351 and similar absence-based tolling statutes).

[510] For example, in *Elkins v. Derby*, 12 Cal. 3d 410, 115 Cal. Rptr. 641, 525 P.2d 81 (1974), the court held that equitable tolling suspends the running of the statute of limitations when an injured person has a choice of several fora or procedures available to remedy the injury and, reasonably and in good faith, pursues one against the defendant. Moreover, where exhaustion of an administrative remedy is mandatory prior to filing a lawsuit, equitable tolling is automatic during the period of the administrative process. *Id.* at 414.

[511] 21 Cal. 3d 313, 146 Cal. Rptr. 224, 578 P.2d 941 (1978). The three elements necessary to establish the doctrine of equitable tolling are (1) timely notice to the defendant, (2) lack of prejudice to the defendant, and (3) reasonable and good faith conduct on the part of the plaintiff. *Id.* at 319.

to exercise pendant jurisdiction, where the plaintiff had timely filed these claims against the defendants in the federal court and subsequently filed them in state court. And, under certain circumstances, a defendant may be equitably estopped from asserting an applicable statute of limitations where the defendant's fraudulent conduct has induced the plaintiff to delay filing an action until after the expiration of the limitations period. For example, in one case, the court held that the defendant, whose promise of settlement fraudulently induce plaintiff to delay filing her civil action, was equitably estopped from asserting the statute of limitations defense.[512]

[6] Cross-Complaints

The California *cross-complaint* is a multi-purpose pleading device which permits a party defending against a cause of action to assert his or her own cause of action against an opposing party, a co-party, or some other person not already a party to the action.[513] The California cross-complaint serves the same functions as the counterclaim, cross-claim, and third-party impleader in federal court.[514] The California Legislature opted for the "one-term-fits-all" approach in 1971 when it eliminated technical limitations of prior methods of countersuits and replaced them with a single form of pleading.[515] A cross-complaint must be filed and served as a separate document, and must comply with the same form and content rules applicable to a complaint. Once served, a cross-defendant must timely respond to the cross-complaint by an answer, a demurrer, or some other appropriate motion in order to avoid a default judgment.

---

[512] *Muraoka v. Budget Rent-a-Car*, 160 Cal. App. 3d 107, 206 Cal. Rptr. 476 (1984); *see, e.g., Bernson v. Browning-Ferris Indus. of Cal., Inc.*, 7 Cal. 4th 926, 30 Cal. Rptr. 2d 440, 873 P.2d 613 (1994) (holding defendant equitably estopped from raising the statute of limitations defense where defendant fraudulently concealed the cause of action against defendant and the plaintiff exercised reasonable diligence, but could not discover the relevant information within the limitations period).

[513] Cal Code Civ. Proc. §§ 428.10–428.80. California cross-complaints are discussed in more detail in the materials on joinder of claims and parties in § 9.11, *infra*.

[514] Counterclaims, cross-claims, and third-party impleader claims in federal court are discussed in §§ 9.03, 9.04 & 9.06, *infra*.

[515] *See, e.g.*, Cal Code Civ. Proc. § 428.80 (counterclaims abolished and deemed cross-complaints); Jack H. Friedenthal, *Joinder of Claims, Counterclaims, and Cross-Complaints: Suggested Revisions of the California Provisions*, 23 Stan. L. Rev. 1, 17–39 (1970).

Chapter 9

COMPLEX PLEADING AND PRACTICE

§ 9.01 OVERVIEW

[1] Definitions of Complex Litigation

The simplest case consists of one claim brought by a single plaintiff against a single defendant. Any expansion of the number of claims (and possibly the number of parties) beyond this minimal configuration represents a form of complex litigation.

It is most useful to approach complex litigation by focusing on claims rather than parties. It is possible to increase the number of claims adjudicated in a case without necessarily increasing the number of parties.[1] The case is complicated by expansion of a claim *and* a party whenever the added claim requires for its binding adjudication the presence of an additional party before the court.[2]

Most of this chapter treats complex litigation in this traditional sense. The term has also taken on a second meaning: to describe litigation scattered over many states (often in both state and federal courts) that arises from a common event or wrong.[3] The wrong might stem from an air crash or from a disease attributed to a substance like asbestos. We conclude the chapter with a review of recent developments in this area.

[2] Reasons for Complex Litigation

Complicating civil litigation with multiple claims, multiple claimants, or multiple parties claimed against, carries inevitable risks. Possibilities for delay and confusion arise when multiple claims compete for attention. This is even more likely to be true when multiple plaintiffs or defendants separately exercise their litigation prerogatives through discovery, pretrial motions and trial of the case. "Additional parties always take additional time. Even if they have no witnesses of their own, they are the source of additional questions, objections, briefs, arguments, motions and the like which tend to make the proceeding a Donnybrook

---

[1] Claim joinder, counterclaim and crossclaim rules perform this function and are the subject of Part A of this chapter, *infra*.

[2] Claim expansion which also requires party expansion occurs through permissive and compulsory joinder, impleader, interpleader, intervention, and class actions — treated in Part B of this chapter, *infra*.

[3] AMERICAN LAW INSTITUTE, COMPLEX LITIGATION: STATUTORY RECOMMENDATIONS AND ANALYSIS, Chapter 2 (1994).

Fair."[4] Given these risks, complex litigation requires offsetting justifications, and there are at least two. First, complex litigation can promote judicial efficiency; and second, it can promote just adjudication by avoiding prejudice to parties and absentees that could arise if claims or parties are excluded from an adjudication.

[a] Judicial Efficiency

Delayed and laborious as complex litigation may be in the short run, a multiple-claim or multiple-party lawsuit is usually preferable to multiple lawsuits. When it averts multiple lawsuits, complex litigation becomes the lesser of two evils, expediting resolution of the entire controversy and avoiding the drain on party and judicial resources caused by inefficient, often redundant litigation.[5]

The wisdom of this objective is most evident when the lawsuit averted would have gone over much of the same ground. Many procedural devices for joining additional claims or parties thus require a nexus between the subject matter of successive claims.[6] Even where claims are unrelated, however, litigating both in one case may promote more efficient use of judicial resources.[7]

[b] Avoiding Prejudice to a Party or Absentee

The substantive rights of either an absentee or a party may be prejudiced if the absentee is not made an additional party in the case. Prejudice in this sense is different from the prejudice of added expense and delay of protracted litigation. For example, substantive prejudice is a concern when an absentee runs the risk of being adversely affected by the outcome in a case without an opportunity to influence that outcome as only parties can.[8] Another example occurs when an existing party suffers from the court's failure to have before it all those involved in the controversy, creating for that party the prospect of conflicting judgments and multiple liability.[9] In both examples, justifications for adding a party go beyond mere judicial efficiency.

---

[4] *Crosby Steam Gage & Valve Co. v. Manning, Maxwell & Moore Inc.*, 51 F. Supp. 972, 973 (D. Mass. 1943).

[5] Courts are motivated by the same concerns in giving preclusive effect to their judgments. The trend is toward giving judgments greater preclusive effect, penalizing piecemeal litigation and delay. *See generally* Chapter 15, *infra*.

[6] *See* for example, discussion of compulsory counterclaims, crossclaims, and required parties in §§ 9.03, 9.04 & 9.05[2], *infra*.

[7] This is the assumption underlying claim joinder and permissive counterclaims. *See* §§ 9.08[1], 9.02 & 9.03, *infra*.

[8] This problem is addressed by Rule 24(a), governing intervention of right. *See* § 62[A], *infra*.

[9] A problem addressed, for example, by Rule 19(a), governing joinder of required parties. *See* § 9.05[2], *infra*.

[3] How the Federal Rules of Civil Procedure Facilitate Expansion of Claims and Parties

Like other aspects of civil procedure, the law of claim and party joinder has undergone substantial change. The courts of the United States, the fifty states, and the District of Columbia each administer their own law in the field. For our primary model when discussing complex litigation, we will use the Federal Rules of Civil Procedure.

The approach of the federal rules is typical of approaches taken elsewhere.[10] The objective is to combine received traditions[11] with an appreciation of the practical necessities of modern civil litigation into a more or less cohesive body of rules. These rules seek to sort, authorize and limit structural devices which enlarge litigation from the minimum configuration of one plaintiff, one defendant and one claim. However, the rules alone cannot alter the jurisdiction of federal courts or venue of federal actions.[12]

In this chapter, we will examine claim and party expansion situations usually taken up by rules.[13] We will consider the functional effect of each rule, justification for its use and limitation, and special problems or issues.

PART A.
Adding Claims Without Adding Parties

In this Part we will consider multiclaim procedure: rules governing claim joinder, counterclaims, and crossclaims. These procedural devices add claims to the litigation, but do not, by themselves, authorize the addition of parties.[14] Each of the multiclaim rules we will consider has the purpose of reducing delay, needless repetition, and expense in civil litigation by reducing the possibility of multiple lawsuits. The function of multiclaim rules, then, is to promote the adjudication of as many claims as possible in the first instance.

---

[10] Most state procedural systems use the approach and often a good deal of the language of the Federal Rules of Civil Procedure. *See generally* John B. Oakley & Arthur F. Coon, *The Federal Rules in State Court: A Survey of State Court Systems of Civil Procedure*, 61 WASH. L. REV. 1367 (1986); § 2 n.4 and accompanying text, *supra*. *See also* John B. Oakley, *A Fresh Look at the Federal Rules in State Courts*, 3 NEV. L.J. 354 (2003) (updating his earlier article by studying state adoption of recent federal amendments).

[11] Multiclaim and multiparty rules have their antecedents in English law, often in equity practice. For one example, see Geoffrey C. Hazard, Jr., *Indispensable Party: The Historical Origin of a Procedural Phantom*, 61 COLUM. L. REV. 1254 (1961).

[12] Rule 82. Until recently, the federal courts extended the reach of federal subject matter jurisdiction and venue through common law. *See* §§ 9.03, 9.04 & 9.05[2], *infra*. Much of that law has now been codified. *See generally* § 5.08, *supra*.

[13] Beyond the federal rules of civil procedure, statutes governing interpleader and multidistrict consolidation of pretrial proceedings are of sufficient general importance to be covered in this chapter. *See* §§ 9.07 & 9.10[2], *infra*.

[14] Thus, while Rule 13(h) indicates that one may join a party in order to make a counterclaim or crossclaim, the provision makes clear that such expansion must separately satisfy rules pertaining to party joinder (one of the multiparty rules discussed in Part B, *infra*).

§ 9.02 CLAIM JOINDER[15]

Rule 18 governs claim joinder, the process by which one who has made a claim may join further claims with it against the same opponent. In addition, once an additional party has been brought into the litigation on the authority of one of the party joinder rules, Rule 18 permits joinder of additional claims against such a party.[16] Rules of civil procedure treating aspects of complex litigation are usually two-sided in their effect. They authorize, but also limit, claim or party expansion.[17] Rule 18 is an exception. It authorizes claim joinder without limitation.[18] Rule 18(a) states that "[a] party asserting a claim" of any kind "may join as independent or alternate claims, as many claims as it has against an opposing party."[19] A claimant wishing to assert entirely unrelated claims against the same party finds no obstacle in Rule 18. For two reasons, however, possibilities for multiple claim adjudication in federal court are not as great as the bare language of Rule 18 might suggest.

First, Rule 18 does not insulate claims from difficulties unrelated to the joinder rules. A federal rule of civil procedure cannot "extend or limit the jurisdiction of the district courts or the venue of actions in those courts."[20] Consider the following example. Federal plaintiff A wishes to make two unrelated claims against defendant B. The first falls within the court's general federal question jurisdiction.[21] The second is based on state law. Absent either diversity of citizenship between A and B or the requisite jurisdictional amount,[22] there is no original federal subject matter jurisdiction over the second claim. Supplemental jurisdiction requires a close relationship between the subject matter of the two claims.[23] Rule 18 may appear to

---

[15] *See generally* MOORE §§ 18.01–18.23; 6A WRIGHT & MILLER §§ 1581–1594; Benjamin Kaplan, *Continuing Work of the Civil Committee: 1966 Amendments of the Federal Rules of Civil Procedure (II)*, 81 HARV. L. REV. 591, 591–98 (1968); William W. Blume, *A Rational Theory for Joinder of Causes of Action and Defences, and for the Use of Counterclaims*, 26 MICH. L. REV. 1 (1927).

[16] *See, e.g.,* 7 WRIGHT & MILLER § 1655 ("If the requirements for joinder of parties [under Rule 20] have been satisfied . . . Rule 18 [claim joinder] may be invoked independently to permit plaintiff to join as many other claims as the plaintiff has against the multiple defendants.").

[17] See for example, limitations placed or on the availability of crossclaims discussed in § 9.04, or on party joinder discussed in § 9.05 *infra*.

[18] *Cf.* Arthur F. Greenbaum, *Jacks or Better to Open: Procedural Limitations on Co-Party and Third-Party Claims*, 74 MINN. L. REV. 507, 532 (1990) (noting acceptance of the view that Rule 18 enables one to "raise any claim against another party after raising a qualifying claim."). Rule 13 similarly permits counterclaims without limitation. *See* § 9.03, *infra*.

[19] Elements of a "claim" are defined in Rule 8(a). For discussion of claim pleading under the federal rules, *see* §§ 8.04 & 8.06[2], *supra*. Most state procedural systems employ the same approach and much of the same language as federal Rule 18. *E.g.,* ALA. CODE R. CIV. P. 18; DEL. CODE ANN. R. CIV. P. 18; KY. REV. STAT. ANN. R. CIV. P. 18.01.

[20] Rule 82. The reference is to federal subject matter jurisdiction. *Cf. Snyder v. Harris*, 394 U.S. 332, 337 (1969) (even if expansion of federal diversity jurisdiction might otherwise be implied from an amendment making class actions more available under Rule 23, such expansion was prohibited under Rule 82).

[21] 28 U.S.C. § 1331, *discussed in* § 5.03, *supra*.

[22] The prerequisites for general diversity jurisdiction under 28 U.S.C. § 1332, discussed in §§ 5.04–5.06, *supra*.

[23] 28 U.S.C. § 1367, *discussed in* § 5.11, *supra*.

authorize both claims, but it will not save the second from dismissal for lack of subject matter jurisdiction.

Second, Rule 18 merely allows parties to plead claim joinder. It does not guarantee that the claims will be tried together. "The Rule addresses pleadings, not trials. The district judge may order separate trials of claims or issues."[24]

The availability of other means for regulating the entry and trial of multiple claims explains in part why Rule 18 contains no limitation on claim joinder. A further reason can be found in the fact that prior attempts to distinguish between permissibly and impermissibly joined claims proved unsatisfactory. Common law and code distinctions were often difficult to administer,[25] generating unproductive litigation. The original Rule 18 attacked the problem by largely eliminating the possibility of impermissible claims. The process was completed with amendment of paragraph (a) of the rule in 1966.[26]

§ 9.03   COMPULSORY AND PERMISSIVE COUNTERCLAIMS[27]

When a party claims against one who previously claimed against him, the claim back is called a counterclaim.[28] Rule 13 divides these into *compulsory counterclaims* under paragraph (a) and *permissive counterclaims* under paragraph (b).[29]

---

[24] *Moore* § 18.02[6]. "The district court has broad authority to proceed with separate trials for a variety of reasons, including the prevention of embarrassment, delay, prejudice or expense." *Moore* § 18.02[6]. *See, e.g., Long & Foster Real Estate, Inc. v. NRT Mid-Atlantic, Inc.*, 357 F. Supp. 2d 911 (E.D. Va. 2005).

[25] 6A *Wright & Miller* § 1581.

[26] Prior to the amendment, the language of the rule "led some courts to conclude that the rules regulating joinder of parties were intended to be superimposed on Rule 18(a) and encouraged them to apply special restrictions to the joinder of claims in multiparty situations." 6A *Wright & Miller* § 1583.

[27] *See generally Moore* §§ 13.10–13.50; 6 *Wright & Miller* §§ 1401–1430; Kevin M. Clermont, *Common-Law Compulsory Counterclaim Rule: Creating Effective and Elegant Res Judicata Doctrine*, 79 Notre Dame L. Rev. 1745 (2004); Michael D. Conway, Comment, *Narrowing the Scope of Rule 13(a)*, 60 U. Chi. L. Rev. 141, 141–42 (1993); John E. Kennedy, *Counterclaims Under Federal Rule 13*, 11 Hous. L. Rev. 255 (1974); Charles A. Wright, *Estoppel By Rule: The Compulsory Counterclaim Under Modern Pleading*, 38 Minn. L. Rev. 423 (1954).

[28] Counterclaims evolved from the common law claims of *recoupment* and *set-off*. Charles E. Clark, Handbook of the Law of Code Pleading 633–36 (2d ed. 1947). By recoupment, defendant was entitled to defeat or reduce the plaintiff's recovery by pleading a claim against him arising out of the same transaction as the plaintiff's claim. By set-off, defendant was permitted to plead a transactionally unrelated claim against the plaintiff, provided that it was a claim for a liquidated sum. *See generally* Joseph H. Koffler & Allison Reppy, Handbook of Common Law Pleading § 278 (1969); Benjamin J. Shipman, Handbook of Common-Law Pleading §§ 209–10 (3d ed. 1923).

[29] Many state procedural systems also maintain the distinction (*e.g.*, Fla. R. Civ. P. 1.170(a) & (b); Ind. Code Ann. Ct. R. Trial 13(A) & (B); N.M. Stat. Ann. R. Civ. P. Dist. Ct. 1-013(A) & (B)), but some do not. New York is an example of the latter. *See* David Siegel, New York Practice § 224, at 384 (5th ed. 2011); McKinney's Consolidated Laws of New York, vol. 7B (2006) ("All counterclaims are permissive in New York: D can use his claim as a counterclaim or save it and sue on it separately."); David Siegel, New York Practice § 224 (4th ed. 2004).

Important consequences can turn on this distinction, as we shall see. However, the status of a counterclaim as compulsory or permissive has nothing to do with its availability to a party under the joinder rules. The scope for counterclaims under Rule 13 is unlimited,[30] like that for claim joinder under Rule 18.[31] But Rule 13 is also like Rule 18 in that satisfaction of the rule offers no guarantee that the counterclaim will be adjudicated at the same time as the preceding claim, or at all. The counterclaim must conform to the requirements of venue and federal subject matter jurisdiction,[32] and the court presented with the counterclaim is free "to order separate trial of a particular issue if this is in fact more convenient or desirable."[33]

The difference between compulsory and permissive counterclaims is important for two reasons. First, the status of a claim as permissive may confer an advantage in the realm of preclusion law. Compulsory counterclaims take their name from the fact that parties having them must either "use em or lose em" — plead or forfeit them, at least in future actions in the same court system.[34] In contrast, one may plead a permissive counterclaim or reserve it for future litigation.[35] Second, permissive counterclaims are more likely to encounter jurisdictional obstacles. A counterclaim beyond original federal court jurisdiction cannot be brought within the language of the supplemental jurisdiction statute[36] unless it is so related in subject matter to plaintiff's claim that it would also meet the test for compulsory counterclaims.[37] Merely permissive counterclaims thus are often ineligible for supplemental jurisdiction.

Counterclaims are permissive unless they meet the compulsory-counterclaim test of Rule 13(a). The test involves several prerequisites.[38] However, just one, "that

---

[30] "It is immaterial whether the counterclaim is legal or equitable, in contract or in tort, or even whether it has any connection with plaintiff's claim." WRIGHT § 79, at 564.

[31] See § 9.02, *supra*.

[32] See § 9.02, *supra*.

[33] WRIGHT § 79.

[34] This is sometimes called preclusion by rule and is discussed in § 15.03[3], *infra*.

[35] "The defendant or party who did not choose the forum or control the litigation, although bound on those matters actually litigated, should not be bound on those claims that, under the law of the first forum, he was not compelled to litigate." Eugene F. Scoles, *Interstate Preclusion by Prior Litigation*, 74 Nw. U. L. Rev. 742, 754 (1979).

[36] 28 U.S.C. § 1367, discussed in § 5.11, *supra*.

[37] Prior to enactment of the statute in 1990, the same distinction limited the availability of ancillary jurisdiction. The doctrine of ancillary jurisdiction tracked compulsory counterclaim, crossclaim and impleader definitions found in the Federal Rules of Civil Procedure. *Owen Equip. & Erection Co. v. Kroger*, 437 U.S. 365, 375 & n.18 (1978). It appears that these applications of ancillary jurisdiction have been preserved and codified under § 1367. See §§ 5.08–5.11, *supra*.

[38]

In an action in personam, a claim defendant has against plaintiff is a compulsory counterclaim if it meets four conditions. It must: (1) arise "out of the transaction or occurrence that is the subject matter of the opposing party's claim;" (2) be matured and owned by the pleader at the time the pleading is served; (3) not require for its adjudication the presence of third parties of whom the court cannot acquire personal jurisdiction; and (4) not have been, at the time the original action was commenced, the subject matter of another pending action.

WRIGHT § 79 (footnotes omitted). *See, e.g., Critical-Vac Filtration Corp. v. Minuteman Int'l Inc.*, 233 F.3d the claim arise out of the transaction or occurrence that is the subject of the opposing party's claim," has posed problems.[39] At least four different definitions of the required transactional nexus have been suggested in the cases: a "same issue" test; a "same evidence" test; a *"res judicata"* test; and a "logical relationship" test.[40] The "same-issue" test suffers a timing problem, since it is hard to know what the issues of law and fact are before the plaintiff has replied to the counterclaim. The *"res judicata"* test asks whether a judgment in the case would bar a subsequent suit on a reserved counterclaim. But "[t]his is no test at all," Professor Wright notes, because, absent a compulsory counterclaim rule, counterclaims can be sued upon independently.[41] The "same-evidence" test is more useful because it assures that compulsory joinder of the counterclaim will produce real economies by preventing duplicative discovery and trial of the same evidence in successive lawsuits. Yet it fails to reach counterclaims which are logically part of the existing controversy between the parties, but which require different proof. In addition, both the same-issue and same-evidence tests are ambiguous because they do not indicate how close to identical the issues or evidence need be.

Most federal courts therefore have adopted a fourth, more generous logical relationship test: whether the counterclaim is logically related to the existing claim against the prospective counterclaimant.[42] For example, plaintiff debtor sued her lender on a truth-in-lending cause of action in *Plant v. Blazer Financial Services, Inc.*[43] The lender counterclaimed with a state law cause of action on the debt. Because the parties were not diverse, the counterclaim could only be heard if it was compulsory and therefore within the court's supplemental (then termed, ancillary) jurisdiction. Although a truth-in-lending claim and a debt counterclaim pose different issues of law and fact and involve substantially different evidence,[44] the court of appeals applied the logical relationship test to affirm the judgment on the counterclaim. "Applying the logical relationship test literally to the counterclaim in this case clearly suggests its compulsory character," reasoned the court, "because a single aggregate of operative facts, the loan transaction, gave rise to both plaintiff's and defendant's claim."[45]

697, 702 (2d Cir. 2000); *Sparrow v. Mazda Am. Credit*, 385 F. Supp. 2d 1063, 1068 (E.D. Cal. 2005).

[39] WRIGHT § 79. *Cf.* Michael D. Conway, Comment, *Narrowing the Scope of Rule 13(a)*, 60 U. CHI. L. REV. 141, 141–42 (1993) (different interpretations of the requirement persist).

[40] *See* WRIGHT § 79.

[41] WRIGHT § 79. *See generally* § 15.03[3] (preclusion by rule), *infra*.

[42] 6 WRIGHT & MILLER § 1410. *See, e.g., Eon Labs, Inc. v. SmithKline Beecham Corp.*, 298 F. Supp. 2d 175, 179 (D. Mass. 2003).

[43] 598 F.2d 1357 (5th Cir. 1979).

[44] *See, e.g., Whigham v. Beneficial Fin. Co.*, 599 F.2d 1322, 1323–24 (4th Cir. 1979) (noting these differences in holding the debt counterclaim not compulsory).

[45] *Plant*, 598 F.2d at 1361. *Cf. Moore v. New York Cotton Exch.*, 270 U.S. 593, 610 (1926) ("[The transaction] is the one circumstance without which neither party would have found it necessary to seek relief."). The *Plant* court noted a split in the courts on the issue whether a counterclaim on the debt is compulsory in truth-in-lending suits, but also attributed it primarily to judicial concern about the chilling effect of such counterclaims on private enforcement of federal truth-in-lending policy. *But see Peterson v. United Accounts, Inc.*, 638 F.2d 1134 (8th Cir. 1981) (despite some overlap of issues, there is no logical relationship between collection claim and truth-in-lending counterclaim).

"The hallmark of [the logical relationship] approach is its flexibility."[46] In this respect and in its ultimate reach, the logical relationship test for compulsory counterclaims is very similar to the "transactional relationship" test for modern claim preclusion.[47] This is not surprising. The ultimate concern of both compulsory counterclaim rules and the law of claim preclusion is the appropriate scope of a lawsuit.

§ 9.04   CROSSCLAIMS[48]

When a party claims against a co-party (rather than an opposing party) the claim is called a crossclaim. Crossclaims in federal court are governed by Rule 13(g), which states:

> A pleading may state as a crossclaim any claim by one party against a coparty if the claim arises out of the transaction or occurrence that is the subject matter either of the original action or of a counterclaim, of if the claim relates to any property that is the subject matter of the original action.[49]

Most federal courts have interpreted the "transaction-or-occurrence" requirement to mean that there must be a logical relationship[50] between the crossclaim and either the original action or a counterclaim.[51]

Like compulsory counterclaims, crossclaims are generally within federal courts' supplemental jurisdiction.[52] They differ, however, in an important respect. While the holder of a compulsory counterclaim must plead or risk forfeiting it, one may either plead a crossclaim or reserve it for further litigation; crossclaims are never compulsory under Rule 13(g).[53]

A crossclaim arguably makes co-parties opposing parties. This means that, should the target of a crossclaim wish to direct a claim back against the crossclaimant, this claim back would be a counterclaim.[54] For Rule 13 to treat this last claim as a counterclaim rather than as a crossclaim may mean that the claimant

---

[46] 6 *Wright & Miller* § 1410.

[47] *See* § 15.03[2] (discussing the emergence of § 24 of the *Restatement (Second) of Judgments*), *infra*.

[48] *See generally Moore* §§ 13.60–13.80; 6 *Wright & Miller* §§ 1431–1433; John D. Bessler, Note, *Defining "Co-Party" Within Federal Rule of Civil Procedure 13(g): Are CrossClaims Between Original Defendants and Third-Party Defendants Allowable?*, 66 Ind. L.J. 549 (1991).

[49] Many state systems have adopted this approach. *E.g.*, Ala. Code R. Civ. P. 13(g); Minn. Stat. Ann. R. Civ. P. Dist. Ct. 13.07; N.C. Gen. Stat. § 1A-1, R. 13(g).

[50] *See* the discussion of the role of the logical relationship test in determining compulsory counterclaims at § 9.03, notes 42–45 and accompanying text, *supra*.

[51] 6 *Wright & Miller* § 1431.

[52] *See* § 5.11, *supra*.

[53] *Moore* § 13.70[1]. Crossclaims are in this sense like permissive counterclaims. *See* § 9.03 *supra*. *See, e.g., Pouliot v. Paul Arpin Van Lines, Inc.*, 303 F. Supp. 2d 135, 138 (D. Conn. 2004).

[54] *See Moore* § 13.71[1]. The shift follows the language of Rule 13. Both paragraph (a) (compulsory counterclaims) and (b) (permissive counterclaims) describe the claimant's target as the "opposing party." *Cf.* Arthur F. Greenbaum, *Jacks or Better to Open: Procedural Limitations on Co-Party and Third-Party Claims*, 74 Minn. L. Rev. 507, 520–21 (1990) ("[M]ost courts and commentators read the

will lose it if it is compulsory and he fails to plead it.

Consider the following illustration. A, B, C and D enter into various construction and material supply contracts related to a large public works project. A sues B, C and D for breach of one of the contracts.[55] B counterclaims against A for breach of the same contract and pleads a claim against C for breach of a different but related contract. So long as it is sufficiently related to the subject matter of the original claim or counterclaim, B's claim against C is a good crossclaim.[56] If C has a claim against B sufficiently related to B's crossclaim, C must plead it back against B as a compulsory counterclaim. If C has any other claim against B, he has the option of pleading it as a permissive counterclaim.

Rule 13(g) also permits crossclaims against a party on the theory that he "is or may be liable to the crossclaimant for all or part of a claim asserted in the action against the cross-claimant." The rule thus provides a joinder mechanism for contingent or derivative claims.[57]

Rules to incorporate a shifting status based on the actual posture of the parties. Thus, if B brings a crossclaim against C, B then becomes an opposing party to C because they now are formally opposing each other on a claim.").

[55] The procedure permitting A to join B, C and D as multiple defendants is discussed in § 9.05, *infra*.

[56] In a well-known case, the Sixth Circuit ruled on facts like these that the two contracts were sufficiently related to the same construction project to bring the crossclaim within the "transaction or occurrence" test of Rule 13(g). *See Lasa Per L'Industria Del Marmo Societa Per Azioni of Lasa v. Alexander*, 414 F.2d 143 (6th Cir. 1969).

[57] The comparable joinder device for such claims against outsiders is impleader under Rule 14. *See* § 9.06, *infra*.

PART B.
Adding Claims by Adding Parties

§ 9.05 PERMISSIVE AND COMPULSORY PARTY JOINDER[58]

[1] Permissive Joinder

Federal Rule 20 authorizes the permissive[59] joinder of claims by multiple plaintiffs or against multiple defendants. In either case, the rule permits the assertion of "any right to relief" held "jointly, severally, or in the alternative," so long as claims joined to bring multiple parties into the lawsuit are "with respect to or arising out of the same transaction, occurrence, or series of transactions or occurrences and . . . any question of law or fact common to all" plaintiffs or defendants will arise in the action. The object of Rule 20 "is to promote trial convenience and expedite the final determination of disputes, thereby preventing multiple lawsuits."[60] To achieve this purpose, it authorizes party joinder to a substantially greater extent than was possible under common law or code systems.[61]

Common law and code systems generally permitted parties plaintiff to join their claims only with reference to rights held in common (jointly). The distinction between rights held jointly and rights held individually (severally) was often difficult for courts to draw. This restricted and complicated joinder practice.[62] Rule 20 clarified matters and increased judicial efficiency by extending party joinder to

[58] *See generally,* Moore §§ 19.01–19.09, 20.01–20.09; 7 Wright & Miller §§ 1601–1660; John B. Oakley, *Joinder and Jurisdiction in the Federal District Courts: The State of the Union of Rules and Statutes,* 69 Tenn. L. Rev. 35 (2001); Joan Steinman, *Postremoval Changes in the Party Structure of Diversity Cases: The Old Law, the New Law, and Rule 19,* 38 U. Kan. L. Rev. 863, 908–27 (1990); Carl Tobias, *Rule 19 and the Public Rights Exception to Party Joinder,* 65 N.C. L. Rev. 745 (1987); Richard D. Freer, *Rethinking Compulsory Joinder: A Proposal to Restructure Federal Rule 19,* 60 N.Y.U. L. Rev. 1061 (1985); John C. McCoid, *A Single Package for Multiparty Disputes,* 28 Stan. L. Rev. 707 (1976); Benjamin Kaplan, *Continuing Work of the Civil Committee: 1966 Amendments of the Federal Rules of Civil Procedure (I),* 81 Harv. L. Rev. 356, 358–75 (1967); *Developments in the Law — Multiparty Litigation in the Federal Courts,* 71 Harv. L. Rev. 874, 879–97 (1958).

[59] Rule 20 permits but does not require party joinder. In contrast, Rule 19 mandates party joinder whenever feasible. *See* § 9.05[2], *infra.* The distinction created between federal Rules 19 and 20 has its counterpart in many state procedural systems. *E.g.,* Del. Code Ann. R. Civ. P. 19–20; Ky. Rev. Stat. Ann. R. Civ. P. 19.01–20.01; Minn. Stat. Ann. R. Civ. P. Dist. Ct. 19.01–20.01.

[60] 7 Wright & Miller § 1652. *Accord,* Moore § 20.02[1][a]. *See, e.g., John S. Clark Co. v. Travelers Indem. Co.,* 359 F. Supp. 2d 429, 438 (M.D.N.C. 2004); *DirecTV, Inc. v. Barrett,* 220 F.R.D. 630, 631 (D. Kan. 2004).

[61] Friedenthal, Kane & Miller § 6.4. The scheme set out in Rule 20 corresponds more closely to English practice. *See* Moore § 20.03.

[62] *Ryder v. Jefferson Hotel Co.,* 113 S.E. 474 (S.C. 1922), is as an example frequently cited. Plaintiffs, who were husband and wife, alleged that they suffered humiliation and financial loss when ousted from their hotel room by defendant. South Carolina procedure permitted plaintiffs to join their claims only with reference to jointly held interests. A majority of the South Carolina Supreme Court concluded that the Ryder's interests were several, likening them to those of two railroad passengers suing for injuries

both categories of claims.[63] It expanded joinder of parties defendant by permitting joinder of multiple defendants claimed against alternatively.[64]

The test for party joinder under Rule 20 is two-fold. The claims supporting party joinder must (1) arise from the same transaction, occurrence, or series and (2) have in common a question of law or fact. The common question requirement is easier to satisfy, since only one common question of law or fact need exist to connect the claims.[65] A same transaction or occurrence requirement is embedded not just in Rule 20(a) but also Rules 13(a) governing compulsory counterclaims; and 13(g), governing crossclaims.[66] The policies these rules embody are likewise the same: to promote fair and efficient adjudication of related claims.[67] The prevailing interpretation of the requirement in all three settings appears to be the same: a logical relationship between claims.[68] This flexible interpretation of the requirement[69] facilitates joinder.[70]

Should the prerequisites for permissive joinder of parties be as accommodating as those for compulsory counterclaims and crossclaims? While all have the common purpose of promoting judicial efficiency, it is at least arguable that Rule 20 should have more limited application because it encumbers the suit with an additional

---

from a train wreck. The dissent argued that the injury alleged in the case was to a jointly held interest, likening plaintiffs to a partnership.

[63] "Illustratively, suppose a bus collides with an automobile. All of the bus passengers who suffered personal injuries or property damage may join as plaintiffs in a single action against defendant under Rule 20(a), even though their respective claims are several rather than joint." 7 WRIGHT & MILLER § 1654.

[64] "The need for alternative joinder of defendants typically arises when the substance of plaintiff's claim indicates that the plaintiff is entitled to relief from someone, but the plaintiff does not know which of two or more defendants is liable under the circumstances set forth in the complaint." 7 WRIGHT & MILLER § 1654

[65] 7 WRIGHT & MILLER § 1653. See, e.g., Jamison v. Purdue Pharma Co., 251 F. Supp. 2d 1315, 1322-23 (D. Miss. 2003).

[66] See §§ 9.03 & 9.04, supra.

[67] Rule 15(c), governing the relation back of amendments, also includes a "same transaction or occurrence" requirement. Here, the rule backdates amended complaints to the time the original complaint was filed if they arose out of the same transaction or occurrence. Here, however, the rule serves the different end of ensuring adequate prior notice to parties against whom claims are brought after the statute of limitations expires.

[68] "Usually, a court applies the transaction-or-occurrence requirement in a particular case by asking whether there is a logical relationship between the claim involving the party to be joined and the rest of the case." FRIEDENTHAL, KANE & MILLER § 6.4. This is also how the requirement is read concerning compulsory counterclaims and crossclaims. See §§ 9.03 & 9.04, supra. For discussions of alternative tests for transaction or occurrence, see § 9.03, supra.

[69] At the same time, the language of the transaction or occurrence requirement in Rule 20 should at least prevent joinder of claims evolving from entirely different facts, even if identical in type. Most federal courts have so read the rule. See, e.g., Scott v. Fairbanks Capital Corp., 284 F. Supp. 2d 880, 888 (S.D. Ohio 2003); Saval v. BL, Ltd., 710 F.2d 1027 (4th Cir. 1983). "[C]ourts properly refuse joinder when claims, while legally similar, are factually distinct." MOORE § 20.05[3].

[70] Professor Wright notes that "it seems practically desirable to give the broadest possible reading to the permissive language of Rule 20(a)." WRIGHT § 71. But see Robin J. Effron, The Shadow Rules of Joinder, 100 GEO. L.J. 759 (2012) (arguing that excessive flexibility of the rules deprives joinder jurisprudence of much-needed "transparency and consistency")

party as well as an additional claim.[71] On the other hand, Rule 20 only operates at the pleading level. It does not guarantee that multiparty claims joined will be tried at the same time, or that all will be tried in federal court. The limitations of subject matter jurisdiction and venue may pose problems.[72] The burdensome presence of an added party can be avoided, moreover, even when proper jurisdiction and venue exist. "[T]he convenience of the parties and the court can be protected fully, though joinder is allowed, by separate trials, pursuant to Rules 20(b) and 42(b) . . . ."[73]

[2] Compulsory Party Joinder

Compulsory party joinder has its origin in equity practice. Rule 19 governs compulsory party joinder in federal court. We have seen that Rule 20 is not compulsory; it merely determines how much freedom exists under the rules for joinder of plaintiffs or defendants. In that way, Rule 20 creates a ceiling that caps the parties a claimant may include. In contrast, Rule 19 creates a floor to ensure that the case does not proceed without parties needed for a just adjudication.

Rule 19(a) provides a framework for determining whether the absentee is a necessary party: one whose relation to the case is such that he must be joined if he can be. When joinder of a person falling under Rule 19(a) is not feasible, Rule 19(b) provides a framework for determining whether the person's absence is so problematic to the case that it cannot go on without him. Cases under this rule may be subject to as many as three inquiries: (1) whether joinder is required, (2) if joinder is required, whether it is feasible; and (3) if joinder is required but infeasible, whether the case should go on without the absentee.

[a] Required Parties Under Rule 19(a) — When Must Joinable Persons Be Brought In?

The object of rules facilitating expansion of claims and parties in civil litigation is either to reduce delay, needless repetition and expense in civil litigation, or to avoid prejudice to a party or absentee.[74] The multiclaim rules considered earlier share the first objective with Rule 20. Compulsory joinder under Rule 19 also fosters judicial efficiency, but it is most concerned with the second objective. Rule 19(a) calls absentees needed for a just adjudication *required parties* (sometimes referred to as "necessary" parties in the cases). Paragraph (a) sets up three separate categories of required parties, stating that each "must be joined as a party" when joinder is feasible. The three categories are couched in flexible, pragmatic terms.

One is required according to Rule 19(a)(1)(A) if "in that person's absence, the court cannot accord complete relief among existing parties." Emphasis here is on

---

[71] *See* § 9.01, *supra*.

[72] *Moore* §§ 20.07–20.08; John B. Oakley, *Joinder and Jurisdiction in the Federal District Courts: The State of the Union of Rules and Statutes*, 69 Tenn. L. Rev. 35 (2001). In contrast, compulsory counterclaims and crossclaims are sheltered by the supplemental jurisdiction statue, *see* § 9.03, *supra*, and pose no serious venue problems.

[73] *Wright* § 71.

[74] *See* § 9.01, *supra*.

"the desirability of joining those persons in whose absence the court would be obliged to grant partial or hollow rather than complete relief to the parties before the court."[75] In close cases, it may be necessary to determine whether the absence of a person makes likely further lawsuits among those already parties or, whether, instead, "meaningful relief can be granted without the absentee."[76] For example, suppose that a former employer sues his former employee, seeking to enjoin him from working for a new employer, on the grounds that the employee acquired trade secrets from his former employer that he has unlawfully shared with his new employer. The new employer is a required party, because complete relief cannot be accorded among the existing parties: enjoining the former employee from working for his new employer will do nothing to rectify harms caused by the new employer wrongfully exploiting trade secrets it already acquired.

One is also a required party when, according to Rule 19(a)(1)(B)(i), "the person claims an interest relating to the subject of the action and is so situated that disposing of the action in the person's absence may . . . as a practical matter impair or impede the person's ability to protect the interest . . . ." Here the rule "recognizes the importance of protecting the person whose joinder is in question against the practical prejudice to him which may arise through a disposition of the action in his absence."[77] Emphasis on practical impairment means that it is not necessary for the absentee to risk the possibility of being bound by the case in a formal sense.[78] What is necessary is a prospect of detriment to the absentee from the case serious enough to entitle him to an opportunity to influence the outcome in ways only a litigant can.[79] At the same time, one whose interests may be thus impaired by the litigation probably has a right to intervene in the case.[80] An absentee's opportunity to intervene thus may be taken into account in determining prejudice to the absentee in the absence of joinder.[81] Returning to the earlier example of the former employer who seeks to enjoin his former employee from working for a new employer, the new employer is also a required party under Rule 19(a)(1)(B)(i): the new employer has an interest in continuing to receive the services of his new employee, an interest that will be impaired if his employee is enjoined.

Finally, one who "claims an interest relating to the subject of the action" is a required party according to Rule 19(a)(1)(B)(ii) when "disposing of the action in the

---

[75] Rule 19, advisory committee's notes (1966).

[76] *Moore* § 19.03[2][d]. *See, e.g., Wilbur v. Locke*, 423 F.3d 1101, 1112 (9th Cir. 2005).

[77] Rule 19, advisory committee's notes (1966).

[78] Indeed, the constitutional law of due process will usually prevent that from happening. *See* § 15.08[1], *infra.*

[79] Party prerogatives include setting boundaries of materiality through pleadings, developing the facts by discovery, creating parts of the factual record, and appeal.

[80] Intervention of right is usually governed by Rule 24(a)(2), discussed more fully in § 9.08[1], *infra.* The language used in Rules 19(a)(1)(B)(i) and 24(a)(2) to describe practical impairment to interests of the absentee is almost identical. The opportunity of absentees described in Rule 19(a)(1)(B)(i) for timely intervention under Rule 24(a)(2) is limited only when their interests are adequately represented by one already a party, or when their joinder would have defeated diversity jurisdiction.

[81] It would be difficult to reach any other conclusion. When the absentee could intervene but chooses not to, any practical impairment from the litigation seems almost self-inflicted. Unfortunately, the availability of intervention makes it harder to identify a discrete role for Rule 19(a)(1)(B)(i).

person's absence may . . . leave an existing party subject to a substantial risk of incurring double, multiple, or otherwise inconsistent obligations because the interest."[82] The strongest case for Rule 19(a)(1)(B)(ii) joinder is where a party, usually a defendant, risks either double liability or inconsistent judgments. Turning once again to the example of the former employer who seeks to enjoin his former employee from working for a new employer, the new employer is a required party under 19(a)(1)(B)(ii) too: if the former employee is enjoined from working for his new employer, his new employer could bring an action against the employee for breach of their employment contract, subjecting the employee to the risk of inconsistent judgments.

The bank in our illustration may urge B's joinder by also arguing that, even if successive suits do not lead to double liability, they may produce inconsistent judgments. Suppose the bank prevails in A's suit through favorable determination of an issue broad enough to defeat B's claim as well. If B is not made a party to the initial case, B will be entitled to relitigate the issue, resulting in the possibility of inconsistent judgments.[83] In addition, the bank can argue that B's joinder should be required simply to spare the bank the vexation and expense of litigating in two lawsuits rather than one. On the other hand, plaintiff can counter that he should be allowed to pick his defendants.

Every application of joinder under Rule 19(a)(1)(B)(ii) would by definition seem to avert multiplicity of litigation. This feature has been stressed in some cases.[84] It is uncertain, however, how much play this factor will or should have in cases where defendant cannot persuasively argue risk of multiple liability or inconsistent judgments. At some point, what has been called the " 'plaintiff autonomy' prem- ise,"[85] becomes a potent counterforce to claimant joinder. There is considerable tradition and sentiment behind the notion that plaintiffs are entitled to sue whomever they want. This notion explains why, under federal procedure and that of many states, joint tortfeasors are not considered necessary or required parties by reason of their tortfeasor relationship alone.[86]

So long as joinder is feasible, a person required according to Rule 19(a) must be joined in order for the lawsuit to continue.[87] If the person will not enter the lawsuit

---

[82] A party prejudiced in the manner described in Rule 19(a)(1)(B)(ii) will sometimes be able to resort to interpleader to force all competing claimants to make their claims against him in one proceeding. On interpleader, see generally § 9.07, *infra*.

[83] This is not double liability, since the bank will be liable only to B. Yet it seems no more than fair for the bank to have an opportunity to bind both A and B to a determination favorable to the bank in the initial suit. This is especially true since B might have been able subsequently to use offensive non-mutual issue preclusion had the issue in an initial suit between the bank and A alone come out in B's favor. *See* § 15.08[2], *infra*. The prospect of inconsistent judgments has been used to require joinder. *E.g., Lopez v. Martin Luther King, Jr. Hosp.*, 97 F.R.D. 24 (C.D. Cal. 1983).

[84] *E.g., Walsh v. Centeio*, 692 F.2d 1239 (9th Cir. 1982).

[85] JAMES, HAZARD & LEUBSDORF § 10.12.

[86] *E.g., Temple v. Synthes Corp.*, 498 U.S. 5, 7 (1990) ("It has long been the rule that it is not necessary for all joint tortfeasors to be named as defendants in a single lawsuit.").

[87] *See, e.g., Dubay v. Wells*, 437 F. Supp. 2d 656, 659 (E.D. Mich. 2006); *Temple Univ. Hosp., Inc. v. Group Health, Inc.*, 413 F. Supp. 2d 420, 425 (E.D. Pa. 2005). The court "will usually give the plaintiff an

voluntarily, he will in most cases be brought in under the rule as a defendant.[88] This is true whether the person joined is a claimant or one claimed against.[89] If the absentee is a claimant, however, the court may realign an involuntarily joined claimant to determine jurisdiction in diversity cases.[90] In addition, Rule 19(a)(2) provides that an absentee claimant may be made "in a proper case, an involuntary plaintiff." Relatively few absentees, however, are subject to involuntary plaintiff treatment.[91]

[b]   Rule 19(a) — When is Joinder of a Required Party Feasible?

However important a person might be to the lawsuit, his joinder may be infeasible for one of three reasons. Rule 19(a) makes clear that the person can only be joined when "subject to service of process" (when the person served would be subject to personal jurisdiction in a forum state court) and when his joinder "will not deprive the court of subject-matter jurisdiction." Moreover, it also excuses an involuntarily joined party from the case if he "objects to venue and the joinder . . . would make venue improper."

Insurmountable difficulties may arise when it is necessary to serve process beyond the borders of the state where the federal court is sitting. We saw earlier that Congress has limited the personal-jurisdiction authority of federal courts in most cases to that enjoyed by local state courts.[92] Rule 4 relaxes this constraint to a degree regarding joinder of parties required under Rule 19, authorizing process against them (and therefore personal jurisdiction) up to a distance of 100 miles from the federal courthouse. Although useful "in major metropolitan areas that span more than one state," the so-called 100-mile bulge "is of limited importance given the general expansion in availability of extraterritorial service under state long-arm statutes."[93]

Even if Rule 19 had made no reference to the topics, it would have been clear that the rule alone could not create subject matter jurisdiction or venue. A federal rule of civil procedure cannot "extend or limit the jurisdiction of the district courts or the venue of actions in those courts."[94] What is more, express requirements in Rule 19

---

opportunity to add the absentee. If the plaintiff fails to do so, the court may dismiss the action because of plaintiff's noncompliance." MOORE § 19.04[4][a].

[88] MOORE § 19.04[4][b]. *See, e.g., EEOC v. Peabody W. Coal Co.*, 400 F.3d 774, 782 (9th Cir. 2005), *cert. denied*, 546 U.S. 1150 (2006).

[89] Rule 19(a)(2) states that "[a] person who refuses to join as a plaintiff may be made a . . . defendant."

[90] *See, e.g., Keith v. Volpe*, 858 F.2d 467, 476 (9th Cir. 1988). *See generally* § 5.04[2] (diversity between whom?), *supra*.

[91] There must be "a relationship between the plaintiff and the absentee such that the absentee must allow the use of its name as plaintiff to enable the extant plaintiff to secure relief. Courts have found such relationships in cases involving exclusive licensees of patents and beneficial owners of copyrights." MOORE § 19.04[4][b] (footnote omitted).

[92] *See* § 3.01[2][b], *supra*.

[93] MOORE § 19.04[2].

[94] Rule 82. The reference is to federal subject matter jurisdiction. *Cf. Snyder v. Harris*, 394 U.S. 332,

for subject matter jurisdiction and venue forestalled applications of ancillary jurisdiction and ancillary venue[95] that were possible in certain other multiclaim and multiparty settings before the enactment of supplemental jurisdiction.[96] Problems therefore arise from attempts to join one who would destroy diversity jurisdiction[97] or who properly objects to venue.[98]

[c] Rule 19(b) — When Is the Absence of a Person Who Cannot Be Joined So Problematic that the Case Must Be Dismissed?

Rule 19(b) states that when an absentee required under paragraph (a) "cannot be joined,"[99] the court must determine whether, in equity and good conscience, the action should proceed among the existing parties, or should be dismissed." The defense of failure to join a required party can be raised by a pre-answer motion to dismiss under Rule 12(b)(7), in the answer, or by a motion for judgment on the pleadings or at trial.[100] Whereas, Rule 19(a) asks whether it would be bad to proceed without an absentee, Rule 19(b) asks whether it would be so bad that the case should be thrown out if it is not feasible to include the absentee. Rule 19(b) then sets out four factors to be weighed in each case before the court decides whether the case should go on without the absentee. In presenting these considerations, the approach taken in the rule is somewhat unusual. Criteria listed in the rules may be serial[101] or cumulative,[102] but they usually line up in support of a common conclusion. Rule 19(b) instead lists factors supporting opposite results.

The first factor is "the extent to which a judgment rendered in the person's absence might prejudice that person the existing parties . . . ." This is the same concern expressed earlier in subclauses (i) and (ii) of Rule 19(a)(1)(B).[103] Tempering

---

337 (1969) (even if expansion of federal diversity jurisdiction might otherwise be implied from an amendment making class actions more available under Rule 23, the same was prohibited under Rule 82).

[95] *But see* George B. Fraser, *Ancillary Jurisdiction of Federal Courts of Persons Whose Interest May Be Impaired If Not Joined*, 62 F.R.D. 483 (1967) (arguing that the objectives of ancillary jurisdiction would be well served by giving play to the doctrine in Rule 19 joinder situations). Now, under the supplemental jurisdiction statute, federal subject matter jurisdiction is unavailable for most applications of Rule 19. For discussion of the statute, *see* §§ 5.08–5.11, *supra*.

[96] For an explanation of prior doctrines of ancillary jurisdiction in complex litigation, *see* § 9.03, *supra*.

[97] *Provident Tradesmen's Bank & Trust Co. v. Patterson*, 390 U.S. 102 (1968).

[98] *See* WRIGHT & MILLER § 1610.

[99] Technically, the venue hurdle created in Rule 19(a) comes after the absentee has been joined. Joinder in such cases (although temporary and unavailing) is feasible in a narrow sense. Yet it is better to read Rule 19(b) to apply to joinder problems including "limitations on service of process, subject matter jurisdiction, *and* venue." Rule 19, advisory committee's notes (1966) (emphasis added). On feasibility of joinder, see generally § 9.05[2][b], *supra*.

[100] Rule 12(h)(2).

[101] For example, satisfaction of any of the three categories in Rule 19(a) makes an absentee a required party. *See* § 9.05[2][a], *supra*.

[102] For example, satisfaction of all of the four categories of Rule 23(a) is necessary for a class action. *See* § 9.09, *infra*.

[103] For discussion of this concern as manifested in Rules 19(a)(1)(B)(i) & (ii), see § 9.05[2][a], *supra*.

the effect of the first factor is the second factor, "the extent to which any prejudice could be lessened or avoided by . . . protective provisions in the judgment . . . shaping the relief; . . . or other measures . . . ." The third factor, "whether a judgment rendered in the person's absence would be adequate," is the same concern expressed earlier in Rule 19(a)(1).[104] It is counterbalanced by the fourth factor, "whether the plaintiff would have an adequate remedy if the action were dismissed for nonjoinder."

This list of factors offers no reasons for concern about the absence of a party beyond those previously raised in Rule 19(a). It is evident from the manner in which the factors are juxtaposed, however, that reasons for treating an absentee as a required party under Rule 19(a) will not invariably support a decision to dismiss the case when joinder is infeasible. The Supreme Court's decision in *Provident Tradesmen's Bank & Trust Co. v. Patterson*[105] bears this out.

The *Provident* case resulted from a motor vehicle accident which caused multiple deaths and serious injury. Various tort claimants sued the indigent estate of one driver (Cionci) and an insurance company for a declaratory judgment that Cionci was driving the car of one Dutcher with Dutcher's permission. If the car was driven with Dutcher's permission, then Cionci's estate shared with Dutcher coverage on Dutcher's liability insurance policy. That policy had been issued by the insurance company defendant.

The Court concluded that Dutcher's relationship to the lawsuit was such that Rule 19(a) required him to be joined, if joinder was feasible. It was not. Dutcher's citizenship would have destroyed diversity of the parties upon which the lower court's jurisdiction depended. That brought the Court to Rule 19(b). The Court concluded that suit should go on without Dutcher. The case suggests some of the circumstances in which it is possible to continue suit in the absence of one deemed required under Rule 19(a).

First, plaintiffs had fully litigated their case at the trial level without Dutcher (defendants having made no Rule 19 challenge there). Stressing the fourth factor in Rule 19(b), the Court noted the unfairness of forcing plaintiffs to start from scratch in state court. The Court declined to speculate whether a Rule 19 dismissal of plaintiffs' case before trial would have afforded them an "adequate remedy" in state court. "After trial, however, the adequacy of this hypothetical alternative, from the plaintiffs' point of view, was obviously greatly diminished."

Second, plaintiffs undercut perhaps the strongest argument in favor of a Rule 19(b) dismissal by agreeing to limit all of their claims to the amount of the insurance policy issued by the defendant insurance company.[106] The insurer otherwise would have faced the risk of paying twice on the same policy,[107] a form of prejudice from

---

[104] For discussion of this concern as manifested in Rule 19(a)(1), see § 9.05[2][a], *supra*.

[105] 390 U.S. 102 (1968).

[106] 390 U.S. at 116.

[107] Had plaintiffs preserved the option of suing Dutcher in a subsequent lawsuit, Dutcher would have claimed sole protection under the policy and probably would have been able to relitigate the permission issue. 390 U.S. at 115. If successful, Dutcher would prevent the insurer from subtracting from its liability coverage amounts paid out to cover Cionci.

proceeding without Dutcher that would be entitled to considerable weight under the first factor in Rule 19(b).[108]

It is impossible to lay down hard and fast rules about the application of the four factors of Rule 19(b). The United States Supreme Court observed recently in *Republic of Philippines v. Pimentel*[109] that "the issue of joinder can be complex, and determinations are case specific."[110]

§ 9.06 IMPLEADER[111]

Third-party practice, or impleader, reduces the possibility of duplicative litigation. It addresses situations where one outside the litigation may either share or be legally responsible for defendant's liability to plaintiff, such that the outsider can be required to reimburse the defendant for all or part of any judgment against the defendant on the plaintiff's claim.[112] Defendant under such circumstances is often able to bring in (implead) the outsider and thereby settle all legal questions in the initial case.

Consider the following situation — first, without impleader. Customer sues retailer on a product liability claim. The facts of the case are that, if retailer is held liable, he will have a strong argument that the manufacturer should *indemnify* or reimburse him for all or part of that liability.[113] However, the consumer does not join the manufacturer as a co-defendant,[114] nor does the manufacturer seek to intervene.[115]

If the consumer obtains a judgment against the retailer, retailer must thereafter bring a separate lawsuit against the manufacturer for indemnification. Moreover, because the manufacturer was not a party to the consumer's lawsuit, the manufac-

---

[108] This corresponds to a party's risk of double liability, identified in Rule 19(a)(1)(B)(ii) and discussed in § 9.05[2][a], *supra*.

[109] 128 S. Ct. 2180, 2188 (2008). The Court was careful to follow the approach laid out in *Provident*. It concluded, largely on international sovereign immunity grounds, that the case could not proceed in the absence of the Philippine government and of a special Philippine commission. The two parties were required under Rule 19(a) but could not be joined. The court ruled that Rule 19(b) required the case to be dismissed.

[110] 128 S. Ct. at 2188. "[T]o a substantial degree the effective operation of the rule depends on the careful exercise of discretion by the district court." 7 WRIGHT & MILLER § 1608. A survey of cases interpreting the factors appears, *id.*, and in MOORE § 19.05[1][a]. *See, e.g., Erline Co. S.A. v. Johnson*, 440 F.3d 648, 652 (4th Cir. 2006).

[111] *See generally* MOORE §§ 14.01–14.42; 6 WRIGHT & MILLER §§ 1441–1465; Arthur F. Greenbaum, *Jacks or Better to Open: Procedural Limitations on Co-Party and Third-Party Claims*, 74 MINN. L. REV. 507, 525–31 (1990); John C. Feirich, *Third Party Practice*, 1967 ILL. L.F. 236; *Developments in the Law — Multiparty Litigation in the Federal Courts*, 71 HARV. L. REV. 874, 906–13 (1958).

[112] When a co-defendant is in this position, the proper device for asserting this legal responsibility in federal court is a crossclaim. *See* § 9.04 (discussing Rule 13(g)), *supra*.

[113] *See generally* Symposium, *Products Liability: Economic Analysis and the Law*, 38 U. CHI. L. REV. 1 (1970).

[114] For discussion of joinder under Rule 20, see § 9.05[1], *supra*.

[115] For discussion of intervention under Rule 24, see § 9.08, *infra*.

turer is free to relitigate issues determined there which underlie the consumer's judgment against the retailer.[116]

On the other hand, impleader would permit the retailer to join the manufacturer in the initial suit. As a party to the case, the manufacturer will then be bound along with the retailer to an adjudication of issues establishing the consumer's right to recover against the retailer. In addition, the retailer may obtain an adjudication of its indemnification claim in the same lawsuit. Permitting impleader in such cases "will avoid circuity of action and eliminate duplication of suits based on closely related matters."[117]

Impleader enjoys widespread use in federal and many state courts.[118] Rule 14 authorizes it in the former. Within fourteen days after service of the defendant's answer, Rule 14 permits defendant to serve a *third-party complaint* on the outsider.[119] In this capacity, defendant becomes a *third-party plaintiff*, the outsider a *third-party defendant*. The third-party defendant or any other party to the suit may move to strike defendant's impleader, either by arguing that it is beyond the scope of Rule 14, or that the court should use its discretion to refuse impleader even if the rule appears satisfied.[120]

The rule requires that the nature of the third-party claim be such that the third-party defendant "is or may be liable" to the third-party plaintiff "for all or part of the claim against it." For impleader to work, it is often necessary to bring in the third-party defendant before the third-party plaintiff's liability to plaintiff can be established. Rule 14 thus authorizes impleader against one who "*may be liable.*"[121] An eventual judgment for the original plaintiff binds not only the defendant/third-party plaintiff, but also precludes the third party defendant from relitigating issues underlying the third-party plaintiff's liability to the original plaintiff.[122]

---

[116] The manufacturer would be a stranger to the first suit and therefore could not be bound by issue preclusion. *See* § 15.08, *infra*.

[117] 6 WRIGHT & MILLER § 1443. *See, e.g.*, *Irwin v. Mascott*, 94 F. Supp. 2d 1052, 1056 (N.D. Cal. 2000). FRIEDENTHAL, KANE & MILLER § 6.9, note that "[t]he availability of impleader saves the time and cost of duplicating evidence in two proceedings, avoids inconsistent results on related claims based on identical or similar evidence, and eliminates the serious prejudice to the original defendant that might result from a time lag between the plaintiff's judgment against him and a judgment in the defendant's favor against the third-party defendant."

[118] FRIEDENTHAL, KANE & MILLER § 6.9.

[119] Rule 14(a) requires court approval for service of the third-party complaint after the fourteen-day period.

[120] *See* text accompanying notes 133–137, *infra*.

[121] Emphasis added. This language in the rule has long been interpreted to permit impleader even when the claim against the third-party defendant is not yet ripe for suit under applicable substantive law because the third-party plaintiff's liability has yet to be determined. See, e.g., the well-known case, *Jeub v. B/G Foods, Inc.*, 2 F.R.D. 238 (D. Minn. 1942).

[122] Rule 14(a) confers litigant status on the third-party defendant in the case, thereby creating an opportunity for the third-party defendant to join with the third-party plaintiff in attempting to defeat plaintiff's claim. Rule 14(a)(2)(C) states that "[t]he third-party defendant may assert against the plaintiff any defenses that the third-party plaintiff has to the plaintiff's claim."

The heart of impleader is the requirement that the claim supporting it be based on secondary or derivative liability. That is, the third-party plaintiff must seek reimbursement from the third-party defendant for all or part of the former's liability to plaintiff. It is not enough that the impleader claim arose out of the same transaction or occurrence as the original plaintiff's claim; the impleader must, in addition, be contingent or derivative: *If* the defendant is liable to the plaintiff, *then* the third-party defendant is liable to the third-party plaintiff.[123] But "[t]he secondary or derivative liability notion is central and it is irrelevant whether the basis of the third-party claim is indemnity, subrogation, contribution, express or implied warranty, or some other theory."[124] Thus, the rule does not permit defendant to implead an outsider on the theory that the outsider should be liable to plaintiff *instead* of the defendant.[125] Nor does it permit impleader for a claim that the outsider is liable to the defendant for the defendant's own injuries from the outsider's conduct, as they are not derivative from defendant's liability to the plaintiff.[126]

While the defendant/third-party plaintiff's liability is established by a judgment for plaintiff against the defendant/third-party plaintiff, the existence of the contingent or derivative liability is a separate question. The answer to it is not supplied by Rule 14, which merely provides the procedure by which such a duty is asserted as an impleader claim.[127] Instead, the answer must be found in the applicable substantive law. Four common theories of contingent or derivative liability are indemnity, subrogation, contribution and warranty. Their precise elements vary somewhat from jurisdiction to jurisdiction.

A right to *indemnification* either arises out of an express contractual provision whereby one party agrees to indemnify (or "hold harmless") another for certain liabilities, or by implication.[128] A right to indemnification will be implied when a person without fault is held legally liable for damages caused by the fault of another.[129]

Subrogation is the succession of one person to the rights of another.[130] "Subrogees are generally joint tortfeasors or innocent insurers who have compen-

---

[123] *See, e.g., Lewis v. Cimarron Valley R.R.*, 162 F. Supp. 2d 1220, 1227 (D. Kan. 2001); *National Bank of Can. v. Artex Indus., Inc.*, 627 F. Supp. 610, 613 (S.D.N.Y. 1986). *See generally* 6 WRIGHT & MILLER § 1446.

[124] 6 WRIGHT & MILLER § 1446 (citing illustrative cases).

[125] 6 WRIGHT & MILLER § 1444; FRIEDENTHAL, KANE & MILLER § 6.9. Rule 14(c) excepts.

[126] If, however, defendant pleads a proper impleader claim for secondary or derivative liability against an outsider, then defendant can join any other claims he has against the defendant pursuant to Rule 18, including any claim for his own injuries caused by the outsider.

[127] *See, e.g., Assicurazioni Generali S.p.A. v. Terranova*, 40 Fed. R. Serv. 2d (Callaghan) 850, 852 (S.D.N.Y. 1984) ("Rule 14 provides only a procedural means of adding a [third-party] defendant; it does not confer any substantive rights on the [third-party] plaintiff.").

[128] *See, e.g., Terranova*, 40 Fed. R. Serv. 2d at 852 (*construing* New York law); *Anderson v. Dreibelbis*, 104 F.R.D. 415 (E.D. Pa. 1984) (*construing* Pennsylvania law), *aff'd*, 787 F.2d 580 (3d Cir. 1986).

[129] *Terranova*, 40 Fed. R. Serv. 2d at 852; *Anderson*, 104 F.R.D. at 416–17.

[130] *See, e.g., Terranova*, 40 Fed. R. Serv.2d at 853. "[S]ubrogation is of two kinds, 'legal' and 'conventional.' The former is grounded in equity and arises by operation of law, which gives to a third

sated the insured for an injury resulting from the negligence of a third-party."[131] An insurer sued by its insured on an insurance policy may therefore implead the negligent third party on a subrogation theory to the extent that the insurer is or may be liable to its insured on the policy.

The right of *contribution* typically arises among joint tortfeasors, two or more persons who are jointly or severally liable in tort for the same injury.[132] If a defendant tortfeasor is liable to pay plaintiff damages for plaintiff's injuries, other joint tortfeasors may be liable to the defendant for all or part of the damages the defendant owes plaintiff.

Finally, a *warranty*, in the impleader context, is an express or implied statement or representation typically made by a seller to a buyer or others in the chain of product distribution regarding the character of or title to the product.

Thus, in our hypothetical product liability suit, the retailer may in most jurisdictions implead the manufacturer either on the basis of an express indemnification clause in a sales contract or on the implied indemnity theory that the retailer is or may be liable to the consumer for defects in the product which are the fault of the manufacturer. Alternately, he may base his impleader on a theory of contribution, if he and the manufacturer are jointly or severally liable for causing the consumer's injury. Finally, he may invoke warranty, on the theory that the manufacturer expressly or impliedly warranted the product to be free of defects and should therefore reimburse the retailer for any liability arising from a product defect.

Since Rule 14 focuses on an easily defined and demonstrable source of judicial inefficiency, it is not surprising that federal courts have usually given it a sympathetic reading. At the same time, the rule is permissive rather than compulsory. Parties claimed against are not obliged to implead an outsider, and whether particular applications of the rule should be permitted when impleader is sought is a matter best left to the sound discretion of the court.[133] In exercising its discretion, a federal court will balance potential savings of time and resources through impleader[134] against any problems posed by addition of the third-party defendant. In some cases these problems will be sufficient to defeat impleader.

---

person who has been compelled to pay a remedy against one who, in justice, ought to pay. 'Conventional' subrogation is grounded upon contract, express or implied." *Insurance Co. of N. Am. v. Medical Protective Co.*, 768 F.2d 315, 320 (10th Cir. 1985).

[131] *Terranova*, 40 Fed. R. Serv. 2d at 853 (*construing* New York law).

[132] 40 Fed. R. Serv. 2d at 852–53 (*construing* New York law); *Anderson*, 104 F.R.D. at 416 (*construing* Pennsylvania law).

[133] 6 *WRIGHT & MILLER* § 1443. *See, e.g., Dishong v. Peabody Corp.*, 219 F.R.D. 382, 385 (E.D. Va. 2003).

[134] Prejudice to the defendant from proceeding in the absence of the outsider does not seem to play a very large role in justifying impleader. Yet the possibility of prejudice can be quite real. Recall the possibility for the retailer of conflicting judgments in the hypothetical opening this section. However, the appropriate response in such cases may be for defendant to argue compulsory joinder of the outsider under Rule 19(a), or dismissal of the case under Rule 19(b) if joinder is not feasible. *See* § 9.05[2], *supra*.

For example, the added presence of a third-party defendant may unduly delay trial for plaintiff.[135] Or in a *respondeat superior* claim of negligence, the employer-defendant could prejudice the plaintiff by impleading a shallow-pocket employee whose presence might prompt a sympathetic jury to return a smaller verdict on the underlying claim against the deep-pocket employer.[136] There may also be "a lack of similarity between the issues and evidence required to prove the main and third-party claims . . . ."[137] Many of these problems, however, can be cured without disallowing the impleader by ordering separate trials under Rule 42, should the prejudice be a factor come trial.[138]

Rule 14 authorizes inclusion of third-party defendants without confronting extrinsic difficulties of personal jurisdiction, subject matter jurisdiction and venue which could actually prevent the third-party defendants from entering the suit. A federal court usually enjoys only as much personal jurisdiction as the courts of the forum state.[139] Rule 4(k)(1)(b) supplements this for process under Rules 14 and 19 with the so-called 100-mile bulge — an added reach of 100 miles from the federal courthouse[140] — which may be inadequate to reach a prospective third-party defendant. The picture is brighter for federal subject matter jurisdiction and venue, however. Impleader claims that would not be within the original subject matter jurisdiction of federal courts now appear covered by the supplemental jurisdiction statute.[141] Similarly, venue does not appear to pose much of a problem in the impleader setting.[142]

---

[135] For discussion of this point and illustrative cases, see 6 WRIGHT & MILLER § 1443. *See, e.g., Riccitelli v. Water Pik Technologies, Inc.*, 203 F.R.D. 62, 63 (D.N.H. 2001).

[136] *See, e.g., Goodhart v. United States Lines Co.*, 26 F.R.D. 163 (S.D.N.Y. 1960) (impleader of employee is denied when it could serve only to suggest to the jury that the employee will pay the judgment or to threaten the employee with bankruptcy unless he testifies favorably to the employer). For further discussion of this point and illustrative cases, see 6 WRIGHT & MILLER § 1443.

[137] 6 WRIGHT & MILLER § 1443. *See, e.g., Dishong v. Peabody Corp.*, 219 F.R.D. 382, 385 (E.D. Va. 2003).

[138]

> [T]he court always must remain flexible in its approach to an attempted impleader and should bear in mind that means other than dismissal may be available to prevent prejudice or confusion. Thus, if it appears that the action may become unduly complex because unrelated issues or evidence are present, or if knowledge of the identity or existence of a third party may cause prejudice to any litigant, the proper remedy is for the court to permit impleader and then to order separate trials pursuant to Rule 42 if any of these concerns becomes a reality.

6 WRIGHT & MILLER § 1443.

[139] *See* § 3.01[2][b], *supra.*

[140] A more detailed explanation appears at § 9.05[2][b], *supra.*

[141] *See* § 5.11, *supra.*

[142] "The prevailing interpretation of the federal venue rule is that if venue is properly established for the original action, the third-party defendant cannot object that venue would have been improper if the action had originally included him or her as a defendant." JAMES, HAZARD & LEUBSDORF § 10.18. Recent statutory developments in federal venue have, if anything, made the possibility of venue for impleader claims more secure. *See* § 6.01, *supra.*

§ 9.07 INTERPLEADER[143]

"Interpleader is a form of joinder open to one who does not know to which of several claimants he or she is liable, if liable at all."[144] Interpleader resembles impleader[145] in that it protects one claimed against from multiple and possibly inconsistent lawsuits,[146] and it resembles permissive joinder[147] in that it permits a party to sort out its legal relationships with a number of opposing parties simultaneously.[148]

Absent interpleader, the party claimed against might have to defend against competing claimants in different courts, perhaps in different parts of the country. This might lead to multiple liability, inconsistent judgments,[149] or (at the very least) the vexation of multiple lawsuits.[150] Interpleader permits one (called a stakeholder) to avoid this by forcing all claimants to proceed against him in one lawsuit.[151]

Although many states authorize interpleader, interpleader in federal court is often preferable, at least in cases where the party claimed against faces the prospect of litigation spread across more than one state. This is not because of any advantage offered by the Federal Rules of Civil Procedure. Federal Rule 22, covering interpleader, provides little not already afforded by the rules of a majority of state courts.[152] Rather, it is because Rule 22 is usually overshadowed by an

---

[143] *See generally* Moore §§ 22.01–22.04; 7 Wright & Miller §§ 1701–21; Paula J. McDermott, Comment, *Can Statutory Interpleader Be Used As a Remedy By the Tortfeasor in Mass Tort Litigation?*, 90 Dick. L. Rev. 439 (1985); Mark W. Smith, Comment, *Deference to State Courts in Federal Interpleader Actions*, 47 U. Chi. L. Rev. 824 (1980); Geoffrey C. Hazard, Jr., & Myron Moskovitz, *An Historical and Critical Analysis of Interpleader*, 52 Cal. L. Rev. 706 (1964); *Developments in the Law — Multiparty Litigation in the Federal Courts*, 71 Harv. L. Rev. 874, 913–28 (1958).

[144] Wright § 74. It "is a procedural device used to resolve conflicting claims to money or property. It enables a person or entity in possession of a tangible res or fund of money (the 'stakeholder') to join in a single suit two or more 'claimants' asserting mutually exclusive claims to that stake." Moore § 22.02[1].

[145] *See* § 9.06 (Rule 14), *supra.*

[146] James, Hazard & Leubsdorf § 10.19.

[147] *See* § 9.05[1] (Rule 20(a)), *supra.*

[148] Interpleader is most like the part of Rule 20(a) "allowing the joinder of plaintiffs in the alternative when they are uncertain which of them has the right to relief and the joinder of defendants in the alternative when it is uncertain which of them is liable." 7 Wright & Miller § 1702.

[149] Multiple liability and inconsistent judgments, the most troublesome byproducts of an excessive number of lawsuits, are described at § 9.05[2][a], *supra.*

[150] Professor Wright suggested that the possibility of vexatious multiple lawsuits can alone be sufficient to justify interpleader. Wright § 74. *Treinies v. Sunshine Mining Co.*, 308 U.S. 66 (1939), is a famous example of interpleader as a response to the concerns listed in the text. Two factions claimed right of ownership to the same block of mining company stock. One claimed on the strength of a Washington court judgment, the other on an Idaho judgment. Uncertain which judgment to honor, the mining company cleared the air by interpleading both claimants in a single action in federal court.

[151] *See, e.g., Estate of Ellington v. EMI Music Publ'g*, 282 F. Supp. 2d 192 (S.D.N.Y. 2003); *Aon Corp. Accidental Death & Dismemberment Plan v. Hohlweck*, 223 F. Supp. 2d 510, 513-14 (S.D.N.Y. 2002). Interpleader is most frequently used as a basis for commencing suit, but it can be initiated in ongoing litigation through a counterclaim, crossclaim or third party claim. *See generally* 7 Wright & Miller § 1708.

[152] The language of the state rules is often nearly identical. *E.g.*, Fla. R. Civ. P. 1.240; N.M. Stat. Ann. R. Civ. P. Dist. Ct. 1-022; Wis. Stat. Ann. § 803.07.

additional procedural remedy available only in federal court: statutory inter-pleader.[153] Congress created a special enclave of subject matter jurisdiction within the interpleader statute,[154] complemented the arrangement with a statute creating special venue possibilities,[155] and (most significant in creating an advantage over interpleader actions in state court) liberalized service of process and, therefore, personal jurisdiction.[156]

Whether proceeding by statute or Rule 22, the stakeholder deposits with the court the stake (fund) — property or money[157] — which is the target of the competing claims against the stakeholder. The stakeholder may then seek inter-locutory relief, enjoining maintenance of other suits against him with respect to the fund during the federal interpleader action.[158] There are two stages to federal interpleader adjudications.

> In the "first stage," the court determines whether interpleader is appro-priate on the facts of the case. If so, in the "second stage," the court adjudicates the adverse claims and distributes the stake.[159]

The stakeholder may be either disinterested or interested. If disinterested, he takes the position that one or more of the claimants is entitled to the fund — stage two of the interpleader action will determine which. A disinterested stakeholder participates only in stage one. After a hearing, the court decides if the stakeholder is entitled to an interpleader remedy. If he is, he is excused from further involvement in the case, leaving the fund with the court to be fought over by rival claimants.[160] However, the stakeholder's lack of interest in the stake is no longer a prerequisite for interpleader. An interested stakeholder may remain to participate in stage two of the interpleader action, claiming that he is obligated to no one and, in effect, competing with the rival claimants for the fund.

State Farm Fire & Casualty Co. v. Tashire[161] offers a good illustration of the scope of federal interpleader. Stakeholder State Farm filed an interpleader action

---

[153] *See* 28 U.S.C. § 1335.

[154] Section 1335 requires diversity of citizenship between only two or more of the adverse claimants (called *minimal diversity*) *see* § 5.04[2], *supra* and, at least $500 in controversy, measured by the value of the stake. In contrast, a federal interpleader action brought solely under Rule 22 would have to qualify either under the general diversity statute, 28 U.S.C. § 1332, requiring complete diversity of citizenship between the stakeholder and all of the claimants, and more than $75,000 in controversy, or under some federal question jurisdictional grant. *See* WRIGHT § 74.

[155] Statutory interpleader has its own venue statute, 28 U.S.C. § 1397, permitting suit in any district where a claimant resides.

[156] 28 U.S.C. § 2361 authorizes service of process on all competing claimants in any judicial district of the United States. "Thus, in statutory interpleader actions, only those claimants who cannot be found or who reside outside of the United States are beyond the reach of the statute." FRIEDENTHAL, KANE & MILLER § 16.12.

[157] The stakeholder will usually be permitted to give a bond in lieu of money. MOORE § 22.03[1][b].

[158] *See, e.g., Star Ins. Co. v. Cedar Valley Express, LLC*, 273 F. Supp. 2d 38 (D.D.C. 2002). Injunctive authority in statutory interpleader cases is explicit in 28 U.S.C. § 2361. 7 WRIGHT & MILLER § 1717.

[159] MOORE § 22.03[1][a] (footnote omitted).

[160] *See* MOORE § 22.03[2][a].

[161] 386 U.S. 523 (1967).

in Oregon federal court based on both the statute and Rule 22, in response to claims made on a $20,000 insurance policy. Its insured had been operating a truck when he collided with a bus in California. The accident resulted in two deaths, injuries to many people, and lawsuits seeking more than $1,000,000 in damages from the insured and the bus company, among others. The federal district court directed claimants to make all of their claims against the stakeholder, its insured, the bus company, and the bus driver in the interpleader action. Reversing, the federal court of appeals viewed the case as altogether inappropriate for interpleader. The Supreme Court reversed in turn, holding that statutory interpleader was available to State Farm to confine to one lawsuit all claims made on the $20,000 policy. The Court refused, however, to resurrect interpleader on the scale attempted by the district court. It noted that "State Farm's interest in this case, which is the fulcrum of the interpleader procedure, is confined to its $20,000 fund."[162] The insurer

> should not be allowed to determine that dozens of tort plaintiffs must be compelled to press their claims — even those claims which are not against the insured and which in no event could be satisfied out of the meager insurance fund — in a single forum of the insurance company's choosing. There is nothing in the statutory scheme, and very little in the judicial and academic commentary upon that scheme, which requires that the tail be allowed to wag the dog in this fashion.[163]

§ 9.08 INTERVENTION[164]

The party joinder devices we have examined so far are available only to one already a party in the case. Intervention differs in that it provides a means for outsiders to make themselves parties. Federal court interventions usually are governed by Rule 24, which has its counterpart in most state procedural systems.[165] The rule contemplates both intervention of right under 24(a) and permissive intervention under 24(b).

[1] Intervention of Right

Rule 24(a) states that:

---

[162] 386 U.S. at 535.

[163] 386 U.S. at 535. "We recognize," added the *Tashire* Court, "that our view of interpleader means that it cannot be used to solve all the vexing problems of multiparty litigation arising out of a mass tort. But interpleader was never intended to perform such a function, to be an all-purpose bill of peace." 386 U.S. at 535.

[164] *See generally* MOORE §§ 24.01–24.24; 7C WRIGHT & MILLER §§ 1901–1923; Amy M. Gardner, *An Attempt to Intervene in the Confusion: Standing Requirements for Rule 24 Intervenors*, 69 U. CHI. L. REV. 681 (2002); Carl Tobias, *Standing to Intervene*, 1991 WIS. L. REV. 415; Gene R. Shreve, *Questioning Intervention of Right — Toward a New Methodology of Decisionmaking*, 74 NW. U. L. REV. 894 (1980); Symposium, *Problems of Intervention in Public Law Litigation*, 13 U.C. DAVIS L. REV. 211 (1980); Edward J. Brunet, *A Study in the Allocation of Scarce Judicial Resources: The Efficiency of Federal Intervention Criteria*, 12 GA. L. REV. 701 (1978); David C. Shapiro, *Some Thoughts on Intervention Before Courts, Agencies, and Arbitrators*, 81 HARV. L. REV. 721 (1968).

[165] *E.g.*, IND. CODE ANN. CT. R. TRIAL 24; N.C. GEN. STAT. § 1A-1 T. 24; MINN. STAT. ANN. R. CIV. P. DIST. CT. 24.

on timely motion, the court must permit anyone to intervene who: (1) is given an unconditional right to intervene by a federal statute; or (2) claims an interest relating to the property or transaction that is the subject of the action, and is so situated that disposing of the action may as a practical matter impair or impede the movant's ability to protect its interest, unless existing parties adequately represent that interest.

Most applications for intervention of right are made under Rule 24(a)(2).[166] To qualify, the applicant must satisfy three requirements.

First, the applicant must demonstrate that the lawsuit carries a possibility of detriment to him serious enough to entitle him to an opportunity to participate in ways that only a litigant can.[167] It is no longer necessary for the applicant to demonstrate that the lawsuit is capable of binding him in a formal sense.[168] Rule 24(a)(2) contemplates merely "practical" impairment. The Supreme Court has noted that the applicant need only have a "significantly protectable interest."[169] However, the scope of absentee interests protected through intervention of right has proven difficult to define precisely.[170]

Second, the applicant must demonstrate a substantial possibility that none of the present parties will adequately represent the applicant's interest. A successful applicant will thereafter make or defend against a claim,[171] generally aligning himself with one already a party. The adequacy question thus boils down to whether the existing party can be expected to represent the applicant's interests adequately in the course of representing his own. If so, the applicant has no right to intervene under Rule 24(a)(2). When the applicant's stake in the outcome is no greater than that of an existing party with whom the applicant would be aligned, and when that existing party is not in collusion with an opposing party, incompetent, or hostile toward the applicant, representation by the existing party often will be deemed adequate and intervention of right will be denied.[172]

---

[166] The function of subdivision (1) of Rule 24(a) is to note provisions for intervention of right appearing elsewhere in federal statutes. For examples, *see Moore* § 24.02. Absent acknowledgement in Rule 24 of the existence of prior federal statutes governing intervention, the latter might have been extinguished by the rule because the Rules Enabling Act, 28 U.S.C. § 2072, states that "[a]ll laws in conflict" with the federal rules "shall be of no further force or effect after such rules have taken effect."

[167] Party prerogatives include setting boundaries of relevancy through pleadings, developing facts by discovery and creating parts of the factual record, and appealing adverse judgments.

[168] The Supreme Court had given this narrow reading to an earlier version of Rule 24 in *Sam Fox Publishing Co. v. United States*, 366 U.S. 683 (1961), prompting amendment of the rule in 1966.

[169] *Diamond v. Charles*, 476 U.S. 54, 68 (1986).

[170] Professor Shapiro noted that "[t]he range of possible interests may defy adequate classification, spreading over a spectrum that is extremely hard to chart." Note 164, *supra*, at 740. Examples include the possible *stare decisis* impact of the case on the applicant, *e.g., Atlantis Dev. Corp. v. United States*, 379 F.2d 818, 822 (5th Cir. 1967), and possible frustration of the applicant's opportunity to obtain future injunctive relief. *E.g., Stallworth v. Monsanto Co.*, 558 F.2d 257, 268 (5th Cir. 1977).

[171] Rule 24(c) requires the applicant's motion to intervene to "be accompanied by a pleading that sets out the claim or defense for which intervention is sought."

[172] *See, e.g., United States v. City of Miami*, 278 F.3d 1174, 1178-79 (11th Cir. 2002); *Delaware Valley Citizens' Council for Clean Air v. Pennsylvania*, 674 F.2d 970 (3d Cir. 1982). In some cases, the argument for inadequate representation will be that the interest of the applicant in the outcome is, upon careful

Third, the application must be timely. Rule 24 sets no deadline for interventions. Absentees may move to intervene after trial of the case and even on appeal. Since, however, the intervener has no right to relitigate issues resolved before intervention,[173] the later the intervener enters the litigation, the fewer opportunities the intervener will have to influence the outcome. Moreover, it is generally true that interventions become increasingly difficult to justify as the case unfolds.[174] Two questions recur when the timeliness of the application is an issue: whether the court and those already parties will suffer from the fact the application did not come earlier,[175] and whether the applicant can be faulted for applying so late.[176] The latter point can be resolved in favor of intervention when, for example, applicant's earlier motion would have failed because representation by an existing party then seemed adequate.[177]

[2] Permissive Intervention

Rule 24(b) states in part that "[o]n timely motion, the court may permit anyone to intervene who . . . has a claim or defense that shares with the main action a common question of law or fact."[178] The present-day function of Rule 24(b)(1)(B) seems confined to promoting judicial economy. Therefore, permissive intervention is warranted only when savings of party and judicial resources from avoiding an extra lawsuit outweigh costs from the added presence of the intervener.[179] Concern

---

examination, more focused or more intense than that of the existing party with whom the applicant would be aligned. Consider, for example, the facts of a well-known intervention case, *Ford Motor Co. v. Bisanz Bros., Inc.*, 249 F.2d 22 (8th Cir. 1957). Plaintiffs sued to shut down a railroad spur as a private nuisance. Ford sought to intervene on the side of the railroad defendant on the ground that it could not continue to operate one of its plants if it could not use the spur. The court ruled that Ford was entitled to intervention as of right. Ford had far more to lose from elimination of the spur than did the railroad. Therefore, while there was no suggestion that the railroad would be less than diligent in protecting *its* interests, the railroad's stake in the outcome did not give it the same incentive that Ford had to litigate vigorously.

[173] *Cf. Arizona v. California*, 460 U.S. 605, 615 (1983) ("Of course, permission to intervene does not carry with it the right to relitigate matters already determined in the case, unless those matters would otherwise be subject to reconsideration.").

[174] Thus, "[t]here is considerable reluctance on the part of the courts to allow intervention after the action has gone to judgment and a strong showing will be required of the applicant." 7C WRIGHT & MILLER § 1916.

[175] For a survey of federal decisions on this point, see *id. See also Doe #1 v. Glickman*, 256 F.3d 371, 376 (5th Cir. 2001).

[176] For a survey of federal decisions on this point, see 7C WRIGHT & MILLER § 1916. *See, e.g., Long Island Trucking, Inc. v. Brooks Pharmacy*, 219 F.R.D. 53, 55 (E.D.N.Y. 2003).

[177] *Smuck v. Hobson*, 408 F.2d 175 (D.C. Cir. 1969), is a noted example. Applicants' interests were at least arguably represented by the defendant until defendant decided not to appeal an adverse ruling by the federal district court. The court of appeals granted intervention, thus avoiding a Catch-22 interplay of the adequacy-of-representation and timeliness concerns which would have shut off the possibility of intervention altogether.

[178] Rule 24(b)(1)(A) recognizes the possibility of a statutory "conditional right to intervene." The functional relationship between (b)(1)(A) and (b)(1)(B) is thus the same as that between (a)(1) and (a)(2) described at note 166, *supra*.

[179] *See* Shreve, note 164, *supra*, at 908–09:

A grant of intervention may adversely affect the original parties in a number of ways.

over the latter is clear from Rule 24(b)(3): "In exercising its discretion, the court must consider whether the intervention will unduly delay or prejudice the adjudication of the original parties' rights."[180]

Rule 24 permits applicants to seek to intervene permissively or as a matter of right in the alternative. Since intervention of right is narrower in scope, adding a request for permissive intervention provides the applicant with a fall-back position.

[3] Comparing Intervention of Right and Permissive Intervention

If an application for intervention falls within Rule 24(a), the paragraph provides that it "must" be granted. If the applicant merely satisfies 24(b), intervention "may" (or may not) be granted. The reason for different treatment can be found in the interests of the applicant in intervening that are reflected in each paragraph. Intervention of right under Rule 24 (a) secures participation in the case for one whose substantive interests may be compromised.[181] Permissive intervention under Rule 24(b) rarely does more than advance the interest of the applicant and possibly the court in more cost-efficient litigation.[182]

The impact of the distinction on an applicant's chances for successful intervention is two-fold. First, the greater premium Rule 24(a) places on interventions is likely to influence the federal district court as initial decisionmaker. Second, while a decision denying permissive intervention is insulated from review by the trial court's discretion,[183] the decision that the applicant is not entitled to

---

Intervention forces the nominal co-party to relinquish partial management of the case. Moreover, the intervener may complicate the original parties' preparation and litigation of the case by maintaining a separate position on existing issues or by adding new claims, parties, or witnesses. Thus, the existing parties' expectations of an expeditious adjudication and an orderly resolution of their claims . . . may be defeated by the delays and complications accompanying intervention. In addition, the complications resulting from intervention may so strain the resources of the original parties that their continued ability to participate is jeopardized, and the forum becomes correspondingly less accessible.

In times of crowded dockets, the court may also have a concern in keeping the case from becoming too burdensome and, in the interests of justice, seeing that the reasonable concerns of existing parties are protected. Related are the interests of the original parties and the court in settling cases, and the concern that an intervener might effectively block settlement.

Reprinted by special permission of the Northwestern University Law Review, © 1980 by Northwestern University School of Law, volume 74.

[180] Quoting this passage, the Supreme Court observed: "Particularly in a complex case . . . , a district judge's decision on how best to balance the rights of the parties against the need to keep the litigation from becoming unmanageable is entitled to great deference." *Stringfellow v. Concerned Neighbors in Action*, 480 U.S. 370, 380 (1987).

[181] Minus reference to the possibility of inadequate representation, the relationship of the absentee to the lawsuit is the same as that described in Rule 19(a)(1)(B) of one who must be joined if feasible. *See* § 9.05[2][a], *supra*.

[182] It is thus comparable to permissive party joinder under Rule 20. *See* § 9.05[1], *supra*.

[183] *E.g., Reid v. Illinois State Bd. of Educ.*, 289 F.3d 1009, 1020 (7th Cir. 2002); *County of Orange v. Air Cal.*, 799 F.2d 535 (9th Cir. 1986) ("If there is no right to intervene under Rule 24(a), it is wholly discretionary with the court whether to allow intervention under Rule 24(b) and even though there is a common question of law or fact, or the requirements of Rule 24(b) are otherwise satisfied, the court may

intervene of right is open to a considerable measure of appellate redecision.[184]

The distinction may in addition affect the court's willingness to attach conditions when it grants a motion to intervene. Limitations on the nature and degree of the applicant's participation are not uncommon in permissive interventions under Rule 24(b), but the propriety of similarly limiting 24(a) interveners of right is open to question.[185]

§ 9.09   CLASS ACTIONS[186]

Parties brought in through the joinder devices we have considered so far share active participation with all other parties in the case. Modern rules of procedure, consolidated litigation,[187] even specially constructed courtrooms,[188] may enable courts to accommodate many active participants in a single case.

---

refuse to allow intervention."). *See* 7C *Wright & Miller* § 1913 (citing numerous examples).

[184] *See, e.g., Trans. Chem. Ltd. v. China Nat'l Mach. Imp. & Exp. Corp.*, 332 F.3d 815, 822 (5th Cir. 2003). Most federal courts of appeal have regarded the Rule 24(a)(2) questions of whether the applicant risks practical impairment from the outcome of the case and whether applicant's interests are adequately represented by an existing party to be open to reexamination on appeal. "[T]he appellate court can substitute its judgment for that of the trial court if it regards the urgency as great enough to warrant a determination that intervention should be allowed as of right." *James, Hazard & Leubsdorf* § 10.17. *But see United States v. Hooker Chems. & Plastics*, 749 F.2d 968, 990 (2d Cir. 1984) (noting the traditional distinction between reviewing standards for (a) and (b) intervention denials but stating, "it is now the rule in this circuit that denials of motions to intervene as of right under Rule 24(a)(2) also are to be reviewed under an abuse of discretion standard.").

Refusals to grant intervention based on untimeliness are regarded as discretionary, whether the application is grounded on (a) or (b) of Rule 24. Therefore, a finding that an application to intervene of right is untimely "will be reviewed only for an abuse of discretion." 7C *Wright & Miller* § 1916.

[185] *See* Shapiro, note 164, *supra*, at 759. Courts refused to limit Rule 24(a) interventions in *Spangler v. United States*, 415 F.2d 1242 (9th Cir. 1969), and *Exchange Nat'l Bank of Chi. v. Abramson*, 45 F.R.D. 97 (D. Minn. 1968). *But see Harris v. General Coach Works*, 37 F.R.D. 343 (E. D. Mich. 1964) (appearing to limit a Rule 24(a) intervener).

[186] The literature on class actions is voluminous. *See, e.g., Moore* §§ 23.01–23.88; 7A-7B *Wright & Miller* §§ 1751–1807; *Herbert B. Newberg, Newberg on Class Actions* (5th ed. 2002); Tobias B. Wolff, *Preclusion in Class Action Litigation*, 105 Colum. L. Rev. 717 (2005); Elizabeth J. Cabraser, *The Class Action Counterreformation*, 57 Stan. L. Rev. 1475 (2005); Theodore Eisenberg & Geoffrey Miller, *The Role of Opt-Outs and Objectors in Class Action Litigation: Theoretical and Empirical Issues*, 57 Vand. L. Rev. 1529 (2004); John C. Coffee, Jr., *Class Action Accountability: Reconciling Exit, Voice, and Loyalty in Representative Litigation*, 100 Colum. L. Rev. 370 (2000); Rhonda Wasserman, *Dueling Class Actions*, 80 B.U. L. Rev. 461 (2000); Linda Silberman, *The Vicissitudes of the American Class Action — With a Comparative Eye*, 7 Tul. J. of Int'l & Comp. L. 201 (1999); Geoffrey C. Hazard, Jr., John L. Gedud & Stephen Sowle, *An Historical Analysis of the Binding Effect of Class Suits*, 146 U. Pa. L. Rev. 1849 (1998); David C. Shapiro, *Class Actions: The Class as Party and Client*, 73 Notre Dame L. Rev. 913 (1998); Symposium, *The Institute of Judicial Administration Research Conference on Class Actions*, 71 N.Y.U. L. Rev. 1 (1996); John C. Coffee, Jr., *Class Wars: The Dilemma of the Mass Tort Class Action*, 95 Colum. L. Rev. 1343 (1995).

[187] *See* § 9.10, *infra*.

[188] *See Megacourtroom*, Time, March 18, 1985 at 67 (discussing the construction of a "megacourt-room" for Manville Corp. asbestos litigation).

There are limits, however. Exercise of the prerogatives of party participation[189] is time-consuming. All joinder can proliferate the number of pleadings and briefs, complicate proof, and slow litigation down; the "mega-joinder" of a class action may often amplify these effects. Procedural safeguards offered for dividing cases or trials that have grown too large[190] or for staggering the adjudication of claims within a case[191] provide only limited protection. Courts must draw the line somewhere,[192] protecting those already parties and themselves from congestion which would overwhelm the case.

The special contribution of the class action device is to facilitate adjudication of additional claims without enlarging the number of active parties. This usually works by designating parties[193] to litigate not only for themselves but also as representatives for a group (the class). At least where class representation has been adequate,[194] class members will be bound by the outcome of the case.[195] That is, they will fare on issues common to the class as does their class representative. However, only their class representative will be an active litigant. Class members will remain passive, unless they exclude themselves from the lawsuit, thereby enabling them to litigate separately (*opt out*),[196] or appear in the litigation to litigate

---

[189] *See* § 9.08, *supra.*

[190] *See* § 9.02, *supra.*

[191] Federal Rule 54(b) provides, "[w]hen an action presents more than one claim for relief . . . , or when multiple parties are involved, the court may direct entry of a final judgment as to one or more, but fewer than all, claims or parties. . . ." *See* § 13.03[2] (finality in multi-party and multi-claim cases), *infra.* Many state procedural systems have similar provisions allowing partial adjudication. *E.g.*, IND. CODE ANN. CT. R. TRIAL 54(B); KY. REV. STAT. ANN. R. CIV. P. 54.02; MINN. STAT. ANN. R. CIV. P. DIST. CT. 54.02.

[192] *See* for example, discussion of concerns weighing against permissive intervention at § 9.08, *supra.*

[193] There can be and often is more than one class representative. For convenience, however, we will use the singular form.

[194] *See* Susan P. Koniak, *How Like a Winter? The Plight of Absent Class Members Denied Adequate Representation*, 79 NOTRE DAME L. REV. 1787 (2004); Linda S. Mullenix, *Taking Adequacy Seriously: The Inadequate Assessment of Adequacy in Litigation and Settlement Classes*, 57 VAND. L. REV. 1687 (2004); Patrick Woolley, *The Availability of Collateral Attack for Inadequate Representation in Class Suits*, 79 TEX. L. REV. 383 (2000).

[195] *See* Tobias B. Wolff, *Preclusion in Class Action Litigation*, 105 COLUM. L. REV. 717 (2005); Samuel Issacharoff, *Preclusion, Due Process, and the Right to Opt Out of Class Actions*, 77 NOTRE DAME L. REV. 1057 (2002).

[196] Federal Rule 23 and the class action provisions of most states have a mechanism for class members with discrete claims to exclude themselves from class actions, avoiding preclusive effects of a judgment later in the case. The process is often called "opting out." For critique and illustration of current practice, *see* Theodore Eisenberg & Geoffrey Miller, *The Role of Opt-Outs and Objectors in Class Action Litigation: Theoretical and Empirical Issues*, 57 VAND. L. REV. 1529 (2004); Steve Baughman, Note, *Class Actions in the Asbestos Context: Balancing the Due Process Considerations Implicated by the Right to Opt Out*, 70 TEX. L. REV. 211 (1991); Mark W. Friedman, Note, *Constrained Individualism in Group Litigation: Requiring Class Members to Make a Good Cause Showing Before Opting Out of a Federal Class Action*, 100 YALE L.J. 745 (1990).

A class member who opts out probably will be unable to exploit through nonmutual offensive issue preclusion a judgment thereafter rendered in favor of the class. 7AA WRIGHT & MILLER § 1789. This is because, by opting out of the class, the party knowingly foregoes an earlier opportunity to litigate the issue.

actively along with the class representative.[197]

[1] Due Process Requirements Common to Federal and State Class Actions

One source of law limits federal and state class actions alike: the constitutional law of due process. The function of the modern class action in federal and most state courts is to bind the class members by the outcome as though they were active parties in the case.[198] This raises due process considerations, since one cannot be bound without participating in a judicial proceeding unless one's interests are adequately represented.

Hansberry v. Lee[199] continues to be of central importance in elaborating the constitutional standard. There, an African American family acquired property in a community where homeowners were subject to an agreement prohibiting their homes from being occupied by blacks. Local homeowners sought to enforce the agreement against the family, arguing that the agreement had been upheld in prior litigation against a white homeowner who had sought to lease his property to a black tenant. The homeowners argued that the judgment in the prior case was res judicata against the family, even though the family had not been a party in the earlier action. *Hansberry* established a principle essential for true class actions, that (under the right circumstances) class action judgments could bind passive class members.[200] Yet the due process ruling in *Hansberry* also imposed important limits on class actions. The Court stated that it was "justified in saying that there has been a failure of due process only in those cases where it cannot be said that the procedure adopted, fairly insures the protection of the interests of absent parties who are to be bound by it."[201] Thus, "members of a class not present as parties to the litigation may be bound by the judgment where they are in fact adequately represented by parties who are present."[202] In this case, however, if the class was defined as present and future homeowners subject to the agreement, the

---

[197] Federal Rule 23(d)(1)(B)(iii) raises possibilities that class members might either appear or intervene in the action. The rule does not explain how the two differ. Professors Wright and Miller suggest that courts may be reluctant to complicate class actions by permitting extensive use of either device. 7B WRIGHT & MILLER § 1799. *But cf. Devlin v. Scardelletti*, 536 U.S. 1 (2002) (holding that an unnamed class member may appeal approval of a class action settlement without intervening).

[198] "Class actions rest on a relatively simple proposition: self-selected class representatives and their lawyers, properly supervised by the court, can represent class members as a group sufficiently well to overcome members' individual rights to be heard." Bryant G. Garth, *Studying Civil Litigation Through the Class Action*, 62 IND. L.J. 497, 497 (1987). "The fascination of foreign scholars with class actions is fairly easy to explain: this principle of representation remains unacceptable to almost the entire legal world outside of the United States." *Id.*

[199] 311 U.S. 32 (1940). For useful analysis and background, see Jay Tidmarsh, *The Story of Hansberry: The Rise of the Modern Class Action, in* CIVIL PROCEDURE STORIES, Ch. 6 (Kevin Clermont, ed., 2d ed. 2008).

[200] "[T]here is scope within the framework of the Constitution for holding in appropriate cases that a judgment rendered in a class suit is *res judicata* as to members of the class who are not formal parties to the suit." 311 U.S. at 42.

[201] 311 U.S. at 42.

[202] 311 U.S. at 42–43.

plaintiff homeowners who sought to enforce the agreement in the prior action did not adequately represent the interests of the African American homeowner who wished to challenge the agreement in the present action. And there was no basis upon which to argue that the defendant in the former action had been sued in a representative capacity.

When is an absent class member "adequately represented?" In answering this question, due process doctrine places greatest reliance on the opinion held prior to the proceeding by the person to be bound. A passive class member may be thought to express his own favorable opinion on adequacy of representation when he knowingly permits the class representative to act for him. He likely will be bound by the class judgment in such cases — even if the representation of the class representative turns out to be lackluster.[203] But, even if the work of the class representative will be superlative, the class member is entitled whenever possible to decide before the fact whether he wants to entrust his interests to that person. Naturally, the class member is only able to control how his interests will be represented if made aware of the case prior to adjudication. That is why in due process doctrine the concept of adequate representation is closely tied to that of notice.

The classic statement on the extent of notice required for binding adjudications appears in *Mullane v. Central Hanover Bank & Trust Co.*[204]

> An elementary and fundamental requirement of due process in any proceeding which is to be accorded finality is notice reasonably calculated, under all the circumstances, to apprise interested parties of the pendency of the action and afford them an opportunity to present their objections. The notice must be of such nature as reasonably to convey the required information, and it must afford a reasonable time for those interested to make their appearance. But if with due regard for the practicalities and peculiarities of the case these conditions are reasonably met, the constitutional requirements are satisfied.[205]

This is a pragmatic approach to notice. *Mullane* holds that actual notice to those to be bound by the litigation is always required where practicable.[206] Furthermore, *Mullane* indicates that those for whom individual notice is impracticable may only be bound under special circumstances. That is, notice to them must be attempted by the best alternative means (possibly publication), and there must be a strong showing that they will be adequately represented by one before the court.[207]

---

[203] 311 U.S. at 43 (class members are bound "where they actually participate in the conduct of the litigation in which members of the class are present as parties").

[204] 339 U.S. 306 (1950). On *Mullane* and this topic generally, see § 4.02[1] (special due process concerns arising from class actions), *supra*.

[205] 339 U.S. at 314–15 (citations omitted).

[206] 339 U.S. at 318.

[207] Because the Court required mail notice to trust beneficiaries whose addresses were known, it was comfortable excusing such personal notice for beneficiaries whose addresses were not known or were ascertainable only at considerable expense. It reasoned that

> [t]his type of trust presupposes a large number of small interests. The individual interest does

Finally, class actions, like all actions, are also subject to due process limitations on personal jurisdiction. These are no different for defendants in class actions than in any other actions. But classes can also be made up of plaintiffs. The class representatives, of course, submit to the personal jurisdiction of the court by filing the action. But does the court have to have personal jurisdiction over the passive class members — those who neither serve as representatives nor intervene or even appear? Some state courts had refused to entertain nationwide class actions because of what they perceived to be the lack of minimum contacts[208] between the forum and nonresident passive members of the plaintiff class.[209] But in *Phillips Petroleum Company v. Shutts*,[210] the Supreme Court gave state courts the green light by ruling that the relationship between the forum and members of the plaintiff class did not have to meet the stringent due process requirements applied to the relationship between a forum and defendants.[211] The passive class members are adequately protected by their representatives, the rules for class certification and their supervision by the judge, and, in certain class actions (those under Rule 23(b)(3), as we shall see), by the opportunity to refuse to participate in the class by "opting out." In short, "[u]nlike a defendant in a civil suit, a class-action plaintiff is not required to fend for himself. The court and named plaintiffs protect his interests."[212]

---

not stand alone but is identical with that of a class. The rights of each in the integrity of the fund and the fidelity of the trustee are shared by many other beneficiaries. Therefore notice reasonably certain to reach most of those interested in objecting is likely to safeguard the interests of all since any objection sustained would inure to the benefit of all. We think that under such circumstances reasonable risks that notice might not actually reach every beneficiary are justifiable.

339 U.S. at 319.

[208] On the function of the minimum contacts test in regulating personal jurisdiction, see § 3.06, *supra*.

[209] *E.g.*, *Feldman v. Bates Mfg. Co.*, 362 A.2d 1177 (N.J. Super. Ct. App. Div. 1976); *Klemow v. Time*, 352 A.2d 12 (Pa.), *cert. denied*, 429 U.S. 828 (1976).

[210] 472 U.S. 797 (1985).

[211] The Court stated that "[b]ecause States place fewer burdens upon absent class plaintiffs than they do upon absent defendants in nonclass suits, the Due Process Clause need not and does not afford the former as much protection from state-court jurisdiction as it does the latter." 472 U.S. at 811. *See* note 270 & accompanying text, *infra*. On the significance of *Shutts* state class actions, see Kurt A. Schwarz, Note, *Due Process and Equitable Relief in State: Multistate Class Actions After* Phillips Petroleum Co. v. Shutts, 68 Tex. L. Rev. 415 (1989); Diane P. Wood, *Adjudicatory Jurisdiction and Class Actions*, 62 Ind. L.J. 597 (1987); Arthur R. Miller & David Crump, *Jurisdiction and Choice of Law in Multistate Class Actions After* Phillips Petroleum Co. v. Shutts, 96 Yale L.J. 1 (1986); John E. Kennedy, *The Supreme Court Meets the Bride of Frankenstein:* Phillips Petroleum Co. v. Shutts *and the State Multistate Class Action*, 34 U. Kan. L. Rev. 255 (1985).

[212] *Phillips Petroleum Co. v. Shutts*, 472 U.S. 797, 809 (1985). The Supreme Court subsequently questioned whether its *Shutts* ruling should apply in class actions where members did not receive notice or a clear opportunity to opt out of the class. *Ortiz v. Fibreboard Corp.*, 527 U.S. 815, 847–48 (1999). The minimum contacts requirement may reappear in such cases.

[2] Class Actions Under Rule 23

Most federal court class actions are governed by Rule 23.[213] Plaintiff is usually the class representative.[214] The class representative pleads an individual claim, but also pleads the existence of a class and a claim or claims on behalf of class members. Rule 23(c)(1) provides for certification of the case as a class action, stating that, "[a]t an early practicable time after a person sues or is sued as a class representative, the court must determine by order whether to certify the action as a class action." Filing a complaint alleging the existence of the class and pleading class claims will usually toll the applicable statute of limitations against members of the putative class.[215]

The burden is on plaintiff to demonstrate that the requirements of Rule 23 have been met. To succeed under the rule, a case must (1) satisfy two requirements that are at best implicit in the Rule, (2) conform to the four express requirements of paragraph (a); and (3) fit into one of the categories in Rule 23(b).

Rule 23(a) states:

> One or more members of a class may sue or be sued as representative parties on behalf of all members only if (1) the class is so numerous that joinder of all members is impracticable; (2) there are questions of law or fact common to the class; (3) the claims or defenses of the representative parties are typical of the claims or defenses of the class; and (4) the representative parties will fairly and adequately protect the interests of the class.

Rule 23 presupposes that the class can be defined.[216] It must describe a group that genuinely exists, and it must do so with sufficient clarity to inform the court and the party opposing the class of the stakes in the litigation. The representative must also be a member of the class.[217]

---

[213] Prior to its 1966 amendment, Rule 23 also governed actions now treated by Rules 23.1 and 23.2. Rule 23.1 deals with shareholder derivative actions. Rule 23.2 "enables a representative suit to be brought by or against the association itself." Moore § 23.2.02.

[214] Much less frequently, plaintiff sues *against*, rather than on behalf of a class. Defendant-class actions are, as one commentator put it, "as rare as unicorns." John C. Coffee, Jr., *Class Action Accountability: Reconciling Exit, Voice, and Loyalty in Representative Litigation*, 100 Colum. L. Rev. 370, 388 (2000). *See also* John Bronsteen & Owen Fiss, *The Class Action Rule*, 78 Notre Dame L. Rev. 1419, 1422 (2003).

[215] Usually, the statute of limitations will either resume running or begin running anew if certification is eventually denied, depending on the statute. *See, e.g., Chardon v. Fumero Soto*, 462 U.S. 650 (1983) (the statute of limitations began running anew after class certification was denied). *See generally* Rhonda Wasserman, *Tolling: The American Pipe Tolling Rule and Successive Class Actions*, 58 Fla. L. Rev. 803, 813-33 (2006).

[216] *See* Manual for Complex Litigation (Fourth) § 21.222 (2004).

[217] 7A Wright & Miller § 1761. *Cf. General Tel. Co. of the Sw. v. Falcon*, 457 U.S. 147, 156 (1982) ("We have repeatedly held that a class representative must be part of the class.") (quoting *East Texas Motor Freight Sys. v. Rodriguez*, 431 U.S. 395, 403 (1977)). This also satisfies the requirement under Article III of the United States Constitution that the class representative have standing. *Ortiz v. Fibreboard Corp.*, 527 U.S. 815 (1999).

If the plaintiff satisfies these implicit requirements, he must also satisfy the express requirements set out seriatim in the subdivisions of Rule 23(a). Subdivisions (1) and (2) pose rudimentary questions about the appropriateness of the case as a class action. The first subdivision concerns what is sometimes called the "numerosity" requirement.[218] If the group offered as a class is so small that active participation of each member is feasible, there is no need for the class action device — permissive joinder under Rule 20 will be adequate to the task.[219] The second subdivision concerns what is sometimes called the "commonality" requirement.[220] If the group does not share issues in common, there is no material in the case for a class-wide adjudication.[221]

The Supreme Court's decision in *Wal-Mart Stores, Inc. v. Dukes*,[222] complicates analysis of the commonality requirement. There, the plaintiffs alleged that Wal-Mart discriminated against female employees by giving local store managers discretion over pay and promotion decisions, which the company knew local managers would exercise in favor of male employees. A five-member majority of the Court characterized the commonality requirement as follows:

> Commonality requires the plaintiff to demonstrate that the class members "have suffered the same injury" . . . "What matters to class certification . . . is not the raising of common 'questions' — even in droves — but, rather the capacity of a classwide proceeding to generate common *answers* apt to drive the resolution of the litigation. Dissimilarities within the proposed class are what have the potential to impede the generation of common answers."[223]

Armed with that standard, the majority concluded that the proposed class action failed to satisfy the commonality requirement: plaintiffs failed to identity, to the Court's satisfaction, "a common mode of exercising discretion that pervades the entire company."[224] Even if plaintiffs could show that promotion patterns for female employees in all 3400 Wal-Mart stores were below national and regional averages, the commonality requirement would not be satisfied because some store managers would argue that disparities at their stores were attributable to non-discriminatory factors.[225]

---

[218] *E.g., General Tel. Co. of the Sw. v. Falcon*, 457 U.S. 147, 156 (1982).

[219] "The question of what constitutes impracticability . . . depends on the particular facts of each case and no arbitrary rules regarding the size of classes have been established by the courts." 7A WRIGHT & MILLER § 1762.

[220] *E.g., General Tel. Co. of the Sw. v. Falcon*, 457 U.S. 147, 156 (1982).

[221] *See, e.g., Trevizo v. Adams*, 455 F.3d 1155, 1163 (10th Cir. 2006). "It is important to note that this provision does not require that all the questions of law and fact raised by the dispute be common . . . . All that can be divined from the rule itself is that the use of the plural 'questions' suggests that more than one issue of law or fact must be common to members of the class." 7A WRIGHT & MILLER § 1763.

[222] 131 S. Ct. 2541, 2547 (2011).

[223] *Id.* at 2551, *quoting* Richard A. Nagareda, *Class Certification in the Age of Aggregate Proof*, 84 N.Y.U.L. Rev. 97, 132 (2009).

[224] *Id.* at 2554–55.

[225] *Id.* at 2555.

Rule 23(a)(2) is a threshold requirement for maintaining all class actions, which by its terms requires only that "there are questions of law or fact common to the class." By concluding that common questions are absent because dissimilarities are present, the Court arguably conflated Rules 23(a)(2) with 23(b)(3). The latter section imposes a more exacting commonality requirement on one form of class action, by requiring that "questions of law or fact common to the class members predominate over any questions affecting only individual members." The dissent argued that by bootstrapping 23(b)(3) requirements to its analysis of 23(a)(2), the Court made it more difficult for plaintiffs to satisfy the commonality requirement in other types of class action to which Rule 23(b)(3) requirements do not apply.[226]

The purpose of subdivision (3) (the "typicality" requirement) and subdivision (4) (the "adequacy of representation" requirement) of Rule 23(a) is to assure that representation of the passive class members' interests will be good enough[227] to make it fair to bind them by the result in the case.[228] Thus, under subdivision (3), the claims of class representatives must be typical of the class as a whole, to avoid class representatives pursuing objectives in tension with the objectives of the class members they represent. Subdivision (4) in turn requires that class representatives will "fairly and adequately" protect class interests, which requires qualified counsel and a consonance of interests among class representatives and members. If subdivisions (3) and (4) had been omitted from Rule 23(a), the constitutional law of due process doubtless would have required federal courts to supplement the rule with these requirements.[229] As it is, Rule 23 not only reflects due process requirements, but secures a greater measure of protection for class members by advancing nonconstitutional policies of procedural fairness.[230] This is evident from the "stricter rules for the appointment of class attorneys, awarding attorney's fees, and approving settlements"[231] adopted in the 2003 amendments to Rule 23.[232]

---

[226] *Id.* at 2561 (Ginsburg, dissenting); *see also* Robin J. Effron, *The Shadow Rules of Joinder*, 100 Geo. L.J. 759 (2012) (discussing the Court's implied conflation of Rules 23(a)(2) and 23(b)(3) in *Wal-Mart*).

[227] *See, e.g., Steinberg v. Nationwide Mut. Ins. Co.*, 224 F.R.D. 67, 75 (E.D.N.Y. 2004). "Quality of representation embraces both the competence of the legal counsel of the representatives and the stature and interest of the named parties themselves." 7A Wright & Miller § 1766.

[228] Of the two, subsection (4) reflects this purpose most clearly. Subsection (3) does not appear to add much, although it "assures that the claims of the named parties are similar enough to the claims of the class so that the representative will adequately represent them." 7A Wright & Miller § 1764.

[229] *Cf.* 7A Wright & Miller § 1765 ("The binding effect of all class action decrees raises substantial due process questions that are directly relevant to Rule 23(a)(4).").

[230] It is difficult and (from the standpoint of administering Rule 23) unnecessary to determine precisely where constitutional requirements end and prudential, rule-based requirements begin. For discussion of the adequate representation requirement in class actions, *see* Ronan E. Degnan, *Foreward: Adequacy of Representation in Class Actions*, 60 Cal. L. Rev. 705 (1972); Daneil J. Steininger, Note, *Class Actions: Defining the Typical and Representative Plaintiff Under Subsections (a)(3) and (4) of Federal Rule 23*, 53 B.U. L. Rev. 406 (1973). Christopher J. Roche, Note, *A Litigation Association Model to Aggregate Mass Tort Claims for Adjudication*, 91 Va. L. Rev. 1463 (2005).

[231] Edward F. Sherman, *Class Actions After the Class Action Fairness Act of 2005*, 80 Tul. L. Rev. 1593, 1595 n.8 (2006).

[232] Federal Rule 23(d)-(h). Of particular note is paragraph (e) regulating settlement. This, along with 28 U.S.C. §§1711–1715 (part of the Class Action Fairness Act of 2005) were intended to address prior

In addition to meeting the threshold requirements of Rule 23(a), a class action must also fall within one of the four categories contained in paragraph (b) of the rule.[233] The first two categories are embedded in Rule 23(b)(1) which "permits a class action when this is necessary to avoid possible adverse effects on the opponents of the class or on absent members of the class."[234] Class actions under Rule 23(b)(1)(A) are designed to avert prejudice to the party opposing the class "if inconsistent results in individual adjudications establish incompatible standards of conduct to which he must adhere, as in a suit by taxpayers to invalidate municipal action or in a suit involving the rights and duties of riparian owners."[235] Class actions under Rule 23(b)(1)(B) protect absent class members from the relative disadvantage of pursuing their interests in individual lawsuits, "as in a suit to compel reorganization of a fraternal association or a suit by stockholders to compel declaration of a dividend."[236] The latter category also includes actions presenting multiple claims against a common limited pool of assets. The justification for class actions under (b)(1) is generally understood to be narrower than that of merely promoting judicial economy. Thus, "subdivision (b)(1)(A) is applicable when practical necessity forces the opposing party to act in the same manner toward the individual class members and thereby makes inconsistent adjudications in separate actions unworkable or intolerable."[237]

The third category is in Rule 23(b)(2), authorizing a class action when "the party opposing the class has acted or refused to act on grounds that apply generally to the class, so that final injunctive relief or corresponding declaratory relief is appropriate respecting the class as a whole . . . ." Rule 23(b)(2) has figured prominently in federal suits directed against state or local officials, where relief sought often is declaratory[238] or injunctive. While (b)(2) was created "essentially as a tool for facilitating civil rights actions,"[239] it is not limited to such cases.[240]

The accepted reading of Rule 23(b)(2) is that "[t]he subdivision does not extend to cases in which the appropriate final relief relates exclusively or predominantly to

---

unfair settlements "that resulted in large fees to attorneys with little benefit to class members." Sherman, *supra*, note 232 at 1594–95. Problems associated with class action settlements have evoked considerable commentary. *See* John Bronsteen, *Class Action Settlements: An Opt-In Proposal*, 2005 U. ILL. L. REV. 903 (205); Howard M. Erichson, *A Typology of Aggregate Settlements*, 80 NOTRE DAME L. REV. 1769 (2005); Lisa M. Mezzetti & Whitney R. Case, *The Coupon Can Be the Ticket: The Use of "Coupon" and Other Non-Monetary Redress in Class Action Settlements*, 18 GEO. J. LEGAL ETHICS 1431 (2005); Allan Kanner & Tibor Nagy, *Exploding the Blackmail Myth: A New Perspective on Class Action Settlements*, 57 BAYLOR L. REV. 681 (2005).

[233] For a useful explanation and critique of the various categories in paragraph (b), see John Bronsteen & Owen Fiss, *The Class Action Rule*, 78 NOTRE DAME L. REV. 1419, 1427-39 (2003).

[234] *WRIGHT* § 72.

[235] *WRIGHT* § 72.

[236] *WRIGHT* § 72.

[237] 7AA *WRIGHT & MILLER* § 1773. For discussion of the scope and application of Rule 23(b)(1), see *Ortiz v. Fibreboard Corp.*, 527 U.S. 815 (1999).

[238] *See* Andrew Brandt, *"Much to Gain and Nothing to Lose": Implications of the History of the Declaratory Judgment for the (b)(2) Class Action*, 58 ARK. L. REV. 767 (2006).

[239] *MOORE* § 23.43[1][b].

[240] *See* Advisory Committee Note to the 1966 amendment to Rule 23.

money damages."[241] Note that this standard does not necessarily exclude from (b)(2) cases seeking damages as well as declaratory or injunctive relief.[242] The question is whether the damages portion of the remedial package predominates. One study concluded that "cases involving claims for both money damages and injunctive or declaratory relief present significant difficulties of classification" under Rule 23.[243]

In *Wal-Mart Stores, Inc. v. Dukes*, the Supreme Court was unanimous in its conclusion that claims for backpay did not qualify for certification under Section (b)(2).[244] The Court ducked the broader question of whether (b)(2) "applies only to requests for such injunctive or declaratory relief and does not authorize the class certification of monetary claims at all," but concluded that "at a minimum, claims for *individualized* relief (like the backpay at issue here) do not satisfy the Rule."[245]

Rule 23(b)(3) creates a final, significant category of class actions.[246] It authorizes the device when, in the language of (b)(3), "the court finds that the questions of law or fact common to class members predominate over any questions affecting only individual members, and that a class action is superior to other available methods for fairly and efficiently adjudicating the controversy."[247] Subdivision (b)(3) has greater scope than (b)(1) or (2) in one respect and less in another. On the one hand, Rule 23 (b)(1) and (2) demand a closer relationship among class interests than the requirement in Rule 23(a)(3) where just the predominance of common questions of law or fact is enough.[248] On the other hand, the court may certify (b)(1) and (2) classes without the finding required under (b)(3) that the class action is superior to other forms of adjudication.

Despite these differences in description, the categories created in Rule 23(b) are not mutually exclusive. Some class actions appropriate to (b)(1) or (2) also appear to

---

[241] Rule 23 advisory committee's notes (1966). On distinctions between damages, injunctions and declaratory judgments, see Chapter 14, *infra*.

[242] Thus, "certification under Rule 23(b)(2) may be allowed in actions involving some damages as long as they are incidental, such as back pay claims in employment-discrimination suits seeking to end certain practices of the employer." 7AA WRIGHT & MILLER § 1775. *See, e.g., Parker v. Time Warner Entm't Co., L.P.*, 331 F.3d 13, 18 (2d Cir. 2003).

[243] ABA Section of Litigation, *Report and Recommendations of the Special Committee on Class Action Improvements* (1986), at 197. The Committee went on to note that "an artful pleader can endeavor to make the declaratory or injunctive relief appear to 'predominate.'" *Id.*

[244] 131 S. Ct. 2541, 2547 (2011).

[245] *Id.* at 2557.

[246] "The great bulk of reported cases in which class actions have been allowed under the revised rule have been (b)(3) actions." WRIGHT § 72.

[247] To aid in resolving these issues, Rule 23(b)(3) identifies four considerations:

(A) the class members' interests in individually controlling the prosecution or defense of separate actions; (B) the extent and nature of any litigation concerning the controversy already begun by or against class members; (C) the desirability or undesirability of concentrating the litigation of the claims in the particular forum; and (D) the likely difficulties in managing a class action.

[248] Members of a 23(b)(2) class must be united in their request for an injunction or declaratory judgment. Satisfaction of (b)(1) will only be possible when the interests of individual class members, although discrete, resemble one another to a large degree.

fit within (b)(3).[249] In such cases, certification under (b)(1) or (b)(2) can offer advantages over certification under (b)(3). This is because Rule 23(c)(2) requires notice to be sent to members of a (b)(3) class and gives them the opportunity to request exclusion from ("opt out of") the class.[250]

The first part of Rule 23(c)(2)[251] appears to have been written under *Mullane's* due process influence, insisting on reasonable notice when it is practical. Unfortunately, (c)(2) thereafter loses much of its *Mullane*-like flexibility, mandating individual notice to all class members whose names and addresses are known — without reference to practicability.[252] Once it read (c)(2) to require notice in the manner indicated above,[253] the Supreme Court found it unnecessary to reach the question whether due process required such notice as well.[254] Federal class actions under Rule 23(b)(1) and (2) are not subject to (c)(2), but only to the general limitations of due process,[255] as are state class actions.[256]

Finally, it is now clear that the requirements posed by subdivisions (a) and (b) of Rule 23 also apply to classes certified solely for purposes of settlement.[257]

[3] Reconciling Judicial Economy and Public Law Enforcement (b)(3) Class Actions

A major goal in drafting Rule 23(b)(3) was one we have encountered previously in this chapter — judicial economy.[258] If only judicial economy was involved, the arguments for and against Rule 23(b)(3) certifications would follow a familiar pattern. The argument for certification would be that efficiency would result from

---

[249] *See, e.g.,* 7AA WRIGHT & MILLER § 1772 (raising the possibility of "an action . . . under both Rule 23(b)(1) and Rule 23(b)(3).").

[250] *See* 7AA WRIGHT & MILLER § 1772. On notice in (b)(3) actions, see § 9.09[2][c], *infra.* On opt-out procedure, see note 196, *supra.*

[251] "In any class action maintained under subdivision (b)(3), the court shall direct to the members of the class the best notice practicable under the circumstances."

[252] At the same time, Rule 23(c)(2) does not reduce notice flexibility under *Mullane* for (b)(3) class members whose names and addresses cannot be ascertained. Concerning this group, "it should be remembered that Rule 23(c)(2) only directs the court to give 'the best notice practicable under the circumstances.'" 7AA WRIGHT & MILLER § 1786. When some class members are individually notified, notice by publication to those whose whereabouts are unknown will often suffice. 7AA WRIGHT & MILLER § 1786.

[253] *Eisen v. Carlisle & Jacquelin,* 417 U.S. 156 (1974), discussed at note 271 and accompanying text, *infra.*

[254] *See* Adolf Homburger, *State Class Actions and the Federal Rule,* 71 COLUM. L. REV. 609, 646 (1971) (arguing "there is nothing in *Hansberry* or *Mullane* to suggest a constitutional prohibition against dispensation with notice in any kind of class suit if procedural fairness and adequacy of representation are safeguarded in other ways").

[255] NEWBERG, note 186, *supra,* § 8.05.

[256] *See Shutts,* 472 U.S. at 811–12

[257] *Ortiz v. Fibreboard,* 527 U.S. 815 (1999); *Amchem Prods. v. Windsor,* 521 U.S. 591 (1997).

[258] "Subdivision (b)(3) encompasses those cases in which a class action would achieve economies of time, effort, and expense, and promote uniformity of decision as to persons similarly situated, without sacrificing procedural fairness or bringing about other undesirable results." Rule 23 advisory committee's notes (1966).

simultaneous adjudication of elements of individual claims common to the class, while the counter-argument would be that maintenance of a class action would confuse and delay the case in ways counterproductive to judicial economy and prejudicial to interests of those opposing the class.[259]

The picture for (b)(3) class actions is complicated, however, by the recurrent suggestion that class actions perform a function apart from promoting judicial economy — that of providing a means for private citizens to sue in the public interest. Thus viewed, Rule 23(b)(3) should be given maximum play when class representatives can, as private attorneys general, protect members of the public who are unable to protect themselves. Government lawyers litigate to protect the public, but they labor with limited resources and limited authority to obtain compensation for those who have been wronged by violation of federal law. Seeking damages for himself and a group of people similarly wronged, the class representative supplements the role of government lawyers. He becomes a kind of private attorney general, blurring the line between public and private litigation. The Supreme Court noted with apparent approval this use of (b)(3): "The policy at the very core of the class action mechanism is to overcome the problem that small recoveries do not provide the incentive for any individual to bring a solo action prosecuting his or her rights. A class action solves this problem by aggregating the relatively paltry potential recoveries into something worth someone's (usually an attorney's) labor."[260]

But it is possible to argue that, since the private attorney-general theory has greatest application when class members' damage claims are too small to be viable as individual lawsuits,[261] use of the idea to justify (b)(3) class actions stands the rule on its head. That is, assuming that (b)(3) was intended to promote judicial economy,[262] it would seem to have the opposite effect when used to facilitate litigation which could not exist otherwise.[263]

---

[259] The same pattern would be followed, for example, in arguments for and against permissive intervention. *See* § 9.08[2], *supra*.

[260] *Amchem Products, Inc. v. Windsor*, 521 U.S. 591, 617 (1997) (quoting *Mace v. Van Ru Credit Corp.*, 109 F.3d 338, 344 (7th Cir. 1997). *Accord Phillips Petroleum Co. v. Shutts*, 472 U.S. 797, 809 (1985); *Deposit Guar. Nat'l Bank v. Roper*, 445 U.S. 326, 339 (1980).

For discussion of private-attorney-general interpretations of paragraph (b)(3), see Howard M. Erichson, *Mississippi Class Actions and the Inevitability of Mass Aggregate Litigation*, 24 Miss. C. L. Rev. 285 (2005); William B. Rubenstein, *On What a "Private Attorney General" Is — And Why It Matters*, 57 Vand. L. Rev. 2129 (2004); Daniel J. Meltzer, *Deterring Constitutional Violations by Law Enforcement Officials: Plaintiffs and Defendants as Private Attorneys General*, 88 Colum. L. Rev. 247 (1988); Carl Cheng, *Important Rights and the Private Attorney General Doctrine*, 73 Cal. L. Rev. 1929 (1985).

[261] Rule 23(b)(3) class actions in federal court "have been especially popular in antitrust and securities fraud cases, when individual persons allegedly injured are in a poor position to seek redress, either because they do not know enough or because the cost of suit is disproportionate to each individual claim." Wright § 72. It is certainly true that many claims of class members or even class representatives in such cases would not support the cost of a separate lawsuit. For example, the individual damage claim of Mort Eisen, class representative in the multimillion dollar case, *Eisen v. Carlisle & Jacquelin*, 417 U.S. 156 (1974), was for $70.

[262] *See* Rule 23(b)(3) advisory committee's notes (1966).

[263] One commentator wrote of the private-attorney-general argument, "this purpose is enunciated

[4]   Small-Claim, Large-Class Actions

[a]   Comparative Availability of Federal and State Class Actions

Procedural opportunities for one filing suit in state court often are about the same as they would be in federal court. A federal forum offers a clear advantage in a few situations.[264] However, a suit brought on behalf of a nationwide class — especially when individual class claims are small — may fare better in the courts of some states than in federal court.[265]

First, states seem less inclined to follow the federal rules model when treating class actions,[266] and several have promulgated class rules more accommodating than Federal Rule 23.[267] Second, even state courts presented with language in their class action rules identical to Rule 23 are not bound by federal court interpretations of the latter,[268] and are in any event free from the constraints of subject matter

---

nowhere in Rule 23. Furthermore, in practice such a principle — if embodied within (b)(3) — would produce a direct conflict with the professed purpose of economy of time, expense and effort." Thomas J. Weithers, *Amended Rule 23: A Defendant's Point of View*, 10 B.C. IND. & COM. L. REV. 515, 518 (1969); *cf. Eisen v. Carlisle & Jacquelin*, 391 F.2d 555, 572 (2d Cir. 1968) (Lumbard, C.J., dissenting) ("The appropriate action for this Court is to affirm the district court and put an end to this Frankenstein monster posing as a class action."). *But see* Tom Ford, *Federal Rule 23: A Device for Aiding the Small Claimant*, 10 B.C. IND. & COM. L. REV. 501, 504 (1969) (one of the purposes of revised Rule 23 is "taking care of the smaller guy") (quoting Professor Kaplan, Reporter for the Advisory Committee).

[264] See for example, the discussion of statutory interpleader in § 9.07, *supra.*

[265] At the same time, class actions can succeed under Federal Rule 23(b)(3), particularly when a governmental entity is willing to litigate on behalf of the class, or when the size of individual class claims increases. Multistate class actions are at times easier to maintain in federal court because the courts of some states are still reluctant to take them on. Moreover, antitrust and certain other federal claims can be heard only in federal court. *See* § 5.01[2], *supra.* States, however, may take jurisdiction over class actions based on state antitrust law. *See generally* Herbert Hovenkamp, *State Antitrust in the Federal Scheme*, 58 IND. L.J. 375 (1983).

[266] According to a leading study, "only a minority of states have embraced the system and philosophy of the Federal Rules wholeheartedly enough to permit classification as true federal replicas." John B. Oakley & Arthur F. Coon, *The Federal Rules in State Courts: A Survey of State Court Systems of Civil Procedure*, 61 WASH. L. REV. 1367, 1369 (1986). A number of states pick and choose models among the federal rules, adopting some (perhaps most), but not all. In this regard, Rule 23 appears to be among those most frequently passed over. For example North Carolina and Wisconsin modeled their intervention rules closely upon Federal Rule 24, but ignored Federal Rule 23. For more on how states approach the subject, see Robert A. Skirnick & Patricia I. Avery, *The State Court Class Action — A Potpourri of Differences*, 20 FORUM 750 (1985).

[267] Florida amended its class action law "to eliminate problems in the federal rule through court decisions." Fla. R. Civ. P. 1.240 committee's note (1980). Like Florida, New York also rejected the federal approach and adopted more liberal class action law. N.Y. CIV. PRAC. L. & R. ART. 9.

[268] The meaning of even identical language in a state rule raises a question of state rather than federal law. Under such circumstances, federal court interpretations of the federal rules (even those by the United States Supreme Court) are no more than persuasive precedent. The best and final authority on the meaning of all state law is the highest state court. *See* § 7.06[1], *supra.* At the same time, federal rule decisions can be quite persuasive when a state court is looking at the same language in its own rule. The following response of an Indiana court may be typical.

> Indiana . . . Rule 23 is the general rule governing class actions. With two exceptions it follows the federal rule, F.R.C.P. 23, verbatim. In addition, our civil code study commission

jurisdiction which further limit federal class actions.[269]

[b]   Problems Small-Claim, Large-Class Actions Pose in Federal Court

The Supreme Court's decision in *Eisen v. Carlisle & Jacquelin*[270] sharply curtailed Rule 23(b)(3) litigation involving small claims in federal court. The Court read Rule 23(c)(2) to require individual notice of the action at the representative's expense to each member of a (b)(3) class whose name and address was available to the class representative, and to prevent shifting any of the cost of notice to the party opposing the clases. Later, in *Oppenheimer Fund, Inc. v. Sanders*,[271] the Supreme Court ruled that the class representative was also required to pay the party opposing the class the latter's expenses in compiling the names and addresses of the class for the representative. Resulting expense dampened the private-attorney-general movement in federal court.[272] However, since *Eisen* and *Oppenheimer* were not constitutional law decisions, they do not control class actions in state courts. States are free to adopt class rules philosophically opposed to *Eisen*.[273]

The availability of class actions under Federal Rule 23(b)(3) is also limited by the reluctance of many federal courts to certify class actions if the process of distributing damages to individual class members seems too complicated or if the prospect of actual reimbursement to class members seems too uncertain. Federal courts must take these factors into account,[274] and obstacles to class certification increase when classes become larger and the size of individual claims smaller. Yet certification may be warranted even in such cases, when it is possible to determine (without examining individual class claims) both the liability of the opposing party to the entire class[275] and the total amount of damages inflicted upon the class.[276]

---

comments direct the bar, with approval, to the note of the Advisory Committee to the federal rule.

For these reasons, and because this is an area of complex litigation where the bench and bar are greatly benefited by a broad body of interpretive law, we will, as far as possible, adopt the federal interpretation of the language of the rule.

Bowen v. Sonnenburg, 411 N.E.2d 390, 396–97 (Ind. Ct. App. 1980); *accord Wal-Mart Stores, Inc. v. Rhodus*, 808 N.E.2d 1198, 1207-08 (Ind. Ct. App. 2004).

[269] The Class Action Fairness Act, discussed in the next subsection, however, has served to make class actions more available in federal courts.

[270] 417 U.S. 156 (1974).

[271] 437 U.S. 340 (1978).

[272] Costs generated by *Eisen* and *Oppenheimer* will be beyond the means of most class representatives and are in any event greatly disproportionate to the value of the representative's personal claim.

[273] *See e.g.*, N.Y. CIV. PRAC. L. & R., Art. 9.

[274] The interests of members of Rule 23(b)(1) and (2) classes tend to be closely tied. "But in an action under Rule 23(b)(3) the members are loosely bound together by common questions of law or fact and considerations of convenience. Even the damages they seek generally are individual in character and disparate in amount." 7AA *WRIGHT & MILLER* § 1784. The requirement in Rule 23(b)(3) that class issues predominate in the case and concern in (b)(3)(D) over "difficulties likely to be encountered in the management of a class action" make the rule sensitive to possible difficulties in distributing damage awards to individual members of the class. 7AA *WRIGHT & MILLER* § 1784.

[275] The feasibility of proving defendants wrong class-wide will depend on the facts and plaintiff's

Certification in this setting may turn on the legitimacy of so-called fluid recovery.

Fluid recovery is a means of disposing of the portion of class-wide damages which goes unclaimed by class members by directing that it be spent in the public interest in a way at least generally responsive to concerns raised in the case.[277] Small-claim, large-class actions may proceed from adjudication of defendant's liability to the class to class-wide assessment of damages and the creation of a fund.[278] After attorney's fees and litigation and administrative expenses are deducted, the balance of the fund theoretically goes to class members in proportion to the value of their individual claims. But most small-claim, large-class actions offer the likelihood that a substantial portion of the class fund will go unclaimed. This may be because many members of the class are unknown and may not learn of the existence of a class award or because the sum involved may be so small that some class members will not bother to apply for their individual recoveries. Most lower federal courts have refused to administer class actions offering the prospect of substantial unclaimed recovery, "unless it is part of a distribution arising out of a settlement."[279] In contrast, some state courts have been more willing to employ fluid

---

theory of liability. Antitrust cases are frequently susceptible to such proof. *See* note 247, *infra*. On the other hand, proof of class-wide fraud under § 10(b) of the Securities Exchange Act of 1934 may be more problematic. *See generally* Note, *The Impact of Class Actions on Rule 10b-5*, 38 U. Chi. L. Rev. 337 (1971).

[276] For example, consider the antitrust case where plaintiff's class is the public with whom the defendants transacted business during a given period. Whether plaintiff's class has been wronged as a matter of antitrust law, and, if so, in what amount, are not simple questions. At the procedural level, however, these issues are often quite susceptible to class-wide resolution, *e.g.*, resolution without the necessity of examining a single individual class claim. Common issues would include whether defendants engaged in price-fixing and, if so, the amount of their total charges to the class during the relevant period, and the differential between those charges and the charges defendants would have made in the absence of price-fixing.

[277] On the topic of fluid recovery, see *Developments*, note 143, *supra* at 1516–23; Michael Malina, *Fluid Class Recovery as a Consumer Remedy in Antitrust Cases*, 47 N.Y.U. L. Rev. 477 (1972). Cases utilizing the device include *Gordon v. Boden*, 586 N.E.2d 461 (Ill. App. Ct. 1991) (damages from sale of adulterated orange juice products available either to fund a charitable project to benefit class or to reduce the price of future product sales); *Bruno v. Superior Court*, 179 Cal. Rptr. 342 (Cal. Ct. App. 1981) (profits from illegal milk prices applied to lower the price of milk in the future); *Market St. Ry. v. Railroad Comm'n*, 171 P.2d 875 (Cal. 1946) (profits from illegal train fares directed to upgrade train facilities). These cases share features common to most fluid recovery cases: (1) the fund is fluidly distributed only after an attempt is made to reach and compensate class members directly for their actual harm; and (2) the means chosen to dispose of the fund is calculated to provide some advantage to members of the class who were not individually compensated. That is, those wronged through past purchase of milk or train tickets are among those most likely to share in the advantage of reduced prices in the future. Of course, the process is inexact. Reduced prices in the future will be a windfall for those members of the class who did make individual claims against the fund and for members of the public not wronged in the past. Iowa, North Dakota and New Jersey have codified their law of fluid recovery. *See* Newberg, note 186, *supra*, § 13.49.

[278] "Devising a plan to distribute a lump sum recovery is beneficial because it may eliminate the need for separate trials on damage issues. In a case involving an extremely large plaintiff class whose members only have small individual claims, the savings in time and expense for all will be considerable." 7AA Wright & Miller § 1784.

[279] 7AA Wright & Miller § 1784. A well-known example of the latter is *West Virginia v. Chas. Pfizer & Co.*, 440 F.2d 1079 (2d Cir. 1971), *cert. denied*, 404 U.S. 871 (1971), an antitrust case in which the court administered a settlement fund of $100,000,000.

recovery.[280]

The actual notice requirement of Rule 23(c)(2) and the reluctance of federal judges to employ fluid recovery combine to restrict the availability of small-claim, large-class actions in federal court. This led to more careful consideration of possible advantages from filing a class action in state rather than federal court. Several state courts have willingly provided a sanctuary for nation-wide class actions that are difficult or impossible to bring in federal court.[281]

On the other hand, Congress enabled litigants to sidestep state-court class actions more easily when it enacted the Class Action Fairness Act of 2005[282] ("CAFA"). Class action authority Edward Sherman explained the impetus for the legislation:

> In recent years, federal courts had been perceived by both plaintiff and defendant lawyers as less sympathetic to class actions and to plaintiff's cases than certain state courts. As federal court judges became more critical of class actions, class action attorneys increasingly filed in state courts. Businesses especially complained that an undue proportion of class actions were filed in certain "magnet venue" state courts . . . where judges, usually elected, were more likely to certify a class action and the juries were likely to be more pro-plaintiff. In addition, corporations that do business in multiple states complained that they were subjected to national or multistate class actions in state courts that could thereby establish legal standards that would govern their activities throughout the country.

The Class Action Fairness Act sought to ameliorate these problems by making a federal forum more accessible for high-stakes class actions. In cases arising out of state law, the Act relaxed the traditional jurisdictional requirement of complete diversity of citizenship between the parties. Subject to enumerated exceptions, it authorized the federal district courts to hear class actions with only minimal diversity — if at least one class member was a citizen of a different state than any defendant — provided that the amount in controversy exceeded $5 million.[283] To

---

[280] See the discussion of state decisions in note 269, *supra.*

[281] "[R]ecent United States Supreme Court cases restricting access to the federal courts in class actions suits have made it necessary for state courts to hear nation-wide class actions." *Shutts v. Phillips Petroleum Co.*, 679 P.2d 1159, 1169 (Kan. 1984), *rev'd on other grounds, Phillips Petroleum Co. v. Shutts*, 472 U.S. 797 (1985). *See also Miner v. Gillette Co.*, 428 N.E.2d 478 (Ill. 1981); *Schlosser v. Allis-Chalmers Corp.*, 271 N.W.2d 879 (Wis. 1978); *Anthony v. General Motors Corp.*, 109 Cal. Rptr. 254 (Cal. Ct. App. 1973); *Paley v. Coca Cola Co.*, 209 N.W.2d 232 (Mich. 1973). *Cf.* G. ALAN TARR & MARY CORNELIA PORTER, STATE SUPREME COURTS IN STATE AND NATION 45 (1988) (noting that a number of states, "either through legislation or court decisions, have developed guidelines on class actions that are considerably more liberal than those prevailing in the federal courts.").

[282] The Act created 28 U.S.C. §§ 1453 & 1711–1715 and amended 28 U.S.C. §§ 1332, 1335, and 1603. For analyses of the CAFA, see Richard L. Marcus, *Assessing CAFA's Stated Jurisdictional Policy*, 156 U. PA. L. REV. 1765 (2008); Adam N. Steinman, *"Less" is "More"? Textualism, Intentionalism, and a Better Solution to the Class Action Fairness Act's Appellate Deadline Riddle*, 92 IOWA L. REV. 1183 (2007); Edward F. Sherman, *Class Actions After the Class Action Fairness Act of 2005*, 80 TUL. L. REV. 1593 (2006); Anna Andreeva, *Class Action Fairness Act of 2005: The Eight-Year Saga is Finally Over*, 59 U. MIAMI L. REV. 385 (2005).

[283] 28 U.S.C. § 1332(d)(2).

make it easier for defendants to remove class actions to federal court, the Act relaxed removal requirements in diversity cases by: enabling home state defendants to remove class actions; permitting any defendant to remove without the consent of co-defendants; and authorizing removal more than one year after commencement of the action.[284]

[5] Class Actions in Global Perspective[285]

The diminishing importance of national boundaries has affected civil procedure[286] as it has other subjects. Class actions are beginning to obtain global dimensions. Special problems arise for U.S. courts in such cases. These include concerns over the proper administration of class actions under Federal Rule 23 regarding international notice, the wish of foreign members of the class to be included or excluded, global settlement, and the enforcement of class judgments abroad. Such actions can also raise special questions about personal jurisdiction and federal subject matter jurisdiction.

---

[284] 28 U.S.C. § 1453(b).

[285] Aspects of the subject have interested commentators. *See, e.g.*, Hannah L. Buxbaum, *Multinational Class Actions Under Federal Securities Law: Managing Jurisdictional Conflict*, 46 COLUM. J. TRANSNAT'L L. 14 (2007); Note, *Actualizing the Trope of Internationalism in Class Action Theory*, 118 HARV. L. REV. 2914 (2005); Ilana T. Buschkin, *The Viability of Class Action Lawsuits in a Global Economy — Permitting Foreign Claimants to be Members of Class Action Lawsuits in the U.S. Federal Courts*, 90 CORNELL L. REV. 1563 (2005); Edward F. Sherman, *American Class Actions: Significant Features and Developing Alternatives in Foreign Legal Systems*, 215 F.R.D. 130 (2003); Debra Lyn Bassett, *U.S. Class Actions Go Global: Transnational Class Actions and Personal Jurisdiction*, 72 FORDHAM L. REV. 41 (2003).

[286] *See* Gene R. Shreve, *Civil Procedure: Other Disciplines, Globalization, and Simple Gifts*, 92 MICH. L. REV. 1401 (1994).

§ 9.10 CONSOLIDATING CASES — CURRENT LAW AND POSSIBILITIES FOR THE FUTURE

[1] Intradistrict Consolidation — Rule 42(a)[287]

Federal Rule 42(a) authorizes the court to "join for hearing or trial" cases pending within the same judicial district that "involve a common question of law or fact." A number of states have essentially the same rule.[288]

The object of Rule 42(a) is to promote judicial economy.[289] Judicial economy has been a recurrent theme in this chapter. Yet Rule 42(a) functions in relative isolation. It does not appear in the pleading or parties sections of the federal rules, as do the other rules we have considered. It has also been suggested that "it would be a mistake to assume that the standard for consolidation is the same as that governing original joinder of parties or claims."[290]

Therefore, one cannot simply assume that Rule 42(a) provides a means of reconstructing litigation along lines possible under federal joinder rules before the cases were filed. The availability of consolidation is in one respect more restricted than joinder, since "in a suit between a single plaintiff and a single defendant, plaintiff may join all of his claims, no matter how unrelated they may be, against the defendant. If the plaintiff brings separate actions, however, only those actions having a common question of law or fact may be consolidated."[291] In another respect, consolidation is less restricted.

> [M]ore than one party can be joined on a side under Rule 20(a) only if there is asserted on behalf of or against all of them one or more claims for relief arising out of the same transaction or occurrence or series of transactions or occurrences. This is in addition to the requirement that there be some question of law or fact common to all the parties. But the common question by itself is enough to permit consolidation, even if the claims arise out of independent transactions.[292]

---

[287] *See generally* MOORE §§ 42.10–42.15; Elizabeth J. Cabraser. *The Class Action Counterreformation*, 57 STAN. L. REV. 1475, 1493-99 (2005); Joan Steinman, *The Effects of Case Consolidation on the Procedural Rights of Litigants: What They Are, They Might Be Part I: Justiciability and Jurisdiction (Original and Appellate)*, 42 UCLA L. REV. 717 (1995); Joan Steinman, . . . *Part II: Non-Jurisdictional Matters*, 42 UCLA L. REV. 967 (1995); Richard L. Marcus, *Confronting the Consolidation Conundrum*, 1995 BYU L. REV. 879; 9A WRIGHT & MILLER §§ 2382–86; MANUAL FOR COMPLEX LITIGATION (THIRD) § 31.11 (1995); Gaylord A. Virden, *Consolidation Under Rule 42 of the Federal Rules of Civil Procedure*, 141 F.R.D. 169 (1992). *Cf.* Theodore Goldberg & Tybe A. Brett, *Consolidation of Individual Plaintiff Personal Injury-Toxic Tort Actions*, 11 J.L. & COM. 59 (1991) (discussing applications of Rule 42(a) in asbestos injury litigation); Charles Silver, *Comparing Class Actions and Consolidations*, 10 REV. LITIG. 495 (1991) (comparing Rules 23 and 42(a)).

[288] *E.g.*, DEL. CODE ANN. R. CIV. P. 42; MINN. STAT. ANN. R. CIV. P. DIST. CT. R. 42.01; N.M. STAT. ANN. R. CIV. P. DIST. CT. 1-042.

[289] "The obvious virtue of consolidation is that it increases the productivity of the judicial system by arranging for simultaneous resolution of issues or entire actions." FRIEDENTHAL, KANE & MILLER § 6.2.

[290] 9A WRIGHT & MILLER § 2382.

[291] 9A WRIGHT & MILLER § 2382.

[292] 9A WRIGHT & MILLER § 2382.

Orders granting or denying Rule 42(a) motions to consolidate are interlocutory and hence difficult to appeal.[293] The federal court's authority to consolidate exists only when two or more cases present a common issue of law or fact. Presence of a common issue empowers the court to order consolidation but does not require it to do so. This is an area where considerable discretion should and does exist. "[I]t is for the court to weigh the saving of time and effort that consolidation would produce against any inconvenience, delay or expense that it would cause."[294]

A federal trial judge has authority under Rule 42(a) to consolidate only cases pending within her judicial district. She may not use the rule to consolidate cases pending in more than one district.[295] The Judicial Panel on Multidistrict Litigation may order consolidation of such cases for pretrial purposes,[296] however, and a trial judge may weigh the possibility of consolidation in deciding whether to transfer a case to another district.[297]

[2] Federal Multidistrict Litigation Under Section 1407[298]

Section 1407(a) of Title 28 reads in part: "When civil actions involving one or more common questions of fact are pending in different districts, such actions may be transferred to any district for coordinated or consolidated pretrial proceedings." By authorizing multidistrict consolidation, Section 1407 exceeds Rule 42(a) in scope. However, it is more narrow than Rule 42(a) in two respects. Section 1407 applies literally only to pretrial proceedings[299] and only to cases having common questions of fact.[300] Moreover, it authorizes transfers only when they "will be for the convenience of the parties and witnesses and will promote the just and efficient conduct of such actions."[301]

---

[293] MOORE § 42.12[1]. See generally § 13.03 (final judgment rule), infra.

[294] 9A WRIGHT & MILLER § 2383. Weighing against consolidation are possibilities of juror confusion, delay, administrative difficulties and prejudice to a party. MOORE § 42.10[5]. See, e.g., Solvent Chem. Co. v. E.I. Dupont De Nemours & Co., 242 F. Supp. 2d 196, 221 (W.D.N.Y. 2002).

[295] MOORE § 42.11[1]. See In re Penn Cent. Commercial Paper Litig., 62 F.R.D. 341 (S.D.N.Y. 1974), aff'd, 515 F.2d 505 (2d Cir. 1975).

[296] 28 U.S.C. § 1407. See § 9.10[2], infra.

[297] 28 U.S.C. § 1404. See generally § 6.02[2] (venue transfer), supra.

[298] See generally 15 WRIGHT & MILLER §§ 3861–3867; MANUAL, note 217, supra, § 20.13; Richard L. Marcus, Cure-All For an Era of Dispersed Litigation? Toward a Maximalist Use of the Multidistrict Litigation Panel's Transfer Power, 82 TULANE L. REV. 2245 (2008); Symposium, Multidistrict Litigation and Aggregation Alternatives, 31 SETON HALL L. REV. 877 (2001).

[299] Rule 42(a) contemplates joint hearing or trial and has been read to cover pretrial as well as trial proceedings. "If one of the purposes of consolidation for trial be to expedite the proceedings and avoid needless time and expense to the litigants and to the court, such objectives are as desirable and as attainable in the period utilized in preparing for trial." MANUAL, note 217, supra, § 31.11 (quoting MacAlister v. Guterma, 263 F.2d 65, 68 (2d Cir. 1958)).

[300] Rule 42(a) encompasses actions that "involve a common question of law or fact" (emphasis added).

[301] 28 U.S.C. § 1407(a). For additional discussion comparing Rule 42(a) with § 1407, see Diana E. Murphy, Unified and Consolidated Complaints in Multidistrict Litigation, 132 F.R.D. 597 (1991); Gregory R. Harris, Note, Consolidation and Transfer in the Federal Courts: 28 U.S.C. Section 1407 Viewed in Light of Rule 42(a) and 28 U.S.C. Section 1404(a), 22 HASTINGS L.J. 1289 (1971).

Congress enacted Section 1407 in response to the confusion and repetition generated by multiple antitrust suits in the electronics industry in the 1960s.[302] Section 1407 creates a "judicial panel on multidistrict litigation"[303] which decides when cases should be consolidated for pretrial proceedings and to which judge they should be transferred. The section has been invoked most frequently in antitrust cases and "common disaster (air crash) actions, patent and trademark suits, products liability actions and securities law violation actions."[304] Section 1407 has been quite useful in expediting and reducing the expense of discovery. The section also permits judges to whom cases have been transferred (*transferee* courts) to consider a variety of pretrial motions, including motions capable of terminating all or part of the consolidated litigation.[305]

Section 1407(a) requires return to the courts of origin (*transferor* courts) of transferred cases which are still alive when multidistrict proceedings are over.[306] In practice, however, transferee courts had frequently retained the cases for consolidated trial. "Federal courts had achieved this result either by securing the consent of the parties or by invoking Section 1404(a), the general transfer provision"[307] to effect a "self-assignment" of the case for trial. In *Lexecon v. Milberg Weiss*,[308] however, the Supreme Court put an end to the practice, holding that self-assignment by a § 1407 transferee court is prohibited by the plain language of § 1407.[309]

---

[302] Comment, *The Judicial Panel on Multidistrict Litigation: Time for Rethinking*, 140 U. Pa L. Rev. 711, 1001 (1991).

[303] The panel "shall consist of seven circuit and district judges . . . no two of whom shall be from the same circuit." 28 U.S.C. § 1407(d).

[304] 15 Wright & Miller § 3862 (*quoting* from the legislative history of § 1407). *See also* C. Clyde Atkins, *An Apologia for Transfer of Aviation Disaster Cases Under Section 1407* 38 J. Air L. & Com. 205 (1972). *See, e.g., Allen v. Bayer Corp.*, 460 F.3d 1217, 1230 (9th Cir. 2006).

[305] "Although the transferee judge has no jurisdiction to conduct a trial in the transferred cases, the judge may terminate actions by ruling on motions to dismiss, for summary judgment, or pursuant to settlement, and may enter consent decrees." Manual, note 217, *supra*, § 20.132.

[306] "Each action so transferred shall be remanded by the panel at or before the conclusion of such pretrial proceedings to the district from which it was transferred unless it shall have been previously terminated . . . ." 28 U.S.C. § 1407(a).

[307] 15 Wright & Miller § 3862. On § 1404 transfer, see § 6.02[2], *supra*. On the whole, "the great majority of cases transferred by the Panel under section 1407 have been disposed of by transferee courts and not remanded to their original districts." *The Judicial Panel*, note 303, *supra*, at 1001–02. The Federal Courts Study Committee has recommended that § 1407 be amended to expressly authorize "consolidated trial as well as pretrial proceedings . . . ." Report of the Federal Courts Study Committee 45 (1990).

[308] 523 U.S. 26 (1998).

[309] *See* text quoted in note 307, *supra* (which uses the mandatory "shall"). *See also* Courtney E. Silver, *Procedural Hassles in Multidistrict Litigation: A Call for Reform of 28 U.S.C. § 1407 and the Lexecon Result*, 70 Ohio St. L.J. 455 (2009) (one law student's cogent criticism of the *Lexecon* decision).

§ 9.11 JOINDER OF PARTIES AND CLAIMS IN THE CALIFORNIA COURTS

[1] Introduction to California Joinder Statutes

The California joinder statutes reflect the same policies evident in the federal joinder rules: promotion of judicial efficiency and just adjudication by avoiding prejudice to parties and absentees that could arise if claims or parties are excluded from the lawsuit. In many instances, the joinder standards stated in the California statutes are modeled after the Federal Rules of Civil Procedure. However, despite this similarity in standards, in one sense joinder in the California courts is more liberal than federal court joinder. Unlike the federal courts, whose subject matter jurisdiction over claims and parties is limited by the United States Constitution and statutes, the California courts essentially have no jurisdictional restrictions. Consequently, in order to achieve judicial efficiency and avoid prejudice, it may be preferable to bring some complex multi-party/multi-claim litigation in state court rather than in federal court.

[2] Permissive Joinder of Parties

[a] Permissive Joinder of Plaintiffs

The California statutes permit joinder of plaintiffs if they assert any right to relief "arising out of the same transaction, occurrence, or series of transactions or occurrences and if any question of law or fact common to all these persons will arise in the action."[310] This statutory standard is liberally construed so as to permit joinder of plaintiffs in one lawsuit and thereby promote judicial efficiency.[311] The broad test for permissive joinder of plaintiffs in the California statutes, as well as for permissive joinder of defendants discussed below, is essentially the same as that of Rule 20(a) of the Federal Rules of Civil Procedure. Misjoinder of plaintiffs or defendants may be raised by demurrer or by answer.[312] Because misjoinder is not a jurisdictional defect, the objection is waived if not raised.[313]

[b] Permissive Joinder of Defendants

Permissive joinder of defendants is proper where the complaint asserts against them any right to relief "arising out of the same transaction, occurrence, or series of transactions or occurrences and if any question of law or fact common to all

---

[310] Cal. Code Civ. Proc. § 378.

[311] See, e.g., Anaya v. Superior Court, 160 Cal. App. 3d 228, 206 Cal. Rptr. 520 (1984) (holding numerous employees of oil company are permitted to join in one lawsuit seeking damages for exposure to toxic chemicals over the course of 20 years); State Farm Fire & Cas. Co. v. Superior Court, 45 Cal. App. 4th 1093, 53 Cal. Rptr. 2d 229 (1996) (ruling group of insured homeowners, whose homes were destroyed by an earthquake, were properly joined as plaintiffs).

[312] Cal. Code Civ. Proc. § 430.10(d).

[313] Cal. Code Civ. Proc. § 430.80.

defendants will arise in the action."[314] For example, in one case, the joinder of 300 homeowners as defendants in an action brought by the plaintiff insurance company to declare the plaintiff not liable for storm damage was held inappropriate because claims did not arise from the "same transaction or occurrence."[315]

Beyond efficiency, there are important advantages to joining all co-defendants in one lawsuit where each defendant blames another defendant for the plaintiff's injuries. This is particularly true in multi-party tort litigation, where each defendant denies negligence, but argues that the plaintiff's injuries were caused by another defendant's negligence. If the plaintiff pursues separate actions against each defendant, there is a risk that the plaintiff will recover nothing even though the jury finds that her injuries were caused by *some* defendant's negligence. For example, assume that plaintiff is seriously injured in a collision with an automobile driven by Smith who, in turn, claims that the accident was precipitated by an unsafe lane change by a truck driven by Jones. In one lawsuit, plaintiff sues (only) defendant Smith to recover personal injury damages caused by Smith's alleged negligence. At trial, defendant Smith persuades the jury that Jones, not Smith, was negligent. Consequently, the jury finds in favor of Smith and against the plaintiff. Plaintiff then files a separate negligence action against Jones. Defendant Jones persuades the new jury that Smith, not Jones, was negligent and plaintiff loses again. This unhappy result likely would have been avoided if plaintiff had joined both Smith and Jones as defendants in one lawsuit.

[3] Permissive Joinder of Claims

California Code of Civil Procedure § 427.10 provides that a plaintiff who alleges a cause of action against one or more defendants "may unite with such cause any other causes which he has . . . against any such defendants." This provision effectively eliminates misjoinder of claims as a defense so long as joinder of parties is proper. The unlimited joinder of claims authorized by section 427.10 is the same as that of Rule 18(a) of the Federal Rules of Civil Procedure.

[4] Compulsory Joinder of Parties

California's compulsory joinder statute — Code of Civil Procedure § 389—is virtually identical to Rule 19 of the Federal Rules of Civil Procedure.[316] Section 389 requires joinder of any person who is subject to service of process and whose

---

[314] CAL. CODE CIV. PROC. § 379; *see, e.g., Farmers Ins. Exch. v. Adams*, 170 Cal. App. 3d 712, 216 Cal. Rptr. 287 (1985); *Colusa Air Pollution Control Dist. v. Superior Court*, 226 Cal. App. 3d 880, 277 Cal. Rptr. 110 (1991) (upholding joinder of regional district air pollution control agencies in a lawsuit challenging adoption by defendants of different regional regulations banning plaintiffs' product, pursuant to statewide proposals, because the adoption of local regulations by each district defendant constituted a series of occurrences).

[315] *Farmers Ins. Exch. v. Adams*, 170 Cal. App. 3d 712, 722–23, 216 Cal. Rptr. 287 (1985).

[316] Federal cases interpreting the federal rule may be relevant to § 389 determinations. *See, e.g., Copley v. Copley*, 126 Cal. App. 3d 248, 296, 178 Cal. Rptr. 842 (1981); *Kraus v. Willow Park Public Golf Course*, 73 Cal. App. 3d 354, 368, n.9, 140 Cal. Rptr. 744 (1977). For example, in *Union Carbide Corp. v. Superior Court*, 36 Cal. 3d 15, 201 Cal. Rptr. 580, 679 P.2d 14 (1984), an anti-trust defendant argued that unless other potential claimants were joined, defendant would be subject to a "substantial risk" of

joinder will not deprive the court of subject matter jurisdiction, and who meets one of the pragmatic criteria stated in § 389(a): (1) in that person's absence, complete relief cannot be accorded existing parties or (2) the absent person claims an interest relating to the subject of the litigation and is so situated that disposition of the action in his absence may as a practical matter impair or impede his ability to protect that interest, or may leave existing parties subject to substantial risk of incurring double or inconsistent obligations by reason of this claimed interest. In such circumstances, the trial court should not dismiss, but should order joinder of the missing person.[317]

A number of prior California court decisions provide useful guidelines as to whether certain categories of persons must be joined under section 389(a). For example, in an action seeking either to enforce or set aside a contract, all contracting parties generally must be joined.[318] However, a plaintiff may proceed against only one tortfeasor; section 389(a) does not require joinder of all tortfeasors in one action.[319] Normally, all partners are regarded as indispensable parties in an action for dissolution of a partnership;[320] and a corporation is an indispensable party in a stockholder derivative action.[321] Where litigation challenges the propriety of government action which confers a benefit on a third person, that person often has been considered an indispensable party.[322] Some special statutes provide for mandatory joinder of certain parties. For example, the California Vehicle Code § 17152 requires that in a negligence action against the owner of vehicle, the driver shall be made a party defendant; and Family Code §§ 2060–2065 mandate joinder of an employee pension benefit plan in a dissolution of marriage proceeding in which either party claims an interest.

If joinder is not possible, then the trial court must consider factors such as those contained in section 389(b) to determine whether, as an exercise of equitable

---

multiple liability within the meaning of § 389(a). The California Supreme Court, by reference to federal cases applying Rule 19(a)(1)(B)(ii), construed "substantial risk" to mean more than a theoretical possibility that an absent party might assert a claim for the same loss. "The risk must be substantial as a practical matter." *Id.* at 21. For discussion of federal Rule 19(a), see § 9.05[2], *supra.*

[317] *See, e.g., Conrad v. Unemployment Ins. Appeals Bd.*, 47 Cal. App. 3d 237, 241, 120 Cal. Rptr. 803 (1975); *Deltakeeper v. Oakdale Irrigation Dist.*, 94 Cal. App. 4th 1092, 1100–05, 115 Cal. Rptr. 2d 244 (2001).

[318] *See, e.g., Vanoni v. Cnty. of Sonoma*, 40 Cal. App. 3d 743, 746–47, 115 Cal. Rptr. 485 (1974); *Northrop Corp. v. McDonnell Douglas Corp.*, 705 F.2d 1030, 1042–46 (9th Cir.), *cert. denied*, 464 U.S. 849 (1983). If all such contracting parties cannot be joined, the court has jurisdiction to proceed against the existing defendants as if they were the only defendants. *See* CAL. CODE CIV. PROC § 410.70.

[319] *See, e.g., Country Wide Home Loans v. Superior Court*, 69 Cal. App. 4th 785, 82 Cal. Rptr. 2d 63 (1999); *Temple v. Synthes Corp.*, 498 U.S. 5, 7 (1990) (holding that under federal Rule 19(a) plaintiff not required to join all joint tortfeasors as defendants in a single lawsuit).

[320] *See Kraus v. Willow Park Public Golf Course*, 73 Cal. App. 3d 354, 369, 140 Cal. Rptr. 744 (1977).

[321] *Stockton v. Ortiz*, 47 Cal. App. 3d 183, 191–92, 120 Cal. Rptr. 456 (1975).

[322] *Sierra Club, Inc. v. Cal. Coastal Comm'n*, 95 Cal. App. 3d 495, 157 Cal. Rptr. 190 (1979) (concluding developer of a real estate project is an indispensible party to an action brought by Sierra Club to set aside a permit authorizing the project); *Beresford Neighborhood Ass'n v. City of San Mateo*, 207 Cal. App. 3d 1180, 1189, 255 Cal. Rptr. 434 (1989) (following *Sierra Club*'s reasoning, but noting that joinder not necessary when challenge is to a general plan which applies equally to all developments in the area).

discretion, the action should proceed with the existing parties or should be dismissed.[323] The section 389(b) factors are essentially the same as those stated in federal Rule 19(b).[324] Only if the trial court determines dismissal appropriate is the absent person regarded as "indispensable."[325] Therefore, the term "indispensible party" refers to the conclusion that may be reached after considering the section 389(b) factors and is, of itself, of little analytical value.[326]

The defense of nonjoinder of parties is usually raised by demurrer or by answer.[327] The issue of nonjoinder may be raised for the first time on appeal, but is properly limited to the argument that the absence of a party precluded the trial court from rendering any effective judgment between the parties before it.[328]

[5] Interpleader

Interpleader is a device which permits the stakeholder, who may be liable to several claimants but does not know which ones, to join all claimants in a single action and require them to litigate their respective claims to property or funds held by the stakeholder. Classic interpleader occurs where the stakeholder has no interest in the property or fund sought to be interpleaded, and seeks joinder of all adverse claimants to force them to litigate their claims among themselves.[329] Once the court determines that interpleader is proper and the stakeholder deposits the

---

[323] *See, e.g., Tracy Press, Inc. v. Superior Court*, 164 Cal. App. 4th 1290, 1297–1302, 80 Cal. Rptr. 3d 464 (2008); *Deltakeeper, supra* (holding that in a proceeding challenging an environmental impact report for a project involving a joint district water purchase agreement, the trial court erred in dismissing for failure to join all of the water purchasers as indispensable parties because the nonjoined parties' interests were adequately represented by the existing parties and there was no adequate remedy if the action was dismissed as the statute of limitations had run for joining more parties); *People ex rel. Lungren v. Cmty. Redev. Agency*, 56 Cal. App. 4th 868, 65 Cal. Rptr. 2d 786 (1997) (holding trial court abused its discretion in dismissing a complaint filed by the Attorney General against a city's community redevelopment agency to set aside a contract between the agency and an American Indian tribe under which the agency would transfer real property to the tribe for development of a gaming casino, where the tribe could not be joined because of its sovereign immunity).

[324] For an explanation of these federal Rule 19(b) factors, see § 9.05[2][c], *supra.*

[325] *See, e.g., Save Our Bay, Inc. v. San Diego Unified Port Dist.*, 42 Cal. App. 4th 686, 49 Cal. Rptr. 2d 847 (1996) (affirming dismissal of a mandate proceeding brought by an environmental organization challenging the adequacy of an environmental impact report for a marine project where the landowner, whose land had to be acquired to complete the project, was an indispensable party who could not be joined because a statutory 30-day limitation period for joining the landowner had expired).

[326] *See, e.g., Marriage of Mena*, 212 Cal. App. 3d 12, 18, n.5, 260 Cal. Rptr. 314 (1989).

[327] CAL. CODE CIV. PROC. § 430.10(d).

[328] *See, e.g., County of Alameda, supra*, 14 Cal. App. 4th at 1105, n.5 (ruling failure to join indispensable party may be raised for first time on appeal only where the trial court was unable to render effective judgment between the parties before it); *Jermstad v. McNelis*, 210 Cal. App. 3d 528, 538, 258 Cal. Rptr. 519 (1989) (holding claim of error in failing to join absent party is not recognizable on appeal unless appropriately raised in the trial court or there is some compelling reason of equity or policy which warrants belated consideration).

[329] *See, e.g., Pacific Loan Mgmt. Corp. v. Superior Court*, 196 Cal. App. 3d 1485, 242 Cal. Rptr. 547 (1987) ("The true test of suitability for interpleader is the stakeholder's disavowal of interest in the property sought to be interpleaded, coupled with the perceived ability of the court to resolve the entire controversy as to entitlement to that property without need for the stakeholder to be a party to the suit."); *Dial 800 v. Fesbinder*, 118 Cal. App. 4th 32, 12 Cal. Rptr. 3d 711 (2004) (holding interpleader action

property or funds with the clerk, the court may discharge the disinterested stakeholder from liability to any of the claimants.[330] Interpleader is also available in California where the stakeholder claims an interest in all or a portion of the deposited property.[331]

The purpose of interpleader is to join all claims against the stakeholder in one action, and thereby prevent a multiplicity of suits and double liability or double vexation.[332] Therefore, interpleader is available not only to a plaintiff who files a separate interpleader action, but also to a defendant in certain circumstances.[333] A defendant may file a cross-complaint in interpleader, or may bring a separate interpleader action against the claimants.[334] Regardless of how an interpleader action is commenced, a trial court has the power to restrain all parties to the interpleader action from instituting or further prosecuting any other proceedings in any other California court which may affect the rights or obligations of parties to the interpleader.[335] This also means that a court exercising interpleader jurisdiction may enjoin the enforcement of a prior judgment which may affect interpleaded property or funds.[336]

Interpleader is available in federal court, either by federal statute or by federal rule, in situations nearly identical to those contained in the California interpleader statute, with even clearer indication that a stakeholder need not be disinterested.[337] The federal statutory scheme provides federal court jurisdiction over interpleader actions involving $500 or more in controversy based on "minimal diversity" between claimants (*i.e.*, only one claimant must be a citizen of a state different from that of the other claimants), authorizes nationwide service of process on all claimants, allows venue in a judicial district where any claimant resides, and relaxes the requirements for personal jurisdiction.[338] Because of these procedural advantages to proceeding in federal court under the liberal federal interpleader statutes, typically only those interpleader actions that lack federal subject matter

---

by companies against individuals claiming ownership interest in companies' shares was proper where companies were disinterested stakeholders).

[330] CAL. CODE CIV. PROC. § 386(a) & (b).

[331] *See* CAL. CODE CIV. PROC. § 386(b) ("The applicant or interpleading party may deny liability in whole or in part to any or all claimants."); *City of Morgan Hill v. Brown*, 71 Cal. App. 4th 1114, 1122–23, 84 Cal. Rptr. 2d 361 (1999) (observing that § 386 broadened the scope of interpleader).

[332] *See City of Morgan Hill, supra,* 71 Cal. App. 4th at 1122–23 (discussing the purposes of interpleader); *Hancock Oil Co. v. Hopkins,* 24 Cal. 2d 497, 508, 150 P.2d 463 (1944).

[333] *See, e.g., Cantu v. Resolution Trust Corp.,* 4 Cal. App. 4th 857, 6 Cal. Rptr. 2d 151 (1992); *Surety Co. of the Pac. v. Piver,* 149 Cal. App. 3d Supp. 29, 197 Cal. Rptr. 531 (1983).

[334] *See* CAL. CODE CIV. PROC. §§ 386(a) & (b); 386.6.

[335] CAL. CODE CIV. PROC. § 386(f).

[336] *See, e.g., Surety Co. of the Pac. v. Piver, supra,* 149 Cal. App. 3d at Supp. 31 (various claimants to a particular fund or property permitted to proceed to judgments in a proper forum of their choice, but may be restrained in the interpleader action as to enforcement of those judgments).

[337] 28 U.S.C. § 1335; FED. R. CIV. P. 22.

[338] *See* WRIGHT & MILLER, FEDERAL PRACTICE AND PROCEDURE: CIVIL 3d § 1710–§ 1712 (West 2001 & Supp. 2012); *see also* Herbert Hovenkamp, *Personal Jurisdiction and Venue in the Federal Courts: A Policy Analysis,* 67 IOWA L. REV. 485 (1982). Interpleader in the federal courts is discussed in § 9.07, *supra.*

jurisdiction (*i.e.*, cases where all the claimants are citizens of the same state) are brought in a California state court.

[6] Joinder by Cross-Complaints, Generally

[a] The California Cross-Complaint — A Multi-Purpose Joinder Device

The California *cross-complaint* is a multi-purpose pleading device which permits a party defending against a cause of action to assert her own affirmative cause of action against an opposing party, a co-party, or some other person not already a party to the action.[339] The California cross-complaint serves the same functions as the familiar counterclaim, cross-claim, and third-party impleader in federal court. The California Legislature opted for the one-term-fits-all approach in 1971 when it eliminated technical limitations of prior methods of countersuits and replaced them with a single form of pleading.[340]

[b] Cross-Complaints Against an Opposing Party

One type of cross-complaint is where one party (usually the defendant) asserts a cause of action back against an opposing party (usually the plaintiff) — in other words, a counterclaim in federal court terminology. As with counterclaims under federal Rule 13, the distinction between a compulsory and a permissive cross-complaint is important for purposes of preclusion law. Code of Civil Procedure § 426.10 and § 426.30 set forth the general preclusion rules for failure to plead a *compulsory cross-complaint.* Under section 426.30(a), if a party against whom a complaint has been filed and served fails to allege in a cross-complaint any "related cause of action" which he has against the plaintiff, "such party may not thereafter in any other action assert against the plaintiff the related cause of action not pleaded." In other words, a "related cause of action" must be alleged as a (compulsory) cross-complaint or its assertion in another lawsuit will be barred.

A "related cause of action" is defined as "a cause of action which arises out of the same transaction, occurrence or series of transactions or occurrences as the cause of action which the plaintiff alleges in his complaint."[341] This definition employs the same type of transactional standard utilized by federal Rule 13(a) in defining a compulsory counterclaim. Like a majority of federal courts, the California courts apply the expansive "logical relationship" test when interpreting the transactional standard. The relevant inquiry under this test is whether the claims of plaintiff and defendant involve common issues of law and fact such that a cross-complaint will

---

[339] CAL. CODE CIV. PROC. §§ 428.10–428.80.

[340] *See, e.g.*, CAL. CODE CIV. PROC. § 428.80 (counterclaims abolished and deemed cross-complaints); Jack H. Friedenthal, *Joinder of Claims, Counterclaims, and Cross-Complaints: Suggested Revisions of the California Provisions*, 23 STAN. L. REV. 1, 17–39 (1970); *1970 Law Revision Commission Report*, pp. 518–51.

[341] CAL. CODE CIV. PROC. § 426.10(c). Section 426.10(a) defines "complaint" to mean a complaint or cross-complaint; section 426.10(b) defines "plaintiff" to mean a person who files a complaint or a cross-complaint.

avoid duplication of time and effort with respect to litigation of these issues.[342] This broadly inclusive interpretation informs the prudent practitioner to plead a cross-complaint that is arguably, even if not clearly, a compulsory one.

Normally, a party must file a cross-complaint against any party who filed a complaint or cross-complaint against her before or at the same time as the answer.[343] However, some measure of forgiveness is available. Code of Civil Procedure § 426.50 authorizes relief from an excusable failure to timely plead a cross-complaint, and directs that such authority "shall be liberally construed to avoid forfeiture of causes of action." Absent a finding of bad faith, section 426.50 does not permit a trial court to deny a motion to file a late compulsory cross-complaint.[344]

Leave of court is required to file a cross-complaint that does not allege "related cause of action" — in other words, a *permissive cross-complaint*. Permission to file a permissive cross-complaint is solely within the trial court's discretion.[345]

[c] Statutes of Limitations

Ordinarily, a statute of limitations will apply to a cross-complaint in the same fashion as it applies to an independent action.[346] However, when an original complaint was filed before the statute of limitations on a cross-complaint had elapsed, the cross-complaint will relate back to the date of the complaint for statute of limitation purposes.[347] This relation-back rule applies only when the cross-complaint is a "related cause of action" — one which arises out of the same transaction or occurrence alleged in the complaint.[348]

---

[342] *Currie Med. Specialties, Inc. v. Newell Bowen*, 136 Cal. App. 3d 774, 777, 186 Cal. Rptr. 543 (1982) (ruling overlap of relevant issues regarding nature of contractual relationship central to both claims satisfied the logical relation test); *Saunders v. New Capital for Small Bus., Inc.*, 231 Cal. App. 2d 324, 41 Cal. Rptr. 703 (1964); *Ranchers Bank v. Pressman*, 19 Cal. App. 3d 612, 97 Cal. Rptr. 78 (1971). For additional discussion of the "logical relation" test, see § 9.03, *supra*.

[343] CAL. CODE CIV. PROC. § 428.50(a). Other types of cross-complaints (*i.e.*, third party and co-party) may be filed at any time before the court has set a date for trial, and even later with leave of court. CAL. CODE CIV. PROC. § 428.50(b) & (c).

[344] *See, e.g., Silver Org. Ltd. v. Frank*, 217 Cal. App. 3d 94, 265 Cal. Rptr. 681 (1990) (holding trial court erred in denying defendant's motion to file compulsory cross-complaint on eve of trial where insufficient evidence of bad faith); *Crocker Nat. Bank v. Emerald*, 221 Cal. App. 3d 852, 862–64, 270 Cal. Rptr. 699 (1990) (denying mandatory relief under § 426.50 because related cause of action did not exist at time defendant answered plaintiff's complaint).

[345] *Crocker Nat. Bank, supra*, 221 Cal. App. 3d at 864 (finding no abuse of discretion by trial court in denying leave to file permissive cross-complaint several years after bases for cross-complaint known to defendant where no explanation given by defendant for failure to seek leave earlier); *Orient Handel v. United States Fid. & Guar. Co.*, 192 Cal. App. 3d 684, 701, 237 Cal. Rptr. 667 (1987) (explaining that permission to file a permissive cross-complaint is solely within the trial court's discretion).

[346] *Liberty Mut. Ins. Co. v. Fales*, 8 Cal. 3d 712, 715, n.4, 106 Cal. Rptr. 21, 505 P.2d 213 (1973).

[347] *See, e.g., Sidney v. Superior Court*, 198 Cal. App. 3d 710, 244 Cal. Rptr. 31 (1988).

[348] *See Sidney v. Superior Court, supra*, 198 Cal. App. 3d at 714–17.

[d]   Cross-Complaint vs. Affirmative Defense

A cross-complaint shares some of the attributes of an affirmative defense, but the two are quite distinct procedural devices. An affirmative defense may provide a partial or complete bar to recovery on an opposing party's complaint or cross-complaint. In contrast, a cross-complaint permits the pleader to obtain relief regardless of the opposing party's recovery, and that relief may be different than, or in excess of, the opposing party's recovery. A cross-complaint is not limited to seeking relief from an opposing party but, as will be discussed below, may also be used to assert a cause of action against a co-party or a wholly new party.

[e]   Res Judicata Compared

Under the doctrine of res judicata (claim preclusion), a valid and final judgment on the merits in favor of a defendant constitutes a complete bar to further litigation by the plaintiff on the same cause of action.[349] The California res judicata doctrine defines a "cause of action" as the remedial right in favor of a plaintiff for the violation of one "primary right," and permits a plaintiff to bring a separate lawsuit against the same defendant for violation of each separate primary right.[350]

A single factual transaction may give rise to the violation of more than one primary right and therefore give a plaintiff the potential of two separate lawsuits against a single defendant. Under established primary rights precedent, for example, one tortious act may violate two primary rights and create two separate causes of action: one for injury to person and a second for damages to property.[351] A typical example is negligence litigation arising out of the crash of two cars, where one driver sues the other. The resulting personal injury to the plaintiff driver is a separate cause of action from the property damage to plaintiff's car, and may be pursued in two separate lawsuits.

In contrast, the California's cross-complaint statutes utilize a "transactional" standard — not a primary rights standard — in defining compulsory cross-complaints.[352] In some circumstance, the transactional cross-complaint standard may have an impact on the primary rights approach to res judicata. Consider the following typical occurrence. Sam Saguaro's car collided with Laura Lorry's truck. Both parties suffered personal injuries, and both vehicles were totaled. Plaintiff Saguaro sued defendant Lorry in superior court for personal injury damages, alleging his injuries were caused by defendant's negligence. Defendant answered and cross-complained against plaintiff, seeking damages for her own personal injuries and alleging they were caused by plaintiff's negligence. The jury found plaintiff Saguaro 5% negligent and defendant Lorry 95% negligent, and awarded appropriate damages.

---

[349] California's res judicata (claim preclusion) doctrine and primary rights theory are discussed in more detail in § 15.16, *infra*.

[350] *See, e.g., Slater v. Blackwood*, 15 Cal. 3d 791, 126 Cal. Rptr. 225, 543 P.2d 593 (1975); *Holmes v. David H. Bricker, Inc.*, 70 Cal. 2d 786, 76 Cal. Rptr. 431, 452 P.2d 647 (1969).

[351] *See Holmes, supra*, 70 Cal. 2d at 788–89.

[352] Cal. Code Civ. Proc. §§ 426.30(a), 426.10(c).

Plaintiff Saguaro then files a subsequent lawsuit against defendant Lorry seeking damages for the destruction of his car. Because plaintiff's second suit is based on a separate primary right, his cause of action is not barred by res judicata. However, plaintiff's second action is barred by rule preclusion under California's compulsory cross-complaint statutes — Code of Civil Procedure § 426.10(c) and § 426.30(a) — which define a "complaint" to also mean a cross-complaint and a "plaintiff" to also mean a person who files a cross-complaint. In other words, once the defendant filed her cross-complaint, the plaintiff must plead any "related cause of action" he has against the defendant. Because plaintiff Saguaro failed to file a cross-complaint, he forfeited his cause of action for property damages. This result would be the same if defendant Lorry had won the first lawsuit. Thus, the compulsory cross-complaint statutes may effectively replace the California's primary rights approach to res judicata with a transactional standard in such typical cases.

[7] Cross-Complaint Against a New Party or a Co-Party

[a] New Party Cross-Complaints, Generally

The California cross-complaint statutes authorize an existing party to file a cross-complaint which adds new parties if the cause of action asserted in the cross-complaint arises out of the same transaction or occurrence as the cause brought against the cross-complainant, or if the cross-complaint asserts a claim or interest in the controversy which is the subject of the cause brought against him.[353] The cross-complainant ("third-party plaintiff") may join any person as cross-complainant or cross-defendant, subject only to California's liberal permissive party joinder standards.[354] Moreover, the cross-complainant may join any other cause of action he has against any cross-defendants.[355]

Rule 14(a) of the Federal Rules of Civil Procedure authorizes a third-party impleader practice that is narrower than the new party cross-complaint practice set forth in the California statutes, because federal Rule 14(a) limits impleader to the assertion of third-party claims where liability is in some way dependent on the outcome of the main claim and is secondary or derivative thereto.[356] Like their

[353] Cal. Code Civ. Proc. § 428.10(b).

[354] Cal. Code Civ. Proc. § 428.20; see § 378 (joinder of plaintiffs) § 379 (joinder of defendants). Section 428.20 reiterates the propriety of filing such a cross-complaint against a previously unnamed party, and section 428.70 explicitly confirms the fact that a cross-complaint may be founded on a claim of total or partial indemnity by defining a "third-party plaintiff" as one who files a cross-complaint claiming "the right to recover all or part of any amount for which he may be held liable" on the original complaint.

[355] Cal. Code Civ. Proc. § 428.30. Also, the third-party defendant may file a "special answer alleging against the person who asserted the cause of action against the third-party plaintiff any defenses which a third-party plaintiff has to such cause of action." Cal. Code Civ. Proc. § 428.70(b). The "special answer" is designed to protect the third-party defendant from the defendant's failure or neglect to assert a proper defense to the plaintiff's action, through collusion or otherwise, by allowing the third-party defendant to assert any defenses available to the original defendant directly against the plaintiff. See 10 Cal. Law Division Comm'n Report (1971), p. 555; Administrative Mgmt. Serv., Inc. v. Fid. & Deposit Co., 129 Cal. App. 3d 484, 181 Cal. Rptr. 141 (1982).

[356] E.g., Stewart v. American Int'l Oil & Gas Co., 845 F.2d 196, 199–200 (9th Cir. 1988). This limitation

federal rule counterpart, the purpose of California's new party cross-complaint statutes is to reduce the possibility of duplicative litigation. This is particularly important in personal injury disputes involving multiple tortfeasors, as discussed below.

[b] Cross-Complaints and Equitable Indemnity

To understand the importance of cross-complaints in multi-party tort litigation, a brief primer on negligence and joint tortfeasors may be helpful. California follows the tort rule of comparative negligence, under which an injured individual's recovery is proportionately diminished, rather than completely eliminated, when the injured individual is partially responsible for the injury. Subject to some important statutory exceptions,[357] California also follows the doctrine of "joint and several liability" whereby each tortfeasor whose negligence is a proximate cause of an indivisible injury remains individually liable for all compensable damages attributed to that injury.[358] This doctrine recognizes that the wronged party may sue one or all of such concurrent (or "joint") tortfeasors to obtain recovery for his injuries, but that the tortfeasors should be left to determine the allocation of loss among themselves. In apportioning liability among concurrent tortfeasors, California permits partial equitable indemnity, under which liability among multiple tortfeasors is apportioned on a comparative fault basis.[359]

A typical use of the cross-complaint joinder device is to assert a claim for partial equitable indemnity against an existing co-defendant or against a new, third-party defendant.[360] This use permits a court to resolve all potential liability issues between plaintiffs and defendants, and among defendants, in one lawsuit. For example, assume that a plaintiff sues defendants A and B and C for injuries caused by the three defendants' concurrent negligence. The defendants file cross-complaints for equitable indemnity against each other. The jury awards $100,000 in damages and allocates fault as follows: defendant A (20%), defendant B (30%), and

---

on the use of impleader in federal court under federal Rule 14 is discussed in § 9.06 *supra*. As a practical matter, California's broader standard is of little consequence because nearly all new party cross-complaints are based on derivative liability, typically claims for equitable indemnity against concurrent tortfeasors.

[357] One important statutory exception is expressed in California Civil Code §§ 1431–1431.5, which modifies the common law rule of joint and several liability by making each defendant's liability for "non-economic" damages several and not joint in comparative fault cases. Civil Code § 1431.2(a) states: "Each defendant shall be liable only for the amount of non-economic damages allocated to that defendant in direct proportion to that defendant's percentage of fault." "Non-economic damages" are defined to mean subjective, non-monetary losses such as pain, suffering, loss of consortium, and injury to reputation; "economic damages" to mean objectively verifiable monetary losses, such as medical expenses and loss of earnings. CAL. CIV. CODE § 1431.2(b).

[358] *Summers v. Tice*, 33 Cal. 2d 80, 199 P.2d 1 (1948); *American Motorcycle Ass'n v. Superior Court*, 20 Cal. 3d 578, 146 Cal. Rptr. 182, 578 P.2d 899 (1978).

[359] *American Motorcycle Ass'n, supra*, 20 Cal. 3d at 591–604.

[360] *See, e.g., American Motorcycle Ass'n, supra; Lyly & Sons Trucking Co. v. State of California*, 147 Cal. App. 3d 353, 195 Cal. Rptr. 116 (1983). Code of Civil Procedure § 428.70 specifically applies to those new party cross-complaints which include claims for indemnity or contribution, and defines the person asserting such claims by cross-complaint as the "third-party plaintiff" and the person alleged in the cross-complaint to be liable to the third-party plaintiff as the "third-party defendant."

defendant C (50%). Under the doctrine of joint and several liability, the plaintiff can recover the entire $100,000 from one (or more) of the defendants. If defendant A pays the entire $100,000 to plaintiff, defendant A can then recover $30,000 from defendant B and $50,000 from defendant C based on defendant A's cross-complaint against them for partial equitable indemnity.

Now assume that the same plaintiff sued only defendant A for injuries caused by the negligence of defendant A and the other concurrent tortfeasors. Defendant A can then file a new-party cross-complaint for equitable indemnity against both defendants B and C, who in turn can file cross-complaints for equitable indemnity against each other. Once again, assuming the jury awards plaintiff $100,000 in damages and allocates fault as before, the plaintiff will recover $100,000 from defendant A and defendant A will then recover $30,000 from defendant B and $50,000 from defendant C based on defendant A's cross-complaint against them for partial equitable indemnity. In this manner, the new-party cross-complaint statutes permit resolution of all the negligence and indemnity claims among the various parties to take place in one, rather than in two or three, lawsuits.

[8] Intervention

[a] Permissive Intervention

California Code of Civil Procedure § 387(a) provides that any "interested" person *may* intervene in an action. The California courts interpret this broad authority for *permissive intervention* to include several limitations. One is that the intervener's interest must not already be represented by existing parties. Another is that the intervener's interest must be "direct and immediate," and not "indirect and consequential."[361] In other words, as one court explained, the interest "must be of such direct and immediate character that the intervener will either gain or lose by the direct legal operation and effect of the judgment."[362] However, the intervener need neither claim a pecuniary interest nor a specific legal or equitable interest in the subject matter of the litigation.

The line between a "direct and immediate" interest which satisfies section 387(a), and an "indirect and consequential" one which is insufficient for permissive intervention, is not always readily apparent. As one court astutely observed, "[the] point at which one's interest . . . becomes direct, and not consequential, is not easily fixed."[363] Whether the intervener's interest is sufficiently direct must be decided on the facts of each case.[364]

---

[361] *E.g., Simpson Redwood Co. v. State*, 196 Cal. App. 3d 1192, 1200–01, 242 Cal. Rptr. 447 (1987); *Lincoln Nat'l Life Ins. Co. v. State Bd. of Equalization*, 30 Cal. App. 4th 1411, 36 Cal. Rptr. 2d 397 (1994).

[362] *Knight v. Alefosio*, 158 Cal. App. 3d 721, 205 Cal. Rptr. 42 (1984).

[363] *Simpson Redwood, supra*, 196 Cal. App. 3d at 1201.

[364] For example, in *Highland Dev. Co. v. City of Los Angeles*, 170 Cal. App. 3d 169, 179–80, 215 Cal. Rptr. 881 (1985), the court analyzed the facts presented by each community group seeking intervention and concluded that some, but not all, groups opposed to the construction of an apartment building adjacent to an historic district possessed the requisite direct interest for intervention in litigation between the developer and the city over the right to a city construction permit.

Granting or denying leave to intervene under section 387(a) is in the discretion of the trial court.[365] Even if an applicant establishes the requisite interest in the litigation, a trial court may deny permissive intervention. As one court recently noted, "[t]he permissive intervention statute balances the interests of others who will be affected by the judgment against the interests of the original parties in pursuing their litigation unburdened by others."[366] How this balance is struck in a particular case is left to the sound discretion of the trial court.

Despite these apparent limitations, the California courts frequently advise that Code of Civil Procedure § 387(a) should be liberally construed in favor of intervention.[367] Sometimes this leads to interesting results. For example, in *Bustop v. Superior Court*,[368] the Court of Appeal held that a group of white parents opposed to mandatory busing of students had sufficient interest "in a sound educational system and in the operation of that system in accordance with the law" to permit intervention in an action where a school district was required to formulate a desegregation plan. According to the court, such a plan would have a "direct social, educational and economic impact" on all students and parents in the district. After this ruling, another organization entitled BEST (Better Education for Students Today) also sought intervention in the trial court. BEST's complaint in intervention disavowed any position toward any integration plan, but asserted that its members were well-intentioned citizens who would certainly have developed positions on the issues by the time they got to court. The trial court permitted BEST to intervene![369]

The California courts are willing to permit intervention by environmental groups despite their lack of pecuniary or legal interest. For example, in *People ex rel. Rominger v. County of Trinity*,[370] the Court of Appeal found that the trial court abused its discretion in not permitting the Sierra Club to intervene in litigation between the State of California and the defendant County. The State sought declaratory and injunctive relief, alleging that the County's ordinance prohibiting aerial spraying of phenoxy herbicides was preempted by state law. The Sierra Club sought to intervene, alleging, among other grounds, that its members would be specifically harmed if spraying resumed in the County. The Sierra Club asserted that its members use these forest lands and exposure to these chemicals would harm them. The Court of Appeal concluded that the Sierra Club, as representative of its members who use the resources of the County, has a direct and immediate,

---

[365] *See, e.g., Lincoln Nat'l Life Ins. Co. v. State Bd. of Equalization*, 30 Cal. App. 4th 1411, 36 Cal. Rptr. 2d 397 (1994) (explaining that unless a special statute prohibits intervention, the trial court's discretion to permit intervention should be liberally construed in favor of intervention); *City of Malibu v. Cal. Coastal Comm'n*, 128 Cal. App. 4th 897, 27 Cal. Rptr. 3d 501 (2005) (finding no abuse of discretion and affirming trial court's denial of permissive intervention); *Bustop v. Superior Court*, 69 Cal. App. 3d 66, 72–73, 137 Cal. Rptr. 793 (1977) (finding abuse of discretion by trial court in refusing to permit intervention).

[366] *Royal Indem. Co. v. United Enter., Inc.*, 162 Cal. App. 4th 194, 203–04, 75 Cal. Rptr. 3d 481 (2008).

[367] *Simpson Redwood, supra*, 196 Cal. App. 3d at 1201.

[368] *Bustop, supra*, 69 Cal. App. 3d at 71.

[369] For a criticism of the reasoning in *Bustop* as an improper extension of the permissive intervention statute, see Stephen C. Yeazell, *Intervention and the Idea of Litigation: A Commentary on the Los Angeles School Case*, 25 U.C.L.A. L. Rev. 244 (1977).

[370] 147 Cal. App. 3d 655, 195 Cal. Rptr. 186 (1983).

rather than consequential and remote, interest in this litigation.[371]

[b]   Federal Court Permissive Intervention, Compared

Federal Rule 24(b) permits intervention, upon timely application and in the trial court's discretion, when an applicant's claim or defense and the existing action have "a question of law and fact in common." This permissive intervention standard is broader than that of section 387(a) in that the federal rule does not require that an applicant have any direct personal interest in the subject of the litigation.[372] However, federal court justiciability doctrines, particularly the doctrine of standing, may impose a similar interest requirement.[373] And, as with all federal joinder devices, a federal court must have subject matter jurisdiction of persons and claims sought to be added by Rule 24 intervention.

[c]   Intervention of Right

In 1977, the California Legislature enacted Code of Civil Procedure § 387(b), which added *intervention of right* to traditional permissive intervention. Section 387(b) is modeled after Rule 24(b) of the Federal Rules of Civil Procedure. Like the federal rule, in the absence of a statute which confers an unconditional right to intervene, a person seeking leave to intervene of right must demonstrate that disposition of the action in his absence will practically impair his ability to protect his interest relating to the property or transaction which is the subject of the action, that none of the present parties will adequately represent his interest, and that the application to intervene is timely.[374]

Although there are numerous federal court decisions construing federal Rule 24(b), there are relatively few California appellate decisions discussing intervention of right.[375] The existence of a number of special statutes conferring an unconditional right to intervene, plus the liberal approach to permissive intervention under section 387(a), may explain why there are so few California cases construing section 387(b).

---

[371] *Rominger, supra*, 147 Cal. App. 3d at 663. *See also Simpson Redwood, supra*, 196 Cal. App. 3d at 1200 (analyzing several factors and holding that a group interested in preservation of old growth redwoods should be permitted to intervene in quiet title action regarding boundaries of state park).

[372] *See* WRIGHT, MILLER & KANE, FEDERAL PRACTICE AND PROCEDURE: CIVIL § 1911 (3d ed. West 2001 & Supp. 2012).

[373] *See, e.g., Warth v. Seldin*, 422 U.S. 490 (1975) (intervening plaintiff must demonstrate a distinct and palpable injury to itself caused by defendant in order to satisfy standing doctrine).

[374] Intervention of right under federal Rule 24(a) is discussed in § 9.08, *supra*.

[375] *See, e.g., Hodge v. Kirkpatrick Dev., Inc.*, 130 Cal. App. 4th 540, 30 Cal. Rptr. 3d 303 (2005) (ruling an insurance company has the right to intervene in a construction defect lawsuit brought by insureds against third-party tortfeasors, where the insurance company obtained partial subrogation rights against the third parties by paying a portion of the insured's claims for property damages to their house); *California Physicians' Serv. v. Superior Court*, 102 Cal. App. 3d 91, 162 Cal. Rptr. 266 (1980) (construing "transaction" and "interest impairment" in § 387).

[9] Intervention Procedures

[a] Status of Intervener

An intervener becomes an actual party to the action, either a plaintiff or defendant (unless adverse to both), with all of the same procedural rights and remedies of the original parties. Although the California courts often state that an intervener "must take the proceedings as it finds them at the time of intervention," an intervener is not limited by every procedural decision made by the original parties. For example, an intervener may move to disqualify a judge, even if the parties are content to try the lawsuit in that court; may object to the jurisdiction of the court or that pleadings do not state a cause of action; and may not be deprived of its right to jury trial by the parties' waiver.[376] An intervener may also pursue affirmative relief not sought by the plaintiff,[377] and may appeal an adverse judgment even where the original party defaults.[378]

[b] Timely Application

A party seeking intervention, whether permissive or of right, must make a "timely application" to the court.[379] What constitutes a timely application varies with the circumstances of each case, and ultimately depends on the court's discretion. For example, in one case, the court permitted class members to intervene to remove the class representative, even though the action was pending on appeal. The court noted that "intervention is possible, if otherwise appropriate, at any time, even after judgment."[380] However, intervention may be denied where there is an unreasonable delay after learning of the action.[381]

---

[376] *See, e.g., Deutschmann v. Sears Roebuck & Co.*, 132 Cal. App. 3d 912, 916, 183 Cal. Rptr. 573 (1982), and cases cited therein.

[377] *E.g., Belt-Cas. Co. v. Furman*, 218 Cal. 359, 23 P.2d 293 (1933).

[378] *E.g., Jade K. v. Viguri*, 210 Cal. App. 3d 1459, 1468, 258 Cal. Rptr. 907 (1989). A person who is legally aggrieved by a judgment, and has an "immediate, pecuniary, and substantial" interest in the judgment, may become a party and obtain a right to appeal by moving to vacate the judgment or by moving for a new trial. *Lippman v. City of Los Angeles*, 234 Cal. App. 3d 1630, 286 Cal. Rptr. 406 (1991); *County of Alameda v. Carleson*, 5 Cal. 3d 730, 736–37, 97 Cal. Rptr. 385, 488 P.2d 953 (1971).

[379] CAL. CODE CIV. PROC. § 387(a) & (b).

[380] *Mallick v. Superior Court*, 89 Cal. App. 3d 434, 437, 152 Cal. Rptr. 503 (1979).

[381] *E.g., Sanders v. Pac. Gas & Elec. Co.*, 53 Cal. App. 3d 661, 668, 126 Cal. Rptr. 415 (1975). For example, in *Northern Cal. Psychiatric Soc'y. v. City of Berkeley*, 178 Cal. App. 3d 90, 223 Cal. Rptr. 609 (1986), the Court of Appeal ruled that a coalition's motion to intervene was not timely where the coalition had been involved in the litigation for six months as amicus but did not seek to intervene until after a summary judgment motion was fully briefed and argued, and the trial court had already indicated its intention to grant summary judgment. But in *Jade K. v. Viguri*, 210 Cal. App. 3d 1459, 1468, 258 Cal. Rptr. 907 (1989), another Court of Appeal considered timely an insurance company's complaint in intervention seeking to vacate and appeal a default entered against its insured because the insurance company was never notified of the default.

§ 9.12   CLASS ACTIONS IN THE CALIFORNIA COURTS

[1]   California Class Actions, Generally

[a]   Introductory Note

The *class action* is the ultimate joinder device. One or more named plaintiffs may represent the interests of hundreds or thousands of absentee class members and obtain a class judgment that will bind those absentees by res judicata.[382] The principal purpose of class actions is efficiency and economy of litigation — class treatment permits a trial court to resolve numerous claims in one lawsuit rather than in several individual actions. But judicial economy is not the sole consideration. Dispute resolution by means of a class action must be fair to the absentee class members, who are passive participants in the litigation but may be bound by the outcome. Therefore, as a matter of fundamental due process, the class representative must adequately protect the interests of the absentee class members. Both the California and the federal requirements for class actions reflect this tension between judicial economy and fairness.[383]

Another justification for class actions is to deter and redress wrongdoing, especially in cases where small recoveries do not provide a financial incentive for an individual plaintiff to bring a separate action. The California courts recognize the importance of this purpose, as demonstrated by their hospitable treatment of small-claim, large-class actions. As succinctly stated by the California Supreme Court: "The problems which arise in the management of a class action involving numerous small claims do not justify a judicial policy that would permit the defendant to retain the benefits of its wrongful conduct and to continue that conduct with impunity."[384] By comparison, the federal courts apply rules that are somewhat hostile, or at best indifferent, to the maintenance of small-claim, large-class actions. In this area more than any other, the California policy toward class actions differs from that of the federal courts.

[b]   No Comprehensive California Class Action Statute

Despite the obvious importance of class actions and their concomitant potential for procedural problems, the California Legislature has yet to enact a comprehensive statute which specifically governs all applications of the class action device.

---

[382] *See, e.g., Daar v. Yellow Cab Co.*, 67 Cal. 2d 695, 63 Cal. Rptr. 724, 433 P.2d 732 (1967) (upholding certification of a class action by taxicab customer against taxicab company on behalf of all others similarly situated to recover excessive charges would be res judicata on thousands of class members); *Lazar v. Hertz Corp.*, 143 Cal. App. 3d 128, 191 Cal. Rptr. 849 (1983) (affirming class action on behalf of approximately 5,000,000 rental car customers); *Cartt v. Superior Court*, 50 Cal. App. 3d 960, 124 Cal. Rptr. 376 (1975) (certifying consumer class action on behalf of over 700,000 credit card holders).

[383] Due process and the federal class action standards are discussed in § 9.09, *supra*.

[384] *Linder v. Thrifty Oil Co.*, 23 Cal. 4th 429, 446, 97 Cal. Rptr. 2d 179, 2 P.3d 27 (2000); *see also Vasquez v. Superior Court*, 4 Cal. 3d 800, 808, 94 Cal. Rptr. 796, 484 P.2d 964 (1971) (explaining the importance of consumer fraud class actions because the amount of individual recovery would be insufficient to justify bringing a separate action and thus an unscrupulous seller retains the benefits of its wrongful conduct).

Instead, the California courts rely on a general statute that authorizes representative actions but contains no standards and a specific statute that provides standards for consumer fraud class actions.[385] In addition, recently adopted California Rules of Court now govern many aspects of class action management, including motions to certify or decertify a class, case conferences, notice to class members, orders in the conduct of class actions, discovery from unnamed class members, and settlement and dismissals of class actions.[386]

In the absence of controlling California authority, the California Supreme Court directs trial courts to utilize the procedures of Rule 23 of the Federal Rules of Civil Procedure to ensure fairness in the resolution of class action lawsuits.[387] Consequently, the California courts often cite federal court interpretations of federal Rule 23 as authority when determining state court class action procedural issues. You might therefore expect that the California courts' treatment of the class action device would be identical to that of the federal courts. In many applications, that expectation is reality. But in a few important areas, the California courts' approach differs markedly from that of the federal courts. This is particularly evident with respect to the procedural rules applicable to small-claim, large-class actions.

[c] California's Class Action Prerequisites, Generally

The party seeking class certification must establish the existence of an "ascertainable class" and a "well-defined community of interest" among the class members. An "ascertainable class" is required in order to give notice to putative class members as to whom the judgment will bind. The vague "community of interest" requirement embodies three factors similar to those of federal Rule 23(a) and (b)(3): (1) common questions of law or fact must predominate over individual questions, (2) class representatives must have claims or defenses typical of the class, and (3) class representatives must adequately represent the interests of the class.[388] The general California rule is that certification of a proposed class should be based on these prerequisites and not upon the trial court's preliminary assessment of whether the cause of action alleged on behalf of the class has sufficient merit.[389]

---

[385] CAL. CODE CIV. PROC. § 382, CAL. CIV. CODE § 1781. Civil Code § 1781 is part of the California Consumer Legal Remedies Act, Civil Code § 1750 *et seq.* The California Supreme Court has suggested that section 1781 and Rule 23 of the Federal Rules of Civil Procedure be used as procedural guidelines to ensure fairness in class action suits. *Richmond v. Dart Indus., Inc.*, 29 Cal. 3d 462, 469, n.7, 174 Cal. Rptr. 515, 629 P.2d 23 (1981); *Vasquez v. Superior Court*, 4 Cal. 3d 800, 821, 94 Cal. Rptr. 796, 484 P.2d 964 (1971).

[386] *See* CAL. CT. R. 3.760–3.771.

[387] *City of San Jose v. Superior Court*, 12 Cal. 3d 447, 453, 115 Cal. Rptr. 797, 525 P.2d 701 (1974) (trial courts should be procedurally innovative and incorporate class action procedures from outside sources, specifically Rule 23, Fed. R. Civ. P.); *La Sala v. Am. Sav. & Loan Ass'n*, 5 Cal. 3d 864, 872, 97 Cal. Rptr. 849, 489 P.2d 1113 (1971).

[388] *E.g., Richmond v. Dart Indus., supra,* 29 Cal. 3d at 470; *Daar v. Yellow Cab Co., supra,* 67 Cal. 2d at 704.

[389] *See Linder, supra,* 23 Cal. 4th at 439–40 (ruling the question of class certification is essentially a procedural one that does not ask whether an action is legally or factually meritorious); *Medrazo v. Honda of N. Hollywood,* 166 Cal. App. 4th 89, 82 Cal. Rptr. 3d 1 (2008) (holding the trial court erred in denying class certification based on its resolution of the merits of defendant's proposed defense).

[2] The "Ascertainable Class" Requirement

Whether a class is ascertainable may be determined by examining the class definition, the size of the class, and the means available for identifying class members.[390] If the existence of an ascertainable class has been shown, however, there is no need to identify its individual members in order to bind all members by the judgment.[391] Some fairly broad class definitions have satisfied the "ascertainable class" requirements. For example, in one case, the California Court of Appeal upheld a class defined by the plaintiff's complaint as "composed of all persons in the State of California who rented automobiles from Hertz during the period commencing November 1, 1976, and ending November 1, 1980 and who were charged a refueling service charge for returning their rented automobiles without having refilled the fuel tank."[392] And in another case, the Court of Appeal found ascertainable a class defined as "all persons nationwide subscribing to Sprint since January 1, 1981, who were charged for one or more unanswered long distance calls."[393]

[3] The "Community of Interest" Requirement

This broadly-stated pragmatic requirement embodies several related factors, whose application varies with the facts and circumstances of each individual case. Each of these factors is discussed below.

[a] Common Questions of Law or Fact Must Predominate Over Individual Issues

The main purpose of this requirement is to assure that maintenance of a class action will further judicial economy. A class action cannot be maintained where each member's right to recovery depends on facts peculiar to his or her case "because the community of interest requirement is not satisfied if every member of the alleged class would be required to litigate numerous and substantial questions determining his individual right to recover."[394] However, this factor does not require a common or identical recovery as a prerequisite to a class action.[395] Nor is a class action

[390] *Reyes v. San Diego Cnty. Bd. of Supervisors*, 196 Cal. App. 3d 1263, 1274, 242 Cal. Rptr. 339 (1987); *Sevidal v. Target Corp.*, 189 Cal. App. 4th 905, 918–22, 117 Cal. Rptr. 3d 66 (2010); *Cohen v. DIRECTV, Inc.*, 178 Cal. App. 4th 966, 975–78, 101 Cal. Rptr. 3d 37 (2009).

[391] *Daar v. Yellow Cab, supra*, 67 Cal. 2d at 706.

[392] *Lazar v. Hertz Corp., supra*, 143 Cal. App. 3d at 137.

[393] *Clothesrigger, Inc. v. GTE Corp.*, 191 Cal. App. 3d 605, 617, 236 Cal. Rptr. 605 (1987); *see also Daar v. Yellow Cab Co., supra*, 67 Cal. 2d at 701–09 (certifying class of all persons who used Yellow Cab taxicab services in Los Angeles during a four-year period and were charged more than the approved rate); *Wershba v. Apple Computer, Inc.*, 91 Cal. App. 4th 224, 110 Cal. Rptr. 2d 145 (2001) (affirming certification and settlement of a nationwide class action alleging that defendant Apple Computer, a California corporation, had rescinded its policy of free technical phone support to its approximately 2.4 million customers in violation of California's consumer protection law).

[394] *City of San Jose v. Superior Court*, 12 Cal. 3d 447, 459, 115 Cal. Rptr. 797, 525 P.2d 701 (1974).

[395] *Daar v. Yellow Cab Co., supra*, 67 Cal. 2d at 707–09; *Richmond v. Dart Indus., Inc.*, 29 Cal. 3d 462, 470, 174 Cal. Rptr. 515, 629 P.2d 23 (1981) (ordering certification of class even where not all class members seek the same type of relief).

inappropriate simply because each member of the class may at some point be required to make an individual showing as to eligibility for recovery or the amount of damages.[396] The fact that each member of the class must prove his separate claim to a portion of any recovery is only one factor to be considered in determining whether a class action is proper.[397] However, where individual issues regarding *liability and damages* substantially predominate over common factual questions, class action treatment is rarely appropriate.[398]

This common questions factor usually precludes class certification of mass tort actions seeking personal injuries.[399] Even though mass tort actions may involve questions of law and fact common to the entire class of injured claimants, the efficiency achieved by determining those questions in one lawsuit is usually outweighed by the need to resolve individualized issues of liability, causation, and damages as to each class member. In such cases, some of the benefits of the class action device may be achieved by coordination of individual lawsuits.[400]

However, the California courts are more willing to find this common questions factor satisfied in consumer rights cases, even though the alleged class-wide fraud or other unfair conduct involved numerous separate and individual transactions.[401]

[396] *Sav-On Drug Stores, Inc. v. Superior Court*, 34 Cal. 4th 319, 332–35, 17 Cal. Rptr. 3d 906, 96 P.3d 194 (2004); *Employment Dev. Dept. v. Superior Court*, 30 Cal. 3d 256, 266, 178 Cal. Rptr. 612, 637 P.2d 575 (1981).

[397] *Vasquez v. Superior Court, supra*, 4 Cal. 3d at 809; *Sav-On Drug Stores, supra*, 34 Cal. 4th at 334–35; *see Evans v. Lasco Bathware, Inc.*, 178 Cal. App. 4th 1417, 1427–32, 101 Cal. Rptr. 3d 354 (2009) (reviewing cases and concluding a trial court has the discretion to deny class certification when it concludes the fact and extent of each class member's injury requires individualized inquiries that defeat predominance).

[398] *Lockheed Martin Corp. v. Superior Court*, 29 Cal. 4th 1096, 131 Cal. Rptr. 2d 1, 63 P.3d 913 (2003) (reversing certification of a medical monitoring class consisting of over 50,000 residents who had consumed drinking water allegedly contaminated by the defendants' discharges of toxic chemicals over several decades because plaintiffs failed to demonstrate by substantial evidence that these common issues of causation and damages predominate over the individual ones); *City of San Jose, supra*, 12 Cal. 3d at 458–63 (holding nuisance and inverse condemnation action by homeowners for diminution of market value of their property due to flight pattern of municipal airport inappropriate for class treatment because recovery is predicated on facts peculiar to each prospective plaintiff).

[399] *See, e.g., Basurco v. 21st Century Ins. Co.*, 108 Cal. App. 4th 110, 133 Cal. Rptr. 2d 367 (2003); *Clausing v. San Francisco Unified Sch. Dist.*, 221 Cal. App. 3d 1224, 271 Cal. Rptr. 72 (1990); *see also Jolly v. Eli Lilly & Co.*, 44 Cal. 3d 1103, 1123, 245 Cal. Rptr. 658, 751 P.2d 923 (1988) (noting mass tort actions for personal injury are rarely appropriate for class certification because their major elements — liability, proximate cause, and damages — may vary widely as to each individual claimant).

[400] *See* CAL. CODE CIV. PROC. § 404 *et seq.* (coordination proceedings); CAL. CT. R. 3.500–3.550.

[401] *See, e.g., Vasquez v. Superior Court, supra*, 4 Cal. 3d at 811–15 (holding consumers may maintain a class action seeking rescission of installment contracts to purchase merchandise based on alleged fraudulent misrepresentations; facts justified inference of class-wide misrepresentations and reliance such that individual proof unnecessary); *Massachusetts Mut. Life Ins. Co. v. Superior Court*, 97 Cal. App. 4th 1282, 119 Cal. Rptr. 2d 190 (2002) (affirming in a consumer fraud action the trial court's certification of a class consisting of 33,000 people who, over a period of 15 years, purchased a particular type of life insurance product from the defendant where the purchases by each class member gave rise to an inference of common reliance on defendant's alleged material misrepresentations); *McAdams v. Monier, Inc.*, 182 Cal. App. 4th 174, 180–87, 105 Cal. Rptr. 3d 704 (2010) (reversing denial of certification of consumer class action that alleged manufacturer had misrepresented the quality of its roof tiles; inference of common reliance was adequate to show each class member was misled); *but see Kavruck v.*

This favorable treatment is likely due to the strong remedial policy reflected in California's consumer protection statutes.

Another relevant consideration is whether class action treatment will result in substantial benefits to both the litigants and the court. This flexible factor overlaps with the common questions factor, and generally requires consideration of whether common questions are sufficiently pervasive such that class treatment is more advantageous than multiple individual suits.[402] Sometimes equated with the "superiority" factor of federal Rule 23(b)(3), this factor requires that a class action must be "superior to other available methods for the fair and efficient adjudication of the controversy," including consideration of "the difficulties likely to be encountered in the management of a class action."[403]

[b] The Class Representative Must Adequately Represent the Interests of the Class

This factor reflects a basic due process concern: Absentee members of a class should not be bound by a class judgment unless their interests were in fact adequately represented by the class representative.[404] Fairness, not judicial economy, is the goal here. The California courts have developed several related inquiries to assist in the determination of whether class certification is appropriate based on this factor.

Are the Interests of the Representative Party in Conflict with the Interests of the Class? Antagonism *per se* among members of a class does not automatically preclude the certification of a class action.[405] In other words, the existence of *some* conflict between the interests of the class representative and the class members will not necessary preclude class certification. If the vast majority of the class do not oppose the suit, the minority may have its views presented either as a subclass or as interveners, or may simply opt out of the class.[406] However, when the vast majority of a class perceives its interest as diametrically opposed to that of the named representatives, a trial court cannot equitably grant the named plaintiffs the right to pursue the litigation on behalf of the entire class.[407]

Blue Cross of Cal., 108 Cal. App. 4th 773, 134 Cal. Rptr. 2d 152 (2003) (denial of class certification proper where action for fraud against health insurance company required proof of oral representations on a subscriber-by-subscriber basis).

[402] *See Vasquez, supra,* 4 Cal. 3d at 810; *City of San Jose, supra,* 12 Cal. 3d at 460.

[403] *See, e.g., Dean Witter Reynolds, Inc. v. Superior Court,* 211 Cal. App. 3d 758, 773, 259 Cal. Rptr. 789 (1989) (finding class treatment of unfair competition claims not demonstrably superior to individual action where statute empowered court to grant injunctive relief, including restitution, in favor of absent persons without certifying a class, but denied compensatory damages); *Lazar v. Hertz Corp., supra,* 143 Cal. App. 3d at 143–44 (holding consumer class action is superior to alternative of asserting claims against fund deposited by defendant within federal Department of Energy).

[404] *Hansberry v. Lee,* 311 U.S. 32 (1940); *City of San Jose, supra,* 12 Cal. 3d at 463.

[405] *Richmond v. Dart Indus., Inc.,* 29 Cal. 3d 462, 472–75, 174 Cal. Rptr. 515, 629 P.2d 23 (1981).

[406] *Richmond, supra,* 29 Cal. 3d at 472–75. *See generally* Deborah L. Rhode, *Class Conflicts in Class Actions,* 34 STAN. L. REV. 1183 (1982).

[407] *Richmond, supra,* 29 Cal. 3d at 471.

The California Supreme Court addressed these concerns in *Richmond v. Dart Industries, Inc.*,[408] where a group of homeowners brought an action against the defendant developer alleging that the defendant had failed to plan and provide for adequate water supply and sewage treatment facilities. The complaint sought compensatory and punitive damages, rescission and declaratory relief. Plaintiffs filed a class certification motion requesting that the trial court grant them the right to represent all of the record owners in the housing development. The defendant opposed the class certification motion, introducing into evidence a survey which showed that approximately 6% of the potential class members might be antagonistic to the suit. Resting its decision primarily on the results of the survey, the trial court denied the motion for class certification.

The California Supreme Court reversed, holding that antagonism *per se* by members of a class does not automatically preclude class certification and that the small number of potential class members who might be antagonistic to the suit was insufficient to defeat class certification. In so holding, the court noted that minority interests could be adequately protected by representatives of subclasses, or by opting out of the class and intervening. As to the prayer for rescission and punitive damages, the court held that the seeking of common relief is not a prerequisite to a class suit and that the trial court, which had continuing jurisdiction to decertify the class, could act if evidence of actual conflicting interests within the class was presented at a later date.

As *Richmond v. Dart Industries, Inc.* demonstrates, the California courts rarely deny class certification where potential conflicts of interests can be removed by modification of the class definition, by sub-classes, or by some other appropriate procedural device.[409] However, where the conflict is widespread and unavoidable, class certification must be denied.[410] In such circumstances, the named representative cannot fairly and adequately protect the interests of all class members.

Is the Class Representative a Member of the Class She Purports to Represent?
Under certain circumstances, class certification may be denied when the class

---

[408] 29 Cal. 3d 462, 174 Cal. Rptr. 515, 629 P.2d 23 (1981).

[409] *See, e.g., Daniels v. Centennial Group, Inc.*, 16 Cal. App. 4th 467, 21 Cal. Rptr. 2d 1 (1993) (finding potential conflict between class representatives and the class over claim of rescission of partnership consolidation as opposed to damages can be avoided by subclasses or by certifying a class as to damage relief only); *Aguiar v. Cintas Corp. No. 2*, 144 Cal. App. 4th 121, 50 Cal. Rptr. 3d 135 (2006) (holding class action alleging defendant employer violated living wage ordinance applicable to employees who worked at least 20 hours per week was proper because the putative class can be divided into subclasses of those employees who worked at least 20 hours per week and those who did not); *National Solar Equip. Owners' Ass'n v. Grumman Corp.*, 235 Cal. App. 3d 1273, 1 Cal. Rptr. 2d 325 (1991) (ruling conflict not irreconcilable; can be cured by the time class seeks certification through redefinition of class, subclasses, or exclusions).

[410] *See, e.g., Knox v. Streatfield*, 79 Cal. App. 3d 565, 145 Cal. Rptr. 39 (1978) (holding class action on behalf of all owners of a subdivision to enforce restrictions against those owners allegedly in violation held inappropriate due to conflict of interests between violating and nonviolating members of the class); *Seastrom v. Neways, Inc.*, 149 Cal. App. 4th 1496, 57 Cal. Rptr. 3d 903 (2007) (holding in an action against a manufacturer of an oral spray for illegally selling the spray without a prescription, the distributors of the oral spray could not represent a class consisting of all persons who purchased the spray without a prescription because the distributors made commissions on the sale of the product to class members and are therefore potential defendants).

representative does not suffer the same injury as the members of the class.[411] This consideration is not inflexibly applied. For example, a named plaintiff may properly represent a proposed class even though not strictly a member of the class, so long as there is a sufficient community of interests between the plaintiff and the class.[412] More importantly, a defendant's grant of individual relief to the named plaintiffs in a class action does not, in itself, necessarily render the plaintiffs unfit to represent the class.[413] According to the California courts, even if the named plaintiffs receive all the benefits they seeks in the complaint, such success does not divest them of the duty to continue the action for the benefit of others similarly situated.[414] Whether this is a wise policy, in light of the named plaintiff's lack of stake in the litigation, is open to question.

The Claims of the Class Representative Must Be Typical of the Claims of the Class. This factor restates the various considerations embodied in the requirement that the representative party must adequately represent the interest of the class. For example, named plaintiffs do not adequately represent the class members when they "fail to raise claims or seek relief reasonably expected to be raised by members of the class and thus pursue a course which, even should the litigation be resolved in favor of the class, would deprive class members of many elements of damage."[415] In one recent case, the court concluded that the plaintiffs, by limiting a homeowners' class action to recovery of the cost of replacing defective shower pans, were not adequate class representatives because that recovery would forfeit additional recoveries, such as consequential damages to other parts of the house.[416]

The Plaintiff's Attorney Must Be Qualified to Conduct the Proposed Class Action Litigation. Adequacy of counsel is particularly important in class actions which involve complex procedural and substantive issues, requiring high levels of competency and resources. However, this consideration is rarely mentioned as a

---

[411] *See, e.g., Stephens v. Montgomery Ward,* 193 Cal. App. 3d 411, 422, 238 Cal. Rptr. 602 (1987) (ruling the plaintiff saleswoman in a department store chain, who had been promoted to department manager twice before, was not an appropriate representative for a class of female employees alleging that defendant failed to promote women to department manager positions); *Fuhrman v. Cal. Satellite Sys.,* 179 Cal. App. 3d 408, 425, 231 Cal. Rptr. 113 (1986) (ruling the plaintiff, who never received defendant's satellite cable television signals, could not represent class of consumers who did receive the defendant's signals, in action for emotional distress caused by defendant's letters threatening unlawful receipt of signals).

[412] *See, e.g., Daniels, supra,* 16 Cal. App. 4th at 473; *Wershba v. Apple Computer, Inc.,* 91 Cal. App. 4th 224, 238–39, 110 Cal. Rptr. 2d 145 (2001).

[413] *Kagan v. Gibraltar Sav. & Loan Ass'n,* 35 Cal. 3d 582, 200 Cal. Rptr. 38, 676 P.2d 1060 (1984); *La Sala v. American Sav. & Loan Ass'n,* 5 Cal. 3d 864, 97 Cal. Rptr. 849, 489 P.2d 1113 (1971). In other words, a class action does not become moot simply because the representative plaintiff's individual claim is moot. *Johnson v. Hamilton,* 15 Cal. 3d 461, 465, 125 Cal. Rptr. 129, 541 P.2d 881 (1975).

[414] *See La Sala, supra,* 5 Cal. 3d at 871 (directing trial court to determine whether named plaintiff will continue to fairly and adequately protect interest of the class); *Wallace v. GEICO Gen. Ins. Co.,* 183 Cal. App. 4th 1390, 108 Cal. Rptr. 3d 375 (2010) (explaining the proper procedure in a "pickoff" situation is for the trial court to consider whether the named plaintiff will continue fairly to represent the class in light of the individual relief offer by the defendant); Jean Wegman Burns, *Standing and Mootness in Class Actions: A Search for Consistency,* 22 U.C. Davis L. Rev. 1239 (1989).

[415] *City of San Jose, supra,* 12 Cal. 3d at 464.

[416] *Evans v. Lasco Bathware, Inc.,* 178 Cal. App. 4th 1417, 1432–34, 101 Cal. Rptr. 3d 354 (2009).   •

significant factor by the California courts in their class action certification deci-sions.[417] The adequacy of class counsel should perhaps receive greater scrutiny, as it now does under federal Rule 23(g). Often a class action owes its existence to an attorney who has an economic incentive (in the form of a large attorney fees award) to bring the action on behalf of a class as opposed to an individual party (or not at all). Therefore, the quality of the class representative's attorney may be far more important than the attributes of the named plaintiff.

[4]   California Class Action Procedures

[a]   Raising the Class Action Issue

Although the trial court may decide the issue of class certification on demurrer, the preferable procedure is for the trial court to make the class action determina-tion subsequent to the pleading stage, after notice and a certification hearing.[418] This determination may be made on motion of either plaintiff or defendant, or on the court's own motion.[419] Although the trial court may properly delay the class certification decision until after the pleading stages of litigation, as a general rule, the court must resolve class certification issues before reaching a decision on the merits.[420] From a defendant's viewpoint, it is very important to know whether the action will be certified as a class action before final determination of the substantive issues. If not certified until trial, the defendant faces the risk of "one-way intervention," where class members opt out if the plaintiff loses on the merits but intervene if the plaintiff wins.[421]

[b]   Appellate Review of Class Determination

Under California decisional law, a trial court order denying class certification to an entire class is an immediately appealable order.[422] However, an order which denies class certification as to some causes of action but grants it as to others is not

---

[417] See, e.g., Miller v. Woods, 148 Cal. App. 3d 862, 874, 196 Cal. Rptr. 69 (1983) (noting and applying, without significant discussion, that in order for the representative to adequately represent the class, the representative's attorney must be qualified, experienced, and generally able to conduct the proposed litigation); McGhee v. Bank of Am., 60 Cal. App. 3d 442, 450, 131 Cal. Rptr. 482 (1976) (observing briefly that there is no indication plaintiffs' attorneys are not qualified to act as attorneys for the class).

[418] See, e.g., Gutierrez v. Cal. Commerce Club, Inc., 187 Cal. App. 4th 969, 976–80, 114 Cal. Rptr. 3d 611 (2010) (as a general principle, class suitability should not be determined at the pleading stage); Prince v. CLS Transp., Inc., 118 Cal. App. 4th 1320, 13 Cal. Rptr. 3d 725 (2004) (reversing trial court's order sustaining a demurrer to the class action allegations in a complaint brought by employees seeking class recovery for nonpayment of overtime compensation and observing that it is only in mass tort actions, or other actions equally unsuited to class action treatment, that class suitability can and should be determined at the pleading stage); but see TJX Companies, Inc. v. Superior Court, 87 Cal. App. 4th 747, 104 Cal. Rptr. 2d 810 (2001) (collecting cases where class issue decided by demurrer).

[419] City of San Jose, supra, 12 Cal. 3d at 453.

[420] Fireside Bank v. Superior Court, 40 Cal. 4th 1069, 1083–84, 56 Cal. Rptr. 3d 861, 155 P.3d 268 (2007); Green v. Obledo, 29 Cal. 3d 126, 172 Cal. Rptr. 206, 624 P.2d 256 (1981).

[421] See Fireside Bank, supra, 40 Cal. 4th at 1078–82 (discussing "one-way intervention").

[422] Daar v. Yellow Cab Co., supra, 67 Cal. 2d at 699 (holding order appealable because it effectively terminated the entire action as to all members of the class); In re Baycol Cases I and II, 51 Cal. 4th 751,

appealable as a matter of right, but may be reviewed by discretionary extraordinary writ.[423] The California approach to appellate review of class action denials differs from the federal approach. Under Rule 23(f) of the Federal Rules of Civil Procedure, a United States Court of Appeals "may in its discretion permit an appeal from an order of a district court granting or denying class action certification." If the Court of Appeals declines to permit an interlocutory appeal, the district court's class certification order is reviewable only on appeal from the subsequent final judgment on the merits.[424]

In many cases, the federal approach may be preferable to California's because, under federal Rule 23(f), the court of appeals is given the unfettered discretion whether to permit the interlocutory appeal — permission that need not be granted in routine cases. Moreover, the California approach may create some unanticipated problems. The failure to appeal a trial court's order denying class certification may preclude subsequent motions to certify, even if based on new evidence.[425] Although bringing new motions on new evidence after a court has initially certified a class is appropriate, successive motions after a court has initially denied certification is not.[426]

[5]   Favorable Treatment of Small-Claimant Class Actions

[a]   Notice to Class Members

Due to the absence of a comprehensive class action statute, the California courts generally follow federal Rule 23(b) & (c) to determine whether a certified class is the type which requires mandatory notice to the absentee members of the class.[427] Consequently, mandatory notice to members of the class is required for those classes which satisfy only the definitions of federal Rule 23(b)(3). Unless due process requires otherwise, notice is discretionary as to federal Rule 23(b)(1) and (b)(2) classes.[428]

---

122 Cal. Rptr. 3d 153, 248 P.3d 681 (2011) (ruling where an order terminates class claims but individual claims survive, the order terminating class claims is immediately appealable under the "death knell" doctrine adopted in *Daar*).

[423] *See, e.g., Vasquez, supra,* 4 Cal. 3d at 806–07; *Blue Chip Stamps v. Superior Court,* 18 Cal. 3d 381, 134 Cal. Rptr. 393, 556 P.2d 755 (1976) (issuing writ of mandamus directing trial court to vacate order which certified class against defendant).

[424] *Coopers & Lybrand v. Livesay,* 437 U.S. 463 (1978).

[425] *Stephen v. Enter. Rent-A-Car,* 235 Cal. App. 3d 806, 1 Cal. Rptr. 2d 130 (1991).

[426] *Stephen, supra,* 235 Cal. App. 3d at 811–14; *see Safaie v. Jacuzzi Whirlpool Bath, Inc.,* 192 Cal. App. 4th 1160, 122 Cal. Rptr. 3d 344 (2011) (holding that despite claimed change in governing law, plaintiff could not renew his class certification motion after affirmance of the prior decertification order by appellate court on writ review).

[427] *E.g., Bell v. Am. Title Ins. Co.,* 226 Cal. App. 3d 1589, 277 Cal. Rptr. 583 (1991); *Frazier v. City of Richmond,* 184 Cal. App. 3d 1491, 228 Cal. Rptr. 376 (1986); *Lowry v. Obledo,* 111 Cal. App. 3d 14, 23, 169 Cal. Rptr. 732 (1980).

[428] FED. R. CIV. P. 23(c)(2) & (d); *but see Phillips Petroleum Co. v. Shutts,* 472 U.S. 797 (1985) (requiring notice and an opportunity to opt out in any class action exclusively or predominantly for money damages).

[b] Nature of Required Notice: Individual vs. Publication

When a California court determines that *some* notice to the class as certified is required, the court does not necessarily follow federal Rule 23(c) to determine the precise nature of the class notice. Instead, the court would apply the manner of notice requirements of California Civil Code § 1781(d), which authorizes notice by publication if personal notification is unreasonably expensive in consumer fraud class actions, and Civil Code § 1781(e), which governs the content of class notice with respect to requests for exclusion.[429] The California courts construe section 1781(d) as requiring individual mailed notice to class members where members of the class have a substantial damage claim such that members may decide to "opt out" of the class and pursue their independent remedies.[430] However, when membership in the class is huge and damages per member minimal, notice by publication may be adequate.[431]

The California Rules of Court also provides important guidance on the procedures and content of notice to class members in all class actions. With respect to the manner of giving notice, these rules require the court to consider the interests of the class, the type of relief requested, the stake of the individual class members, the cost of notifying class members, the resources of the parties, the possible prejudice to class members who do not receive notice, and the binding effect of the judgment on class members.[432] Rule 3.766(f) then provides:

> If personal notification is unreasonably expensive or the stake of the individual class members is insubstantial, or if it appears that all members of the class cannot be notified personally, the court may order a means of notice reasonably calculated to apprise the class members of the pendency of the action — for example, publication in a newspaper or magazine; broadcasting on television, radio, or the Internet; or posting or distribution through a trade or professional association, union, or public interest group.

[c] Federal Notice Rule Not Binding

With respect to the type of notice required for members of the class, the California courts view federal Rule 23 as useful, but not binding, and have declined to follow the construction of federal Rule 23(c)(2) in *Eisen v. Carlisle & Jacquelin*.[433] In *Eisen*, the United States Supreme Court held that federal Rule 23(c)(2) requires, for any class action maintained under Rule 23(b)(3), individual notice mailed to all class members who are identifiable through reasonable effort. The *Eisen* court ruled that publication notice would not be adequate notice even though the cost of providing individual notice to 2,250,000 class members was prohibitively

---

[429] *E.g., Cartt v. Superior Court*, 50 Cal. App. 3d 960, 970–75, 124 Cal. Rptr. 376 (1975); *Cooper v. Am. Sav. & Loan Ass'n*, 55 Cal. App. 3d 274, 283–85, 127 Cal. Rptr. 579 (1976).

[430] *Cooper, supra*, 55 Cal. App. 3d at 285.

[431] *Cooper, supra*, 55 Cal. App. 3d at 284–86; *Cartt, supra*, 50 Cal. App. 3d at 971–73. *See* Cal. Ct. R. 3.766(f), reproduced *infra*.

[432] Cal. Ct. R. 3.766(e).

[433] 417 U.S. 156 (1974). *See, e.g., Cartt, supra*, 50 Cal. App. 3d at 966–76; *Cooper, supra*, 55 Cal. App. 3d at 283.

high and no individual class member had a large enough damage claim to justify litigation of a separate claim.

In contrast to the federal view, the California Rules of Court permit notice by publication even where the names and addresses of the class members may be ascertained through reasonable effort, if personal notification is unreasonably expensive or the stake of the individual class members is insubstantial. However, any such use of publication must also satisfy due process which, is this context, generally authorizes something less than individual notice when individual notice is impracticable.[434]

[d] Who Pays the Cost of Class Notice

Another important difference between the California and the federal practice concerns the issue of who pays for the cost of class notice. The California Legislature has specifically authorized trial courts in consumer fraud class actions to impose the cost of notice to the class upon either the plaintiff or the defendant.[435] The California Supreme Court extended this rule to all class actions in *Civil Service Employees Insurance Co. v. Superior Court*, where it held that California trial courts clearly possess the authority to impose notice costs on either party in a class action.[436] The Court also held that the imposition of class notice costs on a defendant was consistent with due process if, prior to the trial court order, the defendant had a full hearing on the issue of who should bear the cost of notifying the class during the pendency of the suit.[437]

In contrast to the California rule, the federal rules do not authorize a federal court to impose the cost of class notice on the defendant. The United States Supreme Court in *Eisen v. Carlisle & Jacquelin*,[438] held that federal Rule 23 does not authorize departure from the usual rule that a plaintiff must initially bear the cost of notice to the class. The California Supreme Court in *Civil Service Employees* refused to follow *Eisen*, finding *Eisen*'s interpretation of a federal rule of court not binding on the California courts.

The issue of whether a trial court may impose the cost of class notice on the defendant is extremely important in large-class, small-claims actions. The *Eisen* ruling discourages such actions in federal court because the cost of maintaining the class action may be prohibitive. The California approach encourages such actions,

---

[434] *See Cartt, supra,* 50 Cal. App. 3d at 979–76; *see also Mullane v. Central Hanover Bank & Trust Co.,* 339 U.S. 306 (1950); Linda J. Lopez, Note, Cartt v. Superior Court: *Notice and Consumer Class Actions in California,* 64 CAL. L. REV. 1222 (1976). The due process requirements for notice generally are discussed in more detail in § 4.01 & § 4.02, *supra,* and for notice in the context of federal court class actions in § 9.09[1], *supra.*

[435] CAL. CIV. CODE § 1781(d).

[436] 22 Cal. 3d 362, 374–81, 149 Cal. Rptr. 360, 584 P.2d 497 (1978).

[437] *Civil Serv. Emp., supra,* 22 Cal. 3d at 379–81. *See also* CAL. CT. R. 3.766(b) & (c). The factors relevant to this allocation of class notice cost decision include the trial court's preliminary view of the strength of the plaintiff's claim, the cost of class notice in relation to the amount of the potential recovery for each individual class member, and which party is more capable of affording the financial burden of notice. *See Civil Serv. Emp., supra,* 22 Cal. 3d at 380–81; *Cartt, supra,* 50 Cal. App. 3d at 974–75.

[438] 417 U.S. 156, 177–79 (1974); *see* § 9.09[4], *supra* (discussing *Eisen*).

particularly where the class presents a strong case on the merits. Whether one approach is preferable depends on a normative assessment of the propriety and worth of small-claim, large-class actions.[439]

[e] Right to Opt Out of Class

The main purpose of providing proper notice of the pendency of a class action is to advise class members of their options: (1) to remain members of the class represented by plaintiff's counsel and become bound by a favorable or unfavorable judgment in the action, or (2) to intervene in the action through counsel of their own choosing, or (3) to "opt out" of the class action and pursue their own independent actions.[440] A class member will be bound by the class action judgment unless that member affirmatively requests exclusion.[441]

A broader constitutional issue is whether an individual class member has a due process right to opt out of any class action which seeks money damages on behalf of the class. In *Phillips Petroleum Co. v. Shutts*,[442] a class action for money damages brought in a Kansas state court on behalf of thousands of class members, many of whom were not Kansas residents, the United States Supreme Court held that before a court can bind an absent nonresident plaintiff to a class action judgment, due process requires at a minimum that an absent plaintiff be provided with an opportunity to remove himself from the class by executing and returning an "opt out" form to the court.[443] However, the Court expressly limited its holding to those class actions which seek to bind known plaintiffs concerning "claims wholly or predominantly for money judgments." Following the ruling in *Shutts*, the California courts determine whether class members are constitutionally entitled to notice and the right to opt out based on whether the appropriate relief sought by the class action is exclusively or predominantly for money damages.[444]

---

[439] For more discussion of these contrasting rules, see James R. McCall, *Due Process and Consumer Protection: Concepts and Realities in Procedure and Substance — Class Action Issues*, 25 HASTINGS L.J. 1351 (1974).

[440] *Home Sav. & Loan Ass'n v. Superior Court*, 42 Cal. App. 3d 1006, 1010, 117 Cal. Rptr. 485 (1974); CAL. CIV. CODE § 1781(e); FED. R. CIV. P. 23(c)(2). *See* CAL. CT. R. 3.766(b)–(d).

[441] FED. R. CIV. P. 23(c)(2); CAL. CIV. CODE § 1781(e).

[442] 472 U.S. 797 (1985).

[443] *Shutts*, 472 U.S. at 812.

[444] *E.g., Bell v. Am. Title Ins. Co.*, 226 Cal. App. 3d 1589, 1609–11, 277 Cal. Rptr. 583 (1991) (holding *Shutts'* due process holding does not apply to a class action seeking injunctive relief even though the class also sought restitution and price rollbacks, because the class claims are not predominantly for monetary relief). For commentary on *Shutts*, see Arthur R. Miller & David Crump, *Jurisdiction and Choice of Law in Multistate Class Actions After* Phillips Petroleum Co. v. Shutts, 96 YALE L.J. 1, 38–57 (1986); Brian Wolfman & Alan B. Morrison, *What the Shutts Opt-Out Right Is and What It Ought To Be*, 74 U.M.K.C. L. REV. 729 (2006).

[6] Class Action Settlements

A class action shall not be dismissed without appropriate notice to class members and approval of the court.[445] Unlike its passive role in an individual action, in a class action the trial court must actively scrutinize the terms of a proposed settlement to make sure the interests of the absentee class members are adequately protected. A trial court has broad discretion to determine whether a class action settlement is fair, but should consider the following relevant factors, identified by the California Court of Appeal in *Dunk v. Ford Motor Co.*:

> The strength of plaintiffs' case, the risk, expense, complexity and likely duration of further litigation, the risk of maintaining class action status through trial, the amount offered in settlement, the extent of discovery completed and the state of the proceedings, the experience and views of counsel, the presence of a governmental participant, and the reaction of the class members to the proposed settlement. The list of factors is not exhaustive and should be tailored to each case. Due regard should be given to what is otherwise a private consensual agreement between the parties.[446]

The *Dunk* court applied these factors and upheld the settlement of a nationwide class action brought against Ford Motor Company for alleged defects in the doors of certain cars, under which each class member would receive a coupon redeemable for $400 off the price of any new Ford vehicle. The *Dunk* factors have been frequently applied by other California courts in determining the propriety of a proposed class action settlement.[447] When applying these and other relevant factors, the trial court must receive evidence and independently satisfy itself that the consideration being received for the release of the class members' claims is reasonable in light of the strengths and weaknesses of the claims and the risks of the particular litigation.[448]

---

[445] CAL CODE CIV. PROC. § 581(k); CAL. CIV. CODE § 1781(f); CAL. CT. R. 3.769 & 3.770. Dismissal of class actions is one area where generally applicable state law exists to guide litigants and trial courts. In order to provide absentee class members an opportunity to object to a proposed class action settlement, Code of Civil Procedure § 581(k) requires notice to the class and court approval prior to dismissal of an action determined to be a class action. Rules 3.769 and 3.770 also govern settlement and dismissal of class actions, including the manner of notice to class members of a proposed class settlement or dismissal. *See, e.g., Wershba v. Apple Computer, Inc.*, 91 Cal. App. 4th 224, 110 Cal. Rptr. 2d 145 (2001) (affirming settlement of a nationwide class action alleging that defendant Apple Computer had rescinded its policy of free technical phone support to its customers in violation of California's consumer protection law, and approving methods of notice which included notice e-mailed directly to more than 2.4 million class members and also published in USA Today and MacWorld, as well as the posting of notice by Apple on its internet homepage); *Cellphone Termination Fee Cases*, 186 Cal. App. 4th 1380, 1390–93, 113 Cal. Rptr. 3d 510 (2010) (upholding notice of proposed class settlement that included short-form publication and mail notice that directed class members to a settlement website to learn more information about the terms of the proposed settlement).

[446] *Dunk v. Ford Motor Co.*, 48 Cal. App. 4th 1794, 1801, 56 Cal. Rptr. 2d 483 (1996).

[447] *See, e.g., 7-Eleven Owners for Fair Franchising v. Southland Corp.*, 85 Cal. App. 4th 1135, 102 Cal. Rptr. 2d 777 (2000) (applying the fairness factors identified in *Dunk*, and affirming the trial court's approval of the settlement of a national class); *Wershba, supra*, 91 Cal. App. 4th 224; *Clark v. Am. Residential Serv. LLC*, 175 Cal. App. 4th 785, 96 Cal. Rptr. 3d 441 (2009).

[448] *Kullar v. Foot Locker Retail, Inc.*, 168 Cal. App. 4th 116, 127–33, 85 Cal. Rptr. 3d 20 (2008); *Clark,*

[7]   Class Action Remedies

A trial court in a class action has the same authority to award the full range of legal and equitable remedies as the court would have in an individual action. In addition, the California courts have authority to award "fluid class" relief in appropriate cases.

[a]   Fluid Class Recovery

Fluid class recovery is a means of disposing of the portion of class-wide damages which goes unclaimed by class members by directing that it be spent in the public interest in a way at least generally responsive to concerns raised in the case. In *State v. Levi Strauss & Co.*,[449] the California Supreme Court approved a class action settlement which included fluid class relief. The class action in *Levi Strauss* was brought by the attorney general against the defendant manufacturer of jeans, seeking monetary relief for millions of consumers who allegedly were overcharged on jeans purchased during the early 1970s. The trial court approved a class settlement which included a cash refund distribution plan for individual claimants (over one million individual claims were subsequently received). On appellate review, the Supreme Court also approved the establishment of a "consumer trust fund" to further the purposes of the state consumer protection laws and provide indirect compensation to class members.[450]

In *Levi Strauss*, the California Supreme Court endorsed the propriety of fluid recovery in consumer class actions, and stated some guidelines for its use. After the defendant's total damage liability is paid over to a class fund and the individual class members are afforded an opportunity to collect their individual shares by proving their particular damages, any residue remaining after individual claims have been paid is distributed by one of several practical procedures: "The principal methods include a rollback of the defendant's prices, escheat to a governmental body for either specified or general purposes, establishment of a consumer trust fund, and claimant fund sharing."[451]

Subsequently, in 1993, the California Legislature enacted Code of Civil Procedure § 384, which specifically endorses the concept of fluid class recovery. Section 384(a) states that the intent of the Legislature in enacting this section is "to ensure that the unpaid residuals in class action litigation are distributed, to the extent possible, in a manner designed to either further the purposes of the underlying causes of action, or to promote justice for all Californians." Section 383(b) expressly authorizes a court to distribute any unpaid residual derived from a class action judgment "to nonprofit organizations or foundations to support projects that will benefit the class or similarly situated persons, or that promote the law consistent with the objectives and purposes of the underlying cause of action."

---

supra, 175 Cal. App. 4th at 798–804; *Munoz v. BCI Coca-Cola Bottling Co.*, 186 Cal. App. 4th 399, 408–11, 112 Cal. Rptr. 3d 324 (2010).

[449] 41 Cal. 3d 460, 224 Cal. Rptr. 605, 715 P.2d 564 (1986).

[450] *Levi Strauss*, *supra*, 41 Cal. 3d at 475.

[451] *Levi Strauss*, *supra*, 41 Cal. 3d at 472–76.

The availability of fluid class recovery is particularly important in small-claim, large-class actions, such as *Levi Strauss*. Most federal courts disapprove of the use of fluid class recovery as a possible remedy in class actions, and therefore are unwilling to certify a class where it is likely a substantial portion of a class fund will go unclaimed.[452] In contrast, by endorsing fluid class recovery, section 384 encourages certification of small-claim, large-class actions in the California courts.[453]

[b] Attorney Fees

The class action attorney may obtain payment of attorney fees from a portion of a class action settlement. Any such attorney fees agreement must be disclosed to the members of the class, and approved by the court as part of the settlement process.[454] If the class action is not settled but proceeds to trial, a successful class attorney may be entitled to an award of statutory attorney fees in an amount which reflects the nature of the class-wide services rendered.[455] It is this potential for a large financial reward that makes proceeding as a class action, as opposed to an individual action, attractive to plaintiffs' attorneys.

---

[452] *See, e.g., Eisen v. Carlisle & Jacquelin*, 479 F.2d 1005, 1017–18 (2d Cir. 1973), *vacated on other grounds*, 417 U.S. 156 (1974); § 9.09[4][b], *supra* (discussing fluid class recovery in federal courts).

[453] The fluid class recovery has produced much scholarly discussion, most of which supports such relief in appropriate cases. *See, e.g.*, James R. McCall, Patricia Sturdevant, Laura Kaplan & Gail Hillebrand, *Greater Representation for California Consumers — Fluid Recovery, Consumer Trust Funds, and Representative Actions*, 46 Hastings L.J. 797 (1995); Gail Hillebrand & Daniel Torrence, *Claims Procedures in Large Consumer Class Actions and Equitable Distribution of Benefits*, 28 Santa Clara L. Rev. 747 (1988); Martin R. Redish, Peter Julian & Samantha Zyontz, *Cy Pres Relief and the Pathologies of the Modern Class Action: A Normative and Empirical Analysis*, 62 Fla. L. Rev. 617 (2010).

[454] *See Rebney v. Wells Fargo Bank*, 220 Cal. App. 3d 1117, 1142–44, 269 Cal. Rptr. 844 (1990); *see* Cal. Ct. R. 3.769(b).

[455] *See Rebney, supra*, 220 Cal. App. 3d at 1142–43; *Miller v. Woods*, 148 Cal. App. 3d 862, 875, 196 Cal. Rptr. 69 (1983); Cal. Code Civ. Proc. § 1021.5. For discussion of the role of the class action counsel, see Jonathan R. Macy & Geoffrey P. Miller, *The Plaintiffs' Attorney's Role in Class Action and Derivative Litigation: Economic Analysis and Recommendations for Reform*, 58 U. Chi. L. Rev. 1 (1991); Bryant Garth, Ilene H. Nagel & S. Jay Plager, *The Institution of the Private Attorney General: Perspectives from an Empirical Study of Class Action Litigation*, 61 S. Cal. L. Rev. 353 (1988); John C. Coffee, *Understanding the Plaintiff's Attorney: The Implications of Economic Theory for Private Enforcement of Law Through Class Actions and Derivative Actions*, 86 Colum. L. Rev. 669 (1986).

Chapter 10

DISCOVERY

§ 10.01   OVERVIEW

Before filing a complaint, most plaintiffs and their lawyers make some effort to gather facts about the events that gave rise to suit. The lawyer ordinarily will interview the client and obtain information from the client's agents. He may also interview witnesses. But this kind of self-help can only advance the fact gathering so far for several reasons. Many of the most important facts are often within the knowledge and control of the prospective defendant. A wary prospective defendant may stonewall the lawyer who tries to interview him. Ex parte (without the presence of the other party's lawyer) interviews also require the lawyer to walk a tight ethical line — typically, ethics rules prohibit such interviews without the opposing lawyer's permission. Ethical rules in many jurisdictions prohibit the lawyer from stating or implying that he is disinterested, misstating the facts, engaging in conduct to embarrass, delay or burden a third person, or, in a few jurisdictions, giving advice or secretly taping the interview.[1] After the complaint has been filed, these rules prohibit him from communicating at all about the subject of suit with a party represented by a lawyer without that lawyer's consent (unless authorized by law).[2] This prohibition poses especially difficult problems of interpretation when the party is an organization and the witness is a present or former employee.[3]

Formal discovery of facts under court rules picks up where self-help leaves off and avoids most of these problems. Liberalization of such discovery was the most dramatic procedural reform brought by the Federal Rules of Civil Procedure in 1938.

> No longer can the time-honored cry of "fishing expedition" serve to preclude a party from inquiring into the facts underlying his opponent's case. Mutual knowledge of all relevant facts gathered by both parties is essential to proper litigation. To that end, either party may compel the

---

[1] *See generally* Model Rules of Professional Conduct Rule 3.1 cmt. 1, Rules 4.1, 4.3, & 4.4 (2007) (hereinafter ABA Model Rules); Donald J. Farage, *Ex Parte Interrogation: Invasive Self-Help Discovery*, 94 Dick. L. Rev. 1 (1989).

[2] ABA Model Rules, note 1, *supra*, Rule 4.2.

[3] *See, e.g.*, Susan J. Becker, *Conducting Informal Discovery of a Party's Former Employees: Legal and Ethical Concerns and Constraints*, 51 Md. L. Rev. 239 (1992); Eugene P. Gurr, *Ethics of Conducting Ex Parte Interviews*, 3 St. John's J. Legal Comment. 234 (1988); John E. Iole & John D. Goetz, *Ethics or Procedure? A Discovery-Based Approach to Ex Parte Contacts with Former Employees of a Corporate Adversary*, 68 Notre Dame L. Rev. 81 (1992).

other to disgorge whatever facts he has in his possession.[4]

Liberal discovery permitted the de-emphasis of pleading and more liberal amendment. It made trial preparation more effective. Along with liberal joinder and broadened preclusion, liberal discovery was intended to promote judicial efficiency by making it easier to dispose of the entire controversy in one lawsuit.[5] The federal discovery rules proved so useful that a majority of states adopted them,[6] including some that have otherwise retained their own procedural rules.[7]

We therefore use the federal discovery rules as a model for the discussion of formal discovery. Part A explores *what* information can be discovered under the federal rules (the scope of discovery). Part B considers *how* such information can be discovered and used at trial (the mechanics of discovery). After discussing required disclosures, we survey the principal discovery methods, including depositions (oral or written examinations of live witnesses), interrogatories (written questions answered in writing), requests for production of documents and things or for entry upon land, and physical or mental examinations.[8] Finally, Part C considers the judicial *control* of discovery and discovery abuse.

The reported, visible law of discovery is relatively straightforward. Problems arise almost exclusively in its application, usually out of sight of the national reporters and law services.[9] Discovery rulings are often by magistrates rather than judges and rarely generate extensive trial (much less appellate) opinions.[10] As a result, lower court decisions should often be viewed as fact-bound rulings rather than as legal precedents. Moreover, litigants often negotiate discovery disputes outside the court, as they are encouraged and authorized to do by Rule 29. "The very existence of the rules encourages lawyers to use more efficient and economical means to exchange information [including] [b]ilateral trading of documents, cooperative bartering of information, [and] mutual alteration of procedures."[11]

Litigants use discovery for overlapping purposes. The most significant is to prepare for trial and to avert surprise. Discovery permits a plaintiff who has commenced suit on the barest of facts to flesh out and, with liberal amendment, even

[4] *Hickman v. Taylor*, 329 U.S. 495, 507 (1947) (citation omitted).

[5] On the interrelation of pleading, complex litigation, discovery and preclusion in modern civil procedure, see JAMES, HAZARD & LEUBSDORF § 11.16; Gene R. Shreve, *Preclusion and Federal Choice of Law*, 64 TEX. L. REV. 1209, 1215 (1986).

[6] *See* FRIEDENTHAL, KANE & MILLER § 7.1.

[7] *See, e.g.*, VA. RULES ANN. 4:1–4:12 (West 2012) (adopting federal discovery rules almost verbatim, while otherwise retaining vestiges of code and common law pleading); FLA. R. CIV. P. 1.280–1.380 (patterned on federal discovery provisions as amended in 1970).

[8] Requests for admission are an additional discovery method, but are primarily used at the close of discovery as a pretrial device. They are therefore discussed as such in § 12.02, *infra*.

[9] "Thankfully, most of the mountainous volume of the District Courts' pre-trial activity never reaches the pages of a reporter or the files of a computer." *Union City Barge Line, Inc. v. Union Carbide Corp.*, 823 F.2d 129, 134 n.10 (5th Cir. 1987).

[10] This is in part because of the general federal rule against interlocutory appellate review. *See* §§ 13.02 & 13.03, *infra*.

[11] ROGER S. HAYDOCK & DAVID F. HERR, DISCOVERY PRACTICE § 1.1 (4th ed. 2002). *See generally id.* (5th ed. 2010 Supp.).

alter his case for trial.[12] It also affords parties opposing claims the same opportunity to prepare for trial. In addition, discovery helps to streamline the trial itself by permitting pretrial authentication of documents, "nailing down" the likely testimony of witnesses, and creating a storehouse of recollection-refreshing and impeaching material.[13]

On the other hand, the removal of all surprise at trial is not necessarily beneficial. Judge Aldrich observed:

> Not merely may too many rehearsals, in the form of too much discovery, take the bloom off the opening night, but this absence of freshness may make the performance sterile. A certain amount of surprise is often the catalyst which precipitates the truth. Alternatively it may serve as a medium by which the court or jury may gauge the accuracy of the account.[14]

Realizing this, the experienced litigator seeks both to prepare as thoroughly as possible for trial and to preserve as much surprise as possible in her case. These dual purposes coexist uneasily and often strain the discovery rules.

A second purpose of discovery is to preserve evidence for trial. When witnesses are likely to be unavailable for trial, due to age, illness or location beyond the reach of the trial court, their testimony can be preserved by deposition. The discoverer with this purpose cannot simply fish for information. She must be concerned about the content and admissibility of the elicited testimony at trial because she has no second chance at the witness.[15]

Third, discovery can be used to narrow or eliminate issues. By ascertaining whether and which issues are genuinely disputed, discovery can set up Rule 12(b) dismissals, summary judgment, and issue-narrowing or eliminating pretrial orders that can substantially simplify trial.[16] Perhaps even more important in light of litigation statistics, this use of discovery may even encourage settlement.[17] The discoverer with this objective may, contrary to the usual practice, *invite* discovery of the strengths of her case.

But the sheer burden of discovery can also extort settlement, particularly when the resources of the parties are unequal.[18] Discovery thus can have a fourth (and

---

[12] At the same time, liberal discovery, pleading, and amendment rules can combine to invite frivolous litigation by making it easier for plaintiff's counsel to file first and closely examine the claim later. Attorney certification requirements and sanctions for improper certification offer some protection against this. *See* Rule 11 (certification for pleadings and motion papers) discussed in § 8.05[2], *supra*, and Rule 26(g) (certification of discovery requests, responses and objections), discussed in § 10.13[1], *infra*.

[13] *See, e.g.*, HAYDOCK & HERR, note 11, *supra*, § 1.1; JAMES, HAZARD, & LEUBSDORF § 5.2.

[14] *Margeson v. Boston & Me. R.R.*, 16 F.R.D. 200, 201 (D. Mass. 1954).

[15] *See* HAYDOCK & HERR, note 11, *supra*, § 3.4.2.

[16] *Id.* § 1.1.

[17] *But cf. MOORE* § 26.02 (noting that discovery may discourage settlement and that settlement pressures may encourage withholding of unfavorable matter in discovery).

[18] *See id.*

illicit) purpose: harassment, delay and attrition.[19] The Supreme Court has noted that

> to the extent that . . . [discovery] permits a plaintiff with a largely groundless claim to simply take up the time of a number of other people, with the right to do so representing an *in terrorem* increment of settlement value, rather than a reasonably founded hope that the process will reveal relevant evidence, it is a social cost rather than a benefit.[20]

Considerable uncertainty remains over the prevalence of the problem and the most effective cure.[21] But without looking at empirical evidence on that prevalence, the Supreme Court worried in *Twombly* that "the threat of discovery expense will push cost-conscious defendants to settle even anemic cases before reaching" summary judgment or trial.[22] Indeed, it was partly this worry that drove the *Twiqbal* pleading revolution: as the Court said in *Twombly*, "it is only by taking care to require allegations that reach the level suggesting conspiracy that we can hope to avoid the potentially enormous expense of discovery in cases with no 'reasonably founded hope that the [discovery] process will reveal relevant evidence' to support a § 1 claim."[23]

The discoverer's mix of purposes — including any tactical purpose to bludgeon the adversary into settlement — determines the scope, frequency, and methods of the discovery she will pursue. We shall see that most discovery goes on without court involvement. When a party does ask for judicial intervention (either to block or coerce discovery), a comparison of the benefits of proper discovery against the costs of improper or excessive discovery suggests how much and what kind of control a court should impose. Read the remaining sections of this chapter with this comparison in mind.

---

[19] *See Herbert v. Lando*, 441 U.S. 153, 202 (1979) (Marshall, J., dissenting) (libel case in which defendant's editor was deposed intermittently for one year, yielding 3000 pages of testimony and 240 exhibits in 26 volumes of transcript).

[20] *Blue Chip Stamps v. Manor Drug Stores*, 421 U.S. 723, 741 (1975).

[21] *See* § 10.12 (abuse of discovery), *infra*.

[22] *Bell Atl. Corp. v. Twombly*, 550 U.S. 544, 559 (2007).

[23] *Id.* at 560 (citations omitted). Application of the *Twiqbal* plausibility pleading standard therefore can place the plaintiff in a "catch-22" when crucial evidence is exclusively within the defendant's control: she cannot survive a motion to dismiss without that evidence, but she cannot discover the evidence without surviving a motion to dismiss. *See* § 8.04[1][d], *supra*.

PART A.
Scope of Discovery

§ 10.02   IN GENERAL

Rule 26(b) describes what may be discovered under the federal rules[24] and effectively erects a presumption of discoverability.[25] A party may discover any matter that is (1) "relevant to any party's claim or defense," "reasonably calculated to lead to discovery of admissible evidence," but neither (2) privileged nor (3) prepared or acquired in anticipation of litigation or for trial, unless (4) discovery has been otherwise limited by a protective order of the court. A special showing is required for discovery of *work product* prepared or acquired in anticipation of litigation or for trial. Sections 10.03 to 10.06 successively treat each of these aspects of the scope of discovery, except that the discussion of protective orders has been deferred to § 10.13[3] in Part C on the control of discovery.

§ 10.03   THE FADING FEDERAL PRESUMPTION OF DISCOVERABILITY

[1]   Relevant to the Claim or Defense of Any Party

Rule 26(b)(1) originally fixed the scope of discovery as "relevant to the subject matter." One appellate court paraphrased it as "any matter that bears on, or that reasonably could lead to other matter that could bear on, any issue that is or may be in the case, . . . not limited to issues raised by the pleadings . . . [or] to [the] merits of a case."[26] In antitrust or business tort litigation, for example, virtually any matter involving the industry of which the parties are part arguably satisfied that standard. In securities fraud litigation, theoretically any factor that may affect the market for the stock at issue would satisfy that standard. In light of the generality with which discovery requests can be framed under the rules, some questioned whether the original relevant-to-the-subject-matter standard imposed any practical limit on federal discovery.

Heeding these doubts, the rulemakers changed the relevancy standard in 2000 by differentiating party-controlled discovery from court-authorized discovery. For the former, the standard was changed to "relevant to the claim or defense of any

---

[24] What *must* be discovered (required disclosures) is discussed in Part B, section 10.07, together with other general aspects of the mechanics of discovery. Limitations on the permissible scope of discovery apply to required disclosures.

[25] Disputes concerning the scope of discovery are usually resolved in favor of allowing discovery. This outcome reflects in part judges' and magistrates' awareness that orders allowing discovery are far less likely to be reversed on an eventual appeal than orders limiting or prohibiting it. HAYDOCK & HERR, note 11, *supra*, § 1.4.

[26] *Oppenheimer Fund, Inc. v. Sanders*, 437 U.S. 340, 351 & n.12 (1978) (citations omitted). *Compare Kelly v. Nationwide Mut. Ins. Co.*, 188 N.E.2d 445 (Ohio C.P. 1963) (applying relevancy-to-the-issues standard under former Ohio rules).

party."[27] This standard is narrower than the original standard because it is tied to the pleadings (which assert the claims or defenses of the parties), but also arguably broader than the alternative standard "relevant to the issues," which had initially been adopted by some states[28] and urged by some critics of the original rule. At the same time, the rulemakers authorized the court, on good cause shown, to allow discovery under the original "relevant-to-the-subject-matter" discovery standard.[29] Thus, the default scope of discovery was somewhat narrowed, but a party could ask the court to allow broader discovery for good cause.

Whether the change in the relevancy standard for party-controlled discovery has made much difference, standing alone, is questionable. The Advisory Committee itself admitted that the dividing line between the standards "cannot be defined with precision." It then proceeded to suggest that in a negligence or product liability suit arising from one incident, other "incidents of the same type, or involving the same product, could be properly discovered under the revised standard."[30] Ironically, however, it was precisely in products liability suits that some defense lawyers said that the old standard was abused to cast a dragnet for remotely relevant information about other incidents and the same type of products. The Advisory Committee's own explanations, therefore, lend some credence to the prediction that this "semantic change [is] unlikely to have much salutary effect on the conduct of discovery in the hurly-burly world of litigation."[31] A survey of the cases agrees; "[t]he amendment does not effect a dramatic change in the scope of discovery."[32]

On the other hand, the change in the relevancy standard for party-controlled discovery should not be viewed in isolation from the authorization for court-controlled discovery under the old relevancy standard. Responding to the common complaint of litigators that courts have failed to intervene in discovery disputes early or often enough, the Advisory Committee explained that the latter part of the amendment "is designed to involve the court more actively in regulating the breadth of sweeping or contentious discovery."[33] Courts may incrementally enforce the "claim or defense" standard more often, given the safety valve of broader discovery for good cause shown, and thus sometimes play a more active role in managing more sweeping discovery. Considering both of these effects of the rule amendment, at least one commentator has concluded that it reversed the presumption of discoverability:

> Instead of assuming that any matter relevant to the subject matter is discoverable, with the burden on the party opposing discovery to show non-relevance, burden, or privilege, the presumption is that information

---

[27] Rule 26(b)(1).

[28] *E.g.*, Ohio. *See Kelly*, 188 N.E.2d 445 (discussing old and new Ohio rules).

[29] Rule 26(b)(1).

[30] Rule 26(b)(1) advisory committee's notes (2000).

[31] John S. Beckerman, *Confronting Civil Discovery's Fatal Flaws*, 84 MINN. L. REV. 505, 510–11 (2000).

[32] WRIGHT & MILLER § 2008 (2008 Pocket Part).

[33] Rule 26(b)(1) advisory committee's notes (2000).

beyond "claims or defenses" is *not* discoverable. The burden is newly placed on the party seeking discovery either to convince the judge that the information sought falls within the core definition of relevance or to make an undefined and "flexible" showing that there is good cause to allow further discovery.[34]

Finally, as a corollary of the amendment's effect on discovery, some commentators predicted that it would impact pleading. They speculated that the "claim or defense" standard would cause plaintiffs to draft more particularized allegations in order to obtain needed discovery, threatening abandonment of notice pleading and a return to "fact pleading"[35] with all of its problems[36] and attendant motion practice.[37] Any such impact of the amendment will presumably only be reinforced by the Supreme Court's ambiguous endorsement of the plausibility standard of pleading in the *Twiqbal* cases.[38]

Skepticism about the semantic precision of the amendment may be beside the point. The change was really intended as a signal to the parties to try to confine discovery to the pleadings and to the court to watch closely if more is sought. Even if the change failed to supply a bright line for changing the scope of discovery in individual cases, it probably succeeded on the Advisory Committee's terms if it caused a change in the mindset of litigators and the courts that reduces the breadth of discovery at the margins.[39]

A better approach may be to limit directly the amount of discovery, or to emphasize and expand the courts' discretionary powers to control discovery on an ad hoc basis. The rulemakers have done both. In 1993 and again in 2000, they amended the discovery rules to impose quantitative limits on depositions and interrogatories, as we discuss in Part B. They also authorized courts to limit discovery pursuant to Rule 26(b)(2) when "the burden or expense of the proposed discovery outweighs its likely benefit." The rule had previously been amended in 1983 to give the courts the power to control "the frequency or extent of use" of discovery.[40]

---

[34] Elizabeth G. Thornburg, *Giving the "Haves" a Little More: Considering the 1998 Discovery Proposals*, 52 SMU L. Rev. 229, 251–52 (1999) (emphasis in original) (commenting on relevancy standard in 1998 proposal identical to that adopted in 2000). *See also* Jeffrey W. Stempel, *Politics and Sociology in Civil Rulemaking: Errors of Scope*, 52 Ala. L. Rev. 529, 584–86 (2001) (agreeing that rule change shifts "burden of uncertainty" from those opposing discovery to those seeking it, and finding change "misguided" for this and other reasons).

[35] *See, e.g.*, Beckerman, note 31, *supra*, at 541; Carl Tobias, *Congress and the 2000 Federal Civil Rules Amendments*, 22 Cardozo L. Rev. 75, 83 (2000).

[36] *See* § 8.03[3] (discussing the specificity of fact pleading).

[37] Gregory P. Joseph, *Civil Rules II*, Nat'l L.J., April 24, 2000, A17 ("It would be reasonable to anticipate more Rule 12 motion practice, including Rule 12(f) motions to strike . . . which now may have a discernible impact on the scope of discovery.").

[38] *See* § 8.04[1][d], *supra*.

[39] *See generally* Christopher C. Frost, *The Sound and the Fury or the Sound of Silence: Evaluating the Pre-Amendment Predictions and Post-Amendment Effects of the Discovery Scope-Narrowing Language in the 2000 Amendments to Federal Rule of Civil Procedure 26(b)(1)*, 37 Ga. L. Rev. 1039 (2003).

[40] *See* § 10.13[2] (managerial orders), *infra*.

[2]   Reasonably Calculated to Lead to the Discovery of Admissible Evidence

Rule 26(b)(1) provides that "[r]elevant information need not be admissible at the trial if the discovery appears reasonably calculated to lead to the discovery of admissible evidence." What a witness has heard about the issues in the case ("I heard Joe say that he thought the car ran a red light"), for example, is usually hearsay which may be inadmissible at trial unless it falls within an exception to the evidentiary rule against hearsay or constitutes an admission by a party. It is still discoverable, however, because it may lead to the discovery of the identity of fact witnesses (witnesses to the incident giving rise to the claim — like Joe, if he saw the car — and others with personal knowledge of relevant facts)[41] or other facts that might themselves be admissible. Similarly, information about a subsequent repair may be inadmissible at trial to prove negligence because of the public policy to encourage such repairs.[42] Nevertheless, it is discoverable as relevant to a claim in a negligence action.[43]

[3]   Examples and Problem Areas

[a]   Information Already in the Discoverer's Possession

Even when the discoverer already knows or possesses certain information, he is entitled to discover it from his adversary. A party is entitled to discover what the other parties know and contend, in order to facilitate his own preparation and possible settlement. Moreover, knowledge is not the same thing as proof, which is what will be required at trial. A party is entitled to whatever jury impact he can get from proving the facts through evidence produced by his adversary. A court always retains the power, however, to intervene in particular cases when discovery becomes "*unreasonably* cumulative or duplicative . . . [or] the party seeking discovery has had ample opportunity to obtain the information by discovery in the action."[44] If the opposing party has already admitted a fact, for example, a court might conclude that discovery of the fact is "unreasonably cumulative," or that the burden or expense of such discovery outweighs its likely benefit.[45]

---

[41] Rule 26(a)(1) requires initial disclosure of the identity of fact witnesses, and Rule 26(a)(3) requires pretrial disclosure of the identity of trial witnesses (persons who will be called to testify). Prior to the 1993 amendment mandating such disclosures, some courts ruled that a party is not entitled to discover the identity of trial witnesses. They reasoned that the discoveree often does not know her trial witnesses until the eve of trial, or that the identity of such witnesses should be protected as work product under Rule 26(b)(3). Some state courts still follow this reasoning, although many require the mutual identification of trial witnesses in connection with a final pretrial conference. *See, e.g., Ladner v. Ladner,* 436 So. 2d 1366, 1372 (Miss. 1983) (construing state discovery rule modeled on Rule 26(b)). *See generally* § 12.03 (pretrial conference), *infra.*

[42] Fed. R. Evid. 407 advisory committee's note.

[43] *See, e.g., Culligan v. Yamaha Motor Corp., U.S.A.,* 110 F.R.D. 122, 124 (S.D.N.Y. 1986).

[44] Rule 26(b)(2)(C)(i) & (ii) (emphasis supplied). *See* § 10.13[2] (managerial orders), *infra.*

[45] *See* Rule 26(b)(2)(C)(i) & (iii). *But see Cornet Stores v. Superior Court,* 492 P.2d 1191 (Ariz. 1972) (stipulation that plaintiff was highest paid manager will not foreclose discovery of pay of other managers in wrongful discharge action).

[b]   Impeachment Material

Except for required disclosures under Rule 26(a)(1)-(3)[46] discovery is not limited to direct substantive evidence, but includes material that may impeach an opponent's witnesses.

Discovery of material that may impeach the discoverer's own witnesses has been more troublesome to the courts. Some have held that discovery is ordinarily not proper "where the only purpose . . . is to prevent effective cross-examination."[47]

Discovery of surveillance evidence, often movies made by defendant's representatives of plaintiff at work or play after the accident in a personal injury case, furnishes a good example. Many courts resist the plaintiff's discovery of surveillance movies made of him, reasoning that such movies, created after commencement of the litigation, have nothing to do with the merits, contain information already intimately and better known to the plaintiff, and serve as a possible check on a "fertile field for fraud and magnification."[48] Moreover, impeachment material is gathered or developed in preparation for trial, and thus may fall within the spirit, if not always the letter, of Rule 26(b)(3)'s protection for work product.[49]

The trend in the modern cases, however, is to require discovery of even impeachment material. One important reason is that the assumption that matter useful for impeachment has nothing to do with the merits is not always reliable. The same matter can be used both to advance a party's substantive position and to impeach.[50]

A second and more commonly articulated reason is that impeachment material poses its own risk of fraud and magnification. In *Boldt v. Sanders*,[51] for example, one of the plaintiffs in a personal injury action denied having suffered any prior accidents or personal injuries and sought discovery from defendant of any information that would contradict that denial. Defendant's objection rested on "the premise that defendant's evidence which plaintiffs seek to elicit constitutes the unblemished truth which, if prematurely disclosed, will prevent defendant from revealing to the jury the sham and perjury inherent in plaintiffs' claims."[52] The court rejected this premise, posing the equally plausible hypothetical that the defendant "has resorted to fraud and perjury in fabricating pictures of what purport to be plaintiff's physical activities subsequent to the accident, and has manufactured evidence to prove that plaintiff sustained his injuries in prior accidents."[53] Absent a principled basis for choosing between these possibilities, the

---

[46] *See* § 10.07, *infra.*

[47] *Stone v. Marine Transp. Lines, Inc.*, 23 F.R.D. 222, 226 (D. Md. 1959).

[48] *Zimmerman v. Superior Court*, 402 P.2d 212, 219 (Ariz. 1965) (Struckmeyer, J., dissenting).

[49] *See DiMichel v. South Buffalo Ry. Co.*, 604 N.E.2d 63 (N.Y. 1992), *cert. denied sub nom Poole v. Consol. Rail Corp.*, 510 U.S. 816 (1993). *See generally* § 10.05 (work product), *infra.*

[50] *See* WRIGHT § 81.

[51] 111 N.W.2d 225 (Minn. 1961).

[52] *Id.* at 227.

[53] *Id.*.

court fell back on the general rule of mutual discoverability.[54]

[c] Opinions and Contentions

Discovery is not limited to facts, but may also include opinions held by non-experts[55] and contentions regarding the facts or the application of law to the facts. This scope of discovery is expressly set out in Rule 33(a)(2) concerning interrogatories and Rule 36(a)(1) concerning requests for admissions, because they are most often used to probe opinions or contentions. But it is also implicit in Rule 26(b)(1)'s generic statement of the scope of discovery.[56] The only limitation is that the discoveree may defer responding until she has completed discovery of her own and thus had an opportunity to form informed opinions and contentions.[57]

The discoverer, however, may not ask what the law is, because the parties' legal conclusions are considered irrelevant. Only the court can say what the law is.[58] Similarly, the discoverer is not entitled to the discoveree's rank speculation on hypothetical facts, unrelated to the facts or to the application of the law to the facts in the case.[59] Relevancy is probably also at the bottom of this restriction because untrammeled speculation by a witness or a party is arguably not relevant to anything.

[d] Insurance and Other Information About Financial Assets

Rule 26(a)(1) expressly requires disclosure of insurance agreements available to satisfy any or all of any eventual judgment, even though they remain inadmissible at trial. Prior to the 1970 amendment to the rule, some federal courts had denied discovery on relevancy grounds, and many states still do.[60] But the existence of insurance can be relevant to the issue of ownership. More important, it almost always bears significantly on settlement negotiations. It was chiefly to advance the social policy of encouraging settlement that the 1970 amendment made insurance agreements expressly discoverable.

Other information concerning the discoveree's financial position might also be useful in settlement negotiations, but is far less open to discovery. In support of the

---

[54] Many courts have qualified that rule with regard to impeachment material, however, by giving the discoveree the opportunity to depose the discoverer first before having to disclose the impeachment material. *See, e.g., Daniels v. Nat'l R.R. Passenger Corp.*, 110 F.R.D. 160, 161 (S.D.N.Y. 1986).

[55] For discussion of the discovery of opinions held by experts, see § 10.06, *infra*.

[56] *See* MOORE §§ 26.41, 26.43.

[57] *See* Rules 33(b) & 36(a).

[58] *See, e.g., O'Brien v. Int'l Bhd. of Elec. Workers*, 443 F. Supp. 1182 (N.D. Ga. 1977) (an interrogatory requesting an explanation as to why provisions of a union constitution are not deprived of effect by a federal statute seeks purely legal conclusions).

[59] MOORE § 26.41.

[60] *See* JAMES, HAZARD, & LEUBSDORF § 5.8 (noting arguments against relevancy in an action against the insured); Annotation, *Pretrial Examination or Discovery to Ascertain from Defendant in Action for Injury, Death, or Damages, Existence and Amount of Liability Insurance and Insurer's Identity*, 13 A.L.R.3D 822 (1967 & 2000 Supp).

1970 amendment, the Advisory Committee observed that insurance is an asset created specifically to satisfy claims, the insurer often controls the lawsuit, the information is usually available only from the insured or the insurer, and no privacy concerns are implicated by its discoverability.[61] None of these considerations in allowing discovery of insurance agreements applies to routine discovery of other financial assets. A party's general assets are obviously not created for the express purpose of satisfying a legal claim and are usually invested with significant privacy interests.

Accordingly, unless the amount of a party's assets is itself a relevant issue in the case (as it would be in an action to enforce a money judgment or in an action for punitive damages set in relation to the amount of the assets or net worth),[62] discovery of assets other than insurance, and of related information such as tax returns and bank statements, is sometimes denied. Even when assets are relevant and discoverable, privacy concerns may warrant postponing discovery until the discoveree has had an opportunity to contest the claim to which the assets are relevant.[63]

[4]   Electronic Information[64]

Rule 34 was originally called "Discovery and Production of Documents and Things for Inspection, Copying, or Photographing." While "documents" could be (and was) construed to include various kinds of electronically stored information ("ESI"), the phrase was not ideally suited to the task. Neither were the rules themselves, as they understandably reflected the paper-based mind set of the original rulemakers.

Technology has long since overtaken that mindset. Information that was maintained and communicated by paper is now maintained in spreadsheets, emails, websites, and text messages, stored on floppy discs, CD-ROMs, laser discs, thumb drives, zip drives, and DVDs, at the office and at home, on local and on distant servers, on networked computers and stand-alone laptops, and on PDAs, and MP3 players. Most data is created and stored electronically and never reduced to hard copies, and even hard copies, in turn, are now scanned and digitized (and often destroyed after being electronically preserved).[65] ESI includes metadata (data about the data embedded in the file, containing markers that may show changes, author identity, and creation and modification dates) that is not usually reflected in

---

[61] Rule 26(b)(2) advisory committee's note (1970).

[62] *See, e.g.*, *Renshaw v. Ravert*, 82 F.R.D. 361, 363 (E.D. Pa. 1979) (punitive damages).

[63] *See, e.g.*, *Larriva v. Montiel*, 691 P.2d 735, 737–38 (Ariz. Ct. App. 1984) (discoverer must first make *prima facie* showing that he will be entitled to present punitive damages claim to jury).

[64] *See, e.g.*, MICHAEL R. ARKFELD, THE LAW STUDENT'S GUIDE TO ELECTRONIC DISCOVERY AND EVIDENCE (13 ed. 2012-13) (hereinafter *Arkfeld Guide*); MAYER BROWN LLP, ELECTRONIC DISCOVERY DESKBOOK (2012); MICHAEL R. ARKFELD, ARKFELD ON ELECTRONIC DISCOVERY AND EVIDENCE (3d ed. 2011); John K. Rabiej, *Discovery of Electronically Stored Information, in MOORE* ch. 37A; SHIRA A. SCHEINDLIN, E-DISCOVERY: THE NEWLY AMENDED FEDERAL RULES OF CIVIL PROCEDURE (2006); THE SEDONA CONFERENCE, THE SEDONA PRINCIPLES: BEST PRACTICES, RECOMMENDATIONS & PRINCIPLES FOR ADDRESSING ELECTRONIC DOCUMENT PRODUCTION (Jonathan M. Redgrave et al. eds., 2005).

[65] *See generally MOORE* § 37A.02[1]–[4].

a printout of the data and of which the naive author may therefore be unaware, other hidden data (comments, highlights, etc.), residual deleted data (data that has been "deleted" but resides on the computer until overwritten by a new file),[66] "backup tapes" maintained for archival or data-recovery purposes, and "legacy data" (data that can be used only by superseded computer systems or software).[67] In 2005, it was reported that "more than 90% of all corporate information . . . is electronic; North American businesses exchange over 2.5 trillion e-mails per day; . . . less than 1% of all communication will ever appear in paper form; and, on average, a 1000-person corporation will generate nearly 2 million e-mails annually."[68] Some data experts estimated that 1.8 zettabytes (1.8 trillion gigabytes) contained within 500 quadrillion files would be created and replicated in 2011.[69] In 2013 and beyond, these figures are conservative.

This explosion of ESI causes a raft of problems for "E-discovery." First, data retention policies test traditional understandings about data preservation and the application of so-called "litigation holds" to preserve documents during the pendency of suit. Second, both the volume and variety of ESI have raised new questions about the phrasing of E-discovery requests and the format of production. Third, although the availability of ESI often dramatically lowers *search costs*,[70] its sheer volume, coupled with problems of formatting, often raises *production costs*, raising new and thorny questions of discovery cost allocation.

In an early response to some of these problems, the rulemakers changed a few rules in 2006 to take account of E-discovery. But those who look to the rule changes concerning "E-discovery" for detailed guidance in particular cases will be disappointed. Instead, the rulemakers mainly empowered the courts and the parties to develop detailed solutions themselves, in light of what one landmark case identifies as the essential predicate for resolving any E-discovery dispute: "understanding the responding party's computer system, both with respect to active and stored data."[71]

Below, we briefly consider how the rules and the courts have responded to each of these E-discovery problems.

---

[66] *Moore* § 37A.03[1]–[3].

[67] Rule 34 advisory committee's note (2006).

[68] Harvey L. Kaplan, *Electronic Discovery in the 21st Century: Is Help on the Way?*, 733 PLI/Lit 65, 67 (2005) (citations omitted).

[69] *See* John Gantz & David Reinsel, *Extracting Value from Chaos* (IDC iView, Working Paper No. IDC 1142, 2011), *available at* http://www.emc.com/collateral/analyst-reports/idc-extracting-value-from-chaos-ar.pdf.

[70] The Supreme Court foresaw this impact as early as 1978. *See Oppenheimer Fund, Inc. v. Sanders*, 437 U.S. 340, 362 (1978) ("[A]lthough it may be expensive to retrieve information stored in computers when no program yet exists for the particular job, there is no reason to think that the same information could be extracted any less expensively if the records were kept in less modern forms. Indeed, one might expect the reverse to be true, for otherwise computers would not have gained such widespread use in the storing and handling of information.").

[71] *Zubulake v. UBS Warburg LLC*, 217 F.R.D. 309 (S.D.N.Y. 2003).

[a] The Duty to Preserve ESI

Although ESI can usually be easily preserved, it is also volatile: it can be overridden, destroyed, modified, or manipulated. Many ESI users still use backup tapes for temporary storage, and then re-cycle them, in some cases thereby modifying or destroying old data. Others may leave preservation of some ESI — such as email in certain accounts — to the discretion of individual employees. Still others may deliberately adopt ESI retention and purging policies that periodically destroy ESI to make space for newer data, or even to eliminate potential evidence.

Preserving ESI as possible evidence poses two questions: *when* does a duty to preserve attach, and *what* evidence must be preserved?[72] The duty attaches "at the time that litigation was reasonably anticipated" by the party possessing the ESI.[73] Thus, the duty often attaches well before the filing of a complaint. The duty may be triggered by prelitigation correspondence, notice of a claim or demand, oral requests, or even prior industry experience of events usually leading to litigation.[74] In a gender discrimination case, for example, that duty was triggered well before the plaintiff filed a complaint with the EEOC, when the defendant company's emails showed that its managers recognized the possibility that she might sue.[75]

The duty to preserve requires a party to suspend ESI destruction and to place a "litigation hold" on any ESI a party "knows, or reasonably should know, is relevant to the action, is reasonably calculated to lead to the discovery of admissible evidence, is reasonably likely to be requested during discovery and/or is the subject of a pending discovery request."[76] Yet the scope of the duty to preserve is itself reasonable. Thus, one court emphasized that the anticipation of litigation did not obligate an organization to preserve "every shred of paper, every e-mail or electronic document, and every back-up tape."[77] On the other hand, it may well include time-relevant ESI — such as emails — of "key players," those persons who were most directly involved in the litigation-provoking events or transactions. Of course, the discovering party can help particularize the duty to preserve by making a specific hold request, even before discovery, and making particularized production requests after litigation commences. Indeed, the failure to do so may itself be a factor in deciding what ESI a party was reasonably expected to preserve.

Rule 37(e) provides a safe harbor of sorts by forbidding the court from imposing sanctions, "[a]bsent exceptional circumstances, . . . on a party for failing to provide electronically stored information lost as a result of a routine, good-faith operation of an electronic information system." Yet the harbor is lined with shoals: when litigation is reasonably anticipated — that is, the duty to preserve has attached — then "good faith" may require the party "to modify or suspend certain features of

---

[72] *Zubulake v. UBS Warburg LLC*, 220 F.R.D. 212 (S.D.N.Y. 2003) (*Zubulake IV*). *Zubulake IV* is one of a series of E-discovery decisions issued by Judge Shira Scheindlin of the United States District Court for the Southern District of New York, which have become leading precedents in the subject.

[73] *Id.* at 217.

[74] *Arkfeld Guide, supra* note 64, at 7-343.

[75] *Zubulake IV*, 220 F.R.D. at 218–19.

[76] *Id.* at 217 (footnotes omitted).

[77] *Id.*

that routine operation to prevent the loss of information."[78]

[b]   Formulating E-Discovery Requests and Formats

Because of the variety, disorganization, and volume of ESI, special care must often be taken in formulating requests for litigation holds and discovery. For this reason, Rule 26(f) expressly contemplates that the parties meet and confer to discuss issues about preserving and disclosing ESI, "including the form or forms in which it should be produced," and address those issues in their discovery plan. Rule 16(b)(3) also expressly provides for the court's scheduling order to address discovery of ESI.

E-discovery rules require parties and courts to pay special attention to the form of both the request and production of information. For example, if a plaintiff were to request all of a defendant's e-mails pertaining to dealings with Acme Corporation, it makes sense to permit the defendant to use the search terms "Acme Corporation" to conduct an automated search of his e-mail database for pertinent messages. The alternative would be to require the defendant to read through (potentially) thousands of e-mails for relevant information — a truly burdensome task by any standard. As any search engine user is aware, however, selecting the right terms is key to any search. If the case concerned 2008 dealings with Acme's widget division, a simple search for "Acme" would certainly be overbroad; messages outside of the relevant date range would be returned, as would messages related to Acme's non-widget dealings. Courts have responded to this dilemma by encouraging collaboration between parties to create appropriate search parameters.[79]

The "searchability" of the electronic documents produced can also be a point of contention between parties. For instance, electronic documents are often produced in Portable Document Format (these are typically referred to as "PDFs"). The logic behind the widespread use of PDFs is that, ideally, they provide users with "a convenient, efficient mechanism enabling documents to be reliably viewed and printed anywhere," that is, regardless of the viewer's operating system or software budget.[80] Must such documents also be produced in a format that is search-enabled? A 1,000-page PDF without search capability is little better than 1,000 pages of text on paper when it comes to finding snippets of pertinent information. Courts have, therefore, sometimes invoked Rule 34(b)(2)(E)(ii)'s requirement for production "in a reasonably usable form" to require production of electronic documents in searchable PDF form.[81] Requesting searchable documents from the outset seems to be the best practice, however, because some courts hold that, in the absence of a specific request for searchable electronic files, Rule 34(b)(2)(E)(ii) simply requires that the responding party produce documents in the form in which

---

[78] FED. R. CIV. PROC. 37 advisory committee's note (2006).

[79] *See, e.g., Lapin v. Goldman, Sachs & Co.,* 2009 U.S. Dist. LEXIS 9140 (S.D.N.Y. Jan. 23, 2009) (requiring cooperation between parties to devise e-mail search terms).

[80] *See* ADOBE SYS. INC., PDF REFERENCE 23 (6th ed. 2006), *available at* http://www.adobe.com/content/dam/Adobe/en/devnet/acrobat/pdfs/pdf_reference_1-7.pdf.

[81] *See AccessData Corp. v. ALSTE Techs. GmbH,* 2010 U.S. Dist. LEXIS 4566 (D. Utah Jan. 21, 2010).

they are typically maintained" — i.e., "native format."[82]

Another issue of occasional dispute in electronic discovery requests is the treatment of "metadata." Metadata is, essentially, the hidden record associated with an electronic file that contains data pertaining to the file's authorship, creation and modification dates, and other (sometimes highly relevant) historical information. In *National Day Laborer Organizing Network v. United States Immigration and Customs Enforcement Agency*,[83] the court reached the sensible conclusion that metadata is an inextricable part of an electronic record which must be produced with ESI, even if it was not separately identified in the production request.[84]

[c]   Cost Allocation in E-Discovery

The existence of ESI does not mean that relevant information in it is easily accessible. For example, recovery of data from the backup tapes still used by many data-collectors:

> [C]an be singularly time-consuming and costly to review. The data from such tapes must first be decompressed and then processed into a reviewable format. Further, because the information contained on a backup tape may be recorded in a serpentine fashion, the tape drive must shuttle back and forth through the entire tape repeatedly to get to the data. This shuttling process occurs at a glacial pace when compared to the speed with which computers normally retrieve data. Additionally, because backup tapes often lack a directory or catalogue of the information they contain, a party may need to search an entire tape — or perhaps all of an opponent's tapes — to locate a single file. . . . Restoring backup tapes for review can easily cost millions of dollars.[85]

Demanding that a party restore backup tapes can therefore give the plaintiff in a suit against a corporate defendant "a gigantic club with which to beat his opponent into settlement. No corporate president in her right mind would fail to settle a lawsuit for $100,000 if the restoration of backup tapes would cost $300,000. While that scenario might warm the cockles of certain lawyers' hearts, no one would accuse it of being just."[86]

For this reason, in one case, the court invoked Rule 26(c) to fashion an order initially requiring the defendant to restore emails on backup tapes for only a

---

[82] *Cf. Secure Energy, Inc. v. Coal Synthetics*, 2010 U.S. Dist. LEXIS 13532 (E.D. Mo. Feb. 17, 2010) ("[T]here is no requirement under the federal rules of civil procedure for Defendants to produce [electronic files] in [a particular] format when Plaintiffs failed to specific [sic] a format in their requests.").

[83] 827 F. Supp. 2d 242 (S.D.N.Y. Dec. 7, 2011).

[84] *See id.* The order was later withdrawn after the parties resolved their discovery dispute, and other courts have disagreed. *See, also D'Onofrio v. SFX Sports Grp., Inc.*, 247 F.R.D. 43, 48 (D.D.C. 2008) (denying a motion to compel metadata because it was not included in the requesting party's initial discovery request).

[85] John H. Beisner, *Discovering a Better Way: The Need for Effective Civil Litigation Reform*, 60 Duke L.J. 547, 565 (2010) (citations omitted).

[86] *McPeek v. Ashcroft*, 202 F.R.D. 31, 34 (D.D.C. 2001).

time-limited period to see what it cost and whether — in terms of relevant evidence — it was worth it. Based on the results of this "test run," the court would then revisit the order and reconsider the traditional allocation of production costs to the producing party.[87]

Another early landmark case, *Zubulake v. UBS Warburg LLC*,[88] adopted a more refined test for distributing the costs of production. The court rejected the argument that costs should be shifted to the responding party in every E-discovery dispute. "The presumption is that the responding party must bear the expense of complying with discovery requests," the court asserted, and there is no exception for E-discovery.[89] Cost-shifting, however, could be considered when electronic discovery places an undue burden on the responding party. In an E-discovery dispute, the cost of production depends primarily on whether the data is kept in an accessible or inaccessible format[90] which, in turn, depends largely on the media upon which it is stored. The court then found that active e-mail files and those stored on easily searchable optical disks were reasonably accessible, but those on the backup tapes were not. The court then considered whether costs should be shifted to the discovering party, taking into account the specificity of the discovery request; the availability of such information from other sources; the total cost of production, compared to the amount in controversy and the resources of each party; the relative ability of each party to control costs and its incentive to do so; the importance of the issues at stake in the litigation; and the relative benefits to the parties of obtaining the information.

The 2006 rule amendment effectively reflected these innovative approaches to E-discovery by providing that a party may resist E-discovery by showing that the ESI "is not reasonably accessible because of undue burden or cost." A court may nonetheless order E-discovery, after considering the limitations of Rule 26(b)(2)(B) (which track many of the *Zubulake* factors).

§ 10.04   THE NON-DISCOVERABILITY OF PRIVILEGED MATTER

Discovery in every jurisdiction extends only to unprivileged matters.[91] *Privilege* is a legal term of art. It refers to the protection from disclosure that the common law, statute, or rule[92] affords particular communications in order to promote relationships to which confidential communication is essential. Although their elements vary, most privileges require the communications for which the privilege

---

[87] *Id.*

[88] 217 F.R.D. 309 (S.D.N.Y. 2003).

[89] *Id.* at 317 (quotation omitted)

[90] "Examples of inaccessible paper documents could include (a) documents in storage in a difficult to reach place; (b) documents converted to microfiche and not easily readable; or (c) documents kept haphazardly, with no indexing system, in quantities that make page-by-page searches impracticable. But in the world of electronic data, thanks to search engines, any data that is retained in a machine readable format is typically accessible." *Id.* at 318 (citation omitted).

[91] *See, e.g.*, Rule 26(b)(1).

[92] *See, e.g.*, FED. R. EVID. 501 (incorporating federal common law).

is sought (1) to have been made with an expectation of confidentiality, that is (2) essential to a socially approved relationship or purpose and (3) has not been waived by disclosure of the contents of the communications to persons outside the relationship.[93] The attorney-client, doctor-patient, priest-penitent, spousal privilege, and the privilege against self-incrimination are commonly recognized privileges.[94] A privilege that will bar evidence at trial will also prevent disclosure of the same evidence in discovery. This is because violation of the confidence compromises the relationship in either event — disclosure during discovery would destroy confidentiality even if the disclosed matter were ruled inadmissible at trial.

Privileges are narrowly construed in light of the rules' preference for liberal disclosure.[95] The proponent of a privilege has the burden of establishing its existence. This ordinarily requires her to lay a foundation for the existence of the privilege by supplying enough information about the circumstances of the communication to show that it is privileged — a "privilege log." This foundation requirement is codified in Rule 26(b)(5). The 1993 Advisory Committee cautions that a party's failure to supply this information will not only subject it to sanctions under Rule 37, but may also waive the privilege.[96]

Although detailed discussion of particular privileges belongs to the law of evidence rather than to civil procedure, it is useful to develop the attorney-client privilege as an example. Probably the classic judicial statement of the privilege is found in *United States v. United Shoe Machinery Corp.*:[97]

> The privilege applies only if (1) the asserted holder of the privilege is or sought to become a client; (2) the person to whom the communication was made (a) is a member of the bar of a court, or his subordinate and (b) in connection with this communication is acting as a lawyer; (3) the communication relates to a fact of which the attorney was informed (a) by his client (b) without the presence of strangers (c) for the purpose of securing primarily either (i) an opinion on law or (ii) legal services or (iii) assistance in some legal proceeding, and not (d) for the purpose of committing a crime or tort; and (4) the privilege has been (a) claimed and (b) not waived by the client.

---

[93] *See, e.g.*, HAYDOCK & HERR, note 11, *supra*, § 2.1.

[94] Litigants, and occasionally courts, loosely and inaccurately describe as "privileges" the protection accorded to trial preparation materials, which are discoverable upon the proper special showing, *see* §§ 10.05 & 10.06, *infra*, or to materials like trade secrets or membership lists, which are discoverable but often subject to discovery limitations established by a court order to protect their confidentiality. *See* § 10.13[3], *infra*.

[95] *MOORE* § 26.47[1].

[96] Because preparing the privilege log can itself be burdensome, and because waiver is a harsh sanction, some courts have reserved the sanction for unjustifiably delayed, boilerplate privilege logs and have endorsed a "holistic reasonableness analysis" for other inadequacies in the log. *See Burlington N. & Santa Fe Ry. Co. v. U.S. Dist. Court for the Dist. of Mont.*, 408 F.3d 1142, 1149 (9th Cir.) (rejecting a per se waiver rule, but upholding waiver where boilerplate privilege log was filed five months late), *cert. denied*, 546 U.S. 939 (2005).

[97] 89 F. Supp. 357, 358–59 (D. Mass. 1950). *See generally* EDNA S. EPSTEIN, THE ATTORNEY-CLIENT PRIVILEGE AND THE WORK PRODUCT DOCTRINE (5th ed. 2007); JOHN W. GERGACZ, ATTORNEY-CORPORATE CLIENT PRIVILEGE (3d ed. 2000); PAUL R. RICE ET AL., ATTORNEY-CLIENT PRIVILEGE IN THE UNITED STATES (2d ed. 1999).

It is the communication itself, not the underlying facts, that is privileged.[98] Thus a client cannot cloak evidence with the privilege simply by telling it to his lawyer. The privilege is unavailable if third parties were present at the communication, destroying its confidentiality, or if the client has waived it by subsequent disclosure.[99] Finally, the privilege is not available to protect communications made for improper purposes.[100]

The possibility of waiver always haunts lawyers in the discovery process and usually prompts tedious privilege reviews of documents before disclosures are made, as well as the mandated preparation of a privilege log for the withheld documents. Nevertheless, mistakes are made and privileged material may be inadvertently disclosed. These risks are particular acute in the disclosure of ESI.

> With electronically stored information, difficulties [of wasteful privilege review] may become more acute due to volume of such material and the informality that attends the use of some forms of electronic communication such as e-mail. In addition, the possibility that computer programs may retain draft language, marginal notes and other items not apparent to the reader introduces further complexities for the privilege-review process.[101]

However, Federal Rule of Evidence 502 declares that inadvertent disclosures are not waivers, *provided* that the holder of the privilege took reasonable steps to prevent disclosure (even though they failed) and acted promptly to rectify the error. Rule 26(b)(5)(B) sets out procedures for the return (clawback) of inadvertently disclosed privileged or otherwise protected matter.[102] The producing party must notify the recipient of the claim of privilege after an inadvertent disclosure. The recipient must then return the putatively privileged matter, sequester, or destroy it, and may not use or disclose it until any dispute about the availability of the privilege is resolved.

In practice, savvy litigators privatize the problem and control the risks of inadvertent disclosure of ESI by entering into pre-production clawback (return) and "quick-peek" agreements (an agreement that lets the discovering party see the entire data file before production and specify which parts he wants, and then lets the producing party conduct a privilege review on just this smaller data set before producing).[103]

---

[98] *See, e.g., Upjohn Co. v. United States,* 449 U.S. 383, 395–96 (1981).

[99] Indeed, one court has even held the privilege waived by the clients' discarding of privileged documents in a trash dumpster from which they were removed by an enterprising if pungent third party. *Suburban Sew 'N Sweep, Inc. v. Swiss-Bernina, Inc.,* 91 F.R.D. 254 (N.D. Ill. 1981).

[100] *See generally* RICE, note 97, *supra,* §§ 8.2–8.15.

[101] WRIGHT & MILLER § 2051.1.

[102] Some courts have treated inadvertently disclosed metadata like privileged matter which the discovering party must return. *See generally* Andrew M. Perlman, *The Legal Ethics of Metadata Mining,* 43 AKRON L. REV. 785 (2010).

[103] *Arkfeld Guide, supra* note 64, at 7-149.

§ 10.05   WORK PRODUCT[104]

Work product can be defined preliminarily as information prepared or obtained in anticipation of litigation or preparation for trial. In the landmark case of *Hickman v. Taylor*,[105] the Supreme Court recognized a common law qualified immunity of work product from discovery. The rulings in this case were subsequently codified and enlarged by Rule 26(b)(3). Subdivision 1 of this section discusses *Hickman*; Subdivision 2 defines work product more thoroughly in terms of Rule 26(b)(3); Subdivision 3 discusses how the immunity is asserted during discovery; and Subdivision 4 discusses how it is overcome.

[1] *Hickman v. Taylor* and Work Product Immunity

Originally, the federal rules of civil procedure contained no provisions regarding discovery of work product. A few lower federal courts recognized a federal common law[106] protection for such materials. In 1947, the Supreme Court endorsed and explained this common law protection in *Hickman v. Taylor*.

Hickman arose out of the accidental sinking of a tugboat and the resulting death of five crew members. Three days after the sinking, the tug owners and their underwriters employed attorney Fortenbaugh and his firm to defend them against potential suits by the decedents' representatives and to sue a third party for damages to the tug. After a public hearing before the United States Steamboat Inspectors at which the surviving crew members testified, Fortenbaugh privately took written statements from the survivors. He also interviewed other fact witnesses and made memoranda of the interviews.

A decedent's representative ultimately sued the tug owners and filed interrogatories directed to them. One interrogatory asked whether statements of the surviving crew members had been taken and required any written statements to be attached to the answers[107] and any oral statements to be set forth in detail.[108] Additional interrogatories sought the content of any other oral or written statements, memoranda or reports made concerning the subject matter of the suit.

The tug owners admitted in answers prepared by Fortenbaugh that statements had been taken, but declined to set forth the answers' contents in part on the ground that they were "privileged matter obtained in preparation for litigation."[109] The district court ruled that the written witness statements taken by Fortenbaugh

---

[104] *See generally* EPSTEIN, note 97, *supra*; Elizabeth G. Thornburg, *Rethinking Work Product*, 77 VA. L. REV. 1515 (1991); Jeff A. Anderson et al., *The Work Product Doctrine*, 68 CORNELL L. REV. 760 (1983); Annotation, *Development, Since Hickman v. Taylor, of Attorneys Work Product" Doctrine*, 35 A.L.R.3D 412 (1971 & 1993 Supp.).

[105] 329 U.S. 495 (1947).

[106] For discussion of specific federal common law, see § 7.07, *supra*.

[107] Technically, this part of the plaintiff's discovery request was improper. Document production from a party is ordinarily obtained by filing a request for production of documents pursuant to Rule 34. *See* § 10.10[1] (procedures for production requests), *infra*.

[108] *Hickman*, 329 U.S. at 499.

[109] *Id.*

were not privileged and ordered Fortenbaugh to produce them.[110] When he refused, he was ordered imprisoned for contempt. The Court of Appeals reversed, ruling that the information was "work product" and as such privileged from discovery. The Supreme Court affirmed on somewhat different reasoning.

The Court first rejected Fortenbaugh's claim of privilege. It noted that the attorney-client privilege extends neither to information obtained from third parties outside the attorney-client relationship nor to all material prepared by counsel for his own use in prosecuting his client's case.[111] The purpose of the attorney-client privilege is to encourage full disclosure of information between an attorney and her client by protecting the confidentiality of their communications.[112] That purpose did not apply to the materials Fortenbaugh had prepared.

This conclusion, however, did not answer the discovery question presented by the case. The Court held that discovery of attorney Fortenbaugh's work product "contravenes the public policy underlying the orderly prosecution and defense of legal claims," absent any showing of necessity beyond mere relevance or any claim that denial of discovery would cause undue prejudice.[113]

> In performing his various duties, however, it is essential that a lawyer work with a certain degree of privacy, free from unnecessary intrusion by opposing parties and their counsel. Proper preparation of a client's case demands that he assemble information, sift what he considers to be the relevant from the irrelevant facts, prepare his legal theories and plan his strategy without undue and needless interference. . . . This work is reflected, of course, in interviews, statements, memoranda, correspondence, briefs, mental impressions, personal beliefs, and countless other tangible and intangible ways — aptly though roughly termed by the Circuit Court of Appeals in this case as the "work product of the lawyer." Were such materials open to opposing counsel on mere demand, much of what is now put down in writing would remain unwritten.[114]

The Court made clear, however, that the immunity accorded work product is qualified. When the discoverer goes beyond a bare demand, and shows that production is "essential to the preparation" of his case and that denial of discovery would cause hardship because "witnesses are no longer available or can be reached only with difficulty," production of "relevant and non-privileged facts . . . in an

---

[110] This order was also improper. Interrogatories and requests for production of documents could only be directed at parties, and Fortenbaugh was not a party. The only proper procedure for obtaining documents from a non-party was to take her deposition and, in that connection, to serve her with a *subpoena duces tecum. Id.* The Supreme Court noted this but it did not figure in the Court's holding. *Id.* at 504–05.

[111] *Id.* at 508.

[112] *See* § 10.04 (privilege), *supra. See generally* MOORE § 26.70[8] (comparing the attorney-client privilege and the protection of attorney work product).

[113] *Hickman,* 329 U.S. at 509–10. It follows that the work product protection is broader than the attorney-client privilege. WRIGHT & MILLER § 2023 (2008 Pocket Part).

[114] 329 U.S. at 510. *But see* Thornburg, note 104, *supra,* at 1526–32 (arguing that the adversary system itself provides sufficient inducement for thorough, written preparation, without the need for work product immunity).

attorney's file" should be allowed.[115] The plaintiff in *Hickman* had made no such showing. On the contrary, his counsel admitted that he wanted the witness statements "only to help prepare himself to examine witnesses and to make sure that he [had] overlooked nothing."[116] He had ready access to the surviving crew members' prior public testimony before the Steamboat Inspectors and apparently to the witnesses themselves. Moreover, the Court emphasized, he could employ interrogatories to the tug owners to obtain any relevant and non-privileged facts known to them, including any facts learned by their attorney.[117]

Finally, the Court implied that although a showing of necessity and hardship would be sufficient to require production of the written witness statements, it might not be enough to require production of oral witness statements taken by Fortenbaugh, "whether presently in the form of his mental impressions or memoranda."[118] It reasoned that in addition to the previously discussed policy arguments for protection, there is special concern about making the attorney a witness, by forcing him to testify to the contents of oral witness statements he has taken. As Justice Jackson noted in his concurring opinion,

> [t]he lawyer who delivers such statements often would find himself branded a deceiver afraid to take the stand to support his own version of the witness's conversation with him, or else he will have to go on the stand to defend his own credibility — perhaps against that of his chief witness or possibly even his client.[119]

Discoverability of such statements could thus transform the attorney from officer of the court into ordinary witness, contrary to the standards of the profession.[120]

Hickman stood as the common law foundation for the qualified immunity of attorney work product for twenty-three years. Finally, the 1970 amendments to the federal rules codified and enlarged much of the common law doctrine.

[2] Defining Work Product

Rule 26(b)(3) enlarges the common law protection from attorney work product to "documents and tangible things . . . prepared in anticipation of litigation or for trial by or for another party or [his] representative." Where the rule applies, it supplants the common law doctrine of *Hickman*. But *Hickman* still controls the discovery of intangible materials that literally fall outside the rule,[121] and its spirit

---

[115] 329 U.S. at 511.

[116] *Id.* at 513.

[117] *Id.*

[118] *Id.* at 512.

[119] *Id.* at 517.

[120] *ABA Model Rules*, note 1, *supra*, Rule 3.7. *But see* Thornburg, note 104, *supra*, at 1540–44 (arguing that the problem is more imaginary than real because attorneys can have others interview witnesses, tape-record the interview, or simply depose the witnesses).

[121] The rule expressly extends protection only to tangible work product. *See* MOORE § 26.70[2]. But the courts interpret *Hickman* to require work product protection for both tangible and intangible work product. *See In re Cendant Corp. Sec. Litig.*, 343 F.3d 658, 662 (3d Cir. 2003).

animates the rule.

[a] Documents and Tangible Things

The Court in *Hickman* emphasized that although the written witness statements and Fortenbaugh's memoranda were not discoverable on a bare demand, the discoverer was free to obtain the facts gleaned by Fortenbaugh by putting interrogatories — written questions — to his clients. Rule 26(b)(3) rather crudely reflects this distinction between the documents assembled by the client or his representatives, and the underlying facts themselves, by protecting only "documents and tangible things." The qualified immunity for work product does not protect against discovery of facts contained in the work product, including the identity of fact witnesses or the existence of the protected documents and things, "if a litigant can figure out the right question to ask."[122]

In application, however, the distinction is not so clean. Since the rule could be easily circumvented if a discoverer could require the discoveree to describe in detail the contents of protected documents, courts deny such discovery on the theory that it is "the equivalent to discovery of the documents themselves" and therefore prohibited by the rule,[123] or that it violates the broader common law rule of *Hickman*.[124] The distinction is subtle; you may obtain the facts in the document, but may not require the discoveree to recreate the document for you. The distinction is also logical. By its organization and fact selection, the written presentation of the facts often reflects tactical or strategic emphases and priorities that are at the heart of the immunity, even though the bare facts themselves are not. The same reasoning is sometimes given for the denial of discovery of what questions an attorney privately put to a witness.[125]

A similar concern for circumvention of the rule has led some courts to restrict discovery of even the facts themselves when that discovery is sought from the parties' attorneys, rather than from their clients or other witnesses. Not only does the deposition of an opposing attorney unnecessarily make a witness of the attorney (contrary to *Hickman*'s admonition), but it inevitably targets the attorney's mental impressions and legal theories by forcing her to reveal what she thought important enough to remember. Accordingly, the Court of Appeals for the Eighth Circuit upheld an attorney's refusal during her deposition to acknowledge even the existence of trial preparation materials.[126] It reasoned that

---

[122] Thornburg, note 104, *supra*, at 1520. *See generally* WRIGHT § 82.

[123] *See, e.g., Peterson v. United States*, 52 F.R.D. 317, 322 (S.D. Ill. 1971).

[124] *Cf. Gilhuly v. Johns-Manville Corp.*, 100 F.R.D. 752 (D. Conn. 1983); *Bercow v. Kidder, Peabody & Co.*, 39 F.R.D. 357 (S.D.N.Y. 1965).

[125] *See, e.g., Ford v. Philips Elecs. Instruments Co.*, 82 F.R.D. 359, 360 (E.D. Pa. 1979) (discovery denied "[i]nsofar as defendant's question attempted to elicit from the witness the specific questions that plaintiff's counsel posed to him, or even the area of the case to which he directed the majority of his questions," but not "insofar as it was directed to the substance of the witness' knowledge of relevant facts").

[126] *Shelton v. Am. Motors Corp.*, 805 F.2d 1323 (8th Cir. 1986). *See generally* Kathleen Waits, *Opinion Work Product: A Critical Analysis of Current Law and a New Analytical Framework*, 73 ORE. L. REV. 385 (1994) (criticizing *Shelton*); Brian R. Pioske, Comment, *Suppose You Want to Depose Opposing*

[i]n cases that involve reams of documents and extensive document discovery, the selection and compilation of documents is often more crucial than legal research. We believe [that the attorney's] selective review of [her client's] numerous documents was based upon her professional judgment of the issues and defenses involved in this case. . . . Moreover, . . . any recollection [she] may have of the existence of documents in [her client's] possession likely would be limited to those documents she has selected as important to her legal theories concerning this case.[127]

In addition, the court more generally disapproved of the increasingly popular device of deposing opposing counsel and emphasized that henceforth it should be limited to cases in which the discoverer can make the kind of showing of substantial need and undue hardship required by Rule 26(b)(3) for discovery of tangible trial work product.[128]

In short, although Rule 26(b)(3) expressly only protects tangible work product, in the form of documents and other tangible things, the common law declared by *Hickman* extends such protection to some intangible work product as well when it would advance the policies articulated in *Hickman*. Some commentators have urged a distinction between "direct" intangible work product, such as a lawyers testimony about her trial strategy, and "indirect" intangible work product, such as a lawyers selection of documents to use at a deposition (from which strategy could at best be inferred circumstantially[129]), arguing that only the former ordinarily deserves protection, but the courts have yet to adopt this distinction or any other consistent framework for treating intangible work product.[130]

[b] Prepared in Anticipation of Litigation or for Trial[131]

Because qualified work product immunity is designed to promote "the public policy underlying the orderly prosecution and defense of legal claims,"[132] the immunity is limited by Rule 26(b)(3) to materials "prepared in anticipation of litigation or for trial." Litigation need not be pending, but a mere contingency is insufficient. One court has asserted that "the lawyer must at least have had a subjective belief that litigation was a real possibility, and that belief must have been objectively reasonable."[133] Most courts add that the primary purpose of preparing

---

Counsel: Shelton v. American Motors Corp., 73 MINN. L. REV. 1116 (1989) (arguing that courts should only limit and not prohibit depositions of opposing counsel).

[127] *Shelton*, 805 F.2d at 1329 (citations omitted).

[128] *Id.* at 1327. *See generally* Steven W. Simmons, Note, *Deposing Opposing Counsel Under the Federal Rules: Time for a Unified Approach*, 38 WAYNE L. REV. 1959 (1992).

[129] *See* James Holmes, *The Disruption of Mandatory Disclosure with the Work Product Doctrine: An Analysis of a Potential Problem and a Proposed Solution*, 73 TEX. L. REV. 177, 188 (1994).

[130] Waits, note 126, *supra*. *See* § 10.05[4][c] (discussing opinion work product), *infra*.

[131] *See generally* Sherman L. Cohn, *The Work Product Doctrine: Protection Not Privilege*, 71 GEO. L.J. 917, 925–29 (1985); Robert H. Oberbillig, *Work Product Discovery: A Multifactor Approach to the Anticipation of Litigation Requirement of Federal Rule of Civil Procedure 26(b)(3)*, 66 IOWA L. REV. 1277 (1981).

[132] *Hickman*, 329 U.S. at 509.

[133] *In re Sealed Case*, 146 F.3d 881, 884 (D.C. Cir. 1998).

the documents must have been to assist in such litigation.[134] Thus, documents prepared for ordinary business purposes (*e.g.*, a routine accident report), public regulatory requirements (*e.g.*, statutorily-required report to police of automobile accidents involving injuries), or other nonlitigation purposes (*e.g.*, self-evaluation) are not protected.[135]

Purpose alone, however, is often unhelpful as a test for the applicability of the immunity. For example, because it is the ordinary course of business for an insurer to investigate claims in anticipation of litigation, the purpose test alone is unavailing to classify claims investigation materials. Instead, the court must also consider all the circumstances of preparation, including who prepared the materials and precisely when they were prepared in relation to anticipated litigation.[136] A few courts have therefore rejected the primary purpose standard as too narrow in favor of the formulation "prepared because of" the prospect of litigation, which encompasses some business documents not intended to assist in the litigation.[137] A memorandum prepared to assess the effects of possible litigation on the desirability of a merger would qualify as work product under this standard, for example, even though it was not prepared primarily to assist in litigation.

Carver v. Allstate Insurance Co.[138] is illustrative. In an action to recover proceeds under a fire insurance policy and statutory penalties for the insurer's bad faith refusal to pay, the insured sought discovery of daily investigative reports or "diary sheets" prepared by the insurer's claims adjusters. The court allowed discovery of the diary sheets prepared by the initial claims adjuster during the first two months after the fire. It reasoned that such reports are not primarily prepared for the contingency of litigation but rather for the routine business purpose of deciding whether to pay or resist the claim.

However, the court denied discovery of the diary sheets of a second claims adjuster to whom the claim was assigned after the first claims adjuster determined that the claim would be substantial and that the origins of the fire were suspicious. At that point, all the circumstances indicated that the insurer's activities shifted from "mere claims evaluation to a strong anticipation of litigation."[139] The court acknowledged that although an insurer always works in anticipation of litigation, at some point the probability of litigation becomes substantial and imminent, triggering the qualified immunity for materials prepared thereafter.

---

[134] *See, e.g., Janicker v. George Wash. Univ.,* 94 F.R.D. 648 (D.D.C. 1982).

[135] *See generally* Rule 26(b)(3) advisory committee's note (1970); Thomas Wilson, Note, *The Work Product Doctrine: Why Have an Ordinary Course of Business Exception?,* 1988 COLUM. BUS. L. REV. 587.

[136] *See* WRIGHT § 82.

[137] *United States v. Adlman,* 134 F.3d 1194 (2d Cir. 1998). *See, e.g.,* Eric C. McNamara, *Business Planning as It Should Be: Why Adlman Should Be the Standard When Interpreting the Work Product Doctrine,* 34 VAL. U. L. REV. 201 (1999); Charles M. Yablon & Steven S. Sparling, *United States v. Adlman: Protection for Corporate Work Product?,* 64 BROOK. L. REV. 627 (1998).

[138] 94 F.R.D. 131 (S.D. Ga. 1982).

[139] *Id.* at 134.

[c] By a Party or His Representative

Although *Hickman* dealt just with materials prepared by an attorney, preparation of materials in anticipation of litigation or for trial routinely and necessarily requires the assistance of non-attorneys, as well the parties themselves. Rule 26(b)(3) thus expressly extends the qualified immunity to materials prepared by a party or a party's representative, "including [his] attorney, consultant, surety, indemnitor, insurer, or agent."[140] This enlargement of the literal original common law rule accounts in part for Rule 26(b)(3)'s abandonment of the phrase "attorney work product" in favor of "trial preparation materials."

[3] Asserting the Qualified Immunity

While the burden rests on the discoverer to overcome a properly asserted qualified immunity for work product,[141] the discoveree must first lay a proper foundation for the immunity. As previously noted in connection with claims of privilege,[142] this requirement is codified in Rule 26(b)(5). Disregarding the requirement risks sanctions as well as waiver of the immunity. The rule does not specify what information must be provided. "Details concerning time, persons, general subject matter, etc., may be appropriate if only a few items are withheld, but may be unduly burdensome when voluminous documents are claimed to be privileged or protected, particularly if the items can be described by categories."[143] This advice of the Advisory Committee must be taken cautiously because the case law is hostile to blanket claims of privilege.[144]

[4] Overcoming the Qualified Immunity

Once qualified work product immunity has been properly asserted, the burden of overcoming it shifts to the discoverer and depends upon whether the work product consists of *witness statements* requested by the witness, other *factual work product*, or *opinion work product*.

[a] Witness Statements Requested by the Witness

Although witness statements qualify as work product, Rule 26(b)(3)(C) expressly provides that a party or witness may on demand obtain a copy of his own substantially verbatim statement[145] concerning the subject matter of the action.

---

[140] Materials prepared by a party's expert are covered by Rule 26(a)(2) (testimonial expert's written report) or Rule 26(b)(4) (other experts). *See* § 10.06, *infra.*

[141] *See* § 10.05[4], *infra.*

[142] *See* § 10.04 (non-discoverability of privileged matters), *supra.*

[143] Rule 26(b)(5) advisory committee's note (1993).

[144] *See, e.g., Eureka Fin. Corp. v. Hartford Accident & Indem. Co.*, 136 F.R.D. 179, 182 (E.D. Cal. 1991). A court may also disregard an untimely establishment of foundation for the immunity. *Peat, Marwick, Mitchell & Co. v. West*, 748 F.2d 540, 541–42 (10th Cir. 1984), *cert. dismissed*, 469 U.S. 1199 (1985).

[145] *See* Kathleen Waits, *Work Product Protection for Witness Statements: Time for Abolition*, 1985 Wis. L. Rev. 305 (criticizing applicability of this provision only to a witness's own statement).

The 1970 Advisory Committee gave a partial explanation of this exception to qualified immunity in terms of the importance of a person's statement, which is admissible against him at trial as an admission. Since a person who gives a statement without insisting on a copy often does so without benefit of counsel, in ignorance of its legal consequences, and "at a time when he functions at a disadvantage," the Committee reasoned that its discoverability would increase fairness.[146]

[b] Factual Work Product

The immunity for factual work product can be overcome only upon a showing by the discoverer of "substantial need for the materials to prepare [its] case" and that it "cannot without undue hardship, obtain their substantial equivalent by other means."[147] Although the cases do not always sharply distinguish these requirements, they are logically discrete.

Substantial need refers to the importance of the materials to the discoverer's case. *Hickman* itself demonstrates that substantial need means more than that the materials will help the discoverer make sure that he has overlooked nothing, because the Court rejected that showing. Such need, the "natural desire to learn the details of his adversary's preparations for trial," is present in every case and cannot be the substantial need required to overcome the immunity.[148] Nor, obviously, will mere relevance to a claim or defense suffice, or else substantial need would be redundant with the generic scope of discovery.[149] But the stronger the relevance and importance to the discoverer's claim or defense-in-chief, the more likely a court is to find this requirement satisfied.[150]

Hickman also demonstrates that *undue hardship* from denial of discovery cannot exist when a party has other reasonable access to the information. There the discoverer had access to contemporaneous sworn testimony and to the witnesses themselves. When matter is unavailable to the discoverer because the witnesses have died, moved beyond the reach of compulsory process, lost their memories, deviated from their prior testimony, or refused to cooperate, undue hardship can be established.[151] Similarly, the physical disappearance or alteration of evidence reflected in work product, such as photographs of skid marks or conditions at the

---

[146] Rule 26(b)(3) advisory committee's notes (1970). *See generally* § 10.03[3][b] (discoverability of impeachment material), *supra.*

[147] Rule 26(b)(3).

[148] *Alltmont v. United States*, 177 F.2d 971, 978 (3d Cir. 1949), *cert. denied*, 339 U.S. 967 (1950) (pre-rule decision).

[149] *See* § 10.03[1] (relevancy), *supra.*

[150] *See, e.g., Wheeling-Pittsburgh Steel Corp. v. Underwriters Labs., Inc.*, 81 F.R.D. 8 (N.D. Ill. 1978) (statistical data on damages could not be properly analyzed without discovery of work product consisting of methodology used in computing damages). *See generally* WRIGHT & MILLER § 2025.

[151] Rule 26(b)(3) advisory committee's note (1970). *See In re Int'l Sys. & Controls Corp. Sec. Litig.*, 693 F.2d 1235 (5th Cir. 1982) (noting memory loss and cost of obtaining information elsewhere as appropriate particularized showings to make out undue hardship). *See generally* Missy K. Atwood, Comment, *Rule 166b: The Discovery of Work Product Based on Substantial Need and Undue Hardship*, 42 BAYLOR L. REV. 573, 579–87 (1990) (surveying federal cases).

scene of an accident, may establish undue hardship — indeed, impossibility — in obtaining the substantial equivalent by other means.[152] More generally, any time that important facts are exclusively in the control of the discoveree, the undue hardship requirement should be satisfied.[153]

[c] Opinion Work Product[154]

Hickman implied that special protection was due an attorney's mental impressions and legal theories — what might be termed *opinion work product*. Rule 26(b)(3)(B) gave expression to this implication by providing that in ordering discovery of work product after the required showing has been made, the court "must protect against disclosure of the mental impressions, conclusions, opinions, or legal theories of a party's attorney or other representative concerning the litigation." The Rule therefore does not limit opinion work product just to opinions by an attorney, though it does not seemingly include opinions by parties themselves.

Many courts and commentators have read this clause to confer an absolute protection on opinion work product, citing the mandatory verb "shall" in the original rule (now a "must").[155] When factual and opinion work product are intermixed, a court can often protect the latter by inspecting the materials *in camera* (out of the presence of counsel seeking discovery) and ordering disclosure only of segregable factual materials.

Arguably, however, Rule 26(b)(3) does not expressly prohibit disclosure of opinion work product; it only commands the courts to "protect against disclosure." In *Upjohn Co. v. United States*,[156] the Supreme Court suggested that opinion materials merit "special protection" and cited Rule 26(b)(3) and *Hickman* for the proposition that such materials cannot be disclosed "simply" on the usual showing of substantial need and undue hardship.[157] The Court did not reach the question of what further showing might suffice. Lower federal courts have on rare occasions allowed discovery of even opinion work product when attorneys or other representatives are charged with coercion, malpractice, fraud, or crime, or when their opinions and impressions are pivotal to bad faith, limitations, laches, or estoppel issues in the lawsuit.[158] The additional showing that these cases apparently have in

---

[152] *See, e.g., Rackers v. Siegfried*, 54 F.R.D. 24 (W.D. Mo. 1971) (ordering discovery of insurance adjuster's measurements of skid marks).

[153] *See* MOORE § 26.70[5].

[154] Waits, note 145, *supra*; Note, *Protection of Opinion Work Product Under the Federal Rules of Civil Procedure*, 64 VA. L. REV. 333 (1978); Warren H. Smith, Comment, *The Potential for Discovery of Opinion Work Product Under Rule 26(b)(3)*, 64 IOWA L. REV. 103 (1978).

[155] *See, e.g., Duplan Corp. v. Moulinage et Retorderie de Chavanoz*, 509 F.2d 730 (4th Cir. 1974), *cert. denied*, 420 U.S. 997 (1975); *United States v. Chatham City Corp.*, 72 F.R.D. 640, 643 n.3 (S.D. Ga. 1976). *See generally* WRIGHT § 82.

[156] 449 U.S. 383 (1981).

[157] *Id.* at 401.

[158] *See, e.g., Holmgren v. State Farm Mut. Auto. Ins. Co.*, 976 F.2d 573 (9th Cir. 1992) (bad faith denial of insurance claim); *In re Sealed Case*, 676 F.2d 793, 807 (D.C. Cir. 1982) (crime/fraud); *Byers v. Burleson*, 100 F.R.D. 436, 439 (D.D.C. 1983) (limitations); *Donovan v. Fitzsimmons*, 90 F.R.D. 583 (N.D. Ill. 1981) (reliance on advice-of-counsel defense); *Bird v. Penn Cent. Co.*, 61 F.R.D. 43, 47 (E.D. Pa. 1973)

common is that the attorney's or other representative's opinions are themselves an issue in the lawsuit, for which evidence is unavailable by other means.

§ 10.06   EXPERTS[159]

[1]   In General

In *Hickman*, Justice Jackson observed that "[d]iscovery was hardly intended to enable a learned profession to perform its functions . . . on wits borrowed from the adversary."[160] Nor was discovery intended to enable attorneys to prepare for trial with experts borrowed from their adversaries. Indeed, the concern about freeloading discovery is especially acute in the case of experts retained in anticipation of litigation because of the substantial fees experts often demand. On the other hand, the complexity and importance of expert testimony at trial also presents a very real risk of surprise to opposing parties who have not had discovery of the expert.

The rules balance these concerns by differentiating between, on one hand, experts expected to testify at trial (*testifying experts*) and, on the other hand, those merely retained or specially employed in anticipation of trial who are not, however, expected to testify (*non-testifying experts*). Rule 26(a)(2) requires disclosure of the identity and expected testimony of the testifying experts and Rule 26(b)(4)(A) permits their depositions.[161] Rule 26(b)(4) conditionally protects the non-testifying experts from discovery absent a special showing.

Neither part of the rule, however, protects against discovery of an expert who acquires his information as an actor or viewer in the transactions or occurrences that give rise to the lawsuit.[162] Thus, the police officer who responds to the accident scene, the doctor who attends in the emergency room, and the mechanic who services the car whose brakes failed, are all just ordinary fact witnesses, subject to orthodox discovery under the rules, even though they may also be experts.[163]

(laches). *See generally* G. Michael Halfenger, Comment, *The Attorney Misconduct Exception to the Work Product Doctrine*, 58 U. Chi. L. Rev. 1079 (1991).

[159] *See generally* Kathleen M. Brennan, *Must the Show Go On? Defining When One Party May Call or Compel an Opposing Party's Consultative Expert to Testify*, 78 Minn. L. Rev. 1191 (1994); Michael H. Graham, *Expert Witness Testimony and the Federal Rules of Evidence: Insuring Adequate Assurance of Trustworthiness*, 1986 U. Ill. L. Rev. 43; Michael H. Graham, *Discovery of Experts Under Rule 26(b)(4) of the Federal Rules of Civil Procedure: Parts I & II*, 1976 U. Ill. L.F. 895, 1977 U. Ill. L.F. 169.

[160] 329 U.S. at 516 (Jackson, J., concurring).

[161] Discovery of reports of physical or mental examinations conducted pursuant to Rule 35 is governed separately by its provisions. *See* § 10.11 (procedure for taking physical and mental examinations), *infra*.

[162] Rule 26(b)(4) advisory committee's note (1970).

[163] *See, e.g., Nelco Corp. v. Slater Elec., Inc.*, 80 F.R.D. 411 (E.D.N.Y. 1978) (expert may be deposed as an "actor" in the events that are the subject of the litigation). Of course, the rule shields only the facts and opinions held by the expert. " 'It does not . . . excuse the party from disgorging what facts he may have in his possession' " or allow him to insulate those facts from discovery by giving them to an expert. *Marine Petroleum Co. v. Champlin Petroleum Co.*, 641 F.2d 984, 994 (D.C. Cir. 1980) (*quoting* J. Moore, Moore's Federal Practice ¶ 26.66[2] (2d ed. 1979)).

Rule 26 does not address per se the issue of discovery of experts who have been consulted in anticipation of litigation but not retained or specially employed.[164] The 1970 Advisory Committee's notes suggest that the omission was intentional, and that discovery of such experts, or even of their identity, is precluded.[165] The omission of any provision for discovery of generally employed non-testifying experts arguably creates the same inference. Some courts, however, have rejected that inference for such a "party-expert" on the grounds that he is more partisan than professionally objective.[166] If such an expert learned facts and acquired opinions in anticipation of litigation, however, any materials that he has generated reflecting those facts and opinions would presumably be independently protected from discovery by ordinary work product immunity.[167]

A 1991 amendment to Rule 45 may have modified this law by acknowledging the possibility of discovery of "unretained experts,"[168] subject to motions to quash or modify discovery or trial subpoenas. Prior to the amendment, some courts treated unretained and unconsulted experts as ordinary witnesses who are not exempt from the citizen's duty to give evidence. But the problem of freeloading noted above applies to such experts with special force. "[C]ompulsion to give evidence may threaten the intellectual property of [such] experts denied the opportunity to bargain for the value of their services," noted the 1991 Advisory Committee. Rule 45(c), therefore, now allows for motions to quash or modify any subpoena that requires "disclosing an unretained expert's opinion or information that does not describe specific occurrences in dispute and results from the expert's study that was not requested by a party" unless the requesting party can show substantial need for such testimony and undue hardship and assures that she will reasonably compensate the expert.

[2]   Testifying Experts

The 1970 Advisory Committee concluded that any prohibition of discovery from the testifying expert "produces in acute form the very evils that discovery has been created to prevent." The complexity of expert testimony and frequent prior experience of the testifying expert with the rigors of cross-examination require particularly careful preparation by the cross-examiner.[169] If a discovery bar

---

[164] *See* Brennan, note 159, *supra.*

[165] The 1970 Advisory Committee said that the rule "precludes discovery against experts who were informally consulted in preparation for trial, but not retained or specially employed. As an ancillary procedure, a party may on a proper showing require the other party to name experts retained or specially employed, but not those formally consulted."

[166] *See, e.g., Kan.-Neb. Natural Gas Co. v. Marathon Oil Co.,* 109 F.R.D. 12, 15–16 (D. Neb. 1985). For an especially thoughtful discussion of the issue, see also *Va. Elec. & Power Co. v. Sun Shipbuilding & Dry Dock Co.,* 68 F.R.D. 397, 406–10 (E.D. Va. 1975). *See generally* James R. Pielemeier, *Discovery of Non-Testifying "In-House" Experts Under Federal Rule of Civil Procedure 26,* 58 Ind. L.J. 597, 625 (1983) (arguing that "discovery of in-house experts should be treated in the same manner as discovery of 'retained or specially employed' experts" under Rule 26(b)(4)).

[167] *See* § 10.05 (work product), *supra.*

[168] Rule 45(c).

[169] These characteristics of expert testimony are aggravated in federal court by Federal Rule of Evidence 702, which permits an expert to give his opinion without prior disclosure of the underlying

handicaps that preparation, the careful lawyer will often compensate by going slow, over-preparing expert rebuttal testimony, or seeking a continuance to prepare in mid-trial, all in derogation of Rule 1's goal of a "just, speedy and inexpensive determination of every action and proceeding."

Rule 26 originally accommodated these concerns by allowing limited discovery of the testifying expert by interrogatories, with a possibility of discovery by deposition on court order. Because lawyers usually draft the answers to interrogatories, however,[170] this mode of discovery was often insufficient to prepare for the examination of expert witnesses. On the other hand, parties often overcame this problem by agreeing to reciprocal deposition discovery of their expert witnesses.

The 1993 amendment solved the problem by rule, and the solution has been preserved in subsequent amendments. Rule 26(a)(2) requires parties at least ninety days before trial (or at times directed by the court) to disclose the identity and report the expected testimony of their testifying experts. The required report must include a complete statement of the expert's opinion, as well as the basis and reasons for the opinion, any underlying data and supporting exhibits, the expert's qualifications and publications within the preceding ten years, the expert's compensation, and a listing of other cases in which the expert has testified in the preceding four years. The report, then, is intended to be the functional equivalent of the expert witness' testimony. It also includes precisely the kinds of information needed to cross-examine the witness effectively at trial. Rule 26(b)(4) also allows a party to depose a testifying expert without leave of court after the report is provided. These two discovery devices are expected to work together; a complete report may obviate or at least shorten the deposition of the expert witness.

Before the 2010 amendments, parties often sought discovery of their adversary's communications with their testimonial experts, including guidance letters and rough drafts. The potential discoverability of this material sometimes led to artificially constrained communications and satellite litigation. Rule 26(b)(4)(C) now protects communications between the party's lawyer and such experts, except those relating to compensation, facts, data, or assumptions provided by the lawyer to the expert that he considered in forming his opinion.

[3]   Retained or Specially Employed Non-Testifying Experts

There is less need for discovering facts known and opinions held by an expert who is not expected to testify at trial, at least when a party can reasonably consult or retain a comparable expert. Rule 26(b)(4) therefore permits discovery by interrogatories or deposition of "retained or specially employed" non-testifying experts only "on showing exceptional circumstances under which it is impracticable for the party to obtain facts or opinions on the same subject by other means." The discoverer can meet this burden by showing that the expert had a unique and irreplicable opportunity to view the scene or to conduct tests relevant to the

---

facts, contrary to the common law procedure. The opposing party may therefore have to bring out the factual predicate on cross-examination, a procedure with traps for the unprepared.

[170] *See* Rule 26(a)(2) advisory committee's note (1993); § 10.09[2], *infra.*

subject matter,[171] or, more rarely, that the expert is one of a kind. The mere fact that no other expert will hold precisely the same opinion is insufficient, if comparable experts are practically available to the discoverer.[172] Any court-ordered discovery of such a non-testifying expert is ordinarily conditioned on fee sharing.[173]

PART B.
Mechanics of Discovery

§ 10.07   REQUIRED DISCLOSURES AND OTHER GENERAL MECHANICS

Each of the federal modes of discovery has distinctive characteristics, explored in the succeeding sections. But most discovery also shares several common features, unless exempted by local rule, court order, or party stipulation under Rule 29. The parties (1) must begin the discovery process with a mandatory planning conference, (2) make certain disclosures thereafter without being asked in most cases, and (3) supplement the required disclosures and specified discovery responses at appropriate intervals.

[1] Mandatory Discovery Conference and Discovery Plans

Rule 29 has long permitted the parties to stipulate to the mechanics of most discovery, partly in the (often forlorn) hope that discovery could proceed cooperatively without a need for judicial intervention. In 1993, Rule 26(f) was amended to require the parties to confer as soon as practicable[174] to discuss the case and possibilities for settlement, to arrange for required disclosures, to discuss E-discovery issues (including "litigation holds" on data storage), and to develop a discovery plan incorporating these and other agreements for subsequent discovery. The term of art is "meet and confer," and a "meet-and-confer" is often handled by telephone or videoconference. Rule 26(d) forbids parties from taking any discovery prior to the meet-and-confer.[175]

---

[171] *See, e.g., Delcastor, Inc. v. Vail Assocs., Inc.*, 108 F.R.D. 405 (D. Colo. 1985) (expert's opinion concerning cause of mudslide is discoverable where he was the only expert to have examined mudslide area immediately following the slide).

[172] *Marine Petroleum Co.*, 641 F.2d at 996 (the rule's reference to the "same subject" is not to the particular expert's testimony itself, but rather to its subject matter).

[173] *See* Rule 26(b)(4)(C).

[174] Tracing the amended rule's circumlocutory statement of timing requirements suggests that parties will ordinarily have to meet within sixty-nine days of the appearance of a defendant or ninety-nine days after the complaint has been served. *Compare* Rule 16(b) (mandating issuance of discovery scheduling order within ninety days after the appearance of, or 120 days after the complaint was served on, any defendant), *with* Rule 26(f) (mandating planning conference at least twenty-one days before a scheduling order is due).

[175] Rule 27, however, permits discovery by deposition even before litigation commences in order to *perpetuate* (preserve) testimony regarding "any matter cognizable in" (within the subject matter jurisdiction of) a United States court. A person seeking such pre-complaint discovery must establish that

Within 14 days after the meet-and-confer, the parties must submit a report of their plan to the court. The rules anticipate that the plan will be incorporated into the scheduling order that the court is required by Rule 16(b) to issue within 120 days after the complaint has been served.

The mandatory meet-and-confer requirement was clearly intended to encourage cooperative discovery and thereby reduce the need for subsequent judicial intervention into the discovery process. A 2011 survey of 10,000 lawyers in civil cases confirmed that it has had some success. Seventy-two percent reported that they had participated in meet-and-confers to plan discovery (92% in cases in which the judge held a Rule 16(b) scheduling conference), and about the same percentage said that the meeting helped them arrange initial disclosures. Over half said it helped them to develop a proportionate discovery plan and to better understand the opposing party's claims or defenses.[176] Forty percent reported discussing E-discovery in the early met-and-confer, including preservation obligations.

[2]   Required Disclosures[177]

The 1993 rule amendments adopted provisions for self-executing discovery of three kinds: initial disclosures of basic information, disclosures of expert testimony (discussed above in section 10.06[2]), and pretrial disclosures of trial evidence. The provisions for required disclosures have teeth: a party who without substantial justification fails to disclose material subject to required disclosure is precluded under Rule 37(c)(1) from using that material as evidence at trial.

[a]   Initial Disclosures

Rule 26(a)(1) requires initial disclosure (within fourteen days after the Rule 26(f) discovery conference) of the basic information needed in most cases to prepare for trial or to assess settlement, except in eight categories of cases which historically involve little or no discovery.[178] This basic information is usually targeted anyway by discovery requests (if discovery is taken at all). The requirement is intended merely

---

the matter would be within the subject matter jurisdiction of a federal court, that he is presently unable for good cause to bring an action in any court, and that there is a substantial danger that the testimony sought would become unavailable before a complaint can be filed. *See, e.g.*, *In re Boland*, 79 F.R.D. 665 (D.D.C. 1978). Generally it is not sufficient reason that he does not know whether a claim exists; pre-action discovery is not intended to be a fishing expedition for a claim. *Id.* at 668 n.3. Rule 27(a) also requires the discoverer to describe the subject matter of the intended action, the facts he seeks to establish and why, and the identities of prospective adverse parties who are entitled to notice of pre-action depositions.

[176] EMERY G. LEE III, FED. JUDICIAL CTR., EARLY STAGES OF LITIGATION ATTORNEY SURVEY (2012).

[177] *See generally* Kuo-Chang Huang, *Mandatory Disclosure: A Controversial Device with No Effects*, 21 PACE L. REV. 203 (2000); Griffin B. Bell et al., *Automatic Disclosure in Discovery — The Rush to Reform*, 27 GA. L. REV. 1 (1992); Ralph K. Winter, *Foreword: In Defense of Discovery Reform*, 58 BROOKLYN L. REV. 263 (1992); Samuel Issacharof & George Loewenstein, *Unintended Consequences of Mandatory Disclosure*, 73 TEX. L. REV. 753 (1995); Thomas M. Mengler, *Eliminating Abusive Discovery Through Disclosure: Is It Again Time for Reform?*, 138 F.R.D. 155 (1991); Linda S. Mullenix, *Hope Over Experience: Mandatory Informal Discovery and the Politics of Rulemaking*, 69 N.C. L. REV. 795 (1991); William W. Schwarzer, *The Federal Rules, the Adversary Process, and Discovery Reform*, 50 U. PITT. L. REV. 703, 721–23 (1989).

[178] Rule 26(a)(1)(B) (including, for example, petitions for habeas corpus, actions to quash adminis-

to "accelerate the exchange of basic information" and "eliminate the paper work involved in requesting" it, according to the 1993 Advisory Committee.

Basic information covered by Rule 26(a)(1) includes the identity of possible fact witnesses, and identification of documents and reasonably accessible electronically stored information[179] in the possession, custody or control of a party, "that the disclosing party may use to support its claim or defenses, unless the use would be solely for impeachment." This is an important limitation: the rule does not require a party to disclose a document that would be a "smoking gun" for its adversary, but only documents that it would use to support its own case. Parties need not actually produce these documents; the purpose of initial disclosure is only to identify them to help the parties refine subsequent discovery requests. Moreover, voluminous documents may be identified by category. As to ESI, the required disclosure rule does not obligate a party to undertake an exhaustive review of its ESI, as its purpose is chiefly to enable opposing parties "to make an informed decision" about what information they might need to examine."[180] Instead, federal judges are told that it would suffice for a party to "identify the nature of its computer systems, including its backup system, network system, and e-mail system and the software applications used by them."[181] In short, initial disclosures under Rule 26(a)(1)(A)(i) and (ii) are the functional equivalent of responses to interrogatories asking a party to identify witnesses and documents or other tangible things relevant to allegations in the pleadings.[182] Rules 26(a)(1)(A)(iii) and (iv) require parties also to disclose computations of damages and to produce underlying documents and other evidence, as well as insurance agreements that may be used to satisfy all or part of a judgment which may be entered in the action.

The "use-to-support" relevancy standard for initial disclosures was added by amendment in 2000 to replace the more problematical original standard: "relevant to disputed facts alleged with particularity in the pleadings." The original standard was always somewhat at odds with the liberal "notice pleading" requirements of Rule 8,[183] and also with the usual chronology of litigation, in which it is the answer (often coming after initial disclosures are due) which places pleaded facts in dispute. Moreover, the original standard was also criticized for placing lawyers in an awkward conflict by forcing them to disclose unfavorable information to their adversaries.[184] The new standard alleviates these concerns. The amended rule specifically addresses the timing problem by providing that a party may object that initial disclosures are "not appropriate in [the] action" and then await the court's

---

trative subpoenas, and actions by the United States to recover benefit payments or collect student loans).

[179] The 2006 E-discovery amendments expressly provide that a party need not provide discovery of electronically data "from sources the party identifies as not reasonably accessible because of undue burden or cost." Rule 26(b)(2)(B). *See* § 10.03[e] (using pre-amendment decision in *Zubulake* as an example).

[180] BARBARA J. ROTHSTEIN, RONALD J. HEDGES & ELIZABETH C. WIGGINS, FEDERAL JUDICIAL CENTER, MANAGING DISCOVERY OF ELECTRONIC INFORMATION: A POCKET GUIDE FOR JUDGES 12 (2012).

[181] *Id.*

[182] Rule 26(a)(1) advisory committee's note (1993).

[183] Rule 9 identifies only a few categories of allegations which must be pled with particularity. *See* § 8.04[4] (discussing special pleading requirements).

[184] *See, e.g.*, Bell, note 177, *supra*, at 46 n.175.

ruling before making the disclosures. A party is no longer required to disclose to an adversary unfavorable information that it does not intend to use.[185] This not only reduces any alleged conflict for the disclosing lawyer, it also substantially narrows the scope[186] — and therefore burden — of the initial disclosures.

[b]   Pretrial Disclosures

In addition to the required disclosure of expert witness testimony (discussed in section 10.06[2]), the parties must exchange lists of trial witnesses and trial exhibits at least thirty days before trial. This disclosure includes not only witnesses and exhibits that a party expects to present at trial, but also those that the party may use if the need arises (other than any held in reserve solely for impeachment purposes). Fourteen days after the required exchange, the parties must serve and file any evidentiary objections they have to the materials that have been listed by the opposing parties. Objections not made (other than objections under Federal Rules of Evidence 402 (relevancy) and 403 (prejudice)) are waived.

These exchanges are not really discovery at all; they are more accurately viewed as part of the trial process. Indeed, before the 1993 amendment, many courts required such exchanges in connection with the final pretrial conference.[187] Such exchanges not only facilitate trial preparation, but also permit *in limine* (at the threshold of trial) rulings on the evidence that help streamline trial.

[3]   Supplementation of Discovery

The typical litigator has several cases pending at the same time. In each there may be substantial discovery. The burden of continuously reviewing old discovery responses for accuracy and updating them whenever new information becomes available would be great. On the other hand, a failure to supplement an incorrect, misleading or obsolete discovery response may give rise to the very surprise at trial that discovery was intended partly to avoid.

Rule 26(e) originally struck a compromise between these two concerns by imposing a quite limited duty of supplementation on party-discoverees. That compromise was partly undone by the 1993 rule amendments, which require a party to correct or complete its required disclosures (as well as any deposition given by its expert witness), if the additional or corrective information has not already been made known to other parties. This expanded duty to supplement is as broad as the scope of required disclosures. It obligates a lawyer to keep track of all information that might make previous disclosures incomplete or incorrect in any respect.

Rule 26(e) extends the same duty to prior responses to an interrogatory, request for production, or request for admission. The lawyer must therefore also monitor

---

[185] Rule 26(a)(1) advisory committee notes (2000). "Use" is not limited to trial; it includes any use at pretrial conferences or to support a motion. Bell, note 177, *supra*, at 46 n.175.

[186] Carl Tobias, *Congress and the 2000 Federal Civil Rules Amendments*, 22 Cardozo L. Rev. 75, 79 (2000).

[187] *See* § 12.03[2] (procedures for pretrial conferences), *infra*.

the completeness and correctness of such responses throughout the lawsuit. Only responses given in deposition (except depositions by expert witnesses) are exempted, presumably on the theory that these are often given by non-party witnesses and that monitoring them would be extremely burdensome, if not impossible.

Ordinarily, only incurably prejudicial breaches of the rule will support sanctions or constitute grounds for relief from judgment.[188] A common sanction for breach of the duty to supplement is exclusion at trial of evidence withheld by the discoveree.[189] This sanction is inappropriate, however, if a continuance and opportunity for mid-trial discovery can enable the discoverer to overcome his surprise and prepare effective cross-examination and rebuttal.[190]

§ 10.08 DEPOSITIONS

[1] Procedure for Taking

A deposition is the recorded examination of a live witness under oath by oral or written questions before a qualified oath administrator,[191] who is usually a court reporter.[192] The deposition may be recorded by sound, sound-and-visual, or stenographic means at the expense of the taker. In a Rule 30 deposition upon oral questions, an attorney asks the questions and the deponent answers spontaneously, like an examination of a witness at trial. In a Rule 31(a) deposition upon written questions, the discoverer serves his direct questions on the deponent and the other parties in advance, after which any cross, redirect or recross questions[193] are served. The oath administrator reads the written questions to the deponent, who answers them live, if not quite spontaneously (given the prior opportunity to rehearse the answers). Interrogatories differ from the deposition upon written

---

[188] *See, e.g., Johnson v. H. K. Webster, Inc.*, 775 F.2d 1, 7–8 (1st Cir. 1985). For discussion of the rule of prejudicial error, see § 13.09[1], *infra*.

[189] *See, e.g., Scott & Fetzer Co. v. Dile*, 643 F.2d 670 (9th Cir. 1981) (failure to list 20 of 23 trial witnesses and 26 of 51 exhibits in response to interrogatories prejudicially denied the discoverer the right to prepare effective cross-examination and rebuttal and requires their exclusion, especially where the undisclosed witnesses included an expert witness and were used to support a previously undisclosed theory of the case).

[190] *See, e.g., Moore v. Boating Indus. Ass'ns*, 754 F.2d 698 (7th Cir. 1985); *Lewis Refrigeration Co. v. Sawyer Fruit, Vegetable & Cold Storage Co.*, 709 F.2d 427 (6th Cir. 1983); *Gebhard v. Niedzwiecki*, 122 N.W.2d 110, 115 (Minn. 1963) (suggesting that preclusion is proper when the violation is willful and the discoveree seeks to benefit from it "at a time when the harm cannot be undone").

[191] *See* Rule 28 (persons before whom depositions may be taken).

[192] Depositions traditionally have been recorded by a court reporter. Rule amendments eventually liberalized the requirements for taking of depositions by non-stenographic means. *See* Rules 30(b)(3)–(4). The parties no longer need to agree to non-stenographic means or obtain a court order; such means are available *unless* the court orders otherwise. Parties must still stipulate to or obtain a court order for taking depositions by telephone or other remote electronic means. *See* Rule 30(b)(4).

[193] Direct examination is a party's questioning of his own witness. Cross-examination is questioning of a witness called by an opposing party. Redirect is direct examination of a witness after cross-examination. Recross is cross-examination of a witness after redirect. *See generally* McCormick on Evidence § 4 (J. Strong, 4th ed. 1992).

questions partly in that answers to interrogatories are written and often prepared by a party's attorney.[194]

A party does not ordinarily need leave of court to take a deposition unless the deposition would exceed the seven-hour durational limit set by Rule 30(d)(1), or the ten-deposition numerical limit established by Rule 30(a)(2)(A)(i), or the deponent is being noticed for a second deposition. The procedure for orally deposing a party under Rule 30 is simply to serve the party-deponent and all other parties with reasonable written notice of the time and place of the deposition and identity of the party-deponent,[195] as well as a Rule 34 request for production of documents when documents are sought in connection with the deposition.[196] A party must comply with the notice or seek a protective order[197] because, by the initial service of process on her, she has already been subjected to the personal jurisdiction of the court and therefore brought within the reach of properly invoked procedural rules.

This is not true of a non-party witness, however. To compel the attendance at deposition of a non-party witness, the discoverer must first procure the issuance of a *subpoena*[198] from the court for the district in which the deposition will be taken.[199] The non-party witness may ask the court to quash or modify the subpoena if it allows insufficient time for compliance, necessitates excessive travel, requires disclosure of protected or confidential information, or subjects the witness to undue burden.[200]

Under Rule 30(b)(6), a party may name as a deponent in his notice and subpoena a corporation, agency, partnership or other legal entity and describe the matters on which examination is requested. The entity must then designate one or more officers, directors, managing agents, or other persons with relevant knowledge to testify on its behalf. As noted below[201] the deposition of a person so designated may be offered at trial as direct evidence against the designating entity. Rule 30(b)(6)'s legislative history suggests that it was intended simply as a device to facilitate the discovery of appropriate witnesses who could provide further discovery regarding an institutional litigant, in order "to defeat a shield of obfuscation and inefficiency that could be thrown up by . . . [such a] litigant."[202] Instead, it has sometimes been misused to force such litigants to create a witness

---

[194] *See* § 10.09 (interrogatories), *infra.*

[195] Rule 30(b)(1). The notice must be accompanied by the direct questions in the case of a deposition upon written questions. Rule 31(a).

[196] Rule 30(b)(2).

[197] *See* § 10.13[3] (protective orders), *infra.*

[198] *See* Rule 45. A *subpoena duces tecum* must be used if document production is sought in connection with the deposition.

[199] Rules 30(a) & 45. Many states provide for the issuance of subpoenas for depositions to be used in proceedings pending in other states. *See e.g.*, Ariz. R. Civ. Proc. 30(h) (2001); Me. R. Civ. Proc. 30(h) (2001).

[200] Rule 45(c)(3).

[201] *See* § 10.08[2] (use and value of depositions), *infra.*

[202] Kent Sinclair & Roger P. Fendrich, *Discovering Corporate Knowledge and Contentions: Rethinking Rule 30(b)(6) and Alternative Mechanisms*, 50 Ala. L. Rev. 651, 749 (1999).

who can give a "grand synthesis" of evidence to bind the litigant.[203] On the other hand, courts have held that the designating party has a duty to prepare its designee to answer questions on the described matters — you can't just designate a stone.[204]

The chief difference between the conduct of a deposition upon oral questions and examination of a witness at trial is the absence of the trial judge. Consequently, objections to the competency of the witness or to the competency, relevancy, or materiality of testimony are preserved until trial, when the judge can rule upon them. Rule 32(d)(3)(A) expressly states that they are not waived by a failure to make them at the deposition. In contrast, objections to errors which "might have been corrected at that time" are waived if not seasonably made before or during the deposition.[205] These include objections to the qualifications of the presiding officer; to errors and irregularities in the notice; to the manner of taking the deposition; to the oath or affirmation; to the conduct of the parties; or to the form of the questions. For example, "when did you stop beating your wife [or husband]?" is objectionable as to form, for it assumes a predicate. But the objection could be obviated by reforming the question as several separate questions: "Did you beat your wife [husband]?; [if yes] did you stop?; [if yes] when?"[206] If the objecting party could defer the objection to this question until the deposition is offered at trial, it could deprive the examiner of an opportunity to reform the question. Consequently, if no objection is made to the form of the question at the time of the deposition, the objection is waived and lost should the resulting testimony be offered at trial.

Despite the preservation of most objections until the proffer of deposition testimony as evidence at trial, some lawyers assert them during the deposition anyway, not only to create a technically unnecessary record, but sometimes also to educate the witness or obstruct the examination. Indeed, some lawyers instruct the witness not to answer some questions that do not call for privileged information, in effect daring the examiner to halt the deposition to seek judicial assistance. Amendments to Rule 30 now discourage both tactics by requiring objections to be made concisely and in a "nonargumentative and nonsuggestive manner," and by forbidding instructions not to answer except when necessary to preserve a privilege, comply with a court order, or to present a motion to limit or terminate the deposition.[207] Rule 30(d)(3) authorizes a court to grant such a motion upon a showing that the examination is being conducted oppressively or in bad faith.[208]

---

[203] *Id.*

[204] *See Int'l Ass'n of Machinists & Aerospace Workers v. Werner-Matsuda Corp.*, 390 F. Supp. 2d 479 (D. Md. 2005); WRIGHT & MILLER § 2103 (2008 Pocket Part).

[205] Rules 32(d)(3)(A) & (B).

[206] *See generally* McCORMICK ON EVIDENCE, note 193, *supra*, at § 5-7.

[207] Rule 30(c)(2).

[208] Indeed, some courts have held that the Rule 30(d) procedure is the exclusive remedy and censured a lawyer who directed his client not to answer obnoxious questions when that direction was not necessary to preserve any privilege. *See Redwood v. Dobson*, 476 F.3d 462, 469 (7th Cir. 2007) ("instructions not to respond that neither shielded a privilege nor supplied time to apply for a protective order were

The amended rule does not deal directly with a similar deposition tactic: mid-deposition coaching of deponents in private lawyer-client discussions. Some courts, however, are inferring authority from the rules to combat this tactic.[209] Complaining that "[t]he witness comes to the deposition to testify, not to indulge in a parody of Charlie McCarthy [the puppet used by famous ventriloquist, Edgar Bergen], with lawyers coaching or bending the witness's words to mold a convenient record," one court has prohibited private lawyer-client discussions during depositions and deposition recesses, except for the limited purpose of deciding whether to assert a privilege.[210] This court's order, like amended Rule 30(c)(2), reflects the proposition that "[i]n general, counsel should not engage in any conduct during a deposition that would not be allowed in the presence of a judicial officer."[211]

At the completion of the deposition, a transcript of the recorded examination may be prepared by a court reporter or by any party, according to Rule 30(e). On request by the deponent or a party, the transcript is submitted to the deponent for correction and signature. The presiding officer is then responsible for sealing the deposition with her certificate and filing it in the court in which the action is pending or sending it to the lawyer who noticed (that is, served the notice of) the deposition, along with the originals or copies of any documents marked for identification during the deposition.[212]

[2]   Use and Value of Depositions

Under Rule 32(a) any or all of a deposition may be used at trial, as if the witness were then present and testifying, against any party who had notice of the deposition and a reasonable opportunity to obtain counsel or to move for a protective order. The proponent of the deposition testimony may offer it in stenographic form, or in nonstenographic form if he also provides the court and the parties with a transcript. Indeed, Rule 32(c) allows any party to a jury trial to demand that deposition testimony offered as substantive evidence be presented in nonstenographic form, when it is available. When a party offers only part of a deposition in evidence, she designates the relevant part and submits it to the judge in a bench trial or causes it to be read or played to the jury in a jury trial. Under Rule 32(a)(6), an adverse party may require the proponent to introduce additional parts "that in fairness should be considered with the part introduced."

---

unprofessional and violated the Federal Rules of Civil Procedure as well as the ethical rules that govern legal practice.").

[209] On deposition ethics generally, see Fern C. Bomchill, *Restoring Civility*, 58 Fed. Law. 3 (Nov./Dec. 2011); A. Darby Dickerson, *The Law and Ethics of Civil Depositions*, 57 Md. L. Rev. 273 (1998); Janeen Kerper & Gary L. Stuart, *Rambo Bites the Dust: Current Trends in Deposition Ethics*, 22 J. Legal Prof. 103 (1997–1998); Jean M. Cary, *Rambo Depositions: Controlling an Ethical Cancer in Civil Litigation*, 25 Hofstra L. Rev. 561 (1996). Some jurisdictions have adopted voluntary "civility codes" to deal with this and related problems of "Rambo" tactics in civil litigation, *see, e.g.*, D.C. Bar Voluntary Standards for Civility in Professional Conduct (1997), but there is yet little evidence that they have changed the adversarial dynamics which seem to breed such tactics.

[210] *Hall v. Clifton Precision*, 150 F.R.D. 525, 528 (E.D. Pa. 1993).

[211] Rule 30(d) advisory committee's note (1993).

[212] Rule 30(f).

Hearsay is an out-of-court statement offered in evidence to prove the truth of the matter stated.[213] The rule against the admissibility of hearsay would thus appear to prohibit the offer of deposition testimony at trial unless it falls within one of the rule's many exceptions. By providing that the deposition is to be tested for admissibility as if it were given live, however, Rule 32(a) is itself an exception to the rule against hearsay.[214] The rule echoes the Federal Rules of Evidence by permitting the use of deposition testimony to impeach or contradict the deponent as a witness,[215] or as an admission of an adverse party or officer, director, managing agent or designated deponent of an adverse party.[216] In addition, Rule 32(a) permits the use of deposition testimony at trial when the deponent is unavailable because of death, illness, age, imprisonment or is beyond the reach of process.

However, Rule 32 only overcomes the initial hearsay hurdle to the use of a deposition at all. Even when a deposition clears this first hurdle, the rules of evidence still apply to admission of its contents.

> Speaking metaphorically, a deposition is like a box that contains certain evidence. The court must make two determinations. The first is a procedural one: whether to admit the box itself into the trial. In making this assessment, the court applies . . . [Rule 32 or its state equivalent]. Once the court has decided that the deposition meets these procedural requirements, the court then must address the ancillary evidentiary issues such as whether the contents of the box qualifies as admissible evidence. This step is akin to opening the box, assessing its content and then ruling on its admissibility.[217]

The availability of a deposition in lieu of live testimony helps to make it the most valuable method of discovery. So does its flexibility. The contemporaneity of the examination upon oral questions permits the discoverer to frame follow-up questions, pursue new and unanticipated leads, observe demeanor, and pin down witnesses in order to foreclose factual arguments or at least lay a foundation for later impeachment.[218] Finally, the deposition usually is the only method of discovery available against non-party witnesses to elicit testimonial evidence.[219]

---

[213] FED. R. EVID. 801(c).

[214] WRIGHT § 84.

[215] Compare Rule 32(a)(2) with FED. R. EVID. 801(d)(1) (prior inconsistent statement is not hearsay).

[216] Compare Rule 32(a)(3) with Fed. R. Evid. 801(d)(2) (admission by party-opponent is not hearsay). Who is a managing agent for purposes of this provision is decided pragmatically, depending on the scope of the deponent's job responsibilities, assigned discretion and identification with an employer's interests. See generally HAYDOCK & HERR, note 11, supra, § 3.10.1; cf. M. Minnette Massey, Depositions of Corporations: Problems and Solutions — Fed. R. Civ. P. 30(b)(6), 1986 ARIZ. ST. L.J. 81.

[217] Shives v. Furst, 521 A.2d 332, 335–36 (Md. Ct. Spec. App. 1987). See WRIGHT & MILLER § 2142.

[218] See generally HAYDOCK & HERR, note 11, supra, § 3.1.1; Hall, 150 F.R.D. at 528 (noting that depositions serve the purpose of "the memorialization, the freezing, of a witness's testimony at an early stage of the proceedings").

[219] A subpoena can be used to require a non-party witness to produce documents for inspection. See Rule 45.

On the other hand, the chief drawback of depositions is their expense. Not only do they consume enormous amounts of attorney time in preparation, travel and taking, but court reporter fees and travel expenses can also mount quickly, putting extensive deposition discovery beyond the reach of many litigants. In addition, a deposition can educate the deponent, provide a useful rehearsal of examination at trial for the deponent and opposing parties, and of course, elicit and perpetuate unhelpful testimony.[220] On balance, however, almost all practitioners would agree that these drawbacks of deposition discovery are outweighed by its advantages.

§ 10.09 INTERROGATORIES

[1] Procedure for Asking

Interrogatories are written questions directed to a party, who must answer them in writing and under oath, or (by his attorney) object with particularity. Although the client often supplies all or part of the underlying facts, his attorney usually prepares the answers and the client signs. If the answering party is an entity, an officer or employee of the entity signs on its behalf. The lawyer may also object to an interrogatory, and interpose a written objection instead of answering. If the objection is to the entire set of interrogatories on grounds of undue burden, it can also be made by a motion for a protective order under Rule 26(c).[221]

Interrogatories target not just what is known by the discoveree, but also what is reasonably obtainable by him — "the collective knowledge" of the recipient.[222] The rule expressly states that an institutional party "must furnish the information available to the party," but a party who is a natural person cannot answer with an "empty head" either, because Rule 26(g) imposes a duty of reasonable inquiry on the person who signs answers, analogous to Rule 11's duty for persons who sign other written submissions to court.[223] In short, an answering party is charged with knowledge of what his agents know, or what is in records available to him, or even what others have told him on which he intends to rely in his suit.[224]

On the other hand, interrogatories do not require the answering party to do the requesting party's work for him by undertaking elaborate investigations, discovery and data compilation.[225] The standard is reasonableness under the circumstances. Moreover, when the answer to an interrogatory can be ascertained from the answering party's business records (including ESI) as easily by the requesting party from those records as by the answering party, the latter has the option under Rule 33(d) of specifying the relevant records and making them available in lieu of

---

[220] *See generally* HAYDOCK & HERR, note 11, *supra*, § 3.1.2.

[221] MOORE § 33.175.

[222] HAYDOCK & HERR, note 11, *supra*, § 4.6.1.

[223] *See* § 10.13[1] (certification), *infra*.

[224] WRIGHT § 86. *See, e.g., Brunswick Corp. v. Suzuki Motor Co.*, 38 Fed. R. Serv. 2d (Callaghan) 1246, 1248 (E.D. Wis. 1983); *Riley v. United Air Lines, Inc.*, 32 F.R.D. 230, 233 (S.D.N.Y. 1962). Rule 26(b)'s limits on the scope of discovery still apply, including the qualified immunity for work product. *See* § 10.05, *supra*.

[225] *See, e.g., La Chemise Lacoste v. Alligator Co.*, 60 F.R.D. 164 (D. Del. 1973).

answer. The specification requirement precludes the tactic of referring the discoverer to an undifferentiated haystack of records in which the needle may be buried.

There are no special limitations on the form or subject of interrogatories apart from the generic limitations of Rule 26(b). But under Rule 33(b)(2) a court may postpone the time for answering *contention interrogatories*[226] which require the answering party to apply the law to the facts (e.g., "Do you contend that the plaintiff assumed the risk of the collision?"), because he may not know what his contentions will be until completion of discovery or a late pre-trial conference.[227] Were the rule otherwise, the answering party might be forced into a premature statement of what his legal contentions *will be*, evoking shades of the now-discarded theory of the pleadings.[228] In contrast, requiring the party after discovery and on the eve of trial to state what his contentions *are* at that point is not only fairer but conducive to issue-narrowing and surprise-avoidance at trial. Indeed, the parties are sometimes required to exchange their contentions in pre-trial briefs anyway,[229] whether or not contention interrogatories are pending.

The 1970 Advisory Committee concluded that interrogatories had generated a greater percentage of objections and motions than any other discovery method. Probably the most common objection is that they are *unduly burdensome*. The reason for the frequency of this objection is obvious. The answering party is ordinarily inclined to read interrogatories narrowly and against their drafter. Knowing this, and not sure what information is out there, the requesting party drafts numerous and sweeping interrogatories to defeat narrow constructions. As a result, just the sheer number of interrogatories can create an undue burden on the answering party. That burden may even be aggravated by indiscriminate use of *pattern* or *form interrogatories* — standardized, formbook interrogatories for particular kinds of cases[230] — and by multiplication of interrogatories by means of elaborate definitions. Overbreadth is also a common ground for an undue burden objection. Yet a litany of terms like "overly broad, burdensome, oppressive and irrelevant" does not satisfy Rule 33(b)(4)'s requirement that the grounds for the objection be stated with specificity. The answering party should specify by affidavit his claim of undue burden.[231]

---

[226] *See In re Convergent Techs. Sec. Litig.*, 108 F.R.D. 328, 332 (N.D. Cal. 1985) (defining different kinds of contention interrogatories).

[227] *Id.* at 333–34.

[228] *See* § 8.03[2] (theory of pleadings), *supra*.

[229] *See* § 12.03[1] (pretrial), *infra*.

[230] *See, e.g., Robbins v. Camden City Bd. of Educ.*, 105 F.R.D. 49 (D.N.J. 1985) (259 interrogatories were repetitious and objectionable as a result of discoverer's nonspecific use of several sets of pattern interrogatories); *Blank v. Ronson Corp.*, 97 F.R.D. 744, 745 (S.D.N.Y. 1983) (sanctions may be appropriate when interrogatories have been produced by "some word-processing machine's memory of prior litigation"). There is nothing wrong with the discriminating use of pattern interrogatories as long as they are tailored to the facts of the particular case. *See* HAYDOCK & HERR, note 11, *supra*, § 4.4.4.

[231] *See, e.g., Roesberg v. Johns-Manville Corp.*, 28 Fed. R. Serv. 2d (Callaghan) 1170 (E.D. Pa. 1980); *In re Folding Carton Antitrust Litig.*, 83 F.R.D. 260, 264 (N.D. Ill. 1979).

The 1993 amendments to the discovery rules were intended to reduce the need for and abuse of interrogatory practice. "Because Rule 26(a)(1)–(3) requires disclosure of much of the information previously obtained by [interrogatories]," the 1993 Advisory Committee reasoned, "there should be less occasion to use [them]." In addition, a party may now ask no more than twenty-five interrogatories (including all discrete subparts) without leave of court.[232] Finally, Rule 33(b) now requires a party not only to state the grounds for objections with specificity, but to answer "to the extent [the interrogatory] is not objected to."

[2] Use and Value of Interrogatories

Rule 33(c) provides that answers to interrogatories may be used to the extent permitted by the rules of evidence. They can therefore usually be used *against* the answering party as a party admission, but not *by* him as substantive evidence. They do not ordinarily bind or limit proof by the answering party, who may depart from them, modify them, or attempt to explain them away at trial.[233] But in the exceptional case of the requesting party's reasonable and detrimental reliance on the answers, the courts have used concepts of estoppel or preclusion to give greater effect to interrogatory answers by holding the answering party to them.[234]

The chief appeal of discovery by interrogatories is that they are a cheap way to access the collective knowledge of a party. Some have called them the poor man's deposition. For two reasons, however, this tag is unwarranted. First, their economy is one-sided and therefore often only temporary. It is cheap for the requesting party to prepare a set of interrogatories, but often time-consuming and expensive for the attorney for the answering party to draft answers to them. Once reciprocal discovery by interrogatories is initiated, these costs are reversed. Second, the attorney will often find some colorable objection to the most difficult interrogatories or draft answers that are as unhelpful as he can make them. Consequently, a federal judge has described interrogatories as "useless because any lawyer who can't answer interrogatories without giving [an] opponent useful information is not worth his salt."[235]

This critique is exaggerated. The attorney's role in drafting answers will usually make interrogatories ineffective to discover subjective and interpretative information, including state of mind, or complex information that will require

---

[232] Rule 33(a). How much this numerical limitation will reduce litigation about interrogatories is unclear. In the past such numerical limits have generated arid controversies about how multi-part interrogatories should count towards the limit. The Advisory Committee tried to anticipate this problem by noting that "a question asking about communications of a particular type should be treated as a single interrogatory even though it requests that the time, place, persons present, and contents be stated separately for each such communication."

[233] Rule 33(b) advisory committee's note (1970).

[234] *See generally* Moore § 37.96. *Cf., e.g., Zielinski v. Philadelphia Piers, Inc.*, 139 F. Supp. 408 (E.D. Pa. 1956) (relying on estoppel-type theory to preclude defendant from introducing evidence on an issue as to which plaintiff was misled by defendant's interrogatory answers), discussed in § 8.08[1], *supra*.

[235] Quoted in Brazil, *View from the Front Line: Observations by Chicago Lawyers About the System of Civil Discovery*, 1980 A.B.A. Found. Res. J. 217, 233. *See also In re Convergent Techs.*, 108 F.R.D. at 338.

explanation.[236] On the other hand, well-drafted interrogatories can be effectively used to pinpoint the existence and location of witnesses and evidence not already disclosed pursuant to Rule 26(a), to make more specific the factual basis for pleading allegations, and (towards the end of the discovery period) to narrow the issues.

§ 10.10   PRODUCTION AND ENTRY REQUESTS

[1]   Procedure for Making

Rule 34(a) authorizes the discoverer to request that a party produce and permit the inspection and copying of documents or ESI, or the copying, testing, or sampling of things, or entry upon land. A request must designate the documents, things or land with reasonable particularity and specify the time, place and manner of production or entry.[237] At the specified time and place, the discoveree must either permit inspection or entry, or object by item, specifying her grounds. A mere "litany of . . . boilerplate objections," however, is insufficient because it fails to show specifically how a discovery request is burdensome or oppressive by affidavit or other evidence substantiating the objections.[238] An objection to a requested form for producing ESI is expressly allowed.[239]

A Rule 34 production request embraces not only that which is in the possession of the discoveree but also documents and property within her custody or control.[240] *Control* means that the discoveree has a legal right to the document or thing or to enter upon the land.[241] The discoveree cannot avoid production by giving possession of a document or thing to an agent, such as her attorney. The rule thus embraces items in the actual or constructive possession of the discoveree, whether or not she owns them.

The requested documents or things must be described with sufficient clarity for a party of ordinary intelligence to understand what is meant and for the court to determine whether the items have been produced.[242] This task may be made somewhat easier by the disclosures required by Rule 26(a).[243] The 1993 Advisory Committee reasoned that these required disclosures will enable parties to "frame

---

[236] HAYDOCK & HERR, note 11, *supra*, § 4.6.

[237] *See* Form 50.

[238] *See, e.g., St. Paul Reinsurance Co., Ltd. v. Commercial Fin. Corp.*, 198 F.R.D. 508, 514 (N.D. Iowa 2000) (imposing Rule 26(g) sanction for such objections, by requiring objecting lawyer to write and submit for publication an article explaining why they were improper).

[239] Rule 34(b)(2)(D). *See* § 10.03[4][b], *supra*.

[240] *See, e.g., Weck v. Cross*, 88 F.R.D. 325 (N.D. Ill. 1980). *See generally* Note, *Meaning of "Control" in Federal Rules of Civil Procedure 34 Defined to Protect Policy Underlying Trading with Enemy Act*, 107 U. PA. L. REV. 103 (1958).

[241] *See Searock v. Stripling*, 736 F.2d 650, 653–54 (11th Cir. 1984).

[242] *See In re Hunter Outdoor Prods., Inc.*, 21 Bankr. 188 (Bankr. D. Mass. 1982) (specification inadequate when it requires discoveree to form subjective opinion in order to determine what is requested). *See generally* HAYDOCK & HERR, note 11, *supra*, § 5.8.

[243] *See* § 10.07[2], *supra*.

their document requests in a manner likely to avoid squabbles resulting from the wording of the requests." Rule 34(b) also expressly permits designation of items by category.

The practice is to arrange categories by subject matter and to cross-reference all documents identified by required disclosures or in answers to any prior interrogatories. The discoveree should ordinarily produce or object in kind, by item or category, but the practice is often to produce documents *en masse*. The 1980 amendment to Rule 34(b) prohibited the deliberate burial of potentially useful documents among the undifferentiated mass by requiring the discoveree to produce documents "as they are kept in the usual course of business" or by the categories of the request.

This requirement, however, had uncertain application to ESI. Did it mean "native forms," including metadata, or the form in which the responding party itself used the data? Did it include the code for interpreting that data, if one is needed? Rule 34's reference to "translation . . . by the responding party into a reasonably usable form" suggests an affirmative answer, but production of codes may raise trade secret issues calling for protective orders from the court. Can the producing party simply produce the ESI in hard copy form, denying the requesting party the ability to manipulate the data without, at least, incurring the burden of manually inputting the hard copy data back into electronic form?

Rule 34(b)(2)(E) now attempts to answer these questions by providing that if the requesting party does not specify a form of production, "a party must produce it in a form or forms in which it is ordinarily maintained or in a reasonably usable form or forms," but need not produce it in more than one form.[244]

That helps, but it is unlikely to resolve the infinite number of permutations that evolving ESI will throw up. Here again, the rules look primarily to the court and the parties themselves, in discovery conference, to work out the answers.[245]

Production requests and requests for entry upon land may be directed only to parties. But Rule 45 allows the issuance of subpoenas for document production by non-parties. Prior to the amendment of this rule in 1991, the primary method of obtaining documents from non-parties was deposing the custodian of the documents. This cumbersome technique is no longer necessary. A subpoena to compel production of documents by a non-party independent of any deposition is now essentially the equivalent of a Rule 34 request for production of documents by a party. The chief differences lie in the geographic reach of subpoenas (limited to places within the district of the issuing court, within 100 miles of the place of production or inspection therein, or a place allowed by relevant state or federal statute or state court rule)[246] and in the procedure for objecting to a subpoena

---

[244] *See generally* WRIGHT & MILLER § 2219 (2008 Pocket Part). For example, in *Autotech Techs. Ltd. P'ship v. AutomationDirect.com, Inc.*, 248 F.R.D. 556 (N.D. Ill. 2008), the defendant had not specified the form of the data, and plaintiff responded by producing it in PDF and paper format. Realizing belatedly that this format deprived it of the metadata, defendant moved to compel production of an electronic copy in "native format" — with the metadata. Citing the new rule, the court denied the motion.

[245] *See generally supra* § 10.03[4].

[246] Rule 45(b)(2) & (c)(3)(B)(iii).

(motions to quash or modify).[247]

[2] Use and Value of Production and Entry Requests

The fruits of production and entry requests can be used at trial subject to the rules of evidence. The practice is often to procure the producing party's agreement at the time of production to the use of copies in lieu of the originals at trial, obviating one evidentiary objection.

The production request is the most frequently used discovery device, as well as one which generates a high percentage of discovery problems.[248] Production requests are widely used as a step in discovery prior to depositions. They can be highly productive relative to their cost, although, like interrogatories, they generate a large number of undue burden objections. In addition, production requests frequently provoke objections of attorney-client privilege and work product immunity, leading to motions to compel and attendant hearings with occasional *in camera* inspection of the disputed documents by a judge or magistrate. Finally, as discussed above, requests for ESI have produced their own rising flood of issues and costs, at the same time that the ubiquity of ESI has made such requests even more valuable in many cases.

§ 10.11 PHYSICAL AND MENTAL EXAMINATIONS

[1] Procedure for Taking

When the physical or mental condition of a party (or person in the custody or legal control of a party) is in controversy, a court may on motion and for good cause shown order her to undergo a physical or mental examination under Rule 35. Together with Rule 27 (prelitigation deposition), discovery that exceeds the numerical limits on depositions or interrogatories, and discovery of matters going beyond claims or defenses, this discovery method requires a court order and a showing of good cause. These requirements and the limitation of examinations to conditions in controversy reflect the strong privacy interest counterbalancing this form of discovery.[249] The same privacy interest is reflected in Rule 37(b)(2)(A)(vii), which makes contempt of court available for disobedience of any discovery order *except* a Rule 35 order. Similar concerns have created considerable variety among the states in their rules for discovery by physical or mental examination.[250]

---

[247] Rule 45(c). Of course, a person responding to a subpoena may withhold a document on a claim of privilege or work product, provided that the claim is made expressly and with sufficient foundation to enable the discoverer to contest the claim. Rule 45(d)(2).

[248] *FJC Survey*, note 176, *supra*, at 554 (reporting that higher percentage of lawyers reported problems in document discovery than in initial disclosures, expert disclosure, or depositions).

[249] The Supreme Court has ruled that these interests do not make Rule 35 "substantive" for purposes of compliance with the Rules Enabling Act. *Sibbach v. Wilson & Co.*, 312 U.S. 1 (1941). *See* §§ 7.04[2]–[3] (state law and federal rules of civil procedure), *supra*.

[250] *See, e.g.*, CAL. CIV. PROC. CODE § 2032 (2001) (expressly includes agents of a party, unlike Rule 35); Md. R. Civ. Proc. 2-423 (1993) (providing that court order may regulate filing and distribution of

Rule 35(a) limits those who are subject to discovery by examination to parties or persons in a party's *custody or legal control*.[251] In light of the privacy concern, the legal control limitation of Rule 35(a) has been read much more narrowly than the roughly comparable provision of Rule 34 for requests for production and entry. Minor children are in the custody of their parents for purposes of examination when the parents sue for injuries to their children.[252] It is less clear whether a wife is within the legal control of her husband when he sues for injuries to her.[253] But a party's agent, such as a driver/employee in a personal injury action arising from a traffic accident, is usually not within the party's legal control.[254]

The showing that the condition is in controversy must establish more than relevancy. The condition is usually put in controversy by the pleadings. A complaint to recover for personal injuries is the classic illustration, putting in controversy the related condition of the plaintiff. But the requisite controversy is also shown when the condition contributes to the accident, bears on performance of a contract or other obligation, is the subject of an alleged libel to which truth is asserted as a defense, or is asserted as a defense of incompetency.[255]

The Supreme Court decision in *Schlagenhauf v. Holder*[256] illustrates the in-controversy requirement and how it is satisfied. In a complicated personal injury litigation arising out of a bus and truck collision, the defendant truck owners cross-claimed against the defendant bus company and its driver. The truck owner alleged that the bus company knew that its driver's eyes and vision were impaired. The truck owner's attorney filed an affidavit stating that the bus driver had seen red lights for ten to fifteen seconds before the accident and had been involved in a prior accident. On these allegations, the district court ordered a battery of physical, visual, and mental examinations. The court of appeals denied a petition for a writ of mandamus[257] against the trial judge.

On *certiorari*, the Supreme Court emphasized that the requirements of Rule 35(a) "are not met by mere conclusory allegations of the pleadings . . . but require an affirmative showing by the movant."[258] Applying this principle, the Court found that nothing in the pleadings or the affidavit showed that the bus

---

examination findings and examiner's testimony at trial instead of federal rule of reciprocity discussed *infra*).

[251] When the examinee is a non-party in the custody or legal control of a party, the order actually issues to the party, who is merely obligated to use good faith efforts to produce the attendance of the examinee at the examination. Rule 35(a) advisory committee's note (1970).

[252] *See* WRIGHT & MILLER § 2233.

[253] *Id.* (concluding that she is).

[254] Although some commentators have argued the contrary, see HAYDOCK & HERR, note 11, *supra*, § 6.2.1, the legislative history of Rule 35 suggests that agents are not within its scope. *See Schlagenhauf v. Holder*, 379 U.S. 104, 115 n.12 (1964). In many cases involving agents, however, the discoverer can avail himself of the rule by naming the agent as a defendant.

[255] *See, e.g.*, cases cited in MOORE § 35.03; WRIGHT & MILLER § 2232.

[256] 379 U.S. 104 (1964).

[257] *See* § 13.04[3] (mandamus), *infra*.

[258] 379 U.S. at 118.

driver's general physical or mental condition was in controversy.[259] The Court suggested that the allegation in the cross-claim that the bus driver's eyes and vision were impaired, in conjunction with the affidavit, might have supported the eye examination had it been ordered alone. But the Court nevertheless vacated the eye examination order, too, in light of the necessity for remanding the case anyway for reconsideration of the other orders.

Weighing the in-controversy and good cause requirements, the Court noted that "[t]he ability of the movant to obtain the desired information by other means is also relevant."[260] Accordingly, courts have analogized *good cause* to the undue hardship requirement for overcoming the qualified immunity of work product under Rule 26(b)(3), and thus measured it by the reasonable availability of the information from other sources.[261] In *Crider v. Sneider*,[262] for example, a defendant's loss of recollection due to traumatic amnesia did not establish good cause for a physical examination under a state discovery rule like Rule 35 because information about the accident could be discovered from other sources.

An order to submit to examination should specify the conditions and scope of the examination. One of the reasons for vacating the orders for multiple examinations in *Schlagenhauf* was that they were framed too generally, possibly leaving the internal medicine examination to include blood tests, cardiograms, or X-ray examinations — some of which were irrelevant under any theory of the case.[263] In specifying the condition and scope of the examination, a court must balance the discovering party's needs against the privacy interest and safety of the examinee.[264]

Rule 35(b) establishes a rule of reciprocity for the exchange of examination reports. The examinee is entitled to the report of the examination upon request. In exchange, she must produce any prior reports of examinations of the same condition, and she waives any privilege she has regarding the testimony of anyone who has or will examine her concerning that condition.

The actual practice under Rule 35 and comparable state provisions is less formal. Usually the parties stipulate to physical and mental examinations and the exchange of relevant examination reports without seeking any court order.[265]

---

[259] Justice Black dissented with a characteristically pithy argument that when a bus driver has had a prior accident, it is fair to ask, "What is the matter with the driver? Is he blind or crazy?" *Id.* at 123 (Black, J., concurring in part and dissenting in part).

[260] *Id.* at 118.

[261] *Compare Anson v. Fickel*, 110 F.R.D. 184 (N.D. Ind. 1986) (good cause found where discoverer had already tried to obtain information by other means), *with Marroni v. Matey*, 82 F.R.D. 371 (E.D. Pa. 1979) (good cause lacking where no such showing made).

[262] 256 S.E.2d 335 (Ga. 1979).

[263] *Schlagenhauf*, 379 U.S. at 121 n.16.

[264] *Wright* § 88.

[265] *Id.*

[2]   Use and Value of Physical and Mental Examinations

Examination results may be used at trial subject to the rules of evidence. In most cases, the physician-patient privilege is waived in personal injury cases by a party-examinee's proffer of evidence, or, in some states, by statute. The examining doctor typically qualifies as an expert, and other experts may also testify on the basis of the examination when it is the kind upon which experts in the field reasonably rely.[266]

A physical or mental examination is an expensive form of discovery because the discoverer must pay the fees of the examining doctor. Yet it is often essential. No one has raised doubts of the value of Rule 35, although some have argued for its extension to non-parties, such as agents and spouses, in particular cases.[267]

PART C.
Control of Discovery

§ 10.12   THE ABUSE OF DISCOVERY[268]

Discovery abuse is a chronic complaint of litigators. It is also the rallying cry of rule reformers and a major justification for periodic amendments to the discovery rules. Yet there is no corresponding consensus about what discovery abuse is or how often it occurs, let alone what should be done about it. Litigators are likely to describe it, "quite simply, [as] what your opponent is doing to you."[269] The 1983 Advisory Committee identified the problems as over-discovery and evasion.[270]

Over-discovery (or runaway discovery) can be redundant discovery. It can also be discovery that is disproportionate to the nature and complexity of the claims and defenses, the amount in controversy, the social significance of the issues, and the relative resources of the parties.[271] *Evasion* consists of conduct calculated to prevent, distort, or stall disclosure of information legitimately sought through discovery.[272] At its worst, it may lead to modification or destruction of evidence:

---

[266] *See generally* FED. R. EVID. 702–705. Use of such trial experts is subject to the required disclosure requirements of Rule 26(a)(2). *See* § 10.07[2], *supra*.

[267] *See* JAMES, HAZARD & LEUBSDORF § 5.6.

[268] *See generally* Beckerman, note 31, *supra*; John H. Beisner, *Discovering a Better Way: The Need for Effective Civil Litigation Reform*, 60 DUKE L.J. 547 (2010); Charles Yablon, *Stupid Lawyer Tricks: An Essay on Discovery Abuse*, 96 COLUM. L. REV. 1618 (1996); Wayne D. Brazil, *Civil Discovery: How Bad Are the Problems?*, 67 A.B.A.J. 450 (1981); PAUL CONNOLLY, EDITH HOLLEMAN & MICHAEL KUHLMAN, JUDICIAL CONTROLS AND THE CIVIL LITIGATION PROCESS: DISCOVERY (Federal Judicial Center 1978); Randy L. Agnew, Note, *Recent Changes in the Federal Rules of Civil Procedure: Prescriptions to Ease the Pain?*, 15 TEX. TECH. L. REV. 887 (1984) (hereinafter *Recent Changes*).

[269] ARTHUR R. MILLER, THE AUGUST 1983 AMENDMENTS TO THE FEDERAL RULES OF CIVIL PROCEDURE: PROMOTING EFFECTIVE CASE MANAGEMENT AND LAWYER RESPONSIBILITY 31 (1984).

[270] Rule 26(b) advisory committee's note (1983).

[271] *See* text accompanying § 10.03[1] n.26 (noting that over-discovery involves both discovery breadth and depth), *supra*.

[272] *See* Brazil, note 268, *supra*, at 451; *Recent Changes*, note 268, *supra*, at 909.

spoliation. Spoliation is "the destruction or significant alteration of evidence, or the failure to preserve property for another's use as evidence in pending or reasonably foreseeable litigation."[273] A more granulated identification of actions that provoke sanctions lists:

- testifying falsely in deposition;
- failure to timely respond to written discovery;
- spoliation of evidence;
- changing records [some would call this a form of spoliation];
- communicating directly with the opposing party;
- obstructive behavior at deposition;
- abuse of process;
- late disclosure of witnesses;
- unprofessional conduct towards opposing counsel and the court.[274]

The 1983 Advisory Committee did not address the prevalence of these problems. However, other studies have suggested that, while they are common in large and complex cases, they do not permeate the majority of federal filings.[275] A 1997 survey of lawyers by the Federal Judicial Center indicated that 61% of the lawyers in complex cases reported discovery problems, compared to 50% of lawyers in "somewhat complex cases" and 33% in non-complex cases.[276] It also found that lawyers in high-stakes cases were twice as likely to report multiple discovery problems as lawyers in low-stakes cases.[277] Lawyers hired for complex high-stakes cases probably view discovery as simply another tool for conflict.

The line separating over-discovery and evasion from vigorous advocacy is therefore difficult to draw. Some of what may be portrayed as the former may be inherent in an open-ended and party-regulated discovery scheme. Judge Easterbrook has observed that:

> Lawyers cannot limit their search for information in discovery, because they do not know what they are looking for. They do not know when to stop, because they never know when they have enough . . . . When the stakes are high — and often the stakes for corporations are many times the ad damnum of the complaint — it is worthwhile to invest the legal resources needed to produce even a small change in the probable outcome. Lawyers practicing in good faith, therefore, engage in extensive discovery; anything

---

[273] *Zubulake IV*, 220 F.R.D. at 216.

[274] Edward R. Blumberg, *Ten Scenarios That Provoke Motions for Sanctions — And How to Avoid Them*, 81 U.S.L.W. 545 (2012).

[275] *See, e.g.*, Brazil, note 268, *supra*, at 452; CONNOLLY et al., note 268, *supra*, at xi.

[276] *FJC Survey*, note 176, *supra*, at 554–55. *See also* Robert L. Nelson, *The Discovery Process as a Circle of Blame: Institutional, Professional, and Socio-Economic Factors That Contribute to Unreasonable, Inefficient, and Amoral Behavior in Corporate Litigation*, 67 FORDHAM L. REV. 773 (1998) (explaining discovery abuse in high-stakes corporate litigation).

[277] *FJC Survey*, note 176, *supra*, at 555.

less is foolish.[278]

If the client can afford it, a lawyer may heed the ethical admonition to represent clients with "zeal in advocacy"[279] by pursuing discovery with a vengeance. The adversary process also encourages the aggressive lawyer to pursue remote but possible discovery targets or to assert every colorable ambiguity or objection in response to discovery requests. Reciprocity and cooperation are, after all, not hallmarks of the hotly contested lawsuit; the litigation process has been described as "inherently partisan and contentious," which makes the expectation of cooperation in discovery "a striking anomaly."[280] And, regrettably, there is a greater tendency for over-discovery and evasion when lawyers are compensated by the hour.[281]

On the other hand, over-discovery and evasion may also result from premeditated abuse. *Predatory discovery*[282] is intended less to uncover information than to delay, harass, embarrass, or financially burden the discoveree. Evasion for the same purposes becomes *obstruction* of discovery or deliberate spoliation. Predatory discovery and obstruction are correctly viewed as the abuse of discovery, often characterized by rule violations and by unethical conduct.[283]

While there is no bright line separating systemically caused over-discovery and evasion from improperly motivated predatory discovery and obstruction, the distinction may still be worth drawing because these problems suggest somewhat different solutions. The systemic origins of over-discovery and evasion suggest systemic solutions: changes in attitudes and economic incentives of the bar, generic limitations on discovery, and managerial controls by the courts, at least in large and complex cases. Most of these limitations and controls would be applied at the start of and during discovery to avoid over-discovery and evasion. This was the approach of the 1993 discovery rule reforms, although they were not limited to large and complex cases. In contrast, predatory discovery and obstruction are less open to cure from front-end limitations and controls. Given their improper purposes and bad faith, they may require more and tougher sanctions for discovery rule violations.

§ 10.13 FRONT-END CONTROLS: PREVENTING THE ABUSE OF DISCOVERY

The federal rules take three approaches to preventing discovery abuse. First, they require parties or their attorneys to certify to the reasonable basis, proper purpose, and proportionality of discovery requests and responses. Second, they

---

[278] Frank H. Easterbrook, *Discovery as Abuse*, 69 B.U. L. Rev. 635, 641 (1989) (footnote omitted).

[279] *ABA Model Rules*, note 1, *supra*, Rule 1.3 comment.

[280] Beckerman, note 31, *supra*, at 521.

[281] *See generally Recent Changes*, note 268, *supra*, at 909–11.

[282] The phrase is from *Marrese v. Am. Acad. of Orthopaedic Surgeons*, 726 F.2d 1150, 1162 (7th Cir. 1984) (en banc).

[283] *Cf.* ABA Model Rules, note 1, *supra*, Rules 3.2–3.4. *See generally* Robert E. Sarazen, Note, *An Ethical Approach to Discovery Abuse*, 4 Geo. J. Legal Ethics 459 (1990).

permit and encourage judicial management of discovery by pretrial conferences and managerial orders regulating discovery. Finally, they authorize the issuance of protective orders against specific hardships from discovery.

[1] Certification Requirements

Rule 26(g) imposes two different kinds of certification requirements on discovery initiatives. It requires an attorney or unrepresented party to certify that to the best of the signer's knowledge, information or belief, formed after reasonable inquiry, the disclosure under Rule 26(a)(1) or (3) is "complete and correct as of the time it is made." The 1993 Advisory Committee cautioned, however, that the rule does not require exhaustive inquiry so early in the case. Instead, the type of investigation that is required in connection with Rule 26(a) disclosures will depend upon

> the number and complexity of the issues; the location, nature, number, and availability of potentially relevant witnesses and documents; the extent of past working relationships between the attorney and the client, particularly in handling related or similar litigation [e.g., is client a repeat player?]; and of course how long the party has to conduct an investigation, either before or after the filing of the case.[284]

In addition, Rule 26(g) imposes a certification requirement for discovery requests, responses and objections paralleling that of Rule 11. The purpose of this certification requirement is to deter over-discovery and evasion by making "each attorney . . . stop and think about the legitimacy of a discovery request, a response thereto, or an objection."[285] By signing such a request or response, the attorney certifies that "to the best of [his] knowledge, information[] and belief formed after a reasonable inquiry," the discovery paper is (if a disclosure), "complete and correct as of the time it is made," "consistent with these rules and warranted" by law, "not interposed for any improper purpose," and not dispropor-tionate to the needs of the case.[286]

The reasonable basis-in-law and proper-purpose certifications generally track those required by Rule 11.[287] An attorney is not required, however, to certify to the truthfulness of her client's factual responses to a discovery request.[288]

It is doubtful whether these certification requirements had really added much to the deterrence of predatory discovery or obstruction of discovery,[289] since the discovery rules have always implicitly prohibited such conduct. But the additional certification that discovery is not disproportionate to "the needs of the case, the discovery already had . . . , the amount in controversy, and the importance of the

---

[284] Rule 26(g) advisory committee's note (1993).

[285] Rule 26(g) advisory committee's note (1983).

[286] Rule 26(g).

[287] *See* § 8.05[2] (certification), *supra.*

[288] Rule 26(g) advisory committee's note (1983).

[289] *See* § 10.12 (discovery abuse), *supra.*

issues," may awaken some attorneys to the impropriety of over-discovery. According to one authority,

> [i]t is no longer sufficient, as a precondition for conducting discovery, to show that the information sought "appears reasonably calculated to lead to the discovery of admissible evidence." After satisfying this threshold requirement counsel *also must* make a common sense determination, taking into account all the circumstances, that the information sought is of sufficient potential significance to justify the burden the discovery probe would impose, that the discovery tool selected is the most efficacious of the means that might be used to acquire the desired information (taking into account cost effectiveness and the nature of the information being sought), and that the timing of the probe is sensible, *i.e.*, that there is no other juncture in the pretrial period when there would be a clearly happier balance between the benefit derived from and the burdens imposed by the particular discovery effort.[290]

This certification requirement incorporates this common sense determination into discovery even in the absence of appropriate managerial orders by the court under Rule 26(b)(1).[291]

Rule 26(g) mandates appropriate sanctions against the person who certifies in violation of the rule, the party on whose behalf the corresponding disclosure, request, or response was made, or both.[292] In practice, violations of Rule 26(g) will usually be accompanied by violations of other discovery rules subject to sanction under Rule 37, and Rule 26(g) sanctions can be decided simultaneously with Rule 37 sanctions.[293] The 1993 Advisory Committee emphasized, however, that Rule 11 no longer applies to such violations.

[2] Managerial Orders

Section 10.12 suggests that one reason for over-discovery and evasion is that discovery is an open-ended party-regulated adversarial process. One obvious response is more judicial regulation. The 1980 and 1983 amendments to the rules provided this by authorizing and encouraging early judicial intervention by pretrial conference, and by empowering the court (sometimes the district court judge, but perhaps more often, a magistrate judge), as educated by such conferences, to issue managerial discovery orders.[294] The 1993 amendments strengthened the courts' managerial powers because the Advisory Committee believed that "there [was] a

---

[290] *In re Convergent Techs. Sec. Litig.*, 108 F.R.D. 328, 331 (N.D. Cal. 1985) (Brazil, Mag.) (emphasis in original).

[291] *See* § 10.13[2] (managerial orders), *infra*.

[292] *See, e.g., Appeal of Licht & Semonoff*, 796 F.2d 564 (1st Cir. 1986) (dismissing, for lack of jurisdiction, appeal of unreported decision that Rule 26(g) was violated by use of depositions to harass opponents in proxy contest and to gain information for that contest, rather than to advance the lawsuit).

[293] *See, e.g., Perkinson v. Houlihan's/D.C., Inc.*, 108 F.R.D. 667 (D.D.C. 1985); *Tise v. Kule*, 37 Fed. R. Serv. 2d (Callaghan) 846 (S.D.N.Y. 1983). *See generally* § 10.14[2] (nature and incidence of sanctions), *infra*.

[294] *See Stillman v. Nickel Odeon, S.A.*, 102 F.R.D. 286, 287 (S.D.N.Y. 1984) (the amendments

greater need for early judicial involvement to consider the scope and timing of the disclosure requirements of Rule 26(a) and the presumptive limits on discovery imposed" by the rules. The 2000 amendments reinforced the court's powers, by making it the gatekeeper for discovery of matters beyond the claims or defenses in the case, yet relevant to the subject matter.[295] Some states have accomplished the same ends more indirectly by fixing discovery time limits by rule for civil actions,[296] often categorized by their complexity or amount in controversy.

The courts have long had the power under Rule 16 to hold pretrial conferences and issue orders which encompass discovery, and Rule 16(b) contemplates that the court may hold a discovery conference after the parties have conferred and submitted a discovery plan.[297] Whether or not a discovery conference is held by the court, it "shall" enter an order identifying issues for discovery purposes, limiting and scheduling discovery (including required disclosures), determining other matters incidental to discovery, such as cost allocation, and limiting the time by which the parties must complete discovery.[298]

Against reduction of over-discovery and evasion that such rules might provide must be balanced the risk that they will prompt over-management, especially in routine and relatively simple litigation. Rule 16(b) thus provides that local rules may exempt categories of inappropriate cases. Whether this will be sufficient to prevent unwarranted application of the rule's requirements remains to be seen.

If Rules 26(g) and 16(b) supply the occasion for managerial intervention by the courts into discovery, Rule 26(b)(1) supplies the tools "to enable the court to keep tighter rein on the extent of discovery," according to the 1993 Advisory Committee. Rules 30 and 33 presumptively limit the number of depositions and interrogatories, and Rule 26(b)(2) allows courts by local rule or order to alter these limits, as well to limit the length of depositions or the number of requests for admissions. Perhaps more important, Rule 26(b)(2)(C) also provides that the "court must limit the frequency or extent of discovery" if it determines that the discovery sought is excessive for any of three overlapping reasons.

Rule 26(b)(2)(C)(i) requires the court to limit discovery which is unreasonably cumulative or duplicative or is obtainable from a less burdensome and expensive source. Under this provision, courts have prohibited discovery by interrogatories when the discoverer has already obtained the same information from the subject by depositions.[299]

---

encourage courts to take a "strong supervisory role in discovery and to consider innovative cost-shifting concepts").

[295] *See* § 10.03[1], *supra.*

[296] *See, e.g.*, D.C. Super. Ct. R. 26(d).

[297] Rule 26(f) formerly required such a conference on motion by a party. The 1993 amendment deleted the requirement, apparently on the assumption that the mandatory planning conference of the parties would substitute for it and generate a discovery plan on which the court can base the still-required discovery scheduling order. *See* § 10.07[1], *supra.*

[298] *See generally* § 12.03 (pretrial conference), *infra.*

[299] *See, e.g.*, *Cont'l Ill. Nat'l Bank & Trust Co. v. WH Venture*, 1986 U.S. Dist. LEXIS 28237 (E.D. Pa. Mar. 13, 1986) (magistrate's decision) (stating that ordinarily "a motion to compel answers to subsequent interrogatories seeking to elicit the same information as obtained by way of the earlier

Rule 26(b)(2)(C)(ii) requires the court to limit discovery when the discoverer has had ample prior opportunity to discover the information sought. This rule has been used to justify court-imposed time limits on discovery.[300]

Finally, Rule 26(b)(2)(C)(iii) requires the court to limit discovery when "the burden or expense of the proposed discovery outweighs its likely benefit, considering the needs of the case, the amount in controversy, the parties' resources, the importance of the issues at stake in the litigation, and the importance of the discovery in resolving the issues." The rule thus gives a federal court the power to "limit unnecessarily expensive discovery."[301] When this limitation should be imposed depends on the facts of the case. In *TIE/Communications, Inc. v. Bumper Products Corp.*,[302] the discoverer sought to re-depose a corporate employee after having failed to inquire into a subject during the first deposition "due to inadvertence." Refusing to block the deposition, the court considered that the subject involved $100,000, 30% of the damages claimed, that the parties would have to get together anyway for other employee depositions, and that the party opposing discovery had shown no special hardship.

Historically, the courts did not make much use of the managerial power that Rule 26(b)(2)(C)(i)–(iii) requires them to exercise. Stressing the difficulty trial courts face balancing discovery benefits against burdens, one appellate judge has said that unless the imbalance is dramatic, "past habit is likely to cause the court to permit it."[303] But the 2000 amendment to the rule expressly cross-references the Rule 26(b)(2) managerial power in Rule 26(b)(1) to remind the courts of their authority and obligation, and the Supreme Court has itself emphasized that what is now Rule 26(b)(2)(C)(iii) "vests the trial court with broad discretion to tailor discovery narrowly and to dictate the sequence of discovery."[304] Perhaps such pointed reminders will yet overcome "past habit."

Finally, the 2006 rule amendments separately authorized similar cost-benefit analysis for the production of ESI that is not reasonably accessible because of undue burden or cost. If the responding party shows this kind of inaccessibility under Rule 26(b)(2)(B), the requesting party must show good cause for discovery using the cost-benefit formula of Rule 26(b)(2)(C). If the court grants discovery, it may specify conditions for the discovery, which may include cost-shifting.[305] Thus, the growing dominance of ESI in modern life — and, therefore, in big stakes litigation — is breathing new life into Rule 26(b)(2)(C)'s cost-benefit analysis.

---

depositions should be denied," but allowing interrogatory discovery to enable discoverer to close gaps in deponents' answers).

[300] *See, e.g., Slomiak v. Bear Stearns & Co.*, 597 F. Supp. 676 (S.D.N.Y. 1984).

[301] *Brock v. Frank V. Panzarino, Inc.*, 109 F.R.D. 157, 160 (E.D.N.Y. 1986) (properly rejecting this argument as a way around Rule 26(b)(3)'s protection of witness statements).

[302] 1987 U.S. Dist. LEXIS 10037 (E.D. Pa. Nov. 6, 1987).

[303] Winter, note 177, *supra*, at 265.

[304] *Crawford-El v. Britton*, 523 U.S. 574, 598 (1998).

[305] *See* § 10.03[44][c] (discussing *Zubulake* and factors it suggested for deciding cost-shifting for discovery of electronically stored information that is not reasonably accessible).

[3] Protective Orders Against Specific Hardship[306]

Upon motion and for good cause shown, almost all jurisdictions authorize the entry of orders protecting against burdensome or oppressive discovery. Rule 26(c), for example, authorizes the federal courts to issue *protective orders* on motion and the movant's certification that she has conferred in good faith with other parties to resolve the dispute. Protective orders are not materially different from what we have termed *managerial orders*,[307] but protective orders have traditionally been issued to protect against specific hardships from discovery[308] rather than to manage and control over-discovery. In deciding a motion for a protective order, the court must balance hardship to the discoveree if discovery is allowed as sought against the hardship to the discoverer if discovery is denied or restricted.[309] Most commonly, parties seek protective orders against unduly burdensome or invasive discovery.

Discovery can be unduly burdensome because of the location or condition of the discoveree. For example, because there are no geographic limitations on the location of opposing-party depositions, they are sometimes noticed for locations distant from the residence of the party-deponent. A protective order changing the location of the deposition or conditioning it on payment of travel expenses may be appropriate.[310] Or the age or health of a deponent may make a scheduled all-day deposition unduly burdensome and present good cause for shortening it, spacing it, or preventing it in favor of a less burdensome discovery method such as interrogatories.[311]

Discovery may be unduly invasive when it probes matter that, though unprivileged, is confidential. Predatory discovery, in fact, probes such matter more to embarrass and harass the discoveree than to obtain information.[312] As a result, parties often argue confidentiality when they seek a protective order.[313] In commercial litigation, for example, confidentiality is often invoked to protect trade

---

[306] *See generally* Jacqueline S. Guenego, Note, *Trends in Protective Orders Under Federal Rule of Civil Procedure 26(c): Why Some Cases Fumble While Others Score*, 60 Fordham L. Rev. 541 (1991); Richard L. Marcus, *Myth and Reality in Protective Order Litigation*, 69 Cornell L. Rev. 1 (1983).

[307] *See* § 10.13[2], *supra*.

[308] *See Cipollone v. Liggett Grp., Inc.*, 785 F.2d 1108, 1121 (3d Cir. 1986) (stressing burden on movant to show particular need for protection).

[309] *See Marrese*, 726 F.2d at 1159.

[310] *See, e.g., Haviland & Co. v. Montgomery Ward & Co.*, 31 F.R.D. 578, 580 (S.D.N.Y. 1962).

[311] *Id.; see generally* A. Darby Dickerson, *Deposition Dilemmas: Vexatious Scheduling and Errata Sheets*, 12 Geo. J. Legal Ethics 1 (1998) (discussing protective orders and other responses to vexatious deposition scheduling).

[312] *See, e.g., Seattle Times Co. v. Rhinehart*, 467 U.S. 20 (1984) (noting that such discovery implicates not only privacy interests but also litigants' interests in unimpeded access to the courts if they are forced to forgo pursuit of their claims rather than give up their privacy); *Marrese*, 726 F.2d at 1162 (finding a "hint of predatory discovery" in plaintiff's request for membership information as a basis for deposing members who voted against his application).

[313] *See* Laurie K. Dore, *Secrecy by Consent: The Use and Limits of Confidentiality in the Pursuit of Settlement*, 74 Notre Dame L. Rev. 283 (1999).

secrets or customer lists from competitors.³¹⁴ It has also been invoked to protect against unconditional discovery of financial information, group membership information, peer review information in connection with tenure, promotion and other personnel decisions, and institutional self-critiques.³¹⁵ However, the courts have been vigilant in requiring a specific showing of hardship from discovery of confidential matters and have rejected conclusory assertions by the discoveree of embarrassment or unfairness.³¹⁶

Prohibition of discovery is just one of eight different types of protective orders that Rule 26(c) describes. This mix reflects the rule's strong preference for orders restricting discovery rather than denying it altogether. A court may impose conditions on the location, method, scope, and sequence of discovery, or on any other incident of discovery as required to give sufficient protection to the movant. When the asserted hardship is invasion of confidentiality, for example, the court may restrict disclosure to particular parties or their attorneys and prohibit dissemination of the discovered information. In commercial litigation, *umbrella protective orders* are commonplace, extending protection against dissemination to any document that the discoveree designates confidential without any individualized review by the court.³¹⁷

In *Seattle Times Co. v. Rhinehart*,³¹⁸ the Supreme Court rejected a First Amendment challenge to the entry of a protective order restricting dissemination of information obtained by discovery. There, the defendant newspaper in a defamation action sought discovery of the plaintiff religious group's membership and donor lists, candidly acknowledging that such information might be disseminated in newspaper articles. The Court first emphasized that litigants have no First Amendment right of access to information made available only for purposes of trying a suit and that such discovery is not a traditionally public source of information.³¹⁹ It then found that "the prevention of abuse that can attend the coerced production of information under a state's discovery rule is sufficient justification for the authorizing of protective orders."³²⁰

---

³¹⁴ *See* James R. McKown, *Discovery of Trade Secrets*, 10 SANTA CLARA COMPUTER & HIGH TECH. L.J. 35 (1994).

³¹⁵ *See generally* MOORE §§ 12.101, 26.104, 26.105 (listing cases). *Cf. Granger v. Nat'l R.R. Passenger Corp.*, 116 F.R.D. 507, 508 (E.D. Pa. 1987) (applying "critical self-analysis doctrine" to protect recommendations in railroad's accident analysis).

³¹⁶ *See, e.g., Cipollone*, 649 F. Supp. 664 (rejecting as unspecific cigarette manufacturers' sweeping claims that discovery of information regarding their knowledge of the health risks of smoking might prove embarrassing, detrimental to the market price of their stock, and helpful to their competitors or other plaintiffs).

³¹⁷ *See, e.g.*, Dore, note 313, *supra*; Richard L. Marcus, *The Discovery Confidentiality Controversy*, 1991 U. ILL. L. REV. 457 (1991); Marcus, note 306, *supra*, at 9; Arthur R. Miller, *Confidentiality, Protective Orders, and Public Access to the Courts*, 105 HARV. L. REV. 427 (1991).

³¹⁸ 467 U.S. 20 (1984).

³¹⁹ *Id.* at 32.

³²⁰ *Id.* at 35–36.

On the other hand, the Supreme Court has long acknowledged the public's common law right of access to judicial proceedings and judicial records.[321] If documents under a protective order are actually filed in court or submitted into evidence, the strong presumption of access must be balanced against competing interests to determine whether disclosure will be made. Moreover, even in *Seattle Times*, the Court emphasized that the particular protective order for discovery materials was limited in nature and did not restrict the dissemination of information gained outside the discovery process. Other courts have noted that First Amendment interests of discoverers and the public can sometimes be accommodated by properly limited protective orders, requiring, for example, *in camera* inspection of the information by the trial judge, *redaction* (deletion) of names or other especially private information prior to disclosure, or postponement of discovery of private matter until the discoveree has had the opportunity to test the discoverer's *prima facie* claims or defenses.[322] One court has tried to craft a compromise between protection and public access, by holding that material filed with discovery motions under an umbrella protection order is "not subject to the common-law right of access, whereas discovery material filed in connection with pretrial motions that require judicial resolution of the merits is subject to the common-law right."[323]

§ 10.14 BACK-END CONTROLS: SANCTIONS

[1] The Predicate for Sanctions

All procedural systems authorize sanctions against parties and attorneys who violate the discovery rules or discovery orders. Governing law in federal court includes Rules 37 and 26(g), a statute,[324] and common law.[325] Under Rule 37, no party may move for an order compelling discovery or for sanctions without certifying that it has tried in good faith to resolve the discovery dispute with other parties without court action.[326] Sanctions most commonly result from a party's defiance of a prior discovery order. Accordingly, Rule 37(b) authorizes sanctions for a failure to comply with an order to compel discovery or equivalent discovery order.[327] Rules 26(g), 37(c) and 37(d), however, permit the imposition of sanctions without an intervening discovery order in some circumstances. When a discovery

---

[321] *Nixon v. Warner Comm. Inc.*, 435 U.S. 589 (1978).

[322] *See, e.g., Marrese*, 726 F.2d at 1160.

[323] *Chicago Tribune Co. v. Bridgestone/Firestone, Inc.*, 263 F.3d 1304 (2001) (per curiam). *See generally* Richard L. Marcus, *A Modest Proposal: Recognizing (at Last) That the Federal Rules Do Not Declare That Discovery Is Presumptively Public*, 81 Chi.-Kent L. Rev. 331 (2006).

[324] *See* 28 U.S.C. § 1927 (2012).

[325] *See Roadway Express, Inc. v. Piper*, 447 U.S. 752, 764–67 (1980).

[326] Rule 37(e) now provides that no sanctions will lie for a failure to provide electronically stored information "lost as a result of routine, good-faith operation of an electronic information system." This rule thus reinforces the importance of an early discovery conference in which the parties discuss a "litigation hold" on relevant electronic information.

[327] Equivalent discovery orders include Rule 35 orders providing for physical or mental examinations and arguably Rule 16(b) scheduling orders, although they are not mentioned in Rule 37(b).

order has been violated, or the facts warrant bypassing the usual predicate of a discovery order, the court may impose sanctions tailored to the offense.

The discoverer may move under Rule 37(a)[328] for an order compelling discovery either when the discoveree objects to discovery or responds evasively or incompletely. In the former circumstances, this motion tests any objections that the discoveree has interposed to the requested discovery.[329] If the motion to compel is granted, Rule 37(a)(5) requires the court to award the movant attorney's fees and other expenses incurred in making the motion unless it finds that opposition to the motion was "substantially justified."[330] If the motion is denied, then the discoveree has a similar opportunity for reimbursement and the court may issue a protective order in his favor. "The great operative principle of Rule 37(a)(4) is that the loser pays."[331]

Violation of an order compelling discovery or of an equivalent discovery order, whether or not willful,[332] is the predicate for discovery sanctions under Rule 37(b). Evincing a general hesitancy about imposing discovery sanctions,[333] the courts have been strict in rejecting arguments that general managerial or pretrial orders not expressly compelling discovery can satisfy Rule 37(b)'s predicate of a discovery order.[334]

When the discoveree simply refuses to respond — fails to appear at all for her deposition, or to serve any response to interrogatories or production requests — the predicate of a discovery order is eliminated. Rule 37(d) then permits the discoverer to move directly for sanctions short of contempt and for all expenses caused by the failure of discovery, not just those incurred in making the Rule 37(d) motion. Efficiency is the rationale for this shortcut to sanctions. Requiring a court order to compel a response, followed in all likelihood by a second motion to test objections made in the compelled response, would intolerably delay discovery in many cases and invite abuse.[335] Rule 37(d) therefore, provides that a failure to respond is not excused upon the ground that the discovery is objectionable, unless the discoveree has applied for a protective order. The proper way to object to

---

[328] A motion seeking an order against a party must be filed in the court where the action is pending. Motions against non-parties must be filed in the court for the district where the discovery is being, or is to be, taken. Rule 37(a)(2).

[329] *See* Rule 33(a).

[330] "Making a motion, or opposing a motion, is 'substantially justified' if the motion raised an issue about which reasonable people could genuinely differ on whether a party was bound to comply with a discovery rule." WRIGHT & MILLER § 2288.

[331] *Id.*

[332] *See Societe Internationale Pour Participations Industrielles et Commerciales, S.A. v. Rogers,* 357 U.S. 197 (1958). The violator's *scienter* — state of mind — does go to the severity of sanctions, however. *See* § 10.14[2] (nature and incidence of sanctions), *infra.*

[333] *See* § 10.14[2] (incidence of sanctions), *infra.*

[334] *See, e.g., Salahuddin v. Harris,* 782 F.2d 1127 (2d Cir. 1986) (neither Rule 30(a) order *allowing* deposition nor "implied orders" provide the predicate for Rule 37(b) sanctions).

[335] MOORE § 37.90. "Rule 37(d) deals, then, with failure to make the initial response required by the Rules, while subdivisions (a) and (b) provide a method of resolving differences between the parties and enforcing the court's determinations." *Salahuddin,* 782 F.2d 1127.

discovery is to apply for such an order under Rule 26(c) or to make the objections in a written response or at the deposition.

An order compelling discovery is not a prerequisite for sanctions in some additional situations. Rule 37(f) provides for the award of expenses against an attorney who fails to participate in good faith in the framing of a discovery plan under Rule 26(f). Rule 37(c) provides a self-executing sanction for a party's prejudicial failure to disclose information required to be disclosed by Rule 26(a), by precluding that party from using the information as evidence at trial. More importantly, Rule 26(g) requires appropriate sanctions against an attorney or party for violation of its certification requirement.[336] Because most violations of the discovery rules can also be construed as violations of the certification requirement, Rule 26(g) may encourage federal courts to impose discovery sanctions more often without an intervening order compelling discovery.[337]

Rule 26(g) also supplies the sole authority under the rules for imposing sanctions for over-discovery. A limiting order under Rule 26(b)(2)(C)(i)–(iii) or 26(c) need not precede these sanctions,[338] although it is likely that some courts will infer the necessity of one due to the novelty of the offense[339] and their accustomed sanctions practice.

[2] The Nature and Incidence of Sanctions

Courts have long had discretion to impose discovery sanctions under rules like Rule 37(b) and 37(d).[340] Often, however, they have been reluctant to exercise that discretion. This created a climate conducive to discovery abuse.

> The typical pattern of sanctioning that emerges from the reported cases is one in which the delay, obfuscation, contumacy, and lame excuses on the part of litigants and their attorneys are tolerated without any measured remedial action until the court is provoked beyond endurance. At that point the court punishes one side or the other with a swift and final termination of the lawsuit by dismissal or default. This "all or nothing" approach to sanctions results in considerable laxity in the day-to-day application of the rules. Attorneys are well aware that sanctions will be imposed only in the most flagrant situations.[341]

---

[336] *See also* § 12.02[1] (requests for admissions), *infra*, discussing sanction of expenses for unjustified refusals to admit under Rule 36.

[337] *See, e.g., St. Paul Reinsurance Co., Ltd. v. Commercial Fin. Corp.*, 198 F.R.D. 508 (N.D. Iowa 2000) (imposing Rule 26(g) sanction *sua sponte*, without prior order compelling discovery, on discoveree for making boilerplate and frivolous objections).

[338] *See, e.g., Hayes v. Nat'l Gypsum Co.*, 1984 U.S. Dist. LEXIS 24865 (E.D. Pa. Jan. 13, 1984) (awarding expenses incurred by discoveree because of duplicative discovery, despite the absence of any court-ordered limit on same).

[339] *See* § 10.13[2] (managerial orders), *supra*.

[340] Both of these subprovisions provide that the court "may" issue an order for sanctions.

[341] Robert E. Rodes, Jr., Kenneth F. Ripple & Carol Mooney, Sanctions Imposable for Violations of the Federal Rules of Civil Procedure 85 (Fed. Jud. Ctr. 1981). Copyright © 1981 by the Federal Judicial Center. Reprinted with permission. *See also* Brazil, note 268, *supra*, at 456 (noting that

For two reasons, this historical reluctance may be abating. First, the Supreme Court has taken notice of it and reminded the trial courts that the purpose of sanctions is to deter as well as to punish.[342] Second, Rule 26(g) imposes mandatory sanctions for violation of the discovery certification requirements.[343] Since virtually any discovery abuse or discovery rule violation can be construed as a violation of the certification requirement, Rule 26(g)'s mandate may carry well beyond its literal boundaries into Rule 37.

At the same time, courts retain discretion to decide the severity of the sanction even under Rule 26(g). Limited only by the due process requirement that the sanction be proportionate to the offense,[344] or that the same be "just" and "appropriate" in the language of the Rules, federal courts may choose from a range of Rule 37(b) sanctions varying in severity.[345] The court may award discovery expenses against the violator, deem established facts that were the object of discovery,[346] prevent the violator from presenting certain evidence or supporting or opposing certain claims or defenses, instruct the jury that it can draw inferences adverse to the violator,[347] strike all or part of the pleadings, hold the violator of a discovery order (other than one for a physical or mental examination) in contempt,[348] dismiss the action, or render judgment by default. These same options are available for the increasingly common phenomenon of spoliation of ESI.[349]

The sanctions of dismissal or default are the most severe,[350] presupposing correspondingly severe abuse of discovery. Accordingly, the courts have suggested that "willfulness, bad faith, or . . . fault" must be found before dismissal or entry of default is appropriate, even though no such scienter requirement attaches to the underlying finding that a discovery rule or order has been violated.[351]

---

attorneys believe that courts fail miserably in imposing sanctions).

[342] *NHL v. Metro. Hockey Club, Inc.*, 427 U.S. 639 (1976) (*per curiam*). *See also Roadway Express*, 447 U.S. 752.

[343] Rule 26(g) advisory committee's note (1983).

[344] *See Ins. Corp. of Ireland, Ltd. v. Compagnie des Bauxites de Guinee*, 456 U.S. 694 (1982).

[345] *See generally* Joel Slawotsky, *Rule 37 Discovery Sanctions — The Need for Supreme Court Ordered National Uniformity*, 104 Dick. L. Rev. 471 (2000) (surveying sanction practice and finding that relatively unguided discretion has led to disuniformity).

[346] *Id.* (jurisdictional facts).

[347] *See Zubulake IV*, 220 F.R.D. at 216 ("The spoliation of evidence germane to proof of an issue at trial can support an inference that the evidence would have been unfavorable to the party responsible for its destruction.") (quotation omitted).

[348] *See* Greg Neibarger, *Chipping Away at the Stone Wall: Allowing Federal Courts to Impose Non-Compensatory Monetary Sanctions Upon Errant Attorneys Without a Finding of Contempt*, 33 Ind. L. Rev. 1045 (2000) (proposing other non-monetary sanctions in addition to contempt for discovery abuse).

[349] *See Zubulake IV*, 220 F.R.D. 212. *See generally* Charles W. Adams, *Spoliation of Electronic Evidence: Sanctions Versus Advocacy*, 18 Mich. Telecomm. Tech. L. Rev. 1 (2011) (summarizing a number of key electronic discovery decisions made by Judge Scheindlin).

[350] *See, e.g., TWA, Inc. v. Hughes*, 449 F.2d 51 (2d Cir. 1971) (default judgment for $145 million against Howard Hughes for his failure to comply with order to appear for deposition), *rev'd on other grounds sub nom., Hughes Tool Co. v. TWA*, 409 U.S. 363 (1973).

[351] *Societe Internationale*, 357 U.S. at 212. *See also Cine Forty-Second St. Theatre Corp. v. Allied*

The question whether these severe sanctions are appropriate is further complicated when they are levied for transgressions by the attorney rather than the party. The courts have always been reluctant to penalize parties on the merits for the acts of their attorneys, at least absent the client's knowledge or complicity.[352] For example, before the drastic sanction of dismissal is imposed for discovery misconduct of an attorney, the Court of Appeals for the Third Circuit has required the trial court to consider whether the party is responsible for the conduct, the degree of the party's responsibility, the resulting prejudice to the opposing party, whether the attorney has had a history of dilatory discovery tactics, whether the conduct was willful or in bad faith, whether other effective sanctions short of dismissal are viable, and whether the party's claim or defense is "meritorious."[353]

§ 10.15   DISCOVERY IN THE CALIFORNIA STATE COURTS

[1]   Introductory Note

In 1986, the California Legislature adopted the Civil Discovery Act, which clarified the earlier discovery statutes, incorporated existing case law, and implemented many recommendations to bring California discovery principles closer to those of the Federal Rules of Civil Procedure. As a result, the current rules of discovery in the California courts are, for the most part, nearly identical to those in the federal courts. However, as will be discussed below, some significant differences still exist.

[2]   Scope of Discovery Under the California Civil Discovery Act

The scope of pretrial discovery in California is very broad. Unless otherwise limited by an order of the court, any party may obtain discovery regarding "any matter, not privileged, that is relevant to the subject matter involved in the pending action."[354] The scope of discovery encompasses relevant matter that "either is itself admissible in evidence or appears to be reasonably calculated to lead to the discovery of admissible evidence."[355] In accordance with the liberal policies

---

Artists Pictures Corp., 602 F.2d 1062, 1065 (2d Cir. 1979).

[352] *See generally* Charles B. Renfrew, *Discovery Sanctions: A Judicial Perspective*, 67 CAL. L. REV. 264, 273–74 (1979). *But see Link v. Wabash R.R. Co.*, 370 U.S. 626, 633 (1962) (a litigant chooses counsel at his peril).

[353] *Poulis v. State Farm Fire & Cas. Co.*, 747 F.2d 863, 868–70 (3d Cir. 1984). *See also Scarborough v. Eubanks*, 747 F.2d 871 (3d Cir. 1984). In these companion cases (ironically involving the same attorney) the court, respectively, affirmed dismissal for a pattern of dilatory conduct that prejudiced the opposing party, but reversed dismissal for a failure to abide court-ordered deadlines, when no prejudice resulted and the opposing party also missed them. *See also Bluitt v. Arco Chem. Co.*, 777 F.2d 188, 190–91 (5th Cir. 1985).

[354] CAL. CODE CIV. PROC. § 2017.010.

[355] CAL. CODE CIV. PROC. § 2017.010. For example, in *Norton v. Superior Court*, 24 Cal. App. 4th 1750, 30 Cal. Rptr. 2d 217 (1994), the defendant in a malpractice action sought discovery of documents stating the terms of plaintiffs' recovery from their insurer — evidence which was inadmissible to mitigate damages under the collateral source rule. The Court of Appeal held that the documents might lead to the

underlying the discovery procedures, "doubts as to relevance should generally be resolved in favor of permitting discovery."[356] The trial court may exercise control over the scope, frequency, or extent of use of discovery methods pursuant to a motion for a protective order when the court determines the discovery sought is unreasonably burdensome, expensive, or intrusive.[357]

California's "relevant to the subject matter" standard is broader than the "relevant to any party's claim or defense" standard applicable to party-controlled discovery in the federal courts.[358] In opting for a liberal standard, the drafters of the Civil Discovery Act believed that a narrower definition of relevance would produce an increase both in objections on relevance grounds and in the need for court intervention to resolve these disputes.[359] Unfortunately, however, a liberal standard may encourage unfettered "fishing expeditions" and abusive over-discovery. To discourage such practices, the Act imposes numerical limitations on depositions and interrogatories, and requires court approval before resort to some types of discovery, such as physical and mental examinations.

In addition to providing broad guidelines regarding the scope of discovery, the Civil Discovery Act specifically addresses certain controversial discovery issues. For example, the Act expressly allows discovery of insurance coverage. A party may obtain discovery of the existence and contents of insurance policies, including the identity of the carrier, the nature and limits of the coverage, and whether the insurance carrier is disputing coverage of the claim involved in the action.[360] However, because purpose of discovery of insurance information is to facilitate pretrial settlement and not to prove liability at trial, discovery of this information does not make it admissible at trial.[361]

[3] Protection of Privileged Information

[a] Privileges, Generally

The Civil Discovery Act limits the scope of discovery to matters which are not privileged. The laws of privilege are provided by the California Constitution, the Evidence Code, other statutes, and decisional law. Essentially, any privilege which

---

discovery of admissible evidence, and ordered the trial court to inspect the documents in order to make this determination.

[356] *Pacific Tel. & Tel. v. Superior Court*, 2 Cal. 3d 161, 173, 84 Cal. Rptr. 718, 465 P.2d 854 (1970). "Absent a showing that substantial interests will be impaired by allowing discovery, liberal policies of discovery rules will generally counsel against overturning a trial court's decision *granting* discovery and militate in favor of overturning a decision to *deny* discovery." *Flagship Theatres of Palm Desert v. Century Theatres, Inc.*, 198 Cal. App. 4th 1366, 1383, 131 Cal. Rptr. 3d 519 (2011).

[357] CAL. CODE CIV. PROC. §§ 2017.020, 2019.030.

[358] FED. R. CIV. P. 26(b)(1). For discussion of the scope of discovery in federal courts, see §§ 10.02–10.03, *supra*.

[359] *See* 2 JAMES E. HOGAN & GREGORY S. WEBER, CALIFORNIA CIVIL DISCOVERY §§ 11.1–11.3 (2d ed. 2005 & Supp. 2012) (hereinafter, HOGAN & WEBER).

[360] CAL. CODE CIV. PROC. § 2017.210.

[361] CAL. CODE CIV. PROC. § 2017.210. *See Catholic Mut. Relief Society v. Superior Court*, 42 Cal. 4th 358, 366, 64 Cal. Rptr. 3d 434, 165 P.3d 154 (2007).

protects against disclosure at trial also applies to discovery. While the term "privilege" is used generally to refer to information protected from disclosure, it is more accurate to divide the subject into (1) those matters which are truly privileged and entitled to absolute protection and (2) those matters which are entitled to qualified protection and subject to compelled disclosure in the interests of justice.

With respect to the assertion of a claim of privilege in discovery proceedings, the key change in the Civil Discovery Act is its codification of the decisional law holding that a failure to object on the grounds of privilege will operate as a waiver of the privilege.[362] Conversely, the assertion of a privilege during discovery may bar introduction at trial of the evidence withheld.[363] A thorough examination of privileges is beyond the scope of these materials. To understand the scope and limitations of a particular privilege, one should review the applicable statutory and decisional law.

[b]   Absolute Privileges

The California Evidence Code codifies the *absolute privileges* which include the attorney-client privilege,[364] the spousal privilege, the physician-patient privilege,[365] the psychotherapist-patient privilege,[366] the clergyman-penitent privilege, and the mediation privilege. Unless some statutory exception applies or the privilege is waived, information covered by one of these privileges is protected from disclosure regardless of its relevance to the issues and the need for disclosure.[367]

---

[362] CAL. CODE CIV. PROC. §§ 2025.460(a), 2028.050(a), & 2030.290(a); 2 HOGAN & WEBER § 12.1.

[363] *See Xebec Dev. Partners, Ltd. v. Nat. Union Fire Ins. Co.*, 12 Cal. App. 4th 501, 15 Cal. Rptr. 2d 726 (1993) (holding plaintiff who asserted attorney-client privilege as to certain billing materials during discovery cannot waive the privilege at trial to prove amount of recoverable attorneys' fees because too late to cure prejudice to defendant).

[364] CAL. EVID. CODE § 952 *et seq.*

[365] CAL. EVID. CODE §§ 990–992 *et seq.* (defining the scope of the physician-patient privilege). The California courts are highly protective of medical information about nonparties, despite the clear relevance the information may have to pending litigation. *See, e.g., Marcus v. Superior Court*, 18 Cal. App. 3d 22, 95 Cal. Rptr. 545 (1971) (holding in a medical malpractice case where the doctor claimed he had performed the procedure at issue on numerous other patients, that the plaintiff was properly denied discovery of those patients' names); *Henard v. Superior Court*, 26 Cal. App. 3d 129, 133, 102 Cal. Rptr. 721 (1972) (holding in a products liability action involving an adverse drug reaction, that the plaintiff was properly denied discovery of the names of other doctors who had prescribed the drug and reported adverse reactions).

[366] CAL. EVID. CODE §§ 1010–1028. One important exception to the psychotherapist-patient privilege is the "dangerous patient" exception set out in Evidence Code § 1024. *See People v. Wharton*, 53 Cal. 3d 522, 280 Cal. Rptr. 631, 809 P.2d 290 (1991) (ruling that psychotherapist's warning to patient's intended victim was not covered by the privilege where there was reasonable cause for psychotherapist to believe that the patient was dangerous and disclosure of the communication was necessary to prevent any harm); *Menendez v. Superior Court*, 3 Cal. 4th 435, 11 Cal. Rptr. 2d 92, 834 P.2d 786 (1992) (holding dangerous patient exception is applicable to communications during a session which caused psychologist to reasonably believe that patients were dangerous to the psychologist and his wife and lover, and that disclosure was necessary to prevent any harm).

[367] *Rittenhouse v. Superior Court*, 235 Cal. App. 3d 1584, 1 Cal. Rptr. 2d 595 (1991); *see* 2 HOGAN & WEBER § 12.1; WEIL, BROWN, RYLAARSDAM & EDMON, CIVIL PROCEDURE BEFORE TRIAL ¶ 8:110.1 (The Rutter Group 2012).

[c] The Attorney-Client Privilege

Confidential communications between client and lawyer are privileged from disclosure.[368] However, this absolute privilege is subject to several statutory exceptions. For example, the Evidence Code provides an exception where the client consults the attorney to obtain advice in perpetrating a crime or fraud, and also where the attorney is sued for malpractice.[369] Moreover, the attorney-client privilege is waived "if any holder of the privilege, without coercion, has disclosed a significant part of the communication or has consented to such disclosure made by anyone."[370] Likewise, a failure to include an objection to discovery expressly based on the attorney-client privilege in the initial response to a discovery request may constitute a waiver of that privilege.[371] And, of course, although the attorney-client privilege protects the communication between the attorney and the client, it does not prevent discovery of the underlying facts that are the subject of the communication.[372]

Recently, in *Costco Wholesale Corp. v. Superior Court*,[373] the California Supreme Court made some important, basic rulings regarding discovery and the attorney-client privilege. In *Costco*, defendant Costco asked its attorney for legal advice regarding whether certain warehouse managers were exempt from California's wage and overtime laws. The attorney interviewed some employees as part of her investigation, and then sent her client, Costco, a 22-page opinion letter incorporating her findings with her legal conclusions. In a subsequent labor law class action, the plaintiffs, Costco employees, sought discovery of the opinion letter arguing that it contained unprivileged matter. The trial court conducted an *in camera* review of the letter, redacted the letter to conceal what it believed to be privileged, and

---

[368] CAL. EVID. CODE § 954. The attorney-client privilege can be claimed by a corporate client, *Costco Wholesale Corp. v. Superior Court*, 47 Cal. 4th 725, 101 Cal. Rptr. 3d 758, 219 P.3d 736 (2009), and may even apply to statements made to someone who is not an attorney, such as an insurance claims representative, where the "dominant purpose" of the communication is for use by an attorney to defend against possible litigation. *See, e.g., Soltani-Rastegar v. Superior Court*, 208 Cal. App. 3d 424, 256 Cal. Rptr. 255 (1989) (holding statements given to insurer for purpose of defending against claims are protected from discovery by attorney-client privilege even though litigation was only a threat on the horizon and attorneys had not yet been selected to meet that threat); *Scripps Health v. Superior Court*, 109 Cal. App. 4th 529, 135 Cal. Rptr. 2d 126 (2003) (ruling in a wrongful death action that the attorney-client privilege applies to confidential occurrence reports prepared by the defendant hospital regarding the deceased's condition during his hospital stay privilege because their dominant purpose was for attorney review in anticipation of litigation).

[369] CAL. EVID. CODE § 956; *see State Farm Fire & Cas. Co. v. Superior Court*, 54 Cal. App. 4th 625, 643–49, 62 Cal. Rptr. 2d 834 (1997) (applying the crime/fraud exception to the attorney-client privilege).

[370] CAL. EVID. CODE § 912(a).

[371] *See Scottsdale Ins. Co. v. Superior Court*, 59 Cal. App. 4th 263, 69 Cal. Rptr. 2d 112 (1997) (ruling insurer waived its attorney-client privilege with respect to documents sought to be produced because the insurer failed to include an objection based on the privilege in its initial response); *but see Korea Data Sys. Co. v. Superior Court*, 51 Cal. App. 4th 1513, 59 Cal. Rptr. 2d 925 (1997) (finding no waiver of attorney-client privilege occurred where a reference to that privilege was asserted in a timely response to discovery requests, even though the objections were general and nonspecific).

[372] *See, e.g., Costco Wholesale Corp. v. Superior Court*, 47 Cal. 4th 725, 733, 101 Cal. Rptr. 3d 758, 219 P.3d 736 (2009); *Aerojet-General Corp. v. Transp. Indem. Ins.*, 18 Cal. App. 4th 996, 1004, 22 Cal. Rptr. 2d 862 (1993).

[373] 47 Cal. 4th 725, 101 Cal. Rptr. 3d 758, 219 P.3d 736 (2009).

ordered the defendant to disclose the remainder. The California Supreme Court reversed the trial court's order. First, the Court emphasized that the privilege attaches to a confidential communication between the attorney and the client and bars discovery even though the communication includes otherwise unprivileged material or contains factual matter rather than legal advice. Because the privilege protects the *transmission* of information, a communication covered by the privilege does not become unprivileged just because it contains material that could be discovered by some other means.

Second, the Court ruled that the Evidence Code does not permit a trial judge to order an *in camera* review of the information alleged to be protected by the attorney-client privilege. Because this privilege protects a transmission between attorney and client regardless of its content, there is no need to examine its content in order to rule on a claim of privilege.[374] Finally, the Court explained that a party claiming the attorney-client privilege is not required to demonstrate that its ability to present its case would be prejudiced by disclosure of the privilege information. Because the fundamental purpose of the privilege is the preservation of the confidential relationship between attorney and client, the primary harm in the discovery of privileged material is the disruption of that relationship.

[d] Qualified Privileges

In addition to the absolute privileges, California recognizes several *qualified privileges* which will protect certain sensitive information unless the interests of justice compel disclosure. These qualified areas of protection include the newsgatherer's immunity, the medical staff privilege, the trade secret privilege, the taxpayer's privilege, and the constitutional protection of privacy.[375]

[e] The Right of Privacy

A frequently invoked and potentially far-reaching qualified privilege is the right to privacy protected by Article I, section 1, of the California Constitution. In determining whether to require disclosure of information protected by this privilege, a court must balance the right of a civil litigant to discover relevant facts with the right of the information possessor to maintain reasonable privacy.[376] The difficult task of striking a balance between these competing interests often requires

---

[374] *Costco Wholesale, supra*, 47 Cal. 4th at 739.

[375] *See generally* HOGAN & WEBER § 12.34.

[376] *See, e.g., John B. v. Superior Court*, 38 Cal. 4th 1177, 45 Cal. Rptr. 3d 316, 137 P.3d 153 (2006) (balancing husband's right of privacy against wife's right to discover relevant facts, and concluding that husband's medical records and prior sexual history were discoverable in order to confirm or refute wife's allegations that husband knowingly or negligently infected wife with HIV); *Valley Bank of Nevada v. Superior Court*, 15 Cal. 3d 652, 125 Cal. Rptr. 553, 542 P.2d 977 (1975) (balancing interests of litigants and of nonparty bank customers with respect to discovery of customers' bank records); *Johnson v. Superior Court*, 80 Cal. App. 4th 1050, 95 Cal. Rptr. 2d 864 (2000) (donor's right of privacy in his identity and medical history outweighed by public policy interest in health of children, in action by parents and their children against sperm bank alleging transmission of kidney disease to the children by the sperm donor). For an example of the right to privacy applied in the context of a mental examination ordered pursuant to the Civil Discovery Act, see *Vinson v. Superior Court*, 43 Cal. 3d 833, 239 Cal. Rptr. 292, 740 P.2d 404 (1987).

an *in camera* inspection of documents (*i.e.*, a review of the documents by the judge in private to determine whether they should be released, in whole or in part, to the requesting party) to protect privacy interests during the discovery process, as well as a protective order to limit disclosure of information only for purposes related to the lawsuit and only to persons having a legitimate interest in that information for such purposes.[377] Some typical applications of the constitutional right of privacy are discussed below.

The California Supreme Court created a privilege to protect tax returns in recognition of the sensitivity of private financial information and the policy of facilitating collection of taxes.[378] While this privilege has been broadly construed, by statute it does not apply in child and spousal support proceedings.[379] Numerous reported decisions have recognized that a patient has a privacy interest in a doctor's medical records pertaining to the patient's physical or mental condition.[380] The courts must strike a balance between the party's need to discover relevant information and the patient's right to privacy.[381] The problem of inadequate safeguards of consumer records has been specifically addressed in the Civil Discovery Act, requiring notice to the consumer or the consumer's written authorization to release personal documents.[382] Also, in any type of action, a confidential settlement agreement reached in a related case may be protected from

---

[377] *See, e.g., Valley Bank of Nevada, supra,* 15 Cal. 3d at 658 (advising trial courts to employ procedural devices such as *in camera* hearings, partial disclosures, and sealing of documents when fashioning a discovery order that will accommodate considerations of both disclosure and confidentiality); *Babcock v. Superior Court,* 29 Cal. App. 4th 721, 725–28, 35 Cal. Rptr. 2d 462 (1994) (requiring *in camera* inspection and a protective order with respect to personal financial records in a dissolution of marriage action). In *Babcock, supra,* 29 Cal. App. 4th at 728, n.1, the court noted that an example of a prototypical protective order is that disclosure of sensitive information is upon condition that the materials could only be discussed by counsel in consulting with their clients and that copies not be given to the clients, and nor would any person be permitted to use such information for any purposes other than the current litigation.

[378] *Schnabel v. Superior Court,* 5 Cal. 4th 704, 718–23, 21 Cal. Rptr. 2d 200, 854 P.2d 1117 (1993) (collecting cases); *Webb v. Standard Oil of Cal.,* 49 Cal. 2d 509, 319 P.2d 621 (1957); *Sav-On Drugs, Inc. v. Superior Court,* 15 Cal. 3d 1, 123 Cal. Rptr. 283, 538 P.2d 739 (1975).

[379] CAL. FAM. CODE § 3552.

[380] *See, e.g., Lantz v. Superior Court,* 28 Cal. App. 4th 1839, 34 Cal. Rptr. 2d 358 (1994) (collecting cases).

[381] *See Irwin Mem'l Blood Bank v. Superior Court,* 229 Cal. App. 3d 151, 279 Cal. Rptr. 911 (1991) (ruling no depositions of blood donors allowed in an action for negligent screening of blood donors); *Johnson v. Superior Court,* 80 Cal. App. 4th 1050, 95 Cal. Rptr. 2d 864 (2000) (holding in an action by parents and their children against a sperm bank alleging the transmission of a serious kidney disease to the children by the sperm donor, that the donor's constitutional right of privacy in his medical history and identity was outweighed by the public policy expressed in the Family Code which provides for disclosure of insemination records under certain circumstances and by the state's compelling interest in the health and welfare of children).

[382] CAL. CODE CIV. PROC. §§ 1985.3, 2020.410(d) &.510(c). For a good review of the jurisprudence of the constitutional right of privacy, as applied in the context of a consumer class action, see *Pioneer Elec. (USA), Inc. v. Superior Court,* 40 Cal. 4th 360, 53 Cal. Rptr. 3d 513, 150 P.3d 198 (2007) (applying balancing test to determine the extent to which the right of privacy protects purchasers from having their identifying information disclosed to the plaintiff in a consumer rights class action against the defendant seller, where the plaintiff needs the information to facilitate communication with potential class members).

disclosure by the right of privacy.[383]

Information about a person's sexual history is frequently the subject of a privacy claim. Code of Civil Procedure § 2017.220 specifically protects a plaintiff in a sexual harassment case from disclosure of this information. But the issue arises in other cases where the statute does not apply.[384] For example, in an action brought by one spouse against the other spouse alleging that the defendant knowingly or negligently transmitted the HIV virus to the plaintiff, the constitutional right of privacy did not preclude the plaintiff from discovering information about the defendant's sexual conduct before and during the marriage.[385]

The identity of members of clubs and organizations is another difficult area. For example, in litigation concerning the scope of anti-abortion protesters' rights to engage in activities outside Planned Parenthood's facilities, one court concluded that Planned Parenthood should not be ordered to disclose, even pursuant to a protective order, the names, residential addresses, and telephone numbers of staff and volunteers who had knowledge relevant to the litigation.[386] However, a public interest organization seeking an award of attorney fees under the private attorney general statute may be required to disclose the identities of, and donations by, the contributors to its litigation fund.[387]

Employment and personnel information has been found to be outside the scope of discovery. For example, in a wrongful termination case, the plaintiff was denied access to information in the personnel files of other employees absent a showing of compelling need.[388] The protection of this information has also been applied to

---

[383] *See Hinshaw, Winkler, Draa, Marsh & Still v. Superior Court*, 51 Cal. App. 4th 233, 58 Cal. Rptr. 2d 791 (1996) (holding plaintiffs in a legal malpractice action were not entitled to discovery of confidential settlement agreements reached in the original case in which they were dropped by their attorney, because of the policy favoring settlements and the speculative nature of measuring plaintiffs' damages by these settlements); Walter W. Heiser, *Public Access to Confidential Discovery: The California Perspective*, 35 W. St. U. L. Rev. 55 (2007) (discussing access to pretrial settlements and discovery where the settling parties agreed that the settlement will remain confidential and that any information obtained through discovery will not be disclosed to third parties).

[384] *See, e.g., Boler v. Superior Court*, 201 Cal. App. 3d 467, 247 Cal. Rptr. 185 (1987) (applying the constitutional right of privacy and holding defendant in sexual harassment case not required to disclose names of all past employees with whom he had intimate relations); *Morales v. Superior Court*, 99 Cal. App. 3d 283, 160 Cal. Rptr. 194 (1979) (holding plaintiff husband seeking damages for wrongful death of his wife must disclose the frequency of extramarital encounters, but not the names and addresses of the other parties).

[385] *See John B. v. Superior Court*, 38 Cal. 4th 1177, 45 Cal. Rptr. 3d 316, 137 P.3d 153 (2006) (balancing husband's right to privacy against wife's right to discovery of relevant facts, and concluding that husband's medical records and sexual history were discoverable in order to confirm or refute wife's allegations that husband knowingly or negligently infected wife with HIV).

[386] *Planned Parenthood Golden Gate v. Superior Court*, 83 Cal. App. 4th 347, 99 Cal. Rptr. 2d 627 (2000) (finding the privacy interests at stake were particularly strong because the consequences of disclosure of this private information were profound, and therefore outweighed the need for discovery).

[387] *See Save Open Space Santa Monica Mountains v. Superior Court*, 84 Cal. App. 4th 235, 100 Cal. Rptr. 2d 725 (2000) (finding need for discovery outweighed associational privacy interests, where evidence sought was crucial to court's analysis of attorney fees request).

[388] *Perez v. Cnty. of Santa Clara*, 111 Cal. App. 4th 671, 3 Cal. Rptr. 2d 867 (2003) (holding in action by nurse alleging disparate disciplinary treatment based on race, the trial court properly granted a

information about a party to the action.[389] The need to protect employment and personnel information has heightened significance in certain professions. For this reason, the law extends additional protection to police personnel files[390] and to medical board proceedings.[391]

[4] Protection of Attorney's Work Product

[a] Introductory Note

In addition to protecting information within the scope of traditional privilege law, California's Civil Discovery Act provides a specific scheme for protecting the work product of attorneys, insurers, consultants, and agents both in anticipation of litigation and for trial.[392] This protection reflects California's policy of providing incentive for thorough preparation, promoting investigation of both strengths and weaknesses of a case, and preventing one party from taking unfair advantage of another's efforts. To further this policy, the Act provides both absolute and qualified work product protection.

[b] Absolute Work Product Protection

Absolute protection is provided to "[a]ny writing that reflects an attorney's impression, conclusions, opinions, or legal research or theories."[393] The absolute work product privilege extends to an attorney's written notes about a witness's statements; when a witness's statement and the attorney's impressions are inextricably intertwined, absolute protection is afforded to all of the attorney's notes.[394]

There are (only) three recognized exceptions to this absolute privilege: The State Bar may discover attorney work product where disciplinary charges are pending,[395] no privilege exists in an action between an attorney and her client if work product is relevant to the attorney's alleged breach of duty,[396] and, when an attorney is

---

protective order restricting plaintiff's access to personnel records of other nurses at correctional facility); *Harding Lawson Assoc. v. Superior Court*, 10 Cal. App. 4th 7, 12 Cal. Rptr. 2d 538 (1992).

[389] *See Kahn v. Superior Court*, 188 Cal. App. 3d 752, 233 Cal. Rptr. 662 (1987) (affirming denial of discovery of information sought by plaintiff about the tenure discussions in a case alleging wrongful denial of tenure because to allow discovery would impede full and candid discussions of candidates' qualifications).

[390] Cal. Evid. Code § 1043 & Cal. Penal Code § 832.7.

[391] Cal. Evid. Code § 1157; *see, e.g., Fox v. Kramer*, 22 Cal. 4th 531, 93 Cal. Rptr. 2d 497, 994 P.2d 343 (2000) (ruling Evidence Code § 1157(a) makes a hospital's peer review committee records immune from discovery).

[392] Cal. Code Civ. Proc. § 2018.010–2018.080.

[393] Cal. Code Civ. Proc. § 2018.030(a). The term "writing" includes handwriting, printing, photographing, transmitting by electronic mail, and any other form of communication or representation, including letters, pictures, sounds, or combinations thereof, and any record thereby created, regardless of the manner in which the record has been stored. Cal. Code Civ. Proc. § 2018.030(b) (adopting the definition set forth in Evidence Code § 250).

[394] *Rico v. Mitsubishi Motors, supra*, 42 Cal. 4th 807, 814, 68 Cal. Rptr. 3d 758, 171 P.3d 1092 (2007).

[395] Cal. Code Civ. Proc. § 2018.070.

[396] Cal. Code Civ. Proc. § 2018.080.

suspected of knowingly participating in a crime or fraud, there is no work product protection in any official investigation by a law enforcement agency or by a public prosecutor if the services of the lawyer were obtained to aid anyone to commit a crime or fraud.[397] However, no crime-fraud exception to this absolute privilege applies in private civil litigation.[398]

[c] Qualified Work Product Protection and Witness Statements

Conditional protection is afforded to any other attorney work product, which is only discoverable where "the court determines that denial of discovery will unfairly prejudice the party seeking discovery in preparing that party's claim or defense or will result in an injustice."[399] The Civil Discovery Act does not define "work product" for purposes of this qualified privilege and the determination of what is "work product" must be made by individual courts on a case-by-case basis.[400] This *ad hoc* approach has been particularly problematic when applied to discovery requests for witness statements and related information. Recently in *Coito v. Superior Court*,[401] the California Supreme Court attempted to provide some clarification.

The plaintiffs in *Coito*, wrongful death claimants, sought to compel production of recorded witness interviews conducted by investigators employed by the attorney for defendant, as well as the names and addresses of any individuals from whom written or recorded statements had been obtained by defense counsel. On appellate review, the California Supreme Court addressed two important questions: What work product protection, if any, should be accorded (1) witness statements obtained by an attorney and (2) information concerning the identity of witnesses from whom the attorney has obtained statements. To answer these questions, the *Coito* Court first determined what constitutes "work product" in general. The discovery statutes describe when the absolute work product privilege applies, but do not otherwise describe or define "work product" for purposes of the qualified work product privilege. Prior to *Coito*, the majority of the lower courts had concluded that only

---

[397] Cal. Code Civ. Proc. § 2018.050.

[398] *Rico v. Mitsubishi Motors Corp.*, 42 Cal. 4th at 820; *see BP Alaska Exploration, Inc. v. Superior Court*, 199 Cal. App. 3d 1240, 245 Cal. Rptr. 682 (1988) (holding the crime-fraud exception in Evidence Code § 954 applies only to communications shielded by the attorney-client privilege; no similar statute applies to documents protected by the absolute work product privilege).

[399] Cal. Code Civ. Proc. § 2018.030(b).

[400] *See Coito v. Superior Court*, 54 Cal. 4th 480, 142 Cal. Rptr. 3d 607, 278 P.3d 860 (2012). At least one court has held that a list of intended witnesses is protected attorney work product during the pretrial discovery stage of litigation. *City of Long Beach v. Superior Court*, 64 Cal. App. 3d 65, 134 Cal. Rptr. 468 (1976); *see Snyder v. Superior Court*, 157 Cal. App. 4th 1530, 69 Cal. Rptr. 3d 600 (2007) (holding general order of the Los Angeles superior court, which required identification of witnesses in asbestos-exposure cases, is invalid because it requires a plaintiff to disclose the identities of certain nonexpert witnesses without a motion or a showing of prejudice or injustice); *but see In re Jeanette H.*, 225 Cal. App. 3d 25, 275 Cal. Rptr. 9 (1990) (requiring parties to exchange witness lists in a trial-setting conference, as opposed to during pretrial discovery, does not violate the protection accorded to attorneys' work product).

[401] *Coito v. Superior Court*, 54 Cal. 4th 480, 142 Cal. Rptr. 3d 607, 278 P.3d 860 (2012).

"derivative" or interpretative material — material created by or derived from an attorney's evaluation of the law or facts — constitutes work product; whereas "nonderivative" material — material that is only evidentiary in nature — does not constitute work product. The Supreme Court rejected this distinction.

In defining "work product," the *Coito* Court did not announce a black-letter rule. Instead, it indicated that whether material constitutes "work product" should be decided on a case-by-case basis by relying upon the policies underlying the work product statute.[402] The main policies are to prevent attorneys from taking undue advantage of their adversary's industry and efforts, and to encourage attorneys to prepare their cases thoroughly and to investigate not only the favorable but the unfavorable aspects of those cases. Obviously, this is a very flexible test.

However, the *Coito* Court demonstrated how this policy-based test applies to the two questions before it and then announced an important general rule: witness statements obtained as a result of an attorney-directed interview are entitled as a matter of law to *at least* qualified work product protection. They may also be entitled to absolute protection if their disclosure would reveal the attorney's mental impressions.[403] Information as to the identity of witnesses from whom an attorney has obtained statement is not automatically entitled to any work product protection.[404] The party invoking the privilege must persuade the trial court that either the absolute or the qualified work product privilege applies.[405] These rulings provide relatively clear guidance to lower courts and litigants as to these two types of materials. Unfortunately, the Supreme Court's flexible policy-based test leaves room for considerable disagreement as to what other materials constitute "work product," leaving it up to the lower courts to make such determinations on a case-by-case basis.

---

[402] *Coito, supra*, 54 Cal. 4th at 489, 496–97, 499–502. The Supreme Court emphasized that the determination of whether the work product privilege applies, and if so which one, may require the trial court make an *in camera* inspection. *Id.* at 496, 500 & 502.

[403] *Coito, supra*, 54 Cal. 4th at 495–96. The absolute privilege applies not only when a witness's statements are "intertwined with explicit comments of the attorney stating his or her impressions of the witness, the witness's statements, or other issues in the case"; but also "when the questions the attorney chose to ask provide a window into the attorney's theory of the case or the attorney's evaluation of what issues are most important," and in some cases even "the very fact that the attorney has chosen to interview a particular witness may disclose important tactical or evaluative information, perhaps especially so in cases involving a multitude of witnesses." *Id.* at 496.

[404] *Coito, supra*, 54 Cal. 4th at 501–02. The Supreme Court noted that where an attorney takes statements from all or almost all known witnesses to an incident, reflecting neither the attorney's mental impressions nor the attorney's industry and effort in selecting which witnesses to ask for a statement, compelling a list of these witnesses is unlikely to violate the work product privilege. *Id.* at 501–02.

[405] *Coito, supra*, 54 Cal. 4th at 499–501. The Supreme Court explained: "In order to invoke the privilege, defendant must persuade the trial court that disclosure would reveal the attorney's tactics, impressions, or evaluation of the case (absolute privilege) or would result in opposing counsel taking undue advantage of the attorney's industry or efforts (qualified privilege)." *Id.* at 486.

[5]   Comparison to Federal Work Product Doctrine

[a]   Expanded Scope and Protection

The California work product doctrine differs significantly from the federal work product doctrine. While the two doctrines have common origins,[406] the Civil Discovery Act expands the scope of protection and protects an attorney's impressions and opinions absolutely. The California rule protects any document prepared by an attorney in connection with his or her work as an attorney, regardless of whether litigation is contemplated.[407] In contrast, the federal work product rule covers only materials "prepared in anticipation of litigation or for trial."[408]

The California rule provides that "[a]ny writing that reflects an attorney's impressions, conclusions, opinions, or legal research or theories shall not be discoverable under any circumstances."[409] In contrast, the federal work product rule offers, arguably, something less than absolute protection. It permits discovery of regular work product materials on a showing of substantial need where the party seeking discovery cannot obtain equivalent materials without undue hardship.[410] Federal Rule 26(b)(3) then provides that in ordering discovery of such materials when the required showing has been made, the court "must protect against disclosure of the mental impressions, conclusions, opinions or legal theories of a party's attorney . . . concerning the litigation." The strength of this added protection for opinion documents is unclear. The United States Supreme Court has suggested that perhaps only a stronger showing of necessity and unavailability is required.[411]

[b]   Inadvertent Disclosure of Privileged Information

Document production pursuant to a discovery request may involve massive numbers of documents, particularly when they are stored in an electronic format. A question sometimes arises as to what action is required of an attorney who receives privileged documents through inadvertence. According to the California Supreme Court, an attorney in these circumstances may not examine the documents any more closely than is necessary to ascertain that the documents are privileged.[412] Once it becomes apparent that the content is privileged, the attorney must immediately notify opposing counsel and try to resolve the situation. A violation of

---

[406] The United States Supreme Court decision in *Hickman v. Taylor*, 329 U.S. 495 (1947), is the basis for both the federal doctrine stated in Rule 26(b)(3) of the Federal Rules of Civil Procedure and for the California doctrine codified in Code of Civil Procedure § 2018.030. *See Coito, supra*, 54 Cal. 4th at 489–94 (discussing the origins of the California work product doctrine).

[407] *Rumac v. Bottomley*, 143 Cal. App. 3d 810, 815, 192 Cal. Rptr. 104 (1983).

[408] FED. R. CIV. P. 26(b)(3).

[409] CAL. CODE CIV. PROC. § 2018.030(a).

[410] FED. R. CIV. P. 26(b)(3). For discussion of the work product doctrine in federal courts, see § 10.05, *supra*.

[411] *Upjohn Co. v. United States*, 449 U.S. 383, 402 (1981). For more discussion of the protection offered attorney mental impressions under federal Rule 26(b)(3), see § 10.05[4][c], *supra*.

[412] *Rico v. Mitsubishi Motors Corp.*, 42 Cal. 4th 807, 817, 68 Cal. Rptr. 3d 758, 171 P.3d 1092 (2007).

this standard of professional conduct may be remedied by disqualification of the attorney from representation of the party in the litigation.[413]

The approach to such inadvertent disclosures appears to be different in the federal courts, where the duty to take corrective action is placed on the privilege-holder. Pursuant to Rule 26(b)(5)(B) of the Federal Rules of Civil Procedure, if privileged information is inadvertently produced in discovery, the party making the claim of privilege may notify the party that received the information of the claim of privilege. After being so notified, that party must promptly return, sequester, or destroy the specified information, and take other remedial measures, until the claim of privilege is resolved. Pursuant to recent legislation, California now follows the federal procedure in one specific area — inadvertent release of electronically stored information that may be subject to a claim of privilege or work product protection.[414]

§ 10.16 INDIVIDUAL DISCOVERY DEVICES IN THE CALIFORNIA COURTS

California's Civil Discovery Act authorizes the same individual discovery devices as the Federal Rules of Civil Procedure: interrogatories, inspections of documents, depositions, medical examinations, and expert witness disclosures.[415] However, unlike federal Rule 26(a)(1), the California Act does not require parties to provide initial disclosures of information that the disclosing party may use to support its claims or defenses. Instead, this information may be obtained by interrogatories to an opposing party or by some other appropriate discovery device.

[1] Interrogatories

The Civil Discovery Act provides for written interrogatories to a party, but imposes a presumptive limit of 35 specially prepared interrogatories in addition to any number of official form interrogatories.[416] The Act authorizes legal contention interrogatories calling for an opinion that relates to fact or the application of law to fact.[417] While contention interrogatories are expressly allowed, continuing

---

[413] *Rico, supra*, 42 Cal. 4th at 819–20.

[414] Cal. Code Civ. Proc. § 2031.285.

[415] For discussion of each of these discovery devices in federal courts, see § 10.08 (depositions), § 10.09 (interrogatories), § 10.10 (production and entry requests), and § 10.11 (physical and mental examinations), *supra*.

[416] Cal. Code Civ. Proc. §§ 2030.010–.310, 2030.030. The California Judicial Council has approved official form interrogatories which contain questions designed to obtain certain basic, general information about an opposing party's case. Cal. Code Civ. Proc. §§ 2033.710–.740. Use of these form interrogatories is optional; and if used, they may be supplemented by interrogatories specially prepared by the party and tailored for the specific case.

[417] Cal. Code Civ. Proc. § 2030.010(b). Although the practice of using contention interrogatories is well-established in California, asking legal contention questions during a deposition is not allowed. *E.g.*, *Pember v. Superior Court*, 66 Cal. 2d 601, 58 Cal. Rptr. 567, 427 P.2d 167 (1967) (reaffirming the propriety of contention interrogatories but disapproving the use of contention questions at a deposition of a layperson); *Rifkind v. Superior Court*, 22 Cal. App. 4th 1255, 27 Cal. Rptr. 2d 822 (1994) (legal contention questions during a deposition are unfair because they ask the deponent to sort out the factual material

interrogatories are expressly prohibited.[418] "Continuing" interrogatories, such as those required by Rule 26(e) of the Federal Rules of Civil Procedure in federal courts, ask the responding party to update the answers with information acquired in the future. Unlike federal Rule 26(e), the Civil Discovery Act prohibits placing this burden on the responding party and requires instead that the propounding party seek updated information through supplemental interrogatories.[419] Implicit in the California law is the view that it is unfair to require the responding party to constantly review and supplement prior answers.[420]

Within 30 days, unless extended by court order or by stipulation, the responding party must respond in writing under oath separately to each interrogatory by "(1) an answer containing the information sought to be discovered, (2) an exercise of the party's option to produce writings, or (3) an objection to the particular interrogatory."[421] Each answer "shall be as complete and straightforward as the information reasonably available to the responding party permits."[422] A party cannot always discharge the duty to respond by simply denying personal knowledge, but rather has an obligation to undertake a reasonable inquiry.[423] This obligation requires the responding party to provide information which can be obtained from sources under its control.[424] This includes nonprivileged information known to counsel, even if the party has no personal knowledge of the information.[425] If dissatisfied with the answers to interrogatories, the propounding party may move to compel further responses.[426]

---

in the cases according to specific legal contentions, and do this by memory and on the spot).

[418] CAL. CODE CIV. PROC. § 2030.060(g).

[419] CAL. CODE CIV. PROC. § 2030.070. One exception to this approach is allowed for governmental entities defending personal injury actions. CAL. GOV'T CODE § 985(c). This provision requires plaintiffs to update information about collateral source benefits (*i.e.*, the receipt of insurance payments).

[420] *See* 1 HOGAN & WEBER § 5.7.

[421] CAL. CODE CIV. PROC. § 2030.210(a).

[422] CAL. CODE CIV. PROC. § 2030.210(b).

[423] This duty is expressly stated in Code of Civil Procedure § 2030.220(c), which provides that if a party lacks personal knowledge, that party "shall make a reasonable and good faith effort to obtain information by inquiry to other natural persons or organizations, except where the information is equally available to the propounding party."

[424] *Deyo v. Kilbourne*, 84 Cal. App. 3d 771, 149 Cal. Rptr. 499 (1979).

[425] *See Smith v. Superior Court*, 189 Cal. App. 2d 6, 11 Cal. Rptr. 165 (1961).

[426] *See* CAL. CODE CIV. PROC. § 2030.300 (setting forth the procedure for compelling further responses). Unless notice of this motion is given within 45 days of the service of the response, the propounding party waives the right to compel a further response. CAL. CODE CIV. PROC. § 2030.300(c).

[2] Inspections of Documents, Electronically Stored Information, and Other Tangible Things

[a] Inspections, Generally

The Civil Discovery Act provides that any party may obtain discovery by inspecting documents, electronically stored information, tangible things, land, and other property in the possession, custody, or control of any other party.[427] The Act also specifically provides for discovery from a nonparty.[428] These provisions may be used to compel nonparties to permit inspection of records, documents, electronically stored information, and tangible things, but not land or property.[429]

[b] Discovery of Electronically Stored Information

Most information today is in electronic rather than in paper form. Information created, stored, and used with computer technology may be critical to success or failure of a case. Consequently, the discovery of electronically stored information ("ESI") has become an important, and controversial, feature of modern litigation. Electronic discovery has created difficult problems for courts when the burden and costs of accessing the information makes such discovery unreasonable. One of the main issues is under what circumstances, and to what extent, should the requesting party pay the expense of information retrieval and production in a usable form. In response to this and other issues, the Federal Rules of Civil Procedure were revised effective 2006 to clarify the discovery process with respect to electronically stored discovery.[430]

---

[427] CAL. CODE CIV. PROC. §§ 2031–2031.060. Section 2031.010(d) authorizes a party to demand entry on land or property of another party. Because the Civil Discovery Act is permissive and not exclusive, property open to the public can be examined without recourse to formal discovery provided the examination can be conducted in a lawful fashion. *See Pullin v. Superior Court*, 81 Cal. App. 4th 1161, 97 Cal. Rptr. 2d 447 (2000) (holding trial court in a slip and fall case erred in excluding testimony about a test performed on the defendant supermarket's floor by a forensic safety engineer on plaintiff's behalf without resort to any statutory discovery device).

[428] CAL. CODE CIV. PROC. §§ 2020.010–.510. Both sections 2020.010–.030 (inspection subpoenas as to nonparties) and 2031.010–.060 (inspection demands on parties) require that records sought to be produced be designated either by specifically describing each individual item or by reasonably particularizing each category of items. *See Calcor Space Facility, Inc. v. Superior Court*, 53 Cal. App. 4th 216, 61 Cal. Rptr. 2d 567 (1997) (finding unreasonably burdensome the plaintiff's request to a nonparty gun mount manufacturer to produce all materials in its possession relating to gun mounts and dating back nearly 10 years).

[429] In contrast to the right to inspect the land and property of a party, the Civil Discovery Act does not provide for the inspection of the land and property of a nonparty. CAL. CODE CIV. PROC. § 2020.020. In 1991, the federal discovery rules were amended to permit inspection of land and property. FED. R. CIV. P. 34(c) & 45(a). Professor James E. Hogan, Reporter for the Discovery Act, acknowledges the frequent need for such discovery, for example in cases where employees are injured on the job as a result of defective machinery or in litigation arising out of an airplane crash. 1 HOGAN & WEBER § 7.5. Professor Hogan recommends that California should follow the recent federal example and fill the statutory gap by making controlled access to nonparty premises a feature of the California discovery system. *Id.* at § 7.5.

[430] *See, e.g.*, FED. R. CIV. P. 26(b)(2), 34(a) & (b)(1). For discussion of discovery of ESI in the federal courts, see § 10.03[4], *supra*.

In 2009, the California Legislature adopted the Electronic Discovery Act, thereby amending the Civil Discovery Act in order to modernize California's discovery law with respect to ESI. These new provisions provide comprehensive procedures for the handling of demands for the inspection, copying, testing, or sampling of ESI. With respect to the important issue of whether the requesting party should pay the expense of information retrieval and production in a usable form, the Act provides: "If the court finds good cause for the production of electronically stored information from a source that is not reasonably accessible, the court may set conditions for the discovery of the electronically stored information, including allocation of the expense of discovery."[431]

Moreover, pursuant to California's Civil Discovery Act, a court must limit the frequency or extent of discovery of ESI, even from a source that is reasonably accessible, if the court determines that any of the following conditions exist: (1) it is possible to obtain the information from some other source that is more convenient, less burdensome, or less expensive; (2) the discovery sought is unreasonably cumulative or duplicative; (3) the party seeking discovery has had ample opportunity by discovery in the action to obtain the information sought; or (4) the likely burden or expense of the proposed discovery outweighs the likely benefit, taking into account the amount in controversy, the resources of the parties, the importance of the issues in the litigation, and the importance of the requested discovery in resolving the issues.[432]

These provisions reflect the strong influence of the federal rules and federal decisions with respect to cost allocation and management of ESI discovery. Likewise, the California and federal standards for retention of ESI are the same — the duty to preserve attaches at the time that litigation was reasonably anticipated by the party possessing the ESI.[433] Similar to federal Rule 37(e), the Civil Discovery Act also contains a safe harbor provision which, absent exceptional circumstances, protects a party from sanctions for failing to provide ESI that has been "lost, damaged, altered, or overwritten as the result of the routine, good faith operation of an electronic information system."[434]

---

[431] Cal. Code Civ. Proc. §§ 2031.060(e), 2031.310(e).

[432] Cal. Code Civ. Proc. §§ 2020.220(i), 2025.480(g), 2031.060(f), 2031.310(f).

[433] See CEB, California Civil Discovery Practice §§ 4.6–4.13 (4th ed. 2012); § 10.03[4][a], supra. Once the duty to preserve attaches, a party may, at a minimum, face discovery sanctions for deliberate destruction of ESI. E.g., R.S. Creative, Inc. v. Creative Cotton, Ltd., 75 Cal. App. 4th 486, 89 Cal. Rptr. 2d 353 (1999) (affirming dismissal of plaintiff's complaint as sanction for repeated efforts to thwart discovery, including the deliberate destruction of evidence by deletion of plaintiff's computer files). To prevent alteration or destruction of ESI, a party may seek a preservation order in the form of an injunction at the outset of litigation. See Dodge, Warren & Peters Ins. Serv., Inc. v. Riley, 105 Cal. App. 4th 1414, 130 Cal. Rptr. 2d 385 (2003) (affirming preliminary injunction that required the preservation of defendant's electronic evidence and allowed expert to copy all of it, including computer hard drives and disks, to recover deleted files).

[434] Cal. Code Civ. Proc. §§ 2017.020(c), 2023.030(f), 2025.410(c).

[3] Depositions

California's Civil Discovery Act provides for oral depositions of parties and nonparties in California, in another state, and in another country, as well as written depositions.[435] The Act provides for stenographic, audio-taped, and videotaped depositions. In addition to answering questions, a deponent may be compelled to perform a re-enactment of an incident during a videotape deposition — a particularly useful discovery technique when defending a personal injury lawsuit.[436]

With respect to a deponent who is not a natural person, if a deposition notice describes matters on which examination is requested, the deponent must designate the officers, directors, employees, or agents who are the most qualified to testify on its behalf as to those matters at the deposition. The burden is on the corporate defendant to produce the right witnesses and to provide them with the knowledge of the information sought, including any necessary documentation as requested in the deposition notice.[437] A plaintiff may not depose the head of a corporation — a so-called "apex" deposition — when there is no showing the corporate head had any involvement in the lawsuit against the corporation, and prior to the plaintiff's exhaustion of less intrusive means of discovery.[438] A similar general rule applies to a deposition of the head of an agency or other top governmental executives.[439]

The Civil Discovery Act sets out the rules governing the use of depositions at trial. Unless another use is authorized by the Evidence Code, the deposition of a nonparty is generally only used to impeach or contradict live testimony. However, the deposition of a party or party-affiliated deponent may be used by the opponent for any purpose — either as substantive evidence or for impeachment — regardless of whether the deponent testifies at trial. Finally, the deposition of any deponent (party, party-affiliated, or nonparty) may be used at trial where the deponent is unavailable or other exceptional circumstances justify its use.

---

[435] CAL. CODE CIV. PROC. §§ 2025.010–.620, 2028.010–.080, 2026.010, 2027.010.

[436] *Emerson Elec. Co. v. Superior Court*, 16 Cal. 4th 1101, 68 Cal. Rptr. 2d 883, 946 P.2d 841 (1997) (requiring plaintiff to reenact, during a videotaped deposition, an accident with a radial saw manufactured by the defendant).

[437] CAL. CODE CIV. PROC. § 2025.230; *see Maldonado v. Superior Court*, 94 Cal. App. 4th 1390, 115 Cal. Rptr. 2d 137 (2002) (holding defendant company's selection of witnesses to represent the company at depositions who knew little about the topics specified in the deposition notices and who appeared without the necessary documentation was inexcusable and such behavior may justify monetary sanctions).

[438] *See, e.g., Liberty Mut. Ins. Co. v. Superior Court*, 10 Cal. App. 4th 1282, 13 Cal. Rptr. 2d 363 (1992) (holding that when a plaintiff seeks to depose a corporate president or other official at the highest level of corporate management, and that official moves for a protective order to prohibit the deposition, the trial court should first determine whether the plaintiff has shown good cause that the official has unique or superior personal knowledge of discoverable information).

[439] *See, e.g., Nagle v. Superior Court*, 28 Cal. App. 4th 1465, 1468, 34 Cal. Rptr. 2d 281 (1994) (holding that top governmental officials are normally not subject to depositions unless they have direct personal factual information pertaining to material issues in an action and, even then, only upon a showing that the information cannot be obtained through other sources and through much less burdensome means).

[4] Medical Examinations

California's Civil Discovery Act provides for discovery by physical and mental examination of a party, an agent of a party, or a person in the custody or control of a party where that person's mental or physical condition is in controversy in a civil action. The procedures for obtaining a medical examination fall into two categories: (1) those for the routine examination of a plaintiff in a personal injury action, and (2) those for other examinations by court order.

[a] Noticed Examination of Plaintiff in Personal Injury Action

The Act provides a simplified procedure for the defendant in a personal injury action to obtain a physical examination of the plaintiff without obtaining a prior court order, so long as the examination does not include a procedure that is "painful, protracted, or intrusive."[440] The automatic physical examination does not include a mental examination. This is true even where the plaintiff has put his or her mental state in issue by alleging mental distress and emotional suffering.[441]

[b] Court-Ordered Mental and Physical Examinations

Except for the one automatic physical examination in a personal injury action, a party who would like to obtain discovery by a medical examination must obtain leave of court. The Civil Discovery Act permits the physical or mental examination of a party in any action in which the mental or physical condition of that party is "in controversy." However, unless the parties agree to the examination, a trial court will order such an examination only upon a showing of "good cause."[442] The Act provides specific rules for the conduct of a physical examination. A representative of an examinee or a party producing the examinee is entitled to attend and observe a physical examination, and to record the examination stenographically or by audiotape.

A party whose mental condition is "in controversy" may be ordered to submit to a mental examination upon a showing of good cause. Typically, a personal injury plaintiff's mental condition is "in controversy" when he or she seeks damages for mental and emotional injuries, and the existence or extent of those injuries is in dispute.[443] Psychiatric examinations raise a variety of privacy concerns not present

---

[440] CAL. CODE CIV. PROC. § 2032.220(a).

[441] See Roberts v. Superior Court, 9 Cal. 3d 330, 107 Cal. Rptr. 309, 508 P.2d 309 (1973); Reuter v. Superior Court, 93 Cal. App. 3d 332, 337–40, 155 Cal. Rptr. 525 (1979). A mental examination is subject to the requirements of Code of Civil Procedure § 2032.310 and § 2032.320, requiring leave of court on a showing of "good cause."

[442] CAL. CODE CIV. PROC. §§ 2032.020, 2032.310 & 2032.320. A showing of "good cause" requires the moving party to produce specific facts justifying discovery and that the inquiry is relevant to the subject matter of the action. Vinson v. Superior Court, 43 Cal. 3d 833, 840–44, 239 Cal. Rptr. 292, 740 P.2d 404 (1987) (ruling that although good cause shown for psychiatric examination of plaintiff claiming emotional distress damages caused by sexual harassment, defendants did not establish specific facts justifying inquiry into plaintiff's sexual history and practices).

[443] Vinson, supra, 43 Cal. 3d at 839–40 (ruling sexual harassment plaintiff's mental condition is "in

in physical examinations. Not surprisingly, the Civil Discovery Act and the California courts impose some special limitations on court-ordered mental examinations. In contrast to physical examinations, neither counsel nor court reporters are generally allowed to attend mental examinations.[444] However, the trial court has discretion to permit counsel to attend if there is some showing of special need. Although neither counsel nor a court reporter may be present at a mental examination, both the examiner and the examinee have the right to record the entire examination on audiotape.[445]

[5] Exchange of Information About Trial Experts

[a] Expert Witness Disclosures

One general goal of California's Civil Discovery Act is to require pretrial disclosure of information regarding expert witnesses who will testify at trial in order to permit the opposing party to depose the designated expert and to designate additional experts if necessary. This goal is reflected in Code of Civil Procedure § 2034.210, which provides for the compulsory exchange of the identity of expert witnesses who will testify at trial and of the general nature of their testimony. After the initial trial date is set, this exchange may be initiated by either side.

The disclosure required by section 2034.210 is limited to experts who will be called to testify at trial. For such "retained experts" (i.e., experts retained by a party for the purpose of expressing an opinion at trial), the disclosure must include an expert witness declaration setting out the expert's qualifications, the general substance of the expected testimony, a representation that the expert is ready to testify, and a statements of the expert's fees for deposition testimony. For treating physicians who are regarded as percipient witnesses (i.e., witnesses whose testimony recounts facts they perceived), the identity must be disclosed if they will be called to express an opinion, but an expert declaration is not required.[446]

---

controversy" where she seeks damages for emotional distress and defendants deny they caused her mental injuries); *Doyle v. Superior Court*, 50 Cal. App. 4th 1878, 1886, 58 Cal. Rptr. 2d 476 (1996) (ruling mental examinations are not authorized for the purpose of testing a person's credibility, and are only relevant to assess current mental condition and not emotional distress suffered in the past).

[444] *Vinson, supra*, 43 Cal. 3d at 844–47 (ruling plaintiff had no absolute right to the presence of her attorney during the mental examination); *Edwards v. Superior Court*, 16 Cal. 3d 905, 910, 130 Cal. Rptr. 14, 549 P.2d 846 (1976); *see Toyota Motor Sales, U.S.A., Inc. v. Superior Court*, 189 Cal. App. 4th 1391, 117 Cal. Rptr. 3d 321 (2010) (holding trial court abused its discretion in permitting plaintiff's counsel to be present in an adjoining room during a psychiatric examination because evidence indicated that such contemporaneous monitoring would interfere with the examiner's ability to establish the necessary rapport with the plaintiff).

[445] Cal. Code Civ. Proc. § 2032.530(a); *see Golfland Entm't Ctr., Inc. v. Superior Court*, 108 Cal. App. 4th 739, 133 Cal. Rptr. 2d 828 (2003) (ruling defendant entitled to audiotape entire mental examination as opposed to only select parts as ordered by the trial court).

[446] *See* Cal. Code Civ. Proc. § 2034.210; *Schreiber v. Estate of Kiser*, 22 Cal. 4th 31, 91 Cal. Rptr. 2d 293, 989 P.2d 720 (1999) (failure of treating physician to submit an expert witness declaration did not preclude physician's opinion testimony at trial regarding cause of plaintiff's injuries).

The identities and opinions of consulting experts who will not be called to testify at trial are protected by the work product privilege.[447] But once such an expert is designated as a trial witness, the privilege may be considered waived as to earlier reports by that expert, even those tendered while the witness was only a consultant.[448] However, a party may withdraw its designation of an expert trial witness, who is not yet deposed and who remains as the party's consultant, and thereby preclude the deposition of that expert and that expert's retention by an adverse party.[449]

In general, the procedures and expert witness disclosures required by the Civil Discovery Act are similar to those required in federal court under the Federal Rules of Civil Procedure, but some differences exist.[450] The federal rules impose a mandatory duty to disclose information about expert witnesses without waiting for a formal discovery request; under the Act, until a demand is made, the parties need not comply with the disclosure and exchange requirements. Also, the federal rules require disclosure of more detailed information about an expert witness than do the California statutes.

[b]   Failure to Comply with Expert Witness Disclosure Requirements

If a party has unreasonably failed to comply with the requirements for expert disclosure with respect to a witness, the trial court upon objection is required to exclude from evidence the expert testimony of that witness.[451] This rule applies where a party fails to list an expert, fails to submit a required declaration, fails to produce discoverable reports, or fails to make the expert available for deposition. Also, an expert witness may be precluded from testifying at trial on subjects not adequately disclosed in the expert's declaration.[452]

---

[447] Cal. Code Civ. Proc. § 2018.030. *See* Raoul D. Kennedy & James C. Martin, California Expert Witness Guide §§ 8.18 & 10.6 (2d ed. 2011) (collecting cases).

[448] *See County of Los Angeles v. Superior Court*, 222 Cal. App. 3d 647, 271 Cal. Rptr. 698 (1990); *National Steel Prod. Co. v. Superior Court*, 164 Cal. App. 3d 476, 210 Cal. Rptr. 535 (1985); 2 Hogan & Weber § 12.12; CEB, *California Civil Discovery Practice* § 3.59, § 11.5 (4th ed. 2012).

[449] *County of Los Angeles v. Superior Court, supra*, 222 Cal. App. 3d at 657–78 (holding the work product doctrine prevented the plaintiff from deposing defendant's expert-consultant who will not testify for the defendant at trial, and precluded the plaintiff attorney's attempt to retain this same expert to testify for the plaintiff).

[450] For discussion of discovery from experts in the federal courts, see § 10.06, *supra*.

[451] Cal. Code Civ. Proc. § 2034.300; *see, e.g., Waicis v. Superior Court*, 226 Cal. App. 3d 283, 276 Cal. Rptr. 45 (1990) (finding no abuse of discretion for trial court to disqualify properly designated expert witness from testifying at trial where it found the expert had repeatedly been uncooperative in allowing his disposition to be taken).

[452] *Bonds v. Roy*, 20 Cal. 4th 140, 83 Cal. Rptr. 2d 289, 973 P.2d 66 (1999) (holding a trial court may preclude an expert witness from testifying at trial on a subject whose general substance was not previously described in the expert witness declaration).

[c] Testimony of Undesignated Experts

In a limited number of circumstances, a party may call an expert who the party has not designated. First, a party may call an expert to testify who has been designated by some other party to the case so long as the witness has been deposed. Second, an undesignated expert may be called as a rebuttal witness for the purpose of "impeachment." In this context, the term impeachment has been narrowly construed to include testimony pertaining to the falsity or nonexistence of any fact used as the foundation for any opinion by any other party's expert witness, but not to include testimony that contradicts the opinion.[453]

A party who wishes to call at trial an expert who was not designated when expert witness information was exchanged and who is intended to take the place of a previously designated but now unavailable expert must make a motion to augment that party's expert witness list to include the new expert.[454] A replacement expert will not be permitted to testify, over objection, when the party seeking to call the replacement expert has failed to make an augmentation motion.

§ 10.17 ENFORCEMENT OF DISCOVERY REQUESTS IN THE CALIFORNIA COURTS

[1] Introductory Note

A central precept of California's Civil Discovery Act is that civil discovery should be essentially self-executing. However, court intervention may become necessary to prevent or to remedy discovery abuses. To this end, the sections of the Civil Discovery Act providing for specific discovery devices also provide for protective orders, motions to compel discovery responses, and sanctions for discovery misconduct.[455]

[2] Motion to Compel Discovery

The party seeking discovery may move for an order compelling discovery when the responding party objects to discovery, responds evasively or incompletely, or simply refuses to respond. For most types of discovery, the procedure for obtaining an order compelling discovery follows the same sequence. First, the parties are required to meet and confer to attempt to informally resolve the dispute. If the

---

[453] *See, e.g., Fish v. Guevara*, 12 Cal. App. 4th 142, 145, 15 Cal. Rptr. 2d 329 (1993) (holding an undisclosed expert may testify to facts which contradict the factual basis for the opinions of other experts but may not give opinion testimony which contradicts the opinions of other experts); *Howard Contracting, Inc. v. G.A. MacDonald Const. Co.*, 71 Cal. App. 4th 38, 52–54, 83 Cal. Rptr. 2d 590 (1998) (ruling trial court properly excluded testimony of undisclosed expert witness which contradicted an opinion expressed by defendant's expert about accepted accounting practices).

[454] Cal. Code Civ. Proc. § 2034.610; *see Richaud v. Jennings*, 16 Cal. App. 4th 81, 92, 19 Cal. Rptr. 2d 790 (1993) (observing that an augmentation motion allows the opponent to explain the prejudice created, the proponent to demonstrate good cause for any delay, and the court to minimize any continuances and disruption of the litigation).

[455] For discussion of prevention of discovery abuses and discovery sanctions in the federal courts, see §§ 10.12–10.14, *supra*.

informal negotiation is unsuccessful, the dissatisfied party may move to compel discovery by court order, with the losing party being subject to mandatory monetary sanctions unless the court finds "substantial justification" for that party's position or other circumstances which would make the imposition of sanctions unjust.[456] Finally, disobedience of a court order compelling discovery may lead to the imposition of additional, more drastic sanctions depending on the discovery device involved.[457]

[3] The Meet-and-Confer Requirement

Before filing a motion to compel, counsel for the moving party must make a serious attempt to obtain "an informal resolution of each issue."[458] To encourage parties to work out their discovery differences and avoid burdensome court involvement, the Civil Discovery Act requires that counsel for both sides undertake a reasonable and good faith attempt to talk the matter over, compare their views, consult, and deliberate. The level of effort at informal resolution depends on the circumstances. Greater effort may be warranted in a larger, more complex discovery context; more modest effort may suffice in a simpler, more narrowly focused case. For example, exchanging brief letters that state positions but offer no concessions, or bickering over objections during a deposition, may be insufficient.[459] But, where the discovery issue is relatively simple and scheduling conflicts make scheduling a face-to-face meeting or a telephonic conference difficult, an off-the-record discussion during a deposition immediately after an objection may be sufficient.[460] Underscoring the importance of the obligation to attempt informal resolution of discovery disputes, the Act requires the court to impose monetary sanctions on any party or attorney who fails to meet-and-confer, regardless of the outcome of the particular discovery motion.[461]

---

[456] CAL. CODE CIV. PROC. §§ 2025.450 &.480, 2030.290 &.300, 2031.300 &.310, 2032.240, 2033.290 & 2034.730; *see Sexton v. Superior Court*, 58 Cal. App. 4th 1403, 68 Cal. Rptr. 2d 708 (1997) (holding the 45-day time period within which to make a motion to compel discovery is jurisdictional in the sense that its expiration renders the court without authority to rule on the motion other than to deny it).

[457] CAL. CODE CIV. PROC. §§ 2025.480, 2030.290, 2031.320 & 2032.420.

[458] CAL. CODE CIV. PROC. §§ 2016.040, 2025.450, 2031.310. *See Townsend v. Superior Court*, 61 Cal. App. 4th 1431, 72 Cal. Rptr. 2d 333 (1998) (holding a good faith attempt at informal resolution entails something more than bickering with deponent's counsel at a deposition, and therefore directing the trial court to set aside an order compelling answers to deposition questions).

[459] *See Obregon v. Superior Court*, 67 Cal. App. 4th 424, 79 Cal. Rptr. 2d 62 (1998) (concluding that the plaintiff should have made greater effort than a single brief letter to defendant after defendant's objections to plaintiff's grossly overbroad interrogatories); *Townsend v. Superior Court*, 61 Cal. App. 4th 1431, 72 Cal. Rptr. 2d 333 (1998) (finding counsels' heated arguments and lack of informal negotiation over various objections during a deposition did not satisfy the meet-and-confer requirement, and therefore directing trial court to set aside its order compelling discovery).

[460] *Stewart v. Colonial W. Agency, Inc.*, 87 Cal. App. 4th 1006, 105 Cal. Rptr. 2d 115 (2001).

[461] CAL. CODE CIV. PROC. §§ 2023.010(i), 2023.020.

[4] Discovery Sanctions

In addition to monetary sanctions, the Civil Discovery Act authorizes, in ascending order of severity: (1) evidence sanctions prohibiting the introduction of certain evidence; (2) issue sanctions establishing certain facts in the action; (3) case-terminating sanctions striking a pleading, dismissing an action or rendering default judgment; and (4) contempt sanctions treating the misuse of discovery as contempt of court. The legislative intent is that a drastic sanction should not be appropriate in the first instance where a party has failed to respond to a discovery demand, because that would constitute a disproportionate punishment.[462] Several appellate decisions emphasize the need for the trial court to tailor the sanction to fit the misconduct.[463] For example, one court held that an issue or evidence sanction would be appropriate for failure to appear at a deposition, not a case-terminating sanction;[464] another held that an issue sanction was appropriate where objections to production of documents were meritless.[465]

More drastic sanctions are available after the general obligation to participate in discovery has been transformed into a court order. Several recent appellate decisions demonstrate that imposition of case-terminating sanctions may be appropriate where lesser sanctions would not bring about compliance with discovery orders.[466] For example, in one case, the Court of Appeal not only affirmed the trial court's order striking the defendants' answer and entering a default judgment as a sanction for their repeated discovery obstruction and refusals to comply with various discovery orders, but also imposed monetary sanctions on the defendants and their attorneys for prosecuting a frivolous appeal of the discovery sanctions.[467] In another case, the appellate court affirmed the

---

[462] *See Ruvalcaba v. Gov't Emp. Ins. Co.*, 222 Cal. App. 3d 1579, 272 Cal. Rptr. 541 (1990) (holding dismissal of action is inappropriate where there was no prior court order directing the plaintiff to comply).

[463] For examples of the imposition of an evidence and an issue sanction tailored to specific discovery misuse, see *Juarez v. Boy Scouts of America, Inc.*, 81 Cal. App. 4th 377, 97 Cal. Rptr. 2d 12 (2000) (prohibiting plaintiff from producing at trial the evidence he repeatedly refused to produce during discovery); *Vallbona v. Springer*, 43 Cal. App. 4th 1525, 1541–49, 51 Cal. Rptr. 2d 311 (1996) (prohibiting defendants from introducing certain documents into evidence, and admissions imposed as to certain issues, where the defendants willfully failed to respond to the plaintiff's request for production of documents).

[464] *See McArthur v. Bockman*, 208 Cal. App. 3d 1076, 256 Cal. Rptr. 522 (1989).

[465] *Estate of Ivy*, 22 Cal. App. 4th 873, 879, 28 Cal. Rptr. 2d 16 (1994).

[466] *See, e.g., Liberty Mut. Fire Ins. Co. v. LcL Adm'rs, Inc.*, 163 Cal. App. 4th 1093, 78 Cal. Rptr. 3d 200 (2008) (upholding trial court's order striking defendant's answer and cross-complaint where defendant filed evasive answers to interrogatories, and repeatedly ignored meet-and-confer letters and two orders compelling further responses to interrogatories); *Lang v. Hochman*, 77 Cal. App. 4th 1225, 92 Cal. Rptr. 2d 322 (2000) (upholding default against defendants and dismissal of defendants' cross-complaint as sanctions for inexcusable failure to comply with three discovery orders, where trial court had progressively sanctioned defendants but defendants still did not produce requested documents); *R.S. Creative, Inc. v. Creative Cotton, Ltd.*, 75 Cal. App. 4th 486, 89 Cal. Rptr. 2d 353 (1999) (affirming dismissal of plaintiff's complaint as sanction for repeated efforts to thwart discovery, including the violation of two discovery orders and deliberate destruction of evidence by deletion of plaintiff's computer files).

[467] *Collison & Kaplan v. Hartunian*, 21 Cal. App. 4th 1611, 26 Cal. Rptr. 2d 786 (1994). Likewise, in

dismissal of the plaintiff's complaint where the plaintiff refused to testify at his first deposition, disrupted and unilaterally terminated the second deposition, and violated the trial court's order to appear for his third deposition and to provide supplemental answers to interrogatories.[468] And in one recent decision, the Court of Appeal even found an abuse of discretion by the trial court for *not* striking the defendant's answer and entering a default judgment as a sanction for the defendant's flagrant discovery misconduct, where monetary and issue sanctions had not deterred the defendant from misusing the discovery process.[469]

Attorneys, not the parties they represent, are responsible for most discovery abuses. Therefore, the Civil Discovery Act authorizes a court to impose discovery sanctions, in appropriate circumstances of misuse, on a party or on an attorney, or on both. However, unlike monetary sanctions against a party, which are based on the party's misuse of the discovery process, monetary sanctions against a party's attorney require a finding that the attorney advised that conduct.[470]

American Home Assurance Co. v. Societe Commerciale Toutelectric, 104 Cal. App. 4th 406, 435–37, 128 Cal. Rptr. 2d 430 (2002), the court affirmed an order striking the defendant's answer and entering a $25 million default judgment as a sanction for willful failure to meet discovery obligations.

[468] *Parker v. Wolters Kluwer United States, Inc.*, 149 Cal. App. 4th 285, 57 Cal. Rptr. 3d 18 (2007).

[469] *Doppes v. Bentley Motors, Inc.*, 174 Cal. App. 4th 967, 991–97, 94 Cal. Rptr. 3d 802 (2009).

[470] Cal. Code Civ. Proc. § 2023.030. In *Ghanooni v. Super Shuttle*, 20 Cal. App. 4th 256, 24 Cal. Rptr. 2d 501 (1993), for example, the court held that imposition of monetary sanctions jointly on plaintiff and plaintiff's counsel for plaintiff's refusal to submit to certain X-rays constituted an abuse of discretion where plaintiff's refusal was not based on advice of her attorney.

Chapter 11

DISPOSITION WITHOUT TRIAL

§ 11.01 OVERVIEW

All procedural systems provide a variety of alternatives for obtaining judgment before trial. If a defendant fails to respond to a pleading within the time designated for response, he is in *default* and subject to entry of a *default judgment*, discussed in section 11.02. If defendant responds by successfully attacking the pleading, it may be dismissed, under Rule 12(b) or be subject to a motion for judgment on the pleadings under Rule 12(c), as previously discussed in section 8.07. When materials outside the pleadings are submitted in support of some motions attacking the pleadings, the motions are converted to motions for *summary judgment*, discussed in section 11.03. Summary judgment is available to either party whenever it can show that there is no genuinely triable dispute of material fact and that it is entitled to judgment as a matter of law. Finally, when the plaintiff elects to withdraw his action before a final judgment on the merits, he may seek a *voluntary dismissal* or *nonsuit*. Alternatively, if he simply abandons the action by failing to prosecute or disobeys court orders or rules, he is subject to *involuntary dismissal* or *compulsory nonsuit*. Dismissals and nonsuits are discussed in Section 11.04.[1]

§ 11.02 DEFAULT

Our procedural systems rely principally on the parties to move cases along. A party's complete failure to respond to a pleading exposes an adversary to costly delay and uncertainty. Almost all systems therefore make *default judgments* available as a protection for the rights of the claimant. At the same time, all procedural systems prefer dispositions on the merits to default judgments.[2] Rule 55 is quite typical in reconciling these concerns by assuring that the unresponsive party is aware of the risk of such a judgment. The usual pattern under the rule begins when the default — failure to plead or otherwise respond within the time set

---

[1] Motions to dismiss a complaint under Rule 12 are discussed in § 8.07, *supra*.

[2] *See, e.g., Varnes v. Glass Bottle Blowers Ass'n*, 674 F.2d 1365 (11th Cir. 1982); *Ellingsworth v. Chrysler*, 665 F.2d 180 (7th Cir. 1981). Default judgments are common, nevertheless. In the general trial courts of Maine and Delaware, for example, approximately 3% and 15% of civil cases, respectively, ended in default judgments. State of Maine, Administrative Office of the Courts, 1987 Annual Report 90 (1988); Administrative Office of the Courts, 1982 Annual Report of the Delaware Judiciary 79 (1983), cited in Hillard M. Sterling & Philip G. Schrag, *Default Judgments Against Consumers: Has the System Failed?*, 67 Denver U. L. Rev. 357 (1990). A recent study of federal district court statistics revealed a default rate of 5.4%. *See* Gillian K. Hadfield, *Where Have All the Trials Gone? Settlements, Nontrial Adjudications, and Statistical Artifacts in the Changing Disposition of Federal Civil Cases*, 1 J. Empirical Legal Stud. 705, 730 (2004).

by the rules — is formally noted in some fashion, as by a clerk's entry on the docket sheet. Only after *entry of default* may the court, in its discretion and often pursuant to notice to the defaulting party and sometimes a hearing on damages, enter a *default judgment.* In short, be careful to distinguish default and entry of default from a default judgment.

[1]   Entering a Default

A party is in default and subject to the rules governing default judgments when he has "failed to plead or otherwise defend," as he would, for example, by filing an answer or moving to dismiss the complaint.[3] Default is a corollary to the strict time limits most systems impose for responding to pleadings.[4] When a party *has* responded within the time limit by pleading or attacking the complaint, his subsequent failure to appear for trial does not, without more, place him in default. By pleading, he places the case at issue, obligating his adversary to present his proof in order to recover a judgment.[5]

Rule 55 authorizes the clerk to enter a default when it appears from the docket or is shown by affidavit of the claimant. *Entry of default* is simply a notation of the fact of default and an interlocutory — interim — step towards the entry of a default judgment. It cuts off the defaulting party's right to further notice, unless he has appeared in the litigation.[6]

Rule 55(c) authorizes the court in its discretion to set aside a docket entry of default upon good cause shown. The court may consider the defaulting party's willfulness, any prejudice to the adversary should the entry of default be set aside, and the existence of any meritorious defense to the claim.[7] The courts' preference for merits dispositions, however, usually makes them lenient towards the defaulting party on motions to set aside the entry of default where he evinces a desire to correct the default.[8] Moreover, because no default judgment has yet been entered, setting aside the entry of default usually upsets no reliance interests.

---

[3] *See, e.g.*, Rule 55(a). *See generally* Carl B. Schultz, *Sanctioning Defendants' Non-Willful Delay: The Failure of Rule 55 and a Proposal for Its Reform*, 23 U. Rich. L. Rev. 203, 204 (1989).

[4] *See, e.g.*, Rule 12(a) (requiring a party against whom a claim is pled to answer, reply or move against the pleading under Rule 12 within twenty-one days after service).

[5] *See, e.g., Coulas v. Smith*, 395 P.2d 527 (Ariz. 1964) (rules governing default judgments are inapplicable to judgment entered against a defendant who answered the complaint and a crossclaim, but then failed to appear at trial). *See generally Bass v. Hoagland*, 172 F.2d 205 (5th Cir.), *cert. denied*, 338 U.S. 816 (1949). Most courts are also empowered by rule, statute, or inherent power to enter punitive default judgments against parties who violate rules or orders of the court. *See, e.g.*, Rules 11, 16, 26(g), and 37.

[6] Moore § 55.12[1]. *See* § 11.02[2] (defining appearance), *infra.*

[7] Moore § 55.70[2].

[8] *Id.* § 55.50[1]; Wright & Miller § 2692.

[2] Entering a Default Judgment

Judgment may follow entry of default in two ways. Clerks have authority under Rule 55(b)(1) to enter default judgments, but only if the defaulting party is not an unrepresented minor or incompetent, that party has not appeared in the action, and the claimant shows by affidavit that the relief sought is a liquidated (arithmetically ascertainable) sum. Only the court may enter judgment in all other cases. When the defaulting party has appeared, notice and possibly a hearing will be necessary.[9]

An *appearance* is any action that demonstrates sufficient interest by the defaulting party in the litigation to suggest that he might contest the award of relief by default judgment, and therefore could benefit from notice of application for such a judgment. A party usually appears formally by filing a *praecipe* or notice of appearance by his attorney, or by making other submissions to the court during the lawsuit. In part to encourage settlement efforts by parties, the courts have also found the necessary appearance from participation in protracted settlement negotiations, correspondence, or other communications inconsistent with the complete abandonment of the litigation and disregard for judicial process.[10]

After any required notice, Rule 55(b)(2) authorizes the court to conduct a hearing on the proper measure of relief. The judicial hearing is not a trial in most systems, and there is no right to a jury. The federal rules and some states, however, entitle the non-defaulting party who previously claimed a jury to a jury trial on damages.[11] The court will typically first inspect the record to confirm that the defendant was properly served. The default establishes all well-pleaded facts as true and forecloses any offer of proof by the defaulting party as to liability. However, the defaulting party does not admit conclusions of law. A default is not "an absolute confession by the defendant of his liability and of the plaintiff's right to recover," but merely "an admission of the facts cited in the Complaint, which by themselves may or may not be sufficient to establish a defendant's liability."[12] To enter the default judgment on the admitted facts, the court must therefore, in effect, first decide a phantom motion to dismiss for failure to state a claim.[13] Defendant also may offer evidence on the measure of relief. Courts use their discretion to determine whether to enter a default judgment at all, what proof to allow, and how much and what kind of relief they will grant.[14]

---

[9] *See* Rule 55(b)(2).

[10] *See generally* Moore § 55.21. If, however, during informal communications, the defaulting party was clearly informed of his adversary's intent to seek a default judgment, then the court will usually not find an appearance entitling the defaulting party to notice under Rule 55(b)(2). *Compare Wilson v. Moore & Associates, Inc.*, 564 F.2d 366 (9th Cir. 1977) (plaintiff's counsel warned defendant by letter that failure to answer would place him in default; no appearance), *with Lutomski v. Panther Valley Coin Exch.*, 653 F.2d 270 (6th Cir. 1981) (informal contacts regarding proper amount of damage constituted an appearance).

[11] *See, e.g.*, Rule 55(b)(2); VA. SUP. CT. R. 3:19(c) (West 2012).

[12] *Pitts ex rel. Pitts v. Seneca Sports, Inc.*, 321 F. Supp. 2d 1353, 1357 (S.D. Ga. 2004).

[13] *See, e.g., Caruso v. Krieger*, 698 S.W.2d 760 (Tex. App. 1985); Moore § 55.12[1].

[14] The relief is subject to Rule 54(c)'s limitation of the relief to the kind or amount sought in the pleaded demand for relief. *See* § 8.06[3] (demand for relief), *supra*.

Virgin Records America, Inc. v. Lacey[15] provides a typical example. The plaintiff sued the defendant for illegally downloading copyrighted music. When the defendant had not responded or appeared three months after service, the plaintiff asked the clerk to enter a default, and subsequently moved for entry of a default judgment. The court noted that the record contained a return of service, showing that the defendant had been properly served. It also found that, because the defendant had not appeared in the action, "she is entitled to no further notice at this time." It then found that the default admitted the complaint's allegations of repeated music downloads without the plaintiff's permission, and of the plaintiff's copyright ownership of the downloaded music. The court held that these facts sufficiently established the plaintiff's claim to relief. It then found that plaintiff was entitled to statutory damages of $750 per download (which required no evidentiary hearing inasmuch as the amount was set by statute and the plaintiff's stipulation), as well as injunctive relief against continued downloading.

Like other final judgments, default judgments are subject to timely post-judgment attack under Rule 60(b).[16] Courts are particularly apt to grant a motion to vacate a default judgment when the defaulting party was served constructively rather than in person,[17] or was denied notice of the application for judgment to which his prior appearance entitled him. Relevant factors are otherwise the same as those considered on a motion to set aside entry of default, with one important difference. The systemic interest in finality of judgments[18] enters into the equation as a counterweight to leniency. Doubts are still resolved in favor of the defaulting party,[19] but the courts are less lenient in vacating a default judgment than they are in finding good cause to set aside an interlocutory entry of default.[20]

---

[15] 510 F. Supp. 2d 588 (S.D. Ala. 2007).

[16] *See* § 12.11[2][b] (motions to vacate judgment within one year), *infra.* The Supreme Court has held that due process forbids states from conditioning such relief on the existence of a meritorious defense if the default was entered without proper notice to defendant. *Peralta v. Heights Med. Ctr., Inc.*, 485 U.S. 80 (1988).

[17] *See, e.g.*, N.Y. Civ. Prac. L. & R. § 317 (McKinney, Westlaw through 2007 legislation); Va. Code Ann. § 8.01-322 (West 2012).

[18] *See* § 13.01 (overview of appeal), *infra.*

[19] *Hritz v. Woma Corp.*, 732 F.2d 1178, 1185 (3d Cir. 1984). *See generally* Schultz, note 3, *supra*, at 213–14, 216–20 (finding that courts frequently reject default as an inappropriate sanction for non-willful delay).

[20] Wright & Miller § 2692. *See generally* Mary Kay Kane, *Relief from Federal Judgments: A Morass Unrelieved By a Rule*, 30 Hastings L.J. 41 (1978) (urging amendment to Rule 55(c) to make explicit that the standard for relief from entry of default is more lenient than the standard for relief from default judgment).

§ 11.03   SUMMARY JUDGMENT

[1]   Purposes

At one time, pleadings were only open to facial attack (an attack on the sufficiency of allegations appearing on the face of the pleading).[21] The truth and sufficiency of facts supporting a pleading could only be tested at trial.[22] Summary judgment evolved to intercept *before* trial factually insufficient claims or defenses — those which would probably suffer a motion for a directed verdict (now termed judgment as a matter of law in federal courts)[23] — *at* trial. The Supreme Court, in fact, has characterized summary judgments as pretrial equivalents of directed verdicts.[24] The summary judgment motion permits a party to go behind the allegations in the pleadings to show that there is no genuine dispute of material fact in the evidence that would necessitate or justify the expense of trial, and to argue that the court should enter judgment for him on some or all claims and defenses as a matter of law. Like the motion for directed verdict, it is consistent with the right to jury trial because it tests whether there is any genuine factual dispute for the jury to resolve. "Summary judgment distinguishes the merely formal existence of a dispute as framed in the pleadings from the actual substantive existence of a controversy requiring trial."[25]

By forcing the parties to preview their trial evidence and to relate it to their legal theories, a motion for summary judgment may result in what is effectively a form of discovery. This is because the risk of judgment posed by a motion for summary judgment may force the parties to sift the typically undifferentiated mass of evidence produced by normal discovery methods to identify their material evidence in opposition to the motion. "The very intimation of mortality when summary judgment is at issue assures us that the motion will be rebutted with every factual and legal argument available."[26]

A related (but alone insufficient) purpose of summary judgment is educating the parties and the court about the case. Often a motion for summary judgment presents the first occasion for the parties to pull the case together, set priorities in their claims and defenses, relate the facts unearthed by discovery to their legal theories, and assess overall strengths and weaknesses. Even when existence of a factual dispute causes it to fail, the motion may promote settlement by alerting the

---

[21] *See* § 8.07[1] (motion practice in general), *supra.*

[22] *See* Charles E. Clark, Code Pleading § 80 (2d ed. 1947); John A. Bauman, *Evolution of the Summary Judgment Procedure,* 31 Ind. L.J. 329 (1956).

[23] *See* § 12.09[1] (directed verdicts), *infra.*

[24] *See Anderson v. Liberty Lobby, Inc.,* 477 U.S. 242, 250 (1986) (the standard governing summary judgment "mirrors the standard for a directed verdict . . ."); *cf.* § 12.09[3][c] (discussing how motions for summary judgment and directed verdict bear a functional resemblance to motions to dismiss for failure to state a claim, for judgment on the pleadings, and for judgment notwithstanding the verdict).

[25] Moore § 56.02[1].

[26] *Georgia S. & Fla. Ry. Co. v. Atl. Coast Line R.R. Co.,* 373 F.2d 493, 498 (5th Cir.), *cert. denied,* 389 U.S. 851 (1967). *See also* Clark, note 21, *supra,* § 13.02.

nonmovant and the court to the weakness of the nonmovant's case.[27] Alternatively, the motion may at least simplify eventual trial by illuminating the genuine issues.

On the other hand, historically the movant often paid a price for such education by having to preview his *own* evidence. Thus, commentators cautioned that

> [T]he decision to make a summary judgment motion involves a balancing of the possible damage to the movant's case by educating the opponent through supporting documents against the possible benefit of termination of the case through a favorable ruling on the motion and the possible advantage of learning more about the opponent's case through his supporting affidavits.[28]

In addition, an unsuccessful summary judgment motion may evoke a legal ruling that will haunt the movant later in the case.[29]

A trio of decisions by the Supreme Court in 1986, however, changed the price of summary judgment for some movants. Today a defendant who would not have the burden of production at trial may be able to move for summary judgment on little more than a bare motion, placing almost the entire cost of summary judgment on the plaintiff.[30] This possibility invites abuse of the motion as a tool for discovery, or worse, harassment. One appellate court has commented that the motion "has often been used improperly: as a discovery device; to educate the trial judge; in the hope, however faint, of quick victory; and in the expectation, frequently realized, of retarding the progress of a suit and making litigation more expensive."[31] Rule 11[32] (or its state procedural equivalent) acts as a control on such abuse in theory, but it is unclear how effective for this purpose it is in practice.

---

[27] *See* William P. McLauchlan, *An Empirical Study of the Federal Summary Judgment Rule*, 6 J. LEGAL STUD. 427, 458 (1977); *cf.* WILLIAM W. SCHWARZER ET AL., THE ANALYSIS AND DECISION OF SUMMARY JUDGMENT MOTIONS 69 (1991).

[28] ROBERT McC. FIGG, RALPH C. McCULLOUGH & JAMES L. UNDERWOOD, CIVIL TRIAL MANUAL 2 526 (ALI-ABA student 2d ed. 1980). Copyright © 1980 by the American Law Institute. Reprinted with permission of the American Law Institute — American Bar Association Committee on Continuing Professional Education. *See also* John E. Kennedy, *Federal Summary Judgment: Reconciling Celotex v. Catrett with Adickes v. Kress and the Evidentiary Problem Under Rule 56*, 6 REV. LITIG. 227, 253 (1987).

[29] *See* § 15.14 (law of the case), *infra*.

[30] *See* § 11.03[3][b] (relationship to trial burdens), *infra*.

[31] *Professional Managers, Inc. v. Fawer, Brian, Hardy & Zatzkis*, 799 F.2d 218, 221–22 (5th Cir. 1986).

[32] *See* § 8.05[2], *supra*; Beverly Dyer, *A Genuine Ground in Summary Judgment for Rule 11*, 99 YALE L.J. 411 (1989).

[2] Procedure

[a] Initial Motion

A motion for summary judgment may be filed by any party, although it is in practice primarily a defendant's device.[33] The motion asserts that there is no triable or "genuine" dispute as to any material fact and that the moving party is entitled to judgment as a matter of law.[34] Clarifying a matter that was previously ambiguous, a 2010 amendment to Rule 56 now expressly states that a party may move for "partial summary judgment" on any claim or defense, or part of a claim or defense.[35]

While it is customary for the movant to support the motion with affidavits, they are not required. Rule 56(c)(1) expressly provides that a party may use a broad range of materials in the record. A court only has to consider cited material, though it has the right to look at other material in the record.[36] In other words, it has no duty to search the record itself; it is the parties' burden to cite the supporting material in the record that it wants the court to consider. In addition, many federal courts have adopted local rules requiring the movant to accompany its motion with a statement of undisputed material facts, citing to supporting materials or the record.[37] Some states have also taken this approach.[38]

Though the permissible supporting materials include "depositions, documents, electronically stored information, affidavits or declarations, stipulations, admissions, interrogatory answers, or other materials,"[39] the opposing party may object that a particular cited matter "cannot be presented in a form that would be admissible in evidence."[40] The summary judgment motion looks prospectively to

---

[33] McLauchlan, note 27, *supra*, at 441.

[34] *See, e.g.*, Rule 56(a); CAL. CIV. PROC. CODE § 437c(c) (West 2012). *See* § 11.03[3] (the standard for summary judgment), *infra*.

[35] *See* Rule 56(a).

[36] Rule 56(c)(3).

[37] Note, *Court Examination of the Discovery File on a Motion for Summary Judgment*, 79 MICH. L. REV. 321, 325 n.19 (1980) (listing 28 district courts that have adopted such rules) (hereinafter cited as *Court Examination*). While such local rules are probably consistent with Rule 56 (*see* § 1.02, *supra*, and Rule 83), a local "procedure" adopted by individual judges requiring advance screening of summary judgment motions was found inconsistent and therefore invalid in *Brown v. Crawford County*, 960 F.2d 1002 (11th Cir. 1992). The Court of Appeals there noted that a survey had identified no fewer than thirty federal courts with local rules that conflict with Rule 56. *Brown*, 960 F.2d at 1009 n.10 (*citing Local Rules Project* 140 (1989)).

A later study of summary judgment motion practice in a sampling of federal courts revealed very few differences between courts that had adopted such rules and those that had not. JOE CECIL & GEORGE CORT, REPORT ON SUMMARY JUDGMENT PRACTICE ACROSS DISTRICTS WITH VARIATIONS IN LOCAL RULES at 1 (FEDERAL JUDICIAL CENTER, AUG. 13, 2008).

[38] *See, e.g.*, CAL. CIV. PROC. CODE § 437c(b) (West 2012).

[39] Rule 56(c)(1)(A). *See generally* Edward Brunet, *Summary Judgment Materials*, 147 F.R.D. 647 (1993).

[40] Rule 56(c)(2). *See, e.g., Duplantis v. Shell Offshore, Inc.*, 948 F.2d 187 (5th Cir. 1991); *Canada v. Blain's Helicopters, Inc.*, 831 F.2d 920, 925 (9th Cir. 1987); *Aguilera v. Cook County Police & Corr. Merit Bd.*, 760 F.2d 844, 849 (7th Cir.), *cert. denied*, 474 U.S. 907 (1985); *Brown v. Trans World Airlines, Inc.*,

what can be proven at trial.[41] Generally insisting that admissible evidence be offered in support of (or opposition to) summary judgment ensures that "trial would [not be] futile on account of lack of competent evidence."[42] Thus, for example, material grounded in rumor, conclusory allegations without support in the record, legal argument, and inferences or opinions not grounded in observation or first-hand experience, and mere speculation or conjecture will not support summary judgment.[43] Nor can a party simply cite its own pleadings (unless they are verified and the allegations are made on personal knowledge, effectively converting the pleading into an affidavit). The very purpose of summary judgment is "to separate what is formal or pretended in denial or averment from what is genuine and substantial, so that only the latter may subject a suitor to the burden of a trial."[44]

On the other hand, Rule 56(c)(2) recognizes that not all evidence at the summary judgment stage will yet be in a form that would be admissible at trial. In *Celotex Corp. v. Catrett*,[45] the Supreme Court, in discussing the burden on the party opposing a motion for summary judgment said, "We do not mean that the nonmoving party must produce evidence in a form that would be admissible at trial in order to avoid summary judgment."[46] There, the plaintiff had opposed summary judgment by offering a letter from a Mr. Hoff (an executive at her former husband's employer) discussing the employer's use of the defendant's product. Arguably the unauthenticated letter would not, in that form, be admissible at trial. On remand, the lower court cited the foregoing passage from *Celotex* in finding that:

> [T]he record, dispassionately viewed, reflects the existence of a witness who can testify with respect to Mr. Catrett's exposure to Firebar. Thus, even if the Hoff letter itself would not be admissible at trial, Mrs. Catrett has gone on to indicate that the substance of the letter is reducible to admissible evidence in the form of trial testimony.[47]

Apart from this example, and affidavits and unsworn declarations (which the rule itself lists), it is unclear what other kinds of evidence will be considered at summary judgment even if not then in admissible form.[48] In any case, defects in supporting

---

746 F.2d 1354, 1358–59 (8th Cir. 1984). *See generally* Brunet, note 39, *supra*, at 653–55.

[41] *See* James J. Duane, *The Four Greatest Myths About Summary Judgment*, 52 Wash. & Lee L. Rev. 1523, 1535–41 (1996).

[42] *Kern v. Tri-State Ins. Co.*, 386 F.2d 754, 756 (8th Cir. 1967); *See* William W. Schwarzer, *Summary Judgment: A Proposed Revision of Rule 56*, 110 F.R.D. 213, 220 (1987).

[43] *See, e.g., Hogue v. City of Fort Wayne*, 599 F. Supp. 2d 1009, 1016 (N.D. Ind. 2009); Schwarzer, note 42, *supra*.

[44] *Richard v. Credit Suisse*, 152 N.E. 110, 111 (N.Y. 1926) (Cardozo, J.). Verified pleadings, *see* § 8.05[1] (verification), *supra*, however, are sworn statements which may be treated as affidavits, if they are made upon personal knowledge by a competent affiant and present admissible facts. *See, e.g., Forts v. Malcolm*, 426 F. Supp. 464, 466 (S.D.N.Y. 1977).

[45] 477 U.S. 317 (1986) (emphasis added).

[46] *Id.* at 324.

[47] *Catrett v. Johns-Manville Sales Corp.*, 826 F.2d 33, 38 (D.C. Cir. 1987) (footnote omitted).

[48] *See, e.g., Offshore Aviation v. Transcon Lines, Inc.*, 831 F.2d 1013, 1015 n.1 (11th Cir. 1987); *Bushman v. Halm*, 798 F.2d 651, 654 n.5 (3d Cir. 1986). *See generally* Melissa L. Nelken, *One Step Forward, Two Steps Back: Summary Judgment After Celotex*, 40 Hastings L.J. 53, 56, 60–62 (1988)

materials are waived if not challenged, just as they would be at trial.[49] This principle, too, is illustrated in *Celotex* on remand, for the court there also disregarded the movant's objection to the Hoff letter in part because the movant had failed to object in the district court.

Oral testimony, of course, is a form of evidence that would be admissible at trial. But, though such evidence has been considered in connection with a motion for summary judgment in rare cases, and Rule 43(c) authorizes the court to hear it, its routine acceptance would convert a summary judgment hearing into a trial.[50] Rule 56 and all but one state therefore permit the use of affidavits (sworn written statements) to support summary judgment motions. Affidavits must be made on personal knowledge by someone competent to testify.[51] They must "set out facts that would be admissible in evidence."[52] Hearsay, speculation, conclusions of law, conclusory ultimate facts, and promises that the necessary evidence will be offered at trial therefore cannot support a motion for summary judgment, even when presented by an otherwise proper affidavit.[53]

When evidentiary material is offered in support of a Rule 12(b)(6) motion to dismiss for failure to state a claim or a Rule 12(c) motion for judgment on the pleadings, these federal rules provide that the Rule 12 motion shall be treated as a Rule 56 summary judgment motion. In addition, when evidentiary material in the record suggests the availability of summary judgment, a federal court may grant summary judgment *sua sponte* (on its own, without motion).[54] Fair notice to the opposing party and an opportunity to respond are prerequisites for either the conversion of a Rule 12 motion to a summary judgment motion or *sua sponte* action by the court, as Rule 56(f) now expressly provides.

(noting, before the 2010 rule change, that majority's statements in *Celotex* regarding formal requirements for evidence on summary judgment invited lower court confusion).

[49] *See, e.g., Catrett v. Johns-Manville Sales Corp.*, 826 F.2d at 37; McCORMICK'S HANDBOOK OF THE LAW OF EVIDENCE § 4, at 140 (J. Strong 4th ed. 1992). *But see* SCHWARZER, note 27, *supra*, at 51 (criticizing the waiver rule).

[50] *See Stewart v. RCA Corp.*, 790 F.2d 624 (7th Cir. 1986) (asserting that although what is now Rule 43(c) gives judges full menu of methods for gathering evidence to resolve disputes, Rule 56 is not intended to resolve disputes).

[51] Kent Sinclair & Patrick Hanes, *Summary Judgment: A Proposal for Procedural Reform in the Core Motion Context*, 36 WM. & MARY L. REV. 1633, app. B (1995).

[52] Rule 56(c)(4). *See, e.g., Sitts v. United States*, 811 F.2d 736 (2d Cir. 1987).

[53] *See, e.g., Leonard v. Dixie Well Service & Supply, Inc.*, 828 F.2d 291 (5th Cir. 1987) (bare statement that plaintiff was a "[s]eaman" when that is the issue will not suffice); *Campbell v. Fort Worth Bank & Trust*, 705 S.W.2d 400 (Tex. App. 1986, *writ ref'd n.r.e.*) (averments "to the best of my knowledge" do not represent the required personal knowledge). *See generally* Brunet, note 39, *supra*, at 658–59.

[54] Rule 56(f)(3). *See United States v. Grayson*, 879 F.2d 620 (9th Cir. 1989) (approving *sua sponte* summary judgment, even without notice to losing party, when that party has "full and fair opportunity to ventilate the issues"); *Portsmouth Square, Inc. v. Shareholders Protective Comm.*, 770 F.2d 866 (9th Cir. 1985) (affirming trial court's *sua sponte* summary judgment based on plaintiff's inability to establish genuine dispute of material fact in pretrial brief and supporting evidentiary materials). *See generally Celotex Corp.*, 477 U.S. at 326 ("[d]istrict courts are widely acknowledged to possess the power to enter summary judgments *sua sponte*, so long as the losing party was on notice . . . .") (dictum).

[b]   Responses to the Motion

Within a time set by the parties or the court,[55] the non-movant may respond to a summary judgment motion in three ways and may also cross-move for summary judgment.

First, he may present an affidavit under Rule 56(d) showing why he cannot now present facts in opposition to summary judgment.[56] Because most jurisdictions permit defendants to file summary judgment motions at any time, a rule like Rule 56(d) is necessary to give the plaintiff time to undertake discovery.[57] When plaintiff files such an affidavit, the court may either deny the motion for summary judgment or defer it to allow the opposing party time to obtain affidavits or take discovery in opposition to summary judgment. The reasonableness of the non-moving party's request for time is a crucial factor in the exercise of the court's discretion.[58] It is an abuse of discretion for a court to grant summary judgment without affording the opposing party a reasonable opportunity to take discovery pertinent to the motion, even when that party has not filed a Rule 56(d) affidavit.[59] "If the documents or other discovery sought would be relevant to the issues presented by the motion for summary judgment," one appellate court has said, "the opposing party should be allowed the opportunity to utilize the discovery process to gain access to the requested materials."[60]

Second, even when a party could file materials in opposition to the motion, he does not *have* to; he can do nothing. Summary judgment casts the burden of production upon the movant to make a *prima facie* showing that there is no genuine dispute of material fact. That burden must be satisfied before the burden shifts to the opposing party.[61] "A right to judgment as a matter of law is not established

---

[55] Rule 56 sets no time for the non-moving party to file an opposition. The Advisory Committee explained that "Scheduling orders or other pretrial orders can regulate timing to fit the needs of the case." Rule 56 advisory committee's note. Many state rules provide an even longer response time in recognition of the time which a party may need to gather materials in opposition to summary judgment. *See, e.g.*, CAL. CIV. PROC. CODE § 437c(a) (West 2012) (75 days). A court may properly disregard untimely submissions. *See Lujan v. Nat'l Wildlife Fed'n*, 497 U.S. 871, 894–97 (1990). In practice, the parties will usually agree to a response time for the non-moving party.

[56] *See generally* JOHN F. BRUNET, SUMMARY JUDGMENT: FEDERAL LAW & PRACTICE § 7.02 (3d ed. 2006); John F. Lapham, Note, *Summary Judgment Before the Completion of Discovery: A Proposed Revision of Federal Rule of Civil Procedure 56(f)*, 24 U. MICH. J.L. REFORM 253, 267–81 (1990).

[57] *See, e.g.*, CAL. CIV. PROC. CODE § 437c(h) (West 2012); N.Y. CIV. PRAC. L. & R. § 3212(f) (McKinney, Westlaw through 2007 legislation).

[58] *Compare Littlejohn v. Shell Oil Co.*, 483 F.2d 1140 (5th Cir.) (*en banc*), *cert. denied*, 414 U.S. 1116 (1973) (abuse of discretion in the district court's refusal of a continuance pursuant to what is now Rule 56(d), when the 56(d) affidavit demonstrated that the evidence was in the control of the movants and there were complicating factors regarding agreements between counsel about the timing of discovery), *with Walters v. City of Ocean Springs*, 626 F.2d 1317 (5th Cir. 1980) (grant of summary judgment affirmed when the opposing party had ample time to discover allegedly essential non-party witnesses).

[59] *See, e.g.*, *Snook v. Trust Co. of Ga. Bank*, 859 F.2d 865 (11th Cir. 1988).

[60] *Id.* at 870.

[61] *See Celotex Corp.*, 477 U.S. at 330–31 (Brennan, J., dissenting). *See generally* § 11.03[3][b] (relation of summary judgment standard to trial burdens), *infra*; Linda S. Mullenix, *Summary Judgment:*

merely because the opposing party fails to respond."[62] In *Adickes v. S.H. Kress & Co.*,[63] for example, the Supreme Court reversed a summary judgment in favor of the defendant restaurant in a civil rights action despite plaintiff's failure to oppose the motion with admissible materials. The case arose from the plaintiff's arrest for vagrancy. Although the defendant denied a conspiracy, evidence in the record that the arresting policeman had been in defendant's restaurant permitted the inference that he and the defendant had conspired to deny the plaintiff service, creating a genuine dispute of material fact.

If, on the other hand, the movant meets her burden of production and the opposing party does nothing, then Rule 56(e)(3) authorizes grant of summary judgment. To avoid summary judgment in such a case, the opposing party may not rely merely on allegations or denials of his pleading, but must support his assertion that a material fact is genuinely disputed by citing to the record.

"The purpose of Rule 56 is to enable a party who believes there is no genuine dispute as to a specific fact essential to the other side's case to demand at least one sworn averment of that fact before the lengthy process of litigation continues."[64] Indeed, when local "point-counterpoint"[65] rules require the movant to file a statement of undisputed material facts, the opposing party is usually required to deny specifically those facts that he contends are genuinely disputed and to file a counter-statement citing to the record, or the court may accept movant's statement as admitted.[66]

Finally, the opposing party is free to make a cross-motion for summary judgment. He does not concede the absence of genuine issues on the initial motion by doing so. The filing of cross-motions does not require the court to grant either; it may deny both. Each stands on its own bottom.[67]

Taming the Beast of Burdens, 10 AM. J. TRIAL ADVOC. 433, 441 (1987). Of course, the nonmoving party will rarely take the risk of not responding.

[62] MOORE § 56.10[3][b] (2d ed. 1994); Rule 56 advisory committee's note ("summary judgment cannot be granted by default even if there is a complete failure to respond to the motion"). But this is not the same thing as saying that a non-movant is subject to summary judgment if she does not respond after the movant has made a requisite showing under the rule.

[63] 398 U.S. 144 (1970). *Adickes* also suggested that the moving party had to "foreclose the possibility" that the nonmovant might prevail at trial. *Id.* at 157. *See* Samuel Issacharoff & George Loewenstein, *Second Thoughts About Summary Judgment*, 100 YALE L.J. 73, 80 & n.39 (1990) (citing cases). The Court subsequently rejected this implication. *See Celotex Corp.*, 477 U.S. 317; § 11.03[3][b], *infra*.

[64] *Lujan*, 497 U.S. at 888. *See generally* Brunet, note 39, *supra*, at 661–63. The rule's insistence on evidentiary support in the record for a factual assertion may preclude reliance on an expert's affidavit if the affiant fails to state specifically the factual basis on which it rests. *Compare Mid-State Fertilizer Co. v. Exchange Nat'l Bank*, 877 F.2d 1333, 1339 (7th Cir. 1989) (so ruling), *with Bulthuis v. Rexall Corp.*, 777 F.2d 1353, 1356 (allowing consideration of such an affidavit, subject to moving party's right to request disclosure of underlying facts), *amended on other grounds*, 789 F.2d 1315 (9th Cir. 1985). *See generally* SCHWARZER, note 27, *supra*, at 52–57; Edward Brunet, *The Use and Misuse of Expert Testimony in Summary Judgment*, 22 U.C. DAVIS L. REV. 93 (1988).

[65] Approximately a third of the districts have local rules requiring a specific point-counterpoint exchange between the movant and the opposing party. Hon. Diane P. Wood, *Summary Judgment and the Law of Unintended Consequences*, 36 OKLA. CITY U. L. REV. 231, 242–43 (2011).

[66] *See, e.g., Wienco, Inc. v. Katahn Assocs., Inc.*, 965 F.2d 565 (7th Cir. 1992). *Cf.* Rule 56(e)(2).

[67] *See* SCHWARZER, note 27, *supra*, at 73.

[c] Disposition and Appeal

To grant summary judgment, a court must conclude that the movant has met its burden of showing that the material facts are undisputed and that it is entitled to judgment as a matter of law.[68] An evidentiary hearing will not usually attend this determination, although the court may hear oral arguments on the motion. The court need consider only the materials cited in the record, and if the responding party fails to provide support for its assertion that a fact is disputed, the court may consider it undisputed.[69]

If the court finds that the movant has met his burden, it may enter judgment on a claim or defense. It may enter judgment on the issue of liability alone, even though the amount of damages remains for trial.[70] The court should state its reasons for granting or denying the motion.

If the ruling does not obviate trial, Rule 56(g) also authorizes the court to enter an order stating material facts that are undisputed. The purpose of this provision "is to salvage constructive results of the court's denial of a properly-brought but unsuccessful summary judgment motion."[71] But the salvage operation depends on the court's comparison of the cost of eliminating some fact disputes by summary disposition with the cost of resolving those disputes by other means, including trial.[72] Most trial courts have been reluctant to hazard Rule 56(g) orders in cases that will be tried anyway.

A litigation-ending summary judgment order is immediately appealable. An order denying summary judgment is not. An order granting partial summary judgment is interlocutory. It is therefore not ordinarily appealable in the federal system,[73] although a court may direct entry of a final judgment as to one or more but fewer than all the claims or parties in conformity with Rule 54(b).[74]

When summary judgment is appealable, the appellate court decides for itself (*de novo*) whether the record, when viewed most favorably to the loser,[75] reveals any genuine issue of material fact and whether the prevailing party was entitled to judgment as a matter of law.[76]

---

[68] *See* § 11.03[3][b] (relation of standard for summary judgment to trial burdens), *infra*.

[69] Rule 56(e)(2).

[70] *See* Rule 56(a); *Leasing Serv. Corp. v. Graham*, 646 F. Supp. 1410 (S.D.N.Y. 1986); *see generally* SCHWARZER, note 27, *supra*, at 71 (noting possibility that such partial judgments may encourage settlement).

[71] *SFM Corp. v. Sundstrand Corp.*, 102 F.R.D. 555, 558 (N.D. Ill. 1984). "There is no such thing as a Rule [56(g)] motion"; 56(g) orders are the residual of properly-brought summary judgment motions, not proper ends by themselves. *Id. See generally* WRIGHT & MILLER § 2737.

[72] Rule 56 advisory committee's note.

[73] *See* § 13.03[1] (the final judgment rule in general), *infra*.

[74] *See* § 13.03[2] (finality in multi-claim and multi-party cases), *infra*.

[75] *See, e.g., Walters*, 626 F.2d at 1322.

[76] *See* SCHWARZER, note 27, *supra*, at 79; § 13.10[2][a] (*de novo* review standard), *infra*.

[3]   The Standard for Summary Judgment

[a]   In General

Rule 56(a) codifies the traditional summary judgment standard, stating that judgment shall be rendered if the movant "shows that there is no genuine dispute as to any material fact and the movant is entitled to judgment as a matter of law." Most state rules phrase the standard similarly or identically.[77] Because the primary purpose of summary judgment is to avoid an unnecessary trial, the court searches for a genuine dispute the resolution of which at trial might affect the outcome of the lawsuit. If it finds such a dispute, its inquiry is at an end and summary judgment must be denied. The court's function is to determine whether there is such a dispute, not to resolve it. A party is entitled to *try* the genuine disputes of material fact and cannot be deprived of the protections of the trial process by summary resolution of such disputes, even by a judge in a case where no jury has been requested. That is, a party is entitled to *try* factual disputes whether the fact finder is the judge or the jury.

Disputes of material fact are those "that might affect the outcome of the suit under the governing law."[78] A *material* fact is an essential element of claim or defense for purposes of summary judgment.[79] In a creditor's action on a guaranty, for example, whether the debtor has complied with the underlying agreement by submitting timely financial reports is clearly a material fact because the answer to it can decide the lawsuit.[80] In contrast, whether the parties had reached an oral agreement is immaterial to summary judgment when such an agreement would be unenforceable under the statute of frauds. Whether there was such an agreement or there was not does not matter to the outcome, because it is unenforceable in any case.[81]

A *genuine dispute* is one that a reasonable jury could resolve against the movant.[82] The Supreme Court has declared that the standard for summary judgment mirrors the standard for directed verdict (now judgment as a matter of law in federal courts), "which is that the trial judge must direct a verdict if, under the governing law, there can be but one reasonable conclusion as to the verdict."[83] Thus, summary judgment should be granted if the evidence is such that it would require a directed verdict (or judgment as a matter of law) for the movant at trial.[84]

---

[77] *See, e.g.,* CAL. CIVIL PROC. CODE § 437c(c) (West 2012) ("there is no triable issue as to any material fact and that the moving party is entitled to judgment as a matter of law").

[78] *Anderson,* 477 U.S. at 248. SCHWARZER, note 27, *supra,* at 43–44. Whether something is a fact is often a difficult question in itself. *Id.* at 13–37; § 13.10[2][a], *infra.*

[79] Martin B. Louis, *Federal Summary Judgment Doctrine: A Critical Analysis,* 83 YALE L.J. 745, 747 (1974). *Cf.* § 8.06[2] (the burden of pleading a claim), *supra.*

[80] *United Brands Co. v. Intermediate Credit Corp.,* 426 F. Supp. 856 (S.D.N.Y. 1977).

[81] *Soar v. NFL Players Ass'n,* 438 F. Supp. 337 (D.R.I. 1975), *aff'd,* 550 F.2d 1287 (1st Cir. 1977).

[82] *Anderson,* 477 U.S. at 248.

[83] *Id.* at 250. *See also* Rule 50(a).

[84] *Anderson,* 477 U.S. at 250 (citation omitted). *But see* Kennedy, note 28, *supra,* at 232–34 (arguing differences between the standards); Mullenix, note 61, *supra,* at 467–68 (same); § 11.03[3][d], *infra.*

Summary judgment decisions regularly repeat the formula that the judge should not herself weigh the evidence and determine the truth of the matter, but should only determine whether there is a genuine dispute for trial. After paying lip service to this formula, the Supreme Court in *Anderson v. Liberty Lobby, Inc.*[85] implicitly recognized that some weighing of the evidence is unavoidable because the judge decides whether the dispute is one that a jury could *reasonably* resolve against the movant. The *Anderson* Court restated the inquiry as "whether the evidence presents a sufficient disagreement to require submission to a jury or whether it is so one-sided that one party must prevail as a matter of law."[86] The Court added that the standard for summary judgment "necessarily implicates the substantive evidentiary standard of proof that would apply at the trial on the merits."[87] In the normal civil case, the judge must therefore determine whether a reasonable jury could resolve the dispute for the non-movant by a preponderance of the evidence.[88]

As one district judge has explained, "a directed verdict analysis necessarily involves a qualitative evaluation of the evidence, and a decision as to whether a rational fact finder could find in the nonmovant's favor. Such an analysis necessarily calls for a decision of fact, and places the judge in the fact finder's shoes."[89] After *Anderson*, this analysis applies not only to directed verdict, but to summary judgment.

Whether *Anderson* did more than restate the old cliches about summary judgment is unclear. Federal courts still pay lip service to the following laundry list of considerations assembled by the Court of Appeals for the Fourth Circuit:

> [The non-movant] is . . . entitled, as on a motion for a directed verdict, to have the credibility of his evidence as forecast assumed, his version of all that is in dispute accepted, all internal conflicts in it resolved favorably to him, the most favorable of possible alternative inferences from it drawn in his behalf; and finally, to be given the benefit of all favorable legal theories invoked by the evidence so considered.[90]

Anderson did not purport to invalidate these considerations; it only added the evaluative component of reasonableness to each of them. The non-movant still benefits from doubts about the material facts, but only from the reasonable, and not just from the "slightest doubts."[91] Yet, in a companion summary judgment decision,

---

[85] 477 U.S. 242 (1986).

[86] *Id.* at 251–52.

[87] *Id.* at 252.

[88] *See* § 12.04 (burdens of proof), *infra.* Accordingly, *Anderson* ultimately held that when the more rare clear and convincing standard of proof, 477 U.S. at 252, applies to the issue of actual malice in a defamation case, the proper inquiry on a motion for summary judgment is "whether the evidence presented is such that a reasonable jury might find that actual malice had been shown with convincing clarity," *id.* at 257.

[89] Charles R. Richey, *Thoughts on Summary Judgment in Employment Discrimination Cases*, 1 FED. JURIST 4 (1989) (emphasis in original). Judge Richey decided *Celotex* in the trial court.

[90] *Charbonnages de France v. Smith*, 597 F.2d 406, 414 (4th Cir. 1979).

[91] Courts have occasionally embraced the "slightest doubt" test for summary judgment, to the nearly universal opprobrium of academic commentators. *See, e.g., WRIGHT* § 99; *WRIGHT & MILLER* § 2727; Louis, note 79, *supra*, at 760–62. This gloss on Rule 56(a) should not survive *Anderson. See* Alan Steven

Matsushita Electric Industrial Co. v. Zenith Radio Corp.,[92] the Court implied that summary judgment is proper even when there are equally plausible competing inferences. This may be technically correct. Yet some courts may take it as an invitation to invade the fact finder's province when the court finds one inference more plausible than another.

Once the trial judge determines that there is no genuine dispute of material fact, she has still to decide whether the movant is entitled to judgment as a matter of governing law. Modern pleading jurisdictions usually have dispensed with the doctrine that a party is bound by the legal theory presented in his pleadings,[93] and the court will decide the legal question by any available theory — whether or not pleaded.[94] Mere difficulty of the legal question is not grounds for postponing its decision if the record is sufficiently complete.[95] It is not, after all, a genuine dispute about the law that is reserved for trial, but only a genuine dispute about the material facts. Yet novel or constitutionally sensitive questions of law are often best decided upon the fuller record made at trial. Courts thus arguably have discretion to deny summary judgment "where there is reason to believe that the better course would be to proceed to a full trial,"[96] notwithstanding the Rule's directive that the court "shall" grant summary judgment if the movant meets its burden.

Although we have been using the jury case as our model, the rules of summary judgment theoretically apply to nonjury cases with equal force. A party is entitled to *try* genuinely disputed facts, whether before a judge (bench trial) or a jury (jury trial). Some commentators and courts, however, argue that a party can be deprived of a bench trial by summary judgment "when the question for decision concerns drawing inferences from undisputed evidence, or interpreting and evaluating evidence to derive legal conclusions, [because] a trial *may* not add to the judge's ability to decide."[97] They even urge summary judgment in such cases when the judge needs a fuller record, because she can then simply hold "a limited evidentiary hearing" under Rule 43(c) "to develop the record."[98] This argument either assumes that the opportunity to hear all the evidence in context adds nothing to the accuracy

---

Childress, *A New Era for Summary Judgments: Recent Shifts at the Supreme Court*, 6 Rev. Litig. 263, 280 (1987).

[92] 475 U.S. 574, 596–97 (1986). *See generally* Schwarzer, note 27, *supra*, at 64–68; Marcy J. Levine, Comment, *Summary Judgment: The Majority View Undergoes a Complete Reversal in the 1986 Supreme Court*, 37 Emory L.J. 171, 196 (1988); Jack H. Friedenthal, *Cases on Summary Judgment: Has There Been a Material Change in Standards?*, 63 Notre Dame L. Rev. 770, 784–87 (1988).

[93] *See* §§ 8.03[2] (theory of pleadings under the codes) & 8.04[2] (under modern pleading), *supra*.

[94] *See* Wright & Miller § 2725.

[95] *Id.*

[96] *Anderson*, 477 U.S. at 255 (*citing Kennedy v. Silas Mason Co.*, 334 U.S. 249 (1948)). *See generally* Wright & Miller § 2725; *Petition of Bloomfield S.S. Co.*, 298 F. Supp. 1239, 1242 (S.D.N.Y. 1969), *aff'd on other grounds*, 422 F.2d 728 (2d Cir. 1970) ("Such relief is always discretionary, and in cases posing complex issues of fact and unsettled questions of law, sound judicial administration dictates that the court withhold judgment until the whole factual structure stands upon a solid foundation of a plenary trial where the proof can be fully developed, questions answered, issues clearly focused and facts definitively found.").

[97] Schwarzer, note 27, *supra*, at 39 (emphasis added). *Accord Nunez v. Superior Oil Co.*, 572 F.2d 1119, 1123–24 (5th Cir. 1978).

[98] Schwarzer, note 27, *supra*, at 39. *See also* Richey, note 897, *supra*, at 7.

of the fact-finding, or that the nonmoving party may be obliged to make the full record in advance of trial. Both assumptions are controversial,[99] and the latter, coupled with a Rule 43(c) evidentiary hearing, converts the summary judgment hearing into trial-before-trial.[100] The argument also ignores or at least blurs the Advisory Committee's distinction between what Rule 52(c) calls a "judgment on partial findings" in bench trials and summary judgment. These judgments are subject to different standards of appellate review.[101]

[b] Relationship to Trial Burdens

The analogy of summary judgment to directed verdict (or judgment as a matter of law at trial) works well when the movant is the party with the burden of production[102] at trial. His burden on summary judgment is then aligned with his trial burden: to show that there is no genuine dispute concerning all the material factual elements of his claim or affirmative defense.[103] This kind of summary judgment motion can be called a *proof-of-the-elements* motion for summary judgment, made by a claimant for judgment on her claim or, probably more often, by defendant for judgment on an affirmative defense (for which a defendant bears the burden of production at trial).

Lundeen v. Cordner[104] is a well-known example. The suit involved competing claims for proceeds of a life insurance policy. An intervenor claimed that the decedent had intended to change the beneficiaries in intervenor's favor. Governing law did not require the change to be written into the policy in order to be effective, so long as the insured's intent was proven. The intervenor supported her motion for summary judgment with an affidavit of a neutral witness attesting to decedent's stated intent to change the beneficiaries and to the contents of the change, and with other supporting documentation. The opposing party could point to no specific facts in rebuttal. The court granted summary judgment because the movant, on whom

---

[99] *See* Jeffrey W. Stempel, *A Distorted Mirror: The Supreme Court's Shimmering View of Summary Judgment, Directed Verdict, and the Adjudication Process*, 49 Ohio St. L.J. 95, 99, 177–78 (1988) (context of full trial improves accuracy of fact-finding); § 13.10[2][b] (suggesting same rationale for deference to trial court fact-finding).

[100] *See Stewart v. RCA Corp.*, 790 F.2d 624, 628 (7th Cir. 1986) ("If [a judge could make a factual finding at a Rule [43(c)] hearing], it would be the end of the difference between summary judgment and trial . . . ."); Wright & Miller § 2416 ("The purpose of summary judgment in giving a speedy adjudication in cases that present no genuine issue is defeated if the hearing on the motion becomes a preliminary trial."); Brunet, note 39, *supra*, at 649–52.

[101] Judgment entered under Rule 52(c) differs from a summary judgment under Rule 56 in the nature of the evaluation made by the court. A judgment on partial findings is entered against a party based on the court's determination of disputed facts against the party only after the party has been fully heard on the issue. The finding is reversible only if the appellate court finds it to be clearly erroneous. A summary judgment, in contrast, is based upon a finding that the material facts are undisputed (not on the court's resolution of a genuine dispute) and that the movant is entitled to judgment as a matter of law. Such findings and rulings of law are not shielded by the "clear error" standard of review. *See* Rule 52(c) advisory committee's notes (1991); § 12.10 (bench trials), *infra. But see* Schwarzer, note 27, *supra*, at 79–81 (suggesting clearly-erroneous review for finding of "ultimate facts" by summary judgment).

[102] *See* § 12.04 (burdens of proof), *infra.*

[103] *See generally* Louis, note 79, *supra*, at 747; Schwarzer, note 27, *supra*, at 45–46.

[104] 354 F.2d 401 (8th Cir. 1966).

the burden of production would fall at trial, established that there was no genuine dispute concerning all of the essential elements of her claim.

The analogy between summary judgment and directed verdict (or judgment as a matter of law at trial) breaks down, however, when the movant would *not* have the burden of production at trial. Were the case to go to trial, the motion for directed verdict would there come after the non-movant has put on its case, and the movant could simply argue deficiencies in that case. But before trial, the non-movant attacked by summary judgment has yet to put on a case. How can the movant then satisfy his burden of production?

If the analogy to directed verdict (or judgment as a matter of law at trial) held, the movant in these circumstances could satisfy his burden by a naked motion putting the opposing party to her proof.[105] We might call this a *no-evidence* motion for summary judgment. However, permitting such a motion would invite use of summary judgment as a tool of harassment. The movant would be able to force a preview of the opposing party's evidence without paying the price of previewing his own.[106]

An alternative is to require the movant to support the motion with evidence completely negating the existence of an essential element of the opposing party's case. We might call this a *disproof-of-an-element* motion for summary judgment. In the oft-cited case of *Dyer v. MacDougall*,[107] for example, the defendant to a defamation claim won summary judgment by presenting affidavits of all the persons present at the alleged slander, denying that it took place. This alternative, however, shifts the burden of production from the opposing party (who would have it at trial) to the movant. It may thwart the primary purpose of summary judgment by letting a party who has no evidence that would survive a motion for directed verdict or judgment as a matter of law at trial remain in the shadows, while a summary judgment movant struggles to prove a negative. For this reason, some commentators have proposed that a summary judgment movant who would not have the burden of production at trial need show only enough evidence to permit — not

---

[105] *See* David P. Currie, *Thoughts on Directed Verdicts and Summary Judgments*, 45 U. Chi. L. Rev. 72, 79 (1977) (urging this construction of movant's burden in order to accomplish summary judgment's purpose of determining whether there is sufficient evidence to justify trial). Texas has expressly authorized a "no-evidence motion" for summary judgment in its summary judgment rule:

> No-Evidence Motion. After adequate time for discovery, a party without presenting summary judgment evidence may move for summary judgment on the ground that there is no evidence of one or more essential elements of a claim or defense on which an adverse party would have the burden of proof at trial. The motion must state the elements as to which there is no evidence. The court must grant the motion unless the respondent produces summary judgment evidence raising a genuine issue of material fact.

Tex. R. Civ. P. 166(a)(i). *See generally* Charles T. Frazier Jr. et al., *Celotex Comes to Texas: No-Evidence Summary Judgments and Other Recent Developments in Summary Judgment Practice*, 32 Tex. Tech. L. Rev. 111 (2000).

[106] *See* § 11.03[1], *supra*, regarding this built-in control on summary judgment. Rule 11's certification requirements might deter some harassment, *cf.* Stuart R. Pollak, *Liberalizing Summary Adjudication: A Proposal*, 36 Hastings L.J. 419, 428–29 (1985) (urging the adoption of certification requirements in California summary judgment practice in order to reduce the likelihood of such harassment), but summary judgment practice might still be substantially unbalanced.

[107] 201 F.2d 265 (2d Cir. 1952).

require — the jury to find in his favor.[108]

The Supreme Court addressed but did not clearly resolve this issue in *Celotex Corporation v. Catrett*.[109] Celotex was defendant in a products liability suit brought by a survivor of a victim of asbestosis. It moved for summary judgment on the ground that plaintiff had failed to produce any evidence that Celotex's products were the cause of the asbestosis — a no-evidence motion for summary judgment. The trial court granted summary judgment, and the court of appeals reversed on the grounds that the movant had failed to adduce any affirmative evidence in support of its motion. The Supreme Court reversed and remanded.

Eight Justices rejected the first alternative discussed above, agreeing that, even if a party would not have the burden of production at trial, its case for summary judgment must consist of more than the naked no-evidence motion. They agreed that such a movant must at least identify those portions of the discovery record at summary judgment that demonstrate the absence of a genuine issue of material fact.[110] At least seven Justices also appeared to reject the alternative at the other extreme: that such a movant can *only* satisfy his summary judgment burden by submitting a disproof-of-an-element motion supported by affirmative evidence negating an essential element of the non-movant's case.[111]

The 2010 rule amendments recognize both of the later alternatives. Rule 56(c)(1) permits a party to show that a fact is or is not genuinely disputed by citing to materials in the record, thus encompassing the disproof-of-an-element motion. Rule 56(c)(1)(B) also provides that a party may "show[] . . . that an adverse party cannot produce admissible evidence to support the fact," thus encompassing the no-evidence motion.

The rule, however, does not elaborate on just *how* a party would make the no-evidence showing. The rule's silence probably reflects the Supreme Court's own uncertainty.

Celotex left unclear how much more than a naked no-evidence motion for summary judgment was required of a movant who would not have the burden of production at trial. Celotex had supported its motion for summary judgment by noting that the plaintiff had failed in answers to interrogatories to identify any witnesses who could testify about the decedent's exposure to Celotex's asbestos products. Four Justices thought this enough to satisfy Celotex's burden of production on summary judgment and remanded for the Court of Appeals to decide whether plaintiff's opposing evidence was admissible.[112] Three Justices thought that plaintiff's identification elsewhere in the record of a possible witness on the

---

[108] *See* Louis, note 79, *supra*, at 748, 753–59.

[109] 477 U.S. 317 (1986). *See generally* Adam N. Steinman, *The Irrepressible Myth of Celotex: Reconsidering Summary Judgment Burdens Twenty Years After the Trilogy*, 63 WASH. & LEE L. REV. 81 (2006).

[110] 477 U.S. at 324 (Rehnquist, C.J., writing for the Court), 327 (White, J.), 331 (Brennan, Blackmun, and Burger, JJ., dissenting).

[111] *Id.* at 324 (Rehnquist, C.J., writing for the Court), 337 (Brennan, Blackmun, and Burger, JJ., dissenting).

[112] *Id.* at 328.

issue of exposure obligated Celotex to attack the adequacy of the witness's evidence, despite the plaintiff's failure to supply it by affidavit or otherwise.[113] Justice White voted to remand for the Court of Appeals to address this point.[114]

One commentator has suggested a means for reconciling the apparently divergent views of the Justices in *Celotex* regarding application of the *Celotex* principles. She suggests that if, during discovery prior to a summary judgment motion, the nonmoving party has identified sources of evidence for elements of its case, then the movant is obliged to track down that evidence by its own discovery before seeking summary judgment. Thus, had the plaintiff in *Celotex* identified during discovery the two possible witnesses who could support her case, the defendant would have been obliged to depose them or take other additional discovery prior to making its motion for summary judgment. This solution seeks to avoid the problem of forcing a nonmoving party to depose her own witnesses in order to avoid no-evidence summary judgment, without relaxing the requirement for admissible evidence.[115]

[c]   Particular Issues: Credibility and State of Mind

Numerous courts have said that summary judgment is inappropriate in cases involving issues of credibility and state of mind.[116] They offer different reasons for this view, emphasizing that demeanor is crucial in such cases and uniquely for the fact-finder to assess; that the facts are in the control of the movant where his credibility or state of mind is relevant; that self-interest infuses the statements of the parties and alone raises a triable issue of fact; and that parties opposing summary judgment in such cases are entitled to the incentive to truth provided by the formality of trial.[117]

These points may be valid in particular cases. Nonetheless, summary judgment cases are sufficiently varied to elude this kind of treatment by formula.[118] The better approach is to examine credibility and state of mind objections critically on

---

[113] *Id.* at 336–39.

[114] *Id.* at 328–29. On remand, the Court of Appeals again held that summary judgment was inappropriate. It found that Celotex waived its objections to admissibility of the plaintiff's evidence by failing to make timely objection below, and then concluded that the evidence raised a genuine issue of material fact concerning causation. *Catrett v. Johns-Manville Sales Corp.*, 826 F.2d 33 (D.C. Cir. 1987), *cert. denied*, 484 U.S. 1066 (1988).

[115] *See generally* Nelken, note 48, *supra*, at 75–76.

[116] *See, e.g., Hutchinson v. Proxmire*, 443 U.S. 111, 120 n.9 (1979) (asserting that issue of actual malice "does not readily lend itself to summary disposition"). *See generally* J. Palmer Lockard, *Summary Judgment in Pennsylvania: Time for Another Look at Credibility Issues*, 35 Duq. L. Rev. 625 (1997) (criticizing Pennsylvania rule restricting summary judgment where supporting evidence is testimonial); David A. Sonenshein, *State of Mind and Credibility in the Summary Judgment Context: A Better Approach*, 78 Nw. U. L. Rev. 774, 780 (1983) (citing illustrative cases); Daniel P. Collins, Note, *Summary Judgment and Circumstantial Evidence*, 40 Stan. L. Rev. 491 (1988).

[117] For example, in the oft-cited case of *Poller v. Columbia Broadcasting System, Inc.*, 368 U.S. 464, 473 (1962), the Supreme Court cautioned that summary judgment "should be used sparingly in complex antitrust litigation where motive and intent play leading roles, the proof is largely in the hands of the alleged conspirators, and hostile witnesses thicken the plot."

[118] *See First Nat'l Bank of Ariz. v. Cities Serv. Co.*, 391 U.S. 253 (1968). *See* Wright & Miller § 2725.

a case-by-case basis. As Professor Moore has said, "[h]ere, on last analysis, a problem of judging is involved."[119]

Lundeen[120] again provides an illustration. Movant there offered two affidavits by an employee of the company for whom the insured had worked before his death, attesting to the insured's stated intent to change the beneficiaries of an insurance policy purchased by the company. In opposition, the adverse party argued that the employee-affiant's story was so vital that the case should proceed to trial where his demeanor could be observed during his testimony and where he could be cross-examined.

Affirming the grant of summary judgment for the movant, the appellate court reasoned that the same argument could be leveled at any affidavit offered in support of summary judgment. "[I]f plaintiff's position is correct that an affiant's credibility is always an issue for the trial court, then the granting of a summary judgment would be virtually impossible when it is based in any way upon an affidavit."[121] The court's reasoning is persuasive. To accept plaintiff's bald argument would negate the role contemplated for affidavits in Rule 56 and unduly restrict the availability of summary judgments.

Instead, credibility should be put at issue by a showing of facts raising a genuine dispute. While the opposing party in *Lundeen* apparently did not attempt such a showing, the appellate court approved summary judgment only after conducting an unsuccessful search of the record for a genuine dispute of credibility. It noted that the employee-affiant was competent and in a position to observe the facts related in his affidavits. He appeared to be an unbiased witness without personal or financial interest in the litigation. His affidavits were "positive, internally consistent, unequivocal, and in full accord with the documentary exhibits."[122] There was therefore not the slightest indication that he might be impeached by cross-examination or might supply useful information for the opposing party. Finally, that party had made no effort to secure his deposition, which suggested that even she believed there was little to gain from cross-examination.[123]

To block summary judgment, matters of credibility and state of mind should be placed specifically in dispute by the traditional modes of impeachment: "bias, interest, prejudice, corruption, defects in testimonial capacity, prior bad acts bearing on veracity, prior convictions, poor character for veracity, and prior

---

[119] J. MOORE, MOORE'S FEDERAL PRACTICE ¶ 56.15[1.-0] (2d ed. 1994).

[120] 354 F.2d 401, discussed in § 11.03[3][b], *supra*.

[121] 354 F.2d at 409.

[122] Reserved.

[122] *Lundeen*, 354 F.2d at 408.

[123] The affiant was overseas and a deposition upon oral questions would have imposed a substantial expense on the opposing party that would otherwise fall on the movant, who would have had to call the affiant as her witness or offer his deposition at trial to meet her burden of production. Such considerations of relative cost and convenience may fairly be considered in ruling on a summary judgment motion in the circumstances, but it is incumbent on the opposing party to make them known by a Rule 56(f) affidavit. In any event, the opposing party in *Lundeen* did not avail itself of even less expensive discovery options, like a deposition upon written questions. *See* § 10.08[1] (procedure for taking depositions), *supra*.

inconsistent statements."[124] The interest of a party-affiant or deponent does not invariably raise an issue of credibility; nor is the control of relevant information by the movant always a sufficient reason for the inability of the opposing party to specify facts suggesting impeachment. Interest and lack of access together may in particular cases establish a genuine dispute.[125]

The allocation of the burden of production at trial is also relevant to credibility issues. When the non-movant would have the burden of production at trial, she may not defeat summary judgment simply by raising a dispute about the credibility of the movant's denials of material facts. The reason is that she is not by that showing relieved of her own burden of showing evidence from which a reasonable jury could find in her favor.

> It is axiomatic that a party is not permitted to prove a positive proposition by first offering a witness who refutes the proposition, and then impeaching that witness. The jury cannot on this basis find that the positive proposition is a proven fact . . . . [A] contrary rule would permit the jury to *find* a fact . . . despite the absence of any affirmative evidence of that fact in the record.[126]

On the other hand, when the movant would also have the burden of production at trial, specifically established disputes about credibility should be enough to defeat summary judgment.[127]

[d]   Assessment

To assess summary judgment, we need to consider what the courts do, what they say, and what effect their actions and rhetoric have on the "just, speedy and inexpensive determination of every action and proceeding."[128]

Prior to the Supreme Court's *Anderson-Celotex-Matsushita* trilogy of summary judgment opinions in 1986, the traditional view was that summary judgment was rarely granted and that grants were often reversed.[129] Open judicial hostility to summary judgment was not uncommon.[130] But in each of the trilogy cases, the

---

[124] Sonenshein, note 116, *supra*, at 798-01. This obligation is, of course, subject to any reasonable explanation by an opposing party for its inability to present the necessary facts to establish a genuine issue. *See* Rule 56(f).

[125] *See, e.g., Wilmington Trust Co. v. Mfrs. Life Ins. Co.*, 624 F.2d 707 (5th Cir. 1980) (reversing summary judgment for insurer with burden of proof, when it rested on subjective testimony of the insurer's own employee and when the facts were within the insurer's exclusive knowledge).

[126] Sonenshein, note 116, *supra*, at 789. Reprinted by special permission of the Northwestern University Law Review, © 1983 by Northwestern University School of Law, vol. 78. *See Anderson*, 477 U.S. at 256-57.

[127] *See, e.g., Wilmington Trust Co.*, 624 F.2d 707.

[128] Rule 1.

[129] *See, e.g.*, McLauchlan, note 27, *supra*, at 449 (reporting 49% reversal rate in sample of federal courts); Sonenshein, note 116, *supra*, at 775 n.5 (50% in California; 81.2% in Florida; 50% in Fifth Circuit; 70% of cases that reached Texas Supreme Court) (citations omitted); Kennedy, note 28, *supra*, at 254 n.112.

[130] *See, e.g., Wells v. Oppenheimer & Co.*, 101 F.R.D. 358, 359 (S.D.N.Y. 1984) (Knapp, J.) ("motions

Supreme Court ruled in support of summary judgment, and in *Celotex*, the Court sang its praises:

> Summary judgment procedure is properly regarded not as a disfavored procedural shortcut, but rather as an integral part of the Federal Rules as a whole, which are designed "to secure the just, speedy and inexpensive determination of every action." Fed. Rule Civ. Proc. 1. . . . Rule 56 must be construed with due regard not only for the rights of persons asserting claims and defenses that are adequately based in fact to have those claims and defenses tried to a jury, but also for the rights of persons opposing such claims and defenses to demonstrate in the manner provided by the Rule, prior to trial, that the claims and defenses have no factual basis.[131]

Depending on their affection for trial, commentators heralded or bemoaned the dawn of a new era in summary judgment. They predicted, and some found in the short term, a surge in the filing and success of summary judgment motions, especially motions by defendants.[132]

These predictions have not come to pass in the long term, however. A study of summary judgment from 1975 to 2000 in six federal district courts showed that the rate at which summary judgment motions were filed was about 21% at the conclusion of the period, while the rate of cases with motions granted in whole or in part, and the rate at which cases are terminated by summary judgment, was about 12% and 8%, respectively.[133] The same survey showed that the likelihood of a case containing one or more summary judgment motions increased from 12% in 1975 to 17% in 1986 — the year of the trilogy — and remained fairly steady at about 19% since then.[134] Although this is was a 40% increase in filings, most of it occurred *before* the trilogy, and it reflects, in part, the increase in filings of civil rights cases that have always experienced a high rate of summary judgment practice. Moreover,

---

for summary judgment in this Circuit [2d] were usually a waste of time and should be discouraged"), *vacated*, 106 F.R.D. 258 (S.D.N.Y. 1985). One district judge in New Orleans acknowledged the Fifth Circuit's hostility by posting the sign, "No Spitting, No Summary Judgments!" Childress, note 91, *supra*, at 264.

[131] 477 U.S. at 327 (citation omitted).

[132] *See, e.g.*, Issacharoff & Lowenstein, note 63, *supra*, at 88–89; Stempel, note 99, *supra*, at 99 (stating that the trilogy "effected major changes in summary judgment doctrine and practice"); Gregory A. Gordillo, Note, *Summary Judgment and Problems in Applying the Celotex Trilogy Standard*, 42 Clev. St. L. Rev. 263 (1994); John J.P. Howley, Note, *Summary Judgment in Federal Court: New Maxims for a Familiar Rule*, 34 N.Y.L. Sch. L. Rev. 201, 203 (1989) (asserting that new doctrine announced in trilogy "has virtually eliminated trial in certain types of cases").

[133] Joe S. Cecil et al., *A Quarter-Century of Summary Judgment Practices in Six Federal District Courts*, 4 J. Empirical Legal Stud. 861, 896 (2007).

[134] *Id.* at 861. These findings cast some doubt on the long-term significance of reported spikes in summary judgment filings in product liability, antitrust, libel, and civil rights (particularly employment discrimination) cases after the trilogy. *See* Ann C. McGinley, *Credulous Courts and the Tortured Trilogy: The Improper Use of Summary Judgment in Title VII and ADEA Cases*, 34 B.C. L. Rev. 203 (1993); Patricia M. Wald, *Summary Judgment at Sixty*, 76 Tex. L. Rev. 1897, 1938 (1998) (noting that employment discrimination lawyers widely report more frequent grant of summary judgment in employment discrimination cases than in others); Howley, note 132, *supra*, at 213–14 n.99, 218–19 n.125. *See also* Theresa M. Beiner, *The Misuse of Summary Judgment in Hostile Environment Cases*, 34 Wake Forest L. Rev. 71 (1999) (finding excessive use of summary judgment in sexual harassment cases).

there was no statistically significant difference in outcomes between plaintiffs' and defendants' motions.[135]

These findings at first seem inconsistent with a reported substantial shift in federal case dispositions from disposition by trial to disposition by summary judgment. One report found that in 1973, there were an average of 14 summary judgment dispositions per volume of the *Federal Reporter* compared to an average of 52 trial dispositions, while the comparable numbers for 1997–98 (eleven years after the trilogy) had changed to 47 summary judgment dispositions compared to 20 trial dispositions.[136] Reporting on "summary judgment at 60" in the D.C. Circuit, Judge Wald also noted that 22% of case terminations in that circuit in 1996–97 were by summary judgment compared to about 3% by trial, leading her to speculate that "summary judgment may in fact be the more commonly used mode of disposition on the merits, outnumbering settlement by court-annexed arbitration, mediation, early neutral evaluation, and other settlement techniques," as well as trial.[137] It is not clear, however, whether such statistics reflect significant increases in the rate of summary judgment or just a decline in the trial rate, due as much to settlement (and attendant dismissal) as summary judgment. "Summary judgment is but one of several dispositive motions that may result in the drop in the trial rate."[138]

If summary judgment has not increased by as much (or at all) after the trilogy as most scholars and commentators had predicted, should it have? Advocates of summary judgment certainly tout it as an efficient tool for clearing dockets and avoiding trial costs.[139] But this accounting is incomplete. It omits the cost of preparing and, more significantly, of opposing the summary judgment motion itself, including some costs (especially to plaintiff) that would not be incurred in trial (*e.g.*, deposing your own witnesses). It also omits the costs of denied motions.[140] As one federal appellate judge has noted:

> Enormous resources go into the preparation of summary judgment motions; courts labor over them for extended periods of time before issuing a

---

[135] Cecil, note 133, *supra*, at 861.

[136] Paul W. Mollica, *Federal Summary Judgment at High Tide*, 84 Marq. L. Rev. 141, 144, 218–19 (2000). *See also* Martin H. Redish, *Summary Judgment and the Vanishing Trial: Implications of the Litigation Matrix*, 57 Stan. L. Rev. 1329, 1330 (2005) ("Changes in the law of summary judgment quite probably explain at least a large part of the dramatic reduction in federal trials.").

[137] Wald, note 134, *supra* at 1915. Because of the number of cases to which the federal government is party, and the possibility that statutory issues are more significant in such cases than in private cases, the D.C. Circuit's experience may not be typical.

[138] Cecil et al., note 133, *supra*, at 906. In any case, assessments based on reported dispositions are unreliable, because many dispositions are not published, especially denials. *Id.* at 4.

[139] *Id.* (implying that summary judgment eases docket pressures). *But see* McLauchlan, note 27, *supra*, at 456–58 (finding little time-saving in summary judgment). Federal judges also report that prompt rulings on motions for summary judgment are among the two most effective methods for controlling groundless litigation. Elizabeth C. Wiggins et al., *The Federal Judicial Center's Study of Rule 11*, 2 FJC Directions 31 (1991).

[140] Richard L. Marcus, *Completing Equity's Conquest? Reflections on the Future of Trial Under the Federal Rules of Civil Procedure*, 50 U. Pitt. L. Rev. 725, 774–75 (1989); Stempel, note 99, *supra*, at 171, 191 & n.449.

ruling; and appellate courts are inundated with appeals from disappointed parties who insist that the trial court overlooked a critical disputed issue of fact or misapplied the law.[141]

It may also be that the costs of the so-called new summary judgment may not be evenly distributed. *Celotex* seemed to lower the price of summary judgment for defendant-movants who would not have the burden of proof at trial.

> Something close to a one page form motion by defendant can throw on the plaintiff the responsibility to dredge, structure, collate and cross-reference all materials in the file to make them available to the judge before trial. Because the material must be reduced to a coherently structured written form, this task can sometimes take as long or longer than actually trying the case.[142]

The low cost to defendant-movants of making a "put-up-or-shut-up" motion (usually a no-evidence motion) and the corresponding high price to plaintiffs could alter the balance of power, and, some have suggested, discourage settlement.[143] On the other hand, this result may simply compensate for unfair advantages plaintiffs enjoyed with notice pleading and essentially unlimited discovery (or *did* enjoy before the *Twiqbal* decisions declared the plausible pleading standard).

The question remains whether any "new" summary judgment even at the reported rates intrudes seriously on trial by converting once "summary" proceedings into a full dress trial rehearsal. The possible costs of downgrading trial[144] include diminished accuracy from the loss of demeanor evidence, spontaneity, and whatever comprehensibility oral testimony affords; loss of participant satisfaction; loss of public interest and access; and loss of confidence in the reliability of judgment because of the substitution of unaccountable federal judges for juries of peers. Some commentators also suggest that litigants pay a price in constitutional rights to try their factual disputes.[145]

These critiques all suggest that Supreme Court rhetoric should not be allowed to obscure the fact that summary judgment and directed verdict are not, after all, the same. "The crucial difference between summary judgment and the directed

---

[141] Wood, note 65, *supra*, at 232.

[142] D. Michael Risinger, *Another Step in the Counter-Revolution: A Summary Judgment on the Supreme Court's New Approach to Summary Judgment*, 54 BROOKLYN L. REV. 35, 41 (1988).

[143] *See, e.g.*, Risinger, note 142, *supra*, at 39; Issacharoff & Lowenstein, note 63, *supra*, at 75; Stempel, note 99, *supra*, at 161–62, 180–81. *See generally* John Bronsteen, *Against Summary Judgment*, 75 GEO. WASH. L. REV. 522 (2007) (asserting that summary judgment imposes extra costs by discouraging settlement and creates a pro-defendant bias).

[144] *See generally* Marcus, note 140, *supra*, at 757–83; Stempel, note 99, *supra*, at 171–73, 191.

[145] *See, e.g.*, Suja A. Thomas, *The Fallacy of Dispositive Procedure*, 50 B.C. L. REV. 759 (2009) (expressing doubt that courts can actually apply a reasonable juror standard); Mollica, note 136, *supra* at 181–205 (arguing that many applications of summary judgment "press against tolerable constitutional limits" established by due process as well as the Seventh Amendment); *see also* Suja A. Thomas, *Why Summary Judgment Is Unconstitutional*, 93 VA. L. REV. 139 (2007). *Cf.* Jeffrey W. Stempel, *Taking Cognitive Illiberalism Seriously: Judicial Humility, Aggregate Efficiency, and Acceptable Justice*, 43 LOY. U. CHI. L.J. 627 (2012) (arguing that aggressive use of summary judgment risks sacrifices of justice with little or no efficiency gain).

verdict, . . . is that before trial *all* the evidence is not available to the judge for consideration. The directed verdict standard requires that the judge assess what a reasonable jury could find on *all* the evidence, which is not the case at summary judgment."[146] Directed verdict rests on a known record; summary judgment on a predicted record.[147] As Judge Wald put it, summary judgment in her circuit is "something more like a gestalt verdict based on an early snapshot of the case,"[148] "applying legal principles to incomplete, often anemic, factual scenarios."[149]

The reliability of fact finding, and often even of law-deciding, is greater the larger the data base.[150] One commentator notes that "the largest increase in the data base and its reliability occurs between summary judgment and directed verdict at the close of the plaintiff's case."[151] To the extent that the new summary judgment, by so emphatically equating summary judgment and directed verdict, "permits courts to conclude a case as though they did so upon a much richer data base than actually possessed," it may be "bad science and probability theory, as well as bad law."[152]

§ 11.04   DISMISSAL OR NONSUIT

[1]   Voluntary Dismissal or Nonsuit

There are times when plaintiff would like to withdraw suit. This happens whenever plaintiff's case seems likely to lead to a binding adjudication that will defeat or compromise his claim and when it seems reasonable to expect a more favorable result from suit brought at a different time or place.[153] If such a plaintiff can obtain dismissal *without prejudice* to his opportunity to litigate the same claim later,[154] he will voluntarily dismiss his claim.

The common law treated plaintiff as master of his case and therefore permitted him to dismiss or take a *nonsuit* without prejudice at any time before verdict.[155] Today plaintiff's right to dismiss is balanced against the investment of resources made by the other parties and by the court in the lawsuit. Consequently, most systems confine plaintiff's unilateral right to break off the case to the early stages

---

[146] Mullenix, note 61, *supra*, at 474.

[147] Risinger, note 142, *supra*, at 37–38.

[148] Wald, note 134, *supra*, at 1917.

[149] *Id.* at 1944.

[150] *See* Stempel, note 99, *supra*, at 176–77 (analogizing from statistics).

[151] *Id.* at 177.

[152] *Id.*

[153] For example, when a defendant has asserted a limitations defense that appears to be good in the forum, *see generally* Susan Clark Taylor, Note, *Rule 41(a)(2) Dismissals: Forum Shopping for a Statute of Limitations*, 20 Mem. St. U. L. Rev. 629 (1990), or a troublesome party has intervened or been impleaded, or the court or the jury is likely to rule against the plaintiff.

[154] *See* Chapter 15 (respect for final judgments), *infra*.

[155] *See* Benjamin J. Shipman, Common Law Pleading §§ 328–329 (3d ed. 1923). In some states, the right to dismiss is still essentially absolute until trial. *See* James T. Ferrini & Richard R. Winter, *Voluntary Dismissals — From Shield to Sword by the Convergence of Improvident Actions*, 21 J. Marshall L. Rev. 549 (1988) (so characterizing Illinois law).

of litigation, prior to the substantial investment of resources in trial,[156] or even prior to the point at which issues are joined. Federal Rule 41(a)(1)(A) adopts the latter point of no return, providing that plaintiff may dismiss once without leave of court by filing notice of dismissal before an answer or motion for summary judgment is served upon him. Thus, a Rule 12(b) motion to dismiss the complaint does not cut off plaintiff's right to such *notice dismissal* unless the motion is converted into a summary judgment motion by the offer of supporting materials outside the pleadings.[157]

After an issue is joined by the service of an answer or motion for summary judgment, plaintiff may voluntarily dismiss only by stipulation of the parties or by order of the court upon such terms and conditions as it deems proper.[158] However, trial courts usually allow such dismissals unless doing so would unavoidably inflict plain legal prejudice on other parties.[159] Prejudice to defendant must ordinarily consist of more than "the mere prospect of a second law suit,"[160] since that prospect is generally present when a plaintiff seeks voluntary dismissal. Furthermore, the court can often alleviate or remove prejudice to other parties by conditioning voluntary dismissal on plaintiff's reimbursement of the parties' costs, production of discovery materials, or fulfillment of other terms.[161] The Supreme Court has asserted that the parties could make their compliance with a settlement agreement one of the judicially-enforceable conditions of voluntary dismissal.[162]

---

[156] *See generally* Annotation, *Time When Voluntary Nonsuit or Dismissal May Be Taken as of Right Under Statute So Authorizing at Any Time Before "Trial," "Commencement of Trial," "Trial of the Facts," or the Like*, 1 A.L.R. 3D 711 (1965) (discussing rules that permit voluntary dismissal as of right prior to trial or "commencement of trial").

[157] *See generally* §§ 8.07[1] discussing conversion of Rule 12(b)(6) and 12(c) motions to Rule 56 motions) & 11.03[2] (procedure for summary judgment), *supra*. Rule 41(a)(1)(A) is usually (but not always) applied strictly. *See, e.g., American Soccer Co. v. Score First Enters.*, 187 F.3d 1108 (9th Cir. 1999) (even when court treats a hearing as one for summary judgment, the "point of no return" is not reached unless formal motion is filed); *Santiago v. Victim Servs. Agency*, 753 F.2d 219 (2d Cir. 1985) (motion for a preliminary injunction does not cut off plaintiff's right to notice dismissal). The Supreme Court has held, however, that even a voluntary dismissal as of right does not deprive a court of power to impose Rule 11 sanctions on the plaintiff for filing the dismissed action. *Cooter & Gell v. Hartmarx Corp.*, 496 U.S. 384 (1990).

[158] Rule 41(a)(2).

[159] *See, e.g., Paulucci v. City of Duluth*, 826 F.2d 780 (8th Cir. 1987) (denying dismissal, citing absence of explanation for it and prejudice from continuing uncertainty over title to land). *See generally* Lawrence Mentz, Note, *Voluntary Dismissal by Order of Court — Federal Rules of Civil Procedure Rule 41(a)(2) and Judicial Discretion*, 48 NOTRE DAME L. REV. 446 (1972); MOORE § 41.40[5].

[160] *See, e.g., Phillips v. Illinois Cent. Gulf R.R.*, 874 F.2d 984, 987 (5th Cir. 1989); *see generally* MOORE § 41.40[5][c]. *Compare* § 8.10[1] (making same observation with respect to amendment), *supra*. Courts are divided, however, about whether the loss of a good limitations defense is clear legal prejudice to defendant. Some balance the equities when this prejudice is present by considering also plaintiff's diligence and conduct in seeking dismissal and defendant's expenditure of time and money. *See generally* Taylor, note 153, *supra*, at 638–54.

[161] *See, e.g., Radiant Tech. Corp. v. Electrovert USA Corp.*, 122 F.R.D. 201 (N.D. Tex. 1988) (identifying factors to be considered in allowing conditional dismissal, as well as in denying dismissal); *see generally* MOORE § 41.40[10].

[162] *Kokkonen v. Guardian Life Ins. Co. of Am.*, 511 U.S. 375, 381 (1994) (dictum).

Unless the court specifies otherwise, an initial voluntary dismissal is without prejudice to plaintiff's reinstitution of the action. It leaves the parties in the same position they were in prior to suit, but for the passage of time.[163] Federal courts are empowered by Rule 41(d)(1), however, to require a plaintiff who reinstitutes his action to reimburse the parties for the costs of the previously dismissed action.

Many jurisdictions follow a two-dismissal rule, by which a second voluntary dismissal is *with prejudice* to reinstitution.[164] The second thus operates as an adjudication upon the merits with whatever preclusive effect is given judgments by the law of the rendering jurisdiction.[165]

[2] Involuntary Dismissal or Compulsory Nonsuit

We have noted that a default judgment is available in most jurisdictions for the defendant's failure to respond to claims against him or as a penalty for his disobedience of various procedural rules.[166] *Involuntary dismissal* or *compulsory nonsuit* is an analogous remedy for the defendant when the plaintiff fails to prosecute her claims[167] or to obey court rules or orders.[168]

Rule 41(b) does not define a failure to prosecute, but rules locally adopted by federal courts often do.[169] Disobedience that would justify dismissal also often consists of litigation delays, or of failures to appear, respond, or take other required action.[170] Because these matters threaten the trial court's control over its docket, it follows that it may draw on its inherent powers to dismiss plaintiff's action *sua sponte* (on its own initiative).[171]

Involuntary dismissal is a harsh sanction. In exercising discretion to dismiss a claim for want of prosecution or for plaintiff's disobedience of a court rule or order, courts should consider the degree of plaintiff's personal responsibility for the inaction or disobedience, the actual prejudice to defendant, and the availability of

---

[163] Of course, the passage of time is sometimes significant because it may raise the bar of limitations to reinstitution of the action. Some jurisdictions therefore provide by statute for the tolling of the statute of limitations during the pendency of the dismissed or nonsuited action, provided that it is reinstituted within a stated period after the dismissal. *See, e.g.,* VA. CODE ANN. § 8.01-229(E) (West 2012).

[164] *See, e.g.,* Rule 41(a)(1)(B).

[165] *See generally* Chapter 15 (respect for final judgments), *infra.*

[166] *See* § 11.02, *supra.*

[167] *See Ad West Mktg., Inc. v. Hayes,* 745 F.2d 980 (5th Cir. 1984) (failure of attorney representing the plaintiff corporation and two of the cross-defendants to appear for trial justified involuntary dismissal of plaintiff's claims and default judgment against cross-defendants). *See generally* Russell G. Vineyard, Note, *Dismissal with Prejudice for Failure to Prosecute: Visiting the Sins of the Attorney Upon the Client,* 22 GA. L. REV. 195 (1987).

[168] The Supreme Court has excepted the disobedience of discovery rules and orders from operation of Rule 41(b), however, on the theory that discovery sanctions are governed by Rule 37. *Societe Internationale Pour Participations Industrielles et Commerciales v. Rogers,* 357 U.S. 197, 207 (1958).

[169] *See MOORE* § 41.51[1] (listing federal cases based on locally adopted rules). State rules or statutes also treat this. *See, e.g.,* D.C. SUPER. CT. R. 41(b); FLA. R. CIV. P. 1.420(e) (inaction for one year).

[170] *See generally MOORE* § 41.52[3] (citing examples).

[171] *See, e.g., Link v. Wabash R.R. Co.,* 370 U.S. 626, 629 (1962); *Boudwin v. Graystone Ins. Co.,* 756 F.2d 399 (5th Cir. 1985).

lesser sanctions.[172] While Rule 41(b) does not require notice and hearing, they are desirable prior to an order of involuntary dismissal.

Rule 41(b) involuntary dismissals also formerly provided a means for federal courts to decide cases midway through bench (nonjury) trials. Now this purpose is served by motions for judgment on partial findings under Rule 52.[173] In states that have not followed this federal rule change, however, a motion to dismiss at the close of plaintiff's case is still used to present the question of whether, on the facts and the law, plaintiff has met his burden of production.[174] This kind of motion differs from its cousin, the motion for directed verdict in jury cases, because the latter only tests whether plaintiff's evidence could reasonably lead to a favorable verdict.[175] The greater demand placed on plaintiff by a motion for involuntary dismissal reflects the added fact-finding power judges assume in bench trials. Judges may resolve close questions of fact (including issues of credibility) against the plaintiff at the close of his case-in-chief that would otherwise go to juries in a jury case.[176] Involuntary dismissals simply save time by permitting judges to cut bench trials short when an outcome adverse to the plaintiff has become clear and he has been fully heard.[177]

Involuntary dismissals and compulsory nonsuits are with prejudice to reinstitution of the action in the same court, unless otherwise provided or unless grounded on failure of a precondition to suit.[178] Rule 41(b) expressly identifies jurisdiction, proper venue, or joinder of a party under Rule 19, as such preconditions. Dismissals based on plaintiff's failure to satisfy these conditions do not operate as adjudications upon the merits. In this regard, "jurisdiction" is sometimes expansively construed to include dismissals based on the failure of other preconditions, such as posting of security bonds or filing of good cause certificates in certain immigration proceedings.[179]

---

[172] *See, e.g., Boudwin,* 756 F.2d 399; *Scarborough v. Eubanks,* 747 F.2d 871 (3d Cir. 1984). *See generally* Vineyard, note 167, *supra,* at 206–14.

[173] *See* § 12.10 (bench trials), *infra.*

[174] *See* § 12.04[3] (trial burdens), *infra.*

[175] *See* § 12.09[1] (directed verdicts), *infra.*

[176] The judge's view of the facts in a jury trial is comparatively insignificant. When the evidence is rationally capable of supporting a verdict for either side, the jury's conclusion is largely immune from court interference. *See* § 12.09, *infra.*

[177] Rule 52(c).

[178] *See Semtek Int'l Inc. v. Lockheed Martin Corp.,* 531 U.S. 497, 505 (2001) (holding that Rule 41(b) dismissal without prejudice bars refiling *in same court,* but that preclusive effect in other courts depends upon the state or federal law of preclusion that applies in the dismissing court).

[179] *See generally* MOORE § 41.50[7][c]. *Cf. Saylor v. Lindsley,* 391 F.2d 965 (2d Cir. 1968) (dismissal for failure to post bond for security for costs does not operate as adjudication upon the merits despite Rule 41(b)'s express language).

§ 11.05   ALTERNATIVE DISPUTE RESOLUTION

Parties can also resolve their disputes without trial by alternative dispute resolution (ADR). Alternative dispute resolution is as old as formal adjudication, since parties to civil litigation have always had the option of agreeing to *settle* the case. Growing concern, however, about the time and expense of formal adjudication has led to greater interest in dispute resolution by other means. Among the ADR devices now used in addition to traditional settlement negotiation are *mediation*, *arbitration*, and *summary jury trials*.

Congress has required all federal courts to offer some ADR procedures.[180] Many states allow courts to order mandatory ADR for particular kinds of cases.[181] But probably the most common source of ADR is the parties themselves, who contract to use a specified ADR method to resolve disputes under the contract, who agree ad hoc to try an ADR technique before the matter gets to court, or who simply try to negotiate settlement after a suit is filed.

[1]   Settlement

Law students often assume that the object of litigation is to win at trial. If so, most litigators are dismal failures, as fewer than 5% of all civil cases are ever tried, and not all of these actually result in a judgment.[182] One reason for these surprisingly low numbers is that cases settle short of trial, or even at or just after trial, before judgment. This fact suggests the true purpose of most litigation: to resolve the dispute as favorably as possible for your client. Litigation ending in a court judgment is just one means of achieving this purpose, and not always the most efficient.[183] The appeal of settlement is that it can avoid the costs of trial, it can take into account a broader array of interests that can the often-rigid law, and it permits a broader range of outcomes (win/win) than the usually bipolar alternatives (win/lose) at trial. It not only may yield a resolution more satisfying to the parties, but also one that better preserves an ongoing relationship.

A settlement is a contract negotiated among the parties. It usual results in payment of some sum of money by the defendant in return for a *release* of claims by the plaintiff. Because of ethical restrictions on contacting represented parties

---

[180] Alternative Dispute Resolution Act of 1998, 28 U.S.C. §§ 651–658 (2012) ("Each United States district court shall authorize, by local rule adopted under section 2071(a), the use of alternative dispute resolution processes in all civil actions, including adversary proceedings in bankruptcy, in accordance with this chapter, except that the use of arbitration may be authorized only as provided in section 654.").

[181] *See, e.g.*, Alaska Stat. § 25.20.080 (West 2012) (for child custody matters); Mich. Comp. Laws § 600.4951 (West 2012) (for civil actions based on tort); Mont. Code Ann. § 39-71-2401(2011) (for workers' compensation benefit disputes).

[182] *See* § 1.01[4], *supra*. *See* Gillian K. Hadfield, *Exploring Economic and Democratic Theories of Civil Litigation: Differences Between Individual and Organizational Litigants in the Disposition of Federal Civil Cases*, 57 Stan. L. Rev. 1275 (2005) (finding that organizational plaintiffs are more likely to settle their cases than to try them or decide them by other adjudication).

[183] *See, e.g.*, Samuel R. Gross & Kent D. Syverud, *Don't Try: Civil Jury Verdicts in a System Geared to Settlement*, 44 UCLA L. Rev. 1 (1996); David M. Trubeck et al., *The Cost of Ordinary Litigation*, 31 UCLA L. Rev. 72 (1983).

directly,[184] as well as the parties' emotional baggage in some cases, the negotiations are typically conducted by the lawyers. They can start even before the lawsuit, sometimes in response to a demand letter or a "courtesy copy" of the proposed complaint. More commonly, they commence after initial motions to dismiss are decided, significant discovery has occurred, summary judgment is denied, at the final pretrial conference, on the eve of trial, or, as noted, even during trial in response to the evidence. At each of these points in the chronology of a civil lawsuit, the estimated value of a claim changes, in response to court action, discovery, evidence at trial, or simply the accumulating costs of prosecution and defense. Indeed, one of the uses of civil procedure is to influence these costs and thus the settlement potential of a claim.

Settlement discussions are typically held privately and in confidence. Although the court can be instrumental in encouraging settlement,[185] and may even ask the parties' lawyers for general progress reports on settlement discussions, the initiative lies with the parties and the details are typically left to their negotiations. The Federal Rules of Evidence protect the negotiations by making inadmissible offers to compromise as well as most "conduct or . . . statement[s] made during compromise negotiations."[186] The court's approval of a settlement is usually not required except in class actions,[187] and the terms of the settlement are often confidential,[188] although some courts have held that the common law right of access trumps the private interest in confidentiality.[189] Because a settlement agreement is a contract, a party may ask a court to enforce the contract or to award damages from a breach.

[2] Mediation

Mediation has been defined as "a dispute resolution process in which disputants are assisted by a neutral third person (the mediator) to come to a mutually satisfying, self-determined solution."[190] One crucial difference between mediation and adjudication procedures like arbitration or litigation is that the parties maintain control and ultimately decide the final outcome of the mediation for themselves.

In other words, mediation is nothing more than settlement negotiation facilitated by an outsider. Mediation is most likely to succeed in settings where

---

[184] *See* § 10.01 (citing ethical rules), *supra*.

[185] *See* § 12.03[1][b], *infra*.

[186] Fed. R. Evid. 408.

[187] *See* Rule 23(e)(4).

[188] *See* Laurie Kratky Doré, *Secrecy By Consent: The Use and Limits of Confidentiality in the Pursuit of Settlement*, 74 Notre Dame L. Rev. 283 (1999).

[189] *See Bank of Am. Nat'l Trust & Sav. Ass'n v. Hotel Rittenhouse Assocs.*, 800 F.2d 339 (3d Cir. 1986); Cynthia A. Deiters, Note, *A Setback for the Public Policy of Encouraging Settlements*, 1988 J. Disp. Resol. 219.

[190] Nat'l Ctr. for State Courts, Alternative Dispute Resolution (ADR) (2001). Discussion of developments in mediation practice and theory appear in *Symposium*, 2000 J. of Disp. Resol. 245; and *Symposium on the Structure of Court-Connected Mediation Programs*, 14 Ohio St. J. on Disp. Resol. 711 (1999).

opposing parties have good reason to agree but are hostile, alienated or distrustful. The mediator performs a facilitative function by serving as a buffer and go-between for settlement. She may also perform an evaluative function in clarifying for each party its own best interests, although some mediators studiously refrain from doing so.[191]

Parties tend to be more directly involved in mediation because the mediator insists on their presence. Mediation therefore often gives the parties an opportunity to tell their stories more freely than they can in traditional litigation. The flexibility afforded by mediation allows parties to reach individualized and creative solutions, rather than the standardized remedies imposed by the litigation system. Finally, mediation can help promote a sense of accomplishment and community that litigation is not as likely to foster.[192]

[3] Arbitration

Arbitration is closer in form to litigation itself, inasmuch as the neutral third person (the arbitrator) actually considers the case and designates a winner.[193] The appeal of arbitration is a faster and usually less costly decision than one obtained by trial. The arbitration often applies streamlined hearing procedures and allows at best limited discovery. The arbitrator typically does not issue a lengthy opinion explaining her decision, as it is not published and has no precedential value outside (or sometimes within) the arbitration.

"Arbitration is the creature of contract";[194] it rests on the consent of the parties. Whether parties are required to submit to arbitration and, if so, whether the arbitrator's result is binding, usually depends on the nature of the agreement or prior consent of the parties. Thus, if the parties have contracted to submit their disputes to arbitration, they usually must do so before — or instead of — commencing judicial proceedings.[195] Similarly, if the parties have contracted that the arbitrator's decision is binding, it will usually be given preclusive effect in any subsequent case.[196]

---

[191] For a critique of the evaluative and facilitative functions of mediation, see Jeffrey W. Stempel, *The Inevitability of the Eclectic: Liberating ADR from Ideology*, 2000 J. Disp. Resol. 247.

[192] *See* Carrie Menkel-Meadow, Lela P. Love, Andrea K. Schneider & Jean R. Sternlight, Dispute Resolution: Beyond the Adversarial Model 268–71 (2005).

[193] *See* Jacqueline M. Nolan-Haley, Alternative Dispute Resolution in a Nutshell, Ch. 4 (1992).

[194] Edward Brunet, Charles B. Craver & Ellen E. Deason, Alternative Dispute Resolution: The Advocate's Perspective 516 (4th ed. 2011). *See generally* Edward Brunet, *Replacing Folklore Arbitration with a Contract Model of Arbitration*, 74 Tul. L. Rev. 39 (1999).

[195] *See* The Federal Arbitration Act, 9 U.S.C. § 2 (2012) (making contractual arbitration agreements "valid, irrevocable, and enforceable, save upon such grounds as exist at law or in equity for the revocation of any contract."). Section 2 is enforceable in state as well as federal court. *Southland Corp. v. Keating*, 465 U.S. 1 (1984). State laws give similar effect to arbitration agreements. *See, e.g.*, Calif. Code of Civ. Proc. § 1281; Art. 75, N.Y. Civ. Prac. L. & R. § 7501; Tex. Civ. Prac. & Rem. § 171.001.

[196] American Law Institute, Restatement (Second) of Judgments § 84 (1982). "It is well-settled that the doctrines of res judicata and collateral estoppel apply to arbitration awards." Nolan-Haley, note 193, *supra* at 162.

Parties may also contract for judicial review of an arbitral decision. It is, however, unclear how far the parties can go in prescribing the standards by which a court may review the decision. In *Hall Street Associates v. Mattel, Inc.*,[197] the Supreme Court held that the Federal Arbitration Act's provisions for expedited judicial review trumped the arbitration contract, as the FAA provides the "exclusive grounds" for vacatur or modification of an arbitral award.[198] At the same time, the Court cryptically said that "[t]he FAA is not the only way into court for parties wanting review of arbitration awards: they may contemplate enforcement under state statutory or common law."[199]

The arbitration can be administered by a person or a group. The case administrator helps select the arbitrator who will hear the case, arrange the location where the arbitration will be held, and exchange documents before the hearing. Courts and government agencies typically administer nonbinding arbitration, while specialized organizations typically administer binding arbitrations under their own rules.[200]

The Uniform Arbitration Act (UAA) was developed to help states provide uniform rules and procedures for arbitration. Thirty-two states and the District of Columbia have adopted the UAA. In 2000, the National Conference of Commissioners on Uniform State Laws created the Revised Uniform Arbitration Act (RUAA). The RUAA gives more power to arbitrators and attempts to resolve ambiguities in the previous version of the model act. Eight states have adopted the RUAA, and the act is endorsed by the American Arbitration Association, which is one of the nation's oldest and most influential arbitration providers.[201]

Although the creation of arbitration contracts is left to private parties and chiefly to regulation by state law, the Federal Arbitration Act[202] was enacted in part "to ensure judicial enforcement of privately made agreements to arbitrate."[203] The Act does not require arbitration, but merely the judicial enforcement of arbitration contracts on the same footing as other contracts. The Supreme Court has since held that the Act applies to claims brought under the federal courts' diversity jurisdiction and that the enforceability of arbitration agreements cannot be limited by state law.[204] More recently, it held that the Act preempts state laws that prohibit arbitration contracts from disallowing class-wide arbitration.[205] The practical effect is to encourage manufacturers and other institutions with economic

---

[197] 552 U.S. 576 (2008).

[198] *Id.* at 584.

[199] *Id.* at 590.

[200] *See* MENKEL-MEADOW ET AL., note 192, *supra* at 449.

[201] *See* Robert E. Wells, Jr., *Alternative Dispute Resolution — What Is It? Where Is It Now?*, 28 S. ILL. U. L.J. 651, 660 (2004).

[202] 9 U.S.C. § 1 *et seq.* (2012).

[203] *Dean Witter Reynolds, Inc. v. Byrd*, 470 U.S. 213, 219–20 (1985).

[204] *See Southland Corp. v. Keating*, 465 U.S. 1 (1984); *Prima Paint Corp. v. Flood & Conklin Mfg. Co.*, 388 U.S. 395 (1967).

[205] *AT&T Mobility LLC v. Concepcion*, 131 S. Ct. 1740 (2011).

power to require arbitration of class-wide claims, thus effectively precluding class actions on those claims.

Commentators have suggested that the modern trend toward enforcement of contractual arbitration clauses is problematic for several reasons. First, in some cases of boilerplate arbitration provisions, it effectively denies a judicial remedy to those in inferior bargaining positions, like employees,[206] securities investors,[207] or internet consumers.[208] While sometimes a judicial remedy may be more illusory than real, given the costs of litigation, the Supreme Court's *Concepcion* decision may also have the practical effect of denying such parties the less illusory class action remedy.

Second, arbitration allows important decisions to be made privately, which deprives the public of any benefit from the precedential value those decisions would have carried had they been announced by courts.[209] Arbitration can thus be viewed as part of a growing trend towards privatization of dispute resolution, with an attendant loss of transparency, public legitimacy, and law development.[210]

[4] Summary Jury Trials[211]

Summary jury trials are a supplement to normal litigation that can provide the parties with a kind of crystal ball, suggesting the outcome of the case before the labor and expense of formal adjudication is actually undertaken. The parties summarize the evidence gathered in discovery, usually taking less than a day to present the case in the summary jury trial. The parties can also use testimony and argument, but cannot call live witnesses.[212]

The evidence is presented to a small test jury, drawn from the normal jury pool. They hear the evidence and argument by both sides, and reach a consensus non-binding verdict. The verdict is then disclosed to both sides, giving them a sense of how a real jury will evaluate the case and thereby facilitating settlement.[213] The parties even have the opportunity to talk to the jurors to find out more about the reasoning behind the verdict.

---

[206] Jean R. Sternlight, *Rethinking the Constitutionality of the Supreme Court's Preference for Binding Arbitration: A Fresh Assessment of Jury Trial, Separation of Powers, and Due Process Concerns*, 72 TUL. L. REV. 1, 7 (1997).

[207] *Id.* at 7–8.

[208] Elizabeth G. Thornburg, *Going Private: Technology, Due Process, and Internet Dispute Resolution*, 34 U.C. DAVIS L. REV. 151, 184 (2000).

[209] *See* Laurie Kratky Dore, *Public Courts Versus Private Justice: It's Time to Let Some Sun Shine in on Alternative Dispute Resolution*, 81 CHI.-KENT L. REV. 463 (2006) (arguing that because arbitration is more like litigation than like settlement, it requires more transparency and access than settlement negotiations); Keith N. Hylton, *Arbitration: Governance Benefits and Enforcement Costs*, 80 NOTRE DAME L. REV. 489 (2005).

[210] *See* § 12.01[14], *infra.*

[211] *See* § 12.03[1][b], *infra.*

[212] *See* Richard Posner, *The Summary Jury Trial and Other Methods of Alternative Dispute Resolution: Some Cautionary Observations*, 53 U. CHI. L. REV. 366, 369 (1986).

[213] *See* MENKEL-MEADOW ET AL., note 192, *supra*, at 647.

However, the summary jury trial has also been criticized for several reasons. First, the mandated use of summary jury trials for unwilling parties might be an unauthorized use of judicial power. Circuits have split on whether courts can mandate participation in summary jury trials.[214]

Second, jurors usually do not know that their verdict will be advisory rather than binding, leading to ethical questions about how, when, and, if these jurors should be informed about the truth.[215]

Third, some have questioned whether we should be using public courtrooms and resources to encourage private settlements.[216] Given the rate of settlement and the much-reduced role of trial in modern civil litigation, however, this objection may seem quaint.

§ 11.06 DISPOSITION OF CASES WITHOUT TRIAL IN THE CALIFORNIA COURTS

[1] Introductory Note on Pretrial Dispositions

The vast majority of civil cases filed in the California courts are resolved before trial.[217] Some are dismissed by a demurrer to the complaint, perhaps for failure to state a cause of action or because barred by the applicable statute of limitations. But most are disposed of by several other pre-trial mechanisms, such as a default judgment, settlement, voluntary or involuntary dismissal, or summary judgment. Each of these procedures for disposition without trial is discussed below.

[2] Entry of Default and Default Judgment in the California Courts

A plaintiff may obtain a judgment by default against a defendant, properly served with a complaint and summons, who fails to timely file an appropriate responsive paper.[218] Default judgments entered against defendants for failure to timely answer properly served complaints are commonplace in California. Pursuant to California Code of Civil Procedure § 580, the relief granted to the

---

[214] *Compare Cincinnati Gas & Elec. Co. v. Gen. Elec. Co.*, 854 F.2d 900, 904 n.4 (6th Cir. 1988) (noting that courts do "have the power to conduct summary jury trials under either Fed. R. Civ. P. 16 or as a matter of the court's inherent power to manage its cases"), *with Strandell v. Jackson Cnty.*, 838 F.2d 884 (7th Cir. 1987) (holding that Rule 16 does not permit courts to force unwilling parties to participate in settlement negotiations through summary jury trials). *See* § 12.03[1][b], *infra*.

[215] *See* Posner, note 212, *supra* at 386–87 (1986) (arguing that while telling jurors in advance that their verdict is non-binding might make them less serious about the case at hand, a practice of deceiving jurors might lead to jurors in other cases taking their important role less seriously).

[216] *See* MENKEL-MEADOW ET AL., note 192, *supra*.

[217] Approximately 81% of unlimited civil cases, and 93% of limited civil cases, were disposed of before trial by California courts in fiscal year 2010-11. *See 2012 Court Statistics Report of the Judicial Council of California*, Fig. 21.

[218] CAL. CODE CIV. PROC. §§ 585, 586. Likewise, a defendant may obtain a default judgment against another defendant or a plaintiff, properly served with a cross-complaint, who fails to timely file an appropriate responsive paper. CAL. CODE CIV. PROC. §§ 585(e), 587.5.

plaintiff in a default judgment cannot exceed the relief demanded in the complaint. Section 580 embodies a fundamental due process guarantee that defaulting parties receive adequate notice of the maximum judgment that may be assessed against them.[219]

[a]   General Procedures

The procedure utilized to obtain a default judgment is routine in most cases. After the applicable time specified in the summons for responding to the served complaint has expired, the plaintiff must make written application to the clerk of the court for an entry of default, along with the proof of service and return of the original summons, and a declaration stating that a copy of the application has been mailed to the defendant at his or her last known address.[220] In an action to recover actual or punitive damages for personal injury or wrongful death, the process is a little more complex. Complications may arise because the plaintiff is statutorily precluded from stating in the complaint the dollar amount of actual and punitive damages demanded.[221] Consequently, the plaintiff must serve on the defendant a *statement of damages* setting forth the nature and amount of damages being sought, before (usually 30 days) a default may be taken.[222]

[b]   Entry of Default

Generally, an *entry of default* is a prerequisite to a *default judgment*. These two concepts are often lumped together, but are actually two different steps in the default process. When a defendant (or cross-defendant) has not filed the appropriate responsive paper within the prescribed time, the plaintiff (or cross-plaintiff) may request the court clerk to enter the default. Until the time of entry, the defendant may ordinarily file a belated response without consequence. But the entry of default terminates the defendant's right to file an answer or take any other affirmative steps in the litigation until either the default is set aside or a default judgment entered.[223]

[c]   Obtaining Default Judgments

After entry of default by the clerk, the plaintiff (or cross-plaintiff) may then apply for entry of a default judgment. In some actions, the court clerk has statutory authority to enter the default judgment, but in most actions, only the court has the power to enter this judgment. The clerk is authorized to enter a default judgment only in "an action arising upon contract or judgment for recovery of money or

---

[219] *Marriage of Lippel*, 51 Cal. 3d 1160, 1166, 276 Cal. Rptr. 290, 801 P.2d 1041 (1990); *Greenup v. Rodman*, 42 Cal. 3d 822, 826, 231 Cal. Rptr. 220, 726 P.2d 1295 (1986).

[220] CAL. CODE CIV. PROC. §§ 585(a)–(c), 587, 417.10–.30.

[221] CAL. CODE CIV. PROC. § 425.10(b); CAL. CIV. CODE § 3295(e).

[222] CAL. CODE CIV. PROC. § 425.11 (personal injury damages), § 425.115 (punitive damages).

[223] *See, e.g., Devlin v. Kearny Mesa AMC/Jeep/Renault, Inc.*, 155 Cal. App. 3d 381, 385, 202 Cal. Rptr. 204 (1984) (ruling entry of default precluded defendant from participating in subsequent proceedings to determine amount of punitive damages); *Forbes v. Cameron Petroleums, Inc.*, 83 Cal. App. 3d 257, 263, 147 Cal. Rptr. 766 (1978) (holding demurrer or answer filed after entry of default was a legal nullity).

damages," and then only if a defendant has been served other than by publication.[224] Because clerks' judgments are processed without any judicial intervention, the California courts strictly construe the statutory provisions which authorize such judgments. The clerk cannot take evidence or exercise discretion to determine the amount of damages; therefore the contract which forms the basis of a clerk's judgment must provide for some definite fixed amount of damages ascertainable from the contract itself or computable by mathematical calculation from its terms.[225] Consequently, for example, the clerk cannot enter judgment in a contract action requiring any sort of an accounting, such as an action for accounting of the net proceeds from a sales contract or for the assets in a partnership dissolution action.[226]

In all other cases, a plaintiff must apply to the court for a default judgment. Upon application by the plaintiff, "the court shall hear the evidence offered by the plaintiff, and shall render judgment in plaintiff's favor for that relief, not exceeding the amount stated in the complaint" or in the statement of damages in personal injury actions, "as appears by the evidence to be just."[227] To "prove-up" the default for the court, the plaintiff need only introduce evidence sufficient to establish factual support for each element of the alleged cause of action. This is not a difficult task because by defaulting, the defendant admits the truthfulness of the material allegations of the complaint, making introduction of additional evidence to support such allegations unnecessary. Although the court may hold an evidentiary hearing and even utilize a jury to assess damages, the prove-up hearing is usually an informal proceeding. Typically, the court permits the use of affidavits or declarations in lieu of personal testimony so long as the facts stated in the affidavit are within the personal knowledge of the affiant, are stated with particularity, and affirmatively show the affiant's competency to testify.

Of course, a default or default judgment cannot be entered prior to the expiration of the statutory time within which the defendant has to file an answer or other responsive paper. In most actions, the defendant must file a responsive pleading within 30 days after completion of service of the complaint and summons, unless extended by stipulation.[228] The California statutes do not impose any time restrictions as to when the plaintiff must request an entry of default and default judgment once the time for the defendant's responsive pleading has expired, but case management rules of court may require the plaintiff to proceed expeditiously or face possible sanctions.

---

[224] CAL. CODE CIV. PROC. § 585(a) (clerk's judgment).

[225] *Lynch v. Bencini*, 17 Cal. 2d 521, 525–26, 110 P.2d 662 (1941); *Liberty Loan Corp. v. Petersen*, 24 Cal. App. 3d 915, 918, 101 Cal. Rptr. 395 (1972).

[226] *E.g.*, *Crossman v. Vivienda Water Co.*, 136 Cal. 571, 574, 69 P. 220 (1902); *Ely v. Gray*, 224 Cal. App. 3d 1257, 274 Cal. Rptr. 536 (1990).

[227] CAL. CODE CIV. PROC. §§ 585(b) & (c) (court's judgment).

[228] CAL. CODE CIV. PROC. §§ 585, 412.20(a)(3), 1054 (authorizing stipulations); *see also* § 586(a)(1) (30 days within which to respond to amended complaint). Service is deemed complete at the time of delivery in the case of personal service, but is deemed complete later in the case of substituted service or publication. CAL. CODE CIV. PROC. § 415.10 (personal service); § 415.20 (10th day after mailing when substituted service); § 415.40 (10th day after mailing when service by mail on out-of-state defendant); § 415.50, CAL. GOV'T CODE § 6064 (on 28th day of publication when service by publication).

[3]   Relief from Entry of Default and Default Judgments in the California Courts

The California courts recognize a strong public policy in favor of granting relief from defaults and deciding cases on the merits. Accordingly, a defendant (or cross-defendant), unhappy with a default or default judgment entered for failure to timely file a responsive paper, has several procedural options available for requesting relief. Precisely which option the defendant should select depends on the reason for the default and on how promptly the defendant seeks relief.

[a]   Discretionary Relief When No "Actual Notice" to Defendant

California Code of Civil Procedure § 473.5 permits the trial court to vacate a default judgment if "service of a summons has not resulted in actual notice to a party in time to defend the action." A motion for relief under section 473.5 must be made within a reasonable time, but in no event exceeding the earlier of two years after entry of the default judgment or 180 days after service of notice of entry of the default judgment. If the trial court finds that the defaulting party's lack of actual notice was not caused by avoidance of service or inexcusable neglect, the trial court may, in its discretion, set aside the default judgment.

The statutory reference to "actual notice" has been strictly construed, with the aim of implementing the policy of liberally granting relief so that cases may be resolved on their merits.[229] The question of what constitutes "actual notice" often arises in a motion to vacate a default judgment entered after service by publication. Some courts suggest that "actual notice" in this context exists only where the defendant has actual knowledge of the summons as the result of reading the published summons in the newspaper or actually receiving a copy.[230] A defendant who does not receive actual notice of the complaint and summons as a result of service, but acquired knowledge of the lawsuit from some other source, is not precluded from seeking discretionary relief under section 473.5.[231] Moreover, some

---

[229] *See, e.g., Rosenthal v. Garner*, 142 Cal. App. 3d 891, 895, 191 Cal. Rptr. 300 (1983) (ruling that service on an attorney representing defendant in a related prior litigation does not constitute "actual notice" where the attorney did not inform the defendant); *Tunis v. Barrow*, 184 Cal. App. 3d 1069, 1077–80, 229 Cal. Rptr. 389 (1986) (same); *but see Boland v. All Persons*, 160 Cal. 486, 490, 117 P. 547 (1911) (finding defendant, although not personally served, had actual notice of the complaint and summons posted on her front door).

[230] *Olvera v. Olvera*, 232 Cal. App. 3d 32, 40, 283 Cal. Rptr. 271 (1991); *Ellard v. Conway*, 94 Cal. App. 4th 540, 114 Cal. Rptr. 2d 399 (2001); *see also Rosenthal v. Garner, supra*, 142 Cal. App. 3d at 895 (allowing relief under section 473.5 where, in addition to service by publication, plaintiff had sent a copy of the summons and complaint to defendants' counsel, because this imputed knowledge is not equivalent to the actual knowledge required by the statute).

[231] *See, e.g., Olvera v. Olvera, supra*, 232 Cal. App. 3d at 40–41 (ruling defendant served by publication did not have "actual notice" of the complaint and summons even though she knew of the lawsuit as a result of the filing of a lis pendens notice); *Ellard v. Conway, supra*, 94 Cal. App. 4th at 547–48 (explaining that although actual knowledge from a source other than service of summons does not *preclude* a defendant from seeking relief from a default judgment under section 473.5, such knowledge may provide a proper basis for denying relief where the defendants had actual knowledge of the lawsuit in time to defend the action but failed to file an answer due to inexcusable neglect).

cases hold that even if the defendants have received copies of the complaint and summons, they had no actual knowledge when they had neither the English language competency nor business sophistication to understand these documents.[232]

[b] Discretionary Relief When "Excusable Neglect or Mistake"

Code of Civil Procedure § 473(b) permits a court to grant relief from a default or default judgment entered as a result of "mistake, inadvertence, surprise or excusable neglect" on the part of the defendant or the defendant's attorney. The application for such discretionary relief "must be made within a reasonable time, and in no case exceeding six months." The six-month period runs from the date of the entry of the default or from the judgment taken thereafter, depending on whether the defendant seeks to set aside both events or only the subsequent default judgment.

In determining whether neglect was excusable as opposed to inexecusable, the court inquires whether "a reasonably prudent person under the same or similar circumstances might have made the same error."[233] Unless inexcusable neglect is clear, the policy favoring trial on the merits prevails and doubts should be resolved in favor of the request for relief from default.[234] California Courts often note that "when the moving party promptly seeks relief and there is no prejudice to the opposing party, very slight evidence is required to justify relief" from a default judgment.[235] The type of prejudice shown by a plaintiff to justify a trial court's refusal to set aside a default judgment must be something more than the cost and delay of opposing the motion and proceeding to trial — a plaintiff must show substantial evidence of missing witnesses, evidence destroyed, and the like, to establish prejudice.

Examples of circumstances where the court has found excusable neglect sufficient to grant relief under section 473 include cases where settlement discussions lulled defendants into a false sense of security, where default was due to disability or illness of defendant or defendant's attorney, and where due to attorney's change in personnel and consequent misplacement and lack of knowledge of court papers.[236] An attorney's honest mistake of law may constitute excusable

---

[232] *Goya v. P.E.R.U. Enter.*, 87 Cal. App. 3d 886, 151 Cal. Rptr. 258 (1978) (setting aside default for these reasons).

[233] *E.g., Carroll v. Abbott Labs, Inc.*, 32 Cal. 3d 892, 898, 187 Cal. Rptr. 592, 654 P.2d 775 (1982); *Zamora v. Clayborn Contracting Grp., Inc.*, 28 Cal. 4th 249, 258, 121 Cal. Rptr. 2d 187, 47 P.3d 1056 (2002).

[234] *Elston v. City of Turlock*, 38 Cal. 3d 227, 235, 211 Cal. Rptr. 416, 695 P.2d 713 (1985).

[235] *See, e.g., Rogalski v. Nabers Cadillac*, 11 Cal. App. 4th 816, 821, 14 Cal. Rptr. 2d 286 (1992); *Mink v. Superior Court*, 2 Cal. App. 4th 1338, 1343, 4 Cal. Rptr. 2d 195 (1992).

[236] *Beard v. Beard*, 16 Cal. 2d 645, 648, 107 P.2d 385 (1940). *See also Stone v. McWilliams*, 43 Cal. App. 490, 492, 185 P. 478 (1919) (finding no abuse of discretion where trial court set aside default when aged, blind, and illiterate defendant had good defense on merits); *but see Davis v. Thayer*, 113 Cal. App. 3d 892, 170 Cal. Rptr. 328 (1980) (observing the mere fact of defendant's illness insufficient to excuse failure to take any meaningful action to protect themselves from default); *Elston v. City of Turlock*, 38 Cal. 3d 227,

neglect for purposes of discretionary relief under section 473, but only when the attorney acted reasonably and the legal problem posed is complex and debatable.[237]

Even though the policy favors trial on the merits, some showing of excusable neglect or mistake and of a meritorious defense is necessary to set aside a default judgment under section 473. For example, relief from default has been denied where a defendant incorrectly believed service of the complaint and summons was defective but offered no other excuse for failure to timely respond by motion to quash or by answer, where the general "press of business" prevented the defendant's attorney from filing a timely response, where the attorney was distracted by his girlfriend's hospitalization, and where the defendant's attorney mistakenly believed that the clerk's default was not conclusive.[238]

As a general rule, the inexcusable neglect of an attorney is imputed to the client; the client's redress for inexcusable neglect by counsel is an action for malpractice. However, when the attorney's neglect is of such an extreme degree that it amounts to "positive misconduct" — an abandonment by the lawyer of his client, and a *de facto* severance of the attorney-client relationship — the client is not charged with the attorney's negligence.[239] Under such circumstances, the total failure of counsel to represent the client renders unconscionable the application of the general rule charging the client with the attorney's neglect. The distinction between attorney "positive misconduct" (grounds for relief from default) and attorney "inexcusable neglect" (not grounds for relief from default) is difficult to apply.[240] However, the California Supreme Court has made it clear that the "positive misconduct" exception "should be narrowly applied, lest negligent attorneys find the simplest

---

234–35, 211 Cal. Rptr. 416, 695 P.2d 713 (1985) (holding that although attorney's "press of business" insufficient by itself to warrant relief from default, attorney's lack of knowledge of duty to respond because his employees misplaced papers or misinformed him as to relevant dates is sufficient for relief); *but see Henderson v. Pac. Gas & Elec. Co.*, 187 Cal. App. 4th 215, 229–52, 113 Cal. Rptr. 3d 692 (2010) (finding attorney's failure to file timely opposition to summary judgment motion, the preparation of which the attorney delegated to his paralegal, was inexcusable neglect because attorney failed to supervise his employee).

[237] In *State Farm Fire & Cas. Co. v. Pietak*, 90 Cal. App. 4th 600, 611, 109 Cal. Rptr. 2d 256 (2001), the Court of Appeal held that the trial court abused its discretion in denying the defendant insured's request to reopen an interpleader action to assert a cross-complaint against the plaintiff insurance company where the defendant's failure to do so was due to counsel's mistaken conclusion, after a review of the uncertain case law and statutes relevant to the question, that the defendant insured was not required to assert his claims in the interpleader action by way of cross-complaint.

[238] *See, e.g., Elston, supra*, 38 Cal. 3d at 234; *Khourie, Crew & Jaeger v. Sabek, Inc.*, 220 Cal. App. 3d 1009, 269 Cal. Rptr. 687 (1990); *Barragan v. Banco BCH*, 188 Cal. App. 3d 283, 301, 232 Cal. Rptr. 758 (1986).

[239] *Carroll v. Abbott Labs, Inc., supra*, 32 Cal. 3d at 898–900; *Daley v. Cnty. of Butte*, 227 Cal. App. 2d 380, 38 Cal. Rptr. 693 (1964).

[240] *Compare Daley v. County of Butte, supra*, 227 Cal. App. 2d at 392 (finding positive misconduct where the attorney's gross negligence resulted in dismissal for lack of prosecution due to the attorney's failure to appear at pretrial conferences and to communicate with the court, his client, and other counsel, and refusal to sign a substitution of attorney), *with Beeman v. Burling*, 216 Cal. App. 3d 1586, 1603–04, 265 Cal. Rptr. 719 (1990) (finding no positive misconduct where despite the attorney's failure to file answer, to respond to default warning, and to advise the defendant of default judgment, the attorney continued to act, albeit ineffectively, as defendant's representative during ongoing settlement negotiations after the default).

way to gain the twin goals of rescuing clients from defaults and themselves from malpractice liability, is to rise to even greater heights of incompetence and professional irresponsibility."[241]

[c] Mandatory Relief When Motion Accompanied by Attorney's Affidavit of Neglect

The uncertain parameters of discretionary relief from default caused California courts to devote considerable time and resources to resolution of motions to set aside, often with outcomes contrary to the general policy of deciding cases on the merits. In response, Code of Civil Procedure section 473 was amended in 1988 to greatly broaden the grounds for relief from default to now include attorney mistake or neglect, even when the neglect is inexcusable. If the application is accompanied by the attorney's sworn affidavit attesting to his or her mistake or neglect, the court *must* vacate the default or default judgment, unless the court finds that the default was not caused by the attorney's neglect.[242] The court must also direct the attorney to pay reasonable legal fees and costs to opposing counsel or parties, but cannot condition the relief from default on the attorney's payment of such fees, costs, or other sanctions. As with discretionary relief, a motion for mandatory relief must be filed within six months after the default or default judgment sought to be set aside.

Despite the apparent embarrassment associated with such public disclosure, an attorney has considerable incentives to prepare and file an affidavit of neglect in support of a section 473 motion to set aside a default. By obtaining mandatory relief, an attorney acts not only in the best interest of his or her client, but also in the attorney's own interest by eliminating a potential basis of malpractice. Perhaps due to this confluence of interests, motions for mandatory relief are now commonplace and have eliminated use of motions for discretionary relief except in those few cases where a default is caused by the defendant's neglect rather than that of the defendant's attorney.

[d] Equitable Relief Sought After Six Months

After the six-month period has expired, relief from default is no longer available based on the statutory grounds of Code of Civil Procedure section 473. However, independent of this statutory authority, a California court has the inherent equity power to grant relief from a default judgment where there has been "extrinsic fraud or mistake."[243] As might be expected, a court's equitable power to grant relief based on extrinsic fraud or mistake is narrower than its power under section 473.[244]

---

[241] *Carroll v. Abbott Labs, supra*, 32 Cal. 3d at 900.

[242] CAL. CODE CIV. PROC. § 473(b); *see, e.g., Metropolitan Serv. Corp. v. Casa De Palms, Ltd.*, 31 Cal. App. 4th 1481, 37 Cal. Rptr. 2d 575 (1995) (ruling mandatory relief provisions of § 473(b) required the trial court to grant relief if the attorney admits neglect, even inexcusable neglect, within the six-month period, and did not incorporate any additional diligence requirement).

[243] *Rappleyea v. Campbell*, 8 Cal. 4th 975, 981–85, 35 Cal. Rptr. 2d 669, 884 P.2d 126 (1994); *Marriage of Park*, 27 Cal. 3d 337, 342, 165 Cal. Rptr. 792, 612 P.2d 882 (1980); *Weitz v. Yankosky*, 63 Cal. 2d 849, 855, 48 Cal. Rptr. 620, 409 P.2d 700 (1966).

[244] *See Carroll v. Abbott Labs, Inc.*, 32 Cal. 3d 892, 901, n.8, 187 Cal. Rptr. 592, 654 P.2d 775 (1982) (observing that a party who seeks to set aside a default judgment under a court's equity power must

Moreover, when a default *judgment* (as opposed to an entry of default) has been obtained, the strong policy in favor of finality of judgments dictates that equitable relief may be given only in exceptional circumstances.[245]

Extrinsic fraud is a broad concept that tends to encompass almost any set of external circumstances which deprive a party of a fair adversary hearing. The particular circumstances need not qualify as fraudulent or mistaken in the strict legal sense. The clearest examples are in cases where the aggrieved party is kept in ignorance of the proceeding or is in some other way induced not to appear, such as where the husband obtained a default dissolution of marriage against his wife awarding custody of children and most community property to the husband but concealed from the court and the wife's attorney the fact that his wife had been involuntarily deported to another country; where a defendant reasonably relied on a codefendant, insurer, or other third party, to defend; and where the default was due to the incapacity or disability of the party or his attorney.[246]

By contrast, intrinsic fraud or mistake exists where a party has been given notice of the action and has not been prevented from participating therein, but unreasonably neglected to do so.[247] A party's mistake as to the law or the facts is usually an insufficient basis to set aside a default judgment if the party could have reasonably discovered the mistake.[248] For example, where the value of a company was the very subject of the lawsuit, the defendant's alleged misrepresentations about company's financial condition were held intrinsic because the plaintiff conducted no investigation or discovery into the financial condition.[249] Some California courts have criticized the distinction between extrinsic and intrinsic fraud as "quite nebulous" and "hopelessly blurred."[250] Perhaps for this reason, Rule 60(b) of the Federal Rules of Civil Procedure expressly abandoned this distinction and does not distinguish between extrinsic and intrinsic fraud as a ground for setting aside a federal court judgment.

---

make a stronger showing of excusable neglect than is necessary to obtain relief under section 473).

[245] *Rappleyea v. Campbell, supra*, 8 Cal. 4th at 981–82.

[246] *Marriage of Park, supra*, 27 Cal. 3d at 341–47; *Weitz v. Yankosky, supra*, 63 Cal. 2d at 851–58; *Humes v. Margil Ventures, Inc.*, 174 Cal. App. 3d 486, 499, 220 Cal. Rptr. 186 (1985); *Estate of Sanders*, 40 Cal. 3d 607, 614, 221 Cal. Rptr. 432, 710 P.2d 232 (1985).

[247] *Kulchar v. Kulchar*, 1 Cal. 3d 467, 471, 82 Cal. Rptr. 489, 462 P.2d 17 (1969).

[248] *E.g., City of Ontario v. Superior Court*, 2 Cal. 3d 335, 346, 85 Cal. Rptr. 149, 466 P.2d 693 (1970) (observing that ignorance of the law coupled with negligence in ascertaining it will certainly sustain a denial of relief); *Home Ins. Co. v. Zurich Ins. Co.*, 96 Cal. App. 4th 17, 116 Cal. Rptr. 2d 583 (2002) (holding misrepresentation by insurer's attorney that policy limits were $15,000 instead of $500,000, which induced injured party to settle underlying suit for $15,000 after conducting no discovery, is intrinsic because a reasonable investigation and use of discovery would have disclosed the true extent of insurance coverage).

[249] *Heyman v. Franchise Mortg. Acceptance Corp.*, 107 Cal. App. 4th 921, 132 Cal. Rptr. 2d 465 (2003).

[250] *Marriage of Stevenot, supra*, 154 Cal. App. 3d at 1060; *see Marriage of Baltins*, 212 Cal. App. 3d 66, 82, 260 Cal. Rptr. 403 (1989); David E. Smallwood, *Vacating Judgments in California: Time to Abolish the Extrinsic Fraud Rule*, 13 W. St. U. L. Rev. 105–127 (1985) (arguing for abolishment of the extrinsic fraud rule).

[e] Void Judgments

A default judgment can be void for lack of personal or subject matter jurisdiction, improper service of process, or the granting of relief which the trial court had no power to grant.[251] A trial court has the inherent power to set aside a judgment void on its face at any time. For example, a default judgment in excess of the amount stated in the complaint or statement of damages can be collaterally attacked after the six-month period has expired, and may even be challenged for the first time on appeal.[252]

[4] Involuntary Dismissals in the California Courts

[a] Introductory Note on Involuntary Dismissals

In the adversary system, the burden of moving a lawsuit forward through its investigative and decisional stages is placed on the parties and their attorneys, not on the court; the litigation stops unless one party or the other requests the court to compel the opponent to take the next step.[253] California departs from this model in at least one significant way — if a plaintiff fails to prosecute an action diligently, the action is subject to dismissal. California statutes provide for both mandatory and discretionary dismissal.[254] The purpose of these statutes is to promote the trial of cases before evidence is lost or witnesses have forgotten the facts, and to protect defendants from the annoyance of an unmeritorious action remaining undecided for an indefinite period of time. A significant percentage of civil dispositions in the California superior courts are dismissals for delay in prosecution.[255]

In addition to the statutory diligence requirements, several rules of court provide for involuntary dismissal. The most important are the state and local case management rules implementing the Trial Court Delay Reduction Act that frequently impose shorter time limits than the state statutes, and authorize sanctions for failure to comply. In addition, a court has inherent authority to dismiss an action for severe misconduct.[256]

---

[251] *Forbes v. Hyde*, 31 Cal. 342, 355 (1866); *Becker v. S.P.V. Constr. Co.*, 27 Cal. 3d 489, 493, 165 Cal. Rptr. 825, 612 P.2d 915 (1980); *Heidary v. Yadollahi*, 99 Cal. App. 4th 857, 121 Cal. Rptr. 2d 695 (2002).

[252] *Becker, supra*, 27 Cal. 3d at 492–94; *National Diversified Serv., Inc. v. Bernstein*, 168 Cal. App. 3d 410, 417, 214 Cal. Rptr. 113 (1985); *Petty v. Manpower, Inc.*, 94 Cal. App. 3d 794, 798, 156 Cal. Rptr. 622 (1979).

[253] *See* FLEMING JAMES, JR., GEOFFREY C. HAZARD & JOHN LUEBSDORF, CIVIL PROCEDURE § 1.2 (4th ed. 1992) (discussing the roles of the parties and the court in the adversary system).

[254] *See* CAL. CODE CIV. PROC. §§ 583.110–583.430.

[255] California statewide statistics for civil actions indicate the following percentage of dispositions were dismissals for delay in prosecution: 4.7% in 2008-09, 4.2% in 2009-10, and 3.9% in 2010-11. *See 2012 Court Statistics Report of the Judicial Council of California*, Fig. 21.

[256] *See Lyons v. Wickhorst*, 42 Cal. 3d 911, 915, 231 Cal. Rptr. 738, 727 P.2d 1019 (1986) (explaining that a court's inherent power is "tightly circumscribed" by the requirement that a court consider whether the plaintiff's conduct is so severe and deliberate as to constitute extreme circumstances and whether less drastic alternatives are available).

A dismissal for lack of prosecution before trial is without prejudice.[257] Because it is not on the merits, the dismissal has no res judicata (claim preclusion) effect.[258] Consequently, if a cause of action is not barred by the applicable statute of limitations, a party may again litigate it after a dismissal by commencement of a new lawsuit.

[b] Mandatory Dismissals for Lack of Prosecution

Dismissal is mandatory if a plaintiff fails to meet any one of three statutory deadlines: (1) failure to serve the action within three years of filing, (2) failure to bring the case to trial within five years, and (3) failure to bring a case to a new trial within three years.

Under Code of Civil Procedure § 583.210, dismissal is mandatory if the action is not served within three years of filing of the complaint.[259] This provision applies both to named defendants and to fictitious defendants (i.e., a defendant designated as "Doe" defendant in the original complaint as a placeholder for a later-named actual defendant).[260] When new parties are added by an amended complaint, the three-year period begins to run from the filing of the amended complaint.[261] However, where a defendant named in an amended complaint was originally sued under a fictitious name, the three-year period begins ("relates back to") when the original complaint was filed.[262]

Although dismissal for failure to serve within three years is mandatory, the plaintiff can avoid dismissal on a proper showing of tolling or excuse. For example, in computing the time in which service must be made, the time during which the defendant was not amenable to service or the parties were litigating the validity of service is excluded.[263] However, the fact that the defendant is absent from, or concealed within, the state and his whereabouts unknown, or that the defendant is not subject to the court's jurisdiction, does not excuse a failure to serve. The relevant inquiry is whether the party was subject to being served under applicable constitutional and statutory provisions, not whether the defendant was reasonably available as a practical matter for service of process.[264] Therefore, for example, a defendant is amenable to service even though the only available method of service

---

[257] CAL. CODE CIV. PROC. § 581(b)(4).

[258] *Wilson v. Bittick*, 63 Cal. 2d 30, 35–36, 45 Cal. Rptr. 31, 403 P.2d 159 (1965).

[259] Because return of service is required within 60 days of actual service, the plaintiff has an additional 60 days after the three-year period to file the proof of service. CAL. CODE CIV. PROC. § 583.210(b).

[260] *See Nelson v. A.H. Robins Co.*, 149 Cal. App. 3d 862, 197 Cal. Rptr. 179 (1983); *Lesko v. Superior Court*, 127 Cal. App. 3d 476, 179 Cal. Rptr. 595 (1982). California's fictitious ("Doe") defendant doctrine is discussed in § 8.13, *supra*.

[261] *See, e.g., American W. Banker v. Price Waterhouse*, 12 Cal. App. 4th 39, 14 Cal. Rptr. 2d 916 (1993) (new plaintiffs added); *Hennessey's Tavern, Inc. v. Am. Air Filter Co.*, 204 Cal. App. 3d 1351, 251 Cal. Rptr. 859 (1988) (new defendants added).

[262] *See Barrington v. A.H. Robins Co.*, 39 Cal. 3d 146, 216 Cal. Rptr. 405, 702 P.2d 563 (1985).

[263] CAL. CODE CIV. PROC. § 583.240.

[264] *See Watts v. Crawford*, 10 Cal. 4th 743, 42 Cal. Rptr. 2d 81, 896 P.2d 807 (1995).

is by publication.[265]

In addition to these tolling provisions, statutory exceptions to the three-year requirement apply when the parties extend the period by stipulation or when the defendant makes a general appearance within the mandatory three-year period.[266] A general appearance is an act by the defendant recognizing the court's jurisdiction and reflecting the intent to submit to it. Examples include filing a responsive pleading, giving a notice of appearance, agreeing to accept service and requesting an extension of time to plead, and affirmatively engaging in discovery.[267]

[c]   Failure to Bring the Case to Trial within Five Years

Under Code of Civil Procedure § 583.310, dismissal is mandatory if the action is not brought to trial within five years after it is commenced. To determine whether this requirement has been satisfied, the key question is not whether there has actually been a trial but whether the action has been "brought to a stage where a final disposition is to be made of it."[268] Therefore, a defendant is not entitled to an involuntary dismissal on this ground where all the allegations of the complaint have been admitted or the parties have submitted an agreed statement of facts since the defendant has conceded that a trial is not required.[269] For the same reason, any pretrial proceeding resulting in a final judgment within the five-year limit — such as a demurrer, a motion for summary judgment, or binding arbitration — satisfies the requirement.[270]

The burden is on plaintiff to ensure that the action is brought to trial within the five-year period. As the deadline approaches, the plaintiff must move for a trial date *preference* and to specially set the case for trial. Failure to seek a preference may in itself show plaintiff's lack of diligence.[271] Even where the plaintiff brings such a motion, the court has no mandatory duty to provide a preferential trial date and may decline to do so where the plaintiff has failed to show due diligence in prosecuting the action.[272] Although the dismissal for failure to bring a case to trial

---

[265] *Perez v. Smith*, 19 Cal. App. 4th 1595, 24 Cal. Rptr. 2d 186 (1993).

[266] CAL. CODE CIV. PROC. §§ 583.220, 583.230; *see, e.g., Busching v. Superior Court*, 12 Cal. 3d 44, 52, 115 Cal. Rptr. 241, 524 P.2d 369 (1974); *Brookview Condo. Owners' Ass'n v. Heltzer Enter.-Brookview*, 218 Cal. App. 3d 502, 267 Cal. Rptr. 76 (1990).

[267] *See, e.g., General Ins. Co. v. Superior Court*, 15 Cal. 3d 449, 453–56, 124 Cal. Rptr. 745, 541 P.2d 289 (1975); CAL. CODE CIV. PROC. § 1014.

[268] *Berri v. Superior Court*, 43 Cal. 2d 856, 859, 279 P.2d 8 (1955).

[269] *See* CEB, *California Civil Procedure Before Trial, supra* § 39.25 (citing cases).

[270] *Id.* at §§ 39.30–39.34.

[271] *See Tejada v. Blas*, 196 Cal. App. 3d 1335, 242 Cal. Rptr. 538 (1987); *Westinghouse Elec. Corp. v. Superior Court*, 143 Cal. App. 3d 95, 107, 191 Cal. Rptr. 549 (1983).

[272] *See, e.g., Howard v. Thrifty Drug & Discount Stores*, 10 Cal. 4th 424, 440–41, 41 Cal. Rptr. 2d 362, 895 P.2d 469 (1995) (explain that a motion for preferential trial setting raises essentially the same issues as a motion for discretionary dismissal); *Salas v. Sears, Roebuck & Co.*, 42 Cal. 3d 342, 228 Cal. Rptr. 504, 721 P.2d 590 (1986) (ruling there is no mandatory duty to set a preferential trial date; trial court should consider such discretionary factors as the condition of court calendar, dilatory conduct by plaintiff, and prejudice to defendant of an accelerated trial date); *Nye v. 20th Century Ins. Co.*, 225 Cal. App. 3d 1041, 275 Cal. Rptr. 319 (1990) (affirming denial of motion specially set case for trial filed 41 days before

within five years is mandatory, a few statutory exceptions do apply. For example, the time may be extended by stipulation or where bringing the action to trial was "impossible, impracticable, or futile" because no courtroom is available for trial and the plaintiff has exercised reasonable diligence in prosecuting the case.[273] Likewise, in some instances, the exception may apply when the plaintiff's counsel is seriously ill or otherwise disabled.[274]

[d]　Failure to Bring the Case to New Trial Within Three Years

Under Code of Civil Procedure § 583.320, dismissal is mandatory if the plaintiff fails to bring an action to trial within three years after a mistrial, hung jury, order for new trial, or appellate remand. However, this section does not apply where the initial five-year period for bringing an action to trial has not yet expired; the plaintiff gets the benefit of the five-year statute.[275] A plaintiff is entitled to an extension of the three-year deadline on the same grounds as allowed for an extension of the initial five-year period.[276]

[e]　Discretionary Dismissals for Lack of Prosecution

Discretionary dismissal is permitted under Code of Civil Procedure § 583.410 and § 583.420 when a plaintiff fails to meet any one of three statutory deadlines: Failure to serve defendant within two years, failure to bring the case to trial within two years, and failure to bring a case to new trial within two years. California Rules of Court implementing these statutes govern the court's exercise of discretion in ordering dismissals on these grounds and requires the court to be guided by the policies favoring the rights of parties to make stipulations and the disposition of actions on their merits.[277] Moreover, before entering a discretionary dismissal, a

---

expiration of five-year period and noting that plaintiffs who have failed to act diligently will not be allowed to cut in line ahead of diligent litigants).

[273] CAL. CODE CIV. PROC. §§ 583.330(a) & (b), 583.340(c). See, e.g., Coe v. City of Los Angeles, 24 Cal. App. 4th 88, 29 Cal. Rptr. 2d 297 (1994) (holding trial court abused discretion in dismissing action; five-year statute must be tolled by aggregate of court-ordered continuances based upon courtroom unavailability); Chin v. Meier, 235 Cal. App. 3d 1473, 1 Cal. Rptr. 2d 499 (1991) (holding court-ordered continuance because of courtroom unavailability made it impossible for plaintiff to proceed to trial and therefore five-year statute tolled for that period of impossibility).

[274] Compare Sanchez v. City of Los Angeles, 109 Cal. App. 4th 1262, 135 Cal. Rptr. 2d 869 (2003) (finding the fact that attorney for one defendant committed suicide during last six months of statutory period did not make it impracticable or impossible for plaintiffs to bring action to trial), and Sierra Nevada Mem.-Miners Hosp., Inc. v. Superior Court, 217 Cal. App. 3d 464, 266 Cal. Rptr. 50 (1990) (approving dismissal because no causal connection between counsel's physical disabilities and failure to satisfy five-year requirement), with Him v. Superior Court, 184 Cal. App. 3d 35, 228 Cal. Rptr. 839 (1986) (holding five-year period tolled for several weeks due to counsel's illness, where counsel was sole practitioner and illness at end of five-year period), and Tamburina v. Combined Ins. Co. of Am., 147 Cal. App. 4th 323, 54 Cal. Rptr. 3d 175 (2007) (finding stipulated continuances totaling 424 days, attributable to the plaintiff's and his attorney's serious health problems, qualified as a circumstance of impracticability).

[275] CAL. CODE CIV. PROC. § 583.320(b).

[276] CAL. CODE CIV. PROC. §§ 583.310–583.360.

[277] CAL. CT. R. 3.1340, 3.1342(e).

court must consider a variety of factors, such as the availability of parties for service of process, the plaintiff's diligence in effecting service, the extent of settlement discussions, the parties' diligence in discovery and pretrial proceedings, the nature and complexity of the case, the condition of the court's calendar, the interests of justice, and any other relevant facts or circumstances.[278]

[f] Involuntary Dismissals Under California "Fast Track" Rules

In practice, the critical delay-in-prosecution rules are the state-wide *case management rules of court* adopted by the California Judicial Council pursuant to the Trial Court Delay Reduction Act, Government Code §§ 68600–68620, as well as the local delay reduction rules adopted by each superior court. These rules establish time periods that are often dramatically shorter than those set out in the mandatory and discretionary dismissal statutes. For example, under Rule 3.110 of the California Rules of Court, a complaint must be served on all named defendants within 60 days after filing, unless extended by the court. In addition to authorizing shorter time limits, the Act reflects a different policy toward stipulations extending time than the dismissal statutes. The dismissal statutes favor the right of parties to make stipulations in their own interests. In contrast, the Act discourages continuances by stipulation of the parties. To promote the efficient resolution of litigation, the Act limits the parties to a single continuance not to exceed 30 days.[279]

The teeth in the Trial Court Delay Reduction Act are provided by its sanctions provisions. Government Code § 60608(b) authorizes a judge to impose a variety of sanctions for failure to comply with case management ("fast track") rules, including the power to dismiss actions or strike pleadings if it appears that less severe sanctions would not be effective. During the height of reliance on local rules to implement the Act, an issue arose as to whether section 68608(b) preempted Code of Civil Procedure § 575.2, which only authorizes the imposition of sanctions that "adversely affect the party's cause of action or defense" if the failure to comply with local rules is the fault of the party and not the party's attorney. The California Supreme Court subsequently resolved this issue when it held that the limitations on the power to impose case-dispositive sanctions expressed in section 572.2 were applicable to violations of all types of local rules, including local "fast track" rules designed to implement the mandates of the Act.[280]

To promote implementation of the Act, the Judicial Council established the following time goals for disposition of unlimited civil cases (cases with more than $25,000 in controversy) assigned to the case management program: 75% should be disposed within 12 months of filing, 85% within 18 months, and 100% within 24 months.[281] Measured by these standards, California's delay reduction efforts have

---

[278] Cal. Ct. R. 3.1342(e).

[279] Cal. Gov't Code § 68616(d).

[280] *Garcia v. McCutchen*, 16 Cal. 4th 469, 66 Cal. Rptr. 2d 319, 940 P.2d 906 (1997).

[281] Cal. Ct. R. 3.714(b)(1); Standards of Judicial Administration, Cal. Ct. R. App. § 2.1(f)(1). Similar goals apply to limited civil cases (cases for less than $25,000): 90% should be disposed of within 12 months of filing, 98% within 18 months, and 100% within 24 months. Cal. Ct. R. 3.714(b)(2); Standards, § 2.1(f)(2).

been successful. Recent court statistics indicate that 70% of unlimited civil cases were disposed of in less than 12 months of filing, 85% in less than 18 months, and 92% in less than 24 months.[282]

[5] Voluntary Dismissals in the California Courts

Generally, a plaintiff may voluntarily dismiss his or her complaint prior to the actual "commencement of trial."[283] But this right to voluntarily dismiss before trial is not absolute. Limitations on voluntary dismissals have evolved through construction of the term "commencement of trial," and generally arise "where the action has proceeded to a determinative adjudication or to a decision that is tantamount to an adjudication."[284] In other words, the plaintiff's right to dismiss is balanced against the investment of resources made by the other party and by the court in the lawsuit. For example, where a general demurrer (the California equivalent of a motion to dismiss for failure to state a claim) to a complaint is sustained with leave to amend and the plaintiff fails to amend the complaint within the time allotted, the right to voluntarily dismiss the action is cut off.[285] California decisional law reflects the same policy of limiting unilateral dismissals to the early stages of litigation evident in Rule 41(a)(1)(A) of the Federal Rules of Civil Procedure, which permits a plaintiff to dismiss once without leave of court before an answer or motion for summary judgment is served upon him.

A plaintiff has the option, prior to trial, to voluntarily dismiss a lawsuit "with or without prejudice."[286] A dismissal *without prejudice* is not a bar to the filing of a subsequent action, within the applicable statute of limitation period, predicated upon the same cause of action.[287] In contrast, a dismissal *with prejudice* bars a new action on the same subject matter.[288] After the "actual commencement of trial," a voluntary dismissal by plaintiff is with prejudice, unless all the affected parties consent to dismissal without prejudice or the court so orders on a showing of good cause.[289]

In several decisions, the California courts have construed the term "commencement of trial" to limit the right of voluntary dismissal without prejudice

---

[282] *See 2012 Court Statistics Report of the Judicial Council of California*, Superior Courts, Fig. 17-20. Similar success is reported with respect to limited civil cases: 86% were disposed of within 12 months of filing, 95% within 18 months, and 98% within 24 months. *Id.*

[283] Cal. Code Civ. Proc. § 581(b) & (c).

[284] *Cravens v. State Bd. of Equalization*, 52 Cal. App. 4th 253, 256, 60 Cal. Rptr. 2d 436 (1997) (quoting *Harris v. Billings*, 16 Cal. App. 4th 1396, 1402, 20 Cal. Rptr. 2d 718 (1993)); *Zapanta v. Universal Care, Inc.*, 107 Cal. App. 4th 1167, 132 Cal. Rptr. 2d 842 (2003) (discussing several cases).

[285] *Wells v. Marina City Properties, Inc.*, 29 Cal. 3d 781, 785, 176 Cal. Rptr. 104, 632 P.2d 217 (1981); *see Parsons v. Umansky*, 28 Cal. App. 4th 867, 34 Cal. Rptr. 2d 144 (1994) (distinguishing dismissal without prejudice before time to amend has expired from dismissal after the time has lapsed).

[286] Cal. Code Civ. Proc. § 581(b)(1).

[287] *Kuperman v. Great Republic Life Ins. Co.*, 195 Cal. App. 3d 943, 947, 241 Cal. Rptr. 187 (1987).

[288] *See, e.g., Lama v. Comcast Cablevision*, 14 Cal. App. 4th 59, 64, 17 Cal. Rptr. 2d 224 (1993); *Torrey Pines Bank v. Superior Court*, 216 Cal. App. 3d 813, 820, 265 Cal. Rptr. 217 (1989). A plaintiff might intentionally choose to dismiss an action with prejudice pursuant to the terms of a settlement agreement.

[289] Cal. Code Civ. Proc. § 581(e).

in a variety of other pretrial situations.[290] For example, a voluntarily dismissal without prejudice may not be permitted after the trial court has issued a tentative ruling on a general demurrer or a summary judgment motion.[291] After reviewing these decisions, one court observed that "[t]he thread running through all these cases seems to one of fairness: Once the parties commence putting forth the facts of their case before some sort of fact finder . . . or at the pretrial stage a ruling is made on an issue of law or on admitted facts which effectively disposes of the plaintiff's case against him, it is unfair — perhaps a mockery of the system — to allow the plaintiff to dismiss his complaint and refile."[292] Special statutes also may limit voluntary dismissals in certain situations. For example, a class action may not be dismissed unless notice is given to the class and the dismissal is approved by the court.[293] Nor is a plaintiff permitted to dismiss an action when the defendant has filed a cross-complaint seeking affirmative relief.[294]

[6] Alternative Dispute Resolution in California

California statutes encourage parties to use alternative dispute processes such as *settlement, mediation,* and *arbitration* to resolve their disputes without resort to the judicial system or, if an action is already commenced in court, without further pretrial proceedings or a trial. Most of these alternative dispute processes are private and voluntary, and anticipate little or no court involvement. Some are mandatory, such as nonbinding court-annexed ("judicial") arbitration in certain types of cases where the amount in controversy does not exceed $50,000. Each process is designed to be less costly, time-consuming, and stressful than the formal litigation process. Together, they play an essential role in reducing the backlog of cases burdening the judicial system. Some of the more important alternative dispute mechanisms in California are discussed below.

---

[290] *E.g., Vanderkous v. Conley,* 188 Cal. App. 4th 111, 115 Cal. Rptr. 3d 249 (2010) (upholding plaintiff's voluntary dismissal of quiet title action after statement of decision issued ineffective, even though hearing to value defendant's equitable interest in property was still pending); *Gray v. Superior Court,* 52 Cal. App. 4th 165, 60 Cal. Rptr. 2d 428 (1997) (holding plaintiff's right to dismiss is cut off by the commencement of evidentiary proceedings before a referee appointed in a partition action, even though the referee's recommendations are not binding on the appointing court); *Hartbrodt v. Burke,* 42 Cal. App. 4th 168, 49 Cal. Rptr. 2d 562 (1996) (ruling plaintiff may not defeat a defendant's motion for a terminating discovery sanction by filing a voluntary dismissal just before the sanction hearing); *Goldtree v. Spreckels,* 135 Cal. 666, 672–73, 67 P. 1091 (1902) (explaining plaintiff has no right to dismiss without prejudice if a general demurrer has been sustained without leave to amend).

[291] *E.g., Groth Bros. Oldsmobile, Inc. v. Gallagher,* 97 Cal. App. 4th 60, 118 Cal. Rptr. 2d 405 (2002) (allowing a plaintiff to file a voluntary dismissal without prejudice in the face of a tentative ruling that the court will sustain a demurrer without leave to amend "wastes the time and resources of the court and other parties and promotes annoying and continuous litigation," as well as undermines the tentative ruling system); *Mary Morgan, Inc. v. Melzark,* 49 Cal. App. 4th 765, 57 Cal. Rptr. 2d 4 (1996) (holding the plaintiff could not dismiss a case without prejudice after a tentative granting of defendants' summary motions and after the hearing on the motions had commenced but was continued for the exclusive purpose of allowing the plaintiff to produce evidence).

[292] *Gray v. Superior Court, supra,* 52 Cal. App. 4th at 173.

[293] CAL. CODE CIV. PROC. § 581(k).

[294] CAL. CODE CIV. PROC. § 581(i).

[a]　Settlement

The vast majority of civil actions are resolved through *settlement*. Several factors, such as efficiency and certainty of outcome, make settlement desirable to the parties, their attorneys, and the courts. The California courts often acknowledge the importance of the public policy favoring settlements and promote this policy through their decisions.[295] This public policy also manifests itself in pretrial case management rules which mandate settlement conferences in most civil actions.

An attorney cannot surrender any substantive right of a client, nor compromise the client's cause of action, without the client's consent or specific authorization.[296] However, the attorney-client relationship is governed by the general rules of principal and agent.[297] Therefore, a settlement is binding on the client if the attorney had the express, implied, or ostensible authority to make the offer, or if the client subsequently ratifies the settlement.[298] There is a presumption that an attorney has the authority to compromise the client's action, but this presumption is rebuttable.[299] A voluntary dismissal pursuant to a settlement agreement may be set aside where the client proves that the attorney acted beyond the scope of his authority in accepting an offer.[300]

[b]　Offer to Allow Judgment

Code of Civil Procedure § 998 reflects California's policy of encouraging settlements by authorizing any party to serve an offer in writing upon any other party to an action to allow judgment to be taken in accordance with the terms and conditions stated in the offer.[301] If the offer is accepted and the offer with proof of acceptance is filed, the court must enter judgment accordingly.[302] If the offer is not accepted prior to trial or within 30 days after it is made, whichever occurs first, it is deemed withdrawn.[303] An unaccepted offer may also be revoked by the offeror prior to the

---

[295] *See, e.g., Marriage of Assemi*, 7 Cal. 4th 896, 910, 30 Cal. Rptr. 2d 265, 872 P.2d 1190 (1994); Stephen McG. Bundy, *The Policy in Favor of Settlement in an Adversary System*, 44 HASTINGS L.J. 1 (1992).

[296] *See, e.g., Whittier Union High Sch. Dist. v. Superior Court*, 66 Cal. App. 3d 504, 508, 136 Cal. Rptr. 86 (1977); *Bice v. Stevens*, 160 Cal. App. 2d 222, 231–32, 325 P.2d 244 (1958). California Business and Professions Code § 6103.5 requires an attorney to promptly communicate to her client any written offer of settlement made by an opposing party.

[297] *Blanton v. Womancare, Inc.*, 38 Cal. 3d 396, 403, 212 Cal. Rptr. 151, 696 P.2d 645 (1985); *Yanchor v. Kagan*, 22 Cal. App. 3d 544, 549, 99 Cal. Rptr. 367 (1971).

[298] *See, e.g., Navrides v. Zurich Ins. Co.*, 5 Cal. 3d 698, 97 Cal. Rptr. 309, 488 P.2d 637 (1971); *Yanchor, supra*, 22 Cal. App. 3d at 549–50.

[299] *See, e.g., Gagnon Co., Inc. v. Nevada Desert Inn*, 45 Cal. 2d 448, 460–61, 289 P.2d 466 (1955); *Slack v. Slack*, 241 Cal. App. 2d 530, 538, 50 Cal. Rptr. 763 (1966).

[300] *See Whittier Union High Sch. Dist., supra*, 66 Cal. App. 3d at 507–10 (vacating unauthorized voluntary dismissal made by attorney); *Bice, supra*, 160 Cal. App. 2d at 231–34 (same).

[301] *See, e.g., Poster v. Southern Cal. Rapid Transit Dist.*, 52 Cal. 3d 266, 276 Cal. Rptr. 321, 801 P.2d 1072 (1990).

[302] CAL. CODE CIV. PROC. § 998(b)(1).

[303] CAL. CODE CIV. PROC. § 998(b)(2).

expiration of the statutory period.[304] Section 998 provides financial incentives (and corresponding disincentives) to encourage parties to accept an offer and thereby settle the lawsuit. If an offeree does not accept a section 998 offer and subsequently fails to obtain a more favorable judgment, the court may penalize the offeree under section 998 by the withholding or augmenting of allowable costs.[305]

[c] Contractual Arbitration

The California Arbitration Act (CAA) expresses a strong policy in favor of *contractual arbitration* as a speedy and relatively inexpensive means of dispute resolution.[306] Parties to a contract may agree to submit any dispute to arbitration — a process not unlike a private trial but before an arbitrator instead of a judge — and thus bypass the judicial system. In order to avoid the delay and expense associated with judicial involvement, parties typically intend that an arbitrator's decision will be both final and binding. Therefore, as a general rule, an arbitrator's decision cannot be reviewed for errors of fact or law, even if the error appears on the face of the arbitration award and causes substantial injustice to the parties.[307] In other words, by expressly agreeing to arbitration, the parties give up accuracy in decision-making for the perceived benefits of a confidential, faster, and less costly resolution of their dispute. However, because the scope and procedure of arbitration are determined by agreement, the parties may structure the arbitration process to permit judicial review of errors of law, at least as to arbitration governed by the CAA.[308]

Arbitration pursuant to the CAA presents numerous difficult legal questions concerning such topics as when do arbitrators exceed their powers, what remedies are arbitrators authorized to award, when is an arbitration agreement invalid and who determines the validity of the agreement, under what circumstances should an arbitrator be disqualified, and whether or not certain important statutory rights may be vindicated through arbitration as opposed to litigation. These issues are further complicated in some instances because the CAA may be preempted by the provisions of the Federal Arbitration Act (FAA), 9 U.S.C. § 1 *et seq.*, which applies to arbitration agreements in contracts involving interstate commerce.[309] Thorough analysis of these various issues is beyond the scope of the materials.

---

[304] *T.M. Cobb Co. v. Superior Court*, 36 Cal. 3d 273, 204 Cal. Rptr. 143, 682 P.2d 338 (1984).

[305] Cal. Code Civ. Proc. § 998(c)–(e).

[306] Cal. Code Civ. Proc. § 1280 *et seq.*

[307] *Moncharsh v. Heily & Blase*, 3 Cal. 4th 1, 10 Cal. Rptr. 2d 183, 832 P.2d 899 (1992).

[308] *Cable Connection, Inc. v. DIRECTV, Inc.*, 44 Cal. 4th 1334, 82 Cal. Rptr. 3d 229, 190 P.3d 586 (2008).

[309] *E.g., AT&T Mobility v. Concepcion*, ___. U.S. ___, 131 S. Ct. 1740 (2011) (holding the FAA preempts California's rule classifying most class arbitration waivers in consumer contracts as unconscionable); *Perry v. Thomas*, 482 U.S. 483 (1987) (holding FAA, which mandates enforcement of arbitration agreements, preempted California statute which provides that judicial actions for collection of wages may be maintained without regard to the existence of arbitration agreements).

[d]　Judicial Arbitration

The California Judicial Arbitration Act was enacted in 1978 as a means of coping with the increasing cost and complexity of litigation in civil disputes.[310] The Act mandates submission to arbitration of certain categories of unlimited civil actions where the amount in controversy is determined not to exceed a specified amount ($50,000 for each plaintiff as of 2013), authorizes each superior court by local rule to also require arbitration of certain limited civil cases, and permits submission to arbitration upon stipulation by the parties regardless of the amount in controversy. Unlike private contractual arbitration, judicial (or court-annexed) arbitration is compulsory but is not necessarily final or binding. The Act provides that any party may elect to have a *de novo trial* both as to law and facts, and that an arbitration award is final only if a request for a de novo trial or a request for dismissal is not filed within 60 days after the date the arbitrator files the award with the court. When a timely request for a trial is filed with the court, the case is restored to the civil active list and is tried as though no arbitration proceedings had occurred. This lack of finality has led some courts to observe that "judicial arbitration is obviously an inapt term, for the system it describes is neither judicial nor arbitration . . . 'extrajudicial mediation' would be closer to correct."[311]

If there is no request for a de novo trial or for a dismissal, a judgment is entered in the amount of the award and has the same force and effect as a judgment in any civil action, except that it is not subject to appeal.[312] The Act discourages a party, dissatisfied with the arbitration award, from exercising the right to request a de novo trial. A major disincentive is that if the judgment upon the trial de novo is not more favorable in either amount of damages awarded or the type of relief granted for the party electing the trial de novo than the arbitration award, the court shall order that party to pay certain costs and fees, such as the compensation paid to the arbitrator and the other party's costs including certain expert witness fees.[313] According to several surveys, although more than one-half of the cases resulting in a judicial arbitration award were returned to the civil active list after a request for de novo trial, less than 2% of the cases submitted to judicial arbitration were actually tried de novo.[314] A likely explanation for so few de novo trials is that the information obtained through the arbitration process induces the parties to settle their dispute before trial — the request for a trial de novo provides leverage during the negotiations.

Unlike private contractual arbitration, judicial arbitration generates few difficult legal issues. However, one vexing problem is how to deal with a party who simply chooses not to participate in the arbitration process. Knowing that de novo trial is available, a party may decide not to introduce any evidence in support of his case or

---

[310] CAL. CODE CIV. PROC. § 1141.10 *et seq.*; *Blanton v. Womancare, Inc.*, 38 Cal. 3d 396, 401, 212 Cal. Rptr. 151, 696 P.2d 645 (1985).

[311] *Nanfito v. Superior Court*, 2 Cal. App. 4th 315, 319, 2 Cal. Rptr. 2d 876 (1991).

[312] CAL. CODE CIV. PROC. § 1141.23.

[313] CAL. CODE CIV. PROC. § 1141.21(a).

[314] *See* JOHN A. TOKER, CALIFORNIA ARBITRATION AND MEDIATION PRACTICE GUIDE § 7.2 (2003 & Suppl. 2013).

even to refute his opponent's claims, but instead to use the arbitration process solely as a means to discover information about his opponent's case. Addressing this problem in the context of a superior court's dismissal of a trial de novo requested after an unfavorable award, the California Supreme Court in *Lyons v. Wickhorst*[315] recognized the inherent power of a trial court to dismiss actions but held its exercise improper as a sanction for refusal to participate in mandatory arbitration proceedings. The *Lyons* Court noted that only monetary sanctions are authorized for such frivolous or delaying tactics during a judicial arbitration proceeding. Several subsequent decisions have upheld significant monetary sanctions for refusal to participate but have reversed trial court orders striking a motion for trial de novo.[316]

§ 11.07 SUMMARY JUDGMENT IN THE CALIFORNIA COURTS

[1] Introductory Note on California Summary Judgment Practice

California practice employs the motion for summary judgment, which includes a motion for summary adjudication, as a potentially powerful procedural device to probe beneath the pleadings. Pleading motions have limited utility — they accept the facts, or at least the well-pleaded facts, contained in the pleadings as true in testing the sufficiency of claims. Except for novel or badly-pleaded causes of action, a technically skillful pleader will state proper causes of action. Nevertheless, the claim or defenses made to the claim in the pleadings may not be factually substantial enough to warrant a full trial. Summary judgment is the means for weeding out causes of action and defenses that lack merit because they are factually unsupportable.[317]

---

[315] 42 Cal. 3d 911, 231 Cal. Rptr. 738, 727 P.2d 1019 (1986).

[316] *See, e.g., Salowitz Org., Inc. v. Traditional Indus., Inc.*, 219 Cal. App. 3d 797, 268 Cal. Rptr. 493 (1990) (upholding trial court's award of $6,000 as sanction for failure to appear in arbitration proceedings, but reversing involuntary dismissal of de novo trial request); *Zatkin v. Cesare*, 199 Cal. App. 3d 756, 245 Cal. Rptr. 222 (1988) (involuntary dismissal of plaintiff's request for trial de novo held too severe a penalty for failure to fully participate in judicial arbitration even though plaintiff had elected arbitration). For a decision upholding the imposition of a monetary sanction of $2380 on plaintiffs' *attorney* for failure to participate meaningfully in judicial arbitration, see *Rietveld v. Rosebud Storage Partners*, 121 Cal. App. 4th 250, 16 Cal. Rptr. 3d 791 (2004) (based on their attorney's advice, plaintiffs did not attend the arbitration hearing and their attorney did not present any evidence in support of their claims).

[317] The corollary motion for summary adjudication, which may be made by itself or as an alternative to a motion for summary judgment, is used to test the merits of one or more specific causes of action, one or more affirmative defenses, one or more claims for damages, or one or more issues of duty. Cal. Code Civ. Proc. § 437c(f)(1); *see, e.g., Hood v. Superior Court*, 33 Cal. App. 4th 319, 39 Cal. Rptr. 2d 296 (1995) (holding summary adjudication of declaratory relief claim is improper under § 437(f)(1) because it disposed of only certain contract issues implicated in the asserted cause of action, but not the entirety of any cause of action); *Linden Partners v. Wilshire Linden Assoc.*, 62 Cal. App. 4th 508, 73 Cal. Rptr. 2d 708 (1998) (holding a normal and customary contractual performance obligation involved an "issue of duty" within the meaning of § 437c(f)(1), and therefore qualified for summary adjudication treatment).

California's motion for summary judgment is extensively regulated by statute. The awkwardly numbered section 437c of the Code of Civil Procedure now takes up almost three pages of an unannotated code book, all in fine print. The statute has been regularly, almost annually, amended, but its principal standards have remained constant:

> (a) Any party may move for summary judgment in any action or proceeding if it is contended that the action has no merit or that there is no defense to the action or proceeding . . . .

> (b)(1) The motion shall be supported by affidavits, declarations, admissions, answers to interrogatories, depositions, and matters of which judicial notice shall or may be taken . . . .

> (c) The motion for summary judgment shall be granted if all the papers submitted show that there is no triable issue as to any material fact and that the moving party is entitled to a judgment as a matter of law . . . .

In most respects, California summary judgment practice is similar, if not identical, to summary judgment practice in the federal courts under Rule 56 of the Federal Rules of Civil Procedure.[318] However, in some areas, particularly the initial burden imposed on the moving party, the California approach may be somewhat different. The nature and significance of these differences are explored below.

[2] California's Burden-Shifting Approach

[a] Moving Party's Initial Burden, Generally

Pursuant to a trio of recent California Supreme Court decisions, summary judgment practice in the California courts now conforms, largely if not completely, to its federal court counterpart under federal Rule 56.[319] In *Saelzler v. Advanced Group 400*,[320] the California Supreme Court, with little in the way of explanation, described the burden-shifting approach to summary judgment under Code of Civil Procedure § 437c as follows:

> Under the current version of the summary judgment statute, a moving defendant need not support his motion with affirmative evidence negating an essential element of the responding party's case. Instead, the moving defendant may . . . point to *the absence of evidence to support the plaintiff's case.* When that is done, the burden shifts to the plaintiff to present evidence showing there is a triable issue of material fact. If the

---

[318] Summary judgment practice in the federal courts under federal Rule 56 is discussed in § 11.03, *supra.*

[319] *Saelzler v. Advanced Grp. 400*, 25 Cal. 4th 763, 107 Cal. Rptr. 2d 617, 23 P.3d 1143 (2001); *Aguilar v. Atlantic Richfield Co.*, 25 Cal. 4th 826, 107 Cal. Rptr. 2d 841, 24 P.3d 493 (2001); *Guz v. Bechtel Nat'l, Inc.*, 24 Cal. 4th 317, 100 Cal. Rptr. 2d 352, 8 P.3d 1089 (2000); *see* Glenn S. Koppel, *The California Supreme Court Speaks Out on Summary Judgment in Its Own "Trilogy" of Decisions: Has the Celotex Era Arrived?*, 42 Santa Clara L. Rev. 483 (2002).

[320] 25 Cal. 4th 763, 107 Cal. Rptr. 2d 617, 23 P.3d 1143 (2001).

plaintiff is unable to meet her burden of proof regarding an essential element of her case, all other facts are rendered immaterial.[321]

In interpreting section 437c to authorize two methods — the *disproof-of-an-element* motion and the *no-evidence-to-support-an-element* motion — by which a moving defendant may meet its summary judgment burden, the *Saelzler* Court made no reference to any federal decisions interpreting federal Rule 56. However, as a result of the ruling in *Saelzler*, the burden-shifting approach to summary judgment motions in the California courts is now generally the same as the approach delineated in *Celotex Corporation v. Catrett* for federal courts.[322]

The most difficult burden on summary judgment, like the burden at trial, falls to the party with the burden of production and persuasion on the claims or issues in controversy. Thus the party with the burden of production/persuasion (usually the plaintiff) to prevail on its own summary judgment motion, must show that every critical element of a cause of action is established (that there "is no triable issue of fact") *and* that defendant cannot establish any defense to the cause of action. A party without the burden of production/persuasion (most often a defendant) can prevail on summary judgment by demonstrating that the plaintiff cannot prove an essential element of its cause of action, either by showing an absence of evidence in the record to support the essential element or by disproving the essential element, or by taking the more difficult route of establishing an undisputed affirmative defense (for which the defendant bears the burden of production at trial). Because of this variance in burdens, in practice, most summary judgment motions are filed by defendants.

[b] California and Federal Approaches Compared

In *Aguilar v. Atlantic Richfield*,[323] the California Supreme Court explained, endorsed, and then clarified the burden-shifting approach to summary judgment described in *Saelzler v. Advanced Group 400, supra*. The *Aguilar* Court explained that the summary judgment law in California now conforms "largely but not completely" to its federal counterpart. The Court first observed that, like federal law, section 473c no longer requires a defendant moving for summary judgment to conclusively negate an essential element of the plaintiff's cause of action. All that the defendant need do is to show that one or more elements of the cause of action cannot be established by the plaintiff: "In other words, all that the defendant need do is to show that the plaintiff cannot establish at least one element of the cause of action — for example, that the plaintiff cannot prove element X."[324] But then the *Aguilar* Court added an important qualification: Not only must the defendant show that "the plaintiff *does not possess* needed evidence," but "must also show that the plaintiff *cannot reasonably obtain* needed evidence."

The *Aguilar* Court also emphasized that California's summary judgment law diverges from federal law because section 473c "continues to require a defendant

[321] *Saelzler, supra*, 25 Cal. 4th at 780–81 (italics in original).

[322] 477 U.S. 317 (1986). The *Celotex* decision is discussed in detail in § 11.03[3][b], *supra*.

[323] 25 Cal. 4th 826, 107 Cal. Rptr. 2d 841, 24 P.3d 493 (2001).

[324] *Aguilar, supra*, 25 Cal. 4th at 853–54.

moving for summary judgment to present evidence, and not simply point out that the plaintiff does not possess, and cannot reasonably obtain, needed evidence." The defendant must support the motion with evidence including affidavits, declarations, and discovery responses. "The defendant may, but need not, present evidence that conclusively negates an element of the plaintiff's cause of action. The defendant may also present evidence that the plaintiff does not possess, *and cannot reasonably obtain*, needed evidence — as through admissions by the plaintiff following extensive discovery to the effect that he has discovered nothing." But, the *Aguilar* Court concluded, "the defendant *must* indeed present evidence: Whereas, under federal law, 'pointing out through argument' may be sufficient, under state law, it is not."[325]

It is difficult to assess the significance of the *Aguilar* Court's distinction between requiring a moving defendant to "present evidence" as opposed to "simply pointing out through argument." The "must present evidence" requirement may simply be a rejection of the "naked no-evidence" motion and, if so, the *Aguilar* Court's perception that federal law permits this type of motion is inaccurate (or at least outdated).[326] However, lower court decisions applying *Aguilar* emphasize another aspect of this requirement: The moving defendant must not only present evidence that the plaintiff does not possess the needed evidence but also that the plaintiff "cannot reasonably obtain the needed evidence." This aspect of the "must present evidence" requirement has proven to be significant in determining whether a moving defendant, by relying on the plaintiff's factually devoid discovery responses, has met his or her initial summary judgment burden.[327]

[c]   Burden Shifting and "Factually Devoid" Discovery Responses

The extent to which a moving defendant may rely on "factually devoid" discovery responses to sustain its summary judgment burden was clarified in *Scheiding v. Dinwiddie Construction Co.*,[328] a California Court of Appeal decision subsequently

---

[325] *Aguilar, supra*, 25 Cal. 4th at 855.

[326] Pursuant to a 2010 amendment to federal Rule 56(c)(1)(A), a party asserting that a fact cannot be genuinely disputed must support the assertion by citing to particular parts of materials in the record, including affidavits, depositions, interrogatory answers, and other discovery materials. This requirement is consistent with *Celotex*, where eight Justices agreed that, even if a party does not have the burden of production at trial, its case for summary judgment must consist of more than the naked no-evidence motion. *See* § 11.03[3][b], *supra*.

[327] *E.g.*, *McGonnell v. Kaiser Gypsum Co.*, 98 Cal. App. 4th 1098, 120 Cal. Rptr. 2d 23 (2002) (ruling defendant met its summary judgment burden in wrongful death action for occupational exposure to asbestos based on deposition of plaintiffs' decedent showing plaintiffs could not establish causation); *Rio Linda Unified Sch. Dist. v. Superior Court*, 52 Cal. App. 4th 732, 60 Cal. Rptr. 2d 710 (1997) (holding summary judgment for defendant school district was appropriate in a personal injury action because, disregarding the inadmissible hearsay in a deposition to which the defendant objected, the plaintiff produced no evidence that minor plaintiff had in fact fallen from a slide on school property); *Hunter v. Pac. Mech. Corp.*, 37 Cal. App. 4th 1282, 44 Cal. Rptr. 2d 335 (1995) (holding summary judgment was properly entered for a defendant in a personal injury action for occupational exposure to asbestos, where plaintiff's factually vague discovery responses lacked any significant probative evidence on the critical element of causation).

[328] 69 Cal. App. 4th 64, 81 Cal. Rptr. 2d 360 (1999).

quoted with approval by the California Supreme Court in *Saelzler v. Advanced Group 400, supra.* After extensive analysis section 437c, the *Scheiding* Court concluded that the defendant must "show" from the plaintiff's discovery responses that the only reasonable inference is that there is no further evidence available to oppose the motion. In other words, defendant's initial burden is not met by merely showing, based on the discovery responses currently in the record, that there are no facts to support an essential element of plaintiff's claim. Instead, the defendant must "show" that the discovery questions were directed to an essential element of plaintiff's claim and, based on the plaintiff's discovery answers, the only reasonable inference is that the plaintiff can produce no further evidence to support this essential element.

For example, in *Gaggero v. Yura*,[329] the plaintiff sued defendant for specific performance of a real estate sales contract. An essential element of the plaintiff's cause of action is the requirement that he be "ready, willing, and able" to purchase the property. During his deposition, plaintiff unjustifiably refused to answer any questions about his financial ability to purchase the property. Because the record therefore contained no proffered evidence of plaintiff's financial readiness, the trial court granted summary judgment for defendant. The California Court of Appeal reversed, ruling that the absence of evidence to support plaintiff's cause of action is insufficient to meet the defendant's initial summary judgment burden. The defendant had failed to produce evidence that the plaintiff could not reasonably obtain evidence to support his cause of action. The *Gaggero* court explained: Had the defendant obtained an order compelling plaintiff to respond to questions regarding his financial ability to perform under the purchase agreement and had plaintiff then responded by admitting he had no evidence to support this element of his claim, then defendant would have been able to satisfy her burden of submitting evidence that plaintiff could not establish this element of his claim.

The *Gaggero* court distinguished its prior decision in *Union Bank v. Superior Court*,[330] where the plaintiffs, in response to an interrogatory requesting "all facts" that would support a particular element of a claim, stated that they "believed" that a certain series of events occurred. The court in *Union Bank* held that such a response satisfied the defendant's initial burden of demonstrating that the plaintiffs could not establish an element of their claim. When the plaintiffs in *Union Bank* stated mere *beliefs* in response to a question requesting *all facts* supporting an element of their claims, the logical inference was that after discovery they possessed no facts to support that element.[331] However, the *Gaggero* court reasoned, no such logical inference of an absence of facts can be drawn from an objection on privacy grounds even though it was not a proper objection: "For summary judgment purposes, a deposition objection and instruction not to answer are not the equivalent of a factually devoid response, and therefore cannot be used to shift the burden from the moving defendant to the plaintiff" under section 437c.[332]

[329] 108 Cal. App. 4th 884, 134 Cal. Rptr. 2d 313 (2003).
[330] 31 Cal. App. 4th 573, 37 Cal. Rptr. 2d 653 (1995).
[331] *Union Bank, supra*, 31 Cal. App. 4th at 592–93.
[332] *Gaggero v. Yura, supra*, 108 Cal. App. 4th at 893.

The burden imposed on the moving defendant to show that the plaintiff cannot reasonably obtain needed evidence in such cases as *Scheiding* and *Gaggero* seems to go beyond the corresponding burden imposed on a moving defendant in federal court. *Celotex* did not clearly indicate how much more than a naked no-evidence motion for summary judgment is required of the movant, and the current version of Rule 56 does not require the movant to do anything more than cite to particular parts of the record when asserting that an essential element of the plaintiff's claim lacks evidentiary support. The California rule places a duty on a defendant to utilize discovery effectively by asking specific questions designed to conclusively show that the plaintiff is unable to establish an essential element of his or her case.[333] One advantage of this rule, as opposed to the apparent federal practice, is that it discourages a defendant from filing a summary judgment motion unless or until the record is "complete" in the sense that the only logical inference to be drawn from the absence of evidence is that the plaintiff cannot produce the necessary facts.

[3] California Summary Judgment Procedure

The procedure for supporting and opposing papers is elaborately set out in section 437c(b). There must be a *separate statement* setting forth "plainly and concisely all material facts which the moving party contends are undisputed"; each such fact must be followed by a reference to the supporting evidence. The opposing party must then provide a separate statement that responds to each of the moving party's undisputed facts, agreeing or disagreeing with the characterization, and must set forth any other material facts that the opposing party contends are undisputed, along with references to the evidence. If either party has evidentiary objections to the other's summary judgment evidence, they must be made at the hearing on the summary judgment motion or they are waived.

[a] Trial Court Has No Duty to Inquire Beyond the Separate Statement.

In the separate statement required by section 437c(b), the moving party must also specify (1) the issues tendered by the complaint or answer which are pertinent to the summary judgment motion and (2) each of the grounds of law upon which the moving party is relying in asserting that the action has no merit or there is no defense to the action. As a general rule, a party is not entitled to summary judgment based on an undisputed material fact dispositive of the action if the party has not identified in the moving papers how that fact entitles the party to summary judgment as a matter of law. The trial court has no duty to "detect all the issues presented by the complaint and answer and then to search through the allegations of undisputed material facts and identify the legal significance of each fact just in

---

[333] *See Scheiding v. Dinwiddie Constr. Co., supra,* 69 Cal. App. 4th at 80–84 (concluding factually devoid deposition and interrogatory answers were insufficient to shift summary judgment burden because neither discovery device contained questions specifically aimed at establishing a complete lack of evidence to support an essential element of the plaintiff's claim); Koppel, *The California Supreme Court Speaks Out on Summary Judgment in Its Own "Trilogy" of Decisions, supra,* at 549–54 (explaining that the defendant must affirmatively demonstrate an absence of evidence to support the plaintiff's case).

case that significance has been overlooked by the moving party."[334] A contrary rule would impose an undue burden on the trial court, and may expose the trial court to having its summary judgment order overturned on appeal where the moving party belatedly recognizes the legal significance of an undisputed material fact not considered by the trial court.

Although the trial court has no duty to identify a ground for summary judgment not specified in the separate statement, the court need not close its eyes to an unmeritorious claim simply because the operative ground entitling the moving party to summary judgment was not specifically tendered by that party. The trial court has the inherent power to grant summary judgment on a ground not explicitly tendered by the moving party when the parties' separate statements of material facts and supporting evidence demonstrate the absence of a triable issue of material fact put in issue by the pleadings.[335] However, when the trial court grants a summary judgment motion on a ground of law not explicitly tendered by the moving party, due process requires that the party opposing the motion be provided an opportunity to respond to the ground of law identified by the court and be given a chance to show there is a triable issue of fact material to that ground.

[b] Failure to comply with the Statutory Requirements for a Separate Statement

What is the consequence of an opposing plaintiff's failure to comply with the statutory requirement of a separate statement? Some courts hold that the proper response in most instances, if the trial court is not prepared to address the merits of a motion in light of the deficient separate statement, is to give the opposing party an opportunity to file a proper separate statement rather than entering judgment against that party based on its procedural error.[336] Other courts conclude that failure to comply with the separate statement requirement is sufficient grounds to grant a summary judgment motion.[337] Either approach is consistent with section 437c(b)(3), which provides that failure to comply "may constitute a sufficient ground, in the court's discretion, for granting the motion." Of course, the moving party must establish a *prima facie* case of entitlement to summary judgment in order to shift the burden to the nonmoving party to file an opposing separate statement.

---

[334] *Juge v. County of Sacramento*, 12 Cal. App. 4th 59, 67–68, 15 Cal. Rptr. 2d 598 (1993).

[335] *Juge, supra,* 12 Cal. App. 4th at 70.

[336] *See, e.g., Parkview Villas Ass'n, Inc. v. State Farm Fire & Cas. Co.*, 133 Cal. App. 4th 1197, 1211–16, 35 Cal. Rptr. 3d 411 (2005) (holding trial court abused its discretion by granting summary judgment without first giving the plaintiff a chance to cure the deficiencies in its separate statement); *Collins v. Hertz Corp.*, 144 Cal. App. 4th 64, 50 Cal. Rptr. 3d 149 (2006) (affirming summary judgment for defendant where trial court struck portions of plaintiffs' new separate statement, effectively leaving defendant's facts undisputed, after the trial court afforded plaintiffs an opportunity to cure defects in their first separate statement but filed another defective separate statement).

[337] *See, e.g., Whitehead v. Habig*, 163 Cal. App. 4th 896, 77 Cal. Rptr. 3d 679 (2008); *Kulesa v. Castleberry*, 47 Cal. App. 4th 103, 54 Cal. Rptr. 2d 669 (1996); *United Cmty. Church v. Garcin*, 231 Cal. App. 3d 327, 282 Cal. Rptr. 368 (1991).

[c] Summary Judgment Evidence

The evidence that will be used to show there are no triable issues may come from formal and informal discovery, from matters of judicial notice, and on occasion from the opponent's admissions in pleadings. A motion for summary judgment or summary adjudication may be supported by affidavits, declarations, admissions, answers to interrogatories, depositions, and matters of judicial notice. According to section 437c(d), affidavits and declarations must be made "on personal knowledge, shall set forth admissible evidence, and shall show affirmatively that the affiant is competent to testify to the matters stated in the affidavits or declarations."[338] Parties sometimes rely on expert witness testimony to support or oppose a summary judgment motion. An expert witness' declaration may provide the evidentiary basis for or against summary judgment but, pursuant to section 437c(d), only where it satisfies the foundational requirements for admissible expert opinion testimony.[339]

Section 437c does not expressly extend this "admissible evidence" requirement to other sources of summary judgment evidence such as, most notably, discovery responses. However, California case law indicates that, upon timely objection, inadmissible evidence in discovery responses, such as hearsay statements or speculative conclusions in a deposition, will be disregarded in determining whether a party has demonstrated a triable issue of fact.[340]

[d] Continuance to Complete Discovery

Like federal Rule 56(d), Code of Civil Procedure § 473c(h) provides that a motion for summary judgment shall be denied, or a continuance shall be granted, if the nonmoving party has not had an opportunity to complete discovery necessary to oppose the motion. Such a continuance is virtually mandated upon a good faith showing by affidavit that a continuance is needed to obtain facts essential to justify opposition to the summary judgment motion.[341] However, the request for a

---

[338] CAL. CODE CIV. PROC. § 437c(d).

[339] *See, e.g., Kelley v. Trunk*, 66 Cal. App. 4th 519, 78 Cal. Rptr. 2d 122 (1998) (holding summary judgment improper where it was based on an expert witness' declaration that did not disclose the matter relied upon by the expert in forming the opinion expressed; an opinion unsupported by reasons or explanation did not establish the absence of a material fact issue for trial); *Hanson v. Grode*, 76 Cal. App. 4th 601, 90 Cal. Rptr. 2d 396 (1999) (declining to utilize the *Kelley* court's suggestion that even on summary judgment, an expert's declaration must set forth in excruciating detail the factual basis for the opinions stated therein); *St. Mary Med. Ctr. v. Superior Court*, 50 Cal. App. 4th 1531, 58 Cal. Rptr. 2d 182 (1996) (explaining that under proper circumstances, the parties in a summary judgment proceeding should be allowed to depose an expert who supplies an affidavit in support of or in opposition to summary judgment when there is a legitimate question regarding the foundation of the opinion of the expert).

[340] *See, e.g., Rio Linda Unified Sch. Dist. v. Superior Court*, 52 Cal. App. 4th 732, 60 Cal. Rptr. 2d 710 (1997) (holding summary judgment for defendant school district was appropriate in a personal injury action because, disregarding the inadmissible hearsay in a deposition to which the defendant objected, the plaintiff produced no evidence that minor plaintiff had in fact fallen from a slide on school property); *Hunter v. Pac. Mech. Corp.*, 37 Cal. App. 4th 1282, 44 Cal. Rptr. 2d 335 (1995) (holding summary judgment properly entered for a defendant in a personal injury action for occupational exposure to asbestos, where the plaintiff relied on a factually vague deposition that contained only speculation and conjecture and therefore lacked any probative evidence on the critical element of causation).

[341] *See, e.g., Bahl v. Bank of Am.*, 89 Cal. App. 4th 389, 107 Cal. Rptr. 2d 270 (2001) (ruling affiant not

continuance may be denied where the requesting party fails to make a good faith showing as to what facts essential to oppose summary judgment may exist and why such facts could not have been discovered sooner.[342]

---

required to show that essential evidence does exist, but only that it may exist); *Frazee v. Seely*, 95 Cal. App. 4th 627, 115 Cal. Rptr. 2d 780 (2002) (finding an abuse of discretion for trial court to deny a continuance where plaintiff was reasonably diligent but had not been able to complete discovery; "the interests at stake are too high to sanction the denial of a continuance without good reason").

[342] *E.g., Kojababian v. Genuine Home Loans, Inc.*, 174 Cal. App. 4th 408, 418–20, 94 Cal. Rptr. 3d 288 (2009) (finding no abuse of discretion in denying continuance where plaintiff failed to specify information he expected to discover if continuance granted); *Cooksey v. Alexakis*, 123 Cal. App. 4th 246, 19 Cal. Rptr. 3d 810 (2004) (explaining that in determining whether to grant a party responding to a summary judgment motion a continuance for discovery under § 437c(h), the trial court may consider whether that party has been diligent in completing discovery); *Desaigoudar v. Meyercord*, 108 Cal. App. 4th 173, 133 Cal. Rptr. 2d 408 (2003) (affirming denial of continuance where plaintiffs did not provide an affidavit relating to the possibility that essential facts exist or explaining their reasons for not having the evidence).

Chapter 12

TRIAL AND POST-TRIAL MOTIONS

§ 12.01 OVERVIEW: THE TRIAL PROCESS

The incidents of civil trial are similar in most jurisdictions,[1] reflecting the common historical origins of the trial process and the influence of unwritten custom. While federal and most state courts follow rules of evidence regulating proof of facts at trial,[2] rules of civil procedure usually give little attention to the trial process. The Federal Rules of Civil Procedure are typical in their preoccupation with matters before and (to a lesser extent) after trial.

To set the stage for our exploration of procedural issues relating to the trial process, we first briefly summarize that process chronologically. But as we saw in Chapter 1, fewer than 2% of cases in state and federal court are terminated by trial,[3] down from 12% in the 1960s and 20% in 1938.[4] Trial is truly a "vanishing breed" of dispute resolution. Before turning to particular phases of the trial process in greater detail, therefore, we will briefly consider why the jury trial is vanishing and whether this development is good or bad for justice in civil litigation.

[1] Setting the Case For Trial

This initial step in the trial process should in theory await completion of the pretrial process, particularly discovery. However, like Samuel Johnson once said of the prospect of hanging, an early trial date "wonderfully concentrates the mind." Even though only a tiny fraction of federal civil actions now culminate in trial, the role that the *prospect* of an impending trial plays in shaping the pretrial process and settlement negotiations should not be underestimated.[5] Lawyers still need to plan for the possibility of trial. It is also increasingly common for courts to set the trial date early as a reckoning point for setting deadlines, such as the cut-off of discovery and the completion of pretrial motion practice: basically, to force the pace of the litigation.[6] Some jurisdictions set the trial date as soon as issues in the case

---

[1] *See generally* J. Alexander Tanford, *An Introduction to Trial Law*, 51 Mo. L. Rev. 623 (1986).

[2] *See* § 12.08[2], *infra*.

[3] *See* § 1.01[4] text at nn.23–26.

[4] Julianne Davis, *The Vanishing Trial, Revisited*, 31 Litig. J. 1, 2 (2012).

[5] Marc Galanter & Angela Frozena, Pound Civil Justice Institute: 2011 Forum for State Appellate Court Judges, The Continuing Decline of Civil Trials in American Courts, *available at* http://roscoepound.org/docs/2011%20judges%20forum/2011%20Forum%20Galanter-Frozena%20Paper.pdf.

[6] Rule 16(b)(3)(B)(v) permits but does not require the inclusion of the trial date in the initial pretrial scheduling order.

are joined by completion of the pleadings. Commonly the parties advise the court by memorandum that the case is at issue, after which the court places the case on its trial calendar.

[2] Final Pretrial Conference and Order[7]

The use of final pretrial conferences has increased for complex litigation in federal and many state courts. Rule 16 establishes procedure for the former. Parties often exchange briefs (memoranda) at the final pretrial conference, identifying their witnesses and other evidence and delineating their factual and legal contentions. These briefs help the court gauge the time required for trial, streamline the trial itself by flushing out potential evidentiary problems for resolution *in limine* (at the threshold of trial), and may facilitate settlement by previewing the real strength of the parties' trial positions. They may also present an occasion for summary judgment on some or all of the claims.[8]

Information presented in the parties' briefs and further agreements reached during the final pretrial conference provide material for the court's order. The order functions as a kind of program for trial, superseding the pleadings. Often it shrinks the bounds of relevancy set by the pleadings alone.[9] It may also restrict the availability of even relevant evidence at trial by limiting sources of proof to those identified in the order.[10] Parties thereafter seeking enlargement of the final pretrial order bear a considerable burden of justification. Rule 16(e) permits modification of the order "only to prevent manifest injustice."

[3] Jury Selection[11]

The jury is selected on the first day of trial after motions *in limine* and other housekeeping matters have been resolved. Jury selection is a two-step process. The first — assembling the *venire* from which the jury panel of twelve or fewer (plus alternates) is selected — is performed by the clerk's office according to statutory criteria and procedures.[12] The second — questioning (*voir dire*) of the potential jurors (*veniremen*) to select the panel — is performed by counsel, or by the judge with the aid of *voir dire* questions suggested by counsel.

---

[7] *See generally* § 12.03 (pretrial conference), *infra*.

[8] This may happen when the parties have narrowed the issues by requests for admissions (discussed in § 12.02, *infra*) or the court orders them to admit or deny factual assertions in each other's pretrial briefs at the pretrial conference. *See* § 12.03[3], *infra*.

[9] *See* § 12.03[3] (pretrial order and its effect), *infra*; WRIGHT & MILLER § 1527 (noting that the court "might preclude a party from introducing evidence on a claim or defense that is not revealed" at the final pretrial conference).

[10] *See* WRIGHT & MILLER § 1527 (noting that "the court may refuse to allow witnesses not named at the pretrial conference to testify at the trial.").

[11] *See generally* AMER. BAR ASS'N, PRINCIPLES FOR JURIES AND JURY TRIALS (2005), *available at* http://www.americanbar.org/content/dam/aba/migrated/juryprojectstandards/principles.authcheck dam.pdf. On jury trials, *see* §§ 12.06 (the tactical decision whether to claim a jury), 12.07 (obtaining jury trial), 12.08 (judge-jury interaction), & 12.09 (taking the case from the jury), *infra*.

[12] *See, e.g.*, 28 U.S.C. §§ 1861–1869.

The *voir dire* is intended to expose biases or interests of veniremen that would disqualify them for cause. Usually parties are given unlimited *challenges for cause* and a limited number of *peremptory* challenges. The latter permit counsel to keep persons off the jury without offering a reason, although the Supreme Court has ruled that civil litigants may not use their peremptory challenges to exclude jurors on account of their race or gender.[13]

While twelve jurors is the traditional number, use of juries of six has grown among federal and many state courts for civil jury trials.

[4]　Opening Statements

Once the jury has been empaneled, the plaintiff usually gives the first opening statement. Defendant may go first in rare cases where he concedes plaintiff's case-in-chief and has the burden of producing evidence concerning an affirmative defense. In non-jury cases, the judge often dispenses with the formality of opening statements because he or she has already become familiar with the case from presiding over pretrial hearings or from perusing the pleadings.

A well-organized and persuasive opening can go far to influence a fresh and attentive jury.[14] The function of an opening statement is not merely to preview the evidence but to tell the jury the story of a party's case. This is necessary because the presentation of testimony and tangible evidence during the trial is often piecemeal and anachronistic (e.g., out of chronological order). Plaintiff's opening statement thus gives the jury a road map to follow through trial.

For these same reasons, the defendant usually gives her opening statement after the plaintiff. In many jurisdictions, however, the defendant has the option to wait until plaintiff has presented his evidence. A defendant who has waited until then to open can take plaintiff's evidence into account.[15]

---

[13] *See Edmonson v. Leesville Concrete Co.*, 500 U.S. 614 (1991) (race); *J.E.B. v. Alabama*, 511 U.S. 127 (1994) (gender). Three peremptory challenges are permitted in federal courts. 28 U.S.C. § 1870.

[14] One commentator asserts that opening statements determine the outcome in 50–85% of the cases. Weyman I. Lundquist, *Advocacy in Opening Statements*, 8 Litig. 23 (1982). *See also* Neal R. Feigenson, *The Rhetoric of Torts: How Advocates Help Jurors Think About Causation, Reasonableness, and Responsibility*, 47 Hastings L.J. 61, 165 (1995) (noting that "first impressions" in the courtroom "often have a lasting effect"); Thomas A. Pyszczynski & Lawrence S. Wrightsman, *The Effects of Opening Statements on Mock Jurors' Verdicts in a Simulated Criminal Trial*, 11 J. Applied Soc. Psychol. 301 (1981) (finding that mock jurors are heavily influenced by first strong persuasive statement: a lengthy prosecution opening coupled with a brief defense opening tended to yield guilty verdict, while brief prosecution opening coupled with lengthy defense opening tended to yield not-guilty verdict); H.P. Weld & E.R. Danzig, *A Study of the Way in Which a Verdict is Reached by a Jury*, 53 Am. J. Psychol. 518 (1940) (finding that approximately one-quarter of jurors in mock trial reached definite decision early in the trial; for most jurors, degree of certainty oscillated throughout trial according to testimony and lawyers' opening and closing statements).

[15] *See* Salvatore F. Stramondo & Andrew R. Goodspeed, Note, *Defendant's Presentation*, 57 Mass. L.Q. 179 (1972).

[5] Presentation of Plaintiff's Case-in-Chief

After opening statements, the parties proceed with their proof. Testimonial evidence enters by direct examination of a witness by the plaintiff's counsel, followed by cross-examination by the defendant's counsel, and then re-direct and re-cross as necessary. Documents and other tangible exhibits are first marked for identification. Once counsel establishes ("lays") a foundation for such an exhibit with prior evidence or the foundation was conceded by pretrial admission, the exhibit may be offered for admission.

[6] Mid-Trial Motion for Directed Verdict, Involuntary Dismissal or Judgment as a Matter of Law

Whenever a plaintiff has been fully heard on an issue during a jury trial in federal court, the opposing party may move for judgment as a matter of law on the theory that the plaintiff did not proffer sufficient evidence for a reasonable jury to find for him on the issue.[16] This is most often after the plaintiff completes the presentation of his case-in-chief. In many state courts, the motion is called a motion for a directed verdict.[17] When plaintiff's failure to satisfy this burden is sufficiently clear, there is no point in submitting the case to the jury because the judge would have to set aside a verdict for plaintiff on a proper motion for judgment notwithstanding the verdict or, in federal court, for judgment as a matter of law. But if plaintiff has met his burden or if the question is a close one, defendant's motion should be denied[18] without prejudice to defendant's case.

In a non-jury trial, the defendant tests plaintiff's case by a motion for involuntary dismissal or, in federal court, for judgment as a matter of law.[19] Because the trial judge sits as the trier of facts in a non-jury case, this motion — unlike the motion in a jury case — tests the sufficiency *and* weight of the evidence. The judge thus may determine the facts and enter judgment against the plaintiff. On the other hand, because defendant has not yet had the opportunity to put on her evidence, the judge who denies defendant's mid-trial motion in a non-jury case will not ordinarily enter judgment against her at this stage.

[7] Presentation of Additional Evidence

If defendant's mid-trial motion is denied, she puts on her evidence on the issues assigned her. Following her evidence, plaintiff may present rebuttal evidence. Defendant, in turn, may present its rebuttal evidence.

---

[16] Rule 50(a)(1). *See* §§ 12.09[1] and 12.04[2], *infra.*

[17] *See* § 12.09[1], *infra.*

[18] *See* § 12.09[3][b] (discussing the importance of reserving close questions for treatment by judgment n.o.v.), *infra*

[19] *See* §§ 11.04[2], *supra,* & 12.10, *infra.*

[8]   Motions at the Close of All the Evidence

At the close of all the evidence in a jury trial, either party may make a motion for a directed verdict or, in federal court, for judgment as a matter of law. This motion again tests the sufficiency of the opponent's evidence to support a jury verdict.

[9]   Closing Argument

Most jurisdictions permit closing arguments in three parts, with the plaintiff going first and last. Closing argument affords each party an opportunity to put evidence admitted in the case in the best possible light. Counsel may offer the jury conflicting interpretations of the evidence in their closing arguments, but they may not offer conflicting interpretations of law or supplement the record by alluding to facts outside it. The court is the only source of guidance on legal standards by which the jury is to weigh the evidence. Therefore, counsels' closing arguments must be entirely consistent with the court's jury instructions,[20] which usually come later. When they do, the best and most widespread practice is for the court to indicate to counsel prior to closing arguments how it will be instructing the jury.[21]

Unfortunately, some attorneys see in closing argument an opportunity to grandstand, emote, go beyond the evidence, or prey on perceived prejudices of the jury.[22] This behavior can backfire, seeding the trial record with reversible error.

In non-jury cases, post-trial briefs often take the place of closing arguments.

[10]   Instructions to the Jury

In most jurisdictions, the judge instructs the jury after closing arguments, although federal judges have the option to instruct "the jury at any time before the jury is discharged."[23] Usually counsel submit proposed jury instructions, sometimes as early as the final pretrial conference, and the judge advises them of which instructions she will give. Almost all jurisdictions require counsel to object to errors in the instructions before the jury retires. This prevents sandbagging and permits cure of flawed instructions before the jury begins deliberations.

[11]   Jury Deliberation and Verdict

After the jury is instructed, it is placed in the custody of a bailiff. It then deliberates privately and, infrequently, may be *sequestered* (isolated) until it reaches a verdict. At the jury's request and upon notice to the parties, the judge may reread some or all of the instructions or permit the jury to re-examine record evidence or rehear testimony. Jurisdictions and individual judges differ in their

---

[20] *Cf.* Tanford, note 1, *supra*, at 692 (noting that it is improper in closing argument for counsel "to discuss law that is not part of the instructions").

[21] Thus Rule 51(b)(1) states that "must inform the parties of its proposed instructions and proposed action on the requests before instructing the jury and before final jury arguments."

[22] Tanford, note 1, *supra*, at 685–93.

[23] Rule 51(b)(3). *See generally* § 12.08[3] (instructing the jury), *infra*.

tolerance for jury possession of written instructions or trial transcripts in the jury room.

At common law, a twelve-person jury had to reach a unanimous verdict. While unanimity is still required of federal juries, the Supreme Court has approved the use of fewer than twelve jurors. States differ widely in both the number of jurors and the degree of required agreement. However, all are subject to the requirements of due process under the Fourteenth Amendment. The Supreme Court has invoked the Due Process Clause to prohibit six-person, non-unanimous juries in criminal cases.[24] It has yet to define the outer limits of due process in civil state jury cases.

The jury's verdict may take several forms, depending upon the judge's instructions and the jurisdiction. In federal courts, the jury may deliver a traditional *general verdict* finding for or against each party, a *special verdict* answering factual interrogatories framed by the judge, or a combination of these verdicts.[25]

[12]   Challenges to Verdict and the Entry of Judgment

After the jury delivers its verdict, the judge may direct entry of judgment upon it. Most jurisdictions, however, authorize motions for judgment notwithstanding the verdict (judgment n.o.v., called *renewed motion for judgment as a matter of law* in federal court).[26] A party in federal court has until twenty-eight days after the court's entry of judgment on a verdict to renew its motion for judgment as a matter of law, or, alternatively, move for new trial.

In non-jury trials, the court finds the facts and enters judgment accordingly. There is no analogue to a motion for judgment n.o.v., although the parties usually can move for reconsideration or amendment of the judgment[27] within a fixed period of time.

[13]   Other Post-Trial Motions

In addition to the post-verdict and post-judgment motions noted above, courts permit motions for new trial.[28] Historically, new trials have been granted because of prejudicial conduct by jurors or attorneys, judicial errors, or because the verdict was against the weight of the evidence. New trial orders wipe out the jury verdict, but they do not give movant victory on the merits. The trial judge therefore is given

---

[24] *Burch v. Louisiana*, 441 U.S. 130 (1979); *Ballew v. Georgia*, 435 U.S. 223 (1978).

[25] Jury verdicts are discussed in greater detail in § 12.08[4], *infra*.

[26] "N.o.v." is an abbreviation of the Latin phrase *non obstante veredicto*, which means notwithstanding the verdict. See generally § 12.09, *infra*, for extensive discussion of motions for j.n.o.v. and their relation to motions for directed verdicts made earlier in the case (now all called *motions for judgment as a matter of law* in federal court) and to motions for new trial.

[27] *See* § 12.11[2][c], *infra*.

[28] *See* § 12.09[2] (new trials), *infra*.

greater power to grant new trials than to grant judgments n.o.v.[29]

After time for moving for judgment n.o.v., judgment as a matter of law, new trial, reconsideration, or amendment has passed, trial-level attack on the judgment becomes difficult. What remains for the party aggrieved by the judgment is the limited prospect of extraordinary relief. Most jurisdictions permit post-trial motions to set aside judgments. Federal procedure is typical in providing relief because of clerical error[30] or because circumstances suggest that it would be unfair to enforce the judgment.[31] Extraordinary relief provides a fairly reliable means for correcting clerical errors. To a lesser extent, it functions to vacate default judgments. Beyond that, extraordinary relief is usually unavailable — confined, as the term suggests, to *extraordinary* cases. This is consistent with society's interest in the finality of judgments.[32]

[14] Vanishing Civil Trials?

Although the foregoing overview of the trial process often quickens the pulses of eager first-year law students (thinking that now, finally, we'll get to the centerpiece of civil litigation), it is increasingly more the stuff of history than current events. The civil trial is disappearing, if it has not already disappeared as a practical matter.

> In federal courts, the decline in trials has been steep and dramatic. In 1962, there were 5,802 civil trials in the federal courts and 5,097 criminal trials, for a total of 10,899. In 1985, total federal trials had risen to 12,529. By 2002, however, trials had dropped to 4,569 civil trials and 3,574 criminal trials. Thus, our federal courts actually tried fewer cases in 2002 than they did in 1962, despite a fivefold increase in the number of civil filings and more than a doubling of the criminal filings over the same time frame. In 1962, 11.5 percent of federal civil cases were disposed of by trial. By 2002, that figure had plummeted to 1.8 percent.[33]

The trend holds; in 2011, only *1.1 percent* of federal civil cases went to trial.[34] The trend is the same, if not more pronounced, in state courts: from 1976 to 2002, civil jury trials were down by 28 percent (in the 22 states for which data were available) and, in 2002, represented 0.6 percent of the total civil dispositions.

The disappearance of civil trials poses two questions: why are they disappearing, and what are the consequences for civil dispute resolution?

---

[29] On the relationship between judgments n.o.v. (and judgments as a matter of law) and orders for new trial, see §§ 12.09[2][b] & 12.09[3][d], *infra.*

[30] Rule 60(a).

[31] Rule 60(b).

[32] For more extended discussion of Rule 60 and extraordinary relief from judgments, see § 12.11[2][b], *infra.*

[33] Patricia Lee Refo, *The Vanishing Trial*, 30 LITIGATION 1, 1 (2004). *See generally The "Vanishing Trial:" the College, the Profession, the Civil Justice System*, 226 F.R.D. 414 (2005); Marc Galanter, *The Vanishing Trial: An Examination of Trials and Related Matters in Federal and State Courts*, 1 J. EMPIRICAL LEGAL STUD. 459 (2004).

[34] ADMIN. OFFICE OF THE U.S. COURTS, JUDICIAL BUS. OF THE U.S. COURTS, Table C-4, at 149 (2011).

There is wide agreement that there is no single cause. But observers are generally agreed on contributing factors. They include:

- Trial court judges having come to view — indeed, having sometimes been trained to view — their proper office as that of case manager rather than presider over trials.

- Increased use of summary judgment and other dispositive pretrial motions.[35]

- Stricter expert evidence requirements.

- The escalating cost of litigation.

- The rising stakes of civil litigation, coupled with the uncertainty of outcome.

- Increased use of alternative dispute resolution ("ADR"), including arbitration and mediation, voluntary or court-ordered.

- Lack of trial skills and experience among younger lawyers.

- Lack of, or constraints on, judicial resources.

- Pressure from regulators or the financial markets to: (i) resolve promptly loss contingencies; and (ii) eliminate avoidable costs that reduce earnings.

- Compensation incentives to corporate managers to avoid earnings-depressing costs, such as legal fees.

- Tort reform, including caps on compensatory and punitive damages.

- The impact of the Vanishing Trial phenomenon itself on trial judges, who may assume the bench with less trial experience and acquire less courtroom experience in their early years on the bench as they preside over fewer trials.[36]

In particular, the costs and delays of litigation have pressured courts and litigants alike to seek dispositions short of trial to save time and money. Costs of discovery, the "preview" that discovery and pretrial conferences now often provide of the evidence at trial,[37] and the availability of summary judgment,[38] alternative dispute resolution, and settlement negotiation ally to encourage pretrial disposition.

Whether this is an *unholy* alliance, however, is disputed. The purpose of civil litigation, after all, is not trial; it is dispute resolution. Moreover, to the extent that the disappearance of trial is the result of negotiated settlements, it can be viewed as a choice of the parties, often a choice that more flexibly accommodates their diverse interests than could an all-or-nothing final judgment after an expensive trial. On the other hand, this comparison assumes that pretrial dispositional devices

---

[35] As we noted in Chapter 11, there is still dispute about the true extent of any increase in summary judgment. *See supra* § 11.03[3][d].

[36] Ad Hoc Comm. on the Future of Civil Trial, *The "Vanishing Trial:" the College, the Profession, the Civil Justice System*, 226 F.R.D. 414, 414–415 (2005).

[37] *See* Bert. I. Huang, *Trial By Preview*, 113 COLUM. L. REV. ___ (forthcoming 2013).

[38] *See, e.g.*, Stephen B. Burbank, *Vanishing Trials and Summary Judgment in Federal Civil Cases: Drifting Toward Bethlehem or Gomorrah?*, 1 J. EMPIRICAL LEGAL STUD. 591 (2004).

present as level a playing field as trial would. Moreover, "an unfettered commitment to 'efficiency' in the pretrial disposition context — whatever its motivation or however articulated — will erode other systemic values."[39] These systemic values include transparency — the public quality and visibility of trial — partly or wholly lost in "privatized" dispute resolution.[40] Another value is communal resolution of factual disputes by a jury charged with making "commonsense determinations about human behavior, reasonableness, and state of mind based on objective standards, the paradigm being the reasonable person standard,"[41] instead of a judge or an arbitrator. The disappearance of trial may mean a loss of legitimacy, not to mention the loss of an opportunity for citizens to learn from participating in the civil dispute resolution system.

Of course, "trials have never been our principal method of dispute resolution."[42] Yet it does not have to be the *principal* method to exert a healthy influence on our system of civil dispute resolution. It only has to remain one reasonably available and reasonably possible method.

> The importance of the institution is not measured by the number of civil jury trials, which is not great. It is, however, the right to jury trial that makes the rest of the constitutional scheme acceptable. And other institutional arrangements were structured around the concept of a democratic courthouse. . . .

> In its role in civil proceedings, the jury . . . render[s] the legislators who make the controlling law doubly accountable to the people, who first elect their lawmakers and are then called to administer the laws those representatives make. Law departing too far from the common understanding, from common sense, or from commonly shared moral values tends to be modified in its enforcement by civil juries to fit common habits of mind. . . .

> [T]he presence of the jury shapes the function of the American judge. . . .

> It allows the judge to stand, as the independent organ of the law, not only above the parties, hostilely arranged against each other, but also above the whole practical case before the court.

> * * *

> Citizen participation in the disposition of civil cases has been an important, indeed central, and perhaps critical, element in the development of the

---

[39] Arthur R. Miller, *The Pretrial Rush to Judgment: Are the "Litigation Explosion," "Liability Crisis," and Efficiency Clichés Eroding Our Day in Court and Jury Trial Commitments?*, 78 N.Y.U.L. Rev. 982, 1133 (2003).

[40] Refo, note 33, *supra*, at 5 ("The privatization of dispute resolution has a host of consequences. The pleadings, testimony, documents — and the result — are shielded from public view. Indeed, that is one of the reasons litigants turn to private dispute resolution in the first place. Neither the public nor the press has a seat in the private arbitration courtroom. Arbitration decisions contribute nothing to the development of the common law.").

[41] Miller, note 39, *supra*, at 1134.

[42] Refo, note 33, *supra*, at 5.

American legal system. . . . The system has served many purposes, but its enduring purpose has been to secure a greater measure of trust in judicial institutions.[43]

On balance, we think that the robust possibility of trial is still the driver of a just civil dispute resolution system, and that the prospect of vanishing trial is therefore troubling.

PART A.
Narrowing Issues and Allocating Burdens

§ 12.02 REQUESTS FOR ADMISSIONS[44]

[1] Procedure for Requesting Admissions

Many jurisdictions provide a procedure like Federal Rule 36 by which a party may request his adversary to admit the truth of any matters within the scope of discovery. Unless amended or withdrawn by leave of court, admissions are binding at trial[45] and thus relieve their proponent of the time and expense of proving the admitted matter. Although the request for admissions is usually classified as a discovery procedure,[46] it presupposes that the requesting party already has sufficient information about the case to formulate the requested admissions, and it is usually filed at the close of discovery. It is therefore more accurately regarded as a pretrial, issue-narrowing procedure and is so treated here.[47]

The requested admissions must take a declaratory form that is susceptible to the bare response "admit" or "deny." Federal Form 25 offers the following examples: "That each of the following documents, exhibited with this request, is genuine," and "That each of the following statements is true." Under the federal rules, admissions are subject only to the generic limitations of Rule 26(b).[48] They may embrace disputed issues, ultimate issues (negligence, breach, etc.) as well as evidentiary facts, and the application of law to fact, but not pure legal conclusions.[49]

---

[43] *The "Vanishing Trial:" The College, The Profession, The Civil Justice System*, 226 F.R.D. 414, 416 (2005) (quoting Paul D. Carrington, *The Civil Jury and American Democracy*, 13 Duke J. Comp. & Int'l L. 79, 79, 87–88, 93 (2003)) (citations and quotations omitted).

[44] *See generally* Jeffrey S. Kinsler, *Requests for Admission in Wisconsin Procedures: Civil Litigation's Double-Edged Sword*, 78 Marq. L. Rev. 625 (1995); Ted Finman, *The Request for Admissions in Federal Civil Procedure*, 71 Yale L.J. 371 (1962).

[45] *See, e.g.*, Rule 36(b).

[46] Rule 36, for example, appears at Part V of the federal rules, entitled "Depositions and Discovery."

[47] *See* James, Hazard & Leubsdorf § 5.7 ("[i]n some ways, . . . a pleading device that narrows the issues to be tried rather than a discovery device to obtain evidence"); Wright § 89 (not, strictly speaking, a discovery device at all); Roger S. Haydock & David F. Herr, Discovery: Theory, Practice, and Problems § 5.2 (1983) ("more of a trial practice rule").

[48] *See* § 10.03 (scope of federal discovery), *supra*.

[49] Wright § 89. *See, e.g.*, *Williams v. Krieger*, 61 F.R.D. 142 (S.D.N.Y. 1973) (request for admission of pure legal conclusion is improper). *See also* Russell G. Donaldson, Annotation, *Permissible Scope*,

A few courts still disapprove of requests concerning ultimate issues in the case. They do so either on the ground that ultimate issues involve legal conclusions or on the ground that probable denial, followed by a request for expenses under Rule 37(c) should the denying party lose at trial, would circumvent the American rule against awarding attorney's fees to the prevailing party.[50] This reasoning is largely specious, since Rule 37(c) itself exempts a denying party from sanctions for failing to admit when he had "reasonable ground to believe that he might prevail on the matter." There is usually such reasonable ground on the ultimate issues of liability in the ordinary lawsuit.[51]

To ignore requests for admission is unwise, since Rule 36(a) deems failure to reply an admission. If in reasonable doubt of the truth of a requested admission, a party may simply deny. Alternatively, he may object on the ground that the request exceeds the permissible scope of discovery, seek a protective order for any of the reasons listed in Rule 26(c),[52] admit part and deny the balance, qualify his admissions and denials as necessary, or state that after reasonable inquiry the information available to him is insufficient to enable him to admit or deny.[53] To be entitled to the last response, a party may not rely just on his immediate personal knowledge. He must make reasonable inquiry.[54]

Prior to the 1970 amendment to Rule 36, it was unclear whether a defective response to a request for admission relieved the requesting party of the burden of proving the matter at trial.[55] The amended rule permits that party to move before trial to test the sufficiency of answers or objections to requests in order to remove this uncertainty.

An admission obtained under Rule 36, like one appearing in a pleading or by stipulation, takes the admitted matter from the fact-finder and "conclusively establishe[s]" it for purposes of the pending action.[56] No evidence need be proffered to establish the matter admitted, and none will be admitted to refute it, although it is still subject to objections to admissibility.[57] In this respect, admissions are different from the product of the discovery procedures such as

---

Respecting Nature of Inquiry, of Demand for Admissions Under Modern State Civil Rules of Procedure, 42 A.L.R.4TH 489; § 10.03[3][c] (discoverability of contentions), *supra*; § 10.09[1] (contention interrogatories), *supra*.

[50] *See, e.g., Naxon Telesign Corp. v. GTE Info. Sys., Inc.*, 89 F.R.D. 333 (N.D. Ill. 1980). On the American rule generally, see § 14.01[2], *infra*.

[51] *See generally* David L. Shapiro, *Some Problems of Discovery in an Adversary System*, 63 MINN. L. REV. 1055, 1078–92 (1979) (arguing that a party may deny if he reasonably doubts, on the basis of all the admissible evidence known to him, that the requester could prevail at trial).

[52] *See* § 10.13[3] (protective orders against specific hardships), *supra*.

[53] *Compare* Rule 36(a) with Rule 8(b). *Cf.* § 8.08[1] (specific denials), *supra*.

[54] *See, e.g., Al-Jundi v. Rockefeller*, 91 F.R.D. 590, 593–94 (W.D.N.Y. 1981) (blanket assertion that the necessary information is in the knowledge of third persons is insufficient without reasonable inquiry of them). The duty of inquiry is underscored by the certification requirement of Rule 26(g). *See* § 10.13[1] (discovery certification requirement), *supra*.

[55] Rule 36 advisory committee's notes (1970).

[56] Rule 36(b). It supersedes the pleadings *pro tanto*. FRIEDENTHAL KANE & MILLER § 7.10.

[57] *See* WRIGHT & MILLER § 2264.

answers to interrogatories, which are only evidentiary and can therefore be rebutted or even disavowed by the answering party at trial.

Nevertheless, admissions may be withdrawn or amended with leave of court pursuant to Rule 36(b), if it will promote the presentation of the merits and if the party who requested the admission is unable to show prejudice from the amendment.[58] "Although an admission should ordinarily be binding on the party who made it," observes one authority, "there must be room in rare cases for a different result, as when an admission no longer is true because of changed circumstances or through honest error a party has made an improvident admission."[59] Prejudice in this context means more than that the party obtaining the request will now have to convince the fact-finder of the truth. It means preparation prejudice — any difficulty posed for the requesting party in obtaining and making proof beyond that which would have occurred if no admission had been made.[60]

[2] Use and Value of Requests for Admissions

The chief purpose of requests for admissions is not to discover new information, but rather to expedite trial and to reduce the costs of proof.[61] But the leeway afforded by Rule 36 to deny the important issues and the weak sanction provisions of Rule 37(c) have rendered requests for admissions among the least used, most abused, and often disappointing procedural tools.[62] Requests to admit the authenticity of documentary evidence attached to the request are an exception. Because they are easy to frame and hard to evade, these requests are an effective means of avoiding the time and cost of authentication testimony at trial.

§ 12.03 PRETRIAL CONFERENCE[63]

[1] Purposes

In a pretrial conference, lawyers (and sometimes the parties) meet with judge, magistrate[64] or master before trial. Unknown at common law, the pretrial conference was authorized for the federal courts by Rule 16. It is said to be the

---

[58] *See, e.g., Reyes v. Vantage S.S. Co.*, 672 F.2d 556 (5th Cir. 1982) (admission was based on a faulty assumption).

[59] WRIGHT & MILLER § 2264.

[60] *See Brook Vill. N. Assocs. v. General Elec. Co.*, 686 F.2d 66, 70–71 (1st Cir. 1982). *Compare* § 8.10[1] (amendments in general and the prejudice requirement), *supra*.

[61] WRIGHT § 89.

[62] *See, e.g.,* Helen H. Stern Cutner, *Discovery — Civil Litigation's Fading Light: A Lawyer Looks at the Federal Discovery Rules After Forty Years of Use*, 52 TEMP. L.Q. 933, 981 (1979); Shapiro, note 51, *supra*, at 1078. *But see* WRIGHT & MILLER § 2253 (for their purposes, requests are more effective than other discovery).

[63] *See generally* Jeffrey A. Parness & Matthew R. Walker, *Thinking Outside the Civil Case Box: Reformulating Pretrial Conference Laws*, 50 U. KAN. L. REV. 347 (2002); David L. Shapiro, *Federal Rule 16: A Look at the Theory and Practice of Rulemaking*, 137 U. PA. L. REV. 1969 (1989); Wayne D. Brazil, *Improving Judicial Controls Over the Pretrial Development of Civil Actions: Model Rules for Case*

most popular federal rule and has stimulated widespread adoption of similar rules in the states.[65]

A primary purpose of pretrial conferences has always been to simplify, shorten, and possibly avoid trial.[66] The 1983 amendments to Rule 16 added another managerial purpose: to control, expedite and reduce the waste of pretrial litigation generally.[67] In addition, pretrial conferences continue to have the secondary purpose of facilitating settlement. The 1993 amendments reinforced all of these purposes.

[a]　Managerial Purposes

Pretrial conferences alleviate some of the uncertainty inherent in liberalized pleading, joinder, and discovery.

Modern pleading gives notice to the parties of what the case *may* include; pretrial conferences and orders help to define what issues the case *does* include on the eve of trial.[68] The order emerging from the final pretrial conference supersedes the sketchy descriptions of the case allowed in notice pleading jurisdictions.[69] That conference comes after the pleader has had the opportunity to develop his case by discovery. It provides a useful occasion for informing the parties and the judge more precisely about the case, lessening surprise at trial.

There is a significant relationship between pretrial conferences and the discovery process. The 1993 amendments to Rule 16 emphasize that "a major objective of pretrial conferences should be to consider appropriate controls on the extent and timing of discovery."[70] Moreover, broad discovery is permissible today in part because the undifferentiated mass of admissible and inadmissible evidence that it produces can be culled at the pretrial conference. The court can require the parties to specify their factual contentions[71] and their evidence for trial, and it can rule on its admissibility *in limine* (at the threshold of trial).[72]

Management and Sanctions, 1981 Am. B. Found. Res. J. 873; Maurice Rosenberg, The Pretrial Conference and Effective Justice (1964).

[64] *See* 28 U.S.C. §§ 631, 636 (authorizing participation of magistrates in pretrial proceedings), *construed in Mathews v. Weber*, 423 U.S. 261 (1976). *See generally* Arthur L. Sr. Burnett, *Practical, Innovative and Progressive Utilization of United States Magistrates to Improve the Administration of Justice in United States District Courts*, 28 How. L.J. 293 (1985).

[65] Wright § 91.

[66] Moore § 16.03[1].

[67] *See* Rule 16 advisory committee's notes (1983); Moore § 16.03[1].

[68] *Cf.* James, Hazard, & Leubsdorf § 5.19.

[69] *See* §§ 8.01 (history and functions of pleading) & 8.04 (modern notice pleading), *supra*.

[70] Rule 16(c) advisory committee's notes (1993).

[71] *See* Rules 33(a)(2) and 36(a) (permitting postponement until pretrial conference of discovery of contentions regarding application of law to the facts).

[72] *See* Robert E. Bacharach, *Motions in Limine in Oklahoma State and Federal Courts*, 24 Okla. City U. L. Rev. 113 (1999).

The pretrial conference also complements liberal joinder of claims and parties by providing for on-going and anticipatory control of the resulting complexity.[73] It permits courts to schedule or divide cases when necessary, order early presentation of evidence regarding potentially dispositive issues, limit the time allowed for presenting evidence at trial, supervise the complicated and potentially costly discovery of electronically stored information, and address other managerial problems arising in complex litigation.[74]

[b] Facilitating Settlement

Settlement has been a natural by-product of the pretrial conference in many cases because the exchange of contentions, admissions, and evidentiary specifications, and the prospect of an actual trial soon after the conference, make the parties and their lawyers reassess their cases. Some judges have gone further and affirmatively used the pretrial conference to promote settlement. They see judicial initiatives as necessary to compensate for the frequent hesitation of the parties to display weakness by initiating settlement negotiations.[75] On the other hand, outright coercion of settlement is reversible error,[76] and some judges studiously refrain from becoming involved in settlement. The 1993 amendments to Rule 16 apparently endorse the former view by addressing, though not fully resolving, two issues of settlement that have arisen under the rule.

The first is whether a federal judge may order a represented party to attend a settlement conference. Although the former rule only compelled an attorney who will conduct the trial or an unrepresented party to attend the final pretrial conference, a sharply divided Seventh Circuit Court of Appeals sitting *en banc* ruled in *G. Heileman Brewing Co., Inc. v. Joseph Oat Corp.*,[77] that a federal court had inherent authority to compel a represented party to attend a pretrial conference in order to promote settlement. The dissenters argued that the plain language of what was then Rule 16(d) was exclusive,[78] and that compelling parties to attend was tantamount to compelling them to negotiate, which was an abuse of judicial managerial authority.[79] A 1993 amendment to Rule 16 cautiously sides with the *Heileman* majority by explicitly providing that a court may require a party or its representative to be present or reasonably available by telephone to consider possible settlement.[80]

---

[73] See generally Chapter 9 (joinder), *supra*.

[74] See generally THE MANUAL FOR COMPLEX LITIGATION (4th ed. 2004) (recommending at least four pretrial conferences in such cases).

[75] See generally Robert R. Merhige & Alvin B. Rubin, *The Role of the Judge in the Settlement Process*, 75 F.R.D. 203, 205 (1978); Walter E. Craig & Gordon E. Christenson, *The Settlement Process*, 59 F.R.D. 252, 253–55 (1973).

[76] See, e.g., *Kothe v. Smith*, 771 F.2d 667 (2d Cir. 1985); Rule 16 advisory committee's note (1983). *See generally* Carrie Menkel-Meadow, *For and Against Settlement: Uses and Abuses of the Mandatory Settlement Conference*, 33 UCLA L. REV. 485 (1985).

[77] 871 F.2d 648 (7th Cir. 1989).

[78] *Id.* at 658 (Coffey, J., dissenting), at 666 (Manion, J., dissenting).

[79] *Id.* at 665 (Easterbrook, J., dissenting).

[80] Rule 16(c)(1). The 1993 advisory committee's notes add that this explicit authorization "is not

One federal judge, confronted with particularly contentious counsel, is reported to have said, "I cannot order a duel, and thus achieve a salubrious reduction in the number of counsel to put up with. However, a summary jury trial is so ordered."[81] His order presents a second settlement-related issue under Rule 16: whether it authorizes a federal judge to direct a summary jury trial in order to promote settlement. The summary jury trial is an alternative dispute resolution device by which parties summarize their evidence to a small test jury that then reports a non-binding consensus verdict.[82]

Courts that ordered such summary jury trials before the 1993 amendments to Rule 16 relied in part on the then rule's inclusion of "the possibility of settlement or the use of extrajudicial procedures to resolve the dispute" among the permissible subjects of conference, as well as the rule's limited compulsory attendance provision.[83] In *Strandell v. Jackson County*,[84] however, the Seventh Circuit Court of Appeals disagreed, ruling that these provisions of old Rule 16 did not authorize *mandatory* summary jury trial. The 1993 amendments to Rule 16 sidestep this issue by explicitly including as a permissible subject of pretrial conference "settling the case and using special procedures to assist in resolving the dispute *when authorized by statute or local rule*."[85] The underscored qualifier leaves open the issue of a court's inherent authority to mandate summary jury trial.

The foregoing issues, and the rules' caution in approaching them, indicate that there is still no consensus about how much initiative a judge can take to settle the case during pretrial without compromising the neutrality and detachment that has been traditional in our judicial systems,[86] or about whether court-ordered alterna-

---

intended to limit the reasonable exercise of the court's inherent powers," citing *Heileman*. *See also* Civil Justice Reform Act of 1990, 28 U.S.C. § 473(b)(5) (providing that locally adopted plans for reduction of expense and delay may include compulsory attendance requirements).

[81] *Choose Your Weapons*, 78 A.B.A.J. 44 (1992).

[82] *See, e.g.*, § 11.05[4], *supra*; Ann E. Woodley, *Strengthening the Summary Jury Trial: A Proposal to Increase Its Effectiveness and Encourage Uniformity in Its Use*, 12 OHIO ST. J. ON DISP. RESOL. 541 (1997); Shirley A. Wiegand, *A New Light Bulb or the Work of the Devil? A Current Assessment of Summary Jury Trials*, 69 OR. L. REV. 87 (1990); Charles F. Webber, *Mandatory Summary Jury Trial: Playing by the Rules?*, 56 U. CHI. L. REV. 1495 (1989); Richard A. Posner, *The Summary Jury Trial and Other Methods of Alternative Dispute Resolution: Some Cautionary Observations*, 53 U. CHI. L. REV. 366 (1986).

[83] *See, e.g.*, *McKay v. Ashland Oil, Inc.*, 120 F.R.D. 43 (E.D. Ky. 1988); *Arabian American Oil Co. v. Scarfone*, 119 F.R.D. 448 (M.D. Fla. 1988).

[84] 838 F.2d 884 (7th Cir. 1987).

[85] Rule 16(c)(2)(I) (emphasis added). Other "special procedures" include mini-trials, mediation, neutral evaluation, and nonbinding arbitration. *See* Rule 16 advisory committee's notes (1993).

[86] *See generally* Marla Moore, Note, *Mandatory Summary Jury Trials: Too Hasty a Solution to the Growing Problem of Judicial Inefficiency?*, 14 REV. LITIG. 495 (1995); Stephen McG. Bundy, *The Policy in Favor of Settlement in an Adversary System*, 44 HASTINGS L.J. 1 (1992); Steven Flanders, *Blind Umpires — A Response to Professor Resnik*, 35 HASTINGS L.J. 505, 507 (1984); Judith Resnik, *Managerial Judges*, 96 HARV. L. REV. 376 (1982). For views by federal judges, see Charles E. Clark, *Objectives of Pretrial Procedure*, 17 OHIO ST. L.J. 163, 167 (1956) ("Pre-trial used as a club to force settlements will destroy its utility as a stage of the trial process itself."); J. Skelly Wright, *The Pretrial Conference*, 28 F.R.D. 141, 145–47 (1960) ("we try to take the load off . . . the lawyer's back by telling them what we think the case should settle at").

tive dispute resolution is consistent with fair[87] and public[88] process. Even if judicial neutrality can be achieved by assigning different judges to accomplish the managerial and settlement-facilitating purposes of pretrial conferences, the process issues remain, assuring that the settlement-related provisions of Rule 16 will themselves continue to generate litigation.

[c] Assessment

Whether pretrial conferences have successfully accomplished the foregoing purposes is unclear. The evidence that pretrial has shortened trial and reduced congestion is weak, but there is stronger evidence that it has improved the quality of trials by facilitating better presentation of cases and reducing surprise.[89] There is some evidence that it has facilitated settlement, although it is unclear how much of this is a by-product of neutral managerial uses of pretrial and how much the result of more aggressive judicial settlement initiatives.[90] What is clear is that Rule 16 may be changing the adversary system. Instead of leaving its control to the parties by their lawyers, "it directs the sharing of power in handling the processing of a lawsuit."[91] Whether this change is for the better, or whether it is "redefining sub silentio our standards of what constitutes rational, fair, and impartial adjudication" in favor of an inquisitorial model of dispute resolution,[92] is an open question.

[2] Procedures for Pretrial Conferences[93]

Rule 16(a) and most state rules make the holding of pretrial conferences discretionary with the trial judge. The advisory committee in 1983 found that mandatory rules result in the over-regulation of some cases and under-regulation of others.[94] Some jurisdictions accordingly make the conference mandatory only in particular categories of cases.

---

[87] See generally Thomas B. Metzloff, Reconfiguring the Summary Jury Trial, 41 DUKE L.J. 806 (1992); Jennifer O'Hearne, Compelled Participation in Innovative Pretrial Proceedings, 84 Nw. U. L. REV. 290 (1989); Note, Mandatory Mediation and Summary Jury Trial Guidelines for Ensuring Fair and Effective Processes, 103 HARV. L. REV. 1086 (1990).

[88] See Cincinnati Gas & Elec. Co. v. General Elec. Co., 854 F.2d 900 (6th Cir. 1988) (affirming order closing summary jury trial to public), cert. denied, 489 U.S. 1033 (1989). See generally Angela Wade, Note, Summary Jury Trials: A "Settlement Technique" That Places a Shroud of Secrecy on Our Courtrooms?, 23 IND. L. REV. 949 (1990).

[89] See generally STEVEN FLANDERS, CASE MANAGEMENT AND COURT MANAGEMENT IN UNITED STATES DISTRICT COURTS 18–19, 35–37 (1977); ROSENBERG, note 63, supra, at 29–42.

[90] See generally ROSENBERG, note 63, supra, at 49–50; Robert J. Plourde, Pretrial in Maine Under New Rule 16: Settlement, Sanctions, and Sayonara, 34 ME. L. REV. 111, 126 (1982) (suggesting that the dichotomy is false and that settlement is a co-product of management).

[91] Arthur R. Miller & Diana G. Culp, The New Rules of Civil Procedure: Managing Cases, Limiting Discovery, NAT'L L.J., Dec. 5, 1983, at 23–25.

[92] See Resnik, note 86, supra, at 380. See also Todd D. Peterson, Restoring Structural Checks on Judicial Power in the Era of Managerial Judging, 29 U.C. DAVIS L. REV. 41 (1995).

[93] See generally JUDICIAL CONF. OF UNITED STATES, HANDBOOK FOR EFFECTIVE PRETRIAL PROCEDURE (1964), reprinted in 37 F.R.D. 255; Robert F. Peckham, The Federal Judge as a Case Manager: The New Role in Guiding a Case From Filing to Disposition, 69 CAL. L. REV. 770 (1981).

[94] Rule 16 advisory committee's notes (1983).

When only one pretrial conference is held, it is usually scheduled after the completion of discovery, shortly before trial.[95] At that point it is reasonable to make the parties specify issues and evidence and to amend the pleadings. Most rules, like Rule 16, also authorize multiple pretrial conferences in the judge's discretion.

Rule 16(b)(2) also requires the judge to enter a scheduling order within 90 days after the appearance of a defendant or 120 days after the complaint is served, setting time limits for joinder and amendment, motion practice, and completion of discovery, and (optionally) setting the dates for mandatory discovery, pretrial conferences, and trial, subject to modification for good cause.[96] This initial order helps accomplish the stated purpose of "establishing early and continuing control" of the lawsuit.[97]

In addition to now authorizing a court to require the attendance or availability by phone of a party or its representative, Rule 16 requires attorneys to prepare for and attend every pretrial conference and requires at least one of the attorneys who will conduct the trial to attend the final pretrial conference.[98] Backed by sanctions under Rule 16(f),[99] these provisions are aimed at preventing the sabotage of effective pretrial by indifferent preparation or the excuse that the attorney is not authorized to stipulate or to enter into other agreements that might be made at pretrial.

Rule 16(c)(2) supplies a non-exhaustive list of the subjects that may be considered in pretrial.[100] For the final pretrial conference, usually the parties will be asked to submit pretrial briefs.[101] These may state the undisputed facts, identify the disputed facts (often with citation to the discovery record), summarize legal contentions, and list trial witnesses and exhibits. The parties may also be required to make authenticity objections to proposed trial exhibits and are invited to raise other evidentiary objections that could be ruled upon before trial.[102] Now some of these functions of pretrial briefs are fulfilled instead by Rule 26(a)(3), requiring the parties to identify at least thirty days before trial their trial witnesses, exhibits, and other evidence, and to make objections within fourteen days thereafter (at the risk of waiver). Even with this required pretrial disclosure, however, courts may continue to require the parties to propose findings of fact in their pretrial briefs

---

[95] *See* Rule 16(e) (providing that the final pretrial conference shall be held as close to the time of trial as reasonable under the circumstances).

[96] The rule provides that courts may exempt categories of cases from this requirement. Rule 16(b). The Advisory Committee gave social security benefits, *habeas corpus*, and some administrative law cases as examples. Rule 16 advisory committee notes (1983).

[97] Rule 16(a)(2).

[98] Rule 16(c)(1) & (e).

[99] *See also Link v. Wabash R.R. Co.*, 370 U.S. 626 (1962) (affirming dismissal under court's inherent power to punish failure to attend pretrial conferences and other misconduct). *See generally* § 12.03[3] (the pretrial order and its effect), *infra*.

[100] *See generally* MOORE §§ 16.30–16.36; WRIGHT & MILLER § 1525.

[101] WRIGHT & MILLER § 1524.

[102] *See* Edna S. Epstein, *Motions in Limine — A Primer, in* THE LITIGATION MANUAL 642 (American Bar Ass'n 1999).

and to admit or deny each other's proposed findings, as a way of clarifying the issues for trial.[103] Furthermore, to expedite the trial, the court may order early presentation of evidence on a potentially dispositive issue, as noted above, and, more controversially, set reasonable limits on the time allowed for presenting evidence.[104]

By their pretrial briefs, or by formal motion under Rule 15(a), parties often amend their pleadings at pretrial. The imminence of trial creates an incentive to drop borderline claims or defenses for which there was little support from discovery and to sharpen or add others suggested by discovery, eliminating the need to accomplish the same end through disruptive mid-trial amendments. Moreover, it is well-established that the court may itself redefine or even terminate the lawsuit by entering summary judgment on particular claims and defenses, should the pretrial briefs establish the absence of genuine factual dispute.[105]

The pretrial conference, however, is no substitute for discovery or for trial. Although the 1993 amendments authorize inclusion of "controlling and scheduling discovery" as a pretrial conference subject,[106] perhaps impliedly settling the previously unresolved issue of the courts' authority to order discovery pursuant to a pretrial conference,[107] the conference is still not intended as a discovery tool for the parties. It is surely not a device for deciding disputed issues of material fact; it confers no greater power on the court than it already has under the summary judgment rule.[108]

[3] The Pretrial Order and Its Effect

Rule 16(d) requires the court to enter an order after a pretrial conference to preserve the work done there. The order is often prepared by counsel for the approval of the court.[109] Its content varies with the work of the conference. A 1962 study reported that in one-third of federal pretrial conferences, the trial judge failed to file a pretrial order,[110] although that figure has probably declined since the 1983 amendments to Rule 16. In those cases, however, the parties' pretrial memoranda were often given the same effect as a pretrial order.[111]

---

[103] Larry Lempert, *AT&T Case May Become Complex Litigation Model*, LEGAL TIMES OF WASHINGTON, Feb. 4, 1980, at 1.

[104] Rule 16(c)(2)(N) & (O).

[105] Rule 56(f)(3). *See, e.g., Portsmouth Square, Inc. v. S'holders Protective Comm.*, 770 F.2d 866 (9th Cir. 1985) ("The court need not await a formal motion, . . . [as long as] the party against whom judgment was entered had a full and fair opportunity to develop and present facts and legal arguments in support of its position." (citation omitted)). *See also* Rule 16(c) advisory committee's notes (1983).

[106] Rule 16(c)(2)(F).

[107] *See MOORE* § 16.13[2].

[108] *See* § 11.03[1] (summary judgment at court's initiative), *supra*.

[109] *WRIGHT & MILLER* § 1526. The Advisory Committee for the 1983 amendments to Rule 16 were content to leave the question of how a pretrial order should be prepared to the discretion of the presiding judges. Rule 16 advisory committee's notes (1983).

[110] *See* REPORT OF PROCEEDINGS OF THE JUDICIAL CONFERENCE OF THE UNITED STATES 79–80 (1962).

[111] *See Price v. Inland Oil Co.*, 646 F.2d 90, 96 (3d Cir. 1981).

Rule 16(d) provides that the pretrial order "controls the course of action unless the court modifies it." The final pretrial order supersedes the pleadings. Objections to the pleadings, claims and defenses, or issues not incorporated in the order are waived.[112]

> [A] party need offer no proof at trial as to matters agreed to in the order, nor may a party offer evidence or advance theories at trial that are not included in the order or which contradict its terms. Disregard of these principles would bring back the days of trial by ambush and discourage timely preparation by the parties for trial.[113]

The binding effect given the pretrial order thus affords the parties a measure of certainty concerning the real issues for trial and their evidentiary burden.

This contrast between the pretrial order and modern pleading merits emphasis. Under modern federal pleading, a pleader is still not held to just the legal theory identified in the pleadings. A motion to dismiss for failure to state a claim must be denied if the pleading plausibly states a claim that would entitle the pleader to relief on *any* available legal theory. This system is based in part on the presumption that pleaders at the outset often lack sufficient information to articulate details and all possible claims or defenses. Subject to the requirements of "plausibility pleading," modern pleading assumes that parties will be able to ascertain that information by discovery. However, the presumption runs the other way as the parties near the end of the lawsuit. Fairness and trial efficiency then require a higher degree of certainty about what is and what is not at issue.[114]

Exclusion is the typical trial sanction for enlargement of the issues or evidence beyond the pretrial order. Rule 16(f) also authorizes the court to punish disobedience of the pretrial order by striking claims or defenses, dismissing the action, entering a default judgment, or holding the disobedient party in contempt. Thus, the court may refuse to admit into evidence documents that the proponent failed to list in the pretrial order or brief,[115] and it may exclude witnesses that were omitted from final witness lists at pretrial.[116] Similarly, the court may bar a party from asserting a new claim or theory of recovery, if it was omitted from the pretrial order

---

[112] *See, e.g., Simcox v. San Juan Shipyard, Inc.*, 754 F.2d 430, 440 (1st Cir. 1985) (Rule 9(b) objection that complaint did not plead fraud with particularity was waived by failure to object to incorporation of fraud claim in pretrial order); *Syrie v. Knoll Int'l*, 748 F.2d 304, 308 (5th Cir. 1984) (incorporation of unpleaded claim into pretrial order amends the pleadings *pro tanto*).

[113] *United States v. First Nat'l Bank of Circle*, 652 F.2d 882, 886 (9th Cir. 1981).

[114] This is true even though a pretrial order is generally given a liberal construction to include "any of the possible legal or factual theories that might be embraced by its language." WRIGHT & MILLER § 1527. *See, e.g., Miller v. Safeco Title Ins. Co.*, 758 F.2d 364 (9th Cir. 1985) (pretrial order statement of issue as whether a debt was secured by a trust deed construed to include issue whether deed was in the nature of a performance bond). *But see Flannery v. Carroll*, 676 F.2d 126, 129 (5th Cir. 1982) ("District courts are encouraged to construe pre-trial orders narrowly without fear of reversal.").

[115] *See, e.g., Smith v. Rowe*, 761 F.2d 360 (7th Cir. 1985); *United States v. Rayco, Inc.*, 616 F.2d 462 (10th Cir. 1980).

[116] *See, e.g., Spray-Rite Serv. Corp. v. Monsanto Co.*, 684 F.2d 1226 (7th Cir. 1982), *aff'd on other grounds*, 465 U.S. 752 (1984); *Keyes v. Lauga*, 635 F.2d 330 (5th Cir. 1981).

or memorandum.[117]

While final pretrial orders are not ironclad, Rule 16(e) authorizes their modification "only to prevent manifest injustice."[118] In making that determination, the court should consider the comparative prejudice to the parties from modifying or failing to modify the order, the impact of modification on the orderly and efficient conduct of the litigation, and any degree of willfulness, bad faith or inexcusable neglect by the proponent of the modification.[119] For example, modification has been allowed to permit evidence of which the opponent had eleven months' notice despite its omission from the pretrial order,[120] when the opponent mitigated any prejudice to it by effective cross-examination of a previously omitted witness,[121] and when the evidence was newly discovered since the entry of the pretrial order.[122] Modification has been denied when the opponent was lulled into withholding a possible defense by the omission from the pretrial order of an alternative theory of recovery.[123] Of course, when there is no objection to the offer of evidence or claims outside the pretrial order, the court should ordinarily allow it.[124]

Matters pursued at trial that are outside the final pretrial order may also be outside the pleadings. The objecting party actually has two grounds in this situation: Rule 16(e) and the evidentiary grounds of irrelevance or immateriality. The latter are not a very significant addition, however, because Rule 16(e) poses a standard more favorable to the objecting party.[125]

Matters outside the final pretrial order may also be objectionable at trial because they are inconsistent with admissions under Rule 36. Again, Rule 16(e) seems to give more weight to the objection than Rule 36.[126]

---

[117] See, e.g., Allen v. United States Steel Corp., 665 F.2d 689 (5th Cir. 1982); Price v. Inland Oil Co., 646 F.2d 90, 96 (2d Cir. 1981).

[118] A court commits reversible error by amending a pretrial order at trial over objection unless it finds that it is necessary to prevent manifest injustice. See Hale v. Firestone Tire & Rubber Co., 756 F.2d 1322 (8th Cir. 1985).

[119] See First Nat'l Bank of Circle, 652 F.2d at 887 (citations omitted).

[120] See Joubert v. Travelers Indem. Co., 736 F.2d 191, 194 (5th Cir. 1984).

[121] Syvock v. Milwaukee Boiler Mfg. Co., 665 F.2d 149 (7th Cir. 1981).

[122] See MOORE § 16.78[4].

[123] See Flannery, 676 F.2d 126.

[124] See, e.g., Gorby v. Schneider Tank Lines, Inc., 741 F.2d 1015 (7th Cir. 1984); Mechmetals Corp. v. Telex Computer Prods., Inc., 709 F.2d 1287 (9th Cir. 1983). Compare § 8.10[2][a] (conforming amendments by consent at trial), supra.

[125] Compare the standard for mid-trial amendment of pleadings in Rule 15(b)(1) (court should "freely permit an amendment when doing so will aid in presenting the merits" and the objecting party fails to show that the evidence would prejudice it) with the presumption against modifying final pretrial orders in Rule 16(e) (they can be modified "only to prevent manifest injustice"). On mid-trial amendments generally, see § 8.10[2], supra.

[126] Compare the provision in Rule 36(b) for relieving a party of the effects of his admissions (court "may permit withdrawal or amendment of admission if it would promote the presentation of the merits of the action" and the objecting party fails to show that the withdrawal or amendment would prejudice it) with the presumption against modifying final pretrial orders in Rule 16(e) (they can be modified "only to prevent manifest injustice"). On the effect of Rule 36 admissions generally, see § 12.02, supra.

In short, because of greater risk of inefficiency and prejudice, requests for modification or amendment of final pretrial orders will usually receive a less generous reception than earlier requests to amend pleadings or admissions.

§ 12.04   BURDEN OF PROOF

[1]   In General[127]

Plaintiff sues defendant for negligence. If at trial plaintiff fails to produce any evidence of injury, the court should find for defendant. The result is the same whether the issue is tried to the court or the jury; there is nothing for the jury to decide regarding injury. Suppose, however, that the evidence appears to support the positions of plaintiff and defendant to about the same degree. In that event, too, the court in a bench trial should find for defendant. In a jury trial, the issue would be submitted to a jury. But the court could still influence the jury's deliberations by instructing it that if it finds evidence on a critical point evenly balanced, it should return a verdict for defendant.[128]

Loss in either event stems from plaintiff's failure to meet his *burden of proof*. Evidence scholars[129] have modified the term in some settings by substituting more refined (if not always consistent) terminology to describe what is happening in the foregoing hypothetical. The plaintiff who fails to produce evidence on an essential element of his claim has failed the *burden of production* or *burden of going forward*. In a jury case, he has failed to produce sufficient evidence to reach the jury (that is, sufficient to permit a reasonable jury to find for him), and the court should grant a directed verdict or, in federal court, a judgment as a matter of law against him. By contrast, the plaintiff who fails to convince the trier of fact to some pre-established degree of certainty or by a pre-established *standard* of proof of the facts necessary to his claim has failed his *burden of persuasion* or assumed the *risk of nonpersuasion*.[130] In most civil cases, the required standard of proof is a *preponderance of the evidence*: that the facts are more likely than not as the plaintiff contends.

Many of the traditional maxims offered to explain how parties acquire burdens of production and persuasion are of little use. It is said that the burden rests on the party who seeks to disturb the status quo or for whom a particular issue is essential. However, these explanations are only "facile form[s] of statement of the result."[131] It is often defendant who disturbed the status quo outside court; affirmatives can be restated as negatives; and to designate issues as essential begs

---

[127] *See generally* Bruce L. Hay, *Allocating the Burden of Proof*, 72 IND. L.J. 651 (1997); McCORMICK ON EVIDENCE ch. 36 (K. Brown ed., 6th ed. 2006); JOHN MACARTHUR MAGUIRE, EVIDENCE: COMMON SENSE AND COMMON LAW (1947); John T. McNaughton, *Burden of Production of Evidence: A Function of a Burden of Persuasion*, 68 HARV. L. REV. 1382 (1955); *WRIGHT & MILLER* § 5122.

[128] *WRIGHT & MILLER* § 5122.

[129] *See, e.g.*, JAMES BRADLEY THAYER, PRELIMINARY TREATISE ON EVIDENCE 355 (1898).

[130] Some state evidence codes have also adopted such terminology. *See, e.g.*, OR. REV. STAT. §§ 40.105–40.115, rules 305 & 307 (West 2012).

[131] Edmund M. Morgan, *Some Observations Concerning Presumptions*, 44 HARV. L. REV. 906, 910–11

the question. The explanation that the burden of proof follows the burden of pleading[132] is so often contradicted by practice[133] as to be unreliable. Yet, at least initially, the same party usually does assume the burdens of pleading, production, and persuasion. That is because each burden is shaped by the same factors, called by one treatise "the Three P's: Policy, Probability, and Possession of [access to] Proof."[134] We will consider the burdens of production and persuasion in greater detail in the subsections which follow.[135]

[2] The Burden of Production

The plaintiff has the initial burden of production regarding at least some issues. Collectively, they may be called plaintiff's *prima facie* case.[136] Plaintiff must produce sufficient evidence on those issues to enable a reasonable jury, or the judge in a nonjury trial, to find for him absent rebuttal evidence by defendant. If plaintiff does so in a jury trial, the court must deny defendant's motion for a directed verdict or judgment as a matter of law.[137] On the other hand, even if defendant fails to produce any evidence in rebuttal, plaintiff ordinarily would not be entitled to a directed verdict or judgment as a matter of law in *his* favor. Instead the jury usually will be asked to decide whether to accept or reject plaintiff's evidence, at least where acceptance turns on credibility and inference.

It is possible, however, for plaintiff to produce so much evidence that — on the strength of it alone — no reasonable jury could decide against him. In such a case, the burden of production shifts from plaintiff to defendant. It is then defendant who must produce sufficient evidence to meet plaintiff's evidence, or he will suffer a directed verdict. If defendant, in turn, produces so much evidence that no reasonable jury could find against him, the burden of production shifts once again to plaintiff.

This process is depicted in Figure 12-1, a variation on the well-known diagram originally proposed by Professor Wigmore.[138]

(1931). *See also* Edward W. Cleary, *Presuming and Pleading: An Essay on Juristic Immaturity*, 12 STAN. L. REV. 5 (1959).

[132] *See* Ronald J. Allen, *Presumptions in Civil Actions Reconsidered*, 66 IOWA L. REV. 843, 849 (1981).

[133] *See, e.g., Palmer v. Hoffman*, 318 U.S. 109, 117 (1943) (federal rules control burden of pleading, but state law in diversity case controls burden of proof); *Knowles v. Gilchrist Co.*, 289 N.E.2d 879 (Mass. 1972) (bailor has burden of pleading negligent bailment, but once bailor has produced evidence establishing bailment and loss of or damage to bailed good, bailee has burden of proof of due care).

[134] WRIGHT & MILLER § 5122. *See generally* MCCORMICK, note 127, *supra*, § 337 (noting natural tendency to place burdens on party desiring change, special policy concerns such as those disfavoring certain defenses, convenience, fairness, and the judicial estimate of the probabilities as illustrative factors); Cleary, note 131, *supra*, at 8–14.

[135] On the burden of pleading, *see* § 8.06[2] (using *Gomez v. Toledo*, 446 U.S. 635 (1980), to illustrate significance of possession of proof to allocation of burden of pleading), *supra*; § 8.08[2][a] (the burden and affirmative defenses), *supra*.

[136] *See Texas Dep't of Cmty. Affairs v. Burdine*, 450 U.S. 248, 250 (1981).

[137] *See* § 12.09[1] (directed verdict and judgment as a matter of law in general), *infra*.

[138] *See* 9 JOHN HENRY WIGMORE, EVIDENCE § 2487 (3d ed. 1940).

Figure 12-1

If P has the burden of production on an issue, he must produce sufficient evidence to get past X or he will suffer a directed verdict. If he gets past X into the XZ range, the issue will go to the jury. If, however, he produces so much evidence that he passes Z, then the burden of production shifts to D. Unless D now produces enough evidence to pass Z, he will suffer a directed verdict or judgment as a matter of law. Should he produce enough evidence to cross X, then the burden of production shifts back to plaintiff.[139]

The process is essentially similar in a bench (non-jury) trial, as the Supreme Court explained in *Texas Department of Community Affairs v. Burdine*.[140] *Burdine* was a Title VII employment discrimination case.[141] The court of appeals had held that once plaintiff produced evidence establishing a *prima facie* case of discrimination — that plaintiff applied for a position for which she was qualified and was rejected for reasons which gave rise to an inference of discrimination — the defendant had the burden of proving by a preponderance of the evidence the existence of legitimate, non-discriminatory reasons for its employment action. The Supreme Court reversed. It noted that "*prima facie* case . . . may be used by courts to describe the plaintiff's burden of producing enough evidence to permit the trier of fact to infer the fact at issue."[142] Once plaintiff meets her burden, however, it is not the burden of persuasion that shifts to defendant, but only the burden of producing evidence establishing nondiscriminatory reasons for the defendant's employment action.

> The plaintiff retains the burden of persuasion. [If defendant meets its burden, plaintiff] . . . now must have the opportunity to demonstrate that the proffered reason was not the true reason for the employment decision. This burden now merges with the ultimate burden of persuading the court that she had been the victim of intentional discrimination.[143]

In short, the burden of persuasion is generally fixed, but the burden of production may shift back and forth as the evidence unfolds.

---

[139] To visualize the burden of persuasion, see § 12.04[3], *infra*, explaining line Y in Figure 86-1.

[140] 450 U.S. 248 (1981).

[141] *See generally* Robert Belton, *Burdens of Pleading and Proof in Discrimination Cases: Toward a Theory of Procedural Justice*, 34 Vand. L. Rev. 1205 (1981).

[142] 450 U.S. at 254 n.7 (citation omitted). If the judge believes plaintiff's evidence, and defendant produces none, the judge is required to enter judgment for the plaintiff. *Id.* at 254.

[143] *Id.* at 256.

[3] The Burden of Persuasion

The burden of persuasion is the requirement that a party convince the trier of fact of the truth of an issue to a predetermined level of certainty.[144] The function of that level or standard of proof is to "instruct the fact-finder concerning the degree of confidence our society thinks he [or they] should have in the correctness of factual conclusions for a particular type of adjudication."[145] In most civil cases, society is only minimally concerned with outcome, and the level of certainty is usually expressed as a preponderance of the evidence, sometimes also characterized as the *greater weight of the evidence*.[146] The burden of persuasion by a preponderance of the evidence is harder to visualize accurately by diagram, but inserting a Y through the middle of Figure 12-1 may help. To carry his burden of persuasion by a preponderance of the evidence, P must present evidence that will get past Y. If he presents less, or if the evidence is in equipoise at Y, the jury should find against him.

Diagraming the burden in this way can be misleading, however. It suggests a quantitative standard, as does the phrase *greater weight of the evidence*. The preponderance standard refers not to the quantity of evidence — the greater number of witnesses or exhibits — but rather to its convincing force. Weight or movement on the diagramed scale therefore represents the degree of persuasiveness or certainty in the fact-trier's mind that the evidence will produce.

In criminal cases and some civil cases society's greater concern in the outcome increases the burden of persuasion. Society's interest in avoiding erroneous criminal convictions accounts for the requirement that the prosecution must prove guilt *beyond a reasonable doubt*.[147] This demanding standard would move the Y on Figure 12-1 to the right, indicating a much heavier burden for P — the government in a criminal case. The Supreme Court has also required plaintiffs to persuade by *clear and convincing evidence* in some civil cases where interests more significant than money are at stake.[148] This standard falls between preponderance of the evidence and proof beyond a reasonable doubt.[149] Thus, the Y in the figure would not be moved quite as far to the right as it would be in a criminal case. It is uncertain whether juries can differentiate such standards, or whether they apply any of them instead of simply deciding "who is right."[150]

---

[144] Ronald J. Allen, *Presumptions, Inferences, Burden of Proof in Federal Civil Actions — An Anatomy of an Unnecessary Ambiguity and a Proposal for Reform*, 76 Nw. U. L. Rev. 892, 908 (1982).

[145] *In re Winship*, 397 U.S. 358, 370 (1970) (Harlan, J., concurring).

[146] *See generally* McCormick, note 127, *supra*, § 339; Neil Orloff & Jery Stedinger, *A Framework for Evaluating the Preponderance-of-the-Evidence Standard*, 131 U. Pa. L. Rev. 1159 (1983).

[147] *See Santosky v. Kramer*, 455 U.S. 745, 755 (1982).

[148] *Addington v. Texas*, 441 U.S. 418, 424 (1979) (civil commitment). *See also Santosky*, 455 U.S. at 745 (termination of parental rights); *Woodby v. Immigration & Naturalization Serv.*, 385 U.S. 276, 285 (1966) (deportation). At common law in many jurisdictions, fraud and mistake must also be proven by clear and convincing evidence. *See, e.g., Hofmann v. Hofmann*, 446 N.E.2d 499, 506 (Ill. 1983).

[149] One scholar suggested that if preponderance means that a proposition is more probably true than false, clear and convincing means only that it is much more probably true than false. Edmund M. Morgan, *Instructing the Jury Upon Presumptions and Burden of Proof*, 47 Harv. L. Rev. 59, 67 (1933).

[150] *See, e.g.*, Kathleen F. O'Reilly, *Why Some Juries Fail*, 41 D.C.B.J. 69 (1974); Ralph K. Winter, *The*

[4] Presumptions[151]

The subject of presumptions has been aptly described as "one of the most complex topics in the law of evidence" and "a sea of technicality which defies logical analysis."[152] Extended discussion of presumptions is better left to writers of evidence texts. We will confine our attention here to introductory terminology. The term *presumption* is used to describe at least four different concepts.

First, the presumption of innocence is said to apply in criminal trials. This is not really a presumption at all, but a way of saying that the prosecution has the burden of proof and of suggesting that the standard of proof is beyond a reasonable doubt. It would be more accurate to term it an *assumption* than a presumption.

Second, presumption is used generally to refer to a logical inference from the evidence. For example, circumstantial evidence was once treated in the evidence books under the heading "presumptive evidence."[153] Triers of fact draw such inferences all the time. The process does not necessarily relate to burdens of proof.

Third, a presumption may reflect the idea in substantive law that proof of one fact establishes beyond argument the truth of another. Many states, for example, presume the legitimacy of children from proof that they were born to a wife cohabiting with her husband. Such a presumption may or may not be logical, but, in any event, it is not subject to rebuttal, even by evidence of the biological impossibility of paternity.[154] Such *conclusive* or *legal presumptions* are best regarded as part of the substantive law, rather than the law of evidence or procedure.

Finally, the term is used to refer to *rebuttable presumptions* that affect the burden of production and sometimes of persuasion. This happens when plaintiff in establishing one fact is deemed to have established a second, *unless* the defendant offers evidence rebutting the second fact at trial. For example, evidence that a letter has been properly posted creates a rebuttable presumption of delivery to the addressee. The rebuttable presumption thus operates to satisfy the proponent's burden of production, and a court cannot grant a motion for a directed verdict or judgment as a matter of law grounded on non-delivery once posting has been shown, absent rebuttal evidence.[155]

What happens when the opposing party puts on rebuttal evidence is much more controversial. The two leading alternative theories are illustrated by *Legille v. Dann.*[156] To challenge the presumed fact of delivery, defendant offered proof of its routine mail-handling practices. Calling it the majority view, the court adopted the

---

Jury and the Risk of Non-Persuasion, 5 LAW & SOC'Y REV. 335 (1971); MORGAN, note 149, *supra*, at 66–67.

[151] *See generally* JAMES, HAZARD & LEUBSDORF § 7.17; Allen, note 132, *supra*; Charles Nesson, *Rationality, Presumptions and Judicial Comment: A Response to Professor Allen*, 54 HARV. L. REV. 1574 (1981); McCORMICK, note 127, *supra*, §§ 342–45.

[152] WRIGHT & MILLER § 5122.

[153] *Id.*

[154] *See, e.g., Estate of Cornelious*, 674 P.2d 245 (Cal. 1984).

[155] *See* McCORMICK, note 127, *supra*, § 343 (illustrative rebuttable presumptions).

[156] 544 F.2d 1 (D.C. Cir. 1976).

"bursting bubble theory" whereby the production of rebuttal evidence causes the original presumption to "burst" and be without further effect in the case. Thus limited, the effect of the presumption

> is merely to invoke a rule of law compelling the [trier of fact] to reach a conclusion in the absence of evidence to the contrary from the opponent. If the opponent does offer evidence to the contrary (sufficient to satisfy the judge's requirement of some evidence), the presumption disappears as a rule of law, and the case is in the [factfinder's] hands free from any rule.[157]

In short, the presumption affects the production burden only. The majority in *Legille* therefore reversed a grant of summary judgment for the party invoking the presumption of delivery and remanded for trial.[158]

The dissenting judge argued in contrast that the rebuttal evidence was not sufficient to overcome the "strong presumption" of delivery.[159] He would have given the delivery presumption continuing effect, even after some rebuttal evidence was produced. This is consistent with the theory that proof of the basic fact shifts the burden of proof (*i.e.*, burdens of both production and persuasion) to the party against whom the presumption operates.[160] Proponents of this approach criticized the bursting bubble theory for subverting substantive policies underpinning presumptions, giving them too "slight and evanescent" an effect.[161]

There are other theories as well.[162] Moreover, statutes may define the effect of presumptions and thus displace judicial doctrine. The same factors that determine the allocation of burdens of production and persuasion ultimately determine the availability of presumptions.[163]

---

[157] *Id.* at 5–6 (quoting 9 JOHN HENRY WIGMORE, EVIDENCE § 2491 (3d ed. 1940)).

[158] The majority noted that the presumption of delivery and the presumption of procedural regularity

> [B]oth . . . have a common origin in regularity of action. We see nothing suggesting that the methodology buttressing the one is any more or less foolproof than that underpinning the other. We are mindful that some presumptions are founded in part upon exceptionally strong and visible policies, which have been said to persist despite proof rebutting the factual basis for the presumption. The answer here is that from aught that appears the policy reflections are in equilibrium.

Id. at 7 n.39.

[159] *Id.* at 11 (Fahey, J., dissenting).

[160] *See* MORGAN, note 149, *supra*, at 83 ("in situations where a presumption owes its origin to an important social policy, it should operate to fix the burden of persuasion").

[161] Edmund M. Morgan & John MacArthur MaGuire, *Looking Backward and Forward at Evidence*, 50 HARV. L. REV. 909, 913 (1937).

[162] *See, e.g.*, EDMUND M. MORGAN, BASIC PROBLEMS OF STATE AND FEDERAL EVIDENCE 28–30 (J. Weinstein, 5th ed. 1976) (listing eight).

[163] *See* MCCORMICK, note 127, *supra* at § 343.

PART B.
Trial and Judgment

§ 12.05   OVERVIEW

Most civil cases filed never come to trial. Usually they are settled, voluntarily withdrawn, or decided on the merits prior to trial.[164] Yet many cases do require trial. As a more basic matter, the idea and prospect of trial strongly influence the shape of procedure for all civil cases. Pleadings and pretrial proceedings set bounds of inquiry for trial; discovery and less formal means of investigation prepare the parties for trial; and trial can be either a specter that facilitates or an enticement that blocks settlement.[165]

The function of the trial is two-fold: (1) to sift from a controverted factual record the true story — or, at least, the story most likely upon the evidence to be true — and (2) to attach legal significance to that story. The first function culminates in a verdict if performed by a jury or in findings of fact if performed by the judge. The judge always performs the second function, but the manner in which she performs it depends on whether the case is tried with or without a jury. In this Part we will consider some of the ways in which civil procedure is complicated by the fact that some cases are tried through judge-jury collaboration while others are tried by judges alone.

§ 12.06   THE TACTICAL DECISION WHETHER TO DEMAND A JURY TRIAL

The desirability of the jury as a social institution rests on several assumptions: that collective judgment is superior to individual judgment, that an anonymous collective judgment is more easily accepted by the loser than a personalized individual judgment, and that judgment by one's peers is preferable to judgment by non-peers.[166] While these assumptions have come under attack,[167] the public may still have a mild preference for trial by jury.[168]

---

[164] *See* Chapter 11 (pretrial judgments), *supra*.

[165] *See* Samuel R. Gross & Kent D. Syverud, *Don't Try: Civil Jury Verdicts in a System Geared to Settlement*, 44 UCLA L. Rev. 1 (1996) (using empirical evidence to conclude that "[t]he main function of trials is not to resolve disputes but to deter other trials").

[166] For more extended discussion of these considerations, see § 12.08[1], *infra*. The literature on the nature and significance of jury trials is extensive. *See, e.g.*, Symposium, *Jury Reform: Making Juries Work*, 32 U. Mich. J.L. Reform 213 (1999); Symposium, *The American Civil Jury: Illusion and Reality*, 48 DePaul L. Rev. 197 (1998); Valerie P. Hans & Neil Vidmar, Judging the Jury (1986); Ronald C. Wolf, *Trial By Jury: A Sociological Analysis*, 1966 Wis. L. Rev. 820 (1966); Paula DiPerna, Juries on Trial (1984); Jerome Frank, Courts on Trial (1949).

[167] *See, e.g.*, Frank, note 166, *supra*; Fleming James, Jr., *Trial By Jury and the New Federal Rules of Civil Procedure*, 45 Yale L.J. 1022 (1936).

[168] Wolf, note 166, *supra*, at 826 n.14. *But see* Kenneth S. Klein, *Unpacking the Jury Box*, 47 Hastings L.J. 1325 (1996) (noting growing distrust of juries, partly in response to their growing diversity).

However, such concerns are unlikely to figure greatly if at all in a particular decision whether to demand a jury trial. Rather, lawyers decide based upon their personal experiences, subjective and intuitive assessments of the probabilities of success, and highly pragmatic considerations of calendar, cost, and settlement leverage. To place the procedures for obtaining a jury trial in context, it is useful to identify a few of these necessarily ad hoc factors.

Counsel's subjective and intuitive assessment of the role of sentiment and expertise is often a crucial factor in the decision whether to demand a jury trial. When the witnesses for one side are credible, expert, or likely to provoke sympathy, the fact may dictate a strong preference for trial by jury. On the other hand, counsel will often favor a non-jury trial when the evidence and the theory of recovery are complex and technical.[169]

Another factor is the nature of the evidence at the margin, evidence arguably inadmissible. When such evidence is damaging to a party, he would ordinarily prefer a jury trial from which that evidence will be excluded to a non-jury trial in which the marginal evidence will be taken for what it is worth.[170]

Additional factors include calendar and cost. Jury-tried cases take, on average, 40% longer than judge-tried cases.[171] As a result jury trials are harder to schedule and more costly than non-jury trials. The party who seeks a quick result, due to financial need or fear that evidence might be lost, will ordinarily prefer a non-jury trial. Because it is often an injured plaintiff who is in this posture, the demand for a jury trial can work to the defendant's benefit in such circumstances. Even the defendant who is not anxious to go before a jury may consider demanding a jury trial in order to obtain bargaining leverage for a pretrial settlement.

Other factors which may also encourage defendants to demand a jury trial include the requirement for unanimous verdicts and the greater likelihood of reversible errors during jury trials. Where unanimity is required, defendant has but to convince one juror to find for him in order to prevail, a task which may often look more promising than convincing the judge.[172] A defendant anticipating tactical advantages from appeal may also prefer the jury trial because of the opportunities for reversible error in the admission of evidence, instruction of the jury, and jury deliberations,[173] although such reckoning is tempered by awareness of the universal

---

[169] *But see* Kevin M. Clermont & Theodore Eisenberg, *Trial by Jury or Judge: Transcending Empiricism*, 77 Cornell L. Rev. 1124 (1992) (raising doubts about the conventional intuition).

[170] "This practice is based on the theory that the judge, with his knowledge of the rules of evidence, can separate the wheat from the chaff and pay no attention to evidence otherwise inadmissible . . . ." Leighton Bledsoe, *Jury or Non-Jury Trial — A Defense Viewpoint*, 5 Am. Jur. Trials 123, 135 (1966).

[171] Hans Zeisel, Harry Kalven & Bernard Buchholz, Delay in the Court 71–81 (1959). Of course, the proper comparison is not just between trial times, but between the time elapsed from commencement of trial to decision. Jury trials have the virtue of rendering a decision at the close of the trial itself; judges will often delay for months after trial before they render their decisions. Bledsoe, note 170, *supra*, at 141–42. Moreover, part of this delay may result from extensive, and therefore expensive, post-trial briefing by the parties.

[172] Bledsoe, note 170, *supra*, at 141.

[173] Bledsoe, note 170, *supra*, at 133.

rule of greater deference on appeal to jury verdicts than to findings of fact by the judge.[174]

Finally, counsel's assessment of the need for "jury legislation": jury modification (or even nullification) of the letter of the law may be a factor in rare cases. While jury research indicates that judges and juries agree in 75% of all cases, much of their disagreement is due not only to differing assessments of the evidence, but also to the jury's recognition of "values which fall outside the official rules."[175] Juries thus have relaxed the letter of the law by substituting their own notions of comparative negligence for the rule of contributory negligence, or by "improperly" taking into account insurance, collateral benefits, mitigation and ability to pay.[176] Similarly, juries have refused to make findings supporting "technical defenses" based on statutes of frauds or limitations, or on releases or waivers obtained in unequal bargaining situations.[177]

§ 12.07   OBTAINING JURY TRIAL

[1]   The Right to Trial by Jury: The Federal Model

Federal courts and all of their state counterparts give litigants the right in some cases to have the facts tried before a jury.[178] The scope of the right varies from system to system. The United States Constitution does not confer a right to jury trial in *state* civil cases.[179] The courts of each state honor the right to the extent it is created in their constitutions or local statutes.[180] Federal courts rely on the United States Constitution and federal statutes.

The Seventh Amendment provides that "[i]n suits at common law, where the value in controversy shall exceed twenty dollars, the right of trial by jury shall be

---

[174] *See* §§ 13.09[2][b] & [c] (federal standards of review for findings by the court and by the jury), *infra.*

[175] Howard S. Erlanger, *Jury Research in America: Its Past and Future*, 4 Law & Soc. Rev. 345, 349 (1970). *See generally* Arie M. Rubenstein, *Verdicts of Conscience: Nullification and the Modern Jury Trial*, 106 Colum. L. Rev. 959 (2006).

[176] Erlanger, note 175, *supra*, at 350–51. *See generally* Arie M. Rubenstein, *Verdicts of Conscience: Nullification and the Modern Jury Trial*, 106 Colum. L. Rev. 959 (2006); Alan W. Scheflin & Jon M. Van Dyke, *Merciful Juries: The Resilience of Jury Nullification*, 48 Wash. & Lee L. Rev. 165 (1991).

[177] *See* Bledsoe, note 170, *supra*, at 135.

[178] In the broadest sense, jury right also takes in the right of persons to be jurors. "Jury duty is both a civic responsibility and an obligation of all qualified citizens. It is also a constitutional right of citizens recognized by the Supreme Court. *Powers v. Ohio*, 499 U.S. 400 (1991)." Am. Bar Ass'n, Principles for Juries and Jury Trials 10 (2005) *available at* http://www.americanbar.org/content/dam/aba/migrated/juryprojectstandards/principles.authcheckdam.pdf.

[179] *City of Monterey v. Del Monte Dunes at Monterey, Ltd.*, 526 U.S. 687, 719 (1999). In contrast, the Supreme Court has read the Sixth and Fourteenth Amendments to confer a right to jury trial in serious state *criminal* cases. *See, e.g., Duncan v. Louisiana*, 391 U.S. 145 (1968); *Blanton v. City of N. Las Vegas*, 489 U.S. 538 (1989).

[180] *Cf. Friedenthal, Kane & Miller* § 11.7 ("almost all states have . . . constitutional guarantees.").

preserved."[181] In one sense, the Amendment does not *create* a right to jury trial, or "guarantee" such a right in absolute terms.[182] It merely states that the right shall be "preserved." The significance of this distinction is that to some extent the process of determining which issues[183] entitle a litigant to claim a jury turns on history. The reckoning point is English common law in 1791, the year the Amendment was ratified.[184]

The right to a jury trial had been enjoyed to a greater or lesser extent in the colonies,[185] but the right preserved in the Seventh Amendment was that which existed under English law. In a long line of decisions,[186] the Supreme Court has read "common law" in the Seventh Amendment to refer to the jurisdiction of English common-law courts in 1791. These courts dispensed remedies "at law," including damage awards. Litigants in these courts enjoyed extensive rights to trial by jury. England administered at the same time a separate system of chancery or "equity"[187] courts, dispensing equitable remedies, including injunctions.[188] Juries were unavailable in equity proceedings.

The law-equity distinction has been central in determining the scope of the Seventh Amendment.[189] The distinction was significantly blurred, however, by the merger of law and equity proceedings brought about by the adoption of the Federal Rules of Civil Procedure.[190] The merger posed several serious questions

---

[181] There is no federal court right to jury trial, however, when the defendant is the United States. *City of Monterey*, 526 U.S. at 719.

[182] *See* MOORE § 38.10[1].

[183] "[T]he basic decisional unit in determining the existence of a right to jury trial is not the case. It is the particular issue within a case on which jury trial is demanded." 9 WRIGHT & MILLER § 2302.

[184] Not all agree. *See* AKHIL R. AMAR, THE BILL OF RIGHTS: CREATION AND RECONSTRUCTION 89 (1998) (asserting that reckoning point is forum state law); Stanton D. Krauss, *The Original Understanding of the Seventh Amendment Right to Jury Trial*, 33 U. RICH. L. REV. 407, 479–80 (1999) (arguing that reckoning point is in the discretion of Congress).

[185] "Each of the thirteen colonies, as might be expected, had developed an individual style and emphasis, in part because each had begun borrowing from a slightly different state of the English historical development." Edith G. Henderson, *The Background of the Seventh Amendment*, 80 HARV. L. REV. 289, 299 (1966).

[186] *See* the cases cited in MOORE § 38.10[2]. *See also Agfa Corp. v. Creo Prods.*, 451 F.3d 1366, 1373 (Fed. Cir. 2006); *Millsap v. McDonnell Douglas Corp.*, 368 F.3d 1246, 1252 n.4 (10th Cir. 2004).

[187] *See* § 8.02[2] (equity pleading and practice), *supra*.

[188] On the modern-day significance of damage and injunctive remedies, see Chapter 14, *infra*.

[189] *See, e.g.*, *City of Monterey*, 526 U.S. 687. Juries were also unavailable in English admiralty proceedings. In the broadest sense, then, "those actions that are analogous to 18th-century cases tried in courts of equity or admiralty do not require a jury trial." *Tull v. United States*, 481 U.S. 412, 417 (1987). Recent developments in the Supreme Court's Seventh Amendment jurisprudence suggest continued emphasis on the law-equity distinction, but less attention to the particulars of 18th century English practice. *See* note 198, *infra*.

[190] Rule 2 states: "There is one form of action — the civil action." The situation prior to adoption of the Federal Rules has been described as follows:

> Unlike some state systems, there have never been separate law and equity courts in the federal judicial system. But the first Process Act of 1789 introduced separate procedures for actions at law and suits in equity; and two distinct procedures for these civil actions — one applicable on the law side, the other on the equity side of the same court — continued down

about the right to jury trial in federal court. The Court answered three of them in a series of Seventh Amendment decisions establishing the modern trend favoring jury trials.[191]

The first question was whether there is a right to jury trial when the plaintiff brings an equitable claim, and defendant brings a legal counterclaim, or vice versa. The Court answered this question in *Beacon Theatres, Inc. v. Westover*.[192] Plaintiff in *Beacon* sued for equitable relief. Defendant counterclaimed for damages on antitrust grounds, demanding a jury trial. The Supreme Court held that, because the law and equity claims had issues in common, the trial court could not first try the equity portion without a jury. To permit this would "compel Beacon to split its antitrust case, trying part to a judge and part to a jury."[193] The Court apparently assumed that, because common factual issues resolved in the initial equity phase of the case would not be open to relitigation in the later jury phase, a jury trial on them would be lost to the defendant altogether.[194]

A second question was whether there was a right to jury trial in an action in which the plaintiff joins legal and equitable claims,[195] and the equitable claims predominate. The Court addressed this question in *Dairy Queen, Inc. v. Wood*.[196] Plaintiff sued over defendant's alleged failure to make payments due under a trademark licensing contract, seeking an injunction against defendant's continued use of the trademark and an accounting for the sum defendant owed. The Court looked behind plaintiff's labels and concluded that "insofar as the complaint requests a money judgment it presents a claim which is unquestionably legal."[197] The Seventh Amendment "right to trial by jury," said the Court, "cannot be made

---

to 1938 when the Federal Rules became effective.

Moore, 1999 *Rules Pamphlet Part 1*, ¶ 2.3.

[191] *Cf.* WRIGHT § 92 ("The Supreme Court has been zealous to safeguard, perhaps even to enlarge, the function of the jury.").

[192] 359 U.S. 500 (1959). *See generally* John C. McCoid, II, *Procedural Reform and the Right to Jury Trial: A Study of Beacon Theatres, Inc. v. Westover*, 116 U. PA. L. REV. 1 (1967).

[193] 359 U.S. at 508.

[194] *Id.* at 508 & n.10. This assumption of *Beacon* has been tied to the law of prior adjudications. FRIEDENTHAL, KANE & MILLER § 11.5. *Accord Lytle v. Household Mfg., Inc.*, 494 U.S. 545 (1990). Since, however, the effect of the issue determination in the equity phase of the case is felt prior to judgment, it may be more accurate to attribute any prejudicial effect to the law-of-the-case doctrine. *See generally* § 15.14, *infra.* For discussion of relatively rare instances where that doctrine has been applied to settled issues of fact (rather than law), see 18B WRIGHT & MILLER § 4478.

Since *Beacon*, the Court has ruled that a party may be precluded from relitigating facts before a jury in a legal action that were decided against him in a separate and prior equitable action. *Parklane Hosiery Co. v. Shore*, 439 U.S. 322 (1979).

[195] Rule 18 expressly permits the joinder of legal and equitable claims. *See generally* § 9.02, *supra.*

[196] 369 U.S. 469 (1962).

[197] *Id.* at 476. Viewing the plaintiff's "accounting" demand "[a]s an action on a debt allegedly due under a contract, it would be difficult to conceive of an action of a more traditionally legal character." *Id.* at 477 (footnote omitted). In fact, an accounting does trace its origins to equity, but the range of remedies now available under the federal rules, including the appointment of a special master under Rule 53(b) to assist the jury in complicated monetary computations, must be considered in characterizing a claim for purposes of deciding the Seventh Amendment question. *See* McCoid, note 192, *supra*, at 8–9.

to depend upon the choice of words used in the pleadings."[198] Moreover, the right applies "whether the trial judge chooses to characterize the legal issues presented as 'incidental' to the equitable issues or not."[199]

A third question posed by the merger of law and equity was whether jury trial was available for claims asserted by an historically equitable procedure, such as interpleader, a class action, or a derivative action. All these had been adopted by the Federal Rules of Civil Procedure.[200] The Court answered this question in *Ross v. Bernhard.*[201] In *Ross*, plaintiffs brought a shareholder's derivative action under Rule 23.1. The Court of Appeals held that the action was equitable and that none of it could be tried before a jury. Again the Supreme Court reversed. The shareholder derivative device was a creature of equity, and equitable principles still explain why shareholders in such suits can sue on behalf of the corporation. Yet the Court held that "the right to jury trial attaches to those issues in derivative actions as to which the corporation, if it had been suing in its own right, would have been entitled to a jury."[202] The Court added: "[A]s our cases indicate, the 'legal' nature of an issue is determined by considering, first, the pre-merger custom with reference to such questions; second, the remedy sought; and third, the practical abilities and limitations of juries."[203]

Congress has created many causes of action that were unknown to English jurisprudence in 1791. Nothing limits the authority of Congress to supplement the Seventh Amendment by creating a right to trial by jury in federal court whenever it wishes to.[204] But, in determining whether a *constitutional* right to jury trial exists for a statutory cause of action in which Congress has not expressly created a right to jury trial, federal courts have been required to determine whether the issue at hand most closely resembles something adjudicated on the law side or on the equity side of the line in 1791.[205] In *Curtis v. Loether,*[206] the plaintiff sought injunctive relief and damages against the defendant for violating her rights under

[198] 369 U.S. at 477–78.

[199] *Id.* at 473. *Accord Tull*, 481 U.S. at 424–25 (1987). Thus, *Beacon* and *Dairy Queen* together stand for the proposition that if, disregarding the parties' labels, there is any claim or defense in the case — incidental or otherwise — that would be characterized as legal at English common law, it must be tried first to a jury upon timely demand.

[200] *See* Rules 22, 23 & 23.1 respectively.

[201] 396 U.S. 531 (1970). *See generally* Note, *Ross v. Bernhard: The Uncertain Future of the Seventh Amendment*, 81 YALE L.J. 112 (1971); John G. Gibbons, Comment, *From Beacon Theatres to Dairy Queen to Ross: The Seventh Amendment, The Federal Rules, and a Receding Law-Equity Dichotomy*, 48 J. URBAN L. 459 (1971).

[202] 396 U.S. at 532–33.

[203] *Id.* at 538 n.10. The Supreme Court recently extended its holding in *Ross* to the general class action rule, Rule 23. *Ortiz v. Fibreboard Corp.*, 527 U.S. 815, 846 (1999).

[204] For examples, see MOORE § 38.44[3]. *See also Blackmon v. American Home Prods. Corp.*, 328 F. Supp. 2d 647, 657-58 (S.D. Tex. 2004).

[205] *See* notes 185–89 and related text, *supra*. Congress has also created many administrative enforcement schemes and specialized (Article I or legislative) courts in which it has failed to provide for jury trials. In addition to looking for historical analogies to decide the Seventh Amendment question in such cases, the Supreme Court has suggested that "public rights" can constitutionally be enforced in special non-jury proceedings. *See, e.g., Atlas Roofing Co. v. Occupational Safety & Health Review Comm'n*, 430 U.S. 442, 458 (1977). This formulation leaves the question of how one identifies such rights.

the Civil Rights Act of 1968. The plaintiff argued that the Seventh Amendment did not afford defendant the right to a jury trial because the statutory cause of action post-dated 1791. The Court rejected the plaintiff's argument. "It has long been settled that the right extends beyond the common law forms of action recognized at that time," the Court observed, and concluded that the Seventh Amendment guaranteed the defendant a jury trial because the "action involves rights and remedies of the sort typically enforced in an action at law."

Thirteen years later, in *Tull v. United States*,[207] the United States brought suit against a developer for violation of the Clean Water Act. The district court denied defendant's demand for a jury trial. After a bench trial (trial before the judge), the court found that defendant acted in violation of the Act and imposed numerous fines. The Court of Appeals affirmed. The Supreme Court reversed on Seventh Amendment grounds. "Prior to the enactment of the Seventh Amendment," it noted, "English courts had held that a civil penalty suit was a particular species of an action in debt that was within the jurisdiction of the courts of law."[208] The case was thus "clearly analogous to the 18th-century action in debt, and federal courts have rightly assumed that the Seventh Amendment required a jury trial."[209]

Many commentators find the historical approach to defining the scope of the Seventh Amendment troublesome. Even if the content of old English law was clear, analogizing new issues to it would at times be perplexing.[210] Matters are worse because the line between law and equity at that time was not terribly clear.[211] Moreover, sorting cases by historical category obscures useful thought about policies that should shape the contemporary roles of judge and jury. In line with these concerns, the Supreme Court has begun to downplay the importance of divining eighteenth-century English analogies to resolve jury questions under the Seventh Amendment. Rather, "the search for analogs is only preliminary to a more functional question whether the remedy sought is legal or equitable. In *Tull*, in fact, after reviewing and crediting historical analogs in law and equity, the Court concluded that "we need not decide the question" and "reiterate[d] our previously expressed view that characterizing the relief sought is '[m]ore important' than finding a precisely analogous common law cause of action in determining whether the Seventh Amendment guarantees a jury trial." In light of that inquiry, the Court concluded that the relief sought was more equitable in nature, and that the jury right did not attach.[212]

---

[206] 415 U.S. 189 (1974).

[207] 481 U.S. 412 (1987).

[208] *Id.* at 418.

[209] *Id.* Using a similar approach later, in *Feltner v. Columbia Pictures Television*, 523 U.S. 340 (1998), the Supreme Court saw a historic jury analog to the determination of statutory damages under the Copyright Act of 1976 and ruled that a right to jury trial existed under the Seventh Amendment.

[210] Declaratory judgments, for example, posed difficulties of classification. For discussion of developments, see FRIEDENTHAL, KANE & MILLER § 11.5.

[211] JAMES, HAZARD & LEUBSDORF § 8.2.

[212] *See also Chauffeurs, Teamsters and Helpers, Local No. 391 v. Terry*, 494 U.S. 558, 569 (1990) ("The right to a jury trial includes more than the common-law forms of action recognized in 1791; the phrase 'Suits at common law' refers to 'suits in which legal rights [are] to be ascertained and determined,

In short, historical precedents for contemporary causes of action remain the starting point in the Court's Seventh Amendment analysis, and when they provide clear and convincing answers, may remain sufficient to guide the Court's analysis.[213] When, however, the historical record is ambiguous, a more functional analysis may take precedence.[214]

On another front, the growing controversy over the role of juries in complex litigation has created additional pressure on the Supreme Court to address the right to jury trial problem in a manner that takes the demands of contemporary litigation more directly into account. Juries in complex cases may be required to listen to more than a year of testimony and to consider reams of documentary evidence. Jury suffering aside, the situation offers the disagreeable prospect of jury members so overwhelmed that they are incapable of rational decision. Perhaps the Seventh Amendment should not be read to require a jury in such cases.[215] Supreme Court dicta may leave room for this conclusion.[216] Perhaps jury deliberation under such circumstances would produce deliberative incoherence raising countervailing constitutional due process concerns.[217]

The language of the Seventh Amendment, however, may not be broad or general enough to accommodate this policy concern. Nor, for that matter, can we assume that judges as factfinders would necessarily be superior in unraveling

---

in contradistinction to those where equitable rights alone [are] recognized."). Thus, while historical analysis accounting for the law-equity dividing line is likely to remain central to Seventh Amendment decisions, obsession with historical details of 18th century English practice is waning. Writing separately in *Terry*, Justice Brennan urged a complete break. He wrote that "our insistence that the jury trial right hinges in part on a comparison of the substantive right at issue to forms of action used in English courts 200 years ago needlessly convolutes our Seventh Amendment jurisprudence." *Id.* at 575. "I would decide Seventh Amendment questions on the basis of the relief sought. If the relief is legal in nature, *i.e.*, if it is the kind of relief that historically was available from courts of law, I would hold that the parties have a constitutional right to a trial by jury." *Id.*

[213] *City of Monterey*, 526 U.S. 687 (finding a right to a jury in a 1983 action against a city to recover for an unconstitutional taking of property, because the better historical analog was to a suit for damages, and not eminent domain).

[214] *Markman v. Westview Instruments, Inc.*, 517 U.S. 370 (1996) (concluding that the interpretation of a patent claim is better resolved by the judge than a jury, observing that "[w]here history and precedent provide no clear answers, functional considerations also play their part in the choice between judge and jury to define terms of art").

[215] *See Cotten v. Witco Chem. Corp.*, 651 F.2d 274, 276 (5th Cir. 1981) (reversing grant of motion to strike jury demand and stating that *if* "complexity exception" to Seventh Amendment exists it is only for cases so complex that jury could not render rational decision based upon reasonable understanding of evidence), *cert. denied*, 455 U.S. 909 (1982).

[216] The Court held out the possibility in *Beacon* that there might be "imperative circumstances" that would justify trying common issues in a nonjury trial, 359 U.S. at 510–11, and in *Dairy Queen* that there might be "a rare case" in which matters "are of such a 'complicated nature' that only a court of equity can satisfactorily unravel them," 369 U.S. at 478. Its refined historical test from *Ross* also directs the courts to take into account the "practical abilities and limitations of juries" when deciding the Seventh Amendment question. 396 U.S. at 538 n.10. But in *Terry*, the Court reminded courts that it had "never relied on [consideration of a jury's competency] 'as an independent basis for extending the right to a jury trial under the Seventh Amendment.'" 494 U.S. at 565 (quoting *Tull*, 481 U.S. at 418 n.4).

[217] *But see SRI Int'l v. Matsushita Elec. Corp.*, 775 F.2d 1107, 1128 (Fed. Cir. 1985) (dictum) (the due process argument "confuses the route with the destination, for 'due process' is just that, a process . . . . It is not a result.").

complications.[218] The Ninth Circuit noted, in rejecting a complexity exception to the Seventh Amendment, that

> Jurors, if properly instructed and treated with deserved respect, bring collective intelligence, wisdom, and dedication to their tasks, which is rarely equaled in other areas of public service . . . . We do not accept [the view] "that a single judge is brighter than the jurors, collectively functioning together."[219]

As a result, the complexity exception has received mixed reviews in the appellate courts.[220] The Third Circuit has hinted at one,[221] the Ninth has rejected it,[222] and the Second[223] and Fifth Circuits[224] have refused to apply it using language raising doubt whether it exists. The debate rages on,[225] awaiting Supreme Court resolution.

[2] Claiming a Jury Trial

State and federal court litigants are free to waive their right to jury trials. Most systems find waiver in the failure of a party to demand a jury within a requisite period of time.[226] Federal Rule 38 provides an illustration.

Rule 38(a) recites that rights to jury trial created under the Seventh Amendment or by congressional enactment "is preserved to the parties inviolate." Rule 38(b) describes the procedure for demanding a jury:

> On any issue triable of right by a jury, a party may demand a jury trial by: (1) serving the other parties with a written demand — which may be included in a pleading — no later than 10 days after the last pleading directed to the issue is served . . . .[227]

Under Rule 38(d), the failure of a party to make an effective jury demand within the time allowed "waives by jury trial." Waiver occurs whether the right to trial by

---

[218] Nor can we even assume that all factual controversies are capable of rational resolution. *See* § 12.08[1] (the institutional role of juries in difficult cases), *infra*.

[219] *In re U.S. Fin. Sec. Litig.*, 609 F.2d 411, 430–31 (9th Cir. 1979) (*quoting* Patrick E. Higginbotham, *Continuing The Dialogue: Civil Juries and the Allocation of Judicial Power*, 56 TEX. L. REV. 47, 53 (1977)), *cert. denied*, 446 U.S. 929 (1980).

[220] *See* George K. Chamberlin, *Complexity of Civil Action as Affecting Seventh Amendment Right to Trial By Jury*, 54 A.L.R. FED. 733 (1981 and 1999 Supp.).

[221] *In re Japanese Elec. Prods. Antitrust Litig.*, 631 F.2d 1069 (3d Cir. 1980).

[222] *In re U.S. Fin. Sec. Litig.*, 609 F.2d 411.

[223] *City of New York v. Pullman, Inc.*, 662 F.2d 910, 919 (2d Cir. 1981).

[224] *Cotten v. Witco Chem. Corp.*, 651 F.2d 274, 276 (5th Cir. 1981), *cert. denied*, 455 U.S. 909 (1982).

[225] "Much has been written on every side of this argument." WRIGHT § 92. *See generally* Graham C. Lilly, *The Decline of the American Jury*, 72 U. COLO. L. REV. 53 (2001); Joseph Sanders, *Scientifically Complex Cases, Trial by Jury, and the Erosion of Adversarial Processes*, 48 DEPAUL L. REV. 355 (1998); Stephen I. Friedland, *The Competency and Responsibility of Jurors in Deciding Cases*, 85 NW. U. L. REV. 190 (1990); Patrick Devlin, *Equity, Due Process and the Seventh Amendment*, 81 MICH. L. REV. 1571 (1983).

[226] JAMES, HAZARD & LEUBSDORF § 8.5.

[227] Once a party makes an effective jury demand, he may not withdraw it without the consent of the other parties in the case. Rule 38(d).

jury would have been conferred by the Seventh Amendment or by congressional enactment.[228] This contrasts with the traditional reluctance of the Supreme Court to infer waiver of constitutional rights.[229]

There is a ray of hope for a party neglecting to demand a jury trial, in that the trial court has discretion to order one anyway.[230] However, "district judges have been extremely reluctant to exercise this discretion."[231] A party may also amend its pleading to inject a legal issue and start the twenty-eight-day clock running again under Rule 39(a), but the courts look askance at amendments made just to recover a previously waived jury right.[232]

§ 12.08 JUDGE-JURY INTERACTION; VERDICTS

[1] Allocating Issues Between Judge and Jury — An Overview

Unsettled questions about the truth (what did or did not happen) place the case within the sacred preserve of the jury. Jury verdicts should and usually do govern cases where a rational response to the evidence could be a verdict for *either* plaintiff or defendant.

There are at least two arguments for giving juries the last word in such cases.[233] The first is that a group of people (the jury) will be better able to reach the right decision than a single person (judge or juror). The Supreme Court observed:

> Twelve men of the average of the community, comprising men of education and men of little education, men of learning and men whose learning consists only in what they have themselves seen and heard, the merchant, the mechanic, the farmer, the laborer; these sit together, consult, apply their separate experience of the affairs of life to the facts proven, and draw a unanimous conclusion. This average judgment thus given it is the great effort of law to obtain. It is assumed that twelve men know more of the common affairs of life than does one man, that they can draw wiser and safer conclusions from admitted facts thus occurring than can a single judge.[234]

---

[228] A party need not claim a jury to protect his right to jury trial if another party in the case has already claimed one. "[A]ll of the parties to the action who are interested in the issues for which jury trial has been demanded may rely on that demand . . . ." 9 WRIGHT & MILLER § 2318.

[229] See, e.g., Johnson v. Zerbst, 304 U.S. 458, 464 (1938)).

[230] Rule 39(b) states: "the court may, on motion, order a jury trial on any issue for which a jury might have been demanded."

[231] 9 WRIGHT & MILLER § 2321.

[232] See, e.g., American Home Prods. Corp. v. Johnson & Johnson, McNeilab, Inc., 5 Fed. R. Serv. 3d (Callaghan) 581, 584–89 (S.D.N.Y. 1986).

[233] See § 12.06, supra.

[234] Sioux City & Pacific Railroad Co. v. Stout, 84 U.S. 657, 664 (1874). Today, this rationale is least likely to hold up in exceedingly complex cases, where even the Seventh Amendment right to jury trial is under fire. See § 12.07[1], supra.

The second argument reaches a conclusion of jury autonomy from the opposite direction. When the evidence provides reasonable bases for conflicting results, perhaps there is no right result.[235] Yet the need for decision remains, and what the judicial process in such cases lacks in precision it can try to make up for in pageantry. Trial before and decision by a jury gives the loser his "day in court" in the fullest popular sense. It seasons resolution of controversies that the law is powerless to decide[236] with a measure of public opinion.

However, there is a serious limitation on jury power. Matters of law are the exclusive concern of the judge.[237] The law-fact distinction pervades law delineating the trial roles of judge and jury, often circumscribing the latter. The judge's function as guardian of the law authorizes him to decide what facts are worthy of the jury's consideration,[238] how the jury should consider them,[239] and whether, in appropriate cases, the jury's verdict should be erased[240] or even turned around.[241]

[2] Evidentiary Controls

The first opportunity to examine the evidence goes not to the jury but to the judge. When called upon to do so by timely objection, the trial court considers whether the evidence should go to the jury (be admitted). The law of evidence is quite extensive and the subject of a major law school course usually taken after civil procedure.

In setting the scope of discovery,[242] civil procedure gives a less stringent meaning to the term *relevance* than does the law of evidence.[243] Yet relevance in

---

[235] *See* Jerome Michael, *The Basic Rules of Pleading,* 5 RECORD OF N.Y.C.B.A. 175, 199–200 (1950).

[236] The fact that none of the motions for deciding the merits (beginning with demurrer/Rule 12(b)(6) and ending with judgment n.o.v. or judgment as a matter of law) works in such cases means that decision as a pure matter of law never materializes. For a survey and comparison of motions deciding the merits, see § 12.09[3][c], *infra.*

[237] The law-fact distinction is not always easy to draw. *See generally* Mark S. Brodin, *Accuracy, Efficiency, and Accountability in the Litigation Process — The Case for the Fact Verdict,* 59 U. CINN. L. REV. 15 (1990). And, as is generally true with the technique of characterization in legal analysis, it is open to abuse. *Cf.* Joseph Morse, *Characterization: Shadow or Substance,* 49 COLUM. L. REV. 1027 (1949) (noting frailties of characterization associated with conflict of laws). *See* § 13.09[2][a] (fact-law distinction on appeal), *infra.*

[238] *See* § 12.08[2] (evidentiary controls), *infra.* He also decides facts underlying preliminary defenses. *See* §§ 8.07[2][b] & [c], *supra.*

[239] *See* § 12.08[3] (jury instructions), *infra.*

[240] *See* § 12.09[2] (new trials), *infra.*

[241] *See* § 12.09[1][b] (judgments notwithstanding the verdict), *infra.*

[242] Rule 26(b)(1), generally limiting discovery, states that "[r]elevant information need not be admissible at the trial if the discovery appears reasonably calculated to lead to the discovery of admissible evidence." *See* § 10.03 (the federal presumption of discoverability), *supra.*

[243] When evidence offered at trial cannot support any rule of law applicable to the case, to admit it would at best clutter the case with inconsequential fact and at worst induce the jury to render a verdict unsupported by law. The court will exclude such evidence as irrelevant or immaterial. The court may also exclude evidence if it is unreliable (if there is a sufficient possibility that it is not what it is offered to be) or if it is prejudicial (it is likely to inflame or prejudice the jury). *See generally* MCCORMICK ON EVIDENCE ch. 16 (Kenneth S. Brown ed., 6th ed. 2006).

the law of evidence is rooted in civil procedure. The boundaries of relevance at trial are set by the pleadings. These boundaries may narrow as a result of motion practice prior to trial[244] or pretrial orders.[245] Or they may be enlarged by amendment conforming the pleadings to evidence admitted at trial.[246]

In federal courts, the law of evidence is codified in the Federal Rules of Evidence. Although these were originally proposed in the same manner as the Federal Rules of Civil Procedure, under authority of the Rules Enabling Act,[247] congressional concern about the displacement of state laws of privilege[248] led to the revision and enactment of the rules as statutory law.[249]

[3] Instructing the Jury

In nonjury cases, the judge is both the law enforcer and the trier of fact. Since both functions are performed by the same person, fine distinctions separating the two will usually be unnecessary.

Matters are quite different, however, in jury trials. Jurors use the evidence to answer factual questions.[250] But they may not resolve issues about the meaning or application of law. Only the judge does that.[251] Not only is the judge an authority on all legal questions, she must also see to it that the law is enforced. One way in which the judge must maintain legal control is in the way she instructs (charges) the jury.

> Simple, vague instructions allow the jury to decide the case with little guidance . . . . If a judge gives detailed and comprehensive jury instructions relating to the substantive law to be applied by the jury (as opposed to "housekeeping" instructions), the judge is staking out a relatively large perimeter surrounding the "legal" issues that the jury must not cross. Detailed instructions correspondingly diminish the jury's remaining function, finding the "facts" of the case. The more detailed and comprehensive the instructions, the less discretion the jury enjoys to "make law" by

---

[244] For example, from the award of partial summary judgment. On summary judgments, see generally § 11.03, *supra*.

[245] On pretrial orders, *see* § 12.03[3], *supra*.

[246] *See* § 8.10[2], *supra*.

[247] *See* § 1.02 (explaining procedure for creating federal rules of civil procedure), *supra*.

[248] *Cf.* § 7.04 (discussing relation of federal procedural law and state law), *supra*.

[249] After the Supreme Court transmitted the proposed Federal Rules of Evidence to Congress, Congress deferred their effective date until such time as they were enacted into law. Pub. L. No. 93-12; 87 Stat. 9 (March 30, 1973). The proposed rules, as modified by Congress, were subsequently enacted into law. Pub. L. No. 93-595, 88 Stat. 1926 (Jan. 2, 1975).

[250] In federal and many state courts, the judge has the right to comment on the evidence as an aid to the jury. MOORE § 51.10. She may not distort it or add to it, of course, *see Quercia v. United States*, 289 U.S. 466 (1933), and the jury is typically reminded that, as the sole trier of fact, it has the right to disagree with her. *See, e.g., Trezza v. Dame*, 370 F.2d 1006, 1009 (5th Cir. 1967).

[251] The point is explored at greater length in the discussion of directed verdicts, judgments notwithstanding the verdict, and judgments as a matter of law in § 12.09, *infra*.

applying its own notions as to what the statute really says, or as to what elementary fairness requires.[252]

Consider an illustration. At trial in an automobile accident case, the jury is presented with conflicting evidence on the question whether plaintiff's own carelessness was a contributing cause of the accident. The jury, not the judge, must weigh the evidence and answer the question. However, only the judge can determine what the answer to the question means to the outcome of the case.[253] Thus, the judge must not only decide what tort law principle applies but limit the work of the jury to the confines of that principle. Assume that the judge concludes that the governing principle is that contributory negligence is an absolute bar to recovery. She might impose this on the jury by saying in her instructions: "Members of the jury, if you find that plaintiff's carelessness was a contributing cause of the accident, you *must* return a verdict for defendant."

In many jurisdictions, *pattern jury instructions* have been prepared for use in civil cases.[254] The authority of such standardized instructions lies somewhere between the authority of appendix of forms to the Federal Rules of Civil Procedure[255] and form pleadings and interrogatories,[256] depending upon how they were assembled. But even when they were assembled by a committee appointed by the courts, they must be used with caution.

> They may not be swallowed whole. They are intended as an aid to the preparation of appropriate instruction in a particular case. Each case has its own peculiar facts, and formalized instructions must be tailored to the requirements of the facts and the issues.[257]

The parties have the right to propose appropriate jury instructions. Rule 51 treats the manner in which jury instructions are to be prepared and given in federal court. Parties may file written requests for jury instructions and "[t]he court must inform the parties of its proposed instructions and proposed action on the requests before instructing the jury and before final jury arguments." A federal court may instruct the jury before or after argument or both.

---

[252] Ronald W. Eades, *The Problem of Jury Instructions in Civil Cases*, 27 Cumb. L. Rev. 1017, 1018 (1997) (citation omitted).

[253] *But cf.* 9B Wright & Miller § 2503 ("Some of the most famous students of the judicial process have argued that one of the purposes of the jury system is to permit the jury to temper strict rules of law by the demands and necessities of substantial justice, thereby adding a much needed element of flexibility."). *See also* § 12.06, *supra*.

[254] *See, e.g.,* Edward Devitt, Charles B. Blackmar & Michael A. Wolff, Federal Jury Practice and Instructions (4th ed. 1987 and 1992), which is widely used in federal courts. *See generally* Eades, note 252, *supra*, at 1020–23; Robert G. Nieland, Pattern Jury Instructions: A Critical Look at a Modern Movement to Improve the Jury System (1979).

[255] *See* Rule 84 (forms "suffice under [the] rules").

[256] *See* §§ 1.02 (sources of civil procedure) & 10.09[2] (interrogatories), *supra*.

[257] Devitt et al., note 254, *supra*, § 8.03. *See generally* Walter W. Steele, Jr. & Elizabeth G. Thornburg, *Jury Instructions: A Persistent Failure to Communicate*, 67 N.C. L. Rev. 77 (1988).

Whether or not the parties request instructions, a judge has the duty in most jurisdictions to instruct the jury on the applicable law.[258] However, the failure to request specific instructions may operate as a waiver; the judge is charged only with instructing on "the broad general fundamental rules of law."[259] Moreover, Rule 51 is typical in providing that a party may challenge instructions on appeal only if he objected "on the record, stating distinctly the matter objected to and the grounds for the objection." Failure to object usually puts an end to the matter, subject only to a narrow common law power in the appellate courts to correct *plain errors* — errors so egregious that the trial courts should have known them when they saw them.[260]

Errors of law in jury instructions are among the most common grounds for new trials.[261] The appellate courts decide the correctness of the instructions *de novo* (anew).[262] But they view the instructions as a whole, including any curative instructions,[263] and reverse only for prejudicial error.[264]

[4] Verdicts

In the usual civil jury trial, the jury is charged with returning a *general verdict*, that is, a verdict for one side or another supplying no explanation why the jury decided as it did. Such verdicts are in extensive use and can work well in relatively simple cases. Their weakness is that they fail to illuminate the jurors' decision-making process. It is fairly easy for jurors to ignore constraints and admonitions in the charge when they can hide behind a general verdict. It is also difficult to preserve the work of the jury if problems arise with the case on appeal of a general verdict.[265]

The *special verdict* is an alternative intended to address these shortcomings. Jury instructions designed to elicit a special verdict contain a series of short-

---

[258] *See, e.g., Turner Constr. Co. v. Houlihan*, 240 F.2d 435, 439 (1st Cir. 1957). *But see Ouille v. Saliba*, 149 So. 2d 468, 469 (Miss. 1963) (in absence of request for instructions on counterclaim, judge "cannot instruct the jury on his own motion").

[259] *Turner Constr. Co.*, 240 F.2d at 439.

[260] "Actual reversals on the basis of plain error are rare, though they have become more numerous in recent years." 9C WRIGHT & MILLER § 2558. *See* § 13.08[2] (preservation of error below as predicate for review), *infra*.

[261] *See* § 12.09[2][c] (new trials), *infra*.

[262] *See* § 13.09[2][a] (the *de novo* standard of review), *infra*.

[263] *See, e.g., Ayoub v. Spencer*, 550 F.2d 164, 167 (3d Cir.), *cert. denied*, 432 U.S. 907 (1977) ("Our function is to determine whether the charge, taken as a whole and viewed in the light of the evidence, fairly and adequately submits the issues in the case to the jury.").

[264] Rule 61. *See generally* § 13.08[1] (prejudicial effect as predicate for review), *infra*.

[265] "For example, if a prevailing plaintiff asserts several possible theories of recovery, and the appellate court finds the evidence for one of those theories to have been admitted erroneously, a new trial on all issues will be required because there is no way of discovering which theory the jury relied on in reaching the verdict." FRIEDENTHAL, KANE & MILLER § 12.1. In summing up the deficiencies of the general verdict, a recent commentator described it as "the ultimate in 'black box decision-making.' . . . This product of jury deliberations comes into court . . . with no indication whether it is based upon particular findings of fact, or particular interpretation of law, or both, or neither." Brodin, *supra*, note 237, at 34.

answer fact questions.[266] The jurors answer the questions instead of designating a winner. From all the answers, the judge constructs the equivalent of a general verdict. If the answers appear inconsistent, the judge is obliged to "attempt to reconcile the jury's findings, by exegesis if necessary" before either resubmitting them or ordering a new trial.[267]

Parties to complex cases may prefer a special verdict because of the guidance it gives the jury in fact-finding.[268] However, they have no right to have the jury return a special verdict in federal courts. They can only request one.[269] Many trial judges have been reluctant to use the device. Some reluctance may stem from the fact that judges are unfamiliar with it. Some apparently comes from a fear of encroaching upon the independence of the jury.[270] Compared to general verdicts at least, special verdicts do impose tighter controls and may therefore reflect a more suspicious attitude toward juries.[271] Finally, some hesitation to use special verdicts stems from concern about the possibility of inconsistent findings.[272]

Some courts seem receptive to a compromise: a general verdict accompanied with answers to written interrogatories. Federal Rule 49(b) provides this option, again, at the discretion of the court. This verdict form permits jurors to declare a winner but requires them to show their work. However, it is even more vulnerable to inconsistencies than the special verdict, since the jury's answers may be inconsistent not only with each other, but also with the general verdict. Subdivision (b) proposes different solutions for this problem, none of them entirely reassuring.

---

[266] Rule 49(a), governing special verdicts in federal court, refers to "written questions susceptible of a categorical or other brief answer." On the uses and contributions of special verdicts in federal litigation, see *Brodin, supra*, note 237, at 62–84.

[267] *Gallick v. Baltimore & Ohio R.R. Co.*, 372 U.S. 108, 119 (1963). *See generally* Donald Olander, Note, *Resolving Inconsistencies in Federal Special Verdicts*, 53 FORDHAM L. REV. 1089 (1984).

[268] *See* Elizabeth A. Faulkner, *Using the Special Verdict to Manage Complex Cases and Avoid Compromise Verdicts*, 21 ARIZ. ST. L.J. 297 (1989). Another, less common reason for requesting a special verdict may be to isolate particular facts. For example, a public figure who brings a libel action may be as interested in having a jury find that the libel was false as he is in recovering, and more likely to obtain the former, too, given the heavy burden of proving actual malice. For a criticism of these "trial-splitting" devices, *see* Jennifer M. Granholm & William J. Richards, *Bifurcated Justice: How Trial-Splitting Devices Defeat the Jury's Role*, 26 U. TOL. L. REV. 505 (1995) (arguing that special verdicts are improper and are rooted in "a deep-seated distrust of the jury" by judges and litigators).

[269] Rule 49(a) "is permissive, not mandatory. Whether a special or general verdict is to be returned (by the jury) rests in the sound discretion of the trial court." 9B WRIGHT & MILLER § 2505.

[270] FRIEDENTHAL, KANE & MILLER § 12.1.

[271] A special verdict "puts psychological pressure on the jurors to adhere to their legally prescribed functions and to prevent them from deciding cases on grounds they are instructed to ignore." JAMES, HAZARD & LEUBSDORF § 7.23.

[272] *See generally* Shaun P. Martin, *Rationalizing the Irrational: The Treatment of Untenable Federal Civil Jury Verdicts*, 28 CREIGHTON L. REV. 683 (1995). Of course, general verdicts, too, can be inconsistent. Shaun P. Martin, *Rationalizing the Irrational: The Treatment of Untenable Federal Civil Jury Verdicts*, 28 CREIGHTON L. REV. 683 (1995) Motions for j.n.o.v. (judgment as a matter of law in federal courts) or new trial can be used to control the jury in such cases. *See* § 12.09, *infra*.

§ 12.09 TAKING THE CASE FROM THE JURY: MOTIONS FOR JUDGMENT AS A MATTER OF LAW AND FOR NEW TRIAL

[1] Directed Verdicts and Judgments N.O.V. Rephrased as Judgments as a Matter of Law

After trial has begun, a party may move the court to render judgment without letting the case go to a jury verdict, or (if a verdict has been entered) to render judgment overturning the verdict. Traditional terminology for the first such order is *directed verdict* and, for the orders of the second type, *judgment n.o.v.* (or judgment notwithstanding the verdict).

A 1991 amendment to Rule 50 of the Federal Rules of Civil Procedure discarded the two terms in favor of the single phrase, *judgment as a matter of law.* Yet, for several reasons, the change may not be terribly important. First, the amendment will work little if any change in decisionmaking,[273] since the test for a judgment as a matter of law appears to be the same as the test previously applied to both directed verdicts and judgments n.o.v. Second, many state courts will continue for the foreseeable future to be governed by procedural law employing the two older terms. Third, even federal courts may continue to employ them, since directed verdict and judgment n.o.v. are useful to differentiate the two subspecies of the topic covered by the more generic term, judgment as a matter of law.

By whatever name, separate procedural devices for taking the jury out of the picture before or after a verdict still function in all American courts. It continues to be important to grasp their similarities and differences and, for convenience and clarity of discussion, it will be useful to refer to them by their traditional titles, directed verdict and judgment n.o.v.

Motions for directed verdict and for judgment notwithstanding the verdict have much in common. Each is governed by the same legal standard. They can and often do address the same factual record. Appellate courts freely reexamine decisions on both. For all that, we shall see that each makes a discrete contribution as part of a series of motions screening the merits of the case.

---

[273] The Advisory Committee note to the 1991 amendment makes this clear, stating that the new terminology "effects no change in the existing standard. That existing standard was not expressed in the former rule, but was articulated in long-standing case law." For a dissenting view, that the outcome in some cases may be affected by the amendment, see Michael J. Waggoner, *New Rule 50 May End Directed Verdicts for Plaintiffs*, 22 Sw. U. L. Rev. 389 (1993).

The Advisory Committee also stated that the change in terminology was merely a technicality. "If a motion is denominated a motion for directed verdict or for judgment notwithstanding the verdict, the party's error is merely formal. Such a motion should be treated as a motion for judgment as a matter of law in accordance with this rule."

[a]   The Theoretical Justification for Court Intervention in Jury Cases

Recall that the function of the jury is to deliberate, to weigh the evidence in choosing between a result favorable to plaintiff or to defendant. Juries derive their autonomy from the character of the evidence in the case. So long as evidence creates a genuine and substantial controversy over who should win, juries should and do have the last word. Judges have the last word, however, when the evidence supports only one side.[274]

The jury's verdict could coincide with the only right result in such cases. Once, however, the jury loses authority to choose between conflicting results, its presence becomes incidental.

The conclusion that the evidence supports only one result in the case can be as evident to the court before the jury deliberates as after. The first opportunity to end the case thus comes by means of a motion for directed verdict, whereby the court can interpose its decision on the evidence and keep the jury from ever considering the case. The second opportunity comes by means of a motion for judgment n.o.v.[275] (judgment notwithstanding the verdict), whereby the court can reverse a jury verdict unsupported by evidence.

[b]   The Legal Standard Governing Directed Verdicts and Judgments N.O.V.

Each system applies a single legal standard to decide both directed verdicts and judgments n.o.v.[276] Rule 50 provides that a district court may grant such a motion if "the court finds that a reasonable jury would not have a legally sufficient evidentiary basis to find for the party" opposing the motion. But how much evidence is needed to meet such a standard? Courts have answered that question in seemingly different ways, suggesting the possibility of varying tests. For example, one Fifth Circuit case (quoting circuit precedent) declared that imposing judgment under Rule 50 is appropriate only if there is a "complete absence of probative facts

---

[274] That is, they have the authority to resolve the merits of the case in favor of the only litigant whose position is supported by the evidence. "Whether the evidence presented at trial is sufficient to create an issue of fact for the jury or will permit the court to enter judgment as a matter of law is solely a question of law to be determined by the trial court." 9B WRIGHT & MILLER § 2524. In other situations, the judge may not have the last word in this sense but does have the authority to undo the work of the jury by ordering a new trial. See § 12.09[2], *infra*. New trial decisions based on an evaluation of the evidence are governed by a different legal standard from the one governing directed verdicts and judgments n.o.v. discussed in this subsection. 9B WRIGHT & MILLER § 2524.

[275] From the Latin phrase *non obstante veredicto*.

[276] Thus, in federal court, the "standard . . . is the same whether it arises in the procedural context of a motion for judgment as a matter of law prior to the submission of the case to the jury or in the context of a renewed motion for judgment as a matter of law after the jury has returned a verdict." 9B WRIGHT & MILLER § 2524. That standard has been express in Rule 50 since 1991. After technical revisions made by amendment in 2007, Rule 50(a) states that a judgment as a matter of law may be entered "[i]f a party has been fully heard on an issue during a jury trial and the court finds that a reasonable jury would not have a legally sufficient evidentiary basis to find for the party on that issue . . . ."

supporting the nonmovant's position."[277] Another Fifth Circuit case (also quoting circuit precedent) seemed less exacting, observing that judgment under Rule 50 is appropriate "not only when the nonmovant presents no evidence," but also "when there is not a sufficient conflict in substantial evidence to create a jury question."[278]

As a practical matter, however, these differences tend to be illusory, as the courts have steered a middle course. "The court should review the record as a whole," the Supreme Court has said, but "it must disregard all evidence favorable to the moving party that the jury is not required to believe. That is, the court should give credence to the evidence favoring the nonmovant as well as that 'evidence supporting the moving party that is uncontradicted and unimpeached, at least to the extent that that evidence comes from disinterested witnesses.' "[279] On the other hand, the existence of just *any* favorable evidence (no matter how meager) will not protect federal litigants from directed verdicts or judgments n.o.v. The test federal courts usually administer has often been called the *substantial evidence* test. Evidence is substantial in this sense when it is capable of providing a reasonable basis for a juror to find for the party opposing the directed verdict or judgment n.o.v. motion. Or, as one federal circuit court put it, the test

> [I]s whether the evidence is such that, without weighing the credibility of the witnesses or otherwise considering the weight of the evidence, there can be but one conclusion as to the verdict that reasonable men [or women] could have reached.[280]

To call this the substantial evidence test has always been somewhat misleading.[281] It suggests that the motion tests the quality or weight of the evidence, when it really tests whether there is *sufficient* evidence from which a reasonable jury could find against the movant. It is more useful to describe it as a "reasonable juror" test, and the 1991 amendment to Rule 50(a) should encourage this shift in thinking by expressly referring to a "reasonable jury" standard.

[2] New Trial Motions

[a] In General

The most widely used form of judicial control of juries is the order granting a new trial on all or some part of the issues. The power to set aside verdicts and grant new trials was well established in 1791 and is therefore consistent with the

---

[277] *Dance v. Ensco Offshore Co.*, 2009 U.S. App. LEXIS 2973 (5th Cir. Feb. 17, 2009).

[278] *Newsome v. Collin County*, 2006 U.S. App. LEXIS 17874 (5th Cir. July 14, 2006).

[279] *Reeves v. Sanderson Plumbing Prods., Inc.*, 530 U.S. 133, 151 (2000) (quoting 9B WRIGHT & MILLER § 2529).

[280] *Simblest v. Maynard*, 427 F.2d 1, 4 (2d Cir. 1970). The United States Supreme Court has observed that "the standard for a directed verdict under Federal Rule of Civil Procedure 50(a) . . . is that the trial judge must direct a verdict if, under the governing law, there can be but one reasonable conclusion as to the verdict . . . . If reasonable minds could differ as to the import of the evidence, however, a verdict should not be directed." *Anderson v. Liberty Lobby, Inc.*, 477 U.S. 242, 250 (1986).

[281] *See* note 280, *supra*.

constitutional guarantee of jury trial.[282] All jurisdictions permit this control and confer broad (in some circumstances, practically unreviewable) discretion on the trial judge to deploy it. But all also sharply restrict its availability to a short period — twenty-eight days in federal courts[283] — after the verdict is returned or judgment is entered.

The grounds for new trial are as numerous as the sources of possible error in the trial. Some states rules list the grounds,[284] but Federal Rule 59(a)(1) and many state rules simply authorize new trial for "any reason for which a new trial has heretofore been granted in an action at law in federal court." Most grounds for new trial, however, fall into two categories. The first and most troublesome category consists of errors in the jury's evaluation of the evidence. The second consists of errors in the trial process, including errors in the law applied.[285]

[b]   Evaluative Errors: Verdicts That Are Excessive, Inadequate, or Otherwise Against the Weight of the Evidence

When the trial judge concludes that the verdict is excessive, inadequate, or otherwise against the weight of the evidence, she is second-guessing the jury in its evaluation of the evidence.[286] Yet, unlike directed verdict, judgment n.o.v., or judgment as a matter of law, an order for a new trial on the grounds that the verdict is against the weight of the evidence does not deprive the verdict-winner of jury trial. It only forces him to submit his evidence to a new jury. His problem is that he gets "too much jury trial, not too little."[287]

This explains why the test for granting new trial is less restrictive than the test for directed verdict/judgment n.o.v.[288] On the other hand, for the judge to set aside the verdict and order a new trial just because she would have decided the case

---

[282] *Capital Traction Co. v. Hof*, 174 U.S. 1, 13–14 (1899):

> "Trial by jury," in the primary and usual sense of the term at common law and in the American constitutions . . . is a trial by a jury of twelve men in the presence and under the superintendence of a judge empowered to instruct them on law and to advise them on the facts, and . . . to set aside their verdict if, in his opinion, it is against the law or the evidence.

[283] Rule 59(b).

[284] *See, e.g.*, MINN. R. CIV. P. 59.01.

[285] Another, less important category consists of newly discovered evidence that could not, with reasonable diligence, have been discovered and produced at trial. Since such evidence is rarely discovered within the customarily short time periods for seeking new trial, it is probably more commonly advanced in support of a motion for relief from judgment. *See* Rule 60(b)(2), discussed at § 12.11[2][b], *infra*.

[286] Of course, the verdict may be excessive because it exceeds statutory limits. The error is then not evaluative, but an error of law.

[287] FRIEDENTHAL, KANE & MILLER § 12.4.

[288] Indeed, were it the same, no new trial should be granted because the court could enter judgment as a matter of law. WRIGHT § 95. As a result, only a minority of states have adopted a new trial standard that is the same as the reasonable jury standard usually used for directed verdict/judgment n.o.v. *See* JAMES, HAZARD & LEUBSDORF § 7.28.

differently would undercut the jury as fact-finder.[289]

The test for federal and most state courts lies somewhere in between. We say "somewhere" because the test is necessarily approximate. One of the most frequently quoted formulas was stated in *Aetna Casualty & Surety Co. v. Yeats*:[290]

> On such a motion it is the duty of the judge to set aside the verdict and grant a new trial, if he is of opinion that the verdict is against the clear weight of the evidence, or is based upon evidence which is false, or will result in a miscarriage of justice, even though there may be substantial evidence which would prevent direction of a verdict.

This formulation makes it clear that the court may grant a new trial even if it finds "substantial evidence" to support the verdict, because on new trial, unlike directed verdict or j.n.o.v, the court *does* weigh the evidence, not just test it for sufficiency. Another common formula is that the judge must be left with a definite and firm conviction that a mistake has been committed.[291]

In application, this test must take into account the deliberative skill of the jury in the circumstances of the case. The verdict in "a trial that is long and complicated and deals with a subject matter not lying within the ordinary knowledge of jurors . . . should be scrutinized more closely" than the verdict in a simple trial dealing with familiar subject matter.[292] Certainly, the trial judge should be most hesitant to set aside the verdict and order new trial on evidentiary grounds when the key issue in the case was credibility, a matter classically for the jury.

Another kind of evaluative error is that the verdict is excessive or inadequate as a matter of fact.[293] This is logically no different from a weight of the evidence claim. Yet the determination of unliquidated and punitive damages is often so speculative to begin with that judicial intervention on a new trial motion may seem especially problematical. The conditional grant of new trial has often provided a way out, however. The trial judge grants the motion unless the opposing party agrees to a reduction (*remittitur*) or increase (*additur*) of the verdict.[294] In federal courts, the court may order a remittitur if the verdict is so excessive that it "shocks the conscience."[295] The party who consents to such a remittitur waives any right to appellate review of it.[296] The Supreme Court has upheld remittitur against Seventh

---

[289] Although some states have adopted this "thirteenth juror" test for new trial, *see* JAMES, HAZARD, & LEUBSDORF § 7.28, it is doubtful that their judges actually exercise as much discretion as the test seems to confer.

[290] 122 F.2d 350, 352–53 (4th Cir. 1941).

[291] *See* WRIGHT § 95.

[292] *Lind v. Schenley Indus., Inc.*, 278 F.2d 79, 90–91 (3d Cir. 1960).

[293] As opposed to excessive as a matter of law. *See* note 286, *supra*.

[294] He must give the opposing party the option, however, and may not simply fix the proper level of damages himself. *McKinnon v. City of Berwyn*, 750 F.2d 1383, 1389 (7th Cir. 1984). Federal courts are divided on what the proper level should be: the highest reasonable amount, a reasonable amount, or the lowest reasonable amount. *See, e.g., Gorsalitz v. Olin Mathieson Chem. Corp.*, 429 F.2d 1033, 1047 (5th Cir. 1970).

[295] *MOORE* § 59.13[2][g][iii][B].

[296] *Donovan v. Penn Shipping Co.*, 429 U.S. 648 (1977).

Amendment attack, relying on historical grounds and some dubious logic, but has condemned additur as unconstitutional.[297]

In *Gasperini v. Center for Humanities, Inc.*,[298] the Supreme Court added a further wrinkle to remittitur practice in federal diversity cases. There state law authorized trial courts to set aside as excessive any verdict which "deviates materially from what would be reasonable compensation." This is a broader standard than the federal miscarriage-of-justice or "shocks the conscience" standard.[299] The Supreme Court held that the state standard served substantive purposes and therefore controlled in a federal diversity case.

The grant of partial new trial limited to the issue of damages is another possibility when the amount of the verdict has been attacked. In federal court, partial new trial "may not be resorted to unless it clearly appears that the issue to be retried is so distinct and separate from the others that a trial of it alone may be had without injustice."[300] Such orders must be made cautiously, however. A jury that has evaluated damages improperly may well also have evaluated liability improperly. In particular, an inadequate verdict may be a compromise verdict that cannot fairly be set aside only in part.

New trial determinations differ from directed verdicts and judgments n.o.v. not just in availability. Decisions granting or denying directed verdicts or judgments n.o.v. are open to reconsideration on review.[301] In contrast, it is quite difficult to obtain reversal of the court's decision granting or refusing to grant a motion for new trial. In the first place, the grant of a new trial motion — standing alone — is interlocutory. It is not appealable until a final judgment is rendered after a new trial,[302] assuming that the judgment is unfavorable to the party who resisted the new trial.[303] Even then, it is reviewable only for abuse of discretion.[304] When the new trial determination is based on evidentiary grounds, the standard of appellate review for abuse of discretion is extremely narrow.[305]

---

[297] *Compare Dimick v. Schiedt*, 293 U.S. 474, 486 (1935) ("what remains is included in the verdict along with the unlawful excess — in that sense it has been found by the jury — and the remittitur has the effect of merely lopping off an excrescence"), *with Jehl v. Southern Pacific Co.*, 427 P.2d 988 (Cal. 1967) (allowing additur in state court). *See* Sann, *Remittiturs (and Additurs) in Federal Courts: An Evaluation With Suggested Alternatives*, 38 Case W. Res. L. Rev. 157 (1988) (urging elimination of remittitur in federal courts to eliminate inconsistency and inefficiency). David Baldus et al., *Improving Judicial Oversight of Jury Damages Assessments: A Proposal for the Comparative Additur/Remittitur Review of Awards for Nonpecuniary Harms and Punitive Damages*, 80 Iowa L. Rev. 1109 (1995).

[298] 518 U.S. 415, 422 (1996).

[299] *Id.* at 424.

[300] *Gasoline Prods. Co. v. Champlin Ref. Co.*, 283 U.S. 494, 500 (1931).

[301] *See* § 12.09[3], *infra.*

[302] *Allied Chem. Corp. v. Daiflon, Inc.*, 449 U.S. 33, 34, 36 (1980).

[303] *See* § 12.09[3], *infra.*

[304] 518 U.S. at 436.

[305] For a discussion of the standard and its application to new trial determinations, see § 13.09[2][d], *infra.*

[c] Process Errors

There are a variety of errors that may taint the trial process. These include judicial errors in instructing the jury or admitting or commenting on the evidence, and misconduct by parties, counsel, witnesses or jurors, as well as prejudicial happenstance.[306] The judge has discretion to grant a new trial for such errors.[307] This is subject, however, to the possibility that the error may be deemed harmless.[308] No verdict may be set aside and new trial granted unless the error adversely affected the substantial rights of the complaining party. The trial judge's superior ability to assess the prejudicial effect of errors on the trial process explains why he generally enjoys such discretion on ruling on motions for new trial.

Of the sundry errors of trial process which may justify a new trial, jury misconduct merits further discussion. The historic rule at common law was that a juror may not impeach his own verdict.[309] The rule was intended partly to protect the candor of secret jury deliberations and perhaps to protect the institution of jury fact-finding itself from embarrassing disclosure of its imprecision.[310] Since juries typically deliberate in secret, the rule made it extremely difficult to prove jury misconduct in many cases.

Today, most jurisdictions have struck a compromise between the desire to protect candid jury deliberation and the need to control jury misconduct. Almost all jurisdictions use an exclusionary evidentiary rule to protect the mental processes of jurors from disclosure.[311] But "the permissibility of juror testimony hinges upon the purpose for which it is offered."[312] Jurors are often permitted to testify about extraneous information or outside influence that may have tainted the jury's deliberations.[313]

In re Beverly Hills Fire Litigation[314] supplies a good illustration of the modern rule and suggests one test for jury misconduct. There, one of the jurors reported to the jury the results of his home experiment with electrical wiring, in contradiction of expert testimony during the trial. On appeal, the court considered the jurors' testimony about this extraneous information and rejected the verdict winners' arguments that the experimenting juror was only relying on his own general knowledge and common experience. Instead, it found that the juror's actions "went beyond mere general knowledge and was instead a response to the case at hand," prejudicially supplementing the record. It reversed and remanded for a new trial.

---

[306] *See generally* Moore § 59.13.

[307] In theory, there is no discretion in deciding new trial motions based on judicial errors, since they present questions of law. In practice, the assessment of their prejudicial effect invokes a discretion which is entitled to substantial respect on appeal. *See* James, Hazard & Leubsdorf § 7.25. Regarding the appellate review of discretionary orders generally, see § 13.09[2][d], *infra*.

[308] *See* Rule 61.

[309] *See* Comment, *Impeachment of Jury Verdicts*, 25 U. Chi. L. Rev. 360 (1958).

[310] *See generally* James, Hazard & Leubsdorf § 7.27.

[311] Friedenthal, Kane & Miller § 12.5.

[312] *Attridge v. Cencorp Div. of Dover Techs. Int'l, Inc.*, 836 F.2d 113, 117 (2d Cir. 1987).

[313] *See, e.g.*, Fed. R. Evid. 606(b). *See generally* Moore § 59.13[2][e][iii][D].

[314] 695 F.2d 207, 214 (6th Cir. 1982).

In contrast, a closely divided Supreme Court in *United States v. Tanner*[315] held that what the dissenters characterized as "profoundly disturbing" evidence of extensive juror drug and alcohol intoxication *during* deliberations, went to the mental processes of the jury and was therefore inadmissible to impeach the verdict. The majority thus aggressively enforced the federal version of the exclusionary evidentiary rule, notwithstanding a strong argument that drug and alcohol consumption are extraneous and antecedent to the jury's deliberative process.

[3]   The Interplay of Directed Verdicts and Judgments N.O.V. With Other Procedural Law

[a]   The Consistency of Directed Verdicts and Judgments N.O.V. With the Right to Jury Trial

The Seventh Amendment poses two potential challenges to directed verdicts and judgment notwithstanding the verdict. First, do orders that snatch the case away from the jury at trial undermine the right to a jury trial guaranteed by the first clause of the Seventh Amendment? Second, do such orders violate the second clause of the Seventh Amendment, which provides that "no fact tried by a jury, shall otherwise be re-examined in any Court of the United States, than according to the rules of the common law."

Directed verdicts have not posed much of a problem. Early on, the United States Supreme Court appeared to regard the authority of courts to direct verdicts as well-established in common law.[316] By 1943, the Supreme Court observed that Seventh Amendment challenges to federal directed verdicts were "foreclosed by repeated decisions made here consistently for nearly a century."[317] The Supreme Court did read the Seventh Amendment to block judgment n.o.v. in one famous pre-rule decision.[318] However, the Court altered its position in later cases,[319] using the well-accepted rule that directed verdicts were permissible to create something of a legal fiction. A federal judge reserving decision on a motion for directed verdict could later turn around a verdict unsupported by evidence on the theory that he was reviving consideration of the motion for directed verdict.[320] In that way, the judge is not technically reexamining facts tried by the jury, but is reconsidering a motion he first ruled upon before the jury began its deliberations. Rule 50(b) codifies this

---

[315] 483 U.S. 107 (1987). For a trenchant criticism of the case and an analysis of Fed. R. Evid. 606, *see* Edward T. Swaine, Note, *Pre-Deliberations Juror Misconduct, Evidential Incompetence, and Juror Responsibility*, 98 YALE L.J. 187 (1990).

[316] In *Parks v. Ross*, 52 U.S. 362, 373 (1851), the Court noted that "[i]t is undoubtedly the peculiar province of the jury to find all matters of fact, and of the court to decide all questions of law arising thereon. But a jury has no right to assume the truth of any material fact, without some evidence legally sufficient to establish it." That directed verdicts differ "in some major respects" from "the historic jury control devices — the demurrer to the evidence, nonsuit, and a motion for new trial . . . ," FRIEDENTHAL, KANE & MILLER § 12.3, has not troubled the Supreme Court.

[317] *Galloway v. United States*, 319 U.S. 372, 389 (1943).

[318] *Slocum v. New York Life Ins. Co.*, 228 U.S. 364 (1913).

[319] *E.g.*, *Baltimore & Carolina Line, Inc. v. Redman*, 295 U.S. 654 (1935).

[320] *Redman*, 295 U.S. at 658–59.

fiction by making judgments n.o.v. available only to the party who had previously made a motion for a directed verdict under Rule 50(a), specifying the grounds on which the motion is based.[321] And to reinforce the unitary nature of the motion, Rule 50 has dispensed with the terms "directed verdict" and "judgment n.o.v." and substituted the term "judgment as a matter of law" to refer to each. To revisit judgment as a matter of law after the verdict, the court need not expressly reserve decision on the motion before the verdict; the rule provides that "the court is considered to have submitted the action to the jury subject to the court's later deciding the legal questions raised by the motion." The later determination may also be by an appellate court, reversing the trial court's denial of judgment n.o.v.[322] Indeed, the Supreme Court has held that a court of appeals may even direct entry of judgment as a matter of law (instead of remanding) when, after it has excised evidence which was erroneously admitted by the trial court, there is insufficient evidence left to support the jury verdict.[323]

[b] How Directed Verdicts and Judgments N.O.V. Complement Each Other

Since the same legal standard governs both directed verdicts and judgments n.o.v.,[324] and since they often address the same factual record, it is natural to ask why both are necessary.

The principal contribution of judgments n.o.v. is that they make it possible for trial judges to conserve court and party resources. They do this by permitting trial courts to defer acting on the conclusion that the evidence permits only one result until the jury has deliberated and returned its verdict. For two reasons, this is one of the few instances in civil procedure where delay ultimately serves judicial efficiency. First, if the jury eventually finds for the movant, the trial court is spared from making a ruling that is more vulnerable on appeal than a judgment on a jury verdict. Second, deferring a ruling until a motion for judgment n.o.v. reduces the necessity for retrial of the case if appeal is successfully taken,[325] by allowing the jury to return a verdict that can be reinstated on remand.

Consider an example. Defendant moves for a directed verdict in a federal case. The judge concludes that plaintiff has fallen just short of submitting enough

---

[321] Federal courts usually apply the limitation strictly, and the specification requirement added in 1991 effectively rejected earlier cases holding that something less than a formal motion for directed verdict was sufficient to preserve a party's right to move for judgment n.o.v. *See* Moore § 50.40[3]; Rule 50(a) advisory committee's note (1991 amendment). Since Seventh Amendment concerns are local to federal courts, states — even those which typically adopt language of the Federal Rules of Civil Procedure — are free to dispense with the directed verdict prerequisite in their judgment n.o.v. rules. *See, e.g.,* Ind. R. of Trial Proc., Trial Rule 50.

[322] *Cf. Neely v. Martin K. Eby Constr. Co.*, 386 U.S. 317, 322 (1967) ("there is no greater restriction on the province of the jury when an appellate court enters judgment *n.o.v.* than when a trial court does . . . .").

[323] *Weisgram v. Marley Co.*, 528 U.S. 440 (2000).

[324] *See* § 12.09[1][b], *supra*.

[325] *Cf.* Friedenthal, Kane & Miller § 12.3 ("By waiting, the judge avoids disputes about the propriety of a directed verdict, as well as appeals from its grant, and also defers to the jury.").

evidence to meet the substantial evidence standard.[326] However, he denies defendant's motion. By delaying decision until the jury has returned a verdict, the judge allows for the strong possibility that the jury will return a verdict in favor of defendant. If this happens, the court will never have to pass on the highly reviewable question (whether a reasonable jury could find for plaintiff) posed earlier by defendant's motion for directed verdict.[327] Defendant will be content with the jury verdict. Since there will be substantial evidence supporting the verdict, plaintiff cannot successfully attack it. The case is over.[328]

Let us change one element of our hypothetical case. Assume that the jury returns a verdict for plaintiff. Now the judge must act upon his conviction that plaintiff's case is unsupported by substantial evidence by granting defendant's motion for judgment n.o.v. The judgment n.o.v. option also conserves time and effort in this setting. The trial judge's decision to grant defendant's motion for judgment n.o.v. may be affirmed on appeal. But a new trial should not be necessary even if he is reversed. The appellate court can merely reinstate the jury verdict. If, on the other hand, the trial court had granted defendant's motion for a directed verdict, reversal would have required an entirely new trial.[329]

A further justification for the added opportunity for decision provided by judgments n.o.v. may be that the quality of decisions will improve if the court has more time to decide. The court really cannot long delay sending the case to the jury in order to mull over a difficult directed verdict question. The prospect of a motion for judgment n.o.v. permits the court to consider the question for a substantially longer period of time.[330]

Directed verdicts also make a discrete and important contribution. First, judgments n.o.v. would often be impossible if the judicial system did not also recognize the possibility of a directed verdict. A constitutional right to jury trial prevents grant of judgment n.o.v. by either the trial or the appellate court absent an earlier motion for directed verdict in federal courts and in the courts of some states.[331] Second, not all cases profit from delaying decision until after the jury has

---

[326] Or concludes that an unsettled question of law makes the decision whether to grant a directed verdict close, even if the evidence is clear. For example, when the legal definition of a particular claim is unsettled, evidence in the case may clearly support the claim as plaintiff defines it and fail with equal clarity to support the claim as defined by defendant.

[327] Appellate courts freely substitute their judgment for that of trial courts when reviewing directed verdicts. Like trial courts, they must draw all reasonable inferences favorable to the party opposed to the motion. MOORE § 50.92[1].

[328] Cf. 9B WRIGHT & MILLER § 2533 ("If the jury agrees with the court's appraisal of the evidence, and returns a verdict for the party who moved for judgment as a matter of law, the case is at an end.").

[329] "For this reason the appellate courts have repeatedly said that it is usually desirable to take a verdict, and then pass on the sufficiency of the evidence on a post-verdict motion." 9B WRIGHT & MILLER § 2533.

[330] The directed verdict motion flags the question for the court. The motion for judgment n.o.v. in federal court may come as late as 10 days after judgment. Rule 50(b). The trial court may not unduly delay decision on a motion for judgment n.o.v., but has more time to consider it than was practically available to consider the motion for a directed verdict.

[331] On how the Seventh Amendment requires directed verdict motions as predicates for judgments n.o.v. in federal court, see § 12.09[3][a], *supra*. There is a constitutional right to jury trial in the courts

returned a verdict. Directed verdicts make it possible to terminate trial as soon as it becomes clear that the evidence fails to offer a legally permissible choice to the jury. This may be as soon as all the evidence is submitted, when plaintiff has submitted all of his evidence, or, in rare cases, even immediately after plaintiff gives his opening statement.[332]

[c] The Relationship of Directed Verdicts and Motions for Judgments N.O.V. to Earlier Motions for Deciding Cases in Lieu of Trial

Directed verdicts and judgments n.o.v. are the last in a series of five motions used to decide civil cases on the merits and thereby interrupt the ordinary trial process. The first such motion in federal court is a motion to dismiss for failure to state a claim upon which relief can be granted.[333] Motions for judgment on the pleadings[334] and for summary judgment[335] follow.

Apart from the Rule 50 amendments consolidating directed verdicts and judgments n.o.v. into the single term, *judgment as a matter of law*, there are only a few attempts in the federal rules to inform the reader of the interrelationship of these motions.[336] Yet decisions, commentary and language in the rules support the conclusion that all pose the same test: *Do the established facts support a legal rule which should be applied to decide all or part of the case?*[337]

This is the same question posed by trial itself. We could thus administer this test without motions by sending every case to trial and treating every jury verdict as settled fact. If that was our system, however, it would have two major drawbacks. The facts in some cases are established long before trial. To require them to be tried would needlessly burden the party who holds what should be the winning cards and waste judicial resources. Therefore, the first three motions available permit termination of the case before trial begins. Second, treating jury verdicts as established fact may sometimes deny parties substantive justice. The last two motions offer protection here.

---

of most states closely patterned on the Seventh Amendment. *See* FRIEDENTHAL, KANE & MILLER § 11.7.

[332] In spite of the failure of Rule 50 to contemplate the last option, federal "courts continued to hold that they have power to direct a verdict on the opening statement but that the power should not be exercised if there is any doubt about the facts." 9B WRIGHT & MILLER § 2533.

[333] Rule 12(b)(6), *discussed in* § 8.07[2][c], *supra*.

[334] Rule 12(c), *discussed in* § 8.07[1], *supra*.

[335] Rule 56, *discussed in* § 11.03, *supra*.

[336] For example, Rule 12(d) states that when "matters outside the pleadings are presented to and not excluded by the court, the [12(b)(6)] motion shall be treated as one for summary judgment . . . ."

[337] Rule 56(a) governing summary judgments makes explicit reference to the test, stating the court "shall grant summary judgment when affidavits or other types of materials deemed appropriate "show[] that there is no genuine issue as to any material fact and that the movant is entitled to a judgment as a matter of law." After recent amendments, Rule 50(a)(1) makes what was formerly termed directed verdict and judgment available upon a showing that "a reasonable jury would not have a legally sufficient evidentiary basis" to resolve the case differently; and that the movant is therefore entitled to "judgment as a matter of law." *See also* Rule 12(d) (consideration of matters outside the complaint converts a 12(b)(6) motion to one for summary judgment) & Rule 12(c) (consideration of matters outside the pleadings converts a motion for judgment on the pleadings to one for summary judgment).

To better understand when and why it is appropriate to decide cases by motion rather than by the ordinary trial process, it is useful to examine our subject in larger perspective. Civil adjudication has two essential functions. One might be called a *law* function. The law function is to attach the proper legal significance to settled facts. The process of research, argument and deliberation making up the law function is indifferent to how or when facts are settled. Courts conclude civil adjudication by performing the law function and may do so as soon as they deem established those facts supporting a case-ending rule. The other essential in civil adjudication might be called the *fact* function. The fact function is to resolve factual controversies. The fact function often consumes a far larger amount of party and judicial resources than the law function.

The first three motions available to decide the merits (dismissal for failure to state a claim, judgment on the pleadings, and summary judgment) serve to reduce the cost of the fact function of civil adjudication. They do this by creating opportunities for courts to deem facts established as early as possible. The existence of three such motions reflects the realization that the point of the pretrial phase at which facts are established varies from case to case. In a Rule 12(b)(6) motion, defendant challenges plaintiff's legal theory by using as established fact plaintiff's own allegations. When completed pleadings create established fact, either party may move for judgment on the pleadings. When established facts necessary to decision can only be presented from sources outside the pleadings, either party may move for summary judgment.

Substantially less time and effort will be saved by granting a directed verdict, none by granting judgment n.o.v.[338] The rationale for these motions derives instead from the need to preserve rights of the parties under substantive law. Jurors do not consider substantive law as such, but it determines the freedom they are given by the court's instructions to weigh the evidence in reaching a verdict.[339] When the evidence is such that jurors could find for a party only by exceeding that freedom, then a verdict for that party would do violence to the substantive rights of the opposing party.[340] The same concern does not arise in nonjury cases, since legal guardian and fact-finder are one. That explains why directed verdicts and judgments n.o.v. have no real counterpart in bench trials.[341] Motions for deciding cases without (or notwithstanding) trial reflect the procedural judgment that it is not always necessary or desirable to reach the merits through the ordinary process of trial. Trials are indispensable only in those cases where the facts never become established prior to trial, and juries have the last word only where the evidence provides reasonable support for either plaintiff or defendant's conflicting versions of the facts.

---

[338] *Cf.* Robert J. Gregory, *One Too Many Rivers to Cross: Rule 50 Practice in the Modern Era of Summary judgment*, 23 FLA. ST. U. L. REV. 689 (1996) (arguing that relaxation of standards for summary judgment should diminish use of Rule 50 procedures).

[339] *See* § 12.08[3], *supra.*

[340] *See, e.g., Freund v. Nycomed Amersham*, 347 F.3d 752, 761 (9th Cir. 2003). *Cf.* 9B WRIGHT & MILLER § 2522 (declaring Rule 50 to be "essential to the preservation and proper application of the applicable substantive law.").

[341] A federal litigant may move under Rule 41(b) for involuntary dismissal, but the motion is of relatively minor significance. *See* § 11.04 (involuntary dismissals), *supra,* § 912.10 (bench trials), *infra.*

[d] The Interrelationship of Post-Trial Motion Practice and Dispositions on Appeal

In most jurisdictions, the party against whom a verdict is returned may seek judgment n.o.v. or a new trial in the alternative.[342] The verdict-winner in federal court also may move for a new trial twenty-eight days after judgment n.o.v. (judgment as a matter of law) is granted against him.[343] In handling alternative motions, the trial court has a complete range of options. It may grant judgment n.o.v. and a new trial, deny both motions, or grant either motion while denying the other.[344] Each response carries its own implications for appellate review.[345]

When the district court denies judgment n.o.v., but grants new trial, its order is not immediately appealable in the federal system because there is no final judgment.[346] The party may raise the question of the validity of the new trial order only on appeal from an eventual final judgment after the second trial.[347]

When the district court denies judgment n.o.v. and new trial, both decisions are appealable in the normal course. On appeal, the party who prevailed on the motion may argue grounds for a new trial in the event that the appellate court finds error in the denial of the motion for judgment n.o.v.[348] The appellate court may then enter judgment n.o.v., award a new trial, or remand for the trial court to make the new trial determination.[349]

When the district court grants the motion for judgment n.o.v., Rule 50(c) requires it also to rule conditionally on the new trial motion in anticipation of a possible reversal of the judgment n.o.v. on appeal. On appeal, the appellate court will either affirm judgment n.o.v. and end the matter, or reverse. In the event of reversal, when the district court has denied the motion for new trial, the appellate court may order entry of judgment on the verdict, reverse the denial of the motion

---

[342] Rule 50(b). He need not await entry of judgment on the verdict in federal court. Rules 50(b) and 59(b) both require only that the motions be filed no later than twenty-eight days after entry of the judgment.

[343] Rule 50(c)(2).

[344] In rare cases, the court may deny judgment n.o.v. and order a new trial, when only a motion for judgment n.o.v. is before the court. The language of Rule 50(b) seems to provide for this. Yet the practice should be limited to cases where grounds for judgment n.o.v. exist but the court "believes that the defect in the proof might be remedied on a second trial, or if needed evidence was ruled out by some error of the court." 9B *Wright & Miller* § 2538.

[345] For a more extended discussion of this process, see 9B *Wright & Miller* § 2540; Note, *Post-Verdict Motions Under 50: Protecting the Verdict-Winner*, 53 Minn. L. Rev. 358 (1968). On the limitation on federal interlocutory review, *see* § 13.04, *infra*.

[346] *See* § 13.03 (the final judgment rule), *infra*. *Cf. Allied Chem.*, 449 U.S. at 34 (emphasizing unavailability also of *mandamus* to review grant of new trial). An increasing number of state systems, however, do confer appellate jurisdiction over orders granting new trials. *See* Friedenthal, Kane & Miller § 12.4; Rabinowitz, *Appellate Review of Trial Court Orders Granting New Trials*, 8 Rutgers L. Rev. 465 (1954).

[347] *Allied Chem.*, 449 U.S. at 34.

[348] Rule 50(e). *See Neely v. Martin K. Eby Constr. Co.*, 386 U.S. 317 (1967).

[349] Rule 50(e). On the authority of the court of appeals to enter a judgment as a matter of law directly, see *Weisgram v. Marley Co.*, 528 U.S. 440, 447–49 (2000).

for new trial and order a new trial, or remand the case to the trial court for reconsideration of the motion for new trial.[350]

When the district court grants the motion for judgment n.o.v. and conditionally grants new trial as well, there is a final judgment from which to appeal. Although the conditional grant of new trial is still technically nonfinal, it is practical to permit the appellate court to review the new trial order because the case is already before it on appeal of the judgment n.o.v. and it has already become familiar with much of the evidence in the case in ruling on that judgment. Rule 50(c)(1) therefore assumes that the appellate court may reach the new trial order if it reverses the judgment n.o.v.[351] In this event, the appellate court may remand the case to the trial court for new trial,[352] reverse the grant of the motion for new trial and order entry of judgment on the verdict, or remand the case to the trial court for reconsideration of the motion for new trial.[353]

§ 12.10   BENCH TRIALS (NON-JURY CASES)

Some cases are triable only before judges.[354] Others must be tried before a judge because the parties waive their jury claims.[355] Non-jury (bench) trials make up a significant portion of trial litigation.[356] Not only is the bench trial in extensive use, but "it raises . . . fewer procedural problems than does trial to a jury."[357]

The judge in a bench trial is both law enforcer *and* trier of fact. Since these functions are performed by the same person, distinctions between the two do not matter as they do in jury trials. Consequently, directed verdicts and judgments n.o.v., which protect against lawless jury verdicts, have no real counterpart in bench trials. A defendant in a bench trial may move for dismissal, or, in a federal court, for judgment as a matter of law, at the close of plaintiff's submission of evidence,[358] but

---

[350] MOORE § 50.94.

[351] However, use of any federal rule of civil or appellate procedure as authority for relaxing the finality requirement arguably exceeds the strictures of Federal Rule of Civil Procedure 82 and Federal Rule of Appellate Procedure 1(b) that the rules not be construed to expand jurisdiction.

[352] *Montgomery Ward & Co. v. Duncan*, 311 U.S. 243, 254 (1940) ("If the judgment were reversed, the case, on remand, would be governed by the trial judge's award of a new trial.").

[353] MOORE § 50.94[2]. As noted earlier, trial courts enjoy considerable discretion in ordering new trials. *See* § 12.09[2], *supra*. However, perhaps because Rule 50(c)(1) explicitly entertains the possibility of reversal, conditional orders granting new trials appear somewhat more vulnerable. *See, e.g.*, the cases cited in 9B WRIGHT & MILLER § 2540.

[354] The right to a jury trial is protected by constitutional or statutory law, *see* § 12.07[1], *supra*, and "no similar requirement protects trial by the court." *Beacon Theatres, Inc.*, 359 U.S. at 510.

[355] *See* § 12.07[2], *supra*. At the same time, a "court may, if it wishes, submit an issue to an advisory jury on its own initiative, but the verdict of such a jury is advisory only, and the ultimate responsibility for finding the facts remains with the court." WRIGHT & MILLER § 92. Professor Wright adds: "In an action not triable to a jury as of right, the court may, with the consent of both parties, order a trial with a jury whose verdict has the same effect as if trial by jury had been a matter of right." WRIGHT & MILLER § 92.

[356] *Beacon Theatres, Inc.*, 359 U.S. 500 (reporting that more federal cases are tried before judges than before juries).

[357] *Id.* at 644.

[358] *See* Rule 52(c).

unlike the motion for directed verdict, this motion is not to avert mischief by the fact-finder. The person ruling on the motion *is* the fact finder. In fact, under Rule 52(c), either party in a bench trial may move for judgment as a matter of law whenever his opponent has been fully heard with respect to a potentially dispositive issue of fact, and the court may (but need not) enter "judgment on partial findings" at any time it can appropriately make a finding of fact on that issue.[359]

Nor do new trial motions in jury trials have precise counterparts in bench trials. Most errors prompting new trial orders[360] occur only in jury trials.[361] When an error does arise in a bench trial, the court often simply rehears part of the case or reconsiders its decision.[362] Yet bench trials are not easier than jury trials in all respects. They can put quite a strain on judges who must rule on the admissibility of evidence and consider its weight if admitted, at roughly the same time.[363]

Federal Rule 52(a) requires the court to make findings of fact in non-jury cases or when the jury is used only in an advisory capacity. Often the trial court will direct the prevailing party to prepare proposed findings of fact and the loser to object, as appropriate, and then craft its own findings from the submissions. The appellate courts have sharply chastised the trial courts which do this uncritically, citing the "potential for overreaching and exaggeration on the part of attorneys preparing findings of fact when they have already been informed that the judge has decided in their favor."[364] When, however, the trial court provides a framework for the proposed findings by its bench ruling, the loser takes the opportunity to respond to them, and the court does not simply adopt the findings verbatim, the Supreme Court has approved the process.[365]

Rule 52(a)(6) states that, on appeal, "[f]indings of fact, whether based on oral or other evidence, must not be set aside unless clearly erroneous, and the reviewing court must give due regard to the trial court to judge the witnesses' credibility." Thus, judgment in a bench trial differs from summary judgment in that the judge's fact findings in a bench trial are reversible only if clearly erroneous; summary

---

[359] Rule 52(c) advisory committee's notes (1991).

[360] *See* § 12.09[2][a], *supra.*

[361] "Although theoretically new trial motions may be granted in judge as well as jury trials, . . . the type of errors meriting a new trial typically arise only in jury trials. For example, even if the court erroneously receives certain evidence in a nonjury trial, the judge simply may disregard that evidence when rendering judgment, avoiding the need for a new trial." *Friedenthal, Kane & Miller* § 12.4.

[362] Thus, motions for rehearing or for reconsideration are probably more common than motions for new trial in bench trials. Indeed, Rule 59 authorizes new trial in bench trials "for any reason for which rehearing has heretofore been granted in a suit in equity . . . ."

[363] For an examination of bench trials from the perspective of the trial judge, see Roger S. Haydock & John Sonsteng, *Court Trial Empirical Survey: Interview Responses From Trial Judges Explaining Their Experiences and Views Regarding the Trial of Non-jury Cases*, 11 Wm. Mitchell L. Rev. 775 (1985).

[364] *Anderson v. Bessemer City*, 470 U.S. 564, 572 (1985); *Ramey Constr. Co. v. Apache Tribe of Mescalero Reservation*, 616 F.2d 464, 466–68 (10th Cir. 1980) (emphasizing also the effect of judicial origination of findings on the quality of decision-making). *See* Kristen Fjeldstad, *Just the Facts, Ma'am — A Review of the Practice of the Verbatim Adoption of Findings of Fact and Conclusions of Law*, 44 St. Louis U. L.J. 197 (2000).

[365] *Anderson*, 470 U.S. at 572.

judgment is not similarly shielded on review by the clearly erroneous standard because it is based on the judge's determination, *as a matter of law*, that the material facts are without genuine dispute, and questions of law are reviewed de novo on appeal.[366] Section 13.09[2][b], *infra*, discusses standards of appellate review.

§ 12.11   JUDGMENTS

[1]   The Nature and Force of Judgments

Defining the term in a broad sense, Federal Rule 54(a) states that "Judgment . . . includes a decree and any order from which an appeal lies." The rule thus ties judgments to final orders and a small class of interlocutory orders appealable in federal court.[367]

This definition fails to capture the functional significance judgments have in completing the case. In federal court, judgment follows decision. *Decision* describes determinations of fact made by the judge's findings or by jury verdict. *Judgment* "is the pronouncement of that decision and the act that gives it legal effect."[368] The judgment is filed by delivery to the district court clerk and entered through recording by the clerk.[369] While the act of entry is not performed by the court, it is nonetheless important to the force and effect of the judgment.[370]

The significance of a judgment can be twofold. First, judgment either for damages[371] or an injunction[372] gives the judgment-holder leverage over the person against whom the judgment was rendered. The money-judgment-holder has access to special procedures to expedite payment of the award.[373] One ordered to behave a certain way by an injunction must do so or suffer civil and possibly criminal contempt.[374] Second, judgments final and on the merits preclude parties in the future from relitigating issues and whole claims which might otherwise consume time, money and scarce judicial resources.[375]

---

[366] Rule 52(c) advisory committee's notes (1991 amendment).

[367] *See* §§ 13.03–13.05, *supra*.

[368] 10 *Wright & Miller* § 2651.

[369] Rule 58.

[370] "[I]t is crucial to the effectiveness of the judgment and for measuring the time periods for appeal and the filing of various post-trial motions." 10 *Wright & Miller* § 2651.

[371] On damages, see generally § 14.01. *infra*.

[372] On injunctions, see generally § 14.02, *infra*.

[373] On the nature of money-judgment enforcement proceedings, see § 15.02, *infra*.

[374] On the prerequisites for civil and criminal contempt, see § 14.02[2], *infra*.

[375] On the prerequisite to claim preclusion that judgments be final and on the merits, see § 15.05, *infra*.

[2] Resisting the Preclusive Effect of Final Judgments

Parties disadvantaged by judgments must consider what if anything they can do to improve their lot when the judgment has become final — that is to say, when appeal has been unsuccessful or the time for taking an appeal has elapsed. Three approaches are considered below. One can prevail upon a subsequent court presented with the judgment to declare it unenforceable because it is void (collateral attack), one can try to be excused from the judgment (extraordinary relief), or one can try to make the judgment more agreeable (amendment).

[a] Collateral Attack[376]

So strong is the need to resolve controversies and such is the force of preclusion doctrine that parties are not free to relitigate a prior judgment just because it was wrong on the merits.[377]

There are only a few paths of escape, known as points of collateral attack. The most important are the guarantee of notice and the constraint on territorial jurisdiction that is part of the law of constitutional due process. The likelihood that these or the few other grounds for collaterally attacking judgments[378] will be available in a given case is remote.

[b] Extraordinary Relief

When the time for direct attack on the judgment by motion for judgment n.o.v. or for new trial or by appeal has expired, many jurisdictions provide limited extraordinary relief from the judgment by further motion in the trial court. Federal Rule 60 is typical. Rule 60 sorts problems into serious and not-so-serious categories.

Subdivision (a) addresses the second category, correction by the district court of "'clerical' mistakes — mistakes that cause a judgment, order, or other part of the record to reflect something other than what was actually decided or what actually transpired."[379] Subdivision (b) addresses the first category:

> (1) mistake, inadvertence, surprise, or excusable neglect; (2) newly discovered evidence that, with reasonable diligence, could not have been discovered in time to move for a new trial under Rule 59(b); (3) fraud (whether previously called intrinsic or extrinsic), misrepresentation, or misconduct of an opposing party; (4) the judgment is void; (5) the judgment has been satisfied, released, or discharged; it is based on an earlier judgment that has been reversed or vacated; or applying it prospectively is no longer equitable; or (6) any other reason that justifies relief.

---

[376] On the meaning of collateral attack and how it differs from direct attack, see § 3.10, *supra*.

[377] *See, e.g., Milliken v. Meyer*, 311 U.S. 457, 462 (1940); *Federated Dep't Stores, Inc. v. Moitie*, 452 U.S. 394, 398 (1981) (stating that the "*res judicata* consequences of a final, unappealed judgment [are not] altered by the fact that the judgment may have been wrong").

[378] They are discussed in § 3.10[2], *supra*.

[379] MOORE § 60.02[1]. *See generally* Theodore A. Donahue, Jr., *A History and Interpretation of Rule 60(a) of the Federal Rules of Civil Procedure*, 42 DRAKE L. REV. 461 (1993).

Subdivision (c) states that grounds (1)–(3) must be offered no later than a year from judgment.

It is not easy to obtain relief from a judgment under this provision, but easier certainly than it is to attack collaterally the legal sufficiency of the judgment offered for enforcement in a later lawsuit.[380] Space permits only a few specific comments on the grounds listed in Rule 60(b).[381]

Ground (1) is especially suited to relief from default judgments.[382] Rule 55 treats entry of a default and entry of judgment on the default as separate stages. "The court may set aside an entry of default for good cause" when it is unaccompanied by judgment.[383] The void-judgment category of ground (4) is limited to a judgment "void only on grounds of lack of jurisdiction or for some failure of due process in the original proceeding."[384] Finally, despite the open-ended phrasing of ground (6), courts have evinced understandable hesitation in using it. It seems to exist for "unusual cases" and "not for t he purpose of relieving a party from free, calculated, and deliberate choices he has made."[385]

[c]   Amendment

Rule 59(e) gives parties in federal court a brief opportunity to seek amendment of judgment. Rule 59(e) motions resemble in purpose those filed under Rule 60(a).[386] The purpose of each is to give true effect to the judgment by eliminating unwitting error.[387]

---

[380] See the discussion of collateral attack, § 12.11[2][a], *supra*.

[381] The United States Supreme Court reaffirmed the limitation of Rule 60(b) to extraordinary cases in *United States v. Beggerly*, 524 U.S. 38, 47 (1998) ("[U]nder the Rule, an independent action should be available only to prevent a grave miscarriage of justice."). For extended discussion of the grounds, see 11 WRIGHT & MILLER §§ 2851–2864.

[382] See FRIEDENTHAL, KANE & MILLER § 12.6, (noting it "most frequently is invoked successfully in the default setting or when the plaintiff's suit was dismissed for failure to prosecute and judgment was entered by mistake since the party fully intended actively to litigate the dispute."). *See generally* Peter H. Bresnan & James P. Cornelio, Note, *Relief From Default Judgments Under Rule 60(b) — A Study of Federal Case Law*, 49 FORDHAM L. REV. 956 (1981). To succeed in having a default judgment vacated, one may have to demonstrate the existence of a "meritorious defense," 11 WRIGHT & MILLER § 2862, unless the judgment was procured without notice. See *Peralta v. Heights Medical Center, Inc.*, 485 U.S. 80 (1988).

[383] Rule 55(c). See generally § 11.02 (default judgments), *supra*.

[384] FRIEDENTHAL, KANE & MILLER § 12.6.

[385] 11 WRIGHT & MILLER § 2864. "A party remains under a duty to take legal steps to protect his own interests. In particular, it ordinarily is not permissible to use this motion to remedy a failure to take an appeal." *Id.* See, e.g., *Primus Auto Fin. Servs. v. Otto-Wal, Inc.*, 284 F. Supp. 2d 845, 847-48 (N.D. Ohio 2003).

[386] *Discussed in* § 12.11[2][b], *supra*.

[387] Parties cannot use Rule 59(e) or Rule 60(a) to alter the intended effect of a judgment. These motions are confined "to clerical errors or matters of clear oversight, not questions involving the right to additional recovery, or a reduction in an award." *FRIEDENTHAL, KANE & MILLER* § 12.6. Such substantial changes require a motion for new trial made no later than twenty-eight days after entry of judgment, or a motion for relief from the judgment, which may or may not be subject to a one-year time limit depending on the ground for relief used. See § 12.11[2][b], *supra*.

However, the motions differ in several respects. Rule 59(e) motions must be filed within twenty-eight days from entry of judgment. Timely filing keeps the judgment from becoming final for purposes of appeal. A Rule 60(a) motion can be made at any time without affecting the time for appeal.[388] Moreover, while the focus of Rule 60(a) is on clerical mistakes, Rule 59(e) contemplates mistakes by the court.[389]

§ 12.12   TRIAL PROCEEDINGS IN THE CALIFORNIA COURTS

[1]   Introductory Note on the California Trial Process

The civil trial process in California is similar to the process in federal courts and in other states, except that California may place even greater emphasis on pretrial conferences as a means of narrowing issues and reducing delay. As in other jurisdictions, the possibility of a jury trial — a one-time event before a factfinder comprised of ordinary people — influences the entire California civil litigation process. Not only does the reality of the jury trial mandate certain trial, post-trial and appellate procedures, but the possibility of one largely dictates the rules of pleading, discovery, motions and other pretrial proceedings. So pervasive is this influence that even the procedures utilized in nonjury cases mirror those of jury trials. The irony of this influence is that less than one per cent of civil cases in the California courts are disposed by a jury trial, and over 90% of civil cases never come to any type of trial.[390] Instead, they are usually settled, withdrawn, or decided on the merits prior to trial. But the possibility of trial exists in every case, and may be unavoidable in some.

[2]   Pretrial Proceedings in the California Courts

[a]   Delay Reduction and Case Management Rules

One premise of the adversary system is that parties, not judges, are responsible for moving the case forward through the pretrial states of litigation. The California courts have not fully endorsed this model. California's Trial Court Delay Reduction Act and California Rules of Court adopted pursuant to the Act have greatly increased the trial court's supervision of civil litigation prior to trial. These statewide provisions, implemented through local rules, require litigants to complete questionnaires and statements and to attend a variety of pretrial conferences — all designed to expedite disposition of claims and issues.

---

[388] *Moore* § 60.12.

[389] *Boaz v. Mut. Life Ins. Co. of New York*, 146 F.2d 321 (8th Cir. 1944), is frequently offered as an illustration. There the trial court corrected its error, granting defendant's motion to amend the judgment from dismissal of plaintiff's case without prejudice to dismissal with prejudice. The present version of Rule 59(e) codifies this authority. 11 *Wright & Miller* § 2810.1. *See, e.g., Venegas-Hernandez v. Sonolux Records*, 370 F.3d 183, 189 (1st Cir. 2004); *United States v. $23,000 in U. S. Currency*, 356 F.3d 157, 165 n.9 (1st Cir. 2004).

[390] *See 2012 Court Statistics Report of the Judicial Council of California*, Superior Courts, Fig. 21.

[b] Pretrial Conferences

The superior court in each county must adopt local rules consistent with the statewide case management rules, and case disposition time goals, for general civil cases set forth in the California Rules of Court.[391] Pursuant to these rules, the superior court must evaluate each case and, unless an exempt or a complex case, assign it to the local case management program.[392] This program typically includes one or more *case management conferences*, and often includes a *settlement conference*. The court must set an initial case management conference to review the case within 180 days after the filing of the complaint.[393]

Before the date set for the case management conference, the parties must meet and confer to consider matters relevant to the conference. Each party, or both parties jointly if they agree on the terms, must file and serve a *case management statement* which, among other things, describes the case and any damages, requests a jury or nonjury trial, estimates the length of trial, indicates any willingness to engage in alternative dispute resolution or a settlement conference, and indicates the status of discovery and any motions before trial. Counsel for each party must appear at the conference by telephone or in person, must be familiar with the case, and must be prepared to discuss and commit to the party's position on the various subjects for consideration at the conference, as specified in the rules of court. During the conference, the court reviews the case comprehensively and decides whether to assign the case to an alternative dispute process or whether to set the case for trial. The court may also take appropriate action with respect to a variety of other issues, such as whether all parties have been served, any additional parties may be added or pleadings amended, and an early settlement conference should be scheduled. Other matters for discussion include what discovery issues are anticipated and the date by which discovery will be completed, the estimated length of trial, and a date for trial.[394]

After the conference, the court enters a *case management order* setting a schedule for subsequent proceedings and otherwise providing for the management of the case. This order includes such provisions as may be appropriate, such as a date certain for trial, whether the trial will be a jury trial, the dismissal or severance of unserved defendants, the date for any additional case management conferences before trial, and the date for a settlement conference. Importantly, the order issued after the case management conference controls the subsequent course of the action unless it is modified by a later order.[395] In other words, the terms of the order

---

[391] CAL. CT. R. 3.711-3.735. The California Judicial Council established the following time goals for disposition of unlimited civil cases assigned to the case management program: 75% should be disposed within 12 months of filing, 85% within 18 months, and 100% within 24 months. CAL. CT. R. 3.714(b)(1); STANDARDS OF JUDICIAL ADMINISTRATION, CAL. CT. R. APP. § 2.1(f)(1). Similar goals apply to limited civil cases: 90% should be disposed of within 12 months of filing, 98% within 18 months, and 100% within 24 months. CAL. CT. R. 3.714(b)(2); STANDARDS, § 2.1(f)(2).

[392] CAL. CT. R. 3.720-3.727, 3.1380; *see generally* 3 CEB, *California Civil Procedure Before Trial, Case Management Conference and Disposition Time Goals* §§ 40.1-40.93 (4th ed. 2012).

[393] CAL. CT. R. 3.721 & 3.722.

[394] CAL. CT. R. 3.727.

[395] CAL. CT. R. 3.730.

supersede the pleadings and determine the scope of the factual and legal issues for resolution at trial.

Any party may request, or the court on its own motion may order, a judicially supervised *settlement conference*. Prior to this conference, each party must submit to the court and serve on every other party a settlement conference statement containing an itemization of damages by each plaintiff, a good faith offer of settlement by each party, and a statement indentifying and discussing in detail all facts and law pertinent to the issues of liability and damages involved in the case as to that party. Trial counsel, parties, and persons with full authority to settle the case must personally attend the settlement conference, unless excused by the court for good cause. Often, a settlement conference achieves its intended goal. A large percentage of cases settle as a result of the conference, in part because it is supervised by a judge who will not be the trial judge and therefore is a neutral person with experience on the jury value of asserted claims and defenses.[396]

Local rules may also require the parties to attend a final *status conference* a few days before trial to exchange witness and pre-marked exhibits lists and to present any motions *in limine* (at the threshold of trial), jury instructions, special verdict forms, stipulations, and any unusual evidentiary or legal issues anticipated during trial. Parties and their attorneys should, and usually do, take seriously each aspect of the pretrial conference process. Failure to attend pretrial conferences, to timely file required statements and questionnaires, to attend unprepared and not participate in good faith, or to otherwise fail to comply with case management rules may result in the imposition of substantial sanctions.[397]

[c]   Requests for Admissions

The purpose of requests for admission is to expedite the trial process by soliciting and reaching an agreement as to uncontested matters.[398] Requests for admission are usually made near the end of the pretrial phase of a lawsuit, after each party has had an opportunity to discover the basic facts of the case. For the most part, requests for admission in the California courts operate in the same manner as they do in the federal courts under Rule 36 of the Federal Rules of Civil Procedure.[399] A party may serve any other party a request to admit the genuineness of a document, the truth of specific factual matters, or the accuracy of opinions relating to the facts.[400] The responding party must set out an answer or an objection as to each request. Admissions are conclusive at trial — no evidence need be proffered to establish the matter admitted. Unfounded denials may result in the

---

[396] *See* CEB, *California Civil Procedure Before Trial* § 40.71 (4th ed. 2012).

[397] CAL. CT. R. 2.30 (authorizing sanctions for failure to comply with applicable rules); CAL. CODE CIV. PROC. § 575.2 (authorizing sanctions for failure to comply with local rules); CAL. GOV'T CODE § 68608 (authorizing sanctions and encouraging judges to impose sanctions to achieve the purposes of the Trial Court Delay Reduction Act).

[398] *See Cembrook v. Superior Court*, 56 Cal. 2d 423, 15 Cal. Rptr. 127, 364 P.2d 303 (1961) (observing that if a litigant is able to make an admission, the time for doing so is during discovery procedures and not at the trial).

[399] Requests for admissions under federal Rule 36 are discussed in § 12.02, *supra*.

[400] CAL. CODE CIV. PROC. §§ 2033.010-2033.420.

imposition of sanctions in the amount of the costs and attorney fees incurred in proving the matter at trial.[401]

A failure to serve timely responses operates as a waiver to all objections to the requests, including privilege and work product objections.[402] If a party to whom requests have been directed fails to serve a timely response, the requesting party may move for an order that the matters specified in the requests be deemed admitted, as well as for a monetary sanction. If the delinquent party does not serve a proposed response to the admission requests prior to the hearing on the motion, the trial court *must* order that the matters be deemed admitted.[403] A party may be permitted to withdraw or amend an admission deemed admitted due to failure to respond, but only if that party satisfies the heavy burden of showing of mistake, inadvertence, or excusable neglect, and lack of prejudice to the requesting party.[404]

[3] Disqualification of the Trial Judge in the California Courts

[a] Challenge for Cause: Disqualification for Actual or Perceived Bias

An essential component of the adversary system is that the decision-maker — whether a judge or a jury — be fair and impartial. Unless shown to be otherwise, a judge is presumed to be neutral and therefore has a duty to decide a proceeding — often referred to as the "duty to sit." However, a judge may be disqualified upon proof of actual or perceived bias.[405] Disqualification is required, for example, where the judge has personal knowledge of disputed evidentiary facts, served as a lawyer in the case, has a financial interest in the subject of the proceeding, has some relationship with a party or a lawyer, or has a physical inability to properly conduct the proceeding. A judge must also be disqualified where "a person aware of the facts might reasonably entertain a doubt that the judge would be able to be impartial."[406] This potentially broad ground for recusal is interpreted to incorporate an objective standard: A judge faced with a potential ground for disqualification "ought to consider how his participation in a given case looks to the average person on the street."[407] Of course, the average person on the street does not determine whether a judge must be disqualified. That decision is initially made by the judge himself, subject to reconsideration by another judge if the challenged judge refuses to disqualify himself.

---

[401] CAL. CODE CIV. PROC. §§ 2033.410 & 2033.420.

[402] CAL. CODE CIV. PROC. § 2033.280(a).

[403] CAL. CODE CIV. PROC. § 2033.280(c).

[404] *Wilcox v. Birtwhistle*, 21 Cal. 4th 973, 977-83, 90 Cal. Rptr. 2d 260, 987 P.2d 727 (1999).

[405] *See* CAL. CODE CIV. PROC. §§ 170.1-170.9.

[406] CAL. CODE CIV. PROC. § 170.1(a)(6)(c).

[407] *United Farm Workers of Am. v. Superior Court*, 170 Cal. App. 3d 97, 104-105, 216 Cal. Rptr. 4 (1985).

Disqualification for actual or perceived bias rarely occurs, in part because there is a much easier way to disqualify a judge in California. By statute, a party (or each side in a multi-party case) is permitted to make one peremptory challenge to the judge assigned to the case.[408] When a peremptory challenge is made, another judge is automatically assigned to the case. A peremptory challenge may generally be made any time prior to commencement of the trial or hearing, but must also be made within the statutorily prescribed time limits or will be deemed waived.[409] However, a party cannot exercise a peremptory challenge after the commencement of trial, and an otherwise timely peremptory challenge must be denied if the judge has presided at an earlier hearing which involved a determination of contested facts relating to the merits.[410] The reasons for these restrictions are obvious. A peremptory disqualification after commencement a trial would be unduly disruptive, and one after a ruling related to the merits may permit a party to avoid the consequences of an adverse ruling by the simple expedient of getting a new judge.

§ 12.13 TRIAL BY JURY IN THE CALIFORNIA COURTS

[1] Constitutional Right to Jury Trial in California Courts

[a] The "Legal/Equitable" Distinction

The California Constitution *preserves* the right to jury trial in those actions in which there was a right to a jury at common law at the time the California Constitution was first adopted in 1850.[411] Consequently, the determination of the constitutional guarantee turns on an historical analysis.[412] The basic inquiry is whether the "gist" of the action is "legal" and therefore triable by a jury at English or American common law, or "equitable" and therefore to be resolved by the court sitting without a jury.[413] The "legal-equitable" distinction is central in determining whether the right to jury trial exists under the California Constitution, as it is in

---

[408] Cal. Code Civ. Proc. § 170.6(a)(4).

[409] Cal. Code Civ. Proc. § 170.6(a)(2).

[410] Cal. Code Civ. Proc. § 170.6(a)(2); *see, e.g., California Fed. Sav. & Loan Ass'n v. Superior Court,* 189 Cal. App. 3d 167, 234 Cal. Rptr. 414 (1987) (holding the trial judge's ruling on motion for summary adjudication of a "make or break" issue involving contract interpretation bars subsequent peremptory challenge); *School Dist. of Okaloosa Cnty. v. Superior Court,* 58 Cal. App. 4th 1126, 68 Cal. Rptr. 2d 612 (1997) (holding the denial of a motion to quash for lack of personal jurisdiction, like most pretrial motions made in civil cases, does not involve a determination of facts related to the merits of the case).

[411] Cal. Const. art. I, § 16; *see Crouchman v. Superior Court,* 45 Cal. 3d 1167, 1174-1175, 248 Cal. Rptr. 626, 755 P.2d 1075 (1988) (observing that the "common law at the time the Constitution was adopted" includes not only court-made law but also written statutes enacted by Parliament). The Legislature may extend the right to trial by jury to civil actions even though that right is not mandated by the California Constitution. For example, Code of Civil Procedure § 1171 authorizes a jury trial in unlawful detainer actions as to any issue of fact, and the Probate Code authorizes a jury trial in certain proceedings where the Constitution would not likely require one.

[412] *See C&K Eng'g Contractors v. Amber Steel Co.,* 23 Cal. 3d 1, 8-10, 151 Cal. Rptr. 323, 587 P.2d 1136 (1978).

[413] *C&K Eng'g Contractors, supra,* 23 Cal. 3d at 8-9; *People v. One 1941 Chevrolet Coupe,* 37 Cal. 2d 283, 299, 231 P.2d 832 (1951).

determining whether the right exists under the Seventh Amendment in the federal courts.

Most typical civil actions, such as those for damages based on traditional breach of contract or negligence on the one hand, or suits for injunctive relief only on the other, readily fall into one historical category or the other. However, sometimes an action is not so easily classified.[414] For example, in *C&K Engineering Contractors v. Amber Steel Co.*,[415] the plaintiff sought money damages alleging a cause of action for breach of contract based on the doctrine of promissory estoppel. The defendant demanded a jury trial, which was denied by the trial court. The California Supreme Court affirmed, reasoning that although the complaint purports to seek recovery of damages for a breach of contract — in form an action at law in which the right to jury trial would exist — the "gist" of the an action is equitable because promissory estoppel was considered equitable in 1850. *C&K Engineering Contractors v. Amber Steel* demonstrates that the "gist of the action" approach does not focus on the remedy sought but instead on the history of the right asserted, and therefore may mean there is no constitutional right to a jury trial even when a party seeks relief only in the form of money damages. The California approach differs in this regard from the more functional analysis employed by the federal courts when applying the Seventh Amendment, under which the characterization of the relief sought may be more important than finding a historical analogue to the current cause of action.[416]

Where legal and equitable claims are joined in the same action, the parties are entitled to a jury trial on the legal issues.[417] However, a California court will ordinarily resolve the equitable issues first and then, if any legal issues remain, the jury will resolve those issues later.[418] This "equity first" rule is the opposite of the rule employed by the federal courts where the Seventh Amendment generally requires that any claim or defense in the case characterized as "legal" must be tried first to the jury, and the equitable claim later tried to the judge.[419]

---

[414] *See, Shopoff & Cavallo LLP v. Hyon*, 167 Cal. App. 4th 1489, 85 Cal. Rptr. 3d 268 (2008) (holding gist of an interpleader action that seeks to resolve all claims to, and to distribute, interpleaded funds is equitable in nature); *Arciero Ranches v. Meza*, 17 Cal. App. 4th 114, 21 Cal. Rptr. 2d 127 (1993) (ruling defendants entitled to jury trial on cross-complaint seeking injunction to enforce prescriptive easement because gist of such action was considered legal and not equitable in 1850).

[415] 23 Cal. 3d 1, 151 Cal. Rptr. 323, 587 P.2d 1136 (1978).

[416] *See Tull v. United States*, 481 U.S. 412 (1987). The scope of the Seventh Amendment is discussed in § 12.07, *supra*.

[417] *See, e.g., Connell v. Bowes*, 19 Cal. 2d 870, 871, 123 P.2d 456 (1942); *Arciero Ranches v. Meza*, 17 Cal. App. 4th 114, 124, 21 Cal. Rptr. 2d 127 (1993) (citing cases).

[418] *See Arciero Ranches, supra*, 17 Cal. App. 4th at 124 (citing cases); *A-C Co. v. Sec. Pac. Nat'l Bank*, 173 Cal. App. 3d 462, 219 Cal. Rptr. 62 (1985).

[419] *Beacon Theatres, Inc. v. Westover*, 359 U.S. 500 (1959); *see Dairy Queen, Inc. v. Wood*, 369 U.S. 469 (1962).

[b] Waiver of Right to Jury Trial

The California Constitution permits the waiver of jury trial in a civil action "by the consent of the parties expressed as prescribed by statute."[420] Code of Civil Procedure § 631 specifies the ways a jury trial may be waived. These include failure to announce that a jury is required at the time the cause is first set for trial, failure to appear at the trial, failure to deposit jury fees in advance of trial, and waiver by written consent or oral consent in open court. If trial by a jury is demanded by either party and that party later waives a jury trial, section 631 provides any other party with the opportunity to promptly demand a jury trial. A waiver of jury trial is not irrevocable.[421] When relief from a waiver is requested, the court may, in its discretion, allow a trial by jury despite the waiver.[422] Denial of the right to a jury trial constitutes reversible error.[423] Therefore, a party does not waive the right to jury trial by submitting to a nonjury trial after an erroneous denial of a jury, if that party makes a proper and timely objection in the trial court.[424]

[2] Jury Selection in the California Courts

Jury questioning or *voir dire* permits parties to elicit information from potential jurors in order to secure a fair and impartial jury or, more accurately, to remove those potential jurors who are least likely to be fair and impartial. In most civil cases, the trial judge initially examines prospective jurors. Upon completion of the judge's examination, counsel for each party has the right to examine, by oral and direct questioning, any prospective jurors in order to enable counsel to intelligently exercise both *peremptory challenges* and *challenges for cause*.[425] Generally, attorneys in civil jury trials are given considerable freedom and latitude to directly *voir dire* prospective jurors, unless a particular counsel engages in improper questioning. In this context, an improper question is "any question which, as its dominant purpose, attempts to precondition the prospective jurors to a particular result, indoctrinate the jury, or question the prospective jurors concerning the pleadings or the applicable law."[426] In other words, *voir dire* is intended to expose the biases or interests of potential jurors, not to gain favor with the jury by arguing your client's case.

A party may challenge an individual juror for cause for an implied bias or for an actual bias.[427] In addition, each party in civil cases is entitled to six peremptory

---

[420] CAL. CONST. art. I, § 16.

[421] *Taylor v. Union P. R. Corp.*, 16 Cal. 3d 893, 898, 130 Cal. Rptr. 23, 549 P.2d 855 (1976).

[422] CAL. CODE CIV. PROC. § 631(e).

[423] *Cohill v. Nationwide Auto Serv.*, 16 Cal. App. 4th 696, 700, 19 Cal. Rptr. 2d 924 (1993) (citing cases); *Van de Kamp v. Bank of Am.*, 204 Cal. App. 3d 819, 863, 251 Cal. Rptr. 530 (1988).

[424] *Cohill, supra*, 16 Cal. App. 4th at 700-01; *Escamilla v. Cal. Ins. Guar. Ass'n*, 150 Cal. App. 3d 53, 197 Cal. Rptr. 463 (1983) (holding a party who acquiesced without objection in a nonjury trial cannot complain on appeal of the denial of the right to jury trial).

[425] CAL. CODE CIV. PROC. § 222.5.

[426] CAL. CODE CIV. PROC. § 222.5.

[427] CAL. CODE CIV. PROC. § 225(b)(1)(c).

challenges, or eight per side if there are more than two parties.[428] Traditionally, a peremptory challenge may be exercised for any reason and no explanation is necessary. However, United States Supreme Court decisions applying the Fourteenth Amendment hold that a party to a civil lawsuit may not use peremptory challenges to exclude jurors on account of their race or gender.[429] In addition, a California statute now provides that a party "may not use a peremptory challenge to remove a prospective juror on the basis of an assumption that the prospective juror is biased merely because of his or her race, color, religion, sex, national origin, sexual orientation, or similar grounds."[430] However, proving an improper motive for peremptory challenges is difficult because a plausible neutral explanation for exercising the challenge will likely rebut any inference of discrimination.[431]

[3] The Trial Process in the California Courts — The Order of Proceedings

When the jury has been sworn, the trial usually proceeds in the following order: Plaintiff's opening statement, defendant's opening statement unless reserved until after plaintiff has produced its evidence, plaintiff's evidence, defendant's evidence, rebuttal evidence by both parties, plaintiff's main closing argument, defendant's closing argument, plaintiff's concluding argument, and, finally, the judge's instructions to the jury.[432] A slight deviation from this sequence may occur when an answer pleads a defense — such as statute of limitations or res judicata (claim preclusion) — which does not involve the merits but may constitute a bar to trial. In such circumstances, the court may separately try that defense before the trial of the merits.[433] If the court or jury finds in favor of the party asserting the special defense, no further trial is necessary.

[4] Putting the Case to the Jury

[a] Closing Argument

Upon conclusion of the evidence at trial, the attorneys have the right to present closing arguments to the jury. Vigorous and forceful argument is not only expected, but is in keeping with an attorney's ethical obligation to represent the interests of

---

[428] Cal. Code Civ. Proc. § 231(c).

[429] *Edmonson v. Leesville Concrete Co.*, 500 U.S. 614 (1991) (race); *J.E.B. v. Alabama*, 511 U.S. 127 (1994 (gender).

[430] Cal. Code Civ. Proc. § 231.5

[431] *See Batson v. Kentucky*, 476 U.S. 79, 96-98 (1986); Kenneth J. Melilli, *Batson in Practice: What We Have Learned About Batson and Peremptory Challenges*, 71 Notre Dame L. Rev. 447 (1996) (studying several cases and concluding that most attacks on alleged race- and gender-based peremptory challenges have failed).

[432] Cal. Code Civ. Proc. § 607. The order of examination is specified in California Evidence Code § 772.

[433] Cal. Code Civ. Proc. § 597.

his or her client zealously within the bounds of the law.[434] Trial courts accord the attorneys considerable latitude in discussing the facts and the law. An attorney has the right to express opinions based upon fair deductions and reasonable inferences from the evidence given at trial. The argument need not be absolutely logical, but must be based on facts in evidence. Counsel also has the right to state the pertinent law and to apply the law to the facts of the case, so long as the law stated is correct.

Although inappropriate argument may constitute misconduct, the difference between proper and improper argument is difficult to define. Misstatement of the law or facts during argument is clearly improper, but beyond that the line is less clear. The general standards — such as the prohibition on appeals to the prejudice, passions or sympathy of the jury — provide minimal guidance at best. In practice, an attorney's desire to use tactics that are effective with the jury may be more important in determining the content and delivery of a closing argument than the legal or ethical standards as to what constitutes proper or improper argument.

[b] California Jury Instructions

Jury instructions are the means by which a judge communicates the law to be applied by the jury in finding the facts and reaching a verdict. A party is entitled upon request to correct jury instructions as to the law on every theory of the case which is supported by substantial evidence, whether or not that evidence was considered persuasive by the trial court. However, although the trial judge has a responsibility to instruct the jury on all controlling general principles of law, the judge is under no duty in a civil case to instruct on a specific subject if no instruction is proposed.[435]

Generally, counsel for the respective parties must deliver proposed jury instructions to the trial judge, and serve them upon opposing counsel, before the first witness is sworn. Thereafter, counsel may deliver additional proposed instructions upon questions of law developed by the evidence and not disclosed by the pleadings. Before the commencement of closing arguments, the trial judge is required to advise counsel of all instructions to be given so that counsel may refer to them during closing argument. Upon the jury retiring for deliberation, the trial court may, and if requested by the jury shall, supply the jury with a written copy of the instructions.

Jury instructions must clearly and accurately state the applicable legal principles and must not be slanted, unduly repetitious, or argumentative. To better achieve this goal, the California Judicial Council has adopted and approved official pattern jury instructions for use in civil trials, known as *California Civil Jury Instructions* ("CACI"). When CACI does not contain an instruction on a point, the judge may

---

[434] *See* MODEL RULES OF PROFESSIONAL CONDUCT, comment to Rule 1.3; *Gallagher v. Municipal Court*, 31 Cal. 2d 784, 796, 192 P.2d 905 (1948) ("An attorney has the duty to protect the interests of his client. He has a right to press legitimate argument and to protest an erroneous ruling").

[435] CAL. CODE CIV. PROC. § 608. *See, e.g., Agarwal v. Johnson*, 25 Cal. 3d 932, 951, 160 Cal. Rptr. 141, 603 P.2d 58 (1979) (holding that the trial court is under no duty to instruct in absence of specific request, unless there is a complete failure to instruct on controlling legal principles); *Paverud v. Niagara Mach. & Tool Works*, 189 Cal. App. 3d 858, 234 Cal. Rptr. 585 (1987) (ruling the trial court's failure to give instruction on a basic defense, despite lack of request for such instruction, was reversible error).

modify a CACI instruction to submit the issue properly or use a special instruction submitted by a party, but the instruction given should be simple, brief, impartial, and accurate.

A party seeking appellate review of an (allegedly) incorrect jury instruction given by the trial court must prove not only that the instruction was erroneous but also that it was prejudicial and not harmless error.[436] Likewise, a trial court's erroneous refusal to give a specific jury instruction will not require reversal unless the aggrieved party demonstrates actual prejudice.[437] For the same reason, reversible error is not presumed where the trial court instructs the jury on a legal theory for which there was no evidentiary support in the record.[438]

[5] Jury Verdicts in the California Courts

In the California courts, the jury in a civil case must consist of 12 persons unless the parties agree upon a lesser number.[439] Unlike the rule in many other jurisdictions, the California Constitution does not require a unanimous jury in civil cases — a verdict rendered by three-fourths of the jury is sufficient.[440] The verdict of a jury may be either a general or a special verdict. Unlike a general verdict, which merely implies findings on all issues in favor of the plaintiff or defendant, a special verdict requires the jury to make findings with respect to each ultimate fact in the case. The jury must resolve all of the ultimate facts presented in the special verdict, so that "nothing shall remain to the court but to draw from them conclusions of law."[441] When a case is submitted to a jury for special verdicts, the same nine jurors do not have to agree on each special verdict comprising the ultimate verdict.[442]

Generally, the decision whether to submit a general verdict or special verdict to the jury is entirely within the discretion of the trial court. However, use of special verdicts is required in all cases in which issues of punitive damages are presented to the jury so that findings of punitive damages are separate from compensatory damages.[443] The California Supreme Court also recommends the use of special verdicts when the jury is asked to apportion fault on a comparative basis, to assist

---

[436] *See, e.g., Soule v. Gen. Motors Corp.*, 8 Cal. 4th 548, 579-83, 34 Cal. Rptr. 2d 607, 882 P.2d 298 (1994) (holding that error in presenting an inappropriate design defect theory to jury was not sufficiently prejudicial as to require reversal of judgment); *LeMons v. Regents of Univ. of Cal.*, 21 Cal. 3d 869, 876, 148 Cal. Rptr. 355, 582 P.2d 946 (1978) (applying a multi-factor standard for measuring the prejudicial effect of an erroneous instruction).

[437] *Soule, supra*, 8 Cal. 4th at 580 (ruling "there is no rule of automatic reversal or inherent prejudice applicable to any category of civil instructional error, whether of commission or omission").

[438] *See Soule, supra*, 8 Cal. 4th at 580-81.

[439] Cal. Const. art. I, § 16.

[440] Cal. Const. art. I, § 16; Cal. Code Civ. Proc. § 618.

[441] Cal. Code Civ. Proc. § 624.

[442] *Resch v. Volkswagen of Am., Inc.*, 36 Cal. 3d 676, 205 Cal. Rptr. 827, 685 P.2d 1178 (1984) (repudiating the "identical-nine rule").

[443] Cal. Code Civ. Proc. § 625.

the jury with its calculations.[444] However, despite their recommended use in this and in other circumstances, the judicial attitude toward special verdict forms remains lukewarm. Judges are hesitant to use special verdicts because they are concerned about the possibility of inconsistent findings by the jury.

§ 12.14 NON-JURY ("BENCH") TRIALS IN THE CALIFORNIA COURTS

[1] Order of Proceedings

The vast majority (over 96%) of civil trials in the California courts are nonjury or "bench" trials.[445] Ordinarily, unless the court directs otherwise, a nonjury trial of a civil action proceeds in the same order as in a jury trial. The lack of a jury obviously eliminates the need for jury *voir dire*, jury instructions, and other jury-related procedures; and may reduce (but not eliminate) the need for opening statements, closing arguments, sidebar conferences, and strict adherence to some of the rules of evidence. But in most other respects, a nonjury trial follows the familiar sequence of a jury trial.

The trial judge is the trier of fact in a nonjury trial and therefore determines the credibility of witnesses, resolves conflicting evidence, and draws inferences from the evidence.[446] As discussed below, the trial judge must also announce a tentative decision and, if requested, render a statement of decision. Other differences from a jury trial may also apply. For example, in ruling on a motion for new trial, the court may modify the statement of decision or the judgment, may reopen the case for further proceedings and introduction of additional evidence, or may grant a new trial.[447]

[2] Statement of Decision

In a nonjury trial not completed within one day, the superior court must announce a *tentative decision* by written or oral statement.[448] This tentative decision does not constitute the judgment and is not binding on the court.[449] Within 10 days after the court announces its tentative decision, any party may request a

[444] *Daly v. Gen. Motors Corp.*, 20 Cal. 3d 725, 743, 144 Cal. Rptr. 380, 575 P.2d 1162 (1978).

[445] *See 2012 Court Statistics Report of the Judicial Council of California*, Superior Court Dispositions, Fig. 21.

[446] *See, e.g., Hellman v. La Cumbre Golf & Country Club*, 6 Cal. App. 4th 1224, 1229, 8 Cal. Rptr. 2d 293 (1992); *Davis v. Kahn*, 7 Cal. App. 3d 868, 874, 86 Cal. Rptr. 872 (1970).

[447] Cal. Code Civ. Proc. § 662.

[448] Cal. Ct. R. 3.1590(a).

[449] Cal. Ct. R. 3.1590(b); *see, e.g., Marriage of Ditto*, 206 Cal. App. 3d 643, 646, 253 Cal. Rptr. 770 (1988) (ruling that the trial court is not bound by its statement of intended decision and may enter a wholly different judgment than the one tentatively announced); *Slavin v. Borinstein*, 25 Cal. App. 4th 713, 718-719, 30 Cal. Rptr. 2d 745 (1994) (explaining that a trial court has the option to direct that intended decision will become a statement of decision).

statement of decision comprised of findings of fact and conclusions of law.[450] If a party timely requests a statement of decision, the usual practice is for the trial judge to ask the prevailing party to prepare and submit a proposed statement of decision. If another party files objections to the proposed statement, the court may hold a hearing on the proposed statement and the objections before issuing its statement of decision. If a statement of decision is not requested, the court merely prepares a proposed judgment and eventually files the judgment.

The main purpose of a statement of decision is to provide an explanation of the factual and legal basis for the trial court's decision. The statement also enables the parties to determine whether and on what basis review should be sought — findings may demonstrate to a losing party the likely futility of any appeal — and helps to focus the appellate review if an appeal is taken. Moreover, a statement of decision may be essential to the appellant for meaningful review if the judgment is appealed. A finding of fact specified in the statement of decision will not be set aside on appeal where there is *substantial evidence* to support the trial court's finding.[451]

In the absence of a statement of decision, the appellate court must assume that the trial court made whatever factual findings were necessary to support the judgment.[452] This assumption makes reversal on appeal unlikely because the issue before the appellate court is whether substantial evidence supports the implied findings. For example, in *Michael U. v. Jamie B.*,[453] an appeal by adoptive parents of the award of custody of their adopted son to his natural teenage father, the California Supreme Court held that because no statement of decision was requested, the appellate court must assume that the trial court found an award of custody to the natural father would not be detrimental to the son and, consequently, the only issue before the appellate court is whether substantial evidence supports this implied finding. Because of the importance of a statement of decision to the appealing party, a trial judge's failure to prepare a written statement after a timely request usually constitutes reversible error.[454]

A different standard applies to appellate review of nonjury decisions in the federal courts. Pursuant to Rule 52 of the Federal Rules of Civil Procedure, a district court's finding of fact must not be set aside unless "clearly erroneous." The precise meaning of the "clearly erroneous" standard is difficult to determine, but it appears to be somewhat less deferential to a trial court's finding than is California's "substantial evidence" test.[455] Rule 52(a) also *requires* the district court to set forth

---

[450] CAL. CODE CIV. PROC. § 632; CAL. CT. R. 3.1590(d).

[451] *Michael U. v. Jamie B.*, 39 Cal. 3d 787, 792-93, 218 Cal. Rptr. 39, 705 P.2d 362 (1985).

[452] *See, e.g., Slavin v. Borinstein, supra*, 25 Cal. App. 4th at 718; *Marriage of Ditto, supra*, 206 Cal. App. 3d at 647.

[453] 39 Cal. 3d 787, 218 Cal. Rptr. 39, 705 P.2d 362 (1985).

[454] *See, e.g., Whittington v. McKinney*, 234 Cal. App. 3d 123, 285 Cal. Rptr. 586 (1991); *Marriage of Ananeh-Firempong*, 219 Cal. App. 3d 272, 282, 268 Cal. Rptr. 83 (1990).

[455] In *Anderson v. City of Bessemer City*, 470 U.S. 564 (1985), the United States Supreme Court explained that a finding is "clearly erroneous" when "although there is evidence to support it, the reviewing court on the entire evidence is left with the definite and firm conviction that a mistake has been committed." *Id.* at 573. The "clearly erroneous" test is discussed more fully in § 13.09[2][b], *infra*.

findings of fact and conclusions of law which explain its decision; unlike California, no request by a party is necessary.

§ 12.15 JUDICIAL SUPERVISION OF JURY DECISIONS BY THE CALIFORNIA COURTS

[1] Introductory Note

California statutes authorize the traditional motions for nonsuit and directed verdict during trial, and for judgment notwithstanding the verdict (JNOV) after entry of a jury verdict, to test the sufficiency of the evidence to support a jury verdict. The legal standard applicable to each of these procedural devices is essentially the same as for the analogous motion and renewed motion for "judgment as a matter of law" authorized by Rule 50 of the Federal Rules of Civil Procedure. However, unlike federal Rule 50, which requires as a prerequisite to a post-verdict "renewed motion" that the party made the motion for judgment as a matter of law before submission of the case to the jury, a motion for directed verdict is not a prerequisite for a motion for a judgment notwithstanding the verdict in the California courts.[456]

California statutes also authorize motions for new trials on bases that are similar to those available in the federal courts under Rule 59 of the Federal Rules of Civil Procedure. However, in contrast to the procedural simplicity of federal Rule 59, California's new trial statutes contain complicated requirements that have created a procedural minefield for attorneys and judges. Because of their importance to the post-trial supervision of jury decisions, the California new trial statutes are discussed in considerable detail below.

[2] California Nonsuits and Directed Verdicts

A defendant may move for a judgment of *nonsuit* upon completion of the plaintiff's opening statement or after the presentation of plaintiff's evidence in a jury trial.[457] If the motion is granted, the judgment of nonsuit operates as an adjudication on the merits unless the court specifies otherwise.[458] The court may grant the motion as to some or all issues in the action; if granted partially, the trial must proceed as to the remaining issues. If the motion is denied, the defendant still has the right to offer evidence.

---

[456] *See* CAL. CODE CIV. PROC. § 629.

[457] CAL. CODE CIV. PROC. § 581c(a). In California, a trial court may properly grant a motion for nonsuit immediately after the completion of the plaintiff's opening statement "where it appears that counsel for the plaintiff has stated all the facts that he expects to prove and that these would not make a prima facie case." *Dameshghi v. Texaco Refining & Mktg.*, 3 Cal. App. 4th 1262, 1286, 6 Cal. Rptr. 2d 515 (1992) (affirming nonsuit after opening statement); *Freeman v. Lind*, 181 Cal. App. 3d 791, 226 Cal. Rptr. 515 (1986) (affirming nonsuit after plaintiff's opening statement as to two defendants and reversing as to another); *Willis v. Gordon*, 20 Cal. 3d 629, 633, 143 Cal. Rptr. 723, 574 P.2d 794 (1978) (reversing nonsuit because opening statement contained facts from which jury could reasonably draw inference of negligence).

[458] CAL. CODE CIV. PROC. § 581c(c).

A motion for nonsuit is tantamount to a demurrer to the evidence by which a defendant contests the sufficiency of the plaintiff's evidence before presenting his or her own. In making this evaluation of the plaintiff's evidence, the trial court must not weigh the evidence or judge the credibility of witnesses. Instead, the evidence most favorable to the plaintiff must be accepted as true and conflicting evidence must be disregarded.[459] Nonsuit is proper if a plaintiff presents insufficient evidence on an element of the case or if the plaintiff's evidence establishes an affirmative defense that defeats the cause of action.[460] However, where the plaintiff presents substantial evidence in support of each element — thereby creating a factual conflict for resolution by the jury — the motion for nonsuit must be denied.[461]

After all parties have completed the presentation of all their evidence, any party may move for an order directing entry of a verdict in its favor.[462] Except for this difference in timing, a *directed verdict* is equivalent to a nonsuit. The test for directing a verdict is the same as for entering a nonsuit and, as with a nonsuit, the court may grant a directed verdict as to some but not all issues.[463]

[3] Judgment Notwithstanding the Verdict (JNOV)

After a jury verdict, the judge or a party against whom the verdict was rendered may move for a judgment notwithstanding the verdict (JNOV).[464] The trial judge's power to grant a JNOV is the same as its power to grant a nonsuit or to direct a verdict — these powers are merely different aspects of the same judicial function and are governed by the same rules.[465] As with nonsuits and directed verdicts, the trial judge in granting JNOV must not weigh the evidence nor judge the credibility of witnesses.[466]

---

[459] *Nally v. Grace Cmty. Church*, 47 Cal. 3d 278, 291, 253 Cal. Rptr. 97, 763 P.2d 948 (1988).

[460] *See, e.g., Brimmer v. Cal. Charter Med., Inc.*, 180 Cal. App. 3d 678, 225 Cal. Rptr. 752 (1986) (upholding nonsuit as to some defendants because no substantial evidence of their participation in alleged malpractice); *Breazeal v. Henry Mayo Newhall Mem. Hosp.*, 234 Cal. App. 3d 1329, 1337, 286 Cal. Rptr. 207 (1991) (affirming nonsuit granted on grounds that plaintiff's evidence established the affirmative defense of "good samaritan" immunity). After a motion for nonsuit is made, the trial court ordinarily will, if so requested, permit the plaintiff to introduce further evidence to cure the defects in the plaintiff's case. *See Huang v. Garner*, 157 Cal. App. 3d 404, 416-418, 203 Cal. Rptr. 800 (1984) (reversing nonsuit where trial court refused to allow plaintiff to reopen his case).

[461] *Nally, supra*, 47 Cal. 3d at 291.

[462] CAL. CODE CIV. PROC. § 630(a).

[463] CAL. CODE CIV. PROC. § 630(b)-(d). *See, e.g., Newing v. Cheatham*, 15 Cal. 3d 351, 358-359, 124 Cal. Rptr. 193, 540 P.2d 33 (1975) (explaining that directed verdict may be granted against a party when there is no evidence of sufficient substantiality to support a verdict in favor of such party); *Estate of Lances*, 216 Cal. 397, 400, 14 P.2d 768 (1932) (the power of the court to direct a verdict is absolutely the same as the power to grant a nonsuit).

[464] CAL. CODE CIV. PROC. § 629.

[465] *Reynolds v. Willson*, 51 Cal. 2d 94, 99, 331 P.2d 48 (1958); *Hauter v. Zogarts*, 14 Cal. 3d 104, 110-11, 120 Cal. Rptr. 681, 534 P.2d 377 (1975).

[466] *See, e.g., Clemmer v. Hartford Ins. Co.*, 22 Cal. 3d 865, 151 Cal. Rptr. 285, 587 P. 2d 1098 (1978); *Saari v. Jongordon Corp.*, 5 Cal. App. 4th 797, 7 Cal. Rptr. 2d 82 (1992) (holding JNOV motion properly denied where substantial evidence to support jury verdict); *Osborn v. Irwin Mem. Blood Bank*, 5 Cal.

[4] Motion for New Trial in the California Courts

[a] Introductory Note on California's New Trial Statutes

The most frequently employed post-trial motion in the California courts is the *motion for a new trial*. If granted, a new trial order authorizes a *de novo* trial as if the first trial never occurred. The grounds and procedures for new trial motions are set forth in meticulous detail in several California statutes. As will be discussed below, the procedural steps prescribed by these statutes are mandatory and must be strictly followed.

Code of Civil Procedure § 657 specifies the *exclusive* grounds for a new trial motion in the California courts. These enumerated grounds encompass both procedural errors (*e.g.*, jury misconduct and other irregularities in the proceedings) and substantive errors (*e.g.*, insufficiency of the evidence to justify the verdict, excessive damages, and error in law) occurring during trial. Even if one or more grounds exist, a new trial may not be granted unless the error materially affects the substantial rights of the moving party — in other words, unless the error is prejudicial and not harmless.[467] Consequently, the determination of a motion for new trial is addressed to the trial court's discretion.[468]

Section 657 also governs appellate review of new trial orders. An order granting a new trial must be affirmed on appeal if the appellate court finds that it should have been granted upon any ground stated in the motion, whether or not specified as a ground in the order, except that "the order shall not be affirmed upon the ground of the insufficiency of the evidence to justify the verdict or other decision, or upon the ground of excessive or inadequate damages, unless such ground is stated in the order granting the motion."[469] The reason for this limitation on appellate review is that the grounds of "insufficiency of the evidence" and "excessive or inadequate damages" require the trial judge to weigh the evidence, a role unsuitable for the appellate court to undertake in the first instance.

App. 4th 234, 7 Cal. Rptr. 2d 101 (1992) (holding that, in granting a JNOV motion, the court must not weigh conflicting expert opinions).

[467] Cal. Const. art. VI, § 13 ("No judgment shall be set aside, or new trial granted . . . unless, after an examination of the entire cause, including the evidence, the court shall be of the opinion that the error complained of has resulted in a miscarriage of justice"); *see Hasson v. Ford Motor Co.*, 32 Cal. 3d 388, 185 Cal. Rptr. 654, 650 P.2d 1171 (1982) (holding new trial not required where no substantial prejudice resulted from jury misconduct).

[468] *See, e.g., Neal v. Farmers Ins. Exch.*, 21 Cal. 3d 910, 933, 148 Cal. Rptr. 389, 582 P.2d 980 (1978) (observing an appellant court will not reverse a proper order granting a new trial on grounds of excessive damages, or requiring a reduction of the amount as a condition of denying one, unless the trial court clearly abused its discretion); *Weathers v. Kaiser Found. Hosp.*, 5 Cal. 3d 98, 95 Cal. Rptr. 516, 485 P.2d 1132 (1971) (explaining that a motion for new trial for juror misconduct is a matter of discretion for the trial court); *Hand Elec., Inc. v. Snowline Joint Unified Sch. Dist.*, 21 Cal. App. 4th 862, 871, 26 Cal. Rptr. 2d 446 (1994) (noting that on appeal from an order granting a new trial because of misleading jury instruction, sole question is whether trial court abused its discretion).

[469] Cal. Code Civ. Proc. § 657(a).

[b] Motion for New Trial: Procedures

California Code of Civil Procedure § 657 and § 660 impose several important limitations on motions for new trials. An aggrieved party must file a written motion for a new trial designating one or more of the statutory grounds upon which the motion is made. The motion can only be granted on a ground specified in the motion.[470] For example, in one case, an order granting a new trial on the ground of misconduct of counsel was held to be void where the motion only specified the ground of insufficiency of the evidence to justify the verdict.[471]

The motion must be filed within 15 days of the date of mailing the notice of entry of judgment by the clerk or by a party, or within 180 days after entry of judgment, whichever is earliest.[472] Compliance with these statutory time limits is jurisdictional — a court neither has the power to entertain an untimely motion nor to order a new trial *sua sponte* (on its own motion).[473] There is another important time limit, this one on the power of the trial judge to rule on a motion for new trial. Pursuant to section 660, the judge must decide the motion within 60 days after the motion is filed. If the motion is not determined within the 60-day period, "the effect shall be a denial of the motion without further order of the court."[474] A trial court lacks jurisdiction to decide a new trial motion after the 60-day limitation has expired. For example, in one recent case, the appellate court vacated the new trial order and reinstated a $2.4 million judgment because the trial court ruling was on the 61st day after the defendant filed the new trial motion.[475]

[c] The New Trial Order Must State Grounds and Specify Reasons

If a motion for new trial is granted, Code of Civil Procedure § 657 requires the trial judge to state the *grounds* upon which the motion was granted in the new trial order, and to specify the *reasons* for granting the motion within 10 days after the order. The statement of grounds and specification of reasons must be in writing, and the specification of reasons must be more than a mere statement of ultimate facts.[476] The trial court must strictly adhere to these mandatory requirements. A

---

[470] *Malkasian v. Irwin*, 61 Cal. 2d 738, 745, 40 Cal. Rptr. 78, 394 P.2d 822 (1964); *Neal v. Montgomery Elevator Co.*, 7 Cal. App. 4th 1194, 1198, 9 Cal. Rptr. 2d 497 (1992).

[471] *Wagner v. Singleton*, 133 Cal. App. 3d 69, 183 Cal. Rptr. 631 (1982).

[472] CAL. CODE CIV. PROC. § 659. One of the peculiarities of California practice is that a party does not file a "motion," but rather a written "notice of intention to move" for an order, the actual motion presented orally at a hearing. For simplicity, these materials refer to this process as filing a written "motion," the terminology used in federal court and in most other states.

[473] *Sanchez-Corea v. Bank of America*, 38 Cal. 3d 892, 215 Cal. Rptr. 679, 701 P.2d 826 (1985).

[474] CAL. CODE CIV. PROC. § 660.

[475] *Green v. Laibco, LLC*, 192 Cal. App. 4th 441, 446-49, 121 Cal. Rptr. 3d 415 (2011).

[476] *See Stevens v. Parke, Davis & Co.*, 9 Cal. 3d 51, 62, 107 Cal. Rptr. 45, 507 P.2d 653 (1973) (holding the trial court's statement of ultimate fact that "the verdict is excessive, that it is not sustained by the evidence" and was "based upon prejudice and passion on the part of the jury" was an inadequate specification of reasons); *Miller v. Los Angeles County Flood Control Dist.*, 8 Cal. 3d 689, 698, 106 Cal. Rptr. 1, 505 P.2d 193 (1973) (holding the trial court's statement of reasons that "the District completely and adequately discharged any obligation it had in the maintenance of the basin and dam" was

trial court lacks jurisdiction to file the statement of grounds after the 60-day period for ruling on the new trial motion, even though the trial court decided the motion itself within the 60-day limitation.[477] A new trial order that fails to state grounds or specify reasons is defective, but not void.[478] As a consequence, although the new trial order is operative, an appellate court is precluded from affirming the order on the grounds of insufficiency of the evidence or excessive damages.[479] Moreover, as discussed previously, pursuant to section 657, the appellate court is precluded from considering any other ground not designated in the motion for new trial.

An unfortunate consequence of a trial judge's failure to comply with these requirements is that a defendant may be precluded from relying on what may well be his strongest ground — insufficiency of the evidence to support the verdict — in arguing for affirmance of a new trial order on appeal.[480] For example, in *Sanchez-Corea v. Bank of America*,[481] after the jury returned a verdict of over $2 million for the plaintiffs, the defendant moved for a new trial asserting six grounds, including insufficiency of the evidence to support the verdict. On the last day of the 60-day limitation period, the trial judge granted the motion but did not state any grounds or specify any reasons in the new trial order. Several days later, the judge entered a second order explaining that the sole ground for granting the motion was "insufficiency of the evidence." The plaintiffs appealed. The California Supreme Court concluded that the initial new trial order was defective for failure to specify any grounds, and the second order stating grounds was invalid because filed after the 60-day period. Because the initial new trial order was defective but not void, pursuant to section 657 the Supreme Court was precluded from affirming the order on grounds of insufficiency of the evidence even though that was the only ground specified in the invalid second order. After considering the other grounds stated in the defendant's new trial motion, the *Sanchez-Corea* Court concluded that they did not warrant affirming the trial court's order and, accordingly, reversed the new trial order.

The result in *Sanchez-Corea* seems unfair generally, but particularly because section 657 prohibits a trial judge from directing a party to prepare either the order or the specification of reasons.[482] According to the California Supreme Court, these various requirements and limitations on new trial orders are justified by important statutory policies: to promote careful deliberation by the trial judge in the exercise of its broad discretionary power to grant a new trial, and to make a record

---

inadequate to support insufficiency of the evidence ground for new trial).

[477] *Sanchez-Corea, supra,* 38 Cal. 3d at 901-05.

[478] *Oakland Raiders v. Nat'l Football League,* 41 Cal. 4th 624, 634-36, 61 Cal. Rptr. 3d 634, 161 P.3d 151 (2007); *Sanchez-Corea, supra,* 38 Cal. 3d at 900-905.

[479] *See, e.g., Oakland Raiders, supra,* 41 Cal. 4th at 636-38; *Sanchez-Corea, supra,* 38 Cal. 3d at 900-905.

[480] *See, e.g., Sanchez-Corea, supra,* 38 Cal. 3d at 905-906 (even though the trial court's defective order specified insufficiency of the evidence as the sole ground for granting the motion, an appellate court could not affirm the order on that ground).

[481] 38 Cal. 3d 892, 215 Cal. Rptr. 679, 701 P.2d 826 (1985).

[482] Code Civ. Proc. § 657 states "[t]he court shall not direct the attorney for a party to prepare either or both said order and said specification of reasons."

sufficiently precise to permit meaningful appellate review.[483] These policies provide little solace to parties, such as the defendant in *Sanchez-Corea*, who have little or no ability to make sure the trial judge complies with the various statutory requirements.

[5] Grounds for New Trial: Insufficiency of the Evidence and Excessive Damages

[a] Insufficiency of the Evidence to Justify the Verdict

When a trial court determines a motion for new trial made upon the ground of insufficiency of the evidence, Code of Civil Procedure § 657 *requires* the judge to weigh the evidence and judge the credibility of witnesses. In so doing, the court may disbelieve witnesses and draw inferences contrary to those supporting the verdict, and may grant a new trial even though there is sufficient evidence to sustain the jury's verdict on appeal.[484] Nonetheless, pursuant to section 657, a new trial cannot be granted "unless after weighing the evidence the court is convinced from the entire record, including reasonable inferences therefrom, that the . . . jury clearly should have reached a different verdict."

In most cases, a party files a motion for judgment notwithstanding the verdict (JNOV) under Code Civil Procedure § 629 along with a motion for new trial. The standard a trial judge must employ when determining a new trial motion for insufficiency of the evidence differs fundamentally from the standard applicable to a JNOV motion, where the judge is not permitted to weigh the evidence.[485] Because these two standards are different, when a trial court grants a new trial motion for insufficiency of the evidence, it may properly refuse to also grant an accompanying JNOV motion. However, if the court denies a party's new trial motion on the ground of insufficiency of the evidence, it should also deny that party's JNOV motion.

California courts often state that the determination of a new trial motion is addressed to the trial court's discretion, and that a new trial order will not be disturbed on appeal "unless a manifest and unmistakable abuse of discretion clearly appears."[486] That statement is inaccurate with respect to appellate review of an order granting a new trial on the basis of insufficient evidence. As explained by the California Supreme Court in *Lane v. Hughes Aircraft Co.*,[487] an order granting a

---

[483] *See Hasson v. Ford Motor Co.*, 32 Cal. 3d 388, 420, 185 Cal. Rptr. 654, 650 P.2d 1171 (1982) (citing cases).

[484] *Locksley v. Ungureanu*, 178 Cal. App. 3d 457, 463, 223 Cal. Rptr. 737 (1986); *Widener v. Pac. Gas & Elec. Co.*, 75 Cal. App. 3d 415, 440, 142 Cal. Rptr. 304 (1977); *Candido v. Huitt*, 151 Cal. App. 3d 918, 923, 199 Cal. Rptr. 41 (1984).

[485] The court in *Fountain Valley Chateau Blanc Homeowners' Ass'n v. Dept. of Veteran Affairs*, 67 Cal. App. 4th 743, 79 Cal. Rptr. 2d 248 (1998), explained that the difference in these standards reflects the difference in purpose behind these two motions: The purpose of a motion for JNOV is to allow a party to prevail as a matter of law where the relevant evidence is already in; by contrast, the function of a new trial motion for insufficient evidence is to allow a reexamination of an issue of fact. *Id.* at 750-51.

[486] *See, e.g., Neal v. Farmers Ins. Exch.*, 21 Cal. 3d 910, 933, 148 Cal. Rptr. 389, 582 P.2d 980 (1978); *Weathers v. Kaiser Found. Hosp.*, 5 Cal. 3d 98, 95 Cal. Rptr. 516, 485 P.2d 1132 (1971).

[487] 22 Cal. 4th 405, 93 Cal. Rptr. 2d 60, 993 P.2d 388 (2000).

new trial based on insufficiency of the evidence "must be sustained on appeal unless the opposing party demonstrates that no reasonable finder of fact could have found for the movant on [the trial court's] theory."[488] This high degree of deference is called for because the trial court, in ruling on the new trial motion, sits as an independent trier of fact. Therefore, "the trial court's factual determinations, reflected in its decision to grant a new trial, are entitled to the same deference that an appellate court would ordinarily accord a jury's factual determinations." The *Lane* Court also emphasized that "so long as the outcome is uncertain at the close of trial — that is, so long as the evidence can support a verdict if favor of *either* party — a properly constructed new trial order is not subject to reversal on appeal." As a practical matter, this highly deferential standard of appellate review means that, in most cases, an appeal is unwise.

[b] Excessive Damages and Conditional New Trial Orders ("Remittitur")

Section 657 also requires a trial judge to weigh the evidence and judge the credibility of witnesses when determining a motion for new trial based upon the ground of excessive or inadequate damages. In so doing, the trial court may, in its discretion, order a new trial limited to the issue of damages and may condition its order so that the motion is denied if the party in whose favor the verdict has been rendered consents to such reduction of damages "as the court in its independent judgment determines from the evidence to be fair and reasonable."[489] Such a conditional new trial procedure, commonly referred to as "remittitur," is expressly authorized by statute. Trial courts often utilize remittitur when damages are properly awarded but the amount is excessive, and a new trial can be avoided if the nonmoving party consents to a reduction.[490]

[6] Grounds for New Trial: Misconduct During Trial and Other Irregularities

Misconduct during trial — either by the jury, the judge, or the opposing counsel — is often asserted as a ground when moving for a new trial. Any irregularities which deprive a party of a fair and impartial trial may constitute grounds for a new trial.[491] In other words, the misconduct must be prejudicial — an assessment made

---

[488] *Lane, supra,* 22 Cal. 4th at 409.

[489] Cal. Code Civ. Proc. § 662.5(b). Section 662.5(a) authorizes the corresponding process of "additur" for inadequate damages. *See, e.g., Marshall v. Dep't of Water & Power,* 219 Cal. App. 3d 1124, 1137, 268 Cal. Rptr. 559 (1990) (jury award of $1 increased by means of additur to $100,001 after plaintiff moved for new trial). Additur is not authorized in the federal courts. *See Dimick v. Schiedt,* 293 U.S. 474 (1935).

[490] *See, e.g., Hasson v. Ford Motor Co.,* 32 Cal. 3d 388, 418-421, 185 Cal. Rptr. 654, 650 P.2d 1171 (1982) (trial court required plaintiff to consent to a $1,650,000 reduction in damage award in order to avoid a new trial); *Neal v. Farmers Ins. Exchange, supra,* 21 Cal. 3d at 933 (jury verdict of $1.5 million remitted to $750,000); *Grimshaw v. Ford Motor Co.,* 119 Cal. App. 3d 757, 174 Cal. Rptr. 348 (1981) (trial court required plaintiff to remit all but $3.5 million of $125 million punitive damage verdict as a condition of denial of defendant's new trial motion).

[491] *See, e.g., Sabella v. S. Pac. Co.,* 70 Cal. 2d 311, 74 Cal. Rptr. 534, 449 P.2d 750 (1969) (attorney misconduct during closing argument); *Lewis v. Bill Robertson & Sons, Inc.,* 162 Cal. App. 3d 650, 208 Cal.

by the court in each case based on the overall record "taking into account such factors, inter alia, as the nature and seriousness of the remarks and misconduct, the general atmosphere, including the judge's control of the trial, the likelihood of prejudicing the jury, and the efficacy of objection or admonition under all the circumstances."⁴⁹² Even conduct deemed prejudicial may not constitute grounds sufficient for a new trial where the moving party failed to make timely objections and requests that the jury be admonished.⁴⁹³

[a]   Impeachment of Verdict for Juror Misconduct

Code of Civil Procedure § 657 authorizes a new trial where the substantial rights of a party are materially affected by misconduct or irregularity in the proceedings of the jury. However, California Evidence Code § 1150(a) imposes a fundamental restriction on the use of juror testimony to impeach a verdict for juror misconduct: Evidence of objectively verifiable acts of misconduct is admissible, but evidence which describe individual or collective juror subjective mental process, purporting to show how the verdict was reached, is inadmissible. This "objective/subjective" distinction may permit prejudicial error to go unremedied even where jurors have admitted to serious misconduct. But there are strong policy reasons for this distinction, such as preserving the stability of verdicts, deterring harassment of jurors by losing counsel, and assuring the privacy of jury deliberations by foreclosing inquiry into jurors' thought processes.⁴⁹⁴ The same policy concerns are reflected in Rule 606(b) of the Federal Rules of Evidence, which contains an analogous "internal/external" distinction for the admissibility of juror testimony in federal court.⁴⁹⁵

The "objective/subjective" distinction is the basic starting point with respect to impeachment of verdicts for juror misconduct. The distinction has proven difficult to apply in actual cases, at times leading to inconsistent results. For example, in one case, a declaration of the foreperson which evidenced a discussion among the jurors to inflate their verdict to compensate for attorney fees and income taxes was held admissible, as were affidavits from several jurors in another case which established that the jury foreman advised the jury not to worry about the size of the verdict they might return because the trial judge had the power to reduce any excessive award;⁴⁹⁶ but in yet another case, the declaration of a juror describing jury discussion about the amount of any award the plaintiff would have to pay for attorney fees was held inadmissible.⁴⁹⁷ In some cases, declarations of jurors stating

---

Rptr. 699 (1984) (improper commenting on the evidence by judge in jury trial); *Krouse v. Graham*, 19 Cal. 3d 59, 137 Cal. Rptr. 863, 562 P.2d 1022 (1977) (juror misconduct).

⁴⁹² *Dominguez v. Pantalone*, 212 Cal. App. 3d 201, 211, 260 Cal. Rptr. 431 (1989).

⁴⁹³ *See, e.g.*, *Sabella v. S. Pac. Co.*, *supra*, 70 Cal. 2d at 318-321; *Whitfield v. Roth*, 10 Cal. 3d 874, 891-893, 112 Cal. Rptr. 540, 519 P.2d 588 (1974).

⁴⁹⁴ *Hasson v. Ford Motor Co.*, 32 Cal. 3d 388, 414, 185 Cal. Rptr. 654, 650 P.2d 1171 (1982).

⁴⁹⁵ *See Tanner v. United States*, 483 U.S. 107 (1987); § 12.09[2][c], *supra*.

⁴⁹⁶ *Tramell v. McDonnell Douglas Corp.*, 163 Cal. App. 3d 157, 172-173, 209 Cal. Rptr. 427 (1984); *DiRosario v. Havens*, 196 Cal. App. 3d 1224, 1235-1238, 242 Cal. Rptr. 423 (1987).

⁴⁹⁷ *Moore v. Preventive Medicine Med. Group, Inc.*, 178 Cal. App. 3d 728, 740-741, 223 Cal. Rptr. 859 (1986).

that they made up their minds about the case before deliberations were held admissible, but in other cases, similar declarations were held not admissible.[498] In one case, a jury's note, attached to and incorporated by reference on the verdict form, which revealed that the jury misconstrued its duty in apportioning damages was held admissible, but juror declarations revealing how the jury arrived at its damages figures on this verdict form were held inadmissible.[499]

[b] The Objective/Subjective Distinction and "Deliberative Error"

Juror declarations are inadmissible where they describe juror misunderstanding and misinterpretation of the law — in other words, "deliberative error" in the jury's subjective reasoning process.[500] For example, in *Ford v. Bennacka*,[501] the trial court refused to admit proffered juror declarations which disclosed obvious misapplication of basic legal principles by the jury. The jury had returned a verdict for defendant in *Ford*, a personal injury action for negligence involving a motorcycle accident. The plaintiff sought a new trial on grounds of jury misconduct, and submitted declarations from five jurors asserting that the jury had confused the concepts of comparative negligence and preponderance of the evidence. The declarations stated that the jury reached a consensus that both sides were equally negligent, and therefore believed (incorrectly) they must return a verdict for defendant because defendant's negligence did not preponderate over the plaintiff's negligence. The trial court denied the motion and plaintiff appealed. The Court of Appeal held that the proffered declarations were inadmissible because they constituted improper probing of the jurors' subjective mental processes.

Likewise, in *Mesecher v. County of San Diego*,[502] the Court of Appeal held inadmissible several juror declarations which essentially stated that the jurors used a definition of the tort of battery in their deliberations which was more favorable to the plaintiff than the trial court's instructions. Even though the jurors communicated their misunderstanding of the instructions to each other during deliberations, the court viewed these proffered declarations as reflecting the jurors' subjective mental processes and therefore inadmissible.

---

[498] *See Maple v. Cincinnati, Inc.*, 163 Cal. App. 3d 387, 391-394, 209 Cal. Rptr. 451 (1985) (observing that "attempts by judges to straight jacket a jury in its deliberations by an after-the-fact critiquing and criticizing of the language and reasoning used in those deliberations runs directly contrary to our fundamental concept of the jury function"); *but see Grobeson v. City of Los Angeles*, 190 Cal. App. 4th 778, 118 Cal. Rptr. 3d 798 (2010) (holding statement by juror that she had made up her mind during the second week of a five-week trial revealed her mental state but was nevertheless admissible because it also showed she had prejudged the case and thus committed misconduct).

[499] *See Maxwell v. Powers*, 22 Cal. App. 4th 1596, 28 Cal. Rptr. 2d 62 (1994).

[500] *See, e.g., Bell v. Bayerische Motoren Werke Aktiengesellschaft*, 181 Cal. App. 4th 1108, 1124-26, 105 Cal. Rptr. 3d 485 (2010) (holding inadmissible jury declarations describing some of the jurors' purported understanding of the words used in the special verdict form); *Smoketree-Lake Murray, Ltd. v. Mills Concrete Constr. Co.*, 234 Cal. App. 3d 1724, 286 Cal. Rptr. 435 (1991) (ruling juror declaration indicating jurors modified and misapplied instruction on fraud during deliberations inadmissible).

[501] 226 Cal. App. 3d 330, 276 Cal. Rptr. 513 (1990).

[502] 9 Cal. App. 4th 1677, 1683, 12 Cal. Rptr. 279 (1992).

[c] Reliance on Juror Expertise and Personal Experiences; Juror Inattentiveness

Another ground frequently asserted to impeach a verdict is that the jury was improperly influenced by outside information or by jurors' recounting their own outside experiences or expertise. Often, the admission of such juror testimony is held proper, but not in all cases.[503] The courts also struggle with the vexing problem of in what circumstances should a verdict be impeachable when jurors relate their personal experiences during deliberations.[504] A surprising number of verdict impeachment decisions involve jurors performing an experiment. Not all juror experiments constitute juror misconduct. What distinguishes a permissible experiment from an impermissible one is whether the jury conducts the experiment based solely on the evidence presented during trial or on new evidence based on the special expertise of a juror.[505]

The California courts are reluctant to overturn jury verdicts on the ground of inattentiveness during trial. After a survey of numerous cases of such alleged jury misconduct — jurors falling asleep during trial, reading newspapers during trial, consuming alcoholic beverages prior to hearing evidence — the California Supreme Court in *Hasson v. Ford Motor Co.*[506] observed that not one reported case granted a new trial on that ground. The *Hasson* Court itself concluded that misconduct of three jurors consisting of reading a novel and working crossword puzzles during trial proceedings was not sufficiently prejudicial so as to overturn the verdict of $11.5 million awarded plaintiffs.

---

[503] *See, e.g., McDonald v. S. Pac. Transp. Co.*, 71 Cal. App. 4th 256, 83 Cal. Rptr. 2d 734 (1999) (holding that in an action by a train brakeman for injuries suffered in a train yard, the trial court erred in denying plaintiff's motion for a new trial where a juror declaration stated that another juror, a professional transportation consultant, commented at length during deliberations as to why the plaintiff's theory of how due care could have made this workplace safer was unrealistic and impractical); *Elsworth v. Beech Aircraft Corp.*, 37 Cal. 3d 540, 208 Cal. Rptr. 874, 691 P.2d 630 (1984) (holding new trial properly denied in wrongful death action against manufacturer of light plane that crashed where submitted declarations stated two jurors had remarked that they had watched, shortly before commencement of deliberations that lead to large verdict for plaintiffs, a television broadcast of a program criticizing the safety record of light aircraft).

[504] *Compare Enyart v. City of Los Angeles*, 76 Cal. App. 4th 499, 90 Cal. Rptr. 2d 502 (1999) (holding trial court improperly denied defendants' motion for a new trial of a negligence action based on juror misconduct where the declarations of several jurors indicated that three jurors during deliberations had expressed negative generalizations about the conduct and veracity of the defendants City and Los Angeles Police Department; declarations demonstrated that the jurors' negative attitudes were not based solely on the evidence, were the product of bias, and were prejudicial), *with Moore v. Preventive Medicine Med. Group, Inc.*, 178 Cal. App. 3d 728, 223 Cal. Rptr. 859 (1986) (finding no misconduct in medical malpractice verdict where emotional juror discussed her own pain and suffering caused by her own physical deformity).

[505] *See, e.g., Smoketree-Lake Murray, Ltd. v. Mills Concrete Constr. Co.*, 234 Cal. App. 3d 1724, 1745-49, 286 Cal. Rptr. 435 (1991) (holding physical experiment by juror on how concrete was poured based on her own knowledge of concrete construction practice constituted misconduct); *Wagner v. Doulton*, 112 Cal. App. 3d 945, 949-51, 169 Cal. Rptr. 550 (1980) (finding no misconduct where juror made a diagram in the jury room based solely on the evidence received in trial).

[506] 32 Cal. 3d 388, 411-12, 185 Cal. Rptr. 654, 650 P.2d 1171 (1982).

[7] Presumption of Prejudice When Jury Misconduct Proven.

Proof of jury misconduct does not automatically require a new trial. The complaining party must also establish prejudice as a result of the misconduct. Proof of juror misconduct does, however, give rise to a *presumption* of prejudice.[507] This presumption "may be rebutted by an affirmative evidentiary showing that prejudice does not exist or by a reviewing court's examination of the entire record to determine whether there is a reasonable probability of actual harm to the complaining party resulting from the misconduct."[508] Some of the factors to be considered "are the strength of the evidence that the misconduct occurred, the nature and seriousness of the misconduct, and the probability that actual prejudice may have ensued."[509]

A party who moves for a new trial on the ground of juror improprieties must file a "no-knowledge" declaration which states that neither the attorney nor the client was aware of the alleged misconduct prior to the verdict. The policy behind this requirement "is to prevent a party who, personally or through counsel, has discovered some jury misconduct during the proceedings from gambling on the outcome of the jury's deliberations while secretly preserving the error to be raised on a motion for a new trial in the event of an unfavorable verdict."[510]

[8] Federal Court New Trial Motions Compared

There are several differences between the California statutes and the Federal Rules of Civil Procedure regarding new trial motions, some more significant than others. One relatively insignificant difference is that federal Rule 59(a) authorizes a federal trial judge to grant a new trial "for any reason for which a new trial has heretofore been granted in action at law in federal court." This broad authority permits a district court to order a new trial on grounds such as insufficiency of the evidence to support the verdict, excessive damages, newly discovered evidence, misconduct of jury or opposing counsel, and other prejudicial irregularities in the proceedings.[511]

Another difference is more significant. When determining the insufficiency of the evidence to support a verdict, the federal district courts commonly employ some variant of the "verdict is against the great weight of the evidence" standard.[512] Due to Seventh Amendment concerns, the federal courts disagree

---

[507] *In re Stankewitz*, 40 Cal. 3d 391, 402, 220 Cal. Rptr. 382, 708 P.2d 1260 (1985) (ruling that jury misconduct raises a presumption of prejudice, and unless the presumption is rebutted, a new trial should be granted).

[508] *Hasson, supra*, 32 Cal. 3d at 417 (citing cases).

[509] *Hasson, supra*, 32 Cal. 3d at 417.

[510] *Weathers v. Kaiser Found. Hosp.*, 5 Cal. 3d 98, 103, 95 Cal. Rptr. 516, 485 P.2d 1132 (1971).

[511] *See* WRIGHT, MILLER, & KANE FEDERAL PRACTICE AND PROCEDURE: CIVIL §§ 2805-2810 (3d ed. 2012).

[512] *See, e.g., Eyre v. McDonough Power Equip., Inc.*, 755 F.2d 416, 420 (5th Cir. 1985) (ruling that district court is empowered to grant motion for new trial when "verdict is against the great — but not merely the greater — weight of the evidence"); *Kern v. Levolor Lorentzen, Inc.*, 899 F.2d 772, 778 (9th

somewhat on the extent to which a federal trial judge may weigh the evidence and consider the credibility of the witnesses when applying this standard.[513] Consequently, although the federal and California standards are similar, the federal standard for a new trial on the ground of insufficiency of the evidence appears to be more deferential to jury verdicts than is the California standard, which permits the trial judge relatively unfettered power to assess credibility and weigh the evidence.

There are also some significant differences in the procedures governing new trial motions in the federal courts as opposed to in the California state courts. A party has 28 days after entry of judgment to serve a motion for new trial under federal Rule 59(b), as opposed to only 15 days under the California statutes. More importantly, a federal district judge has power to order a new trial on his or her own initiative and, when a party has made a timely motion, the district court may order a new trial for a reason not raised in the motion. Also, unlike the 60-day period in Code of Civil Procedure § 660, federal Rule 59 does not impose any time limit on the district court's power to rule on a party's new trial motion. From the perspective of litigants and trial judges, there is much to be said in favor of the simplicity of federal Rule 59 when contrasted to the complicated requirements of California's new trial statutes.

[9]   Relief from Final Judgment in the California Courts

A *judgment* is the final determination of the rights of the parties in a civil action. Entry of judgment is significant for a number of reasons. First, it triggers the time periods for filing post-trial motions and for taking an appeal. Second, entry of judgment is a necessary condition for taking action to enforce the judgment. And third, a final judgment on the merits binds the parties and precludes them from relitigating the same claims or issues a subsequent lawsuit. After the time for post-trial motions and appeal has passed, or if the motions and an appeal were timely filed but not successful, trial-level attack on a superior court judgment in California becomes very difficult.

Two procedural options are available to a party who seeks post-trial relief from a valid and final judgment. One is a statutory motion to vacate or set aside the judgment; the other is a similar motion addressed to the trial court's inherent equity power. The statutory motion must be filed within six months of the judgment, and requires proof of "mistake, inadvertence, surprise, or excusable neglect."[514] The equitable motion is appropriate after the statutory six-month

---

Cir. 1990) (holding the district court properly determined that the verdicts on liability and damages were not "against the manifest weight of the evidence"); *Brown v. McGraw-Edison Co.*, 736 F.2d 609, 616-617 (10th Cir. 1984) (explaining the new trial standard is whether the verdict is "clearly, decidedly, or overwhelmingly against the weight of the evidence").

[513] *Compare Fineman v. Armstrong World Indus., Inc.*, 980 F.2d 171, 211 (3d Cir. 1992) (explaining that a trial court should not usurp the prime function of the jury as the trier of fact by substituting its judgment of the facts and the credibility of the witnesses for that of the jury), *with Poynter v. Ratcliff*, 874 F.2d 219, 223 (4th Cir. 1989) (ruling a trial judge may weigh the credibility of witnesses and may grant a new trial even if the verdict is supported by substantial evidence).

[514] CAL. CODE CIV. PROC. § 473.

period and requires proof that the judgment was obtained through "extrinsic," as opposed to "intrinsic," fraud or mistake.[515] The disposition of a motion seeking relief on either basis lies within the sound discretion of the trial court, and will not be overturned on appeal unless there has been a clear abuse of discretion.[516]

The California courts apply the same "extrinsic/intrinsic" standard whether relief is sought from a default judgment or from a final judgment entered after a full adversarial trial. However, the standard is not applied in the same manner in both contexts. With respect to a default judgment, the policy favoring trial and disposition on the merits requires very slight evidence of mistake or excusable neglect to justify a trial court setting aside the judgment.[517] The opposite is true with respect to a request for relief from a judgment entered after the litigants have been fully heard on the merits and the court has devoted considerable resources in rendering a decision. A trial court will exercise its power to set aside such a final judgment only when the circumstances are sufficient to overcome the strong policy favoring the finality of judgments. In other words, escape from the preclusive effect of a final judgment will be granted only in "exceptional circumstances."[518]

Extrinsic fraud is a broad concept that tends to encompass almost any set of external circumstances which deprive a party of a fair adversary hearing. The particular circumstances need not qualify as fraudulent or mistaken in the strict legal sense. The clearest examples are cases where the aggrieved party is kept in ignorance of the proceeding or is in some other way induced not to appear. For example, in *Marriage of Park*,[519] the California Supreme Court held that the failure of the husband and his attorney to disclose to the trial court that his wife's nonappearance at trial was because she had been involuntarily deported during the course of the litigation required the judgment awarding child custody and dividing community property be set aside.

By contrast, intrinsic fraud or mistake exists where a party has been given notice of the action and has not been prevented from participating therein, but unreasonably neglected to do so.[520] A party's mistake as to the law or the facts is usually an insufficient basis to set aside a judgment if the party could have reasonably discovered the mistake.[521] For example, where the value of a company

---

[515] *Estate of Sanders*, 40 Cal. 3d 607, 221 Cal. Rptr. 432, 710 P.2d 232 (1985); *Kulchar v. Kulchar*, 1 Cal. 3d 467, 82 Cal. Rptr. 489, 462 P.2d 17 (1969).

[516] *Elston v. City of Turlock*, 38 Cal. 3d 227, 233, 211 Cal. Rptr. 416, 695 P.2d 713 (1985); *Marriage of Connolly*, 23 Cal. 3d 590, 598, 153 Cal. Rptr. 423, 591 P.2d 911 (1979).

[517] *Elston v. City of Turlock, supra*, 38 Cal. 3d at 233; *Rogalski v. Nabers Cadillac*, 11 Cal. App. 4th 816, 821, 14 Cal. Rptr. 286 (1992).

[518] *See, e.g., Carroll v. Abbott Labs, Inc.*, 32 Cal. 3d 892, 901, fn.8, 187 Cal. Rptr. 592, 654 P.2d 775 (1982); *Weitz v. Yankosky*, 63 Cal. 2d 849, 857, 48 Cal. Rptr. 670, 409 P.2d 700 (1966).

[519] 27 Cal. 3d 337, 165 Cal. Rptr. 792, 612 P.2d 882 (1980).

[520] *Kulchar v. Kulchar*, 1 Cal. 3d 467, 471, 82 Cal. Rptr. 489, 462 P.2d 17 (1969).

[521] *E.g., City of Ontario v. Superior Court*, 2 Cal. 3d 335, 346, 85 Cal. Rptr. 149, 466 P.2d 693 (1970) (ruling that ignorance of the law coupled with negligence in ascertaining it will certainly sustain a denial of relief); *Home Ins. Co. v. Zurich Ins. Co.*, 96 Cal. App. 4th 17, 116 Cal. Rptr. 2d 583 (2002) (holding misrepresentation by insurer's attorney that policy limits were $15,000 instead of $500,000, which induced injured party to settle underlying suit for $15,000 after conducting no discovery, was intrinsic

was the very subject of the lawsuit, the defendant's alleged misrepresentations about the company's financial condition were held intrinsic because the plaintiff conducted no investigation or discovery into the financial condition.[522] Some California courts have criticized the distinction between extrinsic and intrinsic fraud as "quite nebulous" and "hopelessly blurred."[523] Perhaps for this reason, Rule 60(b) of the Federal Rules of Civil Procedure expressly abandoned this distinction and does not distinguish between extrinsic and intrinsic fraud as a ground for setting aside a federal court judgment.

---

because a reasonable investigation and use of discovery would have disclosed the true extent of insurance coverage).

[522] *Heyman v. Franchise Mortg. Acceptance Corp.*, 107 Cal. App. 4th 921, 132 Cal. Rptr. 2d 465 (2003).

[523] *Marriage of Stevenot, supra*, 154 Cal. App. 3d at 1060; *see Marriage of Baltins*, 212 Cal. App. 3d 66, 82, 260 Cal. Rptr. 403 (1989); *see* Donald E. Smallwood, *Vacating Judgments in California: Time to Abolish the Extrinsic Fraud Rule*, 13 W. ST. U. L. REV. 105-127 (1985) (arguing for abolishment of the extrinsic fraud rule).

Chapter 13

APPEAL

§ 13.01 OVERVIEW

Appeal is the submission of a lower court's disposition of a matter to the review of a higher court.[1] One purpose of appeal is to *ensure the correctness* of lower court dispositions.[2] This purpose is reflected by the availability in most judicial systems of at least one layer of obligatory review — appeal as of right. Another purpose of appeal is *institutional review* to assure uniformity in the application of law and to furnish guidance to the lower courts. In many judicial systems, this systemic purpose is served by the availability of some form of discretionary appeal — appeal by permission — to the system's highest court, which allows it to pick and choose its cases for optimal institutional benefit.[3] Both of these purposes of appeal may be

---

[1] *Rehearing* serves the same purposes as appeal but submits the disposition to review by the same court, although sometimes a different or fuller panel. *See generally* David W. Louisell & Ronan E. Degnan, *Rehearing in American Appellate Courts*, 44 CAL. L. REV. 627 (1956). A *rehearing en banc* is a special form of rehearing by which the decision by a panel of appellate judges (usually consisting of three judges, selected from among all of an appeals court's judges, and, in the federal system, sometimes including a district judge who is assigned to sit on the panel "by designation") is reheard by all of the judges on an appeals court. *See generally* Richard S. Arnold, *Why Judges Don't Like Petitions for Rehearing*, 3 J. APP. PRAC. & PROCESS 29 (2001). *De novo* review is considered an appeal, but it is a do-over instead of a review for errors in the record made below. The higher court decides the matter anew without regard to the prior disposition by the lower court. A federal *habeas corpus* action effectively submits the state court system's disposition of a criminal case to the review of a federal district court, but that review is only to test the constitutional validity of state detention after the normal course of state appeals, and not to test the accuracy of the state courts' judgments. *See* 28 U.S.C. §§ 2241–2255.

By contrast, neither reconsideration nor removal involves appeal. *Reconsideration* usually refers to the trial or magistrate judge's reconsideration of her own interlocutory decision based on new facts or new law. *Removal* is a procedure for withdrawing the case from the jurisdiction of one court and lodging it with another before any disposition, and therefore is not a form of appeal.

[2] *See generally* Steven Shavell, *The Appeals Process as a Means of Error Correction*, 24 J. LEGAL STUD. 379 (1995).

[3]

> No litigant is entitled to more than two chances, namely, to the original trial and to a review, and the intermediate courts of review are provided for that purpose. When a case goes beyond that, it is not primarily to preserve the rights of the litigants. The Supreme Court's function is for the purpose of expounding and stabilizing principles of law for the benefit of the people of the country, passing upon constitutional questions and other important questions of law for the public benefit. It is to preserve the uniformity of decision among the intermediate courts of appeal.

Testimony by Chief Justice Taft regarding the "Judges' Bill," *quoted in Dick v. New York Life Ins. Co.*, 359 U.S. 437, 448 (1959) (Frankfurter, J., dissenting). *See generally* Craig M. Bradley, *The Uncertainty Principle in the Supreme Court*, 1986 DUKE L.J. 1.

at odds with two other objectives of procedural systems: *efficiency* and *finality*. These objectives call for technical (some would say grudging) application of many procedures for appeal, lest the proceedings of the lower courts be disrupted or their judgments be devalued by too ready appeal. Consequently, the law of appeal can be viewed as a fine balance of concern for correctness and uniformity of disposition on one hand, and efficiency and finality on the other.

Appeal poses five questions: when, where, how, what, and how much? *When* is the question of appealability, discussed in Part A. *Where* and *how* are questions of perfecting the appeal, discussed in Part B. *What* is a question of reviewability: whether a particular issue is reviewable, discussed in Part C. Finally, *how much* is a question of the intensity of review, discussed in Part D.

PART A.
When? Appealability

§ 13.02 APPEALABILITY IN GENERAL

Appealability poses a choice between ordinary appeal of the *final judgment* at the end of the litigation and *interlocutory* appeal of a decision made before final judgment. These alternatives can be compared using the following formula:

> The costs of allowing interlocutory appeals are the costs of an unnecessary extra appeal if the trial judge turns out to have been correct. (The appeal is an extra one because an appeal will still be allowed at the end.) The costs of not allowing interlocutory appeals are those of an unnecessary or an unnecessarily long trial if the trial judge turns out to have been wrong. If we assume that the costs of an unnecessary extra appeal are approximately the same as the costs of the unnecessary or unnecessarily long trial, the overall costs are proportional to the number of times the trial judge is right versus the number of times he is wrong. If trial judges are right more often than they are wrong (measured by eventual reversal when appeal finally occurs), then the general policy should disfavor interlocutory appeals.[4]

In fact, it appears that trial judges are more often right than reversibly wrong, since the substantial majority of trial court rulings are affirmed.[5] Consequently, the

---

[4] STEPHEN C. YEAZELL, CIVIL PROCEDURE 848 (6th ed. 2004). Copyright © by Aspen Law & Business. Reprinted with permission. *See also Richardson-Merrell, Inc. v. Koller*, 472 U.S. 424, 434 (1985) (performing cost-benefit analysis to deny interlocutory appeal of order disqualifying counsel); *Reise v. Board of Regents of Univ. of Wis.*, 957 F.2d 293, 295 (7th Cir. 1992), *cert. denied*, 510 U.S. 892 (1993):

> Because almost all interlocutory appeals from discovery orders would end in affirmance (the district court possesses discretion, and review is deferential), the costs of delay via appeal, and the costs to the judicial system of entertaining these appeals, exceed in the aggregate the costs of the few erroneous discovery orders that might be corrected were appeals available.

[5] *WRIGHT & MILLER* § 3907. For the twelve months ended Sept. 30, 2007, only 8.9% of the appeals terminated on the merits in federal appellate courts were reversals; over 89% were affirmances or dismissals. JUD. BUS. OF THE U.S. CTS. 125–27, Table B-5, at 89 (2011).

federal system and most states limit interlocutory appeals. On the other hand, a few states assess the costs and benefits differently and more often allow interlocutory appeals.[6] Section 13.03, *infra*, uses the federal system to discuss the general policy against interlocutory appeal.

Even in the majority of jurisdictions that disfavor interlocutory appeals, there are exceptions. These include cases in which the costs of error are particularly large and irreversible, the alleged errors involve unresolved questions of law increasing the likelihood of error by the trial judge, or where issues are presented that, as a practical matter, will be lost to a party before appeal from a final judgment can be taken. Interlocutory appeal can have important benefits, as the Supreme Court has explained.

> In certain cases, it may avoid injustice by quickly correcting a trial
> court's error. It can simplify, or more appropriately direct, the future
> course of litigation. And, it can thereby reduce the burdens of future
> proceedings, perhaps freeing a party from those burdens entirely.[7]

Sections 13.04 and 13.05, *infra*, use the federal system to illustrate typical statutory and judge-made exceptions to the general policy against interlocutory appeal.

§ 13.03   FINAL JUDGMENT RULE

[1]   In General

In most jurisdictions, statute or decisional law has made an entry of final judgment a jurisdictional prerequisite to appeal.[8] The court of appeals must satisfy itself that a final judgment was entered below or dismiss the appeal, whether or not the parties raise this issue.[9] The *final judgment rule*, or "rule against piecemeal appeals," is that the parties can only appeal from a final judgment on all claims in the action, whether the alleged errors are in that judgment or in the pretrial or trial procedures leading to it. The rule thus does not go to *whether* such errors may be appealed (a question of reviewability, which we treat below), but only *when*. It serves simply "to combine in one review all stages of the proceeding that effectively may be reviewed and corrected if and when final judgment results."[10]

---

[6] *See, e.g.*, N.Y. Civ. Prac. L. & R. 5701(a)(2)(iv) & (v) (McKinney, through Leg. Sess. 2000) (allowing interlocutory appeal of any order which "involves some part of the merits" or which "affects a substantial right"). *See generally* Harold L. Korn, *Civil Jurisdiction of the New York Court of Appeals and Appellate Division*, 16 Buffalo L. Rev. 307 (1967).

[7] *Johnson v. Jones*, 515 U.S. 304, 309–10 (1995).

[8] *See, e.g.*, 28 U.S.C. § 1291 (granting federal courts of appeals jurisdiction of appeals "from all final decisions" of the district courts). Congress has given the Supreme Court power to define when a district court ruling is final for purposes of appeal under section 1291. 28 U.S.C. § 2072(c). *See generally* Robert J. Martineau, *Defining Finality and Appealability by Court Rule: Right Problem, Wrong Solution*, 54 U. Pitt. L. Rev. 717 (1993).

[9] *Brown Shoe Co. v. United States*, 370 U.S. 294, 305 (1962).

[10] *Cohen v. Beneficial Indus. Loan Corp.*, 337 U.S. 541, 546 (1949).

The cost analysis that underlies all questions of appealability suggests that a primary purpose of the final judgment rule[11] is to avoid extra and unnecessary appeals: interlocutory appeals that might be mooted by the further course of litigation should the trial judge change her interlocutory decision or the interlocutory appellant ultimately prevail, mooting its claims of error. The rule also promotes consolidation of alleged errors in a single appeal, permitting appellate review of each of them in the context of the whole and on the fullest trial court record.[12] At the same time, the rule helps to expedite the proceedings in the trial court by protecting them from appellate interruption. This promotes efficiency and also comity — the institutional goal of "maintaining the appropriate relationship" between the trial and appellate courts[13] and respect for trial court decisions. Finally, the rule guards against tactical abuse of appeal to harass and delay.

Rule 58 makes it easy to identify when a judgment has been entered by requiring judgments to be set forth on a separate document. But whether the judgment is also final has proven a more elusive question. The Supreme Court has declared that a final judgment "ends the litigation on the merits and leaves nothing for the court to do but execute the judgment."[14] Thus, a trial court decision of liability, but not of all damages, is interlocutory. On the other hand, a decision to grant a permanent injunction is final if no other remedy is sought, even though the court nominally retains jurisdiction to ensure compliance. Other applications of the concept are more problematic.[15] The courts have sensibly taken a "pragmatic approach to the question of finality" that precludes the formulation of any precise verbal formula for deciding it.[16] Yet a prominent scholar suggested that the saving grace of the courts' pragmatic approach is that "in almost all situations it is entirely clear" from the nature of the order or the decisional law whether the order is final.[17]

Federal courts carried pragmatism too far in according finality to refusals to certify suits as class actions. The argument was that such decisions sounded a "death knell" for the litigation — effectively ending it — because the plaintiffs found it economically imprudent to pursue their claims individually without the

---

[11] On this and other purposes of the rule, see generally Elizabeth G. Thornburg, *Interlocutory Review of Discovery Orders: An Idea Whose Time Has Come*, 44 Sw. L.J. 1045, 1047–49 (1990); Note, *Appealability in the Federal Courts*, 75 Harv. L. Rev. 351, 351–52 (1961); Wright & Miller § 3907.

[12] Indeed, one scholar traced the final judgment rule at common law to the need for a full record below. *See* Carleton M. Crick, *The Final Judgment as Basis for Appeal*, 41 Yale L.J. 539, 542–43 (1932). *See also* Wright & Miller § 3906.

[13] *Coopers & Lybrand v. Livesay*, 437 U.S. 463, 476 (1978), *quoting Parkinson v. April Indus. Inc.*, 520 F.2d 650, 654 (2d Cir. 1975).

[14] *Catlin v. United States*, 324 U.S. 229, 233 (1945). Requests for attorney's fees are not part of the merits and their pendency does not affect the finality of a decision on the merits. *Budinich v. Becton Dickinson & Co.*, 486 U.S. 196 (1988).

[15] *Compare Catlin*, 324 U.S. at 232–33 (decree of title in condemnation case is not final decision, when question of compensation is still open), *with Brown Shoe Co. v. United States*, 370 U.S. 294, 305 (1962) (order of divestiture in antitrust case is final decision, even though question how divestiture is to be accomplished is still open).

[16] *Brown Shoe*, 370 U.S. at 306.

[17] Wright § 101.

incentive of a possible group recovery.[18] Rejecting this view, the Supreme Court noted in *Coopers & Lybrand v. Livesay*[19] that this logic would apply with equal force to many interlocutory orders in ordinary litigation, from venue decisions to discovery orders and summary judgment, "that may have such tactical economic significance that a defeat is tantamount to a 'death knell' for the entire case."[20] Moreover, whether such orders did sound the death knell would turn on the courts' perception of their impact on the parties in particular cases. The Court concluded that the death-knell doctrine undermined efficient judicial administration by eroding the final judgment rule, while requiring "individualized jurisdictional inquiry" into the financial stamina of the would-be class representatives from case to case.[21]

The *Coopers & Lybrand* Court therefore held "that the fact that an interlocutory order may induce a party to abandon his claim before final judgment is not a sufficient reason for considering it a 'final decision' within the meaning of [28 U.S.C.] § 1291."[22] Interestingly, the rules were amended in 1998 to give appellate courts the discretion to permit an interlocutory appeal from an order granting or denying class-action certification.[23] But *Coopers & Lybrand* may well have sounded the death knell for other applications of this kind of pragmatic approach to appellate jurisdiction.[24]

[2] Finality in Multi-Claim and Multi-Party Cases

Literal application of the final judgment rule in cases involving multiple claims or parties would prohibit appeal of decisions on individual claims until all have been decided. The result could often be to delay for years review and execution of early-decided claims. On the other hand, if immediate appeal of such decisions were allowed, they would have to be clearly identified as final, or parties would be uncertain when to appeal to protect their rights. Rule 54(b) provides the solution in the federal system, authorizing the trial court in multi-claim actions to make "direct entry of a final judgment" on fewer than all of the claims or parties upon "if the court expressly determines that there is no just cause for delay."[25] Rule 54(b) is not an exception to the final judgment rule, but instead a statutory standard for

---

[18] Typically, the prospective individual recovery was insufficient incentive in light of plaintiffs' liability for their own attorney's fees, which might otherwise come out of a class recovery. *See* § 9.09 (class actions), *supra*.

[19] 437 U.S. 463 (1978).

[20] *Id.* at 470.

[21] *Id.* at 473.

[22] *Id.* at 477 (footnote omitted).

[23] Rule 23(f). *See* Aimee G. Mackay, *Appealability of Class Certification Orders Under Federal Rule of Civil Procedure 23(f): Towards a Principled Approach*, 96 Nw. U.L. Rev. 755 (2002).

[24] *But see* Wright & Miller § 3912.

[25] Of course, a party with multiple claims could also "manufacture" a final judgment by voluntarily dismissing (*see* § 11.04[1], *supra*) other claims after a court has ruled on the one it wishes to appeal. *See* Rebecca A. Cochran, *Gaining Appellate Review by "Manufacturing" a Final Judgment Through Voluntary Dismissal of Peripheral Claims*, 48 Mercer L. Rev. 979 (1997).

its application in multi-claim and multi-party cases.[26] It applies to trial court decisions that would have been appealable final judgments standing alone but for the liberal joinder permitted by the federal rules.

A threshold issue for making the Rule 54(b) determination is whether the trial court's order has finally disposed of an individual *claim* in a multi-claim or multi-party case or merely one of several legal *theories* or alternative *requests for relief* on a single claim. The trial court's determination of this issue is not controlling; the appeals court must decide for itself. In *Liberty Mutual Insurance Co. v. Wetzel*,[27] for example, the plaintiff alleged employment discrimination and sought injunctive relief, damages, and attorney's fees. The trial court granted plaintiffs' motion for partial summary judgment and then purported to direct entry of final judgment pursuant to Rule 54(b) on the issue of liability. Defendant appealed.

The Supreme Court ruled that, notwithstanding entry of judgment under Rule 54(b), the trial court had not finally adjudicated a separate claim for purposes of appeal. Treatment of the liability determination as a declaratory judgment[28] would not alter this since Rule 54(b) is *claim* rather than relief-focused. The Court held that a "complaint asserting only one legal right, even if seeking multiple remedies for the alleged violation of that right, states a single claim for relief."[29] Since plaintiffs advanced "but one legal theory" (employment discrimination in violation of federal law) applicable to only one set of facts, and since the ruling on liability left open questions of injunctive relief and damages, Rule 54(b) was inapplicable.[30]

The Court expressly refrained from resolving definitively what constitutes a claim for relief under the rules, but its analysis is reminiscent of the tests for deciding a cause of action for purposes of *res judicata* (claim preclusion in the modern parlance).[31] In the same vein, the Second Circuit Court of Appeals has suggested using the test of whether the action involves theories of recovery that could be separately enforced.[32] The Seventh and D.C. Circuit Courts of Appeals noted the affinity to preclusion, holding that when alleged "claims [are] so closely related that they would fall afoul of the rule against splitting claims [under the law of claim preclusion] if brought separately," they do not qualify as separate claims within the meaning of Rule 54(b).[33]

---

[26] *Sears, Roebuck & Co. v. Mackey*, 351 U.S. 427, 435 (1956). The courts are divided on Rule 54(b)'s application in cases that have been consolidated under Rule 42(a). *See* Jacqueline Gerson, Note, *The Appealability of Partial Judgments in Consolidated Cases*, 57 U. Chi. L. Rev. 169 (1990).

[27] 424 U.S. 737 (1976).

[28] *See* § 14.03 (declaratory relief), *infra*.

[29] *Wetzel*, 424 U.S. at 743 n.4.

[30] *Id.* at 743.

[31] *See* § 15.03, *infra*.

[32] *Rieser v. Baltimore & Ohio R.R.*, 224 F.2d 198, 199 (2d Cir. 1955) (Clark, J.), *cert. denied*, 350 U.S. 1006 (1956).

[33] *Local P-171, Amalgamated Meat Cutters & Butcher Workmen v. Thompson Farms*, 642 F.2d 1065, 1070–71 (7th Cir. 1981) (adding as another "rule[] of thumb" the test whether separate recovery is possible on each claim); *Tolson v. United States*, 732 F.2d 998 (D.C. Cir. 1984).

To understand these tests, consider a suit for personal injuries in which the plaintiff alleges several different bases for relief — simple negligence, gross negligence, breach of implied warranty, and breach of express warranty. Summary judgment on any one such basis would not be appealable as judgment on a separate claim under Rule 54(b), because each is an alternative legal theory applicable to the same basic set of facts, and they all assert but one legal right to freedom from personal injury. If plaintiff pursued an action to judgment on any one of these theories, he would be precluded in most jurisdictions from suing separately upon the rest under the doctrine of claim preclusion; separating the action by theories would be "splitting a cause of action," which is barred by that doctrine. Allowing a litigant, even with the assent of the trial court under Rule 54(b), to define a claim by any single theory of recovery, while other theories of recovery on the same facts remain for decision, would permit evasion of the final judgment rule.

If Rule 54(b) applies, the trial judge must additionally determine that "there is no just reason for delay" in entering final judgment. In part, this involves consideration whether the claims are so interrelated (though separate) that efficient appeal requires review only as a single unit.[34] By this reasoning, for example, there may be just reason for delay when the remaining claims include a possible set-off to the separate claim and therefore ought to be considered together, or when they will inevitably present the same issues on appeal as are presented by the separate claim.[35] Determination of "no just reason for delay" also involves consideration of the equities in the litigation, such as a disparity between the statutory and market rates of interest that would cause a claimant to lose money from any delay in execution on a separate claim.[36]

Since the trial judge can best assess the relevant considerations, both determinations are reviewable only for abuse of discretion.[37] An abuse of discretion occurs, for example, when the trial court finds "no just cause for delay" simply because early appellate review of its ruling on the sufficiency of the evidence might avoid possible retrial of the entire case. The Second Circuit Court of Appeals has held that

> absent any special circumstances indicating that adherence to the normal and federally preferred practice of postponing appeal until after a final judgment has been entered, disposing of all the claims of all the parties, will cause an unusual hardship or work an injustice, the district court's preference to have pretrial appellate review of its assessment of the sufficiency of the evidence to support a given claim is an improper basis for entry of an immediate partial final judgment.[38]

---

[34] *See Curtiss-Wright Corp. v. General Elec. Co.*, 446 U.S. 1, 10 (1980).

[35] *See id.* at 8.

[36] *Id.* at 11.

[37] *See* § 13.10[2][d], *infra.*

[38] *Hogan v. Consolidated Rail Corp.*, 961 F.2d 1021, 1026 (2d Cir. 1992).

§ 13.04 "PRACTICAL CONSTRUCTIONS" OF THE FINAL JUDGMENT RULE

[1] Collateral Order Doctrine[39]

The Supreme Court has said that "[t]he collateral order doctrine is best understood not as an exception to the 'final decision' rule laid down by Congress in 1291, but as a 'practical construction' of it."[40] The Court construed the rule to permit immediate appeal and review of interlocutory orders that are incidental — *collateral* — to the merits and that cannot be effectively preserved for review on appeal from a final judgment. Since they pose no risk of repetitive appellate review, a cost analysis favors interlocutory review.

The leading federal case is *Cohen v. Beneficial Industrial Loan Corp.*[41] The trial court had denied a corporation's motion that the plaintiff be required, pursuant to state statute, to post security for defendant's reasonable expenses in defending a shareholder's derivative action.[42] Acknowledging that the final judgment rule would preclude appeal, the Supreme Court nevertheless reasoned that its purposes would not be served by refusing appeal in the circumstances. The trial court's ruling was final as to the subject it addressed, did not touch on the merits of the case, and would therefore not be merged into the final judgment. The Court noted that final judgment would be too late in any event to review the ruling, because the statutory rights would then have been lost, probably irretrievably.[43] The Court, therefore, held that the

> decision appears to fall in that small class which finally determine claims of right separable from, and collateral to, rights asserted in the action, too important to be denied review and too independent of the cause itself to require that appellate consideration be deferred until the whole case is adjudicated.[44]

The Supreme Court maintains that *Cohen* did not amend the final judgment rule, but only "continued a tradition of giving [it] a 'practical rather than a technical construction.' "[45]

---

[39] *See* Lloyd C. Anderson, *The Collateral Order Doctrine: A New "Serbonian Bog" and Four Proposals for Reform*, 46 Drake L. Rev. 539 (1998).

[40] *Digital Equip. Corp. v. Desktop Direct, Inc.*, 511 U.S. 863, 867 (1994) (internal citations omitted).

[41] 337 U.S. 541 (1949).

[42] *See* Rule 23.1.

[43] 337 U.S. at 546–47. The purpose of the security requirement was to discourage frivolous derivative actions, known as "strike suits," and assure reimbursement to the corporation of the reasonable expenses of a successful defense. Appellate correction of the trial court's error after a final judgment would obviously come too late to accomplish the deterrent effect of the security requirement, and in all likelihood too late to assure the corporation of funds from which to collect its expenses.

[44] *Id.* at 546.

[45] *Firestone Tire & Rubber Co. v. Risjord*, 449 U.S. 368, 375 (1981).

The Court has since refined *Cohen* to impose three strict requirements for invocation of the collateral order doctrine.[46] First, the order must finally and conclusively determine the disputed question. In *Cohen*, the court's denial of defendant's motion conclusively disposed of the question of security; that question could only arise at the front of the case. By contrast, a ruling on class certification is expressly subject under Rule 23(c)(1) to revision before final judgment and therefore "inherently tentative"[47] and unsuitable for interlocutory appeal as a collateral order. An order refusing to disqualify counsel is similarly subject to revision (should conflicts of interest materialize later in the litigation) and is therefore not immediately appealable.[48]

Second, the order must resolve an important issue completely collateral to the merits. It must be collateral, because if enmeshed in the merits, it is likely that it can only be fairly assessed after trial.[49] It must be important in terms of the difficulty of resolution it poses and its effect both upon and beyond the litigation.[50] This requirement prevents appeal of interlocutory decisions that, precisely because they are collateral to the merits, are also insignificant. The order regarding security in *Cohen* met this requirement because it did not touch on the merits and presented a "serious and unsettled question."[51] In contrast, an order refusing to certify a class was not completely collateral, since Rule 23's certification provisions expressly require the court to identify common questions of law or fact and make other determinations that inevitably touch on the merits.[52]

Finally, the order must be effectively unreviewable on appeal from the final judgment, so that the "opportunity for meaningful review will perish unless immediate appeal is permitted."[53] Like the order denying security in *Cohen*, this was true of orders denying summary judgment on the defenses of absolute immunity[54] and double jeopardy,[55] both designed to spare a defendant the rigors of trial, a protection that would obviously be irretrievably lost unless immediate appeal

---

[46] Coopers & Lybrand, 437 U.S. at 468. The Supreme Court has disapproved a purported exercise of pendent appellate jurisdiction to hear otherwise non-appealable issues in connection with a collateral order appeal, although it did not rule out such jurisdiction in all cases. *Swint v. Chambers County Comm'n*, 514 U.S. 35 (1995). *See generally* Joan Steinman, *The Scope of Appellate Jurisdiction: Pendent Appellate Jurisdiction Before and After* Swint, 49 Hastings L.J. 1337 (1998).

[47] *Coopers & Lybrand*, 437 U.S. at 469 n.11.

[48] *Firestone*, 449 U.S. at 377.

[49] *Id.* at 377–78.

[50] *See Will v. Hallock*, 546 U.S. 345, 352 (2006) (stressing significance of importance factor). *See In re Ford Motor Co.*, 110 F.3d 954 (3d Cir. 1997) (discussing importance factor). *But see Under Seal v. Under Seal*, 326 F.3d 479, 480–85 (4th Cir. 2003) (declining to apply the importance factor based on inconsistent treatment of factor in both circuit and Supreme Court precedent).

[51] *Cohen*, 337 U.S. at 546–47.

[52] *Coopers & Lybrand*, 437 U.S. at 468 & n.12. *See also Van Cauwenberghe v. Biard*, 486 U.S. 517 (1988) (denying collateral order appeal of *forum non conveniens* dismissal because it is not completely separate from the merits); *Richardson-Merrell, Inc. v. Koller*, 472 U.S. 424 (1985) (denying collateral order appeal of order to disqualify counsel for conflict because it is based on the possibility that a conflict will infect the proceedings and is therefore intertwined with the merits).

[53] *Firestone*, 449 U.S. at 377–78.

[54] *Helstoski v. Meanor*, 442 U.S. 500, 506–08 (1979). *See also P.R. Aqueduct & Sewer Auth. v. Metcalf*

is allowed. On the other hand, the Court has held that an order compelling discovery as against a claim of privilege is not immediately appealable. Its theory was that the party may defy the order and then challenge it on direct appeal of a resulting contempt citation.[56]

From time to time, courts have intimated that the importance requirement is a distinct fourth requirement for collateral order appeals,[57] a view for which Justice Scalia has expressed support.[58] Without deciding whether it is distinct, the Supreme Court has nevertheless emphasized that it is not an alternative or dispensable requirement, whose absence can be overcome if the other requirements are satisfied. "To the contrary," the Court has declared, "a third *Cohen* question, whether a right is 'adequately vindicable' or 'effectively reviewable,' simply cannot be answered without a judgment about the value of the interests that would be lost through rigorous application of a final judgment requirement."[59] In short, the collateral order appellant must satisfy all requirements, including the importance requirement.

Furthermore, the Supreme Court has repeatedly emphasized that the collateral order doctrine "is a narrow one, and the courts have applied it stringently to assure that it does not swallow the general rule."[60] This grudging approach to collateral order review recognizes:

> the district court's central role in managing ongoing litigation, and seek[s] to avoid the inefficiencies that would be created by permitting a court of appeals to review issues before the district court has had an opportunity to address all of the case's often interrelated questions. But these interests protect more than judicial resources: the Supreme Court has cautioned that the conditions that allow for collateral review "are stringent" in order also to serve "the sensible policy of avoiding the obstruction to just claims that would come from permitting the harassment and cost of a succession of separate appeals from the various rulings to which a litigation may give rise."[61]

In short, the same considerations that support the final judgment rule mandate a narrow construction of collateral orders that are effectively unreviewable on normal appeal.

& *Eddy, Inc.*, 506 U.S. 139 (1993) (authorizing collateral order review of Eleventh Amendment immunity claims).

[55] *Abney v. United States*, 431 U.S. 651, 660–62 (1977).

[56] *Cobbledick v. United States*, 309 U.S. 323, 327 (1940). *See* § 13.05[2], *infra.*

[57] *See, e.g.*, WRIGHT & MILLER § 3911.

[58] *Gulfstream Aerospace Corp. v. Mayacamas Corp.*, 485 U.S. 271, 291–92 (1988) (Scalia, J., concurring).

[59] *Digital Equip. Corp. v. Desktop Direct, Inc.*, 511 U.S. 863, 878–79 (1994). *Accord Will v. Hallock*, 546 U.S. 345 (2006).

[60] MOORE § 202.07[1] (citing cases).

[61] *Linde v. Arab Bank, PLC*, 706 F.3d 92, 104 (2d Cir. 2013) (internal citations omitted).

[2]   Other "Practical Constructions"

"A decision 'final' within the meaning of § 1291 does not necessarily mean the last order possible to be made in a case," the Supreme Court has reminded us.[62] The courts have applied this insight to several orders beyond collateral orders.

They have permitted immediate appeal of criminal contempt orders because of their serious consequences and practical finality.[63] Courting criminal contempt, however, is a risky way to obtain interlocutory appeal since a wrong guess leaves the appellant with a fine or imprisonment. The courts have also allowed non-parties to appeal civil contempt orders on the theory that they have no standing to appeal from an eventual final judgment.[64] Parties, in contrast, must await the final judgment in pending cases.

The Supreme Court suggested in *Gillespie v. United States Steel Corp.*[65] that it might allow interlocutory appeal when it would save time in the circumstances and was in the spirit of the federal discretionary appeal statute, although the trial court had never certified the question under it. Taken for all it is worth, this reasoning does violence to the statutory scheme and is inconsistent with the federal policy disfavoring piecemeal review. It is not surprising that it has met with little approval.[66] The Court has since acknowledged that "[i]f *Gillespie* were extended beyond the unique facts of that case, section 1291 would be stripped of all significance."[67] *Gillespie* may not have much continuing force.

Finally, an early Supreme Court decision adopted a hardship test, allowing interlocutory appeal of an order that would cause "irreparable injury" before final judgment.[68] While the Court itself has not consistently applied this test in its subsequent decisions, the practical construction it has given the requirement for finality — to the point of rationalizing the collateral order doctrine as a mere application of the statutory requirement — points in the direction of such a test.[69]

---

[62] *Gillespie v. United States Steel Corp.*, 379 U.S. 148, 152 (1964).

[63] *See generally* WRIGHT & MILLER § 3917; MOORE § 26.07[2][g].

[64] MOORE § 202.11[9]; WRIGHT & MILLER § 3917. *See generally Shillitani v. United States*, 384 U.S. 364, 369–70 (1966) (explaining that criminal contempt is intended to punish, while civil contempt is intended merely to coerce).

[65] 379 U.S. 148 (1964).

[66] *But see* WRIGHT & MILLER §§ 3905, 3913 (approving "pragmatic approach" of *Gillespie* to allow disposition on the merits of appeals mistakenly taken from non-final decisions).

[67] *Coopers & Lybrand*, 437 U.S. at 477 n.30.

[68] *Forgay v. Conrad*, 47 U.S. (6 How.) 201, 205–06 (1848) (review of an order to transfer property).

[69] *See* WRIGHT § 101, *quoting United States v. Wood*, 295 F.2d 772, 778 (5th Cir. 1961), *cert. denied*, 369 U.S. 850 (1962), to same effect. The irreparable injury test has also been endorsed as part of a balancing approach urged by some commentators. *See* Martin Redish, *The Pragmatic Approach to Appealability in the Federal Courts*, 75 COLUM. L. REV. 89 (1975).

§ 13.05 STATUTORY INTERLOCUTORY APPEAL

[1] Statutory Interlocutory Appeal as of Right

Justification for immediate review of interlocutory orders is greatest when they have immediate and irreparable consequences. Then the cost of possible error outweighs the cost of an extra appeal, because an appeal of a final judgment in the ordinary course would come too late to undo the harm from the error. Many jurisdictions allow interlocutory appeal of such orders by statute. As exceptions to the final judgment rule, such provisions are strictly construed, and the scope of appeal is typically limited to only the issues presented by the interlocutory order.[70] The federal interlocutory appeal provisions are illustrative.

Section 1292(a)(1) authorizes appeal of interlocutory orders granting, modifying, refusing, or otherwise affecting injunctions.[71] Orders granting or denying an interlocutory injunction can be as important to the parties as the court's eventual decision whether to grant a permanent injunction.[72] The court's decision has immediate effect, either requiring a party to take or to refrain from action, or permitting an allegedly harmful action or condition to continue. Costs of error under the circumstances are sufficiently great to justify immediate appellate review.

Section 1292(a)(1) extends to orders addressing motions for preliminary injunctions. Because of the wording of the statute, however, some doubt exists concerning its applicability to temporary restraining orders.[73] Rule 65 provides for both types of interlocutory injunction.[74] Once it seemed settled that temporary restraining orders were not appealable under the statute. But "[t]he cases seem to be edging slowly toward a principle that rulings with respect to temporary restraining orders are appealable on a sufficiently strong showing of potential irreparable injury."[75]

Because the justification for immediate appellate review is practical, the federal courts look to the practical effect of trial court rulings and not to whether they expressly address injunctive relief. Yet "a litigant must show more than that the order has the practical effect of refusing [or granting] an injunction"; he must also show that it might have "serious, perhaps, irreparable, consequence," and that it

---

[70] *See, e.g.,* WRIGHT § 102 (discussing 28 U.S.C. § 1292(a)(1)). Congress has given the Supreme Court rulemaking power to provide for interlocutory appeals not otherwise provided for by the interlocutory appeal statute. 28 U.S.C. § 1292(e). *See generally* Martineau, note 8, *supra.*

[71] 28 U.S.C. § 1292(a). Similar provisions are common in state law as well. *See, e.g.,* MD. CODE ANN., CTS. & JUD. PRO. CODE ANN. § 12-303 (West 2012). On injunctions generally, see § 14.02, *infra.*

[72] *See generally* Susan H. Black, *A New Look at Preliminary Injunctions*, 36 ALA. L. REV. 1 (1984); John Leubsdorf, *The Standard for Preliminary Injunctions*, 91 HARV. L. REV. 525 (1978).

[73] On distinctions between preliminary injunctions and temporary restraining orders generally, see § 14.02[2], *infra*; Bernard J. Nussbaum, *Temporary Restraining Orders and Preliminary Injunctions — The Federal Practice*, 26 SW. L.J. 265 (1972).

[74] *See* § 14.02[2] (provisional equitable relief), *infra.*

[75] WRIGHT § 102. *But see* WRIGHT & MILLER § 2962.

can be " 'effectually challenged' only by immediate appeal."[76] The Supreme Court has thus held that the denial of summary judgment in an action for a permanent injunction did not qualify for immediate appeal, because appellants failed to show that it would cause them irreparable harm during the lawsuit, and because permanent injunctive relief might have been obtained after trial.[77] The Court also concluded that denial of class certification in a sex discrimination suit seeking permanent injunctive relief was not immediately appealable; appellant had not sought preliminary injunctive relief nor made any showing of direct and irreparable consequences from the order.[78] In contrast, one federal circuit court has held that an order refusing to enter a consent decree, though not phrased in terms of injunctive relief, was immediately appealable. The order had the effect of denying an injunction directing defendants to restructure their transfer and promotion policies as provided in the proposed consent order, and it imposed irreparable costs by denying the parties the benefits of their negotiated settlement and exposing them to the burden and uncertainties of litigation.[79]

The federal statute also makes immediately appealable orders appointing receivers, or refusing to wind up receiverships or to direct sales or other disposals of property.[80] The possible immediate and irreversible effect of such orders on property transfers justifies the exception to the final judgment rule. Many states make similar exceptions and expand them to a broader category of judicial orders effecting the transfer or attachment of property and changes in title or custody.[81]

[2] Statutory Interlocutory Appeal by Permission

Many jurisdictions also allow discretionary interlocutory appeal, in part to serve the systemic purposes of uniformity and guidance, and in part to accommodate unusual cases in which the likelihood of error is so great that a cost analysis supports immediate appeal. Section 1292(b), the federal provision for discretionary interlocutory appeal, is perhaps more onerous than the typical state provision, but still provides a useful illustration.

Section 1292(b) poses three requirements. First, the trial court must have issued an order from which appeal is taken. Section 1292(b) is not a provision for certifying questions to obtain advisory opinions.[82] Second, the trial court must exercise its discretion to certify that the order (a) "involves a controlling question of law as to which there is substantial ground for difference of opinion" and (b) "that an immediate appeal from the order may materially advance the ultimate

---

[76] *Carson v. American Brands, Inc.*, 450 U.S. 79, 85 (1981), *quoting Baltimore Contractors, Inc. v. Bodinger*, 348 U.S. 176, 181 (1955).

[77] *Switzerland Cheese Ass'n, Inc. v. E. Horne's Market, Inc.*, 385 U.S. 23 (1966).

[78] *Gardner v. Westinghouse Broad. Co.*, 437 U.S. 478 (1978).

[79] *Carson*, 450 U.S. at 83.

[80] 28 U.S.C. § 1292(a)(2).

[81] *See, e.g.*, MINN. STAT. ANN. R. 103.03(c), (f) (West 2012); VA. CODE ANN. § 8.01-670 (West 2012).

[82] *See, e.g., Nickert v. Puget Sound Tug & Barge Co.*, 480 F.2d 1039, 1041 (9th Cir. 1973). A little-used federal statute authorizes certification of particular questions of law from the courts of appeals to the Supreme Court, 28 U.S.C. § 1254(2), and such provisions are fairly common at the state level.

termination of the litigation."[83] Finally, the court of appeals must also agree in its discretion to allow the appeal.[84]

A section 1292(b) interlocutory appeal differs from an appeal of a Rule 54(b) judgment in two respects: it does not contemplate or require a final judgment on any separate claim in the trial court, and it vests the courts of appeals with complete discretion to take the appeal of a certified question, not just a power of review of the propriety of the trial court certification.

The requirement that the trial court certify a controlling question of law helps to confine discretionary interlocutory appeal to those cases in which the likelihood of trial court error is greatest. For example, when the trial court changes its mind three times on the sufficiency of a novel and potentially absolute defense, there is self-evidently substantial ground for difference of opinion within the meaning of section 1292(b).[85] In contrast, interlocutory orders that lie in the discretion of a trial judge are usually unsuitable for interlocutory review because they do not as clearly pose questions of law, and because their discretionary component makes likelihood of reversible error much smaller.[86] Thus, several circuit courts of appeals have suggested that challenges to trial court discretion in granting or denying federal venue transfers[87] are unsuitable for interlocutory appeal.[88]

Certification that interlocutory appeal will materially advance the litigation speaks to its effect on trial. This varies from case to case, which helps to explain why determinations are discretionary. Section 1292(b) exists only for exceptional cases. Litigation will rarely be advanced by allowing immediate review of orders regarding the sufficiency of pleadings, in light of the ease of amendment, or of any case that is likely to go to trial regardless of the correctness of the interlocutory ruling.[89]

The narrow construction federal courts have given section 1292(b) has severely limited its availability.[90] But the discretion that district courts enjoy as a result may be preferable to greater use of judge-made interlocutory appeal and has the added virtue of statutory legitimation. There may, however, be an argument for revitalizing statutory interlocutory appeal "based primarily upon the need to clarify the law on issues which typically do not reach appellate courts, and upon a recognition that the vast majority of cases terminate before appeal via settlements

---

[83] 28 U.S.C. § 1292(b). If the district court refuses to cooperate, that will usually put an end to the matter. In rare cases, appellant can proceed in the face of the district court's refusal to certify under § 1292(b) by seeking a writ of prohibition or mandamus from the court of appeals. *See* § 13.04[3] (mandamus and prohibition), *infra.*

[84] 28 U.S.C. § 1292(b).

[85] *See, e.g., SEC v. National Student Mktg. Corp.*, 68 F.R.D. 157 (D.D.C. 1975), *aff'd*, 538 F.2d 404 (D.C. Cir. 1976), *cert. denied*, 429 U.S. 1073 (1977).

[86] *See* § 13.10[2][d] (describing deferential appellate review of exercises of discretion), *infra.*

[87] On venue transfers, see § 6.02[2], *supra.*

[88] *See, e.g., Garner v. Wolfinbarger*, 433 F.2d 117 (5th Cir. 1970).

[89] Wright § 102.

[90] *See* Michael E. Solimine, *Revitalizing Interlocutory Appeals in Federal Courts*, 58 Geo. Wash. L. Rev. 1165, 1171–74, 1193–1201 (1991).

or otherwise."[91] Alternatively, the Supreme Court may use its rulemaking power to the same end.[92]

[3] Extraordinary Statutory Review: Mandamus and Prohibition

A few trial court errors may be so costly, either to the parties or to the integrity of the judicial system, that a cost analysis favors immediate appeal even without irreparable harm. Most jurisdictions historically provided interlocutory appeal in these rare cases by petition for a *writ of mandamus* — ordering the trial judge to issue an order or fulfill a mandatory duty — or a *writ of prohibition* — forbidding the trial judge from acting in excess of her jurisdiction. Historical distinctions between the two have faded over time, and in the federal system mandamus is used for both purposes,[93] serving as an extraordinary allowance of statutory[94] review of the propriety of actions in the trial court. It is extraordinary because it is not a substitute for appeal[95] and is therefore only available when there is "no other adequate means to attain" the desired relief from circumstances amounting to "a judicial 'usurpation of power . . . .' "[96]

What circumstances or errors amount to judicial usurpation is neither clear nor uniform across judicial systems. The historical rule was that mandamus extended to "jurisdictional errors," and, indeed, many states authorize it for interlocutory challenges to assertions of subject matter or personal jurisdiction.[97] Another common generalization is that mandamus is in aid of appellate jurisdiction.[98] This explains the availability of mandamus for an order transferring venue out of one federal circuit to another,[99] but in most cases, is no more helpful as an explanation for mandamus than is "jurisdictional error."

Cases in which the Supreme Court has approved of mandamus[100] suggest two categories. One is breach by the trial judge of a clear legal duty. The Court has approved mandamus on this basis when a trial court, on the grounds that it was too busy, abdicated its duty to try a case by referring it to a special master,[101] and

---

[91] Solimine, note 90, *supra*, at 1213.

[92] *See* 28 U.S.C. § 1292(e); Martineau, note 8, *supra*.

[93] *See In re Simons*, 247 U.S. 231, 239 (1918).

[94] 28 U.S.C. § 1651.

[95] *Roche v. Evaporated Milk Ass'n*, 319 U.S. 21, 26 (1943).

[96] *Kerr v. U.S. District Court*, 426 U.S. 394, 402–03 (1976) (citing *Roche*, 319 U.S. at 26).

[97] *See, e.g, World-Wide Volkswagen Corp. v. Woodson*, 585 P.2d 351 (Okla. 1978), *rev'd*, 444 U.S. 286 (1980) (writ of prohibition against exercise of personal jurisdiction over foreign defendants); CAL. CIV. PROC. CODE § 418.10 (West 2012).

[98] *United States v. Beatty*, 232 U.S. 463, 467 (1914).

[99] *In re Fireman's Fund Ins. Cos. v. Pennington*, 588 F.2d 93 (5th Cir. 1979).

[100] *See generally* Annotation, *Mandamus as an Appropriate Remedy to Control Action of Federal Court in Civil Case — Supreme Court Cases*, 57 L. Ed. 2d 1203 (1979).

[101] *La Buy v. Howes Leather Co.*, 352 U.S. 249 (1957). Rule 53(a)(1)(B)(i) now expressly states that a court may appoint a master "to hold trial proceedings and make or recommend findings of fact on issues to be decided without a jury if appointment is warranted by . . . some exceptional condition . . . ,"

when a trial court denied a party its constitutional right to a jury trial.[102] In contrast, the grant of a new trial, even if error, does not occasion mandamus, there being no clear-cut and mandatory standard for granting new trials.[103]

Errors for which appellate review may carry broad precedential significance for judicial administration make up the second category. Thus, while routine discovery orders will almost never qualify for review by mandamus,[104] an interlocutory order presenting a question of first impression about the federal discovery rules may justify a kind of *supervisory mandamus*, on the theory that appellate precedent in such a case can generally improve the administration of justice.[105] Reflecting these categories, the courts of appeals have enunciated their own tests for deciding whether mandamus relief is warranted. The Court of Appeals for the Ninth Circuit, for example, considers whether the petitioner has other adequate means to obtain relief and will be irreparably damaged or prejudiced without mandamus relief, as well as whether the district court order was clearly erroneous as a matter of law, was an oft-repeated error or manifests a persistent disregard of the rules, or raises new and important issues of first impression.[106] The Second Circuit applies a similar test, looking to whether the trial court's order "amount[ed] to a judicial usurpation of power or a clear abuse of discretion."[107]

This standard for error reviewable by mandamus is more deferential than the standard applicable to ordinary appellate review of a final judgment. Thus, the Second Circuit explained, after denying a petition for mandamus because petitioner had not demonstrated a "clear abuse of discretion,"

> Because the writ of mandamus is such an extraordinary remedy, our analysis of whether the petitioning party has a "clear and indisputable" right to the writ is necessarily more deferential to the district court than our review on direct appeal. *Cf. In re Volkswagen of America, Inc.*, 566 F.3d 1349, 1351 (Fed. Cir. 2009) (Mandamus relief is only appropriate "when the petitioner is able to demonstrate that the [district court committed] a 'clear' abuse of discretion [producing] a patently erroneous result. A suggestion that the district court abused its discretion, which might warrant reversal

---

but nothing in the rule or its history authorizes referrals merely because of calendar congestion.

[102] *Beacon Theatres, Inc. v. Westover*, 359 U.S. 500 (1959). *See* Nathan A. Forrester, Comment, *Mandamus as a Remedy for the Denial of Jury Trial*, 58 U. Chi. L. Rev. 769 (1991).

[103] *Allied Chem. Corp. v. Daiflon, Inc.*, 449 U.S. 33 (1980). *See generally* § 12.09[2] (new trial), *supra*. A minority of states expressly authorize interlocutory review of new trial rulings. *See, e.g.*, N.Y. Civ. Prac. L. & R. 5602(b)(2)(iii) (McKinney, WESTLAW through L. 2008); Minn. Stat. Ann. R. 103.03(d) (1993).

[104] *See Kerr*, 426 U.S. 394. *But see* Thornburg, note 11, *supra* (surveying use of mandamus in Texas to review discovery orders and urging interlocutory review of such orders in other courts).

[105] *See, e.g.*, *Schlagenhauf v. Holder*, 379 U.S. 104 (1964) (the appropriate scope of Rule 35); *Colonial Times, Inc. v. Gasch*, 509 F.2d 517 (D.C. Cir. 1975) (question of first impression concerning scope of Rule 30(b)(4)).

[106] *United States v. Fei Ye*, 436 F.3d 1117, 1121–1124 (9th Cir. 2006). A petitioner need not establish all of these factors.

[107] *Linde v. Arab Bank, PLC*, 706 F.3d 92, 107 (2d Cir. 2013).

on a direct appeal, is not a sufficient showing to justify mandamus relief."
(internal quotation marks omitted)).[108]

Mandamus makes the trial judge a litigant by directing the writ at her or her
court by name, but the parties conduct the appeal in substance. Considerations of
comity between the trial and appellate courts reinforce the policy against piecemeal
appeals and the exacting standards for the issuance of the writ to make it truly
extraordinary relief.[109] Courts of appeals often strain to avoid censuring a trial
judge by issuing a writ of mandamus. Instead, even when the error below calls for
correction, an appellate court will typically deny the writ with an opinion expressing
confidence that the trial judge will do what the appellate court describes as the right
thing,[110] or, at worst, will delay issuance of the writ to allow her time to do so.

PART B.
Where and How? Perfecting Appeal

§ 13.06 WHERE? APPELLATE SYSTEMS

Where an appellant takes an appeal is typically determined by statute or
constitutional provision. Systems vary widely from jurisdiction to jurisdiction. A
four-tier court system is common, however.

Appeal from the bottom tier, courts of limited jurisdiction, is usually to courts of
general jurisdiction which re-try the matter *de novo* (anew). Little or no deference
is paid the lower court decision because of the restrictions on its jurisdiction and, in
many cases, on its procedures.[111]

Appeal from a court of general jurisdiction is to a true appellate court. This was
traditionally to the highest court in many states, but a growing number have
created intermediate appellate courts to ease the workload on the highest courts
and free them for review on a discretionary basis. Appeal to an intermediate
appellate court is usually as of right,[112] as it is in the federal system to the circuit
courts of appeals.[113] In some jurisdictions, the decision of the intermediate

---

[108] *Id.* at 108–09 (citation omitted).

[109] *See Kerr*, 426 U.S. at 403.

[110] *See, e.g., id.* at 406; *Colonial Times, Inc. v. Gasch*, 509 F.2d 517 (D.C. Cir. 1975). As an appellate
judge has admitted, "[t]his is but a delicate way of issuing the writ, for the trial court would not lightly
ignore this court's 'suggestion.' " *United States v. Harrod*, 428 A.2d 30, 35 n.1 (D.C. 1981) (Ferren, J.,
concurring, in an opinion in which JJ. Kelly and Mack join). *See generally* Robert S. Berger, *The
Mandamus Power of the United States Courts of Appeals: A Complex and Confused Means of Appellate
Control*, 31 Buffalo L. Rev. 37, 86–87 (1982).

[111] In the Virginia system, for example, the jurisdiction of the district court is limited by amount in
controversy, and the district court rules do not permit full discovery or jury trials. Va. Code Ann.
§§ 16.1-77, 16.1-113 (West 2012). Some courts of general jurisdiction, however, may give great weight to
findings of such inferior courts. *See* 5 Am. Jur. 2d *Appeal and Error* § 822 (1962 & 1993 Supp.) (listing
cases).

[112] *See, e.g.*, Md. Code Ann., Cts. & Jud. Proc. § 12-301 (West 2012).

[113] 28 U.S.C. § 1291. The mounting workload of the federal appellate courts has prompted some calls

appellate court is final for the most fact-bound and routine kinds of cases, such as domestic relations and non-capital criminal cases, subject perhaps to discretionary appeal for constitutional questions.

Appeal from the intermediate appellate court to the highest court is predominantly by permission, with exceptions for a small number of important cases selected by the legislatures, such as administrative law cases involving governmental parties or capital criminal cases.[114] Some systems limit the appellate jurisdiction of the highest court by amounts in controversy or subject; most empower the highest court to select, by *certiorari* or other permission, cases posing serious constitutional issues, conflicts in the lower courts, or other special needs for appellate guidance.[115]

The United States Supreme Court's rules, for example, list the following factors as relevant in granting *certiorari*: inter-circuit conflicts, conflicts between the courts of appeals and state courts of last resort, interstate conflicts on federal questions, conflicts with Supreme Court decisions on federal questions, important and unsettled federal questions, and other federal rulings calling for the exercise of the Supreme Court's power of supervision.[116] The Supreme Court's *certiorari* jurisdiction is thus highly discretionary,[117] so discretionary that the Court has repeatedly stressed that its refusal to grant review by *certiorari* connotes little if anything about the correctness of the decision below.[118]

In addition, the Supreme Court exercises mandatory appellate jurisdiction in a few very limited circumstances.[119]

---

for making appeal to them discretionary. *See* Ronald M. Parker & Ron Chapman, Jr., *Accepting Reality: The Time for Adopting Discretionary Review in the Court of Appeals Has Arrived*, 50 SMU L. REV. 573 (1997). Other options include splitting the workload in some circuits by splitting the circuit, *see* COMMISSION ON STRUCTURAL ALTERNATIVES FOR FEDERAL COURTS OF APPEALS, FINAL REPORT (1998), *discussed in* Carl Tobias, *The Federal Appeals Courts at Century's End*, 34 U.C. DAVIS L. REV. 549 (2000), and truncating appellate procedures (including oral argument) as well as the decisionmaking process itself. *See* FEDERAL JUDICIAL CENTER, CASE MANAGEMENT PROCEDURES IN THE FEDERAL COURTS OF APPEALS 15 (2011) ("All of the courts of appeals have some form of appellate mediation or conference program for resolving appeals by settlement with little or no judicial intervention."); William M. Richman & William L. Reynolds, *Elitism, Expediency, and the New Certiorari: Requiem for the Learned Hand Tradition*, 81 CORNELL L. REV. 273 (1996) (criticizing this trend and endorsing increase in number of appellate judges as a remedy).

[114] *See, e.g.*, VA. CODE ANN. § 8.01-670 (West 2012).

[115] *See, e.g.*, MD. CODE ANN., CTS. & PROC. CODE ANN. § 12-301-305 (West 2012).

[116] SUP. CT. R. 10.

[117] *See generally* ROBERT L. STERN, EUGENE GRESSMAN & STEPHEN SHAPIRO, SUPREME COURT PRACTICE §§ 4.1–4.26 (8th ed. 2002); Saul Brenner, *Granting Certiorari by the United States Supreme Court: An Overview of the Social Science Studies*, 92 LAW LIBR. J. 193 (2000).

[118] *See, e.g., Maryland v. Baltimore Radio Show*, 338 U.S. 912 (1950) (Frankfurter, J.). *See generally* STERN, GRESSMAN & E. SHAPIRO, note 117, *supra*, at §§ 5–7; Peter Linzer, *The Meaning of Certiorari Denials*, 79 COLUM. L. REV. 1227 (1979).

[119] 28 U.S.C. § 1253 (authorizing direct appeal from orders granting or denying interlocutory or permanent injunctions by three-judge courts).

§ 13.07 HOW? PROCEDURAL STEPS IN PERFECTING APPEAL

In most jurisdictions the procedures for perfecting an appeal appear in detail in statutes or rules.[120] Consequently, only the broad general outlines of the typical steps are presented in this section, with illustrative citation to the federal rules of appellate procedure.[121]

The first and (in many jurisdictions) only crucial step in taking an appeal as of right is timely filing of notice of appeal.[122] The appellate court usually has discretion to excuse errors or lateness respecting the taking of all subsequent steps, but not respecting the filing of notice of appeal. This step is therefore said to be jurisdictional — a predicate to the exercise of appellate power in most systems.[123] Appellant usually must file notice with the court rendering the judgment, not the higher court, and must state clearly what party is appealing from what parts of the judgment.[124] Appellant usually must pay a filing fee at that time, post a bond for costs on appeal, and (because the pendency of appeal does not alone automatically stay the enforcement of a judgment) either post a *supersedeas* bond to suspend the enforcement of a money judgment or seek a stay from the lower court of other granted relief.[125] In the federal system, the notice of appeal must be filed within thirty days of the entry of judgment or the date of an order deciding any timely filed post-trial fourteen-day motion[126] in civil actions between private parties.[127]

Second, other parties must file notices of cross-appeal. Timely filing is necessary to preserve any cross-appeal, but the rule is usually framed to allow filing of defensive cross-appeals within a reasonable time after the initial notice of appeal.[128]

---

[120] Such rules include local rules of appellate courts, which have been proliferating in the federal system. *See* Gregory C. Sisk, *The Balkanization of Appellate Justice: The Proliferation of Local Rules in Federal Circuits*, 68 U. COLO. L. REV. 1 (1997).

[121] For more detailed description of appellate procedure generally, see ROBERT L. MARTINEAU, APPELLATE PRACTICE AND PROCEDURE (2d ed. 2005). For federal appellate procedure in particular, see WRIGHT § 104.

[122] When the appeal is discretionary, the appellant must file a petition for permission to appeal with the appellate court, instead of notice of appeal in the trial court.

[123] *But see* Marie A. Hall, *The Jurisdictional Nature of the Time to Appeal*, 21 GA. L. REV. 399 (1986) (arguing that appeal periods should be subject to waiver).

[124] *See* FED. R. APP. P. 3.

[125] *See* FED. R. APP. P. 7 & 8.

[126] *See* FED. R. APP. P. 4(a)(4); § 12.09[1] (directed verdicts, judgments n.o.v., and new trial), *supra*. Rule 60 motions for relief from judgment do not toll the 30-day time period for filing notice of appeal. *See* § 12.11[2][b], *supra*.

[127] *See* FED. R. APP. P. 4(a)(4). An untimely post-trial motion does not postpone the time in which to take appeal, *see, e.g., Hulson v. Atchison, Topeka & Santa Fe Ry. Co.*, 289 F.2d 726 (7th Cir. 1961), although the district court may for "excusable neglect or good cause" grant an extension of time up to thirty days. FED. R. APP. P. 4(a)(5). The circuits are split on the question of whether improper district court permission to file a post-trial motion out of time can ever postpone the time for filing notice of appeal. The arguments for and against are discussed in *Bailey v. Sharp*, 782 F.2d 1366, 1369–74 (7th Cir. 1986) (Easterbrook, J., concurring).

[128] *See* FED. R. APP. P. 4(a)(3) (within 14 days of notice of appeal by any other party or time provided for original notice, whichever is longer).

Third, the appellant must prepare and transmit the record. The record may comprise the transcript, exhibits, and docket from the trial court,[129] but there is substantial variation in what an appellant actually must transmit to the appellate court. Most jurisdictions allow appellant to designate and appellee to cross-designate parts of the record. As an alternative procedure, some provide for appellant's preparation of a narrative summary of the record, subject to appellee's objections and certification of the summary by the trial court.[130]

Fourth, the parties brief the issues. Usually the appellant and appellee file briefs in succession, and appellant is permitted a shorter reply.[131] In some jurisdictions, the parties support their briefs with a joint appendix of key excerpts from the record.[132]

Finally, the parties may be heard in oral argument some time after submission of their briefs.[133] Summary disposition, with little (*e.g.*, ten minutes) or no argument, is an increasingly common response of appellate courts to burgeoning caseloads. Few jurisdictions grant oral argument as of right.

PART C.
What? Reviewability

§ 13.08 WHAT? REVIEWABILITY

Under the final judgment rule, a final judgment is appealable. But its appealability does not assure that any particular claim of error is reviewable. Reviewability of a claim of error turns on whether it prejudiced the appellant, whether the appellant preserved the error by timely request or objection in the lower court, and whether appellant properly presented it in its appeal. Questions of uniformity and systemic guidance aside, appeal is primarily intended to correct improper dispositions by the lower courts when necessary to protect adversely affected parties. The scope of review is therefore restricted to prejudicial errors appealed by aggrieved parties. The systemic goal of efficiency dictates giving the trial court opportunity to correct its own errors and to create a clear record for appeal. The scope of review is therefore further restricted ordinarily to errors that are preserved in the record below. Last, efficiency also requires that the appellant present the error to the appellate court, in order to relieve it of the tedious and wasteful task of searching the record.

---

[129] *See* FED. R. APP. P. 10(a).

[130] *See* VA. SUP. CT. R. 5:11(c) & (d). *See also* FED. R. APP. P. 10(c) (authorizing statement of the evidence in limited circumstances); 10(d) (authorizing agreed statement of facts in lieu of the record).

[131] *See* FED. R. APP. P. 28.

[132] *See* FED. R. APP. P. 30.

[133] *See* FED. R. APP. P. 34.

[1] Prejudicial Effect

The term *prejudicial effect* is used here to embrace two principles of reviewability. First, the appeal must be taken by an aggrieved party.[134] An aggrieved party is one who did not receive the full disposition he requested. Appeal is to correct an improper disposition below, not to make trials error-free nor to make clearer the grounds for initial disposition. Appeal will not usually lie to substitute some other ground for a judgment below or to correct findings unnecessary to the judgment,[135] since they are unlikely to be preclusive[136] and so cannot legally aggrieve a party to the judgment. What findings are necessary to a judgment depends on the substantive law.[137]

These principles are not always easy to apply. Even in damage cases, "amount is not the sole measure of relief to which a party may be entitled."[138] Thus one court has held that a party who recovers a judgment in the amount prayed, but on a theory of indemnification rather than of fraud, may appeal the court's ruling on the fraud theory when that ruling may have collateral effects in subsequent proceedings.[139] The Supreme Court has also allowed an alleged patent infringer to appeal a decree in his favor, when the decree literally incorporated an otherwise immaterial finding that the patent was valid.[140] What these decisions may have in common is a concern for the judgment's possible unfavorable preclusive effects on the appellant of an otherwise favorable judgment.[141]

Second, the errors alleged must have been harmful to the appellant in the sense that they may have materially contributed to the adverse part of the judgment.

---

[134] *Deposit Guar. Nat'l Bank v. Roper*, 445 U.S. 326, 333 (1980). *See generally* MOORE § 205.04[1]; WRIGHT & MILLER § 3902. The party is ordinarily party to the judgment, but proper interveners may also appeal if they are aggrieved. *See, e.g., Smuck v. Hobson*, 408 F.2d 175 (D.C. Cir. 1969). Non-parties may argue on appeal as *amicus curiae* by permission only. *See generally* Note, *The Amicus Curiae*, 55 NW. U. L. REV. 469 (1960).

[135] *Electrical Fittings Corp. v. Thomas & Betts Co.*, 307 U.S. 241, 242 (1939) ("A party may not appeal from a judgment or decree in his favor, for the purpose of obtaining a review of findings he deems erroneous which are not necessary to support the decree.").

[136] *See* § 15.07[3] (adjudication of the issue must have been necessary to judgment), *infra*.

[137] The same question of necessity to the judgment is treated under the law of collateral estoppel or issue preclusion. *See* § 15.07[3], *infra*.

[138] *Aetna Cas. & Sur. Co. v. Cunningham*, 224 F.2d 478, 480 (5th Cir. 1955). *Cf.* Rule 54(c) (". . . every . . . final judgment should grant the relief to which each party is entitled, even if the party has not demanded that relief in the pleadings").

[139] *Aetna Casualty*, 224 F.2d 478.

[140] *Electrical Fittings*, 307 U.S. 241.

[141] The concern in *Aetna* would have been that the finding of no fraud might preclude use of that theory to avoid a later bankruptcy discharge by the judgment debtor, and in *Electrical Fittings* that the finding of patent validity might preclude the judgment winner from asserting a defense to future suits by the patent holder. However, these concerns may be redundant with protections already built into the law of preclusion, which does not usually permit preclusion by judgments that are unreviewable on appeal or by findings that are unnecessary to the judgment. *See* § 15.07[3], *infra*. Commentators have accordingly noted the circularity between the "aggrieved by the judgment" rule and preclusion law. *See, e.g.,* WRIGHT & MILLER § 3902. Perhaps the Court believed in *Electrical Fittings* that incorporation of the finding in the decree would dignify it sufficiently to give it issue-preclusive effect, and therefore justified appellate reformation of the decree.

Congress has given expression to this concept by providing that appellate courts should disregard any errors that "do not affect the substantial rights of the parties."[142] Many errors along the way do not. Errors in the exclusion or admission of evidence are frequently rendered harmless by the cumulative weight of other, properly admitted evidence; error at one stage of an action can often be neutralized by curative action at a later stage.

Yet some errors are so central to the integrity of the fact-finding process, or so unsusceptible to proof of actual prejudice, that harm must be presumed. For example, many cases hold that the taint of the jury by exposure to extraneous evidence outside the record falls into this category.[143] Although the proper standard of harmlessness remains an open question, some courts have suggested that a "more probable than not" standard is most appropriate to civil cases in line with the usual preponderance burden of proof.[144]

[2] Preservation Below[145]

Ordinarily, only errors appearing in the record made below are reviewable. Failure to make a timely objection waives the objection for purposes of reviewability on appeal. This limitation is necessary to give the trial court the opportunity to correct its own errors and thereby moot an appeal; to guard against sandbagging by the parties below (holding claims of error in reserve in case they lose); and to develop and clarify the record on appeal, which may include the trial court's analysis of the objection.[146]

> Our adversarial system endows the parties with the opportunity — and duty — to craft their own legal theories for relief in the district court. It is the significant but limited job of our appellate system to correct errors made by the district court in assessing the legal theories presented to it,

---

[142] 28 U.S.C. § 2111. *See also* Rule 61.

[143] *See, e.g., In re Beverly Hills Fire Litig.*, 695 F.2d 207 (6th Cir. 1982) (juror told jury the results of his own, unsupervised experiment); *Gertz v. Bass*, 208 N.E.2d 113 (Ill. App. Ct. 1965) (bailiff gave jurors a dictionary that defined key terms differently from jury instructions). However, the Supreme Court has held that a juror's mistaken answer to *voir dire* questions, *see generally* § 12.01[3] (selecting a jury), *supra*, is not presumptively harmful absent a showing that the juror answered dishonestly and that an honest answer would have provided a valid basis for a challenge for cause. *McDonough Power Equip., Inc. v. Greenwood*, 464 U.S. 548, 556 (1984).

[144] *See, e.g., Haddad v. Lockheed Calif. Corp.*, 720 F.2d 1454, 1459 (9th Cir. 1983). Professors Wright and Miller endorse the discussion by the Supreme Court in *Kotteakos v. United States*, 328 U.S. 750, 765 (1946) (". . . if one cannot say, with fair assurance, after pondering all that happened without stripping the erroneous action from the whole, that the judgment was not substantially swayed by the error, it is impossible to conclude that substantial rights were not affected."). WRIGHT & MILLER § 2883. *See generally* ROGER J. TRAYNOR, THE RIDDLE OF HARMLESS ERROR (1970).

[145] *See generally* Robert J. Martineau, *Considering New Issues on Appeal: The General Rule and the Gorilla Rule*, 40 VAND. L. REV. 1023 (1987); Rhett R. Dennerline, Note, *Pushing Aside the General Rule in Order to Raise New Issues on Appeal*, 64 IND. L.J. 985 (1989).

[146] *See Pfeifer v. Jones & Laughlin Steel Corp.*, 678 F.2d 453, 456 (3d Cir. 1982), *vacated and remanded*, 462 U.S. 523 (1983). *See generally* Ferdinand Fairfax Stone, *Scope of Review and Record on Appeal*, 2 F.R.D. 317 (1943). *But see* Amanda Frost, *The Limits of Advocacy*, 59 DUKE L.J. 447 (2009) (arguing that trial judges should be more proactive in raising claims and arguments that parties have overlooked or ignored in part to preserve their reviewability on appeal).

not to serve as "a second-shot forum . . . where secondary, back-up theories may be mounted for the first time." Affording plenary appellate review to newly raised legal theories would do much to undermine this adversarial and appellate order. It would force the judicial system to permit costly "do-overs" in the district court anytime a party can conceive a new winning argument on appeal — even when the district court answered perfectly every question of law the parties bothered to put before it. It would also work unfairness on appellees who, no doubt, thought they knew the legal questions at issue in the case by the time of appeal, only to be surprised when a new threat to their victory in the district court emerges from nowhere for the first time in the pages of an appellate brief.[147]

In the federal system, objection need not take the form of formal exception. It is sufficient that a party makes known to the trial court what action he desires the court to take or the general grounds for his objection.[148] However, creation of a strong record for appeal frequently requires more than cursory objection. In this as in other matters of procedure, a lawyer must be guided by tactical common sense and not just the minimum required by the rules.

Some courts have relaxed their rules for so-called *plain errors*.[149] They reason that "[a] litigant surely has the right to assume that a . . . trial judge knows the elementary substantive legal rules, long established by the precedents and . . . will act accordingly, without prompting by the litigant's lawyer."[150] Although the lay litigant may reasonably make the same assumption of his own attorney, concerns for the appearance of justice and the integrity of the legal system make ignorance in the trial judge less tolerable than ignorance in counsel. Yet what errors are plain enough to overcome the normal requirement for objection, not to mention the explicit requirement of Rule 51(c) for objection to jury instructions, is unclear.[151] For example, the Ninth Circuit Court of Appeals has declined to invoke

---

[147] *Richison v. Ernest Group, Inc.*, 634 F.3d 1123, 1130 (10th Cir. 2011) (distinguishing, however, between legal arguments that are waived (intentionally relinquished) and those that are forfeited through neglect, and asserting that new forfeited theories will be considered on appeal "if failing to do so would entrench a plainly erroneous result").

[148] Rule 46. *But see* Catherine Murr Young, Comment, *Should a Motion in Limine or Similar Preliminary Motion Made in the Federal Court System Preserve Error on Appeal Without a Contemporaneous Objection*, 79 Ky. L.J. 177 (1990–1991) (noting that several federal circuits require contemporaneous objection at trial to evidence that objector unsuccessfully sought to exclude by motion *in limine*). The requirement for objection to proposed jury instructions may be slightly more exacting, because the rule is stated separately from the general rule regarding objection and requires objections and the grounds for them to be stated "distinctly." Rule 51. Of course, the lack of objection is excused when there is no opportunity to make one. Rule 46.

[149] *See* Fed. R. Evid. 103(e) (nothing in rule requiring objection to evidence precludes "tak[ing] notice of a plain error affecting a substantial right, even if the claim of error was not properly preserved").

[150] *Troupe v. Chicago, Duluth & Georgian Bay Transit Co.*, 234 F.2d 253, 261 (2d Cir. 1956) (Frank, J., concurring).

[151] As a result, one commentator has criticized the plain error rule as an unpredictable and *ad hoc* "Gorilla Rule." *See* Martineau, note 145, *supra*. He proposes a standard for the review of a new issue on appeal that would be analogous to the standard for Rule 60 motions. *See* Martineau, note 145, *supra*, at 1059–61; § 12.11[2][b], *supra*.

plain error to reach errors in jury instructions in the absence of objection below.[152]

The preservation-below requirement usually applies also to any legal arguments made to *challenge* a judgment. One federal court has explained:

> By requiring parties to present all their legal issues to the district court as well, we preserve the hierarchical nature of the federal courts and encourage ultimate settlement before appeal. It also prevents surprise on appeal and gives the appellate court the benefit of the legal analysis of the trial court.[153]

The same rule is not strictly applied to arguments for *affirmance* of a judgment, however, even though they may also attack the reasoning of the lower court. Instead, any legal argument that is fairly supported by the record may be made in support of the judgment.[154] For example, after an appellate court rejected the fraud theory of recovery that plaintiff advanced below to recover a money judgment, it permitted plaintiff/appellee to argue for the first time on appeal a theory of quasi-contract in support of the judgment. It was enough that the new theory "did not contemplate any factual situation different from that established by the evidence in the trial court."[155]

The different treatment on appeal of arguments attacking and arguments supporting the judgment stems from considerations of economy and finality. Entertaining new arguments to attack the judgment *detracts* from finality by increasing the likelihood of reversal, while entertaining new arguments to support it *promotes* finality and avoids an inefficient remand for the trial court to re-enter the same judgment on an alternative ground.[156] As one court of appeals explained:

> Because of the cost and risk involved anytime we upset a court's reasoned judgment, we are ready to affirm whenever the record allows it. So it is that appellants must always shoulder a heavy burden — they must come ready *both* to show the district court's error and, when necessary, to explain why no other grounds can support affirmance of the district court's decision.[157]

---

[152] *Moore v. Telfon Comm. Corp.*, 589 F.2d 959, 966 (9th Cir. 1978).

[153] *Patterson v. Cuyler*, 729 F.2d 925, 929 (3d Cir. 1984). Courts have made an exception to this requirement when the legal argument first becomes available on appeal as a result of an unanticipated change in the law and is supported by the record. *See, e.g., Carson Prods. Co. v. Califano*, 594 F.2d 453 (5th Cir. 1979).

[154] *Schweiker v. Hogan*, 457 U.S. 569, 585 n.24 (1982); *United States v. American Ry. Express Co.*, 265 U.S. 425, 435 (1924). "Fairly supported in the record" means not just that the record is sufficient, but that it is in "the same basic posture as it would have been" had the argument been made below. FRIEDENTHAL, KANE, & MILLER § 13.4.

[155] *Ward v. Taggart*, 336 P.2d 534, 537–38 (Cal. 1959).

[156] *See, e.g., Southard v. Southard*, 305 F.2d 730, 732 (2d Cir. 1962) (justifying hearing new argument on appeal by inevitability of trial court judgment on that argument and desirability of expediting termination of litigation).

[157] *Richison*, 634 F.3d at 1130.

Arguments in support of the judgment, however, must be distinguished from arguments to enlarge or diminish it.[158] The latter place their proponent in the position of appellant and subject him to the usual requirement of presentation below, as well as the procedural necessity for taking a timely cross-appeal.[159] In *Standard Accident Insurance Co. v. Roberts*,[160] for example, the plaintiffs recovered a judgment against an insurer on an estoppel theory, although the trial court also found no coverage under the insurance contract. On appeal by the insurer, the plaintiffs/appellees argued that the insurer was estopped, that they were covered under the policy, that the contract should have been reformed to cover them, and that they were entitled to reasonable attorneys fees and a statutory penalty. Only the first two arguments were properly made without cross-appeal. Both had been presented below and were, in any event, merely alternative grounds to support the judgment, while the latter two arguments would have modified and expanded the judgment.

[3] Presentation Above

Without more, preservation of the objection or argument in the record below is not sufficient to make it reviewable. Apart from questions of subject matter jurisdiction, which an appellate court must raise at its own initiative,[161] the court will not search the record for error. Instead, the appellant must identify and present the issue in his brief. This requirement obviously promotes efficiency on appeal by sparing the appellate court the rigors of a complete search and by encouraging well-prepared briefs.[162] It also minimizes the likelihood of surprise. In interlocutory appeals, it serves the additional purpose of discouraging a party from injecting "a sham issue as the vehicle to . . . [appeal] at the interlocutory stage for a declaration on an order not otherwise reviewable."[163]

In the Supreme Court, the presentation-above rule is codified as Sup. Ct. R. 14.1(a). It provides that "[o]nly the questions set forth in the petition [for *certiorari*], or fairly included therein, will be considered by the Court." This rule serves two purposes, the Court has explained. It provides respondent with notice of the grounds upon which a petitioner seeks *certiorari* and thus enables the respondent "to sharpen the arguments as to why *certiorari* should not be

---

[158] *See, e.g., American Ry. Express Co.*, 265 U.S. at 435.

[159] *See* § 13.07 (procedural steps in appeal), *supra. See generally* William H. Baughman, Jr., *Federal Cross-Appeals — A Guide and a Proposal*, 42 Ohio St. L.J. 505 (1981); Robert L. Stern, *When to Cross-Appeal or Cross-Petition — Certainty or Confusion?*, 87 Harv. L. Rev. 763 (1974); Annotation, *Effect of Party's Failure to Cross-Appeal on Scope of Appellate Review as to Contentions of a Party Relating to Judgment Below — Supreme Court Cases*, 63 L. Ed. 2d 911 (1981).

[160] 132 F.2d 794 (8th Cir. 1942).

[161] This is a particular concern of federal appellate courts. *See* § 5.01[2] (federal subject matter jurisdiction in general), *supra.*

[162] *Cf. Hospital Corp. of Am. v. FTC*, 807 F.2d 1381, 1392 (3d Cir. 1986) (four out of eighty-five pages in a brief is insufficient to present constitutional argument; "[b]revity may be the soul of wit, but seismic constitutional change is no laughing matter").

[163] *See Garner v. Wolfinbarger*, 433 F.2d 117, 120 (5th Cir. 1970).

granted."[164] It also, of course, helps the Court select the cases in which *certiorari* will be granted, an important consideration for a court that faces over 10,000 petitions for *certiorari* each term.

Like its companions in the law of reviewability, the presentation-above rule is flexible. Many appellate courts assert the power to reach any issue that is sufficiently illuminated to permit decision without further development below — what a disapproving court has described as "a sort of ad hoc pendent jurisdiction."[165] The Tenth Circuit Court of Appeals, for example, has set out criteria for what it unabashedly calls "pendent appellate jurisdiction." These are the sufficiency of the legal and factual development of the pendent issue for review, the overlap between the appealable and the pendent issues, and "whether judicial economy will be better served by resolving the otherwise nonappealable issue, notwithstanding the federal policy against piecemeal appeals."[166]

While pendent appellate jurisdiction may promote efficiency in otherwise proper appeals from final judgments, it is more problematic on interlocutory appeals that are justified on issue-specific grounds.[167] Thus, the Supreme Court has taken a dim view of appellate jurisdiction exercised pendent to a collateral order appeal. At the same time, it has not ruled out all pendent appellate jurisdiction, at least where the pendent issue is "inextricably intertwined" with the independently appealable issue or where review of the pendent issue is "necessary to ensure meaningful review of the [independently appealable issue]."[168] Finally, another exception is for a limited category of plain errors that the appellate courts uncover at their own initiative.[169]

---

[164] *Yee v. City of Escondido*, 503 U.S. 519, 536 (1992).

[165] *Garner*, 433 F.2d at 120. *See generally* Steinman, note 46, *supra.*

[166] *Colorado v. Idarado Mining Co.*, 916 F.2d 1486, 1491 (10th Cir. 1990), *cert. denied*, 499 U.S. 960 (1991).

[167] *Compare, e.g., Energy Action Educ. Found. v. Andrus*, 654 F.2d 735, 745 n.54 (D.C. Cir. 1980) (promotes efficiency), *with* Riyaz A. Kanji, Note, *The Proper Scope of Appellate Jurisdiction in the Collateral Order Context*, 100 Yale L.J. 511 (1990) (urging narrow scope of pendent appellate jurisdiction in collateral order appeals).

[168] *Swint v. Chambers County Comm'n*, 514 U.S. 35, 51 (1995).

[169] *See generally* Allan D. Vestal, *Sua Sponte Consideration in Appellate Review*, 27 Fordham L. Rev. 477 (1959) (also describing other exceptions, including questions of the interpretation of written instruments, important public policy issues, and when justice otherwise demands appellate consideration of an issue in the record).

PART D.
How Much? Intensity of Review

§ 13.09   HOW MUCH? INTENSITY OF REVIEW

[1] In General

Intensity of review refers to how much an appellate court should defer to or substitute judgment for a decision made below. Intensity of review is issue-specific. It is sometimes said that it depends on whether the issue is fact or law, but this is an oversimplification. Fact-law distinctions merely reflect the subtle interaction of the objectives of correctness, finality, and efficiency in shaping intensity of review.

Correctness is best served by adjusting the intensity of review to relative competency. The trial court has all the advantages of being there; it hears all evidence as it comes in, observes the demeanor of witnesses, and experiences nuance and context that are at best imperfectly conveyed by the cold record considered by the appellate court.[170] Hence the trial court, and the jury when it is the fact finder, have a comparative advantage in fact finding that justifies substantial appellate deference to findings of fact made below. In addition, the trial court is experienced in making managerial decisions regarding scheduling, managerial limitations on discovery, continuances, and new trial that are not susceptible to precise rules of decision. Best left to the discretion of the trial judge, such decisions should also be reviewed deferentially. In contrast, the appellate court may be superior to the trial court in researching, interpreting and applying the law, due to its specialization in deciding law questions, its customarily greater library and law clerk resources, and its habit of collegial decision-making. Along with the need for uniformity, these considerations justify appellate substitution of judgment for conclusions of law and, arguably, of mixed law and fact.

But these observations are tempered by consideration of the systemic procedural objectives of finality and efficiency. At least when the trial and appellate courts are equally competent, these objectives support limiting review, in order to increase respect for lower court judgments and to discourage the number and individual burden of appeals.

> The judicial process is at best a less than scientific method of determining the facts. . . . All that can be expected is the opportunity to present to a neutral *factfinder* the parties' respective versions, under rules designed to assure a measure of fairness, and to let that *factfinder* draw inferences. Since certainty is impossible no matter how often the process is repeated, society's interest emphasizes finality at that point.[171]

---

[170] *See* Maurice Rosenberg, *Judicial Discretion of the Trial Court, Viewed from Above*, 22 SYRACUSE L. REV. 635, 660–65 (1971).

[171] *Davis v. United States Steel Supply*, 581 F.2d 335 (3d Cir. 1978), *vacated en banc*, 688 F.2d 166 (3d Cir. 1982) (Gibbons, J. dissenting), *cert. denied*, 460 U.S. 1014 (1983).

Unfortunately many courts have approached the problem of intensity of review with conclusory labels or *standards of review* ("*de novo*," "clearly erroneous," "abuse of discretion"). Students of appellate opinions thus may begin to distrust the standards of review and to conclude that the intensity of review is wholly result-oriented. Indeed, some courts themselves are expressing skepticism. Thus, one circuit reports a split in its ranks

> over whether we must or even can establish fine gradations of judicial review. One school of thought holds that the verbal differences in standards of judicial review (arbitrary and capricious, clearly erroneous, substantial evidence, abuse of discretion, substantial basis, etc.) mark real differences in the degree of deference that the reviewing court should give the findings and rulings of the tribunal being reviewed. The other school holds that the verbal differences are for the most part merely semantic, that there are really only two standards of review — plenary [*de novo*] and deferential — and that differences in deference in a particular case depend on factors specific to the case, such as the nature of the issue, and the evidence, rather than on differences in the stated standard of review.[172]

But perhaps the schools are not so far apart, if it is recognized that "the verbal differences" are just shorthand ways of describing approximately where on a continuum ranging from 100% substitution of judgment to total deference the intensity of review lies for a particular issue.[173] Figure 13-1 presents the resulting spectrum of review[174] in federal courts, showing traditional standards of review above and types of issues below the horizontal line.

---

[172] *Morales v. Yeutter*, 952 F.2d 954, 957 (7th Cir. 1991) (construing standards of review of administrative decisions) (citations omitted).

[173] Childress and Davis remind us that

> [s]tandards of review, though slippery, cannot be dismissed as sheer politics, especially as the court-watcher begins to look at the practical meaning below the surface catchphrase. The ubiquitous standard, either in basic form or as defined and refined, is presented as a meaningful guidepost to frame both the arguments to the appellate court and the court's analytical response. Even when the slogans have no real internal meaning, in many cases it is clear that the issue framing or assignment of power *behind* the words is the turning point of the decision.

1 Steven Alan Childress & Martha A. Davis, Federal Standards of Review § 1.01 (4th ed. 2010) (footnote omitted).

[174] *Cf.* Ellen E. Sward, *Appellate Review of Judicial Fact-Finding*, 40 U. Kan. L. Rev. 1, 5 (1991); Roy A. Schotland, *Scope of Review of Administrative Action — Remarks Before the D.C. Circuit Judicial Conference*, 34 Fed. B.J. 54, 59 (1959).

Figure 13-1

Standards of Review

Types of Issues

Location on the spectrum is assigned in accordance with the above-described objectives of appeal and of the procedural system.[175]

[2] The Principal Federal Standards of Review[176]

[a] *De Novo* — Questions of Law

Considerations of comparative institutional competency, described in section 13.09[1], coupled with systemic needs for uniformity and guidance in the application of law, dictate plenary or *de novo* review of questions of law. That is, the appellate court decides whether decision of a question of law was right or wrong, freely substituting its judgment for that of the lower court. For all other issues, the lower court receives some measure of deference, and appellate review is correspondingly less intensive.

Characterization of an issue on appeal as law or fact thus directly affects the likelihood of reversal. But no one has yet formulated a rule or principle that will unerringly make the distinction between law and fact. One useful test is whether consistency among decisions on the issue is necessary. The question is more likely to be one of law if it requires a fixed standard that applies to the whole community

---

[175] One scholar describes the spectrum by assigning hypothetical probabilities to the likelihood of affirmance under each standard:

Standard of Review	Hypothesized Affirmance Rates
No Review	100%
Arbitrary and Capricious	85–90%
Substantial Evidence	75–85%
Clearly Erroneous	70–80%
De Novo	40–50%

Paul R. Verkuil, *An Outcomes Analysis of Scope of Review Standards*, 44 WM. & MARY L. REV. 679, 689 (2002).

[176] *See generally* CHILDRESS & DAVIS, note 173, *supra*; Kelly Kunsch, *Standard of Review (State and Federal): A Primer*, 18 SEATTLE U. L. REV. 11 (1994).

impartially, because then consistency of decision is necessary, which a court can best supply. Questions of statutory intent, sufficiency of a defense, adequacy of jury instructions, admission of evidence, and choice of law are typical questions of law. In addition, trial court grants of motions to dismiss for failure to state a claim, summary judgment, directed verdict, judgment as a matter of law, and judgment n.o.v. are reviewed *de novo*, since these motions are granted "as a matter of law."[177]

In contrast, ad hoc historical questions do not require or permit consistent decisions. These are also questions to which a jury could bring a wealth of ordinary experience.[178] What, when, where, and how something happened, and whether witnesses are telling the truth, are thus questions of fact. For example, the Supreme Court held in *Pullman-Standard v. Swint*[179] that the question of discriminatory intent or actual motive is a question of fact, even when characterized as an ultimate fact,[180] and therefore not subject to *de novo* appellate review.

The problem of characterization is complicated by mixed questions of fact and law: "questions in which the historical facts are admitted or established, the rule of law is undisputed, and the issue is whether the facts satisfy the statutory standard, or to put it another way, whether the rule of law as applied to the established facts is or is not violated."[181] Supreme Court decisions lend some support to *de novo* review of such questions, but the circuit courts are divided and the Court has not yet ruled definitively.[182] Some commentators have urged deferential review under the clearly-erroneous standard discussed in the next subsection, because the application of law to facts will normally generate little of precedential value. Thus it "does not implicate the central function of an appellate court — to exercise control over the development of law."[183] Others have urged bifurcated review, with *de novo* review of legal conclusions and effects and deferential review of determinations of underlying facts and factual inferences.[184]

A comparable problem is presented by a fact that is "inseparable from the principles through which it was deduced."[185]

At some point, the reasoning by which a fact is "found" crosses the line between application of those ordinary principles of logic and common

---

[177] *See* § 12.09[3][c], *supra*.

[178] *See Nunez v. Superior Oil Co.*, 572 F.2d 1119, 1126 (5th Cir. 1978) (if an inference "requires 'experience with the mainsprings of human conduct' and reference to 'the data of practical human experience'" it is for the jury, *quoting Commissioner v. Duberstein*, 363 U.S. 278, 289 (1960)).

[179] 456 U.S. 273, 289–90 (1982).

[180] *See* § 8.03[3] (specificity of code pleading), *supra*.

[181] *Pullman-Standard*, 456 U.S. at 289–90 n.19. *See, e.g., Bogardus v. Commissioner*, 302 U.S. 34, 38–39 (1937) (whether monetary awards given taxpayer were taxable compensation or tax-free gifts is a mixed question of fact and law).

[182] *Pullman-Standard*, 456 U.S. at 289–90 n.19, citing cases. *See generally* Even Tsen Lee, *Principled Decision Making and the Proper Role of Federal Appellate Courts: The Mixed Questions Conflict*, 64 S. Cal. L. Rev. 235 (1991) (finding a four-way split in the circuits on the issue); Wright & Miller § 2589.

[183] Lee, note 182, *supra*, at 236–37 [footnote omitted].

[184] Childress & Davis, note 173, *supra*, § 2.18.

[185] *Bose Corp. v. Consumers Union of U.S., Inc.*, 466 U.S. 485, 501 n.17 (1984).

experience which are ordinarily entrusted to the finder of fact into the realm of a legal rule upon which the reviewing court must exercise its own independent judgment. Where the line is drawn varies according to the nature of the substantive law at issue. Regarding certain largely factual questions in some areas of the law, the stakes — in terms of impact on future cases and future conduct — are too great to entrust them finally to the judgment of the trier of fact.[186]

They therefore receive *de novo* review on appeal.

The Court has held that the finding of actual malice necessary to establish liability in a libel action by a public figure against a media defendant falls into this category, because of the courts' special responsibility for preserving First Amendment rights and the close relationship between the finding of such constitutional facts and the scope of the right.[187] "The simple fact is that First Amendment questions of 'constitutional fact' compel this Court's *de novo* review," as Justice Brennan put it.[188]

Some of the same considerations counsel *de novo* appellate review of whether a jury award of punitive damages is constitutionally excessive.[189] Unlike jury determinations of compensatory damages, which are essentially factual, the imposition of punitive damages is not factual, but instead an expression of moral condemnation which is subject to substantive limits imposed by the Due Process Clause. The Due Process standard of "gross excessiveness" is a fluid one which takes its meaning from context and case-by-case application. "Independent review" by appeals courts is therefore necessary to control, clarify, and unify the applicable constitutional legal principles, according to the Supreme Court.[190]

One commentator takes issue with the "mixed question," "application of law-to-facts," and "constitutional fact" rubrics federal courts offer to justify *de novo* review of (at least partially) factual matters. He argues that the intensity of review of such matters should reflect "the intellectual processes" by which the particular determination in question has been made: by observation (warranting substantial deference) or by reflection on record evidence (warranting less).[191]

---

[186] *Id.*

[187] *Id.* at 501. Cf. *Baumgartner v. United States*, 322 U.S. 665, 671 (1944) (whether there is clear, unequivocal, and convincing proof of conduct that justifies denaturalization is a question that "cannot escape broad[] social judgments" justifying independent appellate consideration).

[188] *Rosenbloom v. Metromedia, Inc.*, 403 U.S. 29, 54 (1971) (Brennan, J., joined by Burger, C.J., and Blackmun, J.). See *Roth v. United States*, 354 U.S. 476, 497–98 (1957), for a particularly forceful statement by Justice Harlan of the rationale for this rule.

[189] *Cooper Indus., Inc. v. Leatherman Tool Group, Inc.*, 532 U.S. 424, 431 (2001).

[190] *Id.* at 436.

[191] George C. Christie, *Judicial Review of Findings of Fact*, 87 Nw. U. L. Rev. 14, 56 (1992). *See* § 13.09[2][b] (explaining variability in clearly erroneous standard), *infra*.

[b]　Clearly Erroneous — Findings by the Court

Historically, the law judge was viewed as a surrogate for the jury, while the equity judge was viewed as the equivalent of a master. Factual findings by the former thus received the same deference on review as findings by a jury, while findings by the latter received no special weight except insofar as they rested on determinations of credibility that only the trial judge could make.[192] With the merger of law and equity in the federal courts, these historical practices have also been merged into Rule 52(a)(6), which provides that judge-made "[f]indings of fact, whether based on oral or other evidence, must not be set aside unless clearly erroneous, and the reviewing court must give due regard to the trial court's opportunity to judge the witnesses' credibility."

The Supreme Court has stated that a finding is clearly erroneous "when although there is evidence to support it, the reviewing court on the entire evidence is left with the definite and firm conviction that a mistake has been committed."[193] It is not enough for the appellate court to conclude that it would have decided the issue differently. The test is not simply right or wrong, or review would be *de novo*.[194]

How much more is necessary depends not on whether the fact is ultimate or subsidiary,[195] but "on the nature of the materials on which the finding is based"[196] and any other factors that affect the relative competency of trial and appellate courts. Because of the trial judge's unique opportunity to observe the demeanor of witnesses, the presumption of correctness is stronger when the finding is based on oral evidence than when it is based on documentary evidence.[197] Rule 52 expressly reminds the appellate court of this by urging "due regard" for that opportunity. The presumption of correctness becomes stronger as trials become longer and more complex, on the theory that the trial court acquires greater intimacy with the evidence from living with it for weeks or months instead of just a few days or hours.[198] In contrast, the trial court's comparative fact-finding advantage diminishes when the evidence is entirely documentary and the trial short and simple. Then the court of appeals has nearly the same opportunity to acquaint itself with the evidence that the trial court had in making the record. The location of the clearly erroneous standard on the spectrum of review in Figure 13.1 then shifts slightly to the left.

---

[192] *James, Hazard & Leubsdorf* § 12.9; Sward, note 174, *supra*, at 18–20.

[193] *United States v. United States Gypsum Co.*, 333 U.S. 364, 395 (1948).

[194] *See Anderson v. City of Bessemer*, 470 U.S. 564, 573 (1985). On the scope of *de novo* review, see § 13.10[1], *supra*.

[195] *Pullman-Standard*, 456 U.S. at 287 (Rule 52 "does not divide findings into categories"). Categorization of a fact as ordinary fact, mixed question of fact and law, or constitutional fact, on the other hand, can determine whether Rule 52 applies at all. *See* § 13.10[2][a] (*de novo* review), *supra*.

[196] *Baumgartner*, 322 U.S. at 671.

[197] *See Bose Corp.*, 466 U.S. at 497.

[198] 466 U.S. at 497. *See* Jeffrey W. Stempel, *A Distorted Mirror: the Supreme Court's Shimmering View of Summary Judgment, Directed Verdict, and the Adjudication Process*, 49 Ohio St. L.J. 95, 177–78 (1993).

Prior to 1985, some federal courts went a step further and reasoned that the presumption in such circumstances was not just weakened but eliminated. They declined to apply the clearly erroneous standard of review to judge-made findings based solely on documentary evidence, instead reviewing them *de novo*.[199] These courts arguably disregarded the conjunctive "due regard" phrase in Rule 52. Moreover, they were wrong by their own reasoning, because they ignored the superiority in fact finding that a trial judge acquires even in documentary cases from her experience in general and her unavoidable exposure to the whole case in particular.[200] They also ignored the systemic interest in finality, which counsels against *de novo* appellate review of findings even when the trial and appellate courts have the same competency.

In 1985, the Supreme Court put an end to this practice of *de novo* re-decision in *Anderson v. City of Bessemer*.[201] There it emphasized that the clearly erroneous standard applies to *all* judge-made findings, although the strength of the presumption of correctness that it embodies may vary.[202] Rule 52(a) was amended thereafter to make clearer its applicability to all "[f]indings of fact, whether based on oral or documentary evidence" (now phrased as "oral or other evidence").

[c]　Reasonableness — Findings by the Jury and Some Administrative Agencies

The command of the Seventh Amendment ("[N]o fact tried by a jury, shall be otherwise re-examined in any Court of the United States, than according to the rules of the common law") reinforces the considerations noted above and requires more deferential appellate review of jury findings than of judge findings. Logically, too, the jury's greater numbers should enhance its fact-finding ability and dilute its biases, entitling its findings to greater weight on appeal. The standard of review is the same as that employed by the trial judge to decide motions for directed verdict, judgment as a matter of law, or judgment notwithstanding the verdict: whether a reasonable jury could have reached the verdict.[203]

Notwithstanding this deferential standard of review, however, there is significant empirical evidence that federal appellate courts are more aggressive in review of jury verdicts for sufficiency of the evidence. They overturned fully half the verdicts

---

[199] *See, e.g., Davis*, 32 Fed. R. Serv. 2d (Callaghan) at 733 ("the Rule 52(a) 'clearly erroneous' standard does not apply to wholly documentary cases where the record discloses no oral testimony"); *Orvis v. Higgins*, 180 F.2d 537 (2d Cir.), *cert. denied*, 340 U.S. 810 (1950).

[200] "The trial judge's major role is the determination of fact, and with experience in fulfilling that role comes expertise." *Anderson*, 470 U.S. at 574.

[201] 470 U.S. 564.

[202] *Id.*

[203] *See, e.g., Hersch v. United States*, 719 F.2d 873, 877 (6th Cir. 1983); *Williams v. City of Valdosta*, 689 F.2d 964, 970 (11th Cir. 1982) (*citing Boeing Co. v. Shipman*, 411 F.2d 365, 374–75 (5th Cir. 1969) (*en banc*)). *See* § 12.09[1] (taking the case from the jury), *supra*. The standard of review is nominally the same when the trial judge has denied such motions as when he has granted them, but his decision to let the verdict stand may, as a practical matter, add weight to the verdict.

appealed in the one-year period from 1984–1985, for example.[204] A large number of these decisions are aimed at so-called excessive jury verdicts.[205]

Statutes subject many administrative agency findings to a reasonableness standard like the standard for deciding motions attacking the jury's verdict.[206] Just as a jury's findings are given deference in part because of its fact-finding abilities, many administrative agency findings receive special weight because of the agencies' expertise in finding particular kinds of facts.

[d] Abuse of Discretion — Discretionary Orders

Hardest to place on the spectrum of review is the *abuse of discretion* standard for reviewing discretionary orders by the trial court. Certain matters are within the discretion of the trial judge because they are largely ad hoc and situation-specific, closely related to calendar and trial management.[207] Decisions regarding scheduling, amendment by permission, complex joinder, consolidation and separation of claims for trial, order of discovery, order of proof, and sanctions under Rules 11 and 37 are illustrative. A right-or-wrong *de novo* standard of review would be difficult (perhaps impossible) to administer in such cases. Instead, the federal courts apply the abuse of discretion standard, which is tolerant of mistakes in the exercise of acknowledged discretion.

The difficulty in locating this standard on the spectrum of review is well-illustrated by the review of new trial decisions in jury cases. To grant or deny a new trial is in the discretion of the trial judge, who is best positioned to appreciate whether improper influences or argument tainted a jury verdict or whether the verdict is against the weight of the evidence.[208] When a new trial has been denied for any reason, the deference owed the trial court is reinforced by the deference owed a jury verdict, which is left standing when the appellate court affirms the trial court's denial of new trial. On the other hand, when a new trial is granted, and the issue is preserved for review on appeal from an eventual final judgment,[209] the trial judge receives less deference.

> This is because when the jury verdict is set aside usual deference to the trial judge conflicts with deference to the jury on questions of fact. When a new trial is granted on the basis that the verdict is against the weight of the evidence . . . [appellate] review is particularly stringent to protect the litigant's right to a jury trial.[210]

---

[204] Eric Schnapper, *Judges Against Juries — Appellate Review of Federal Civil Verdicts*, 1989 Wis. L. Rev. 237, 238.

[205] *Id.* at 313.

[206] The statutory term of art is "supported by substantial evidence," *see* 5 U.S.C. § 706(2)(E), which has been interpreted to mean rational or reasonable, *see generally* Bernard Schwartz, Administrative Law §§ 10.7–10.11 (3d ed. 1991).

[207] *See* Rosenberg, note 170, *supra*, at 643–53 (noting that thirty of the Federal Rules of Civil Procedure involve some area of trial court discretion).

[208] *See* § 12.09 (new trial), *supra*.

[209] *See* § 13.03[1] (final judgment rule), *supra*.

[210] *Hewitt v. B.F. Goodrich Co.*, 732 F.2d 1554, 1556 (11th Cir. 1984).

In fact, when the trial is simple, the facts highly disputed, and there is no taint from pernicious circumstances, review should be even more intense because of the correspondingly greater likelihood that the jury verdict was sound.[211]

This is only to suggest that the abuse of discretion standard varies in intensity with the breadth of discretion. Accordingly, abuse of discretion really occupies a band in the middle of the spectrum of intensity of review, its precise locus in any particular case depending upon the nature of the discretionary order under review.[212]

[e] No Review — Selective Findings by Administrative Agencies

Placing a "standard of review" at the far left hand point of the spectrum of review seemingly poses an anomaly in that zero substitution of judgment — complete deference — is tantamount to no review. But because the intensity of review is issue-specific, the point is not just hypothetical. It is possible to allow appeal of a decision and still foreclose review of particular issues within it.

This in fact is what Congress has done with respect to certain fact-bound administrative decisions, typically mass justice benefit determinations by social service agencies.[213] Because of the large number of such decisions, their lack of precedential importance, and the arguably reliable adjudicative process by which they are made in the agencies, Congress has made some of the agencies' substantive decisions final and not subject to review outside the agencies. On the other hand, review-denying statutory provisions usually have not been read to foreclose review of associated issues of procedure, regulatory authority, and constitutional law,[214] which are less likely to flood the federal courts and which may carry precedential value.[215]

---

[211] *See, e.g., Williams v. City of Valdosta*, 689 F.2d 964, 974–75 (11th Cir. 1982).

[212] *Cf. Heat & Control, Inc. v. Hester Indus., Inc.*, 785 F.2d 1017, 1022 (Fed. Cir. 1986). *See generally* CHILDRESS & DAVIS, note 173, *supra*, § 4-154 (asserting that "no single level of deference or scrutiny is intended for the phrase *abuse of discretion*" and that it has a "sliding contextual meaning").

[213] *See, e.g.*, 38 U.S.C. § 511(a) (providing that, "The Secretary shall decide all questions of law and fact necessary to a decision by the Secretary under a law that affects the provision of benefits by the Secretary to veterans. . . . [T]he decision of the Secretary as to any such question shall be final and conclusive and may not be reviewed by any other official or by any court, whether by an action in the nature of mandamus or otherwise.").

[214] The denial of federal court review of bona fide constitutional claims would raise serious questions of due process. *See* SCHWARTZ, note 206, *supra* § 8.40.

[215] *See, e.g., Johnson v. Robison*, 415 U.S. 361 (1974) (statutory review-denying provision does not bar review of constitutional claim); *Carter v. Cleland*, 643 F.2d 1, 3, 5 (D.C. Cir. 1980) (statutory review-denying provisions construed narrowly to allow review of issues of regulatory authority for and constitutionality of agency action).

§ 13.10 APPEALS IN THE CALIFORNIA COURTS

[1] Introductory Note on Appealability of Judgments and Orders

The California statutes and rules regarding appealability reflect the same concern for correctness and uniformity of disposition on one hand versus efficiency and finality on the other as is evident in the federal system. As a result, California authorizes appeals from final judgments of trial courts in much the same manner as in the federal courts. However, the California courts assess the costs and benefits of allowing interlocutory appellate review somewhat differently than the federal courts and more often allow such review by appeal or extraordinary writ. Whether California's approach to interlocutory review is preferable to the federal one in terms of judicial efficiency is an open question.

[2] The "One-Final-Judgment-Rule"

California supposedly follows the *one-final-judgment-rule*, the essence of which is that an appeal lies only from a final judgment which terminates the proceeding in the lower court by completely disposing of the matter in controversy.[216] A judgment is "final," so as to be appealable, "when no further judicial action by the court is essential to the final determination of the rights of the parties to the action."[217] As the California Supreme Court has observed: "It is not the form of the decree but the substance and effect of the adjudication which is determinative. As a general test, which must be adapted to the particular circumstances of the individual case, it may be said that where no issue is left for future consideration except the fact of compliance or noncompliance with the terms of the first decree, that decree is final."[218] So stated, this test is somewhat misleading, as illustrated by its application by the Court of Appeal in *UAP-Columbus JV 3261 32 v. Nesbit*.[219]

The plaintiff in *UAP-Columbus* commenced an interpleader action seeking declaratory relief and an allowance of costs and substantial attorney fees under the interpleader statute. On March 19, 1990, the superior court ruled on the interpleader and declaratory relief causes of action, but did not dispose of the request for fees and costs until July 23, 1990. On appeal, the *UAP-Columbus* court concluded the March 19 judgment was final and not interlocutory. According to the court, costs and allowable attorney fees are only incidental to the main action, and are not essential to the final determination of the rights of the parties to the action. Because the defendants' notices of appeal were not timely filed as to the March 19 judgment, their appeals were dismissed as to that judgment. In light of the holding in *UAP-Columbus*, perhaps a more precise definition of "final" judgment would be:

---

[216] *See, e.g., Morehart v. Cnty. of Santa Barbara*, 7 Cal. 4th 725, 741-44, 29 Cal. Rptr. 2d 804, 872 P.2d 143 (1994); *Bank of Am. Nat. Trust & Sav. Ass'n v. Superior Court*, 20 Cal. 2d 697, 701, 128 P.2d 357 (1942); *Kinoshita v. Horio*, 186 Cal. App. 3d 959, 963, 231 Cal. Rptr. 241 (1986).

[217] *UAP-Columbus JV 326132 v. Nesbitt*, 234 Cal. App. 3d 1028, 1035, 285 Cal. Rptr. 856 (1991); *see Morehart, supra*, 7 Cal. 4th at 741-44.

[218] *Lyon v. Goss*, 19 Cal. 2d 659, 670, 123 P.2d 11 (1942).

[219] 234 Cal. App. 3d 1028, 1034, 285 Cal. Rptr. 856 (1991).

If the merits of the action are not yet fully resolved, the judgment is not "final;" but when the merits are fully resolved, the judgment is "final" even though issues ancillary to the merits, such as awarding costs and attorney fees, must still be decided.

The substance and effect of a decree, not its label or form, determine whether it is appealable as a final judgment. This axiom creates some difficult problems for litigants. For example, in *Laraway v. Pasedena Unified School District*,[220] the plaintiff petitioned the superior court for mandamus, declaratory, and injunctive relief seeking certain public records from the defendant school district. The superior court denied the relief requested in the petition in an "Order" dated August 23, 2000. This order did not award any attorney fees or costs. Subsequently, on January 29, 2001, the superior court filed a "Judgment" which reiterated that the court had "ruled by Order dated August 23, 2000" on the petition, set forth the same rulings as contained in the order denying the petition, added a provision that judgment was entered in favor of respondent and against petitioner, and awarded respondent $0 in costs against petitioner. With respect to the maximum 180-day time period within which to file a notice of appeal, the *Laraway* court concluded that the time to appeal began to run on August 23, 2000. The August 23 "Order" constituted a final judgment because it disposed of all the issues between the parties, the court reasoned, whereas the subsequent "Judgment" was merely a repetition of that earlier order and added nothing but an award of $0 in costs. Therefore, the notice of appeal was untimely.

In *Griset v. Fair Political Practices Commission*,[221] the California Supreme Court applied the "substance and effect not form of the decree" standard to determine whether a superior court adjudication was final and appealable. The plaintiffs had alleged four related causes of action, including a petition for writ of mandate, challenging the constitutionality of a statute that required those supporting or opposing a candidate for public office or a ballot measure to identify themselves on any mass mailings to prospective voters. Central to all four causes of action was plaintiffs' allegation that this statute violated the right to free speech under the First Amendment. The superior court denied plaintiffs' mandamus cause of action on the ground that the statute was constitutional, but did not formally rule on the other three causes of action. Plaintiffs appealed, and the court of appeal affirmed.

When the *Griset* case subsequently reached the California Supreme Court, the main issue was whether the court of appeal had jurisdiction to hear plaintiffs' appeal from superior court. The Court first observed that the superior court's ruling was not an appealable *judgment* if it disposed of only one of the causes of action pending between the parties. However, the Court then concluded that superior court's ruling was indeed a final judgment because it disposed of all four causes of action between the parties, even though there was no formal entry of judgment by the superior court. Regardless of its form, the *substance* of the superior court's denial of plaintiffs' petition for a writ of mandate disposed of all

---

[220] 98 Cal. App. 4th 579, 120 Cal. Rptr. 2d 213 (2002).

[221] 25 Cal. 4th 688, 107 Cal. Rptr. 2d 149, 23 P.3d 43 (2001).

issues in the action between plaintiffs and defendant "because it completely resolved plaintiffs' allegation — essential to all of plaintiffs' causes of action — that [the statute] was unconstitutional."[222]

The decisions in *Griset, Laraway,* and *UAP-Columbus* inform California litigants that when the "one-final-judgment-rule" produces an unclear result, they should err on the side of caution and assume a "final" judgment. If this assumption proves wrong, an appeal will be considered premature and will likely be dismissed, but can still be brought later. But, as these decisions illustrate, failure to appeal from a trial court decision that the appellate court views as "final" will preclude any appellate review of that decision.

[3] Appealability of Orders

An order is a written ruling of a trial court which is not included in a judgment. Ordinarily, an order is considered interlocutory and therefore not appealable. However, the California Legislature and courts recognize that some interlocutory orders, due to their immediate and irreparable consequences, are appealable as exceptions to the one-final-judgment-rule. California statutes authorize appeals from several interlocutory orders, such as orders granting or refusing to grant a preliminary injunction, certain postjudgment orders, and some sanction orders.[223] Moreover, as will be discussed below, the California courts have developed significant judgemade exceptions to the one-final-judgment rule. Therefore, as a general test of whether a trial court's decree is appealable or not, the one-final-judgment-rule is obviously inaccurate.

[4] Judge-Made Exceptions to Statutory One-Final-Judgment-Rule

Generally speaking, the right to appeal is governed by statute. California Code of Civil Procedure § 904.1 sets forth the statutory authority for appeals from a superior court to the court of appeal in unlimited civil cases, and section 904.2 delineates when an appeal may be taken to the appellate division of the superior court in a limited civil case. However, the statement often repeated by the California courts — that "the right to appeal is wholly statutory" — is inaccurate. The California courts permit appeals in certain circumstances despite the lack of statutory authority, recognizing at least two judicially-created exceptions to the one-final-judgment-rule.

[a] Ruling On Collateral Matter

Perhaps the most frequently utilized exception to the one-final-judgment-rule is the *collateral order doctrine,* which has been defined by the California Supreme Court as follows: "When a court renders an interlocutory order collateral to the main issue, dispositive of the rights of the parties in relation to the collateral matter, and directing payment of money or performance of an act, direct appeal may be

---

[222] *Griset, supra,* 25 Cal. 4th at 699.

[223] CAL. CODE CIV. PROC. §§ 904.1(a)(2)-(6), (8)-(13); 906.

taken."[224] The California courts have applied the collateral matter doctrine to permit immediate appeal of interlocutory orders in a variety of circumstances, including orders disqualifying an attorney, reducing temporary spousal support, and certain orders for payment of money sanctions.[225]

Although some California courts do not require that the collateral order direct the payment of money or the performance of an act for this exception to apply, most conclude that judicially compelled payment of money or performance of an act is an essential prerequisite.[226] In this regard, California's collateral order doctrine is narrower than the corresponding federal doctrine, which does not appear to impose this additional prerequisite.[227] However, the fact that an interlocutory order directs payment of money or performance of an act does not, by itself, mean that the order comes within California's collateral matter exception. The interlocutory order must also be "collateral" to the merits of the case, i.e., distinct and severable from the general subject of the litigation and therefore not a necessary step to the correct determination of the main issue of the action.

In another regard, California's collateral order doctrine may be broader than the federal doctrine. One requirement of the federal doctrine is that the collateral order must be effectively unreviewable on appeal from the final judgment, so that the opportunity for meaningful review will be lost unless an immediate appeal is permitted.[228] The various cases applying the California doctrine do not emphasize, and in many cases even mention, this "effectively unreviewable on appeal" requirement. Instead, the California courts are more concerned with whether the order is final as to the issues determined and truly collateral to the merits.[229]

---

[224] *In re Marriage of Skelley*, 18 Cal. 3d 365, 368, 134 Cal. Rptr. 197, 556 P.2d 297 (1976).

[225] *In re Marriage of Skelley, supra*, 18 Cal. 3d at 367-70; *I. J. Weinrot & Son, Inc. v. Jackson*, 40 Cal. 3d 327, 331, 220 Cal. Rptr. 103, 708 P.2d 682 (1985); *Meehan v. Hopps*, 45 Cal. 2d 213, 216-217, 288 P.2d 267 (1955).

[226] *See, e.g., Ponce-Bran v. Tr. of the Cal. State Univ.*, 48 Cal. App. 4th 1656, 56 Cal. Rptr. 2d 358 (1996) (holding the trial court's order denying a motion to appoint counsel was not appealable under the collateral order doctrine because the order did not direct the payment of money or the performance of an act); *Mercury Interactive Corp. v. Klein*, 158 Cal. App. 4th 60, 70 Cal. Rptr. 3d 88 (2007) (holding an order directing the unsealing of exhibits previously designated as confidential is appealable because it is a final determination of a collateral matter that directs the performance of an act — unsealing — against the party who filed the exhibits under seal); *Muller v. Fresno Comty. Hosp. & Med. Ctr.*, 172 Cal. App. 4th 887, 91 Cal. Rptr. 3d 617 (2009) (reviewing the conflicting authorities as to whether the order must direct the payment of money or the performance of an act and observing that the California Supreme Court will find the order appealable without reference to these limitations, as long as the Court is satisfied that the order is "truly collateral").

[227] The collateral order doctrine applied in federal courts is discussed in § 13.04[1], *supra*.

[228] *See* § 13.04[1], *supra*.

[229] *See, e.g., Muller, supra*, 172 Cal. App. 4th at 898-905 (reviewing numerous collateral order decisions and concluding that the focus of the doctrine is on whether the order is final and "truly collateral); *Steen v. Fremont Cemetery Corp.*, 9 Cal. App. 4th 1221, 1226-30, 11 Cal. Rptr. 2d 780 (1992) (holding collateral order doctrine inapplicable to an order directing service of class action notice because the order is neither final as to the class notice issues nor collateral to the main action).

[b] Judgment Final as to One Party

When litigation involves multiple parties and a judgment is entered which leaves no issue to be determined as to one party, that party has the right to immediately appeal the judgment even though the litigation is not final as to other parties.[230] For example, dismissal of all causes of action pleaded by one of two plaintiffs constitutes an appealable judgment even though the remaining plaintiff had joined in some of these causes of action. Likewise, an order dismissing fewer than all defendants from an action is a final judgment as to them and thus appealable. This exception to the one-final-judgment-rule is the apparent rationale for numerous California Supreme Court holdings that an order denying a motion to certify a class action is appealable.[231] If an order terminates class claims but individual claims survive, the order terminating class claims is immediately appealable under the "death knell" doctrine. However, an order that certifies a class, but not one as extensive as plaintiff sought, is not an appealable order under this exception.[232]

Except for one significant difference, California's judgment-final-as-to-one-party doctrine is similar to the "directed" final judgment under Rule 54(b) of the Federal Rules of Civil Procedure when multiple parties are involved in a federal court action. Under federal Rule 54(b), the district court *may* direct entry of final judgment as to fewer than all parties "only if the court expressly determines that there is no just cause for delay." In contrast, an express direction by the superior court is not a precondition under the California doctrine — a judgment determining all issues as to fewer than all parties is *automatically* appealable as a final judgment.

California's automatic right to appellate review of class action denials also differs from the discretionary approach to appellate review of such decisions in federal court. Under Rule 23(f) of the Federal Rules of Civil Procedure, a United States Court of Appeals "may in its discretion permit an appeal from an order of a district court granting or denying class action certification." If the Court of Appeals declines to permit an interlocutory appeal, the district court's class certification order is reviewable only on appeal from the subsequent final judgment on the merits.[233] In many cases, the federal approach may be preferable to California's because under federal Rule 23(f) the court of appeals is given the unfettered discretion whether to permit the interlocutory appeal — permission that need not be granted in routine cases. Moreover, the California approach may create some unanticipated problems. Because California follows a "one shot" rule with respect to appellate review of class action denials, if an interlocutory appeal from an order denying class certification is

---

[230] *E.g., Justus v. Atchison,* 19 Cal. 3d 564, 568, 139 Cal. Rptr. 97, 565 P.2d 122 (1977); *Hydrotech Sys., Ltd. v. Oasis Water Park,* 52 Cal. 3d 988, 993, n.3, 277 Cal. Rptr. 517, 803 P.2d 370 (1991).

[231] *E.g., In re Baycol Cases I and II,* 51 Cal. 4th 751, 122 Cal. Rptr. 3d 153, 248 P.3d 681 (2011); *Richmond v. Dart Indus., Inc.,* 29 Cal. 3d 462, 470, 174 Cal. Rptr. 515, 629 P.2d 23 (1981); *Daar v. Yellow Cab Co.,* 67 Cal. 2d 695, 699, 63 Cal. Rptr. 724, 433 P.2d 732 (1967) (ruling that a demurrer sustained as to class action allegations "is tantamount to a dismissal of the action as to all members of the class other than plaintiff").

[232] *See Baycol, supra,* 51 Cal. 4th at 757-758 (ruling the "death knell" doctrine applies to orders that entirely terminate class claims, but not orders that only limit the scope or the number of claims available to the class).

[233] *Cooper & Lybrand v. Livesay,* 437 U. S. 403, 98 S. Ct. 54, 57 L. Ed. 2d 351 (1978).

not taken, the right to appeal later and argue for class action status is forfeited.[234] Consequently, the failure to appeal a trial court's order denying class certification may preclude subsequent motions to certify, even if based on new evidence.

[c] No Interlocutory Appeal from Order Determining "Separate and Independent Issues"

Prior to the California Supreme Court's 1994 decision in *Morehart v. County of Santa Barbara*,[235] the courts of appeal applied a third exception to the one-final-judgment-rule, authorizing an immediate appeal from a judgment on fewer than all issues where those issues are "separate and independent" from other issues still pending in the trial court.[236] The *Morehart* Court repudiated this exception and held that a judgment that disposes of fewer than all causes of action is necessarily interlocutory, and not yet final, as to any parties between whom another cause of action remains pending. The Court's disapproval of this exception to the one-final-judgment-rule seems entirely appropriate — the uncertain parameters of this exception necessitated the expenditure of considerable judicial resources to appealability determinations. To demonstrate this point, the *Morehart* court contrasted the automatic appeal under this exception to the approach under Rule 54(b) of the Federal Rules of Civil Procedure where the federal district court is used as a "dispatcher." Federal Rule 54(b) authorizes the district court in multi-claim actions to "direct entry of a final judgment on fewer than all of the claims" if the court "expressly determines that there is no just cause for delay." Because the district court in effect must state that its decision constitutes a "final judgment," adversely affected parties know that the time for appeal will not begin to run until this designation is made.

Even before the ruling in *Morehart*, the general rule was that, absent one of the exceptions to the one-final-judgment-rule, dismissal of a complaint does not constitute a final appealable judgment with respect to parties as to whom a cross-complaint (the California equivalent of a counterclaim) remains pending, even though the complaint has been fully adjudicated.[237] The same general rule applies when the defendant's cross-complaint against the plaintiff is dismissed but the complaint is still pending.[238] However, a dismissal that adjudicates all issues as to a specific *third-party* cross-defendant constitutes an appealable final judgment because final judgment treatment in such circumstances is consistent with the

---

[234] *See Baycol, supra*, 51 Cal. 4th at 762, n. 8; *Stephen v. Enter. Rent-A-Car*, 235 Cal. App. 3d 806, 1 Cal. Rptr. 2d 130 (1991) (holding the failure to file timely notice of appeal from order denying class action certification bars later appeal of class issues as part of appeal from final judgment in the individual action; review of this order by later appeal not permitted because an immediate appeal of this order might have been taken).

[235] 7 Cal. 4th 725, 29 Cal. Rptr. 2d 804, 872 P.2d 143 (1994).

[236] *See, e.g., Garat v. City of Riverside*, 2 Cal. App. 4th 259, 275-280, 3 Cal. Rptr. 2d 504 (1991); *Day v. Papadakis*, 231 Cal. App. 3d 503, 282 Cal. Rptr. 548 (1991) (citing cases).

[237] *See, e.g., California Dental Ass'n v. Cal. Dental Hygienists' Ass'n*, 222 Cal. App. 3d 49, 59, 271 Cal. Rptr. 410 (1990); *Daon Corp. v. Place Homeowners Ass'n*, 207 Cal. App. 3d 1449, 1456, 255 Cal. Rptr. 448 (1989).

[238] *Sjoberg v. Hastorf*, 33 Cal. 2d 116, 118, 119 P.2d 688 (1948).

"judgment-final-as-to-one-party" doctrine.[239]

[5] The California Appellate System

[a] Appellate Review of Superior Court Cases

An appeal in an "unlimited civil case" in the superior court is to the California Court of Appeal. However, in a "limited civil case" — generally, an action in which the amount in controversy does not exceed $25,000 — appeal is to the appellate division of the superior court.[240] The Court of Appeal has authority to order transfer of such an appeal when the superior court certifies or the Court of Appeal on its own motion determines "that such transfer appears necessary to secure uniformity of decision or to settle important questions of law."[241] However, under the current statutory scheme, a decision of the appellate division of the superior court in a "limited civil case" is not appealable to the Court of Appeal.

[b] Publication of California Appellate Court Opinions

The California Constitution requires decisions on the merits by the California Supreme Court and Courts of Appeal be in writing with the court's reasons stated. All such written opinions of the Supreme Court are published in the Official Reports (*i.e.*, the multi-volume *California Reports*). However, an opinion of the Court of Appeal is published (in the multi-volume *California Appellate Reports*) only if it satisfies one of the criteria specified in the California Rules of Court (*e.g.*, the opinion establishes a new rule of law, address or creates an apparent conflict in the law, involves a legal issue of continuing public interest, etc.). These criteria discourage publication — approximately 18% of the Courts of Appeal opinions in civil appeals are published.[242] Partial publication is also authorized and is frequently utilized. If the Court of Appeal determines that only portions of its opinion meet the standards for publication, it can order publication of only those portions; the unpublished parts are treated as an unpublished opinion.

The general rule is that an unpublished opinion cannot be cited or relied on by a court or a party in any other action or proceeding. This prohibition is subject to limited exceptions, most notably that such opinions may be cited or relied on "when the opinion is relevant under the doctrines of law of the case, res judicata, or collateral estoppel."[243] Because an unpublished opinion cannot be cited, it has no precedential value. Improper citation to an unpublished opinion in an appellate brief

---

[239] *E.g., County of Los Angeles v. Guerrero*, 209 Cal. App. 3d 1149, 1152, n.2, 257 Cal. Rptr. 787 (1989) (ruling that where defendant cross-complains against a third party, the dismissal of the cross-complaint is a final adverse adjudication of cross-complainant's rights against a distinct party, the order is appealable); *Miller v. Silver*, 181 Cal. App. 3d 652, 658, 226 Cal. Rptr. 479 (1986) (holding the dismissal of cross-complaint against a third party, not a defendant or plaintiff, is appealable).

[240] CAL. CODE CIV. PROC. § 904.2.

[241] CAL. CODE CIV. PROC. § 911.

[242] *See* Judicial Council of California, *2012 Court Statistics Report*, Courts of Appeal, Fig. 30.

[243] CAL. CT. R. 8.1115(b)(1); *see, e.g., Hummel v. First Nat. Bank*, 191 Cal. App. 3d 489, 491, 236 Cal. Rptr. 449 (1987) (law of the case); *Los Angeles Police Protective League v. City of Los Angeles*, 102 Cal. App. 4th 85, 91, 124 Cal. Rptr. 2d 911 (2002) (collateral estoppel).

may even result in the imposition of monetary sanctions on the offending attorney.

[c] Review by the California Supreme Court

A party seeking review of a decision of the Court of Appeal must file and serve a petition for review within 10 days after the decision becomes final.[244] The jurisdiction of the California Supreme Court in civil cases is discretionary. The grounds for review are set forth in the California Rules of Court; by far the most important is where review "appears necessary to secure uniformity of decision or to settle an important question of law."[245] Over the past 10 years, the Supreme Court has granted, on average, approximately five percent of the petitions for review.[246] Of course, the denial of the petition for review does not necessarily mean the Supreme Court endorses the correctness of the Court of Appeal's reasoning and decision.

Generally, the immediate effect of a grant of a petition for review on the Court of Appeal's decision is that the opinion is superseded and is not published.[247] When the California Supreme Court decides to grant a petition for review, it then has several options. It may review the entire Court of Appeal decision, or may review and decide only specific issues. With respect to issues not decided, the Supreme Court may order republication of those portions of the lower court's opinion resolving those issues, may leave those portions unpublished, or may transfer the case back to the Court of Appeal to decide the remaining issues. If after granting review the Supreme Court determines that the case involves issues already before the court in another case, it may "grant and hold" the new case until the lead case is decided. It may even transfer the entire case back to the lower court with instructions for further proceedings, a routine practice where a petition for extraordinary writ has been summarily denied by the Court of Appeal. These options, as well as the depublication practice discussed below, provide the Supreme Court with flexibility to accomplish its primary institutional functions — to decide important legal questions and to secure statewide uniformity of decision. The California Supreme Court has the final say on matters of state law, but a party may seek review of a decision involving a federal question by a petition for writ of certiorari before the United States Supreme Court.[248]

[d] Depublication by Supreme Court Order

The California Supreme Court has the power to order depublication of a Court of Appeal opinion previously certified for publication, either on its own motion or pursuant to a request for depublication.[249] The publication and depublication rules empower the Supreme Court to eliminate the precedential effect of an otherwise valid court of appeal decision, and do not require the Court to hear the case or to state reasons for the depublication order. The Supreme Court's depublication

---

[244] CAL. CT. R. 8.500(a) & (e).

[245] CAL. CT. R. 8.500(b).

[246] *See* Judicial Council of California, 2012 *Court Statistics Report*, Supreme Court, Fig. 19.

[247] CAL. CT. R. 8.1105(c).

[248] 28 U.S.C. § 1257(a).

[249] CAL. CT. R. 8.1105(e) & 8.1125(c).

practice has been criticized on a variety of grounds, including that it is ordered without reasons stated and may leave attorneys and lower courts without guidance as to what the Supreme Court considers to be the law.[250] Perhaps as a response to these various concerns, the Supreme Court's exercise of its depublication authority has declined dramatically over the past several years, from over 100 opinions ordered depublished per year in the early 1990s to only 11 opinions in 2010-2011.[251]

[6] Timeliness of Appeals from the Superior Courts

[a] General Time Limits for Appeals

The California Rules of Court set forth the general time limits for filing a notice of appeal in civil actions.[252] These time limits may be extended when a party files a motion for a new trial or certain other post-trial motions, so long as the motion itself is timely filed and valid. Like the federal courts, the California courts are unforgiving in their enforcement of these time limits. The requirement as to the time for filing a notice of appeal is mandatory. An appellate court has no jurisdiction to consider an appeal taken after expiration of the applicable limitation period.[253]

[b] Late Appeals

An appeal from a superior court judgment or order is commenced by filing a notice of appeal within the relevant time limitation specified by the California Rules of Court. As already noted, the timely filing of a notice of appeal is jurisdictional — failure to appeal from an appealable judgment or order within the prescribed time limit bars appellate review of the issues determined by the trial court's ruling. If a

---

[250] See Stephen R. Barnett, *Making Decisions Disappear: Depublication and Stipulated Reversal in the California Supreme Court*, 26 Loy. L.A. L. Rev. 1033 (1993); Joseph R. Grodin, *The Depublication Practice of the California Supreme Court*, 72 Cal. L. Rev. 514 (1984).

[251] See Judicial Council of California, 2012 *Court Statistics Report*, Supreme Court, Fig. 23.

[252] The time for filing a notice of appeal is governed by Rule 8.104(a) of the California Rules of Court, which states:

> (a) *Normal time*. Unless a statute or rule 8.108 provides otherwise, a notice of appeal must be filed on or before the earliest of: (1) 60 days after the superior court clerk serves the party filing the notice of appeal with a document entitled "Notice of Entry" of judgment or a file-stamped copy of the judgment, showing the date either was served; (2) 60 days after the party filling the notice of appeal serves or is served by a party with a document entitled "Notice of Entry" of judgment or a file-stamped copy of the judgment, accompanied by proof of service; or (3) 180 days after entry of judgment.

The use of "judgment" in Rule 8.104(a) includes an appealable order if appeal is from an appealable order. Cal. Rule of Ct. 8.104(e).

[253] *E.g., Hollister Convalescent Hosp., Inc. v. Rico*, 15 Cal 3d 660, 666-674, 125 Cal. Rptr. 757, 542 P.2d 1349 (1975) (explaining that a reviewing court lacks jurisdiction to excuse a late-filed notice of appeal); *Sharp v. Union Pac. R.R. Co.*, 8 Cal. App. 4th 357, 361, 9 Cal. Rptr. 2d 925 (1992) ("neither mistake, inadvertence, accident, misfortune, estoppel nor waiver can afford relief from the jurisdictional necessity of filing a timely notice of appeal"); *Delmonico v. Laidlaw Waste Sys., Inc.*, 5 Cal. App. 4th 81, 6 Cal. Rptr. 2d 599 (1992) (finding appeal untimely when not filed within 60 days after service of notice of entry of judgment despite fact that notice stated incorrect date of entry of judgment).

notice of appeal is filed late, the reviewing court must dismiss the appeal.[254]

This strict jurisdictional requirement makes the consequences of a late appeal far more drastic than those of a premature appeal. It also places a premium on a thorough understanding of what constitutes an appealable judgment or order under the relevant statute or judge-made exceptions to the one-final-judgment-rule. Failure to commence a timely appeal of an interlocutory order made appealable by one of these exceptions will bar later review of the order by appeal taken after final judgment is entered by the trial court.[255] Consequently, when a trial court enters an order adverse to your client which *arguably* (but not clearly) comes within one of these exceptions, a prudent attorney should advise her client about taking an immediately appeal so as to protect the right of appellate review.

[c]   Premature Appeals

The California Rules of Court governing the appellate process expressly address the appropriate treatment of a premature notice of appeal. In some limited circumstances, such as where a notice of appeal is filed after final judgment is rendered but before it is formally entered, the notice of appeal is treated as filed immediately after entry of judgment.[256] Moreover, in rare cases an appellate court may treat a premature appeal as a petition for an extraordinary writ and, in its discretion, consider the issues raised by the premature appeal.[257] For example, a premature appeal may be treated as a petition for writ of mandate where the appealability question is very confusing, the merits of the issues are fully briefed, and judicial economy would not be served by deferring a ruling on the merits.[258]

But the usual rule is that an appeal from a judgment that is not final must be dismissed, unless the violation can be cured by amending the judgment. Where the trial court's failure to dispose of all causes of action results from mistake or inadvertence, an appellate court has the discretion to preserve the appeal by

---

[254] CAL. CT. R. 8.104(b), ("If a notice of appeal is filed late, the reviewing court must dismiss the appeal"); *see Hollister Convalescent Hosp., supra,* 15 Cal. 3d at 666-74 (dismissing appeal because notice of appeal filed one day late).

[255] *E.g., Stephen v. Enter. Rent-A-Car,* 235 Cal. App. 3d 806, 1 Cal. Rptr. 2d 130 (1991) (holding failure to file timely notice of appeal from order denying class action certification bars later appeal of class issues as part of appeal from final judgment in the individual action); *California Dental Ass'n v. Cal. Dental Hygienists'Ass'n,* 222 Cal. App. 3d 49, 60, 271 Cal. Rptr. 410 (1990) (ruling dismissal as to some parties, but not all, in multi-party lawsuit, obligates them to appeal immediately); *United Pac. Ins. Co. v. Hanover Ins. Co.,* 217 Cal. App. 3d 925, 940-43, 266 Cal. Rptr. 231 (1990) (holding that by failing to immediately appeal interim collateral order, defendant acquiesced in the trial court's determination).

[256] CAL. RULE OF CT. 8.104(d)(1). Also, a reviewing court *may* treat a notice of appeal filed after the superior court has announced its intended ruling, but before it has rendered judgment, as filed immediately after entry of judgment. CAL. RULE OF CT. 8.104(d)(2).

[257] *See, e.g., Morehart v. Cnty. of Santa Barbara,* 7 Cal. 4th 725, 744-47, 29 Cal. Rptr. 2d 804, 872 P.2d 143 (1994) (treating premature notice of appeal as a petition for writ of mandamus because of unusual circumstances including the statewide importance of the issues). *Olson v. Cory,* 35 Cal. 3d 390, 197 Cal. Rptr. 843, 673 P.2d 720 (1983) (explaining that although appellate court has power to treat purported appeal as petition for writ of mandate, it should not exercise that power except under unusual circumstances).

[258] *Stonewall Ins. Co. v. City of Palos Verdes Estates,* 46 Cal. App. 4th 1810, 1831-32, 54 Cal. Rptr. 2d 176 (1996).

amending the judgment to reflect the manifest intent of the trial court.[259] Even when a cause of action remained intentionally unresolved by the trial court, the appellant may remove this impasse by voluntarily dismissing the remaining cause of action with prejudice. According to the California Supreme Court, "[w]hen a party expressly waives on appeal the right to litigate an unresolved cause of action that deprived the judgment as entered of finality, the appellate court may give effect to the waiver by amending the judgment to reflect a dismissal of the cause of action with prejudice."[260]

[d]   Cross-Appeals and Protective Cross-Appeals

The first appeal filed in a case is the "appeal," any subsequent appeals by any party are "cross-appeals." The California Rules of Court set forth the time limitations for filing cross-appeals. For example, if an appellant timely appeals from a judgment or appealable order, the time for any other party to appeal from the same judgment or order is extended until 20 days after the superior court clerk serves notification of the first appeal."[261] If a party is dissatisfied with part of a judgment, that party must appeal the adverse aspects of the judgment in order to raise the issues before the appellate court. Absent a cross-appeal, a respondent is limited to defending and preserving the trial court's judgment before the appellate court.

The Rules of Court also authorize the filing of a "protective cross-appeal" by a party who has obtained an order granting a motion for new trial or to vacate the judgment. A cross-appeal from the judgment by the *successful* movant is appropriate in such circumstances in case the order is reversed on appeal and the respondent then wishes to attack the propriety of the underlying judgment in the appellate court. For an analogous reason, a protective cross-appeal is also authorized for a party whose motion for judgment notwithstanding the verdict (JNOV) was denied but motion for new trial was granted. Failure to file a cross-appeal precludes appellate review of the denial of the motion for JNOV, as well as of the underlying judgment.

[7]   California's "Prejudicial Error" Rule

[a]   Standing to Appeal

"Any aggrieved party" may appeal from an adverse judgment.[262] This standing requirement is jurisdictional and cannot be waived.[263] An aggrieved party is one who has an "immediate, pecuniary, and substantial interest" that is "injuriously affected by the judgment."[264] As a general rule, a party who consents to a stipulated

---

[259] *Sullivan v. Delta Air Lines, Inc.*, 15 Cal. 4th 288, 63 Cal. Rptr. 2d 74, 935 P.2d 781 (1997).

[260] *Sullivan, supra*, 15 Cal. 4th at 308-309.

[261] CAL. CT. R. 108(g)(1).

[262] CAL. CODE CIV. PROC. § 902.

[263] *E.g., Rebney v. Wells Fargo Bank*, 220 Cal. App. 3d 1117, 1132, 269 Cal. Rptr. 844 (1990); *Life v. Cnty. of Los Angeles*, 218 Cal. App. 3d 1287, 1292, n.3, 267 Cal. Rptr. 557 (1990).

[264] *E.g., California Ass'n of Psychology Providers v. Rank*, 51 Cal 3d 1, 9-10, 270 Cal. Rptr. 796, 793

judgment or a plaintiff who voluntarily dismisses an action is not an "aggrieved party," unless the consent or dismissal was merely given to facilitate an appeal following an adverse determination of a critical issue.[265] Likewise, a plaintiff who has consented to a remittitur — a reduction of damages awarded in lieu of a new trial — does not have standing to appeal the reduced judgment entered pursuant to the remittitur; but if the defendant appeals the remitted judgment, the plaintiff does have standing to file a cross-appeal even though she consented to the remittitur.[266] And a prevailing party may be considered "aggrieved" and have standing to appeal the unfavorable portions of an otherwise favorable judgment.[267]

[b] Prejudicial vs. Harmless Error

A judgment or order is presumed to be correct; therefore, error must be affirmatively shown by the appellant. Even where error is proven on appeal a corrective ruling is not automatic. The appellate court will reverse or modify only for "prejudicial," as opposed to "harmless," error. This rule usually requires the appellant to prove actual prejudice. Prejudice *per se*, if recognized at all, is limited to a handful of fundamental trial errors. Consequently, an appellant not only has the burden to prove error, but must also demonstrate that the error is prejudicial. As a result of these rules, the goals of accuracy and fairness to litigants are appropriately tempered by concerns for judicial economy and finality of judgments. Adherence to these rules may also explain, at least in part, why California's trial court affirmance rate is usually around 78% for civil appeals decided by an opinion.[268]

The "prejudicial error" rule is based on Article VI, § 13, of the California Constitution and various statutes. The most common judicial statement of the rule

---

P.2d 2 (1990) (ruling the trial court judgment against hospital which diminishes sphere of responsibility of psychiatrists vis-a-vis clinical psychologists, and thus will affect psychiatrists' income and authority at hospital, confers standing to appeal on psychiatrists' associations); *Rebney, supra*, 220 Cal. App. 3d at 1129-32 (holding a party lacks standing to appeal judgment which only injuriously affects other, non-appealing, co-party's interests).

[265] *Norgart v. UpJohn Co.*, 21 Cal. 4th 383, 399-403, 87 Cal. Rptr. 2d 453, 981 P.2d 79 (1999) (finding parties' stipulation permitting the trial court's order granting defendant's motion for summary judgment was not a nonappealable consent judgment because that consent was given only pro forma to facilitate as appeal, and with the understanding on the part of both parties that the plaintiffs did not intend to abandon their right to be heard on appeal); *Ashland Chem. Co. v. Provence*, 129 Cal. App. 3d 790, 793, 181 Cal. Rptr. 340 (1982) (explaining that a plaintiff may appeal voluntary dismissal of complaint after adverse ruling by trial court, because dismissal not really voluntary but to expedite the appeal).

[266] *See, e.g., Neal v. Farmers Ins. Exch.*, 21 Cal. 3d 910, 930-33, 148 Cal. Rptr. 389, 582 P.2d 980 (1978); *Rosenau v. Heimann*, 218 Cal. App. 3d 74, 77, 267 Cal. Rptr. 20 (1990); *Miller v. Nat'l Am. Life Ins. Co.*, 54 Cal. App. 3d 331, 343-45, 126 Cal. Rptr. 731 (1976).

[267] *See, e.g., Liodas v. Sahadi*, 19 Cal. 3d 278, 285, 137 Cal. Rptr. 635, 562 P.2d 316 (1977) (ruling that a party seeking new trial on all issues is an aggrieved party when only a partial new trial is granted as to issue of damages, and may appeal therefrom); *Zarrahy v. Zarrahy*, 205 Cal. App. 3d 1, 4, 252 Cal. Rptr. 20 (1988) (ruling a prevailing party has standing to appeal portions of community property judgment unfavorable to her); *Sturgeon v. Leavitt*, 94 Cal. App. 3d 957, 959, n.1, 156 Cal. App. 3d 957, 959, n.1, 156 Cal. Rptr. 687 (1979) (ruling a party is aggrieved and has standing to appeal when awarded less than originally demanded).

[268] *See* Judicial Council of California, 2012 *Court Statistics Report*, Courts of Appeal, Fig. 25.

comes from *People v. Watson*,[269] where the California Supreme Court quoted portions of Article VI, § 13:

> A "miscarriage of justice" should be declared only when the court, "after an examination of the entire cause, including the evidence," is of the opinion that it is reasonably probable that a result more favorable to the appealing party would have been reached in the absence of the error. * * * The test is necessarily based upon reasonable probabilities rather than upon mere possibilities; otherwise the entire purpose of the constitutional provision would be defeated.

The identification of "prejudicial" as opposed to "harmless" error is not always easy. There are few set rules. Instead several factors may be relevant in determining whether it is "reasonably probable" that a trial judge or jury would have reached a result more favorable to the appealing party in the absence of error. For example, in assessing prejudice from an erroneous jury instruction, the California Supreme Court considered the following factors: "(1) the degree of conflict in the evidence on critical issues; (2) whether respondent's argument to the jury may have contributed to the instruction's misleading effect; (3) whether the jury requested a rereading of the erroneous instruction or of related evidence; (4) the closeness of the jury's verdict; and (5) the effect of other instructions in remedying the error."[270] Moreover, where there are numerous errors, an appellate court may consider their cumulative effect. For example, in one case the California Supreme Court concluded the cumulative effect of the judge's and opposing counsel's improper comments constitutes prejudicial error even though, taken separately, they would not justify reversal.[271]

[c] Prejudice *Per Se* vs. Actual Prejudice

A few types of error are considered "reversible per se" such that prejudice is conclusively presumed and need not be proven. These include denial of the right to a jury trial, undue restriction on right of cross-examination, erroneous sustaining of demurrer without leave to amend, failure to render a statement of decision when timely requested and required in a nonjury trial, and an award of punitive damages entered without evidence of the defendant's financial condition.[272] However, most

---

[269] 46 Cal. 2d 818, 836, 299 P.2d 243 (1953).

[270] *Pool v. City of Oakland*, 42 Cal. 3d 1051, 1069-70, 232 Cal. Rptr. 528, 728 P.2d 1163 (1986) (quoting *LeMons v. Regents of Univ. of Cal.*, 21 Cal. 3d 869, 876, 148 Cal. Rptr. 355, 582 P.2d 946 (1978)); *see Soule v. Gen. Motors Corp.*, 8 Cal. 4th 548, 570-83, 34 Cal. Rptr. 2d 607, 882 P.2d 298 (1994) (applying the *LeMons* factors).

[271] *Delzell v. Day*, 36 Cal. 2d 349, 223 P.2d 625 (1950). *See Johnson v. Tosco Corp.*, 1 Cal. App. 4th 123, 141, 1 Cal. Rptr. 2d 747 (1991) (holding the cumulative effect of jury instructions and erroneous restriction of expert testimony constitutes prejudice).

[272] *See, e.g., Selby Constructors v. McCarthy*, 91 Cal. App. 3d 517, 527, 154 Cal. Rptr. 164 (1979) (denial of right to jury trial); *Fremont Indem. Co. v. Workers Comp. Appeals Bd.*, 153 Cal. App. 3d 965, 971, 200 Cal. Rptr. 762 (1984) (cross examination restrictions); *Deeter v. Angus*, 179 Cal. App. 3d 241, 251, 224 Cal. Rptr. 801 (1986) (demurrer without leave to amend); *In re Marriage of Ananeh-Firempong*, 219 Cal. App. 3d 272, 282, 268 Cal. Rptr. 83 (1990) (failure to render statute of decision); *Adams v. Murakami*, 54 Cal. 3d 105, 284 Cal. Rptr. 318, 813 P.2d 1348 (1991) (punitive damages without financial evidence).

errors, even serious ones such as erroneous admission or exclusion of evidence, attorney or jury misconduct, giving an improper jury instruction, or erroneously refusing to give a jury instruction although supported by the evidence,[273] are not considered *per se* prejudicial. These various applications of the *prejudicial error rule* recognize that many trial errors do not substantially affect the rights of the parties and, accordingly, do not necessitate corrective appellate action.

[8] Scope of Appellate Review Determined by Record

[a] Adequate Record for Appellate Review

A judgment or order of a trial court is presumed to be correct on appeal. A decision of the trial court must be affirmed if found to be correct by the appellate court, even if the reasons stated by the trial court for its decision are erroneous. The party appealing a judgment has the burden of showing reversible error by an adequate record. An appellate court is confined in its review to matters contained in the record of the trial court proceedings, or properly subject to judicial notice.[274] The appellant is responsible not only for preserving matters in the record of the trial court proceedings, but also for assembling a trial court record which provides the appellate court with an adequate basis for determining whether reversal is appropriate.[275] Appellant's responsibility to ensure a sufficient record on appeal has other components, which are discussed below.

[b] Statement of Decision in Nonjury Trial

Upon timely request of any party in a nonjury trial, the trial court must issue a statement of decision explaining the factual and legal bases for its decision as to each principal controverted issue at trial.[276] If the appellant fails to request a statement of decision as to specific issues to obtain an explanation of the trial court's

---

[273] *See, e.g., Clifton v. Ulis*, 17 Cal. 3d 99, 130 Cal. Rptr. 155, 549 P.2d 1251 (1976) (erroneous exclusion of important evidence); *Cassim v. Allstate Ins. Co.*, 33 Cal. 4th 780, 800-805,16 Cal. Rptr. 3d 374, 94 P. 3d 513 (2004) (ruling plaintiff's misconduct during closing argument was harmless error); *Hasson v. Ford Motor Co.*, 32 Cal. 3d 388, 185 Cal. Rptr. 654, 650 P.2d 1171 (1982) (finding presumption of prejudice raised by jurors' reading novels and working crossword puzzles during presentation of evidence rebutted by an affirmative evidentiary showing that prejudice did not exist); *Mitchell v. Gonzales*, 54 Cal. 3d 1041, 1054-1056, 1 Cal. Rptr. 2d 913, 819 P.2d 872 (1991) (holding erroneous proximate cause instruction not automatically prejudicial); *Soule, supra*, 8 Cal. 4th at 570-80 (ruling erroneous refusal of proffered jury instruction not automatically reversible error).

[274] *People v. Collie*, 30 Cal. 3d 43, 57, n. 10, 177 Cal. Rptr. 458, 634 P.2d 534 (1981) (no consideration given to declaration of trial judge proffered during appeal); *Tinsley v. Palo Alto Unified Sch. Dist.*, 91 Cal. App. 3d 871, 891, n. 11, 154 Cal. Rptr. 591 (1979) (court of appeal takes judicial notice of official map indicating school districts).

[275] *See, e.g., Ballard v. Uribe*, 41 Cal. 3d 564, 574, 224 Cal. Rptr. 664, 715 P.2d 624 (1986) (holding appellant's failure to include transcript of jury voir dire and of new trial hearing in record precludes the appellate court from ascertaining whether alleged juror misconduct of concealed bias and alleged error in denying motion for new trial occurred); *Maria P. v. Riles*, 43 Cal. 3d 1281, 1295, 240 Cal. Rptr. 872, 743 P.2d 932 (1987) (ruling appellate court cannot consider alleged error by trial court in method used to calculate attorney fee award because appellant failed to furnish adequate record of attorney fee proceedings).

[276] Cal. Code Civ. Proc. §§ 632, 634.

tentative decision, the appellate court will imply findings to support the judgment. A judgment based on implied findings is difficult to reverse on appeal because the appellate court must assume the trial court made whatever findings were necessary to sustain the judgment. For example in one case, because a defendant did not request a statement of decision on the computation of attorney and accountant fees awarded by the superior court pursuant to a fee-shifting statute, the court of appeal first assumed that the superior court had applied the correct time and hourly rate factors when calculating these fee awards and, therefore, then ruled that the contested amounts were supported by substantial evidence.[277]

[c] Preserving Error for Appeal

The appellant has the responsibility for making an adequate record for appeal in another sense — by taking the necessary actions during trial to preserve the error for appeal. Generally, an issue must be raised in the trial court to be argued on appeal. Likewise, the theory upon which a case is tried must be adhered to on appeal. One major but ill-defined exception is that issues of law, or new legal theories based on undisputed facts, may be raised for the first time on appeal. For example, in one case the California Supreme Court held that although the facts pleaded and proved by plaintiff did not sustain the judgment on the theory of tort advanced in the trial court, they were sufficient under the quasi-contract unjust enrichment theory advanced on appeal.[278]

Not only must an issue be raised in the trial court, but error must be preserved for appellate review by an appropriate challenge during the trial proceedings. Failure to register a timely objection in the proper manner generally waives the issue for appeal.[279] Some trial errors require additional procedural steps — such as a motion to strike, an offer of proof, or a request that the jury be admonished — to preserve them for appeal.[280] For example, in *Sabella v. Southern Pacific Co.*,[281] the California Supreme Court held that to preserve for appeal issues of attorney misconduct during closing argument a party must both object and request that the

---

[277] *In re Marriage of Ananeh-Firempong*, 219 Cal. App. 3d 272, 268 Cal. Rptr. 83 (1990); *see, e.g., Michael U. v. Jamie B.*, 39 Cal. 3d 787, 792-793, 218 Cal. Rptr. 39, 705 P.2d 362 (1985) (ruling in appeal by adoptive parents of award of custody of son to his natural teenage father; because no statement of decision requested, the appellate court must assume that the trial court found an award of custody to natural father would not be detrimental to son).

[278] *Ward v. Taggart*, 51 Cal. 2d 736, 742, 336 P.2d 534 (1959); *see also Fisher v. City of Berkeley*, 37 Cal. 3d 644, 654, n. 3, 209 Cal. Rptr. 682, 693 P.2d 261 (1984) (Supreme Court considers anti-trust issues with respect to validity of rent control ordinance even though raised for first time on appeal, because based on undisputed facts and involves question of great public importance).

[279] *See, e.g., Doers v. Golden Gate Bridge Dist.*, 23 Cal. 3d 180, 184-85, n. 3, 151 Cal. Rptr. 837, 588 P.2d 1261 (1979) (explaining that appellate courts will not consider procedural errors where an objection could have been but was not presented to the lower court, or where acquiescence constitutes waiver or estoppel); CAL. CODE CIV. PROC. § 353(a) (no appellate consideration of erroneous admission of evidence unless record contains objection with specific grounds).

[280] Failure to make an adequate offer of proof generally precludes consideration of the alleged error on appeal. CAL. EVID. CODE § 354(a) (a judgment shall not be reversed by reason of erroneous exclusion of evidence unless "the substance, purpose, and relevance of the excluded evidence" is made part of the record through an offer of proof).

[281] 70 Cal. 2d 311, 74 Cal. Rptr. 534, 449 P.2d 750 (1969).

jury be admonished. By giving the trial judge the opportunity to instruct the jury to disregard the misconduct, the *Sabella* court reasoned, its effect may be removed and the error corrected without the necessity of appeal. In this manner, these seemingly technical requirements promote judicial efficiency and finality of trial judgments.

[9] The California Appellate Procedure — Presentation of Errors

As discussed previously, error must be affirmatively demonstrated by an adequate record on appeal. If conduct alleged as error is not part of the record (*e.g.*, the clerk's transcript, the reporter's transcript, a party's appendix), the appellate court simply has no basis for reviewing the merits of the alleged error. For example, without a transcript of the relevant trial court proceedings in the record, a reviewing court is unable to assess whether error actually occurred during those proceedings.[282] Written briefs are also an essential component of the appellate process. Not only are they the primary vehicle for presenting arguments and persuading the court, but they frame the issues that will be considered by the appellate court. Grounds for appeal not raised in the appellate briefs may be considered waived.[283]

Oral argument is another important component. The California Constitution guarantees the right of oral argument in both the California Supreme Court and the Courts of Appeal. Counsel may waive the right to oral argument, but the Supreme Court and most appellate specialists recommend against such waiver. In one recent case, the California Supreme Court described oral argument as important because "we, like all other courts, rely upon the presentation of oral argument by well-prepared attorneys to assist us in reaching an appropriate resolution of the often difficult questions presented in the cases before us," and found two attorneys in contempt for failure to appear for oral argument before the Court.[284]

[10] Intensity of Review — Standards of Appellate Review in the California Courts

The term "appellate standard of review" refers to the degree of deference an appellate court must grant a particular type of trial court ruling. Generally, a California appellate court must apply one of three available standards of review in assessing the correctness of a trial court determination — independent ("*de novo*")

---

[282] *E.g., Ballard, supra*, 41 Cal. 3d at 574 (ruling the failure of appellant to include transcript of voir dire, hearing on new trial motion, and portion of trial dealing with damages precludes appellate court consideration of alleged error in those trial court proceedings); *see also Cosenza v. Kramer*, 152 Cal. App. 3d 1100, 1102, 200 Cal. Rptr. 18 (1984)(ruling appellant's failure to include complaint in clerk's transcript precludes appellate consideration of alleged pleading defect).

[283] *E.g., Mann v. Cracchiolo*, 38 Cal. 3d 18, 41, 210 Cal. Rptr. 762, 694 P.2d 1134 (1985) (ruling that although plaintiff appealed from certain orders, failure to attack them in opening brief waives appellate consideration); *Elster v. Friedman*, 211 Cal. App. 3d 1439, 1440, n. 1, 260 Cal. Rptr. 148 (1989) (considering point abandoned because not argued in appellant's brief).

[284] *In re Aguilar*, 34 Cal. 4th 386, 390, 18 Cal. Rptr. 3d 874, 97 P.3d 815 (2004).

review, abuse of discretion, or the substantial evidence rule. For the most part, the definitions and, with one exception, the applications of these standards are the same in the California courts as they are in the federal courts.[285]

An appellate court gives no deference to a trial court's determination of a pure question of law, such as the proper interpretation of a statute, but must engage in a *de novo* review of the issue. When a decision is, by law, committed to the discretion of the trial court the appropriate standard of appellate review of such decision is *abuse of discretion*. The precise meaning of this standard is difficult to explain, but a typical general definition is: "The appropriate test for abuse of discretion is whether the trial court exceeded the bounds of reason. When two or more inferences can reasonably be deduced from the facts, the reviewing court has no authority to substitute its decision for that of the trial court."[286] A California appellate court must apply the *substantial evidence rule* when reviewing a trial court's determination of an issue of fact — whether in a jury or nonjury trial — based on whether there was sufficient evidence to support the determination.[287]

[a] California's Substantial Evidence Rule

The "substantial evidence" standard is usually stated as follows:

In reviewing the evidence on appeal all conflicts must be resolved in favor of the respondent, and all legitimate and reasonable inferences indulged in to uphold the verdict if possible. When a verdict is attacked as being unsupported, the power of the appellate court begins and ends with *a determination as to whether there is any substantial evidence, contradicted or uncontradicted, which will support the conclusion reached by the jury*. When two or more inferences can be reasonably deduced from the facts, the reviewing court is without power to substitute its deductions for those of the trial court.[288]

An appellate court does not weigh the evidence, consider the credibility of the witnesses, or resolve conflicts in the evidence, to determine if it is "substantial." The California standard appropriately recognizes that the trial judge or jury, as the fact-finder who hears the evidence as it comes in and observes the demeanor of witnesses, has a comparative advantage in fact finding that justifies substantial appellate deference to findings of fact made below.

[b] Federal and California Appellate Review Standards, Compared

Like the California courts, the federal appellate courts apply the *de novo* review standard when reviewing questions of law, and the substantial evidence test when reviewing factual determinations made by a jury. But unlike the California courts,

[285] The federal standards of appellate review are discussed in § 13.09, *supra*.

[286] *Shamblin v. Brattain*, 44 Cal. 3d 474, 478-79, 243 Cal. Rptr. 902, 749 P.2d 339 (1988).

[287] *E.g., Alderson v. Alderson*, 180 Cal. App. 3d 450, 465, 225 Cal. Rptr. 610 (1986); *Tillery v. Richland*, 158 Cal. App. 3d 957, 962-63, 205 Cal. Rptr. 191 (1984).

[288] *Crawford v. S. Pac. Co.*, 3 Cal. 2d 427, 429, 45 P.2d 183 (1935) (italics added).

the federal courts must apply a different standard — the "clearly erroneous" test — when reviewing factual determinations made by a trial judge in a nonjury case.[289] The federal courts have had considerable difficulty defining and applying the "clearly erroneous" test, and distinguishing it from the substantial evidence test. The California courts avoid such difficulties by simply applying the substantial evidence test to review of *all* trial court factual determinations, whether made by a judge or by a jury.

It is difficult to determine whether, as a practical matter, the "substantial evidence" test produces a significantly different outcome than the "clearly erroneous" test when applied in an actual case. As with any of the various formulas for review of facts — such as the federal "reasonable jury" or "sufficient evidence" standards — the differences may be more "verbal" than meaningful. However, California's substantial evidence test appears to be more deferential to the trial court's finding than the federal clearly erroneous standard.[290] This observation is reinforced by an examination of the federal standard for appellate review of findings by a jury in a jury trial. Because the Seventh Amendment requires more deferential appellate review of jury findings than of judge findings, the federal courts do not apply the clearly erroneous test in that context. Instead, they apply standard of review — whether a reasonable jury could have reached the verdict — that is essentially the same as the substantial evidence rule.[291]

[c] Judicial Review by Administrative Mandamus and the "Independent Judgment" Test

Administrative mandamus refers to the statutory procedure by which a party may obtain judicial review (usually in the superior court) of a California state or local administrative agency's "adjudicatory" decision made after an evidentiary hearing.[292] If the administrative decision "substantially affects a fundamental vested right," the superior court must exercise its "independent judgment" upon the evidence in the administrative record with respect to issues both of law *and* of fact.[293] Under the *independent judgment standard*, where a party claims that the agency findings are not supported by the evidence, the court determines whether the findings are supported by the weight of the evidence.[294] The reviewing court can resolve evidentiary conflicts in a manner different than the agency, draw different inferences from the evidence, and resolve credibility questions contrary to the

---

[289] FED.R. CIV. P. 52(a)(6). The "clearly erroneous" test is discussed more fully in § 13.09[2][b], *supra.*

[290] In *Anderson v. City of Bessemer City*, 470 U.S. 564 (1985), the United States Supreme Court explained that a finding is "clearly erroneous" when "although there is evidence to support it, the reviewing court on the entire evidence is left with the definite and firm conviction that a mistake has been committed." *Id.* at 573.

[291] *See* § 13.09[1] & [2][c], *supra.*

[292] CAL. CODE CIV. PROC. § 1094.5.

[293] *See, e.g., Anton v. San Antonio Cmty. Hosp.*, 19 Cal. 3d 802, 820-21, 140 Cal. Rptr. 442, 567 P.2d 1162 (1977); *Strumsky v. San Diego Cnty. Emp. Retirement Ass'n*, 11 Cal. 3d 28, 112 Cal. Rptr. 805, 520 P.2d 29 (1974); *Bixby v. Pierno*, 4 Cal. 3d 130, 93 Cal. Rptr. 234, 481 P.2d 242 (1971).

[294] CAL. CODE CIV. PROC. § 1094.5(c).

agency's findings where testimony is in conflict.[295] In cases not involving a fundamental vest right, the superior court's role is limited to a determination of whether the agency findings are supported by substantial evidence.[296] Unlike the independent judgment standard, which is less deferential to the agency's decision, the substantial evidence test does not permit the reviewing court to weigh the evidence in the administrative record.

The determination of whether an agency decision "substantially affects a fundamental vested right" is made on a case-by-case basis. According to the California Supreme Court, "[i]n determining whether the right is fundamental the courts do not alone weigh the economic aspect of it, but the effect of it in human terms and the importance of it to the individual in the life situations."[297] Despite this vague guideline, the California courts have developed some general distinctions. In cases involving judicial review of administrative professional licensing decisions, the independent judgment standard applies to review of license revocations and suspensions, but the substantial evidence standard applies to review of initial application denials.[298] However, this distinction has not always held up in nonlicensing cases. For example, the California Supreme Court has held that the independent judgment standard applies to judicial review of administrative decisions denying *applications* for welfare benefits and for unemployment compensation benefits.[299]

The independent judgment standard has been sharply criticized by many scholars and dissenting justices.[300] The general nature of these criticisms is that the

---

[295] *See, e.g., Fukuda v. City of Angels*, 20 Cal 4th 805, 818, 85 Cal. Rptr. 2d 696, 977 P.2d 693 (1999) ("Because the trial court ultimately must exercise its own judgment, that court is free to substitute its own findings after first giving due respect to the agency findings"); *Interstate Brands v. Unemp. Ins. Appeals Bd.*, 26 Cal. 3d 770, 775, n. 2, 163 Cal. Rptr. 619, 608 P.2d 707 (1980) (explain that the trial court may draw its own inferences from the evidence in the record).

[296] CAL. CODE CIV. PROC. § 1094.5(c).

[297] *Bixby v. Pierno*, 4 Cal. 3d 130, 144, 93 Cal. Rptr. 234, 481 P.2d 242 (1971).

[298] *See, Unterthiner v. Desert Hosp. Dist.*, 33 Cal. 3d 285, 294-298, 188 Cal. Rptr. 590, 656 P.2d 554 (1983); (holding the substantial evidence rule applied to decisions denying initial applications by doctors for hospital privileges); *Turner v. Bd. of Tr.*, 16 Cal. 3d 818, 824-825, 129 Cal. Rptr. 443, 548 P.2d 1115 (1976) (holding the denial of an application for a teaching position and the refusal to renew the teaching contract of a probationary or nontenured teacher do not substantial affect a vested fundamental right, but the refusal to retain a tenured teacher does); *Berlinghieri v. Dept. of Motor Vehicles*, 33 Cal. 3d 392, 188 Cal. Rptr. 891, 657 P.2d 383 (1983) (finding the suspension of driver's license by the DMV substantially affects a fundamental vested right).

[299] *Frink v. Prod*, 31 Cal. 3d 166, 177-80, 181 Cal. Rptr. 893, 643 P.2d 476 (1982) (observing that, with respect to the decisions denying applications for welfare benefits, "while the degree to which the right is vested may not be overwhelming, the degree of fundamentalness is"); *Interstate Brands, supra*, 26 Cal. 3d at 777-782 (ruling the independent judgment standard applies when employee seeks judicial review of denials of unemployment compensation benefits and when employers seek judicial review of the granting of benefits).

[300] *See, e.g.*, Sam Walker, *Judicially Created Uncertainty: The Past, Present, and Future of California Writ of Administrative Mandamus*, 24 U.C. DAVIS L. REV. 783-839 (1991); Mary Lu Christie, *Strumsky v. San Diego County Employees Retirement Association: Determining the Scope of Judicial Review of Administrative Decisions in California*, 26 HASTINGS L.J. 1465-1501 (1975); *County of Alameda v. Bd. of Retirement*, 46 Cal. 3d 902, 910-17, 251 Cal. Rptr. 267, 760 P.2d 464 (1988) (dissenting opinion of J. Broussard); *Anton, supra*, 19 Cal. 3d at 831-34 (dissenting opinion of J. Clark).

independent judgment rule defeats the beneficial purposes of administrative adjudication, *i.e.*, agency use of appropriate expertise, economical and speedy determination of disputes, and the recognition that institutional policy should be made by the agency not by the trial court. Moreover, because judicial review generally is limited to a transcript of the agency hearing record, the court's independent judgment on credibility is unlikely to be more accurate than the agency's resolution. For these reasons, California's use of the independent judgment standard is very much a minority view.

§ 13.11   EXTRAORDINARY WRITS IN THE CALIFORNIA COURTS

[1]   Discretionary Appellate Review by Extraordinary Writs, Generally

Extraordinary writs provide a mechanism for potential immediate appellate review of non-appealable, interlocutory trial court decisions. Writs are extraordinary remedies in the sense that they are speedy and discretionary and, unlike appeals, do not authorize review as a matter of right. They also involve foundational prerequisites not necessary for an appeal. An extraordinary writ allows an appellate court to review actions of a superior court when review by appeal is inadequate.[301] In general, the issuance of an extraordinary writ is discretionary. The reviewing court is not required to decide the merits of a writ petition or even state a reason for declining to do so.

Extraordinary writs in California are available to review a wide variety of pretrial orders. Unlike the in federal courts, where such writs are discouraged, extraordinary writ practice is well-established and frequently-employed in the California courts.[302] Few uses are completely off-limits, and new ones are limited only by the practitioner's imagination and creativity. Some uses are fairly routine, such as writ review of discovery orders that allegedly violate an important confidential privilege or present issues of general concern. Other uses are less common, such as writ review of rulings at the pleading stage of a lawsuit.[303] However, despite the frequent resort to extraordinary writ practice in the California courts, the vast majority of writ petitions are denied, and most of these

---

[301] *See, e.g.*, Cal. Code Civ. Proc. §§ 1085, 1086; *see also* CEB, *California Civil Writ Practice* §§ 14.1-14.3, 16.86-16.145 (4th ed. 2012).

[302] Appellate review by extraordinary writs in the federal courts is discussed in § 13.04[3], *supra*.

[303] *See, e.g.*, *Brandt v. Superior Court*, 37 Cal. 3d 813, 210 Cal. Rptr. 211, 693 P.2d 796 (1985) (approving writ review of order striking portions of complaint seeking attorney fees is proper because issue is of widespread interest and courts of appeal are in conflict); *Cianci v. Superior Court*, 40 Cal. 3d 903, 908, n.3, 221 Cal. Rptr. 575, 710 P.2d 375 (1985); *James W. v. Superior Court*, 17 Cal. App. 4th 246, 252, 21 Cal. Rptr. 2d 169 (1993) (granting writ to review demurrers sustained without leave to amend as to some but not all causes of action; trial court directed to vacate order sustaining demurrer on issue of defendants' immunity from suit); *Cuadros v. Superior Court*, 6 Cal. App. 4th 671, 8 Cal. Rptr. 2d 18 (1992) (granting writ directing trial court to set aside order denying petitioner's motion to amend complaint, and to enter new order granting motion to amend).

are summarily denied.[304] The large number of denials demonstrates the appellate courts' hesitancy to use their scarce resources to second guess every ruling of the trial court and to interfere with the orderly administration of justice at the trial and appellate levels.

[2] Primer on California's Extraordinary Writ Practice

A "writ" is an order entered by a higher court directing an inferior court to prevent, perform, or annul certain acts. When a writ is sought from an appellate court the process is referred to as "petitioning" for a writ. Usually there are three parties to a writ proceeding: the petitioner, the respondent, and the real party in interest. The "petitioner" is the party seeking relief from the appellate court, the "respondent" is the inferior tribunal (usually the superior court) whose decision is being challenged by the petitioner, and the "real party in interest" is the party who prevailed in the decision by the trial court. Generally the real party in interest, not the respondent court, is expected to respond to the petition.

There are a number of different types of writs recognized in California. The two most frequently requested appellate writs are the "writ of mandate" — also referred to by the traditional name of "mandamus" — and the "writ of prohibition."[305] Selection of the appropriate writ can be difficult because they overlap in definition and function. Fortunately, the California courts are flexible when it comes to selecting the appropriate writ and rarely refuse relief solely because the petitioner requested the wrong type of writ.

Certain extraordinary writs are referred to as "statutory" writs, as opposed to "common law" writs. A "statutory" writ is not a distinct type of writ, but is simply one where writ review is specifically authorized for a particular situation by a special statute. Such writ review applies to some very important interlocutory decisions, including the denial of a motion to quash service of process (the California equivalent of a motion to dismiss for lack of personal jurisdiction), a decision on a motion to change venue, and a determination with respect to disqualification of a judge.[306] Appellate review by a petition for a writ of mandate is the *exclusive* remedy in such circumstances.[307] (Note also this statutory authority

---

[304] *See, e.g.*, Judicial Council of California, *2012 Court Statistical Report*, California Courts of Appeal, Table 6 (2,034 civil writ petitions denied without opinion in fiscal year 2010-11, 147 disposed of by written opinion; 1,900 denied without opinion in fiscal year 2009-10, 149 disposed of by written opinion); *Omaha Indem. Co. v. Superior Court*, 209 Cal. App. 3d 1266, 258 Cal. Rptr. 66 (1989) (noting that approximately 90% of petitions seeking an extraordinary writ are denied, and that a court rarely gives detailed reasons for its rejection of a petition).

[305] A writ of mandate is authorized by Code of Civil Procedure §§ 1084-1094, a writ of prohibition by §§ 1102-1105, 1107-1108.

[306] Cal. Code Civ. Proc. §§ 418.10(a)(1) & (c) (petition for writ of mandate within 10 days after denial of motion to quash); § 400 (petition for writ of mandate within 20 days after venue decision); §§ 170.3, 170.6 (petition for writ of mandamus within 10 days of disqualification decision).

[307] *See McCorkle v. City of Los Angeles*, 70 Cal. 2d 252, 256-60, 74 Cal. Rptr. 389, 449 P.2d 453 (1969) (denial of motion to quash service of process); *Hennigan v. Boren*, 243 Cal. App. 2d 810, 814-15, 52 Cal. Rptr. 748 (1966) (review of decision on motions to change venue); *People v. Hull*, 1 Cal. 4th 266, 2 Cal. Rptr. 2d 526, 820 P.2d 1036 (1991) (review by mandate is the exclusive means of appellate review of unsuccessful challenge to a judge, whether peremptory or for cause).

for immediate appellate review is a departure from federal court practice, which does not permit interlocutory appeal from personal jurisdiction or venue decisions.)

In addressing the "discretionary" character of extraordinary writs, the California Supreme Court explained that in some situations a reviewing court's discretion is quite restricted: "[W]hen writ review is the exclusive means of appellate review of a final order or judgment, an appellate court may not deny an apparently meritorious writ petition, timely presented in a formally and procedurally sufficient manner, merely because, for example, the petition presents no important issue of law or because the court considers the case less worthy of its attention than other matters."[308] Consequently, it is somewhat misleading to say that all extraordinary writ review is discretionary.

[3] Basic Writ Prerequisites

There are some basic statutory prerequisites common to all writs of mandate and prohibition. First, the petitioner must have no "plain, speedy, and adequate remedy in the ordinary course of law." Generally, writ review is inappropriate if the challenged decision is immediately appealable.[309] An appeal is usually viewed as "adequate" even though it involves far greater expense and time than review by writ. Moreover, review by appeal does not become "inadequate" because a party failed to file a timely notice of appeal.[310]

A second general prerequisite to writ review, similar to inadequacy of remedy at law, is that the petitioner will suffer "irreparable injury" if the writ is not granted. This prerequisite encompasses several related inquiries. One is whether the nature of the harm or prejudice is such that it cannot be corrected on appeal from the subsequent final judgment. For example, the extraordinary writ review is usually held proper in cases where the trial court's discovery order allegedly violates a privilege, because the person seeking to exercise the privilege must either succumb to the trial court's order and disclose privileged information or subject himself to contempt for refusal to obey court's order pending appeal.[311] Although generally the courts will not find "irreparable injury" based on the fact that if the trial court's ruling is wrong and the petitioner will unnecessarily incur the time and expense of going to trial, sometimes the courts will find writ review necessary to prevent an expensive trial and ultimate reversal.[312]

---

[308] *Powers v. City of Richmond*, 10 Cal. 4th 85, 113-14, 40 Cal. Rptr. 2d 839, 893 P.2d 1160 (1995).

[309] *In re Marriage of Skelley*, 18 Cal. 3d 365, 369, 134 Cal. Rptr. 197, 556 P.2d 297 (1976); *Phelan v. Superior Court*, 35 Cal. 2d 363, 370, 217 P.2d 951 (1950).

[310] *See, e.g., Adoption of Alexander S.*, 44 Cal. 3d 857, 865, 245 Cal. Rptr. 1, 750 P.2d 778 (1988); *Andrews v. Police Court*, 21 Cal. 2d 479, 480, 133 P.2d 398 (1943).

[311] *E.g., Sav-On Drugs, Inc. v. Superior Court*, 15 Cal. 3d 1, 123 Cal. Rptr. 283, 538 P.2d 739 (1975) (finding writ review proper when petitioning party asserts discovery order violates a privilege); *Bridgestone/Firestone, Inc. v. Superior Court*, 7 Cal. App. 4th 1384, 9 Cal. Rptr. 2d 709 (1992) (ruling extraordinary writ proper to review discovery order involving trade secrets); *Hiott v. Superior Court*, 16 Cal. App. 4th 712, 20 Cal. Rptr. 2d 157 (1993) (finding writ proper to review motion to compel production of videotape where attorney-client privilege raised).

[312] *See, e.g., Smith v. Superior Court*, 10 Cal. App. 4th 1033, 13 Cal. Rptr. 2d 133 (1992) (holding writ review of trial court's denial of motion to strike emotional distress and punitive damage allegations from

Another inquiry is whether the petitioner has requested the relief from the lower tribunal, and been denied, prior to seeking the relief by writ. A related inquiry is whether there are any alternative proceedings available which may remedy the petitioner's injury. For example, an appellate court is unlikely to entertain a writ where the petitioner has not yet attempted a post-trial motion, such as a motion for new trial or to vacate a judgment; where the erroneous ruling does not preclude a challenge later during the trial process, such as a dismissal or the denial of a motion to sever, *without prejudice*; or where an order can be quickly remedied by the petitioner's own subsequent action, such as where a partial demurrer is sustained with leave to amend. As one appellate court wryly observed, an "irreparable inconvenience" does not constitute an "irreparable injury."[313] A final statutory prerequisite is that the petitioner must be "beneficially interested" in the outcome of the writ proceeding.

The criteria discussed above, "inadequate remedy at law," "irreparable injury," and "beneficial interest" are the basic statutory prerequisites for writ review. The California Supreme Court has stated additional general criteria for determining the propriety of review by extraordinary writ in individual cases. These include: (1) the issue tendered in the writ is of widespread interest, or presents a significant and novel constitutional issue, (2) the trial court's order deprived the petitioner of an opportunity to present a substantial portion of his cause of action, (3) conflicting trial court interpretations of the law require a resolution of the conflict, or (4) that the trial court's order is both clearly erroneous as a matter of law and substantially prejudices the petitioner's case.[314] Unfortunately, the Supreme Court has neglected to explain when and how they apply or how much weight each criterion should be given in a particular case, adding to the inherent uncertainty of writ practice in California.

---

complaint proper because delay and expense of a trial made remedy of appeal inadequate and significant legal issue of importance involved); *Barrett v. Superior Court*, 222 Cal. App. 3d 1176, 1183, 272 Cal. Rptr. 304 (1990) (ruling writ appropriate because if trial court's order is determined incorrect on an appeal, a second trial would be required).

[313] *Omaha Indem. Co. v. Superior Court*, 209 Cal. App. 3d 1266, 1274, 258 Cal. Rptr. 66 (1989).

[314] *See Omaha Indem., supra*, 209 Cal. App. 3d at 1273-74 (listing criteria with supporting California Supreme Court citations).

Chapter 14

REMEDIES

§ 14.01 DAMAGES; SCOPE OF MONETARY RECOVERY[1]

[1] Types of Damage Awards

[a] Compensatory Damages

The objective of most civil actions is recovery of damages, a financial award payable from the defendant to the plaintiff. The most common kind of damage formula attaches a monetary value to the difference between what the plaintiff's situation is, and what it would have been if the defendant had performed a legal duty owed to the plaintiff — for example, if defendant had not breached its contract with plaintiff or had not carelessly caused plaintiff physical injury. When defendant has wronged plaintiff, the measure of the wrong is plaintiff's actual or *compensatory* damages. "The essence of compensatory damages" has thus been described as "restor[ing] the injured party as nearly as possible to the position he would have been in but for the wrong."[2]

This formula requires the fact-finder to resolve two points in plaintiff's favor before awarding damages. First, plaintiff must have suffered harm capable of monetary quantification.[3] Second, the harm must have been caused by defendant's failure to act as he had a legal duty to act toward plaintiff.[4] It is not necessary that harm suffered by plaintiff be susceptible to precise monetary valuation.[5] At the

---

[1] *See generally* Russell L. Weaver, Elaine W. Shoben & Michael B. Kelly, Principles of Remedies Law 148-270 (2d ed. 2011); Dan B. Dobbs, Handbook on the Law of Remedies §§ 3.1–3.12 (2d ed. 1993); Laurens Walker & John Monahan, *Sampling Damages*, 83 Iowa L. Rev. 545 (1998); Robert Cooter & Melvin A. Eisenberg, *Damages for Breach of Contract*, 73 Cal. L. Rev. 1432 (1985). *See also* § 4.02[2] (prejudgment attachments), *supra*, and § 15.02 (enforcement of money judgments), *infra*.

[2] Douglas Laycock, Modern American Remedies 15 (3d ed. 2002).

[3] Thus, valuation of damage to property is "usually based on the idea that the plaintiff's balance sheet shows a loss of net worth as a result of the defendant's tort or breach of contract." Dobbs, note 1, *supra*, § 3.2.

[4] In litigation, however, the sequence is sometimes reversed when issues of duty and breach are first decided as a matter of law, mooting the issue of damages. For example, plaintiff may have a strong case to make at trial that plaintiff suffered harm from defendant's failure to perform under a contract. But plaintiff will never get to make that case if defendant obtains summary judgment because the contract did not comply with the statute of frauds, thus establishing that he owed plaintiff no contractual duty. For discussion of how summary judgments and other procedural devices screen out such cases before trial, see § 12.09[3][c], *supra*.

[5] The best example may be damage recovery for intangible pain and suffering in tort cases. *See*

same time, some wrongs are so difficult to appraise monetarily that courts deny them damage treatment, or permit damages only in insignificant amount.[6] When such wrongs can be foreseen, they are often better suited for treatment by preventative (injunctive)[7] relief.

[b]   Punitive Damages[8]

In some cases, plaintiff can obtain as a substantial element of his total damage recovery a sum unrelated to any actual harm done by defendant. These are *punitive* (exemplary) damages.[9] The object of this form of damages is to deter defendant and others from similar acts in the future. Only exceptional facts will support punitive damages. Usually they must establish either serious and calculated wrong by the defendant or conduct reflecting rank indifference to public safety or welfare, variously carrying the labels of gross negligence, recklessness, or willful and wanton misconduct.

It is more difficult to generalize a formula for punitive damages than for compensatory damages. As noted above, courts or juries set compensatory damages through a somewhat empirical approach, measuring the difference in plaintiff's situation with and without defendant's wrong, or what is necessary to restore the plaintiff to where she would have been had defendant not breached its duty to her. In contrast, punitive damages are more like ad hoc criminal fines. Moreover, while determination of compensatory damages is more or less mandatory upon proof of harm from defendant's wrong, plaintiff has no right to punitive damages.

The United States Supreme Court has also placed significant due process constraints on the availability of punitive damages.[10] The Supreme Court and commentators have attempted to separate the Court's punitive damages decisions

---

Robert L. Rabin, *Pain and Suffering and Beyond: Some Thoughts on Recovery for Intangible Loss*, 55 DePaul L. Rev. 359 (2006); Victor E. Schwartz & Leah Lorber, *Twisting the Purpose of Pain and Suffering Awards: Turning Compensation into "Punishment"*, 54 S.C. L. Rev. 47 (2002).

[6] "A plaintiff who loses her pet cat may suffer something that cannot be measured by the market value of the cat." Dobbs, note 1, *supra*, § 3.2.

[7] *See* § 14.02[1], *infra*.

[8] On punitive damages generally, see Thomas A. Eaton, David B. Mustard & Susette M. Talarico, *The Effects of Seeking Punitive Damages on the Processing of Tort Claims*, 34 J. Legal Stud. 343 (2005).

[9] *See* Stephen C. Yeazell, *Punitive Damages, Descriptive Statistics, and the Economy of Civil Litigation*, 79 Notre Dame L. Rev. 2025 (2004); Colleen P. Murphy, *Judgment as a Matter of Law on Punitive Damages*, 75 Tul. L. Rev. 459 (2000); A. Mitchell Polinsky & Steven Shavell, *Punitive Damages: An Economic Analysis*, 111 Harv. L. Rev. 869 (1998); Stephen Daniels & Joanne Martin, *Myth and Reality in Punitive Damages*, 75 Minn. L. Rev. 1 (1990); Dorsey D. Ellis, Jr., *Fairness and Efficiency in the Law of Punitive Damages*, 56 S. Cal. L. Rev. 1 (1982). For a valuable study of the history of punitive damages in English and American courts, see Thomas B. Colby, *Beyond the Multiple Punishment Problem: Punitive Damages as Punishment for Individual, Private Wrongs*, 87 Minn. L. Rev. 583, 614–29 (2003).

Related are statutory provisions for multiple damages — usually a doubling or trebling of compensatory damages. *See generally* Dobbs, note 1, *supra*, § 3.12.

[10] Despite the broad discretion that States possess with respect to the imposition of . . .

   punitive damages, the Due Process Clause of the Fourteenth Amendment . . . imposes substantive limits on that discretion. That Clause makes the Eighth Amendment's prohibition against excessive fines and cruel and unsual punishments applicable to the States . . . The into two categories: protection of procedural due process and protection of substantive due process:

> The Supreme Court has now ruled that the due process clause of the Fourteenth Amendment requires states to adopt procedures to ensure that punitive damage awards are made through a fair process that include[s] judicial review of jury awards. [The Court] also endorsed the position that the due process clause authorizes review courts to impose a substantive limit on the amount of punitive damages.[11]

In *Honda Motor Co., Ltd. v. Oberg*,[12] the first of three procedural due process cases, the Supreme Court ruled that lack of judicial review of the fairness of a jury's punitive damages award violated due process. Then, in *Cooper Industries, Inc. v. Leatherman Tool Group, Inc.*,[13] the Court required *de novo* appellate review of the trial court's ruling on the constitutionality of a punitive damages award, rather than review merely for abuse of discretion. Finally, in *Philip Morris USA v. Williams*,[14] it rejected, as a violation of procedural due process, a calculation of punitive damages that included harm to nonparties in the case.

Honda also envisioned the possibility that a punitive damages award might be so great as to violate substantive due process. The Supreme Court found such a case in *BMW of North America, Inc. v. Gore*,[15] ruling that the differential between $4,000 in compensatory damages and the judgment of $2 million (after reduction from $4 million by the trial court) in punitive damages was so excessive as to violate substantive due process. Similarly, in *State Farm Mutual Automobile Insurance Co. v. Campbell*,[16] the Court stuck down a $145,000,000 punitive damages award when compensatory damages were only $1,000,000. The Court has declined to issue a specific numerical standard for determining the permissible differential between compensatory and punitive damages in cases arising in state court,[17] but did assert

---

Due Process Claus of its own force also prohibits the States from imposing "grossly excessive" punishments on tortfeasors.

Cooper Indus., Inc. v. Leatherman Tool Group, Inc., 532 U.S. 424, 433–34 (2001).

The appropriate role of the Constitution in regulating punitive damages remains a subject of lively debate. *Compare* A. Benjamin Spencer, *Due Process and Punitive Damages: The Error of Federal Excessiveness Jurisprudence*, 79 S. CAL. L. REV. 1085 (2006) (urging fewer constitutional constraints on punitive damages), *with* Martin H. Redish & Andrew L. Mathews, *Why Punitive Damages are Unconstitutional*, 53 EMORY L.J. 1 (2004) (arguing punitive damages are unconstitutional per se).

[11] RONALD D. ROTUNDA & JOHN E. NOWAK, TREATISE ON CONSTITUTIONAL LAW — SUBSTANCE AND PROCEDURE § 14.6[e] (4th ed. 2007).

[12] 512 U.S. 415 (1994), *discussed in* RONALD D. ROTUNDA & JOHN E. NOWAK, TREATISE ON CONSTITUTIONAL LAW § 14.06[e] (4th ed. 2007).

[13] 532 U.S. 424 (2001), *featured in* R. Shane McLaughlin, *Constitutional Law — Judicial Review — Appellate Courts Must Review De Novo the Constitutionality of Punitive Damages Awards*, 71 MISS. L.J. 711 (2001).

[14] 549 U.S. 346 (2007).

[15] 517 U.S. 559 (1996), *discussed in* Pamela S. Karlan, *"Pricking the Lines": The Due Process Clause, Punitive Damages, and Criminal Punishment*, 88 MINN. L. REV. 880, 905–11 (2004).

[16] 538 U.S. 408 (2003), *discussed in* Joseph J. Chambers, *In re Exxon Valdez: Application of Due Process Constraints on Punitive Damages Awards*, 20 ALASKA L. REV. 195, 212–18 (2003).

[17] In contrast, the Court recently limited punitive damages to the amount of compensatory damages

in *State Farm* that "in practice, few awards exceeding a single-digit ratio between punitive and compensatory damages, to a significant degree, will satisfy due process."[18] This has led two leading constitutional scholars to conclude: "it appears that trial courts will have difficulty justifying any award of punitive damages that is more than 9 times greater than the amount of compensatory damages awarded in a case."[19]

The Court also provided some guidance in *BMW of North America, Inc. v. Gore*[20] for deciding the reasonableness of a jury's award of punitive damages. It held that it depends upon: (1) the reprehensibility of defendant's conduct; (2) the disparity between the actual or potential harm suffered by plaintiff and the award; and (3) the difference between an award and the civil penalties authorized or imposed in similar cases. The dealer's failure to disclose the repainting of the buyer's car was not notably reprehensible: there was no evidence that it had acted in bad faith or that its nondisclosure had affected the car's performance, safety, or even (initially) its appearance. The punitive damages award was 500 times the amount of Gore's actual harm. Finally, the Court noted that the maximum civil penalty set by state legislatures for deceptive trade practices ranged from $2000 to $10,000, giving the dealer no reason to anticipate the $4 million penalty that the jury had imposed. Although the Court was "not prepared to draw a bright line marking the limits of a constitutionally acceptable punitive damages award," it had little difficulty concluding that the four-million-dollar award "transcend[ed] the constitutional limit."[21]

Statutes and rules of civil procedure may also limit punitive damages claims. Statutes may place caps on punitive damages[22] or prohibit them altogether for certain claims. Rules may restrict the discovery of evidence needed to argue punitive damages, the evidence permitted to establish them, or the standard used to supervise them both at the trial court and the appellate levels. Indeed, in *Gore*, three concurring justices emphasized that Alabama's failure to supply either legal or quantitative standards that might "significantly cabin the fairly unbounded discretion" given the jury to decide punitive damages helped to persuade them that

---

in a federal maritime case. *Exxon Shipping Co. v. Baker*, 554 U.S. 471 (2008). The Court took pains to distinguish *Exxon* from the due process cases discussed in the text.

> Today's enquiry differs from due process review because the case arises under federal maritime jurisdiction, and we are reviewing a jury award for conformity with maritime law, rather than the outer limit allowed by due process; we are examining the verdict in the exercise of federal maritime common law authority, which precedes and should obviate any application of the constitutional standard.

Id. at 501–02. *See generally* Maria C. Klutinoty, Exxon Shipping Co. v. Baker: *Why the Supreme Court Missed the Boat on Punitive Damages*, 43 AKRON L. REV. 203 (2010) (arguing that *Exxon* should be limited to maritime law).

[18] 538 U.S. at 424.

[19] RONALD D. ROTUNDA & JOHN E. NOWAK, TREATISE ON CONSTITUTIONAL LAW § 14.06[e] (4th ed. 2007).

[20] 517 U.S. 559 (1996).

[21] *Id.* at 585–86.

[22] For a survey of state statutes imposing caps on punitive damages awards, see *Gore*, 517 U.S. at 614–16 (Appendix to Opinion of Ginsburg, J.).

the $2 million award was unconstitutionally excessive.[23]

[c] Nominal Damages

Like punitive damages, *nominal* damages do not reflect real harm, but in contrast they are quite small.[24] When permitted, nominal damages can make possible litigation in which plaintiff either suffered no actual harm or the harm is impossible to prove.[25] They may also play a role when plaintiff seeks but fails to obtain substantial damage recovery, since award of nominal damages often makes the defendant liable for the court costs.[26]

[2] Added Elements in Financial Awards — Costs, Expenses, and Attorney's Fees

Complaints in damage cases seek compensatory, punitive, or nominal damages (or some combination thereof) in specific amounts, or unspecified amounts in accordance with the proof. (Federal Rule 54(c) provides that a judgment shall grant "the relief to which each party is entitled, even if the party has not demanded that relief in its pleadings.") Most such complaints also request court costs.[27] Expenses awarded as court costs to the winning party (plaintiff or defendant) usually are relatively insignificant. Thus, by statute, costs in federal courts include only fees of the clerk and marshal; fees for printed or electronically recorded transcripts necessarily obtained for use in the case; fees and disbursements for printing and witnesses; fees for copy costs when the copies are necessarily obtained for use in the case; docket fees; and compensation of court - appointed experts and interpreters in some cases.[28] Notably, "taxable costs" do not include the bulk of discovery costs or attorney's fees.[29]

While English courts usually require the losing party to pay the victor's attorney's fees,[30] there is still a strong tradition against that practice in this country.[31] There are, however, two types of exceptions. First, certain forms of litigation (although brought by private parties) are considered sufficiently within

---

[23] *Gore*, 517 U.S. at 595–96.

[24] "Nominal damages are damages in name only, trivial sums such as six cents or $1." Dobbs, note 1, *supra*, § 3.3(2). A useful discussion of nominal damages appears in David Schoenbrod, Angus McBeth, David Levine & David Jung, Remedies Public and Private 482–83 (1990).

[25] *See* Anthony DiSarro, *A Farewell to Harms: Against Presuming Irreparable Injury in Constitutional Litigation*, 35 Harv. J.L. & Pub. Pol'y 743, 792–94 (2012) (discussing prominent role of nominal damages in civil rights cases).

[26] Dobbs, note 1, *supra*, § 3.8, at 193. *See, e.g.,* Rule 54(d), *discussed in* § 14.01[2] *infra*.

[27] Rule 54(d)(1).

[28] 28 U.S.C. § 1920.

[29] Thus, the federal rule expressly prescribes "costs — *other than attorney's fees*." Rule 54(d)(1) (emphasis added).

[30] *Cf. Wright & Miller* § 2665 ("The cardinal principle of the English system has been and continues to be one of total reimbursement.").

[31] Thomas D. Rowe, Jr., *Indemnity or Compensation? The Contract with America, Loser Pays Fee Shifting*, 37 Washburn L.J. 317 (1998); *Symposium on Fee Shifting*, 71 Chi-Kent L. Rev. 415 (1995); *Fogerty v. Fantasy, Inc.*, 510 U.S. 517 (1994); *Key Tronic Corp. v. United States*, 511 U.S. 809 (1994).

the public interest to warrant shifting of attorney's fees by statute from the prevailing party to the losing party as an incentive to suit.[32] Second, the growing expense of legal services and a general apprehension about indiscriminate civil litigation in this country has led to creation of expense-shifting mechanisms in certain procedural rules. These are intended to compensate parties suffering from opponents' litigation abuses and to provide a corresponding incentive for careful and restrained use of civil procedure. Thus, expense-shifting is authorized as a sanction for violations of Rule 11,[33] discovery abuses,[34] and in some circumstances when a party has rejected offers of judgment made prior to trial.[35]

[3] Enforcing Money Judgments

[This topic is discussed in § 15.02, *infra*.]

§ 14.02 EQUITABLE RELIEF; INJUNCTIONS[36]

Injunctions are available in all state and federal courts. They are one of three types of equitable remedies that can be traced to English practice.[37] Injunctions are court decrees which control the behavior of the defendant by ordering him either to act or to refrain from acting in a certain way. While factual analysis for damages remedies is retrospective — looking backward to what defendant did and what it cost the plaintiff — factual analysis for injunctive remedies is prospective — looking forward to what the defendant will do to the plaintiff, absent an injunction and what an injunction would cost the defendant.

---

[32] Since the Supreme Court's decision in *Alyeska Pipeline Service Co. v. Wilderness Society*, 421 U.S. 240 (1975), federal court authority to award attorney fees on this basis has largely been confined to statute. However, the list of such statutes is quite extensive. *Alyeska Pipeline Serv. Co.*, 421 U.S. at 260 n.33. *See, e.g.*, Martha Pacold, Comment, *Attorneys' Fees in Class Actions Governed by Fee-Shifting Statutes*, 68 U. Chi. L. Rev. 1007 (2001).

[33] *See, e.g.*, §§ 8.05[2] (federal Rule 11) & 10.13[1] (federal Rule 26(g)), *supra*.

[34] *See, e.g.*, § 10.14[2] (federal Rule 37), *supra*.

[35] For example, federal Rule 68 states that, at least fourteen days before trial, "a party defending against a claim may serve on an opposing party an offer to allow judgment" in a certain amount. If the offer is refused and "the judgment that the offeree finally obtains is not more favorable than the unaccepted offer, the offeree must pay the costs incurred after the offer was made." On the scope and application of Rule 68, see *Marek v. Chesny*, 473 U.S. 1 (1985); *Delta Air Lines, Inc. v. August*, 450 U.S. 346 (1981). *See generally* Wright & Miller §§ 3001–3005; Thomas D. Rowe, Jr. & David A. Anderson, *One-Way Fee Shifting Statutes and Offer of Judgment Rules: An Experiment*, 36 Jurimetrics J. 255 (1996). What "costs" Rule 68 takes in is unclear, although the Court in *Marek* gave the term broader application than it usually has in Rule 54(d). *See* § 14.01, note 27, *supra*. The rule remains a source of controversy. *See* Peter Margulies, *After Marek, the Deluge: Harmonizing the Interaction Under Rule 68 of Statutes That Do and Do Not Classify Attorney's Fees as "Costs,"* 73 Iowa L. Rev. 413 (1988); Stephen B. Burbank, *Proposals to Amend Rule 68 — Time to Abandon Ship*, 19 Mich. J.L. Reform 425 (1986).

[36] *See generally* Douglas Laycock, The Death of the Irreparable Injury Rule (1991); Gene R. Shreve, *Federal Injunctions and the Public Interest*, 51 Geo. Wash. L. Rev. 382 (1983); Dan B. Dobbs, Handbook on the Law of Remedies §§ 2.1–2.11 (2d ed. 1993); Note, *Developments in the Law — Injunctions*, 78 Harv. L. Rev. 994 (1965); W. de Funiak, Handbook of Modern Equity (1956).

[37] The other two are specific performance and judicial administration of estates. F.W. Maitland, Equity 22 (2d rev. ed. 1936).

[1] The Shape of Equitable Discretion

Equitable remedies evolved to supplement legal remedies. They were a response to appeals for fairness and justice in what were thought to be especially deserving cases, in which the rigidity of the common law prevented it from affording full justice.[38] It continues to be true that equitable remedies rarely exist as a matter of right. The discretion of courts to refuse injunctions is well-established. That discretion takes shape from a set of injunctive prerequisites, often called *equitable jurisdiction*, and from a number of maxims, or *equitable defenses*, further limiting the availability of relief.

The concept of equitable jurisdiction[39] encompasses as many as three requirements. Two are keyed on the character of harm plaintiff will suffer without an injunction. First, harm must be immediate and substantial. If the prospect of substantial harm to plaintiff is remote, plaintiff's request for an injunction will usually be denied.[40] Second, harm must be irreparable.[41] This requirement is sometimes stated another way: that plaintiff has no adequate remedy at law.[42] This reflects the historical notion that equity stepped in only when the common law could not give justice. Third and finally, the controversy must provide a manageable setting for injunctive relief. That is, it must be possible for the court to describe the conduct it intends to regulate with sufficient clarity in the decree that it and the parties will not thereafter become ensnared in difficult issues of interpretation and compliance.[43]

Since courts use fairness and justice to support equitable remedies, additional facts showing that plaintiff has been less than fair in his treatment of defendant may render plaintiff ineligible for an injunction. Maxims like "plaintiff must come

---

[38] Writing on English practice in the sixteenth century, a distinguished commentator wrote that it was the "intent [of] equity . . . to temper and mitigate the rigour of the law." C. St. Germain, Dialogues Between A Doctor of Divinity and A Student in the Laws of England 45 (W. Muchall 18th ed. 1792). *See* 4 W. Holdsworth, A History of English Law 281 (1924) (equity is necessary in order that the law can do complete justice); *see also* Peter Hoffer, The Law's Conscience 8 (1990) (discussing Aristotle's view of the necessity of equity to lessen the severity of law); *see* § 8.02[2] (equity pleading and practice), *supra*.

[39] "[T]he equity jurisdiction of the federal courts is the jurisdiction in equity exercised by the High Court of Chancery in England at the time of the adoption of the Constitution and the enactment of the original Judiciary Act, 1789." *Grupo Mexicano de Desarrollo, S.A. v. Alliance Bond Fund, Inc.*, 527 U.S. 308, 318 (1999).

[40] The classic case illustrating this point is *Fletcher v. Bealy*, 28 Ch. D. 688 (1885) (injunction denied because plaintiff failed to establish that the likelihood of harm to its downstream paper processing operation was both substantial and immediate).

[41] *See generally* Douglas Laycock, *Injunctions and the Irreparable Injury Rule*, 57 Tex. L. Rev. 1065 (1979). Whether the irreparable injury rule still has much life in contemporary injunction cases is a matter of debate. *Compare* Laycock, note 36, *supra* (arguing that the rule has little remaining significance), *with* Gene R. Shreve, *The Premature Burial of the Irreparable Injury Rule*, 70 Tex. L. Rev. 1063 (1992) (maintaining that the rule is alive and influential in modern cases).

[42] Owen Fiss, The Civil Rights Injunction 38 (1978). *See generally* Doug Rendleman, *The Inadequate Remedy at Law Prerequisite for an Injunction*, 33 U. Fla. L. Rev. 346 (1981).

[43] *See* Shreve, note 36, *supra*, at 394. *Cf.* de Funiak, note 36, *supra*, at 24 ("Where the court has the theoretical power to grant an injunction but enforcement is impracticable or impossible, the court will not grant the injunction. It would be derogatory of the dignity of the court to enter orders it could not enforce.").

to the court with clean hands" and "equity aids only the vigilant"[44] thus function as equitable defenses. Courts have also used the technique of "balancing the equities" to deny plaintiffs injunctions, concluding that it would be much harder for defendant to live with the injunction than for plaintiff to live without it.[45]

Finally, courts also consider the public interest in the issuance of the injunction.[46] Thus, in *Winter v. Natural Resources Defense Council, Inc.*,[47] the Supreme Court reversed an injunction requiring the Navy to assess the impact on marine mammals of exercises using underwater sonar pulses, in part because the district court gave insufficient weight to the public interest in continuing the training exercises. In another famous case, a court denied an injunction against continued operation of a polluting cement plant in part because of the potential economic effect on the larger community of shutting down the community's major employer.[48] In short, equitable injunction is not shaped solely by the interests and equities of the immediate parties.

[2] Procedure for Obtaining and Enforcing Injunctions

The procedure for obtaining a final (permanent) injunction is a trial on the merits of the case much like that for a damages remedy. It takes time, however, to reach judgment on plaintiff's prayer for a final injunction. During the interim, defendant may inflict considerable damage on plaintiff or act to moot the case. All procedural systems thus have provision for provisional (interlocutory) injunctive relief.[49] Federal Rule 65 authorizes both temporary restraining orders and preliminary injunctions.[50] Plaintiff may appeal the denial of a final injunction, and, sometimes, denial of an interlocutory injunction.

---

[44] *See generally* HENRY L. McCLINTOCK, HANDBOOK OF THE PRINCIPLES OF EQUITY §§ 26 & 28 (2d ed. 1948) (discussing the development of the clean hands doctrine and the maxim that equity aids only the vigilant). Similar to the latter is the doctrine of laches, "which bars a plaintiff from maintaining a suit if he unreasonably delays in filing suit and as a result harms the defendant." *National R.R. Passenger Corp. v. Morgan*, 536 U.S. 101, 121 (2002).

Not all equitable defenses key on plaintiff's conduct. See for example, discussion of the maxim, "Equity Will Not Enjoin a Crime," in *Developments*, note 36, *supra*, at 1013–18.

[45] *See generally* Elizabeth G. Thornburg, *Litigating the Zero Sum Game: The Effect of Institutional Reform Litigation on Absent Parties*, 66 OR. L. REV. 843 (1987); W. Page Keeton & Clarence Morris, *Notes on "Balancing the Equities"*, 18 TEX. L. REV. 412 (1940); John L. Mechem, *The Peasant in His Cottage: Some Comments on the Relative Hardship Doctrine in Equity*, 28 S. CAL. L. REV. 139 (1955). *Cf.* David S. Schoenbrod, *The Measure of an Injunction: A Principle to Replace Balancing the Equities and Tailoring the Remedy*, 72 MINN. L. REV. 627 (1988) (proposing changes in the approach).

[46] *See* WEAVER ET AL., *supra*, note 1, at 58–59.

[47] 555 U.S. 7 (2008).

[48] *Boomer v. Atl. Cement Co.*, 257 N.E.2d 870 (N.Y. 1970).

[49] The leading work on provisional injunctive relief remains John Leubsdorf, *The Standard for Preliminary Injunctions*, 91 HARV. L. REV. 525 (1978). In addition, *see* Richard R.W. Brooks & Warren F. Schwartz, *Legal Undertainty, Economic Efficiency, and the Preliminary Injunction Doctrine*, 58 STAN. L. REV. 381 (2005); Douglas Lichtman, *Uncertainty and the Standard for Preliminary Relief*, 70 U. CHI. L. REV. 197 (2003); Bart Forsyth, *Preliminary Imprimaturs: Prevailing Party Status Based on Preliminary Injunctions*, 60 WASH. & LEE L. REV. 927 (2003); Morton Denlo, *The Motion for a Preliminary Injunction: Time for a Uniform Federal Standard*, 22 REV. LITIG. 495 (2003).

[50] Many courts look to the following factors in determining whether to grant preliminary injunctions:

What gives interlocutory and final injunctions their force is the prospect that defendants who violate them may be liable for either civil or criminal contempt.[51] Civil contempt adjudications may be either compensatory (producing a sum payable to plaintiff for the violation) or coercive (threatening defendant with damages or incarceration if the violations continue). Criminal contempt sanctions are penal (setting fines payable to the sovereign or fixed jail sentences). Two ways in which this difference manifests itself are in the nature of the proceeding necessary to support a determination of contempt[52] and in the gravamen of the wrong.[53]

Choices presented to a party who is provisionally or permanently enjoined[54] are not limited to compliance or contempt. The party may also seek dissolution or modification of the injunction through appeal, or through rehearing before the court that issued it.[55] This factor can either help or hurt parties who are enjoined.

(1) the significance of the threat of irreparable harm to plaintiff if the injunction is not granted; (2) the state of the balance between this harm and the injury that granting the injunction would inflict on defendant; (3) the probability that plaintiff will succeed on the merits; and (4) and the public interest.

WRIGHT & MILLER § 2948. The same factors undoubtedly influence decisions whether to issue temporary restraining orders. However, proceedings leading to decision on plaintiff's application for a temporary restraining order tend to be more summary in nature and may, under extraordinary circumstances, be conducted *ex parte*. At the same time, neither Rule 65 nor practice under the rule clearly delineate the two. The Supreme Court has, in fact, downplayed the importance of Rule 65 as a means of defining federal equity practice. See *Grupo Mexicano de Desarrollo, S.A. v. Alliance Bond Fund, Inc.*, 527 U.S. 308 (1999). The distinction between a temporary restraining order and a preliminary injunction may affect the appealability of an order denying relief. See § 13.05[1] (statutory appeal as of right), *supra*. On temporary injunctive relief in federal court generally, see WRIGHT & MILLER §§ 2947–2954.

[51] Useful general discussions of civil and criminal contempt and how they differ can be found in Issachar Rosen-Zvi & Talia Fisher, *Overcoming Procedural Boundaries*, 94 VA. L. REV. 79 (2008); Jennifer Fleiscer, *In Defense of Civil Contempt Sanctions*, 36 COLUM. J.L. & SOC. PROBS. 35 (2002); Linda S. Beres, *Games Civil Contemnors Play*, 18 HARV. J.L. & PUB. POLICY 795 (1995); Earl C. Dudley, Jr., *Getting Beyond the Civil/Criminal Distinction: A New Approach to the Regulation of Indirect Contempts*, 79 VA. L. REV. 1025 (1993); Doug Rendleman, *Disobedience and Coercive Contempt Confinement: The Terminally Stubborn Contemnor*, 48 WASH. & LEE L. REV. 185 (1991); Dan B. Dobbs, *Contempt of Court: A Survey*, 56 CORNELL L. REV. 183 (1971); Comment, *Developments*, note 36, *supra*, at 1086–90.

[52] Civil contempt is an adjunct of the main case. It "[i]s prosecuted in the name of the plaintiff, and largely controlled by the plaintiff. He initiates it with a motion, and up to a point he can abandon it or settle it." DOUGLAS LAYCOCK, MODERN AMERICAN REMEDIES — CASES AND MATERIALS 637 (1985). "Criminal contempt," in contrast, "is prosecuted in the name of the sovereign." There are more opportunities for reversible error, since "defendant gets substantially all the protections of criminal procedure." *Id.* at 636.

[53] Criminal contempts represent a kind of defiant disobedience. They are willful in the sense crimes are usually thought of as willful. In contrast, adjudications of civil contempt proceed from the bare fact of noncompliance. *Cf.* ROBERT S. THOMPSON & JOHN A. SEBERT, REMEDIES: DAMAGES, EQUITY AND RESTITUTION § 3.10 (1983) ("Criminal contempts are those which flout the court's authority; civil contempts are those designed to compel enforcement of court orders.").

[54] Here, the "word 'permanent' signifies not the injunction's duration but rather that it is not contingent upon some further finding on the merits." SCHOENBROD ET AL., note 24, *supra*, at 166. "A permanent injunction continues to apply unless it expires by its own terms or is later modified or dissolved by a court of competent jurisdiction." *Id.*

[55] For discussion of processes for clarifying, restricting and dissolving injunctions, see Timothy S. Jost, *From Swift to Stotts and Beyond: Modifications of Injunctions in the Federal Courts*, 64 TEX. L.

On one hand, the concerns of equity and fairness that support issuance of injunctions[56] also support the idea that such parties should have broad court access to argue why injunctions running against them should be dissolved or at least narrowed. Even a court that issued an injunction will often reconsider its decision, particularly in light of new evidence or changed circumstances. In deciding the continued justification for injunctions, courts are more willing than they usually are to revisit matters already decided.[57] On the other hand, the willingness of courts to entertain challenges against the continued operation of injunctions bolsters their authority to impose contempt sanctions against enjoined parties who bypass opportunities for modification or appeal.[58]

§ 14.03 DECLARATORY RELIEF[59]

[1] Nature of Declaratory Relief

All judicial remedies proceed from a determination of the rights and obligations of the parties. Courts would otherwise lack the authority to dispense damage awards and injunctions. What sets declaratory judgments apart is that they *only* determine rights and obligations. That may not seem like a lot, but declaratory judgments actually can accomplish a great deal. For example, the fruits of victory for a party threatened with liability are precisely the same in a declaratory proceeding as in a suit for damages — a favorable judgment precluding further litigation.[60]

REV. 1101 (1986); Note, *The Modification of Consent Decrees in Institutional Reform Litigation*, 99 HARV. L. REV. 1020 (1986); *Developments in the Law*, note 36, *supra* at 1078–91. The same procedure is available to enlarge injunctions.

[56] *See* note 44, *supra.*

[57] This idea finds support in *Miller v. French*, 530 U.S. 327 (2000), and *Agostini v. Felton*, 521 U.S. 203 (1997). The contrasting reluctance of courts, as a general matter, to return to matters they have already ruled upon is clear from the "law of the case" doctrine, discussed at § 15.14, *infra.*

[58] A graphic illustration of the point can be found in *Walker v. City of Birmingham*, 388 U.S. 307 (1967). The Supreme Court denied defendants an opportunity to raise as a defense to contempt proceedings the unconstitutionality of the state anti-parading law upon which the injunction had been based. The Court noted: "This case would arise in quite a different constitutional posture if the petitioners, before disobeying the injunction, had challenged it in the Alabama courts, and had been met with delay or frustration of their constitutional claims." *Walker*, 388 U.S. at 318. For examination of the issues raised in *Walker*, see John R.B. Palmer, *Collateral Bar and Contempt: Challenging a Court Order After Disobeying It*, 88 CORNELL L. REV. 215 (2002); Richard E. Labunski, *The "Collateral Bar" Rule and the First Amendment: The Constitutionality of Enforcing Unconstitutional Orders*, 37 AM. U. L. REV. 323 (1988).

[59] *See generally* WRIGHT & MILLER §§ 2751–71; Samuel L. Bray, *Preventive Adjudication*, 77 U. CHI. L. REV. 1275 (2010); *Developments in the Law — Declaratory Judgments*, 62 HARV. L. REV. 787 (1949).

[60] Thus,

declaratory judgment relief creates means by which rights and obligations may be adjudicated in cases involving an actual controversy that has not reached a stage at which either party may seek a coercive remedy or in which a party entitled to a coercive remedy fails to sue.

MOORE § 57.04[3]. For a survey of issues concerning the precise res judicata effects of declaratory judgments, see Elizabeth L. Hisserich, *The Collision of Declaratory Judgments and Res Judicata*, 48 UCLA L. REV. 159 (2000).

Requests for declaratory judgments are sometimes made in tandem with requests for damages or injunctive relief. The real significance of the remedy, however, lies in situations where only declaratory relief is available. Frequently the plaintiff in such cases is one who expects eventually to be the target of a claim for damages or an injunction. The plaintiff beats his adversary to the courthouse, suing preemptively for a favorable adjudication of an issue underlying defendant's prospective claim.[61] Plaintiff's incentive for bringing the declaratory proceeding is to clear the air and head off a suit against him. The preclusive effect given federal declaratory judgments is typical. "Any such declaration shall have the force and effect of a final judgment or decree and shall be reviewable as such."[62]

[2]   The Federal Model

Federal courts were slower to dispense declaratory judgments than many state courts. The problem was uncertainty whether suit for declaratory relief alone satisfied the case and controversy requirement of Article III of the Constitution. The Supreme Court finally ruled that such suits were permissible, "so long as the case retains the essentials of an adversary proceeding, involving a real, not a hypothetical controversy."[63] Congress soon responded by enacting the Federal Declaratory Judgment Act, conferring authority to render declaratory judgments in cases "of actual controversy."[64]

The line between a potential and an actual controversy is not always clear. The best approach is to examine the facts of each case. The Supreme Court's observations in *Aetna Life Insurance Co. v. Haworth* remain a useful guide:

> The controversy must be definite and concrete, touching the legal relations of parties having adverse legal interests. It must be a real and substantial controversy admitting of specific relief through a decree of a conclusive character, as distinguished from an opinion advising what the law would be upon a hypothetical state of facts. Where there is such a concrete case admitting of an immediate and definitive determination of the legal rights of the parties in an adversary proceeding upon the facts alleged, the judicial function may be appropriately exercised.[65]

Even when the prerequisites for a declaratory judgment are satisfied, federal and many state courts have considerable discretion to withhold the remedy. Reasons for doing so include inability of the declaratory judgment to end the controversy, the public interest in delaying suit, and existence of a pending and related action.[66]

---

[61] In this case, the declaratory judgment action is anticipatory, a kind of preemptive strike. Thus the labels of plaintiff and defendant are the reverse of what they would be if the claimant had been permitted eventually to file suit. *See, e.g., Aetna Life Ins. Co. v. Haworth*, 300 U.S. 227 (1937) (declaratory judgment action filed by insurer against the insured). This reversal may have significant consequences for federal question jurisdiction. *See* § 5.03, *supra*.

[62] 28 U.S.C. § 2201.

[63] *Nashville, Chattanooga, & St. Louis Ry. v. Wallace*, 288 U.S. 249, 264 (1933).

[64] 28 U.S.C. § 2201.

[65] 300 U.S. 227, 240–41 (1937) (citations omitted).

[66] *See Developments — Declaratory Judgments*, note 59, *supra*, at 805–17.

Rule 57 extends coverage of the Federal Rules of Civil Procedure to cases under the Declaratory Judgment Act. "The incidents of pleading, process, discovery, trial, and judgment are the same."[67] The parties to a declaratory judgment action have a right to a jury trial, if that right would have existed in the "kind of action in which the issue involved would have been decided if there were no declaratory-judgment procedure."[68] In the usual reversed parties case,[69] this inquiry would require application of the modified historical test for the right to jury trial[70] to the action that the declaratory judgment defendant would have brought had not the declaratory judgment plaintiff filed first.

§ 14.04   DAMAGES; MONETARY RECOVERY IN THE CALIFORNIA COURTS

[1]   Compensatory Damages

Compensatory damages are generally intended to remedy a personal injury or economic loss that has already occurred. In tort actions, the general measure of compensatory damages in California is "the amount which will compensate for all the detriment proximately caused" by the defendant's wrongful conduct, "whether it could have been anticipated or not."[71] This includes compensation for objectively verifiable monetary losses ("economic damages") such as medical expenses, lost of earnings, cost of replacement or repair or loss in value of property; and for subjective, non-monetary losses ("non-economic damages") such as pain, suffering, emotional distress, loss of society and companionship, loss of consortium, and injury to reputation and humiliation.[72] In breach of contract actions, the general measure of damages is "the amount which will compensate the party aggrieved for all the detriment proximately caused" by the breach. In both types of actions, the purpose of the measure of damages is to make a party whole for the harm suffered (or, perhaps more accurately, as whole as is possible through an award of monetary relief).

[a]   Post-judgment Interest

The fact that a plaintiff obtains a judgment for money damages does not necessarily mean the defendant (the "judgment debtor") will immediately, or ever, satisfy the judgment. The judgment debtor may delay payment by taking an appeal or by not cooperating with the plaintiff's efforts to collect the judgment. However, such delays are not without consequence because during that time the amount of the judgment will, in most cases, be increased by *post-judgment interest*. By authority of the California Constitution, interest automatically accrues upon a

---

[67] WRIGHT & MILLER § 2768.

[68] WRIGHT § 100.

[69] *See* note 61, *supra.*

[70] *See* § 12.07[1], *supra.*

[71] CAL. CIV. CODE § 3333.

[72] CAL. CIV. CODE § 1431.2(b).

money judgment rendered in any court. The Constitution authorizes the Legislature to set the rate of interest which, currently, is 10% per annum.[73] A judgment bears simple, not compound, interest from date of entry until the judgment is satisfied. This means interest continues to accrue even during an appeal. As a consequence, a judgment debtor has little incentive to delay payment of a money judgment by stalling tactics or by a questionable appeal, particularly when the post-judgment interest rate exceeds the market rate.

[b] Prejudgment Interest

Full compensation should include interest not only from the time a money judgment is entered until it is paid, but also from the time the loss is incurred until it results in a judgment. For this reason, several California statutes authorize a party to recover interest as damages — commonly referred to as *prejudgment interest*. This means interest may begin to accrue on an amount sought as money damages *before* the action becomes a final judgment and, in some instances, even *before* the action is commenced in court. The extent of this right varies with the nature of the cause of action and whether the damages sought are liquidated ("certain") or unliquidated ("uncertain"). For example, California Civil Code § 3287(a) provides the general authority for the right to recover prejudgment interest in any action, including actions in tort and in contract, for money damages when the damages are "certain or capable of being made certain by calculation." Damages are deemed "certain" within the meaning of section 3287(a) where there is essentially no dispute between the parties concerning the amount of damages recoverable but where the dispute centers on the issue of liability giving rise to the damage.[74]

Civil Code § 3287(a) reflects legislative consideration of two countervailing policies. One is that interest traditionally has been denied on unliquidated claims because of the general equitable principle that a person who does not know what sum is owed cannot be in default for failure to pay. Thus, no prejudgment interest is assessed against a litigant for failing to pay a sum which is unascertainable prior to judgment. The other is that injured parties should be compensated for the loss of the use of their money during the period between the assertion of a claim and the rendition of judgment. These competing policy considerations have led the Califor-

---

[73] CAL. CONST. art. XV, § 1; CAL. CODE CIV. PROC. § 685.010. The Legislature has not established an interest rate for judgments against public entities so, by default, the constitutional rate of 7% applies. *California Sav. & Loan Assn. v. City of Los Angeles*, 11 Cal. 4th 342, 45 Cal. Rptr. 2d 279, 902 P.2d 297 (1995); *see 311 South Spring Street Co. v. Dept. of Gen. Serv.*, 178 Cal. App. 4th 1009, 101 Cal. Rptr. 3d 176 (2009) (holding an award of post-judgment interest against public entity in excess of 7% rate is void and subject to collateral attack).

[74] *E.g., Stein v. S. Cal. Edison Co.*, 7 Cal. App. 4th 565, 8 Cal. Rptr. 2d 907 (1992) (affirming prejudgment interest in the amount of $46,645 accruing from the date the complaint was filed where the defendant never disputed the amount stated in the complaint but only asked for proof of plaintiff's claims); *Levy-Zentner Co. v. S. Pac. Trans. Co.*, 74 Cal. App. 3d 762, 142 Cal. Rptr. 1 (1977) (affirming prejudgment interest accruing on the date of the plaintiff's request for admission as to the amount of damages caused by a fire, which was the same amount subsequently awarded by the jury, where the defendant never contested the amount of damages); *Cassinos v. Union Oil Co.*, 14 Cal. App. 4th 1770, 18 Cal. Rptr. 2d 574 (1993) (upholding prejudgment in the amount of $1.7 million accruing from the date of the defendant's wrongful act).

nia courts to focus on the *defendant's* knowledge about the amount of the plaintiff's claim. The fact the plaintiff or some omniscient third party knew or could calculate the amount is not sufficient.

Another California statute, Civil Code § 3288, vests the fact-finder — the jury or the judge in a bench trial — with the discretion to award prejudgment interest in non-contract actions even though the damages are not "certain." Under this statute, the fact-finder also has the discretion to determine the date upon which the prejudgment interest begins to accrue, which may be as early as when the loss occurred. Additional California statutes authorize an award of prejudgment interest in a breach of contract action. For example, a party who is entitled to recover damages for breach of obligation to pay a liquidated sum is also entitled to recover prejudgment interest from the date the claim arose.[75] The rate of prejudgment interest is determined by the interest rate stipulated in the contract.[76] If the contract does not stipulate a legal (nonusurious) rate of interest, the obligation bears interest of 10% per annum after a breach.[77]

[2] Punitive Damages

In additional to compensatory damages, a plaintiff in an action other than a breach of contract action may recover *punitive damages* "for sake of example and by way of punishing the defendant."[78] A California court may award punitive damages only where the plaintiff proves by "clear and convincing" evidence that the defendant was guilty of "oppression, fraud, or malice."[79] In addition to these substantive requirements, California statutes impose several procedural constraints on the pleading, discovery, and jury consideration of punitive damages claims. For example, a plaintiff may not seek pretrial discovery with to the respect to the defendant's profits or financial condition unless the trial court enters an order permitting such discovery, and the court may require the plaintiff to prove a prima facie case of liability for punitive damages before evidence of the defendant's financial condition may be introduced at trial.[80] In addition to these statutory limitations, the California courts must comply with the various United States Supreme Court decisions imposing substantive and procedural due process restrictions on the assessment of punitive damages.[81]

---

[75] CAL. CIV. CODE §§ 3287(a), 3302.

[76] CAL. CIV. CODE § 3289(a). *See Roodenburg v. Pavestone Co.*, 171 Cal. App. 4th 185, 89 Cal. Rptr. 3d 558 (2009) (affirming prejudgment interest award of $489,550 calculated by using the 18 % interest rate provided in the contract).

[77] CAL. CIV. CODE § 3289(b).

[78] CAL. CIV. CODE § 3294.

[79] CAL. CIV. CODE § 3294.

[80] CAL. CIV. CODE § 3295.

[81] *See* LELAND M. JOHNS, CALIFORNIA DAMAGES: LAW AND PROOF §§ 18.6-18.25 (5th ed. 2012) (discussing California decisions that applied due process restrictions to the assessment of punitive damages). The due process constraints on punitive damages are discussed in § 14.01[1][b], *supra*.

[3] Attorney Fees

California follows the "American Rule" with respect to the recovery of attorney fees which, in the absence of an established exception, requires that each party is responsible for its own attorney fees, win or lose.[82] However, California recognizes many exceptions to this general rule based on fee-shifting statutes, judge-made equitable doctrines, and contractual agreements. Not only do California statutes authorize parties to allocate attorney fees by agreement, they also make an otherwise one-sided contractual right to recover attorney fees reciprocally binding upon all parties to the contract in an action to enforce the contract or to recover damages for its breach.[83] When combined, all these various bases for recovery of attorney fees from the losing party constitute very significant departures from the American Rule.

Numerous fee-shifting statutes authorize the California courts to award reasonable attorney fees to the prevailing party with respect to specific types of claims, each designed to encourage litigation of those claims by offering the "bounty" of court ordered fees.[84] The most frequently utilized statute is Code of Civil Procedure § 1021.5, the "private attorney general" statute, that authorizes an award of attorney fees to a "successful party" in actions "affecting the public interest" when "the necessity and financial burden of private enforcement are such as to make the award appropriate." The fundamental objectives of section 1021.5 are to encourage suits enforcing important public rights and to financial reward attorneys who successfully prosecute such suits.[85] Section 1021.5 and the various California fee-shifting statutes are independent of the federal fee-shifting statutes which may apply when a party seeks enforcement of the federal statute in state court.[86]

In addition fee-shifting statutes, although perhaps less significant in overall impact, the California courts have created several exceptions to the American Rule based on equitable theories. The most important of these judge-made exceptions is the "common fund" doctrine, under which a successful party whose lawsuit creates

[82] *See, e.g., Serrano v. Unruh*, 32 Cal. 3d 621, 627, 186 Cal. Rptr. 754, 652 P.2d 985 (1982).

[83] Cal. Code Civ. Proc. § 1021 (authorizing parties to a contract to include an agreement as to who will recover attorney fees in the event of subsequent litigation); Cal. Civ. Code § 1717 (a contractual provision making recovery of attorney's fees available for only one party is reciprocally binding and awards attorney fees to "the party prevailing on the contract, whether he or she is the party specified in the contract or not"). Civil Code § 1717 was enacted to establish mutuality of remedy where a contractual provision makes recovery of attorney's fees available for only one party, and to prevent oppressive use of one-sided attorney's fees provisions. *Reynolds Metals Co. v. Alperson*, 25 Cal. 3d 124, 128, 158 Cal. Rptr. 1, 599 P.2d 83 (1979).

[84] Although California Code of Civil Procedure § 1021.5 is the most utilized fee-shifting statute, the California Legislature has enacted over 300 other statutes which authorize an award of attorney fees to the prevailing party. For a discussion of these various statutes by subject, *see* CEB, *California Attorney Fee Awards, Fee-Shifting Statutes* §§ 3.80-3.129 (3d ed. 2012).

[85] *Maria P. v. Riles*, 43 Cal. 3d 1281, 1288-89, 240 Cal. Rptr. 872, 743 P.2d 932 (1987);

[86] *See, e.g., Sokolow v. Cnty. of San Mateo*, 13 Cal. App. 3d 231, 261 Cal. Rptr. 520 (1989) (directing the superior court to award attorney fees under both 42 U.S.C. § 1988 and Cal. Code Civ. Proc. § 1021.5 in civil rights action); *Green v. Obledo*, 161 Cal. App. 3d 678, 207 Cal. Rptr. 830 (1984) (holding superior court must apply federal fee-shifting statute when federal claim brought in state court).

a identifiable fund from which others derive benefit may require those passive beneficiaries to bear their fair share of the litigation expenses. However, unlike other fee-shifting doctrines, the successful party's attorney fees are paid out of the common fund and not by the losing party.[87] The "common fund" doctrine provides the authority for a court to award attorney fees to class counsel from the class recovery in a class action, a common practice in many class action settlements. Consideration of these judge-made exceptions still does not provide a complete picture of attorney fee recovery in California. In appropriate situations, a court may award attorney fees as a sanction for bad faith litigation, for misuse of the discovery process, and for frivolous appeals.

When calculating the amount of an award of attorney fees, the California courts usually follow the "lodestar" method.[88] This method requires the trial court to first determine the lodestar figure by multiplying the time spent on the case by a reasonable hourly rate for each attorney. Once the lodestar amount is determined, the trial court may consider a variety of other factors which may justify either the augmentation or the diminution of the lodestar amount. Most importantly, the lodestar amount may be reduced (*i.e.*, a "negative multiplier") to reflect the relative degree of success achieved by the prevailing party[89] or may be enhanced (*i.e.*, a "positive multiplier") based on several factors, including the novelty and difficulty of the questions involved and the contingent nature of the fee award.[90]

Despite its endorsement and frequent use by the California courts, a positive multiplier is controversial because it may double count factors, such as the difficulty of a legal question and the quality of representation, that are already encompassed in calculation of the lodestar amount. For this and related reasons, the United States Supreme Court has held that, with respect to federal fee-shifting statutes, enhancement of the lodestar may be appropriate only in those rare circumstances where specific evidence shows the lodestar fee, by itself, would be inadequate to attract competent counsel.[91]

---

[87] *See, e.g., Serrano v. Priest*, 20 Cal. 3d 25, 141 Cal. Rptr. 315, 569 P.2d 1303 (1977); *Quinn v. State of Cal.* 15 Cal. 3d 162, 167-68, 124 Cal. Rptr. 1, 539 P.2d 761 (1975).

[88] *See, e.g., Press v. Lucky Stores, Inc.*, 34 Cal. 3d 311, 193 Cal. Rptr. 900, 667 P. 2d 704 (1983); *Serrano v. Priest*, 20 Cal. 3d 25, 141 Cal. Rptr. 315, 569 P. 2d 1303 (1977).

[89] *See, e.g., Californians for Responsible Toxics Mgmt. v. Kizer*, 211 Cal. App. 3d 961, 259 Cal. Rptr. 599 (1989) (upholding trial court's 35% negative multiplier where plaintiff achieved limited success through lawsuit).

[90] *See, e.g., Graham v. DaimlerChrysler Corp.*, 34 Cal. 4th 553, 21 Cal. Rptr. 3d 331, 101 P. 3d 140 (2004) (affirming attorney fee award of $762,830 calculated by enhancing the lodestar amount by a 2.25 multiplier); *Chavez v. Netflix, Inc.*, 162 Cal. App. 4th 43, 73 Cal. Rptr. 3d 413 (2008) (upholding a 2.5 multiplier); *City of Oakland v. Oakland Raiders*, 203 Cal. App. 3d 78, 249 Cal. Rptr. 606 (1988) (affirming award where lodestar amount of $853,756 increased by multiplier to $2 million to account for the extraordinary novelty and complexity of the issues presented).

[91] In *Perdue v. Kenny A.*, 559 U.S. 542 (2010), the United States Supreme Court held that the calculation of attorney fee award under 42 U.S.C. § 1988 — the fee-shifting statute applicable to federal civil rights actions — based on the lodestar may be increased by a multiplier only in "rare" and "exceptional" cases. The *Perdue* Court noted that an enhancement may not be based on a factor that is subsumed in the lodestar calculation, such as the case's novelty or complexity, or the quality of the attorney's performance.

[4]   Recovery of Court Costs by the Prevailing Party

Unlike attorney fees, the general rule is that a successful litigant may recover *court costs* from the losing party. In California, a prevailing party is entitled to recover costs as a matter of right. A "prevailing party" includes "the party with a net monetary recovery, a defendant in whose favor a dismissal is entered, a defendant where neither plaintiff nor defendant obtains any relief, and a defendant as against those plaintiffs who do not recover any relief against that defendant."[92] Costs are recoverable if incurred, whether or not they were actually paid.[93]

The items of costs a prevailing party may recover are somewhat broader in California than in many other jurisdictions. Allowable costs include, among other items, the amounts paid for: filing, motion, and jury fees; taking, videotaping, and transcribing necessary depositions including an original and one copy of those taken by the claimant and one copy of depositions taken by the party against whom costs are allowed, and travel expenses to attend depositions; service of process; fees of expert witnesses ordered by the court; court reporters fees; and models and blowups of exhibits and photocopies of exhibits if they were reasonably helpful to aid the trier of fact.[94] Other items not expressly allowed or prohibited by the cost statutes may nevertheless be recoverable in the discretion of the court.

Costs that are allowable must be reasonable in amount and must be "reasonably necessary to the conduct of the litigation rather than merely convenient or beneficial to its preparation."[95] Technological advances in the conduct of litigation have complicated the "reasonably necessary" determination. For example, in one case the court found that expenses incurred for a graphics communication system (searchable electronic storage of documents and videos for presentation at trial) and for editing of videotape depositions for effective presentation of the testimony to the jury were not "reasonably necessary" because there are alternative "low-tech" methods of presenting this information.[96] However, in a more recent case the court found cost items of $111,063 for hourly billings of personnel to process the raw business data that went into an exhibit and $2,250 for equipment to project documents on a screen during trial were "reasonably necessary" and properly awarded by the trial court.[97]

Costs awarded to the prevailing party may be withheld or augmented pursuant to California Code of Civil Procedure § 998, which authorizes a party to serve upon any other party a written offer to allow judgment to be taken in accordance with the terms and conditions stated in the offer. If the offer made by a defendant is not accepted and the plaintiff fails to obtain a more favorable judgment, the plaintiff shall not recover his or her post-offer costs and shall pay the defendant's costs from

---

[92] CAL. CODE CIV. PROC. §§ 1021, 1032(b).

[93] CAL. CODE CIV. PROC. § 1033.5(c)(1).

[94] CAL. CODE CIV. PROC. § 1033.5

[95] CAL. CODE CIV. PROC. § 1033.5(c)(2) & (3).

[96] *Science Applications Int'l Corp. v. Superior Court*, 39 Cal. App. 4th 1095, 46 Cal. Rptr. 2d 332 (1995).

[97] *El Dorado Meat Co. v. Yosemite Meat & Locker Serv., Inc.*, 150 Cal. App. 4th 612, 58 Cal. Rptr. 3d 590 (2007).

the time of the offer.[98] If an offer made by a plaintiff is not accepted and the defendant fails to obtain a more favorable judgment the court, in its discretion, may require the defendant to pay a reasonable sum to cover the costs of the services of expert witnesses, in addition to plaintiff's costs.[99] The purpose of these financial incentives and corresponding disincentives is to encourage parties to accept an offer and thereby settle the lawsuit.

[5] Enforcement of Money Judgments in the California Courts

A party who obtains a money judgment (referred to as the "judgment creditor") may have won the easiest part of the litigation battle. A successful decision on liability may be of very little benefit to the judgment creditor unless the judgment can be effectively enforced. California's statutes provide a judgment creditor with a variety of procedural mechanisms for enforcement of a judgment. These statutory procedures can be quite complex, and contain many technicalities and exceptions.[100]

A money judgment is enforceable upon entry, and remains enforceable for a period of 10 years after date of entry, renewable for another 10 years.[101] During this period, the judgment creditor has several options available to enforce the judgment, such as levy and forced sale of the judgment debtor's real or personal property and garnishment of the debtor's wages. All property of the judgment debtor is subject to enforcement of a money judgment, except for that property specifically exempted by statute. For example, California statutes recognize a homestead exemption to protect a judgment debtor's "dwelling" (or the debtor's equity in the dwelling) up to the statutory maximum (currently, $75,000 if the judgment debtor is a single person, $100,000 if the judgment debtor or spouse is a member of a family unit, or $175,000 if the judgment debtor or spouse is over 65 years of age, is disabled, or of low income). The enforcement procedures provide a judgment debtor the opportunity to assert these exemptions at appropriate times during the process but, consistent with doctrine of claim preclusion, do not permit the debtor to reexamine the factual or legal underpinnings of the cause of action leading to the underlying judgment.

The various procedures for the enforcement of a money judgment mean very little unless the judgment creditor can ascertain the existence and location of the judgment debtor's assets. The California statutes make some useful discovery devices available to the judgment creditor at any time a money judgment is enforceable, unless the judgment is stayed during appeal. The judgment creditor may propound written interrogatories to the judgment creditor, and may demand production and inspection of documents. Another extremely useful discovery tool is the debtor's examination. Upon proper application by the judgment creditor, the

---

[98] CAL. CODE CIV. PROC. § 998(c).

[99] CAL. CODE CIV. PROC. § 998(d).

[100] For more in-depth analyses, see CEB, *Debt Collection Practice in California* (2d ed. 2012); 8 Witkin, *California Procedure, Enforcement of Judgment* (5th ed. 2008).

[101] CAL. CODE CIV. PROC. §§ 683.010, 683.020.

court may order the judgment debtor to appear before the court at a specific time and place "to furnish information to aid in enforcement of the money judgment."[102] If the judgment debtor fails to appear, the court may punish the judgment debtor for contempt.[103] These examination proceedings function not only as a broad discovery device, but may also result in an order by the court which resolves contested exemption claims, punishes for contempt, forbids transfer or other disposition of property interests, and creates a lien on property or debt.[104]

The various post-judgment enforcement procedures also may mean very little if the defendant has already sold, transferred, or otherwise disposed of his property during the course of the litigation. California's Attachment Law seeks to prevent this by affording the plaintiff the authority to ask the court to "attach" (*e.g.*, seize or bring under the court's control) the defendant's assets at the beginning of the lawsuit.[105] Because prejudgment attachments constitute a deprivation of the defendant's property rights by a branch of the state, the statutory procedures must comply with the constitutional requirements of procedural due process. For example, without a showing of "exigent circumstances" (*e.g.*, imminent transfer or sale), due process will likely require the court to give the defendant advance notice and an opportunity for a hearing in order to contest the propriety of a proposed prejudgment attachment.[106]

§ 14.05   EQUITABLE REMEDIES IN THE CALIFORNIA COURTS

[1]   Injunctive Relief

[a]   Temporary Restraining Orders and Preliminary Injunctions

California statutes provide for interlocutory as well as permanent injunctive relief, in much the same manner as Rule 65 of the Federal Rules of Civil Procedure. A trial court may enter a temporary restraining order (TRO), with or without advance notice to the defendant, to prevent "great or irreparable injury" until the matter can be more fully heard and determined.[107] A TRO is an interim order of limited duration — by statute, ordinarily no more than 15 days, or up to 22 days for good cause shown — designed to preserve the status quo pending a hearing on an application for a preliminary injunction. Like any other injunction, a TRO may be enforced by contempt.

---

[102] CAL. CODE CIV. PROC. § 708.110.

[103] CAL. CODE CIV. PROC. §§ 708.110(e), 708.170.

[104] CAL. CODE CIV. PROC. §§ 708.140-708.205; *see, e.g., Imperial Bank v. Pim Elec., Inc.*, 33 Cal. App. 4th 540, 39 Cal. Rptr. 2d 432 (1995) (ruling the referee properly ordered the judgment debtors to turn over specified assets identified by the debtors during their judgment debtors examinations to satisfy a debt owed to the judgment creditor).

[105] CAL. CODE CIV. PROC. § 481.010 *et seq.*

[106] *See Connecticut v. Doehr*, 501 U.S. 1 (1991).

[107] CAL. CODE CIV. PROC. §§ 526(a)(2), 527(a).

Whether or not the trial court enters a TRO, the plaintiff may apply for a preliminary injunction. Unlike a TRO, a preliminary injunction will not be granted unless the opposing party has notice of, and an opportunity to respond to, the application at a preliminary injunction hearing. In deciding whether to exercise its discretion and issue a preliminary injunction, the trial court must weigh two interrelated factors: (1) the likelihood that the moving party will ultimately prevail on the merits, and (2) the relative interim harm to the parties from the issuance or nonissuance of the injunction.[108] Generalizations regarding "interim harm" are difficult. However, a preliminary injunction is more likely when the plaintiff demonstrates that it is necessary to prevent great or irreparable injury. Of course, what constitutes irreparable injury varies with the circumstances of each case. If the plaintiff may be fully compensated by the payment of damages in the event he or she prevails on the merits, then irreparable injury does not exist. The court must also consider the potential harm to the defendant and to the public if a preliminary injunction is granted.

[b] Permanent Injunctions

A California court has the authority to grant a permanent injunction to restrain the commission or continuance of an act, or the failure to act, upon proof by the plaintiff that he has or will suffer "irreparable injury" caused by the act or inaction for which monetary compensation would not afford adequate relief.[109] If the court grants a permanent injunction and the defendant fails to obey it, the plaintiff may seek an order of contempt to compel compliance. However, as a matter of basic due process, a defendant cannot be found guilty of contempt if the injunction violated is so uncertain that the defendant could not determine what the injunction required him to do or not to do.[110] To be enforceable against a defendant, the injunction order must be directed against that defendant, either by naming the defendant as an individual or by designating a class of persons to which the defendant belongs.[111] Also, a defendant can challenge the validity of the injunction as a defense to a contempt proceeding.[112]

[2] Declaratory Relief

Under California's Declaratory Judgment Act, a party may ask the court for a binding declaration of rights and duties.[113] Under the Act, a party may ask the court for declaratory relief either alone or in conjunction with coercive relief such

---

[108] *Butt v. State of California,* 4 Cal. 4th 668, 677-78, 15 Cal. Rptr. 2d 480, 842 P. 2d 1240 (1992).

[109] *See* Cal. Code Civ. Proc. §§ 525, 526; Cal. Civ. Code § 3422.

[110] *See City of Vernon v. Superior Court,* 38 Cal. 2d 509, 615, 241 P.2d 243 (1952).

[111] *See, e.g., Planned Parenthood Golden Gate v. Garibaldi,* 107 Cal. App. 4th 345, 132 Cal. Rptr. 2d 46 (2003) (holding an injunction order that applies to "all persons with actual notice of this judgment" does not bind a nonparty who has actual notice of the order).

[112] *See, e.g., Welton v. City of L. A.,* 18 Cal. 3d 497, 507-508, 134 Cal. Rptr. 668, 556 P.2d 1119 (1976) (vacating a contempt order because an injunction based on an unconstitutional ordinance exceeded the issuing court's jurisdiction); *In re Berry,* 68 Cal. 2d 137, 65 Cal. Rptr. 273, 436 P.2d 273 (1968) (holding disobedience of an unconstitutional order cannot validly be punished by contempt).

[113] Cal. Code Civ. Proc. § 1060 *et seq.*

as damages, specific performance, or an injunction. Unlike injunctive relief, in which a party is ordered by the court to do or to refrain from doing something, a declaratory judgment merely declares the legal relationship between the parties. A declaratory judgment action may be brought to establish rights once a conflict has arisen, or a party may request declaratory relief as a prophylactic measure before a breach of an obligation occurs.

Declaratory relief promotes judicial economy. A declaratory judgment action provides litigants with a quick, efficient means of resolving a disputed issue. Often a declaratory remedy will end the controversy between the parties. For example, if a court finds that a plaintiff has no rights under a contract, the dispute is resolved and no further litigation is likely. On the other hand, if the court determines that a defendant is in breach of a contract, the defendant will likely comply with the contract rather than risk a subsequent suit for damages or specific performance, since the prior declaratory judgment will serve as a conclusive determination on the issue of defendant's breach.[114] A final judgment in an action seeking only "pure" declaratory relief — an action not also seeking coercive relief — does not preclude any party from obtaining additional relief based on the same facts in a subsequent action.[115]

---

[114] *Mycogen Co. v. Monsanto Co.*, 28 Cal. 4th 888, 897-98, 123 Cal. Rptr. 2d 432, 51 P. 3d 297 (2002).

[115] CAL. CODE CIV. PROC. § 1062; *see Mycogen, supra,* 28 Cal. 4th 888, 896-904 (discussing the parameters of the declaratory judgment exception to claim preclusion stated in § 1062).

Chapter 15

RESPECT FOR FINAL JUDGMENTS

§ 15.01 INTRODUCTION

[1] The Law of Prior Adjudication and Its Cousins

This chapter will examine the manner in which prior adjudications can bind or preclude parties in subsequent lawsuits. The body of law which sets the effect of prior adjudications (judgments) is called *res judicata*[1] or, in modern parlance, *preclusion* doctrine. American courts initially borrowed their law of *res judicata* from English jurisprudence, where the term appears in judicial decisions as early as the thirteenth century.[2] In this country, *res judicata* has always been primarily a creature of judicial doctrine — the common law. Its status as common law gives it flexibility, though often at the expense of clarity and comprehensibility.

Res judicata law has long consisted of two sub-doctrines. The first concerns how a judgment can foreclose subsequent opportunities to bring a claim or cause of action. This used to be referred to as *merger and bar* or simply *res judicata*. While these terms are still employed, the sub-doctrine is increasingly described in modern usage as *claim preclusion*. Part A of this chapter treats claim preclusion. The second sub-doctrine concerns how a judgment can prevent relitigation of a particular issue of fact or law. This used to be referred to as *collateral estoppel by judgment*. That label is in the process of being replaced by the term *issue preclusion*.[3] Part B of the chapter treats issue preclusion. This chapter will usually refer to the two sub-doctrines as claim and issue preclusion.

The content of preclusion doctrine varies within our system of federal and state courts. The Supremacy Clause of the United States Constitution requires all courts

---

[1]

> Res judicata performs the job of delineating the real content of a judgment, doing so by specifying the effects of the decision. Res judicata dictates whether decided matters are subject to reopening, as well as which actually undecided matters nevertheless fall within the bounds of a judgment and so receive treatment as if decided. It thus defines by means of fixing the boundaries of the judgment.

Kevin M. Clermont, *Common-Law Compulsory Counterclaim Rule: Creating Effective and Elegant Res Judicata Doctrine*, 79 Notre Dame L. Rev. 1745 (2004).

[2] Alan D. Vestal, Res Judicata/Preclusion 28–30 (1969).

[3] The modern terminology of claim and issue preclusion has been used by the Supreme Court in several cases. *E.g.*, *Migra v. Warren City Sch. Dist. Bd. of Educ.*, 465 U.S. 75, 77 n.1 (1984). It was adopted by the American Law Institute in Restatement (Second) of Judgments 1 (1982).

to respect federal law guaranteeing due process to litigants[4] and to give full faith and credit to the judgments of other states.[5] But these constraints leave each state judicial system a good deal of freedom to fashion its own rules of preclusion. It is clear, for example, that cases decided by the Supreme Court which determine the content of federal court preclusion doctrine are not binding on state preclusion doctrine.[6] The existence of multiple judicial systems poses the question of what respect the courts of one system owe the judgment of a court in another. Part C addresses questions of inter-system preclusion.

Finally, preclusion by judgment is not the only way in which courts discourage relitigation. *Stare decisis*, "law of the case," and judicial estoppel are other doctrines deployed by courts for the same purpose. Part D surveys these doctrines.

[2]   What's Wrong with Relitigation? The Rationale for Preclusion

Each system determines how much preclusive effect to give its judgments by weighing policies favoring preclusion against concern that the succeeding case be correctly decided. Commonly accepted policies supporting preclusion derive from the fact that repetitive litigation takes its toll on courts, other litigants, and the public. Litigating a claim once is costly enough, in terms of attorneys' fees, discovery costs, judicial resources, and the time of the parties, witnesses, and, in jury trials, jurors. Litigating it twice is economically unjustifiable, especially when dockets are crowded with other actions. Furthermore, repetitive litigation can be an abusive litigation tactic. The objectives of *res judicata* are therefore "to save judicial energy, to prevent harassment of the defendant, to further societal interests in the orderly and expeditious resolution of controversies, and to give repose."[7]

Giving "repose" is especially important.

> The deepest interests underlying the conclusive effect of prior adjudication draw from the purpose to provide a means of finally ending private disputes. The central role of adversary litigation in our society is to provide binding answers. We want to free people from the uncertain prospect of litigation, with all its costs to emotional peace and the ordering of future affairs. Repose is the most important product of *res judicata*.[8]

Another reason for preclusion doctrines is to promote respect for the civil litigation process. If the same or similar claims or issues could be relitigated, the

---

[4] *See* § 15.06, *infra*.

[5] *See* § 15.10, *infra*.

[6] Within constitutional limits, the courts of each state determine how preclusive their judgments will be. Yet Supreme Court cases can be influential by example. *See, e.g.*, the discussion of *Parklane Hosiery Co. v. Shore*, 439 U.S. 322 (1979), at § 15.08[2][b], *infra*.

[7] ARTHUR VON MEHREN & DONALD TRAUTMAN, THE LAW OF MULTISTATE PROBLEMS: CASES AND MATERIALS ON CONFLICT OF LAWS 1459 (1965). For further discussion of the policies of *res judicata*, see Allan D. Vestal, *Rationale of Preclusion*, 9 ST. LOUIS U. L.J. 29, 31–43 (1964).

[8] *WRIGHT & MILLER* § 4403.

process might yield inconsistent results. For example, even reasonable fact finders might come out differently in successive cases on the same record. A party who lost the first time might win the next even without a change in the evidence. Of course, an intelligent observer knows that even the best procedural system carries this possibility. But "[i]t is easier to live with the abstract knowledge that our imperfect trial processes would often produce opposite results in successive efforts than to accept repeated concrete realizations of that fact."[9] By preventing relitigation, the preclusion doctrines "preserv[e] the acceptability of judicial dispute resolution against the corrosive disrespect that would follow if the same matter were twice litigated to inconsistent results."[10]

Concern for correctness of judicial decision is the prudential counterforce to preclusion in all systems. It is out of this concern that "the defense of *res judicata* is universally respected, but actually not very well liked," as Judge Charles E. Clark, the father of the federal rules remarked.[11] A "simplistic emphasis on judicial economy" can blind courts to the injustice, or even inefficiency, of particular applications of preclusion doctrine.[12] Judge Learned Hand observed that *res judicata* "must be treated as a compromise between two conflicting interests: the convenience of avoiding a multiplicity of suits and the adequacy of the remedies afforded for conceded wrongs."[13]

Of course, the primary procedural mechanism for testing the correctness of a judgment is appeal. The law of preclusion accepts judgments not because they are correct (though it makes that assumption), but because they are final; it leaves correctness to appeal. Scholars therefore remind us that "the first lesson one must learn on the subject of *res judicata* is that judicial findings must not be confused with absolute truth,"[14] and courts therefore often say that the incorrectness of a judgment does not diminish its preclusive effect.[15] This maxim is easy to follow when the second suit is merely a replication of the first. The more dissimilar the first and second suits are, however, the more the maxim loses force.

Moreover, respect for the litigation system can also be diminished by perpetuating grievous error by precluding its correction through relitigation. Every system seems to recognize some point where preclusion — although constitutional — is inappropriate because the judgment does not carry a sufficient assurance of correctness to govern the different case as well, and every system has developed a rich, if confusing, set of exceptions to preclusion principles to accommodate concerns for justice in limited circumstances.

---

[9] *Id.*

[10] *Id.*

[11] *Riordan v. Ferguson*, 147 F.2d 983, 988 (2d Cir. 1945) (Clark, J., dissenting).

[12] ROBERT C. CASAD & KEVIN M. CLERMONT, RES JUDICATA: A HANDBOOK ON ITS THEORY, DOCTRINE, AND PRACTICE 30 (2001).

[13] *Lyons v. Westinghouse Elec. Corp.*, 222 F.2d 184, 189 (2d Cir. 1955).

[14] Brainerd Currie, *Mutuality of Collateral Estoppel: Limits of the* Bernhard *Doctrine*, 9 STAN. L. REV. 281, 315 (1957).

[15] *See, e.g., Federated Dep't Stores, Inc. v. Moitie*, 452 U.S. 394, 398–99 (1981).

[3] Litigation Perspectives — Offensive and Defensive Preclusion

The tactical advantages litigants see from preclusion are twofold. First, it is better to win by extending a prior judicial victory to your case than to risk the possibility of losing by litigating afresh. Second, it is quicker and cheaper to cover ground in the case by incorporating by reference an issue of fact or law decided in an earlier case than to have to establish it again.

Either plaintiff or defendant may be in a position to argue preclusion. It simply depends on who profits from the prior adjudication.[16] When a litigant argues claim or issue preclusion in order to advance a claim, that is *offensive* preclusion. When a litigant argues preclusion to defeat a claim, it is *defensive* preclusion.[17] Preclusion arguments must be raised in a timely fashion, or they will be waived.[18] A defendant can plead *res judicata* or estoppel as an affirmative defense (Rule 8(c) has not caught up with the modern terminology of claim or issue preclusion). Either party can move for summary judgment (or partial summary judgment), supported with a certified copy of the prior judgment and, if the basis of the motion is issue preclusion, with evidence that the same issue was actually and fairly litigated in the prior lawsuit (usually excerpts from the record and sometimes pleadings from that lawsuit).

[4] Preclusion Essentials

[a] Claim Preclusion

The basic rule of claim preclusion is that a final judgment on the merits precludes the same parties (and those closely related to them) from litigating the same or a sufficiently similar *claim* (or in common state law parlance, a same cause of action[19]) in a subsequent lawsuit. Though we call it "claim" preclusion, it also precludes relitigation of most defenses that were or could have been litigated in the first lawsuit. Modern claim preclusion is not just a doctrine preventing relitigation, because it extends also to sufficiently similar claims (and defenses) that *could have been litigated* in the first lawsuit, even though they were not.

Section 15.02 of this chapter examines how identical claims are precluded. Section 15.03 treats the preclusion of similar though nonidentical claims and defenses. Section 15.04 discusses the identity-of-parties requirement, while § 15.05

---

[16] It is even possible for *both* plaintiff and defendant to make preclusion arguments in the same case. *See* § 15.06, *infra*.

[17] *Cf. United States v. Mendoza*, 464 U.S. 154, 159 n.4 (1984):

Offensive use of collateral estoppel [issue preclusion] occurs when a plaintiff seeks to foreclose a defendant from relitigating an issue the defendant has previously litigated unsuccessfully in another action against the same or a different party. Defensive use of collateral estoppel occurs when a defendant seeks to prevent a plaintiff from relitigating an issue the plaintiff has previously litigated unsuccessfully in another action against the same or a different party.

[18] *See Arizona v. California*, 530 U.S. 392 (2000).

[19] Courts sometimes use the older term, "cause of action" in place of the term "claim." *E.g., Nevada v. United States*, 463 U.S. 110, 130 (1983).

treats the requirement that judgments be final and on the merits.

[b] Issue Preclusion

The doctrine of issue preclusion gives a final judgment preclusive effect with respect to identical issues in a subsequent case which cannot be said, even in the broadest sense, to involve the same claim. The basic rule of issue preclusion is that a final judgment precludes relitigation of the same *issue* of fact or law, so long as (1) the issue was actually litigated, determined and necessary to the judgment in the prior adjudication, and (2) the circumstances of the particular case do not suggest any reason why it would be unfair to invoke the doctrine. Issue preclusion differs importantly from claim preclusion in three ways. First, it applies even to actions that do not, remotely, involve the same claim, so long as they involve the identical issue of law or fact. Second, it applies only to issues that were actually litigated in the lawsuit. Finally, modern issue preclusion in most (though not all) jurisdictions does not carry the identity-of-parties requirement found in claim preclusion. In some cases, persons who were not parties to the first lawsuit can rely upon it to argue issue preclusion. But due process protects genuine strangers to the original litigation from being bound by issue preclusion.

Section 15.06 of this chapter elaborates on how issue preclusion differs from claim preclusion. Section 15.07 treats the basic requirements for issue preclusion: that the same issue be litigated, determined, and necessary to a prior judgment and that application of the doctrine be fair under the circumstances of the particular case. Section 15.08 considers the possible uses of issue preclusion by and against those not parties to the prior case. The final judgment requirement of issue preclusion receives no separate attention in this Section, since it is substantially the same as the final- judgment requirement for claim preclusion discussed in § 15.05.[20]

[5] Spotting Preclusion Issues

Preclusion questions are easy to spot. They invariably involve two or more lawsuits with overlapping issues or claims. The question is whether the first lawsuit to reach a final judgment on the merits precludes relitigation in the next or later lawsuits of a claim that was or could have been litigated in the first lawsuit, or relitigation of an issue of fact or law that is identical to one actually and fairly litigated, determined, and necessary to the judgment in, the first lawsuit. By "first (or prior) lawsuit," we mean the first to reach a judgment, which is not always the first lawsuit that was commenced.[21]

---

[20] *Cf.* RESTATEMENT (SECOND) OF JUDGMENTS, note 3, *supra*, § 13 cmt. g ("Usually there is no occasion to interpret finality less strictly when the question is one of issue preclusion.").

[21] For claim preclusion, the significant event is when judgment becomes final, not when the case begins. RESTATEMENT (SECOND) OF JUDGMENTS § 14. This means that a suit filed earlier in time may be subject to the preclusive effects of a subsequent suit when the latter is the first to reach final judgment.

PART A.
Claim Preclusion

§ 15.02 PRECLUSION WHEN ORIGINAL AND SUCCESSIVE CLAIMS ARE IDENTICAL; DYNAMICS OF JUDGMENT ENFORCEMENT

"You can't sue someone twice for the same thing." This crude intuition lies at the heart of claim preclusion. The most basic application of claim preclusion prevents parties from pressing a claim or cause of action identical to one presented in a prior adjudication. If the prior case ends with a judgment which is final and on the merits,[22] parties to it[23] are foreclosed from litigating the same claim in any subsequent proceeding. It does not matter whether judgment in the prior suit was for or against the claimant. The judgment makes the claim disappear. When a damage claim is successful, the cause of action represented by the claim becomes a cause of action on the money judgment.[24] The claim is said to have *merged* into the judgment. If the damage claim was unsuccessful, the resulting adverse judgment is said to *bar* another suit on the claim. (Thus, the now largely obsolete label of "merger and bar" was once widely used for claim preclusion.)

The successful claimant becomes a *judgment creditor* and the party who unsuccessfully opposed the judgment becomes a *judgment debtor*. If the judgment debtor fails to satisfy the judgment, the judgment creditor may have to sue again — not in a lawsuit on the claim, but instead in a supplementary proceeding to enforce the judgment, or as much of it as possible.

Thanks to claim preclusion, the plaintiff-judgment creditor holds most of the cards in the enforcement proceeding. Procedures to enforce money-judgments vary.[25] However, most are summary in nature and usually are limited to the same questions: is the defendant in fact the judgment debtor (the person named in the judgment); how much can the judgment debtor pay toward satisfaction of the judgment; and how soon?[26] Judgment enforcement proceedings usually present no

---

[22] The requirement that judgments be final and on the merits is discussed at § 15.05, *infra*.

[23] The identity-of-parties requirement for claim preclusion is discussed at § 15.04, *infra*.

[24] *See* Stephen B. Burbank, *Federal Judgments Law: Sources of Authority and Sources of Rules*, 70 Tex. L. Rev. 1551 (1992); Robert L. Haig & Patricia O. Kahn, *Representing the Judgment Creditor*, 16 Am. J. Tr. Advoc. 1 (1992); James J. Brown, *Collecting a Judgment*, 13 Litig. 31 (Fall 1986). Judgments granting injunctive relief (rather than damages) are enforced differently. *See* § 14.02[2], *supra*.

[25] Rule 69(a) generally requires the supplementary procedure for the enforcement of judgments in federal court to "accord with the procedure of the state where the court is located . . . ." For comparison of procedures in this country with those abroad, see Friedrich K. Juenger, *The Recognition of Money Judgments in Civil and Commercial Matters*, 36 Am. J. Comp. L. 1 (1988).

Even if the judgment debtor has not been sued on the judgment, he may feel pressure to honor it. For example, mere entry of the judgment may act as a lien on real estate held by the judgment debtor in that judicial district. *See, e.g.*, Ind. Code Ann. § 34-55-9-2 (West 2012).

[26] Courts often have authority to compel the judgment debtor to disclose her financial worth and to order that judgment debtor's assets be liquidated or placed in receivership to facilitate payment.

opportunity to reexamine the factual and legal underpinnings of the claim leading to judgment, matters the judgment debtor was free by denials and affirmative defenses to question prior to final judgment. In other words, relitigation of these defenses, too, is barred by the judgment: "In an action upon the judgment, the defendant cannot avail himself of defenses he might have interposed, or did interpose, in the first action."[27] Claim preclusion confines the judgment debtor to a short list of challenges to the validity of the judgment, and it is unlikely that she will be able to raise even these unless the judgment was obtained by default.[28] In short, judgment precludes defendant from improving her position by relitigating the merits.

The claimant may also be disadvantaged by claim preclusion in two ways. First, of course, the initial case may end with a judgment on the merits against her. This will preclude (bar) the claimant from relitigating the claim.[29] Less obviously, claim preclusion may also bring adverse consequences to the claimant if she *wins* in the initial case. The damages awarded her in the proceeding may be less than she sought and than she believes she could establish if given another chance to litigate the claim. Yet she will be unable to sue again because her claim merged into her judgment.[30] In addition, a final judgment on the merits — whether or not in claimant's favor — may preclude her from presenting other claims grounded on the same evidence or events that were the subject of the judgment. The following section discusses how and to what extent judgments preclude such nonidentical claims.

---

[27] RESTATEMENT (SECOND) OF JUDGMENTS § 18 (1982).

[28] The judgment debtor may attack a default judgment on grounds that she failed to receive adequate notice of the initial proceeding or that the court rendering the default judgment lacked personal jurisdiction to do so. RESTATEMENT (SECOND) OF JUDGMENTS § 1 at 30. For discussion of the requirement of adequate notice, *see generally* Chapter 4, *supra*; of personal jurisdiction, *see* Chapter 3, *supra*.

If the defendant participated in the original proceeding instead of taking a default, she may not use these grounds to attack collaterally a judgment otherwise entitled to claim-preclusive effect. For example, if the defendant elects to question personal jurisdiction initially and is unsuccessful, that decision will preclude reexamination of the question when the judgment is presented for enforcement. *See Baldwin v. Iowa State Traveling Men's Ass'n*, 283 U.S. 522, 525–26 (1931); *Stoll v. Gottlieb*, 305 U.S. 165, 172 (1938); § 10[B][2], *supra*. Theoretically, broadened principles of preclusion, *see* § 15.03, *infra*, should also prevent collateral attack if the defendant omitted her jurisdictional challenge when participating in the initial proceeding. The tendency in such cases, however, is for courts to reach the same result simply by noting that defendant's participation in the initial proceeding operated as a consent to jurisdiction. *Cf. Ins. Corp. of Ireland Ltd. v. Compagnie des Bauxites de Guinee*, 456 U.S. 694, 703–04 (1982) (explaining how defendant can waive her due process challenge by participating in the initial case).

In rare cases, resistance may be permitted when the court rendering the judgment lacked subject matter jurisdiction, or when the judgment is (under the local law of the place rendering it) unenforceable for some reason. *See* § 3.04[2], *supra*.

[29] "A valid and final personal judgment rendered in favor of the defendant bars another action by the plaintiff on the same claim." RESTATEMENT (SECOND) OF JUDGMENTS § 19, at 161. The same is true with reference to a judgment rendered in favor of the plaintiff on defendant's counterclaim. *See* § 15.03[3], *infra*.

[30] "The plaintiff cannot thereafter maintain an action on the original claim or any part thereof, although he may be able to maintain an action upon the judgment." RESTATEMENT (SECOND) OF JUDGMENTS § 18(1), at 151–52. The same is true with reference to a judgment rendered in favor of defendant on defendant's counterclaim. *See* § 15.02, *infra*.

§ 15.03 PRECLUSION WHEN ORIGINAL AND SUCCESSIVE CLAIMS ARE NOT IDENTICAL

[1] How and Why Non-Identical Claims are Precluded

Perhaps the most significant feature of claim preclusion is the availability of the doctrine to preclude claims that did not actually appear in the prior adjudication. It has long been accepted that claim preclusion cannot be confined to precluding identical claims.[31] For example, it would be indefensible to permit an automobile accident plaintiff to bring one suit against the other driver for damage to the right fender of plaintiff's car and follow with a second suit for damage to the left fender. All jurisdictions would regard this succeeding property damage claim to be extinguished by judgment in the first suit. This is because the two claims are so related that the doctrine of claim preclusion regards them as parts of what is, in a larger sense, a single claim.

Under modern preclusion law, this expanded concept of a "claim" encompasses all of the alternative legal theories and the full scope of damages or other remedies generated by the facts of the original controversy.[32] Whether all of this broadly conceived claim was actually put forward in the prior case is immaterial. What matters for claim preclusion is whether it *could* have been put forward.[33] If the new material could have been included in a more complete presentation of the initial claim, the succeeding claim is "swallowed by the judgment in the prior suit."[34]

Jones v. Morris Plan Bank of Portsmouth[35] is a familiar casebook example. In the first suit, the bank sued Jones and recovered two delinquent car-installment payments. In the second suit, the court held that the prior adjudication extinguished the bank's further rights under the contract, even though Jones had since missed additional payments. The court read the installment contract as creating a right in bank to sue for the entire unpaid balance as soon as Jones missed a payment (a so-called "acceleration clause"). For purposes of claim preclusion, the scope of bank's "claim" adjudicated in the first case was what it could have sued for (the entire unpaid balance) under the acceleration clause. Thus defined, that claim (or any part of it) disappeared by merging into the first judgment for the two missed installments.[36] The bank was left with its judgment for the two installments, and Jones was left with the car.

---

[31] *E.g., Commissioner v. Sunnen*, 333 U.S. 591, 597 (1948); *Cromwell v. County of Sac*, 94 U.S. 351, 352–53 (1877).

[32] *See* Allan D. Vestal, *Res Judicata/Claim Preclusion: Judgment for the Claimant*, 62 Nw. U. L. Rev. 357, 359–61 (1967); Edward W. Cleary, *Res Judicata Reexamined*, 57 Yale L.J. 339, 343–44 (1948).

[33] "Claim preclusion refers to the effect of a judgment in foreclosing litigation of a matter that never has been litigated, because of a determination that it should have been advanced in an earlier suit." *Migra*, 465 U.S. at 77 n.1.

[34] *Commissioner v. Sunnen*, 333 U.S. 591, 598 (1948).

[35] 191 S.E. 608 (Va. 1937).

[36] *See* § 15.02 (merger generally), *supra*.

The modern extension of claim preclusion from claims that were actually litigated to judgment to related claims that could have been litigated at the same time promotes both finality and efficiency by encouraging a claimant to join together in a single action as many related claims as he has. By holding claimants to the most complete presentation of the claim possible in the initial adjudication, claim preclusion also forecloses switching legal theories of recovery in subsequent litigation. Another casebook favorite, *Roach v. Teamsters Local Union No. 688*,[37] illustrates the point. The plaintiffs sued their union local upon the legal theory that the local breached a duty of fair representation imposed by federal statute. After receiving a disappointing recovery, two of the same plaintiffs brought a second suit against the local, this time under a different federal statute which guaranteed them certain rights as union members. The court held that the first suit precluded the second. "We are convinced," stated the court, "that plaintiffs are attempting to recover for a wrong for which they sought recovery" in the prior case.[38] "A party may not litigate a claim and then, upon unsuccessful disposition, revive the same cause of action with a new theory."[39] Claim preclusion forbids splitting a claim or cause of action by damage (right versus the left fender), remedy (dollars versus injunction), or legal theory (battery versus negligence).

[2] Which Nonidentical Claims Are Precluded?

The extension of claim preclusion to nonidentical but related claims was driven by ever-expanding definitions of the concept of a claim or cause of action. In many jurisdictions, the scope of a cause of action was set either by the evidence or by the nature of the primary right the plaintiff was advancing. However, the publication of the *Restatement (Second) of Judgments* in 1982 prompted a growing number of jurisdictions to embrace a transaction test for the scope of a claim.

[a] Same Evidence or Primary Right

The first *Restatement of Judgments* embraced the *same evidence* test by which claims are deemed the same "if the evidence needed to sustain the second action would have sustained the first action."[40] The difficulty that this test posed is that the evidence is hardly ever completely the same; more often, only much or most of it is the same. But how much overlap is enough? Suppose, for example, that plaintiff sued defendant for his personal injuries in a car accident. After a judgment, plaintiff sues the same defendant for property damages sustained in the same car accident. Clearly, evidence of negligence in the accident would be the same: evidence concerning defendant's breach of his duty of reasonable care in connection with the accident. But evidence of damages would just as clearly be different: evidence of physical injury, medical expenses, and pain and suffering in the first lawsuit versus evidence of damage to plaintiff's car in the second. By a strict application of the

---

[37] 595 F.2d 446 (8th Cir. 1979).

[38] *Id.* at 449.

[39] *Id.* at 450.

[40] RESTATEMENT OF JUDGMENTS § 61 (1942). A few decisions still refer to the test. *See, e.g., Church of New Song v. Establishment of Religion*, 620 F.2d 648, 652 (7th Cir. 1980).

same evidence test, plaintiff would not be claim-precluded from bringing his property damage suit. But by a looser application of the test, requiring only a substantial evidentiary overlap, he would be.

A still narrower test for the scope of a cause of action is the *same right* test, which asks whether the two actions assert infringement of the same right or seek redress for the same legal injury.[41] By this test, our hypothetical plaintiff would not be claim-precluded because his two lawsuits assert different primary rights. The first asserted his primary right to protection from personal injury; the second, his right to protection from property damage. Thus, a California court described its "primary rights theory of causes of action" as:

> the settled rule that conduct that simultaneously causes harm both to the person and to the property of one individual gives rise to two separate and distinct causes of action, one for violation of the right to freedom from legally impermissible interference with the integrity of the person and one for violation of the right to quiet enjoyment of property.[42]

The trouble with this test, however, is that it simply substitutes one abstract inquiry (what is a primary right?) for another (what is the scope of a cause of action?). This test proved imprecise and difficult to apply[43] and has been justly criticized as question-begging.[44] It is also at odds with the modern trend of giving a broader, more functional definition of a claim for purposes of claim preclusion.

Jurisdictions still permitting claim-splitting in accident cases[45] may, therefore, eventually overrule their precedents and adopt the modern approach. This is what the Ohio Supreme Court did in one well-known case, *Rush v. City of Maple Heights*.[46] In *Rush*, the plaintiff suffered a motorcycle accident. She first sued the city for property damage to her motorcycle, alleging that the accident was caused because the city negligently maintained the street. She obtained a final judgment for $100. Thereafter, she sued the city for personal injuries from the same accident and obtained judgment on a verdict for $12,000. The Ohio Supreme Court reversed on the ground that the judgment in the prior case precluded plaintiff's personal injury claim. In so doing, the court abandoned its previous position favoring claim-splitting in accident cases on primary rights grounds.[47] Claim-splitting, it

---

[41] *E.g., Baltimore S.S. Co. v. Phillips*, 274 U.S. 316, 321 (1927) (referring to "single primary right" and to "cause of action" to decide the scope of the judgment).

[42] *Holmes v. David H. Bricker, Inc.*, 452 P.2d 647, 649 (Cal. 1969) (but declining to apply it where plaintiff's claims in both cases were founded on breach of the same express warranty).

[43] *See* CHARLES E. CLARK, CODE PLEADING 134 (2d ed. 1947).

[44] *See* JAMES, HAZARD & LEUBSDORF § 11.9.

[45] Surveys of state jurisdictions permitting claim splitting under these circumstances include Howard M. Erichson, *Interjurisdictional Preclusion*, 96 MICH. L. REV. 945, 974 n.141 (1998); and Andrea G. Nadel, *Simultaneous Injury to Person and Property as Giving Rise to Single Cause of Action*, 24 A.L.R.4TH 646, 685–86 (1983).

[46] 147 N.E.2d 599 (Ohio 1958).

[47] *Vasu v. Kohlers, Inc.*, 61 N.E.2d 707, 712 (Ohio 1945), illustrates the prior position. The Ohio Supreme Court said that: "[I]njuries to both person and property suffered by the same person as a result of the same wrongful act are infringements of different rights, and give rise to distinct causes of action, with the result that the recovery or denial of recovery of compensation for damages to the property is

said, "is in conflict with the great weight of authority in this country and has caused vexatious litigation."[48]

[b]   Same Transaction

The foregoing problems with the same evidence and primary rights tests for defining the scope of a cause of action or, in the vernacular of the federal rules, a claim, led most courts to adopt more expansive and pragmatic definitions. Section 24 of the American Law Institute's *Restatement (Second) of Judgments* exemplifies this modern approach and has been quite influential.[49] Section 24 advances a *transaction* test. It defines the claim precluded by the judgment to include "all rights of the plaintiff to remedies against the defendant with respect to all or any part of the transaction, or series of connected transactions, out of which the [original] action arose." According to the section, "transaction" and "series" of transactions:

> are to be determined pragmatically, giving weight to such considerations as whether the facts are related in time, space, origin, or motivation, whether they form a convenient trial unit, and whether their treatment as a unit conforms to the parties' expectations or business understanding or usage.

Applying this test to the prior hypothetical, it is clear that the plaintiff who first sued for his personal injuries would be claim-precluded by the judgment from suing for property damages from the same accident. Whatever the evidentiary overlap or the primary rights he asserts, both claims arise from the same transaction — the car accident. He therefore should have brought them together in a single proceeding and cannot now assert a new, but transactionally related claim. The transaction test is factually based and pragmatic, and it promotes efficiency because it helps to assure that the facts of the transaction have to be sifted only once. It takes added force from its similarity to the federal rules' formula for joinder of compulsory counterclaims, cross-claims, permissive joinder of parties, and intervention of right, which is copied by many states.[50]

The transaction test is not applied in the same way by all courts that have adopted it (or something like it). For example, some courts "measure the claim by reference to a single transaction or occurrence, all grounds for relief arising out of the conduct complained of, operative facts, or even a 'factual clone.' "[51]

---

no bar to an action subsequently prosecuted for the personal injury."

[48]   147 N.E.2d at 604.

[49]   It is difficult to overstate its influence. Even in draft form, the work's treatment of the law of *res judicata* shaped many judicial decisions. Like the *Restatements* generally, it is a combination of what the law currently seems to be and what the writers would like the law to be. *See* Herbert Wechsler, *Restatements and Legal Change: Problems of Policy in the Restatement Work of the American Law Institute*, 13 St. Louis U. L.J. 185 (1968).

[50]   *See* §§ 9.03 (compulsory counterclaims), 9.04 (cross-claims), 9.05[1] (permissive party joinder); 9.08[1] (intervention of right), *supra*.

[51]   Wright & Miller § 4407.

Section 24 is, however, the most influential contemporary claim preclusion test. Many state jurisdictions have adopted it.[52] Many lower federal courts have incorporated Section 24 into federal preclusion doctrine,[53] and the Supreme Court has discussed the section with apparent approval.[54]

[3]   Preclusion of Defendants

Recall that a final judgment on the merits can preclude not only subsequent claims but also most defenses that were or could have been interposed in the original adjudication.[55] Similarly, a final judgment on the merits of any counterclaim (or cross-claim or third-party claim) asserted by the defendant carries the same claim-preclusive effect as a judgment on plaintiff's claim.[56]

Treatment of counterclaims that were available but were not asserted in the prior adjudication is a different and more complicated matter. Under what circumstances is defendant forced to present his claim as a counterclaim or lose it thereafter through preclusion?

When a defendant who has been claimed against intends to make a claim in return which is based on the same subject matter, it is more efficient for the defendant to add the second claim to the original suit than to bring a new suit upon it later. The time and expense taken up in trying the two claims will be significantly reduced if they can be tried together. If the same party held two claims that were so related, the doctrine of claim preclusion would in most jurisdictions keep him from splitting the claims and withholding one for later suit. A few commentators[57] and courts[58] have therefore also treated a counterclaim sufficiently related to the original claim as within the doctrine of claim preclusion.

But there is a significant countervailing consideration. Unlike the plaintiff, who chose the time and place to bring her claim, the defendant is an involuntary party. If claim preclusion applied to a transactionally related counterclaim, a defendant would be forced to bring it at a time and in a forum of the plaintiff's choosing, not

---

[52] *See, e.g., Hadley v. Cowan*, 804 P.2d 1271, 1276 (Wash. App. 1991); *Post v. Schwall*, 460 N.W.2d 794, 797 (Wis. App. 1990); *Kauhane v. Acutron Co.*, 795 P.2d 276, 279 (Haw. 1990). Professor Friedenthal earlier found that a majority of states had already embraced a "same operative facts" test indistinguishable in most respects from the transaction test of the RESTATEMENT (SECOND) OF JUDGMENTS. Jack H. Friedenthal, *Joinder of Claims, Counterclaims, and Cross-Complaints: Suggested Revision of the California Provisions*, 23 STAN. L. REV. 1, 12-13 (1970).

[53] *E.g., Kale v. Combined Ins. Co. of Am.*, 924 F.2d 1161, 1166 (1st Cir.), *cert. denied*, 502 U.S. 816 (1991); *Aliff v. Joy Mfg. Co.*, 914 F.2d 39, 43 (4th Cir. 1990); *Smith v. Safeco Ins. Co.*, 863 F.2d 403, 404 (5th Cir. 1989).

[54] *Nevada v. United States*, 463 U.S. 110, 130 (1983).

[55] *See* § 15.02, *supra*. To this extent, it can be said that the *res judicata* rule applied to the defendant is the "mirror image" of that applied to plaintiff. FRIEDENTHAL, KANE & MILLER § 14.6.

[56] "A defendant who interposes a counterclaim is, in substance, a plaintiff, as far as the counterclaim is concerned, and the plaintiff is, in substance, a defendant." RESTATEMENT (SECOND) OF JUDGMENTS § 23 comment a (1982).

[57] *E.g., Developments in the Law — Res Judicata*, 65 HARV. L. REV., 818, 831–32 (1952).

[58] *See Great Lakes Rubber Corp. v. Herbert Cooper Co.*, 286 F.2d 631 (3d Cir. 1961), and the decisions cited in WRIGHT & MILLER § 1417.

her own, or find herself precluded from ever bringing it. Because of this unfairness, in many jurisdictions the common law of claim preclusion does not apply to transactionally related counterclaims.[59]

On the other hand, weighing the efficiency of preclusion against the unfairness to defendants, the federal rules and the rules of civil procedure in many other jurisdictions opted for efficiency by making such claims compulsory, overriding the common law. The result is sometimes called *rule preclusion*, or perhaps more accurately, *estoppel by rule*.[60]

For example, Federal Rule 13(a)(1) states:

> A pleading must state as a counterclaim any claim that — at the time of its service — the pleader has against an opposing party if the claim: (A) arises out of the transaction or occurrence that is the subject matter of the opposing party's claim . . . .[61]

A majority of states have adopted a rule like Rule 13(a) as part of their local rules of procedure.[62] The relationship between two claims described in Rule 13(a) is much like that required for claim preclusion.[63] Claim preclusion and compulsory counterclaim rules also share common goals. Each is "designed to settle the entire dispute between the parties in one proceeding as fairly as that may be done" and to "conserve judicial resources."[64]

Even in jurisdictions that have not overridden the common law by adopting a compulsory counterclaim rule, however, the common law's generosity to defendants

---

[59] *See* RESTATEMENT (SECOND) OF JUDGMENTS § 22 (1982)

[60] *See generally* ALAN D. VESTAL, RES JUDICATA/PRECLUSION 150–63 (1969). "In many ways this analysis provides a more apposite and useful approach to the problem of omitted counterclaims than does the doctrine of claim preclusion." WRIGHT & MILLER § 1417.

[61] "Although Rule 13(a) does not explain the consequences of failure to plead a compulsory counterclaim, virtually all courts agree that a party who fails to plead a compulsory counterclaim cannot raise that claim in subsequent litigation." Michael D. Conway, Comment, *Narrowing the Scope of Rule 13(a)*, 60 U. CHI. L. REV. 141, 141 (1993). The rule does not apply when the counterclaim requires "adding another party over whom the court cannot acquire jurisdiction." This provision contemplates territorial jurisdiction and not federal subject matter jurisdiction. Rule 13(a) also protects defendant's refusal to plead the counterclaim if, "when the action was commenced, the claim was the subject of another pending action," or when "the opposing party sued on its claim by attachment or other process that did not establish personal jurisdiction over the pleader on that claim, and the pleader does not assert any counterclaim under this rule." *See generally* § 9.03 (counterclaims), *supra*. The second exception "provides defendant with the option of continuing the prior action rather than advancing it as a counterclaim in the second action without fear of it being barred if the second action results in a judgment before the claim has been adjudicated in the first action." WRIGHT & MILLER § 1411.

[62] *See* John B. Oakley & Arthur F. Coon, *The Federal Rules in State Courts: A Survey of State Court Systems of Civil Procedure*, 61 WASH. L. REV. 1367 (1986). *But see* DAVID SIEGEL, N.Y. CIV. PRAC. L. & R. § 3019 commentary (McKinney 1991). "All counterclaims are permissive in New York: D can use his claim as a counterclaim or save it and sue on it separately. D may save it for separate suit even when it is a related counterclaim, i.e., when it arises out of the same transaction or occurrence as P's claim." DAVID SIEGEL, NEW YORK PRACTICE § 224, at 384 (5th ed. 2011)(citation omitted).

[63] *See, e.g.*, the claim comparison required under § 24 of the RESTATEMENT (SECOND) OF JUDGMENTS, discussed at § 115.03[2], *supra*.

[64] Eugene F. Scoles, *Interstate Preclusion by Prior Litigation*, 74 NW. U. L. REV. 742, 753 (1979).

may be more apparent than real. First, the common law of preclusion gives preclusive effect to defenses which could have been raised in the first suit,[65] and the facts pertaining to some defenses may also present a potential counterclaim. In such circumstances, defendant cannot always safely predict whether he will be barred from suing on the same facts for an affirmative recovery in a later action.[66] Second, even when claim preclusion poses no bar, issue preclusion may defeat the later action by precluding defendant from relitigating issues of fact or law necessary to establish his counterclaim.[67] Finally, some jurisdictions that allow defendants to withhold counterclaims for subsequent suit nevertheless bar subsequent suits which are so closely related to the prior suit that they pose a serious risk of logically irreconcilable judgments.[68] The last problem can even occur for federal court defendants who otherwise satisfy one of the exceptions to federal Rule 13(a).[69]

[4] The "Could-Have-Brought" Requirement: The Prior Court's Power to Hear the Omitted Claim

The extension of claim preclusion beyond the claims that were actually litigated to claims that were not rests not only on a same evidence, same primary right, or, in the modern and majority view, same transaction relationship between the claims, but also on the assumption that the unasserted claims *could have been brought* in the prior court. Claims could have been brought if the first court had subject matter and personal jurisdiction to hear them, and if the first court's joinder rules permitted their joinder. Contrariwise, claim preclusion does not apply when:

> [t]he plaintiff was unable to rely on a certain theory of the case or to seek a certain remedy or form of relief in the first action because of the limitations on the subject matter jurisdiction of the courts or restrictions on their authority to entertain multiple theories or demands for multiple remedies or forms of relief in a single action, and the plaintiff desires in the second action to rely on that theory or to seek that remedy or form of relief.[70]

---

[65] *See* § 15.02 *supra.*

[66] *Compare, e.g., Mitchell v. Federal Intermediate Credit Bank*, 164 S.E. 136 (S.C. 1932) (judgment on debtor's payment defense to suit on a note precluded debtor's independent action to recover excess payment from creditor), *with Virginia-Carolina Chem. Co. v. Kirven*, 215 U.S. 252 (1909) (judgment in seller's action for payment did not preclude purchaser's subsequent action for damages caused by goods sold). *But see generally* RESTATEMENT (SECOND) OF JUDGMENTS § 22 comment d (1982) (mere defensive assertion of facts should not preclude subsequent use of same facts by defendant in suit for affirmative recovery).

[67] *See* § 15.06 (comparing claim and issue preclusion), *infra.*

[68] *See, e.g., University of N. H. v. April*, 347 A.2d 446, 450–51 (N.H. 1975); *Chicot County Drainage Dist. v. Baxter State Bank*, 308 U.S. 371 (1940).

[69] The problem comes when plaintiff's original suit is dismissed before defendant was obligated to assert an otherwise compulsory counterclaim. *See Martino v. McDonald's Sys., Inc.*, 598 F.2d 1079 (7th Cir. 1979) ("counterclaim exception to the *res judicata* rule" does not permit prosecution of a claim that "would nullify rights established by the prior action").

[70] RESTATEMENT (SECOND) OF JUDGMENTS § 26(1)(c) (1982).

For example, when a party is injured by conduct that is both actionable under state law and under a federal statute providing an exclusively federal remedy, an adverse judgment in a state court action should not preclude the plaintiff from pursuing his exclusively federal remedy for the same conduct.[71] He could not have brought the federal claim in his state court action. In *Marrese v. American Academy of Orthopaedic Surgeons*,[72] the Supreme Court said that, "[i]f state preclusion law includes this requirement of prior jurisdictional competency [that is, subject matter jurisdiction of the prior court over the omitted claim], which is generally true, a state judgment will not have claim preclusive effect on a cause of action within the exclusive jurisdiction of the federal courts." It thus left the preclusion question to the rendering state's preclusion law, but acknowledged it is "generally true" that a claim that could not have been brought because of limitations on the first court's subject matter jurisdiction will not be claim-precluded by its judgment. The Court's opinion leaves open the possibility, however, that the plaintiff could be issue-precluded.[73]

Yet the plaintiff in the hypothetical might have brought both claims in *federal* court. Even if the parties are not diverse, the federal court would have federal question subject matter jurisdiction over the federal claim and supplemental jurisdiction over the transactionally related state law claim. An aggressive application of claim preclusion might hold the plaintiff precluded by the state court judgment from asserting the federal claim because he could have brought both claims in a *different* court — the federal court. Arguably, however, this is a stretch too far, as it not only looks to a different possible forum, but, on these facts, assumes that the federal court would have exercised its discretion to hear the supplemental state law claim, rather than dismiss it.[74]

On the other hand, the same reasoning has not barred claim preclusion when a plaintiff has voluntarily sued in a state court of limited jurisdiction (for example, a small claims court), and then tried to sue for additional relief for the same transaction or occurrence in a state court of general jurisdiction. "Although res judicata does not force the plaintiff to abandon the state court system for the federal court system, it does effectively force the plaintiff into an appropriate state court."[75]

[5] Expanding the Reach of Claim Preclusion?

Given the general trend in *res judicata* developments toward greater preclusion,[76] and the urging of many commentators that expansion continue,[77] other courts probably have been tempted in some cases to dispense even with a

---

[71] *Id.* cmt.

[72] 470 U.S. 373, 382 (1985).

[73] *See* FRIEDENTHAL, KANE, & MILLER § 14.12.

[74] *See* 28 U.S.C. § 1367(c) (2012).

[75] ROBERT C. CASAD & KEVIN M. CLERMONT, RES JUDICATA 100 (2001).

[76] *See* § 15.01[2][c], *supra*.

[77] *See, e.g.*, for arguments expanding the scope of claim preclusion, Michael J. Waggoner, *Fifty Years of Bernhard v. Bank of America is Enough: Collateral Estoppel Should Require Mutuality But Res Judicata Should Not*, 12 REV. LITIG. 391 (1993); Robert G. Bone, *Rethinking the "Day in Court" Ideal*

required nexus between a claim actually presented in the prior adjudication and the claim sought to be precluded.[78] It can be argued that such expansion achieves added judicial economy and evokes a familiar theme in claim preclusion doctrine by focusing on what the claimant could have done in the first case.[79]

On balance, however, it may be unwise to so extend claim preclusion. Such an expansion would sometimes force a claimant to join dissimilar claims in the original proceeding, and benefits to litigants and the courts from forced joinder of dissimilar claims are doubtful.

> Where . . . claims are factually quite distinct so that there will be no overlap in presenting evidence to support them, much less is to be saved by trying them together, or including them in a single lawsuit to be tried separately. Indeed, trying them together may cause confusion and prejudice.[80]

Another enlarged form of claim preclusion occurs when a court uses the doctrine to block a claim related to one presented by the same plaintiff in earlier litigation although the subsequent claim was unforeseeable at the time of the original case. This has occurred in latent disease litigation. Harm from asbestos exposure provides an example. "Typically, victims first suffer asbestosis; many years later, some of the same victims also develop cancer."[81] The flexible construction of statutes of limitation in such cases suggest a fair and sensible approach. The statute is tolled until plaintiff has been able to discover the subsequent and more serious consequence of asbestos exposure. That approach would be nullified if plaintiffs were claim-precluded by their failure to bring unforeseen claims.[82]

It is true that, in this setting, the claim making up plaintiff's successive case is often so closely related as to satisfy that requirement for claim preclusion. But to apply claim preclusion disregards another requirement that should be understood as fundamental to the operation of the doctrine — that it was foreseeable to plaintiff

---

and Nonparty Preclusion, 67 N.Y.U. L. Rev. 193 (1992).

[78] Alternatively, the New Jersey Supreme Court has used its so-called "Entire Controversy" Doctrine to preclude plaintiffs from later proceeding against different defendants in a later lawsuit when the subsequent claims were related to a claim made against a different defendant in an earlier case. *See Cogdell v. Hospital Ctr.*, 116 N.J. 7, 560 A.2d 1169 (1989); *Mortgagelinq Corp. v. Commonwealth Land Title Ins. Co.*, 662 A.2d 536 (N.J. 1995). The doctrine has been justly criticized. Symposium, *Entire Controversy Doctrine*, 28 Rutgers L.J. 1 (1996)

[79] *Cf.* Robert Ziff, Note, *For One Litigant's Sole Relief: Unforeseeable Preclusion and the Second Restatement*, 77 Cornell L. Rev. 905, 922 (1992) ("Because the benefits of res judicata depend on the expectation of preclusion shaping litigants' behavior, res judicata only makes sense if it is foreseeable.").

[80] Fleming James, et. al, Civil Procedure § 11.10 (5th ed. 2001). Professor James suggested that fear of claim waiver generated by a rule requiring claimant to join dissimilar claims in the first case might defeat judicial economy by forcing parties to introduce claims that would not otherwise have been litigated. At the same time, consequences from the omission of insufficiently related claims would be too severe: "Hardship from oversight would be greatly multiplied if the parties were bound to think of all the aspects of all possible claims against their adversaries." *Id.* at 556.

[81] Note, *Claim Preclusion in Modern Latent Disease Cases: A Proposal for Allowing Second Suits*, 103 Harv. L. Rev. 1989, 1989 (1990).

[82] *Claim Preclusion in Modern Latent Disease Cases: A Proposal for Allowing Second Suits*, note 81, *supra*, at 1990–98.

when he omitted the claim from the first case that the omitted claim could be the subject of future litigation.[83] Claim preclusion stops making sense and becomes quite unfair when it is used to punish plaintiff's failure to do the impossible.

§ 15.04 THE IDENTITY-OF-PARTIES REQUIREMENT

[1] The Relation Between the Identity-of-Parties Requirement and the Meaning of Claim

The general rule has long been that strangers[84] to a prior adjudication can neither bind nor be bound by claim preclusion.[85] The technical reason for this is that claims are personal and unique to parties; one party's claim is, by definition, different from another party's claim even if they are otherwise the same and arise from the same transaction.[86] This narrow reading of a claim for purposes of claim preclusion does not seem entirely consistent with the rule that non-identical yet similar claims between the same parties are subject to claim preclusion,[87] and it stands in contrast to the widespread use of issue preclusion *by* strangers to the original proceeding.[88]

Perhaps a better contemporary justification of the identity-of-parties limitation on claim preclusion rests on concerns of party fairness. While issue preclusion usually applies only to fully litigated matters,[89] claim preclusion extinguishes unlitigated claims and attaches even to default judgments.[90] It may be only fair to confine the effects of such broad-spectrum preclusion to parties in the first case or those in close relation to them.[91]

---

[83] *See* note 79, *supra.*

[84] In the terminology of *res judicata*/preclusion, those neither parties to nor involved with the prior adjudication are called "strangers" to it.

[85] *See, e.g.,* ALAN D. VESTAL, RES JUDICATA/PRECLUSION 50–51 (1969) (stating American, Canadian and English law to be in accord on the principle that "a judgment against one tortfeasor is not a bar to an action against another.") Notwithstanding this rule, it is possible to bind passive members of a plaintiff class without their active involvement in the case. For discussion of how class actions work and of the special treatment they receive under the Constitution, *see* §§ 4.02[1] (constitutional concerns) & 9.09 (class actions generally), *supra.*

[86] *See, e.g., Developments in the Law — Res Judicata,* 65 HARV. L. REV. 818, 861–62 (1952) ("since a different party is involved in the second action, the cause of action must be different."). *Montana v. United States,* 440 U.S. 147, 154 (1979), makes the same point.

[87] *See* § 15.03, *supra.*

[88] *See* § 15.08[2], *infra.*

[89] *See* § 15.07[2], *infra.*

[90] *See* § 15.05 and related text, *infra.*

[91] *See, e.g., Taylor v. Sturgell,* 128 S. Ct. 2161 (2008) (refusing to use claim preclusion to bind a nonparty to earlier litigation).

[2] The Claim-Preclusive Effect of Judgments Upon Those in Close Relation to Parties

Parties not actually named in the original case may be subject to claim preclusion if they are sufficiently related to original parties. Courts often describe the relationship as *privity*.[92] Privity, however, is merely a conclusory label for situations where courts have been willing to stretch the identity-of-parties requirement in order to find claim preclusion. Professor Vestal wrote: "Involved seems to be the idea that the precluded party's interests were represented in the first suit, or that the precluded party should have no greater interest than did the losing party in the first suit."[93] A classic example of privity is a party's sale or assignment of his interests to a non-party after commencement of the litigation. The transferee of the interest is then considered bound by a judgment affecting the interest.[94] Courts have used the concept of privity to extend preclusion in many other settings.[95]

It is possible to express the principle represented by privity without using the term itself.[96] But, in all cases, it is necessary that the closeness of the relationship bear on the claim which was the subject of the first case. In *Taylor v. Sturgell*,[97] the Supreme Court identified six categories of persons who have a sufficiently close relationship to parties to the first action that they can be precluded by its judgment: first, a person who has agreed to be bound; second, a person who has a pre-existing legal relationship with parties, such as assignor-assignee; third, a person who was adequately represented in the first lawsuit by someone with the same interests, such as a class representative in a certified class action; fourth, a person who had effective control over the first lawsuit; fifth, a person who is merely a proxy or agent for a party in the first lawsuit; and, finally, a person who is foreclosed by a statutory scheme such as bankruptcy from bringing claims. The Court was also emphatic that these established categories were not only narrow,

---

[92] *E.g., Federated Dep't Stores, Inc. v. Moitie*, 452 U.S. 394, 398 (1981) ("A final judgment on the merits of an action precludes the parties or their privies from relitigating issues that were or could have been raised in that action.").

[93] VESTAL, note 85, *supra*, at 121.

[94] *Id.*

[95]

> This same concept is applied in the case of lessor and lessee and mortgagor and mortgagee where the transfer is made after the start of the litigation in Suit I. This same closeness sufficient to ground preclusion is also found in the case of various governmental agencies, guardian and ward, corporation and stockholders, and bankrupt and trustees. In community property states, husband and wife may be held to be in privity. Finally, in the case of a decedent and his successors in interest, the courts have found the closeness so that the label of "privity" may be applied.

VESTAL, note 85, *supra*, at 122–23.

[96] For example, without using the term privity, the American Law Institute's *Restatement (Second) of Judgments* § 48 (1982) describes circumstances under which one member of the family may be precluded by a prior case brought by another family member for damage to a familial relationship. For additional discussion of parties within the reach of mainstream claim preclusion, see Waggoner, note 77, *supra*, at 395–96; Bone, note 77, *supra*, at 197.

[97] 553 U.S. 880 (2008).

but exclusive. It rejected the argument that a person was precluded because he had been "virtually represented" by a friend with similar interests in the first lawsuit.

§ 15.05   THE JUDGMENT MUST BE FINAL AND ON THE MERITS

A lawsuit cannot have preclusive effect until it has been reduced to final judgment.[98] The law governing finality of a judgment is that of the judicial system where the judgment was rendered (although the Supreme Court has said that the claim-preclusive effect of a dismissal by a federal court sitting in diversity should be measured by its forum state's preclusion law).[99] Court systems have different views about what must happen before their judgments become final. Federal courts regard their judgments to be final even if the case is under appeal.[100] In contrast, some state systems do not give finality to their judgments as long as there is a possibility that the outcome will be changed through appeal.[101]

Only judgments on the merits are entitled to claim-preclusive effect. Judgments in favor of the plaintiff are considered to be on the merits. This is true even if the judgment was rendered by default, stipulation between the parties, or summary judgment.[102]

Judgments on the merits for defendants have the same preclusive effect. However, defendants often obtain judgments on defenses that do not reach the merits. For example, the defendant may successfully argue that the court lacks personal jurisdiction over him[103] or that an absentee indispensable to the case cannot be brought before the court.[104] Similarly, a defendant in federal court may successfully question the court's subject matter jurisdiction[105] or venue.[106] In such instances, the case is terminated without prejudice to plaintiff's right to refile in a

---

[98] RESTATEMENT (SECOND) OF JUDGMENTS § 13 (1982).

[99] *Semtek Int'l Inc. v. Lockheed Martin Corp.*, 531 U.S. 497, 508 (2001) ("[N]ationwide uniformity in the substance of the matter is better served by having the same claim-preclusive rule (the state rule) apply whether the dismissal has been ordered by a state or a federal court. This is, it seems to us, a classic case for adopting, as the federally prescribed rule of decision, the law that would be applied by state courts in the State in which the federal diversity court sits.").

[100] "Should the judgment be vacated by the trial court or reversed on appeal, however, *res judicata* falls with the judgment." WRIGHT & MILLER § 4427.

[101] *See, e.g.*, the discussion of Utah state law in *Chavez v. Morris*, 566 F. Supp. 359 (D. Utah 1983).

[102] *Cf.* RESTATEMENT (SECOND) OF JUDGMENTS § 18 comment a (1982) ("It is immaterial whether the judgment was rendered upon a verdict or upon a motion to dismiss or upon consent, confession, or default."). Courts are divided concerning the preclusive effect of dismissals based on the legal insufficiency of pleadings. Federal decisions generally regard such dismissals under Rule 12(b)(6) to be preclusive. *See, e.g., Federated Dep't Stores, Inc. v. Moitie*, 452 U.S. 394, 399 n.3 (1981). Many state decisions (either styling their motions in the manner of the federal rule or in the earlier form of demurrer) take the same view. But some do not. *See, e.g., In re Estate of Cochrane*, 391 N.E.2d 35 (Ill. App. Ct. 1979).

[103] *See* Chapter 3 (territorial jurisdiction), *supra.*

[104] *See* § 9.05[2] (compulsory party joinder), *supra.*

[105] *See* Chapter 5, *supra.*

[106] *See* Chapter 6, *supra.*

court where the defect which led to initial dismissal can be avoided. Orders dismissing such cases are not judgments on the merits and, hence, do not have claim-preclusive effect.

Rule 41(b) of the Federal Rules of Civil Procedure reflects some of these same principles by providing: "Unless the dismissal order states otherwise, a dismissal under this sub-section (b) and any dismissal not under this rule — except one for lack of jurisdiction, improper venue, or failure to join a party under Rule 19 — operates as an adjudication on the merits."[107] However, the Supreme Court has held that the rule does not state any general rule of preclusion, in part because interpreting it as such could in diversity cases threaten to abridge substantive rights in violation of the Rules Enabling Act.[108] Instead, it interpreted the Rule only to bar a dismissed party from refiling in the same federal court unless the dismissal was for one of the listed reasons.[109] The broader claim-preclusive effect of a dismissal in federal court is still decided by federal common law, which measures the effect of dismissal by a federal court sitting in diversity by its forum state law.[110]

PART B.
ISSUE PRECLUSION

§ 15.06 ISSUE AND CLAIM PRECLUSION COMPARED

[1] How Issue Preclusion Supplements Claim Preclusion

The function of issue preclusion (collateral estoppel) is to advance the objectives of *res judicata*[111] beyond the confines of claim preclusion. Thus, it gives a final adjudication preclusive effect in a subsequent case which cannot be said, even in the broadest sense, to share the same claim.

In some cases, issue preclusion operates where claim preclusion obviously could not apply. For example, a criminal proceeding may be capable of generating issue-preclusive effects on a subsequent civil proceeding.[112] The convicted felon may be

---

[107] However, the federal rule has not always been applied literally to other dismissals "in which the merits could not be reached for failure of the plaintiff to satisfy a precondition." *Costello v. United States*, 365 U.S. 265, 286 (1961). For example, in *Saylor v. Lindsley*, 391 F.2d 965 (2d Cir. 1968), the court declined to give claim-preclusive effect to a dismissal "with prejudice" for failure to post a bond for costs, reasoning that the defendant had not been put to the burden of preparing a defense to the first litigation and would therefore not be unduly inconvenienced by having to defend the second.

[108] *Semtek*, 531 U.S. at 503–04.

[109] *Id.* at 506.

[110] *Id.* at 508–509.

[111] *See* § 15.01[1], *supra.*

[112] *E.g., Allen v. McCurry*, 449 U.S. 90 (1980); *White Earth Band of Chippewa Indians v. Alexander*, 683 F.2d 1129 (8th Cir.), *cert. denied*, 459 U.S. 1070 (1982). However, different burdens of proof for civil and criminal proceedings limit the range of issues which are identical in the sense required by claim preclusion. *See generally* RESTATEMENT (SECOND) OF JUDGMENTS § 85 (1982); Susan W. Brenner, *"Crossing Over": The Issue Preclusive Effects of a Civil/Criminal Adjudication Upon a Proceeding of the Opposite*

precluded from relitigating whether he committed the criminal act in a later lawsuit for damages by the victim. In other cases the distinction between issue and claim preclusion is more subtle. Suppose, for example, that a lawyer sues his client for his fees. The client defends on the grounds that the lawyer gave bad advice, but loses. Now the client sues his lawyer for legal malpractice based on the same advice. Absent a compulsory counterclaim rule, the client is not precluded from bringing the malpractice action by the judgment in the first lawsuit. Claim and defense preclusion usually excepts transactionally related counterclaims in order to permit defendants like the client to sue on his claim at a time and in a forum of his own choosing. However, if the quality of the lawyer's advice was actually litigated and decided in the first lawsuit for fees, and the fact finder's determination in that suit that the advice was sound was necessary to the judgment (as it would be if bad advice was a defense to the lawyer's fee claim), then the client is issue-precluded from relitigating the adequacy of the advice. The lawyer can move for summary judgment in the malpractice lawsuit on the grounds that an essential element of the client's claim — the soundness of his advice — was decided adversely to the client by the first lawsuit.[113]

Issue preclusion may have the same effect when a plaintiff brings successive property damage and personal injury lawsuits arising out of the same automobile accident. In the minority of jurisdictions that permit the second suit,[114] issue preclusion may yet defeat the second claim. If plaintiff lost the first property damage suit upon a finding of contributory negligence, issue preclusion may deny him the opportunity to relitigate his own negligence in his subsequent personal injury action. Conversely, if plaintiff established negligence and recovered in the property damage suit, then plaintiff might argue issue preclusion to advance his personal injury claim in the second lawsuit.[115]

Character, 7 N. ILL. U. L. REV. 141 (1987); David L. Shapiro, *Should a Guilty Plea Have Preclusive Effect?*, 70 IOWA L. REV. 27 (1984).

Another example of how issue preclusion operates in a sphere separate from claim preclusion may occur in civil litigation, when a prior court decides the identical issue without addressing the merits of plaintiff's claim. *E.g.*, *Deckert v. Wachovia Student Fin. Servs., Inc.*, 963 F.2d 816 (5th Cir. 1992) (preclusive effect given by a Texas federal court to a prior Texas state court ruling that personal jurisdiction for plaintiff's case was lacking in Texas).

[113] *See, e.g.*, *Felger v. Nichols*, 370 A.2d 141 (Md. 1977).

[114] *See* § 15.03, *supra*.

[115] In that event, defendant might argue claim preclusion, hoping to change the *res judicata* law of the jurisdiction. This is what happened in *Rush v. City of Maple Heights*, 147 N.E.2d 599 (Ohio 1958), discussed in § 15.03[4][a], *supra*. Ohio state trial and intermediate courts ruled in favor of plaintiff on issue preclusion grounds. Given the fairness concerns that should temper applications of issue preclusion, *see* § 15.08[4], *infra*, application of the doctrine against the defendant in *Rush* is open to criticism. The matter became academic when the Ohio Supreme Court reversed and ordered dismissal of the case by invoking *claim* preclusion.

[2] How Guarantees of Procedural Fairness Limit Each Doctrine

A fundamental guarantee of our judicial process is that no one may have his rights extinguished by a judgment unless he has first received a full and fair opportunity for a hearing. This idea provides an important check on *both* claim and issue preclusion.[116] It means that the preclusive weight of a final judgment must be commensurate with the opportunities for litigation which preceded it. Claim preclusion prevents a litigant from raising new issues based on the same transaction, but usually only upon a demonstration that the party to be bound could have raised the new matters in the first case. Issue preclusion extinguishes issues that claim preclusion cannot reach, but only those that were actually litigated in a prior adjudication and necessary to judgment. Finally, for both kinds of preclusion, courts have increasingly been willing to consider the fairness of the procedures and resulting litigation opportunity in the first lawsuit.

§ 15.07 THE SAME ISSUE MUST HAVE BEEN LITIGATED, DETERMINED AND NECESSARY TO THE JUDGMENT IN THE PRIOR CASE

[1] The Identity-of-Issues Requirement

Issue preclusion (collateral estoppel) can operate only if the issues in the original and the succeeding proceeding are identical. Generally, issues of either law or fact qualify.[117] This is true even though stray courts have occasionally suggested that issue preclusion is not available for issues of law[118] and might be available only as to issues of "ultimate" fact.[119]

---

[116] To preclude parties without affording such fairness protections raises serious questions under the Due Process Clauses of the Fifth and Fourteenth Amendments to the United States Constitution. *See* Jack Ratliff, *Offensive Collateral Estoppel and the Option Effect*, 67 Tex. L. Rev. 63, 64 (1988); James R. Pielemeier, *Due Process Limitations on the Application of Collateral Estoppel Against Nonparties to Prior Litigation*, 63 B.U. L. Rev. 383 (1983); Robert C. Casad, *Intersystem Issue Preclusion and the Restatement (Second) of Judgments*, 66 Cornell L. Rev. 510, 517 (1981); Barbara A. Atwood, *State Court Judgments in Federal Litigation: Mapping the Contours of Full Faith and Credit*, 58 Ind. L.J. 59, 69–70 n.54 (1982). See, in addition, the Supreme Court decisions discussed in § 15.08, *infra*.

[117] Restatement (Second) of Judgments § 27 (1982).

[118] *E.g., United States v. Moser*, 266 U.S. 236 (1924). For a critique of this proposition, *see* Friedenthal, Kane & Miller § 14.10. The principle that issues of pure law should not be subject to issue preclusion has been hard to articulate and to apply consistently, particularly because it is often difficult to distinguish among issues of law, fact, and mixed law and fact. On preclusion of issues of law generally, see Restatement (Second) of Judgments § 28(2) (1982); Colin H. Buckley, *Issue Preclusion and Issues of Law: A Doctrinal Framework Based on Rules of Recognition, Jurisdiction and Legal History*, 24 Houston L. Rev. 875 (1987); Geoffrey C. Hazard, Jr., *Preclusion as to Issues of Law: The Legal System's Interest*, 70 Iowa L. Rev. 81, 86–87 (1984).

[119] The leading case for the latter proposition is *The Evergreens v. Nunan*, 141 F.2d 927 (2d Cir.), *cert. denied*, 323 U.S. 720 (1944). The case attaches importance to the difference between ultimate facts (which support conclusions of law) and factual determinations leading up to ultimate facts (which are only conclusions of "evidentiary" or "mediate" fact). This has not been a very effective tool for limiting issue preclusion, since "[t]he line between ultimate and evidentiary facts is often impossible to draw."

Courts have stressed that the identity-of-issue requirement should be taken literally. For example, in *Commissioner v. Sunnen*,[120] the Supreme Court refused to give preclusive effect to a prior Tax Court determination that a wife's income was not taxable to her husband, even though the original and succeeding cases both involved the husband's practice of transferring rights under patent contracts to his wife. The Court observed that collateral estoppel (issue preclusion) "must be confined to situations where the matter raised in the second suit is identical in all respects with that decided in the first proceeding and where the controlling facts and applicable legal rules remain unchanged."[121]

At the same time, litigants cannot escape issue preclusion by dressing up previously litigated issues to make them appear new. This is true even though a litigant can demonstrate that differences in factual support or legal argument might cause the issue to be resolved differently in the succeeding case.

> Thus, for example, if the party against whom preclusion is sought did in fact litigate an issue of ultimate fact and suffered an adverse determination, new evidentiary facts may not be brought forward to obtain a different determination of that ultimate fact. . . . And similarly if the issue was one of law, new arguments may not be presented to obtain a different determination of that issue.[122]

In this way, issue preclusion is like claim preclusion[123] in pressuring litigants to be complete in their initial presentations.

[2]   The Issue Must Have Been Litigated and Determined in the Prior Case

Probably the central feature setting issue preclusion apart from claim preclusion is that the former only precludes matters which were actually litigated and determined in the prior case.[124] "Actually litigated" means that the parties put on evidence, or had the opportunity to offer evidence, on the issue, and "determined" means that the fact finder decided the issue. Trials provide a frequent but not exclusive means for determining issues. "An issue may be submitted and determined on a motion to dismiss for failure to state a claim, a

---

RESTATEMENT (SECOND) OF JUDGMENTS § 27 comment j (1982). For the same reason, the distinction caused problems in code pleading and was abandoned in the federal pleading rules. *See* §§ 8.03[3] (specificity of fact pleading under the codes) & 8.04[1] (specificity of notice pleading), *supra*.

[120]   333 U.S. 591 (1948).

[121]   333 U.S. at 599–600. *Accord, United States v. Watts*, 519 U.S. 148, 156 (1997) ("an acquittal in a criminal case does not preclude the Government from relitigating an issue when it is presented in a subsequent action governed by a lower standard of proof." (quoting *Dowling v. United States*, 493 U.S. 342, 349 (1990)).

[122]   RESTATEMENT (SECOND) OF JUDGMENTS § 27 comment c (1982).

[123]   *See* § 15.03[1], *supra*.

[124]   The parties usually will have raised the issues in their pleadings. However, this will not always be the case. Many systems permit their courts to determine upon the evidence at trial issues which go beyond the pleadings. For example, Rule 15(b) authorizes federal trial courts to grant motions to amend pleadings to conform to the evidence at trial but notes that "failure to amend does not affect the result of the trial of that issue." *See* § 8.10[2], *supra*.

motion for judgment on the pleadings, a motion for summary judgment . . . , a motion for directed verdict or their equivalents, as well as on a judgment entered on a verdict."[125] On the other hand, many courts hold that default judgments, consent judgments and judgments based on stipulations of fact or admissions should not generate issue-preclusive effects because the issues there have not been litigated.[126]

The actually-decided-and-determined requirements reflect the presumption of adversarial justice that litigating an issue makes a correct determination more likely. When the issue was litigated in the first lawsuit, we are more comfortable about holding a party to the issue determination in the next lawsuit by precluding its relitigation. When a party has stipulated to facts or consented to a judgment, on the other hand, we lack the same assurance of correctness, because parties may stipulate or consent for reasons other than the truth of the facts.

Similarly, a party's decision to take a default in the initial case is not necessarily a reflection of the strength of his opponent's case. Reasons why a party may default may include "the smallness of the amount or the value of the property in controversy, the difficulty of obtaining the necessary evidence, the expense of the litigation, and his own situation at the time."[127] To endow default judgments with issue-preclusive effect may also "make a default so perilous that a well-advised defendant will be driven to litigate any petty claim asserted against him if there is the slightest prospect that a buried issue may be foreclosed in a subsequent suit. In the end this could frustrate the very purpose of *res judicata*, to reduce contention and dispute. Instead of more litigation later, there will be more litigating now."[128]

When a judge makes findings in a bench trial or a jury returns a special verdict, answering questions put by the judge, it is usually apparent what issues the fact-finder determined. A general verdict can also support inferences about what the jury found. In a negligence case, for example, we can infer from a general verdict for the plaintiff in a stated amount that the jury found that the defendant breached a duty of reasonable care to the plaintiff, that plaintiff was not contributorily negligent (if contributory negligence is an issue in the case that the jury was instructed to consider), and what amount the jury found necessary to compensate the plaintiff for his injury. But a general verdict for defendant in the same circumstances would be opaque. The jury found for defendant, but was it because it found the defendant non-negligent, it found the plaintiff contributorily negligent, or it found that the plaintiff suffered no compensable damages? When we cannot identify what the fact finder determined on an issue, we don't know what to preclude. This is why it is not enough for issue preclusion that an issue was actually litigated; we must also be able to discern what was decided.

---

[125] RESTATEMENT (SECOND) OF JUDGMENTS § 27 comment d (1982).

[126] *See Arizona v. California*, 530 U.S. 392 (2000) (judgments entered by confession, consent or default should not be entitled to issue-preclusive effect.)

[127] *Cromwell v. County of Sac*, 94 U.S. 351, 356 (1877).

[128] Maurice Rosenberg, *Collateral Estoppel in New York*, 44 ST. JOHN'S L. REV. 165, 177 (1969).

[3]   The Determination of the Issue Must Have Been Necessary to Judgment

[a]   The Function and Purpose of the Necessary-Determination Rule

Not only must the same issue have been litigated and determined in the prior proceeding, but the determination must have been necessary to support the judgment there.[129] This added requirement functions with the others to assure that only those who have had a full and fair prior opportunity to litigate issues will be subject to issue preclusion. Insistence that the adjudication be necessary to the judgment "is a protection, for it means that the issue will be really disputed and that the loser will have put out his best efforts."[130]

It also means that the party to be bound will usually have an opportunity to appeal the initial adjudication and to challenge the correctness of the issue determination, thus providing an added layer of assurance in its correctness. In contrast, determinations which are not necessary to support the judgment are usually not appealable. "Such determinations have the characteristics of dicta, and may not ordinarily be the subject of an appeal by the party against whom they were made."[131] But if such determinations, like dicta, cannot be corrected by appeal, then they should not be used against the adverse party in a subsequent lawsuit. Issue preclusion is and should be limited to determinations necessary to support the judgment because "the interest in providing an opportunity for a considered determination, which if adverse may be the subject of an appeal, outweighs the interest in avoiding the burden of relitigation."[132]

Rios v. Davis[133] provides a classic example. Davis sued Rios for negligence in an automobile collision. The jury found Rios negligent, but also found Davis contributorily negligent, requiring judgment to be entered for Rios. Rios then sued Davis for injuries Rios had received in the same collision. Davis defended on the grounds that the jury's finding in the first case established Rios' contributory negligence and precluded him from relitigating it in the second. The court refused to give the earlier judgment issue-preclusive effect. It said of the first case:

> The finding that Rios was negligent was not essential or material to the judgment and the judgment was not based thereon. . . . Since the judgment was in favor of Rios he had no right or opportunity to complain of or to appeal from the finding that he was guilty of such negligence even if such finding had been without any support whatever in the evidence. The right

---

[129] *See, e.g., United States v. Alaska*, 521 U.S. 1, 13 (1997) (issue preclusion "could only preclude relitigation of issues of fact or law *necessary* to a court's judgment." (emphasis in original)).

[130] *The Evergreens v. Nunan*, 141 F.2d 927, 929 (2d Cir. 1944).

[131] Restatement (Second) of Judgments § 27 cmt. h (1982).

[132] *Id.*

[133] 373 S.W.2d 386 (Tex. Civ. App. 1963).

of appeal is from a judgment and not from a finding.[134]

To determine whether an issue was necessary to support the judgment, ask whether, if the issue had been decided the opposite way, the same judgment would have been entered. If so, then judgment did not depend on the way the issue actually was resolved. Applying this test to the *Rios* case, we find that, once the jury found Davis to be contributorily negligent, Rios had to win. Thus, the same judgment would have been entered in the case no matter what conclusion the jury reached concerning Rios's own negligence.

[b] Alternative Determinations

A special problem arises when alternative issue determinations support the judgment. If each is independently capable of supporting the judgment, then neither is necessary to the judgment in a strict sense. Applying the test above, if either issue had been resolved differently, the judgment would have been unchanged.

The weakest case for issue preclusion is when it is unclear which of two grounds supports the judgment. Preclusion is unwarranted in such cases.[135] The problem is that it is impossible to determine whether a given issue was determined at all.

A classroom case, *Illinois Central Gulf Railroad Co. v. Parks*,[136] illustrates this difficulty. A husband and wife were injured when their car collided with one of defendant's trains. In the first suit, the wife sued for her injuries and the husband sued for loss of the services and companionship of his wife. The wife recovered against the railroad, but the jury returned a general verdict against the husband. In a subsequent lawsuit, the husband sued defendant railroad for his own injuries. The railroad urged claim and issue preclusion. The court rejected both arguments.[137] The railroad based its case for issue preclusion on the possibility that the first jury returned a verdict against the husband because he had been contributorily negligent as driver of the car. The court noted, however, that it was equally possible that the first jury returned a verdict against the husband because the husband proved no damages for loss of his wife's services and companionship. Under this possibility, the contributory negligence issue would not have been determined in the first case at all.[138]

One influential decision denying preclusive effect to a prior adjudication expressly based on alternative grounds is *Halpern v. Schwartz*.[139] *Halpern* rejected the assumption that alternative grounds were as likely as non-alternative grounds

---

[134] *Id.* at 387–88. On the last point, see § 13.08[1] (prejudicial effect as requirement for reviewability), *supra.*

[135] *See* RESTATEMENT (SECOND) OF JUDGMENTS § 27 cmt. i (1982).

[136] 390 N.E.2d 1078 (Ind. Ct. App. 1979).

[137] Whether the husband engaged in a kind of claim-splitting which should have been barred by claim preclusion is an interesting question. Indiana courts appear to be more indulgent on this point than most other jurisdictions. *See* § 15.03, *supra.*

[138] On the issue-preclusion requirement that the issue actually be determined in the prior proceeding, see § 15.07[2], *supra.*

[139] 426 F.2d 102 (2d Cir. 1970).

to be thoroughly litigated prior to judgment.

> First, if the court in the prior case were sure as to one of the alternative grounds and this ground by itself was sufficient to support the judgment, then it may not feel as constrained to give rigorous consideration to the alternative grounds. Second, since there are alternative grounds which could independently support the prior judgment, vigorous review of an asserted error as to one ground probably would not occur. The losing litigant would have little motivation to appeal from an alleged erroneous finding in connection with one of several independent alternative grounds, since even if his claim of error were sustained, the judgment would be affirmed on one of the other grounds.[140]

Some courts continued to adhere to an older rule giving effect to issues decided on alternative grounds.[141] But the *Restatement (Second) of Judgments* endorsed the *Halpern* principle, stating that "[i]f a judgment of a court of first instance is based on determinations of two issues, either of which standing independently would be sufficient to support the result, the judgment is not conclusive with respect to either issue standing alone."[142] At the same time, the *Restatement* regards such determinations as preclusive if both grounds are affirmed on appeal. At this point, "the losing party . . . has obtained an appellate decision on the issue, and thus the balance weighs in favor of preclusion."[143]

[4] Application of Issue Preclusion Must Be Fair in the Given Case

The essential prerequisites for issue preclusion discussed in this section all grow out of a concern for procedural fairness — that litigants have a sufficient opportunity to litigate before they are bound.[144] But issue preclusion's requirement that the same issue be previously determined and necessary to judgment is not always enough to assure procedural fairness.

For example, if a party faced a higher burden of proof in the first lawsuit, was denied effective discovery, or encountered some other procedural burden that made fair litigation of an issue difficult or impossible, it might not be fair to preclude the party from relitigating the issue under different, more favorable procedures. Small claims courts often operate with abbreviated procedures (including limited or no discovery opportunities), for example, that may make it unfair to give their issue determinations preclusive effect in some later cases brought in courts of general subject matter jurisdiction with fuller procedural opportunities. A party who fails to establish fraud by clear and convincing evidence in lawsuit one should not necessarily be precluded from trying to establish it, on

---

[140] *Id.* at 105–06.

[141] *Compare, e.g., Halpern v. Schwartz, 426 F.2d 102 (2d Cir. 1970), with In re Westgate-Cal. Corp.,* 642 F.2d 1174 (9th Cir. 1981); and *Jean Alexander Cosmetics, Inc. v. L'Oreal USA, Inc.,* 458 F.3d 244 (3d Cir. 2006) (giving preclusive effect to an alternate ground supporting a judgment).

[142] RESTATEMENT (SECOND) OF JUDGMENTS § 27 cmt. i (1982) (citing *Halpern* with approval).

[143] *Id.* § 27 cmt. o.

[144] On the importance of procedural fairness to preclusion law, see § 15.06[2], *supra.*

the same or similar facts, in a second lawsuit governed by the general, lower preponderance standard of proof.

For similar reasons, there should be no issue preclusion if

> [T]here is a clear and convincing need for a new determination of the issue . . . because it was not sufficiently foreseeable at the time of the initial action that the issue would arise in the context of a subsequent action, or . . . because the party sought to be precluded, as a result of the conduct of his adversary or other special circumstances, did not have an adequate opportunity or incentive to obtain a full and fair adjudication in the initial action.[145]

Moreover, the trend, explored in the next section, of relaxing the identity-of-parties requirement for issue preclusion has created a greater need for courts to inquire whether invocation of issue preclusion will be fair under the circumstances of the particular case.[146]

[5] Issue Preclusion by Decisions of Administrative Agencies

So far, we have assumed that the rendering forum was a court. The comparisons that issue preclusion requires are intuitively easy when both fora are courts. But the rationale for issue preclusion by judicial judgments can apply also to some decisions of administrative agencies.[147] "When an administrative agency is acting in a judicial capacity and resolved disputed issues of fact properly before it which the parties have had an adequate opportunity to litigate, the courts have not hesitated to apply res judicata [issue preclusion] to enforce repose."[148]

The "when" is the rub. Administrative agencies often do not provide the same procedural opportunities to litigate that courts provide, and appeal of administrative decisions may be sharply limited. But this does not introduce a new variable in the issue preclusion matrix; it only reinforces its insistence on a full and fair opportunity to litigate the identical issue. To decide the issue-preclusive effect of an administrative agency decision, therefore, it is necessary to look closely at the procedural setting and the opportunity the to-be-precluded party had to make its case on the issue, as well as "whether there is any substantive [policy] reason . . . to justify relitigation.[149]

---

[145] RESTATEMENT (SECOND) OF JUDGMENTS § 28(5) (1982).

[146] See § 15.08[2], infra.

[147] RESTATEMENT (SECOND) OF JUDGMENTS § 83 (1982) ("a valid and final adjudicative determination by an administrative tribunal has the same effects under the rules of res judicata, subject to the same exceptions and qualifications, as a judgment of a court," subject to several exceptions).

[148] United States v. Utah Const. & Mining Co., 384 U.S. 394, 422 (1966). See generally RESTATEMENT (SECOND) OF JUDGMENTS § 83 (1982) ("a valid and final adjudicative determination by an administrative tribunal has the same effects under the rules of res judicata, subject to the same exceptions and qualifications, as a judgment of a court," subject to several exceptions); WRIGHT & MILLER § 4475.

[149] ROBERT C. CASAD & KEVIN M. CLERMONT, RES JUDICATA 209 (2010).

§ 15.08   WHO CAN BIND AND BE BOUND BY ISSUE PRECLUSION?

In most jurisdictions, issue preclusion (collateral estoppel) has no counterpart to the identity-of-parties requirement which limits claim preclusion.[150] It is clear, of course, that issue preclusion can operate when the parties in the succeeding case are the same. It is also clear, as a matter of fundamental due process, that issue preclusion should ordinarily not operate *against* one who was a complete stranger to the first case. Under the right circumstances, however, it may also operate *in favor of* one who was neither a party nor in privity with a party in the earlier case.

[1]   The General Rule Against Binding Those Who Were Strangers to the Prior Adjudication

The general rule is that strangers to the prior case cannot be bound by it.[151] After entertaining the possibility of change,[152] the Supreme Court reaffirmed the rule in *Parklane Hosiery Co. v. Shore*, noting that it would be "a violation of due process for a judgment to be binding on a litigant who was not a party or a privy and therefore has never had an opportunity to be heard."[153] This is true even if a stranger forgoes a clear opportunity to participate in the prior adjudication,[154] and even if the quality of the initial adjudication was so high as to suggest that the stranger will not put on a better case when permitted to relitigate the issue.[155] In this context, due process is not satisfied by adequate or even exemplary representation by another litigant in another case. The sentiment — if not the logic — of due process guarantees strangers their own day in court before they can be bound, if for no other reason than to cauterize the wounds of defeat.

---

[150] *See* § 15.09, *supra.*

[151] *See* § 15.06, *supra*, and the authorities surveyed in Jack Ratliff, *Offensive Collateral Estoppel and the Option Effect*, 67 Tex. L. Rev. 63, 64 n.8 (1988).

[152] In *Provident Tradesmens Bank & Trust Co. v. Patterson*, 390 U.S. 102, 114 (1968), the Court wondered whether a person "should be bound by the previous decision because, although technically a nonparty, he had purposely bypassed an adequate opportunity to intervene." *Accord, Richards v. Jefferson City*, 517 U.S. 793 (1996); *Nat'l R.R. Passenger Corp. v. Pa. Pub. Util. Comm.*, 342 F.3d 242 (3d Cir. 2003). For the argument that issue preclusion should attach under such circumstances, see ALI, *Complex Litigation Project* § 5.05 (1993); Louis Touton, Note, *Preclusion of Absent Disputants to Compel Intervention*, 79 Colum. L. Rev. 1551 (1979); Michael A. Berch, *A Proposal to Permit Collateral Estoppel of Nonparties Seeking Affirmative Relief*, 1979 Ariz. St. L.J. 511 (1979).

[153] 439 U.S. 322, 327 n.7 (1979). On how the Due Process Clause of the United States Constitution functions to prevent applications of preclusion which compromise a party's right to a hearing, see § 15.06[2], *supra*. For subsequent applications of the rule that strangers to a civil lawsuit may not be precluded by it, see *Georgia v. South Carolina*, 497 U.S. 376, 392 (1990); *Martin v. Wilks*, 490 U.S. 755 (1989). "A judgment or decree among parties to a lawsuit resolves issues as among them, but it does not conclude the rights of stranger to those proceedings." 490 U.S. at 762.

Notwithstanding this rule, it is possible to bind passive members of a plaintiff class without their active involvement in the case. For discussion of how class actions work and of the special treatment they receive under the Constitution, see §§ 4.02[1] (constitutional concerns) & 9.09 (class actions generally), *supra.*

[154] Probably the worst that will happen to a party who deliberately forgoes prior participation will be that he may later be denied use of nonmutual issue preclusion.

[155] *See, e.g., Humphreys v. Tann*, 487 F.2d 666 (6th Cir. 1973).

Persons who were not party to the first lawsuit are occasionally subject to issue preclusion, but the exceptions to the general rule are narrow and confined to situations in which the persons have close relationships to the parties, just as the Supreme Court has announced for nonparty claim preclusion.[156] But this usually occurs only when they chose to involve themselves significantly in the prior case — whether by becoming unusually active amicus curiae,[157] or by furnishing behind-the-scenes assistance to one of the actual parties. For example, in *Montana v. United States*,[158] the Supreme Court held that the United States was bound by issue preclusion even though it was not a party to the prior adjudication. The Court reached this conclusion by noting that the United States subsidized and controlled the actions of one who was a party there. The United States directed decisions to file and to appeal, paid litigation costs, and reviewed and approved papers filed in that case.

[2] When Strangers to the Prior Adjudication May Bind Those Who Were Parties

One question has dominated modern-day developments in issue preclusion. When, if ever, can strangers to the prior adjudication invoke the doctrine? Once the rule was never. Applying the *mutuality doctrine*, courts held, that since strangers were safe from the adverse effects of a prior adjudication, they could not use it to their advantage.[159] Issue preclusion had to be mutual or not at all. In time, however, courts began to attach importance to the difference between binding total strangers to the prior litigation and binding those subject to a prior adjudication of the issue, albeit against a different party. While a minority of jurisdictions continue to adhere to the mutuality doctrine,[160] most courts have now dispensed with it in favor of nonmutual issue preclusion against those who were parties. They permit strangers to the prior case to invoke issue preclusion against those who were parties, whenever it appears from the circumstances that it is fair to do so, but not the reverse.

[a] The Decline of the Mutuality Doctrine

The mutuality doctrine rests upon two separate propositions. *First*, strangers to a prior adjudication will not be bound by it. *Second*, it is unfair to permit anyone who cannot be bound by a prior adjudication to use it to bind another. That is, one-way preclusion is unfair; the risk of preclusion from the initial case must be mutual.

---

[156] *Taylor v. Sturgell*, 553 U.S. 880 (2008). *See* § 15.04[2], *supra*.

[157] This rarely occurs. "Because the amicus curiae generally lacks party status, or the ability to control the course of the litigation, the private amici can, in most instances, participate in the suit free of the effects of res judicata." Michael K. Lowman, Comment, *The Litigating Amicus Curiae: When Does the Party Begin After the Friends Leave?*, 41 Am. U. L. Rev. 1243, 1260–61 (1992).

[158] 440 U.S. 147 (1979).

[159] *E.g.*, *Bigelow v. Old Dominion Copper Mining & Smelting Co.*, 225 U.S. 111, 127 (1912); *Buckeye Powder Co. v. E. I. DuPont de Nemours Powder Co.*, 248 U.S. 55, 63 (1918).

[160] A study identified eight states that still retained the mutuality doctrine in 1998: Alabama, Florida, Georgia, Kansas, Louisiana, Mississippi, North Dakota, and Virginia. Howard M. Erichson, *Interjurisdictional Preclusion*, 96 Mich. L. Rev. 945, 966–67 (1998) (citing cases).

The first of these two propositions is still true — due process still protects strangers to a prior adjudication from being bound by it.[161] The widespread collapse of the mutuality doctrine occurred because most jurisdictions no longer accept the second proposition. Swelling dockets and a greater appreciation of the benefits of judicial economy led courts to reexamine the assumption that one-way preclusion was invariably unfair. This resulted in a series of significant state and federal decisions repudiating the mutuality doctrine.

The most significant state case was *Bernhard v. Bank of America*.[162] In the first lawsuit, plaintiff, an estate's administratrix, sued her predecessor for failing to include certain funds in his accounting of the assets of the estate. She lost. She then sued the bank in the second lawsuit, claiming that it was indebted to the estate for releasing these same funds without proper authorization. The bank argued that the issue of its authorization had been determined adversely to the plaintiff in the first lawsuit.

The bank was a stranger to the first lawsuit. Thus it could not have been bound[163] had the authorization issue in that case been resolved differently. That is, if the first case determined that the bank released the funds without proper authority, the bank could nonetheless litigate the issue in the second case and attempt to prove that it had been authorized to release the funds. The only way, then, that the California Supreme Court could give preclusive effect to the judgment rendered in the first lawsuit was to dispense with the doctrine of mutuality. It did so, stating that "no satisfactory rationalization has been advanced for the requirement of mutuality."[164]

Two federal cases are also of special importance. In *Blonder-Tongue Laboratories, Inc. v. University of Illinois Foundation*,[165] the Supreme Court extensively criticized the mutuality doctrine.[166] The Court refused to invoke the mutuality requirement in *Blonder-Tongue*, but the breadth of its ruling was uncertain. However, in a subsequent case, *Parklane Hosiery Co. v. Shore*,[167] the Court categorically repudiated the mutuality doctrine and thus ended its use in federal courts.[168]

Parklane faulted the mutuality doctrine for "failing to recognize the obvious difference in position between a party who has never litigated an issue and one who

---

[161] *See* § 15.08[2], *supra.*

[162] 122 P.2d 892 (Cal. 1942).

[163] *See* § 15.08[2], *supra.*

[164] 122 P.2d at 895.

[165] 402 U.S. 313 (1971). For additional discussion of this case, see John B. Corr, *Supreme Court Doctrine in the Trenches: The Case of Collateral Estoppel*, 27 Wm. & Mary L. Rev. 35, 37–39 (1985).

[166] 402 U.S. at 322–27.

[167] 439 U.S. 322 (1979). For an extended discussion of the case and the circumstances surrounding it, see Lewis A. Grossman, *The Story of Parklane: The "Litigation Crisis" and the Efficiency Imperative*, in Civil Procedure Stories 405–43 (Kevin M. Clermont, ed., 2d ed. 2008). In addition, see Maurice J. Holland, *Modernizing Res Judicata: Reflections on the Parklane Doctrine*, 55 Ind. L.J. 615 (1980).

[168] Judith Resnik, *Tiers*, 57 S. Cal. L. Rev. 837, 868 (1984).

has fully litigated and lost."[169] *Parklane* completes the process, begun by *Blonder-Tongue*, of replacing one fairness test with another. The mutuality doctrine rested on the idea that it was invariably unfair to create risk-free opportunities for preclusion, and that benefits of preclusion were spoils of victory earned through the risk of equally adverse consequences had matters in the original suit turned out differently. Rejecting these ideas, *Parklane* declared that henceforth it would be necessary to adduce some particular reason why it would be unfair to bind a party by nonmutual issue preclusion. Attention under this new approach thus shifted from the position of the party wishing to use the doctrine to the position of the party against whom it was invoked.

[b] Limits on Courts' Discretion to Invoke Nonmutual Issue Preclusion

Nonmutual issue preclusion has had its critics. While most endorse defensive nonmutual issue preclusion (to defeat a claim by a prior party against a stranger), many observers were concerned that *offensive* nonmutual issue preclusion (by a stranger to establish a claim against a prior party) might give the stranger an unfair advantage over the prior party.[170]

For example, Professor Brainerd Currie put forth what he called the "multiple claimant anomaly."[171] In his hypothetical case, fifty injured passengers bring successive suits against a railroad arising from the same train accident. In the first case, the railroad wins by establishing that it was not negligent. When the second passenger brings suit, the court will deny the railroad issue-preclusive effect from the prior determination of no negligence, since the second passenger was a stranger to the first suit.[172] The plaintiff in the second suit is thus free to relitigate the question of the railroad's negligence. In Currie's example, twenty-five passenger plaintiffs bring twenty-five successive lawsuits. Each plaintiff is free to relitigate the negligence issue, but each loses. Then, in the twenty-sixth case, a passenger prevails on the negligence issue and recovers. Currie then poses the question:

> Are we to understand that the remaining twenty-four passengers can plead the judgment in the case of No. 26 as conclusively establishing that the railroad was guilty of negligence, while the railroad can make no reference to the first twenty-five cases which it won?[173]

---

[169] 439 U.S. at 327.

[170] *See* Ratliff, note 151, *supra*; Elvin E. Overton, *The Restatement of Judgments, Collateral Estoppel, and Conflict of Laws*, 44 Tenn. L. Rev. 927 (1977); Edwin H. Greenebaum, *In Defense of the Doctrine of Mutuality of Estoppel*, 45 Ind. L.J. 1 (1969); Brainerd Currie, *Mutuality of Collateral Estoppel: Limits of the Bernhard Doctrin e*, 9 Stan. L. Rev. 281 (1957). *Cf.* Waggoner, note 77, *supra* (rejecting nonmutual issue preclusion but advocating nonmutual claim preclusion); Note, *Exposing the Extortion Gap: An Economic Analysis of the Rules of Collateral Estoppel*, 105 Harv. L. Rev. 1940 (1992) (criticizing nonmutual preclusion by contending that it is unfair to subsequent plaintiffs).

[171] Currie, note 170, *supra*, at 285–89.

[172] *See* § 15.08[1], *supra*.

[173] Currie, note 170, *supra*, at 286.

Abuses of nonmutual offensive preclusion might also lead to proliferation of litigation contrary to one purpose of preclusion. For example, passenger B in Currie's hypothetical might forgo an opportunity to join with passenger A in the initial case, taking a "wait and see" attitude. If A wins, B can invoke nonmutual issue preclusion. If A loses, B (a stranger to the first case) is free to relitigate all issues.

The Supreme Court acknowledged all of these concerns in *Parklane*. While it approved offensive nonmutual issue preclusion for that case, it made clear that the doctrine should not always be available. Federal courts have "broad discretion to determine when it should be applied."[174] They must use their discretion to refuse offensive nonmutual issue preclusion when circumstances suggest that use of the doctrine against a party to the prior case would be unfair. The Court stated that offensive nonmutual issue preclusion should be denied when sought by one who deliberately bypassed an opportunity to participate in the original proceeding; when the stake of the party against whom preclusion would be invoked was deceptively small in the original proceeding; when the subsequent proceeding affords significantly more advantageous procedural opportunities for that party; or when there were inconsistent prior judgments.[175]

Of course, *Parklane* is not controlling on state courts.[176] But a large number of state jurisdictions rejecting mutuality have defined and limited offensive nonmutual issue preclusion in ways similar to Supreme Court's opinion. Since *Parklane* relied in part on a draft provision of the *Restatement (Second) of Judgments*, this consensus is not surprising.

That provision, which became Section 29 of the *Restatement (Second)*, expressly rejects the doctrine of mutuality by making issue preclusion available to strangers to the prior adjudication. But Section 29 makes clear that issue preclusion is unavailable if the party who would be bound "lacked full and fair opportunity to litigate the issue in the first action or other circumstances justify affording him an opportunity to relitigate the issue."

Problems of procedural fairness can arise even if the parties in the successive suits are identical.[177] However, Section 29 notes additional problems which may arise when strangers to the first suit attempt to invoke issue preclusion. These include:

> (2) The forum in the second action affords the party against whom preclusion is asserted procedural opportunities in the presentation and determination of the issue that were not available in the first action and could likely result in the issue being differently determined;

---

[174]   439 U.S. at 331.

[175]   *Id.* at 331.

[176]   Subject only to the due process and full faith and credit constraints of federal law, state courts are free to devise their own answers to preclusion questions. *See* § 15.01[1], *supra*.

[177]   *Restatement (Second) of Judgments* Section 28 addresses this. For discussion of Section 28 and how concerns of procedural fairness can prevent application of issue preclusion even when the parties are the same, see § 15.07[4], *supra*. Incorporating Section 28 by reference, Section 29 makes clear that the same factors can be important in ascertaining nonmutual issue preclusion.

(3) The person seeking to invoke favorable preclusion, or to avoid unfavorable preclusion, could have effected joinder in the first action between himself and his present adversary;

(4) The determination relied on as preclusive was itself inconsistent with another determination of the same issue . . . .[178]

Clear acknowledgment in *Parklane* and in Section 29 of situations to which offensive nonmutual issue preclusion should not apply has done much to ease apprehensions over rejection of the mutuality doctrine. For example, both *Parklane*[179] and Section 29[180] seem to offer an answer to the so-called multiple claimant anomaly posed earlier in this discussion. It would clearly be unfair to permit a claimant to exploit one judgment that was inconsistent with twenty-five others, and a court faced with such a case is directed to refuse offensive nonmutual issue preclusion.[181] Courts are similarly directed to deny offensive nonmutual issue preclusion to claimants who have adopted a "wait-and-see" attitude toward the initial case.[182]

---

[178] Other reasons for refusing nonmutual offensive issue preclusion are listed in Section 29 and elsewhere. Partial immunity from issue preclusion extended to government litigants provides an example.

> [B]ecause the government often litigates an issue against different parties in different circuits, an unrestrained use of issue preclusion against the government would allow a decision in one case to bind the government in all subsequent litigation. The result would be to require the government to vigorously contest and appeal every lawsuit in which it is involved, placing an enormous strain on its resources.

LINDA L. SILBERMAN, ALLAN R. STEIN & TOBIAS B. WOLFF, CIVIL PROCEDURE: THEORY AND PRACTICE 888 (2d ed. 2006). For an overview, see Samuel Estreicher & Richard L. Revesz, *Nonacquiesence by Federal Administrative Agencies*, 98 YALE L.J. 679 (1989).

[179] *See* § 15.08[2][a], *supra*.

[180] *See* RESTATEMENT (SECOND) OF JUDGMENTS § 29(3)-(4) (1982), quoted in the text of this sub-section, *supra*.

[181] In addition, *see* RESTATEMENT (SECOND) OF JUDGMENTS § 29 cmt. f (1982):

> Giving a prior determination of an issue conclusive effect in subsequent litigation is justified not merely by avoiding further costs of litigation but also by underlying confidence that the result reached is substantially correct. Where a determination relied on as preclusive is itself inconsistent with some other adjudication of the same issue, that confidence is generally unwarranted.

[182] In addition, *see* RESTATEMENT (SECOND) OF JUDGMENTS § 29 cmt. e (1982):

> A person in such a position that he might ordinarily have been expected to join as plaintiff in the first action, but who did not do so, may be refused the benefits of "offensive" issue preclusion where the circumstances suggest that he wished to avail himself of the benefits of a favorable outcome without incurring the risk of an unfavorable one.

PART C.
Inter-System Preclusion

§ 15.09   INTRAMURAL AND INTER-SYSTEM PRECLUSION COMPARED

Preclusion law is largely common law. Within limits,[183] each judicial court system is free to fashion doctrine determining how much force its judgments should have. When courts of a system are presented with their own judgments, questions concerning the effect of the judgment arise in an *intramural*[184] context. The intramural law that courts apply is their local preclusion law. For federal courts, it is federal common law.

Increasingly, courts must also consider the effect of judgments which were rendered outside their system. Then, questions concerning the effect of the judgment arise in an *inter-system* context.[185] For inter-system cases, which body of preclusion law should determine the force and effect of the judgment? Is it measured by the intramural law of the system rendering the judgment or by the intramural law of the system where the judgment is offered for enforcement?

So long as applicable preclusion law is the same in both systems, the question is academic. The law will often but not always be the same. As noted earlier, systems disagree over whether to permit claim-splitting in traffic accident cases[186] and over whether to refuse nonmutual issue preclusion by invoking the mutuality doctrine.[187] Other differences also exist.[188] When rules conflict, the court where the judgment is presented might have an understandable preference for its own intramural preclusion law. However, federal full faith and credit law severely restricts the

---

[183] The Due Process Clause of the United States Constitution limits the preclusive effect a court can give to one of its judgments. *See* § 15.06 note 116 and related text, *supra*.

[184] *See* Robert C. Casad, *Intersystem Issue Preclusion and the Restatement (Second) of Judgments*, 66 Cornell L. Rev. 510, 511 (1981); Restatement (Second) of Judgments, 2 (introduction) (1982).

[185] An elaboration of many of the points under this heading appears in Gene R. Shreve, *Preclusion and Federal Choice of Law*, 64 Tex. L. Rev. 1209 (1986). On the subject generally, see Howard M. Erichson, *Interjurisdictional Preclusion*, 96 Mich. L. Rev. 945 (1998); Graham C. Lilly, *The Symmetry of Preclusion*, 54 Ohio St. L.J. 289 (1993); Gene R. Shreve, *Judgments from a Choice-of-Law Perspective*, 40 Am. J. Comp. L. 985 (1992); Sanford N. Caust-Ellenbogen, *False Conflicts and Interstate Preclusion: Moving Beyond a Wooden Reading of the Full Faith and Credit Statute*, 58 Ford. L. Rev. 593 (1990); Jean A. Mortland, *Interstate Federalism: Effect of Full Faith and Credit to Judgments*, 16 U. Dayton L. Rev. 47 (1990); Stephen B. Burbank, *Interjurisdictional Preclusion and Federal Common Law: Toward a General Approach*, 70 Cornell L. Rev. 625 (1985); Barbara A. Atwood, *State Court Judgments in Federal Litigation: Mapping the Contours of Full Faith and Credit*, 58 Ind. L.J. 59 (1982); Casad, note 184, *supra*; Ronan E. Degnan, *Federalized Res Judicata*, 85 Yale L.J. 741 (1976).

[186] *See* § 15.03, *supra*.

[187] *See* § 15.08, *supra*.

[188] For example, compare the federal court view that its judgments are final during appeal with the Utah state view that does not attach finality to its judgments under such circumstances. *See* § 15.05, *supra*. And compare the United States Supreme Court's refusal to give issue-preclusive effect to federal default judgments with the opposing view New York has taken concerning the effect of its state judgments. *See* § 15.07, *supra*.

court's freedom to disregard the preclusion law of the place rendering the judgment.[189] This appears to be true whether the effect sought from the judgment is claim or issue preclusion.[190]

A different problem exists when foreign-country judgments are presented in the United States for enforcement. Federal full faith and credit law does not reach such cases. The policy arguments for giving preclusive effect to foreign-country judgments are not as strong. At the same time, it would be unwise simply to ignore foreign-country judgments. American courts generally recognize such judgments, but the content of governing law is relatively indistinct.[191]

§ 15.10 THE FEDERAL FULL FAITH AND CREDIT OBLIGATION THAT JUDGMENTS BE GIVEN AS MUCH EFFECT AS THEY WOULD HAVE WHERE RENDERED

To a large extent, federal full faith and credit law determines the enforceability of judgments rendered by a court in the United States and presented elsewhere in this country for enforcement. Full faith and credit obligations appear in the Full Faith and Credit Clause of the United States Constitution[192] and in the full faith and credit statute.[193] The basic requirement of each is that a judgment must be given as much effect where presented for enforcement as it would have had where rendered. The Full Faith and Credit Clause imposes the rule on states presented with sister-state judgments. The full faith and credit statute protects state judgments in state or federal courts and has been read to protect federal judgments in state court.

[1] Preserving the Preclusive Effect of State Judgments in Sister-State Courts

The Full Faith and Credit Clause of the Constitution[194] contains the requirement that "[f]ull faith and credit shall be given in each State to the public acts, records, and judicial proceedings of every other State." Congress passed the

---

[189] *See* §§ 15.10–15.11, *infra.*

[190] "Although it has been suggested that issue preclusion may operate with less force than does claim preclusion under [the federal full faith and credit statute] the cases do not support such a distinction." Atwood, note 185, *supra*, at 69. *See Migra*, 465 U.S. at 83, and *McDonald v. City of West Branch*, 466 U.S. 284, 291 (1984), each equating claim and issue preclusion for purposes of federal court enforcement of state judgments.

[191] *See* § 15.12, *infra.*

[192] U.S. Const. art. IV, § 1.

[193] 28 U.S.C. § 1738 (2012).

[194] For examination of the Clause, see David E. Engdahl, *The Classic Rule of Faith and Credit*, 118 YALE L.J. 1584 (2009); Katherine C. Pearson, *Common Law Preclusion, Full Faith and Credit, and Consent Judgments: The Analytical Challenge*, 48 CATH. U. L. REV. 419 (1999); Ralph U. Whitten, *The Constitutional Limitations on State-Court Jurisdiction: A Historical-Interpretive Reexamination of the Full Faith and Credit and Due Process Clauses (Part One)*, 14 CREIGHTON L. REV. 499 (1981); Kurt H. Nadelmann, *Full Faith and Credit to Judgments and Public Acts*, 56 MICH. L. REV. 33, 60 (1957);

full faith and credit statute in 1790.[195] The statute's requirement, that all courts in the United States give "such faith and credit" to state "records and judicial proceedings" as they would have in the courts of that state, dates from 1790.[196] Except in child custody cases,[197] the Full Faith and Credit Clause and statute govern the recognition and enforcement of state judgments in other state courts.[198]

Initially, some lower courts read the Full Faith and Credit Clause and statute to require only that judgments be taken as *prima facie* evidence in subsequent proceedings. This view would have left courts free, at the very least, to apply their own preclusion law to determine the effect of judgments rendered elsewhere. However, the Supreme Court rejected the view in *Mills v. Duryee*.[199] Invoking both Clause and statute, the Court held that the obligation of full faith and credit to a New York state judgment required the application of New York preclusion law.[200] Of the full faith and credit statute, Justice Story wrote, "we can perceive no rational interpretation of the act . . . unless it declares a judgment conclusive when a Court of the particular state where it is rendered would pronounce the same decision."[201]

When courts simultaneously invoke the Full Faith and Credit Clause and statute, it is often difficult to determine which is carrying the main weight in decisions to follow the preclusion law of the judgment-rendering state. But it may not be terribly important to distinguish between the two in this context. Perhaps it is enough to collapse both — as one distinguished writer has — into "the full faith and credit requirement."[202] While the area is not free of uncertainty,[203] the basic obligation of federal full faith and credit is firm. State courts must give as much effect to sister-state judgments as they would have where rendered.[204]

James D. Sumner, Jr., *Full Faith and Credit for Judicial Proceedings*, 2 UCLA L. REV. 441 (1955); Max Radin, *The Authenticated Full Faith and Credit Clause: Its History*, 39 ILL. L. REV. 1 (1944).

[195] Act of May 26, 1790 (now codified as 28 U.S.C. § 1738).

[196] Amendments to the Act of 1790, *reviewed in* Lea Brilmayer, *Credit Due Judgments and Credit Due Laws: The Respective Roles of Due Process and Full Faith and Credit in the Interstate Context*, 70 IOWA L. REV. 95, 95 n.2 (1984), have not altered its basic standard.

[197] *See* note 216, *infra*.

[198] The Revised Uniform Enforcement of Foreign Judgments Act (1964) seeks to expedite compliance with federal full faith and credit law and has been adopted by most states.

[199] 11 U.S. (7 Cranch) 481 (1813).

[200] "[I]t is beyond all doubt that the judgment of the Supreme Court of New York was conclusive upon the parties in that state. It must, therefore, be conclusive here also." *Id.* at 484.

[201] *Id.* at 485.

[202] Robert C. Casad, *Intersystem Issue Preclusion and the Restatement (Second) of Judgments*, 66 CORNELL L. REV. 510, 520 (1981).

[203] For example, the Supreme Court has had difficulty developing an intelligible standard for determining the effect of state worker's compensation decrees. *See Thomas v. Wash. Gas Light Co.*, 448 U.S. 261 (1980); *Indus. Comm'n of Wis. v. McCartin*, 330 U.S. 622 (1947); *Magnolia Petroleum Co. v. Hunt*, 320 U.S. 430 (1943). For a discussion of these cases, see WILLIAM M. RICHMAN & WILLIAM L. REYNOLDS, UNDERSTANDING CONFLICT OF LAWS § 117[c][1]–[5] (3d ed. 2002).

[204] *See, e.g., Underwriters Nat'l Assurance Co. v. N.C. Life & Accident & Health Ins. Guar. Ass'n*, 455 U.S. 691 (1982); *Durfee v. Duke*, 375 U.S. 106 (1963); *Fauntleroy v. Lum*, 210 U.S. 230 (1908). *See generally* William L. Reynolds, *The Iron Laws of Full Faith and Credit*, 53 MD. L. REV. 412 (1994).

[2]   Preserving the Preclusive Effect of State Judgments in Federal Court

Congress has always had a variety of legislative options in determining the manner and extent to which it wishes to regulate inter-system preclusion. At one extreme, Congress could have codified intersystem preclusion law, elaborating a precise, systematic scheme to regulate the inter-system enforcement of state and federal judgments.[205] Commentators have suggested that the idea is worth considering,[206] but Congress has never really acted upon it. Except in child-custody cases,[207] Congress has not used its power to extensively regulate inter-system preclusion. At the other extreme, Congress could have done nothing. If the Supreme Court had interpreted the Full Faith and Credit Clause as self-applying,[208] congressional inaction might not have diminished state court obligations to enforce sister-state judgments. But federal courts are beyond the textual reach of the Full Faith and Credit Clause.[209] They are probably under no constitutional compulsion to recognize the effects of state judgments created under state preclusion law.[210] Congressional silence, then, would have left federal courts free to determine how much effect to give to state judgments.

Congress decided instead to steer a middle course. Although the legislative history of the full faith and credit statute[211] is uncertain, it seems clear that Congress intended to impose upon federal courts an obligation to recognize and enforce the judgments of states equivalent to the obligation imposed on states by the Constitution's Full Faith and Credit Clause to recognize and enforce sister-state judgments.[212] This is how the Supreme Court has read the statute.[213] The Court has made clear that, in cases where the statute applies, "Congress has

---

[205] The Full Faith and Credit Clause, U.S. Const. art IV, § 1, expressly authorizes Congress to enact laws elaborating the obligation of states to respect sister-state judgments. Congress' power to impose upon federal courts a duty to recognize state judgments derives from U.S. Const. art. III, § 1. The Commerce Clause (U.S. Const. art. I, § 8) and the Privileges and Immunities Clause (U.S. Const. art. IV, § 2), provide additional support for a broad statutory scheme.

[206] *See, e.g.*, Brainerd Currie, *Full Faith and Credit, Chiefly to Judgments: A Role for Congress*, 1964 Sup. Ct. Rev. 89.

[207] The Parental Kidnapping Prevention Act of 1980, 28 U.S.C. § 1738A, augments § 1738 with reference to state child custody decrees. Discussions of the Act appear in Barbara A. Atwood, *Child Custody Jurisdiction and Territoriality*, 52 Ohio St. L.J. 369 (1991); Russell M. Coombs, *Interstate Child Custody: Jurisdiction, Recognition, and Enforcement*, 66 Minn. L. Rev. 711 (1982).

[208] After early uncertainty, the Supreme Court adopted the view that the clause is self-applying. Robert H. Jackson, *Full Faith and Credit — the Lawyer's Clause of the Constitution*, 45 Colum. L. Rev. 1, 11 (1945); Elliott E. Cheatham, *Res Judicata and the Full Faith and Credit Clause: Magnolia Petroleum Co. v. Hunt*, 44 Colum. L. Rev. 330, 333 (1944).

[209] Art. IV, § 1 of the U.S. Constitution imposes a full faith and credit obligation only upon sister states. The Supreme Court noted that federal courts were "not included within the constitutional provision." *Kremer v. Chem. Constr. Corp.*, 456 U.S. 461, 483–84 n. 24 (1982).

[210] *See* Gene R. Shreve, *Preclusion and Federal Choice of Law*, 64 Tex. L. Rev. 1209, 1223 n.77 (1986).

[211] 28 U.S.C. § 1738 (2012).

[212] Atwood, note 185, *supra*, at 67; Degnan, note 185, *supra*, at 743–44.

[213] *E.g., Davis v. Davis*, 305 U.S. 32, 40 (1939) ("The Act extended the rule of the Constitution to all courts, federal as well as state.").

specifically required all federal courts to give preclusive effect to state-court judgments whenever the courts of the State from which the judgments emerged would do so."[214]

At the same time, important differences flow from the fact that federal courts' obligation to give effect to state judgments is only statutory. Just as Congress did not have to enact the full faith and credit statute, it is free either to repeal it or to lighten its obligations by amending it to create exceptions. Section 1738 itself contains no exceptions to the obligation of federal courts to honor state judgments, but other federal statutes can suspend that obligation.

Congress has sometimes expressly suspended Section 1738.[215] More often, however, the question will be whether suspension not expressly required is nonetheless necessary to effectuate exclusive federal subject-matter jurisdiction. In short, should an exception to the mandate of Section 1738 be implied from congressional grants of exclusive federal jurisdiction? This question has divided commentators[216] and federal courts.[217]

Marrese v. American Acad. of Orthopaedic Surgeons[218] presented the Supreme Court with the issue whether exclusive federal antitrust jurisdiction operates as an exception to Section 1738. The Court declined to answer the question but did suggest that exclusive federal jurisdiction would not invariably create an implied exception.[219] The Court also offered some guidelines for resolving "the more general question . . . whether the concerns underlying a particular grant of exclusive jurisdiction justify a finding of an implied partial repeal of Section 1738."

> Resolution of this question will depend on the particular federal statute as well as the nature of the claim or issue involved in the subsequent federal action. Our previous decisions indicate that the primary consideration must be the intent of Congress.[220]

[214] *Allen v. McCurry*, 449 U.S. 90, 96 (1980).

[215] The most prominent example is the federal *habeas corpus* statute. 28 U.S.C. § 2254 (2012). *See* David P. Currie, *Res Judicata: The Neglected Defense*, 45 U. Chi. L. Rev. 317, 330, 333 (1978).

[216] *Compare, e.g.*, Allan D. Vestal, *Res Judicata/Claim Preclusion: Judgment for the Claimant*, 62 Nw. U. L. Rev. 357, 374–75 (1967), and Note, *The Collateral Estoppel Effect of Prior State Court Findings in Cases Within Exclusive Federal Jurisdiction*, 91 Harv. L. Rev. 1281, 1290–91 (1978) (arguing for preclusion), *with* Stephen B. Burbank, *Afterwords: A Response to Professor Hazard and a Comment on Marrese*, 70 Cornell L. Rev. 659, 664 (1985), and Atwood, note 185, *supra*, at 63 (arguing against preclusion because of the insulating effect of exclusive federal jurisdiction).

[217] *Compare, e.g.*, *RX Data Corp. v. Dep't of Soc. Servs.*, 684 F.2d 192 (2d Cir. 1982), and *Lektro-Vend Corp. v. Vendo Co.*, 660 F.2d 255 (7th Cir. 1981), *cert. denied*, 455 U.S. 921 (1982) (state court judgment denied preclusive effect when federal court had exclusive jurisdiction), *with Nash County Bd. of Educ. v. Biltmore Co.*, 640 F.2d 484 (4th Cir. 1981), and *Derish v. San Mateo-Burlingame Bd. of Realtors*, 724 F.2d 1347 (9th Cir. 1983) (state judgment given preclusive effect notwithstanding exclusive jurisdiction).

[218] 470 U.S. 373 (1985).

[219] *Id.* at 380–81.

[220] 470 U.S. at 386. The Court then cited *Kremer v. Chemical Construction Corp.*, 456 U.S. 461 (1982), and *Brown v. Felsen*, 442 U.S. 127 (1979). In *Kremer*, the Court left open the possibility that jurisdiction over claims under Title VII of the Civil Rights Act of 1964 was exclusive in federal court, but found no support in Title VII or its legislative history for the conclusion that it implied an exception to Section 1738. But the Supreme Court refused in *Brown* to give preclusive effect to a prior state judgment in a

[3] Preserving the Preclusive Effect of Federal Judgments in Other Federal Courts

The preclusive effect to be given to a federal judgment by the court that rendered it, or by any other federal court, is an intramural question of federal preclusion law. The Supreme Court's decisions elaborating federal preclusion doctrine[221] will largely determine the effect of such judgments. However, the Court has held that this doctrine should adopt the preclusion law of the state in which the federal judgment was rendered to decide its effect, when the rendering federal court was sitting in diversity.[222] In other words, in such cases, the federal common law of preclusion borrows the state's preclusion law.

When unresolved differences exist among the federal circuits concerning questions which the Supreme Court has not passed upon, one might expect the law of the federal circuit in which the judgment was rendered to control. However, a statute which authorizes federal court registration of a judgment "for the recovery of money or property" rendered in another federal district court[223] suggests a different result. Section 1963 provides that "judgment so registered shall have the same effect" as if it had been rendered where registered, suggesting that the law of the federal circuit where the federal judgment is presented for enforcement will control.

[4] Preserving the Preclusive Effect of Federal Judgments in State Courts

The Full Faith and Credit Clause of the Constitution and the full faith and credit statute both address state judgments. Neither makes provision for federal judgments in state court. At the same time, "[i]t would be unthinkable to suggest that state courts should be free to disregard the judgments of federal courts, given the basic requirements that state courts honor the judgments of courts in other states and that federal courts must honor state court judgments."[224]

In a series of decisions, the Supreme Court therefore filled the gap by reading the full faith and credit statute to require state courts to respect federal judgments.[225] Congress undoubtedly has the authority to enact legislation protecting federal judgments,[226] but this seems quite beyond the language of

---

subsequent federal bankruptcy proceeding within the federal court's exclusive jurisdiction. The *Brown* Court curiously made no reference to Section 1738, but did declare: "While Congress did not expressly confront the problem created by pre-bankruptcy state-court adjudications, it would be inconsistent with the philosophy of the [federal statutes] to adopt a policy of *res judicata* which takes these [federal bankruptcy] questions away from bankruptcy courts and forces them back into state courts." 442 U.S. at 136.

[221] *E.g., Parklane Hosiery Co. v. Shore,* 439 U.S. 322 (1979). *Parklane* is discussed at § 15.08[2][a], *supra.*

[222] *Semtek,* 531 U.S. at 508–09 (2001).

[223] 28 U.S.C. § 1963 (2012).

[224] WRIGHT & MILLER § 4468.

[225] *E.g., Embry v. Palmer,* 107 U.S. 3, 9–10 (1883); *Stoll v. Gottlieb,* 305 U.S. 165, 170 (1938).

[226] That authority derives, *inter alia,* from Congress' power to create lower federal courts under Art.

section 1738. The Court has never come up with an entirely satisfactory rationale for grafting this requirement onto the statute. After surveying the case law in this area, Professor Ronan Degnan observed that his study did

> not . . . show that the Court was willfully wrong in doing what it did, but that it was wantonly right. By strength of arm and sleight of hand, it achieved a result that is indispensable to federalism. . . . Were there no such rule, it would be necessary to invent one — so invent it the Supreme Court did.[227]

The content of the federal preclusion to be applied by subsequent state (or federal) courts depends on the type of federal judgment offered for enforcement or recognition. Federal question judgments have effect under federal preclusion doctrine. *Parklane* would be an example. As noted above, the preclusive effect of federal diversity judgments must be determined by the intramural preclusion law of the state where the federal court rendering the judgment was sitting.[228]

§ 15.11   ARE OTHER COURTS FREE TO GIVE JUDGMENTS MORE EFFECT THAN THEY WOULD HAVE WHERE RENDERED?

Conflicts of preclusion law among state and federal courts[229] lead to situations in which the local preclusion law of a court where a judgment is presented would give greater preclusive effect to it than would the law of the court rendering the judgment. For example, a federal court, which permits nonmutual issue preclusion, may be presented with a judgment rendered in a state court which still adheres to the limitations of the mutuality doctrine.[230] Under such circumstances, may the federal court disregard the preclusion law of the rendering forum and apply federal doctrine to give issue-preclusive effect to the state judgment? Supreme Court decisions suggest not. Whether sister-state courts can augment the preclusive effect of other state judgments seems a more open question.

[1]   May Federal Courts Give Greater Effect to State Judgments?

There is considerable support for the proposition that the full faith and credit statute[231] prevents federal courts from giving any more preclusive effect to state judgments than they would have under the law of the rendering state. In *Marrese*

III, § 1 of the Constitution. Degnan, note 185, *supra*, at 749.

[227] Degnan, note 185, *supra*, at 749.

[228] *Semtek*, 531 U.S. 497. For additional discussions of *Semtek*, see Patrick Woolley, *The Sources of Federal Preclusion Law After Semtek*, 72 U. Cinn. L. Rev. 527 (2003); Stephen B. Burbank, *Semtek, Forum Shopping, and Federal Common Law*, 77 Notre Dame L. Rev. 1027 (2002). On the creation of federal common law, see § 7.07, *supra*.

[229] *See* § 15.09, *supra*.

[230] For a discussion of these conflicting positions, see § 15.08[2], *supra*.

[231] 28 U.S.C. § 1738 (2012).

v. American Academy of Orthopaedic Surgeons,[232] the Supreme Court stated that Section 1738

> directs a federal court to refer to the preclusion law of the State in which judgment was rendered. "It has long been established that § 1738 does not allow federal courts to employ their own rules of *res judicata* in determining the effect of state judgments. Rather, it goes beyond the common law and commands a federal court to accept the rules chosen by the State from which the judgment was taken."[233]

Later in the opinion, the Court read an earlier case[234] to reject "the view that Section 1738 allows a federal court to give a state court judgment greater preclusive effect than the state courts themselves would give to it."[235] The Supreme Court's decisions have not been entirely consistent.[236] However, in *Marrese* and in one decision since[237] the Court seems determined that federal courts give state judgments no greater preclusive effect than they would have in the state courts where they originated.[238]

[2] May State Courts Give Greater Effect to Sister-State Judgments?

It is clear that the federal full faith and credit statute applies to sister-state as well as federal courts.[239] There is little to suggest that the added application of the Constitution's Full Faith and Credit Clause to state courts[240] increases their obligation to respect sister-state judgments. If anything, Section 1738 imposes a more stringent obligation than does the Full Faith and Credit Clause.[241] So the

---

[232] 470 U.S. 373 (1985).

[233] *Id.* at 380, *quoting Kremer,* 456 U.S. at 481–82.

[234] *Migra,* 465 U.S. 75.

[235] 470 U.S. at 384.

[236] In *Haring v. Prosise,* 462 U.S. 306 (1983), the Court refused to invoke federal doctrine to give greater preclusive effect to a Virginia judgment, but it discussed the possibility at length. *Id.* at 317–23. *Haring* seemed to make clear that, in a deserving case, a federal court could give greater preclusive effect to a state judgment than the state rendering it would. In other cases, the Supreme Court has treated the effect of state judgments in federal court as a matter of federal rather than state law. *Brown,* 442 U.S. 127; *Montana v. United States,* 440 U.S. 147 (1979). In one case, the Court invoked federal doctrine to permit relitigation in apparent disregard of Section 1738's requirement that a state judgment be given as much preclusive effect in federal court. *England v. La. State Bd. of Med. Exam'rs,* 375 U.S. 411 (1964). The Court did not criticize any of these prior cases in its later *Marrese* decision.

[237] *Parsons Steel, Inc. v. First Ala. Bank,* 474 U.S. 518, 523–25 (1986).

[238] For criticism of this position and for the argument that federal courts should give nonmutual, issue-preclusive effect to judgments rendered by states adhering to the mutuality doctrine, see Shreve, note 210, *supra,* at 1251.

[239] RESTATEMENT (SECOND) OF JUDGMENTS § 86 cmt. c (1982). *See, e.g., Underwriters Nat'l Assurance Co.,* 455 U.S. at 694 (1982).

[240] *See* § 15.10, *supra.*

[241] *Cf. Thomas,* 448 U.S. at 270 (where the plurality opinion observes that the essential obligation to give the same effect to sister-state judgments as they would have where rendered, "[if] not compelled by the Full Faith and Credit Clause itself, is surely required by 28 U.S.C. § 1738.") (citation omitted).

legal obligation should be the same for state and federal enforcement courts.

At the same time, the Supreme Court has confined its strongest statements about the deference due to the preclusion law of the rendering states to cases where their judgments were presented in federal court.[242] A few state courts have flatly refused to honor the confines of the preclusion doctrine of the state where the judgment was rendered.[243] Whether or how the Supreme Court will check the impulse of state courts to give greater preclusive effect to sister-state judgments remains to be seen.

[3] Why the Greater-Preclusion Issue Will Rarely Arise Concerning Federal Judgments

Federal doctrine is in the vanguard of the movement to give judgments greater preclusive effect. This is evident from the Supreme Court's rejection of the mutuality doctrine,[244] and from numerous lower federal court decisions giving a broad definition to the "claim" precluded by the federal doctrine of claim preclusion.[245] Therefore, it will be rare for a state court to find the preclusive effect of a federal judgment to be greater under its law than it would be in federal court.

§ 15.12 FOREIGN-COUNTRY JUDGMENTS IN AMERICAN COURTS AND AMERICAN JUDGMENTS ABROAD

[1] Foreign-Country Judgments in American Courts

State and federal courts in the United States take a more receptive view of judgments rendered abroad than the courts of most other nations.[246] It has been suggested that "[m]ost states accord foreign-country judgments essentially the same status as sister-state judgments."[247] This receptiveness is in part a reflection

---

[242] *See* notes 233–35, 237 and related text, *supra.*

[243] *Finley v. Kesling*, 433 N.E.2d 1112, 1116–18 (Ill. App. Ct. 1982) (refusing to honor a mutuality limitation under Indiana law); *Hart v. Am. Airlines, Inc.*, 61 Misc. 2d 41 (N.Y. Sup. Ct. 1969) (refusing to honor a mutuality limitation under Texas law). *But see Columbia Cas. Co. v. Playtex FP, Inc.*, 584 A.2d 1214, 1218 (Del. 1991) (honoring a mutuality limitation under Kansas law). The *Columbia Casualty* court observed that, if Delaware courts were to give "the judgments of a sister state greater preclusive effect than they would have in the rendering jurisdiction," the result would be "at variance with the purpose and spirit of the full faith and credit clause." For further discussion of case developments, see Gene R. Shreve, *Judgments from a Choice-of-Law Perspective*, 40 Am. J. Comp. L. 985 (1992).

[244] *See* § 15.08[2][a], *supra.*

[245] *See* § 15.03, *supra.*

[246] Arthur T. von Mehren & Donald T. Trautman, *Recognition of Foreign Adjudications: A Survey and a Suggested Approach*, 81 Harv. L. Rev. 1601, 1602–03 (1969). For commentary and legal materials on the United States enforcement of foreign judgments generally, see Linda J. Silberman & Andreas F. Lowenfeld, *A Different Challenge for the ALI: Herein of Foreign Country Judgments, an International Treaty and an American Statute*, 75 Ind. L.J. 635 (2000); Jeffrey Rabkin, Note, *Universal Justice: The Role of Federal Courts in International Civil Litigation*, 95 Colum. L. Rev. 2120 (1995); Robert E. Lutz, *Enforcement of Foreign Judgments, Part I: A Selected Bibliography on United States Enforcement of Judgments Rendered Abroad*, 27 Int'l Lawyer 471 (1993).

[247] Eugene F. Scoles & Peter H. Hay, Conflict of Laws § 24.6 (2d ed. 1992).

of a strong tradition of inter-system preclusion within the United States.[248]

But the compulsion behind judgment recognition in the latter context is missing when American courts are presented with foreign country judgments. Neither the Full Faith and Credit Clause of the United States Constitution[249] nor the full faith and credit statute[250] apply to judgments rendered in foreign countries.[251] This is due in part to the limited textual reach of these provisions and in part to the interlocking character that the judgment-rendering and enforcing forums have when both are courts in the United States. That character is lacking in the international setting. Cautioning against treating foreign country judgments under domestic *res judicata* principles, Professors von Mehren and Trautman have noted some fundamental differences between American and foreign courts:

> [O]ne of the purposes of *res judicata* is to maintain the integrity of the domestic judicial system. The case of recognition of internationally foreign judgments is quite different because it may be proper for different legal systems to come to different results on the same set of facts. [And] there are basic differences in the surrounding circumstances. The economic and cultural relationships within a single jurisdiction tend to be closer, and as a result the practical arguments supporting conclusive effects for domestic judgments are stronger. At the same time, shared traditions and experience and the identity of procedures and standards help reduce doubt about the quality of justice represented by a judgment. For these reasons, treating recognition problems as an aspect of *res judicata* tends to lead to a confusion of concepts which should be kept separate.[252]

By the same token, important interests may be served when American courts recognize foreign-country judgments. "[I]f in our highly complex and interrelated world each community exhausted every possibility of insisting on its parochial interests, injustice would result and the normal patterns of life would be disrupted."[253]

---

[248] *See* § 15.10, *supra.*

[249] U.S. Const. art. IV, § 1.

[250] 28 U.S.C. § 1738 (2012).

[251] Hans Smit, *International Res Judicata and Collateral Estoppel in the United States*, 9 UCLA L. Rev. 44 (1962). *See also* William M. Richman & William L. Reynolds, Understanding Conflict of Laws § 122 (3d ed. 2002).

[252] von Mehren & Trautman, note 246, *supra* at 1605–06. Copyright © 1969 by the Harvard Law Review Association. Reprinted with permission.

[253] von Mehren & Trautman, note 246, *supra*, at 1603. The authors suggest that, "at least when judgments emanate from legal systems with well-established legal institutions and traditions," more precise policies supporting recognition of foreign country judgments could be articulated. Their list includes:

> a desire to avoid the duplication of effort and consequent waste involved in reconsidering a matter that has already been litigated; a related concern to protect the successful litigant, whether plaintiff or defendant, from harassing or evasive tactics on the part of his previously unsuccessful opponent; a policy against making the availability of local enforcement the decisive element, as a practical matter, in the plaintiff's choice of forum; an interest in fostering stability and unity in an international order in which many aspects of life are not confined to any single jurisdiction.

Perhaps the "shared tradition" in American courts which may most clearly set their adjudications apart from foreign-country adjudications is that all proceedings must be in accordance with the constitutional requirements of due process.[254] It is therefore not surprising that judgments of common-law countries having a due process tradition close to our own are most open to recognition in American courts. For example, in the well-known case, *Somportex Ltd. v. Philadelphia Chewing Gum Corp.*,[255] the Third Circuit gave effect to an English default judgment.

The *Somportex* court invoked the principle of *comity*, perhaps the most durable of the doctrines addressing the recognition and enforcement of foreign-country judgments.[256] It described comity as

> not a rule of law, but one of practice, convenience, and expediency. Although more than mere courtesy and accommodation, comity does not achieve the force of an imperative or obligation. Rather, it is a nation's expression of understanding which demonstrates due regard both to international duty and convenience and to the rights of persons protected by its own laws. Comity should be withheld only when its acceptance would be contrary or prejudicial to the interest of the nation called upon to give it effect.[257]

Neither Congress nor the executive has acted to create anything approaching comprehensive law governing the recognition of international judgments.[258] Nor has the Supreme Court refined many standards through the development of federal common law.[259] Despite the efforts of individual states,[260] the law remains frag-

---

Id. at 1603–04. Copyright © 1969 by the Harvard Law Review Association. Reprinted with permission.

[254] For discussion of the effect of due process on personal jurisdiction, notice and *res judicata*, see § 15.02, *supra.*

American courts have also refused to enforce foreign judgments that, on the merits, would have been unconstitutional if rendered in the United States. *E.g., Yahoo!, Inc. v. La Ligue Contre Le Racisme et L'Antisemitisme*, 169 F. Supp. 2d 1181 (N.D. Cal. 2001). For discussion of *Yahoo* and other cases, see Mark D. Rosen, Should *"Un-American" Foreign Judgments Be Enforced?*, 88 MINN. L. REV. 783 (2004); Mark D. Rosen, *Exporting the Constitution*, 53 EMORY L.J. 171 (2004).

[255] 453 F.2d 435 (3d Cir. 1971), *cert. denied*, 405 U.S. 1017 (1972). The Court relied in part on *Hilton v. Guyot*, 159 U.S. 113 (1895), a case that provides much of the framework for modern analysis. For an excellent discussion of *Hilton* and its context, see Louise Ellen Teitz, *The Story of Hilton: From Gloves to Globalization, in* CIVIL PROCEDURE STORIES 445–71 (Kevin M. Clermont ed., 2d ed. 2008).

[256] The doctrine of reciprocity, which limits the effect of judgments of countries to the effect United States judgments would have in their courts, has played a more limited and controversial role in this area. For a discussion of comity, reciprocity and other doctrines, see Smit, note 251, *supra*, at 48–56.

[257] 453 F.2d at 440.

[258] "There is no bilateral treaty or multilateral international convention in force between the United States and any other country on reciprocal recognition and enforcement of judgments." *Enforcement of Judgments*, BUREAU OF CONSULAR AFFAIRS, U.S. DEP'T OF STATE, *available at* http://travel.state.gov/law/judicial/judicial_691.html (last visited Mar. 8, 2013).

[259] For discussions of federal common law applicable to the recognition of foreign-country judgments, see Ronald A. Brand, *Enforcement of Foreign Money-Judgments in the United States: In Search of Uniformity and International Acceptance*, 67 NOTRE DAME L. REV. 253 (1991); Albert A. Lindner, Comment, *Judgments Rendered Abroad-State Law or Federal Law?*, 12 VILL. L. REV. 618 (1967).

Approximately thirty states have adopted the Uniform Foreign Money-Judgments Recognition Act. The Act "is intended to standardize as much as possible, in the interests of certitude and convenience, the nation's treatment of foreign country judgments." Richard J. Graving, *The Carefully Crafted 2005* mented.[261] This condition is a special cause for concern, because it can affect how courts abroad enforce judgments from United States courts.[262]

[2]   American Judgments Abroad

While attitudes toward American judgments vary from country to country,[263] there is widespread agreement among commentators that "it has often been much more difficult to enforce U.S. judgments abroad that to enforce foreign judgments in the United States."[264] Simply put, "[m]any countries are quite restrictive when it comes to enforcing judgments rendered by courts in the United States."[265]

Resistance abroad is attributable to many important differences between how civil cases are adjudicated United State and foreign adjudications. Numerous idiosyncrasies of American civil procedure account for what one writer has called "the nasty aroma American litigation seems to elicit in much of the rest of the world."[266] Resistance is in part a reaction to the lack of a national standard in the United States for enforcing foreign judgments.[267] Adding to the problem are many traditional features of American litigation that foreign courts find unfamiliar if not distasteful. The late Friedrich Juenger observed:

Uniform Foreign-Country Money Judgments Recognition Act Cures a Serious Constitutional Defect in Its 1962 Predecessor, 16 MICH. ST. J. INT'L L. 289, 290 (2007). A 2005 rewrite of the Act vitiated its prior reliance on conflicting judicial decisions as its source of international reciprocity law, "[p]roving to foreign countries that the United States will recognize their judgments[.]" *Id.* at 291. Only a handful of states have passed the 2005 version of the law, however. *See id.* at 293.

[260] On the experience of states that have adopted uniform judgment-recognition acts, and on guidelines for state court decisions provided by *The Restatement (Third) of Foreign Relations Law*, see Brand, note 259, *supra*, at 265–80.

[261] BORN & WESTIN, note 261, *supra*, at 938 ("There is presently no federal standard governing the enforcement of judgments rendered by foreign courts in the United States.").

[262] SCOLES & HAY, note 247, *supra* § 24.6. On the fate of United States judgments abroad, *see* Brand, note 259, *supra*, at 281–83; Peter Hay, *The Recognition and Enforcement of American Money-Judgments in Germany — The 1992 Decision of the German Supreme Court*, 40 AM. J. COMP. L. 729 (1992).

[263] For two examples, see Francisco Ramos Romeu, *Litigation Under the Shadow of an Exequatur: The Spanish Recognition of U.S. Judgments*, 38 INT'L LAWYER 945 (2004); and Alessandro Barzaghi, *Recognition and Enforcement of United States Judgments in Italy*, 18 N.Y. INT'L L. REV. 61 (2005).

[264] Louise Ellen Teitz, *The Hague Choice of Court Convention: Validating Party Autonomy and Providing an Alternative to Arbitration*, 53 AM. J. OF COMP. L. 543, 544 (2005).

[265] Linda J. Silberman, *The Impact of Jurisdictional Rules and Recognition Practice on International Business Transactions: The U.S. Regime*, 26 HOUSTON J. OF INT'L L. 327, 351 (2004). Thus, "companies often do not sue in the United States when the assets are elsewhere because they fear the uncertainty of subsequent enforcement of a United States judgment overseas." Louise Ellen Teitz, *The Hague Choice of Court Convention: Validating Party Autonomy and Providing an Alternative to Arbitration*, 53 AM. J. OF COMP. L. 543, 548 (2005).

[266] Richard L. Marcus, *Putting American Procedural Exceptionalism into a Globalized Context*, 53 AM. J. COMP. L. 709, 709–10 (2005). Professor Marcus lists "relaxed pleading, broad discovery, jury trial, limited cost shifting, potentially remarkable awards for pain and suffering or punitive damages, and heavy reliance on private lawyers to enforce public norms, to name several but not all the distinguishing characteristics" of U.S. procedure. For a similar assessment, see Friedrich K. Juenger, *Traveling to The Hague in a Worn-Out Shoe*, 29 PEPP. L. REV. 7, 11 (2001).

[267] *See* § 15.12[2], *supra*.; *see also* note 259, *supra*.

No other country routinely tries civil actions to a jury or authorizes discovery to the extent we do. Most outlaw contingent fees, and many follow the "English rule" that loser pays all. These facets of American practice result in judgments that boggle foreign lawyers' minds.[268]

PART D.
Beyond Preclusion: Additional Doctrines of Repose

Courts employ doctrines in addition to preclusion to reduce frustration and uncertainty generated by recurrent litigation. None of these focus as much as preclusion on the integrity of prior judgments, but they are sufficiently analogous and complementary to preclusion to merit discussion.

§ 15.13 *STARE DECISIS*

[1] The Nature of the Doctrine

When a legal issue arises for the first time, trial and appellate courts have the latitude to choose from among competing rules of law, declaring and applying the one which seems the best. *Stare decisis*[269] denies courts the same flexibility when the legal issue recurs in subsequent cases, binding them instead to the approach of the prior case (precedent). The doctrine has been described by one commentator as fostering a "blind imitation of the past."[270] In stifling a continuing search for the best legal answers, *stare decisis* bears a considerable burden of justification. It is justified by the fact that our judicial process could not cope with the strains which would be caused if legal re-examination was routinely available.

> [R]outine reconsideration of the correctness or propriety of binding precedents would be enormously destructive. Any one at any time can initiate litigation, and if any litigant on the wrong side of the law could force a full dress reconsideration of settled points simply by filing a complaint, it would not only weaken public reliance on the law, but would require judges to hear endless reargument of the same issues.[271]

---

[268] Juenger, *supra* note 266, at 11.

[269] *Stare decisis* defined: "*Stare decisis*" is short for *stare decisis et non quieta movere*, which means 'stand by the thing decided and do not disturb the calm.' . . . At its most basic level . . . *stare decisis* refers simply to a court's practice of following precedent, whether its own or that of a superior court." Amy Coney Barrett, *Stare Decisis and Due Process*, 74 U. Colo. L. Rev. 1011, 1016 (2003).

[270] Oliver W. Holmes, *The Path of the Law*, 10 Harv. L. Rev. 457, 469 (1897).

[271] 1B J. Moore, Moore's Federal Practice ¶ 0.402[3.-1] (2d ed.1979). *Accord* Benjamin Cardozo, The Nature of the Judicial Process 149 (1921):

> [T]he labor of judges would be increased almost to the breaking point if every past decision could be reopened in every case, and one could not lay one's own course of bricks on the secure foundation of the courses laid by others who had gone before him.

Stare decisis thus shares the general aim of preclusion: to minimize the assorted costs of relitigation.[272] In particular, *stare decisis* bears a functional resemblance to the preclusion of issues of law.[273] However, *stare decisis* differs from preclusion in that it "relates to the orderly development of law. It does not relate to the finality of judgments."[274] This makes *stare decisis* both broader and narrower in scope than preclusion.

The rule protecting a stranger to the prior adjudication from the effects of preclusion[275] has no counterpart in the doctrine of *stare decisis*. On the contrary, the very purpose of *stare decisis* is to settle future legal controversies, including those between persons who have no connection to the prior adjudication. The only way one who expects to be a party in future litigation can avert the possible effects of *stare decisis* is to try to influence the legal decision in the initial case through intervention[276] or *amicus curiae* participation. On the other hand, the effects of *stare decisis* are often less definite than those of preclusion, as we discuss below.

[2] The Scope of *Stare Decisis*

[a] Boundaries Set by Legal Analysis

First, the *stare decisis* effect of a case must derive from a well-articulated statement of law that was necessary to explain the decision there. It may be possible to avoid *stare decisis* either by arguing that the court has not yet clearly formed a principle and the law is still in a state of flux,[277] or that the principle offered for *stare decisis* effect is not a rule necessary to explain the decision, but is instead only a rule mentioned in passing — *dictum*.[278]

Second, it may be possible to avoid a rule argued for its *stare decisis* effect by challenging the applicability of the rule to the facts of the succeeding case. "[T]he scope of a rule of law, and therefore its meaning, depends upon a determination of what facts will be considered similar to those present when the rule was first

---

[272] *See* § 15.01[1] (preclusion policies), *supra*.

[273] *See* § 15.07, *supra*.

[274] 1B J. Moore, Moore's Federal Practice ¶ 0.402[2] (2d ed. 1979).

[275] Discussed in § 15.08[1], *supra*.

[276] Some courts have recognized possible prejudice from *stare decisis* as a basis for intervention of right. *See, e.g., Natural Res. Def. Council, Inc. v. U.S. Nuclear Regulatory Comm'n*, 578 F.2d 1341 (10th Cir. 1978), and the cases cited in Gene R. Shreve, *Questioning Intervention of Right — Toward a New Methodology of Decisionmaking*, 74 Nw. U. L. Rev. 894, 906 (1980); Note, *Federal Civil Procedure: Prejudicial Effects of Stare Decisis Can Compel Intervention of Right Under Rule 24(a)*, 1967 Duke L.J. 1251. On intervention generally, see § 9.08, *supra*.

[277] *Cf.* P.S. Atiyah & Robert S. Summers, Form and Substance in Anglo-American Law 120 (1987) ("Whenever the substantive reasoning in a case seems at all dubious, the case must go through a period of evaluative trial before it can be regarded as settled and therefore valid law.").

[278] "A holding consists of those propositions along the chosen decisional path or paths of reasoning that (1) are actually decided, (2) are based upon the facts of the case, (3) lead to the judgment. If not a holding, a proposition stated in a case counts as dicta." Michael Abramowicz & Maxwell Stearns, *Defining Dicta*, 57 Stan. L. Rev. 953, 1065 (2005).

announced."[279] The process of determining whether the facts of two cases are sufficiently similar (apposite) that the first serves as precedent for the second, or sufficiently dissimilar that the first is factually distinguishable and hence without binding effect, is at the heart of legal analysis. One must try to determine what policies supported the rule of the first case and the extent to which those policies are implicated in the facts of the second. Factual differences may take the succeeding case out of the sweep of the prior rule. At the same time, cases are rarely if ever entirely identical. One must be alert to the possibility of extending the prior rule of decision to cover new facts.[280]

[b] Boundaries Set by Judicial Structure

Some courts have little choice but to follow apposite precedent. Others are entirely free to disregard it. Still others reserve the authority occasionally to disregard it. These classifications depend on judicial structure, the institutional relationship between the court making the prior decision and the court considering it as precedent.

Precedent is most coercive on the hierarchical inferiors of the court that decided the prior case. Hierarchy is determined by the tiers in a court system's structure. The federal court system and many state systems consist of a trial tier, an intermediate appellate tier and the highest appellate court.[281] In state systems, the last tier is often (but not always) called the state's *supreme* court.[282] In theory at least, the authority of apposite decisions of hierarchical superiors — sometimes called *controlling* precedent — is nearly absolute.[283] The final authority on the meaning of state law is the highest court of that state.[284] Similarly, the United States Supreme Court is the final arbiter of the meaning of federal law. When federal and state courts decide federal law issues, they are treated as one expanded court system. The Supreme Court's federal law decisions bind federal and state courts alike as controlling precedent.

At the other extreme, precedent may be no more than *persuasive*. This occurs when a decision from one judicial system is offered as precedent in another. Courts may follow such precedent if they agree with it, but they are under no compulsion

---

[279] Edward Levi, An Introduction to Legal Reasoning 2 (1948).

[280] "Not only do new situations arise, but in addition peoples' wants change. The categories used in the legal process must be left ambiguous in order to permit the infusion of new ideas." Levi, note 279, *supra*, at 3.

[281] *See* § 13.06 (appellate systems), *supra*.

[282] *See generally* § 13.06 and § 2.01 (state and federal judicial systems), *supra*.

[283] The principle is widely but not universally honored. Atiyah & Summers suggest that, while lower courts entirely lack the authority to overrule precedents of their hierarchical superiors, note 277, *supra*, at 123, they will sometimes ignore them, "even though the American theory of precedent does not fully acknowledge the practice in so many words." *Id.* at 120. In addition, some decisions are designated by appellate courts as non-precedential and thereby not controlling on lower courts. The practice has become widespread in federal courts of appeal. "Today, the vast majority of opinions from the federal appellate courts are designated as non-precedential." Amy E. Sloan, *A Government of Laws and Not Men: Prohibiting Non-Precedential Opinions by Statute or Procedural Rule*, 79 Ind. L.J. 711, 718 (2004).

[284] Discussed in § 7.06[1], *supra*.

to do so.[285] Thus a New York state court may reject a rule of decision in a factually indistinguishable New Hampshire case. One federal circuit court may similarly reject the precedent of another federal circuit. State courts may even reject the decisions of lower federal courts concerning the meaning of federal law.[286]

The precedential effect that the decision has on the same court that rendered it falls somewhere between controlling and persuasive precedent. Courts do not control themselves by their cases in the way they control the courts that fall below them in a judicial system's hierarchy of courts. American courts borrowed their essential conception of *stare decisis* from England but are less reluctant than English jurists to overrule their own decisions.[287] On the other hand, courts cannot regard their own decisions as lightly as would the courts of other systems. If courts do not give their decisions considerably more weight than persuasive precedent, they will be afflicted with the problems that *stare decisis* was intended to avoid.[288]

The resulting rule is that courts usually, but not invariably, follow their own precedents. When courts do discard their precedents, they are said to *overrule* them. The time at which precedent will fall is often difficult to predict and the process frequently controversial.[289] It is possible, however, to identify some of the circumstances in which it is most likely that a court will overrule its own prior decision:

1. if it is seriously out of keeping with contemporary views of what is right and just;

2. if it has been passed by in the development of the law and no longer fits the general principles that govern like cases and overruling it will not require costly or disruptive readjustment of relationships created in reliance upon it; or

3. if the rule has proved to be unworkable or inconvenient in practice and the court is convinced that a different rule will be substantially better, taking into consideration the dislocation a change may produce.[290]

Courts generally will give greater *stare decisis* effect to their settled interpretations of statutes than to either their constitutional decisions or common law precedents. This view is not universally accepted,[291] but it is defensible. A legislature is presumed to acquiesce in the judicial interpretations of its statutes when it does not overrule them by statutory repeal or amendment. This can be seen as a kind of retrospective legislative intent. Moreover, if courts were more willing to

---

[285] Under a narrower view of *stare decisis*, the influence of persuasive precedent is so slight as to be outside the doctrine. ATIYAH & SUMMERS, note 277, *supra*, at 115.

[286] *See* David L. Shapiro, *State Courts and Federal Declaratory Judgments*, 74 Nw. U. L. REV. 759 (1979).

[287] ATIYAH & SUMMERS, note 277, *supra*, at 123–24.

[288] *See* note 271 and related text, *supra*.

[289] *See, e.g.*, Chief Justice Bell's vigorous dissent to the Pennsylvania Supreme Court's overruling of its decisions limiting recovery for negligently inflicted emotional distress. *Niederman v. Brodsky*, 261 A.2d 84, 90 (Pa. 1970).

[290] 1B J. MOORE, MOORE'S FEDERAL PRACTICE ¶ 0.402[3-1] (2d ed. 1979).

[291] *See, e.g.*, criticism of the idea in CARDOZO, note 271, *supra*, at 148.

reinterpret statutes, this might sap the legislature's initiative to review and periodically revise statutory law. Therefore, "once a decisive interpretation of legislative intent has been made . . . the court should take that direction as given."[292]

§ 15.14 LAW OF THE CASE

The law-of-the-case doctrine inhibits relitigation of issues of law in the same case.[293] It shares with preclusion the purpose of making litigation more efficient. Unlike preclusion, it operates in advance of final judgment. Since courts have discretion to depart from the law-of-the-case doctrine,[294] it is similar in operation to *stare decisis*.[295] However, the long range purpose of the law-of-the-case doctrine is more modest than that of *stare decisis*, since the former settles law only for the case at hand.

The doctrine is important to judicial administration. At trial,

the doctrine of the law of the case is little more than a management practice to permit logical progression toward judgment. Prejudgment orders remain interlocutory and can be reconsidered at any time, but efficient disposition of the case demands that each stage of the litigation build on the last, and not afford an opportunity to reargue every previous ruling.[296]

For the trial judge, the law-of-the-case doctrine is one of self-restraint. It offers no protection to the trial court's legal decisions when they are reviewed by an appellate court. But the converse is not true. This is because the law-of-the-case doctrine gives controlling effect to an appellate court ruling if the case is remanded to an inferior court for further proceedings. The doctrine also imposes self-restraint on the appellate court if the case returns by a further appeal.[297]

As with *stare decisis*, the law-of-the-case doctrine permits some flexibility for courts to reconsider their own prior rulings. One court has suggested that reconsideration would be warranted if "the evidence on a subsequent trial was substantially different, controlling authority has since made a contrary decision of the law applicable to such issues, or the decision was clearly erroneous and would

---

[292] LEVI, note 279, *supra*, at 32. Correspondingly, since Congress cannot overturn the Supreme Court's constitutional decisions, these are entitled to the least *stare decisis* effect. *Agostini v. Felton*, 521 U.S. 203, 235–36 (1997). *See generally* Amy Coney Barrett, *Statutory Stare Decisis in the Courts of Appeals*, 73 GEO. WASH. L. REV. 317, 317 (2005).

[293] *See* John R. Knight, *The Law of the Case Doctrine: What Does It Really Mean?*, 43 FED. LAW. 8 (1996); Joan Steinman, *Law of the Case: A Judicial Puzzle in Consolidated and Transferred Cases in and Multidistrict Litigation*, 135 U. PA. L. REV. 595, 597–613 (1987); Brett T. Parks, *McDonald's Corp. v. Hawkins and "The Law of the Case" Doctrine in Arkansas*, 50 ARK. L. REV. 127 (1997).

[294] The law of the case doctrine "cannot prohibit a court from disregarding an earlier holding in an appropriate case . . . ." *Castro v. United States*, 540 U.S. 375, 384 (2003).

[295] Discussed in § 15.13, *supra*.

[296] 1B J. MOORE, MOORE'S FEDERAL PRACTICE ¶ 0.404[1] (2d ed. 1979).

[297] *Id.*

work a manifest injustice."[298] In addition, a court is more likely to reconsider one of its legal rulings if it made the ruling when considering a motion for a temporary restraining order or under other hurried circumstances. Similarly, "[e]arly pretrial rulings . . . may often be subject to reconsideration as a case progresses toward trial."[299]

§ 15.15 INCONSISTENT FACTUAL POSITIONS — JUDICIAL ESTOPPEL

Some courts have refused to permit a litigant to take inconsistent positions in successive lawsuits. Doctrine supporting this is sometimes called *judicial estoppel*.[300] While federal courts and virtually all state courts permit litigants to make inconsistent positions in their pleadings,

> courts do not relish the prospect that an adept litigant may succeed in proving a proposition in one suit, and then succeed in proving the opposite in a second. At worst, successful assertion of inconsistent positions may impose multiple liability on an adversary or defeat a legitimate right of recovery. At best, the judicial system is left exposed to an explicit demonstration of the frailties that remain in adversary litigation and adjudication.[301]

Scarano v. Central R.R. Co.[302] is a well-known example. In the first case, plaintiff obtained a substantial damage recovery against his employer for disability resulting from a job-related injury. In the second case against his employer, this time for reinstatement, plaintiff reversed his factual position and sought to prove he was fit for work. The court found the record in the first case insufficiently clear to support collateral estoppel (issue preclusion),[303] but nonetheless refused plaintiff an oppor-

---

[298] *White v. Murtha*, 377 F.2d 428, 432 (5th Cir. 1967).

[299] WRIGHT & MILLER § 4478 (quoting *White*, 377 F.2d at 431–32). "Law of the case principles are therefore best understood as rules of sensible and sound practice that permit logical progression toward judgment, but that do not disable a court from altering prior interlocutory decisions in a case." Steinman, note 293, *supra*, at 599.

[300] "Judicial estoppel presently appears under a variety of names, especially in state courts. It is frequently called the doctrine of preclusion against inconsistent positions . . . . Less frequently, courts refer to the doctrine as estoppel by oath." Note, *Judicial Estoppel: The Refurbishing of a Judicial Shield*, 55 GEO. WASH. L. REV. 409, 410 n.8 (1987). *See generally* Kira A. Davis, *Judicial Estoppel and Inconsistent Positions of Law Applied to Fact and Pure Law*, 89 CORNELL L. REV. 191 (2003); Ashley S. Deeks, Comment, *Raising the Cost of Lying: Rethinking Erie for Judicial Estoppel*, 64 U. CHI. L. REV. 873 (1997); Douglas W. Henkin, *Judicial Estoppel — Beating Shields into Swords and Back Again*, 139 U. PA. L. REV. 1711 (1991); Rand G. Boyers, Comment, *Precluding Inconsistent Statements: The Doctrine of Judicial Estoppel*, 80 NW. U. L. REV. 1244 (1986).

[301] WRIGHT & MILLER § 4477. As this quotation suggests, it is necessary not only that the party's successive positions be inconsistent but that "the first position has been accepted by a court." Kira A. Davis, *Judicial Estoppel and Inconsistent Positions of Law Applied to Fact and Pure Law*, 89 CORNELL L. REV. 191, 192 (2003).

[302] 203 F.2d 510 (3d Cir. 1953).

[303] Discussed in § 15.07 (requirements for issue preclusion), *supra*. It usually is and should be a requirement for judicial estoppel that the declarant appears to have profited from the first factual position. That is, the court must have relied upon (or ruled consistently with) the declarant's position in

tunity to prove a lack of disability in the second case. The court said: "Such use of inconsistent positions would most flagrantly exemplify that playing fast and loose with the courts which has been emphasized as an evil the courts should not tolerate."[304] The court went on to say that plaintiff's maneuver "is more than [an] affront to judicial dignity. For intentional self-contradiction is being used as a means of obtaining unfair advantage in a forum provided for suitors seeking justice."[305]

Judicial estoppel is a controversial doctrine and its boundaries are difficult to chart.[306] Litigants should be free to change factual positions in succeeding cases when new evidence has come to light or in other circumstances which suggest good reasons for a change of position and no injustice to the opposing party. As the *Scarano* court noted, "each case must be decided upon its own particular facts and circumstances."[307] Perhaps the most that can be said is that courts have the power to refuse adjudication under the inconsistent position doctrine and may use that power in a sufficiently compelling case.

§ 15.16   CALIFORNIA'S RES JUDICATA (CLAIM PRECLUSION) DOCTRINE

[1]   Introductory Note

The doctrine of res judicata (claim preclusion) describes a set of rules which determine the preclusive effects of final judgment on the merits. The California doctrine has two familiar components. First, a prior judgment precludes parties from relitigating *the same cause of action* in a subsequent proceeding. This aspect of the doctrine is known as "claim preclusion," and is commonly referred to as "res judicata." Second, although a second suit between the same parties on a different cause of action is not precluded by a prior judgment, the first judgment operates as a conclusive adjudication as to such issues in the second action as were actually litigated and determined in the first action. This second aspect is known as "issue preclusion," and is commonly referred to as "collateral estoppel."

California's claim preclusion is largely the product of judge-made law. In developing this doctrine, the courts have sought to promote various efficiency notions and thereby protect both the parties and the courts:

> Res judicata protects parties by eliminating the costs of multiple
> lawsuits, bringing an end to litigation, preventing inconsistent judgments,

---

the first case. 203 F.2d at 510. *Cf. Pegram v. Herdrich*, 530 U.S. 211, 228 n.8 (2000) ("Judicial estoppel generally prevents a party from prevailing in one phase of a case on an argument and then relying on a contradictory argument to prevail in another phase.").

[304]   203 F.2d at 513.

[305]   *Id.*

[306]   It has been described as a "minor but controversial doctrine, which varies widely from jurisdiction to jurisdiction and which is even rejected outright in a good number of states." RICHARD H. FIELD, BENJAMIN KAPLAN & KEVIN M. CLERMONT, MATERIALS FOR A BASIC COURSE IN CIVIL PROCEDURE 715 (9TH ED. 2007).

[307]   203 F.2d at 513, quoting *Galt v. Phoenix Indem. Co.*, 120 F.2d 723, 726 (D.C. Cir. 1941).

encouraging reliance on adjudication, and fostering repose through certainty, stability, and finality of judgments. It protects the courts by conserving judicial resources, promoting efficient judicial administration, and bringing an end to a case so that the court may allocate its limited judicial resources to the resolution of other matters.[308]

Accordingly, the goal of claim preclusion doctrine is to define what rights are extinguished by a final judgment such that parties are barred from pursuing multiple lawsuits to resolve disputes which could have been resolved in one proceeding. A definition broad in scope as to what rights are extinguished obviously furthers this goal more effectively than a less inclusive one. However, the California courts have opted for a narrow view — based on the primary rights theory — of what substantive rights are extinguished by a judgment. As will be discussed below, the primary rights theory sometimes permits parties to litigate aspects of a unitary controversy in two lawsuits even though they could have otherwise presented their entire dispute in one.

[2]   California's Res Judicata (Claim Preclusion) Doctrine, Generally

[a]   The Primary Rights Theory

On a general level, California's claim preclusion doctrine of merger and bar is similar to the doctrine set forth in the *Restatement (Second) of Judgments*.[309] Both doctrines prohibit "claim splitting" and preclude parties from relitigating the same claim (or the same "cause of action," using California terminology) already adjudicated in a prior action between them. Likewise, both doctrines bar a second action on the same cause of action even through in the second action the plaintiff presents different grounds for relief or legal theories than those presented, or seeks new forms of relief not requested, in the prior action.[310] However, despite these general similarities, there is a major difference between the *Restatement* and the California approaches to claim preclusion: The California doctrine relies on the primary rights theory, instead of the *Restatement's* same transaction test, to determine the "same cause of action."[311]

---

[308] Walter W. Heiser, *California's Unpredictable Res Judicata (Claim Preclusion) Doctrine*, 35 SAN DIEGO L. REV. 559, 560-61 (1998).

[309] RESTATEMENT (SECOND) OF JUDGMENTS § 17 & § 25 (1982).

[310] E.g., *Slater v. Blackwood, supra*, 15 Cal. 3d at 795 ("Even where there are multiple legal theories upon which recovery might be predicated, on injury gives rise to only one claim for relief"); *Panos v. Great Western Packing Co.*, 21 Cal. 2d 636, 134 P.2d 242 (1943) (holding that two actions seeking recovery for the same personal injuries suffered by plaintiff constituted one primary right and the same cause of action, even though the plaintiff alleged totally different theories of negligence in the two actions); *Duffy v. City of Long Beach*, 201 Cal. App. 3d 1352, 247 Cal. Rptr. 715 (1988) (holding that the prior action to enjoin the impending demolition of plaintiff's house raised the same cause of action as the present action for damages filed by plaintiff after the actual demolition); *see* Heiser, *California's Unpredictable Res Judicata (Claim Preclusion) Doctrine, supra*, at 564-65 (comparing the *Restatement* and the California doctrines).

[311] The *Restatement* defines a "claim" extinguished by the rules of merger or bar as "all rights of the plaintiff to remedies against the defendant with respect to all or any part of the transaction, or series of

The primary rights theory was developed by Professor John Norton Pomeroy[312] in the nineteenth century, and adopted by the California Supreme Court as early as 1887.[313] Under the primary rights theory advanced by Pomeroy, a "cause of action" consists of a "primary right" possessed by the plaintiff, a corresponding "primary duty" of the defendant, and a wrongful act by the defendant constituting a breach of that duty.[314] Unlike the *Restatement* approach, a single factual transaction, or a single wrongful act by the defendant, can violate two primary rights and create two causes of action.[315]

The central feature of California's claim preclusion doctrine is that a single cause of action cannot be split and made the subject of separate lawsuits.[316] However, where a plaintiff has more than one cause of action against a defendant, the plaintiff may join them in one lawsuit but is not required to do so either by the rules of joinder or of res judicata. In other words, a plaintiff who has two causes of action against a defendant may proceed with two separate lawsuits — a judgment in one lawsuit will have no claim preclusive effect on the other.[317]

[b] Primary Rights Theory — The "Harm Suffered" Approach

The central inquiry under California's claim preclusion doctrine is whether or not two lawsuits involve the "same cause of action." Because California defines a cause of action according to the primary rights theory, the concomitant definition of a "primary right" is of central importance. The most frequently quoted definition of the primary rights theory is from *Agarwal v. Johnson*,[318] where the California Supreme Court indicated that "the significant factor is the harm suffered" as opposed to the particular theory of recovery asserted or remedy sought by the litigant. Even where there are multiple legal theories upon which recovery might be predicated, and several remedies available, one injury gives rise to one cause of

---

connected transactions, out of which the action arose." RESTATEMENT (SECOND) OF JUDGMENTS § 24 (1982). The *Restatement's* same transaction test is discussed in more detail in § 15.03[b], *supra*.

[312] John Norton Pomeroy (1828-1885) was a law professor during the nineteenth century and a prolific legal scholar. In addition to his influential multi-volume treatise on equity jurisprudence and equitable remedies, in which he explained at length the primary rights theory of a cause of action, J. POMEROY, REMEDIES AND REMEDIAL RIGHTS (1876); Professor Pomeroy also published treatises on a wide variety of topics, including the civil procedure in California and other states, code pleading and remedies, constitutional law, wills and trusts, and western water law.

[313] *See Hutchinson v. Ainsworth*, 73 Cal. 452, 455, 15 P. 82 (1887). For an historical analysis of the primary rights theory and res judicata, *see* Heiser, *California's Unpredictable Res Judicata (Claim Preclusion) Doctrine*, *supra*, at 571-76.

[314] *See Crowley v. Katleman*, 8 Cal. 4th 666, 34 Cal. Rptr. 2d 386, 881 P.2d 1083, 1090 (1994); J. POMEROY, REMEDIES AND REMEDIAL RIGHTS § 453, at 487 (1876).

[315] *Agarwal v. Johnson, supra*, 25 Cal. 3d at 954 ("the significant factor is the harm suffered; that the same facts are involved in both suits is not conclusive").

[316] *See, e.g., Slater v. Blackwood*, 15 Cal. 3d 791,795,126 Cal. Rptr. 225, 543 P.2d 593 (1975); *Sawyer v. First City Financial Corp.*, 124 Cal. App. 3d 390, 388, 177 Cal. Rptr. 398 (1981).

[317] *Agarwal v. Johnson*, 25 Cal. 3d 932, 954,160 Cal. Rptr. 141, 603, P.2d 58 (1979) ("Unless the requisite identity of causes of action is established, however, the first judgment will not operate as a bar").

[318] 25 Cal. 3d 932, 160 Cal. Rptr. 141, 603, P.2d 58 (1979).

action. The *Agarwal* court also emphasized that a single wrongful act of the defendant may violate more than one primary right and, therefore, create more than one cause of action.

California courts usually begin a primary rights analysis with the "harm suffered" approach. In some instances, this approach is relatively easy to apply. For example, where a plaintiff brings two lawsuits seeking recovery of damages as compensation for the same personal injury allegedly caused by the defendant's negligence, both actions involve the same primary right.[319] However, in less obvious situations, the harm suffered approach does not always produce logical, or even consistent, results. A classic example is *Sawyer v. First City Financial Corp.*,[320] where the plaintiffs brought two separate lawsuits against the defendants arising from the real estate transaction and seeking recovery of the same unpaid promissory note. In the first action, the plaintiffs (the sellers) alleged several theories of liability based on breach of contract by the defendants (the buyers). After a judgment in favor of the defendants, the plaintiffs pursued their second action, this time alleging the defendants had engaged in a conspiracy to defraud plaintiffs for the purpose of eliminating the defendants' obligation to pay the balance of the purchase price. The trial court dismissed the second action as barred by res judicata, and plaintiffs appealed.

The Court of Appeal in *Sawyer* found that the fraud alleged in the second action "rests upon a completely separate set of facts" and violated a different primary right than the one adjudicated in the breach of contract action. "While the monetary loss may be measurable by the same promissory note amount, and hence in a general sense the same 'harm' has been done in both cases," the *Sawyer* court reasoned, "the plaintiffs have been 'harmed' differently by tortious conduct destroying the value of the note, than by the contractual breach of simply failing to pay it."[321] The court concluded that the two lawsuits are based upon separate causes of action therefore res judicata did not bar the second lawsuit.

Conversely, in *Holmes v. David H. Bricker, Inc.*,[322] the California Supreme Court found one primary right violated even though the plaintiffs suffered two different types of injuries. The plaintiffs in *Holmes* purchased a used car from the defendant dealer, which was warranted to be in good working condition. Less than one month later, the plaintiffs' car crashed causing personal injury to them and to their car. Plaintiffs' initially sued the defendant to recover damages for their personal injuries caused by defective brakes, alleging breach of warranty, and obtained a sizable money judgment. Subsequently, plaintiffs filed a second action to recover damages to their car, again alleging breach of warranty. The trial court sustained defendant's

---

[319] *E.g., Boeken v. Philip Morris USA, Inc.*, 48 Cal. 4th 788, 108 Cal. Rptr. 3d 806, 230 P. 3d 342 (2010) (holding current wrongful death against defendant cigarette manufacturer for loss of consortium after plaintiff's husband's death from lung cancer alleged the same primary right as in plaintiff's prior common law action for loss of consortium brought, and dismissed with prejudice, after plaintiff's husband was diagnosed with lung cancer).

[320] 124 Cal. App. 3d 390, 177 Cal. Rptr. 398 (1981).

[321] *Sawyer, supra,* 124 Cal. App. 3d at 403.

[322] 70 Cal. 2d 786, 76 Cal. Rptr. 431, 452 P.2d 647 (1969).

demurrer to plaintiffs' complaint and dismissed their action as barred by claim preclusion.

On appeal, the plaintiffs argued that injuries to person and to property constituted two causes of action. The California Supreme Court acknowledged its prior decisions that injuries to person and property violate two primary rights and constitute two separate causes of action, but explained that those prior decisions involved *tortious* injury to person and property. In contrast, the plaintiffs' present complaint, which alleged breach of warranty, was *contractual* in nature and, as such, was identical to the breach of warranty alleged in the prior personal injury action. The *Holmes* Court concluded that the judgment in the prior action barred the second action because "[u]nder these circumstances the applicable rule is that all damages for a single breach of contract must be recovered in one action." In other words, a breach of contract that results in injury to person and property violates only one primary right, and therefore gives rise to only one cause of action.

[c]   Primary Rights Determined by Precedent

Despite the general uncertainty in defining a "primary right" under the harm suffered approach, some applications of the theory are (relatively) settled by precedent. Perhaps the most frequently encountered application involves a person who simultaneously suffers both personal injury and property damage caused by the defendant's single tortious act. A typical example is negligence litigation arising out of the crash of two cars, where one driver sues the other. The resulting personal injury to the plaintiff driver is a separate primary right from the property damage to the plaintiff's car, and may be pursued in two separate lawsuits.[323] In contrast, pursuant to the holding in *Holmes v. David H. Bricker, Inc., supra*, a breach of contract that results in injury to person and property violates only one primary right and therefore gives rise to only one cause of action.

Other areas are also (relatively) settled by precedent. One wrongful act which results in injury to several pieces of property traditionally gives rise to only one cause of action, as does one wrongful act which results in multiple personal injuries to a plaintiff.[324] However, a wrongful act which causes injury to real property has been held to constitute a separate primary right from injury to personal property situated on the real property.[325]

The question of whether there are two primary rights, or only one primary right with two theories of recovery, often arises in cases where the defendant's conduct potentially violates both federal and state laws. Several California courts have explicitly ruled on this question, and generally agreed that where both laws are

---

[323] *See Holmes, supra*, 70 Cal. 2d at 788-89 (citing several authorities).

[324] *See, e. g., Sawyer v. First City Fin. Corp., supra*, 124 Cal. App. 3d at 399-400 (citing authorities); *Swartzendruber v. City of San Diego*, 3 Cal. App. 4th 896, 904, 5 Cal. Rptr. 2d 64 (1992) (ruling consequential damages did not support a second cause of action); *Allstate Ins. Co. v. Mel Rapton, Inc.*, 77 Cal. App. 4th 901, 92 Cal. Rptr. 2d 151 (2000) (holding a separate cause of action does not arise for each separate item of personal property damaged by one tortious act).

[325] *McNulty v. Copp*, 125 Cal. App. 2d 697, 271 P.2d 90 (1954).

intended to redress the same harm only one primary right is involved.[326] For example, the courts have held that a prior judgment for the plaintiff in an employment discrimination action under a federal civil rights statute precludes a subsequent action under California's fair employment statute because they both involve the same primary right — the right to be free from invidious discrimination in employment.[327]

[d] "Cause of Action"

Accurate use of the term "cause of action" is particularly important in applying California's res judicata doctrine. This term is used in many ways for many purposes, which makes its use for claim preclusion purposes even more confusing.[328] In the vernacular of lawyers, a "cause of action" most often refers to a "different theory of recovery." For example, many lawyers typically say that a client's personal injury caused by a defective product gives rise to several "causes of action" identified as breach of warranty, breach of contract, strict liability, negligence, fraud, etc. And when they plead such a case, lawyers typically allege each of these as a separate "cause of action" in the complaint. This common use of "cause of action" is incorrect for claim preclusion purposes. In our products liability example, the plaintiff has several legal theories but only one cause of action based on the primary right to protection from injury to person.

[3] Inherent Ambiguity of the Primary Rights Theory

A major criticism of the primary rights theory is its inherent ambiguity.[329] Neither the history nor the standard definitions of the doctrine provide much guidance to a court faced with an application not governed by precedent. A broad characterization of what constitutes a primary right will most likely mean that a plaintiff has only one cause of action; a narrow characterization may mean a greater number of causes of action, and more opportunities for multiple lawsuits. In light of the policy favoring judicial economy, a court is likely to resolve this inherent ambiguity in applying the primary rights doctrine by finding only one cause of action.

---

[326] *E.g., Mattson v. City of Costa Mesa*, 106 Cal. App. 3d 441, 447-48, 164 Cal. Rptr. 913 (1980) (holding plaintiff's state court action seeking damages for unlawful arrest based on state negligence law involves same primary right as plaintiff's claim for damages under federal civil rights statute unfavorably determined by prior federal court jury verdict); *City of Los Angeles v. Superior Court (Levy)*, 85 Cal. App. 3d 143, 153, 149 Cal. Rptr. 320 (1978) (holding plaintiff's state court action on state law grounds against defendant officials seeking damages for unlawful seizure and loss of property involved same primary right as in earlier federal civil rights action seeking damages for same seizure of property).

[327] *E.g., Acuna v. Regents of Univ. of Cal.*, 56 Cal. App. 4th 639, 649-50, 65 Cal. Rptr. 2d 388 (1997); *Johnson v. Am. Airlines, Inc.*, 157 Cal. App. 3d 427, 203 Cal. Rptr. 638 (1984).

[328] *See, e.g., Slater v. Blackwood*, 15 Cal. 3d 791, 795-96, 126 Cal. Rptr. 225, 543 P.2d 593 (1975) (observing that the phrase "cause of action" is often used indiscriminately to mean what it says and to mean *counts* which state differently the same cause of action).

[329] *See* Heiser, *California's Unpredictable Res Judicata (Claim Preclusion) Doctrine, supra*, at 602-603; Robin James, Note, *Res Judicata: Should California Abandon Primary Rights?*, 23 Loy. L.A. L. Rev. 351, 387-402 (1989).

For example, in *Takahashi v. Board of Education*,[330] the California Court of Appeal took a broad view of what constitutes a single primary right. The defendant board of education dismissed plaintiff Takahashi, a public school teacher, on the basis of incompetency in the classroom. Plaintiff requested an administrative hearing to contest this evaluation and her dismissal. Because the administrative agency lacked jurisdiction to award damages, plaintiff did not present any defenses to her dismissal based on violation of her civil or constitutional rights. The agency upheld plaintiff's discharge, and this decision was affirmed by the superior court upon judicial review.

Subsequently, plaintiff filed another action in superior court, alleging wrongful discharge from employment and seeking monetary and injunctive relief. Among other claims, plaintiff alleged her termination was due to her race, sex, age, and ancestry in violation of her federal constitutional and state civil rights. The trial court dismissed the action as barred by claim preclusion. On appeal, the *Takahashi* court affirmed, viewing plaintiff's prior and current lawsuits as alleging the invasion of only one primary right — the contractual right to employment by the defendant school district. According to the court, "each act complained of caused the plaintiff's dismissal (wrongful discharge, conspiracy, unconstitutional discharge, discharge in violation of state civil rights) or was a consequence of the termination (emotional distress, damages)" and therefore is "part and parcel of the violation of the single primary right, the single harm suffered."[331]

Compare the reasoning in *Takahashi* with that of *Craig v. County of Los Angeles*[332] where the court found two primary rights violated in a similar fact situation. Plaintiff Craig sought employment as a harbor patrol officer with the defendant County, but was denied the appointment for improper reasons. Craig filed a writ of mandate to enforce a Civil Service Commission recommendation that he be appointed, which resulted in a court order that Craig be hired by the defendant. Craig then filed a subsequent action in state court, this time seeking damages against defendant for intentional infliction of emotional distress and fraud. Defendant demurred based on claim preclusion, and the trial court dismissed the complaint.

The California Court of Appeal reversed, holding that this damage action involves a different primary right than was involved in the prior mandate proceeding and federal action, and was therefore not barred by claim preclusion. The *Craig* court ruled that the type of harm involved in the prior proceeding is different that the type of wrong in the present case. In the prior action "the harm suffered was the denial of the harbor patrol position despite the Commission's order that he be hired," the court reasoned, but in the present action "the harm suffered included the emotional distress which resulted from respondents' wrongful conduct."[333]

---

[330]   202 Cal. App. 3d 1464, 249 Cal. Rptr. 578 (1988), *cert. denied*, 490 U.S. 1011 (1989).

[331]   *Takahashi, supra*, 202 Cal. App. 3d at 1476. The court also observed that "[p]laintiff's allegations of consequential injuries are not based upon infringement of a separate primary right." *Id.*

[332]   221 Cal. App. 3d 1294, 271 Cal. Rptr. 82 (1990).

[333]   *Craig*, 221 Cal. App. 3d at 1302-03.

It is difficult to assess whether *Takahashi* or *Craig* is the better reasoned decision. Given the inherent ambiguity of the primary rights theory, the result reached by each court is justifiable. What can be said is that *Takahashi* takes a broad, almost transactional view of what constitutes a single primary right, whereas *Craig* takes a more narrow view. Such inconsistent views demonstrate a recurring problem with California's primary rights analysis — its application lacks predictability in cases not governed by established precedent.

[4] Primary Rights Doctrine vs. *Restatement*'s Same Transaction

The *Restatement (Second) of Judgments* defines the "claim" extinguished by a prior judgment to include "all rights of the plaintiff to remedies against the defendant with respect to all or any part of the transactions, or series of related transactions, out of which the action arose."[334] One major advantage of the *Restatement* is that its same transaction standard is less ambiguous and therefore more predictable in application than the primary rights approach. The *Restatement's* standard also provides clearer warning of what matter must be raised in an initial lawsuit or be forever barred, and therefore is both fairer and easier to administer.

A second basic advantage is that the same transaction standard is more inclusive in defining the substantive rights extinguished by a prior judgment, and therefore better achieves the goal of judicial economy. For example, a single transaction or occurrence, such as an automobile accident, that tortiously injures the plaintiff in both person and property gives rise to only one "claim" under the *Restatement* standard, as opposed to two "causes of action" under California's primary rights approach. Therefore, under the *Restatement* an automobile accident would result in only one lawsuit — a final judgment on the merits would bar any subsequent action as constituting claim-splitting. In contrast, under California's primary rights doctrine, the same accident could result in two lawsuits — one to damages for personal injury and another for property damage — and a judgment in the first judgment would not bar the second action.

Few if any advantages result from the primary rights approach, unless adherence to tradition and uncertain precedent is viewed as an advantage. A strong case can be made for the recommendation that the California courts should abandon the primary rights doctrine and adopt the *Restatement's* same transaction approach.[335] California's primary rights theory is mostly judge-made doctrine and therefore could be changed or eliminated by the California Supreme Court. However, the Court has not indicated any desire to do so even through the *Restatement's* transactional approach has been adopted by a majority of states as well as by the federal court when applying federal claim preclusion law. Although

---

[334] RESTATEMENT (SECOND) OF JUDGMENTS § 24 (1982).

[335] *See* Heiser, *California's Unpredictable Res Judicata (Claim Preclusion) Doctrine, supra* (arguing that California's primary rights doctrine is inefficient and unpredictable in application) and James, *Res Judicata: Should California Abandon Primary Rights?, supra.*

distinctly a minority view, the primary rights doctrine remains the law of California.

[5]   Claim Preclusion and Pendant ("Supplemental") Claims

One particularly troublesome application of claim preclusion involves the preclusive effect of a prior federal court judgment on related state law claims that were or could have been raised in the federal court action based on pendent ("supplemental") jurisdiction. If the federal court extended pendent jurisdiction over state law claims and resolved these claims on the merits, then obviously the federal court judgment will preclude relitigation of these state law claims in state court. Less clear is the preclusive effect of a federal court judgment with respect to state law claims that were raised in the federal lawsuit, but over which the federal court declined to exercise pendent jurisdiction.

[a]   The Traditional California Rule

Mattson v. City of Costa Mesa,[336] sets forth the traditional California rule on the preclusive effect of a prior federal court judgment which involved a pendent state claim. In *Mattson*, the plaintiff filed a complaint in federal court, alleging violation of his civil rights under federal law and a nonfederal claim of negligence based on the same facts. The federal court declined to exercise pendent jurisdiction over the state law claim. Following an adverse jury verdict on the federal claim, the plaintiff brought a state law negligence action in superior court alleging the same facts as he had alleged in the federal action. The superior court sustained defendants' demurrer on the ground that the state action was barred by claim preclusion, and the California Court of Appeal affirmed.

The *Mattson* Court reasoned that when a federal court has declined to exercise pendent jurisdiction over a nonfederal claim, the plaintiff is presented with a choice. He may proceed to trial on the federal claim or he may elect to dismiss the federal claim without prejudice and litigate both claims in the state court. If the plaintiff "elects to proceed to trial and judgment in the federal court, his entire cause of action is either merged in or barred by the federal court judgment so that he may not thereafter maintain a second suit on the same cause of action in a state court."[337]

[b]   California's Emerging New Approach

The California courts appear to be developing a new approach to the preclusive effect of a prior federal court judgment when the plaintiff alleged the state claim in the federal lawsuit but the federal court declined to exercise pendent jurisdiction. Several recent court of appeal decisions have declined to follow the *Mattson* rule where the federal court, instead of the plaintiff, splits a cause of action.[338] These courts have held that a federal court's discretionary refusal to exercise pendent

---

[336]   106 Cal. App. 3d 441, 164 Cal. Rptr. 913 (1980).

[337]   *Mattson, supra*, 106 Cal. App. 3d at 454-55.

[338]   *E.g., Harris v. Grimes*, 104 Cal. App. 4th 180, 187-89, 127 Cal. Rptr. 2d 791 (2002); *Lucas v. County of Los Angeles*, 47 Cal. App. 4th 277, 286-87, 54 Cal. Rptr. 2d 655 (1996); *see also City of Simi Valley v. Superior Court*, 111 Cal. App. 4th 1077, 1084, 4 Cal. Rptr. 3d 468 (2003) (indicating *Harris* and *Lucas*

jurisdiction over a state claim does not bar further litigation of the state claim in state court.

This new approach, which is based on the *Restatement (Second) of Judgments*,[339] may be preferable to the *Mattson* rule in terms of fairness to a plaintiff who made a good faith effort to persuade the federal court to exercise pendent jurisdiction. Moreover, the *Restatement* approach is the more recent and widely held pronouncement of the law. However, unlike the *Mattson* rule, the *Restatement* approach does not necessarily promote judicial economy. When both the federal and state claims can be heard in state court, the *Mattson* rule encourages a plaintiff to litigate both claims in state court, the court of general jurisdiction. In contrast, in cases where the *Restatement* approach applies, a plaintiff may be permitted to litigate the federal claim in state court and, subsequently or simultaneously, to litigate the state claim in state court.[340]

[6] Preclusion Based on California's Cross-Complaint Statutes

[a] Compulsory Cross-Complaints

The California "cross-complaint" is a multi-purpose pleading device. One type of cross-complaint is where one party (usually the defendant) asserts a cause of action back against an opposing party (usually the plaintiff) — in other words, a counterclaim in federal court terminology. Code of Civil Procedure § 426.10 and § 426.30 set forth the general preclusion rules for failure to plead a compulsory cross-complaint. Under section 426.30(a), if a party against whom a complaint has been filed and served fails to allege in a cross-complaint any "related cause of action" which he has against the plaintiff, "such party may not thereafter in any other action assert against the plaintiff the related cause of action not pleaded." In other words, a "related cause of action" must be alleged as a (compulsory) cross-complaint or its assertion in another lawsuit will be barred. A "related cause of action" is defined as "a cause of action which arises out of the same transaction, occurrence or series of transactions or occurrences as the cause of action which the plaintiff alleges in his complaint."[341] Thus, California's mandatory cross-claim rule

---

state the general rule); *but see Acuna v. Regents of Univ. of Cal.*, 56 Cal. App. 639, 650-52, 65 Cal. Rptr. 2d 388 (1997) (following the *Mattson* doctrine).

[339] RESTATEMENT (SECOND) OF JUDGMENTS § 25 cmt. e (1982).

[340] A further complication is the role of federal common law, which may dictate a different rule for determining the claim preclusive effect of a prior federal court judgment. The United States Supreme Court has indicated that federal common law determines the preclusive effect afforded a prior federal court judgment in a subsequent state court proceeding. *Semtek Int'l, Inc. v. Lockheed Martin Corp.*, 531 U.S. 497 (2001). Where subject matter jurisdiction in the prior federal action was based on diversity of citizenship, not on federal question jurisdiction, the Court in *Semtek* held that, as a matter of federal common law, the claim-preclusive effect of the federal court judgment should be determined by the claim preclusion law of the state in which the federal diversity court sits. However, the United States Supreme Court has not had occasion to consider the content of the federal common law rule that might be applicable in a *Mattson*-type situation.

[341] CAL. CODE CIV. PROC. § 426.10(c).

is the analogue to the federal compulsory counterclaim rule.[342]

[b] The Effect of Compulsory Cross-Complaints on Primary Rights Analysis

As explained previously, a single factual transaction may give rise to the violation of more than one primary right and therefore give a plaintiff the potential of two separate lawsuits against a single defendant. Under established primary rights precedent, for example, one tortious act may violate two primary rights and create two separate causes of action: one for injury to person and a second for damages to property. A typical example is negligence litigation arising out of the crash of two cars, where one driver sues the other. The resulting personal injury to the plaintiff driver is a separate cause of action from the property damage to plaintiff's car, and may be pursued in two separate lawsuits.

In contrast, the California's cross-complaint statutes utilize a "transactional" standard — not a primary rights standard — in defining compulsory cross-complaints.[343] In some circumstance, the transactional cross-complaint standard may have an impact on the primary rights approach to claim preclusion. Consider the following typical occurrence. Sam Saguaro's car collided with Laura Lorry's truck. Both parties suffered personal injuries, and both vehicles were totaled. Plaintiff Saguaro sued defendant Lorry in superior court for personal injury damages, alleging his injuries were caused by defendant's negligence. Defendant answered and cross-complained against plaintiff, seeking damages for her own personal injuries and alleging they were caused by plaintiff's negligence. The jury found plaintiff Saguaro 5% negligent and defendant Lorry 95% negligent, and awarded appropriate damages.

Plaintiff Saguaro then files a subsequent lawsuit against defendant Lorry seeking damages for the destruction of his car. Because plaintiff's second suit is based on a separate primary right, his cause of action is not barred by claim preclusion. However, plaintiff's second action is barred by California's compulsory cross-complaint statutes, which define a "complaint" to also mean a cross-complaint and a "plaintiff" to also mean a person who files a cross-complaint.[344] In other words, once defendant Lorry filed her cross-complaint in the first lawsuit, plaintiff Saguaro must plead any "related cause of action" he has against the defendant. Because Saguaro failed to file a cross-complaint, he forfeited his cause of action for property damages. This result would be the same if defendant Lorry had won the first lawsuit. The net practical effect of this means that the "same transaction" standard is usually applicable and not the "primary rights" approach in determining what claims *must* be litigated in the typical automobile negligence case. Therefore, it is somewhat misleading in such cases to view California as following a primary rights theory which permits separate lawsuits for different causes of action.

---

[342] FED. R. CIV. P. 13(a).

[343] CAL. CODE CIV. PROC. §§ 426.30(a), 426.10(c).

[344] CAL. CODE CIV. PROC. § 426.10(a).

[7] The Requirement of a Final Judgment on the Merits

The doctrine of claim preclusion applies only to "final" judgments or orders. The California rule is that a judgment is not final for purposes of claim preclusion if it is still open to direct attack by appeal or otherwise.[345] Consequently, an order or judgment is not final for claim preclusion purposes during the pendency of an appeal or, even though no appeal has yet been taken, until the time for appeal has expired. The federal courts and a majority of state courts follow a different rule: a judgment once rendered is final for claim preclusion purposes until reversed on appeal, modified, or set aside. Under this approach, the pendency of an appeal does not suspend the claim preclusive effect of an otherwise final judgment.

To have a claim preclusive effect, a judgment must not only be final but must also be rendered "on the merits." The paradigm "judgment on the merits" is one rendered by a judge or jury after a full trial of the issues of fact and law, and also includes a judgment entered on a directed verdict and a judgment notwithstanding the verdict. When not dealing with the paradigm, the question of whether a decision is on the merits becomes a little more complicated. Generally, a judgment by default is "on the merits" and is conclusive as to all issues pleaded in the complaint.[346] Likewise, a summary judgment that adjudicates the substantive merits of a cause of action will have a claim preclusive effect, as will general demurrer granted for failure to state a cause of action[347] However, a summary judgment or demurrer that disposes of an action without reaching the substantive merits, such as for lack of jurisdiction or because barred by the statute of limitations, is not a judgment on the merits.[348]

[8] Claim Preclusive Effect of Non-Judicial Tribunal Decision

The general rule in California is that the final administrative determination of an administrative agency acting in a judicial capacity will have a claim preclusive effect in any subsequent court proceeding.[349] An administrative agency acts in a judicial capacity when it resolves disputed issues of fact properly before it and provides the parties with an opportunity to present evidence and fully litigate the issues. However, a decision of an administrative agency is not considered final for claim preclusion purposes while subject to direct review in court. Also, although the

---

[345] *E.g., Agarwal v. Johnson*, 25 Cal. 3d 932, 954, n.11, 160 Cal. Rptr. 141, 603 P.2d 58 (1979); *National Union Fire Ins. Co. v. Stites Prof'l Law Corp.*, 235 Cal. App. 3d 1718, 1726, 1 Cal. Rptr. 2d 570 (1991).

[346] *E.g., English v. English*, 9 Cal. 2d 358, 70 P.2d 625 (1937); *see* RESTATEMENT (SECOND) JUDGMENTS § 19 cmt. c (1982). However, a defendant may challenge the res judicata effect of a prior default judgment by a collateral attack on the validity of the rendering court's jurisdiction. *See, e.g., Marriage of Nosbisch*, 5 Cal. App. 4th 629, 635, 6 Cal. Rptr. 2d 817 (1992); *Pennoyer v. Neff*, 95 U.S. 714 (1877).

[347] *E.g., Stuart v. Lilves*, 210 Cal. App. 3d 1215, 1218, 258 Cal. Rptr. 780 (1989) (summary judgment); *See v. Joughin*, 18 Cal. 2d 603, 607, 116 P.2d 777 (1941) (general demurrer).

[348] *E.g., Koch v. Rodlin Enter., Inc.*, 223 Cal. App. 3d 1591, 1595-97, 273 Cal. Rptr. 438 (1990); *Goddard,v. Sec. Title Ins. & Guar. Co.*, 14 Cal. 2d 47, 51-52, 92 P. 2d 804 (1939).

[349] *See, e.g., Hollywood Circle, Inc. v. Dept. of Alcoholic Beverage Control*, 55 Cal. 2d 728, 732-33, 13 Cal. Rptr. 104, 361 P.2d 712 (1961); *Johnson v. City of Loma Linda*, 24 Cal. 4th 61, 69-76, 99 Cal. Rptr. 2d 316, 5 P.3d 874 (2000).

claim preclusion rules are generally applicable to administrative decisions, their enforcement is sometimes more flexible than when applied to judicial decisions.[350]

[9] Sister State Judgments

A judgment rendered by a court of a sister state is entitled to the same claim preclusive effect in California courts as it would have in the courts of the rendering state.[351] This treatment is mandated by the Full Faith and Credit Clause of the United States Constitution,[352] and by federal and state statutes.[353] Any challenge to according full faith and credit to a sister state judgment is limited to a determination of whether the rendering court had fundamental jurisdiction of the case.[354] Full Faith and Credit requires recognition of sister state judgments for purposes of enforcement, as well as for claim preclusion purposes.[355] Enforcement of sister state money judgments in California is governed by the Sister State and Foreign Money Judgments Act.[356]

[10] Pleading, Proof, and Waiver of Claim Preclusion

Claim preclusion must be properly pleaded or proved at trial, or it is waived.[357] The normal and appropriate method of raising claim preclusion is by an affirmative defense. However, claim preclusion can be raised by a general demurrer where the complaint pleads, or the court takes judicial notice of, the former judgment.[358] Likewise, statutory preclusion pursuant to Code of Civil Procedure § 426.30, which bars a cause of action not asserted as a compulsory cross-complaint in a prior action, must be pleaded as an affirmative defense in the subsequent action. Failure to do so constitutes a waiver of this statutory defense.[359]

---

[350] *E.g., George Arakelian Farms, Inc. v. Agric. Labor Relations Bd.*, 49 Cal. 3d 1279, 1290-91, 265 Cal. Rptr. 162, 783 P.2d 749 (1989).

[351] *Underwriters Nat. Assurance Co. v. N. Carolina Guar. Ass'n*, 455 U.S. 691, 705, 102 S. Ct. 1357, 71 L. Ed. 2d 558 (1982); *Durfee v. Duke*, 375 U.S. 106, 109-11, 84 S. Ct. 242, 11 L. Ed. 2d 186 (1963); *St. Sava Mission Corp. v. Serbian E. Orthodox Diocese*, 223 Cal. App. 3d 1354, 1364, 273 Cal. Rptr. 340 (1990).

[352] U.S. CONST. art. IV, § 1. The Full Faith and Credit Clause is discussed in detail in § 15.10 & § 15.11, *supra*.

[353] Full Faith and Credit Act, 28 U.S.C. § 1738; Cal. Code Civ. Proc. § 1913.

[354] *Durfee, supra*, 375 U.S. at 109-11; *St. Sava Mission, supra*; 223 Cal. App. 3d at 1364; *World Wide Imports, Inc. v. Bartel*, 145 Cal. App. 3d 1006, 1010, 193 Cal. Rptr. 830 (1983); Cal. Code Civ. Proc. § 1916.

[355] *E.g., Medical Legal Consulting Serv., Inc. v. Covarrubias*, 214 Cal. App. 3d 80, 89-93, 285 Cal. Rptr. 559 (1991).

[356] Cal. Code Civ. Proc. §§ 1710.10-1710.65. Enforcement of a money judgment rendered by a court in a foreign country is governed by the Uniform Foreign-Country Money Judgments Recognition Act. Cal. Code Civ. Proc. §§ 1713-1724.

[357] *See, e.g., Wolfsen v. Hathaway*, 32 Cal. 2d 632, 638, 198 P.2d 1 (1948); *Road Sprinkler Fitters Local Union No. 669 v. G & G Fire Sprinklers*, 102 Cal. App. 4th 765, 772, n.6, 125 Cal. Rptr. 2d 804 (2002).

[358] *E.g., Flores v. Arroyo*, 56 Cal. 2d 492, 496-97, 15 Cal. Rptr. 87, 364 P.2d 263 (1961); *Carroll v. Puritan Leasing Co.*, 77 Cal. App. 3d 481, 486, 143 Cal. Rptr. 772 (1978); *see* Cal. Evid. Code §§ 452(d), 453 (permitting judicial notice of court records).

[359] *Hulsey v. Koehler*, 218 Cal. App. 3d 1150, 1153, 1158, 267 Cal. Rptr. 523 (1990).

Unlike claim preclusion, no special plea is required to raise issue preclusion because it merely involves conclusive evidence of a fact in issue as opposed to a complete defense.[360] Even if not raised by pleadings or during pretrial proceedings, issue preclusion can be raised for the first time at trial or, in some situations, in a motion to set aside a judgment after trial.

§ 15.17 CALIFORNIA'S COLLATERAL ESTOPPEL (ISSUE PRECLUSION) DOCTRINE

[1] Introductory Note

Collateral estoppel (issue preclusion) bars a party from relitigating an issue of fact or of law if that issue was actually litigated and determined by a valid and final judgment in a previous proceeding. The prior determination of the issue is conclusive in a subsequent action between the parties, or those persons in privity with a party, whether dealing with the same or a different cause of action.[361] Consequently, issue preclusion may be applicable in a subsequent action even though claim preclusion is unavailable.

Issue preclusion may play a more significant judicial economy role in California than in some other jurisdictions. This is because, unlike the majority of other states, California employs the primary rights theory to narrow the scope of claim preclusion. Consider, for example, a situation where a negligence act by a defendant injures the plaintiff's person and property. Under primary rights analysis, the plaintiff is permitted to bring two lawsuits, for example, one to recover damages from the defendant for the personal injuries and a second to recover damages for the property loss. However, if the plaintiff loses the first lawsuit because the defendant was determined not to have been negligent, issue preclusion will prevent the plaintiff from relitigating the issue of negligence in the second action. If the plaintiff wins the first lawsuit, issue preclusion will conclusively establish the defendant's negligence in the second action rendering litigation of that issue unnecessary. Regardless of whether the plaintiff wins or loses the first action in our example, issue preclusion results in some economies for the court and the parties.

Unlike claim preclusion, where the California courts apply their own primary rights theory, the California courts usually rely on the *Restatement (Second) of Judgments* when resolving questions of issue preclusion. Court opinions often quote extensively from relevant sections of the *Restatement*, as well as from the explanations contained in the various section "comments."[362] Nevertheless, as will

---

[360] *Dakins v. Bd. of Pension Comm'r*, 134 Cal. App. 3d 374, 387, 184 Cal. Rptr. 576 (1982); *Solari v. Atlas-Universal Serv., Inc.*, 215 Cal. App. 2d 587, 592-93, 30 Cal. Rptr. 407 (1963).

[361] *See, e.g., George Arakelian Farms, Inc. v. Agric. Labor Relations Bd.*, 49 Cal. 3d 1279, 265 Cal. Rptr. 162, 783 P.2d 749 (1989) (citing § 27, *Restatement Second of Judgments* (1982)).

[362] *E.g., Lucido v. Superior Court*, 51 Cal. 3d 335, 272 Cal. Rptr. 767, 795 P.2d 1223 (1990); *Perez v. City of San Bruno*, 27 Cal. 3d 875, 168 Cal. Rptr. 114, 616 P.2d 1287 (1980); *In re Nathaniel P.*, 211 Cal. App. 3d 660, 259 Cal. Rptr. 555 (1989) (quoting *Restatement* § 28(4)); *Barker v. Hull*, 191 Cal. App. 3d 221, 226, 236 Cal. Rptr. 285 (1987) (quoting § 27, comment d); *Sandoval v. Superior Court*, 140 Cal. App. 3d

be discussed below, the California courts do not always strictly adhere to the *Restatement*'s principles.

[2] The California Issue Preclusion (Collateral Estoppel) Doctrine, Generally

In *Lucido v. Superior Court*,[363] the California Supreme Court identified the "threshold requirements" for issue preclusion under the California doctrine: (1) the issue is identical to that decided in the former proceeding, (2) the issue was actually litigated in the former proceeding, (3) the issue was necessarily decided in the former proceeding, (4) the decision in the former proceeding is final and on the merits, and (5) preclusion is sought against a person who was a party or in privity with a party to the former proceeding. These prerequisites are essentially the same as those stated in section 27 of the *Restatement (Second) of Judgments*.[364]

The *Lucido* Court also distinguished between the "threshold requirements" and the public policy considerations of issue preclusion, which influence whether its application in a particular circumstance would be fair to the parties and constitutes sound judicial policy. According to the Court, these policies are: "preservation of the integrity of the judicial system, promotion of judicial economy, and protection of litigants from harassment by vexatious litigation."[365] In a subsequent decision, the Court further explained the role of these public policy considerations.

> Whether collateral estoppel is fair and consistent with public policy in a particular case depends in part upon the character of the forum that first decided the issue later sought to be foreclosed. In this regard, courts consider the judicial nature of the prior forum, *i.e.*, its legal formality, the scope of its jurisdiction, and its procedural safeguards, particularly including the opportunity for judicial review of adverse rulings.[366]

As these decisions demonstrate, policy considerations play a much larger role in the application of issue preclusion than claim preclusion in the California courts.

In addition, California courts have long recognized a "public interest" exception to the doctrine of collateral estoppel. Even if the formal prerequisites to collateral estoppel are present, an important public interest may permit relitigation of issues determined in a prior judgment. Cases applying this exception usually find the requisite overriding public interest in statutes designed to protect the public, and often involve a government entity as the party in whose favor the exception is

---

932, 190 Cal. Rptr. 29 (1983) (relying on § 29 and comments thereunder).

[363] 51 Cal. 3d 335, 272 Cal. Rptr. 767, 795 P.2d 1223 (1990).

[364] The requirements for collateral estoppel under the *Restatement (Second) of Judgments* § 27 are discussed in § 15.07, *supra*.

[365] *Lucido, supra,* 51 Cal. 3d at 343. In *Lucido*, the court refused to apply issue preclusion even though the threshold requirements were satisfied because to do so would be inconsistent with these public policies, and therefore held that an issue determination favorable to the defendant in a probation revocation hearing did not collaterally estop the prosecution from relitigating the identical issue in a subsequent criminal prosecution.

[366] *Vandenberg v. Superior Court,* 21 Cal. 4th 815, 830, 88 Cal. Rptr. 2d 366, 982 P.2d 229 (1999).

applied.[367]

[3] What is an "Identical Issue" for Purposes of Issue Preclusion?

Issue Preclusion bars relitigation of an issue "identical" to an issue decided in a previous proceeding. One difficulty in applying this requirement is that issues may not be totally identical in the literal sense of same time, place, occurrence, and legal context.[368] As in other jurisdictions, the California courts sometimes must determine whether or not a party is seeking to relitigate an issue previously litigated even though the two proceedings involve different historical transactions,[369] changes in factual circumstances,[370] or raise the issue in a different legal context,[371] sometimes with conflicting results. Such problems are inherent in any attempt to delineate the issues foreclosed by prior litigation and are perhaps an inevitable by-product of the issue preclusion doctrine.

Issue preclusion will not bar relitigation of an issue where the adversary in the second action has a significantly heavier burden of proof than he had in the first

---

[367] *E.g., Arcadia Unified Sch. Dist. v. State Dept. of Ed.*, 2 Cal. 4th 251, 257-59, 5 Cal. Rptr. 2d 545, 825 P.2d 438 (1992) (ruling the California Department of Education is not collaterally estopped from relitigating constitutionality of statute authorizing school districts to charge fees for pupil transportation); *City of Sacramento v. State of Cal.*, 50 Cal. 3d 51, 64-65, 266 Cal. Rptr. 139, 785 P.2d 522 (1990) (ruling the State is not collaterally estopped from relitigating issue of whether the State is required to reimburse local governments for certain unemployment insurance expenses under California Constitution, even though issue determined adversely to State in prior lawsuit); *Chern v. Bank of Am.*, 15 Cal. 3d 866, 872, 127 Cal. Rptr. 110, 544 P.2d 1310 (1978) (applying the exception to permit relitigation of certain banking practices issues based on strong public interest to regulate banking evidenced by applicable federal and state statutes).

[368] *See* Walter W. Heiser, *California's Confusing Collateral Estoppel (Issue Preclusion) Doctrine*, 35 SAN DIEGO L. REV. 509, 535-36 (1998).

[369] Courts sometimes find collateral estoppel inapplicable in a subsequent action involving parallel facts but concerning a different historical transaction. *See, e.g., Chern v. Bank of Am.*, 15 Cal. 3d 866, 127 Cal. Rptr. 110, 544 P.2d 1310 (1976). Other times, courts conclude the fact that issues previously determined in a prior judgment related to a different historical transaction does not "separate the issues or render them non-identical." *E.g., County of Los Angeles v. Cnty. Assessment Appeals Bd.*, 13 Cal. App. 4th 102, 16 Cal. Rptr. 2d 479, 483 (1993); *Frommhagen v. Bd. of Supervisors*, 197 Cal. App. 3d 1292, 243 Cal. Rptr. 390 (1987) (prior judgment upholding validity of county's levy of service charges for 1984-1985 fiscal year bars present action challenging validity of such charges for 1985-1986 with respect to issues not affected by the fact they involve charges levied in different years).

[370] *Compare, e.g., Evans v. Celotex Corp.*, 194 Cal. App. 3d 741, 238 Cal. Rptr. 259 (1987) (holding that a prior judgment which found that a relative's illness was not caused by asbestos exposure collaterally estopped instant wrongful death action despite new facts that relative died after prior judgments and autopsy revealed asbestos exposure was the cause of the relative's illness and death) *with Smith v. ExxonMobil Oil Corp.*, 153 Cal. App. 4th 1407, 1419, n. 7, 64 Cal. Rptr. 3d 69 (2007) (noting the *Evans* court's conclusion can only be justified if the plaintiffs were previously able to obtain and present evidence that death was caused by asbestos, and the biopsy did not provide substantially stronger evidence).

[371] The courts sometimes conclude that collateral estoppel does not apply where the same issue arises in different legal contexts. *See, e.g., Ruffalo v. Patterson*, 234 Cal. App. 3d 341, 285 Cal. Rptr. 647 (1991) (holding that determination in plaintiff's prior dissolution of marriage judgment that certain property was community property did not collaterally estop plaintiff from suing her former attorney for negligently instructing plaintiff to characterize the property as community property).

action.[372] For example, a prior acquittal in a criminal action, where the State failed to prove each element of a crime beyond a reasonable doubt, does not bar relitigation of the same issues by the State against the defendant in a subsequent civil action governed by the lower preponderance of the evidence standard.[373] Likewise, a finding for the State in a civil action does not preclude relitigation of the same issues by the defendant in a related subsequent criminal action. Conversely, a finding for the defendant and against the plaintiff State in a civil action may bar the State from prosecuting the same issue in a subsequent criminal proceeding.[374] And any issue necessarily litigated against the defendant in a prior criminal conviction is conclusively determined against the defendant in a subsequent civil action.[375] However, a prior criminal conviction based on a guilty plea does not have a collateral estoppel effect because a plea may only reflect a compromise and not a full presentation of the issues.[376]

[4] Issues Actually Litigated and Determined

The central feature of California's issue preclusion doctrine is that issues must have been "actually litigated and determined" in the prior action. This seemingly straightforward requirement has produced some problems, many of which can be traced back to the 1940 opinion in *Sutphin v. Spiek*,[377] where the California Supreme Court addressed the general question of under what circumstances is an issue to be deemed decided by a prior judgment. "Obviously," the *Sutphin* Court answered, "if a matter was actually raised by proper pleadings and treated as an issue in the prior case, it is conclusively determined by the first judgment." But, the Court reasoned, the issue preclusion rule goes further and applies to "matters which were raised or could have been raised, on matters litigated or litigable."

Further explaining its reasoning in a supplemental opinion, the *Sutphin* Court denied that it had extended issue preclusion to any issue which could have been raised in the first suit even though not actually determined. Instead, the Court explained that the defendant in *Sutphin* had not in fact actually raised a "new issue" in the second suit. According to the court, the defendant's asserted "new issue" was simply another "legal theory by which the same issue might be differently decided." The Court concluded by observing that the defendant should not be permitted to relitigate an issue determined in an earlier action "whenever defendant can discover a new theory upon which to attack" the prior

---

[372] *See, e.g. In re Nathaniel P.*, 211 Cal. App. 3d 660, 259 Cal. Rptr. 555 (1989) (a finding in a dependency proceeding that a father physically and sexually abused his children under a preponderance of the evidence standard did not preclude relitigation of the same issue by the father in a subsequent action to terminate his parental rights, where the standard is clear and convincing evidence).

[373] *See In re Coughlin*, 16 Cal. 3d 52, 58-59, 127 Cal. Rptr. 337, 545 P.2d 249 (1976); RESTATEMENT (SECOND) OF JUDGMENTS § 28(4) (1982).

[374] *See People v. Sims*, 32 Cal. 3d 468, 485, 186 Cal. Rptr. 77, 651 P.2d 321 (1982).

[375] *Teitelbaum Furs, Inc. v. Dominion Ins. Co.*, 58 Cal. 2d 601, 25 Cal. Rptr. 559, 375 P.2d 439 (1962).

[376] *See Teitelbaum Furs, supra*, 58 Cal. 2d at 605-606; *Pease v. Pease*, 201 Cal. App. 3d 29, 246 Cal. Rptr. 762 (1988) (collecting cases).

[377] 15 Cal. 2d 195, 99 P.2d 652 (1940), *reh'g. denied*, 15 Cal. 2d 195, 101 P.2d 497 (1940).

determination.[378] In other words, issue preclusion will not bar a party from raising a new "issue" in a subsequent proceeding, but will foreclose a party from merely presenting a new factual or legal "theory" with respect to the same "issue" previously litigated.[379]

Quoting from *Sutphin*, the California courts sometimes describe the issue preclusive effect of a prior judgment as precluding relitigation of "matters which were raised or could have been raised, or matters litigated or litigable"[380] To some extent, this may be the result of the *Sutphin* court's use of imprecise language. For example, the *Restatement* makes an analogous distinction between an "ultimate fact" and an "evidentiary fact," commenting "if the party against whom preclusion is sought did in fact litigate an issue of ultimate fact and suffered an adverse determination, new evidentiary facts may not be brought forward to obtain a different determination of that ultimate fact."[381] Unfortunately, some courts invoke *Sutphin's* language to justify affording an issue preclusive effect to issues that *could* have been, but were not actually, litigated in a prior proceeding. Fortunately, this reliance on *Sutphin* is limited to only a few applications, such as the issue preclusive effect of a default judgment and a stipulated judgment.

[5] Issue Preclusive Effect of Default Judgments, Stipulated Judgments, and Voluntary Dismissals With Prejudice

A default judgment constitutes a judgment on the merits and, as such, will have a claim preclusive effect on subsequent actions, so long as the default is a valid judgment. A more problematic question is whether a default judgment also has a issue preclusive effect. The *Restatement* states that in the case of a judgment entered by default, none of the issues are actually litigated.[382] Consequently, the *Restatement* view is that a default judgment has no issue preclusive effect with respect to any issue raised in a subsequent action.

The California courts do not follow the *Restatement* view. Instead, under the California rule, a default judgment will have a issue preclusive effect as to material issues actually raised in the pleadings and necessary to uphold the default judgment.[383] For example, in *County of San Diego v. Hotz*,[384] the court held that an Iowa dissolution degree entered by default which contained express findings

---

[378] *Sutphin v. Speik, supra,* 15 Cal. 2d at 205.

[379] *See* Heiser, *California's Confusing Collateral Estoppel (Issue Preclusion)Doctrine, supra,* 35 SAN DIEGO L. REV. at 540.

[380] *See, e.g., Marriage of Mason,* 46 Cal. App. 4th 1025, 1028, 54 Cal. Rptr. 2d 263 (1996); *Tensor Group v. City of Glendale,* 14 Cal. App. 4th 154, 160, 17 Cal. Rptr. 2d 639 (1993); *Interinsurance Exch. of the Auto. Club v. Superior Court,* 209 Cal. App. 3d 177, 182, 257 Cal. Rptr. 37 (1989).

[381] RESTATEMENT (SECOND) OF JUDGMENTS, § 27 cmt. c (1982).

[382] RESTATEMENT (SECOND) OF JUDGMENTS § 27 cmt. e (1982).

[383] *English v. English,* 9 Cal. 2d 358, 70 P.2d 625 (1937); *Four Star Elec. Inc. v. Feh Const.,* 7 Cal. App. 4th 1375, 10 Cal. Rptr. 2d 1 (1992); *see Murray v. Alaska Airlines, Inc.,* 50 Cal. 4th 860, 871, 114 Cal. Rptr. 3d 241, 237 P. 3d 565 (2010) (indicating in dicta that a default judgment is res judicata as to all issues aptly pleaded in the complaint and the defendant is estopped from denying in a subsequent action any allegations contained in the former complaint).

[384] 168 Cal. App. 3d 605, 214 Cal. Rptr. 658 (1985).

that Hotz was the father of a child precluded defendant Hotz from contesting the issue of paternity in a subsequent action by the County for support and reimbursement of welfare given the child. Issue preclusion will not, however, preclude litigation of available defenses not raised by the defendant in the prior default judgment but sought to be raised by defendant in a later suit on a different cause of action.[385]

In a similar vein, the California rule is that a stipulated or consent judgment has a issue preclusive effect as to the issues put in dispute by the pleadings, unless the parties agree otherwise.[386] In developing this rule, several courts have applied the "raised or could have been raised" rationale of *Sutphin v. Speik* to justify the extension of issue preclusion to a stipulated judgment. In contrast, the view of the *Restatement* is that a stipulated judgment does not have an issue preclusive effect, unless the parties agree otherwise, because the issues were are not actually litigated and determined but rather were resolved by the parties' compromise.[387]

[6]   Issue "Necessarily Decided" in Prior Proceeding

Issue preclusion bars relitigation of an issue determined in a prior proceeding, but only if resolution of that issue was necessary to the prior judgment.[388] In *Lucido v. Superior Court*,[389] the California Supreme Court construed this requirement to mean that the issue must not have been "entirely unnecessary" to the judgment in the prior proceeding. An interesting application of this "necessary" requirement is where a judgment is based on two or more alternative grounds and either ground, standing alone, could support the judgment. With respect to the issue preclusive effect of such a judgment, the California courts have adopted the approach of the *Restatement (Second) of Judgments* and announced the following rule: Where a trial court decides a case on two alternative grounds and the reviewing court affirms based on one of those grounds, declining to consider the other, the judgment is binding for purposes of issue preclusion only on

---

[385] *English v. English, supra*, 9 Cal. 2d at 363.

[386] *See, e.g., California State Auto. Ass'n Interins. Bureau v. Superior Court*, 50 Cal. 3d 658, 664-65, n.2, 667, 268 Cal. Rptr. 284, 788 P.2d 1156 (1990) (collecting cases and ruling that a stipulated judgment may properly be given a collateral estoppel effect as to all issues of liability, unless the scope of such issue preclusion is restricted by the parties); *Wittman v. Chrysler Corp.*, 199 Cal. App. 3d 586, 591-593, 245 Cal. Rptr. 20 (1988) (ruling that a consent judgment had a collateral estoppel effect on issues raised in the pleadings although abandoned by a party).

[387] RESTATEMENT (SECOND) OF JUDGMENTS § 27 cmt. e (1982).

[388] *See, e.g., Bronco Wine Co v. Frank A. Logoluso Farms*, 214 Cal. App. 3d 699, 262 Cal. Rptr. 899 (1989) (finding by court as to amount of contract damages in upholding administrative suspension of defendant's wine producer's license did not preclude court from determining amount of contract damages in subsequent breach of contract action by growers against defendant because finding in first proceeding was unnecessary to that judgment); *Marriage of Rabkin*, 179 Cal. App. 3d 1071, 225 Cal. Rptr. 219 (1986) (holding a statement by trial court in order granting temporary increase in spousal support because marital residence not yet sold — that such sale would constitute a change in circumstances justifying a future modification in spousal support — was unnecessary to that court's decision, so given no collateral estoppel effect).

[389] 51 Cal. 3d 335, 342, 272 Cal. Rptr. 767, 795 P.2d 1223 (1990).

the ground addressed by the appellate court.[390]

[7]　Issue preclusive Effect of Administrative Agency Decisions

In appropriate circumstances, a final decision by an administrative agency will have an issue preclusive, as well as a claim preclusive, effect. In *People v. Sims*,[391] the California Supreme Court held that issue preclusion may be applied to decisions made by administrative agencies when the agency was acting in a "judicial capacity" and resolved disputed issues of fact properly before it which the parties have had a full and fair opportunity to litigate.[392] The *Sims* Court found that an administrative hearing conducted by the state welfare department was a judicial-like adversarial proceeding, and its determinations should be given an issue preclusive effect.

[8]　Final Judgment for Purposes of Issue Preclusion

One of the requirements for issue preclusion is that there must be a "final" judgment on the merits in the previous suit. To be "final" in this context, a judgment must be a firm and stable one, the last word of the rendering court.[393] However, with respect to an administrative agency, a decision is not considered "final" for purposes of issue preclusion unless the decision is free from direct attack by appeal to the superior court or by petition for administrative mandamus because the time for judicial review has expired.[394]

[9]　Issue Preclusion (Collateral Estoppel) and Mutuality

For many years, the California courts and those of all other states required "mutuality" of parties as a prerequisite to issue preclusion.[395] The concept of "mutuality" had many complicated niceties, but in essence the doctrine required

---

[390] *E.g., Zevnik v. Superior Court*, 159 Cal. App. 4th 76, 70 Cal. Rptr. 3d 817 (2008); *Newport Beach Country Club, Inc. v. Founding Members of the Newport Beach Country Club*, 140 Cal. App. 4th 1120, 45 Cal. Rptr. 3d 207 (2006).

[391] 32 Cal. 3d 468, 186 Cal. Rptr. 77, 651 P.2d 321 (1982).

[392] In *Pacific Lumber Co. v. State Water Res. Control Bd.*, 37 Cal. 4th 921, 943, 38 Cal. Rptr. 3d 220. 126 P. 3d 1040 (2006), the California Supreme Court explained more fully that for an administrative decision to have an issue preclusive effect the administrative proceeding must possess a judicial character: "Indicia of proceedings undertaken in a judicial capacity include a hearing before an impartial decision maker; testimony given under oath or affirmation; a party's ability to subpoena, call, examine, and cross-examine witnesses, to introduce documentary evidence, and to make oral and written argument; the taking of a record of the proceeding; and a written statement of reasons for the decision." Another relevant, but not conclusive, factor is whether the administrative decision is subject to judicial review by administrative mandamus. *Id.* at 943, n 12.

[393] *Producers Dairy Delivery Co. v. Sentry Ins. Co.*, 41 Cal. 3d 903, 911, 226 Cal. Rptr. 558, 718 P.2d 920 (1986).

[394] *See People v. Sims, supra,* 32 Cal. 3d at 485-86.

[395] *See generally* E.H. Schopler, Annotation, *Mutuality of Estoppel As Prerequisite of Availability of Doctrine of Collateral Estoppel to a Stranger to the Judgment,* 31 A.L.R.3d 1044-99 (1970) (collecting cases).

that a party *asserting* issue preclusion in a present proceeding must have been the same party, or in privity with a party, in the previous litigation. California was the first jurisdiction to reject the traditional mutuality doctrine, by the landmark 1942 decision of *Bernhard v. Bank of America.*[396]

In *Bernhard*, the California Supreme Court noted that the criteria for determining *who may assert* issue preclusion differ fundamentally from the criteria for determining *against whom* a plea of issue preclusion may be asserted, and then articulated the now familiar inquiries for application of issue preclusion: "Was the issue decided in the prior adjudication identical with the one presented in the action in question? Was there a final judgment on the merits? Was the party *against whom* the plea is asserted a party or in privity with a party to the prior adjudication?"[397] The *Bernhard* decision had an impact far beyond California. The federal courts and most state courts have eliminated the mutuality requirement, especially where, as in *Bernhard*, the prior judgment is invoked *defensively* in a second action against a plaintiff bringing suit on an issue that the plaintiff litigated and lost as plaintiff against a different defendant in a prior action.[398]

The California courts also recognize the more controversial doctrine of *offensive* nonmutual issue preclusion, *i.e.*, where a plaintiff seeks to foreclose a defendant from relitigating issues which the defendant previously litigated and lost against another plaintiff.[399] These courts apply the standards adopted in *Parklane Hosiery Co. v. Shore*,[400] where the United States Supreme Court defined the federal common law doctrine for use in the federal courts. *Parklane* held that the offensive use of nonmutual issue preclusion was permitted in the broad discretion of the trial court based on the following general rule: "[I]n cases where a plaintiff could easily have joined in the earlier action or where, either for the reasons discussed above or for other reasons, the application of offensive estoppel would be unfair to a defendant, a trial judge should not allow the use of offensive issue preclusion."[401]

---

[396] 19 Cal. 2d 807, 122 P.2d 892 (1942).

[397] *Bernhard, supra*, 19 Cal. 2d at 813; *see Producers Dairy Delivery Co. v. Sentry Ins. Co.* 41 Cal. 3d 903, 910, 226 Cal. Rptr. 558, 718 P.2d 920 (1986).

[398] *E.g., Blonder-Tongue Lab. v. Univ. of Ill. Found.*, 402 U.S. 313 (1971); RESTATEMENT (SECOND) OF JUDGMENTS § 29 (1982); *see* § 15.08[2], *supra*.

[399] *See, e.g., Imen v. Glassford*, 201 Cal. App. 3d 898, 247 Cal. Rptr. 514 (1988); *Sandoval v. Superior Court*, 140 Cal. App. 3d 932, 190 Cal. Rptr. 29 (1983); *White Motor Corp. v. Teresinski*, 214 Cal. App. 3d 754, 263 Cal. Rptr. 26 (1989).

[400] 439 U.S. 322 (1979).

[401] *Parklane, supra*, 439 U. S. at 331. The offensive use of nonmutual issue preclusion is discussed more fully in § 15.08[2][b], *supra*.

§ 15.18   WHEN ARE NONPARTIES BOUND BY A PRIOR JUDGMENT

[1]   Nonparty Preclusion — California's Privity Doctrine

Generally, issue and claim preclusion can only be applied against someone who was a party in a prior lawsuit. However, not only are actual parties bound by a prior judgment, but also nonparties who are in "privity" with the actual parties. The concept of "privity" refers to a variety of relationships under which the preclusive effects of a prior judgment extend beyond a party to the prior action and apply to persons having specified relationships to that party, such as successors in interest, persons represented by a fiduciary, members of the class in an action certified as a class action, and persons who have a financial interest in and control of the conduct of the prior lawsuit. Although traditional applications of privity were quite limited, the modern California doctrine is much broader. The California Supreme Court has expanded the concept to any relationship between the party to be precluded and the unsuccessful party in the prior litigation which is "sufficiently close" so as to justify application of claim or issue preclusion.[402]

Obviously, the "sufficiently close" test is imprecise and ambiguous. This flexible standard for nonparty preclusion is limited by due process, which requires that each person be given a full and fair opportunity to litigate, but the parameters of due process are equally vague: "In the context of issue preclusion, due process requires that the party to be estopped must have had an identity or community of interest with, and adequate representation by, the losing party in the first action as well as that the circumstances must have been such that the party to be estopped should reasonably have expected to be bound by the prior adjudication."[403] Even with these due process restrictions, California's privity doctrine provides little guidance to litigants and courts.

The determination of privity under the "sufficiently close" standard is sometimes said to constitute a legal conclusion based on a policy decision.[404] In other words, this standard does not supply a workable test but rather is the conclusion reached by a court when it determines that a nonparty is bound by a prior judgment. According to the California Supreme Court, the privity determination requires a court to balance the rights of the party to be precluded against the need for applying issue or claim preclusion in a particular case "in order to promote judicial economy by minimizing repetitive litigation, to prevent inconsistent judgments which undermine the integrity of the judicial system, or to protect against vexatious litigation."[405] Unfortunately, these general policy considerations add very little in the way of analytical content to the vague

---

[402] *Clemmer v. Hartford Ins. Co.*, 22 Cal. 3d 865, 875, 151 Cal. Rptr. 285, 587 P.2d 1098 (1978).

[403] *Clemmer, supra*, 22 Cal. 3d at 875.

[404] *See Dyson v. State Pers. Bd.*, 213 Cal. App. 3d 711, 723-25, 262 Cal. Rptr. 112 (1989) (explaining that the term "privity" represents a legal conclusion; emphasis in the privity analysis is upon the policy of ending litigation where there has been a fair trial of one's interests).

[405] *Clemmer, supra*, 22 Cal. 3d at 875; *People v. Sims*, 32 Cal. 3d 468, 486-89, 186 Cal. Rptr. 77, 651 P. 2d 321 (1982).

"sufficiently close" concept but they do send a general message to the California courts: in close cases, resolve doubts in favor of a finding of privity.

[2] Federal Nonparty Preclusion Doctrine, Compared

Recently in *Taylor v. Sturgell*,[406] the United States Supreme Court discussed the federal common law doctrine of nonparty preclusion applicable when determining the preclusive effect of a prior federal court judgment in federal question cases. The Supreme Court carefully delineated six limited categories of recognized exceptions to the general rule against nonparty preclusion, but specifically rejected the "virtual representation" or "close enough" exception because it is based an amorphous balancing test, has unclear standards, and does not sufficiently require adequate representation of a nonparty.[407] Although the Supreme Court had no occasion to consider California's privity doctrine, the *Taylor* opinion leaves little doubt that the Court would not include a "sufficiently close" exception to the federal common law general rule against nonparty preclusion.

§ 15.19 CALIFORNIA'S LAW OF THE CASE, JUDICIAL ESTOPPEL, AND STARE DECISIS DOCTRINES

[1] California's Law of the Case Doctrine

The doctrine of "law of the case" is related to issue and claim preclusion but, unlike those doctrines, precludes relitigation of issues within the context of a single case. Where an appellate court in deciding an appeal states a principle or rule of law necessary to the decision, that principle or rule of law becomes the "law of the case" and must be adhered to throughout the litigation's subsequent progress, both in the lower court on remand and upon subsequent appeal to the same appellate court.[408]

Because California's law of the case doctrine is viewed as "merely a rule of procedure" grounded in judicial efficiency, it is subject to several exceptions to avoid an "unjust decision."[409] The most common exception is when there has been an intervening change in the law since the prior appellate decision, typically by a higher court in another case.[410] But not all changes in the law will justify disregarding the established law of the case. The change must be in the *controlling* rule of law.[411] Even then, this exception may not automatically apply. For example,

---

[406] 553 U. S. 880 (2008).

[407] *Taylor*, 553 U.S. at 898-902.

[408] *People v. Shuey*, 13 Cal. 3d 835, 841, 120 Cal. Rptr. 83, 533 P.2d 211 (1975).

[409] *Clemente v. State of Cal.*, 40 Cal. 3d 202, 211-12, 219 Cal. Rptr. 445, 707 P.2d 818 (1985); *see* Joan Steinman, *Law of the Case: A Judicial Puzzle in Consolidated and Transferred Cases and in Multidistrict Litigation*, 135 U. PA. L. REV. 595, 597-618 (1987).

[410] *See, e.g., Clemente, supra*, 40 Cal. 3d at 212-13; *People v. Whitt*, 51 Cal. 3d 620, 638-39, 274 Cal. Rptr. 252, 798 P.2d 849 (1990); *Subsequent Injuries Fund v. Indus. Accident Comm'n*, 53 Cal. 2d 392, 395, 1 Cal. Rptr. 833, 348 P.2d 193 (1960).

[411] *See George Arakelian Farms, Inc. v. Agric. Labor Relations Bd.*, 49 Cal. 3d 1279, 1292, n.9, 265

if the change in controlling law occurs *after* full trial of a case on remand from the first appeal, as a matter of fairness and judicial economy the appellate court may decide not to apply the intervening change in law in a subsequent appeal.[412]

[2] California's Judicial Estoppel Doctrine

Several California decisions have invoked the doctrine of judicial estoppel, which prevents a party from asserting a position in a legal proceeding that is contrary to a position previously taken in the same or some earlier proceeding.[413] For example, in one recent case the appellate court ruled that, even if the parties' settlement agreement was not actually enforceable, the plaintiffs were judicially estopped from denying its enforceability because they represented to the trial court that the case had settled and the trial court terminated the trial and discharged the jury in reliance on plaintiffs' representation.[414]

According to the California Supreme Court, judicial estoppel applies when: "(1) [T]he same party has taken two positions; (2) the positions were taken in judicial or quasi-judicial administrative proceedings; (3) the party was successful in asserting the first position (i.e., the tribunal adopted the position or accepted is as true; (4) the two positions are totally inconsistent; and (5) the first position was not taken as a result of ignorance, fraud, or mistake."[415] However, because judicial estoppel is an equitable doctrine, its application is discretionary even where all necessary elements are present.

[3] The Role of *Stare Decisis* in the California Courts

Like the hierarchy of courts in the federal judicial system, the California judicial system consists of trial courts (the Superior Courts), intermediate appellate courts (the California Courts of Appeal), and a highest court (the California Supreme Court). In explaining the role of *stare decisis*, the California Supreme Court has observed that "all tribunals exercising inferior jurisdiction are required to follow decisions of courts exercising superior jurisdiction" and therefore the "decisions of this court are binding upon and must be followed by all the state courts of

---

Cal. Rptr. 162, 783 P.2d 749 (1989); *Clemente, supra*, 40 Cal. 3d at 212-13.

[412] *See George Arakelian Farms, supra*, 49 Cal. 3d at 1291 ("[J]udicial economy demands that [appellant] demonstrate that failure to apply [an intervening change in case law] would be a manifest misapplication of existing legal principles and would result in a substantial injustice.").

[413] *See, e.g., Levin v. Ligon*, 140 Cal. App. 4th 1456, 45 Cal. Rptr. 3d 560 (2006) (holding ex-husband's prior legal malpractice action in England, which he settled after asserting that he lost his right to any interest in the financial assets held by his former wife and accumulated during their marriage, estopped him from claiming a community property interest in these same assets); *Jackson v. Cnty. of Los Angeles*, 60 Cal. App. 4th 171, 70 Cal. Rptr. 2d 96 (1997) (holding judicial estoppel barred plaintiff's action alleging defendant County violated the Americans with Disability Act by refusing to reinstate plaintiff as a safety police officer, the only job plaintiff wanted and a job whose duties plaintiff admitted involved substantial stress, because plaintiff had previously received a stipulated workers' compensation award based on an agreed finding that he needed a stress-free job).

[414] *Blix St. Records, Inc. v. Cassidy*, 191 Cal. App. 4th 39, 47-51,119 Cal. Rptr. 3d 574 (2010).

[415] *Aguilar v. Lerner*, 32 Cal. 4th 974, 986-87, 12 Cal. Rptr. 3d 287, 88 P. 3d 24 (2004) (*quoting Jackson, supra*, 60 Cal. App. 4th at 183).

California."[416] This is a basic tenet of California's *stare decisis* doctrine. The doctrine also means that all Superior Courts are bound by all published decisions of the California Courts of Appeal, the only qualifications being that the relevant point in the appellate decision must not have been disapproved by the California Supreme Court and must not be in conflict with another appellate decision.

California statutes divide the state geographically into six appellate districts, each containing a Court of Appeal. Three of these districts are subdivided into smaller territorial divisions. For example, the Court of Appeal for the Second Appellate District (made up of Los Angeles, Santa Barbara, San Luis Obispo, and Ventura Counties) contains eight divisions. Another basic feature of California's *stare decisis* doctrine is that decisions of every *division* of the California Courts of Appeal are binding upon all Superior Courts throughout the state.[417] This is simply another application of the basic tenet that courts exercising inferior jurisdiction must accept the law declared by courts of superior jurisdiction. This means, for example, that a Superior Court trial judge sitting in San Francisco is bound by decisions from divisions of the Court of Appeal sitting in Los Angeles (2nd Appellate District) or San Diego (4th Appellate District) just as much as he or she is bound by decisions of an appellate panel sitting in San Francisco (1st Appellate District). California doesn't work the way the federal courts do, where so-called "rules of the circuit" mean that the federal district courts located within one federal appellate circuit are bound by decisions of the federal court of appeals for that circuit but not by decisions of courts of appeals in other circuits.[418]

As in the federal judicial system, there is no "horizontal *stare decisis*" among the six districts of the California Court of Appeal.[419] The court of appeal in one appellate district is not bound by a prior resolution of a legal issue by a court of appeal in another appellate district. However, unlike some federal intermediate appellate courts, such as the sprawling Ninth Circuit, there is also no "intra-district *stare decisis*" among the various divisions within a particular appellate district.[420] For example, Division Seven of the Second Appellate District of the California Court of Appeal is not bound by an earlier decision by Division One of the Second Appellate District with respect to the same legal issue. This lack of horizontal *stare decisis* means that each division and district may resolve a legal issue in a manner that conflicts with another division or district. In such circumstances, the resulting lack of uniformity and judicial economy is outweighed by the flexibility to develop the best answers to recurring legal issues.

---

[416] *Auto Equity Sales, Inc. v. Superior* Court, 57 Cal.2d 450, 455, 20 Cal. Rptr. 321, 369 P.2d 937 (1962).

[417] *Sarti v. Salt Creek, Inc.*, 167 Cal. App. 4th 1187, 1193, 85 Cal. Rptr. 3d 506 (2008).

[418] *See Sarti, supra,* 167 Cal. App. 4th at 1187, 1193, n. 2.

[419] *See Sarti, supra,* 167 Cal. App. 4th at 1187, 1193, n. 3.

[420] *E.g., Jessen v. Mentor Corp.,* 158 Cal.App.4th 1480, 1489, n. 10, 71 Cal. Rptr. 3d 714 (2008) (declining to follow a contrary decision by another division of the Second District on the issue of whether plaintiff's state law claims for negligence, strict liability, and breach of warranty against the defendant medical device manufacturer were preempted by a federal statute).

TABLE OF CASES

[References are to pages]

[References are to pages]

[References are to pages]

[References are to pages]

[References are to pages]

[References are to pages]

[References are to pages]

Dryden v. Tri-Valley Growers 329

Dubay v. Wells. 350

Duberstein; Commissioner v. 674

Dudley v. Dept. of Transp. 321

Duffy v. City of Long Beach 778

Dugar v. Happy Tiger Records, Inc 203

Duncan v. Louisiana 587

Dunk v. Ford Motor Co. 411

Duplan Corp. v. Moulinage et Retorderie de Chavanoz 441

Duplantis v. Shell Offshore, Inc.. 505

Durfee v. Duke 761; 789

Dusenbery v. United States 110

DVI, Inc. v. Superior Court. 103

Dyer v. MacDougall 515

Dyson v. State Pers. Bd. 798

E

E. Chestnut St. Corp. v. Lakefront Realty Corp. . 301

Earl W. Schott, Inc. v. Kalar. 121, 122

East Texas Motor Freight Sys. v. Rodriguez . . . 370

East Texas, V. & G. Railroad v. Grayson. 146

Eastway Constr. Co. v. City of New York 273

Edmonds v. Compagnie Generale Transatlantique 240

Edmonson v. Leesville Concrete Co. 561; 625

Edwards v. Superior Court. 492

EEOC v. Peabody W. Coal Co. 351

Eichenbaum v. Alon 318

Eisen v. Carlisle & Jacquelin. . .375, 376; 378; 408, 409; 413

El Dorado Meat Co. v. Yosemite Meat & Locker Serv., Inc. 719

Electrical Fittings Corp. v. Thomas & Betts Co. . 665

Eleven Owners for Fair Franchising v. Southland Corp. 411

Elfenbein v. Gulf & Western Indus., Inc. 301

Eli Lilly & Co. v. Roussel Corp. 119

Elkins v. Derby. 297; 334

Ellard v. Conway. 123; 535

Ellingsworth v. Chrysler. 499

Ellington, Estate of v. EMI Music Publ'g. 359

Elster v. Friedman 695

Elston v. City of Turlock. 536, 537; 642

Elsworth v. Beech Aircraft Corp. 639

Ely v. Gray. 534

Embry v. Palmer. 764

Emerson Elec. Co. v. Superior Court 490

Employment Development Dept. v. Superior Court 402

Energy Action Educ. Found. v. Andrus 670

England v. Louisiana State Bd. of Medical Examiners. 766

English v. English. 788; 794, 795

Enyart v. City of Los Angeles. 639

Eon Labs, Inc. v. SmithKline Beecham Corp. . . .343

Epic Commc'n, Inc. v. Richwave Tech., Inc . . . 100

Equal Employment Opportunity Comm'n v. Concentra Health Servs., Inc. 261

Erickson v. Pardus. 261

Erie R. R. Co. v. Tompkins. . . .209; 211; 213; 239

Eriline Co. S.A. v. Johnson 354

ESAB Group, Inc. v. Centricut, Inc. 91

Escamilla v. California Ins. Guarantee Assn. 624

Espey v. Wainwright. 301

Espindola v. Nunez. 121, 122

Estate of (see name of party)

Eureka Financial Corp. v. Hartford Acci. & Indem. Co.. 439

Evans v. Celotex Corp.. 792

Evans v. Lasco Bathware, Inc 402; 405

The Evergreens v. Nunan. 746; 749

Ex rel. (see name of relator)

Exchange Nat'l Bank of Chi. v. Abramson 365

Executive Software N. Am., Inc. v. United States Dist. Court 175

Exxon Corp. v. Eagerton. 235

Exxon Mobil Corp. v. Allapattah Services, Inc. . 156; 177, 178

Exxon Shipping Co. v. Baker 705

Eyre v. McDonough Power Equip., Inc. 640

F

F.C. Stiles Contracting Co. v. Home Ins. Co.. . .167

F.T.C. v. Hope Now Modifications, LLC 296

Factor Health Mgmt. v. Superior Court. 105

Factors Etc., Inc. v. Pro Arts, Inc.. . . . . .235, 236

Fairyland Amusement Co. v. Metromedia, Inc.. . .271

Farmers Ins. Exch. v. Adams 386

Farmers Ins. Exch. v. Superior Court 183

Fauntleroy v. Lum. 84; 761

Federated Dep't Stores, Inc. v. Moitie.616; 727; 742, 743

Fei Ye; United States v. 660

Feigler v. Tidex, Inc.. 168

Feinstein v. Massachusetts General Hospital . . . 218

Feldman v. Bates Mfg. Co. 369

Felger v. Nichols. 745

Feltner v. Columbia Pictures Television. 591

Ferens v. John Deere Co.. . . . . .195; 233–235

[References are to pages]

[References are to pages]

I

[References are to pages]

[References are to pages]

[References are to pages]

[References are to pages]

[References are to pages]

[References are to pages]

[References are to pages]

[References are to pages]

[References are to pages]

Z

TABLE OF STATUTES

[References are to pages]

[References are to pages]

[References are to pages]

[References are to pages]

[References are to pages]

[References are to pages]

[References are to pages]

INDEX

[References are to sections.]

[References are to sections.]

[References are to sections.]

[References are to sections.]

[References are to sections.]

[References are to sections.]

[References are to sections.]

[References are to sections.]

NOMINAL DAMAGES
Generally . . . 14.01[1][c]

NON-JURY TRIALS
Order of proceedings . . . 12.14[1]
Statement of decision . . . 12.14[2]

P

PENDENT JURISDICTION
Claim . . . 5.09[1]
Party . . . 5.09[2]
Personal . . . 3.12[1]

PERSONAL JURISDICTION
California courts
    Agency doctrine . . . 3.13[7][a]
    Alter ego doctrine . . . 3.13[7][a]
    California long-arm statute . . . 3.13[1]
    Defense
        Motion to quash, timely requriement for
          . . . 3.13[8][b]
        Waivable due process right
          . . . 3.13[8][a]
        Writ of mandate . . . 3.13[8][c]
    Due process (See subhead: Due process)
    Effects test . . . 3.13[5]
    Forum selection clauses (See subhead: Forum
      selection clauses)
    Nonresident parent corporations (See subhead:
      Nonresident parent corporations)
    Reasonableness factors . . . 3.13[3]
    Representative services doctrine
      . . . 3.13[7][b]
    Stream of commerce . . . 3.13[4]
    Transient jurisdiction . . . 3.13[6]
    Waivable due process right . . . 3.13[8][a]
Consent to, waiver of or (See subhead: Waiver of or
  consent to)
Cyberspace, jurisdiction in . . . 3.12[2]
Due process
    Defense . . . 3.13[8][a]
    Effects test . . . 3.13[5]
    Lower court decisions . . . 3.13[2][c]
    Snowney versus *Harrah's Entertainment, Inc*
      . . . 3.13[2][b]
    Substantial connection test . . . 3.13[2][a]
    Vons Companies, Inc. versus *Seabest Foods,*
      Inc. . . . 3.13[2][a]
Forum selection clauses
    Generally . . . 3.13[9][a]
    Consumer contracts . . . 3.13[9][c]
    Forum non conveniens and . . . 3.13[9][b]
Frontier of, issues on
    Cyberspace, jurisdiction in . . . 3.12[2]
    Globalization and personal jurisdiction
      . . . 3.12[3]
    Pendent or supplemental personal jurisdiction
      . . . 3.12[1]
    Supplemental personal jurisdiction
      . . . 3.12[1]
Globalization and . . . 3.12[3]

PERSONAL JURISDICTION—Cont.
Issues on frontier of (See subhead: Frontier of, is-
  sues on)
Nonresident parent corporations
    Agency doctrine . . . 3.13[7][a]
    Alter ego doctrine . . . 3.13[7][a]
    Representative services doctrine
      . . . 3.13[7][b]
Pendent . . . 3.12[1]
Problems, arise of . . . 3.01[1]
Reach of, law limiting
    Federal courts . . . 3.01[2][b]
    State courts . . . 3.01[2][a]
Shoe's extension of, justifications for . . . 3.03[3]
Supplemental . . . 3.12[1]
Traditional categories of
    Generally . . . 3.01[3]
    In personam jurisdiction . . . 3.01[3][a]
    In rem jurisdiction . . . 3.01[3][b]
    Quasi in rem jurisdiction . . . 3.01[3][c]
Venue, relationship with . . . 6.03
Waiver of or consent to
    Appearances, special and limited . . . 3.11[2]
    Litigating jurisdiction as partial consent or
      waiver . . . 3.11[3]
    Operation of waiver . . . 3.11[1]
    Partial consent or waiver, litigating jurisdiction
      as . . . 3.11[3]
    Pre-litigation consent, jurisdiction by
      . . . 3.11[4]

PLEADING
Generally . . . 8.11
Amendment of
    Generally . . . 8.10
    Before trial, amendment . . . 8.10[1]
    During and after trial
      Generally . . . 8.10[2]
      Consent, conforming amendment by
        . . . 8.10[2][a]
      Objection, conforming amendment over
        . . . 8.10[2][b]
      Tactical dilemma of objecting party
        . . . 8.10[2][c]
    Relation back status
      Responding to amendment
        . . . 8.10[3][c]
      Statutes of limitation and . . . 8.10[3][a],
        [3][b]
    Statutes of limitation and
      Relation back status . . . 8.10[3][a],
        [3][b]
      Responding to amendment
        . . . 8.10[3][c]
Answer (See ANSWER)
California Code pleading
    Generally . . . 8.12[1]
    Amendments to pleadings
      Conform to proof, amendments to
        . . . 8.12[7][b]
      Liberal amendment policy
        . . . 8.12[7][a]
    Complaint (See subhead: Complaint)

[References are to sections.]

[References are to sections.]

[References are to sections.]

[References are to sections.]